# Keeping Our Fingers Crossed

**Jeff Jones, Publisher**

Maybe it's my stage in life but as I throttle down heading into 2018, I seem to spend more time looking back than forward. Being an optimist, I'm not ready to concede reality. At age 64, there is obviously more wake behind me now and fewer adventures on the horizon. By the time this letter gets published in the 2018 edition of the Waterway Guide I will be a first-time grandfather and embarking on adventures I do not yet fully comprehend. For the first time in four generations on my side of the family, a little girl will bless our lives, and it is as exciting and awe inspiring as my first bareboat adventure in the BVIs. Many of you have this perspective and know the adventures of which I speak.

Meanwhile back at the helm….It has been a decade since the "great recession" and like most of you I've ruminated as to where those years went and what the next 10 years will bring. I'm not an economist (just an old ad executive who stayed at a Holiday Inn Express once), but I think it's safe to say that the boating/marine industry suffered as much as most during the past 10 years. Many marinas/yards/captains/boat manufacturers/etc. came through the tough times and are now positioned to conquer whatever the future holds. I know

at WG we are ship shape with sails up ready to continue bringing you digital and print products to make your time on the water safe, productive and enjoyable.

As we approach the third decade of the 21st century (think about that), the boating community has lots of reasons to be optimistic. The economy is experiencing growth meaning more jobs and more disposable income; fuel prices are the lowest in many years meaning more boats and time on the water; and technology is making life on the water easier, better and smarter. Reasonable discussions can now be held as to the level of improvement in weather predictions, climate change and the quality of our waterways. But, in general, improvements are happening. With these more positive macro-economic trends taking shape, businesses across the marine industry should become more prosperous well into the next decade. The WG team is glad to help out along the way.

At WG we too weathered the recession of 2008 and have come through with renewed vigor. Having been at the ownership helm since only 2014, I can say it was tough but necessary to make the changes to get us to where we are today. We have our team in place to carry us into the next decade. We will remain focused on our business model and champion the causes of this wonderful lifestyle.

Hope is not a plan, but we're keeping our fingers crossed for smooth sailing for the next 10 years. Those of us working in this industry and those of you participating in the boating lifestyle deserve nothing less.

Best,

Jeff Jones, Publisher

# DESTINATION

# MARATHON MARINA

*We are closer than you think*

F L O R I D A

EVERGLADES
NATIONAL
PARK

*1018 N. M. from*
**New York**

*100 N. M. from*
**Fort Lauderdale**

*556 N. M. from*
**North Carolin**

GULF
*of*
MEXICO

F L O R I D A   K E Y S

ATLANTIC
OCEAN

*Marathon Marina*

# QUALITY CRUISING, REAL COMMUNITY.

You're not just buying a boat, you're joining our family.

Join us at:
RangerTugs.com
Tugnuts.com

## WATERWAY GUIDE OFFICES

Corporate/Production Office
16273 General Puller Hwy.
P.O. Box 1125
Deltaville, VA 23043
804-776-8999
804-776-6111 (fax)
www.waterwayguide.com

### BOOK SALES

waterwayguide.com/shipstore

Waterway Guide is published annually in seven regional editions— Bahamas, Southern, Atlantic ICW, Chesapeake Bay, Northern, Great Lakes and Cuba—by Waterway Guide Media, LLC © 2018. All rights reserved. Reproduction in whole or part or use of any data compilation without written permission from the publisher is prohibited. The title Waterway Guide is a registered trademark. ISBN Number: 978-0-9985863-0-4 for the Southern 2018 Edition. Purchase and use of Waterway Guide constitutes acceptance of the restrictions set forth herein.

FOUNDED IN 1947

| | |
|---|---|
| Publisher | **JEFF JONES** <br> jjones@waterwayguide.com |
| General Manager/ Editor-in-Chief | **ED TILLETT** <br> etillett@waterwayguide.com |
| Managing Editor | **JANI PARKER** <br> jparker@waterwayguide.com |
| Graphic Design/ Production Manager | **SCOTT MCCONNELL** <br> scott@waterwayguide.com |
| Product Manager | **HEATHER SADEG** <br> heather@waterwayguide.com |
| Book Sales Manager | **LINDA JERNIGAN** <br> linda@waterwayguide.com |
| Marketing & Advertising Traffic Manager | **SANDY HICKEY** <br> sandy@waterwayguide.com |
| Business Development Manager | **GRAHAM JONES** <br> graham@waterwayguide.com |
| Comptroller | **ARTHUR CROWTHER** <br> acrowther@waterwayguide.com |
| Senior Advisor/ Skipper Bob Editor | **TED STEHLE** <br> tstehle@waterwayguide.com |
| News Editor | **LISA SUHAY** <br> lisa@waterwayguide.com |
| Web Master | **MIKE SCHWEFLER** |
| Office Assistant | **LEON HOLZMAN** |
| Intern | **ERIN MALONEY** |

### ADVERTISING SALES

| | |
|---|---|
| Northern, Atlantic ICW, Florida West Coast & the Gulf | **MIKE KUCERA** <br> mkucera@waterwayguide.com |
| Bahamas | **BOB BOWER** <br> bobby@waterwayguide.com |
| Chesapeake Bay | **PATRICK DURHAM** <br> patrick@waterwayguide.com |
| Florida East Coast including the Keys & Great Lakes | **PETE HUNGERFORD** <br> pete@waterwayguide.com |
| National Sales | **GRAHAM JONES** <br> graham@waterwayguide.com |

### CRUISING EDITORS

| | |
|---|---|
| **BAHAMAS** | BO CHESNEY <br> BOB BOWER <br> LUCY & MATT CLAIBORNE |
| **SOUTHERN** | BUD & ELAINE LLOYD <br> TOM & DIANE TASMA <br> TOM DOVE |
| **ATLANTIC ICW** | BUD & ELAINE LLOYD <br> CAPT. GEORGE & PAT HOSPODAR |
| **CHESAPEAKE BAY** | REX & AMY NOEL <br> SCOTT RICHARD BERG <br> JAMES DEAN <br> DEB & DENNIS JANSMA |
| **NORTHERN** | CAPT. GEORGE & PATRICIA HOSPODAR <br> MICHAEL CAMERATA <br> CAPT. DENA HANKINS & JAMES LANE <br> TONY SMITH |
| **GREAT LAKES** | MICHAEL O'REILLY & ANN PHILLIPS <br> CAPT. GEORGE & PATRICIA HOSPODAR <br> CAPT. JOHN JOHNSTON <br> MARY & THERON RODRIGUEZ |

Find us on Facebook

# #BahamasBoating

## 's Better In The Bahamas

he most breathtakingly clear waters on Earth lie just 50 nm off Florida. Our cays,coasts
nd countryside aren't to be missed either. Over 32 ports of entry make it easy.
r special marina deals or to join our boating flings
isit Bahamas.com/boating or call 1.800 32SPORT (7678)
ollow us On: 🅿 📘 ▶️ 🐦 📷

THE ISLANDS OF THE
**bahamas**

016 The Islands Of The Bahamas
otos courtesy of Staniel Cay Yacht Club, The Exumas

# CUTWATER

DISCOVER YOUR INNER EXPLORER

**View all seven trailerable models at CutwaterBoats.com**

C-242C • C-242SC • C-28 • C-30S • C-30CB • C-302C • C-302SC

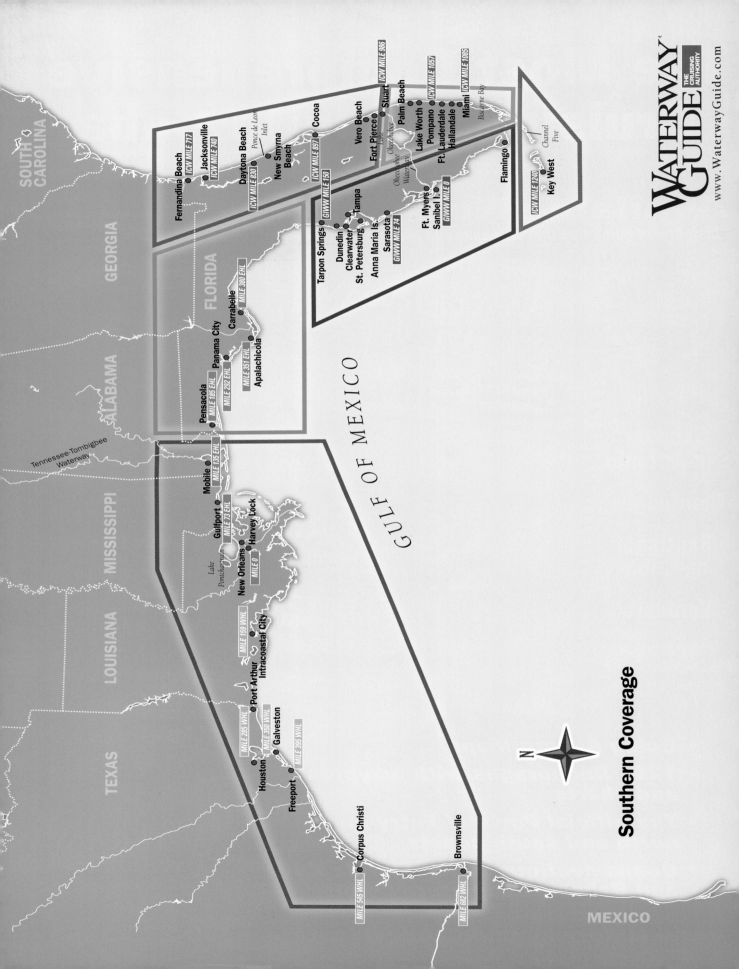

**WATERWAY GUIDE** THE CRUISING AUTHORITY

www.WaterwayGuide.com

SOUTH CAROLINA

GEORGIA

FLORIDA

ALABAMA

MISSISSIPPI

LOUISIANA

TEXAS

MEXICO

GULF OF MEXICO

Tennessee-Tombigbee Waterway

Lake Pontchartrain

**Southern Coverage**

N

Fernandina Beach — *ICW MILE 717*
Jacksonville — *ICW MILE 740*
Daytona Beach — *ICW MILE 830*
*Ponce de Leon Inlet*
New Smyrna Beach
*ICW MILE 897*
Cocoa
*ICW MILE 886*
Vero Beach
Fort Pierce
Stuart
*Lake Okeechobee*
*Okeechobee Waterway*
Palm Beach — *ICW MILE 1057*
Lake Worth
Pompano
Ft. Lauderdale
Hallandale
Miami — *ICW MILE 1085*
*Biscayne Bay*
*Channel Five*
Key West — *ICW MILE 1240*
Flamingo

Tarpon Springs — *GIWW MILE 150*
Dunedin
Clearwater
Tampa
St. Petersburg
Anna Maria Is.
Sarasota — *GIWW MILE 74*
Ft. Myers
Sanibel I.
*GIWW MILE 0*

Carrabelle — *MILE 380 EHL*
Panama City — *MILE 351 EHL*
Apalachicola — *MILE 292 EHL*
Pensacola — *MILE 185 EHL*
Mobile — *MILE 135 EHL*
Gulfport — *MILE 73 EHL*
Harvey Lock
New Orleans — *MILE 0*
*MILE 169 WHL*
Intracoastal City
Port Arthur — *MILE 285 WHL*
Galveston — *MILE 350 WHL*
Houston
Freeport — *MILE 395 WHL*
Corpus Christi — *MILE 545 WHL*
Brownsville — *MILE 682 WHL*

# Contents

2018 Southern Edition, Volume 71, No. 3

## FLORIDA'S UPPER EAST COAST

*Cruising south on the ICW, mariners enter Florida at Mile 714. As you cross Cumberland Sound and the St. Marys River, the broad expanses of the marsh-bordered Georgia ICW give way to the narrower, more protected and more populated Florida route. Below St. Lucie Inlet, the coastline becomes truly tropical, with a profusion of palm trees and exotic flowers. The Florida ICW is well marked and easy to follow.*

## FLORIDA'S LOWER EAST COAST

*More than 300 miles of mostly navigable inland waterways carve through the Fort Lauderdale area, making it the "Venice of America." It is well known as a yachting center and boating amenities and services are readily available. Fort Lauderdale to Miami is known as "Florida's Gold Coast," and it glimmers with glamour and charm.*

## THE FLORIDA KEYS

*Extending in a sweeping southwesterly curve from Miami and the mainland, the Florida Keys offer the cruising boater an environment unlike other Waterway areas. In many ways, the Keys resemble the islands of the Bahamas. However, a main highway and a total of 18.94 miles of bridges tie them together.*

## FLORIDA'S WEST COAST

*Zoologically and geographically, Florida's lower west coast differs substantially from the east. The cruising, too, is entirely different. The sophistication, glamour and luxury so prevalent on the east coast comes in more measured doses here. The pace is slower, the atmosphere more relaxed and the amenities somewhat more limited and spaced farther apart, but the cruising is superb.*

TABLE OF CONTENTS

## FLORIDA'S UPPER GULF COAST

*Florida's Panhandle, stretching from Carrabelle or Apalachicola on the eastern end to Pensacola and Perdido Bay on the west, is sometimes called the Forgotten Coast. It can be reached in one of three ways: From the east, either directly across 130 to 170 miles of the Gulf of Mexico or skirting the Big Bend area just offshore; or from the west from Mobile Bay, from which many Midwestern cruisers come, down the river route.*

## GULF COAST

*The area west from Florida along the Gulf Coast historically has been described as the playground of the South. The region is known for its miles of pure white beaches, scenic landscapes and historic towns. This trip can challenge your boating skills. Expect to encounter a variety of conditions, ranging from open water on Mobile Bay and Mississippi Sound to narrow, sometimes cramped, canals and waterways. Lagoons and bayous often alternate with long and sometimes tedious land cuts.*

## EXTENDED CRUISING

## INDEXES

# THE SOJOURNER PERMIT

Florida has a unique form of short-term registration of a vessel called a Sojourner's Permit. It allows a boater to maintain their homeport state of registration while extending the lawful grace period for registering vessels by an additional 60 days. This is most applicable to those who leave their boats in a marina for the entire winter season.

A Sojourner Permit is required for any vessel owned by a non-Florida resident that is registered in another state or federally documented and that stays in Florida waters for more than 90 days or is used in Florida waters more than 183 days a year. The intent is to ensure that boats used in Florida are registered in Florida, thus making them taxable under Florida's sales and use tax law regarding items purchased out of state but stored or used in Florida. However, under the Sojourner permit, your stay is deemed temporary and no sale tax is collected if you meet <u>all</u> of the following conditions:

• You are a legal resident of another state
• You have owned the boat 6 months or longer
• You have shown no intent to use the boat in Florida at or before the time of purchase
• The boat has been in use 6 months or longer within the taxing jurisdiction of another state.

Florida law requires that a vessel be registered in a U.S. jurisdiction at the time the boat enters Florida waters so as to be eligible for the initial 90-day grace period. Documented vessels from another state may also apply for a Sojourner Permit and will be granted an additional one year of use in Florida waters.

The Sojourner Permit is issued by the individual county tax offices. State law is subject to local interpretation depending on the tax district. Therefore, if you are going to keep a boat in Florida longer than the allotted 90 days, you will want to educate yourself in advance.

Download and complete the forms in advance: The permit required is HSMV 87244, "Application to Register Non Titled Vessels." Refer to the Florida Department of Revenue's "Sales and Use Tax on Boats" at dormyflorida.com for more information.

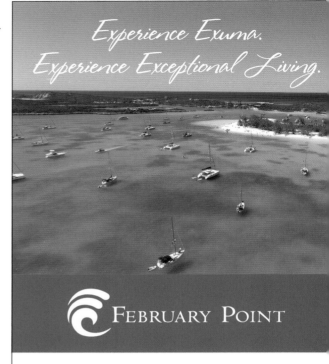

**Marinas**    **Services**    **Anchorages**    **Bridges & Locks**    **Nav Alerts**    **Fuel**

# Waterway Explorer provides
# **6** different icons that overlay
# on the maps as modes
## Modes

## Info Pane with details

*Plan your time on the water with* **Explorer**

# www.waterwayguide.com

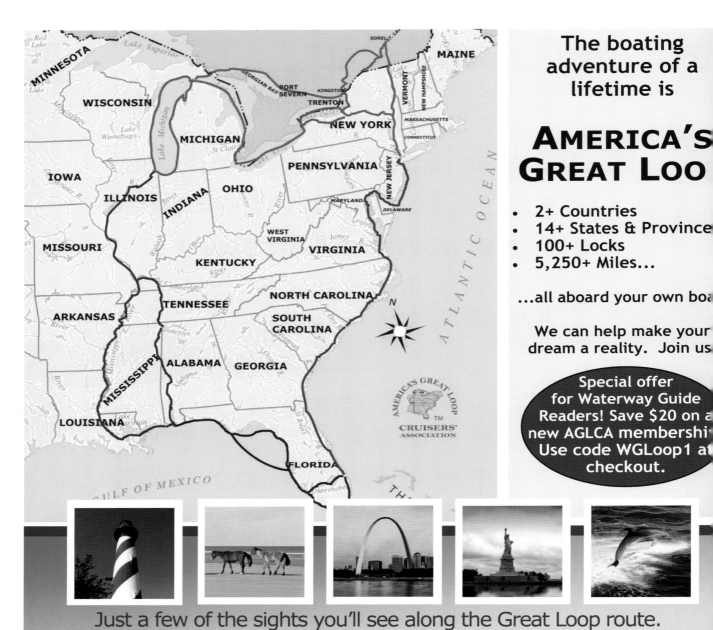

# Cruising Editors

*Waterway Guide's on-the-water Cruising Editors bring us firsthand information about the navigation, news and trends along the waterways we cover. In addition to contributing to the annual guide, they provide daily updates on our companion web site at waterwayguide.com. We are pleased to introduce you to our crew.*

## BAHAMAS

**Bo Chesney** was introduced to sailing in the early 1970s in southern California when his college roommate turned to the football team for "serious ballast" on blustery race days. He fell in love with the sport and has been sailing ever since. In the mid-1980s he moved to the east coast and discovered the Chesapeake Bay. In 2000 he graduated from racing to cruising and spent summers and the time between business trips cruising the Chesapeake Bay with his wife, Joyce. In 2008 they made their first trip north to New England and Maine, followed by their first trip south to the Florida Keys. After Joyce's retirement in 2010, they moved aboard *Dream Catcher*, their Beneteau 49, and have immersed themselves in the cruising lifestyle, spending winters in Florida and the Bahamas. Beginning in 2015, Bo turned his passion for photography and videography into an integral part of his cruising activities, creating promotional videos and documenting the cruising lifestyle. If you run into him, he'd love to hear your story!

**Matt and Lucy Claiborne** met while studying together for their pilot's license and have been sharing adventures ever since. They lived aboard a 31-foot sailboat as newlyweds; then owned a 19-foot runabout while living in Key Largo, which they used for sunset cruises. They upgraded to a 21-foot cuddy cabin, which they used as a platform for diving in the Florida Keys and for week-long camping vacations exploring different parts of Florida's beautiful coasts. Fueled by the desire to be on the water full-time, they sold their house, purchased a 38-foot sailing catamaran (*Independence*) and moved aboard, along with their cocker spaniel Captain Hastings. They are in the middle of a planned three-year cruise and have traveled to Florida, the ICW, the Chesapeake Bay and the Bahamas. They both hold USCG 50-ton Master licenses and love every minute spent on the water.

**Bob Bower** worked at his family business in Nassau for 21 years, where edited the *Bahamas Tourist News*, and the promotion boards' *Bahama Out Islands Travel Guide and Nassau/Paradise Island Tourist News*. Born in Nassau and schooled in the UK, Bob lived in Australia for seven years, where he co-partnered a successful public relations firm in Sydney. For the past two years he served as executive director for the Association of Bahamas Marinas. He also writes for *Fodor's Travel Guides*. Bob loves to travel the Bahama Out Islands and his further journeys have taken him to the Caribbean, Spain, Malta, France, Belgium, Ireland, the UK, the USA and Canada. Since 1987 Bob has resided in Nassau with his wife and three children and loves his faith, reading, chess, travel and photography.

## SOUTHERN & ATLANTIC ICW

**Bud & Elaine Lloyd** are Cruising Editors for the Southern and the Atlantic ICW editions. After being long-time sailors, Bud and Elaine decided that in order to fulfill their dream of living aboard and cruising full time they needed a trawler. *Diamond Girl* was the choice, and after many years they still believe that their decision was good. From their homeport of Long Beach, CA, they cruised all over Southern California and parts of Mexico. Finally they decided that it was time to get serious about fulfilling their dream of cruising, so they put *Diamond Girl* on a ship and sent her to Ft. Lauderdale, FL. They have been cruising on the East Coast for a number of years now and have found the lifestyle even more rewarding than they ever imagined. After 30,000 miles on the ICW, many crossings of Lake Okeechobee, and numerous summers spent on the Chesapeake Bay, they truly enjoy passing along information and sharing some of their favorite spots with the *Waterway Guide*. If you see *Diamond Girl*, knock on the boat and say "hi".

**om and Diane Tasma** have traveled every mile of the CW from Norfolk, VA to its western terminus at Mile 82 WHL in the Port of Brownsville, Texas. Tom grew p in Western Michigan and has had a passion for boats nd sailing since he was a child. Diane grew up in West exas and became an avid boater and sailor when she nd Tom met and married almost 40 years ago. Tom is retired school superintendent from the Houston, TX, rea and Diane is a retired nurse. Much of their cruising as been done on a 32-foot Endeavor and a 41-foot ormosa. They are currently cruising on an Integrity 34 rawler, and keep a 22-foot runabout for easy access to nany waterway adventures. These days they are most ikely to found aboard *"Open Return"* in South Texas, the lorida Keys, or Bahamas.

**Capt. George and Patricia Hospodar** have been oaters for over 40 years and have cruised more than 3,000 miles together aboard two sailboats and their 8-foot Symbol motor yacht, *Reflection*. Since 2008 they nave traveled up and down the Atlantic ICW numerous imes between their home on Barnegat Bay in Brick, NJ, and their "adopted" home at Banana Bay Marina in Marathon, FL, and have completed the America's Great Loop journey twice through the waterways of the U.S. and Canada. George, a retired business owner, has been a 100-ton licensed U.S. Coast Guard Captain for 26 years and is a Past Commodore of the Bristol Sailing Club in Bay Head, NJ, a Past Director of the New Jersey Marine Trades Association and a Past President of the Chesapeake Marine Canvas Fabricators Association. He and Pat (a retired music teacher and choral director) are Platinum lifetime members of the America's Great Loop Cruisers' Association, as well as members of the Marine

Trawler Owners Association and the Marathon Yacht Club. Together they have also authored two popular boating books: *Reflection on America's Great Loop* and *The Great Loop Experience from Concept to Completion*, and they are often featured speakers at boat shows, TrawlerFests and other nautical events. George and Patricia are also Cruising Editors for the Northern and Great Lakes editions of *Waterway Guide*.

## CHESAPEAKE BAY

**Rex and Amy Noel** actively cruised the Chesapeake Bay and as far as Long Island Sound on their first boat, a Hunter Legend 35.5. After seven seasons, they moved up to their current Legend 43, *Xtasea*. They continued to cruise the Bay and extended their range from Pamlico Sound to Nantucket. Rex also had the opportunity to sail (round trip) to Bermuda with friends, adding a little offshore experience. Rex and Amy have been active for 20 years in the Northern Star Hunter Sailing Association, and Rex served as Vice Commodore and Commodore for the club. They are both members of the Seven Seas Cruising Association, and Rex holds a 100-ton USCG Master's license and is a licensed amateur radio operator (KI4GNA). They achieved their dream of cruising to the Bahamas over the winter of 2014 and spent their second winter season in the islands in 2016. While no one can claim to have seen it all, they have poked into many corners of the Chesapeake over the past 30 years and plan to see many more. They enjoy sharing that experience as Cruising Editors for the Southern portion of the Chesapeake.

**Scott Richard Berg** is a lifelong boater and full-time cruiser with five decades of experience on a range of vessels from el Toro prams to a 135-foot Baltic Trader. He operated Chardonnay Boatworks, a full-service marine repair company, for many years from a series of cruising sailboats (all named *Chardonnay*). He is the immediate past president of the Seven Seas Cruising Association, an ABYC Certified Master Technician and holds an Amateur Extra Class radio license. Scott is *Waterway Guide's* Cruising Editor for the Potomac River.

**Debi and Dennis Jansma** are Cruising Editors for the Upper Chesapeake and Delmarva areas. Although they only began their cruising lifestyle recently, both have a long-lived love of the sea and boating. Dennis began sailing as a teenager on a Hobie Cat in Hingham

MA, while Debi grew up helping in marinas managed by her parents along the Erie Canal. The two met in high school in Rumson NJ, and sailed together in the Navesink River. After they married, they became members in the Monmouth Boat Club, where Dennis enjoyed racing Flying Scots.

As their three children grew older, sailing stayed front and center with family vacations on bareboat charters in the U.S. and British Virgin Islands. In 2005, Debi and Dennis moved to the Miami area, seeking a longer sailing season, and joined the Coconut Grove Sailing Club. Both became very active on the CGSC Race Committee, and traded their Flying Scot for a 27-foot Stiletto catamaran to sail on Biscayne Bay. After their youngest left for college, wanderlust set in for real and they started planning to make the liveaboard life reality. They spent three years having their dream boat built, a kit catamaran from Australia called a Fusion 40 (*XYZZY*). They have cruised both coasts of Florida, the East Coast north as far as Kittery, ME, and spent 5 months in the Bahamas during their second winter aboard. Both Debi & Dennis are SSCA members.

## NORTHERN

**Capt. Dena Hankins & James Lane** left Seattle, WA, aboard a William Garden Seawolf ketch in 1999 and have been traveling ever since. They sailed the Puget Sound and the San Juan Islands, the Georgia Strait and the Strait of Juan de Fuca, the northern Pacific Ocean and the San Francisco Bay. There, they downsized to a Gulf 32 pilothouse sloop and jumped the trades to the Big Island of Hawai'i. They sailed throughout the archipelago for a year and sold that boat in Oahu in order to move to the Indian Subcontinent in 2008.

In 2009, they chose the Chesapeake Bay as the restarting point for their circumnavigation, titled "Around the World in 80 Years." They settled aboard their new old boat, a 1961 Philip Rhodes Chesapeake sloop, and gunkholed from Norfolk, VA, to Winter Harbor, ME, and south to Cape Fear, NC. Between extremes, their home towns have included: Baltimore, MD; Portland, ME; Noank, CT (where they crewed on a tall ship); Manhattan, NY; Boston, MA; Wilmington, NC; and Annapolis, MD. As Cruising Editors, they've covered: Maine; Nantucket to Portsmouth, NH; the north shore of the Long Island Sound; the C&D Canal; Northern Chesapeake Bay; and the ICW between Norfolk and Cape Fear. Dena is a multi-published novelist and short-story writer with a 50-ton Master License. James is an accomplished photographer and indefatigable traveler, storyteller and sailor. Together, they can face anything, even a head rebuild, and honestly say they're living the dream.

**Michael Camarata** started his sailing/boating life in the early 1970s when he decided to buy a Sunfish-type sailboat with his future wife, Carol Zipke. A few years later they bought a larger sailing dinghy with TWO sails. This was to set a pattern of larger and more complicated sailing vessels that continued to the vessel they now own and live aboard, a 44-foot sailing (occasionally) catamaran, *Infinite Improbability*, which Michael says is their last upgrade. Michael and Carol's cruising area originally ranged from New York City to Nantucket and north of the Cape Cod Canal. Now, having sold all of their "dirt-based property" the couple roams from southern New England to the Florida Keys and the Bahamas. They live in Mystic, CT, in the summer and Marathon, FL, in the winter. They are both Past Commanders of the Waterbury (Conn) Power Squadron, as well as Senior Navigators in the U.S. Power Squadron.

**Tony Smith** is the Cruising Editor for the Buzzards Bay area in Southeastern Massachusetts. Tony has been on the water his whole life. His parents divorced when he was young and his mother moved back to her home land of Bermuda and his father stayed in Cape Cod; when Tony was with either parent he was sailing somewhere. When he got to college he took summer jobs teaching sailing at either the Royal Bermuda Yacht Club or the New Bedford Yacht Club, depending on which parent he was with.

Tony later owned his own boats. A Pearson Ariel was his first boat, which he sailed from Maine to Nantucket each summer, then a Cal 28, which he sailed in the Chesapeake and later in Florida. Then he bought a small trawler and ran up and down the ICW while filming a video for others wanting to see what the ICW was all about. At present Tony owns and sails a classic 37-year-old Hunter 30 back in the Buzzards Bay area.

## GREAT LAKES

**Michael O'Reilly and Ann Phillips** came to sailing by first messing about with canoes and kayaks while living on the Canadian shore of Lake Superior. Sailing replaced the smaller boats, and over the last 15-plus years they have enjoyed many extended summer cruises. Most recently they completed a cruise through four of the five Great Lakes, and currently plan on exploring Lake Ontario, the St. Lawrence Seaway down to Newfoundland, and beyond. Mike is a long-time freelance journalist, writing mostly about the sciences. With the transition to this new watery life Mike now spends most of his work time writing about traveling, destinations and cruising. Ann is an accomplished photographer. Together they are chronicling their life afloat.

**Mary and Tharon Rodriguez** are Cruising Editors for the fresh waters of Lake Michigan. They both grew up in Northern Michigan but didn't meet until attending Grand Valley State University in Grand Rapids, MI. They love exploring new hobbies and learned to sail on 12-foot lasers on Reed's Lake. Their first sailboat was *Fuzz*, an S2 7.3. In 2015, they got married and have been cruising full-time on their 36-foot Nonsuch, *Tipsy Gypsy*. Their maiden voyage started as a trip around Lake Michigan, then up through the North Channel, throughout the remaining Great Lakes, down the ICW to Florida, finishing all around the Bahamas and back to Florida. They both work full-time aboard, which allows them the freedom of cruising year-round in Lake Michigan from May to October and Florida/Bahamas from November to April. Check out their adventures via land and sea at maryandtharon.com

**Captain John "JJ" Johnston** is Cruising Editor for the Erie Canal and the New York State Canal System. He's from Pittsburgh, PA, but calls Fairport, NY his home canal town. JJ retired from Kodak's motion picture division in 2007 and became a captain on *Sam Patch*, a popular Erie Canal tour boat. Captain JJ also served as Executive Director of CANAL NY, a destination marketing organization, traveling on his 29-foot diesel inboard C Dory, *Penguin,* across NY State, promoting the waterway and learning about its history, operation and navigation. He's motored all 524 miles of the NY canal system, been up and down all 57 locks, overnighted in 42 canal communities and participated in more than 20 canal events.

Captain JJ holds a 100-ton USCG license and is a certified on the water instructor for U.S. Powerboating, the National Safe Boating Council and NYS Boater Safety course. As Captain JJ LLC, he offers charter cruises and provides powerboat training for boat clubs in upstate NY and Ft. Lauderdale, FL.

Captain JJ is a member of the Canal Society of NY and looking forward to the events celebrating the 200th anniversary of the construction of the Erie Canal and helping boaters understand, appreciate and enjoy "Clinton's Ditch."

## Other Contributors

*Waterway Guide* gathers information and photos from a variety of sources, including boaters, marinas, communities and tourism divisions. We would like to thank everyone who contributed to this edition, with special thanks to:

Bill Hezlep
Rudy & Jill Sechez
Tom Dove (St. Johns River)
Brad Whitmore (Cocoa Beach)
James Cash (Dauphine Island)
Hunter Todd (Gulf Coast)

# FREE*
# DIGITAL SUBSCRIPTION

Get all the boat reviews, gadgets and destination articles you've come to enjoy from *Southern Boating* right at your fingertips.

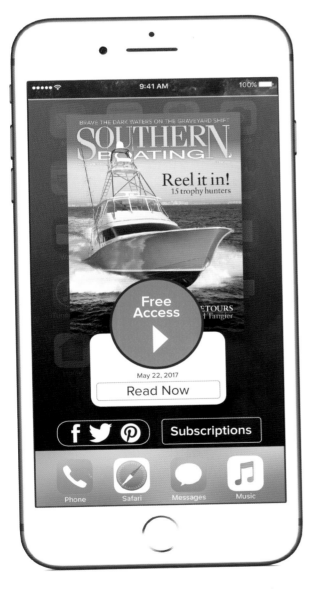

## PLUS

- Love a product? Easily click through to partner sites.

- Exclusive video content only seen in the digital magazine.

- Jump to your favorite section with a single click.

- Instant notifications when an issue is published and ready for download.

- Revisit past archived issues in one convenient place.

Available on iTunes, Google Play and Amazon Kindle

*Offer exclusive to Waterway Guide Readers

Visit *southernboating.com/waterway-guide/* to get your free digital subscription today!

# WATERWAY EXPLORER
# RATINGS & REVIEWS

*Waterway Explorer* **has ratings and reviews. See what others say about Marinas, Anchorages, Bridges/Locks and Navigation Alerts!**

## 1. Marathon Boat Yard Marine Center
☆☆☆☆☆

**Max Length:** 80
**Total/Transient Slips:** 20/5
**Approach/Dockside Depth:** 8.0/20.0
**Fuel:** **pairs:** Hull / Eng

**No stars indicate that this marina is awaiting a review**

## 2. Faro Blanco Res Club
☆☆☆☆☆

**Max Length:** 130
**Total/Transient Slips:** 74/
**Approach/Dockside De**
**Fuel:** Diesel/Gas
**pout:** Yes

Max Length:
Total/Transient Slips: 20/3
Approach/Dockside Depth: 8.0/8.0
Fuel: Diesel/Gas
Pumpout: Yes
Repairs: No

**Yellow stars indicate the rating that this marina got from reviewers**

### Faro Blanco Resort & Yacht Club

**Mile Marker:** between markers 17 and 18

**Marathon, FL 33050**

**Phone:** (305) 743-9018

**Hailing Channel:** 16

☑ Compare to other marinas in the area

 ☆☆☆☆☆
1 Boater Review

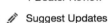 Suggest Updates

↩ Complete Marina Listing

*Be the first to review and rate – or add your comments to the list!*

- # Fill out the review form and post your rating
- # No log in required
- # No private information shared

*Waterway Guide staff and editors validate and verify postings and content to ensure accuracy*

## Reviews: Faro Blanco Resort & Yacht Club

These are observations from the boating community. Waterway Guide information is ver ed regularly and all efforts will be made to validate any ...here. Thank you for taking the time to share comments abou ... erience.

Back to the Waterway Explorer

**Faro Blanco Resort & Yacht Club**

1990 Overseas Highway
Marathon, FL 33050
Florida Bay between markers 17 and 18 48

**Lat / Lon:** N 24° 42.693' / W 081° 06.309'
**Hours:** 7:00 am to 7:00pm
**Contact:** Alain Giudice
**VHF Monitored:** 16
**VHF Working:** 9
**Phone:** (305) 743-9018
**Email:** srudek@faroblancomarina.com
**Website:** faroblancoresort.com

☆☆☆☆☆ (1)
5.00 out of 5 stars

**Review for Faro Blanco Resort & Yacht Club**

**Reviewed by:** Ed, *Adonia*, on Jun 29, 2016
**Boat Type:** Power
**LOA:** 61'
**Draft:** 4.5'

**Rating:** ☆☆☆☆☆

Faro Blanco is a wonderful facility. We were there in May 2016 for the Marlow Marine Cruising Club 20th rendezvous. The staff members were on top of their game. Hospitality, facilities and ambiance are top notch. The docks and slips are all new and no expense has been spared. The Hyatt is also new. Plan on visiting this icon of the Keys. It's a great facility.

View location on the Waterway Guide Explorer

**Name** *(Displayed)*

| |

**Email** *(Not Displayed)*

Email

**Vessel Name** Display? ☐

Vessel Name

**LOA (ft):** **Draft (ft):** **Boat Type:**

| | | | Sail | Power |

**Rating:**
★★★★★

**Comments:**

Type review here. How was the service? Amenities? Ambience? Ease of docking?

☑ Yes, sign me up for the Cruisers' Weekly Update.

**Submit** Review Policies

# SKIPPER'S HANDBOOK

# U.S. Coast Guard

The Coast Guard stands watch at all times to aid vessels of all sizes and the persons on board. The Coast Guard locations listed below cover the areas included in this edition of Waterway Guide. In some areas, you can quickly reach the Coast Guard by dialing *CG on a cellular phone. If you have a question of a non-emergency nature, the Coast Guard prefers that you telephone the nearest station. As always, if there is an emergency, initiate a "MAY DAY" call on VHF Channel 16. The following Coast Guard district offices cover the areas in this book.

## ■ SEVENTH COAST GUARD DISTRICT
**District Office:** Brickell Plaza Federal Building, 909 SE 1st Ave., Miami, FL 33131
305-415-6860, uscg.mil/d7

### FLORIDA (SECTOR JACKSONVILLE)
4200 Ocean St., Atlantic Beach, FL 32233
904-564-7500/7511 or -7512 (emergency)

### FLORIDA (SECTOR MIAMI)
100 MacArthur Causeway, Miami Beach, FL 33139
305-535-4304 or -4472/-4520 (emergency)

### FLORIDA (SECTOR KEY WEST)
100 Trumbo Point Rd., Key West, FL 33040
305-292-877 or -8727 (emergency)

## ■ EIGHTH COAST GUARD DISTRICT
**District Office:** Hale Boggs Federal Building, 500 Poydras Street, New Orleans, LA 70130
504-589-6225, uscg.mil/d8

### GULF COAST (SECTOR ST. PETERSBURG)
600 8th Ave., SE, St. Petersburg, FL 33701
727-824-7534 or -7506 (emergency)

### GULF COAST (SECTOR MOBILE)
1500 15th Street, Brookley Complex, Mobile, AL 36615-1300
251-441-5720 or -6211 (emergency)

### GULF COAST (SECTOR NEW ORLEANS)
200 Hendee Street, New Orleans, LA 70114
504-365-2200 or -2544 (emergency)

### TEXAS (SECTOR HOUSTON/GALVESTON)
13411 Hillard St., Houston, TX 77034
281-464-4800 or -4854 (emergency)

### TEXAS (SECTOR CORPUS CHRISTI)
8930 Ocean Dr., Corpus Christi, TX 78419
361-939-6393 or -6349 (emergency)

*Additional Resources*
*U.S. Coast Guard: uscg.mil*

# Coast Guard Requirements

In addition to aiding boaters in distress, the Coast Guard also enforces maritime law and conducts safety inspections. While a Coast Guard boarding can be unnerving, if you are responsible and prepared, it will only take 15 to 30 minutes and will be a non-event. First, have your boat in order. This includes having your vessel documentation, registration and insurance documents on hand, as well as your passport. Organize this in a binder and keep it in the nav station so you don't have to fumble around looking for documents and paperwork. You will need to acknowledge the location of any weapons on board and show a permit (when required by state law).

As they begin to inspect your boat, the officers will focus on areas with the largest safety concerns, including the following.

**Life Jackets:** All vessels must have one wearable personal floatation device (PFD) for each person on board, as well as a throwable (Type IV) device for boats over 16 feet. Life jackets must be U.S. Coast Guard approved, in good/serviceable condition, of appropriate size and type for intended user and properly stowed.

**Visual Distress Signals:** All vessels 16 feet and over must be equipped with visual distress signals, such as flares or flags, and flares must be up to date (e.g., not expired)

**Sound Producing Devices:** A whistle, horn, siren, etc. capable of a 4-second blast audible for 0.5 mile must be on board for use during periods of reduced visibility. Boats over 39.4 feet and over must also have a bell.

**Navigation Lights:** All boats over 16 feet must have working navigational lights and an independent all-around anchor light.

**Fire Extinguisher:** U.S. Coast Guard-approved, marine-type fire extinguishers are required on boats where a fire hazard could be expected from the engines or fuel system. They must be in good working condition and readily accessible. (Number of units required depends on vessel length.)

**Ventilation:** Boats built after 1 August 1980 with gasoline engines in closed compartments must have a powered ventilation system.

**Backfire Flame Arrester:** All gasoline-powered inboard/outboard or inboard motor boats must be equipped with an approved backfire flame arrester.

**Pollution Placard:** It is illegal to discharge oil or oily waste into any navigable waters of the U.S. Boats over 26 feet must display an oily waste "pollution" placard.

**MARPOL Trash Placard:** It is illegal to dump plastic trash anywhere in the ocean or navigable waters of the U.S. It is also illegal to discharge garbage in the navigable waters of the U.S., including the inland waters and anywhere in the Great Lakes. Vessels of 26 feet or longer must display a durable placard at least 4 by 9 inches in a prominent location, notifying the crew and passengers of the discharge restrictions.

**Navigation Rules:** Boats 39.4 feet and over must have a copy of current navigation rules on board.

**Marine Sanitation Devices:** The discharge of treated sewage is allowed within 3 nm of shore except in designated "No Discharge Zone" areas. The Coast Guard will check that overboard discharge outlets can be sealed (and are, if required).

These requirements are detailed in a **downloadable boater's guide** at uscgboating.org/images/420.PDF. State and local requirements are also considered. If there is a minor violation, they may give you a written warning explaining what needs to be fixed to be in compliance. If you are found with a small violation and correct it quickly, then this will merely be a chance to interact with those whose goal is to keep you as safe as possible on the water.

# VHF Communications

Skippers traveling the U.S. inland waterways use their VHF radios almost every day to contact other vessels and bridge tenders, make reservations at marinas, arrange to pass other vessels safely and conduct other business. Waterway Guide has put together the following information to help remove any confusion as to what frequency should be dialed in to call bridges, marinas, commercial ships or your friend anchored down the creek. Remember to use low power (1 watt) for your radio transmission whenever possible. If you are within a couple of miles of the responding station (bridge, marina or other craft) there is no need to broadcast at 25 watts and disturb the transmissions of others 25 miles away.

## Channel Usage Tips

■ VHF Channel 16 (156.8 MHz) is by far the most important frequency on the VHF-FM band. VHF Channel 16 is the international distress, safety and calling frequency.

■ If you have a VHF radio on your boat, FCC regulations require that you to maintain a watch on either VHF Channel 09 or 16 whenever you are underway and the radio is not being used to communicate on another channel. Since the Coast Guard does not have the capability of announcing an urgent marine information broadcast or weather warning on VHF Channel 09, it recommends that boaters normally keep tuned to and use VHF Channel 16, but no conversations of any length should take place there; its primary function is for emergencies only.

■ The Coast Guard's main working VHF Channel is 22A, and both emergency and non-emergency calls generally are switched to it in order to keep VHF Channel 16 clear. Calling the Coast Guard for a radio check on VHF Channel 16 is prohibited.

■ Radio-equipped bridges in SC, GA and FL use VHF Channel 09, with a few exceptions.

■ Recreational craft typically communicate on VHF Channels 68, 69, 71, 72 or 78A. Whenever possible, avoid calling on VHF Channel 16 altogether by prearranging initial contact directly on one of these channels. No transmissions should last longer than 3 minutes.

Coast Guard radio communication radar tower

■ The Bridge-to-Bridge Radio Telephone Act requires many commercial vessels, including dredges and tugboats, to monitor VHF Channel 13. VHF Channel 13 is also the frequency used by bridges in several states.

Note: The Coast Guard has asked the FCC to eliminate provisions for using VHF **Channel 09** as an alternative calling frequency to VHF Channel 16 when it eliminates watch-keeping on VHF Channel 16 by compulsory-equipped vessels.

## Distress Calls

**MAYDAY:** The distress signal "MAYDAY" is used to indicate that a vessel is threatened by grave and imminent danger and requests immediate assistance.

**PAN PAN:** The urgency signal "PAN PAN" is used when the safety of the ship or person is in jeopardy.

**SÉCURITÉ:** The safety signal "SÉCURITÉ" is used for messages about the safety of navigation or important weather warnings.

VHF Channel 16 is the distress call frequency. The codeword "MAYDAY" is the international alert signal of a life-threatening situation at sea. After a MAYDAY message is broadcast, VHF Channel 16 must be kept free of all traffic, other than those directly involved in the rescue situation, until the rescue has been completed. If you hear a MAYDAY message and no one else is responding, it is your duty to step in to answer the call, relay it to the nearest rescue organization and get to the scene to help. Remember, a MAYDAY distress call can only be used when life is threatened. For example, if you have run on the rocks but no one is going to lose their life, that is NOT a MAYDAY situation.

| VHF Channels | |
|---|---|
| **09** | Used for radio checks and hailing other stations (boats, shoreside operations). Also used to communicate with drawbridges in Florida. |
| **13** | Used to contact and communicate with commercial vessels, military ships and drawbridges. Bridges in several states monitor VHF Channel 13. |
| **16** | *Emergency use only.* May be used to hail other vessels, but once contact is made, conversation should be immediately switched to a working (68, 69, 71, 72, 78A) VHF channel. |
| **22** | Used for U.S. Coast Guard safety, navigation and Sécurité communications. |
| **68** **69** **71** **72** **78A** | Used primarily for recreational ship-to-ship and ship-to-shore communications. |

## How to Make a Distress Call
*Hello All Ships. MAYDAY! MAYDAY! MAYDAY!*

**This is:** Give your vessel name and call sign.

**Our position is:** Read it off the GPS, or give it as something like "two miles southwest of Royal Island." (Your rescuers must be able to find you!)

**We are:** Describe what's happening (e.g., on fire/hit a reef/sinking)

**We have:** Report how many people are on board

**At this time we are:** Say what you're doing about the crisis (e.g., standing by/abandoning ship)

**For identification we are:** Describe your boat: type, length, color, etc. (so your rescuers can more readily identify you)

**We have:** List safety equipment you have e.g., flares/smoke/ocean dye markers/EPIRB

*We will keep watch on Channel 16 as long as we can.*

# Ditch Bag Checklist

## Rescue Items

- [ ] Functioning, registered EPIRB
- [ ] Handheld VHF radio (waterproof or in sealed pouch, with extra batteries)
- [ ] Sea anchor, drogue and line
- [ ] Manual inflation pump
- [ ] Selection of flares (parachute and handheld) and smoke signals
- [ ] Strobe light (may be present in inflatable PFD)
- [ ] Flashlight & batteries (headlamp is ideal)
- [ ] Whistle (may be present in inflatable PFD)
- [ ] Signal mirror
- [ ] Handheld GPS or compass (for position)
- [ ] Small pair of binoculars (to confirm a boat or plane spotting before using flares)

## Survival Items

- [ ] Sponges and bailer (with handle)
- [ ] Patch kit for inflatable dinghy or life raft (or emergency clamps)
- [ ] Water (individually sealed or in collapsible containers)–at least 2 gallons per person
- [ ] Emergency food rations and can opener (if needed)
- [ ] Power Bars
- [ ] Prescription medications
- [ ] Seasickness medications/remedies
- [ ] First aid kit
- [ ] Multipurpose tool or sailor's knife
- [ ] Waterproof matches

## Other Items

- [ ] Solar blanket
- [ ] Heavy-duty coated gloves
- [ ] Duct tape
- [ ] Sewing kit
- [ ] Simple fishing gear (line, jigs, hooks, etc.)
- [ ] Polypropylene line
- [ ] Waterproof sunscreen and zinc oxide
- [ ] Bug repellent
- [ ] Ziploc bags (gallon size)
- [ ] Paper and pen in Ziploc bag
- [ ] Spare prescription glasses and sunglasses (polarized to reduce glare)
- [ ] Laminated copies of passports or license
- [ ] Cash ($50 in small bills)
- [ ] Copy of the yacht's papers (including insurance)

# Customs

perators of small pleasure vessels arriving in the United ates from a foreign port are required to report their rival to Customs and Border Patrol (CBP) immediately. BP has designated specific reporting locations within ie Field Offices that are staffed during boating season or pleasure boats to report their arrival and be inspected y CBP. When clearing back in to the U.S., the master f the boat must call in to the CBP (see numbers under Ports of Entry") so as to be directed to the nearest Port f Entry to satisfy the face-to-face requirement, or to ie nearest designated reporting location for inspection. Only the captain may disembark to make this call; all thers must await clearance onboard.

You may be required to rent a car or take a cab to the earest airport or federal office several miles away for the nspection. These offices are often closed on weekends. f your arrival is after working hours, you are required o stay on board and clear in the next morning. You must clear in within 24 hours of your arrival. Everyone on board, regardless of nationality, has to report in person. U.S. nationals must take their passports or passport cards. All non-U.S. Nationals should take their passports with valid visas and a Green Card, if held. Take your boat papers, either U.S. documentation or state registration with state decal number. You will need o show:

- Registered name of vessel and the declared home port
- Your FCC call sign
- Your hull identification number
- LOA, LWL, beam and draft

Additionally, have a list of firearms and ammunition on board.

## Advance Notice of Arrival (Foreign Vessels)

With limited exceptions, the Coast Guard Advance Notice of Arrival (ANOA) regulations apply to foreign vessels bound for or departing from ports in the United States. The requirement does not apply to U.S. recreational vessels.

There are various methods for submitting an ANOA, but the preferred method is electronically via the web site at the National Vessel Movement Center (NVMC). If the vessel is on a voyage of 96 hours or more, the ANOA

must be received by the NVMC at least 96 hours before the vessel enters a port or place in the U.S. If the voyage is of less than 96 hours, the ANOA must be received by the NVMC before the vessel departs for the U.S. port, but at least 24 hours before entering the port. To access the electronic ANOA, go to enoad.nvmc.uscg.gov. The form can be completed and sent to the NVMC from that link. The NVMC can also be contacted at 800-708-9823 or 304-264-2502.

## Exceptions to Face-to-Face Reporting (U.S. Vessels)
### Small Vessel Reporting System

The Small Vessel Reporting System (SVRS) is a voluntary effort that allows eligible, frequent pleasure boat operators and passengers, who are U.S. Citizens or Lawful Permanent Residents (LPRs) of the United States, to register with CBP. SVRS offers facilitated customs and immigration clearance for recreational low-risk boaters at time of arrival. Enrollment in SVRS is voluntary and allows CBP to expedite the arrival reporting process to boaters who have enrolled in the program. This program satisfies the boat operator's legal requirement to report to a port-of-entry for face-to-face inspection, but boaters must still phone in their arrival.

## Applying for participation in SVRS is an easy three-step process:

1. Complete an online application.
2. Schedule your appointment for an interview by phone or online.
3. Participate in your interview and present your documents to the CBP Officer.

The enrollment system is web-based and can be accessed at svrs.cbp.dhs.gov. New applicants register online and self-schedule an interview with a CBP officer at an authorized reporting location of their choice. Participants receive an email with their Boater Registration (BR) number and password for SVRS.

## NEXUS (entry from Canada)

NEXUS Marine program is a joint Canada–U.S. initiative that offers facilitated customs and immigration clearance for recreational low-risk boaters entering either country through registration into the program. NEXUS is valid for 5 years and satisfies the boat operator's legal requirement to report to a port-of-entry for face-to-face inspection, but boaters must still phone in their arrival.

## Canadian Border Boat Landing Permit (I-68)

Canadian Border Boat Landing Permit (I-68) applicants for admission into the U.S. by small pleasure boats are inspected and issued an I-68 permit for the entire boating season. The I-68 permit allows boaters to enter the U.S. from Canada for recreational purposes with only the need to report to CBP by telephoning in their arrival. Persons who are not U.S. citizens or lawful permanent residents of the United States may use Form I-68 for visits not to exceed 72 hours to visit within 25 miles of the shoreline along the U.S. border with Canada. Designated offices are listed at cbp.gov/travel/pleasure-boats-private-flyers/cbbl.

## OARS (entry from Canada)

Outlying Area Reporting System (OARS) is another northern border method for boaters to report entry to satisfy 19USC and 8CFR requirements into the U.S. from Canada. The OARS program uses videophones, typically located at public marinas, which boaters may use to report to CBP.

Masters must report their arrival to U.S. Customs and Border Protection if having been engaged in any of the below activities:

- After having been at any foreign port or place
- After having had contact with any hovering vessel

## Reporting Procedure

Procedures vary, depending on the port so it is best to call ahead. In most cases, the master or designee may go ashore only to report the arrival to U.S. Customs and Border Protection either in person or by telephone. No other person may leave or board the boat and no baggage or merchandise may be removed or loaded until the report of arrival is made and release granted by a U.S. Customs and Border Protection Officer. Failure to do so can result in civil fines.

## Designated Ports of Entry

### Florida
*(Call 800-432-1216 or 800-451-0393 to report arrivals.)*

| | |
|---|---|
| Fernandina Beach | 904-261-6154 |
| Ft. Myers | 239-561-6205 |
| Jacksonville | 904-360-5020 |
| Panama City | 850-785-4688 |
| Pensacola | 850-433-3205 |
| Cape Canaveral | 321-783-2066 |
| Daytona Beach | 386-248-8043 |
| West Palm Beach | 561-844-1703 |
| Pt. Manatee | 941-729-9301 |
| St. Petersburg | 727-536-7311 |
| Tampa | 813-712-6000 |
| Miami | 305-536-4878 |
| Pt. Everglades | 954-761-2000 |
| Key West | 305-296-5411 |

### Gulf States
*(Report to individual stations or call 1-800-973-2867 after hours.)*

| | |
|---|---|
| Mobile, AL | 251-378-7600 |
| Pascagoula, MS | 228-762-7311 |
| Gulfport, MS | 228-863-6350 |
| New Orleans, LA | 504-623-6600 |
| Morgan City, LA | 985-632-8182 |
| Lake Charles, LA | 337-439-5512 |

### Texas
*(Report to individual stations or call after hours numbers shown following main numbers below.)*

| | |
|---|---|
| Port Arthur | 409-727-0285 / 800-973-2867 |
| Sabine | 409-727-2895 / 800-973-2867 |
| Houston Seaport | 409-766-3581 / 800-973-2867 or 713-454-8002 |
| Freeport | 979-233-3004 / 800-973-2867 or 713-454-8002 |
| Corpus Christi | 361-879-4400 / 800-973-2867 |
| Brownsville | 956-983-5800 / 956-542-6201 |

# Port Security

In the United States, the U.S. Coast Guard and Customs and Border Patrol–both components of the Department of Homeland Security–handle port security. Local law enforcement agencies and the FBI also have a role in port security at the local and regional level. Each year, more than 11 million maritime containers arrive at our seaports. At land borders, another 11 million arrive by truck and 2.7 million by rail. Homeland Security is responsible for knowing what is inside those containers, whether it poses a risk to the American people and ensuring that all proper revenues are collected.

As an example, one in five food items is now imported. American consumers demand fresh limes and blueberries all year round and, as a result, during the winter months in the U.S., nearly 80 percent of the fresh fruits and vegetables on our tables come from other countries. With the ever-increasing amount of trade, the agricultural risks to the United States grow. The threat to crops and livestock is real.

In response to this threat and others, the U.S. Coast Guard has established "protection zones" around all U.S. naval vessels, tank vessels and large-capacity cruise vessels, even when underway. U.S. Navy bases, U.S. Coast Guard bases and some shoreside facilities, such as nuclear power plants, are also in protection zones. Non-military vessels (this means YOU) are not allowed within 100 yards of these protection zones. To do so can rack up serious civil penalties and even imprisonment. These protection zones vary from port to port and from facility to facility, but ignorance of the protection zones is not a viable excuse. Having said that, law-abiding boaters sometimes find themselves unable to comply with the letter of the law without hitting a jetty, for example. In such cases, common sense and good communication should prevail.

Government officials view the recreational boating community as an ally. We can do our part (and perhaps stave off more stringent regulations and surveillance

measures) by becoming familiar with the Coast Guard's America's Waterway Watch program. Think of it as a neighborhood watch program for the waterways.

It is not the intent of America's Waterway Watch to spread paranoia or to encourage spying on one another, and it is not a surveillance program; instead, it is a simple deterrent to potential terrorist activity. The purpose of the program is to allow boaters and others who spend time along the water to help the authorities counter crime and terrorism. To report suspicious behavior, call the National Response Center at 877-249-2824. For immediate danger to life or property, call 911, or call the Coast Guard on Marine VHF-FM Channel 16.

This section includes a list of ports and places that require a little forethought and vigilance on your part. Following the steps in the action plan below will help ensure a trouble-free journey and keep you and your crew out of the headlines.

## Prepare:

■ Before you leave, check the current charts for the area in which you will be traveling and identify any security areas. Security zones are highlighted and outlined in magenta with special notes regarding the specific regulations pertaining to that area.

■ Check the latest *Local Notice to Mariners* (available online at navcen.uscg and posted at some marinas) and identify any potential security areas that may not be shown on the chart.

■ Listen to VHF Channel 16 for any Sécurité alerts from the Coast Guard (departing cruise ships, Naval vessels, fuel tankers, etc.) for the area you will be cruising prior to your departure.

■ Talk to other boaters in your anchorage or marina about the areas where you will be traveling. They may have tips and suggestions on any potential security zones or special areas they may have encountered on their way.

## Stay Alert While Underway:

■ Mind the outlined magenta security areas noted on your charts.

■ Look for vessels with blue or red warning lights in port areas and, if approached, listen carefully and strictly obey all instructions given to you.

■ Keep your VHF radio switched to VHF Channel 16 and keep your ears tuned for bulletins, updates and possible requests for communication.

■ Avoid commercial port operation areas, especially those that involve military, cruise line or petroleum facilities. Observe and avoid other restricted areas near power plants, national monuments, etc.

■ If you need to pass within 100 yards of a U.S. Naval vessel for safe passage, you must contact the U.S. Naval vessel or the Coast Guard escort vessel on VHF Channel 16 to let them know your intentions.

■ If government security or the U.S. Coast Guard hails you, do exactly what they say, regardless of whether or not you feel their instructions have merit.

## Sensitive Southern Ports

■ **PORT OF FERNANDINA, FL**
Provides terminal service to numerous pulp and paper producers located throughout Florida and the southeast. In addition, the Port has expanded in providing steel export services to several steel mills in the southeast.

■ **PORT OF JACKSONVILLE (JAXPORT), FL**
One of the largest and busiest cargo ports in the South Atlantic and also a bustling cruise port.

■ **PORT CANAVERAL, FL**
Major cruise port that is home to several year-round and seasonal cruise lines with a solid and growing cargo market.

■ **PORT OF PALM BEACH, FL**
Important distribution center for commodities and offers on-deck rail via its own locomotive and 5 miles of track.

■ **PORT EVERGLADES, FL**
One of the busiest cruise ports in the world. The Port is a leading container port and south Florida's main seaport for receiving petroleum products, including gasoline, jet fuel and alternative fuels.

■ **PORT MIAMI, FL**
Recognized throughout the world with the dual distinction of being the Cruise Capital of the World and the Cargo Gateway of the Americas.

## PORT OF KEY WEST, FL

Consists of numerous cruise berths as well as a private pier. The City also supports a domestic ferry operation in Key West Bight. These facilities constitute one of the busiest ports-of-call in the nation.

## PORT MANATEE, FL

Multi-purpose deep-water seaport, handling a variety of bulk, containerized and heavy-lift project cargoes. Located on Tampa Bay, the Port is the closest U.S. deep water port to the Panama Canal and has plans for expansion.

## PORT TAMPA BAY, FL

Largest of the Florida ports, as measured by tonnage and land. The Port is major port-of-entry for all types of cargo and cruise passengers and a major center for shipbuilding and repair.

## PORT PANAMA CITY, FL

Provides modern seaport facilities for a variety of bulk and containerized cargo. The Port provides central services to several major manufacturing companies.

## PORT OF PENSACOLA, FL

Known as northwest Florida's gateway to the world, the Port has existed since 1754 due to local and regional business interests. It continues to attract diverse business lines.

## PORT OF MOBILE, AL

Only deep-water port in the State of Alabama. The Port has public, deep water terminals with direct access to 1,500 miles of inland and intracoastal waterways serving the Great Lakes, the Ohio and Tennessee river valleys (via the Tennessee-Tombigbee Waterway) and the Gulf of Mexico.

## PORT OF SOUTH LOUISIANA

Not only the largest port in the US, it is also the largest port in the Western Hemisphere (based on tonnage). Goods can be loaded onto a barge at any point on the Mississippi River and be transferred to overseas destinations at the Port.

## PORT OF HOUSTON, TX

One of the largest seaports in the U.S., which mostly exports petroleum-related products, although it also exports tens of millions of dollars worth of machinery every year, as well as several million tons of cereals, steel and other raw materials to other countries.

## PORT OF GALVESTON, TX

The only port in Texas that serves as a base for cruise ships. The Port also has major tanker traffic.

## PORT OF CORPUS CHRISTI, TX

Provides quick access to the Gulf, the U.S. inland waterway system and the world beyond. This busy Port imports crude oil and gas and exports fuel oil in support of area refineries, as well as other commodities.

## OTHER TEXAS PORTS

Beaumont, Brownsville, Calhoun Port Authority, Freeport, Halingen, Palacious, Port Arthur, Port Isabel, Port Mansfield, Texas City, Victoria and West Calhoun.

| Additional Resources |
|---|
| **Department of Homeland Security:** dhs.gov |
| **U.S. Customs and Border Protection:** cbp.gov |
| **Local Notice to Mariners:** navcen.uscg.gov (then click on "LNMS" on the top menu bar) |
| **Florida Ports Council:** flaports.org |
| **Texas Ports Association:** texasports.org |
| **Atlantic Intracoastal Waterway Association:** atlintracoastal.org |
| **America's Waterway Watch:** americaswaterwaywatch.org |

# State Registration & Fees

Remember that as you cross state lines in your vessel, boating laws will change, as described below. Mandatory education requirements to operate a boat, for example, vary from state to state. It's also important to know that not all states accept out-of-state boater education certification for visitors afloat. In most cases, however, a boater education certificate, issued by your home state and bearing the NASBLA seal, will satisfy the requirements of the state you're visiting, either in your own boat or when operating a friend's boat there.

The bottom line in vessel registration and education is: Know before you go. Make sure you display a valid registration sticker from your home state and follow your host state's regulations. Some specifics are provided here, but this information is subject to change, so visit the individual web sites listed below for additional information and updates.

## Alabama
**Registration Grace Period:** 90 days
**Boat Sales & Use Tax Rate:** 2%
**Boater License:** To legally operate a boat in the state, you must be at least 12 years old and have an operator's license obtained by successfully completing a boater safety course. If you are 12 or 13, you must have a currently licensed boat driver in the vessel. That person must be at least 21 years old, and able to take immediate control of the boat, if necessary.
**Boating Registration:**
outdooralabama.com/boat-registration
**State Tax Department:** revenue.alabama.gov

## Florida
**Registration Grace Period:** 90 days
**Boat Sales & Use Tax Rate:** 6%
**Notes:** Sales tax is capped at $18,000. Vessels brought into the state for repair exempt from registration requirement. Boats are registered at the county level; check with the county tax office.
**Boater License**: Anyone born on or after January 1, 1988 must have proof of the completion of a State-approved boater safety course in order to operate a boat or PWC with a horsepower of 10 or greater.
**Boating Registration:** flhsmv.gov/dmv/FFFVO.pdf
**State Tax Department:** floridarevenue.com

## Louisiana
**Registration Grace Period:** 90 days
**Boat Sales & Use Tax Rate:** 5%
**Boater License:** Anyone born on or after January 1, 1984 must have proof of the completion of a State-approved boater safety course in order to operate a boat or PWC with a horsepower of 10 or greater. Otherwise, you must have with you either someone who is at least 18 years and has completed the course, or someone who is exempt from the requirement. Further, it is unlawful for anyone under 16 years of age to operate a PWC.
**Boating Registration:**
wlf.louisiana.gov/boating/boat-title-and-registration
**State Tax Department:** rev.state.la.us

## Mississippi
**Registration Grace Period:** 60 days
**Boat Sales & Use Tax Rate:** 7%
**Boater License:** Anyone born on or after June 30, 1980 must have proof of the completion of a State-approved boater safety course in order to operate a boat or PWC with a horsepower of 10 or greater.
**Boating Registration:**
mdwfp.com/license/boating-registration
**State Tax Department:** dor.ms.gov

## Texas
**Registration Grace Period:** 90 days
**Boat Sales & Use Tax Rate:** 6.25%
**Boater License:** Anyone born on or after September 1, 1993 proof of the completion of a State-approved boater safety course in order to operate a boat.
**Boating Registration:**
tpwd.state.tx.us/fishboat/boat/owner/titles_and_registration
**State Tax Department:** comptroller.texas.gov/taxes

# Rules of the Road

Anyone planning to cruise our waterways should make themselves familiar with the rules of the road. *Chapman Piloting: Seamanship and Small Boat Handling* and *The Annapolis Book of Seamanship* are both excellent on-the-water references with plentiful information on navigation rules. For those with a penchant for the exact regulatory language, the Coast Guard publication *Navigation Rules: International–Inland* covers both international and U.S. inland rules. (Boats over 39.4 feet are required to carry a copy of the U.S. Inland Rules at all times.) These rules are also available online at navcen.uscg.gov. Click on NavRules on the top menu bar.

The following is a list of common situations you will likely encounter on the waterways. Make yourself familiar with them, and if you ever have a question as to which of you has the right-of-way, let the other vessel go first. Sailors need to remember that a boat under sail with its engine running is considered a motorboat.

## Passing or being passed:

■ If you intend to pass a slower vessel, try to hail them on your VHF radio to let them know you are coming.

■ In close quarters, BOTH vessels should slow down. Slowing down normally allows the faster vessel to pass quickly without throwing a large wake onto the slower boat.

■ Slower boats being passed have the right-of-way and passing vessels must keep clear of these slower vessels.

■ As you pass a slower boat, take a look back to see how they were affected by your wake. Remember: YOU are responsible for your wake. It is the law to slow down, and it is common courtesy.

## At opening bridges:

■ During an opening, boats traveling with the current go first and generally have the right-of-way.

■ Boats constrained by their draft, size or maneuverability (e.g., dredges, tugs and barges) also take priority.

■ Standard rules of the road apply while circling or waiting for a bridge opening.

## Tugs, freighters, dredges and naval vessels:

■ These vessels are usually constrained by draft or their inability to easily maneuver. For this reason, you will almost always need to give them the right-of-way and keep out of their path.

■ You must keep at least 100 yards away from any Navy vessel. If you cannot safely navigate without coming closer than this, you must notify the ship of your intentions over VHF Channel 16.

■ Keep a close watch for freighters, tugs with tows and other large vessels while offshore or in crowded ports. They often come up very quickly, despite their large size.

■ It is always a good practice to radio larger vessels (VHF Channel 13 or 16) to notify them of your location and your intentions. The skippers of these boats are generally appreciative of efforts to communicate with them. This is especially true with dredge boats on all the waterways.

## In a crossing situation:

- When two vessels under power are crossing and a risk of collision exists, the vessel that has the other on her starboard side must keep clear and avoid crossing ahead of the other vessel.

- When a vessel under sail and a vessel under power are crossing, the boat under power is usually burdened and must keep clear. The same exceptions apply as per head-on meetings.

- On the Great Lakes and western rivers (e.g., the Mississippi River system), a power-driven vessel crossing a river shall keep clear of a power-driven vessel ascending or descending the river.

## Power vessels meeting any other vessel:

- When two vessels under power (either sailboats or powerboats) meet "head-to-head," both are obliged to alter course to starboard.

- Generally, when a vessel under power meets a vessel under sail (i.e., not using any mechanical power), the powered vessel must alter course accordingly.

- Exceptions are vessels not under command, vessels restricted in ability to maneuver, vessels engaged in commercial fishing or those under International Rules, such as a vessel constrained by draft.

## Two sailboats meeting under sail:

- When each has the wind on a different side, the boat with the wind on the port side must keep clear of the boat with the wind on the starboard side.

- When both have the wind on the same side, the vessel closest to the wind (windward) will keep clear of the leeward boat.

- A vessel with wind to port that sees a vessel to windward but cannot determine whether the windward vessel has wind to port or starboard will assume that windward vessel is on starboard tack and keep clear.

# Reference Materials

## NOAA Charts & Corrections

**Print on Demand Paper Charts:** Updated weekly and available from NOAA-certified agents. Orders shipped next business day. For a complete list, see: nauticalcharts.noaa.gov/staff/print_agents.html.

**PDF Nautical Charts:** Updated weekly. Available at charts.noaa.gov/PDFs/PDFs.shtml.

**Raster Nautical Charts:** Full-color digital images of NOAA paper charts. Compatible with most marine navigation software and available for free at charts.noaa.gov/InteractiveCatalog/nrnc.shtml.

**Booklet Charts:** Reduced in scale and divided into pages for convenience, but otherwise contains all the information of the full-scale nautical chart. Updated weekly. Available at nauticalcharts.noaa.gov/staff/BookletChart.html.

**USCG *Local Notice to Mariners*:** Provides timely marine safety information for the correction of all US Government navigation charts and publications from a wide variety of sources, both foreign and domestic. Divided by district. Updated weekly and available in .pdf format at navcen.uscg.gov. (Select LNMs tab at top of page.)

## Navigation

- *NAVIGATION RULES, INTERNATIONAL— INLAND*, U.S. Dept. of Homeland Security. The US Coast Guard requires all vessels over 12 meters [39 feet] carry this book of the national and international rules of the road. Can be downloaded as a .pdf from navcen.uscg.gov.

- *U.S. Coast Pilot (1-5)*, NOAA. Includes piloting information for coasts, bays, creeks and harbors. Also includes tide tables and highlights restricted areas. Updated weekly and can be downloaded as a .pdf at nauticalcharts.noaa.gov/nsd/cpdownload.htm.

- *A Boaters Guide to the Federal Requirements for Recreational Boats*, U.S. Coast Guard. Can be downloaded as a .pdf from uscgboating.org.

**NOAA Chart No 1. Symbols, Abbreviations and Terms, NOAA/DoD can be downloaded as a .pdf from nauticalcharts.noaa.gov.**

## Maintenance

- *Boatowner's Mechanical & Electrical Manual*, Nigel Calder

- *Boatowner's Illustrated Electrical Handbook*, Charlie Wing

- *Boat Mechanical Systems Handbook*, David Gerr

## Seamanship

- *The Annapolis Book of Seamanship (4th Edition)*, John Rousmaniere

- *The Art of Seamanship*, Ralph Naranjo

- *Boater's Pocket Reference*, Thomas McEwen

- *Boat Owners Mechanical and Electrical Manual (4th Edition)*, Nigel Calder

- *Chapman Piloting & Seamanship (67th Edition)*, Charles B. Husick

- *Eldridge Tide and Pilot Book* (annual), Robert E. and Linda White

- *Heavy Weather Sailing (6th Edition)*, Peter Bruce

- *Nigel Calder's Cruising Handbook*, Nigel Calder

- *Offshore Cruising Encyclopedia*, Steve and Linda Dashew

- *World Cruising Essentials*, Jimmy Cornell

## First Aid & Medical

- *Advanced First Aid Afloat (5th Edition)*, Dr. Peter F. Eastman

- *DAN Pocket Guide to First Aid for Scuba Diving*, Dan Orr & Bill Clendenden

- *First Aid at Sea*, Douglas Justin and Colin Berry

- *Marine Medicine: A Comprehensive Guide (2nd Edition)*, Eric Weiss and Michael Jacobs

- *On-Board Medical Emergency Handbook: First Aid at Sea*, Spike Briggs and Campbell Mackenzie

# Useful Apps

## General Reference

- **BOAT LIGHTS ($3.99):**
Simple app for identifying navigation lights, shapes and sounds on the water

- **BOAT RAMPS (FREE):**
Quickly locate directions to more than 35,000 boat ramps throughout the U.S.

- **BOATERS POCKET REFERENCE ($4.99):**
Offers how-to information on piloting and navigation, communication, boating regulations, weather and more

- **COMPLETE BOATING LOGBOOK ($4.99):**
Includes logbook, fuel log, expense log, maintenance log, vessel log, shopping list and to do list

## Marinas & Facilities

- **WATERWAY GUIDE MARINAS APP (FREE):**
Detailed listings for over 3,700 marinas and boatyards; set preferences and GPS mapping to filter out only the locations that can best serve your vessel

## Tides

- **AYE TIDES ($7.99):**
Displays tides and/or currents for over 12,500 locations worldwide; does not require a network connection

- **NOAA BUOY AND TIDE DATA ($1.99):**
Provides tide and weather data from NOAA's National Data Buoy Center

- **TIDES NEAR ME (FREE):**
Focuses on nearby stations and current tidal conditions

- **USA TIDES (FREE):**
Choose tides (data or graph) for any station and any date; includes tide events as well as sunrise, sunset, moonrise and moonset

## Safety

- **BOATUS (FREE) or SEATOW (FREE):**
Share your location and call for assistance with either of these apps

- **BOAT SAFE (FREE):**
Create a plan and email to participants or emergency contacts

- **DRAG QUEEN ANCHOR ALARM (FREE) or ANCHOR WATCH ($0.99):**
Both provide alarms if anchor drag is detected based on your phone's GPS

- **BOAT BEACON ($12.99):**
Uses real-time AIS data; only AIS ship tracking app to provide collision warnings and share your boat's position

- **MARINE TRAFFIC ($4.99) or SHIP FINDER ($6.99):**
Uses real-time AIS data to target location of other vessels

- **MAN OVER-BOARD ($4.99):**
Shows the position of a man overboard (latitude and longitude) and the direction and distance back

- **SOS & MORSE (FREE):**
Turns your cell phone into a signaling device

# Talking About the Weather

Every day on the water can't entail balmy breezes, abundant sunshine and consistently warm weather; however, staying out of bad weather is relatively easy if you plan ahead. The National Weather Service (NWS) provides mariners with continuous broadcasts of weather warnings, forecasts, radar reports and buoy reports over VHF-FM and Single Side Band (SSB) radio. Reception range for VHF radios is usually up to 40 miles from the antenna site, although Florida stations are frequently picked up in the near Bahamas. There are almost no areas on the U.S. coast where a good quality, fixed-mount VHF cannot pick up one or more coastal VHF broadcasts. Also, there is no substitute for simply looking at the sky, and either stay put or seek shelter if you don't like what you see.

## SSB Offshore Weather

SSB reports are broadcast from station NMN in Chesapeake, VA and from station NMG in New Orleans, LA. The broadcasts are not continuous, so refer to the latest schedules and frequency lists (see sidebar) to catch them. SSB reports provide the best source of voice offshore weather information. Two major broadcasts alternate throughout the day. The High Seas Forecast provides information for mariners well offshore, including those crossing the North Atlantic Ocean. Coastal cruisers will be more interested in the Offshore Forecast, which includes information on waters more than 50 miles from shore. The forecast is divided into regions.

| Weather Apps |
|---|
| Boating Weather ($1.99) |
| Buoy Weather (FREE) |
| Marine Weather by AccuWeather (FREE) |
| NOAA SuperRes Radar HD ($2.99) |
| PredictWind (FREE) |
| Storm Radar (FREE) |
| Weather Underground (FREE) |
| Windfinder (FREE) |
| Windyty (FREE) |

| Weather Online |
|---|
| Accuweather (accuweather.com) |
| Windfinder (windfinder.com) |
| Buoy Weather (buoyweather.com) |
| National Hurricane Center (nhc.noaa.gov) |
| National Weather Service (weather.gov) |
| NOAA Marine Forecasts (nws.noaa.gov/om/marine) |
| Passage Weather (passageweather.com) |
| Predict Wind (predictwind.com) |
| Sailflow (sailflow.com) |
| The Weather Channel (weather.com) |
| Weather Underground (wunderground.com/MAR) |

## SSB Weather Frequencies

| UTC | Chesapeake, VA NMN Frequencies (kHz) | New Orleans, LA NMG Frequencies (kHz) |
|---|---|---|
| 0330 (Offshore) | 4426.0, 6501.0, 8764.0 | 4316.0, 8502.0, 12788.0 |
| 0515 (High Seas) | 4426.0, 6501.0, 8764.0 | 4316.0, 8502.0, 12788.0 |
| 0930 (Offshore) | 4426.0, 6501.0, 8764.0 | 4316.0, 8502.0, 12788.0 |
| 1115 (High Seas) | 6501.0, 8764.0, 13089.0 | 4316.0, 8502.0, 12788.0 |
| 1530 (Offshore) | 6501.0, 8764.0, 13089.0 | 4316.0, 8502.0, 12788.0 |
| 1715 (High Seas) | 8764.0, 13089.0, 17314.0 | 4316.0, 8502.0, 12788.0 |
| 2130 (Offshore) | 6501.0, 8764.0, 13089.0 | 4316.0, 8502.0, 12788.0 |
| 2315 (High Seas) | 6501.0, 8764.0, 13089.0 | 4316.0, 8502.0, 12788.0 |

*(UTC, or Coordinated Universal Time, is equivalent to Greenwich Mean Time)*

## VHF-FM/NOAA Weather Frequencies

| | |
|---|---|
| WX1 | 162.550 MHz |
| WX2 | 162.400 MHz |
| WX3 | 162.475 MHz |
| WX4 | 162.425 MHz |
| WX5 | 162.450 MHz |
| WX6 | 162.500 MHz |
| WX7 | 162.525 MHz |

# Lightning Safety

Water and metal are excellent conductors of electricity, making boating in a thunderstorm a risky prospect. Several coastal Florida cities are among the most lightning-prone in the U.S., according to the World Meteorological Organization (WMO). Some of the cities that made the "Top 10" and average number of thunderstorms per year are: Fort Myers (88 days), Tampa (82.7 days), Tallahassee (82.5 days), West Palm Beach (76.8 days), Daytona Beach (73.4 days) and Miami (72.3 days). But Florida isn't alone in this dubious honor: Lake Charles, Louisiana, also made the top of the list (75.8 days), as did Mobile, Alabama (75.5 days). While the odds of a given boat being hit are small, the consequences are severe and deadly. Do not try and play the odds!

The best advice if you are out on the water and skies are threatening is get back to land and seek safe shelter, but that's not always practical for cruisers who live aboard or are not near land.

## Reading the Skies

Thunderstorms occur when air masses of different temperatures meet over inland or coastal waters. An example of this would be when air with a high humidity that is warm near the ground rises and meets cooler air, which condenses and creates water droplets. This releases energy, which charges the atmosphere and creates lightning. This is why thunderstorms are a daily occurrence between March and October near southern waterways.

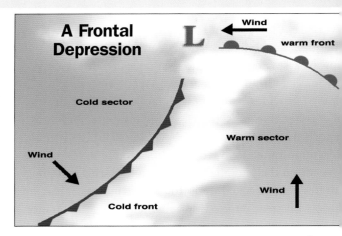

The trigger of change is a depression. Here, in a cold front, counterclockwise flow of cold air comes in from the northwest. Warm air is sucked in from the south, which rises above the cold air, causing wind sheer and rain. The wind veers. A falling barometer is one of the warnings of a developing front.

A tell-tale sign of a thunderstorm is cumulonimbus clouds: those tall clouds with an anvil-shaped (flat) top. Thunderstorms can also precede even a minor cold front. Keep in mind that thunderstorms generally move in an easterly direction so if you see a storm to the south or southwest of you, start preparing!

## Don't Wait Until It's Too Late

Almost all lightning will occur within 10 miles of its parent thunderstorm, but it can strike much farther than that. Also, the current from a single flash will easily travel for long distances. Because of this, if you see lightning or hear thunder, you CAN get struck!

he ability to see lightning will depend on the time of ay, weather conditions and obstructions, but on a clear ight it is possible to see a strike more than 10 miles way. Thunder can also be heard for about 10 miles, rovided there is no background noise, such as traffic, ind or rain.

If you see lightning, you can determine the distance y timing how long it takes for you to hear the thunder. he old rule that every 5 seconds of time equals 1 mile f distance works well. So if it takes 20 seconds to hear hunder after you see lighting, then the storm is 4 miles way. This is the time to drop anchor and "hunker down."

## afety Tips

ightning tends to strike the tallest object and boats on he open water fit this profile to a tee. The lightning will y to take the most direct path to the water, which is sually down the mast on a sailboat or the VHF antenna n a powerboat. However, both sailboats and powerboats ith cabins–especially those with lightning protection stems properly installed–are relatively safe, provided ou keep a few things in mind:

### If You Are Struck

1. Check people first. Many individuals struck by lightning or exposed to excessive electrical current can be saved with prompt and proper cardiopulmonary resuscitation (CPR). Contrary to popular belief, there is no danger in touching persons after they have been struck by lightning.

2. Check the bilge as strikes can rupture through-hull fittings and punch holes in hulls. Props and rudders are natural exit points on power boats.

3. Check electronics and the compasses. Typically everything in the path of the lightning is destroyed on the way down to the water, including instruments, computers and stereos.

4. Consider a short haul to check the bottom thoroughly. Lightning strikes sometimes leave traces of damage that may only be seen when the boat is out of the water.

- Before the storm strikes, lower, remove or tie down all antennas, fishing rods and flag poles.

- Stay down below and in the center of the cabin. Avoid keel-stepped masts and chain plates (on sailboats) and large metal appliances, such as microwaves or TVs. Remove any metal jewelry.

- Disconnect the power and antenna leads to all electronics, including radios. Do not use the VHF radio unless absolutely necessary.

- If you are stuck on deck, stay away from metal railings, the wheel, the mast and stays (on sailboats) or other metal fittings. Do not stand between the mast and stays as lightning can "side-flash" from one to the other.

- Stay out of the water. Don't fish or dangle your feet overboard. Salt water conducts electricity, which means that it can easily travel through the water toward you.

- Don't think your rubber-soled deck shoes will save you; while rubber is an electric insulator, it's only effective to a certain point. The average lightning bolt carries about 30,000 amps of charge, has 100 million volts of electric potential and is about 50,000°F.

## Don't Rush Back Out

Because electrical charges can linger in clouds after a thunderstorm has passed, experts agree that you should wait at least 30 minutes after a storm before resuming activities. And remember: If you can hear thunder, you can still be struck by lightning!

### *NOAA National Severe Storms Laboratory: nssl.noaa.gov*

# Hurricanes

While all coastal areas of the country are vulnerable to the effects of a hurricane (especially from June through November), the Gulf Coast, Southern and Mid-Atlantic states typically have been the hardest hit. But northern locales aren't immune; several destructive hurricanes have dealt a blow to areas in New England over the last 100 years, including Hurricane Sandy in 2012 and Matthew in 2016. While hurricanes can create vast swaths of devastation, ample preparation can help increase your boat's chances of surviving the storm.

According to the National Weather Service, a mature hurricane may be 10 miles high with a great spiral several hundred miles in diameter. Winds are often well above the 74 mph required to classify as hurricane strength, especially during gusts. Hurricane damage is produced by four elements: tidal surge, wind, wave action and rain.

■ Tidal surge is an increase in ocean depth prior to the storm. This effect, amplified in coastal areas, may cause tidal heights in excess of 15 to 20 feet above normal. Additionally, hurricanes can produce a significant negative tidal effect as water rushes out of the waterways after a storm.

■ Wind gusts can exceed reported sustained winds by 25 to 50 percent. So, for example, a storm with winds of 150 mph might have gusts of more than 200 mph, according to the National Weather Service.

■ Wave action is usually the most damaging element of a hurricane for boaters. The wind speed, water depth and the amount of open water determine the amount of wave action created. Storm surges can transform narrow bodies of water into larger, deeper waters capable of generating extreme wave action.

■ Rainfall varies but hurricanes can generate anywhere from 5 to 20 inches or more of rain.

If your boat is in a slip, you have three options: Leave it where it is (if it is in a safe place); move it to a refuge area; or haul it and put it on a trailer or cradle. Some marinas require mandatory evacuations during hurricane alerts. Check your lease agreement, and talk to your dockmaster before a hurricane if you are uncertain. Keep in mind that many municipalities close public mooring fields in advance of the storm. In some localities, boaters may be held liable for any damage that their boat inflicts to marina piers or property; check locally for details. Because

of this, rivers, canals, coves and other areas away from large stretches of open water are best selected as refuges.

Consult your insurance agent if you have questions about coverage. Many insurance agencies have restricted or canceled policies for boats that travel or are berthed in certain hurricane-prone areas. Review your policy and check your coverage, as many insurance companies will not cover boats in hurricane-prone areas during the June through November hurricane season. Riders for this type of coverage are notoriously expensive.

## Natural Seasickness Remedies

| |
|---|
| **Take slow, deep breaths.** This helps with upset stomach and dizziness. |
| **Focus on the horizon.** Keep your body still and head facing forward and watch a stationary object. Taking the helm always helps. |
| **Ginger can help.** Eat ginger snaps, drink ginger tea or ginger ale or digest ginger in capsule form ahead of time. |
| **Peppermint works too.** Sucking on a peppermint candy, drinking peppermint tea or breathing in peppermint oil dabbed on a cloth can help with stomach issues. |
| **Acupuncture wristbands** apply pressure to specific points in your wrist and can reduce nausea. |

## Hurricane Categorization

| CATEGORY | PRESSURE | WIND SPEED | SURGE |
|---|---|---|---|
| **1** | Above 980 mb (Above 28.91 in.) | 64–82 knots (74–95 mph) | 4–5 ft. (1–1.5 m) |
| *Visibility much reduced. Maneuvering under engines just possible. Open anchorages untenable. Danger of poorly secured boats torn loose in protected anchorages.* | | | |
| **2** | 965–979 mb (28.50–28.91 in.) | 83-95 knots (96–110 mph) | 6–8 ft. (1.5–2.5 m) |
| *Visibility close to zero. Boats in protected anchorages at risk, particularly from boats torn loose. Severe damage to unprotected boats and boats poorly secured and prepared.* | | | |
| **3** | 945–964 mb (27.91–28.50 in.) | 96–113 knots (111–130 mph) | 9–12 ft. (2.5–3.5 m) |
| *Deck fittings at risk and may tear loose, anchor links can fail and unprotected lines will chafe through. Extensive severe damage.* | | | |
| **4** | 920–944 mb (27.17–27.91 in.) | 114–135 knots (131–155 mph) | 13–18 ft. (3.5–5.4 m) |
| *Very severe damage and loss of life.* | | | |
| **5** | Below 920 mb (Below 27.17 in.) | Above 135 knots (131–155 mph) | Above 18 ft. (Above 5.4 m) |
| *Catastrophic conditions with catastrophic damage.* | | | |

## Preparing Your Boat

- Have a hurricane plan made up ahead of time to maximize what you can get done in amount of time you will have to prepare (no more than 12 hours in some cases). You won't want to be deciding how to tie up the boat or where to anchor when a hurricane is barreling down on you. Make these decisions in advance!

- Buy hurricane gear in advance (even if there is no imminent storm). When word of a hurricane spreads, local ship stores run out of storm supplies (anchors and line, especially) very quickly.

- Strip everything that isn't bolted down off the deck of the boat (canvas, sails, antennas, bimini tops, dodgers, dinghies, dinghy motors, cushions, unneeded control lines on sailboats), as this will help reduce windage and damage to your boat. Remove electronics and valuables and move them ashore.

- Any potentially leaky ports or hatches should be taped up. Dorades (cowls) should be removed and sealed with deck caps.

- Make sure all systems on board are in tip-top shape in case you have to move quickly. Fuel and water tanks should be filled, bilge pumps should be in top operating condition and batteries should be fully charged.

You will need many lengths of line to secure the boat; make certain it is good stretchy nylon (not Dacron). It is not unusual to string 600 to 800 feet of dock line on a 40-foot-long boat in preparation for a hurricane. If you can, double up your lines (two for each cleat), as lines can and will break during the storm. Have fenders and fender boards out and make sure all of your lines are protected from chafe.

- If you are anchored out, use multiple large anchors; there is no such thing as an anchor that is too big. If you can, tie to trees with a good root system, such as mangroves or live oaks. Mangroves are particularly good because their canopy can have a cushioning effect. Be sure mooring lines include ample scope to compensate for tides 10 to 20 feet above normal.

- Lastly, do not stay aboard to weather out the storm. Many people have been seriously injured (or worse) trying to save their boats during a hurricane. Take photos of the condition in which you left your boat and take your insurance papers with you.

## Returning Safely After the Storm

- Before hitting the road, make sure the roads back to your boat are open and safe for travel. Beware of dangling wires, weakened docks, bulkheads, bridges and other structures.

- Check your boat thoroughly before attempting to move it. If returning to your home slip, watch the waters for debris and obstructions. Navigate carefully as markers may be misplaced or missing.

- If your boat is sunk, arrange for engine repairs before floating it, but only if it is not impeding traffic. Otherwise, you will need to remove it immediately. Contact your insurance company right away to make a claim.

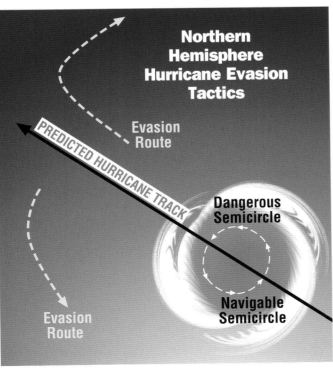

**Northern Hemisphere Hurricane Evasion Tactics**

Evasion Route

PREDICTED HURRICANE TRACK

Dangerous Semicircle

Navigable Semicircle

Evasion Route

> *NOAA Hurricane Resource Center:*
> *hurricanes.noaa.gov*
>
> *National Hurricane Center:*
> *nhc.noaa.gov*
>
> *BoatU.S. Hurricane Resource Page:*
> *boatus.com/hurricanes*

# Health Hazards

**Dietary Distress:** The major health risk while cruising is not tropical disease, but the bad luck of ingesting a bad piece of shellfish, exotic fruit or too many rum punches. If your body is not accustomed to some of these foods, or if the foods have been cleaned improperly, you may suffer diarrhea. If you tend to have digestive problems, always opt for bottled water and avoid ice, unpasteurized milk and uncooked food such as fresh salads.

**Sun Exposure:** Getting too much sun can be a real issue in southern locales. You must, of course, take the usual precautions against sunburn and sunstroke that you would anywhere. Apply sunscreen (SPF 30 if possible) 30 minutes prior to going out, even if it's overcast. Don't forget your lips, hands, tip of your ears and the back of your neck. Your time in the sun should be wisely limited. If you do burn, try these remedies:

- Apply cold compresses with plain water, witch hazel, oatmeal or a mixture of 1 cup fat-free milk and 4 cups water

- Make a cornstarch paste (with water) and apply directly to the burn

- Apply yogurt to sunburned areas

- Cover burned eyelids with tea bags soaked in cool water

- Take a cool bath with vinegar (1 cup/tub) or baking soda (generous sprinkle)

- Slather on bath oil and lotions

**Dehydration:** It's easy to get dehydrated, and it can make you feel lousy. Plan to drink at least one gallon of drinking water per person per day; 4 ounces of water every 20 minutes is recommended. Remember that drinking alcohol will speed dehydration.

**Swimmer's Ear:** Often overlooked, swimmer's ear can be a very painful malady. Anyone who snorkels or free dives, especially without head gear, is susceptible. The trick to avoiding it is to dry out your ears, not with a towel, but a good soak in a drying solution. You can use one of the many over-the-counter products made for this, or you can make your own solution of 50 percent white vinegar and 50 percent rubbing alcohol. The trick is to leave the solution in your ear canal a full 5 minutes. Do this each time you get in the water. For divers, a visit to your physician to have earwax removed before you depart for the islands is a wise idea.

Sand Crab

**Jellyfish & Portuguese Man-of-War Stings:** There
is always risk of being stung by jellyfish, and now
Portuguese Man-of-War are showing up as far north as
the Chesapeake Bay. Treatment starts with immediate
removal of any tentacles that are still sticking to the
skin. Lift them off (don't scrape with a knife) using a
stick or pair of tweezers. Rinse the area with seawater
(not fresh water) and then apply vinegar or isopropyl
alcohol, if you have it. Treat the affected area with
a topical anesthetic or use a sunburn preparation
containing Lidocaine or Benzocaine. If the pain
continues, apply Hydrocortisone 0.5% cream.

**Sea Lice:** Sea lice or jellyfish larvae often come
from seagrass that has been kicked up or disturbed,
bringing the larvae to the surface. In contact with the
human skin, both sea lice and jellyfish larvae parasites
burrow into the upper layers of the skin causing a rash,
sometimes tenderness, sometimes small pimples, but
always irritation and itching. Remove swimsuit and
wash the affected area thoroughly in fresh water as soon
as possible. Watch for infection. Sometimes the smallest
pimple can become infected easily in the saltwater
environment.

**Crabs:** Crabs will run away from you (albeit sideways)
unless you step on one, in which case it will likely pinch
your toe. This can really hurt and even become infected.
Clean well with fresh water and use a topical ointment
like Neosporin.

**Stingrays:** Contrary to popular belief, stingrays do
not attack but will lash out with their venomous stinger
when threatened. The stinger (or spine) is at the base of
their tails (closer to the body). Most injuries occur when
stingrays are stepped on in shallow water. There can be
up to four spines (or barbs) in the groove along the tail.
The stinger also contains venom that can cause severe
pain and swelling. Medical attention is definitely needed
in the case of a stingray-related injury.

**Sharks:** The most likely place to confront sharks is on
the east coast of Florida, although they have been known
to roam into the Chesapeake Bay, up the coast as far north
as Maine and even up the Mississippi River! Use common
sense to avoid an encounter with a shark: Don't swim at
night, avoid shiny jewelry or brightly colored clothing,
don't swim if bleeding and don't swim near fishermen. If
attacked, do whatever it takes to get away!

Man-of War

Stingrays

Sharks

# Pets on Board

If you want to bring your four-legged first mate with you on the boat, be sure to plan ahead for a safe voyage. Here are some suggestions.

**1. PRACTICE MAKES PERFECT.**

If your Rover hasn't been boating, introduce him to your boat by bringing him aboard while the boat is docked. Start the engine on the boat so he gets used to the noise and vibrations. Keep the first trip short and check for signs of seasickness.

**2. HAVE A PET OVERBOARD PLAN.**

Discuss what to do if Kitty falls in or Rover abandons ship. Practice swimming and rescue drills with your pet on a nice day and make a game of it. A coiled line or carpet strip makes it easier for a cat to climb onboard; a swim ladder or platform works better for a dog. In a pinch, even a fishing net with a long handle will work for a small dog or cat.

**3. LIFE JACKETS FOR ALL.**

All pets should have life jackets or harnesses when on board and make sure the life jacket has a handle should Rover or Kitty have to be retrieved from the water, and that it's a bright color for maximum visibility. Have your pet wear the life jacket or harness at home beforehand to get used to it.

**4. WELCOMING PETS ONBOARD.**

Provide steps or telescoping ramps for getting Rover and Kitty on and off the boat. Swim platforms and floating ramps are more easily accessed when returning to the boat from the water than a swim ladder.

**5. KEEPING PETS ONBOARD.**

Childproof netting can keep Rover and Kitty confined and on board when that dolphin swims by, beckoning them to come for a swim. A tether works equally well. Throw rugs with non-skid backing are useful in the cabin and cockpit, and you can lay indoor/outdoor carpeting in your dinghy to create more traction. AstroTurf on the deck can serve dual purposes, as it is grippy and will help keep pets on deck, plus it can be used for other purposes…giving a whole new meaning to the term "poop deck"!

**6. KEEP YOUR PET HYDRATED.**

When 85-pound Rover has the sun beating on him and no place to go, he can become overheated. If he starts to pant profusely and his tongue turns purple, get him into the shade and cool him off, as these are signs of heat exhaustion. Rub him down from head to toe with water or ice and provide cool drinking water. (This goes for Kitty too.)

**7. PACK A FIRST AID KIT.**

Bring necessary medications, antibiotic ointment and sunscreen. (Yes, little pink noses and feet can get sunburn!) Water-loving dogs tend to have issues with their ears after swimming so pack ear cleanser with a drying agent.

## 8. SECURE CONTAINERS.

All types of pets like to stick their noses in open containers so make sure gasoline jogs, motor oil, cleaning products and bait containers have secure lids. Even that beer that Rover so aptly fetches could cause alcohol poisoning if ingested.

## 9. AVOID ANGLING FOR A "DOG FISH."

It is not uncommon for a dog or cat to be hooked by a zealous fisherman. Be sure pets stay clear of lines and the fish. If your pet does get hooked, don't try to remove it yourself; seek veterinary attention. It's not just the hook that's an issue; ingesting yards of fishing line can cause an internal blockage, necessitating a trip to the vet and sometimes surgery. When not fishing, be sure gear is put away. Also avoid letting crabs scurry about on deck; they look like wind-up play toys to Rover and Kitty!

## 10. CHECK AHEAD.

Some marinas do not allow pets, and many parks and wildlife areas do not permit pets ashore. Always carry your pet's rabies vaccination certificate and health records when on land.

*Suggested App: Pet First Aid by American Red Cross (FREE)*

SKIPPER'S HANDBOOK

# What's in Your Tackle Box?

A good tackle box is the angler's suitcase and while the contents may vary, most will include the essentials: bobbers, sinkers, leaders, weights, swivels, hooks and excess line. But your tackle box should include more than just what goes in the water. Here are some other items you should stock.

Florida requires a **fishing license** for both freshwater and saltwater fishing. The easiest way to get a license is online, but the licenses are available through sporting goods stores and are available at the county offices. Just do not wet your lines in Florida without it.

| | Tackle Box Items | |
|---|---|---|
| 1 | **Polarized sunglasses:** | To handle the glare off the water. |
| 2 | **Gloves:** | For protection from cuts and bites. |
| 3 | **Cloth:** | Fish are slimy and smell bad; you will want a (preferably moist) rag handy. |
| 4 | **Sunscreen:** | The fish should be broiled, not you. Use sunscreen that is sweat-proof and with a high protection factor. An umbrella will work too, if it's not too windy. |
| 5 | **Bug spray:** | The fish are there because they feed on the mosquito larvae; the mosquitoes, in turn, feed on you! |
| 6 | **Hook file:** | To keep hooks and knife nice and sharp. |
| 7 | **Sharp stainless steel knife:** | For cleaning fish, cutting lines, slicing up bait and opening cans. (Nail clippers also work well for cutting lines.) |
| 8 | **Needle nose pliers:** | To remove hooks from fish (and you). |
| 9 | **First aid kit:** | Include a few adhesive bandages, an antiseptic salve, some gauze, and a small spool of waterproof medical tape.  A pain reliever is good to have as well. |
| 10 | **Raincoat:** | If you carry one, it won't rain! |

# Lionfish as Game Fish

Lionfish are an edible, venomous fish invading Florida and Bahamian waters. They can be found in the Atlantic, Caribbean and Gulf of Mexico and are voracious eaters of valuable game fish, crustaceans and, perhaps, even coral. Lionfish are usually found floating in a stationary position around coral heads, swaying beautifully with their mouths open and ready to feed. Game fish and crustaceans don't even seem to register that they are in danger; scientists think that they fool prey into thinking they are sea fans, seagrass or seaweed. Researchers have discovered that in just five weeks, lionfish can reduce the number of young native fish on a reef by as much as 80 percent. The ramifications for grouper, lobster, shrimp and similar fishery resources are grave.

In response, Reef Environmental Education Foundation (REEF) organizes lionfish derbies in the Bahamas and Florida to collect and remove as many lionfish as possible. Teams collect lionfish by netting or spearing while SCUBA diving, free diving, or snorkeling. At the end of the derby, each fish is measured and prizes are awarded for teams catching the most, biggest and smallest lionfish. The public is invited to watch scoring, taste free lionfish samples, watch filleting and dissection demonstrations and ask questions about lionfish. Visit reef.org/lionfish/derbies for details.

It is important to note that lionfish are venomous, not poisonous. Eating the cooked fish is a gastronome's delight, not a gourmet danger, and is another way to minimize their impact. Order lionfish when offered or cook your own. REEF has published "The Lionfish Cookbook" (2nd edition), which is a unique blend of 45 recipes, background on the lionfish invasion and its impacts and a section on how to safely catch handle and prepare the fish. Lionfish range from bluegill size, all the way to 18 inches long. A lionfish "sting" can be as painful as a stingray's or as mellow as a honeybee's. If you do get stung, remove the spine if it is stuck in your flesh and immerse the digit in the hottest water that you can possibly stand as soon as possible. The pain does not last as long as a stingray's (nor is there the possibility of an embedded sheath), but it is just as nasty in the immediate sense.

# Onboard Waste & No Discharge Zones

Up until the late 1980s, many boaters simply discharged their untreated sewage overboard into the water. After a revision to the Clean Water Act was passed in 1987, the discharge of untreated sewage into U.S. waters within the three-mile limit was prohibited. Shortly thereafter, pump-out stations became a regular feature at marinas and fuel docks throughout the U.S. waterways.

Simply stated, if you have a marine head installed on your vessel and are operating in coastal waters within the U.S. three-mile limit (basically all of the waters covered in the guide you are now holding), you need to have a holding tank, and you will obviously need to arrange to have that tank pumped out from time to time.

Government regulation aside, properly disposing of your waste is good environmental stewardship. While your overboard contribution to the waterways may seem small in the grand scheme of things, similar attitudes among fellow boaters can quickly produce unsavory conditions in anchorages and small creeks. The widespread availability of holding tank gear and shoreside pump-out facilities leaves few excuses for not doing the right thing.

## No Discharge Zones

■ No Discharge means exactly what the name suggests: No waste, even waste treated by an onboard Type I marine sanitation device (MSD), may be discharged overboard. All waste must be collected in a holding tank and pumped out at an appropriate facility.

■ Keep in mind that there are some areas that forbid overboard discharge of any waste, including gray water from showers or sinks. Familiarize yourself with local regulations before entering new areas to ensure you don't get hit with a fine.

## The Law

■ If you have a marine head onboard and are operating on coastal waters within the U.S. three-mile limit (basically all of the waters covered in this Guide), you need to have an approved holding tank or Type I MSD. In a No Discharge area even a Type I MSD system must have a holding tank.

■ All valves connected to your holding tank or marine head that lead to the outside (both Y-valves AND seacocks) must be wire-tied, padlocked or absent of the valve handle and in the closed position. Simply having them closed without the (non-releasable) wire ties will not save you from a fine if you are boarded.

■ You may discharge waste overboard from a Type I MSD in all areas except those designated as No-Discharge Zones. A Type I MSD treats waste by reducing bacteria and visible solids to an acceptable level before discharge overboard.

■ While small and inconvenient for most cruisers, "Port-A-Potties" meet all the requirements for a Type III MSD, as the holding tank is incorporated into the toilet itself.

## Pump-Out Station and Holding Tank Basics

■ Some marinas are equipped with pump-out facilities, normally located at the marina's fuel dock. Check the marina listing tables throughout this guide for the availability of pump-out services at each facility. Some marinas charge a fee for the service.

■ Several municipalities and local governments have purchased and staffed pump-out boats that are equipped to visit boats on request, especially those at anchor. Radio the local harbormaster to see if this service is available in the area you are visiting. There is normally a small fee involved.

bacteria content. Raritan's Electro Scan and Groco's Thermopure systems are examples of Type I MSDs. Not permitted in No Discharge Zones.

- Type II MSD: Type II MSDs provide a higher level of waste treatment than Type I units and are larger as a result. They employ biological treatment and disinfection. These units are usually found on larger vessels due to their higher power requirements. These may not be discharged in No-Discharge Zones.

- Type III MSD: Regular holding tanks store sewage until the holding tank can either be pumped out to an onshore facility or at sea beyond the U.S. boundary waters (i.e., three miles offshore).

### Additional Resources
**BoatU.S. Guide to Overboard Discharge:**
boatus.com/foundation/guide/environment_7.html

**EPA Listing of No-Discharge Zones:**
water.epa.gov/polwaste/vwd/vsdnozone.cfm

- You will want to keep an eye out on your holding tank level while you are cruising, especially if you are getting ready to enter an area where you many not have access to proper pump-out services for a few days. Plan a fuel stop or marina stay to top off the fuel and water tanks and empty the other tank before you set out into the wild.

## Marine Sanitation Devices

- Type I MSD: Treats sewage before discharging it into the water using maceration. The treated discharge must not show any visible floating solids and must meet specified standards for

# GPS Waypoints

The following list provides selected waypoints for the waters covered in this book. The latitude/longitude readings are taken from government light lists and must be checked against the appropriate chart and light list for accuracy. Some waypoints listed here are lighthouses and should not be approached too closely as they may be on land, in shallow water or on top of a reef. Many buoys must be approached with caution, as they are often located near shallows or obstructions. The positions of every aid to navigation should be updated using the Coast Guard's *Local Notice to Mariners*, which is available online at: navcen.uscg.gov/lnm.

The U.S. Coast Guard will continue to provide Differential GPS (DGPS) correction signals for those who need accuracy of 10 meters or less, even though most GPS receivers now come with an internal capability for receiving differential signals.

> *Prudent mariners will not rely solely on these waypoints to navigate. Every available navigational tool should be used at all times to determine your vessel's position.*

| Florida East Coast | | |
|---|---|---|
| **LOCATION** | **LATITUDE** | **LONGITUDE** |
| St. Marys Entrance Lighted Buoy STM | N 30° 42.900' | W 081° 14.650' |
| St. Johns Lighted Buoy STJ | N 30° 23.583' | W 081° 19.133' |
| St. Augustine Lighted Whistle Buoy STA | N 29° 54.917' | W 081° 15.283' |
| Ponce de Leon Inlet Lighted Bell Buoy 2 | N 29° 04.767' | W 080° 53.483' |
| Cape Canaveral App. Chnl. Lig. Buoy 8 | N 28° 23.867' | W 080° 33.433' |
| Fort Pierce Inlet Lighted Buoy 2 | N 27° 28.650' | W 080° 15.417' |
| St. Lucie Entrance Lighted Buoy 2 | N 27° 10.017' | W 080° 08.383' |
| Lake Worth Inlet Lighted Buoy LW | N 26° 46.367' | W 080° 00.600' |

| Location | Latitude | Longitude |
|---|---|---|
| Boca Raton Inlet North Jetty Light 2 | N 26° 20.167' | W 080° 04.183' |
| Hillsboro Inlet Entrance Lighted Buoy HI | N 26° 15.133' | W 080° 04.467' |
| Port Everglades Lighted Buoy PE | N 26° 05.500' | W 080° 04.767' |
| Bakers Haulover Inlet Jetty Light | N 25° 53.933' | W 080° 07.183' |
| Miami Lighted Buoy M | N 25° 46.100' | W 080° 05.000' |

| Florida Keys | | |
|---|---|---|
| **LOCATION** | **LATITUDE** | **LONGITUDE** |
| Biscayne National Park N. Lig. Buoy N | N 25° 38.733' | W 080° 05.367' |
| Fowey Rocks Light | N 25° 35.433' | W 080° 05.800' |
| Triumph Reef Light 2TR | N 25° 28.267' | W 080° 06.917' |
| Pacific Reef Light | N 25° 22.267' | W 080° 08.517' |
| Carysfort Reef Light | N 25° 13.317' | W 080° 12.683' |
| Elbow Reef Light 6 | N 25° 08.667' | W 080° 15.500' |
| Molasses Reef Light 10 | N 25° 00.717' | W 080° 22.583' |
| Davis Reef Light 14 | N 24° 55.550' | W 080° 30.167' |
| Alligator Reef Light | N 24° 51.100' | W 080° 37.133' |
| Tennessee Reef Light | N 24° 44.767' | W 080° 46.933' |
| Coffins Patch Light 20 | N 24° 40.550' | W 080° 57.500' |
| Sombrero Key Light | N 24° 37.667' | W 081° 06.650' |
| Big Pine Shoal Light 22 | N 24° 34.117' | W 081° 19.550' |
| Looe Key Light 24 | N 24° 32.800' | W 081° 24.150' |
| American Shoal Light | N 24° 31.500' | W 081° 31.167' |
| Pelican Shoal Light 26 | N 24° 30.367' | W 081° 35.983' |
| Stock Island Approach Channel Light 32 | N 24° 28.483' | W 081° 44.533' |
| Key West Ent. Lighted Whistle Buoy KW | N 24° 27.683' | W 081° 48.033' |
| Key West NW Chan. Ent. Lig. Bell Buoy 1 | N 24° 38.867' | W 081° 53.967' |
| Sand Key Light | N 24° 27.233' | W 081° 52.650' |
| Cosgrove Shoal Light | N 24° 27.467' | W 082° 11.100' |
| Twenty-Eight Foot Shoal Light | N 24° 25.800' | W 082° 25.533' |

| | | |
|---|---|---|
| Halfmoon Shoal Light WR2 | N 24° 33.500' | W 082° 28.433' |
| Rebecca Shoal Light | N 24° 34.733' | W 082° 35.117' |
| Dry Tortugas Light | N 24° 38.000' | W 082° 55.233' |
| New Ground Rocks Light | N 24° 40.000' | W 082° 26.650' |
| Ellis Rock Light | N 24° 38.950' | W 082° 11.033' |
| Smith Shoal Light | N 24° 43.100' | W 082° 55.300' |

## Florida Bay and West Coast

| LOCATION | LATITUDE | LONGITUDE |
|---|---|---|
| Bullfrog Banks Light BB | N 24° 50.733' | W 081° 20.567' |
| Arsenic Bank Light 1 | N 24° 52.250' | W 080° 53.017 |
| East Cape Light 2 | N 25° 05.000' | W 081° 04.967' |
| Northwest Cape Light 4 | N 25° 12.833' | W 081° 11.750' |
| Little Shark River Entrance Light 1 | N 25° 19.350' | W 081° 09.233' |
| Broad Creek Light 6 | N 25° 26.317' | W 081° 12.200' |
| Lostmans River Light 8 | N 25° 32.567' | W 081° 14.983' |
| Pavilion Key Light 10 | N 25° 40.917' | W 081° 21.400' |
| Cape Romano Shoals Light | N 25° 41.300' | W 081° 38.783' |
| Indian Key Pass Light 1 | N 25° 47.983' | W 081° 28.067' |
| Coon Key Light | N 25° 52.900' | W 081° 37.933' |
| Capri Pass Light 2 | N 25° 58.500' | W 081° 46.267' |
| Gordon Pass Shoal Light | N 26° 05.483' | W 081° 48.683' |
| San Carlos Bay Light SC | N 26° 25.133' | W 081° 57.550' |
| Sanibel Island Light | N 26° 27.183' | W 082° 00.850' |
| Charlotte Harbor Ent. Lig. Bell Buoy 2 | N 26° 39.850' | W 082° 19.567' |
| Venice Inlet Light 1 | N 27° 06.767' | W 082° 28.217' |
| Big Sarasota Pass Light 1 | N 27° 15.567' | W 082° 33.767' |
| New Pass Entrance Light NP | N 27° 18.917' | W 082° 35.883' |
| Longboat Pass Approach Light LP | N 27° 25.850' | W 082° 41.850' |
| Southwest Channel Ent. Lig. Bell Buoy 1 | N 27° 32.333' | W 082° 48.600' |
| Tampa Bay Lighted Buoy T | N 27° 35.317' | W 083° 00.717' |

| | | |
|---|---|---|
| Pass-A-Grille Entrance Light PG | N 27° 40.583' | W 082° 46.017' |
| Johns Pass Light JP | N 27° 46.500' | W 082° 48.033' |
| Clearwater Pass Channel Light 1 | N 27° 58.267' | W 082° 50.850' |
| Anclote Anchorage South Ent. Light 1 | N 28° 08.283' | W 082° 51.950' |
| Anclote River Entrance Light 1 | N 28° 10.383' | W 082° 49.533' |
| Anclote Anchorage North Ent. Light 2 | N 28° 15.050' | W 082° 52.900' |
| Homosassa Bay Entrance Light 2 | N 28° 41.433' | W 082° 48.650' |
| Crystal River Lighted Buoy 2 | N 28° 47.517' | W 082° 58.583' |
| Withlacoochee River Entrance Light 1 | N 28° 58.133' | W 082° 49.717' |
| Cedar Keys Main Channel Light 1 | N 29° 04.000' | W 083° 04.550' |
| Cedar Keys NW Channel App. Light 2 | N 29° 08.483' | W 083° 07.850' |
| Suwannee River, Alligator Pass Light 2 | N 29° 14.583' | W 083° 11.783' |
| Suwannee R., McGriff Pass Daybeacon 1 | N 29° 18.583' | W 083° 12.017' |
| Steinhatchee River Light 1 | N 29° 39.383' | W 083° 27.433' |
| St. Marks River Lighted Buoy SM | N 30° 04.300' | W 084° 10.800' |
| Carrabelle Channel Lighted Bell Buoy 2 | N 29° 44.550' | W 084° 39.200' |
| St. George Island W Jetty Lig. Buoy 1 | N 29° 36.167' | W 084° 57.217' |
| St. Joseph Bay Lig. & Ent. Rg. A Rear Lig. | N 29° 55.100' | W 085° 22.833' |
| St. Andrew Bay Ent. Lig. Whistle Buoy SA | N 30° 05.500' | W 085° 46.433' |
| Choctawhatchee Bay Ent. Lig. Whi. By CB | N 30° 22.250' | W 086° 30.900' |
| Pensacola Bay Ent. Lig. Gong Buoy 1 | N 30° 16.267' | W 087° 17.550' |

## Alabama

| LOCATION | LATITUDE | LONGITUDE |
|---|---|---|
| Perdido Pass Ent. Lig. Whistle Buoy PP | N 30° 15.517' | W 087° 33.400' |
| Mobile Entrance Lighted Horn Buoy M | N 30° 07.517' | W 088° 04.117' |

## Mississippi

| LOCATION | LATITUDE | LONGITUDE |
|---|---|---|
| Petit Bois Island Obstruction Light 2 | N 30° 13.400' | W 088° 29.200' |
| Horn Island Pass Lig. Whistle Buoy HI | N 30° 08.500' | W 088° 34.649' |
| Dog Keys Pass Lighted Gong Buoy 1 | N 30° 12.933' | W 088° 47.450' |
| Gulfport Ship Chan. Lig. Whistle Buoy GP | N 30° 07.167' | W 088° 52.645' |

## Louisiana

| LOCATION | LATITUDE | LONGITUDE |
|---|---|---|
| Chandeleur Light | N 30° 02.800' | W 088° 52.700' |
| Old Harbor Island Lighted Buoy 1 | N 29° 46.600' | W 089° 03.717' |
| Pass a Loutre N Pass Lig. Bell Buoy 2 | N 29° 14.283' | W 088° 57.467' |
| South Pass Lighted Bell Buoy 2 | N 28° 58.717' | W 089° 06.517' |
| Southwest Pass Ent. Lig. Whistle Buoy SW | N 28° 52.650' | W 089° 25.917' |
| Barataria Pass Lighted Whistle Buoy BP | N 29° 13.967' | W 089° 54.117' |
| Belle Pass Entrance Lighted Bell Buoy 2 | N 29° 04.267' | W 090° 13.667' |
| Point Au Fer Reef Light | N 29° 22.333' | W 091° 23.067' |
| Atchafalaya Channel Ent. Lig. Bell Buoy A | N 29° 10.000' | W 091° 33.900' |
| Sabine Bank Channel Lig. Whistle Buoy SB | N 29° 25.017' | W 093° 40.017' |

## Texas

| LOCATION | LATITUDE | LONGITUDE |
|---|---|---|
| Galveston Bay Ent. Lig. Whistle Buoy GA | N 29° 09.483' | W 094° 25.900' |
| Freeport Ent. Lighted Whistle Buoy FP | N 28° 52.617' | W 095° 14.150' |
| Colorado River W Jetty Entrance Light 1 | N 28° 35.467' | W 095° 59.067' |
| Matagorda Ship App. Lig. Wh. Buoy MSC | N 28° 25.300' | W 096° 05.217' |
| Aransas Pass Ent. Lig. Whistle Buoy AP | N 27° 47.567' | W 096° 57.367' |
| Pt Mansfield Chan. Ent. Lig. Wh. Buoy PM | N 26° 33.867' | W 097° 15.383' |
| Brazos Santiago Pass Ent. Lig. Wh. By BS | N 26° 03.933' | W 097° 06.583' |

## BAHAMAS

| LOCATION | LATITUDE | LONGITUDE |
|---|---|---|
| Memory Rock Light | N 26° 56.800' | W 079° 06.800' |
| Indian Cay Light | N 26° 43.000' | W 079° 00.100' |
| Settlement Point Light | N 26° 41.500' | W 078° 59.900' |
| Freeport, Pinder Point Light | N 26° 31.500' | W 078° 46.400' |
| Great Stirrup Cay Light | N 25° 49.700' | W 077° 54.000' |
| Nassau, Paradise Island Light | N 25° 05.200' | W 077° 21.100' |
| Great Isaac Light | N 26° 01.800' | W 079° 05.400' |
| North Rock Light | N 25° 48.100' | W 079° 15.700' |
| North Bimini Island Light | N 25° 43.700' | W 079° 18.000' |
| Gun Cay Light | N 25° 34.500' | W 079° 18.800' |
| South Riding Rock Light | N 25° 13.800' | W 079° 09.000' |

# Float Plan

BoatU.S.

## 1. Phone Numbers

Coast Guard:_____

Marine Police:_____

Local TowBoatU.S. Company:_____

## 2. Description of the Boat

Boat Name:_____ Hailing Port:_____

Type:_____ Model Year:_____

Make:_____ Length:_____ Beam:_____ Draft:_____

Color, Hull:_____ Cabin:_____ Deck:_____ Trim:_____ Dodger:_____

Other Colors:_____ # of Masts:_____

Distinguishing Features:_____

Registration No:_____ Sail No:_____

Engine(s) Type:_____ Horsepower:_____ Cruising Speed:_____

Fuel Capacity, Gallons:_____ Cruising Range:_____

### Electronics/Safety Equipment Aboard

VHF Radio:_____ Cell Phone:_____ CB:_____ SSB:_____

Frequency Monitored:_____ Loran:_____ SatNav:_____

Depth Sounder:_____ Radar:_____ GPS:_____

Raft:_____ Dinghy:_____ EPIRB:_____ A/B/C/406M
(Indicate Type)

## 3. Trip Details

Owner/Skipper (Filing Report):_____

Phone:_____ Age:_____

Address:_____

**Additional Persons Aboard, Total:_____**

Name:_____ Age:_____

Address:_____ Phone:_____

Boating Experience:_____

Name:_____ Age:_____

Address:_____ Phone:_____

Boating Experience:_____

Name:_____ Age:_____

Address:_____ Phone:_____

Boating Experience:_____

Name:_____ Age:_____

Address:_____ Phone:_____

Boating Experience:_____

Name:_____ Age:_____

Address:_____ Phone:_____

Boating Experience:_____

Departure Date/Time:_____ Return No Later Than:_____

Depart From:_____

**Marina (Home Port):**_____ Phone:_____

Auto Parked At:_____

Model/color:_____ Lic. #_____

**Destination Port:** _____

_____ ETA:_____ No Later Than:_____

Phone:_____

**Anticipated Stopover Ports:**_____

_____ ETA:_____ No Later Than:_____

Phone:_____

_____ ETA:_____ No Later Than:_____

Phone:_____

_____ ETA:_____ No Later Than:_____

Phone:_____

_____ ETA:_____ No Later Than:_____

Phone:_____

_____ ETA:_____ No Later Than:_____

Phone:_____

**Plan Filed With:**_____

Name:_____ Phone:_____

Get in the habit of filing a Float Plan. It can assure quicker rescue in the event of a breakdown, stranding or weather delay. Fill out the permanent data in Sections 1 and 2. Then, make enough copies to last for the season. If you file a Float Plan with someone not at your home, such as a harbormaster or boating friend, be sure to notify them as soon as you return. Don't burden friends or authorities with unnecessary worry and responsibility if you are safe.

Check your *BoatU.S. Towing Guide.* Some listed companies will accept a verbal Float Plan via telephone or VHF.

StationId:8720086
Source:NOAA/NOS/CO-OPS
Station Type:Subordinate
Time Zone:LST/LDT
Datum:mean lower low water (MLLW) which is the chart datum of soundings

**NOAA Tide Predictions**

## Amelia City, South Amelia River, Florida, 2017

**Times and Heights of High and Low Waters**

### October

| Day | Time | ft | cm | Day | Time | ft | cm |
|---|---|---|---|---|---|---|---|
| 1 Su | 12:18 AM | 1.1 | 34 | 16 M | 12:59 AM | 0.4 | 12 |
|  | 06:06 AM | 5.3 | 162 |  | 07:09 AM | 6.1 | 186 |
|  | 12:26 PM | 1.0 | 30 |  | 01:22 PM | 0.3 | 9 |
|  | 06:43 PM | 5.9 | 180 |  | 07:34 PM | 6.4 | 195 |
| 2 M | 01:06 AM | 0.9 | 27 | 17 Tu | 01:51 AM | 0.3 | 9 |
|  | 07:00 AM | 5.6 | 171 |  | 08:03 AM | 6.4 | 195 |
|  | 01:18 PM | 0.8 | 24 |  | 02:17 PM | 0.2 | 6 |
|  | 07:33 PM | 6.1 | 186 |  | 08:24 PM | 6.4 | 195 |
| 3 Tu | 01:53 AM | 0.6 | 18 | 18 W | 02:39 AM | 0.2 | 6 |
|  | 07:50 AM | 5.9 | 180 |  | 08:52 AM | 6.5 | 198 |
|  | 02:08 PM | 0.5 | 15 |  | 03:08 PM | 0.2 | 6 |
|  | 08:20 PM | 6.3 | 192 |  | 09:09 PM | 6.3 | 192 |
| 4 W | 02:37 AM | 0.3 | 9 | 19 Th | 03:24 AM | 0.1 | 3 |
|  | 08:37 AM | 6.2 | 189 |  | 09:37 AM | 6.6 | 201 |
|  | 02:57 PM | 0.3 | 9 |  | 03:55 PM | 0.2 | 6 |
|  | 09:05 PM | 6.4 | 195 |  | 09:52 PM | 6.2 | 189 |
| 5 Th | 03:21 AM | 0.1 | 3 | 20 F | 04:05 AM | 0.2 | 6 |
|  | 09:23 AM | 6.5 | 198 |  | 10:19 AM | 6.6 | 201 |
|  | 03:44 PM | 0.1 | 3 |  | 04:38 PM | 0.3 | 9 |
|  | 09:49 PM | 6.4 | 195 |  | 10:33 PM | 6.0 | 183 |
| 6 F | 04:04 AM | -0.1 | -3 | 21 Sa | 04:44 AM | 0.3 | 9 |
|  | 10:09 AM | 6.7 | 204 |  | 11:00 AM | 6.5 | 198 |
|  | 04:30 PM | 0.0 | 0 |  | 05:19 PM | 0.5 | 15 |
|  | 10:35 PM | 6.4 | 195 |  | 11:12 PM | 5.8 | 177 |
| 7 Sa | 04:47 AM | -0.3 | -9 | 22 Su | 05:21 AM | 0.5 | 15 |
|  | 10:56 AM | 6.8 | 207 |  | 11:39 AM | 6.3 | 192 |
|  | 05:16 PM | 0.0 | 0 |  | 05:59 PM | 0.7 | 21 |
|  | 11:21 PM | 6.3 | 192 |  | 11:51 PM | 5.6 | 171 |
| 8 Su | 05:31 AM | -0.3 | -9 | 23 M | 05:58 AM | 0.7 | 21 |
|  | 11:45 AM | 6.9 | 210 |  | 12:17 PM | 6.1 | 186 |
|  | 06:05 PM | 0.1 | 3 |  | 06:40 PM | 0.9 | 27 |
| 9 M | 12:10 AM | 6.2 | 189 | 24 Tu | 12:30 AM | 5.4 | 165 |
|  | 06:18 AM | -0.2 | -6 |  | 06:35 AM | 0.9 | 27 |
|  | 12:36 PM | 6.8 | 207 |  | 12:57 PM | 5.9 | 180 |
|  | 06:57 PM | 0.2 | 6 |  | 07:22 PM | 1.1 | 34 |
| 10 Tu | 01:01 AM | 6.0 | 183 | 25 W | 01:11 AM | 5.3 | 162 |
|  | 07:10 AM | 0.0 | 0 |  | 07:16 AM | 1.1 | 34 |
|  | 01:30 PM | 6.7 | 204 |  | 01:38 PM | 5.8 | 177 |
|  | 07:55 PM | 0.5 | 15 |  | 08:09 PM | 1.3 | 40 |
| 11 W | 01:56 AM | 5.9 | 180 | 26 Th | 01:54 AM | 5.1 | 155 |
|  | 08:08 AM | 0.2 | 6 |  | 08:02 AM | 1.3 | 40 |
|  | 02:28 PM | 6.6 | 201 |  | 02:23 PM | 5.6 | 171 |
|  | 08:57 PM | 0.6 | 18 |  | 08:59 PM | 1.4 | 43 |
| 12 Th | 02:54 AM | 5.7 | 174 | 27 F | 02:41 AM | 5.1 | 155 |
|  | 09:12 AM | 0.4 | 12 |  | 08:56 AM | 1.4 | 43 |
|  | 03:30 PM | 6.5 | 198 |  | 03:12 PM | 5.6 | 171 |
|  | 10:01 PM | 0.7 | 21 |  | 09:52 PM | 1.4 | 43 |
| 13 F | 03:58 AM | 5.7 | 174 | 28 Sa | 03:33 AM | 5.1 | 155 |
|  | 10:17 AM | 0.5 | 15 |  | 09:54 AM | 1.4 | 43 |
|  | 04:35 PM | 6.4 | 195 |  | 04:06 PM | 5.5 | 168 |
|  | 11:04 PM | 0.6 | 18 |  | 10:44 PM | 1.3 | 40 |
| 14 Sa | 05:05 AM | 5.7 | 174 | 29 Su | 04:29 AM | 5.2 | 158 |
|  | 11:22 AM | 0.5 | 15 |  | 10:53 AM | 1.3 | 40 |
|  | 05:39 PM | 6.3 | 192 |  | 05:04 PM | 5.6 | 171 |
|  |  |  |  |  | 11:35 PM | 1.0 | 30 |
| 15 Su | 12:03 AM | 0.5 | 15 | 30 M | 05:28 AM | 5.4 | 165 |
|  | 06:10 AM | 5.9 | 180 |  | 11:50 AM | 1.1 | 34 |
|  | 12:24 PM | 0.4 | 12 |  | 06:01 PM | 5.7 | 174 |
|  | 06:40 PM | 6.4 | 195 |  |  |  |  |
|  |  |  |  | 31 Tu | 12:25 AM | 0.8 | 24 |
|  |  |  |  |  | 06:25 AM | 5.7 | 174 |
|  |  |  |  |  | 12:46 PM | 0.8 | 24 |
|  |  |  |  |  | 06:54 PM | 5.9 | 180 |

### November

| Day | Time | ft | cm | Day | Time | ft | cm |
|---|---|---|---|---|---|---|---|
| 1 W | 01:14 AM | 0.5 | 15 | 16 Th | 01:12 AM | 0.2 | 6 |
|  | 07:18 AM | 6.1 | 186 |  | 07:30 AM | 6.4 | 195 |
|  | 01:40 PM | 0.5 | 15 |  | 01:49 PM | 0.3 | 9 |
|  | 07:45 PM | 6.1 | 186 |  | 07:43 PM | 5.8 | 177 |
| 2 Th | 02:02 AM | 0.1 | 3 | 17 F | 01:56 AM | 0.2 | 6 |
|  | 08:08 AM | 6.5 | 198 |  | 08:13 AM | 6.4 | 195 |
|  | 02:32 PM | 0.2 | 6 |  | 02:34 PM | 0.3 | 9 |
|  | 08:34 PM | 6.2 | 189 |  | 08:24 PM | 5.7 | 174 |
| 3 F | 02:49 AM | -0.2 | -6 | 18 Sa | 02:37 AM | 0.2 | 6 |
|  | 08:57 AM | 6.8 | 207 |  | 08:53 AM | 6.4 | 195 |
|  | 03:22 PM | -0.1 | -3 |  | 03:16 PM | 0.3 | 9 |
|  | 09:22 PM | 6.3 | 192 |  | 09:04 PM | 5.6 | 171 |
| 4 Sa | 03:36 AM | -0.4 | -12 | 19 Su | 03:15 AM | 0.2 | 6 |
|  | 09:46 AM | 7.1 | 216 |  | 09:32 AM | 6.3 | 192 |
|  | 04:11 PM | -0.2 | -6 |  | 03:55 PM | 0.4 | 12 |
|  | 10:11 PM | 6.4 | 195 |  | 09:43 PM | 5.5 | 168 |
| 5 Su | 03:23 AM | -0.6 | -18 | 20 M | 03:51 AM | 0.4 | 12 |
|  | 09:36 AM | 7.2 | 219 |  | 10:10 AM | 6.2 | 189 |
|  | 04:00 PM | -0.3 | -9 |  | 04:33 PM | 0.5 | 15 |
|  | 10:01 PM | 6.3 | 192 |  | 10:21 PM | 5.3 | 162 |
| 6 M | 04:10 AM | -0.6 | -18 | 21 Tu | 04:27 AM | 0.5 | 15 |
|  | 10:28 AM | 7.2 | 219 |  | 10:47 AM | 6.0 | 183 |
|  | 04:50 PM | -0.2 | -6 |  | 05:10 PM | 0.7 | 21 |
|  | 10:53 PM | 6.2 | 189 |  | 11:00 PM | 5.2 | 158 |
| 7 Tu | 05:00 AM | -0.4 | -12 | 22 W | 05:03 AM | 0.7 | 21 |
|  | 11:21 AM | 7.1 | 216 |  | 11:25 AM | 5.9 | 180 |
|  | 05:43 PM | 0.0 | 0 |  | 05:49 PM | 0.8 | 24 |
|  | 11:47 PM | 6.0 | 183 |  | 11:39 PM | 5.1 | 155 |
| 8 W | 05:53 AM | -0.2 | -6 | 23 Th | 05:40 AM | 0.9 | 27 |
|  | 12:17 PM | 6.9 | 210 |  | 12:04 PM | 5.7 | 174 |
|  | 06:39 PM | 0.2 | 6 |  | 06:30 PM | 0.9 | 27 |
| 9 Th | 12:43 AM | 5.9 | 180 | 24 F | 12:21 AM | 5.0 | 152 |
|  | 06:52 AM | 0.1 | 3 |  | 06:23 AM | 1.0 | 30 |
|  | 01:14 PM | 6.6 | 201 |  | 12:46 PM | 5.6 | 171 |
|  | 07:40 PM | 0.4 | 12 |  | 07:16 PM | 1.0 | 30 |
| 10 F | 01:43 AM | 5.8 | 177 | 25 Sa | 01:06 AM | 5.0 | 152 |
|  | 07:56 AM | 0.3 | 9 |  | 07:13 AM | 1.1 | 34 |
|  | 02:13 PM | 6.4 | 195 |  | 01:31 PM | 5.4 | 165 |
|  | 08:43 PM | 0.5 | 15 |  | 08:06 PM | 1.0 | 30 |
| 11 Sa | 02:45 AM | 5.7 | 174 | 26 Su | 01:55 AM | 5.0 | 152 |
|  | 09:03 AM | 0.5 | 15 |  | 08:11 AM | 1.2 | 37 |
|  | 03:15 PM | 6.2 | 189 |  | 02:21 PM | 5.4 | 165 |
|  | 09:44 PM | 0.5 | 15 |  | 08:59 PM | 0.9 | 27 |
| 12 Su | 03:50 AM | 5.7 | 174 | 27 M | 02:49 AM | 5.1 | 155 |
|  | 10:08 AM | 0.6 | 18 |  | 09:13 AM | 1.1 | 34 |
|  | 04:17 PM | 6.0 | 183 |  | 03:16 PM | 5.4 | 165 |
|  | 10:41 PM | 0.4 | 12 |  | 09:51 PM | 0.7 | 21 |
| 13 M | 04:53 AM | 5.9 | 180 | 28 Tu | 03:47 AM | 5.3 | 162 |
|  | 11:09 AM | 0.5 | 15 |  | 10:14 AM | 0.9 | 27 |
|  | 05:16 PM | 5.9 | 180 |  | 04:15 PM | 5.4 | 165 |
|  | 11:35 PM | 0.3 | 9 |  | 10:44 PM | 0.4 | 12 |
| 14 Tu | 05:51 AM | 6.0 | 183 | 29 W | 04:47 AM | 5.6 | 171 |
|  | 12:07 PM | 0.5 | 15 |  | 11:14 AM | 0.6 | 18 |
|  | 06:09 PM | 5.9 | 180 |  | 05:14 PM | 5.5 | 168 |
|  |  |  |  |  | 11:36 PM | 0.1 | 3 |
| 15 W | 12:25 AM | 0.2 | 6 | 30 Th | 05:45 AM | 6.0 | 183 |
|  | 06:43 AM | 6.2 | 189 |  | 12:12 PM | 0.3 | 9 |
|  | 01:00 PM | 0.4 | 12 |  | 06:11 PM | 5.7 | 174 |
|  | 06:58 PM | 5.9 | 180 |  |  |  |  |

### December

| Day | Time | ft | cm | Day | Time | ft | cm |
|---|---|---|---|---|---|---|---|
| 1 F | 12:29 AM | -0.2 | -6 | 16 Sa | 01:28 AM | 0.1 | 3 |
|  | 06:41 AM | 6.4 | 195 |  | 07:48 AM | 6.0 | 183 |
|  | 01:08 PM | 0.0 | 0 |  | 02:11 PM | 0.2 | 6 |
|  | 07:05 PM | 5.8 | 177 |  | 07:56 PM | 5.2 | 158 |
| 2 Sa | 01:20 AM | -0.6 | -18 | 17 Su | 02:10 AM | 0.0 | 0 |
|  | 07:34 AM | 6.8 | 207 |  | 08:28 AM | 6.0 | 183 |
|  | 02:01 PM | -0.3 | -9 |  | 02:52 PM | 0.1 | 3 |
|  | 07:57 PM | 6.0 | 183 |  | 08:37 PM | 5.2 | 158 |
| 3 Su | 02:12 AM | -0.8 | -24 | 18 M | 02:49 AM | 0.0 | 0 |
|  | 08:27 AM | 7.0 | 213 |  | 09:07 AM | 6.0 | 183 |
|  | 02:53 PM | -0.6 | -18 |  | 03:31 PM | 0.1 | 3 |
|  | 08:50 PM | 6.1 | 186 |  | 09:16 PM | 5.1 | 155 |
| 4 M | 03:02 AM | -1.0 | -30 | 19 Tu | 03:26 AM | 0.1 | 3 |
|  | 09:20 AM | 7.2 | 219 |  | 09:45 AM | 5.9 | 180 |
|  | 03:44 PM | -0.7 | -21 |  | 04:07 PM | 0.2 | 6 |
|  | 09:43 PM | 6.1 | 186 |  | 09:55 PM | 5.1 | 155 |
| 5 Tu | 03:53 AM | -1.0 | -30 | 20 W | 04:02 AM | 0.1 | 3 |
|  | 10:13 AM | 7.1 | 216 |  | 10:22 AM | 5.8 | 177 |
|  | 04:35 PM | -0.6 | -18 |  | 04:43 PM | 0.2 | 6 |
|  | 10:37 PM | 6.0 | 183 |  | 10:33 PM | 5.0 | 152 |
| 6 W | 04:44 AM | -0.9 | -27 | 21 Th | 04:37 AM | 0.3 | 9 |
|  | 11:07 AM | 7.0 | 213 |  | 10:59 AM | 5.7 | 174 |
|  | 05:27 PM | -0.5 | -15 |  | 05:19 PM | 0.3 | 9 |
|  | 11:32 PM | 5.9 | 180 |  | 11:12 PM | 4.9 | 149 |
| 7 Th | 05:38 AM | -0.6 | -18 | 22 F | 05:13 AM | 0.4 | 12 |
|  | 12:01 PM | 6.7 | 204 |  | 11:36 AM | 5.6 | 171 |
|  | 06:21 PM | -0.3 | -9 |  | 05:57 PM | 0.4 | 12 |
|  |  |  |  |  | 11:52 PM | 4.9 | 149 |
| 8 F | 12:28 AM | 5.8 | 177 | 23 Sa | 05:54 AM | 0.5 | 15 |
|  | 06:36 AM | -0.2 | -6 |  | 12:15 PM | 5.4 | 165 |
|  | 12:55 PM | 6.4 | 195 |  | 06:38 PM | 0.5 | 15 |
|  | 07:19 PM | -0.1 | -3 |  |  |  |  |
| 9 Sa | 01:26 AM | 5.6 | 171 | 24 Su | 12:34 AM | 4.9 | 149 |
|  | 07:38 AM | 0.1 | 3 |  | 06:40 AM | 0.6 | 18 |
|  | 01:51 PM | 6.1 | 186 |  | 12:56 PM | 5.3 | 162 |
|  | 08:19 PM | 0.1 | 3 |  | 07:24 PM | 0.4 | 12 |
| 10 Su | 02:26 AM | 5.5 | 168 | 25 M | 01:20 AM | 4.9 | 149 |
|  | 08:44 AM | 0.3 | 9 |  | 07:35 AM | 0.7 | 21 |
|  | 02:48 PM | 5.8 | 177 |  | 01:42 PM | 5.2 | 158 |
|  | 09:18 PM | 0.2 | 6 |  | 08:15 PM | 0.4 | 12 |
| 11 M | 03:27 AM | 5.5 | 168 | 26 Tu | 02:11 AM | 5.0 | 152 |
|  | 09:48 AM | 0.5 | 15 |  | 08:37 AM | 0.7 | 21 |
|  | 03:47 PM | 5.5 | 168 |  | 02:34 PM | 5.1 | 155 |
|  | 10:14 PM | 0.2 | 6 |  | 09:10 PM | 0.2 | 6 |
| 12 Tu | 04:29 AM | 5.6 | 171 | 27 W | 03:08 AM | 5.2 | 158 |
|  | 10:49 AM | 0.5 | 15 |  | 09:41 AM | 0.6 | 18 |
|  | 04:45 PM | 5.3 | 162 |  | 03:33 PM | 5.0 | 152 |
|  | 11:06 PM | 0.2 | 6 |  | 10:06 PM | 0.0 | 0 |
| 13 W | 05:26 AM | 5.7 | 174 | 28 Th | 04:11 AM | 5.5 | 168 |
|  | 11:45 AM | 0.5 | 15 |  | 10:44 AM | 0.4 | 12 |
|  | 05:39 PM | 5.2 | 158 |  | 04:37 PM | 5.1 | 155 |
|  | 11:56 PM | 0.1 | 3 |  | 11:02 PM | -0.3 | -9 |
| 14 Th | 06:18 AM | 5.8 | 177 | 29 F | 05:15 AM | 5.8 | 177 |
|  | 12:38 PM | 0.4 | 12 |  | 11:45 AM | 0.1 | 3 |
|  | 06:28 PM | 5.2 | 158 |  | 05:40 PM | 5.2 | 158 |
|  |  |  |  |  | 11:59 PM | -0.6 | -18 |
| 15 F | 12:43 AM | 0.1 | 3 | 30 Sa | 06:17 AM | 6.2 | 189 |
|  | 07:05 AM | 5.9 | 180 |  | 12:45 PM | -0.2 | -6 |
|  | 01:27 PM | 0.3 | 9 |  | 06:40 PM | 5.4 | 165 |
|  | 07:14 PM | 5.2 | 158 |  |  |  |  |
|  |  |  |  | 31 Su | 12:56 AM | -0.9 | -27 |
|  |  |  |  |  | 07:15 AM | 6.5 | 198 |
|  |  |  |  |  | 01:42 PM | -0.5 | -15 |
|  |  |  |  |  | 07:37 PM | 5.6 | 171 |

Heights are referred to mean lower water which is the chart datum of sounding. All times are local. Daylight Saving Time has been used when needed. Additional tide tables are available online from NOAA at www.tidesandcurrents.noaa.gov/tide_predictions.shtml.

**SKIPPER'S HANDBOOK**

StationId: 8720086
Source: NOAA/NOS/CO-OPS
Station Type: Subordinate
Time Zone: LST_LDT
Datum: MLLW

## NOAA Tide Predictions

# AMELIA CITY, SOUTH AMELIA RIVER, FL,2018

### Times and Heights of High and Low Waters

## January

| | Time | ft | cm | | Time | ft | cm |
|---|---|---|---|---|---|---|---|
| **1** M | 01:52 AM | -1.1 | -34 | **16** Tu | 02:23 AM | -0.1 | -3 |
| | 08:12 AM | 6.8 | 207 | | 08:42 AM | 5.7 | 174 |
| | 02:38 PM | -0.8 | -24 | | 03:05 PM | 0.0 | 0 |
| | 08:34 PM | 5.7 | 174 | | 08:50 PM | 4.9 | 149 |
| **2** Tu ○ | 02:46 AM | -1.3 | -40 | **17** W ● | 03:02 AM | -0.2 | -6 |
| | 09:06 AM | 6.9 | 210 | | 09:21 AM | 5.7 | 174 |
| | 03:30 PM | -0.9 | -27 | | 03:42 PM | -0.1 | -3 |
| | 09:29 PM | 5.8 | 177 | | 09:30 PM | 4.9 | 149 |
| **3** W | 03:38 AM | -1.3 | -40 | **18** Th | 03:39 AM | -0.2 | -6 |
| | 10:00 AM | 6.9 | 210 | | 09:58 AM | 5.7 | 174 |
| | 04:20 PM | -0.9 | -27 | | 04:17 PM | -0.1 | -3 |
| | 10:23 PM | 5.8 | 177 | | 10:09 PM | 4.9 | 149 |
| **4** Th | 04:30 AM | -1.2 | -37 | **19** F | 04:15 AM | -0.1 | -3 |
| | 10:52 AM | 6.8 | 207 | | 10:35 AM | 5.6 | 171 |
| | 05:10 PM | -0.8 | -24 | | 04:52 PM | 0.0 | 0 |
| | 11:17 PM | 5.8 | 177 | | 10:47 PM | 4.9 | 149 |
| **5** F | 05:23 AM | -0.9 | -27 | **20** Sa | 04:52 AM | 0.0 | 0 |
| | 11:44 AM | 6.5 | 198 | | 11:11 AM | 5.5 | 168 |
| | 06:02 PM | -0.6 | -18 | | 05:27 PM | 0.0 | 0 |
| | | | | | 11:25 PM | 4.9 | 149 |
| **6** Sa | 12:11 AM | 5.7 | 174 | **21** Su | 05:31 AM | 0.1 | 3 |
| | 06:19 AM | -0.5 | -15 | | 11:48 AM | 5.3 | 162 |
| | 12:35 PM | 6.1 | 186 | | 06:06 PM | 0.0 | 0 |
| | 06:55 PM | -0.4 | -12 | | | | |
| **7** Su | 01:05 AM | 5.5 | 168 | **22** M | 12:06 AM | 4.9 | 149 |
| | 07:18 AM | -0.1 | -3 | | 06:16 AM | 0.2 | 6 |
| | 01:26 PM | 5.7 | 174 | | 12:28 PM | 5.2 | 158 |
| | 07:51 PM | -0.2 | -6 | | 06:50 PM | 0.0 | 0 |
| **8** M ◑ | 02:00 AM | 5.4 | 165 | **23** Tu | 12:50 AM | 5.0 | 152 |
| | 08:20 AM | 0.2 | 6 | | 07:08 AM | 0.3 | 9 |
| | 02:18 PM | 5.3 | 162 | | 01:12 PM | 5.0 | 152 |
| | 08:46 PM | 0.0 | 0 | | 07:39 PM | 0.0 | 0 |
| **9** Tu | 02:57 AM | 5.3 | 162 | **24** W ◐ | 01:40 AM | 5.1 | 155 |
| | 09:22 AM | 0.4 | 12 | | 08:09 AM | 0.4 | 12 |
| | 03:12 PM | 5.0 | 152 | | 02:03 PM | 4.9 | 149 |
| | 09:41 PM | 0.1 | 3 | | 08:35 PM | -0.1 | -3 |
| **10** W | 03:56 AM | 5.2 | 158 | **25** Th | 02:37 AM | 5.2 | 158 |
| | 10:22 AM | 0.5 | 15 | | 09:14 AM | 0.4 | 12 |
| | 04:07 PM | 4.8 | 146 | | 03:02 PM | 4.8 | 146 |
| | 10:33 PM | 0.1 | 3 | | 09:35 PM | -0.2 | -6 |
| **11** Th | 04:53 AM | 5.2 | 158 | **26** F | 03:42 AM | 5.4 | 165 |
| | 11:18 AM | 0.5 | 15 | | 10:20 AM | 0.2 | 6 |
| | 05:02 PM | 4.7 | 143 | | 04:08 PM | 4.8 | 146 |
| | 11:23 PM | 0.1 | 3 | | 10:36 PM | -0.4 | -12 |
| **12** F | 05:46 AM | 5.3 | 162 | **27** Sa | 04:52 AM | 5.6 | 171 |
| | 12:10 PM | 0.4 | 12 | | 11:24 AM | 0.0 | 0 |
| | 05:54 PM | 4.7 | 143 | | 05:17 PM | 4.9 | 149 |
| | | | | | 11:37 PM | -0.6 | -18 |
| **13** Sa | 12:12 AM | 0.1 | 3 | **28** Su | 05:59 AM | 5.9 | 180 |
| | 06:35 AM | 5.5 | 168 | | 12:26 PM | -0.2 | -6 |
| | 12:59 PM | 0.3 | 9 | | 06:22 PM | 5.1 | 155 |
| | 06:42 PM | 4.7 | 143 | | | | |
| **14** Su | 12:58 AM | 0.1 | 3 | **29** M | 12:37 AM | -0.9 | -27 |
| | 07:20 AM | 5.6 | 171 | | 07:00 AM | 6.3 | 192 |
| | 01:45 PM | 0.2 | 6 | | 01:25 PM | -0.5 | -15 |
| | 07:27 PM | 4.8 | 146 | | 07:22 PM | 5.4 | 165 |
| **15** M | 01:42 AM | 0.0 | 0 | **30** Tu | 01:36 AM | -1.2 | -37 |
| | 08:02 AM | 5.7 | 174 | | 07:58 AM | 6.5 | 198 |
| | 02:27 PM | 0.1 | 3 | | 02:20 PM | -0.8 | -24 |
| | 08:09 PM | 4.9 | 149 | | 08:19 PM | 5.6 | 171 |
| | | | | **31** W ○ | 02:31 AM | -1.3 | -40 |
| | | | | | 08:52 AM | 6.7 | 204 |
| | | | | | 03:12 PM | -1.0 | -30 |
| | | | | | 09:13 PM | 5.8 | 177 |

## February

| | Time | ft | cm | | Time | ft | cm |
|---|---|---|---|---|---|---|---|
| **1** Th | 03:24 AM | -1.4 | -43 | **16** F | 03:18 AM | -0.3 | -9 |
| | 09:43 AM | 6.7 | 204 | | 09:34 AM | 5.7 | 174 |
| | 04:01 PM | -1.1 | -34 | | 03:49 PM | -0.3 | -9 |
| | 10:06 PM | 5.9 | 180 | | 09:45 PM | 5.2 | 158 |
| **2** F | 04:16 AM | -1.3 | -40 | **17** Sa | 03:55 AM | -0.3 | -9 |
| | 10:33 AM | 6.5 | 198 | | 10:11 AM | 5.6 | 171 |
| | 04:49 PM | -1.0 | -30 | | 04:23 PM | -0.3 | -9 |
| | 10:58 PM | 5.9 | 180 | | 10:23 PM | 5.3 | 162 |
| **3** Sa | 05:06 AM | -1.0 | -30 | **18** Su | 04:33 AM | -0.3 | -9 |
| | 11:22 AM | 6.2 | 189 | | 10:48 AM | 5.5 | 168 |
| | 05:36 PM | -0.8 | -24 | | 04:59 PM | -0.3 | -9 |
| | 11:48 PM | 5.8 | 177 | | 11:02 PM | 5.3 | 162 |
| **4** Su | 05:58 AM | -0.6 | -18 | **19** M | 05:14 AM | -0.2 | -6 |
| | 12:09 PM | 5.9 | 180 | | 11:25 AM | 5.4 | 165 |
| | 06:24 PM | -0.5 | -15 | | 05:38 PM | -0.3 | -9 |
| | | | | | 11:42 PM | 5.4 | 165 |
| **5** M | 12:38 AM | 5.6 | 171 | **20** Tu | 05:58 AM | -0.1 | -3 |
| | 06:53 AM | -0.2 | -6 | | 12:06 PM | 5.2 | 158 |
| | 12:55 PM | 5.5 | 168 | | 06:21 PM | -0.2 | -6 |
| | 07:14 PM | -0.2 | -6 | | | | |
| **6** Tu | 01:27 AM | 5.4 | 165 | **21** W | 12:26 AM | 5.4 | 165 |
| | 07:50 AM | 0.2 | 6 | | 06:50 AM | 0.1 | 3 |
| | 01:42 PM | 5.1 | 155 | | 12:50 PM | 5.1 | 155 |
| | 08:07 PM | 0.0 | 0 | | 07:10 PM | -0.2 | -6 |
| **7** W ◐ | 02:19 AM | 5.2 | 158 | **22** Th | 01:16 AM | 5.4 | 165 |
| | 08:49 AM | 0.4 | 12 | | 07:49 AM | 0.2 | 6 |
| | 02:31 PM | 4.7 | 143 | | 01:41 PM | 4.9 | 149 |
| | 09:00 PM | 0.2 | 6 | | 08:07 PM | -0.1 | -3 |
| **8** Th | 03:13 AM | 5.0 | 152 | **23** F ◐ | 02:13 AM | 5.4 | 165 |
| | 09:47 AM | 0.6 | 18 | | 08:53 AM | 0.3 | 9 |
| | 03:24 PM | 4.5 | 137 | | 02:40 PM | 4.8 | 146 |
| | 09:53 PM | 0.4 | 12 | | 09:10 PM | -0.2 | -6 |
| **9** F | 04:10 AM | 5.0 | 152 | **24** Sa | 03:20 AM | 5.5 | 168 |
| | 10:42 AM | 0.6 | 18 | | 10:00 AM | 0.2 | 6 |
| | 04:20 PM | 4.4 | 134 | | 03:48 PM | 4.8 | 146 |
| | 10:46 PM | 0.4 | 12 | | 10:14 PM | -0.3 | -9 |
| **10** Sa | 05:07 AM | 5.0 | 152 | **25** Su | 04:32 AM | 5.6 | 171 |
| | 11:35 AM | 0.6 | 18 | | 11:05 AM | 0.1 | 3 |
| | 05:16 PM | 4.4 | 134 | | 05:00 PM | 4.9 | 149 |
| | 11:37 PM | 0.3 | 9 | | 11:19 PM | -0.4 | -12 |
| **11** Su | 06:00 AM | 5.1 | 155 | **26** M | 05:42 AM | 5.9 | 180 |
| | 12:26 PM | 0.5 | 15 | | 12:07 PM | -0.1 | -3 |
| | 06:08 PM | 4.5 | 137 | | 06:07 PM | 5.2 | 158 |
| **12** M | 12:27 AM | 0.2 | 6 | **27** Tu | 12:22 AM | -0.7 | -21 |
| | 06:49 AM | 5.3 | 162 | | 06:45 AM | 6.1 | 186 |
| | 01:13 PM | 0.3 | 9 | | 01:06 PM | -0.4 | -12 |
| | 06:57 PM | 4.7 | 143 | | 07:08 PM | 5.5 | 168 |
| **13** Tu | 01:14 AM | 0.1 | 3 | **28** W | 01:22 AM | -0.9 | -27 |
| | 07:33 AM | 5.5 | 168 | | 07:42 AM | 6.4 | 195 |
| | 01:56 PM | 0.1 | 3 | | 02:01 PM | -0.7 | -21 |
| | 07:42 PM | 4.9 | 149 | | 08:04 PM | 5.8 | 177 |
| **14** W | 01:58 AM | -0.1 | -3 | | | | |
| | 08:15 AM | 5.6 | 171 | | | | |
| | 02:36 PM | 0.0 | 0 | | | | |
| | 08:25 PM | 5.0 | 152 | | | | |
| **15** Th ● | 02:39 AM | -0.2 | -6 | | | | |
| | 08:55 AM | 5.7 | 174 | | | | |
| | 03:13 PM | -0.2 | -6 | | | | |
| | 09:05 PM | 5.2 | 158 | | | | |

## March

| | Time | ft | cm | | Time | ft | cm |
|---|---|---|---|---|---|---|---|
| **1** Th | 02:18 AM | -1.1 | -34 | **16** F | 03:14 AM | -0.1 | -3 |
| | 08:34 AM | 6.5 | 198 | | 09:25 AM | 5.7 | 174 |
| | 02:51 PM | -0.9 | -27 | | 03:40 PM | -0.2 | -6 |
| | 08:57 PM | 6.0 | 183 | | 09:38 PM | 5.6 | 171 |
| **2** F ○ | 03:10 AM | -1.2 | -37 | **17** Sa ● | 03:55 AM | -0.2 | -6 |
| | 09:24 AM | 6.5 | 198 | | 09:58 AM | 5.7 | 174 |
| | 03:39 PM | -1.0 | -30 | | 04:17 PM | -0.3 | -9 |
| | 09:47 PM | 6.1 | 186 | | 10:19 PM | 5.7 | 174 |
| **3** Sa | 04:00 AM | -1.1 | -34 | **18** Su | 04:35 AM | -0.3 | -9 |
| | 10:11 AM | 6.3 | 192 | | 10:45 AM | 5.7 | 174 |
| | 04:23 PM | -0.9 | -27 | | 04:54 PM | -0.4 | -12 |
| | 10:35 PM | 6.1 | 186 | | 10:59 PM | 5.8 | 177 |
| **4** Su | 04:48 AM | -0.8 | -24 | **19** M | 05:16 AM | -0.4 | -12 |
| | 10:56 AM | 6.0 | 183 | | 11:24 AM | 5.6 | 171 |
| | 05:07 PM | -0.7 | -21 | | 05:32 PM | -0.4 | -12 |
| | 11:22 PM | 6.0 | 183 | | 11:39 PM | 5.9 | 180 |
| **5** M | 05:36 AM | -0.5 | -15 | **20** Tu | 05:58 AM | -0.3 | -9 |
| | 11:40 AM | 5.7 | 174 | | 12:05 PM | 5.5 | 168 |
| | 05:51 PM | -0.4 | -12 | | 06:13 PM | -0.4 | -12 |
| **6** Tu | 12:07 AM | 5.7 | 174 | **21** W | 12:22 AM | 5.9 | 180 |
| | 06:25 AM | -0.1 | -3 | | 06:44 AM | -0.2 | -6 |
| | 12:23 PM | 5.3 | 162 | | 12:48 PM | 5.3 | 162 |
| | 06:36 PM | 0.0 | 0 | | 06:57 PM | -0.3 | -9 |
| **7** W | 12:52 AM | 5.5 | 168 | **22** Th | 01:09 AM | 5.9 | 180 |
| | 07:16 AM | 0.3 | 9 | | 07:36 AM | 0.0 | 0 |
| | 01:06 PM | 5.0 | 152 | | 01:36 PM | 5.2 | 158 |
| | 07:24 PM | 0.3 | 9 | | 07:49 PM | -0.2 | -6 |
| **8** Th | 01:38 AM | 5.2 | 158 | **23** F | 02:01 AM | 5.8 | 177 |
| | 08:11 AM | 0.6 | 18 | | 08:34 AM | 0.2 | 6 |
| | 01:52 PM | 4.7 | 143 | | 02:29 PM | 5.0 | 152 |
| | 08:15 PM | 0.6 | 18 | | 08:48 PM | -0.1 | -3 |
| **9** F | 02:27 AM | 5.0 | 152 | **24** Sa ◐ | 02:59 AM | 5.7 | 174 |
| | 09:07 AM | 0.8 | 24 | | 09:38 AM | 0.3 | 9 |
| | 02:41 PM | 4.5 | 137 | | 03:29 PM | 5.0 | 152 |
| | 09:09 PM | 0.7 | 21 | | 09:53 PM | 0.0 | 0 |
| **10** Sa | 03:22 AM | 4.9 | 149 | **25** Su | 04:06 AM | 5.7 | 174 |
| | 10:02 AM | 0.8 | 24 | | 10:43 AM | 0.3 | 9 |
| | 03:36 PM | 4.4 | 134 | | 04:37 PM | 5.0 | 152 |
| | 10:05 PM | 0.7 | 21 | | 11:00 PM | 0.0 | 0 |
| **11** Su | 05:21 AM | 4.9 | 149 | **26** M | 05:17 AM | 5.7 | 174 |
| | 11:55 AM | 0.8 | 24 | | 11:47 AM | 0.3 | 9 |
| | 05:35 PM | 4.5 | 137 | | 05:48 PM | 5.1 | 155 |
| | 11:59 PM | 0.7 | 21 | | | | |
| **12** M | 06:18 AM | 5.0 | 152 | **27** Tu | 12:05 AM | -0.2 | -6 |
| | 12:46 PM | 0.7 | 21 | | 06:26 AM | 5.8 | 177 |
| | 06:31 PM | 4.6 | 140 | | 12:48 PM | -0.1 | -3 |
| | | | | | 06:55 PM | 5.4 | 165 |
| **13** Tu | 12:52 AM | 0.5 | 15 | **28** W | 01:08 AM | -0.4 | -12 |
| | 07:11 AM | 5.2 | 158 | | 07:27 AM | 6.0 | 183 |
| | 01:34 PM | 0.5 | 15 | | 01:45 PM | -0.3 | -9 |
| | 07:24 PM | 4.9 | 149 | | 07:54 PM | 5.7 | 174 |
| **14** W | 01:43 AM | 0.4 | 12 | **29** Th | 02:08 AM | -0.6 | -18 |
| | 07:59 AM | 5.4 | 165 | | 08:23 AM | 6.2 | 189 |
| | 02:19 PM | 0.3 | 9 | | 02:39 PM | -0.5 | -15 |
| | 08:12 PM | 5.1 | 155 | | 08:48 PM | 6.1 | 186 |
| **15** Th | 02:30 AM | 0.1 | 3 | **30** F | 03:04 AM | -0.7 | -21 |
| | 08:43 AM | 5.6 | 171 | | 09:13 AM | 6.2 | 189 |
| | 03:01 PM | 0.0 | 0 | | 03:28 PM | -0.7 | -21 |
| | 08:56 PM | 5.4 | 165 | | 09:38 PM | 6.3 | 192 |
| | | | | **31** Sa ○ | 03:55 AM | -0.8 | -24 |
| | | | | | 10:01 AM | 6.2 | 189 |
| | | | | | 04:13 PM | -0.7 | -21 |
| | | | | | 10:26 PM | 6.3 | 192 |

Heights are referred to mean lower water which is the chart datum of sounding. All times are local. Daylight Saving Time has been used when needed. Additional tide tables are available online from NOAA at www.tidesandcurrents.noaa.gov/tide_predictions.shtml.

StationId: 8720086
Source: NOAA/NOS/CO-OPS
Station Type: Subordinate
Time Zone: LST_LDT
Datum: MLLW

**NOAA Tide Predictions**

# AMELIA CITY, SOUTH AMELIA RIVER, FL,2018

### Times and Heights of High and Low Waters

## April

| Day | Time | ft | cm | Day | Time | ft | cm |
|---|---|---|---|---|---|---|---|
| 1 Su | 04:42 AM | -0.7 | -21 | 16 M | 04:14 AM | -0.4 | -12 |
| | 10:46 AM | 6.0 | 183 | | 10:17 AM | 5.7 | 174 |
| | 04:56 PM | -0.6 | -18 | | 04:26 PM | -0.5 | -15 |
| | 11:11 PM | 6.3 | 192 | ● | 10:34 PM | 6.3 | 192 |
| 2 M | 05:28 AM | -0.5 | -15 | 17 Tu | 04:58 AM | -0.5 | -15 |
| | 11:29 AM | 5.7 | 174 | | 11:01 AM | 5.6 | 171 |
| | 05:37 PM | -0.4 | -12 | | 05:07 PM | -0.6 | -18 |
| | 11:53 PM | 6.1 | 186 | | 11:19 PM | 6.4 | 195 |
| 3 Tu | 06:12 AM | -0.3 | -9 | 18 W | 05:43 AM | -0.4 | -12 |
| | 12:10 PM | 5.4 | 165 | | 11:46 AM | 5.5 | 168 |
| | 06:17 PM | -0.1 | -3 | | 05:51 PM | -0.5 | -15 |
| 4 W | 12:35 AM | 5.9 | 180 | 19 Th | 12:07 AM | 6.4 | 195 |
| | 06:57 AM | 0.1 | 3 | | 06:31 AM | -0.3 | -9 |
| | 12:51 PM | 5.2 | 158 | | 12:34 PM | 5.4 | 165 |
| | 06:58 PM | 0.2 | 6 | | 06:39 PM | -0.4 | -12 |
| 5 Th | 01:16 AM | 5.6 | 171 | 20 F | 12:57 AM | 6.3 | 192 |
| | 07:43 AM | 0.4 | 12 | | 07:24 AM | -0.1 | -3 |
| | 01:32 PM | 4.9 | 149 | | 01:26 PM | 5.3 | 162 |
| | 07:41 PM | 0.6 | 18 | | 07:33 PM | -0.2 | -6 |
| 6 F | 01:58 AM | 5.4 | 165 | 21 Sa | 01:51 AM | 6.1 | 186 |
| | 08:32 AM | 0.7 | 21 | | 08:22 AM | 0.0 | 0 |
| | 02:15 PM | 4.7 | 143 | | 02:22 PM | 5.2 | 158 |
| | 08:30 PM | 0.8 | 24 | | 08:34 PM | 0.0 | 0 |
| 7 Sa | 02:44 AM | 5.2 | 158 | 22 Su | 02:50 AM | 6.0 | 183 |
| | 09:25 AM | 0.9 | 27 | | 09:25 AM | 0.1 | 3 |
| | 03:02 PM | 4.6 | 140 | | 03:23 PM | 5.2 | 158 |
| | 09:24 PM | 1.0 | 30 | ◐ | 09:41 PM | 0.1 | 3 |
| 8 Su | 03:35 AM | 5.0 | 152 | 23 M | 03:54 AM | 5.8 | 177 |
| | 10:19 AM | 0.9 | 27 | | 10:28 AM | 0.1 | 3 |
| | 03:55 PM | 4.5 | 137 | | 04:29 PM | 5.2 | 158 |
| ◐ | 10:21 PM | 1.0 | 30 | | 10:48 PM | 0.1 | 3 |
| 9 M | 04:31 AM | 4.9 | 149 | 24 Tu | 05:01 AM | 5.8 | 177 |
| | 11:12 AM | 0.9 | 27 | | 11:30 AM | 0.0 | 0 |
| | 04:53 PM | 4.6 | 140 | | 05:37 PM | 5.4 | 165 |
| | 11:19 PM | 1.0 | 30 | | 11:53 PM | 0.0 | 0 |
| 10 Tu | 05:30 AM | 5.0 | 152 | 25 W | 06:06 AM | 5.8 | 177 |
| | 12:02 PM | 0.8 | 24 | | 12:27 PM | -0.1 | -3 |
| | 05:52 PM | 4.8 | 146 | | 06:40 PM | 5.7 | 174 |
| 11 W | 12:14 AM | 0.8 | 24 | 26 Th | 12:55 AM | -0.1 | -3 |
| | 06:27 AM | 5.1 | 155 | | 07:06 AM | 5.8 | 177 |
| | 12:51 PM | 0.6 | 18 | | 01:22 PM | -0.3 | -9 |
| | 06:47 PM | 5.0 | 152 | | 07:38 PM | 5.9 | 180 |
| 12 Th | 01:07 AM | 0.6 | 18 | 27 F | 01:53 AM | -0.2 | -6 |
| | 07:18 AM | 5.3 | 162 | | 07:59 AM | 5.8 | 177 |
| | 01:37 PM | 0.3 | 9 | | 02:13 PM | -0.4 | -12 |
| | 07:37 PM | 5.4 | 165 | | 08:29 PM | 6.2 | 189 |
| 13 F | 01:57 AM | 0.3 | 9 | 28 Sa | 02:47 AM | -0.4 | -12 |
| | 08:06 AM | 5.5 | 168 | | 08:49 AM | 5.8 | 177 |
| | 02:21 PM | 0.1 | 3 | | 03:01 PM | -0.5 | -15 |
| | 08:24 PM | 5.7 | 174 | | 09:17 PM | 6.3 | 192 |
| 14 Sa | 02:45 AM | 0.1 | 3 | 29 Su | 03:37 AM | -0.4 | -12 |
| | 08:51 AM | 5.6 | 171 | | 09:35 AM | 5.7 | 174 |
| | 03:04 PM | -0.2 | -6 | | 03:45 PM | -0.4 | -12 |
| | 09:08 PM | 6.0 | 183 | | 10:02 PM | 6.3 | 192 |
| 15 Su | 03:30 AM | -0.2 | -6 | 30 M | 04:23 AM | -0.4 | -12 |
| | 09:34 AM | 5.7 | 174 | | 10:18 AM | 5.6 | 171 |
| | 03:45 PM | -0.4 | -12 | | 04:27 PM | -0.3 | -9 |
| | 09:51 PM | 6.2 | 189 | ○ | 10:44 PM | 6.3 | 192 |

## May

| Day | Time | ft | cm | Day | Time | ft | cm |
|---|---|---|---|---|---|---|---|
| 1 Tu | 05:06 AM | -0.3 | -9 | 16 W | 04:40 AM | -0.6 | -18 |
| | 11:00 AM | 5.4 | 165 | | 10:38 AM | 5.6 | 171 |
| | 05:06 PM | -0.1 | -3 | | 04:45 PM | -0.8 | -24 |
| | 11:25 PM | 6.1 | 186 | | 11:02 PM | 6.7 | 204 |
| 2 W | 05:47 AM | -0.1 | -3 | 17 Th | 05:28 AM | -0.6 | -18 |
| | 11:40 AM | 5.2 | 158 | | 11:29 AM | 5.5 | 168 |
| | 05:44 PM | 0.1 | 3 | | 05:33 PM | -0.8 | -24 |
| | | | | | 11:54 PM | 6.6 | 201 |
| 3 Th | 12:04 AM | 5.9 | 180 | 18 F | 06:18 AM | -0.5 | -15 |
| | 06:29 AM | 0.2 | 6 | | 12:22 PM | 5.4 | 165 |
| | 12:20 PM | 5.0 | 152 | | 06:24 PM | -0.6 | -18 |
| | 06:23 PM | 0.4 | 12 | | | | |
| 4 F | 12:43 AM | 5.6 | 171 | 19 Sa | 12:47 AM | 6.5 | 198 |
| | 07:11 AM | 0.4 | 12 | | 07:12 AM | -0.4 | -12 |
| | 01:00 PM | 4.8 | 146 | | 01:17 PM | 5.4 | 165 |
| | 07:03 PM | 0.6 | 18 | | 07:21 PM | -0.4 | -12 |
| 5 Sa | 01:24 AM | 5.4 | 165 | 20 Su | 01:43 AM | 6.3 | 192 |
| | 07:56 AM | 0.6 | 18 | | 08:09 AM | -0.2 | -6 |
| | 01:43 PM | 4.7 | 143 | | 02:14 PM | 5.3 | 162 |
| | 07:48 PM | 0.9 | 27 | | 08:23 PM | -0.1 | -3 |
| 6 Su | 02:07 AM | 5.2 | 158 | 21 M | 02:40 AM | 6.1 | 186 |
| | 08:44 AM | 0.8 | 24 | | 09:10 AM | -0.1 | -3 |
| | 02:28 PM | 4.6 | 140 | | 03:15 PM | 5.3 | 162 |
| | 08:40 PM | 1.0 | 30 | | 09:29 PM | 0.0 | 0 |
| 7 M | 02:53 AM | 5.1 | 155 | 22 Tu | 03:40 AM | 5.8 | 177 |
| | 09:35 AM | 0.8 | 24 | | 10:11 AM | -0.1 | -3 |
| | 03:18 PM | 4.6 | 140 | | 04:18 PM | 5.4 | 165 |
| | 09:37 PM | 1.1 | 34 | ◐ | 10:35 PM | 0.1 | 3 |
| 8 Tu | 03:45 AM | 5.0 | 152 | 23 W | 04:41 AM | 5.7 | 174 |
| | 10:26 AM | 0.8 | 24 | | 11:09 AM | -0.2 | -6 |
| | 04:13 PM | 4.7 | 143 | | 05:21 PM | 5.5 | 168 |
| ◐ | 10:36 PM | 1.0 | 30 | | 11:39 PM | 0.1 | 3 |
| 9 W | 04:40 AM | 5.0 | 152 | 24 Th | 05:42 AM | 5.5 | 168 |
| | 11:16 AM | 0.6 | 18 | | 12:04 PM | -0.3 | -9 |
| | 05:10 PM | 4.9 | 149 | | 06:22 PM | 5.7 | 174 |
| | 11:34 PM | 0.9 | 27 | | | | |
| 10 Th | 05:37 AM | 5.0 | 152 | 25 F | 12:39 AM | 0.0 | 0 |
| | 12:05 PM | 0.4 | 12 | | 06:39 AM | 5.4 | 165 |
| | 06:06 PM | 5.2 | 158 | | 12:56 PM | -0.3 | -9 |
| | | | | | 07:17 PM | 5.9 | 180 |
| 11 F | 12:29 AM | 0.7 | 21 | 26 Sa | 01:35 AM | 0.0 | 0 |
| | 06:32 AM | 5.1 | 155 | | 07:32 AM | 5.4 | 165 |
| | 12:53 PM | 0.2 | 6 | | 01:46 PM | -0.3 | -9 |
| | 06:59 PM | 5.5 | 168 | | 08:07 PM | 6.1 | 186 |
| 12 Sa | 01:23 AM | 0.4 | 12 | 27 Su | 02:28 AM | -0.1 | -3 |
| | 07:24 AM | 5.3 | 162 | | 08:21 AM | 5.3 | 162 |
| | 01:40 PM | -0.1 | -3 | | 02:32 PM | -0.3 | -9 |
| | 07:49 PM | 5.9 | 180 | | 08:53 PM | 6.2 | 189 |
| 13 Su | 02:14 AM | 0.1 | 3 | 28 M | 03:16 AM | -0.2 | -6 |
| | 08:13 AM | 5.4 | 165 | | 09:06 AM | 5.2 | 158 |
| | 02:26 PM | -0.4 | -12 | | 03:17 PM | -0.3 | -9 |
| | 08:37 PM | 6.2 | 189 | | 09:37 PM | 6.2 | 189 |
| 14 M | 03:04 AM | -0.2 | -6 | 29 Tu | 04:01 AM | -0.2 | -6 |
| | 09:01 AM | 5.5 | 168 | | 09:49 AM | 5.1 | 155 |
| | 03:13 PM | -0.6 | -18 | | 03:58 PM | -0.2 | -6 |
| | 09:24 PM | 6.5 | 198 | ○ | 10:18 PM | 6.1 | 186 |
| 15 Tu | 03:52 AM | -0.5 | -15 | 30 W | 04:43 AM | -0.1 | -3 |
| | 09:49 AM | 5.5 | 168 | | 10:30 AM | 5.0 | 152 |
| | 03:58 PM | -0.8 | -24 | | 04:37 PM | 0.0 | 0 |
| ● | 10:12 PM | 6.6 | 201 | | 10:57 PM | 5.9 | 180 |
| | | | | 31 Th | 05:22 AM | 0.0 | 0 |
| | | | | | 11:11 AM | 4.9 | 149 |
| | | | | | 05:15 PM | 0.1 | 3 |
| | | | | | 11:36 PM | 5.8 | 177 |

## June

| Day | Time | ft | cm | Day | Time | ft | cm |
|---|---|---|---|---|---|---|---|
| 1 F | 06:01 AM | 0.2 | 6 | 16 Sa | 06:03 AM | -0.8 | -24 |
| | 11:51 AM | 4.8 | 146 | | 12:08 PM | 5.5 | 168 |
| | 05:52 PM | 0.3 | 9 | | 06:11 PM | -0.8 | -24 |
| 2 Sa | 12:15 AM | 5.6 | 171 | 17 Su | 12:35 AM | 6.6 | 201 |
| | 06:41 AM | 0.3 | 9 | | 06:56 AM | -0.7 | -21 |
| | 12:32 PM | 4.7 | 143 | | 01:05 PM | 5.5 | 168 |
| | 06:31 PM | 0.5 | 15 | | 07:08 PM | -0.6 | -18 |
| 3 Su | 12:54 AM | 5.4 | 165 | 18 M | 01:30 AM | 6.3 | 192 |
| | 07:22 AM | 0.5 | 15 | | 07:52 AM | -0.5 | -15 |
| | 01:14 PM | 4.6 | 140 | | 02:02 PM | 5.5 | 168 |
| | 07:13 PM | 0.7 | 21 | | 08:10 PM | -0.3 | -9 |
| 4 M | 01:34 AM | 5.2 | 158 | 19 Tu | 02:24 AM | 6.0 | 183 |
| | 08:05 AM | 0.6 | 18 | | 08:51 AM | -0.4 | -12 |
| | 01:58 PM | 4.6 | 140 | | 03:00 PM | 5.5 | 168 |
| | 08:01 PM | 0.9 | 27 | | 09:14 PM | 0.0 | 0 |
| 5 Tu | 02:17 AM | 5.1 | 155 | 20 W | 03:20 AM | 5.7 | 174 |
| | 08:52 AM | 0.6 | 18 | | 09:49 AM | -0.4 | -12 |
| | 02:44 PM | 4.6 | 140 | | 04:00 PM | 5.5 | 168 |
| | 08:56 PM | 0.9 | 27 | ◐ | 10:19 PM | 0.1 | 3 |
| 6 W | 03:04 AM | 5.0 | 152 | 21 Th | 04:16 AM | 5.5 | 168 |
| | 09:41 AM | 0.5 | 15 | | 10:44 AM | -0.3 | -9 |
| | 03:34 PM | 4.8 | 146 | | 05:00 PM | 5.6 | 171 |
| ◐ | 09:55 PM | 0.9 | 27 | | 11:21 PM | 0.2 | 6 |
| 7 Th | 03:54 AM | 4.9 | 149 | 22 F | 05:14 AM | 5.2 | 158 |
| | 10:31 AM | 0.3 | 9 | | 11:37 AM | -0.3 | -9 |
| | 04:28 PM | 4.9 | 149 | | 05:58 PM | 5.7 | 174 |
| | 10:54 PM | 0.8 | 24 | | | | |
| 8 F | 04:49 AM | 4.9 | 149 | 23 Sa | 12:18 AM | 0.2 | 6 |
| | 11:20 AM | 0.1 | 3 | | 06:09 AM | 5.1 | 155 |
| | 05:24 PM | 5.2 | 158 | | 12:28 PM | -0.3 | -9 |
| | 11:52 PM | 0.6 | 18 | | 06:52 PM | 5.8 | 177 |
| 9 Sa | 05:46 AM | 4.9 | 149 | 24 Su | 01:13 AM | 0.1 | 3 |
| | 12:10 PM | -0.1 | -3 | | 07:02 AM | 5.0 | 152 |
| | 06:20 PM | 5.6 | 171 | | 01:16 PM | -0.2 | -6 |
| | | | | | 07:42 PM | 5.9 | 180 |
| 10 Su | 12:48 AM | 0.3 | 9 | 25 M | 02:04 AM | 0.1 | 3 |
| | 06:42 AM | 5.0 | 152 | | 07:50 AM | 4.9 | 149 |
| | 01:01 PM | -0.3 | -9 | | 02:03 PM | -0.2 | -6 |
| | 07:14 PM | 5.9 | 180 | | 08:27 PM | 5.9 | 180 |
| 11 M | 01:44 AM | 0.0 | 0 | 26 Tu | 02:52 AM | 0.0 | 0 |
| | 07:37 AM | 5.2 | 158 | | 08:36 AM | 4.9 | 149 |
| | 01:52 PM | -0.6 | -18 | | 02:48 PM | -0.1 | -3 |
| | 08:07 PM | 6.3 | 192 | | 09:10 PM | 5.9 | 180 |
| 12 Tu | 02:38 AM | -0.3 | -9 | 27 W | 03:36 AM | 0.0 | 0 |
| | 08:30 AM | 5.3 | 162 | | 09:20 AM | 4.8 | 146 |
| | 02:43 PM | -0.8 | -24 | | 03:30 PM | -0.1 | -3 |
| | 09:00 PM | 6.5 | 198 | | 09:51 PM | 5.9 | 180 |
| 13 W | 03:30 AM | -0.6 | -18 | 28 Th | 04:18 AM | 0.0 | 0 |
| | 09:23 AM | 5.4 | 165 | | 10:02 AM | 4.8 | 146 |
| ● | 03:35 PM | -1.0 | -30 | ○ | 10:31 PM | 5.8 | 177 |
| | 09:53 PM | 6.7 | 204 | | | | |
| 14 Th | 04:21 AM | -0.7 | -21 | 29 F | 04:56 AM | 0.0 | 0 |
| | 10:17 AM | 5.5 | 168 | | 10:43 AM | 4.7 | 143 |
| | 04:26 PM | -1.1 | -34 | | 04:48 PM | 0.1 | 3 |
| ○ | 10:46 PM | 6.8 | 207 | | 11:10 PM | 5.7 | 174 |
| 15 F | 05:11 AM | -0.8 | -24 | 30 Sa | 05:34 AM | 0.1 | 3 |
| | 11:12 AM | 5.5 | 168 | | 11:24 AM | 4.7 | 143 |
| | 05:17 PM | -1.0 | -30 | | 05:26 PM | 0.2 | 6 |
| | 11:41 PM | 6.7 | 204 | | 11:48 PM | 5.5 | 168 |

SKIPPER'S HANDBOOK

Heights are referred to mean lower water which is the chart datum of sounding. All times are local. Daylight Saving Time has been used when needed. Additional tide tables are available online from NOAA at www.tidesandcurrents.noaa.gov/tide_predictions.shtml.

StationId: 8720086
Source: NOAA/NOS/CO-OPS
Station Type: Subordinate
Time Zone: LST_LDT
Datum: MLLW

## NOAA Tide Predictions

## AMELIA CITY, SOUTH AMELIA RIVER, FL,2018

### Times and Heights of High and Low Waters

### July

| Day | Time | ft | cm |
|---|---|---|---|
| 1 Su | 06:11 AM | 0.2 | 6 |
| | 12:04 PM | 4.7 | 143 |
| | 06:03 PM | 0.4 | 12 |
| 2 M | 12:26 AM | 5.4 | 165 |
| | 06:49 AM | 0.3 | 9 |
| | 12:46 PM | 4.6 | 140 |
| | 06:44 PM | 0.5 | 15 |
| 3 Tu | 01:05 AM | 5.3 | 162 |
| | 07:28 AM | 0.3 | 9 |
| | 01:28 PM | 4.7 | 143 |
| | 07:29 PM | 0.7 | 21 |
| 4 W | 01:45 AM | 5.1 | 155 |
| | 08:11 AM | 0.3 | 9 |
| | 02:11 PM | 4.8 | 146 |
| | 08:21 PM | 0.8 | 24 |
| 5 Th | 02:28 AM | 5.0 | 152 |
| | 08:58 AM | 0.2 | 6 |
| | 02:58 PM | 4.9 | 149 |
| | 09:18 PM | 0.8 | 24 |
| 6 F ◑ | 03:14 AM | 4.9 | 149 |
| | 09:48 AM | 0.1 | 3 |
| | 03:49 PM | 5.1 | 155 |
| | 10:18 PM | 0.7 | 21 |
| 7 Sa | 04:07 AM | 4.9 | 149 |
| | 10:40 AM | 0.0 | 0 |
| | 04:45 PM | 5.4 | 165 |
| | 11:18 PM | 0.5 | 15 |
| 8 Su | 05:04 AM | 4.9 | 149 |
| | 11:33 AM | -0.3 | -9 |
| | 05:44 PM | 5.7 | 174 |
| 9 M | 12:17 AM | 0.3 | 9 |
| | 06:05 AM | 4.9 | 149 |
| | 12:28 PM | -0.5 | -15 |
| | 06:44 PM | 6.0 | 183 |
| 10 Tu | 01:16 AM | 0.0 | 0 |
| | 07:05 AM | 5.1 | 155 |
| | 01:23 PM | -0.7 | -21 |
| | 07:42 PM | 6.3 | 192 |
| 11 W | 02:13 AM | -0.3 | -9 |
| | 08:04 AM | 5.2 | 158 |
| | 02:19 PM | -0.9 | -27 |
| | 08:39 PM | 6.6 | 201 |
| 12 Th ○ | 03:08 AM | -0.6 | -18 |
| | 09:01 AM | 5.4 | 165 |
| | 03:15 PM | -1.1 | -34 |
| | 09:35 PM | 6.8 | 207 |
| 13 F ● | 04:02 AM | -0.8 | -24 |
| | 09:59 AM | 5.6 | 171 |
| | 04:09 PM | -1.2 | -37 |
| | 10:31 PM | 6.8 | 207 |
| 14 Sa | 04:53 AM | -0.9 | -27 |
| | 10:56 AM | 5.7 | 174 |
| | 05:03 PM | -1.1 | -34 |
| | 11:25 PM | 6.8 | 207 |
| 15 Su | 05:45 AM | -0.9 | -27 |
| | 11:53 AM | 5.7 | 174 |
| | 05:57 PM | -0.9 | -27 |
| 16 M | 12:19 AM | 6.6 | 201 |
| | 06:37 AM | -0.8 | -24 |
| | 12:49 PM | 5.7 | 174 |
| | 06:53 PM | -0.6 | -18 |
| 17 Tu | 01:11 AM | 6.3 | 192 |
| | 07:30 AM | -0.6 | -18 |
| | 01:44 PM | 5.7 | 174 |
| | 07:53 PM | -0.3 | -9 |
| 18 W | 02:03 AM | 6.0 | 183 |
| | 08:25 AM | -0.5 | -15 |
| | 02:40 PM | 5.7 | 174 |
| | 08:55 PM | 0.0 | 0 |
| 19 Th ◑ | 02:55 AM | 5.6 | 171 |
| | 09:21 AM | -0.3 | -9 |
| | 03:36 PM | 5.6 | 171 |
| | 09:58 PM | 0.2 | 6 |
| 20 F | 03:48 AM | 5.3 | 162 |
| | 10:15 AM | -0.2 | -6 |
| | 04:32 PM | 5.6 | 171 |
| | 10:57 PM | 0.3 | 9 |
| 21 Sa | 04:42 AM | 5.0 | 152 |
| | 11:08 AM | -0.1 | -3 |
| | 05:29 PM | 5.6 | 171 |
| | 11:54 PM | 0.4 | 12 |
| 22 Su | 05:36 AM | 4.9 | 149 |
| | 11:58 AM | 0.0 | 0 |
| | 06:23 PM | 5.6 | 171 |
| 23 M | 12:47 AM | 0.4 | 12 |
| | 06:29 AM | 4.8 | 146 |
| | 12:47 PM | 0.1 | 3 |
| | 07:13 PM | 5.7 | 174 |
| 24 Tu | 01:37 AM | 0.4 | 12 |
| | 07:19 AM | 4.8 | 146 |
| | 01:34 PM | 0.1 | 3 |
| | 07:59 PM | 5.7 | 174 |
| 25 W | 02:24 AM | 0.3 | 9 |
| | 08:06 AM | 4.8 | 146 |
| | 02:20 PM | 0.1 | 3 |
| | 08:43 PM | 5.8 | 177 |
| 26 Th | 03:09 AM | 0.2 | 6 |
| | 08:50 AM | 4.8 | 146 |
| | 03:04 PM | 0.1 | 3 |
| | 09:24 PM | 5.8 | 177 |
| 27 F ○ | 03:50 AM | 0.2 | 6 |
| | 09:33 AM | 4.9 | 149 |
| | 03:45 PM | 0.1 | 3 |
| | 10:05 PM | 5.8 | 177 |
| 28 Sa | 04:28 AM | 0.1 | 3 |
| | 10:15 AM | 4.9 | 149 |
| | 04:25 PM | 0.2 | 6 |
| | 10:44 PM | 5.7 | 174 |
| 29 Su | 05:05 AM | 0.1 | 3 |
| | 10:57 AM | 4.9 | 149 |
| | 05:02 PM | 0.2 | 6 |
| | 11:22 PM | 5.7 | 174 |
| 30 M | 05:40 AM | 0.2 | 6 |
| | 11:37 AM | 5.0 | 152 |
| | 05:40 PM | 0.4 | 12 |
| | 11:59 PM | 5.5 | 168 |
| 31 Tu | 06:16 AM | 0.2 | 6 |
| | 12:17 PM | 5.0 | 152 |
| | 06:19 PM | 0.5 | 15 |

### August

| Day | Time | ft | cm |
|---|---|---|---|
| 1 W | 12:36 AM | 5.4 | 165 |
| | 06:53 AM | 0.2 | 6 |
| | 12:58 PM | 5.0 | 152 |
| | 07:02 PM | 0.6 | 18 |
| 2 Th | 01:15 AM | 5.3 | 162 |
| | 07:34 AM | 0.2 | 6 |
| | 01:40 PM | 5.1 | 155 |
| | 07:51 PM | 0.7 | 21 |
| 3 F | 01:56 AM | 5.2 | 158 |
| | 08:19 AM | 0.2 | 6 |
| | 02:25 PM | 5.3 | 162 |
| | 08:48 PM | 0.7 | 21 |
| 4 Sa ◑ | 02:42 AM | 5.1 | 155 |
| | 09:10 AM | 0.1 | 3 |
| | 03:16 PM | 5.4 | 165 |
| | 09:48 PM | 0.7 | 21 |
| 5 Su | 03:34 AM | 5.0 | 152 |
| | 10:05 AM | 0.0 | 0 |
| | 04:13 PM | 5.6 | 171 |
| | 10:50 PM | 0.6 | 18 |
| 6 M | 04:33 AM | 5.0 | 152 |
| | 11:03 AM | -0.1 | -3 |
| | 05:15 PM | 5.9 | 180 |
| | 11:52 PM | 0.4 | 12 |
| 7 Tu | 05:36 AM | 5.0 | 152 |
| | 12:02 PM | -0.3 | -9 |
| | 06:20 PM | 6.1 | 186 |
| 8 W | 12:52 AM | 0.2 | 6 |
| | 06:41 AM | 5.2 | 158 |
| | 01:01 PM | -0.6 | -18 |
| | 07:23 PM | 6.4 | 195 |
| 9 Th | 01:51 AM | -0.1 | -3 |
| | 07:44 AM | 5.4 | 165 |
| | 02:01 PM | -0.8 | -24 |
| | 08:22 PM | 6.7 | 204 |
| 10 F | 02:48 AM | -0.4 | -12 |
| | 08:44 AM | 5.7 | 174 |
| | 02:58 PM | -0.9 | -27 |
| | 09:18 PM | 6.9 | 210 |
| 11 Sa ● | 03:42 AM | -0.6 | -18 |
| | 09:42 AM | 5.9 | 180 |
| | 03:54 PM | -1.0 | -30 |
| | 10:13 PM | 6.9 | 210 |
| 12 Su ○ | 04:33 AM | -0.8 | -24 |
| | 10:38 AM | 6.1 | 186 |
| | 04:48 PM | -0.9 | -27 |
| | 11:06 PM | 6.8 | 207 |
| 13 M | 05:23 AM | -0.8 | -24 |
| | 11:34 AM | 6.2 | 189 |
| | 05:41 PM | -0.7 | -21 |
| | 11:58 PM | 6.6 | 201 |
| 14 Tu | 06:12 AM | -0.7 | -21 |
| | 12:28 PM | 6.2 | 189 |
| | 06:35 PM | -0.4 | -12 |
| 15 W | 12:48 AM | 6.3 | 192 |
| | 07:02 AM | -0.5 | -15 |
| | 01:20 PM | 6.1 | 186 |
| | 07:32 PM | -0.1 | -3 |
| 16 Th | 01:37 AM | 6.0 | 183 |
| | 07:54 AM | -0.2 | -6 |
| | 02:13 PM | 6.0 | 183 |
| | 08:30 PM | 0.3 | 9 |
| 17 F | 02:26 AM | 5.6 | 171 |
| | 08:47 AM | 0.0 | 0 |
| | 03:05 PM | 5.8 | 177 |
| | 09:30 PM | 0.5 | 15 |
| 18 Sa ◑ | 03:16 AM | 5.3 | 162 |
| | 09:41 AM | 0.3 | 9 |
| | 03:59 PM | 5.7 | 174 |
| | 10:29 PM | 0.7 | 21 |
| 19 Su | 04:07 AM | 5.0 | 152 |
| | 10:34 AM | 0.4 | 12 |
| | 04:53 PM | 5.6 | 171 |
| | 11:24 PM | 0.8 | 24 |
| 20 M | 05:01 AM | 4.9 | 149 |
| | 11:26 AM | 0.5 | 15 |
| | 05:48 PM | 5.6 | 171 |
| 21 Tu | 12:16 AM | 0.8 | 24 |
| | 05:54 AM | 4.9 | 149 |
| | 12:16 PM | 0.5 | 15 |
| | 06:39 PM | 5.7 | 174 |
| 22 W | 01:05 AM | 0.8 | 24 |
| | 06:46 AM | 4.9 | 149 |
| | 01:05 PM | 0.5 | 15 |
| | 07:28 PM | 5.7 | 174 |
| 23 Th | 01:53 AM | 0.7 | 21 |
| | 07:35 AM | 5.0 | 152 |
| | 01:53 PM | 0.5 | 15 |
| | 08:13 PM | 5.9 | 180 |
| 24 F | 02:37 AM | 0.5 | 15 |
| | 08:21 AM | 5.2 | 158 |
| | 02:38 PM | 0.4 | 12 |
| | 08:55 PM | 5.9 | 180 |
| 25 Sa | 03:18 AM | 0.4 | 12 |
| | 09:05 AM | 5.3 | 162 |
| | 03:21 PM | 0.4 | 12 |
| | 09:36 PM | 6.0 | 183 |
| 26 Su ○ | 03:57 AM | 0.3 | 9 |
| | 09:48 AM | 5.4 | 165 |
| | 04:01 PM | 0.3 | 9 |
| | 10:15 PM | 6.0 | 183 |
| 27 M | 04:33 AM | 0.3 | 9 |
| | 10:29 AM | 5.5 | 168 |
| | 04:40 PM | 0.4 | 12 |
| | 10:54 PM | 5.9 | 180 |
| 28 Tu | 05:08 AM | 0.2 | 6 |
| | 11:09 AM | 5.5 | 168 |
| | 05:18 PM | 0.4 | 12 |
| | 11:31 PM | 5.8 | 177 |
| 29 W | 05:43 AM | 0.2 | 6 |
| | 11:48 AM | 5.6 | 171 |
| | 05:57 PM | 0.5 | 15 |
| 30 Th | 12:09 AM | 5.6 | 171 |
| | 06:20 AM | 0.3 | 9 |
| | 12:29 PM | 5.6 | 171 |
| | 06:40 PM | 0.6 | 18 |
| 31 F | 12:48 AM | 5.5 | 168 |
| | 07:00 AM | 0.3 | 9 |
| | 01:11 PM | 5.7 | 174 |
| | 07:28 PM | 0.7 | 21 |

### September

| Day | Time | ft | cm |
|---|---|---|---|
| 1 Sa | 01:30 AM | 5.4 | 165 |
| | 07:46 AM | 0.3 | 9 |
| | 01:57 PM | 5.8 | 177 |
| | 08:23 PM | 0.8 | 24 |
| 2 Su | 02:17 AM | 5.3 | 162 |
| | 08:39 AM | 0.3 | 9 |
| | 02:50 PM | 5.9 | 180 |
| | 09:25 PM | 0.8 | 24 |
| 3 M ◑ | 03:11 AM | 5.2 | 158 |
| | 09:38 AM | 0.3 | 9 |
| | 03:49 PM | 6.0 | 183 |
| | 10:28 PM | 0.8 | 24 |
| 4 Tu | 04:11 AM | 5.2 | 158 |
| | 10:40 AM | 0.2 | 6 |
| | 04:55 PM | 6.1 | 186 |
| | 11:31 PM | 0.6 | 18 |
| 5 W | 05:18 AM | 5.3 | 162 |
| | 11:43 AM | 0.0 | 0 |
| | 06:02 PM | 6.3 | 192 |
| 6 Th | 12:32 AM | 0.4 | 12 |
| | 06:26 AM | 5.5 | 168 |
| | 12:45 PM | -0.2 | -6 |
| | 07:06 PM | 6.6 | 201 |
| 7 F | 01:31 AM | 0.1 | 3 |
| | 07:30 AM | 5.8 | 177 |
| | 01:46 PM | -0.4 | -12 |
| | 08:06 PM | 6.8 | 207 |
| 8 Sa | 02:28 AM | -0.1 | -3 |
| | 08:29 AM | 6.1 | 186 |
| | 02:44 PM | -0.6 | -18 |
| | 09:01 PM | 6.9 | 210 |
| 9 Su ● | 03:21 AM | -0.4 | -12 |
| | 09:25 AM | 6.4 | 195 |
| | 03:40 PM | -0.6 | -18 |
| | 09:53 PM | 7.0 | 213 |
| 10 M | 04:11 AM | -0.5 | -15 |
| | 10:20 AM | 6.6 | 201 |
| | 04:33 PM | -0.6 | -18 |
| | 10:44 PM | 6.8 | 207 |
| 11 Tu | 04:58 AM | -0.5 | -15 |
| | 11:12 AM | 6.6 | 201 |
| | 05:24 PM | -0.4 | -12 |
| | 11:33 PM | 6.6 | 201 |
| 12 W | 05:45 AM | -0.4 | -12 |
| | 12:03 PM | 6.6 | 201 |
| | 06:15 PM | -0.1 | -3 |
| 13 Th | 12:21 AM | 6.3 | 192 |
| | 06:31 AM | -0.1 | -3 |
| | 12:52 PM | 6.4 | 195 |
| | 07:07 PM | 0.3 | 9 |
| 14 F | 01:07 AM | 5.9 | 180 |
| | 07:19 AM | 0.2 | 6 |
| | 01:41 PM | 6.2 | 189 |
| | 08:01 PM | 0.6 | 18 |
| 15 Sa | 01:54 AM | 5.6 | 171 |
| | 08:09 AM | 0.6 | 18 |
| | 02:29 PM | 6.0 | 183 |
| | 08:57 PM | 0.9 | 27 |
| 16 Su ◑ | 02:41 AM | 5.3 | 162 |
| | 09:02 AM | 0.8 | 24 |
| | 03:20 PM | 5.8 | 177 |
| | 09:54 PM | 1.1 | 34 |
| 17 M | 03:30 AM | 5.1 | 155 |
| | 09:56 AM | 1.0 | 30 |
| | 04:12 PM | 5.7 | 174 |
| | 10:49 PM | 1.2 | 37 |
| 18 Tu ◑ | 04:23 AM | 5.0 | 152 |
| | 10:50 AM | 1.1 | 34 |
| | 05:07 PM | 5.6 | 171 |
| | 11:40 PM | 1.2 | 37 |
| 19 W | 05:17 AM | 5.0 | 152 |
| | 11:43 AM | 1.1 | 34 |
| | 06:01 PM | 5.7 | 174 |
| 20 Th | 12:30 AM | 1.1 | 34 |
| | 06:12 AM | 5.1 | 155 |
| | 12:34 PM | 1.0 | 30 |
| | 06:52 PM | 5.8 | 177 |
| 21 F | 01:17 AM | 1.0 | 30 |
| | 07:03 AM | 5.3 | 162 |
| | 01:24 PM | 0.9 | 27 |
| | 07:39 PM | 5.9 | 180 |
| 22 Sa | 02:01 AM | 0.8 | 24 |
| | 07:51 AM | 5.6 | 171 |
| | 02:11 PM | 0.7 | 21 |
| | 08:23 PM | 6.0 | 183 |
| 23 Su | 02:43 AM | 0.6 | 18 |
| | 08:36 AM | 5.8 | 177 |
| | 02:55 PM | 0.6 | 18 |
| | 09:04 PM | 6.1 | 186 |
| 24 M | 03:23 AM | 0.5 | 15 |
| | 09:19 AM | 5.9 | 180 |
| | 03:37 PM | 0.5 | 15 |
| | 09:45 PM | 6.1 | 186 |
| 25 Tu ○ | 04:00 AM | 0.3 | 9 |
| | 10:00 AM | 6.1 | 186 |
| | 04:17 PM | 0.4 | 12 |
| | 10:24 PM | 6.1 | 186 |
| 26 W | 04:36 AM | 0.3 | 9 |
| | 10:41 AM | 6.2 | 189 |
| | 04:57 PM | 0.4 | 12 |
| | 11:03 PM | 6.0 | 183 |
| 27 Th | 05:13 AM | 0.2 | 6 |
| | 11:21 AM | 6.2 | 189 |
| | 05:38 PM | 0.5 | 15 |
| | 11:43 PM | 5.9 | 180 |
| 28 F | 05:51 AM | 0.2 | 6 |
| | 12:03 PM | 6.3 | 192 |
| | 06:21 PM | 0.6 | 18 |
| 29 Sa | 12:25 AM | 5.7 | 174 |
| | 06:33 AM | 0.3 | 9 |
| | 12:48 PM | 6.3 | 192 |
| | 07:10 PM | 0.7 | 21 |
| 30 Su | 01:10 AM | 5.6 | 171 |
| | 07:21 AM | 0.4 | 12 |
| | 01:37 PM | 6.3 | 192 |
| | 08:05 PM | 0.8 | 24 |

Heights are referred to mean lower water which is the chart datum of sounding. All times are local. Daylight Saving Time has been used when needed. Additional tide tables are available online from NOAA at www.tidesandcurrents.noaa.gov/tide_predictions.shtml.

SKIPPER'S HANDBOOK

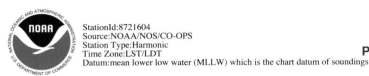

StationId:8721604
Source:NOAA/NOS/CO-OPS
Station Type:Harmonic
Time Zone:LST/LDT
Datum:mean lower low water (MLLW) which is the chart datum of soundings

**NOAA Tide Predictions**

## PORT CANAVERAL (TRIDENT PIER),Florida,2017

### Times and Heights of High and Low Waters

## October

| Day | Time | ft | cm | Day | Time | ft | cm |
|---|---|---|---|---|---|---|---|
| **1** Su | 04:51 AM | 3.5 | 107 | **16** M | 05:45 AM | 4.2 | 128 |
| | 10:52 AM | 0.9 | 27 | | 11:48 AM | 0.5 | 15 |
| | 05:21 PM | 4.1 | 125 | | 06:09 PM | 4.4 | 134 |
| | 11:33 PM | 0.9 | 27 | | | | |
| **2** M | 05:39 AM | 3.7 | 113 | **17** Tu | 12:20 AM | 0.4 | 12 |
| | 11:43 AM | 0.7 | 21 | | 06:36 AM | 4.4 | 134 |
| | 06:06 PM | 4.2 | 128 | | 12:42 PM | 0.4 | 12 |
| | | | | | 06:57 PM | 4.3 | 131 |
| **3** Tu | 12:16 AM | 0.7 | 21 | **18** W | 01:04 AM | 0.4 | 12 |
| | 06:25 AM | 4.0 | 122 | | 07:24 AM | 4.5 | 137 |
| | 12:32 PM | 0.5 | 15 | | 01:31 PM | 0.4 | 12 |
| | 06:49 PM | 4.3 | 131 | | 07:41 PM | 4.2 | 128 |
| **4** W | 12:58 AM | 0.5 | 15 | **19** Th ● | 01:45 AM | 0.3 | 9 |
| | 07:10 AM | 4.3 | 131 | | 08:08 AM | 4.6 | 140 |
| | 01:18 PM | 0.4 | 12 | | 02:15 PM | 0.5 | 15 |
| | 07:33 PM | 4.4 | 134 | | 08:23 PM | 4.1 | 125 |
| **5** Th ○ | 01:39 AM | 0.3 | 9 | **20** F | 02:23 AM | 0.3 | 9 |
| | 07:55 AM | 4.5 | 137 | | 08:50 AM | 4.6 | 140 |
| | 02:05 PM | 0.3 | 9 | | 02:57 PM | 0.5 | 15 |
| | 08:17 PM | 4.4 | 134 | | 09:04 PM | 4.0 | 122 |
| **6** F | 02:21 AM | 0.1 | 3 | **21** Sa | 03:00 AM | 0.4 | 12 |
| | 08:42 AM | 4.7 | 143 | | 09:31 AM | 4.6 | 140 |
| | 02:51 PM | 0.2 | 6 | | 03:39 PM | 0.7 | 21 |
| | 09:03 PM | 4.4 | 134 | | 09:44 PM | 3.8 | 116 |
| **7** Sa | 03:03 AM | 0.0 | 0 | **22** Su | 03:38 AM | 0.5 | 15 |
| | 09:29 AM | 4.9 | 149 | | 10:10 AM | 4.5 | 137 |
| | 03:40 PM | 0.2 | 6 | | 04:22 PM | 0.8 | 24 |
| | 09:49 PM | 4.3 | 131 | | 10:23 PM | 3.6 | 110 |
| **8** Su | 03:49 AM | 0.0 | 0 | **23** M | 04:17 AM | 0.7 | 21 |
| | 10:18 AM | 5.0 | 152 | | 10:50 AM | 4.4 | 134 |
| | 04:33 PM | 0.3 | 9 | | 05:06 PM | 0.9 | 27 |
| | 10:37 PM | 4.2 | 128 | | 11:03 PM | 3.5 | 107 |
| **9** M | 04:38 AM | 0.1 | 3 | **24** Tu | 05:00 AM | 0.8 | 24 |
| | 11:08 AM | 5.0 | 152 | | 11:31 AM | 4.2 | 128 |
| | 05:29 PM | 0.4 | 12 | | 05:53 PM | 1.1 | 34 |
| | 11:28 PM | 4.1 | 125 | | 11:45 PM | 3.3 | 101 |
| **10** Tu | 05:33 AM | 0.2 | 6 | **25** W | 05:47 AM | 1.0 | 30 |
| | 12:02 PM | 4.9 | 149 | | 12:14 PM | 4.1 | 125 |
| | 06:29 PM | 0.6 | 18 | | 06:43 PM | 1.2 | 37 |
| **11** W | 12:23 AM | 3.9 | 119 | **26** Th | 12:30 AM | 3.2 | 98 |
| | 06:32 AM | 0.3 | 9 | | 06:38 AM | 1.1 | 34 |
| | 01:00 PM | 4.7 | 143 | | 01:02 PM | 3.9 | 119 |
| | 07:31 PM | 0.7 | 21 | | 07:33 PM | 1.2 | 37 |
| **12** Th ◑ | 01:24 AM | 3.8 | 116 | **27** F ◐ | 01:22 AM | 3.2 | 98 |
| | 07:35 AM | 0.4 | 12 | | 07:31 AM | 1.2 | 37 |
| | 02:04 PM | 4.6 | 140 | | 01:55 PM | 3.8 | 116 |
| | 08:34 PM | 0.7 | 21 | | 08:24 PM | 1.2 | 37 |
| **13** F | 02:32 AM | 3.7 | 113 | **28** Sa | 02:19 AM | 3.2 | 98 |
| | 08:39 AM | 0.5 | 15 | | 08:26 AM | 1.2 | 37 |
| | 03:13 PM | 4.5 | 137 | | 02:51 PM | 3.8 | 116 |
| | 09:36 PM | 0.7 | 21 | | 09:13 PM | 1.1 | 34 |
| **14** Sa | 03:43 AM | 3.8 | 116 | **29** Su | 03:19 AM | 3.3 | 101 |
| | 09:44 AM | 0.5 | 15 | | 09:21 AM | 1.1 | 34 |
| | 04:18 PM | 4.4 | 134 | | 03:46 PM | 3.9 | 119 |
| | 10:35 PM | 0.6 | 18 | | 10:02 PM | 0.9 | 27 |
| **15** Su | 04:48 AM | 4.0 | 122 | **30** M | 04:15 AM | 3.5 | 107 |
| | 10:48 AM | 0.5 | 15 | | 10:17 AM | 0.9 | 27 |
| | 05:17 PM | 4.4 | 134 | | 04:37 PM | 3.9 | 119 |
| | 11:31 PM | 0.5 | 15 | | 10:49 PM | 0.7 | 21 |
| | | | | **31** Tu | 05:05 AM | 3.8 | 116 |
| | | | | | 11:11 AM | 0.8 | 24 |
| | | | | | 05:25 PM | 4.1 | 125 |
| | | | | | 11:35 PM | 0.5 | 15 |

## November

| Day | Time | ft | cm | Day | Time | ft | cm |
|---|---|---|---|---|---|---|---|
| **1** W | 05:54 AM | 4.2 | 128 | **16** Th | 06:06 AM | 4.4 | 134 |
| | 12:04 PM | 0.5 | 15 | | 12:17 PM | 0.5 | 15 |
| | 06:12 PM | 4.1 | 125 | | 06:16 PM | 3.7 | 113 |
| **2** Th | 12:21 AM | 0.2 | 6 | **17** F | 12:16 AM | 0.2 | 6 |
| | 06:41 AM | 4.5 | 137 | | 06:47 AM | 4.4 | 134 |
| | 12:54 PM | 0.3 | 9 | | 12:59 PM | 0.5 | 15 |
| | 06:59 PM | 4.2 | 128 | | 06:57 PM | 3.6 | 110 |
| **3** F | 01:05 AM | 0.0 | 0 | **18** Sa ● | 12:53 AM | 0.2 | 6 |
| | 07:29 AM | 4.8 | 146 | | 07:27 AM | 4.4 | 134 |
| | 01:44 PM | 0.1 | 3 | | 01:38 PM | 0.5 | 15 |
| | 07:47 PM | 4.2 | 128 | | 07:37 PM | 3.5 | 107 |
| **4** Sa | 01:50 AM | -0.2 | -6 | **19** Su | 01:30 AM | 0.3 | 9 |
| | 08:18 AM | 5.1 | 155 | | 08:05 AM | 4.4 | 134 |
| | 02:33 PM | 0.1 | 3 | | 02:17 PM | 0.6 | 18 |
| | 08:37 PM | 4.2 | 128 | | 08:16 PM | 3.4 | 104 |
| **5** Su ○ | 01:36 AM | -0.3 | -9 | **20** M | 02:07 AM | 0.4 | 12 |
| | 08:08 AM | 5.2 | 158 | | 08:44 AM | 4.3 | 131 |
| | 02:24 PM | 0.0 | 0 | | 02:56 PM | 0.6 | 18 |
| | 08:27 PM | 4.2 | 128 | | 08:55 PM | 3.3 | 101 |
| **6** M | 02:25 AM | -0.3 | -9 | **21** Tu | 02:45 AM | 0.5 | 15 |
| | 08:59 AM | 5.2 | 158 | | 09:22 AM | 4.2 | 128 |
| | 03:17 PM | 0.1 | 3 | | 03:38 PM | 0.7 | 21 |
| | 09:19 PM | 4.1 | 125 | | 09:35 PM | 3.2 | 98 |
| **7** Tu | 03:17 AM | -0.2 | -6 | **22** W | 03:26 AM | 0.6 | 18 |
| | 09:51 AM | 5.1 | 155 | | 10:01 AM | 4.1 | 125 |
| | 04:14 PM | 0.2 | 6 | | 04:22 PM | 0.8 | 24 |
| | 10:12 PM | 4.0 | 122 | | 10:16 PM | 3.1 | 94 |
| **8** W | 04:14 AM | 0.0 | 0 | **23** Th | 04:11 AM | 0.7 | 21 |
| | 10:45 AM | 4.9 | 149 | | 10:41 AM | 3.9 | 119 |
| | 05:14 PM | 0.3 | 9 | | 05:08 PM | 0.8 | 24 |
| | 11:09 PM | 3.8 | 116 | | 10:59 PM | 3.1 | 94 |
| **9** Th | 05:15 AM | 0.2 | 6 | **24** F | 05:00 AM | 0.8 | 24 |
| | 11:43 AM | 4.7 | 143 | | 11:24 AM | 3.8 | 116 |
| | 06:16 PM | 0.4 | 12 | | 05:55 PM | 0.8 | 24 |
| | | | | | 11:46 PM | 3.0 | 91 |
| **10** F ◑ | 12:12 AM | 3.7 | 113 | **25** Sa | 05:52 AM | 0.9 | 27 |
| | 06:20 AM | 0.4 | 12 | | 12:11 PM | 3.7 | 113 |
| | 12:46 PM | 4.4 | 134 | | 06:43 PM | 0.8 | 24 |
| | 07:18 PM | 0.5 | 15 | | | | |
| **11** Sa | 01:21 AM | 3.7 | 113 | **26** Su ◐ | 12:40 AM | 3.1 | 94 |
| | 07:26 AM | 0.5 | 15 | | 06:47 AM | 0.9 | 27 |
| | 01:52 PM | 4.2 | 128 | | 01:03 PM | 3.6 | 110 |
| | 08:17 PM | 0.5 | 15 | | 07:31 PM | 0.7 | 21 |
| **12** Su | 02:33 AM | 3.8 | 116 | **27** M | 01:38 AM | 3.2 | 98 |
| | 08:32 AM | 0.6 | 18 | | 07:44 AM | 0.9 | 27 |
| | 02:57 PM | 4.1 | 125 | | 01:58 PM | 3.6 | 110 |
| | 09:14 PM | 0.4 | 12 | | 08:19 PM | 0.5 | 15 |
| **13** M | 03:38 AM | 3.9 | 119 | **28** Tu | 02:36 AM | 3.4 | 104 |
| | 09:37 AM | 0.6 | 18 | | 08:41 AM | 0.7 | 21 |
| | 03:56 PM | 4.0 | 122 | | 02:52 PM | 3.6 | 110 |
| | 10:07 PM | 0.4 | 12 | | 09:07 PM | 0.3 | 9 |
| **14** Tu | 04:33 AM | 4.1 | 125 | **29** W | 03:31 AM | 3.8 | 116 |
| | 10:37 AM | 0.6 | 18 | | 09:39 AM | 0.6 | 18 |
| | 04:47 PM | 3.9 | 119 | | 03:46 PM | 3.7 | 113 |
| | 10:54 PM | 0.3 | 9 | | 09:56 PM | 0.1 | 3 |
| **15** W | 05:22 AM | 4.3 | 131 | **30** Th | 04:23 AM | 4.1 | 125 |
| | 11:30 AM | 0.6 | 18 | | 10:36 AM | 0.3 | 9 |
| | 05:33 PM | 3.8 | 116 | | 04:38 PM | 3.7 | 113 |
| | 11:37 PM | 0.2 | 6 | | 10:46 PM | -0.2 | -6 |

## December

| Day | Time | ft | cm | Day | Time | ft | cm |
|---|---|---|---|---|---|---|---|
| **1** F | 05:14 AM | 4.5 | 137 | **16** Sa | 06:26 AM | 4.0 | 122 |
| | 11:31 AM | 0.1 | 3 | | 12:41 PM | 0.4 | 12 |
| | 05:29 PM | 3.8 | 116 | | 06:32 PM | 3.1 | 94 |
| | 11:35 PM | -0.5 | -15 | | | | |
| **2** Sa | 06:05 AM | 4.8 | 146 | **17** Su | 12:27 AM | 0.0 | 0 |
| | 12:24 PM | -0.1 | -3 | | 07:04 AM | 4.1 | 125 |
| | 06:21 PM | 3.9 | 119 | | 01:18 PM | 0.3 | 9 |
| | | | | | 07:12 PM | 3.0 | 91 |
| **3** Su ○ | 12:24 AM | -0.6 | -18 | **18** M ● | 01:04 AM | 0.0 | 0 |
| | 06:57 AM | 5.0 | 152 | | 07:42 AM | 4.1 | 125 |
| | 01:16 PM | -0.2 | -6 | | 01:55 PM | 0.3 | 9 |
| | 07:14 PM | 3.9 | 119 | | 07:51 PM | 3.0 | 91 |
| **4** M | 01:14 AM | -0.7 | -21 | **19** Tu | 01:42 AM | 0.0 | 0 |
| | 07:49 AM | 5.1 | 155 | | 08:20 AM | 4.0 | 122 |
| | 02:07 PM | -0.3 | -9 | | 02:32 PM | 0.3 | 9 |
| | 08:08 PM | 3.9 | 119 | | 08:31 PM | 3.0 | 91 |
| **5** Tu | 02:06 AM | -0.7 | -21 | **20** W | 02:20 AM | 0.1 | 3 |
| | 08:42 AM | 5.1 | 155 | | 08:57 AM | 4.0 | 122 |
| | 03:01 PM | -0.3 | -9 | | 03:11 PM | 0.3 | 9 |
| | 09:02 PM | 3.9 | 119 | | 09:10 PM | 3.0 | 91 |
| **6** W | 02:59 AM | -0.6 | -18 | **21** Th | 03:00 AM | 0.2 | 6 |
| | 09:35 AM | 5.0 | 152 | | 09:35 AM | 3.9 | 119 |
| | 03:57 PM | -0.2 | -6 | | 03:51 PM | 0.3 | 9 |
| | 09:57 PM | 3.8 | 116 | | 09:49 PM | 2.9 | 88 |
| **7** Th | 03:57 AM | -0.4 | -12 | **22** F | 03:42 AM | 0.3 | 9 |
| | 10:28 AM | 4.7 | 143 | | 10:13 AM | 3.7 | 113 |
| | 04:55 PM | -0.1 | -3 | | 04:34 PM | 0.4 | 12 |
| | 10:54 PM | 3.7 | 113 | | 10:30 PM | 2.9 | 88 |
| **8** F | 04:58 AM | -0.2 | -6 | **23** Sa | 04:28 AM | 0.4 | 12 |
| | 11:24 AM | 4.4 | 134 | | 10:52 AM | 3.6 | 110 |
| | 05:55 PM | 0.0 | 0 | | 05:18 PM | 0.4 | 12 |
| | 11:55 PM | 3.6 | 110 | | 11:15 PM | 2.9 | 88 |
| **9** Sa | 06:03 AM | 0.1 | 3 | **24** Su | 05:18 AM | 0.5 | 15 |
| | 12:22 PM | 4.1 | 125 | | 11:34 AM | 3.5 | 107 |
| | 06:53 PM | 0.1 | 3 | | 06:03 PM | 0.3 | 9 |
| **10** Su ◑ | 01:02 AM | 3.5 | 107 | **25** M | 12:04 AM | 3.0 | 91 |
| | 07:08 AM | 0.3 | 9 | | 06:12 AM | 0.5 | 15 |
| | 01:24 PM | 3.8 | 116 | | 12:21 PM | 3.3 | 101 |
| | 07:50 PM | 0.1 | 3 | | 06:49 PM | 0.2 | 6 |
| **11** M | 02:12 AM | 3.5 | 107 | **26** Tu ◐ | 12:59 AM | 3.1 | 94 |
| | 08:14 AM | 0.4 | 12 | | 07:10 AM | 0.5 | 15 |
| | 02:28 PM | 3.5 | 107 | | 01:14 PM | 3.2 | 98 |
| | 08:44 PM | 0.1 | 3 | | 07:38 PM | 0.1 | 3 |
| **12** Tu | 03:18 AM | 3.6 | 110 | **27** W | 01:58 AM | 3.3 | 101 |
| | 09:18 AM | 0.5 | 15 | | 08:09 AM | 0.4 | 12 |
| | 03:28 PM | 3.3 | 101 | | 02:12 PM | 3.2 | 98 |
| | 09:36 PM | 0.1 | 3 | | 08:28 PM | -0.1 | -3 |
| **13** W | 04:14 AM | 3.8 | 116 | **28** Th | 02:57 AM | 3.6 | 110 |
| | 10:19 AM | 0.5 | 15 | | 09:10 AM | 0.3 | 9 |
| | 04:20 PM | 3.2 | 98 | | 03:10 PM | 3.2 | 98 |
| | 10:24 PM | 0.1 | 3 | | 09:21 PM | -0.3 | -9 |
| **14** Th | 05:02 AM | 3.9 | 119 | **29** F | 03:55 AM | 3.9 | 119 |
| | 11:14 AM | 0.5 | 15 | | 10:11 AM | 0.1 | 3 |
| | 05:07 PM | 3.1 | 94 | | 04:08 PM | 3.3 | 101 |
| | 11:08 PM | 0.1 | 3 | | 10:16 PM | -0.6 | -18 |
| **15** F | 05:45 AM | 4.0 | 122 | **30** Sa | 04:50 AM | 4.3 | 131 |
| | 12:00 PM | 0.4 | 12 | | 11:10 AM | -0.1 | -3 |
| | 05:50 PM | 3.1 | 94 | | 05:04 PM | 3.4 | 104 |
| | 11:48 PM | 0.0 | 0 | | 11:10 PM | -0.8 | -24 |
| | | | | **31** Su | 05:45 AM | 4.6 | 140 |
| | | | | | 12:05 PM | -0.3 | -9 |
| | | | | | 06:00 PM | 3.5 | 107 |

Heights are referred to mean lower water which is the chart datum of sounding. All times are local. Daylight Saving Time has been used when needed. Additional tide tables are available online from NOAA at www.tidesandcurrents.noaa.gov/tide_predictions.shtml.

SKIPPER'S HANDBOOK

StationId: 8721604
Source: NOAA/NOS/CO-OPS
Station Type: Primary
Time Zone: LST_LDT
Datum: MLLW

# NOAA Tide Predictions

## Trident Pier, FL,2018

### Times and Heights of High and Low Waters

## January

| Day | Time (h m) | Height (ft) | Height (cm) | Day | Time (h m) | Height (ft) | Height (cm) |
|---|---|---|---|---|---|---|---|
| 1 M | 12:04 AM | -1.0 | -30 | 16 Tu | 12:42 AM | -0.2 | -6 |
|  | 06:41 AM | 4.7 | 143 |  | 07:20 AM | 3.7 | 113 |
|  | 01:01 PM | -0.5 | -15 |  | 01:32 PM | 0.1 | 3 |
|  | 06:56 PM | 3.5 | 107 |  | 07:27 PM | 2.8 | 85 |
| 2 Tu ○ | 12:57 AM | -1.1 | -34 | 17 W | 01:20 AM | -0.2 | -6 |
|  | 07:35 AM | 4.8 | 146 |  | 07:57 AM | 3.8 | 116 |
|  | 01:53 PM | -0.6 | -18 |  | 02:08 PM | 0.0 | 0 |
|  | 07:52 PM | 3.6 | 110 |  | 08:06 PM ● | 2.8 | 85 |
| 3 W | 01:51 AM | -1.1 | -34 | 18 Th | 01:59 AM | -0.2 | -6 |
|  | 08:28 AM | 4.8 | 146 |  | 08:34 AM | 3.7 | 113 |
|  | 02:45 PM | -0.6 | -18 |  | 02:44 PM | 0.0 | 0 |
|  | 08:47 PM | 3.6 | 110 |  | 08:45 PM | 2.9 | 88 |
| 4 Th | 02:45 AM | -0.9 | -27 | 19 F | 02:38 AM | -0.2 | -6 |
|  | 09:20 AM | 4.6 | 140 |  | 09:11 AM | 3.7 | 113 |
|  | 03:39 PM | -0.5 | -15 |  | 03:22 PM | 0.0 | 0 |
|  | 09:41 PM | 3.6 | 110 |  | 09:24 PM | 2.9 | 88 |
| 5 F | 03:41 AM | -0.7 | -21 | 20 Sa | 03:19 AM | -0.1 | -3 |
|  | 10:11 AM | 4.4 | 134 |  | 09:47 AM | 3.6 | 110 |
|  | 04:34 PM | -0.4 | -12 |  | 04:01 PM | 0.0 | 0 |
|  | 10:37 PM | 3.5 | 107 |  | 10:04 PM | 2.9 | 88 |
| 6 Sa | 04:40 AM | -0.4 | -12 | 21 Su | 04:03 AM | 0.0 | 0 |
|  | 11:02 AM | 4.0 | 122 |  | 10:25 AM | 3.5 | 107 |
|  | 05:29 PM | -0.3 | -9 |  | 04:42 PM | 0.0 | 0 |
|  | 11:34 PM | 3.4 | 104 |  | 10:46 PM | 3.0 | 91 |
| 7 Su | 05:42 AM | -0.1 | -3 | 22 M ◑ | 04:51 AM | 0.1 | 3 |
|  | 11:56 AM | 3.7 | 113 |  | 11:05 AM | 3.3 | 101 |
|  | 06:24 PM | -0.2 | -6 |  | 05:26 PM | -0.1 | -3 |
|  |  |  |  |  | 11:33 PM | 3.0 | 91 |
| 8 M ◑ | 12:36 AM | 3.3 | 101 | 23 Tu | 05:45 AM | 0.2 | 6 |
|  | 06:45 AM | 0.1 | 3 |  | 11:49 AM | 3.2 | 98 |
|  | 12:52 PM | 3.3 | 101 |  | 06:13 PM | -0.1 | -3 |
|  | 07:17 PM | -0.2 | -6 |  |  |  |  |
| 9 Tu | 01:42 AM | 3.3 | 101 | 24 W ◐ | 12:26 AM | 3.2 | 98 |
|  | 07:48 AM | 0.3 | 9 |  | 06:43 AM | 0.2 | 6 |
|  | 01:52 PM | 3.0 | 91 |  | 12:41 PM | 3.0 | 91 |
|  | 08:09 PM | -0.1 | -3 |  | 07:02 PM | -0.2 | -6 |
| 10 W | 02:48 AM | 3.3 | 101 | 25 Th | 01:25 AM | 3.3 | 101 |
|  | 08:52 AM | 0.4 | 12 |  | 07:43 AM | 0.2 | 6 |
|  | 02:53 PM | 2.8 | 85 |  | 01:40 PM | 2.9 | 88 |
|  | 09:00 PM | 0.0 | 0 |  | 07:56 PM | -0.3 | -9 |
| 11 Th | 03:46 AM | 3.4 | 104 | 26 F | 02:29 AM | 3.5 | 107 |
|  | 09:53 AM | 0.5 | 15 |  | 08:46 AM | 0.1 | 3 |
|  | 03:49 PM | 2.7 | 82 |  | 02:43 PM | 2.9 | 88 |
|  | 09:49 PM | 0.0 | 0 |  | 08:53 PM | -0.5 | -15 |
| 12 F | 04:36 AM | 3.5 | 107 | 27 Sa | 03:31 AM | 3.8 | 116 |
|  | 10:49 AM | 0.4 | 12 |  | 09:50 AM | 0.0 | 0 |
|  | 04:39 PM | 2.6 | 79 |  | 03:46 PM | 3.0 | 91 |
|  | 10:36 PM | 0.0 | 0 |  | 09:52 PM | -0.7 | -21 |
| 13 Sa | 05:21 AM | 3.6 | 110 | 28 Su | 04:32 AM | 4.1 | 125 |
|  | 11:37 AM | 0.3 | 9 |  | 10:52 AM | -0.2 | -6 |
|  | 05:24 PM | 2.7 | 82 |  | 04:46 PM | 3.1 | 94 |
|  | 11:21 PM | -0.1 | -3 |  | 10:52 PM | -0.9 | -27 |
| 14 Su | 06:02 AM | 3.6 | 110 | 29 M | 05:29 AM | 4.3 | 131 |
|  | 12:18 PM | 0.3 | 9 |  | 11:50 AM | -0.4 | -12 |
|  | 06:06 PM | 2.7 | 82 |  | 05:44 PM | 3.3 | 101 |
|  |  |  |  |  | 11:49 PM | -1.1 | -34 |
| 15 M | 12:02 AM | -0.2 | -6 | 30 Tu | 06:25 AM | 4.5 | 137 |
|  | 06:41 AM | 3.7 | 113 |  | 12:44 PM | -0.6 | -18 |
|  | 12:56 PM | 0.2 | 6 |  | 06:41 PM | 3.4 | 104 |
|  | 06:47 PM | 2.7 | 82 |  |  |  |  |
|  |  |  |  | 31 W ○ | 12:44 AM | -1.2 | -37 |
|  |  |  |  |  | 07:19 AM | 4.5 | 137 |
|  |  |  |  |  | 01:35 PM | -0.7 | -21 |
|  |  |  |  |  | 07:37 PM | 3.6 | 110 |

## February

| Day | Time (h m) | Height (ft) | Height (cm) | Day | Time (h m) | Height (ft) | Height (cm) |
|---|---|---|---|---|---|---|---|
| 1 Th | 01:38 AM | -1.2 | -37 | 16 F | 01:38 AM | -0.3 | -9 |
|  | 08:11 AM | 4.5 | 137 |  | 08:07 AM | 3.7 | 113 |
|  | 02:25 PM | -0.7 | -21 |  | 02:13 PM | -0.2 | -6 |
|  | 08:31 PM | 3.7 | 113 |  | 08:20 PM | 3.1 | 94 |
| 2 F | 02:31 AM | -1.0 | -30 | 17 Sa | 02:18 AM | -0.3 | -9 |
|  | 09:01 AM | 4.3 | 131 |  | 08:44 AM | 3.6 | 110 |
|  | 03:14 PM | -0.7 | -21 |  | 02:50 PM | -0.2 | -6 |
|  | 09:23 PM | 3.7 | 113 |  | 09:00 PM | 3.2 | 98 |
| 3 Sa | 03:24 AM | -0.8 | -24 | 18 Su | 02:59 AM | -0.3 | -9 |
|  | 09:49 AM | 4.1 | 125 |  | 09:21 AM | 3.6 | 110 |
|  | 04:04 PM | -0.6 | -18 |  | 03:27 PM | -0.2 | -6 |
|  | 10:15 PM | 3.6 | 110 |  | 09:40 PM | 3.3 | 101 |
| 4 Su | 04:20 AM | -0.5 | -15 | 19 M | 03:43 AM | -0.2 | -6 |
|  | 10:36 AM | 3.7 | 113 |  | 09:59 AM | 3.4 | 104 |
|  | 04:55 PM | -0.5 | -15 |  | 04:08 PM | -0.2 | -6 |
|  | 11:07 PM | 3.5 | 107 |  | 10:22 PM | 3.4 | 104 |
| 5 M | 05:17 AM | -0.2 | -6 | 20 Tu | 04:31 AM | -0.1 | -3 |
|  | 11:24 AM | 3.4 | 104 |  | 10:39 AM | 3.3 | 101 |
|  | 05:45 PM | -0.3 | -9 |  | 04:52 PM | -0.2 | -6 |
|  |  |  |  |  | 11:08 PM | 3.4 | 104 |
| 6 Tu | 12:01 AM | 3.4 | 104 | 21 W | 05:25 AM | 0.0 | 0 |
|  | 06:16 AM | 0.1 | 3 |  | 11:24 AM | 3.1 | 94 |
|  | 12:14 PM | 3.0 | 91 |  | 05:40 PM | -0.3 | -9 |
|  | 06:36 PM | -0.2 | -6 |  |  |  |  |
| 7 W ◐ | 01:00 AM | 3.2 | 98 | 22 Th | 12:00 AM | 3.5 | 107 |
|  | 07:15 AM | 0.3 | 9 |  | 06:23 AM | 0.1 | 3 |
|  | 01:09 PM | 2.7 | 82 |  | 12:16 PM | 3.0 | 91 |
|  | 07:26 PM | 0.0 | 0 |  | 06:33 PM | -0.3 | -9 |
| 8 Th | 02:03 AM | 3.2 | 98 | 23 F ◐ | 12:59 AM | 3.5 | 107 |
|  | 08:15 AM | 0.5 | 15 |  | 07:24 AM | 0.2 | 6 |
|  | 02:10 PM | 2.5 | 76 |  | 01:17 PM | 2.8 | 85 |
|  | 08:17 PM | 0.1 | 3 |  | 07:31 PM | -0.3 | -9 |
| 9 F | 03:05 AM | 3.2 | 98 | 24 Sa | 02:05 AM | 3.6 | 110 |
|  | 09:15 AM | 0.5 | 15 |  | 08:27 AM | 0.1 | 3 |
|  | 03:11 PM | 2.4 | 73 |  | 02:23 PM | 2.8 | 85 |
|  | 09:10 PM | 0.1 | 3 |  | 08:32 PM | -0.4 | -12 |
| 10 Sa | 04:00 AM | 3.2 | 98 | 25 Su | 03:12 AM | 3.8 | 116 |
|  | 10:13 AM | 0.5 | 15 |  | 09:32 AM | 0.0 | 0 |
|  | 04:06 PM | 2.4 | 73 |  | 03:29 PM | 3.0 | 91 |
|  | 10:02 PM | 0.1 | 3 |  | 09:35 PM | -0.5 | -15 |
| 11 Su | 04:49 AM | 3.3 | 101 | 26 M | 04:15 AM | 4.0 | 122 |
|  | 11:04 AM | 0.4 | 12 |  | 10:35 AM | -0.1 | -3 |
|  | 04:54 PM | 2.5 | 76 |  | 04:33 PM | 3.1 | 94 |
|  | 10:52 PM | 0.0 | 0 |  | 10:38 PM | -0.7 | -21 |
| 12 M | 05:32 AM | 3.4 | 104 | 27 Tu | 05:14 AM | 4.1 | 125 |
|  | 11:47 AM | 0.4 | 12 |  | 11:33 AM | -0.3 | -9 |
|  | 05:39 PM | 2.6 | 79 |  | 05:32 PM | 3.4 | 104 |
|  | 11:37 PM | -0.1 | -3 |  | 11:37 PM | -0.8 | -24 |
| 13 Tu | 06:13 AM | 3.5 | 107 | 28 W | 06:10 AM | 4.2 | 128 |
|  | 12:26 PM | 0.1 | 3 |  | 12:26 PM | -0.5 | -15 |
|  | 06:20 PM | 2.8 | 85 |  | 06:28 PM | 3.6 | 110 |
| 14 W | 12:19 AM | -0.2 | -6 |  |  |  |  |
|  | 06:52 AM | 3.6 | 110 |  |  |  |  |
|  | 01:02 PM | 0.2 | 6 |  |  |  |  |
|  | 07:01 PM | 2.9 | 88 |  |  |  |  |
| 15 Th ● | 12:59 AM | -0.3 | -9 |  |  |  |  |
|  | 07:30 AM | 3.7 | 113 |  |  |  |  |
|  | 01:38 PM | -0.1 | -3 |  |  |  |  |
|  | 07:41 PM | 3.0 | 91 |  |  |  |  |

## March

| Day | Time (h m) | Height (ft) | Height (cm) | Day | Time (h m) | Height (ft) | Height (cm) |
|---|---|---|---|---|---|---|---|
| 1 Th | 12:33 AM | -0.9 | -27 | 16 F | 01:35 AM | -0.2 | -6 |
|  | 07:02 AM | 4.3 | 131 |  | 07:57 AM | 3.6 | 110 |
|  | 01:14 PM | -0.6 | -18 |  | 02:02 PM | -0.1 | -3 |
|  | 07:22 PM | 3.8 | 116 |  | 08:13 PM | 3.4 | 104 |
| 2 F ○ | 01:25 AM | -0.3 | -9 | 17 Sa ● | 02:16 AM | -0.3 | -9 |
|  | 07:52 AM | 4.2 | 128 |  | 08:36 AM | 3.7 | 113 |
|  | 02:01 PM | -0.7 | -21 |  | 02:39 PM | -0.2 | -6 |
|  | 08:13 PM | 3.9 | 119 |  | 08:53 PM | 3.6 | 110 |
| 3 Sa | 02:16 AM | -0.8 | -24 | 18 Su | 02:57 AM | -0.3 | -9 |
|  | 08:41 AM | 4.1 | 125 |  | 09:15 AM | 3.6 | 110 |
|  | 02:46 PM | -0.6 | -18 |  | 03:16 PM | -0.3 | -9 |
|  | 09:02 PM | 3.9 | 119 |  | 09:34 PM | 3.7 | 113 |
| 4 Su | 03:07 AM | -0.6 | -18 | 19 M | 03:40 AM | -0.3 | -9 |
|  | 09:24 AM | 3.8 | 116 |  | 09:55 AM | 3.6 | 110 |
|  | 03:31 PM | -0.5 | -15 |  | 03:55 PM | -0.3 | -9 |
|  | 09:50 PM | 3.9 | 119 |  | 10:16 PM | 3.9 | 119 |
| 5 M | 03:58 AM | -0.3 | -9 | 20 Tu | 04:26 AM | -0.2 | -6 |
|  | 10:08 AM | 3.5 | 107 |  | 10:36 AM | 3.5 | 107 |
|  | 04:16 PM | -0.3 | -9 |  | 04:37 PM | -0.3 | -9 |
|  | 10:37 PM | 3.7 | 113 |  | 11:00 PM | 3.9 | 119 |
| 6 Tu | 04:50 AM | -0.1 | -3 | 21 W | 05:16 AM | -0.1 | -3 |
|  | 10:52 AM | 3.2 | 98 |  | 11:19 AM | 3.3 | 101 |
|  | 05:03 PM | -0.1 | -3 |  | 05:23 PM | -0.3 | -9 |
|  | 11:24 PM | 3.5 | 107 |  | 11:48 PM | 3.9 | 119 |
| 7 W | 05:44 AM | 0.2 | 6 | 22 Th | 06:10 AM | 0.0 | 0 |
|  | 11:37 AM | 2.9 | 88 |  | 12:07 PM | 3.2 | 98 |
|  | 05:51 PM | 0.0 | 0 |  | 06:15 PM | -0.2 | -6 |
| 8 Th | 12:15 AM | 3.4 | 104 | 23 F | 12:40 AM | 3.9 | 119 |
|  | 06:39 AM | 0.4 | 12 |  | 07:09 AM | 0.1 | 3 |
|  | 12:27 PM | 2.6 | 79 |  | 01:01 PM | 3.0 | 91 |
|  | 06:42 PM | 0.2 | 6 |  | 07:12 PM | -0.2 | -6 |
| 9 F | 01:12 AM | 3.2 | 98 | 24 Sa ◐ | 01:40 AM | 3.8 | 116 |
|  | 07:35 AM | 0.5 | 15 |  | 08:10 AM | 0.2 | 6 |
|  | 01:25 PM | 2.5 | 76 |  | 02:03 PM | 2.9 | 88 |
|  | 07:34 PM | 0.3 | 9 |  | 08:13 PM | -0.2 | -6 |
| 10 Sa | 02:13 AM | 3.1 | 94 | 25 Su | 02:46 AM | 3.8 | 116 |
|  | 08:31 AM | 0.6 | 18 |  | 09:13 AM | 0.2 | 6 |
|  | 02:24 PM | 2.4 | 73 |  | 03:12 PM | 3.0 | 91 |
|  | 08:29 PM | 0.4 | 12 |  | 09:18 PM | -0.2 | -6 |
| 11 Su | 04:14 AM | 3.1 | 94 | 26 M | 03:55 AM | 3.8 | 116 |
|  | 10:27 AM | 0.6 | 18 |  | 10:16 AM | 0.1 | 3 |
|  | 04:28 PM | 2.5 | 76 |  | 04:20 PM | 3.1 | 94 |
|  | 10:24 PM | 0.3 | 9 |  | 10:23 PM | -0.3 | -9 |
| 12 M | 05:08 AM | 3.2 | 98 | 27 Tu | 04:59 AM | 3.9 | 119 |
|  | 11:20 AM | 0.5 | 15 |  | 11:17 AM | 0.0 | 0 |
|  | 05:20 PM | 2.6 | 79 |  | 05:24 PM | 3.4 | 104 |
|  | 11:18 PM | 0.2 | 6 |  | 11:28 PM | -0.4 | -12 |
| 13 Tu | 05:55 AM | 3.3 | 101 | 28 W | 05:58 AM | 4.0 | 122 |
|  | 12:06 PM | 0.4 | 12 |  | 12:14 PM | -0.2 | -6 |
|  | 06:07 PM | 2.8 | 85 |  | 06:22 PM | 3.6 | 110 |
| 14 W | 12:07 AM | 0.1 | 3 | 29 Th | 12:28 AM | -0.5 | -15 |
|  | 06:37 AM | 3.4 | 104 |  | 06:52 AM | 4.0 | 122 |
|  | 12:48 PM | 0.2 | 6 |  | 01:04 PM | -0.4 | -12 |
|  | 06:50 PM | 3.0 | 91 |  | 07:16 PM | 3.8 | 116 |
| 15 Th | 12:53 AM | 0.0 | 0 | 30 F | 01:22 AM | -0.5 | -15 |
|  | 07:18 AM | 3.5 | 107 |  | 07:42 AM | 4.0 | 122 |
|  | 01:26 PM | 0.0 | 0 |  | 01:50 PM | -0.5 | -15 |
|  | 07:32 PM | 3.2 | 98 |  | 08:06 PM | 4.0 | 122 |
|  |  |  |  | 31 Sa ○ | 02:13 AM | -0.5 | -15 |
|  |  |  |  |  | 08:30 AM | 3.9 | 119 |
|  |  |  |  |  | 02:33 PM | -0.5 | -15 |
|  |  |  |  |  | 08:54 PM | 4.1 | 125 |

Heights are referred to mean lower water which is the chart datum of sounding. All times are local. Daylight Saving Time has been used when needed. Additional tide tables are available online from NOAA at www.tidesandcurrents.noaa.gov/tide_predictions.shtml.

SKIPPER'S HANDBOOK

StationId: 8721604
Source: NOAA/NOS/CO-OPS
Station Type: Primary
Time Zone: LST_LDT
Datum: MLLW

## NOAA Tide Predictions

## Trident Pier, FL, 2018

### Times and Heights of High and Low Waters

### APRIL

| Day | Time | ft | cm |
|---|---|---|---|
| 1 Su | 03:01 AM | -0.5 | -15 |
| | 09:15 AM | 3.7 | 113 |
| | 03:15 PM | -0.5 | -15 |
| | 09:40 PM | 4.1 | 125 |
| 2 M | 03:48 AM | -0.3 | -9 |
| | 09:58 AM | 3.5 | 107 |
| | 03:56 PM | -0.3 | -9 |
| | 10:24 PM | 4.1 | 125 |
| 3 Tu | 04:35 AM | -0.1 | -3 |
| | 10:40 AM | 3.3 | 101 |
| | 04:38 PM | -0.1 | -3 |
| | 11:06 PM | 3.9 | 119 |
| 4 W | 05:23 AM | 0.1 | 3 |
| | 11:21 AM | 3.1 | 94 |
| | 05:22 PM | 0.1 | 3 |
| | 11:49 PM | 3.7 | 113 |
| 5 Th | 06:13 AM | 0.3 | 9 |
| | 12:04 PM | 2.9 | 88 |
| | 06:09 PM | 0.3 | 9 |
| 6 F | 12:35 AM | 3.5 | 107 |
| | 07:04 AM | 0.5 | 15 |
| | 12:51 PM | 2.7 | 82 |
| | 06:59 PM | 0.4 | 12 |
| 7 Sa | 01:25 AM | 3.3 | 101 |
| | 07:55 AM | 0.6 | 18 |
| | 01:44 PM | 2.5 | 76 |
| | 07:53 PM | 0.5 | 15 |
| 8 Su ☽ | 02:21 AM | 3.2 | 98 |
| | 08:48 AM | 0.6 | 18 |
| | 02:44 PM | 2.5 | 76 |
| | 08:48 PM | 0.6 | 18 |
| 9 M | 03:21 AM | 3.2 | 98 |
| | 09:40 AM | 0.6 | 18 |
| | 03:46 PM | 2.6 | 79 |
| | 09:44 PM | 0.5 | 15 |
| 10 Tu | 04:17 AM | 3.2 | 98 |
| | 10:31 AM | 0.5 | 15 |
| | 04:41 PM | 2.8 | 85 |
| | 10:39 PM | 0.5 | 15 |
| 11 W | 05:08 AM | 3.3 | 101 |
| | 11:18 AM | 0.4 | 12 |
| | 05:30 PM | 3.0 | 91 |
| | 11:32 PM | 0.3 | 9 |
| 12 Th | 05:53 AM | 3.4 | 104 |
| | 12:02 PM | 0.2 | 6 |
| | 06:15 PM | 3.3 | 101 |
| 13 F | 12:21 AM | 0.1 | 3 |
| | 06:36 AM | 3.5 | 107 |
| | 12:44 PM | 0.0 | 0 |
| | 06:58 PM | 3.5 | 107 |
| 14 Sa | 01:07 AM | 0.0 | 0 |
| | 07:18 AM | 3.5 | 107 |
| | 01:23 PM | -0.2 | -6 |
| | 07:41 PM | 3.8 | 116 |
| 15 Su | 01:52 AM | -0.2 | -6 |
| | 08:01 AM | 3.6 | 110 |
| | 02:02 PM | -0.3 | -9 |
| | 08:25 PM | 4.0 | 122 |
| 16 M ● | 02:36 AM | -0.3 | -9 |
| | 08:45 AM | 3.6 | 110 |
| | 02:43 PM | -0.4 | -12 |
| | 09:09 PM | 4.2 | 128 |
| 17 Tu | 03:22 AM | -0.3 | -9 |
| | 09:29 AM | 3.5 | 107 |
| | 03:25 PM | -0.5 | -15 |
| | 09:55 PM | 4.3 | 131 |
| 18 W | 04:10 AM | -0.3 | -9 |
| | 10:15 AM | 3.4 | 104 |
| | 04:11 PM | -0.5 | -15 |
| | 10:42 PM | 4.4 | 134 |
| 19 Th | 05:02 AM | -0.2 | -6 |
| | 11:02 AM | 3.3 | 101 |
| | 05:01 PM | -0.4 | -12 |
| | 11:32 PM | 4.3 | 131 |
| 20 F | 05:59 AM | -0.1 | -3 |
| | 11:54 AM | 3.2 | 98 |
| | 05:57 PM | -0.3 | -9 |
| 21 Sa | 12:26 AM | 4.2 | 128 |
| | 06:58 AM | 0.0 | 0 |
| | 12:50 PM | 3.1 | 94 |
| | 06:58 PM | -0.2 | -6 |
| 22 Su ☾ | 01:25 AM | 4.0 | 122 |
| | 07:58 AM | 0.1 | 3 |
| | 01:54 PM | 3.1 | 94 |
| | 08:01 PM | -0.1 | -3 |
| 23 M | 02:30 AM | 3.9 | 119 |
| | 08:59 AM | 0.1 | 3 |
| | 03:04 PM | 3.1 | 94 |
| | 09:07 PM | 0.0 | 0 |
| 24 Tu | 03:38 AM | 3.8 | 116 |
| | 09:59 AM | 0.0 | 0 |
| | 04:13 PM | 3.3 | 101 |
| | 10:13 PM | 0.0 | 0 |
| 25 W | 04:41 AM | 3.7 | 113 |
| | 10:57 AM | -0.1 | -3 |
| | 05:15 PM | 3.5 | 107 |
| | 11:17 PM | -0.1 | -3 |
| 26 Th | 05:38 AM | 3.7 | 113 |
| | 11:50 AM | -0.2 | -6 |
| | 06:10 PM | 3.8 | 116 |
| 27 F | 12:17 AM | -0.1 | -3 |
| | 06:30 AM | 3.7 | 113 |
| | 12:39 PM | -0.3 | -9 |
| | 07:01 PM | 4.0 | 122 |
| 28 Sa | 01:11 AM | -0.2 | -6 |
| | 07:19 AM | 3.6 | 110 |
| | 01:23 PM | -0.4 | -12 |
| | 07:49 PM | 4.1 | 125 |
| 29 Su | 02:00 AM | -0.2 | -6 |
| | 08:05 AM | 3.5 | 107 |
| | 02:04 PM | -0.4 | -12 |
| | 08:34 PM | 4.2 | 128 |
| 30 M ○ | 02:45 AM | -0.2 | -6 |
| | 08:49 AM | 3.3 | 101 |
| | 02:43 PM | -0.3 | -9 |
| | 09:16 PM | 4.2 | 128 |

### MAY

| Day | Time | ft | cm |
|---|---|---|---|
| 1 Tu | 03:29 AM | -0.1 | -3 |
| | 09:31 AM | 3.2 | 98 |
| | 03:23 PM | -0.2 | -6 |
| | 09:58 PM | 4.1 | 125 |
| 2 W | 04:12 AM | 0.0 | 0 |
| | 10:12 AM | 3.0 | 91 |
| | 04:03 PM | 0.0 | 0 |
| | 10:38 PM | 4.0 | 122 |
| 3 Th | 04:57 AM | 0.2 | 6 |
| | 10:53 AM | 2.9 | 88 |
| | 04:45 PM | 0.1 | 3 |
| | 11:19 PM | 3.8 | 116 |
| 4 F | 05:43 AM | 0.3 | 9 |
| | 11:35 AM | 2.8 | 85 |
| | 05:31 PM | 0.3 | 9 |
| 5 Sa | 12:01 AM | 3.6 | 110 |
| | 06:31 AM | 0.4 | 12 |
| | 12:19 PM | 2.7 | 82 |
| | 06:21 PM | 0.5 | 15 |
| 6 Su | 12:46 AM | 3.4 | 104 |
| | 07:19 AM | 0.5 | 15 |
| | 01:09 PM | 2.6 | 79 |
| | 07:14 PM | 0.6 | 18 |
| 7 M | 01:36 AM | 3.3 | 101 |
| | 08:08 AM | 0.5 | 15 |
| | 02:04 PM | 2.6 | 79 |
| | 08:08 PM | 0.6 | 18 |
| 8 Tu ☽ | 02:29 AM | 3.2 | 98 |
| | 08:56 AM | 0.5 | 15 |
| | 03:02 PM | 2.7 | 82 |
| | 09:03 PM | 0.6 | 18 |
| 9 W | 03:24 AM | 3.2 | 98 |
| | 09:43 AM | 0.4 | 12 |
| | 03:59 PM | 2.9 | 88 |
| | 09:58 PM | 0.5 | 15 |
| 10 Th | 04:16 AM | 3.2 | 98 |
| | 10:29 AM | 0.2 | 6 |
| | 04:50 PM | 3.1 | 94 |
| | 10:53 PM | 0.4 | 12 |
| 11 F | 05:05 AM | 3.2 | 98 |
| | 11:15 AM | 0.0 | 0 |
| | 05:37 PM | 3.4 | 104 |
| | 11:46 PM | 0.2 | 6 |
| 12 Sa | 05:52 AM | 3.3 | 101 |
| | 12:00 PM | -0.2 | -6 |
| | 06:24 PM | 3.8 | 116 |
| 13 Su | 12:37 AM | 0.0 | 0 |
| | 06:39 AM | 3.4 | 104 |
| | 12:44 PM | -0.4 | -12 |
| | 07:10 PM | 4.1 | 125 |
| 14 M | 01:26 AM | -0.2 | -6 |
| | 07:26 AM | 3.4 | 104 |
| | 01:28 PM | -0.6 | -18 |
| | 07:57 PM | 4.3 | 131 |
| 15 Tu ● | 02:15 AM | -0.3 | -9 |
| | 08:15 AM | 3.4 | 104 |
| | 02:13 PM | -0.7 | -21 |
| | 08:46 PM | 4.5 | 137 |
| 16 W | 03:04 AM | -0.4 | -12 |
| | 09:05 AM | 3.4 | 104 |
| | 03:00 PM | -0.7 | -21 |
| | 09:35 PM | 4.6 | 140 |
| 17 Th | 03:55 AM | -0.4 | -12 |
| | 09:55 AM | 3.4 | 104 |
| | 03:50 PM | -0.7 | -21 |
| | 10:26 PM | 4.6 | 140 |
| 18 F | 04:49 AM | -0.3 | -9 |
| | 10:48 AM | 3.3 | 101 |
| | 04:44 PM | -0.6 | -18 |
| | 11:18 PM | 4.5 | 137 |
| 19 Sa | 05:46 AM | -0.3 | -9 |
| | 11:42 AM | 3.3 | 101 |
| | 05:43 PM | -0.4 | -12 |
| 20 Su | 12:13 AM | 4.3 | 131 |
| | 06:45 AM | -0.2 | -6 |
| | 12:41 PM | 3.2 | 98 |
| | 06:46 PM | -0.3 | -9 |
| 21 M | 01:11 AM | 4.1 | 125 |
| | 07:45 AM | -0.2 | -6 |
| | 01:45 PM | 3.2 | 98 |
| | 07:51 PM | -0.1 | -3 |
| 22 Tu ☾ | 02:13 AM | 3.8 | 116 |
| | 08:42 AM | -0.2 | -6 |
| | 02:54 PM | 3.3 | 101 |
| | 08:56 PM | 0.0 | 0 |
| 23 W | 03:17 AM | 3.6 | 110 |
| | 09:38 AM | -0.2 | -6 |
| | 04:02 PM | 3.4 | 104 |
| | 10:01 PM | 0.1 | 3 |
| 24 Th | 04:18 AM | 3.5 | 107 |
| | 10:32 AM | -0.3 | -9 |
| | 05:02 PM | 3.6 | 110 |
| | 11:05 PM | 0.1 | 3 |
| 25 F | 05:14 AM | 3.3 | 101 |
| | 11:23 AM | -0.3 | -9 |
| | 05:56 PM | 3.8 | 116 |
| 26 Sa | 12:04 AM | 0.1 | 3 |
| | 06:05 AM | 3.2 | 98 |
| | 12:10 PM | -0.3 | -9 |
| | 06:44 PM | 3.9 | 119 |
| 27 Su | 12:57 AM | 0.0 | 0 |
| | 06:53 AM | 3.1 | 94 |
| | 12:54 PM | -0.3 | -9 |
| | 07:29 PM | 4.0 | 122 |
| 28 M | 01:45 AM | 0.0 | 0 |
| | 07:39 AM | 3.0 | 91 |
| | 01:35 PM | -0.3 | -9 |
| | 08:12 PM | 4.0 | 122 |
| 29 Tu ○ | 02:28 AM | 0.0 | 0 |
| | 08:22 AM | 2.9 | 88 |
| | 02:14 PM | -0.2 | -6 |
| | 08:53 PM | 4.0 | 122 |
| 30 W | 03:09 AM | 0.1 | 3 |
| | 09:05 AM | 2.9 | 88 |
| | 02:53 PM | -0.1 | -3 |
| | 09:33 PM | 4.0 | 122 |
| 31 Th | 03:49 AM | 0.1 | 3 |
| | 09:46 AM | 2.8 | 85 |
| | 03:33 PM | 0.0 | 0 |
| | 10:12 PM | 3.9 | 119 |

### JUNE

| Day | Time | ft | cm |
|---|---|---|---|
| 1 F | 04:31 AM | 0.2 | 6 |
| | 10:27 AM | 2.7 | 82 |
| | 04:15 PM | 0.1 | 3 |
| | 10:52 PM | 3.7 | 113 |
| 2 Sa | 05:14 AM | 0.2 | 6 |
| | 11:08 AM | 2.7 | 82 |
| | 04:59 PM | 0.2 | 6 |
| | 11:31 PM | 3.6 | 110 |
| 3 Su | 05:59 AM | 0.3 | 9 |
| | 11:51 AM | 2.6 | 79 |
| | 05:47 PM | 0.4 | 12 |
| 4 M | 12:13 AM | 3.4 | 104 |
| | 06:44 AM | 0.3 | 9 |
| | 12:37 PM | 2.6 | 79 |
| | 06:38 PM | 0.5 | 15 |
| 5 Tu | 12:57 AM | 3.3 | 101 |
| | 07:29 AM | 0.3 | 9 |
| | 01:26 PM | 2.6 | 79 |
| | 07:31 PM | 0.5 | 15 |
| 6 W ☽ | 01:44 AM | 3.2 | 98 |
| | 08:14 AM | 0.2 | 6 |
| | 02:20 PM | 2.7 | 82 |
| | 08:24 PM | 0.5 | 15 |
| 7 Th | 02:34 AM | 3.1 | 94 |
| | 08:58 AM | 0.1 | 3 |
| | 03:16 PM | 2.9 | 88 |
| | 09:19 PM | 0.5 | 15 |
| 8 F | 03:27 AM | 3.1 | 94 |
| | 09:43 AM | 0.0 | 0 |
| | 04:09 PM | 3.2 | 98 |
| | 10:15 PM | 0.4 | 12 |
| 9 Sa | 04:19 AM | 3.1 | 94 |
| | 10:30 AM | -0.2 | -6 |
| | 05:00 PM | 3.6 | 110 |
| | 11:12 PM | 0.2 | 6 |
| 10 Su | 05:10 AM | 3.1 | 94 |
| | 11:19 AM | -0.4 | -12 |
| | 05:50 PM | 3.9 | 119 |
| 11 M | 12:07 AM | 0.0 | 0 |
| | 06:02 AM | 3.2 | 98 |
| | 12:08 PM | -0.6 | -18 |
| | 06:41 PM | 4.2 | 128 |
| 12 Tu | 01:01 AM | -0.2 | -6 |
| | 06:54 AM | 3.2 | 98 |
| | 12:57 PM | -0.8 | -24 |
| | 07:32 PM | 4.5 | 137 |
| 13 W ● | 01:53 AM | -0.4 | -12 |
| | 07:48 AM | 3.3 | 101 |
| | 01:48 PM | -0.9 | -27 |
| | 08:25 PM | 4.6 | 140 |
| 14 Th | 02:45 AM | -0.5 | -15 |
| | 08:42 AM | 3.3 | 101 |
| | 02:39 PM | -0.9 | -27 |
| | 09:18 PM | 4.7 | 143 |
| 15 F | 03:38 AM | -0.5 | -15 |
| | 09:37 AM | 3.4 | 104 |
| | 03:33 PM | -0.9 | -27 |
| | 10:11 PM | 4.7 | 143 |
| 16 Sa | 04:33 AM | -0.5 | -15 |
| | 10:33 AM | 3.4 | 104 |
| | 04:29 PM | -0.8 | -24 |
| | 11:04 PM | 4.5 | 137 |
| 17 Su | 05:30 AM | -0.5 | -15 |
| | 11:29 AM | 3.4 | 104 |
| | 05:30 PM | -0.6 | -18 |
| | 11:57 PM | 4.3 | 131 |
| 18 M | 06:28 AM | -0.4 | -12 |
| | 12:28 PM | 3.4 | 104 |
| | 06:33 PM | -0.3 | -9 |
| 19 Tu | 12:53 AM | 4.0 | 122 |
| | 07:24 AM | -0.4 | -12 |
| | 01:31 PM | 3.4 | 104 |
| | 07:37 PM | -0.1 | -3 |
| 20 W ☾ | 01:51 AM | 3.7 | 113 |
| | 08:19 AM | -0.4 | -12 |
| | 02:37 PM | 3.4 | 104 |
| | 08:41 PM | 0.0 | 0 |
| 21 Th | 02:52 AM | 3.4 | 104 |
| | 09:12 AM | -0.3 | -9 |
| | 03:43 PM | 3.5 | 107 |
| | 09:45 PM | 0.2 | 6 |
| 22 F | 03:52 AM | 3.2 | 98 |
| | 10:04 AM | -0.3 | -9 |
| | 04:43 PM | 3.6 | 110 |
| | 10:48 PM | 0.2 | 6 |
| 23 Sa | 04:48 AM | 3.0 | 91 |
| | 10:53 AM | -0.3 | -9 |
| | 05:36 PM | 3.7 | 113 |
| | 11:47 PM | 0.3 | 9 |
| 24 Su | 05:39 AM | 2.9 | 88 |
| | 11:41 AM | -0.2 | -6 |
| | 06:23 PM | 3.8 | 116 |
| 25 M | 12:40 AM | 0.2 | 6 |
| | 06:27 AM | 2.8 | 85 |
| | 12:25 PM | -0.2 | -6 |
| | 07:07 PM | 3.9 | 119 |
| 26 Tu | 01:26 AM | 0.2 | 6 |
| | 07:12 AM | 2.8 | 85 |
| | 01:07 PM | -0.2 | -6 |
| | 07:49 PM | 3.9 | 119 |
| 27 W | 02:07 AM | 0.2 | 6 |
| | 07:56 AM | 2.7 | 82 |
| | 01:48 PM | -0.2 | -6 |
| | 08:30 PM | 3.9 | 119 |
| 28 Th ○ | 02:46 AM | 0.2 | 6 |
| | 08:39 AM | 2.7 | 82 |
| | 02:28 PM | -0.1 | -3 |
| | 09:09 PM | 3.8 | 116 |
| 29 F | 03:24 AM | 0.2 | 6 |
| | 09:21 AM | 2.7 | 82 |
| | 03:08 PM | 0.0 | 0 |
| | 09:48 PM | 3.8 | 116 |
| 30 Sa | 04:04 AM | 0.2 | 6 |
| | 10:02 AM | 2.7 | 82 |
| | 03:49 PM | 0.1 | 3 |
| | 10:26 PM | 3.7 | 113 |

Heights are referred to mean lower water which is the chart datum of sounding. All times are local. Daylight Saving Time has been used when needed. Additional tide tables are available online from NOAA at www.tidesandcurrents.noaa.gov/tide_predictions.shtml.

SKIPPER'S HANDBOOK

StationId: 8721604
Source: NOAA/NOS/CO-OPS
Station Type: Primary
Time Zone: LST_LDT
Datum: MLLW

**NOAA Tide Predictions**

## Trident Pier, FL,2018

### Times and Heights of High and Low Waters

## July

| Day | Time | ft | cm |
|---|---|---|---|
| **1** Su | 04:44 AM | 0.2 | 6 |
| | 10:42 AM | 2.7 | 82 |
| | 04:32 PM | 0.2 | 6 |
| | 11:04 PM | 3.6 | 110 |
| **2** M | 05:26 AM | 0.2 | 6 |
| | 11:23 AM | 2.7 | 82 |
| | 05:17 PM | 0.3 | 9 |
| | 11:42 PM | 3.5 | 107 |
| **3** Tu | 06:08 AM | 0.2 | 6 |
| | 12:06 PM | 2.8 | 85 |
| | 06:06 PM | 0.4 | 12 |
| **4** W | 12:22 AM | 3.4 | 104 |
| | 06:50 AM | 0.2 | 6 |
| | 12:51 PM | 2.8 | 85 |
| | 06:57 PM | 0.5 | 15 |
| **5** Th | 01:05 AM | 3.2 | 98 |
| | 07:33 AM | 0.1 | 3 |
| | 01:41 PM | 3.0 | 91 |
| | 07:50 PM | 0.5 | 15 |
| **6** F ◐ | 01:52 AM | 3.1 | 94 |
| | 08:17 AM | 0.0 | 0 |
| | 02:35 PM | 3.2 | 98 |
| | 08:45 PM | 0.4 | 12 |
| **7** Sa | 02:44 AM | 3.0 | 91 |
| | 09:03 AM | -0.1 | -3 |
| | 03:31 PM | 3.4 | 104 |
| | 09:43 PM | 0.4 | 12 |
| **8** Su | 03:39 AM | 3.0 | 91 |
| | 09:52 AM | -0.3 | -9 |
| | 04:27 PM | 3.7 | 113 |
| | 10:41 PM | 0.2 | 6 |
| **9** M | 04:36 AM | 3.0 | 91 |
| | 10:44 AM | -0.5 | -15 |
| | 05:21 PM | 4.0 | 122 |
| | 11:40 PM | 0.1 | 3 |
| **10** Tu | 05:32 AM | 3.1 | 94 |
| | 11:39 AM | -0.7 | -21 |
| | 06:16 PM | 4.3 | 131 |
| **11** W | 12:38 AM | -0.1 | -3 |
| | 06:28 AM | 3.2 | 98 |
| | 12:33 PM | -0.8 | -24 |
| | 07:11 PM | 4.6 | 140 |
| **12** Th ○ | 01:32 AM | -0.3 | -9 |
| | 07:25 AM | 3.3 | 101 |
| | 01:28 PM | -1.0 | -30 |
| | 08:06 PM | 4.7 | 143 |
| **13** F ● | 02:26 AM | -0.4 | -12 |
| | 08:23 AM | 3.5 | 107 |
| | 02:22 PM | -1.0 | -30 |
| | 09:01 PM | 4.7 | 143 |
| **14** Sa | 03:19 AM | -0.5 | -15 |
| | 09:20 AM | 3.6 | 110 |
| | 03:18 PM | -0.9 | -27 |
| | 09:54 PM | 4.7 | 143 |
| **15** Su | 04:12 AM | -0.5 | -15 |
| | 10:16 AM | 3.6 | 110 |
| | 04:15 PM | -0.8 | -24 |
| | 10:46 PM | 4.5 | 137 |
| **16** M | 05:07 AM | -0.5 | -15 |
| | 11:13 AM | 3.7 | 113 |
| | 05:14 PM | -0.5 | -15 |
| | 11:38 PM | 4.3 | 131 |
| **17** Tu | 06:02 AM | -0.5 | -15 |
| | 12:10 PM | 3.7 | 113 |
| | 06:16 PM | -0.3 | -9 |
| **18** W | 12:30 AM | 3.9 | 119 |
| | 06:57 AM | -0.4 | -12 |
| | 01:09 PM | 3.6 | 110 |
| | 07:19 PM | 0.0 | 0 |
| **19** Th ◑ | 01:24 AM | 3.6 | 110 |
| | 07:50 AM | -0.3 | -9 |
| | 02:12 PM | 3.6 | 110 |
| | 08:22 PM | 0.2 | 6 |
| **20** F | 02:22 AM | 3.3 | 101 |
| | 08:42 AM | -0.2 | -6 |
| | 03:16 PM | 3.6 | 110 |
| | 09:23 PM | 0.4 | 12 |
| **21** Sa | 03:22 AM | 3.0 | 91 |
| | 09:32 AM | -0.1 | -3 |
| | 04:17 PM | 3.7 | 113 |
| | 10:25 PM | 0.5 | 15 |
| **22** Su | 04:20 AM | 2.9 | 88 |
| | 10:22 AM | 0.0 | 0 |
| | 05:11 PM | 3.7 | 113 |
| | 11:23 PM | 0.5 | 15 |
| **23** M | 05:13 AM | 2.8 | 85 |
| | 11:11 AM | 0.0 | 0 |
| | 05:59 PM | 3.8 | 116 |
| **24** Tu | 12:16 AM | 0.5 | 15 |
| | 06:01 AM | 2.8 | 85 |
| | 11:58 AM | 0.0 | 0 |
| | 06:43 PM | 3.8 | 116 |
| **25** W | 01:01 AM | 0.5 | 15 |
| | 06:47 AM | 2.8 | 85 |
| | 12:43 PM | 0.0 | 0 |
| | 07:25 PM | 3.8 | 116 |
| **26** Th | 01:42 AM | 0.4 | 12 |
| | 07:30 AM | 2.8 | 85 |
| | 01:25 PM | 0.0 | 0 |
| | 08:05 PM | 3.9 | 119 |
| **27** F | 02:19 AM | 0.3 | 9 |
| | 08:13 AM | 2.9 | 88 |
| | 02:05 PM | 0.0 | 0 |
| | 08:44 PM | 3.9 | 119 |
| **28** Sa | 02:56 AM | 0.3 | 9 |
| | 08:54 AM | 3.0 | 91 |
| | 02:45 PM | 0.1 | 3 |
| | 09:22 PM | 3.9 | 119 |
| **29** Su | 03:33 AM | 0.3 | 9 |
| | 09:35 AM | 3.0 | 91 |
| | 03:25 PM | 0.1 | 3 |
| | 09:59 PM | 3.8 | 116 |
| **30** M | 04:10 AM | 0.3 | 9 |
| | 10:15 AM | 3.1 | 94 |
| | 04:07 PM | 0.2 | 6 |
| | 10:35 PM | 3.8 | 116 |
| **31** Tu | 04:49 AM | 0.2 | 6 |
| | 10:55 AM | 3.1 | 94 |
| | 04:50 PM | 0.3 | 9 |
| | 11:12 PM | 3.6 | 110 |

## August

| Day | Time | ft | cm |
|---|---|---|---|
| **1** W | 05:29 AM | 0.2 | 6 |
| | 11:35 AM | 3.2 | 98 |
| | 05:37 PM | 0.4 | 12 |
| | 11:50 PM | 3.5 | 107 |
| **2** Th | 06:10 AM | 0.2 | 6 |
| | 12:19 PM | 3.3 | 101 |
| | 06:28 PM | 0.5 | 15 |
| **3** F | 12:31 AM | 3.4 | 104 |
| | 06:53 AM | 0.2 | 6 |
| | 01:07 PM | 3.4 | 104 |
| | 07:22 PM | 0.6 | 18 |
| **4** Sa ◑ | 01:18 AM | 3.3 | 101 |
| | 07:39 AM | 0.1 | 3 |
| | 02:00 PM | 3.6 | 110 |
| | 08:18 PM | 0.6 | 18 |
| **5** Su | 02:11 AM | 3.2 | 98 |
| | 08:28 AM | 0.0 | 0 |
| | 02:58 PM | 3.8 | 116 |
| | 09:16 PM | 0.5 | 15 |
| **6** M | 03:09 AM | 3.1 | 94 |
| | 09:22 AM | -0.1 | -3 |
| | 03:59 PM | 4.0 | 122 |
| | 10:17 PM | 0.5 | 15 |
| **7** Tu | 04:10 AM | 3.2 | 98 |
| | 10:18 AM | -0.3 | -9 |
| | 04:58 PM | 4.3 | 131 |
| | 11:18 PM | 0.3 | 9 |
| **8** W | 05:10 AM | 3.3 | 101 |
| | 11:17 AM | -0.5 | -15 |
| | 05:56 PM | 4.5 | 137 |
| **9** Th | 12:16 AM | 0.1 | 3 |
| | 06:09 AM | 3.5 | 107 |
| | 12:16 PM | -0.6 | -18 |
| | 06:52 PM | 4.7 | 143 |
| **10** F | 01:12 AM | -0.1 | -3 |
| | 07:08 AM | 3.7 | 113 |
| | 01:13 PM | -0.7 | -21 |
| | 07:48 PM | 4.8 | 146 |
| **11** Sa ● | 02:05 AM | -0.3 | -9 |
| | 08:06 AM | 3.9 | 119 |
| | 02:08 PM | -0.8 | -24 |
| | 08:42 PM | 4.8 | 146 |
| **12** Su ○ | 02:56 AM | -0.4 | -12 |
| | 09:03 AM | 4.0 | 122 |
| | 03:03 PM | -0.7 | -21 |
| | 09:34 PM | 4.7 | 143 |
| **13** M | 03:47 AM | -0.4 | -12 |
| | 09:58 AM | 4.1 | 125 |
| | 03:59 PM | -0.5 | -15 |
| | 10:25 PM | 4.5 | 137 |
| **14** Tu | 04:39 AM | -0.3 | -9 |
| | 10:52 AM | 4.1 | 125 |
| | 04:56 PM | -0.2 | -6 |
| | 11:14 PM | 4.3 | 131 |
| **15** W | 05:31 AM | -0.2 | -6 |
| | 11:46 AM | 4.1 | 125 |
| | 05:56 PM | 0.1 | 3 |
| **16** Th | 12:03 AM | 3.9 | 119 |
| | 06:23 AM | -0.1 | -3 |
| | 12:41 PM | 4.0 | 122 |
| | 06:56 PM | 0.3 | 9 |
| **17** F | 12:54 AM | 3.6 | 110 |
| | 07:15 AM | 0.1 | 3 |
| | 01:39 PM | 3.9 | 119 |
| | 07:57 PM | 0.6 | 18 |
| **18** Sa ◑ | 01:49 AM | 3.3 | 101 |
| | 08:07 AM | 0.2 | 6 |
| | 02:41 PM | 3.8 | 116 |
| | 08:56 PM | 0.7 | 21 |
| **19** Su | 02:49 AM | 3.1 | 94 |
| | 08:58 AM | 0.3 | 9 |
| | 03:43 PM | 3.8 | 116 |
| | 09:55 PM | 0.8 | 24 |
| **20** M | 03:49 AM | 3.0 | 91 |
| | 09:50 AM | 0.4 | 12 |
| | 04:39 PM | 3.8 | 116 |
| | 10:52 PM | 0.9 | 27 |
| **21** Tu | 04:46 AM | 3.0 | 91 |
| | 10:41 AM | 0.5 | 15 |
| | 05:29 PM | 3.8 | 116 |
| | 11:44 PM | 0.3 | 9 |
| **22** W | 05:35 AM | 3.0 | 91 |
| | 11:31 AM | 0.5 | 15 |
| | 06:14 PM | 3.9 | 119 |
| **23** Th | 12:29 AM | 0.8 | 24 |
| | 06:21 AM | 3.1 | 94 |
| | 12:18 PM | 0.4 | 12 |
| | 06:56 PM | 4.0 | 122 |
| **24** F | 01:09 AM | 0.7 | 21 |
| | 07:03 AM | 3.2 | 98 |
| | 01:02 PM | 0.3 | 9 |
| | 07:35 PM | 4.0 | 122 |
| **25** Sa | 01:46 AM | 0.6 | 18 |
| | 07:45 AM | 3.3 | 101 |
| | 01:43 PM | 0.3 | 9 |
| | 08:14 PM | 4.1 | 125 |
| **26** Su ○ | 02:22 AM | 0.5 | 15 |
| | 08:26 AM | 3.4 | 104 |
| | 02:23 PM | 0.3 | 9 |
| | 08:51 PM | 4.1 | 125 |
| **27** M | 02:58 AM | 0.4 | 12 |
| | 09:06 AM | 3.6 | 110 |
| | 03:02 PM | 0.3 | 9 |
| | 09:28 PM | 4.0 | 122 |
| **28** Tu | 03:34 AM | 0.4 | 12 |
| | 09:46 AM | 3.7 | 113 |
| | 03:43 PM | 0.4 | 12 |
| | 10:05 PM | 4.0 | 122 |
| **29** W | 04:11 AM | 0.4 | 12 |
| | 10:25 AM | 3.7 | 113 |
| | 04:26 PM | 0.5 | 15 |
| | 10:42 PM | 3.9 | 119 |
| **30** Th | 04:49 AM | 0.4 | 12 |
| | 11:06 AM | 3.8 | 116 |
| | 05:13 PM | 0.6 | 18 |
| | 11:21 PM | 3.7 | 113 |
| **31** F | 05:31 AM | 0.4 | 12 |
| | 11:49 AM | 3.9 | 119 |
| | 06:04 PM | 0.7 | 21 |

## September

| Day | Time | ft | cm |
|---|---|---|---|
| **1** Sa ◑ | 12:04 AM | 3.6 | 110 |
| | 06:17 AM | 0.4 | 12 |
| | 12:37 PM | 4.0 | 122 |
| | 06:59 PM | 0.7 | 21 |
| **2** Su | 12:51 AM | 3.5 | 107 |
| | 07:07 AM | 0.3 | 9 |
| | 01:32 PM | 4.1 | 125 |
| | 07:56 PM | 0.8 | 24 |
| **3** M ◑ | 01:46 AM | 3.4 | 104 |
| | 08:02 AM | 0.3 | 9 |
| | 02:32 PM | 4.2 | 128 |
| | 08:56 PM | 0.7 | 21 |
| **4** Tu | 02:48 AM | 3.4 | 104 |
| | 08:59 AM | 0.2 | 6 |
| | 03:37 PM | 4.3 | 131 |
| | 09:58 PM | 0.7 | 21 |
| **5** W | 03:53 AM | 3.5 | 107 |
| | 10:00 AM | 0.1 | 3 |
| | 04:39 PM | 4.5 | 137 |
| | 10:59 PM | 0.5 | 15 |
| **6** Th | 04:56 AM | 3.7 | 113 |
| | 11:02 AM | -0.1 | -3 |
| | 05:39 PM | 4.7 | 143 |
| | 11:57 PM | 0.3 | 9 |
| **7** F | 05:57 AM | 3.9 | 119 |
| | 12:03 PM | -0.2 | -6 |
| | 06:35 PM | 4.8 | 146 |
| **8** Sa | 12:52 AM | 0.1 | 3 |
| | 06:54 AM | 4.2 | 128 |
| | 01:01 PM | -0.3 | -9 |
| | 07:29 PM | 4.9 | 149 |
| **9** Su ● | 01:43 AM | 0.0 | 0 |
| | 07:50 AM | 4.4 | 134 |
| | 01:56 PM | -0.3 | -9 |
| | 08:21 PM | 4.8 | 146 |
| **10** M | 02:32 AM | -0.1 | -3 |
| | 08:45 AM | 4.5 | 137 |
| | 02:49 PM | -0.3 | -9 |
| | 09:12 PM | 4.7 | 143 |
| **11** Tu | 03:19 AM | -0.1 | -3 |
| | 09:37 AM | 4.6 | 140 |
| | 03:42 PM | -0.1 | -3 |
| | 10:00 PM | 4.5 | 137 |
| **12** W | 04:06 AM | 0.0 | 0 |
| | 10:28 AM | 4.6 | 140 |
| | 04:36 PM | 0.2 | 6 |
| | 10:47 PM | 4.2 | 128 |
| **13** Th | 04:54 AM | 0.1 | 3 |
| | 11:18 AM | 4.5 | 137 |
| | 05:32 PM | 0.4 | 12 |
| | 11:34 PM | 3.9 | 119 |
| **14** F | 05:44 AM | 0.3 | 9 |
| | 12:08 PM | 4.4 | 134 |
| | 06:29 PM | 0.7 | 21 |
| **15** Sa | 12:22 AM | 3.6 | 110 |
| | 06:35 AM | 0.5 | 15 |
| | 01:01 PM | 4.2 | 128 |
| | 07:26 PM | 0.9 | 27 |
| **16** Su ◑ | 01:14 AM | 3.4 | 104 |
| | 07:28 AM | 0.7 | 21 |
| | 01:58 PM | 4.0 | 122 |
| | 08:23 PM | 1.1 | 34 |
| **17** M | 02:12 AM | 3.2 | 98 |
| | 08:21 AM | 0.8 | 24 |
| | 03:00 PM | 3.9 | 119 |
| | 09:19 PM | 1.2 | 37 |
| **18** Tu | 03:15 AM | 3.1 | 94 |
| | 09:15 AM | 0.9 | 27 |
| | 04:00 PM | 3.9 | 119 |
| | 10:14 PM | 1.2 | 37 |
| **19** W | 04:14 AM | 3.0 | 91 |
| | 10:09 AM | 0.9 | 27 |
| | 04:53 PM | 3.9 | 119 |
| | 11:04 PM | 1.1 | 34 |
| **20** Th | 05:06 AM | 3.3 | 101 |
| | 11:02 AM | 0.9 | 27 |
| | 05:39 PM | 4.0 | 122 |
| | 11:50 PM | 1.0 | 30 |
| **21** F | 05:52 AM | 3.5 | 107 |
| | 11:51 AM | 0.8 | 24 |
| | 06:21 PM | 4.1 | 125 |
| **22** Sa | 12:31 AM | 0.9 | 27 |
| | 06:35 AM | 3.6 | 110 |
| | 12:36 PM | 0.7 | 21 |
| | 07:00 PM | 4.1 | 125 |
| **23** Su | 01:09 AM | 0.7 | 21 |
| | 07:16 AM | 3.8 | 116 |
| | 01:18 PM | 0.6 | 18 |
| | 07:39 PM | 4.2 | 128 |
| **24** M | 01:45 AM | 0.6 | 18 |
| | 07:56 AM | 4.0 | 122 |
| | 01:59 PM | 0.5 | 15 |
| | 08:17 PM | 4.2 | 128 |
| **25** Tu ○ | 02:21 AM | 0.5 | 15 |
| | 08:36 AM | 4.1 | 125 |
| | 02:40 PM | 0.5 | 15 |
| | 08:56 PM | 4.2 | 128 |
| **26** W | 02:57 AM | 0.4 | 12 |
| | 09:17 AM | 4.3 | 131 |
| | 03:21 PM | 0.5 | 15 |
| | 09:35 PM | 4.1 | 125 |
| **27** Th | 03:34 AM | 0.4 | 12 |
| | 09:57 AM | 4.4 | 134 |
| | 04:05 PM | 0.6 | 18 |
| | 10:14 PM | 4.0 | 122 |
| **28** F | 04:14 AM | 0.4 | 12 |
| | 10:40 AM | 4.5 | 137 |
| | 04:53 PM | 0.7 | 21 |
| | 10:56 PM | 3.9 | 119 |
| **29** Sa | 04:58 AM | 0.5 | 15 |
| | 11:25 AM | 4.5 | 137 |
| | 05:45 PM | 0.8 | 24 |
| | 11:42 PM | 3.8 | 116 |
| **30** Su | 05:47 AM | 0.5 | 15 |
| | 12:14 PM | 4.5 | 137 |
| | 06:41 PM | 0.8 | 24 |

Heights are referred to mean lower water which is the chart datum of sounding. All times are local. Daylight Saving Time has been used when needed. Additional tide tables are available online from NOAA at www.tidesandcurrents.noaa.gov/tide_predictions.shtml.

StationId:8723178
Source:NOAA/NOS/CO-OPS
Station Type:Harmonic
Time Zone:LST/LDT
Datum:mean lower low water (MLLW) which is the chart datum of soundings

**NOAA Tide Predictions**

# GOVERNMENT CUT, MIAMI HARBOR ENTRANCE,Florida,201

### Times and Heights of High and Low Waters

*SKIPPER'S HANDBOOK*

## October

| Day | Time | ft | cm |
|---|---|---|---|
| 1 Su | 05:41 AM | 2.5 | 76 |
| | 11:42 AM | 0.7 | 21 |
| | 06:16 PM | 2.7 | 82 |
| 2 M | 12:10 AM | 0.8 | 24 |
| | 06:35 AM | 2.7 | 82 |
| | 12:29 PM | 0.6 | 18 |
| | 07:04 PM | 2.8 | 85 |
| 3 Tu | 12:53 AM | 0.6 | 18 |
| | 07:24 AM | 2.9 | 88 |
| | 01:13 PM | 0.5 | 15 |
| | 07:49 PM | 3.0 | 91 |
| 4 W | 01:34 AM | 0.4 | 12 |
| | 08:11 AM | 3.0 | 91 |
| | 01:56 PM | 0.4 | 12 |
| | 08:32 PM | 3.1 | 94 |
| 5 Th ○ | 02:15 AM | 0.3 | 9 |
| | 08:57 AM | 3.2 | 98 |
| | 02:39 PM | 0.3 | 9 |
| | 09:14 PM | 3.1 | 94 |
| 6 F | 02:57 AM | 0.1 | 3 |
| | 09:43 AM | 3.3 | 101 |
| | 03:23 PM | 0.3 | 9 |
| | 09:58 PM | 3.2 | 98 |
| 7 Sa | 03:41 AM | 0.1 | 3 |
| | 10:29 AM | 3.3 | 101 |
| | 04:08 PM | 0.3 | 9 |
| | 10:42 PM | 3.2 | 98 |
| 8 Su | 04:27 AM | 0.0 | 0 |
| | 11:18 AM | 3.3 | 101 |
| | 04:56 PM | 0.4 | 12 |
| | 11:30 PM | 3.1 | 94 |
| 9 M | 05:17 AM | 0.1 | 3 |
| | 12:09 PM | 3.2 | 98 |
| | 05:48 PM | 0.5 | 15 |
| 10 Tu | 12:21 AM | 3.0 | 91 |
| | 06:11 AM | 0.2 | 6 |
| | 01:04 PM | 3.1 | 94 |
| | 06:46 PM | 0.6 | 18 |
| 11 W | 01:17 AM | 2.9 | 88 |
| | 07:12 AM | 0.3 | 9 |
| | 02:04 PM | 3.0 | 91 |
| | 07:51 PM | 0.7 | 21 |
| 12 Th ◑ | 02:20 AM | 2.9 | 88 |
| | 08:19 AM | 0.4 | 12 |
| | 03:08 PM | 3.0 | 91 |
| | 09:00 PM | 0.8 | 24 |
| 13 F | 03:28 AM | 2.8 | 85 |
| | 09:29 AM | 0.5 | 15 |
| | 04:14 PM | 2.9 | 88 |
| | 10:08 PM | 0.7 | 21 |
| 14 Sa | 04:37 AM | 2.9 | 88 |
| | 10:36 AM | 0.5 | 15 |
| | 05:17 PM | 3.0 | 91 |
| | 11:10 PM | 0.6 | 18 |
| 15 Su | 05:43 AM | 2.9 | 88 |
| | 11:36 AM | 0.5 | 15 |
| | 06:15 PM | 3.0 | 91 |
| 16 M | 12:05 AM | 0.5 | 15 |
| | 06:42 AM | 3.0 | 91 |
| | 12:31 PM | 0.4 | 12 |
| | 07:07 PM | 3.1 | 94 |
| 17 Tu | 12:55 AM | 0.4 | 12 |
| | 07:34 AM | 3.1 | 94 |
| | 01:20 PM | 0.4 | 12 |
| | 07:53 PM | 3.1 | 94 |
| 18 W | 01:41 AM | 0.3 | 9 |
| | 08:20 AM | 3.2 | 98 |
| | 02:05 PM | 0.4 | 12 |
| | 08:36 PM | 3.1 | 94 |
| 19 Th ● | 02:23 AM | 0.2 | 6 |
| | 09:03 AM | 3.2 | 98 |
| | 02:47 PM | 0.4 | 12 |
| | 09:16 PM | 3.1 | 94 |
| 20 F | 03:04 AM | 0.2 | 6 |
| | 09:44 AM | 3.2 | 98 |
| | 03:28 PM | 0.5 | 15 |
| | 09:53 PM | 3.0 | 91 |
| 21 Sa | 03:43 AM | 0.3 | 9 |
| | 10:22 AM | 3.1 | 94 |
| | 04:08 PM | 0.6 | 18 |
| | 10:30 PM | 2.9 | 88 |
| 22 Su | 04:21 AM | 0.4 | 12 |
| | 11:00 AM | 3.0 | 91 |
| | 04:47 PM | 0.7 | 21 |
| | 11:07 PM | 2.8 | 85 |
| 23 M | 04:59 AM | 0.5 | 15 |
| | 11:39 AM | 2.9 | 88 |
| | 05:26 PM | 0.8 | 24 |
| | 11:45 PM | 2.7 | 82 |
| 24 Tu | 05:39 AM | 0.6 | 18 |
| | 12:20 PM | 2.8 | 85 |
| | 06:07 PM | 0.9 | 27 |
| 25 W | 12:26 AM | 2.6 | 79 |
| | 06:21 AM | 0.7 | 21 |
| | 01:03 PM | 2.7 | 82 |
| | 06:53 PM | 1.0 | 30 |
| 26 Th | 01:11 AM | 2.5 | 76 |
| | 07:08 AM | 0.8 | 24 |
| | 01:51 PM | 2.6 | 79 |
| | 07:46 PM | 1.1 | 34 |
| 27 F ◐ | 02:03 AM | 2.4 | 73 |
| | 08:03 AM | 0.9 | 27 |
| | 02:44 PM | 2.5 | 76 |
| | 08:45 PM | 1.1 | 34 |
| 28 Sa | 03:01 AM | 2.4 | 73 |
| | 09:04 AM | 0.9 | 27 |
| | 03:41 PM | 2.5 | 76 |
| | 09:45 PM | 1.0 | 30 |
| 29 Su | 04:03 AM | 2.4 | 73 |
| | 10:05 AM | 0.9 | 27 |
| | 04:38 PM | 2.6 | 79 |
| | 10:40 PM | 0.9 | 27 |
| 30 M | 05:04 AM | 2.6 | 79 |
| | 11:01 AM | 0.8 | 24 |
| | 05:32 PM | 2.7 | 82 |
| | 11:30 PM | 0.7 | 21 |
| 31 Tu | 06:01 AM | 2.7 | 82 |
| | 11:52 AM | 0.7 | 21 |
| | 06:23 PM | 2.8 | 85 |

## November

| Day | Time | ft | cm |
|---|---|---|---|
| 1 W | 12:16 AM | 0.5 | 15 |
| | 06:54 AM | 2.9 | 88 |
| | 12:41 PM | 0.5 | 15 |
| | 07:11 PM | 2.9 | 88 |
| 2 Th | 01:01 AM | 0.3 | 9 |
| | 07:44 AM | 3.1 | 94 |
| | 01:27 PM | 0.4 | 12 |
| | 07:58 PM | 3.0 | 91 |
| 3 F | 01:46 AM | 0.1 | 3 |
| | 08:33 AM | 3.3 | 101 |
| | 02:14 PM | 0.3 | 9 |
| | 08:45 PM | 3.1 | 94 |
| 4 Sa ○ | 02:32 AM | -0.1 | -3 |
| | 09:21 AM | 3.4 | 104 |
| | 03:01 PM | 0.3 | 9 |
| | 09:32 PM | 3.2 | 98 |
| 5 Su | 02:19 AM | -0.2 | -6 |
| | 09:10 AM | 3.4 | 104 |
| | 02:49 PM | 0.3 | 9 |
| | 09:21 PM | 3.2 | 98 |
| 6 M | 03:08 AM | -0.2 | -6 |
| | 10:01 AM | 3.4 | 104 |
| | 03:40 PM | 0.3 | 9 |
| | 10:12 PM | 3.1 | 94 |
| 7 Tu | 04:00 AM | -0.1 | -3 |
| | 10:53 AM | 3.3 | 101 |
| | 04:34 PM | 0.4 | 12 |
| | 11:06 PM | 3.0 | 91 |
| 8 W | 04:56 AM | 0.0 | 0 |
| | 11:48 AM | 3.2 | 98 |
| | 05:33 PM | 0.5 | 15 |
| 9 Th | 12:04 AM | 2.9 | 88 |
| | 05:58 AM | 0.2 | 6 |
| | 12:46 PM | 3.0 | 91 |
| | 06:37 PM | 0.5 | 15 |
| 10 F ◑ | 01:07 AM | 2.8 | 85 |
| | 07:04 AM | 0.3 | 9 |
| | 01:48 PM | 2.9 | 88 |
| | 07:45 PM | 0.6 | 18 |
| 11 Sa | 02:14 AM | 2.8 | 85 |
| | 08:13 AM | 0.4 | 12 |
| | 02:51 PM | 2.8 | 85 |
| | 08:51 PM | 0.5 | 15 |
| 12 Su | 03:21 AM | 2.8 | 85 |
| | 09:18 AM | 0.5 | 15 |
| | 03:52 PM | 2.8 | 85 |
| | 09:51 PM | 0.4 | 12 |
| 13 M | 04:26 AM | 2.8 | 85 |
| | 10:18 AM | 0.5 | 15 |
| | 04:49 PM | 2.8 | 85 |
| | 10:45 PM | 0.3 | 9 |
| 14 Tu | 05:23 AM | 2.9 | 88 |
| | 11:11 AM | 0.5 | 15 |
| | 05:40 PM | 2.8 | 85 |
| | 11:34 PM | 0.2 | 6 |
| 15 W | 06:14 AM | 2.9 | 88 |
| | 11:59 AM | 0.5 | 15 |
| | 06:26 PM | 2.8 | 85 |
| 16 Th | 12:18 AM | 0.2 | 6 |
| | 07:00 AM | 3.0 | 91 |
| | 12:43 PM | 0.4 | 12 |
| | 07:08 PM | 2.8 | 85 |
| 17 F | 12:59 AM | 0.1 | 3 |
| | 07:41 AM | 3.0 | 91 |
| | 01:24 PM | 0.5 | 15 |
| | 07:48 PM | 2.8 | 85 |
| 18 Sa ● | 01:38 AM | 0.1 | 3 |
| | 08:20 AM | 3.0 | 91 |
| | 02:04 PM | 0.5 | 15 |
| | 08:25 PM | 2.7 | 82 |
| 19 Su | 02:16 AM | 0.2 | 6 |
| | 08:57 AM | 2.9 | 88 |
| | 02:42 PM | 0.5 | 15 |
| | 09:02 PM | 2.7 | 82 |
| 20 M | 02:53 AM | 0.2 | 6 |
| | 09:34 AM | 2.8 | 85 |
| | 03:19 PM | 0.6 | 18 |
| | 09:39 PM | 2.6 | 79 |
| 21 Tu | 03:30 AM | 0.3 | 9 |
| | 10:12 AM | 2.8 | 85 |
| | 03:57 PM | 0.6 | 18 |
| | 10:17 PM | 2.5 | 76 |
| 22 W | 04:07 AM | 0.4 | 12 |
| | 10:52 AM | 2.7 | 82 |
| | 04:36 PM | 0.7 | 21 |
| | 10:58 PM | 2.4 | 73 |
| 23 Th | 04:45 AM | 0.5 | 15 |
| | 11:33 AM | 2.6 | 79 |
| | 05:18 PM | 0.8 | 24 |
| | 11:42 PM | 2.3 | 70 |
| 24 F | 05:28 AM | 0.6 | 18 |
| | 12:17 PM | 2.5 | 76 |
| | 06:05 PM | 0.8 | 24 |
| 25 Sa ◑ | 12:30 AM | 2.3 | 70 |
| | 06:17 AM | 0.6 | 18 |
| | 01:05 PM | 2.4 | 73 |
| | 06:58 PM | 0.8 | 24 |
| 26 Su ◐ | 01:25 AM | 2.3 | 70 |
| | 07:15 AM | 0.7 | 21 |
| | 01:56 PM | 2.4 | 73 |
| | 07:56 PM | 0.7 | 21 |
| 27 M | 02:25 AM | 2.3 | 70 |
| | 08:17 AM | 0.7 | 21 |
| | 02:51 PM | 2.4 | 73 |
| | 08:54 PM | 0.6 | 18 |
| 28 Tu | 03:26 AM | 2.4 | 73 |
| | 09:18 AM | 0.6 | 18 |
| | 03:47 PM | 2.5 | 76 |
| | 09:48 PM | 0.4 | 12 |
| 29 W | 04:27 AM | 2.5 | 76 |
| | 10:15 AM | 0.5 | 15 |
| | 04:42 PM | 2.6 | 79 |
| | 10:40 PM | 0.2 | 6 |
| 30 Th | 05:24 AM | 2.7 | 82 |
| | 11:09 AM | 0.4 | 12 |
| | 05:36 PM | 2.7 | 82 |
| | 11:31 PM | -0.1 | -3 |

## December

| Day | Time | ft | cm |
|---|---|---|---|
| 1 F | 06:18 AM | 2.9 | 88 |
| | 12:01 PM | 0.2 | 6 |
| | 06:28 PM | 2.8 | 85 |
| 2 Sa | 12:20 AM | -0.3 | -9 |
| | 07:11 AM | 3.0 | 91 |
| | 12:51 PM | 0.1 | 3 |
| | 07:20 PM | 2.9 | 88 |
| 3 Su ○ | 01:10 AM | -0.4 | -12 |
| | 08:02 AM | 3.2 | 98 |
| | 01:41 PM | 0.0 | 0 |
| | 08:11 PM | 2.9 | 88 |
| 4 M | 02:01 AM | -0.5 | -15 |
| | 08:53 AM | 3.2 | 98 |
| | 02:32 PM | 0.0 | 0 |
| | 09:03 PM | 3.0 | 91 |
| 5 Tu | 02:52 AM | -0.5 | -15 |
| | 09:44 AM | 3.2 | 98 |
| | 03:25 PM | 0.0 | 0 |
| | 09:57 PM | 2.9 | 88 |
| 6 W | 03:46 AM | -0.4 | -12 |
| | 10:36 AM | 3.1 | 94 |
| | 04:20 PM | 0.0 | 0 |
| | 10:51 PM | 2.9 | 88 |
| 7 Th | 04:42 AM | -0.3 | -9 |
| | 11:30 AM | 3.0 | 91 |
| | 05:18 PM | 0.1 | 3 |
| | 11:49 PM | 2.7 | 82 |
| 8 F | 05:41 AM | -0.1 | -3 |
| | 12:25 PM | 2.8 | 85 |
| | 06:19 PM | 0.1 | 3 |
| 9 Sa | 12:49 AM | 2.6 | 79 |
| | 06:44 AM | 0.1 | 3 |
| | 01:22 PM | 2.7 | 82 |
| | 07:23 PM | 0.2 | 6 |
| 10 Su ◑ | 01:52 AM | 2.5 | 76 |
| | 07:49 AM | 0.2 | 6 |
| | 02:20 PM | 2.6 | 79 |
| | 08:25 PM | 0.2 | 6 |
| 11 M ◐ | 02:57 AM | 2.5 | 76 |
| | 08:52 AM | 0.3 | 9 |
| | 03:19 PM | 2.5 | 76 |
| | 09:24 PM | 0.1 | 3 |
| 12 Tu | 04:00 AM | 2.4 | 73 |
| | 09:52 AM | 0.4 | 12 |
| | 04:16 PM | 2.4 | 73 |
| | 10:18 PM | 0.1 | 3 |
| 13 W | 04:58 AM | 2.5 | 76 |
| | 10:46 AM | 0.4 | 12 |
| | 05:09 PM | 2.4 | 73 |
| | 11:07 PM | 0.0 | 0 |
| 14 Th | 05:50 AM | 2.5 | 76 |
| | 11:35 AM | 0.4 | 12 |
| | 05:57 PM | 2.4 | 73 |
| | 11:52 PM | 0.0 | 0 |
| 15 F | 06:36 AM | 2.5 | 76 |
| | 12:20 PM | 0.3 | 9 |
| | 06:40 PM | 2.4 | 73 |
| 16 Sa | 12:34 AM | 0.0 | 0 |
| | 07:17 AM | 2.6 | 79 |
| | 01:01 PM | 0.3 | 9 |
| | 07:21 PM | 2.4 | 73 |
| 17 Su | 01:14 AM | -0.1 | -3 |
| | 07:57 AM | 2.6 | 79 |
| | 01:41 PM | 0.3 | 9 |
| | 08:00 PM | 2.4 | 73 |
| 18 M ● | 01:52 AM | -0.1 | -3 |
| | 08:34 AM | 2.6 | 79 |
| | 02:19 PM | 0.3 | 9 |
| | 08:38 PM | 2.4 | 73 |
| 19 Tu | 02:29 AM | -0.1 | -3 |
| | 09:12 AM | 2.5 | 76 |
| | 02:56 PM | 0.3 | 9 |
| | 09:16 PM | 2.3 | 70 |
| 20 W | 03:05 AM | 0.0 | 0 |
| | 09:49 AM | 2.5 | 76 |
| | 03:33 PM | 0.3 | 9 |
| | 09:55 PM | 2.3 | 70 |
| 21 Th | 03:41 AM | 0.0 | 0 |
| | 10:27 AM | 2.4 | 73 |
| | 04:10 PM | 0.3 | 9 |
| | 10:35 PM | 2.2 | 67 |
| 22 F | 04:18 AM | 0.1 | 3 |
| | 11:06 AM | 2.4 | 73 |
| | 04:48 PM | 0.3 | 9 |
| | 11:17 PM | 2.1 | 64 |
| 23 Sa | 04:57 AM | 0.2 | 6 |
| | 11:46 AM | 2.3 | 70 |
| | 05:30 PM | 0.3 | 9 |
| 24 Su | 12:03 AM | 2.1 | 64 |
| | 05:42 AM | 0.3 | 9 |
| | 12:29 PM | 2.2 | 67 |
| | 06:18 PM | 0.3 | 9 |
| 25 M | 12:53 AM | 2.1 | 64 |
| | 06:34 AM | 0.3 | 9 |
| | 01:15 PM | 2.2 | 67 |
| | 07:11 PM | 0.3 | 9 |
| 26 Tu ◐ | 01:49 AM | 2.1 | 64 |
| | 07:34 AM | 0.3 | 9 |
| | 02:07 PM | 2.2 | 67 |
| | 08:10 PM | 0.1 | 3 |
| 27 W | 02:50 AM | 2.1 | 64 |
| | 08:37 AM | 0.3 | 9 |
| | 03:04 PM | 2.2 | 67 |
| | 09:09 PM | 0.0 | 0 |
| 28 Th | 03:54 AM | 2.2 | 67 |
| | 09:40 AM | 0.3 | 9 |
| | 04:04 PM | 2.2 | 67 |
| | 10:08 PM | -0.2 | -6 |
| 29 F | 04:57 AM | 2.4 | 73 |
| | 10:40 AM | 0.2 | 6 |
| | 05:05 PM | 2.3 | 70 |
| | 11:04 PM | -0.4 | -12 |
| 30 Sa | 05:56 AM | 2.6 | 79 |
| | 11:37 AM | 0.0 | 0 |
| | 06:04 PM | 2.5 | 76 |
| | 11:59 PM | -0.6 | -18 |
| 31 Su | 06:52 AM | 2.7 | 82 |
| | 12:31 PM | -0.1 | -3 |
| | 07:00 PM | 2.6 | 79 |

Heights are referred to mean lower water which is the chart datum of sounding. All times are local. Daylight Saving Time has been used when needed. Additional tide tables are available online from NOAA at www.tidesandcurrents.noaa.gov/tide_predictions.shtml.

StationId: 8723178
Source: NOAA/NOS/CO-OPS
Station Type: Primary
Time Zone: LST_LDT
Datum: MLLW

**NOAA Tide Predictions**

# MIAMI BEACH, GOVERNMENT CUT, FL,2018

### Times and Heights of High and Low Waters

## January

| Day | Time | ft | cm |
|---|---|---|---|
| 1 M | 12:54 AM | -0.7 | -21 |
| | 07:47 AM | 2.8 | 85 |
| | 01:26 PM | -0.2 | -6 |
| | 07:56 PM | 2.7 | 82 |
| 2 Tu ○ | 01:47 AM | -0.8 | -24 |
| | 08:39 AM | 2.9 | 88 |
| | 02:19 PM | -0.3 | -9 |
| | 08:50 PM | 2.7 | 82 |
| 3 W | 02:40 AM | -0.8 | -24 |
| | 09:29 AM | 2.9 | 88 |
| | 03:11 PM | -0.3 | -9 |
| | 09:43 PM | 2.7 | 82 |
| 4 Th | 03:33 AM | -0.7 | -21 |
| | 10:19 AM | 2.9 | 88 |
| | 04:05 PM | -0.3 | -9 |
| | 10:36 PM | 2.7 | 82 |
| 5 F | 04:27 AM | -0.6 | -18 |
| | 11:10 AM | 2.7 | 82 |
| | 05:00 PM | -0.3 | -9 |
| | 11:31 PM | 2.5 | 76 |
| 6 Sa | 05:22 AM | -0.4 | -12 |
| | 12:00 PM | 2.6 | 79 |
| | 05:56 PM | -0.2 | -6 |
| 7 Su | 12:26 AM | 2.4 | 73 |
| | 06:20 AM | -0.2 | -6 |
| | 12:52 PM | 2.4 | 73 |
| | 06:54 PM | -0.2 | -6 |
| 8 M ◑ | 01:24 AM | 2.3 | 70 |
| | 07:19 AM | 0.0 | 0 |
| | 01:45 PM | 2.3 | 70 |
| | 07:53 PM | -0.1 | -3 |
| 9 Tu | 02:24 AM | 2.2 | 67 |
| | 08:20 AM | 0.2 | 6 |
| | 02:40 PM | 2.1 | 64 |
| | 08:51 PM | -0.1 | -3 |
| 10 W | 03:25 AM | 2.1 | 64 |
| | 09:19 AM | 0.3 | 9 |
| | 03:36 PM | 2.0 | 61 |
| | 09:46 PM | -0.1 | -3 |
| 11 Th | 04:25 AM | 2.1 | 64 |
| | 10:15 AM | 0.3 | 9 |
| | 04:31 PM | 2.0 | 61 |
| | 10:37 PM | -0.1 | -3 |
| 12 F | 05:20 AM | 2.1 | 64 |
| | 11:06 AM | 0.3 | 9 |
| | 05:23 PM | 2.0 | 61 |
| | 11:25 PM | -0.1 | -3 |
| 13 Sa | 06:08 AM | 2.1 | 64 |
| | 11:53 AM | 0.2 | 6 |
| | 06:10 PM | 2.0 | 61 |
| 14 Su | 12:09 AM | -0.2 | -6 |
| | 06:52 AM | 2.2 | 67 |
| | 12:37 PM | 0.2 | 6 |
| | 06:54 PM | 2.0 | 61 |
| 15 M | 12:51 AM | -0.2 | -6 |
| | 07:33 AM | 2.2 | 67 |
| | 01:17 PM | 0.1 | 3 |
| | 07:36 PM | 2.1 | 64 |
| 16 Tu | 01:30 AM | -0.2 | -6 |
| | 08:12 AM | 2.3 | 70 |
| | 01:56 PM | 0.1 | 3 |
| | 08:16 PM | 2.1 | 64 |
| 17 W ● | 02:07 AM | -0.3 | -9 |
| | 08:50 AM | 2.3 | 70 |
| | 02:33 PM | 0.1 | 3 |
| | 08:56 PM | 2.1 | 64 |
| 18 Th | 02:43 AM | -0.3 | -9 |
| | 09:27 AM | 2.3 | 70 |
| | 03:09 PM | 0.0 | 0 |
| | 09:35 PM | 2.1 | 64 |
| 19 F | 03:19 AM | -0.2 | -6 |
| | 10:04 AM | 2.3 | 70 |
| | 03:45 PM | 0.0 | 0 |
| | 10:15 PM | 2.1 | 64 |
| 20 Sa | 03:55 AM | -0.2 | -6 |
| | 10:41 AM | 2.2 | 67 |
| | 04:21 PM | 0.0 | 0 |
| | 10:55 PM | 2.1 | 64 |
| 21 Su | 04:33 AM | -0.1 | -3 |
| | 11:19 AM | 2.2 | 67 |
| | 05:01 PM | 0.0 | 0 |
| | 11:39 PM | 2.0 | 61 |
| 22 M | 05:16 AM | 0.0 | 0 |
| | 11:59 AM | 2.1 | 64 |
| | 05:45 PM | -0.1 | -3 |
| 23 Tu | 12:27 AM | 2.0 | 61 |
| | 06:05 AM | 0.0 | 0 |
| | 12:42 PM | 2.0 | 61 |
| | 06:37 PM | -0.1 | -3 |
| 24 W ◑ | 01:20 AM | 2.0 | 61 |
| | 07:02 AM | 0.1 | 3 |
| | 01:32 PM | 2.0 | 61 |
| | 07:35 PM | -0.2 | -6 |
| 25 Th | 02:22 AM | 2.0 | 61 |
| | 08:06 AM | 0.2 | 6 |
| | 02:30 PM | 2.0 | 61 |
| | 08:38 PM | -0.2 | -6 |
| 26 F | 03:28 AM | 2.1 | 64 |
| | 09:13 AM | 0.1 | 3 |
| | 03:36 PM | 2.0 | 61 |
| | 09:43 PM | -0.4 | -12 |
| 27 Sa | 04:35 AM | 2.2 | 67 |
| | 10:18 AM | 0.1 | 3 |
| | 04:43 PM | 2.1 | 64 |
| | 10:45 PM | -0.5 | -15 |
| 28 Su | 05:39 AM | 2.3 | 70 |
| | 11:19 AM | -0.1 | -3 |
| | 05:47 PM | 2.2 | 67 |
| | 11:44 PM | -0.7 | -21 |
| 29 M | 06:37 AM | 2.5 | 76 |
| | 12:16 PM | -0.2 | -6 |
| | 06:47 PM | 2.4 | 73 |
| 30 Tu | 12:40 AM | -0.8 | -24 |
| | 07:31 AM | 2.6 | 79 |
| | 01:11 PM | -0.4 | -12 |
| | 07:43 PM | 2.5 | 76 |
| 31 W ○ | 01:34 AM | -0.8 | -24 |
| | 08:22 AM | 2.7 | 82 |
| | 02:03 PM | -0.5 | -15 |
| | 08:36 PM | 2.6 | 79 |

## February

| Day | Time | ft | cm |
|---|---|---|---|
| 1 Th | 02:26 AM | -0.8 | -24 |
| | 09:11 AM | 2.8 | 85 |
| | 02:55 PM | -0.6 | -18 |
| | 09:28 PM | 2.6 | 79 |
| 2 F | 03:17 AM | -0.8 | -24 |
| | 09:58 AM | 2.7 | 82 |
| | 03:45 PM | -0.6 | -18 |
| | 10:18 PM | 2.6 | 79 |
| 3 Sa | 04:07 AM | -0.6 | -18 |
| | 10:44 AM | 2.6 | 79 |
| | 04:35 PM | -0.5 | -15 |
| | 11:08 PM | 2.5 | 76 |
| 4 Su | 04:58 AM | -0.4 | -12 |
| | 11:30 AM | 2.5 | 76 |
| | 05:26 PM | -0.4 | -12 |
| | 11:58 PM | 2.3 | 70 |
| 5 M | 05:49 AM | -0.2 | -6 |
| | 12:16 PM | 2.3 | 70 |
| | 06:18 PM | -0.3 | -9 |
| 6 Tu | 12:50 AM | 2.2 | 67 |
| | 06:43 AM | 0.0 | 0 |
| | 01:04 PM | 2.1 | 64 |
| | 07:12 PM | -0.2 | -6 |
| 7 W ◐ | 01:44 AM | 2.0 | 61 |
| | 07:40 AM | 0.1 | 3 |
| | 01:54 PM | 1.9 | 58 |
| | 08:09 PM | -0.1 | -3 |
| 8 Th | 02:41 AM | 1.9 | 58 |
| | 08:39 AM | 0.3 | 9 |
| | 02:49 PM | 1.8 | 55 |
| | 09:06 PM | 0.0 | 0 |
| 9 F | 03:41 AM | 1.8 | 55 |
| | 09:37 AM | 0.3 | 9 |
| | 03:47 PM | 1.8 | 55 |
| | 10:01 PM | 0.0 | 0 |
| 10 Sa | 04:41 AM | 1.8 | 55 |
| | 10:33 AM | 0.3 | 9 |
| | 04:45 PM | 1.8 | 55 |
| | 10:54 PM | 0.0 | 0 |
| 11 Su | 05:35 AM | 1.9 | 58 |
| | 11:24 AM | 0.3 | 9 |
| | 05:38 PM | 1.8 | 55 |
| | 11:42 PM | -0.1 | -3 |
| 12 M | 06:23 AM | 2.0 | 61 |
| | 12:10 PM | 0.2 | 6 |
| | 06:27 PM | 1.9 | 58 |
| 13 Tu | 12:25 AM | -0.2 | -6 |
| | 07:06 AM | 2.1 | 64 |
| | 12:52 PM | 0.1 | 3 |
| | 07:12 PM | 2.0 | 61 |
| 14 W | 01:06 AM | -0.2 | -6 |
| | 07:46 AM | 2.2 | 67 |
| | 01:31 PM | 0.0 | 0 |
| | 07:54 PM | 2.1 | 64 |
| 15 Th ● | 01:44 AM | -0.3 | -9 |
| | 08:24 AM | 2.3 | 70 |
| | 02:08 PM | -0.1 | -3 |
| | 08:34 PM | 2.2 | 67 |
| 16 F | 02:21 AM | -0.3 | -9 |
| | 09:02 AM | 2.3 | 70 |
| | 02:43 PM | -0.1 | -3 |
| | 09:14 PM | 2.2 | 67 |
| 17 Sa | 02:57 AM | -0.3 | -9 |
| | 09:38 AM | 2.3 | 70 |
| | 03:19 PM | -0.2 | -6 |
| | 09:54 PM | 2.2 | 67 |
| 18 Su | 03:33 AM | -0.3 | -9 |
| | 10:15 AM | 2.3 | 70 |
| | 03:55 PM | -0.2 | -6 |
| | 10:35 PM | 2.2 | 67 |
| 19 M | 04:12 AM | -0.2 | -6 |
| | 10:52 AM | 2.2 | 67 |
| | 04:35 PM | -0.3 | -9 |
| | 11:18 PM | 2.2 | 67 |
| 20 Tu | 04:55 AM | -0.1 | -3 |
| | 11:32 AM | 2.2 | 67 |
| | 05:19 PM | -0.3 | -9 |
| 21 W | 12:05 AM | 2.2 | 67 |
| | 05:43 AM | 0.0 | 0 |
| | 12:16 PM | 2.1 | 64 |
| | 06:09 PM | -0.3 | -9 |
| 22 Th | 12:58 AM | 2.1 | 64 |
| | 06:39 AM | 0.1 | 3 |
| | 01:06 PM | 2.0 | 61 |
| | 07:08 PM | -0.3 | -9 |
| 23 F ◑ | 01:59 AM | 2.1 | 64 |
| | 07:43 AM | 0.2 | 6 |
| | 02:07 PM | 2.0 | 61 |
| | 08:14 PM | -0.3 | -9 |
| 24 Sa | 03:07 AM | 2.1 | 64 |
| | 08:52 AM | 0.2 | 6 |
| | 03:16 PM | 2.0 | 61 |
| | 09:23 PM | -0.3 | -9 |
| 25 Su | 04:16 AM | 2.2 | 67 |
| | 10:00 AM | 0.1 | 3 |
| | 04:28 PM | 2.1 | 64 |
| | 10:29 PM | -0.4 | -12 |
| 26 M | 05:22 AM | 2.3 | 70 |
| | 11:04 AM | 0.0 | 0 |
| | 05:35 PM | 2.3 | 70 |
| | 11:30 PM | -0.5 | -15 |
| 27 Tu | 06:21 AM | 2.4 | 73 |
| | 12:02 PM | -0.2 | -6 |
| | 06:36 PM | 2.4 | 73 |
| 28 W | 12:27 AM | -0.6 | -18 |
| | 07:14 AM | 2.6 | 79 |
| | 12:56 PM | -0.4 | -12 |
| | 07:31 PM | 2.6 | 79 |

## March

| Day | Time | ft | cm |
|---|---|---|---|
| 1 Th | 01:20 AM | -0.7 | -21 |
| | 08:03 AM | 2.7 | 82 |
| | 01:46 PM | -0.5 | -15 |
| | 08:22 PM | 2.7 | 82 |
| 2 F ○ | 02:10 AM | -0.7 | -21 |
| | 08:50 AM | 2.7 | 82 |
| | 02:35 PM | -0.6 | -18 |
| | 09:11 PM | 2.7 | 82 |
| 3 Sa | 02:58 AM | -0.6 | -18 |
| | 09:34 AM | 2.7 | 82 |
| | 03:22 PM | -0.6 | -18 |
| | 09:57 PM | 2.7 | 82 |
| 4 Su | 03:45 AM | -0.5 | -15 |
| | 10:17 AM | 2.6 | 79 |
| | 04:08 PM | -0.5 | -15 |
| | 10:43 PM | 2.6 | 79 |
| 5 M | 04:31 AM | -0.3 | -9 |
| | 10:58 AM | 2.5 | 76 |
| | 04:53 PM | -0.4 | -12 |
| | 11:28 PM | 2.4 | 73 |
| 6 Tu | 05:18 AM | -0.1 | -3 |
| | 11:40 AM | 2.3 | 70 |
| | 05:40 PM | -0.3 | -9 |
| 7 W | 12:14 AM | 2.2 | 67 |
| | 06:06 AM | 0.1 | 3 |
| | 12:23 PM | 2.1 | 64 |
| | 06:30 PM | -0.1 | -3 |
| 8 Th | 01:02 AM | 2.1 | 64 |
| | 06:58 AM | 0.3 | 9 |
| | 01:09 PM | 1.9 | 58 |
| | 07:23 PM | 0.1 | 3 |
| 9 F ◐ | 01:54 AM | 1.9 | 58 |
| | 07:55 AM | 0.4 | 12 |
| | 02:01 PM | 1.8 | 55 |
| | 08:21 PM | 0.2 | 6 |
| 10 Sa | 02:52 AM | 1.8 | 55 |
| | 08:55 AM | 0.5 | 15 |
| | 03:00 PM | 1.8 | 55 |
| | 09:20 PM | 0.2 | 6 |
| 11 Su | 04:53 AM | 1.8 | 55 |
| | 10:54 AM | 0.5 | 15 |
| | 05:03 PM | 1.8 | 55 |
| | 11:17 PM | 0.2 | 6 |
| 12 M | 05:53 AM | 1.9 | 58 |
| | 11:49 AM | 0.4 | 12 |
| | 06:03 PM | 1.8 | 55 |
| 13 Tu | 12:09 AM | 0.1 | 3 |
| | 06:45 AM | 2.0 | 61 |
| | 12:37 PM | 0.3 | 9 |
| | 06:56 PM | 2.0 | 61 |
| 14 W | 12:55 AM | 0.0 | 0 |
| | 07:31 AM | 2.1 | 64 |
| | 01:20 PM | 0.2 | 6 |
| | 07:44 PM | 2.1 | 64 |
| 15 Th | 01:37 AM | -0.1 | -3 |
| | 08:13 AM | 2.2 | 67 |
| | 02:00 PM | 0.0 | 0 |
| | 08:28 PM | 2.2 | 67 |
| 16 F | 02:16 AM | -0.1 | -3 |
| | 08:53 AM | 2.3 | 70 |
| | 02:37 PM | -0.1 | -3 |
| | 09:10 PM | 2.4 | 73 |
| 17 Sa ● | 02:55 AM | -0.2 | -6 |
| | 09:32 AM | 2.4 | 73 |
| | 03:14 PM | -0.2 | -6 |
| | 09:52 PM | 2.5 | 76 |
| 18 Su | 03:33 AM | -0.2 | -6 |
| | 10:10 AM | 2.4 | 73 |
| | 03:51 PM | -0.3 | -9 |
| | 10:33 PM | 2.5 | 76 |
| 19 M | 04:12 AM | -0.2 | -6 |
| | 10:48 AM | 2.4 | 73 |
| | 04:30 PM | -0.3 | -9 |
| | 11:15 PM | 2.5 | 76 |
| 20 Tu | 04:53 AM | -0.2 | -6 |
| | 11:28 AM | 2.4 | 73 |
| | 05:11 PM | -0.4 | -12 |
| 21 W | 12:00 AM | 2.5 | 76 |
| | 05:37 AM | -0.1 | -3 |
| | 12:10 PM | 2.3 | 70 |
| | 05:58 PM | -0.3 | -9 |
| 22 Th | 12:49 AM | 2.4 | 73 |
| | 06:27 AM | 0.0 | 0 |
| | 12:57 PM | 2.3 | 70 |
| | 06:50 PM | -0.3 | -9 |
| 23 F | 01:42 AM | 2.4 | 73 |
| | 07:23 AM | 0.2 | 6 |
| | 01:52 PM | 2.2 | 67 |
| | 07:51 PM | -0.2 | -6 |
| 24 Sa ◑ | 02:43 AM | 2.3 | 70 |
| | 08:28 AM | 0.2 | 6 |
| | 02:55 PM | 2.1 | 64 |
| | 08:59 PM | -0.1 | -3 |
| 25 Su | 03:50 AM | 2.3 | 70 |
| | 09:38 AM | 0.2 | 6 |
| | 04:06 PM | 2.1 | 64 |
| | 10:09 PM | -0.1 | -3 |
| 26 M | 04:59 AM | 2.3 | 70 |
| | 10:47 AM | 0.2 | 6 |
| | 05:18 PM | 2.2 | 67 |
| | 11:16 PM | -0.2 | -6 |
| 27 Tu | 06:04 AM | 2.4 | 73 |
| | 11:50 AM | 0.0 | 0 |
| | 06:25 PM | 2.4 | 73 |
| 28 W | 12:17 AM | -0.3 | -9 |
| | 07:02 AM | 2.5 | 76 |
| | 12:47 PM | -0.1 | -3 |
| | 07:24 PM | 2.5 | 76 |
| 29 Th | 01:13 AM | -0.3 | -9 |
| | 07:54 AM | 2.6 | 79 |
| | 01:40 PM | -0.3 | -9 |
| | 08:17 PM | 2.7 | 82 |
| 30 F | 02:04 AM | -0.4 | -12 |
| | 08:41 AM | 2.7 | 82 |
| | 02:27 PM | -0.4 | -12 |
| | 09:06 PM | 2.8 | 85 |
| 31 Sa ○ | 02:51 AM | -0.4 | -12 |
| | 09:25 AM | 2.7 | 82 |
| | 03:12 PM | -0.5 | -15 |
| | 09:51 PM | 2.8 | 85 |

Heights are referred to mean lower water which is the chart datum of sounding. All times are local. Daylight Saving Time has been used when needed. Additional tide tables are available online from NOAA at www.tidesandcurrents.noaa.gov/tide_predictions.shtml.

**SKIPPER'S HANDBOOK**

StationId: 8723178
Source: NOAA/NOS/CO-OPS
Station Type: Primary
Time Zone: LST_LDT
Datum: MLLW

**NOAA Tide Predictions**

## MIAMI BEACH, GOVERNMENT CUT, FL,2018

### Times and Heights of High and Low Waters

## April

| | Time | ft | cm | | Time | ft | cm |
|---|---|---|---|---|---|---|---|
| **1** Su | 03:37 AM | -0.3 | -9 | **16** M ● | 03:07 AM | -0.1 | -3 |
| | 10:07 AM | 2.7 | 82 | | 09:40 AM | 2.6 | 79 |
| | 03:56 PM | -0.5 | -15 | | 03:23 PM | -0.4 | -12 |
| | 10:35 PM | 2.7 | 82 | | 10:11 PM | 2.8 | 85 |
| **2** M | 04:20 AM | -0.2 | -6 | **17** Tu | 03:50 AM | -0.1 | -3 |
| | 10:48 AM | 2.6 | 79 | | 10:23 AM | 2.6 | 79 |
| | 04:38 PM | -0.4 | -12 | | 04:06 PM | -0.4 | -12 |
| | 11:16 PM | 2.6 | 79 | | 10:57 PM | 2.8 | 85 |
| **3** Tu | 05:03 AM | -0.1 | -3 | **18** W | 04:35 AM | -0.1 | -3 |
| | 11:27 AM | 2.5 | 76 | | 11:07 AM | 2.6 | 79 |
| | 05:20 PM | -0.3 | -9 | | 04:52 PM | -0.4 | -12 |
| | 11:58 PM | 2.5 | 76 | | 11:44 PM | 2.7 | 82 |
| **4** W | 05:46 AM | 0.1 | 3 | **19** Th | 05:22 AM | 0.0 | 0 |
| | 12:06 PM | 2.3 | 70 | | 11:54 AM | 2.5 | 76 |
| | 06:03 PM | -0.1 | -3 | | 05:42 PM | -0.4 | -12 |
| **5** Th | 12:39 AM | 2.4 | 73 | **20** F | 12:35 AM | 2.7 | 82 |
| | 06:30 AM | 0.3 | 9 | | 06:15 AM | 0.1 | 3 |
| | 12:46 PM | 2.2 | 67 | | 12:45 PM | 2.4 | 73 |
| | 06:48 PM | 0.1 | 3 | | 06:37 PM | -0.3 | -9 |
| **6** F | 01:23 AM | 2.2 | 67 | **21** Sa | 01:30 AM | 2.6 | 79 |
| | 07:18 AM | 0.4 | 12 | | 07:14 AM | 0.2 | 6 |
| | 01:30 PM | 2.0 | 61 | | 01:43 PM | 2.4 | 73 |
| | 07:38 PM | 0.2 | 6 | | 07:39 PM | -0.1 | -3 |
| **7** Sa | 02:11 AM | 2.1 | 64 | **22** Su ◐ | 02:30 AM | 2.5 | 76 |
| | 08:11 AM | 0.5 | 15 | | 08:19 AM | 0.2 | 6 |
| | 02:19 PM | 1.9 | 58 | | 02:47 PM | 2.3 | 70 |
| | 08:33 PM | 0.3 | 9 | | 08:47 PM | 0.0 | 0 |
| **8** Su ◑ | 03:04 AM | 2.0 | 61 | **23** M | 03:34 AM | 2.4 | 73 |
| | 09:10 AM | 0.6 | 18 | | 09:27 AM | 0.2 | 6 |
| | 03:16 PM | 1.9 | 58 | | 03:57 PM | 2.3 | 70 |
| | 09:33 PM | 0.4 | 12 | | 09:56 PM | 0.0 | 0 |
| **9** M | 04:03 AM | 1.9 | 58 | **24** Tu | 04:40 AM | 2.4 | 73 |
| | 10:11 AM | 0.6 | 18 | | 10:34 AM | 0.1 | 3 |
| | 04:19 PM | 1.9 | 58 | | 05:07 PM | 2.4 | 73 |
| | 10:33 PM | 0.4 | 12 | | 11:02 PM | 0.0 | 0 |
| **10** Tu | 05:03 AM | 2.0 | 61 | **25** W | 05:42 AM | 2.4 | 73 |
| | 11:07 AM | 0.5 | 15 | | 11:34 AM | 0.0 | 0 |
| | 05:22 PM | 1.9 | 58 | | 06:11 PM | 2.5 | 76 |
| | 11:28 PM | 0.3 | 9 | | | | |
| **11** W | 05:59 AM | 2.1 | 64 | **26** Th | 12:01 AM | 0.0 | 0 |
| | 11:57 AM | 0.4 | 12 | | 06:39 AM | 2.5 | 76 |
| | 06:20 PM | 2.1 | 64 | | 12:28 PM | -0.1 | -3 |
| | | | | | 07:09 PM | 2.6 | 79 |
| **12** Th | 12:17 AM | 0.2 | 6 | **27** F | 12:55 AM | -0.1 | -3 |
| | 06:49 AM | 2.2 | 67 | | 07:30 AM | 2.6 | 79 |
| | 12:42 PM | 0.2 | 6 | | 01:18 PM | -0.2 | -6 |
| | 07:11 PM | 2.2 | 67 | | 08:00 PM | 2.7 | 82 |
| **13** F | 01:02 AM | 0.1 | 3 | **28** Sa | 01:44 AM | -0.1 | -3 |
| | 07:34 AM | 2.3 | 70 | | 08:16 AM | 2.6 | 79 |
| | 01:23 PM | 0.1 | 3 | | 02:04 PM | -0.3 | -9 |
| | 07:58 PM | 2.4 | 73 | | 08:47 PM | 2.7 | 82 |
| **14** Sa | 01:44 AM | 0.0 | 0 | **29** Su | 02:30 AM | -0.1 | -3 |
| | 08:17 AM | 2.4 | 73 | | 08:59 AM | 2.6 | 79 |
| | 02:03 PM | -0.1 | -3 | | 02:47 PM | -0.3 | -9 |
| | 08:43 PM | 2.6 | 79 | | 09:30 PM | 2.8 | 85 |
| **15** Su | 02:26 AM | 0.0 | 0 | **30** M ○ | 03:14 AM | -0.1 | -3 |
| | 08:59 AM | 2.5 | 76 | | 09:40 AM | 2.6 | 79 |
| | 02:42 PM | -0.3 | -9 | | 03:29 PM | -0.3 | -9 |
| | 09:27 PM | 2.7 | 82 | | 10:11 PM | 2.7 | 82 |

## May

| | Time | ft | cm | | Time | ft | cm |
|---|---|---|---|---|---|---|---|
| **1** Tu | 03:55 AM | 0.0 | 0 | **16** W | 03:29 AM | -0.1 | -3 |
| | 10:19 AM | 2.5 | 76 | | 10:00 AM | 2.6 | 79 |
| | 04:09 PM | -0.3 | -9 | | 03:46 PM | -0.6 | -18 |
| | 10:51 PM | 2.6 | 79 | | 10:39 PM | 2.9 | 88 |
| **2** W | 04:36 AM | 0.1 | 3 | **17** Th | 04:18 AM | -0.1 | -3 |
| | 10:57 AM | 2.4 | 73 | | 10:49 AM | 2.6 | 79 |
| | 04:49 PM | -0.1 | -3 | | 04:36 PM | -0.5 | -15 |
| | 11:30 PM | 2.5 | 76 | | 11:30 PM | 2.8 | 85 |
| **3** Th | 05:17 AM | 0.2 | 6 | **18** F | 05:09 AM | -0.1 | -3 |
| | 11:35 AM | 2.3 | 70 | | 11:40 AM | 2.6 | 79 |
| | 05:30 PM | 0.0 | 0 | | 05:29 PM | -0.5 | -15 |
| **4** F | 12:09 AM | 2.4 | 73 | **19** Sa | 12:22 AM | 2.8 | 85 |
| | 05:58 AM | 0.3 | 9 | | 06:04 AM | 0.0 | 0 |
| | 12:15 PM | 2.2 | 67 | | 12:35 PM | 2.5 | 76 |
| | 06:11 PM | 0.1 | 3 | | 06:26 PM | -0.3 | -9 |
| **5** Sa | 12:50 AM | 2.3 | 70 | **20** Su | 01:16 AM | 2.7 | 82 |
| | 06:42 AM | 0.5 | 15 | | 07:04 AM | 0.1 | 3 |
| | 12:57 PM | 2.1 | 64 | | 01:34 PM | 2.4 | 73 |
| | 06:56 PM | 0.2 | 6 | | 07:28 PM | -0.2 | -6 |
| **6** Su | 01:35 AM | 2.2 | 67 | **21** M | 02:14 AM | 2.6 | 79 |
| | 07:31 AM | 0.5 | 15 | | 08:08 AM | 0.1 | 3 |
| | 01:45 PM | 2.0 | 61 | | 02:37 PM | 2.4 | 73 |
| | 07:47 PM | 0.4 | 12 | | 08:34 PM | -0.1 | -3 |
| **7** M | 02:23 AM | 2.1 | 64 | **22** Tu ◐ | 03:14 AM | 2.5 | 76 |
| | 08:26 AM | 0.6 | 18 | | 09:13 AM | 0.1 | 3 |
| | 02:38 PM | 1.9 | 58 | | 03:44 PM | 2.3 | 70 |
| | 08:44 PM | 0.4 | 12 | | 09:40 PM | 0.0 | 0 |
| **8** Tu ◑ | 03:16 AM | 2.0 | 61 | **23** W | 04:15 AM | 2.4 | 73 |
| | 09:24 AM | 0.6 | 18 | | 10:16 AM | 0.0 | 0 |
| | 03:38 PM | 1.9 | 58 | | 04:50 PM | 2.4 | 73 |
| | 09:43 PM | 0.4 | 12 | | 10:43 PM | 0.1 | 3 |
| **9** W | 04:12 AM | 2.0 | 61 | **24** Th | 05:15 AM | 2.4 | 73 |
| | 10:20 AM | 0.5 | 15 | | 11:13 AM | -0.1 | -3 |
| | 04:40 PM | 2.0 | 61 | | 05:53 PM | 2.4 | 73 |
| | 10:40 PM | 0.4 | 12 | | 11:41 PM | 0.1 | 3 |
| **10** Th | 05:08 AM | 2.1 | 64 | **25** F | 06:11 AM | 2.4 | 73 |
| | 11:11 AM | 0.3 | 9 | | 12:06 PM | -0.2 | -6 |
| | 05:40 PM | 2.1 | 64 | | 06:49 PM | 2.5 | 76 |
| | 11:33 PM | 0.3 | 9 | | | | |
| **11** F | 06:01 AM | 2.2 | 67 | **26** Sa | 12:34 AM | 0.1 | 3 |
| | 11:58 AM | 0.2 | 6 | | 07:02 AM | 2.4 | 73 |
| | 06:35 PM | 2.3 | 70 | | 12:55 PM | -0.2 | -6 |
| | | | | | 07:40 PM | 2.5 | 76 |
| **12** Sa | 12:23 AM | 0.2 | 6 | **27** Su | 01:22 AM | 0.1 | 3 |
| | 06:51 AM | 2.3 | 70 | | 07:49 AM | 2.4 | 73 |
| | 12:43 PM | 0.0 | 0 | | 01:40 PM | -0.3 | -9 |
| | 07:26 PM | 2.5 | 76 | | 08:25 PM | 2.6 | 79 |
| **13** Su | 01:10 AM | 0.1 | 3 | **28** M | 02:07 AM | 0.1 | 3 |
| | 07:39 AM | 2.4 | 73 | | 08:32 AM | 2.4 | 73 |
| | 01:28 PM | -0.2 | -6 | | 02:22 PM | -0.3 | -9 |
| | 08:15 PM | 2.6 | 79 | | 09:08 PM | 2.6 | 79 |
| **14** M | 01:56 AM | 0.0 | 0 | **29** Tu ○ | 02:50 AM | 0.1 | 3 |
| | 08:26 AM | 2.5 | 76 | | 09:13 AM | 2.4 | 73 |
| | 02:12 PM | -0.4 | -12 | | 03:03 PM | -0.3 | -9 |
| | 09:03 PM | 2.8 | 85 | | 09:47 PM | 2.6 | 79 |
| **15** Tu ● | 02:42 AM | -0.1 | -3 | **30** W | 03:31 AM | 0.1 | 3 |
| | 09:12 AM | 2.6 | 79 | | 09:52 AM | 2.3 | 70 |
| | 02:58 PM | -0.5 | -15 | | 03:43 PM | -0.2 | -6 |
| | 09:51 PM | 2.8 | 85 | | 10:26 PM | 2.5 | 76 |
| | | | | **31** Th | 04:11 AM | 0.2 | 6 |
| | | | | | 10:30 AM | 2.3 | 70 |
| | | | | | 04:22 PM | -0.1 | -3 |
| | | | | | 11:04 PM | 2.4 | 73 |

## June

| | Time | ft | cm | | Time | ft | cm |
|---|---|---|---|---|---|---|---|
| **1** F | 04:50 AM | 0.2 | 6 | **16** Sa | 04:55 AM | -0.2 | -6 |
| | 11:09 AM | 2.2 | 67 | | 11:27 AM | 2.6 | 79 |
| | 05:00 PM | 0.0 | 0 | | 05:16 PM | -0.6 | -18 |
| | 11:43 PM | 2.4 | 73 | | | | |
| **2** Sa | 05:30 AM | 0.3 | 9 | **17** Su | 12:06 AM | 2.8 | 85 |
| | 11:49 AM | 2.1 | 64 | | 05:51 AM | -0.2 | -6 |
| | 05:40 PM | 0.1 | 3 | | 12:23 PM | 2.6 | 79 |
| | | | | | 06:13 PM | -0.4 | -12 |
| **3** Su | 12:22 AM | 2.3 | 70 | **18** M | 12:59 AM | 2.7 | 82 |
| | 06:11 AM | 0.4 | 12 | | 06:50 AM | -0.2 | -6 |
| | 12:30 PM | 2.0 | 61 | | 01:21 PM | 2.5 | 76 |
| | 06:21 PM | 0.2 | 6 | | 07:13 PM | -0.3 | -9 |
| **4** M | 01:04 AM | 2.2 | 67 | **19** Tu | 01:53 AM | 2.6 | 79 |
| | 06:55 AM | 0.4 | 12 | | 07:51 AM | -0.1 | -3 |
| | 01:16 PM | 2.0 | 61 | | 02:21 PM | 2.4 | 73 |
| | 07:06 PM | 0.3 | 9 | | 08:16 PM | -0.1 | -3 |
| **5** Tu | 01:47 AM | 2.1 | 64 | **20** W ◐ | 02:49 AM | 2.5 | 76 |
| | 07:44 AM | 0.4 | 12 | | 08:52 AM | -0.1 | -3 |
| | 02:05 PM | 1.9 | 58 | | 03:23 PM | 2.4 | 73 |
| | 07:57 PM | 0.3 | 9 | | 09:19 PM | 0.0 | 0 |
| **6** W | 02:34 AM | 2.1 | 64 | **21** Th ◐ | 03:46 AM | 2.4 | 73 |
| | 08:36 AM | 0.4 | 12 | | 09:52 AM | -0.1 | -3 |
| | 03:00 PM | 1.9 | 58 | | 04:27 PM | 2.3 | 70 |
| | 08:53 PM | 0.4 | 12 | | 10:19 PM | 0.1 | 3 |
| **7** Th | 03:25 AM | 2.1 | 64 | **22** F | 04:44 AM | 2.3 | 70 |
| | 09:30 AM | 0.3 | 9 | | 10:48 AM | -0.1 | -3 |
| | 03:59 PM | 2.0 | 61 | | 05:28 PM | 2.3 | 70 |
| | 09:52 PM | 0.4 | 12 | | 11:17 PM | 0.2 | 6 |
| **8** F | 04:18 AM | 2.1 | 64 | **23** Sa | 05:40 AM | 2.3 | 70 |
| | 10:23 AM | 0.2 | 6 | | 11:41 AM | -0.2 | -6 |
| | 04:59 PM | 2.1 | 64 | | 06:25 PM | 2.3 | 70 |
| | 10:49 PM | 0.3 | 9 | | | | |
| **9** Sa | 05:13 AM | 2.1 | 64 | **24** Su | 12:09 AM | 0.2 | 6 |
| | 11:15 AM | 0.0 | 0 | | 06:32 AM | 2.2 | 67 |
| | 05:58 PM | 2.2 | 67 | | 12:29 PM | -0.2 | -6 |
| | 11:44 PM | 0.2 | 6 | | 07:16 PM | 2.4 | 73 |
| **10** Su | 06:08 AM | 2.2 | 67 | **25** M | 12:58 AM | 0.2 | 6 |
| | 12:06 PM | -0.2 | -6 | | 07:20 AM | 2.2 | 67 |
| | 06:54 PM | 2.4 | 73 | | 01:15 PM | -0.2 | -6 |
| | | | | | 08:02 PM | 2.4 | 73 |
| **11** M | 12:36 AM | 0.1 | 3 | **26** Tu | 01:43 AM | 0.2 | 6 |
| | 07:02 AM | 2.3 | 70 | | 08:05 AM | 2.2 | 67 |
| | 12:56 PM | -0.4 | -12 | | 01:58 PM | -0.2 | -6 |
| | 07:48 PM | 2.6 | 79 | | 08:44 PM | 2.4 | 73 |
| **12** Tu | 01:28 AM | 0.0 | 0 | **27** W | 02:26 AM | 0.2 | 6 |
| | 07:55 AM | 2.4 | 73 | | 08:47 AM | 2.2 | 67 |
| | 01:46 PM | -0.5 | -15 | | 02:39 PM | -0.2 | -6 |
| | 08:40 PM | 2.7 | 82 | | 09:24 PM | 2.4 | 73 |
| **13** W ● | 02:18 AM | -0.1 | -3 | **28** Th ○ | 03:07 AM | 0.2 | 6 |
| | 08:48 AM | 2.5 | 76 | | 09:27 AM | 2.2 | 67 |
| | 02:37 PM | -0.6 | -18 | | 03:18 PM | -0.2 | -6 |
| | 09:31 PM | 2.8 | 85 | | 10:02 PM | 2.4 | 73 |
| **14** Th | 03:09 AM | -0.2 | -6 | **29** F | 03:46 AM | 0.2 | 6 |
| | 09:40 AM | 2.6 | 79 | | 10:06 AM | 2.2 | 67 |
| | 03:28 PM | -0.7 | -21 | | 03:57 PM | -0.1 | -3 |
| | 10:22 PM | 2.9 | 88 | | 10:40 PM | 2.4 | 73 |
| **15** F | 04:01 AM | -0.2 | -6 | **30** Sa | 04:25 AM | 0.2 | 6 |
| | 10:33 AM | 2.6 | 79 | | 10:45 AM | 2.2 | 67 |
| | 04:21 PM | -0.7 | -21 | | 04:34 PM | -0.1 | -3 |
| | 11:14 PM | 2.9 | 88 | | 11:17 PM | 2.3 | 70 |

Heights are referred to mean lower water which is the chart datum of sounding. All times are local. Daylight Saving Time has been used when needed. Additional tide tables are available online from NOAA at www.tidesandcurrents.noaa.gov/tide_predictions.shtml.

SKIPPER'S HANDBOOK

StationId: 8723178
Source: NOAA/NOS/CO-OPS
Station Type: Primary
Time Zone: LST_LDT
Datum: MLLW

**NOAA Tide Predictions**

# MIAMI BEACH, GOVERNMENT CUT, FL,2018

### Times and Heights of High and Low Waters

## July

| Day | Time | ft | cm | Day | Time | ft | cm |
|---|---|---|---|---|---|---|---|
| 1 Su | 05:03 AM | 0.2 | 6 | 16 M | 05:33 AM | -0.3 | -9 |
| | 11:25 AM | 2.1 | 64 | | 12:06 PM | 2.7 | 82 |
| | 05:11 PM | 0.0 | 0 | | 05:56 PM | -0.4 | -12 |
| | 11:55 PM | 2.3 | 70 | | | | |
| 2 M | 05:41 AM | 0.3 | 9 | 17 Tu | 12:36 AM | 2.8 | 85 |
| | 12:06 PM | 2.1 | 64 | | 06:29 AM | -0.3 | -9 |
| | 05:50 PM | 0.1 | 3 | | 01:01 PM | 2.6 | 79 |
| | | | | | 06:53 PM | -0.2 | -6 |
| 3 Tu | 12:34 AM | 2.2 | 67 | 18 W | 01:27 AM | 2.6 | 79 |
| | 06:21 AM | 0.3 | 9 | | 07:26 AM | -0.2 | -6 |
| | 12:49 PM | 2.0 | 61 | | 01:58 PM | 2.5 | 76 |
| | 06:31 PM | 0.2 | 6 | | 07:51 PM | 0.0 | 0 |
| 4 W | 01:14 AM | 2.2 | 67 | 19 Th | 02:19 AM | 2.5 | 76 |
| | 07:04 AM | 0.3 | 9 | | 08:24 AM | -0.1 | -3 |
| | 01:35 PM | 2.0 | 61 | | 02:57 PM | 2.4 | 73 |
| | 07:17 PM | 0.3 | 9 | | 08:51 PM | 0.2 | 6 |
| 5 Th | 01:56 AM | 2.1 | 64 | 20 F | 03:13 AM | 2.4 | 73 |
| | 07:51 AM | 0.2 | 6 | | 09:22 AM | -0.1 | -3 |
| | 02:26 PM | 2.0 | 61 | | 03:57 PM | 2.3 | 70 |
| | 08:10 PM | 0.3 | 9 | | 09:51 PM | 0.3 | 9 |
| 6 F | 02:42 AM | 2.1 | 64 | 21 Sa | 04:09 AM | 2.2 | 67 |
| | 08:44 AM | 0.2 | 6 | | 10:19 AM | 0.0 | 0 |
| | 03:22 PM | 2.1 | 64 | | 04:58 PM | 2.3 | 70 |
| | 09:09 PM | 0.3 | 9 | | 10:49 PM | 0.4 | 12 |
| 7 Sa | 03:34 AM | 2.1 | 64 | 22 Su | 05:06 AM | 2.2 | 67 |
| | 09:40 AM | 0.1 | 3 | | 11:13 AM | 0.0 | 0 |
| | 04:23 PM | 2.1 | 64 | | 05:56 PM | 2.3 | 70 |
| | 10:10 PM | 0.3 | 9 | | 11:43 PM | 0.4 | 12 |
| 8 Su | 04:31 AM | 2.1 | 64 | 23 M | 06:01 AM | 2.1 | 64 |
| | 10:38 AM | -0.1 | -3 | | 12:03 PM | 0.0 | 0 |
| | 05:25 PM | 2.3 | 70 | | 06:49 PM | 2.3 | 70 |
| | 11:10 PM | 0.3 | 9 | | | | |
| 9 M | 05:31 AM | 2.2 | 67 | 24 Tu | 12:32 AM | 0.4 | 12 |
| | 11:35 AM | -0.2 | -6 | | 06:52 AM | 2.2 | 67 |
| | 06:26 PM | 2.4 | 73 | | 12:50 PM | 0.0 | 0 |
| | | | | | 07:36 PM | 2.3 | 70 |
| 10 Tu | 12:08 AM | 0.2 | 6 | 25 W | 01:18 AM | 0.4 | 12 |
| | 06:32 AM | 2.3 | 70 | | 07:38 AM | 2.2 | 67 |
| | 12:30 PM | -0.4 | -12 | | 01:34 PM | 0.0 | 0 |
| | 07:24 PM | 2.6 | 79 | | 08:18 PM | 2.4 | 73 |
| 11 W | 01:03 AM | 0.0 | 0 | 26 Th | 02:01 AM | 0.3 | 9 |
| | 07:31 AM | 2.4 | 73 | | 08:22 AM | 2.2 | 67 |
| | 01:25 PM | -0.6 | -18 | | 02:16 PM | 0.0 | 0 |
| | 08:20 PM | 2.7 | 82 | | 08:58 PM | 2.4 | 73 |
| 12 Th | 01:58 AM | -0.1 | -3 | 27 F | 02:42 AM | 0.3 | 9 |
| | 08:28 AM | 2.6 | 79 | | 09:03 AM | 2.3 | 70 |
| | 02:19 PM | -0.7 | -21 | | 02:55 PM | 0.0 | 0 |
| | 09:13 PM | 2.8 | 85 | | 09:36 PM | 2.5 | 76 |
| 13 F | 02:51 AM | -0.2 | -6 | 28 Sa | 03:21 AM | 0.3 | 9 |
| | 09:23 AM | 2.7 | 82 | | 09:43 AM | 2.3 | 70 |
| | 03:13 PM | -0.7 | -21 | | 03:32 PM | 0.0 | 0 |
| | 10:04 PM | 2.9 | 88 | | 10:14 PM | 2.5 | 76 |
| 14 Sa | 03:44 AM | -0.3 | -9 | 29 Su | 03:58 AM | 0.3 | 9 |
| | 10:18 AM | 2.8 | 85 | | 10:22 AM | 2.3 | 70 |
| | 04:06 PM | -0.7 | -21 | | 04:08 PM | 0.0 | 0 |
| | 10:55 PM | 2.9 | 88 | | 10:50 PM | 2.5 | 76 |
| 15 Su | 04:38 AM | -0.3 | -9 | 30 M | 04:34 AM | 0.2 | 6 |
| | 11:12 AM | 2.8 | 85 | | 11:02 AM | 2.3 | 70 |
| | 05:00 PM | -0.6 | -18 | | 04:44 PM | 0.1 | 3 |
| | 11:45 PM | 2.9 | 88 | | 11:27 PM | 2.4 | 73 |
| | | | | 31 Tu | 05:09 AM | 0.2 | 6 |
| | | | | | 11:42 AM | 2.3 | 70 |
| | | | | | 05:21 PM | 0.2 | 6 |

## August

| Day | Time | ft | cm | Day | Time | ft | cm |
|---|---|---|---|---|---|---|---|
| 1 W | 12:04 AM | 2.4 | 73 | 16 Th | 12:56 AM | 2.8 | 85 |
| | 05:46 AM | 0.2 | 6 | | 06:55 AM | -0.1 | -3 |
| | 12:23 PM | 2.3 | 70 | | 01:30 PM | 2.7 | 82 |
| | 06:00 PM | 0.2 | 6 | | 07:22 PM | 0.2 | 6 |
| 2 Th | 12:42 AM | 2.3 | 70 | 17 F | 01:46 AM | 2.6 | 79 |
| | 06:27 AM | 0.2 | 6 | | 07:50 AM | 0.1 | 3 |
| | 01:08 PM | 2.3 | 70 | | 02:25 PM | 2.6 | 79 |
| | 06:45 PM | 0.3 | 9 | | 08:20 PM | 0.4 | 12 |
| 3 F | 01:22 AM | 2.3 | 70 | 18 Sa | 02:37 AM | 2.4 | 73 |
| | 07:13 AM | 0.2 | 6 | | 08:48 AM | 0.2 | 6 |
| | 01:57 PM | 2.3 | 70 | | 03:22 PM | 2.4 | 73 |
| | 07:36 PM | 0.4 | 12 | | 09:19 PM | 0.6 | 18 |
| 4 Sa | 02:07 AM | 2.3 | 70 | 19 Su | 03:32 AM | 2.3 | 70 |
| | 08:06 AM | 0.2 | 6 | | 09:46 AM | 0.3 | 9 |
| | 02:52 PM | 2.3 | 70 | | 04:22 PM | 2.3 | 70 |
| | 08:35 PM | 0.5 | 15 | | 10:18 PM | 0.7 | 21 |
| 5 Su | 02:59 AM | 2.2 | 67 | 20 M | 04:30 AM | 2.2 | 67 |
| | 09:06 AM | 0.1 | 3 | | 10:42 AM | 0.3 | 9 |
| | 03:54 PM | 2.3 | 70 | | 05:21 PM | 2.3 | 70 |
| | 09:39 PM | 0.5 | 15 | | 11:14 PM | 0.7 | 21 |
| 6 M | 04:00 AM | 2.3 | 70 | 21 Tu | 05:28 AM | 2.2 | 67 |
| | 10:08 AM | 0.0 | 0 | | 11:36 AM | 0.4 | 12 |
| | 04:59 PM | 2.4 | 73 | | 06:16 PM | 2.4 | 73 |
| | 10:44 PM | 0.4 | 12 | | | | |
| 7 Tu | 05:06 AM | 2.3 | 70 | 22 W | 12:05 AM | 0.7 | 21 |
| | 11:11 AM | -0.1 | -3 | | 06:22 AM | 2.3 | 70 |
| | 06:04 PM | 2.5 | 76 | | 12:24 PM | 0.3 | 9 |
| | 11:46 PM | 0.3 | 9 | | 07:05 PM | 2.4 | 73 |
| 8 W | 06:12 AM | 2.5 | 76 | 23 Th | 12:52 AM | 0.6 | 18 |
| | 12:11 PM | -0.2 | -6 | | 07:11 AM | 2.4 | 73 |
| | 07:05 PM | 2.7 | 82 | | 01:09 PM | 0.3 | 9 |
| | | | | | 07:48 PM | 2.5 | 76 |
| 9 Th | 12:44 AM | 0.2 | 6 | 24 F | 01:35 AM | 0.5 | 15 |
| | 07:14 AM | 2.6 | 79 | | 07:56 AM | 2.4 | 73 |
| | 01:09 PM | -0.4 | -12 | | 01:51 PM | 0.3 | 9 |
| | 08:01 PM | 2.9 | 88 | | 08:28 PM | 2.6 | 79 |
| 10 F | 01:40 AM | 0.0 | 0 | 25 Sa | 02:15 AM | 0.5 | 15 |
| | 08:13 AM | 2.8 | 85 | | 08:38 AM | 2.5 | 76 |
| | 02:04 PM | -0.5 | -15 | | 02:29 PM | 0.2 | 6 |
| | 08:54 PM | 3.0 | 91 | | 09:07 PM | 2.7 | 82 |
| 11 Sa | 02:34 AM | -0.1 | -3 | 26 Su | 02:52 AM | 0.4 | 12 |
| | 09:08 AM | 2.9 | 88 | | 09:18 AM | 2.6 | 79 |
| | 02:57 PM | -0.5 | -15 | | 03:06 PM | 0.2 | 6 |
| | 09:44 PM | 3.1 | 94 | | 09:44 PM | 2.7 | 82 |
| 12 Su | 03:26 AM | -0.2 | -6 | 27 M | 03:28 AM | 0.4 | 12 |
| | 10:02 AM | 3.0 | 91 | | 09:58 AM | 2.6 | 79 |
| | 03:50 PM | -0.4 | -12 | | 03:42 PM | 0.2 | 6 |
| | 10:33 PM | 3.1 | 94 | | 10:20 PM | 2.7 | 82 |
| 13 M | 04:18 AM | -0.3 | -9 | 28 Tu | 04:02 AM | 0.3 | 9 |
| | 10:54 AM | 3.0 | 91 | | 10:37 AM | 2.7 | 82 |
| | 04:41 PM | -0.3 | -9 | | 04:17 PM | 0.3 | 9 |
| | 11:21 PM | 3.0 | 91 | | 10:57 PM | 2.7 | 82 |
| 14 Tu | 05:09 AM | -0.2 | -6 | 29 W | 04:37 AM | 0.3 | 9 |
| | 11:45 AM | 3.0 | 91 | | 11:17 AM | 2.7 | 82 |
| | 05:34 PM | -0.2 | -6 | | 04:54 PM | 0.3 | 9 |
| | | | | | 11:33 PM | 2.7 | 82 |
| 15 W | 12:08 AM | 2.9 | 88 | 30 Th | 05:14 AM | 0.3 | 9 |
| | 06:02 AM | -0.2 | -6 | | 11:59 AM | 2.7 | 82 |
| | 12:37 PM | 2.8 | 85 | | 05:34 PM | 0.4 | 12 |
| | 06:27 PM | 0.0 | 0 | | | | |
| | | | | 31 F | 12:11 AM | 2.6 | 79 |
| | | | | | 05:55 AM | 0.3 | 9 |
| | | | | | 12:43 PM | 2.6 | 79 |
| | | | | | 06:19 PM | 0.5 | 15 |

## September

| Day | Time | ft | cm | Day | Time | ft | cm |
|---|---|---|---|---|---|---|---|
| 1 Sa | 12:53 AM | 2.5 | 76 | 16 Su | 01:59 AM | 2.6 | 79 |
| | 06:42 AM | 0.3 | 9 | | 08:09 AM | 0.5 | 15 |
| | 01:33 PM | 2.6 | 79 | | 02:43 PM | 2.6 | 79 |
| | 07:10 PM | 0.6 | 18 | | 08:42 PM | 0.9 | 27 |
| 2 Su | 01:40 AM | 2.5 | 76 | 17 M | 02:53 AM | 2.5 | 76 |
| | 07:37 AM | 0.3 | 9 | | 09:08 AM | 0.7 | 21 |
| | 02:29 PM | 2.6 | 79 | | 03:41 PM | 2.5 | 76 |
| | 08:10 PM | 0.7 | 21 | | 09:43 PM | 1.0 | 30 |
| 3 M | 02:36 AM | 2.5 | 76 | 18 Tu | 03:51 AM | 2.4 | 73 |
| | 08:40 AM | 0.4 | 12 | | 10:08 AM | 0.7 | 21 |
| | 03:33 PM | 2.6 | 79 | | 04:40 PM | 2.5 | 76 |
| | 09:18 PM | 0.7 | 21 | | 10:42 PM | 1.0 | 30 |
| 4 Tu | 03:41 AM | 2.5 | 76 | 19 W | 04:52 AM | 2.4 | 73 |
| | 09:48 AM | 0.3 | 9 | | 11:04 AM | 0.7 | 21 |
| | 04:40 PM | 2.6 | 79 | | 05:37 PM | 2.5 | 76 |
| | 10:26 PM | 0.7 | 21 | | 11:35 PM | 0.9 | 27 |
| 5 W | 04:51 AM | 2.6 | 79 | 20 Th | 05:49 AM | 2.5 | 76 |
| | 10:55 AM | 0.2 | 6 | | 11:55 AM | 0.7 | 21 |
| | 05:46 PM | 2.8 | 85 | | 06:28 PM | 2.6 | 79 |
| | 11:30 PM | 0.5 | 15 | | | | |
| 6 Th | 06:00 AM | 2.7 | 82 | 21 F | 12:22 AM | 0.8 | 24 |
| | 11:57 AM | 0.1 | 3 | | 06:40 AM | 2.6 | 79 |
| | 06:47 PM | 2.9 | 88 | | 12:40 PM | 0.6 | 18 |
| | | | | | 07:13 PM | 2.7 | 82 |
| 7 F | 12:29 AM | 0.4 | 12 | 22 Sa | 01:05 AM | 0.7 | 21 |
| | 07:02 AM | 2.9 | 88 | | 07:27 AM | 2.7 | 82 |
| | 12:55 PM | 0.0 | 0 | | 01:22 PM | 0.6 | 18 |
| | 07:42 PM | 3.1 | 94 | | 07:54 PM | 2.8 | 85 |
| 8 Sa | 01:24 AM | 0.2 | 6 | 23 Su | 01:44 AM | 0.6 | 18 |
| | 08:00 AM | 3.1 | 94 | | 08:10 AM | 2.8 | 85 |
| | 01:49 PM | -0.1 | -3 | | 02:00 PM | 0.5 | 15 |
| | 08:33 PM | 3.2 | 98 | | 08:33 PM | 2.9 | 88 |
| 9 Su | 02:16 AM | 0.0 | 0 | 24 M | 02:20 AM | 0.5 | 15 |
| | 08:53 AM | 3.2 | 98 | | 08:51 AM | 2.9 | 88 |
| | 02:41 PM | -0.1 | -3 | | 02:37 PM | 0.5 | 15 |
| | 09:21 PM | 3.3 | 101 | | 09:11 PM | 2.9 | 88 |
| 10 M | 03:06 AM | -0.1 | -3 | 25 Tu | 02:55 AM | 0.4 | 12 |
| | 09:44 AM | 3.3 | 101 | | 09:32 AM | 3.0 | 91 |
| | 03:31 PM | -0.1 | -3 | | 03:14 PM | 0.5 | 15 |
| | 10:08 PM | 3.3 | 101 | | 09:48 PM | 2.9 | 88 |
| 11 Tu | 03:54 AM | -0.1 | -3 | 26 W | 03:30 AM | 0.4 | 12 |
| | 10:33 AM | 3.3 | 101 | | 10:12 AM | 3.0 | 91 |
| | 04:20 PM | 0.0 | 0 | | 03:51 PM | 0.5 | 15 |
| | 10:53 PM | 3.2 | 98 | | 10:26 PM | 2.9 | 88 |
| 12 W | 04:42 AM | -0.1 | -3 | 27 Th | 04:07 AM | 0.3 | 9 |
| | 11:22 AM | 3.2 | 98 | | 10:53 AM | 3.0 | 91 |
| | 05:08 PM | 0.2 | 6 | | 04:30 PM | 0.5 | 15 |
| | 11:38 PM | 3.1 | 94 | | 11:05 PM | 2.9 | 88 |
| 13 Th | 05:31 AM | 0.1 | 3 | 28 F | 04:46 AM | 0.3 | 9 |
| | 12:10 PM | 3.1 | 94 | | 11:37 AM | 3.0 | 91 |
| | 05:58 PM | 0.4 | 12 | | 05:12 PM | 0.6 | 18 |
| | | | | | 11:46 PM | 2.8 | 85 |
| 14 F | 12:23 AM | 2.9 | 88 | 29 Sa | 05:30 AM | 0.3 | 9 |
| | 06:20 AM | 0.2 | 6 | | 12:23 PM | 3.0 | 91 |
| | 12:58 PM | 2.9 | 88 | | 05:58 PM | 0.7 | 21 |
| | 06:49 PM | 0.6 | 18 | | | | |
| 15 Sa | 01:10 AM | 2.7 | 82 | 30 Su | 12:31 AM | 2.8 | 85 |
| | 07:13 AM | 0.4 | 12 | | 06:19 AM | 0.4 | 12 |
| | 01:49 PM | 2.7 | 82 | | 01:15 PM | 2.9 | 88 |
| | 07:44 PM | 0.8 | 24 | | 06:52 PM | 0.8 | 24 |

Heights are referred to mean lower water which is the chart datum of sounding. All times are local. Daylight Saving Time has been used when needed. Additional tide tables are available online from NOAA at www.tidesandcurrents.noaa.gov/tide_predictions.shtml.

**SKIPPER'S HANDBOOK**

StationId:8723970
Source:NOAA/NOS/CO-OPS
Station Type:Harmonic
Time Zone:LST/LDT
Datum:mean lower low water (MLLW) which is the chart datum of soundings

**NOAA Tide Predictions**

# VACA KEY, USCG STATION, FLORIDA BAY,Florida,201

### Times and Heights of High and Low Waters

## October

| Day | Time | ft | cm | Day | Time | ft | cm |
|---|---|---|---|---|---|---|---|
| **1** Su | 01:06 AM | 1.0 | 30 | **16** M | 12:57 AM | 1.1 | 34 |
| | 03:28 AM | 0.9 | 27 | | 04:02 AM | 0.9 | 27 |
| | 09:55 AM | 1.2 | 37 | | 12:34 PM | 1.2 | 37 |
| | 04:14 PM | 0.5 | 15 | | 04:36 PM | 0.7 | 21 |
| **2** M | 01:42 AM | 1.1 | 34 | **17** Tu | 01:33 AM | 1.2 | 37 |
| | 04:23 AM | 0.9 | 27 | | 05:04 AM | 0.8 | 24 |
| | 11:02 AM | 1.2 | 37 | | 01:43 PM | 1.3 | 40 |
| | 05:01 PM | 0.6 | 18 | | 05:21 PM | 0.8 | 24 |
| **3** Tu | 02:12 AM | 1.1 | 34 | **18** W | 02:05 AM | 1.2 | 37 |
| | 05:10 AM | 0.9 | 27 | | 05:55 AM | 0.7 | 21 |
| | 12:28 PM | 1.2 | 37 | | 02:40 PM | 1.3 | 40 |
| | 05:43 PM | 0.7 | 21 | | 06:02 PM | 0.9 | 27 |
| **4** W | 02:35 AM | 1.1 | 34 | **19** Th ● | 02:29 AM | 1.3 | 40 |
| | 05:53 AM | 0.8 | 24 | | 06:39 AM | 0.6 | 18 |
| | 02:18 PM | 1.3 | 40 | | 03:33 PM | 1.3 | 40 |
| | 06:23 PM | 0.8 | 24 | | 06:41 PM | 0.9 | 27 |
| **5** Th ○ | 02:31 AM | 1.2 | 37 | **20** F | 01:58 AM | 1.3 | 40 |
| | 06:37 AM | 0.7 | 21 | | 07:21 AM | 0.5 | 15 |
| | 03:17 PM | 1.3 | 40 | | 04:21 PM | 1.3 | 40 |
| | 07:02 PM | 0.9 | 27 | | 07:20 PM | 0.9 | 27 |
| **6** F | 02:19 AM | 1.2 | 37 | **21** Sa | 02:11 AM | 1.3 | 40 |
| | 07:22 AM | 0.6 | 18 | | 08:03 AM | 0.4 | 12 |
| | 04:09 PM | 1.3 | 40 | | 05:08 PM | 1.2 | 37 |
| | 07:41 PM | 0.9 | 27 | | 07:59 PM | 0.9 | 27 |
| **7** Sa | 02:47 AM | 1.3 | 40 | **22** Su | 02:48 AM | 1.4 | 43 |
| | 08:09 AM | 0.5 | 15 | | 08:45 AM | 0.4 | 12 |
| | 05:00 PM | 1.3 | 40 | | 05:54 PM | 1.1 | 34 |
| | 08:21 PM | 0.9 | 27 | | 08:39 PM | 0.9 | 27 |
| **8** Su | 03:22 AM | 1.4 | 43 | **23** M | 03:30 AM | 1.4 | 43 |
| | 08:58 AM | 0.4 | 12 | | 09:29 AM | 0.3 | 9 |
| | 05:54 PM | 1.2 | 37 | | 06:40 PM | 1.1 | 34 |
| | 09:02 PM | 1.0 | 30 | | 09:20 PM | 0.9 | 27 |
| **9** M | 04:01 AM | 1.4 | 43 | **24** Tu | 04:12 AM | 1.4 | 43 |
| | 09:50 AM | 0.3 | 9 | | 10:13 AM | 0.3 | 9 |
| | 06:59 PM | 1.1 | 34 | | 07:33 PM | 1.0 | 30 |
| | 09:44 PM | 1.0 | 30 | | 10:03 PM | 0.9 | 27 |
| **10** Tu | 04:42 AM | 1.5 | 46 | **25** W | 04:56 AM | 1.3 | 40 |
| | 10:43 AM | 0.3 | 9 | | 11:00 AM | 0.2 | 6 |
| | 08:18 PM | 1.0 | 30 | | 08:40 PM | 1.0 | 30 |
| | 10:29 PM | 0.9 | 27 | | 10:49 PM | 0.9 | 27 |
| **11** W | 05:25 AM | 1.5 | 46 | **26** Th | 05:42 AM | 1.3 | 40 |
| | 11:39 AM | 0.3 | 9 | | 11:49 AM | 0.3 | 9 |
| **12** Th ◐ | 06:13 AM | 1.4 | 43 | **27** F ◑ | 06:30 AM | 1.2 | 37 |
| | 12:37 PM | 0.4 | 12 | | 12:41 PM | 0.3 | 9 |
| **13** F | 07:06 AM | 1.4 | 43 | **28** Sa | 07:22 AM | 1.2 | 37 |
| | 01:38 PM | 0.4 | 12 | | 01:35 PM | 0.4 | 12 |
| | | | | | 11:35 PM | 1.0 | 30 |
| **14** Sa | 08:07 AM | 1.3 | 40 | **29** Su | 01:51 AM | 0.9 | 27 |
| | 02:41 PM | 0.5 | 15 | | 08:20 AM | 1.1 | 34 |
| | | | | | 02:32 PM | 0.5 | 15 |
| **15** Su | 12:17 AM | 1.1 | 34 | **30** M | 12:14 AM | 1.1 | 34 |
| | 02:49 AM | 0.9 | 27 | | 02:59 AM | 0.9 | 27 |
| | 09:18 AM | 1.2 | 37 | | 09:26 AM | 1.1 | 34 |
| | 03:42 PM | 0.6 | 18 | | 03:28 PM | 0.6 | 18 |
| | | | | **31** Tu | 12:45 AM | 1.1 | 34 |
| | | | | | 03:59 AM | 0.9 | 27 |
| | | | | | 10:44 AM | 1.1 | 34 |
| | | | | | 04:19 PM | 0.7 | 21 |

## November

| Day | Time | ft | cm | Day | Time | ft | cm |
|---|---|---|---|---|---|---|---|
| **1** W | 01:04 AM | 1.1 | 34 | **16** Th | 12:08 AM | 1.2 | 37 |
| | 04:50 AM | 0.8 | 24 | | 04:52 AM | 0.5 | 15 |
| | 01:39 PM | 1.2 | 37 | | 01:39 PM | 1.1 | 34 |
| | 05:05 PM | 0.8 | 24 | | 04:29 PM | 0.8 | 24 |
| | | | | | 11:11 PM | 1.2 | 37 |
| **2** Th | 12:05 AM | 1.2 | 37 | **17** F | 05:30 AM | 0.4 | 12 |
| | 05:36 AM | 0.7 | 21 | | 02:31 PM | 1.1 | 34 |
| | 02:40 PM | 1.2 | 37 | | 05:09 PM | 0.9 | 27 |
| | 05:47 PM | 0.9 | 27 | | 11:43 PM | 1.3 | 40 |
| **3** F | 12:34 AM | 1.3 | 40 | **18** Sa ● | 06:06 AM | 0.3 | 9 |
| | 06:21 AM | 0.5 | 15 | | 03:19 PM | 1.1 | 34 |
| | 03:36 PM | 1.2 | 37 | | 05:48 PM | 0.9 | 27 |
| | 06:26 PM | 1.0 | 30 | | | | |
| **4** Sa ○ | 01:09 AM | 1.3 | 40 | **19** Su | 12:24 AM | 1.3 | 40 |
| | 07:07 AM | 0.4 | 12 | | 06:43 AM | 0.2 | 6 |
| | 04:28 PM | 1.2 | 37 | | 04:05 PM | 1.0 | 30 |
| | 07:06 PM | 1.0 | 30 | | 06:26 PM | 0.9 | 27 |
| **5** Su | 01:51 AM | 1.4 | 43 | **20** M | 01:10 AM | 1.3 | 40 |
| | 06:54 AM | 0.3 | 9 | | 07:22 AM | 0.2 | 6 |
| | 04:20 PM | 1.2 | 37 | | 04:49 PM | 1.0 | 30 |
| | 06:46 PM | 1.0 | 30 | | 07:05 PM | 0.9 | 27 |
| **6** M | 01:36 AM | 1.5 | 46 | **21** Tu | 01:56 AM | 1.3 | 40 |
| | 07:42 AM | 0.2 | 6 | | 08:03 AM | 0.1 | 3 |
| | 05:13 PM | 1.1 | 34 | | 05:32 PM | 0.9 | 27 |
| | 07:28 PM | 1.0 | 30 | | 07:47 PM | 0.8 | 24 |
| **7** Tu | 02:24 AM | 1.5 | 46 | **22** W | 02:43 AM | 1.2 | 37 |
| | 08:32 AM | 0.2 | 6 | | 08:45 AM | 0.1 | 3 |
| | 06:07 PM | 1.1 | 34 | | 06:13 PM | 0.9 | 27 |
| | 08:13 PM | 1.0 | 30 | | 08:31 PM | 0.8 | 24 |
| **8** W | 03:13 AM | 1.5 | 46 | **23** Th | 03:28 AM | 1.2 | 37 |
| | 09:24 AM | 0.2 | 6 | | 09:30 AM | 0.1 | 3 |
| | | | | | 06:53 PM | 0.9 | 27 |
| | | | | | 09:19 PM | 0.8 | 24 |
| **9** Th | 04:02 AM | 1.4 | 43 | **24** F | 04:14 AM | 1.1 | 34 |
| | 10:17 AM | 0.2 | 6 | | 10:16 AM | 0.1 | 3 |
| | 08:02 PM | 1.0 | 30 | | 05:52 PM | 0.9 | 27 |
| | 10:02 PM | 0.9 | 27 | | 10:13 PM | 0.8 | 24 |
| **10** F ◑ | 04:53 AM | 1.4 | 43 | **25** Sa | 05:02 AM | 1.1 | 34 |
| | 11:12 AM | 0.3 | 9 | | 11:05 AM | 0.2 | 6 |
| | 08:56 PM | 1.0 | 30 | | 06:30 PM | 0.9 | 27 |
| | 11:10 PM | 0.9 | 27 | | 11:14 PM | 0.7 | 21 |
| **11** Sa | 05:48 AM | 1.2 | 37 | **26** Su ◐ | 05:53 AM | 1.0 | 30 |
| | 12:09 PM | 0.4 | 12 | | 11:56 AM | 0.3 | 9 |
| | 09:44 PM | 1.0 | 30 | | 07:14 PM | 0.9 | 27 |
| **12** Su | 12:26 AM | 0.8 | 24 | **27** M | 12:19 AM | 0.7 | 21 |
| | 06:50 AM | 1.1 | 34 | | 06:51 AM | 0.9 | 27 |
| | 01:06 PM | 0.5 | 15 | | 12:49 PM | 0.4 | 12 |
| | 10:27 PM | 1.0 | 30 | | 07:59 PM | 0.9 | 27 |
| **13** M | 01:48 AM | 0.7 | 21 | **28** Tu | 01:26 AM | 0.7 | 21 |
| | 08:07 AM | 1.0 | 30 | | 07:57 AM | 0.9 | 27 |
| | 02:04 PM | 0.6 | 18 | | 01:43 PM | 0.5 | 15 |
| | 11:07 PM | 1.1 | 34 | | 08:42 PM | 1.0 | 30 |
| **14** Tu | 03:06 AM | 0.7 | 21 | **29** W | 02:29 AM | 0.7 | 21 |
| | 11:40 AM | 1.0 | 30 | | 11:30 AM | 0.8 | 24 |
| | 02:58 PM | 0.7 | 21 | | 02:35 PM | 0.6 | 18 |
| | 11:42 PM | 1.1 | 34 | | 09:22 PM | 1.0 | 30 |
| **15** W | 04:07 AM | 0.6 | 18 | **30** Th | 03:25 AM | 0.5 | 15 |
| | 12:44 PM | 1.1 | 34 | | 12:43 PM | 0.9 | 27 |
| | 03:46 PM | 0.8 | 24 | | 03:23 PM | 0.7 | 21 |
| | | | | | 09:58 PM | 1.1 | 34 |

## December

| Day | Time | ft | cm | Day | Time | ft | cm |
|---|---|---|---|---|---|---|---|
| **1** F | 04:16 AM | 0.3 | 9 | **16** Sa | 05:16 AM | 0.0 | 0 |
| | 01:43 PM | 1.0 | 30 | | 02:22 PM | 0.7 | 21 |
| | 04:07 PM | 0.8 | 24 | | 04:38 PM | 0.6 | 18 |
| | 10:33 PM | 1.2 | 37 | | 11:05 PM | 1.0 | 30 |
| **2** Sa | 05:04 AM | 0.2 | 6 | **17** Su | 05:48 AM | 0.0 | 0 |
| | 02:38 PM | 1.0 | 30 | | 03:09 PM | 0.7 | 21 |
| | 04:49 PM | 0.8 | 24 | | 05:17 PM | 0.6 | 18 |
| | 11:11 PM | 1.2 | 37 | | 11:51 PM | 1.0 | 30 |
| **3** Su ○ | 05:51 AM | 0.1 | 3 | **18** M ● | 06:22 AM | -0.1 | -3 |
| | 03:29 PM | 1.0 | 30 | | 03:53 PM | 0.7 | 21 |
| | 05:31 PM | 0.9 | 27 | | 05:57 PM | 0.6 | 18 |
| | 09:33 PM | 1.3 | 40 | | | | |
| **4** M | 06:38 AM | 0.0 | 0 | **19** Tu | 12:41 AM | 1.0 | 30 |
| | 04:18 PM | 0.9 | 27 | | 06:59 AM | -0.1 | -3 |
| | 06:14 PM | 0.8 | 24 | | 04:33 PM | 0.7 | 21 |
| | | | | | 06:37 PM | 0.6 | 18 |
| **5** Tu | 12:59 AM | 1.3 | 40 | **20** W | 01:31 AM | 1.0 | 30 |
| | 07:26 AM | 0.0 | 0 | | 07:38 AM | -0.1 | -3 |
| | | | | | 05:09 PM | 0.7 | 21 |
| | | | | | 07:20 PM | 0.6 | 18 |
| **6** W | 01:59 AM | 1.3 | 40 | **21** Th | 02:20 AM | 1.0 | 30 |
| | 08:15 AM | 0.0 | 0 | | 08:19 AM | -0.1 | -3 |
| | 05:49 PM | 0.8 | 24 | | 05:37 PM | 0.7 | 21 |
| | 07:51 PM | 0.7 | 21 | | 08:06 PM | 0.5 | 15 |
| **7** Th | 02:54 AM | 1.3 | 40 | **22** F | 03:08 AM | 0.9 | 27 |
| | 09:04 AM | 0.0 | 0 | | 09:02 AM | -0.1 | -3 |
| | 06:32 PM | 0.8 | 24 | | 05:17 PM | 0.6 | 18 |
| | 08:47 PM | 0.7 | 21 | | 08:56 PM | 0.5 | 15 |
| **8** F | 03:47 AM | 1.2 | 37 | **23** Sa | 03:54 AM | 0.9 | 27 |
| | 09:55 AM | 0.1 | 3 | | 09:47 AM | -0.1 | -3 |
| | 07:14 PM | 0.8 | 24 | | 05:21 PM | 0.7 | 21 |
| | 09:50 PM | 0.6 | 18 | | 09:50 PM | 0.4 | 12 |
| **9** Sa | 04:39 AM | 1.1 | 34 | **24** Su | 04:41 AM | 0.8 | 24 |
| | 10:46 AM | 0.2 | 6 | | 10:33 AM | -0.1 | -3 |
| | 07:57 PM | 0.8 | 24 | | 05:53 PM | 0.7 | 21 |
| | 11:01 PM | 0.6 | 18 | | 10:48 PM | 0.4 | 12 |
| **10** Su ◑ | 05:32 AM | 0.9 | 27 | **25** M | 05:31 AM | 0.7 | 21 |
| | 11:37 AM | 0.3 | 9 | | 11:20 AM | 0.0 | 0 |
| | 08:39 PM | 0.8 | 24 | | 06:31 PM | 0.7 | 21 |
| | | | | | 11:50 PM | 0.3 | 9 |
| **11** M | 12:17 AM | 0.5 | 15 | **26** Tu ◐ | 06:27 AM | 0.6 | 18 |
| | 06:32 AM | 0.8 | 24 | | 12:09 PM | 0.1 | 3 |
| | 12:30 PM | 0.3 | 9 | | 07:11 PM | 0.7 | 21 |
| | 09:20 PM | 0.8 | 24 | | | | |
| **12** Tu | 01:40 AM | 0.4 | 12 | **27** W | 12:53 AM | 0.2 | 6 |
| | 10:18 AM | 0.7 | 21 | | 07:33 AM | 0.5 | 15 |
| | 01:24 PM | 0.4 | 12 | | 12:59 PM | 0.3 | 9 |
| | 09:52 PM | 0.9 | 27 | | 07:52 PM | 0.8 | 24 |
| **13** W | 03:03 AM | 0.3 | 9 | **28** Th | 01:57 AM | 0.1 | 3 |
| | 11:34 AM | 0.7 | 21 | | 11:31 AM | 0.5 | 15 |
| | 02:18 PM | 0.5 | 15 | | 01:50 PM | 0.4 | 12 |
| | 09:04 PM | 0.9 | 27 | | 08:32 PM | 0.8 | 24 |
| **14** Th | 04:04 AM | 0.2 | 6 | **29** F | 02:58 AM | 0.0 | 0 |
| | 12:37 PM | 0.7 | 21 | | 09:11 PM | 0.9 | 27 |
| | 03:09 PM | 0.6 | 18 | | | | |
| | 09:42 PM | 1.0 | 30 | | | | |
| **15** F | 04:43 AM | 0.1 | 3 | **30** Sa | 03:54 AM | -0.1 | -3 |
| | 01:32 PM | 0.7 | 21 | | 09:49 PM | 1.0 | 30 |
| | 03:56 PM | 0.6 | 18 | | | | |
| | 10:22 PM | 1.0 | 30 | | | | |
| | | | | **31** Su | 04:45 AM | -0.1 | -3 |
| | | | | | 10:30 PM | 1.0 | 30 |

Heights are referred to mean lower water which is the chart datum of sounding. All times are local. Daylight Saving Time has been used when needed. Additional tide tables are available online from NOAA at www.tidesandcurrents.noaa.gov/tide_predictions.shtml.

**SKIPPER'S HANDBOOK**

StationId: 8723970
Source: NOAA/NOS/CO-OPS
Station Type: Primary
Time Zone: LST_LDT
Datum: MLLW

**NOAA Tide Predictions**

## Vaca Key, FL, 2018

**Times and Heights of High and Low Waters**

### January

| Date | Time | ft | cm |
|---|---|---|---|
| 1 M | 05:36 AM | -0.2 | -6 |
|  | 09:24 PM | 1.1 | 34 |
| 2 Tu ○ | 06:24 AM | -0.2 | -6 |
| 3 W | 12:36 AM | 1.0 | 30 |
|  | 07:11 AM | -0.2 | -6 |
| 4 Th | 01:45 AM | 1.0 | 30 |
|  | 05:22 PM | 0.6 | 18 |
|  | 07:36 PM | 0.4 | 12 |
| 5 F | 02:44 AM | 1.0 | 30 |
|  | 08:46 AM | -0.2 | -6 |
|  | 05:54 PM | 0.5 | 15 |
|  | 08:35 PM | 0.3 | 9 |
| 6 Sa | 03:37 AM | 0.9 | 27 |
|  | 09:33 AM | -0.1 | -3 |
|  | 06:19 PM | 0.5 | 15 |
|  | 09:39 PM | 0.3 | 9 |
| 7 Su | 04:28 AM | 0.7 | 21 |
|  | 10:20 AM | 0.0 | 0 |
|  | 06:12 PM | 0.6 | 18 |
|  | 10:48 PM | 0.2 | 6 |
| 8 M ◑ | 05:19 AM | 0.6 | 18 |
|  | 11:08 AM | 0.0 | 0 |
|  | 06:17 PM | 0.6 | 18 |
| 9 Tu | 12:00 AM | 0.1 | 3 |
|  | 06:14 AM | 0.4 | 12 |
|  | 11:56 AM | 0.1 | 3 |
|  | 06:51 PM | 0.7 | 21 |
| 10 W | 01:17 AM | 0.0 | 0 |
|  | 10:06 AM | 0.3 | 9 |
|  | 12:47 PM | 0.2 | 6 |
|  | 07:32 PM | 0.7 | 21 |
| 11 Th | 02:34 AM | -0.1 | -3 |
|  | 11:23 AM | 0.3 | 9 |
|  | 01:40 PM | 0.2 | 6 |
|  | 08:17 PM | 0.7 | 21 |
| 12 F | 03:39 AM | -0.2 | -6 |
|  | 12:26 PM | 0.4 | 12 |
|  | 02:33 PM | 0.3 | 9 |
|  | 09:03 PM | 0.7 | 21 |
| 13 Sa | 04:23 AM | -0.2 | -6 |
|  | 01:21 PM | 0.4 | 12 |
|  | 03:21 PM | 0.3 | 9 |
|  | 09:49 PM | 0.7 | 21 |
| 14 Su | 04:56 AM | -0.3 | -9 |
|  | 10:37 PM | 0.7 | 21 |
| 15 M | 05:28 AM | -0.3 | -9 |
|  | 11:27 PM | 0.7 | 21 |
| 16 Tu | 06:01 AM | -0.3 | -9 |
| 17 W ● | 12:20 AM | 0.7 | 21 |
|  | 06:36 AM | -0.3 | -9 |
|  | 04:10 PM | 0.4 | 12 |
|  | 06:13 PM | 0.3 | 9 |
| 18 Th | 01:14 AM | 0.7 | 21 |
|  | 07:14 AM | -0.3 | -9 |
|  | 04:39 PM | 0.4 | 12 |
|  | 06:57 PM | 0.3 | 9 |
| 19 F | 02:05 AM | 0.7 | 21 |
|  | 07:55 AM | -0.3 | -9 |
|  | 04:54 PM | 0.4 | 12 |
|  | 07:44 PM | 0.2 | 6 |
| 20 Sa | 02:53 AM | 0.7 | 21 |
|  | 08:37 AM | -0.3 | -9 |
|  | 04:31 PM | 0.4 | 12 |
|  | 08:34 PM | 0.2 | 6 |
| 21 Su | 03:40 AM | 0.6 | 18 |
|  | 09:20 AM | -0.2 | -6 |
|  | 04:46 PM | 0.5 | 15 |
|  | 09:27 PM | 0.1 | 3 |
| 22 M | 04:27 AM | 0.6 | 18 |
|  | 10:04 AM | -0.2 | -6 |
|  | 05:17 PM | 0.5 | 15 |
|  | 10:23 PM | 0.0 | 0 |
| 23 Tu ◑ | 05:16 AM | 0.5 | 15 |
|  | 10:48 AM | -0.1 | -3 |
|  | 05:51 PM | 0.5 | 15 |
|  | 11:22 PM | -0.1 | -3 |
| 24 W ◑ | 06:11 AM | 0.3 | 9 |
|  | 11:33 AM | 0.0 | 0 |
|  | 06:29 PM | 0.6 | 18 |
| 25 Th | 12:23 AM | -0.2 | -6 |
|  | 09:55 AM | 0.2 | 6 |
|  | 12:18 PM | 0.1 | 3 |
|  | 07:08 PM | 0.6 | 18 |
| 26 F | 01:27 AM | -0.2 | -6 |
|  | 07:48 PM | 0.7 | 21 |
| 27 Sa | 02:31 AM | -0.3 | -9 |
|  | 08:30 PM | 0.7 | 21 |
| 28 Su | 03:32 AM | -0.4 | -12 |
|  | 09:15 PM | 0.8 | 24 |
| 29 M | 04:28 AM | -0.4 | -12 |
|  | 10:09 PM | 0.8 | 24 |
| 30 Tu | 05:19 AM | -0.3 | -9 |
|  | 11:19 PM | 0.8 | 24 |
| 31 W ○ | 06:06 AM | -0.3 | -9 |
|  | 03:36 PM | 0.4 | 12 |
|  | 05:36 PM | 0.3 | 9 |

### February

| Date | Time | ft | cm |
|---|---|---|---|
| 1 Th | 12:37 AM | 0.8 | 24 |
|  | 06:51 AM | -0.3 | -9 |
|  | 04:08 PM | 0.4 | 12 |
|  | 06:31 PM | 0.2 | 6 |
| 2 F | 01:48 AM | 0.7 | 21 |
|  | 07:35 AM | -0.2 | -6 |
|  | 04:37 PM | 0.4 | 12 |
|  | 07:27 PM | 0.1 | 3 |
| 3 Sa | 02:46 AM | 0.7 | 21 |
|  | 08:19 AM | -0.2 | -6 |
|  | 04:56 PM | 0.4 | 12 |
|  | 08:25 PM | 0.0 | 0 |
| 4 Su | 03:37 AM | 0.6 | 18 |
|  | 09:03 AM | -0.2 | -6 |
|  | 04:48 PM | 0.4 | 12 |
|  | 09:25 PM | -0.1 | -3 |
| 5 M | 04:23 AM | 0.5 | 15 |
|  | 09:48 AM | -0.1 | -3 |
|  | 04:57 PM | 0.5 | 15 |
|  | 10:27 PM | -0.2 | -6 |
| 6 Tu | 05:09 AM | 0.3 | 9 |
|  | 10:32 AM | -0.1 | -3 |
|  | 05:27 PM | 0.5 | 15 |
|  | 11:31 PM | -0.3 | -9 |
| 7 W ◗ | 05:57 AM | 0.2 | 6 |
|  | 11:18 AM | -0.1 | -3 |
|  | 06:06 PM | 0.5 | 15 |
| 8 Th | 12:35 AM | -0.3 | -9 |
|  | 09:51 AM | 0.1 | 3 |
|  | 12:06 PM | 0.0 | 0 |
|  | 06:49 PM | 0.5 | 15 |
| 9 F | 01:41 AM | -0.4 | -12 |
|  | 07:37 PM | 0.5 | 15 |
| 10 Sa | 02:45 AM | -0.4 | -12 |
|  | 08:27 PM | 0.5 | 15 |
| 11 Su | 03:41 AM | -0.4 | -12 |
|  | 09:19 PM | 0.5 | 15 |
| 12 M | 04:25 AM | -0.4 | -12 |
|  | 10:13 PM | 0.5 | 15 |
| 13 Tu | 05:00 AM | -0.4 | -12 |
|  | 02:27 PM | 0.3 | 9 |
|  | 04:30 PM | 0.2 | 6 |
|  | 11:10 PM | 0.5 | 15 |
| 14 W | 05:35 AM | -0.3 | -9 |
|  | 03:02 PM | 0.3 | 9 |
|  | 05:13 PM | 0.2 | 6 |
| 15 Th ● | 12:10 AM | 0.5 | 15 |
|  | 06:11 AM | -0.3 | -9 |
|  | 03:31 PM | 0.3 | 9 |
|  | 05:56 PM | 0.2 | 6 |
| 16 F | 01:08 AM | 0.5 | 15 |
|  | 06:48 AM | -0.3 | -9 |
|  | 03:52 PM | 0.3 | 9 |
|  | 06:41 PM | 0.1 | 3 |
| 17 Sa | 02:01 AM | 0.5 | 15 |
|  | 07:27 AM | -0.2 | -6 |
|  | 03:46 PM | 0.4 | 12 |
|  | 07:27 PM | 0.0 | 0 |
| 18 Su | 02:50 AM | 0.5 | 15 |
|  | 08:08 AM | -0.2 | -6 |
|  | 03:42 PM | 0.4 | 12 |
|  | 08:16 PM | -0.1 | -3 |
| 19 M | 03:37 AM | 0.5 | 15 |
|  | 08:50 AM | -0.2 | -6 |
|  | 04:06 PM | 0.5 | 15 |
|  | 09:07 PM | -0.2 | -6 |
| 20 Tu | 04:24 AM | 0.4 | 12 |
|  | 09:31 AM | -0.1 | -3 |
|  | 04:37 PM | 0.5 | 15 |
|  | 10:01 PM | -0.3 | -9 |
| 21 W | 05:12 AM | 0.3 | 9 |
|  | 10:13 AM | -0.1 | -3 |
|  | 05:11 PM | 0.5 | 15 |
|  | 10:57 PM | -0.4 | -12 |
| 22 Th ◗ | 06:08 AM | 0.2 | 6 |
|  | 10:55 AM | 0.0 | 0 |
|  | 05:48 PM | 0.6 | 18 |
|  | 11:57 PM | -0.4 | -12 |
| 23 F ◗ | 06:28 AM | 0.6 | 18 |
| 24 Sa | 12:59 AM | -0.4 | -12 |
|  | 07:12 PM | 0.6 | 18 |
| 25 Su | 02:04 AM | -0.4 | -12 |
|  | 08:03 PM | 0.6 | 18 |
| 26 M | 03:08 AM | -0.4 | -12 |
|  | 09:01 PM | 0.6 | 18 |
| 27 Tu | 04:07 AM | -0.4 | -12 |
|  | 10:09 PM | 0.6 | 18 |
| 28 W | 04:58 AM | -0.3 | -9 |
|  | 02:22 PM | 0.3 | 9 |
|  | 04:34 PM | 0.2 | 6 |
|  | 11:32 PM | 0.6 | 18 |

### March

| Date | Time | ft | cm |
|---|---|---|---|
| 1 Th | 05:43 AM | -0.2 | -6 |
|  | 02:54 PM | 0.3 | 9 |
|  | 05:30 PM | 0.1 | 3 |
| 2 F ○ | 01:15 AM | 0.6 | 18 |
|  | 06:25 AM | -0.1 | -3 |
|  | 03:23 PM | 0.4 | 12 |
|  | 06:25 PM | 0.0 | 0 |
| 3 Sa | 02:27 AM | 0.6 | 18 |
|  | 07:07 AM | -0.1 | -3 |
|  | 03:43 PM | 0.4 | 12 |
|  | 07:18 PM | -0.1 | -3 |
| 4 Su | 03:17 AM | 0.5 | 15 |
|  | 07:48 AM | -0.1 | -3 |
|  | 03:40 PM | 0.4 | 12 |
|  | 08:12 PM | -0.1 | -3 |
| 5 M | 03:57 AM | 0.5 | 15 |
|  | 08:30 AM | 0.0 | 0 |
|  | 03:43 PM | 0.5 | 15 |
|  | 09:06 PM | -0.3 | -9 |
| 6 Tu | 04:30 AM | 0.3 | 9 |
|  | 09:13 AM | 0.0 | 0 |
|  | 04:11 PM | 0.6 | 18 |
|  | 10:01 PM | -0.4 | -12 |
| 7 W | 05:04 AM | 0.2 | 6 |
|  | 09:56 AM | 0.0 | 0 |
|  | 04:46 PM | 0.6 | 18 |
|  | 10:55 PM | -0.4 | -12 |
| 8 Th | 05:44 AM | 0.1 | 3 |
|  | 10:40 AM | 0.0 | 0 |
|  | 05:27 PM | 0.6 | 18 |
|  | 11:51 PM | -0.4 | -12 |
| 9 F ◗ | 06:12 PM | 0.5 | 15 |
| 10 Sa | 12:49 AM | -0.4 | -12 |
|  | 07:01 PM | 0.5 | 15 |
| 11 Su | 01:48 AM | -0.4 | -12 |
|  | 08:54 PM | 0.4 | 12 |
| 12 M | 03:48 AM | -0.4 | -12 |
|  | 09:51 PM | 0.4 | 12 |
| 13 Tu | 04:41 AM | -0.3 | -9 |
|  | 02:13 PM | 0.3 | 9 |
|  | 04:26 PM | 0.2 | 6 |
|  | 10:52 PM | 0.4 | 12 |
| 14 W | 05:25 AM | -0.2 | -6 |
|  | 02:48 PM | 0.3 | 9 |
|  | 05:15 PM | 0.2 | 6 |
| 15 Th | 12:00 AM | 0.5 | 15 |
|  | 06:03 AM | -0.2 | -6 |
|  | 03:19 PM | 0.4 | 12 |
|  | 05:59 PM | 0.2 | 6 |
| 16 F | 01:17 AM | 0.5 | 15 |
|  | 06:41 AM | -0.1 | -3 |
|  | 03:42 PM | 0.4 | 12 |
|  | 06:42 PM | 0.1 | 3 |
| 17 Sa ● | 02:28 AM | 0.5 | 15 |
|  | 07:18 AM | -0.1 | -3 |
|  | 03:48 PM | 0.4 | 12 |
|  | 07:25 PM | 0.0 | 0 |
| 18 Su | 03:21 AM | 0.5 | 15 |
|  | 07:57 AM | 0.0 | 0 |
|  | 03:33 PM | 0.5 | 15 |
|  | 08:11 PM | -0.1 | -3 |
| 19 M | 04:07 AM | 0.5 | 15 |
|  | 08:36 AM | 0.0 | 0 |
|  | 03:53 PM | 0.5 | 15 |
|  | 08:59 PM | -0.2 | -6 |
| 20 Tu | 04:52 AM | 0.5 | 15 |
|  | 09:16 AM | 0.1 | 3 |
|  | 04:23 PM | 0.6 | 18 |
|  | 09:48 PM | -0.3 | -9 |
| 21 W | 05:38 AM | 0.4 | 12 |
|  | 09:57 AM | 0.1 | 3 |
|  | 04:57 PM | 0.6 | 18 |
|  | 10:41 PM | -0.4 | -12 |
| 22 Th | 06:30 AM | 0.3 | 9 |
|  | 10:37 AM | 0.1 | 3 |
|  | 05:33 PM | 0.7 | 21 |
|  | 11:35 PM | -0.5 | -15 |
| 23 F | 09:14 AM | 0.2 | 6 |
|  | 11:18 AM | 0.1 | 3 |
|  | 06:12 PM | 0.7 | 21 |
| 24 Sa ◗ | 12:33 AM | -0.5 | -15 |
|  | 06:55 PM | 0.7 | 21 |
| 25 Su | 01:33 AM | -0.4 | -12 |
|  | 07:46 PM | 0.7 | 21 |
| 26 M | 02:37 AM | -0.3 | -9 |
|  | 08:45 PM | 0.6 | 18 |
| 27 Tu | 03:41 AM | -0.2 | -6 |
|  | 09:54 PM | 0.6 | 18 |
| 28 W | 04:40 AM | -0.1 | -3 |
|  | 02:04 PM | 0.4 | 12 |
|  | 04:32 PM | 0.2 | 6 |
|  | 11:23 PM | 0.6 | 18 |
| 29 Th | 05:30 AM | -0.1 | -3 |
|  | 02:37 PM | 0.4 | 12 |
|  | 05:33 PM | 0.1 | 3 |
| 30 F | 02:11 AM | 0.6 | 18 |
|  | 06:14 AM | 0.0 | 0 |
|  | 03:07 PM | 0.5 | 15 |
|  | 06:27 PM | 0.1 | 3 |
| 31 Sa ○ | 03:11 AM | 0.6 | 18 |
|  | 06:55 AM | 0.1 | 3 |
|  | 03:30 PM | 0.5 | 15 |
|  | 07:18 PM | 0.0 | 0 |

Heights are referred to mean lower water which is the chart datum of sounding. All times are local. Daylight Saving Time has been used when needed. Additional tide tables are available online from NOAA at www.tidesandcurrents.noaa.gov/tide_predictions.shtml.

**SKIPPER'S HANDBOOK**

StationId: 8723970
Source: NOAA/NOS/CO-OPS
Station Type: Primary
Time Zone: LST_LDT
Datum: MLLW

**NOAA Tide Predictions**

## Vaca Key, FL, 2018

### Times and Heights of High and Low Waters

## April

| Day | Time | ft | cm | Day | Time | ft | cm |
|---|---|---|---|---|---|---|---|
| 1 Su | 04:03 AM | 0.6 | 18 | 16 M | 04:06 AM | 0.6 | 18 |
| | 07:34 AM | 0.1 | 3 | | 07:22 AM | 0.3 | 9 |
| | 03:32 PM | 0.6 | 18 | | 02:30 PM | 0.7 | 21 |
| | 08:07 PM | -0.1 | -3 | ● | 07:54 PM | -0.1 | -3 |
| 2 M | 04:51 AM | 0.5 | 15 | 17 Tu | 04:54 AM | 0.6 | 18 |
| | 08:14 AM | 0.2 | 6 | | 08:01 AM | 0.3 | 9 |
| | 03:27 PM | 0.6 | 18 | | 03:04 PM | 0.7 | 21 |
| | 08:55 PM | -0.2 | -6 | | 08:41 PM | -0.3 | -9 |
| 3 Tu | 05:38 AM | 0.5 | 15 | 18 W | 05:44 AM | 0.6 | 18 |
| | 08:55 AM | 0.2 | 6 | | 08:40 AM | 0.3 | 9 |
| | 03:54 PM | 0.7 | 21 | | 03:41 PM | 0.8 | 24 |
| | 09:43 PM | -0.3 | -9 | | 09:30 PM | -0.4 | -12 |
| 4 W | 06:24 AM | 0.4 | 12 | 19 Th | 06:41 AM | 0.5 | 15 |
| | 09:37 AM | 0.1 | 3 | | 09:21 AM | 0.3 | 9 |
| | 04:30 PM | 0.7 | 21 | | 04:20 PM | 0.8 | 24 |
| | 10:31 PM | -0.4 | -12 | | 10:21 PM | -0.4 | -12 |
| 5 Th | 07:22 AM | 0.3 | 9 | 20 F | 07:52 AM | 0.4 | 12 |
| | 10:19 AM | 0.1 | 3 | | 10:02 AM | 0.3 | 9 |
| | 05:10 PM | 0.7 | 21 | | 05:00 PM | 0.9 | 27 |
| | 11:20 PM | -0.4 | -12 | | 11:15 PM | -0.4 | -12 |
| 6 F | 08:43 AM | 0.2 | 6 | 21 Sa | 05:44 PM | 0.8 | 24 |
| | 11:03 AM | 0.1 | 3 | | | | |
| | 05:52 PM | 0.7 | 21 | | | | |
| 7 Sa | 12:10 AM | -0.4 | -12 | 22 Su | 12:10 AM | -0.4 | -12 |
| | 06:37 PM | 0.6 | 18 | ◐ | 06:32 PM | 0.8 | 24 |
| 8 Su | 01:03 AM | -0.4 | -12 | 23 M | 01:08 AM | -0.3 | -9 |
| ◐ | 07:27 PM | 0.5 | 15 | | 07:28 PM | 0.7 | 21 |
| 9 M | 01:58 AM | -0.3 | -9 | 24 Tu | 02:08 AM | -0.2 | -6 |
| | 08:22 PM | 0.5 | 15 | | 12:01 PM | 0.4 | 12 |
| | | | | | 02:06 PM | 0.3 | 9 |
| | | | | | 08:33 PM | 0.6 | 18 |
| 10 Tu | 02:56 AM | -0.2 | -6 | 25 W | 03:09 AM | 0.0 | 0 |
| | 12:52 PM | 0.3 | 9 | | 12:40 PM | 0.5 | 15 |
| | 03:03 PM | 0.3 | 9 | | 03:25 PM | 0.3 | 9 |
| | 09:22 PM | 0.5 | 15 | | 09:54 PM | 0.6 | 18 |
| 11 W | 03:52 AM | -0.1 | -3 | 26 Th | 04:06 AM | 0.1 | 3 |
| | 01:29 PM | 0.4 | 12 | | 01:16 PM | 0.6 | 18 |
| | 04:07 PM | 0.3 | 9 | | 04:35 PM | 0.2 | 6 |
| | 10:30 PM | 0.5 | 15 | | | | |
| 12 Th | 04:42 AM | 0.0 | 0 | 27 F | 01:20 AM | 0.6 | 18 |
| | 02:00 PM | 0.5 | 15 | | 04:56 AM | 0.2 | 6 |
| | 04:59 PM | 0.2 | 6 | | 01:48 PM | 0.6 | 18 |
| | | | | | 05:34 PM | 0.1 | 3 |
| 13 F | 12:07 AM | 0.5 | 15 | 28 Sa | 02:22 AM | 0.6 | 18 |
| | 05:26 AM | 0.1 | 3 | | 05:40 AM | 0.3 | 9 |
| | 02:25 PM | 0.5 | 15 | | 02:14 PM | 0.7 | 21 |
| | 05:43 PM | 0.2 | 6 | | 06:24 PM | 0.0 | 0 |
| 14 Sa | 02:22 AM | 0.6 | 18 | 29 Su | 03:17 AM | 0.7 | 21 |
| | 06:06 AM | 0.2 | 6 | | 06:21 AM | 0.3 | 9 |
| | 02:32 PM | 0.5 | 15 | | 02:15 PM | 0.7 | 21 |
| | 06:25 PM | 0.1 | 3 | | 07:08 PM | -0.1 | -3 |
| 15 Su | 03:16 AM | 0.6 | 18 | 30 M | 04:08 AM | 0.6 | 18 |
| | 06:44 AM | 0.2 | 6 | | 07:00 AM | 0.4 | 12 |
| | 02:04 PM | 0.6 | 18 | | 02:00 PM | 0.8 | 24 |
| | 07:09 PM | 0.0 | 0 | ○ | 07:51 PM | -0.2 | -6 |

## May

| Day | Time | ft | cm | Day | Time | ft | cm |
|---|---|---|---|---|---|---|---|
| 1 Tu | 04:56 AM | 0.6 | 18 | 16 W | 05:07 AM | 0.7 | 21 |
| | 07:40 AM | 0.4 | 12 | | 07:24 AM | 0.5 | 15 |
| | 02:33 PM | 0.8 | 24 | | 02:15 PM | 0.9 | 27 |
| | 08:34 PM | -0.2 | -6 | | 08:24 PM | -0.3 | -9 |
| 2 W | 05:43 AM | 0.5 | 15 | 17 Th | 05:58 AM | 0.6 | 18 |
| | 08:20 AM | 0.3 | 9 | | 08:05 AM | 0.5 | 15 |
| | 03:13 PM | 0.8 | 24 | | 03:02 PM | 1.0 | 30 |
| | 09:17 PM | -0.3 | -9 | | 09:13 PM | -0.3 | -9 |
| 3 Th | 06:30 AM | 0.5 | 15 | 18 F | 03:49 PM | 1.0 | 30 |
| | 09:01 AM | 0.3 | 9 | | 10:03 PM | -0.3 | -9 |
| | 03:54 PM | 0.8 | 24 | | | | |
| | 10:01 PM | -0.4 | -12 | | | | |
| 4 F | 07:20 AM | 0.4 | 12 | 19 Sa | 04:37 PM | 1.0 | 30 |
| | 09:43 AM | 0.3 | 9 | | 10:55 PM | -0.3 | -9 |
| | 04:37 PM | 0.8 | 24 | | | | |
| | 10:47 PM | -0.4 | -12 | | | | |
| 5 Sa | 08:19 AM | 0.4 | 12 | 20 Su | 05:26 PM | 0.9 | 27 |
| | 10:27 AM | 0.3 | 9 | | 11:48 PM | -0.2 | -6 |
| | 05:21 PM | 0.8 | 24 | | | | |
| | 11:34 PM | -0.4 | -12 | | | | |
| 6 Su | 06:07 PM | 0.7 | 21 | 21 M | 06:18 PM | 0.8 | 24 |
| 7 M | 12:23 AM | -0.3 | -9 | 22 Tu | 12:42 AM | -0.1 | -3 |
| | 06:56 PM | 0.6 | 18 | | 10:23 AM | 0.5 | 15 |
| | | | | | 12:45 PM | 0.4 | 12 |
| | | | | ◐ | 07:15 PM | 0.7 | 21 |
| 8 Tu | 01:15 AM | -0.2 | -6 | 23 W | 01:38 AM | 0.0 | 0 |
| | 11:17 AM | 0.4 | 12 | | 11:06 AM | 0.6 | 18 |
| | 01:22 PM | 0.4 | 12 | | 02:05 PM | 0.3 | 9 |
| ◐ | 07:51 PM | 0.6 | 18 | | 08:23 PM | 0.6 | 18 |
| 9 W | 02:09 AM | -0.1 | -3 | 24 Th | 02:34 AM | 0.1 | 3 |
| | 11:58 AM | 0.4 | 12 | | 11:45 AM | 0.6 | 18 |
| | 02:34 PM | 0.4 | 12 | | 03:27 PM | 0.3 | 9 |
| | 08:54 PM | 0.5 | 15 | | | | |
| 10 Th | 03:04 AM | 0.0 | 0 | 25 F | 12:11 AM | 0.5 | 15 |
| | 12:31 PM | 0.6 | 18 | | 03:29 AM | 0.3 | 9 |
| | 03:41 PM | 0.3 | 9 | | 12:21 PM | 0.7 | 21 |
| | 10:08 PM | 0.5 | 15 | | 04:39 PM | 0.2 | 6 |
| 11 F | 03:57 AM | 0.2 | 6 | 26 Sa | 01:22 AM | 0.6 | 18 |
| | 12:54 PM | 0.6 | 18 | | 04:20 AM | 0.3 | 9 |
| | 04:36 PM | 0.3 | 9 | | 12:49 PM | 0.8 | 24 |
| | | | | | 05:34 PM | 0.1 | 3 |
| 12 Sa | 01:29 AM | 0.6 | 18 | 27 Su | 02:21 AM | 0.6 | 18 |
| | 04:44 AM | 0.4 | 12 | | 05:06 AM | 0.4 | 12 |
| | 11:45 AM | 0.6 | 18 | | 12:05 PM | 0.8 | 24 |
| | 05:23 PM | 0.2 | 6 | | 06:17 PM | 0.0 | 0 |
| 13 Su | 02:30 AM | 0.6 | 18 | 28 M | 03:14 AM | 0.6 | 18 |
| | 05:27 AM | 0.4 | 12 | | 05:48 AM | 0.4 | 12 |
| | 12:16 PM | 0.7 | 21 | | 12:29 PM | 0.9 | 27 |
| | 06:07 PM | 0.0 | 0 | | 06:55 PM | -0.1 | -3 |
| 14 M | 03:25 AM | 0.7 | 21 | 29 Tu | 04:04 AM | 0.6 | 18 |
| | 06:06 AM | 0.5 | 15 | | 06:28 AM | 0.5 | 15 |
| | 12:51 PM | 0.8 | 24 | ○ | 07:32 PM | -0.2 | -6 |
| | 06:51 PM | -0.1 | -3 | | | | |
| 15 Tu | 04:16 AM | 0.7 | 21 | 30 W | 04:51 AM | 0.6 | 18 |
| | 06:45 AM | 0.5 | 15 | | 07:07 AM | 0.5 | 15 |
| | 01:31 PM | 0.9 | 27 | | 01:52 PM | 0.9 | 27 |
| ● | 07:37 PM | -0.2 | -6 | | 08:11 PM | -0.2 | -6 |
| | | | | 31 Th | 05:36 AM | 0.6 | 18 |
| | | | | | 07:47 AM | 0.5 | 15 |
| | | | | | 02:38 PM | 0.9 | 27 |
| | | | | | 08:51 PM | -0.3 | -9 |

## June

| Day | Time | ft | cm | Day | Time | ft | cm |
|---|---|---|---|---|---|---|---|
| 1 F | 06:19 AM | 0.5 | 15 | 16 Sa | 03:30 PM | 1.1 | 34 |
| | 08:28 AM | 0.4 | 12 | | 09:44 PM | -0.2 | -6 |
| | 03:24 PM | 0.9 | 27 | | | | |
| | 09:32 PM | -0.3 | -9 | | | | |
| 2 Sa | 07:01 AM | 0.5 | 15 | 17 Su | 07:15 AM | 0.6 | 18 |
| | 09:11 AM | 0.4 | 12 | | 09:17 AM | 0.4 | 12 |
| | 04:09 PM | 0.9 | 27 | | 04:23 PM | 1.0 | 30 |
| | 10:16 PM | -0.3 | -9 | | 10:33 PM | -0.1 | -3 |
| 3 Su | 07:41 AM | 0.5 | 15 | 18 M | 07:55 AM | 0.6 | 18 |
| | 09:57 AM | 0.4 | 12 | | 10:17 AM | 0.4 | 12 |
| | 04:55 PM | 0.8 | 24 | | 05:15 PM | 1.0 | 30 |
| | 11:01 PM | -0.3 | -9 | | 11:23 PM | -0.1 | -3 |
| 4 M | 08:20 AM | 0.5 | 15 | 19 Tu | 08:34 AM | 0.6 | 18 |
| | 10:49 AM | 0.4 | 12 | | 11:24 AM | 0.4 | 12 |
| | 05:41 PM | 0.8 | 24 | | 06:08 PM | 0.8 | 24 |
| | 11:47 PM | -0.2 | -6 | | | | |
| 5 Tu | 07:09 AM | 0.5 | 15 | 20 W | 12:13 AM | 0.0 | 0 |
| | 11:47 AM | 0.4 | 12 | | 09:13 AM | 0.6 | 18 |
| | 06:30 PM | 0.7 | 21 | | 12:38 PM | 0.3 | 9 |
| | | | | ◐ | 07:04 PM | 0.7 | 21 |
| 6 W | 12:36 AM | -0.1 | -3 | 21 Th | 01:04 AM | 0.1 | 3 |
| | 07:50 AM | 0.5 | 15 | | 09:49 AM | 0.7 | 21 |
| | 12:52 PM | 0.4 | 12 | | 01:58 PM | 0.3 | 9 |
| ◐ | 07:24 PM | 0.6 | 18 | | 10:38 PM | 0.5 | 15 |
| 7 Th | 01:27 AM | 0.0 | 0 | 22 F | 01:57 AM | 0.2 | 6 |
| | 08:35 AM | 0.6 | 18 | | 09:14 AM | 0.7 | 21 |
| | 02:00 PM | 0.3 | 9 | | 03:22 PM | 0.2 | 6 |
| | 08:27 PM | 0.5 | 15 | | | | |
| 8 F | 02:19 AM | 0.2 | 6 | 23 Sa | 12:08 AM | 0.5 | 15 |
| | 09:20 AM | 0.6 | 18 | | 02:51 AM | 0.3 | 9 |
| | 03:07 PM | 0.3 | 9 | | 09:48 AM | 0.8 | 24 |
| | 09:46 PM | 0.5 | 15 | | 04:37 PM | 0.1 | 3 |
| 9 Sa | 03:11 AM | 0.2 | 6 | 24 Su | 01:15 AM | 0.5 | 15 |
| | 10:02 AM | 0.7 | 21 | | 03:44 AM | 0.4 | 12 |
| | 04:06 PM | 0.2 | 6 | | 10:28 AM | 0.9 | 27 |
| | | | | | 05:28 PM | 0.0 | 0 |
| 10 Su | 01:27 AM | 0.6 | 18 | 25 M | 02:12 AM | 0.6 | 18 |
| | 04:00 AM | 0.4 | 12 | | 04:33 AM | 0.4 | 12 |
| | 10:41 AM | 0.8 | 24 | | 11:08 AM | 0.9 | 27 |
| | 04:58 PM | 0.1 | 3 | | 06:04 PM | -0.1 | -3 |
| 11 M | 02:28 AM | 0.6 | 18 | 26 Tu | 03:04 AM | 0.6 | 18 |
| | 04:45 AM | 0.5 | 15 | | 05:18 AM | 0.5 | 15 |
| | 11:18 AM | 0.9 | 27 | | 11:50 AM | 0.9 | 27 |
| | 05:46 PM | 0.0 | 0 | | 06:38 PM | -0.1 | -3 |
| 12 Tu | 03:23 AM | 0.7 | 21 | 27 W | 03:51 AM | 0.6 | 18 |
| | 05:27 AM | 0.6 | 18 | | 05:59 AM | 0.5 | 15 |
| | 11:56 AM | 1.0 | 30 | | 12:35 PM | 0.9 | 27 |
| | 06:33 PM | -0.1 | -3 | | 07:12 PM | -0.1 | -3 |
| 13 W | 12:39 PM | 1.0 | 30 | 28 Th | 04:36 AM | 0.6 | 18 |
| ● | 07:19 PM | -0.2 | -6 | | 06:39 AM | 0.5 | 15 |
| | | | | | 01:23 PM | 0.9 | 27 |
| | | | | ○ | 07:47 PM | -0.2 | -6 |
| 14 Th | 01:34 PM | 1.1 | 34 | 29 F | 05:17 AM | 0.6 | 18 |
| | 08:07 PM | -0.2 | -6 | | 07:19 AM | 0.5 | 15 |
| | | | | | 02:13 PM | 0.9 | 27 |
| | | | | | 08:25 PM | -0.2 | -6 |
| 15 F | 02:34 PM | 1.1 | 34 | 30 Sa | 05:55 AM | 0.6 | 18 |
| | 08:55 PM | -0.2 | -6 | | 08:01 AM | 0.5 | 15 |
| | | | | | 03:02 PM | 0.9 | 27 |
| | | | | | 09:05 PM | -0.2 | -6 |

Heights are referred to mean lower water which is the chart datum of sounding. All times are local. Daylight Saving Time has been used when needed. Additional tide tables are available online from NOAA at www.tidesandcurrents.noaa.gov/tide_predictions.shtml.

StationId: 8723970
Source: NOAA/NOS/CO-OPS
Station Type: Primary
Time Zone: LST_LDT
Datum: MLLW

**NOAA Tide Predictions**

# Vaca Key, FL,2018

### Times and Heights of High and Low Waters

## July

| | Time | Height ft | cm | | Time | Height ft | cm |
|---|---|---|---|---|---|---|---|
| **1** Su | 06:26 AM<br>08:45 AM<br>03:49 PM<br>09:47 PM | 0.6<br>0.5<br>0.9<br>-0.2 | 18<br>15<br>27<br>-6 | **16** M | 06:29 AM<br>09:06 AM<br>04:18 PM<br>10:08 PM | 0.7<br>0.5<br>1.1<br>0.1 | 21<br>15<br>34<br>3 |
| **2** M | 06:35 AM<br>09:34 AM<br>04:35 PM<br>10:30 PM | 0.6<br>0.4<br>0.9<br>-0.1 | 18<br>12<br>27<br>-3 | **17** Tu | 06:52 AM<br>10:07 AM<br>05:09 PM<br>10:54 PM | 0.7<br>0.4<br>0.9<br>0.2 | 21<br>12<br>27<br>6 |
| **3** Tu | 06:03 AM<br>10:26 AM<br>05:21 PM<br>11:14 PM | 0.6<br>0.4<br>0.8<br>-0.1 | 18<br>12<br>24<br>-3 | **18** W | 06:46 AM<br>11:13 AM<br>06:00 PM<br>11:41 PM | 0.7<br>0.3<br>0.8<br>0.2 | 21<br>9<br>24<br>6 |
| **4** W | 06:32 AM<br>11:22 AM<br>06:10 PM | 0.7<br>0.4<br>0.7 | 21<br>12<br>21 | **19** Th | 06:55 AM<br>12:23 PM<br>06:55 PM | 0.8<br>0.3<br>0.6 | 24<br>9<br>18 |
| **5** Th | 12:00 AM<br>07:09 AM<br>12:23 PM<br>07:03 PM | 0.0<br>0.7<br>0.3<br>0.6 | 0<br>21<br>9<br>18 | **20** F | 12:29 AM<br>07:29 AM<br>01:38 PM<br>10:37 PM | 0.3<br>0.8<br>0.2<br>0.5 | 9<br>24<br>6<br>15 |
| **6** F | 12:48 AM<br>07:50 AM<br>01:26 PM<br>08:05 PM | 0.1<br>0.7<br>0.3<br>0.5 | 3<br>21<br>9<br>15 | **21** Sa | 01:20 AM<br>08:11 AM<br>02:56 PM<br>11:57 PM | 0.4<br>0.9<br>0.1<br>0.5 | 12<br>27<br>3<br>15 |
| **7** Sa | 01:37 AM<br>08:42 AM<br>02:31 PM | 0.3<br>0.8<br>0.2 | 9<br>24<br>6 | **22** Su | 02:14 AM<br>08:58 AM<br>04:12 PM | 0.4<br>0.9<br>0.1 | 12<br>27<br>3 |
| **8** Su | 12:08 AM<br>02:27 AM<br>09:14 AM<br>03:34 PM | 0.5<br>0.4<br>0.8<br>0.1 | 15<br>12<br>24<br>3 | **23** M | 01:02 AM<br>03:11 AM<br>09:47 AM<br>05:08 PM | 0.6<br>0.5<br>0.9<br>0.0 | 18<br>15<br>27<br>0 |
| **9** M | 09:56 AM<br>04:32 PM | 0.9<br>0.0 | 27<br>0 | **24** Tu | 01:57 AM<br>04:06 AM<br>10:36 AM<br>05:45 PM | 0.6<br>0.5<br>0.9<br>0.0 | 18<br>15<br>27<br>0 |
| **10** Tu | 10:36 AM<br>05:25 PM | 1.0<br>-0.1 | 30<br>-3 | **25** W | 02:46 AM<br>04:54 AM<br>11:25 AM<br>06:17 PM | 0.6<br>0.5<br>1.0<br>0.0 | 18<br>15<br>30<br>0 |
| **11** W | 11:18 AM<br>06:14 PM | 1.1<br>-0.1 | 34<br>-3 | **26** Th | 03:30 AM<br>05:38 AM<br>12:14 PM<br>06:49 PM | 0.7<br>0.6<br>1.0<br>0.0 | 21<br>18<br>30<br>0 |
| **12** Th | 12:09 PM<br>07:02 PM | 1.1<br>-0.1 | 34<br>-3 | **27** F | 04:11 AM<br>06:18 AM<br>01:06 PM<br>07:23 PM | 0.7<br>0.6<br>1.0<br>0.0 | 21<br>18<br>30<br>0 |
| **13** F ● | 01:15 PM<br>07:48 PM | 1.2<br>-0.1 | 37<br>-3 | **28** Sa | 04:47 AM<br>06:59 AM<br>01:58 PM<br>07:59 PM | 0.7<br>0.6<br>1.0<br>0.0 | 21<br>18<br>30<br>0 |
| **14** Sa | 02:22 PM<br>08:35 PM | 1.2<br>0.0 | 37<br>0 | **29** Su | 05:18 AM<br>07:41 AM<br>02:48 PM<br>08:37 PM | 0.7<br>0.6<br>1.0<br>0.1 | 21<br>18<br>30<br>3 |
| **15** Su | 05:59 AM<br>08:09 AM<br>03:23 PM<br>09:21 PM | 0.7<br>0.5<br>1.1<br>0.0 | 21<br>15<br>34<br>0 | **30** M | 05:35 AM<br>08:26 AM<br>03:36 PM<br>09:17 PM | 0.7<br>0.5<br>1.0<br>0.1 | 21<br>15<br>30<br>3 |
| | | | | **31** Tu | 05:06 AM<br>09:14 AM<br>04:22 PM<br>09:59 PM | 0.7<br>0.5<br>1.0<br>0.1 | 21<br>15<br>30<br>3 |

## August

| | Time | Height ft | cm | | Time | Height ft | cm |
|---|---|---|---|---|---|---|---|
| **1** W | 05:22 AM<br>10:04 AM<br>05:09 PM<br>10:42 PM | 0.8<br>0.4<br>0.9<br>0.2 | 24<br>12<br>27<br>6 | **16** Th | 05:34 AM<br>10:56 AM<br>05:58 PM<br>11:07 PM | 1.0<br>0.3<br>0.8<br>0.5 | 30<br>9<br>24<br>15 |
| **2** Th | 05:53 AM<br>10:58 AM<br>05:57 PM<br>11:25 PM | 0.8<br>0.3<br>0.8<br>0.3 | 24<br>9<br>24<br>9 | **17** F | 06:05 AM<br>11:59 AM<br>06:49 PM<br>11:53 PM | 1.0<br>0.3<br>0.7<br>0.5 | 30<br>9<br>21<br>15 |
| **3** F | 06:29 AM<br>11:54 AM<br>06:50 PM | 0.9<br>0.3<br>0.7 | 27<br>9<br>21 | **18** Sa ◑ | 06:44 AM<br>01:04 PM<br>10:25 PM | 1.1<br>0.2<br>0.6 | 34<br>6<br>18 |
| **4** Sa ◐ | 12:10 AM<br>06:48 AM<br>12:55 PM<br>07:52 PM | 0.4<br>0.9<br>0.2<br>0.6 | 12<br>27<br>6<br>18 | **19** Su | 12:44 AM<br>07:29 AM<br>02:12 PM | 0.5<br>1.1<br>0.2 | 15<br>34<br>6 |
| **5** Su | 12:55 AM<br>07:49 AM<br>01:58 PM | 0.5<br>0.9<br>0.1 | 15<br>27<br>3 | **20** M | 08:19 AM<br>03:22 PM | 1.0<br>0.2 | 30<br>6 |
| **6** M | 08:33 AM<br>03:03 PM | 1.0<br>0.1 | 30<br>3 | **21** Tu | 12:42 AM<br>02:42 AM<br>09:13 AM<br>04:26 PM | 0.7<br>0.6<br>1.0<br>0.2 | 21<br>18<br>30<br>6 |
| **7** Tu | 09:18 AM<br>04:05 PM | 1.1<br>0.1 | 34<br>3 | **22** W | 01:34 AM<br>03:45 AM<br>10:08 AM<br>05:14 PM | 0.7<br>0.7<br>1.0<br>0.2 | 21<br>21<br>30<br>6 |
| **8** W | 10:06 AM<br>05:03 PM | 1.1<br>0.1 | 34<br>3 | **23** Th | 02:19 AM<br>04:39 AM<br>11:04 AM<br>05:50 PM | 0.8<br>0.7<br>1.0<br>0.2 | 24<br>21<br>30<br>6 |
| **9** Th | 10:59 AM<br>05:55 PM | 1.2<br>0.1 | 37<br>3 | **24** F | 02:59 AM<br>05:24 AM<br>12:01 PM<br>06:22 PM | 0.8<br>0.7<br>1.1<br>0.3 | 24<br>21<br>34<br>9 |
| **10** F | 12:02 PM<br>06:42 PM | 1.2<br>0.1 | 37<br>3 | **25** Sa | 03:35 AM<br>06:04 AM<br>12:58 PM<br>06:55 PM | 0.9<br>0.7<br>1.1<br>0.3 | 27<br>21<br>34<br>9 |
| **11** Sa ● | 04:11 AM<br>07:08 AM<br>01:14 PM<br>07:27 PM | 0.8<br>0.7<br>1.2<br>0.2 | 24<br>21<br>37<br>6 | **26** Su ○ | 04:06 AM<br>06:44 AM<br>01:54 PM<br>07:30 PM | 0.9<br>0.7<br>1.1<br>0.4 | 27<br>21<br>34<br>12 |
| **12** Su | 04:44 AM<br>07:06 AM<br>02:26 PM<br>08:11 PM | 0.8<br>0.6<br>1.2<br>0.3 | 24<br>18<br>37<br>9 | **27** M | 04:27 AM<br>07:25 AM<br>02:46 PM<br>08:07 PM | 0.9<br>0.7<br>1.1<br>0.4 | 27<br>21<br>34<br>12 |
| **13** M | 05:12 AM<br>08:00 AM<br>03:29 PM<br>08:54 PM | 0.8<br>0.6<br>1.2<br>0.3 | 24<br>18<br>37<br>9 | **28** Tu | 04:14 AM<br>08:09 AM<br>03:33 PM<br>08:46 PM | 0.9<br>0.6<br>1.1<br>0.5 | 27<br>18<br>34<br>15 |
| **14** Tu | 05:30 AM<br>08:57 AM<br>04:23 PM<br>09:38 PM | 0.9<br>0.5<br>1.1<br>0.4 | 27<br>15<br>34<br>12 | **29** W | 04:12 AM<br>08:55 AM<br>04:19 PM<br>09:26 PM | 1.0<br>0.5<br>1.1<br>0.5 | 30<br>15<br>34<br>15 |
| **15** W | 05:24 AM<br>09:55 AM<br>05:11 PM<br>10:22 PM | 0.9<br>0.4<br>1.0<br>0.4 | 27<br>12<br>30<br>12 | **30** Th | 04:39 AM<br>09:43 AM<br>05:05 PM<br>10:08 PM | 1.1<br>0.4<br>1.0<br>0.5 | 34<br>12<br>30<br>15 |
| | | | | **31** F | 05:12 AM<br>10:34 AM<br>05:53 PM<br>10:49 PM | 1.1<br>0.3<br>1.0<br>0.6 | 34<br>9<br>30<br>18 |

## September

| | Time | Height ft | cm | | Time | Height ft | cm |
|---|---|---|---|---|---|---|---|
| **1** Sa | 05:49 AM<br>11:29 AM<br>06:46 PM<br>11:31 PM ◑ | 1.1<br>0.3<br>0.8<br>0.6 | 34<br>9<br>24<br>18 | **16** Su ◑ | 06:06 AM<br>12:26 PM<br>10:06 PM | 1.3<br>0.3<br>0.8 | 40<br>9<br>24 |
| **2** Su | 06:27 AM<br>12:27 PM | 1.1<br>0.2 | 34<br>6 | **17** M | 12:08 AM<br>06:52 AM<br>01:26 PM | 0.8<br>1.2<br>0.3 | 24<br>37<br>9 |
| **3** M ◐ | 07:09 AM<br>01:28 PM | 1.2<br>0.2 | 37<br>6 | **18** Tu | 07:43 AM<br>02:28 PM | 1.2<br>0.3 | 37<br>9 |
| **4** Tu | 07:56 AM<br>02:33 PM | 1.2<br>0.2 | 37<br>6 | **19** W | 12:14 AM<br>02:17 AM<br>08:39 AM<br>03:32 PM | 0.9<br>0.8<br>1.1<br>0.4 | 27<br>24<br>34<br>12 |
| **5** W | 08:48 AM<br>03:38 PM | 1.2<br>0.3 | 37<br>9 | **20** Th | 01:02 AM<br>03:29 AM<br>09:39 AM<br>04:28 PM | 0.9<br>0.8<br>1.1<br>0.4 | 27<br>24<br>34<br>12 |
| **6** Th | 09:47 AM<br>04:39 PM | 1.3<br>0.3 | 40<br>9 | **21** F | 01:43 AM<br>04:29 AM<br>10:43 AM<br>05:13 PM | 1.0<br>0.8<br>1.1<br>0.5 | 30<br>24<br>34<br>15 |
| **7** F | 10:53 AM<br>05:32 PM | 1.3<br>0.4 | 40<br>12 | **22** Sa | 02:19 AM<br>05:14 AM<br>11:54 AM<br>05:49 PM | 1.0<br>0.8<br>1.2<br>0.6 | 30<br>24<br>37<br>18 |
| **8** Sa | 02:55 AM<br>05:11 AM<br>12:10 PM<br>06:18 PM | 1.0<br>0.8<br>1.3<br>0.5 | 30<br>24<br>40<br>15 | **23** Su | 02:51 AM<br>05:52 AM<br>01:32 PM<br>06:24 PM | 1.1<br>0.8<br>1.2<br>0.7 | 34<br>24<br>37<br>21 |
| **9** Su | 03:27 AM<br>06:07 AM<br>01:54 PM<br>07:01 PM ● | 1.0<br>0.7<br>1.3<br>0.6 | 30<br>21<br>40<br>18 | **24** M | 03:14 AM<br>06:30 AM<br>02:34 PM<br>06:59 PM | 1.1<br>0.8<br>1.2<br>0.7 | 34<br>24<br>37<br>21 |
| **10** M | 03:55 AM<br>07:00 AM<br>03:16 PM<br>07:41 PM | 1.0<br>0.7<br>1.3<br>0.7 | 30<br>21<br>40<br>21 | **25** Tu ○ | 03:09 AM<br>07:09 AM<br>03:17 PM<br>07:35 PM | 1.1<br>0.7<br>1.2<br>0.8 | 34<br>21<br>37<br>24 |
| **11** Tu | 04:14 AM<br>07:52 AM<br>04:13 PM<br>08:22 PM | 1.1<br>0.6<br>1.3<br>0.7 | 34<br>18<br>40<br>21 | **26** W | 02:53 AM<br>07:52 AM<br>03:58 PM<br>08:13 PM | 1.2<br>0.6<br>1.2<br>0.8 | 37<br>18<br>37<br>24 |
| **12** W | 04:08 AM<br>08:45 AM<br>05:03 PM<br>09:04 PM | 1.1<br>0.5<br>1.2<br>0.7 | 34<br>15<br>37<br>21 | **27** Th | 03:21 AM<br>08:36 AM<br>04:39 PM<br>08:52 PM | 1.2<br>0.5<br>1.2<br>0.8 | 37<br>15<br>37<br>24 |
| **13** Th | 04:15 AM<br>09:38 AM<br>05:52 PM<br>09:47 PM | 1.2<br>0.4<br>1.1<br>0.7 | 37<br>12<br>34<br>21 | **28** F | 03:55 AM<br>09:23 AM<br>05:23 PM<br>09:32 PM | 1.3<br>0.4<br>1.1<br>0.8 | 40<br>12<br>34<br>24 |
| **14** F | 04:46 AM<br>10:33 AM<br>07:02 PM<br>10:31 PM | 1.3<br>0.3<br>1.0<br>0.7 | 40<br>9<br>30<br>21 | **29** Sa | 04:32 AM<br>10:13 AM<br>06:13 PM<br>10:12 PM | 1.3<br>0.3<br>1.1<br>0.9 | 40<br>9<br>34<br>27 |
| **15** Sa | 05:23 AM<br>11:29 AM<br>08:42 PM<br>11:17 PM | 1.3<br>0.3<br>0.9<br>0.7 | 40<br>9<br>27<br>21 | **30** Su | 05:10 AM<br>11:06 AM<br>08:40 PM<br>10:54 PM | 1.4<br>0.3<br>1.0<br>0.9 | 43<br>9<br>30<br>27 |

Heights are referred to mean lower water which is the chart datum of sounding. All times are local. Daylight Saving Time has been used when needed. Additional tide tables are available online from NOAA at www.tidesandcurrents.noaa.gov/tide_predictions.shtml.

**SKIPPER'S HANDBOOK**

StationId:8726520
Source:NOAA/NOS/CO-OPS
Station Type:Harmonic
Time Zone:LST/LDT
Datum:mean lower low water (MLLW) which is the chart datum of soundings

**NOAA Tide Predictions**

## ST. PETERSBURG, Florida, 2017

### Times and Heights of High and Low Waters

## October

| Day | Time | ft | cm | Day | Time | ft | cm |
|---|---|---|---|---|---|---|---|
| 1 Su | 12:50 AM | 1.9 | 58 | 16 M | 12:59 AM | 2.0 | 61 |
| | 05:30 AM | 1.5 | 46 | | 06:27 AM | 1.1 | 34 |
| | 11:26 AM | 2.3 | 70 | | 12:36 PM | 2.3 | 70 |
| | 06:34 PM | 0.5 | 15 | | 07:01 PM | 0.6 | 18 |
| 2 M | 01:13 AM | 2.0 | 61 | 17 Tu | 01:20 AM | 2.1 | 64 |
| | 06:20 AM | 1.3 | 40 | | 07:16 AM | 0.8 | 24 |
| | 12:23 PM | 2.4 | 73 | | 01:32 PM | 2.3 | 70 |
| | 07:12 PM | 0.5 | 15 | | 07:34 PM | 0.7 | 21 |
| 3 Tu | 01:32 AM | 2.0 | 61 | 18 W | 01:39 AM | 2.2 | 67 |
| | 07:02 AM | 1.1 | 34 | | 07:58 AM | 0.6 | 18 |
| | 01:12 PM | 2.4 | 73 | | 02:20 PM | 2.2 | 67 |
| | 07:45 PM | 0.6 | 18 | | 08:01 PM | 0.9 | 27 |
| 4 W | 01:50 AM | 2.1 | 64 | 19 Th | 01:57 AM | 2.3 | 70 |
| | 07:41 AM | 0.8 | 24 | | 08:36 AM | 0.4 | 12 |
| | 01:57 PM | 2.4 | 73 | | 03:04 PM | 2.1 | 64 |
| | 08:15 PM | 0.7 | 21 | ● | 08:25 PM | 1.0 | 30 |
| 5 Th | 02:09 AM | 2.2 | 67 | 20 F | 02:15 AM | 2.4 | 73 |
| | 08:21 AM | 0.6 | 18 | | 09:11 AM | 0.3 | 9 |
| ○ | 02:42 PM | 2.4 | 73 | | 03:44 PM | 2.0 | 61 |
| | 08:44 PM | 0.8 | 24 | | 08:47 PM | 1.2 | 37 |
| 6 F | 02:30 AM | 2.4 | 73 | 21 Sa | 02:35 AM | 2.5 | 76 |
| | 09:02 AM | 0.4 | 12 | | 09:46 AM | 0.2 | 6 |
| | 03:29 PM | 2.3 | 70 | | 04:25 PM | 1.9 | 58 |
| | 09:12 PM | 1.0 | 30 | | 09:09 PM | 1.3 | 40 |
| 7 Sa | 02:56 AM | 2.5 | 76 | 22 Su | 02:58 AM | 2.5 | 76 |
| | 09:46 AM | 0.3 | 9 | | 10:23 AM | 0.2 | 6 |
| | 04:19 PM | 2.2 | 67 | | 05:07 PM | 1.8 | 55 |
| | 09:40 PM | 1.2 | 37 | | 09:32 PM | 1.4 | 43 |
| 8 Su | 03:25 AM | 2.6 | 79 | 23 M | 03:25 AM | 2.6 | 79 |
| | 10:36 AM | 0.2 | 6 | | 11:03 AM | 0.2 | 6 |
| | 05:16 PM | 2.1 | 64 | | 05:56 PM | 1.8 | 55 |
| | 10:09 PM | 1.3 | 40 | | 09:59 PM | 1.4 | 43 |
| 9 M | 04:00 AM | 2.7 | 82 | 24 Tu | 03:57 AM | 2.5 | 76 |
| | 11:32 AM | 0.1 | 3 | | 11:48 AM | 0.2 | 6 |
| | 06:24 PM | 1.9 | 58 | | 06:55 PM | 1.7 | 52 |
| | 10:38 PM | 1.5 | 46 | | 10:30 PM | 1.5 | 46 |
| 10 Tu | 04:41 AM | 2.7 | 82 | 25 W | 04:35 AM | 2.4 | 73 |
| | 12:37 PM | 0.2 | 6 | | 12:41 PM | 0.3 | 9 |
| | 07:56 PM | 1.7 | 52 | | 08:12 PM | 1.7 | 52 |
| | 11:10 PM | 1.6 | 49 | | 11:14 PM | 1.6 | 49 |
| 11 W | 05:30 AM | 2.6 | 79 | 26 Th | 05:21 AM | 2.3 | 70 |
| | 01:53 PM | 0.2 | 6 | | 01:43 PM | 0.4 | 12 |
| | | | | | 09:38 PM | 1.7 | 52 |
| 12 Th | 06:36 AM | 2.5 | 76 | 27 F | 12:30 AM | 1.6 | 49 |
| | 03:15 PM | 0.3 | 9 | | 06:22 AM | 2.2 | 67 |
| ☽ | 11:31 PM | 1.8 | 55 | ☾ | 02:50 PM | 0.4 | 12 |
| | | | | | 10:38 PM | 1.8 | 55 |
| 13 F | 01:54 AM | 1.7 | 52 | 28 Sa | 02:25 AM | 1.6 | 49 |
| | 08:10 AM | 2.4 | 73 | | 07:48 AM | 2.0 | 61 |
| | 04:31 PM | 0.3 | 9 | | 03:53 PM | 0.4 | 12 |
| | | | | | 11:16 PM | 1.8 | 55 |
| 14 Sa | 12:07 AM | 1.8 | 55 | 29 Su | 04:03 AM | 1.4 | 43 |
| | 04:01 AM | 1.6 | 49 | | 09:28 AM | 2.0 | 61 |
| | 10:00 AM | 2.3 | 70 | | 04:49 PM | 0.5 | 15 |
| | 05:33 PM | 0.4 | 12 | | 11:44 PM | 1.9 | 58 |
| 15 Su | 12:34 AM | 1.9 | 58 | 30 M | 05:12 AM | 1.2 | 37 |
| | 05:27 AM | 1.4 | 43 | | 10:54 AM | 2.0 | 61 |
| | 11:28 AM | 2.3 | 70 | | 05:36 PM | 0.5 | 15 |
| | 06:22 PM | 0.5 | 15 | | | | |
| | | | | 31 Tu | 12:09 AM | 2.0 | 61 |
| | | | | | 06:03 AM | 0.9 | 27 |
| | | | | | 12:01 PM | 2.0 | 61 |
| | | | | | 06:17 PM | 0.6 | 18 |

## November

| Day | Time | ft | cm | Day | Time | ft | cm |
|---|---|---|---|---|---|---|---|
| 1 W | 12:31 AM | 2.1 | 64 | 16 Th | 06:53 AM | 0.1 | 3 |
| | 06:48 AM | 0.7 | 21 | | 01:27 PM | 1.7 | 52 |
| | 12:59 PM | 2.1 | 64 | | 06:13 PM | 1.0 | 30 |
| | 06:53 PM | 0.7 | 21 | | | | |
| 2 Th | 12:54 AM | 2.2 | 67 | 17 F | 12:13 AM | 2.3 | 70 |
| | 07:30 AM | 0.4 | 12 | | 07:29 AM | 0.0 | 0 |
| | 01:52 PM | 2.1 | 64 | | 02:12 PM | 1.7 | 52 |
| | 07:26 PM | 0.9 | 27 | | 06:37 PM | 1.1 | 34 |
| 3 F | 01:18 AM | 2.4 | 73 | 18 Sa | 12:33 AM | 2.4 | 73 |
| | 08:12 AM | 0.1 | 3 | | 08:02 AM | -0.1 | -3 |
| | 02:44 PM | 2.0 | 61 | ● | 02:53 PM | 1.6 | 49 |
| | 07:56 PM | 1.0 | 30 | | 07:00 PM | 1.2 | 37 |
| 4 Sa | 01:45 AM | 2.5 | 76 | 19 Su | 12:56 AM | 2.4 | 73 |
| | 08:56 AM | -0.1 | -3 | | 08:35 AM | -0.2 | -6 |
| ○ | 03:37 PM | 2.0 | 61 | | 03:33 PM | 1.6 | 49 |
| | 08:26 PM | 1.2 | 37 | | 07:23 PM | 1.3 | 40 |
| 5 Su | 01:15 AM | 2.7 | 82 | 20 M | 01:22 AM | 2.5 | 76 |
| | 08:42 AM | -0.3 | -9 | | 09:10 AM | -0.2 | -6 |
| | 03:33 PM | 1.8 | 55 | | 04:12 PM | 1.5 | 46 |
| | 07:54 PM | 1.3 | 40 | | 07:49 PM | 1.3 | 40 |
| 6 M | 01:50 AM | 2.7 | 82 | 21 Tu | 01:52 AM | 2.4 | 73 |
| | 09:33 AM | -0.3 | -9 | | 09:46 AM | -0.2 | -6 |
| | 04:36 PM | 1.7 | 52 | | 04:54 PM | 1.5 | 46 |
| | 08:23 PM | 1.4 | 43 | | 08:19 PM | 1.3 | 40 |
| 7 Tu | 02:29 AM | 2.7 | 82 | 22 W | 02:27 AM | 2.4 | 73 |
| | 10:29 AM | -0.3 | -9 | | 10:27 AM | -0.1 | -3 |
| | 05:51 PM | 1.6 | 49 | | 05:41 PM | 1.5 | 46 |
| | 08:55 PM | 1.5 | 46 | | 08:59 PM | 1.3 | 40 |
| 8 W | 03:15 AM | 2.7 | 82 | 23 Th | 03:06 AM | 2.3 | 70 |
| | 11:31 AM | -0.2 | -6 | | 11:12 AM | -0.1 | -3 |
| | 07:24 PM | 1.6 | 49 | | 06:34 PM | 1.5 | 46 |
| | 09:38 PM | 1.5 | 46 | | 09:53 PM | 1.3 | 40 |
| 9 Th | 04:09 AM | 2.5 | 76 | 24 F | 03:53 AM | 2.1 | 64 |
| | 12:38 PM | 0.0 | 0 | | 12:02 PM | 0.0 | 0 |
| | 08:51 PM | 1.6 | 49 | | 07:29 PM | 1.5 | 46 |
| | 11:06 PM | 1.6 | 49 | | 11:13 PM | 1.3 | 40 |
| 10 F | 05:21 AM | 2.3 | 70 | 25 Sa | 04:51 AM | 2.0 | 61 |
| | 01:48 PM | 0.1 | 3 | | 12:56 PM | 0.1 | 3 |
| ☽ | 09:39 PM | 1.7 | 52 | | 08:17 PM | 1.6 | 49 |
| 11 Sa | 01:23 AM | 1.5 | 46 | 26 Su | 12:53 AM | 1.3 | 40 |
| | 07:03 AM | 2.0 | 61 | | 06:08 AM | 1.8 | 55 |
| | 02:53 PM | 0.2 | 6 | ☾ | 01:51 PM | 0.2 | 6 |
| | 10:12 PM | 1.8 | 55 | | 08:57 PM | 1.7 | 52 |
| 12 Su | 03:16 AM | 1.2 | 37 | 27 M | 02:28 AM | 1.1 | 34 |
| | 08:57 AM | 1.9 | 58 | | 07:43 AM | 1.6 | 49 |
| | 03:48 PM | 0.4 | 12 | | 02:44 PM | 0.3 | 9 |
| | 10:40 PM | 1.9 | 58 | | 09:32 PM | 1.8 | 55 |
| 13 M | 04:32 AM | 0.9 | 27 | 28 Tu | 03:41 AM | 0.8 | 24 |
| | 10:27 AM | 1.8 | 55 | | 09:18 AM | 1.6 | 49 |
| | 04:34 PM | 0.6 | 18 | | 03:33 PM | 0.5 | 15 |
| | 11:06 PM | 2.0 | 61 | | 10:03 PM | 1.9 | 58 |
| 14 Tu | 05:28 AM | 0.6 | 18 | 29 W | 04:40 AM | 0.5 | 15 |
| | 11:38 AM | 1.8 | 55 | | 10:40 AM | 1.6 | 49 |
| | 05:13 PM | 0.7 | 21 | | 04:18 PM | 0.6 | 18 |
| | 11:30 PM | 2.1 | 64 | | 10:33 PM | 2.1 | 64 |
| 15 W | 06:14 AM | 0.3 | 9 | 30 Th | 05:30 AM | 0.2 | 6 |
| | 12:36 PM | 1.8 | 55 | | 11:51 AM | 1.6 | 49 |
| | 05:45 PM | 0.9 | 27 | | 04:59 PM | 0.8 | 24 |
| | 11:52 PM | 2.2 | 67 | | 11:04 PM | 2.2 | 67 |

## December

| Day | Time | ft | cm | Day | Time | ft | cm |
|---|---|---|---|---|---|---|---|
| 1 F | 06:17 AM | -0.2 | -6 | 16 Sa | 07:19 AM | -0.4 | -12 |
| | 12:54 PM | 1.6 | 49 | | 02:24 PM | 1.3 | 40 |
| | 05:36 PM | 0.9 | 27 | | 05:59 PM | 1.1 | 34 |
| | 11:36 PM | 2.4 | 73 | | | | |
| 2 Sa | 07:04 AM | -0.4 | -12 | 17 Su | 12:04 AM | 2.2 | 67 |
| | 01:53 PM | 1.6 | 49 | | 07:53 AM | -0.5 | -15 |
| | 06:11 PM | 1.0 | 30 | | 03:04 PM | 1.3 | 40 |
| | | | | | 06:27 PM | 1.1 | 34 |
| 3 Su | 12:11 AM | 2.5 | 76 | 18 M | 12:32 AM | 2.2 | 67 |
| | 07:51 AM | -0.6 | -18 | | 08:26 AM | -0.5 | -15 |
| ○ | 02:51 PM | 1.5 | 46 | ● | 03:38 PM | 1.3 | 40 |
| | 06:44 PM | 1.1 | 34 | | 06:56 PM | 1.1 | 34 |
| 4 M | 12:49 AM | 2.6 | 79 | 19 Tu | 01:03 AM | 2.2 | 67 |
| | 08:40 AM | -0.7 | -21 | | 08:58 AM | -0.5 | -15 |
| | 03:49 PM | 1.5 | 46 | | 04:08 PM | 1.3 | 40 |
| | 07:17 PM | 1.2 | 37 | | 07:28 PM | 1.1 | 34 |
| 5 Tu | 01:30 AM | 2.7 | 82 | 20 W | 01:36 AM | 2.2 | 67 |
| | 09:30 AM | -0.7 | -21 | | 09:32 AM | -0.5 | -15 |
| | 04:48 PM | 1.4 | 43 | | 04:36 PM | 1.3 | 40 |
| | 07:55 PM | 1.2 | 37 | | 08:06 PM | 1.0 | 30 |
| 6 W | 02:16 AM | 2.6 | 79 | 21 Th | 02:14 AM | 2.2 | 67 |
| | 10:23 AM | -0.6 | -18 | | 10:07 AM | -0.4 | -12 |
| | 05:49 PM | 1.3 | 40 | | 05:06 PM | 1.3 | 40 |
| | 08:43 PM | 1.2 | 37 | | 08:53 PM | 1.0 | 30 |
| 7 Th | 03:07 AM | 2.4 | 73 | 22 F | 02:55 AM | 2.1 | 64 |
| | 11:16 AM | -0.5 | -15 | | 10:44 AM | -0.4 | -12 |
| | 06:48 PM | 1.3 | 40 | | 05:39 PM | 1.3 | 40 |
| | 09:50 PM | 1.2 | 37 | | 09:50 PM | 1.0 | 30 |
| 8 F | 04:05 AM | 2.2 | 67 | 23 Sa | 03:41 AM | 1.9 | 58 |
| | 12:11 PM | -0.3 | -9 | | 11:23 AM | -0.2 | -6 |
| | 07:40 PM | 1.4 | 43 | | 06:16 PM | 1.4 | 43 |
| | 11:27 PM | 1.2 | 37 | | 10:58 PM | 0.9 | 27 |
| 9 Sa | 05:16 AM | 1.9 | 58 | 24 Su | 04:36 AM | 1.7 | 52 |
| | 01:06 PM | 0.0 | 0 | | 12:06 PM | -0.1 | -3 |
| | 08:24 PM | 1.5 | 46 | | 06:55 PM | 1.5 | 46 |
| 10 Su | 01:21 AM | 1.0 | 30 | 25 M | 12:19 AM | 0.8 | 24 |
| | 06:52 AM | 1.6 | 49 | | 05:43 AM | 1.5 | 46 |
| ☾ | 02:00 PM | 0.2 | 6 | | 12:51 PM | 0.1 | 3 |
| | 09:02 PM | 1.6 | 49 | | 07:36 PM | 1.6 | 49 |
| 11 M | 03:03 AM | 0.8 | 24 | 26 Tu | 01:45 AM | 0.7 | 21 |
| | 08:42 AM | 1.4 | 43 | | 07:09 AM | 1.3 | 40 |
| | 02:50 PM | 0.4 | 12 | ☾ | 01:39 PM | 0.2 | 6 |
| | 09:37 PM | 1.8 | 55 | | 08:16 PM | 1.7 | 52 |
| 12 Tu | 04:18 AM | 0.5 | 15 | 27 W | 03:04 AM | 0.4 | 12 |
| | 10:20 AM | 1.3 | 40 | | 08:50 AM | 1.2 | 37 |
| | 03:36 PM | 0.6 | 18 | | 02:28 PM | 0.4 | 12 |
| | 10:10 PM | 1.9 | 58 | | 08:57 PM | 1.8 | 55 |
| 13 W | 05:16 AM | 0.2 | 6 | 28 Th | 04:13 AM | 0.1 | 3 |
| | 11:39 AM | 1.3 | 40 | | 10:30 AM | 1.2 | 37 |
| | 04:18 PM | 0.8 | 24 | | 03:17 PM | 0.6 | 18 |
| | 10:41 PM | 2.0 | 61 | | 09:39 PM | 2.0 | 61 |
| 14 Th | 06:02 AM | -0.1 | -3 | 29 F | 05:13 AM | -0.2 | -6 |
| | 12:43 PM | 1.3 | 40 | | 11:56 AM | 1.2 | 37 |
| | 04:55 PM | 0.9 | 27 | | 04:05 PM | 0.8 | 24 |
| | 11:10 PM | 2.1 | 64 | | 10:21 PM | 2.2 | 67 |
| 15 F | 06:43 AM | -0.3 | -9 | 30 Sa | 06:07 AM | -0.5 | -15 |
| | 01:38 PM | 1.3 | 40 | | 01:07 PM | 1.2 | 37 |
| | 05:29 PM | 1.0 | 30 | | 04:51 PM | 0.9 | 27 |
| | 11:37 PM | 2.2 | 67 | | 11:05 PM | 2.3 | 70 |
| | | | | 31 Su | 06:58 AM | -0.8 | -24 |
| | | | | | 02:08 PM | 1.2 | 37 |
| | | | | | 05:34 PM | 1.0 | 30 |
| | | | | | 11:51 PM | 2.4 | 73 |

Heights are referred to mean lower water which is the chart datum of sounding. All times are local. Daylight Saving Time has been used when needed. Additional tide tables are available online from NOAA at www.tidesandcurrents.noaa.gov/tide_predictions.shtml.

SKIPPER'S HANDBOOK

StationId: 8726520
Source: NOAA/NOS/CO-OPS
Station Type: Primary
Time Zone: LST_LDT
Datum: MLLW

## NOAA Tide Predictions

# St Petersburg, Tampa Bay, FL, 2018

### Times and Heights of High and Low Waters

## January

| Day | Time | ft | cm | Day | Time | ft | cm |
|---|---|---|---|---|---|---|---|
| **1** M | 07:49 AM | -0.9 | -27 | **16** Tu | 12:19 AM | 2.1 | 64 |
| | 03:10 PM | 1.2 | 37 | | 08:13 AM | -0.7 | -21 |
| | 06:14 PM | 1.0 | 30 | | 03:26 PM | 1.1 | 34 |
| | | | | | 06:45 PM | 0.9 | 27 |
| **2** Tu ○ | 12:35 AM | 2.5 | 76 | **17** W ● | 12:55 AM | 2.1 | 64 |
| | 08:38 AM | -1.0 | -30 | | 08:44 AM | -0.6 | -18 |
| | 03:58 PM | 1.2 | 37 | | 03:45 PM | 1.1 | 34 |
| | 06:59 PM | 1.0 | 30 | | 07:22 PM | 0.9 | 27 |
| **3** W | 01:23 AM | 2.5 | 76 | **18** Th | 01:31 AM | 2.1 | 64 |
| | 09:25 AM | -0.9 | -27 | | 09:14 AM | -0.6 | -18 |
| | 04:41 PM | 1.2 | 37 | | 04:02 PM | 1.1 | 34 |
| | 07:50 PM | 1.0 | 30 | | 08:03 PM | 0.8 | 24 |
| **4** Th | 02:14 AM | 2.4 | 73 | **19** F | 02:09 AM | 2.0 | 61 |
| | 10:11 AM | -0.8 | -24 | | 09:44 AM | -0.5 | -15 |
| | 05:18 PM | 1.2 | 37 | | 04:21 PM | 1.2 | 37 |
| | 08:50 PM | 0.9 | 27 | | 08:49 PM | 0.7 | 21 |
| **5** F | 03:07 AM | 2.2 | 67 | **20** Sa | 02:50 AM | 1.9 | 58 |
| | 10:55 AM | -0.6 | -18 | | 10:15 AM | -0.4 | -12 |
| | 05:54 PM | 1.2 | 37 | | 04:45 PM | 1.3 | 40 |
| | 10:01 PM | 0.8 | 24 | | 09:40 PM | 0.6 | 18 |
| **6** Sa | 04:05 AM | 1.9 | 58 | **21** Su | 03:35 AM | 1.8 | 55 |
| | 11:38 AM | -0.3 | -9 | | 10:47 AM | -0.3 | -9 |
| | 06:29 PM | 1.3 | 40 | | 05:13 PM | 1.4 | 43 |
| | 11:23 PM | 0.8 | 24 | | 10:39 PM | 0.5 | 15 |
| **7** Su | 05:11 AM | 1.6 | 49 | **22** M | 04:27 AM | 1.6 | 49 |
| | 12:20 PM | -0.1 | -3 | | 11:22 AM | -0.1 | -3 |
| | 07:07 PM | 1.4 | 43 | | 05:46 PM | 1.5 | 46 |
| | | | | | 11:47 PM | 0.4 | 12 |
| **8** M ◑ | 12:55 AM | 0.6 | 18 | **23** Tu | 05:30 AM | 1.4 | 43 |
| | 06:33 AM | 1.3 | 40 | | 11:59 AM | 0.1 | 3 |
| | 01:02 PM | 0.2 | 6 | | 06:24 PM | 1.6 | 49 |
| | 07:46 PM | 1.5 | 46 | | | | |
| **9** Tu | 02:27 AM | 0.4 | 12 | **24** W ◑ | 01:05 AM | 0.3 | 9 |
| | 08:18 AM | 1.1 | 34 | | 06:52 AM | 1.1 | 34 |
| | 01:44 PM | 0.4 | 12 | | 12:03 PM | 0.3 | 9 |
| | 08:27 PM | 1.7 | 52 | | 07:06 PM | 1.7 | 52 |
| **10** W | 03:47 AM | 0.1 | 3 | **25** Th | 02:29 AM | 0.1 | 3 |
| | 10:09 AM | 1.0 | 30 | | 08:43 AM | 1.0 | 30 |
| | 02:29 PM | 0.6 | 18 | | 01:24 PM | 0.6 | 18 |
| | 09:08 PM | 1.8 | 55 | | 07:54 PM | 1.8 | 55 |
| **11** Th | 04:50 AM | -0.1 | -3 | **26** F | 03:49 AM | -0.2 | -6 |
| | 11:42 AM | 1.0 | 30 | | 10:49 AM | 1.0 | 30 |
| | 03:17 PM | 0.8 | 24 | | 02:15 PM | 0.8 | 24 |
| | 09:49 PM | 1.9 | 58 | | 08:48 PM | 1.9 | 58 |
| **12** F | 05:42 AM | -0.3 | -9 | **27** Sa | 04:59 AM | -0.5 | -15 |
| | 12:53 PM | 1.1 | 34 | | 12:30 PM | 1.0 | 30 |
| | 04:06 PM | 0.9 | 27 | | 03:14 PM | 0.9 | 27 |
| | 10:29 PM | 1.9 | 58 | | 09:46 PM | 2.1 | 64 |
| **13** Sa | 06:26 AM | -0.5 | -15 | **28** Su | 06:00 AM | -0.7 | -21 |
| | 01:47 PM | 1.1 | 34 | | 01:36 PM | 1.1 | 34 |
| | 04:51 PM | 1.0 | 30 | | 04:18 PM | 1.0 | 30 |
| | 11:07 PM | 2.0 | 61 | | 10:45 PM | 2.2 | 67 |
| **14** Su | 07:05 AM | -0.6 | -18 | **29** M | 06:54 AM | -0.9 | -27 |
| | 02:29 PM | 1.2 | 37 | | 02:22 PM | 1.2 | 37 |
| | 05:33 PM | 1.0 | 30 | | 05:19 PM | 1.0 | 30 |
| | 11:44 PM | 2.0 | 61 | | 11:43 PM | 2.3 | 70 |
| **15** M | 07:41 AM | -0.6 | -18 | **30** Tu | 07:42 AM | -1.0 | -30 |
| | 03:01 PM | 1.2 | 37 | | 02:57 PM | 1.2 | 37 |
| | 06:10 PM | 1.0 | 30 | | 06:17 PM | 0.9 | 27 |
| | | | | **31** W ○ | 12:37 AM | 2.3 | 70 |
| | | | | | 08:26 AM | -0.9 | -27 |
| | | | | | 03:25 PM | 1.2 | 37 |
| | | | | | 07:11 PM | 0.8 | 24 |

## February

| Day | Time | ft | cm | Day | Time | ft | cm |
|---|---|---|---|---|---|---|---|
| **1** Th | 01:30 AM | 2.3 | 70 | **16** F | 01:33 AM | 2.0 | 61 |
| | 09:07 AM | -0.8 | -24 | | 08:46 AM | -0.4 | -12 |
| | 03:51 PM | 1.2 | 37 | | 03:09 PM | 1.3 | 40 |
| | 08:06 PM | 0.7 | 21 | | 08:08 PM | 0.6 | 18 |
| **2** F | 02:21 AM | 2.2 | 67 | **17** Sa | 02:11 AM | 1.9 | 58 |
| | 09:43 AM | -0.6 | -18 | | 09:11 AM | -0.3 | -9 |
| | 04:15 PM | 1.2 | 37 | | 03:25 PM | 1.4 | 43 |
| | 09:03 PM | 0.5 | 15 | | 08:49 PM | 0.4 | 12 |
| **3** Sa | 03:12 AM | 2.0 | 61 | **18** Su | 02:51 AM | 1.8 | 55 |
| | 10:17 AM | -0.4 | -12 | | 09:38 AM | -0.2 | -6 |
| | 04:40 PM | 1.3 | 40 | | 03:46 PM | 1.5 | 46 |
| | 10:02 PM | 0.4 | 12 | | 09:35 PM | 0.3 | 9 |
| **4** Su | 04:04 AM | 1.7 | 52 | **19** M | 03:36 AM | 1.7 | 52 |
| | 10:49 AM | -0.1 | -3 | | 10:05 AM | 0.0 | 0 |
| | 05:08 PM | 1.5 | 46 | | 04:12 PM | 1.6 | 49 |
| | 11:06 PM | 0.3 | 9 | | 10:27 PM | 0.2 | 6 |
| **5** M | 05:03 AM | 1.4 | 43 | **20** Tu | 04:28 AM | 1.5 | 46 |
| | 11:20 AM | 0.2 | 6 | | 10:35 AM | 0.2 | 6 |
| | 05:40 PM | 1.6 | 49 | | 04:43 PM | 1.8 | 55 |
| | | | | | 11:27 PM | 0.1 | 3 |
| **6** Tu ◑ | 12:18 AM | 0.3 | 9 | **21** W | 05:31 AM | 1.3 | 40 |
| | 06:15 AM | 1.1 | 34 | | 10:47 AM | 0.4 | 12 |
| | 11:51 AM | 0.4 | 12 | | 05:19 PM | 1.8 | 55 |
| | 06:16 PM | 1.6 | 49 | | | | |
| **7** W ◑ | 01:37 AM | 0.1 | 3 | **22** Th | 12:39 AM | 0.0 | 0 |
| | 07:55 AM | 0.9 | 27 | | 06:58 AM | 1.1 | 34 |
| | 12:25 PM | 0.6 | 18 | | 11:36 AM | 0.7 | 21 |
| | 06:59 PM | 1.7 | 52 | | 06:03 PM | 1.9 | 58 |
| **8** Th | 02:58 AM | 0.0 | 0 | **23** F ◐ | 02:03 AM | -0.1 | -3 |
| | 10:08 AM | 0.9 | 27 | | 09:14 AM | 1.0 | 30 |
| | 01:05 PM | 0.8 | 24 | | 12:07 PM | 0.9 | 27 |
| | 07:50 PM | 1.7 | 52 | | 06:59 PM | 2.0 | 61 |
| **9** F | 04:11 AM | -0.2 | -6 | **24** Sa | 03:31 AM | -0.3 | -9 |
| | 12:01 PM | 1.0 | 30 | | 08:08 PM | 2.0 | 61 |
| | 02:05 PM | 1.0 | 30 | | | | |
| | 08:49 PM | 1.8 | 55 | | | | |
| **10** Sa | 05:11 AM | -0.3 | -9 | **25** Su | 04:47 AM | -0.5 | -15 |
| | 01:03 PM | 1.1 | 34 | | 09:28 PM | 2.1 | 64 |
| | 03:26 PM | 1.0 | 30 | | | | |
| | 09:50 PM | 1.8 | 55 | | | | |
| **11** Su | 06:01 AM | -0.4 | -12 | **26** M | 05:49 AM | -0.6 | -18 |
| | 01:40 PM | 1.2 | 37 | | 01:31 PM | 1.2 | 37 |
| | 04:37 PM | 1.1 | 34 | | 04:24 PM | 1.1 | 34 |
| | 10:46 PM | 1.8 | 55 | | 10:44 PM | 2.2 | 67 |
| **12** M | 06:43 AM | -0.5 | -15 | **27** Tu | 06:41 AM | -0.7 | -21 |
| | 02:07 PM | 1.2 | 37 | | 01:54 PM | 1.3 | 40 |
| | 05:32 PM | 1.0 | 30 | | 05:36 PM | 1.0 | 30 |
| | 11:35 PM | 1.9 | 58 | | 11:49 PM | 2.2 | 67 |
| **13** Tu | 07:19 AM | -0.5 | -15 | **28** W | 07:25 AM | -0.7 | -21 |
| | 02:29 PM | 1.2 | 37 | | 02:16 PM | 1.3 | 40 |
| | 06:15 PM | 0.9 | 27 | | 06:34 PM | 0.8 | 24 |
| **14** W | 12:17 AM | 2.0 | 61 | | | | |
| | 07:51 AM | -0.5 | -15 | | | | |
| | 02:44 PM | 1.2 | 37 | | | | |
| | 06:53 PM | 0.8 | 24 | | | | |
| **15** Th ● | 12:56 AM | 2.0 | 61 | | | | |
| | 08:19 AM | -0.5 | -15 | | | | |
| | 02:57 PM | 1.2 | 37 | | | | |
| | 07:30 PM | 0.7 | 21 | | | | |

## March

| Day | Time | ft | cm | Day | Time | ft | cm |
|---|---|---|---|---|---|---|---|
| **1** Th | 12:46 AM | 2.2 | 67 | **16** F | 01:53 AM | 1.9 | 58 |
| | 08:02 AM | -0.5 | -15 | | 08:42 AM | -0.1 | -3 |
| | 02:35 PM | 1.4 | 43 | | 03:00 PM | 1.5 | 46 |
| | 07:26 PM | 0.6 | 18 | | 08:28 PM | 0.5 | 15 |
| **2** F | 01:38 AM | 2.1 | 64 | **17** Sa ● | 02:32 AM | 1.9 | 58 |
| | 08:35 AM | -0.4 | -12 | | 09:07 AM | 0.0 | 0 |
| | 02:54 PM | 1.5 | 46 | | 03:13 PM | 1.6 | 49 |
| | 08:15 PM | 0.4 | 12 | | 09:05 PM | 0.3 | 9 |
| **3** Sa | 02:26 AM | 2.0 | 61 | **18** Su | 03:12 AM | 1.9 | 58 |
| | 09:04 AM | -0.1 | -3 | | 09:32 AM | 0.1 | 3 |
| | 03:13 PM | 1.6 | 49 | | 03:30 PM | 1.8 | 55 |
| | 09:03 PM | 0.2 | 6 | | 09:44 PM | 0.1 | 3 |
| **4** Su | 03:13 AM | 1.8 | 55 | **19** M | 03:55 AM | 1.8 | 55 |
| | 09:31 AM | 0.1 | 3 | | 09:56 AM | 0.3 | 9 |
| | 03:34 PM | 1.7 | 52 | | 04:11 PM | 1.9 | 58 |
| | 09:52 PM | 0.1 | 3 | | 10:28 PM | 0.0 | 0 |
| **5** M | 04:02 AM | 1.6 | 49 | **20** Tu | 04:42 AM | 1.6 | 49 |
| | 09:55 AM | 0.3 | 9 | | 10:21 AM | 0.5 | 15 |
| | 03:58 PM | 1.8 | 55 | | 04:19 PM | 2.1 | 64 |
| | 10:44 PM | 0.1 | 3 | | 11:18 PM | -0.1 | -3 |
| **6** Tu | 04:55 AM | 1.4 | 43 | **21** W | 05:38 AM | 1.5 | 46 |
| | 10:19 AM | 0.5 | 15 | | 10:47 AM | 0.7 | 21 |
| | 04:27 PM | 1.9 | 58 | | 04:51 PM | 2.2 | 67 |
| | 11:41 PM | 0.0 | 0 | | | | |
| **7** W | 06:02 AM | 1.2 | 37 | **22** Th | 12:16 AM | -0.2 | -6 |
| | 10:43 AM | 0.7 | 21 | | 06:49 AM | 1.3 | 40 |
| | 04:59 PM | 1.9 | 58 | | 11:11 AM | 0.9 | 27 |
| | | | | | 05:29 PM | 2.2 | 67 |
| **8** Th | 12:46 AM | 0.0 | 0 | **23** F | 01:26 AM | -0.2 | -6 |
| | 07:40 AM | 1.0 | 30 | | 08:37 AM | 1.1 | 34 |
| | 11:05 AM | 0.9 | 27 | | 11:29 AM | 1.0 | 30 |
| | 05:39 PM | 1.9 | 58 | | 06:17 PM | 2.2 | 67 |
| **9** F ◑ | 02:02 AM | 0.0 | 0 | **24** Sa ◐ | 02:48 AM | -0.2 | -6 |
| | 06:31 PM | 1.8 | 55 | | 07:19 PM | 2.1 | 64 |
| **10** Sa | 03:20 AM | -0.1 | -3 | **25** Su | 04:15 AM | -0.3 | -9 |
| | 07:42 PM | 1.8 | 55 | | 08:46 PM | 2.1 | 64 |
| **11** Su | 05:28 AM | -0.1 | -3 | **26** M | 05:29 AM | -0.3 | -9 |
| | 01:44 PM | 1.3 | 40 | | 01:34 PM | 1.4 | 43 |
| | 04:05 PM | 1.2 | 37 | | 04:16 PM | 1.3 | 40 |
| | 10:10 PM | 1.8 | 55 | | 10:26 PM | 2.0 | 61 |
| **12** M | 06:23 AM | -0.2 | -6 | **27** Tu | 06:27 AM | -0.4 | -12 |
| | 02:02 PM | 1.3 | 40 | | 01:48 PM | 1.5 | 46 |
| | 05:35 PM | 1.2 | 37 | | 05:50 PM | 1.1 | 34 |
| | 11:25 PM | 1.8 | 55 | | 11:51 PM | 2.1 | 64 |
| **13** Tu | 07:08 AM | -0.3 | -9 | **28** W | 07:15 AM | -0.3 | -9 |
| | 02:21 PM | 1.4 | 43 | | 02:06 PM | 1.5 | 46 |
| | 06:32 PM | 1.0 | 30 | | 06:55 PM | 0.9 | 27 |
| **14** W | 12:24 AM | 1.9 | 58 | **29** Th | 12:58 AM | 2.1 | 64 |
| | 07:44 AM | -0.3 | -9 | | 07:54 AM | -0.2 | -6 |
| | 02:36 PM | 1.4 | 43 | | 02:24 PM | 1.6 | 49 |
| | 07:15 PM | 0.9 | 27 | | 07:46 PM | 0.6 | 18 |
| **15** Th | 01:11 AM | 1.9 | 58 | **30** F | 01:54 AM | 2.0 | 61 |
| | 08:15 AM | -0.2 | -6 | | 08:26 AM | 0.0 | 0 |
| | 02:49 PM | 1.5 | 46 | | 02:41 PM | 1.8 | 55 |
| | 07:53 PM | 0.7 | 21 | | 08:32 PM | 0.3 | 9 |
| | | | | **31** Sa ○ | 02:44 AM | 1.9 | 58 |
| | | | | | 08:53 AM | 0.2 | 6 |
| | | | | | 02:58 PM | 1.9 | 58 |
| | | | | | 09:15 PM | 0.2 | 6 |

Heights are referred to mean lower water which is the chart datum of sounding. All times are local. Daylight Saving Time has been used when needed. Additional tide tables are available online from NOAA at www.tidesandcurrents.noaa.gov/tide_predictions.shtml.

SKIPPER'S HANDBOOK

StationId: 8726520
Source: NOAA/NOS/CO-OPS
Station Type: Primary
Time Zone: LST_LDT
Datum: MLLW

**NOAA Tide Predictions**

# St Petersburg, Tampa Bay, FL, 2018

### Times and Heights of High and Low Waters

SKIPPER'S HANDBOOK

## April

| Day | Time | ft | cm |
|---|---|---|---|
| **1** Su | 03:30 AM | 1.8 | 55 |
| | 09:17 AM | 0.4 | 12 |
| | 03:17 PM | 2.0 | 61 |
| | 09:56 PM | 0.0 | 0 |
| **2** M | 04:15 AM | 1.7 | 52 |
| | 09:39 AM | 0.6 | 18 |
| | 03:37 PM | 2.1 | 64 |
| | 10:38 PM | -0.1 | -3 |
| **3** Tu | 05:01 AM | 1.5 | 46 |
| | 10:00 AM | 0.8 | 24 |
| | 04:01 PM | 2.2 | 67 |
| | 11:22 PM | -0.1 | -3 |
| **4** W | 05:53 AM | 1.4 | 43 |
| | 10:21 AM | 0.9 | 27 |
| | 04:29 PM | 2.2 | 67 |
| **5** Th | 12:10 AM | -0.1 | -3 |
| | 06:58 AM | 1.3 | 40 |
| | 10:41 AM | 1.0 | 30 |
| | 05:01 PM | 2.2 | 67 |
| **6** F | 01:06 AM | -0.1 | -3 |
| | 08:35 AM | 1.2 | 37 |
| | 10:57 AM | 1.2 | 37 |
| | 05:40 PM | 2.1 | 64 |
| **7** Sa | 02:12 AM | 0.0 | 0 |
| | 06:30 AM | 2.0 | 61 |
| **8** Su | 03:24 AM | 0.0 | 0 |
| | 07:42 PM | 1.9 | 58 |
| **9** M | 04:33 AM | 0.0 | 0 |
| | 12:47 PM | 1.5 | 46 |
| | 03:51 PM | 1.4 | 43 |
| | 09:22 PM | 1.8 | 55 |
| **10** Tu | 05:30 AM | 0.0 | 0 |
| | 01:02 PM | 1.5 | 46 |
| | 05:22 PM | 1.2 | 37 |
| | 10:53 PM | 1.8 | 55 |
| **11** W | 06:16 AM | 0.0 | 0 |
| | 01:19 PM | 1.6 | 49 |
| | 06:19 PM | 1.0 | 30 |
| **12** Th | 12:01 AM | 1.8 | 55 |
| | 06:54 AM | 0.1 | 3 |
| | 01:34 PM | 1.7 | 52 |
| | 07:03 PM | 0.8 | 24 |
| **13** F | 12:56 AM | 1.9 | 58 |
| | 07:27 AM | 0.2 | 6 |
| | 01:47 PM | 1.8 | 55 |
| | 07:41 PM | 0.5 | 15 |
| **14** Sa | 01:43 AM | 1.9 | 58 |
| | 07:55 AM | 0.3 | 9 |
| | 02:02 PM | 1.9 | 58 |
| | 08:19 PM | 0.3 | 9 |
| **15** Su | 02:29 AM | 1.8 | 55 |
| | 08:21 AM | 0.4 | 12 |
| | 02:19 PM | 2.1 | 64 |
| | 08:57 PM | 0.1 | 3 |
| **16** M ● | 03:15 AM | 1.8 | 55 |
| | 08:46 AM | 0.6 | 18 |
| | 02:40 PM | 2.2 | 67 |
| | 09:38 PM | -0.1 | -3 |
| **17** Tu | 04:03 AM | 1.7 | 52 |
| | 09:10 AM | 0.8 | 24 |
| | 03:06 PM | 2.4 | 73 |
| | 10:23 PM | -0.3 | -9 |
| **18** W | 04:58 AM | 1.6 | 49 |
| | 09:35 AM | 0.9 | 27 |
| | 03:37 PM | 2.5 | 76 |
| | 11:14 PM | -0.3 | -9 |
| **19** Th | 06:02 AM | 1.4 | 43 |
| | 09:58 AM | 1.1 | 34 |
| | 04:14 PM | 2.5 | 76 |
| **20** F | 12:12 AM | -0.3 | -9 |
| | 07:30 AM | 1.3 | 40 |
| | 10:16 AM | 1.2 | 37 |
| | 04:57 PM | 2.5 | 76 |
| **21** Sa | 01:21 AM | -0.3 | -9 |
| | 05:49 PM | 2.4 | 73 |
| **22** Su ◐ | 02:37 AM | -0.2 | -6 |
| | 07:00 AM | 2.2 | 67 |
| **23** M | 03:52 AM | -0.2 | -6 |
| | 12:24 PM | 1.5 | 46 |
| | 02:38 PM | 1.5 | 46 |
| | 08:42 PM | 2.0 | 61 |
| **24** Tu | 04:58 AM | -0.1 | -3 |
| | 12:34 PM | 1.6 | 49 |
| | 04:48 PM | 1.3 | 40 |
| | 10:30 PM | 1.9 | 58 |
| **25** W | 05:51 AM | 0.0 | 0 |
| | 12:52 PM | 1.7 | 52 |
| | 06:05 PM | 1.0 | 30 |
| | 11:55 PM | 1.9 | 58 |
| **26** Th | 06:35 AM | 0.1 | 3 |
| | 01:12 PM | 1.8 | 55 |
| | 07:02 PM | 0.6 | 18 |
| **27** F | 01:03 AM | 1.9 | 58 |
| | 07:10 AM | 0.3 | 9 |
| | 01:31 PM | 2.0 | 61 |
| | 07:49 PM | 0.4 | 12 |
| **28** Sa | 02:00 AM | 1.8 | 55 |
| | 07:39 AM | 0.5 | 15 |
| | 01:49 PM | 2.1 | 64 |
| | 08:31 PM | 0.1 | 3 |
| **29** Su | 02:50 AM | 1.7 | 52 |
| | 08:04 AM | 0.7 | 21 |
| | 02:08 PM | 2.3 | 70 |
| | 09:10 PM | 0.0 | 0 |
| **30** M ○ | 03:37 AM | 1.6 | 49 |
| | 08:25 AM | 0.9 | 27 |
| | 02:28 PM | 2.4 | 73 |
| | 09:47 PM | -0.1 | -3 |

## May

| Day | Time | ft | cm |
|---|---|---|---|
| **1** Tu ● | 04:22 AM | 1.5 | 46 |
| | 08:45 AM | 1.0 | 30 |
| | 02:51 PM | 2.4 | 73 |
| | 10:24 PM | -0.2 | -6 |
| **2** W | 05:07 AM | 1.4 | 43 |
| | 09:06 AM | 1.1 | 34 |
| | 03:17 PM | 2.5 | 76 |
| | 11:03 PM | -0.2 | -6 |
| **3** Th | 05:58 AM | 1.4 | 43 |
| | 09:28 AM | 1.2 | 37 |
| | 03:47 PM | 2.5 | 76 |
| | 11:47 PM | -0.2 | -6 |
| **4** F | 07:00 AM | 1.3 | 40 |
| | 09:51 AM | 1.2 | 37 |
| | 04:22 PM | 2.4 | 73 |
| **5** Sa | 12:36 AM | -0.1 | -3 |
| | 05:03 PM | 2.3 | 70 |
| **6** Su | 01:31 AM | 0.0 | 0 |
| | 05:54 PM | 2.1 | 64 |
| **7** M | 02:32 AM | 0.0 | 0 |
| | 10:56 AM | 1.5 | 46 |
| | 01:11 PM | 1.5 | 46 |
| | 07:02 PM | 1.9 | 58 |
| **8** Tu ◐ | 03:31 AM | 0.0 | 0 |
| | 11:22 AM | 1.6 | 49 |
| | 03:22 PM | 1.4 | 43 |
| | 08:34 PM | 1.8 | 55 |
| **9** W | 04:26 AM | 0.2 | 6 |
| | 11:45 AM | 1.7 | 52 |
| | 04:51 PM | 1.2 | 37 |
| | 10:10 PM | 1.7 | 52 |
| **10** Th | 05:13 AM | 0.3 | 9 |
| | 12:06 PM | 1.8 | 55 |
| | 05:52 PM | 0.9 | 27 |
| | 11:29 PM | 1.7 | 52 |
| **11** F | 05:53 AM | 0.4 | 12 |
| | 12:25 PM | 1.9 | 58 |
| | 06:41 PM | 0.6 | 18 |
| **12** Sa | 12:35 AM | 1.7 | 52 |
| | 06:29 AM | 0.5 | 15 |
| | 12:45 PM | 2.1 | 64 |
| | 07:23 PM | 0.3 | 9 |
| **13** Su | 01:33 AM | 1.7 | 52 |
| | 07:01 AM | 0.7 | 21 |
| | 01:06 PM | 2.2 | 67 |
| | 08:05 PM | 0.1 | 3 |
| **14** M | 02:28 AM | 1.7 | 52 |
| | 07:30 AM | 0.8 | 24 |
| | 01:31 PM | 2.4 | 73 |
| | 08:47 PM | -0.2 | -6 |
| **15** Tu ● | 03:23 AM | 1.6 | 49 |
| | 07:57 AM | 1.0 | 30 |
| | 01:59 PM | 2.6 | 79 |
| | 09:32 PM | -0.4 | -12 |
| **16** W | 04:20 AM | 1.6 | 49 |
| | 08:23 AM | 1.1 | 34 |
| | 02:32 PM | 2.7 | 82 |
| | 10:21 PM | -0.5 | -15 |
| **17** Th | 05:23 AM | 1.5 | 46 |
| | 08:48 AM | 1.2 | 37 |
| | 03:10 PM | 2.8 | 85 |
| | 11:14 PM | -0.5 | -15 |
| **18** F | 06:38 AM | 1.4 | 43 |
| | 09:13 AM | 1.3 | 40 |
| | 03:53 PM | 2.7 | 82 |
| **19** Sa | 12:11 AM | -0.5 | -15 |
| | 04:43 PM | 2.6 | 79 |
| **20** Su | 01:13 AM | -0.4 | -12 |
| | 05:43 PM | 2.4 | 73 |
| **21** M | 02:17 AM | -0.2 | -6 |
| | 10:36 AM | 1.5 | 46 |
| | 12:48 PM | 1.5 | 46 |
| | 07:01 PM | 2.2 | 67 |
| **22** Tu ◐ | 03:19 AM | 0.0 | 0 |
| | 11:01 AM | 1.6 | 49 |
| | 03:10 PM | 1.4 | 43 |
| | 08:43 PM | 1.9 | 58 |
| **23** W ◑ | 04:15 AM | 0.1 | 3 |
| | 11:26 AM | 1.8 | 55 |
| | 04:52 PM | 1.1 | 34 |
| | 10:28 PM | 1.8 | 55 |
| **24** Th | 05:03 AM | 0.3 | 9 |
| | 11:52 AM | 1.9 | 58 |
| | 06:04 PM | 0.7 | 21 |
| | 11:55 PM | 1.7 | 52 |
| **25** F | 05:43 AM | 0.6 | 18 |
| | 12:17 PM | 2.1 | 64 |
| | 06:58 PM | 0.4 | 12 |
| **26** Sa | 01:07 AM | 1.6 | 49 |
| | 06:17 AM | 0.8 | 24 |
| | 12:40 PM | 2.2 | 67 |
| | 07:44 PM | 0.2 | 6 |
| **27** Su | 02:08 AM | 1.6 | 49 |
| | 06:46 AM | 0.9 | 27 |
| | 01:03 PM | 2.4 | 73 |
| | 08:25 PM | 0.0 | 0 |
| **28** M | 03:02 AM | 1.5 | 46 |
| | 07:11 AM | 1.1 | 34 |
| | 01:26 PM | 2.5 | 76 |
| | 09:02 PM | -0.2 | -6 |
| **29** Tu ○ | 03:51 AM | 1.5 | 46 |
| | 07:34 AM | 1.2 | 37 |
| | 01:50 PM | 2.5 | 76 |
| | 09:37 PM | -0.2 | -6 |
| **30** W | 04:36 AM | 1.4 | 43 |
| | 07:56 AM | 1.2 | 37 |
| | 02:17 PM | 2.6 | 79 |
| | 10:12 PM | -0.3 | -9 |
| **31** Th | 05:19 AM | 1.4 | 43 |
| | 08:21 AM | 1.3 | 40 |
| | 02:47 PM | 2.6 | 79 |
| | 10:49 PM | -0.2 | -6 |

## June

| Day | Time | ft | cm |
|---|---|---|---|
| **1** F | 06:03 AM | 1.4 | 43 |
| | 03:21 PM | 2.5 | 76 |
| | 11:28 PM | -0.2 | -6 |
| **2** Sa | 06:49 AM | 1.4 | 43 |
| | 09:26 AM | 1.3 | 40 |
| | 04:00 PM | 2.5 | 76 |
| **3** Su | 12:11 AM | -0.1 | -3 |
| | 07:38 AM | 1.4 | 43 |
| | 10:16 AM | 1.4 | 43 |
| | 04:44 PM | 2.4 | 73 |
| **4** M | 12:56 AM | -0.1 | -3 |
| | 08:26 AM | 1.5 | 46 |
| | 11:27 AM | 1.4 | 43 |
| | 05:35 PM | 2.2 | 67 |
| **5** Tu | 01:43 AM | 0.0 | 0 |
| | 09:09 AM | 1.6 | 49 |
| | 01:01 PM | 1.4 | 43 |
| | 06:37 PM | 2.0 | 61 |
| **6** W ◑ | 02:32 AM | 0.2 | 6 |
| | 09:45 AM | 1.7 | 52 |
| | 02:41 PM | 1.3 | 40 |
| | 07:56 PM | 1.8 | 55 |
| **7** Th | 03:19 AM | 0.3 | 9 |
| | 10:18 AM | 1.8 | 55 |
| | 04:08 PM | 1.1 | 34 |
| | 09:27 PM | 1.6 | 49 |
| **8** F | 04:05 AM | 0.5 | 15 |
| | 10:48 AM | 2.0 | 61 |
| | 05:17 PM | 0.8 | 24 |
| | 10:57 PM | 1.6 | 49 |
| **9** Sa | 04:48 AM | 0.6 | 18 |
| | 11:17 AM | 2.1 | 64 |
| | 06:13 PM | 0.5 | 15 |
| **10** Su | 12:17 AM | 1.5 | 46 |
| | 05:27 AM | 0.8 | 24 |
| | 11:47 AM | 2.3 | 70 |
| | 07:04 PM | 0.2 | 6 |
| **11** M | 01:29 AM | 1.5 | 46 |
| | 06:04 AM | 1.0 | 30 |
| | 12:18 PM | 2.5 | 76 |
| | 07:52 PM | -0.1 | -3 |
| **12** Tu | 02:35 AM | 1.5 | 46 |
| | 06:38 AM | 1.1 | 34 |
| | 12:53 PM | 2.6 | 79 |
| | 08:40 PM | -0.4 | -12 |
| **13** W ● | 03:39 AM | 1.5 | 46 |
| | 07:10 AM | 1.2 | 37 |
| | 01:31 PM | 2.8 | 85 |
| | 09:29 PM | -0.5 | -15 |
| **14** Th | 04:41 AM | 1.5 | 46 |
| | 07:42 AM | 1.3 | 40 |
| | 02:13 PM | 2.9 | 88 |
| | 10:19 PM | -0.6 | -18 |
| **15** F | 05:42 AM | 1.4 | 43 |
| | 08:17 AM | 1.4 | 43 |
| | 02:59 PM | 2.9 | 88 |
| | 11:10 PM | -0.5 | -15 |
| **16** Sa | 06:43 AM | 1.4 | 43 |
| | 09:01 AM | 1.4 | 43 |
| | 03:49 PM | 2.8 | 85 |
| **17** Su | 12:03 AM | -0.4 | -12 |
| | 07:38 AM | 1.4 | 43 |
| | 10:03 AM | 1.4 | 43 |
| | 04:45 PM | 2.6 | 79 |
| **18** M | 12:55 AM | -0.3 | -9 |
| | 08:24 AM | 1.5 | 46 |
| | 11:30 AM | 1.4 | 43 |
| | 05:48 PM | 2.4 | 73 |
| **19** Tu | 01:46 AM | 0.0 | 0 |
| | 09:03 AM | 1.6 | 49 |
| | 01:16 PM | 1.3 | 40 |
| | 07:05 PM | 2.1 | 64 |
| **20** W ◐ | 02:35 AM | 0.2 | 6 |
| | 09:40 AM | 1.8 | 55 |
| | 03:04 PM | 1.1 | 34 |
| | 08:39 PM | 1.8 | 55 |
| **21** Th | 03:22 AM | 0.5 | 15 |
| | 10:15 AM | 1.9 | 58 |
| | 04:36 PM | 0.8 | 24 |
| | 10:21 PM | 1.6 | 49 |
| **22** F | 04:05 AM | 0.7 | 21 |
| | 10:49 AM | 2.1 | 64 |
| | 05:48 PM | 0.5 | 15 |
| | 11:55 PM | 1.5 | 46 |
| **23** Sa | 04:45 AM | 0.9 | 27 |
| | 11:23 AM | 2.3 | 70 |
| | 06:45 PM | 0.3 | 9 |
| **24** Su | 01:14 AM | 1.5 | 46 |
| | 05:22 AM | 1.1 | 34 |
| | 11:55 AM | 2.4 | 73 |
| | 07:33 PM | 0.1 | 3 |
| **25** M | 02:21 AM | 1.5 | 46 |
| | 05:56 AM | 1.2 | 37 |
| | 12:26 PM | 2.5 | 76 |
| | 08:14 PM | -0.1 | -3 |
| **26** Tu | 03:17 AM | 1.5 | 46 |
| | 06:27 AM | 1.3 | 40 |
| | 12:57 PM | 2.5 | 76 |
| | 08:52 PM | -0.1 | -3 |
| **27** W | 04:04 AM | 1.5 | 46 |
| | 06:57 AM | 1.3 | 40 |
| | 01:27 PM | 2.6 | 79 |
| | 09:27 PM | -0.2 | -6 |
| **28** Th ○ | 04:42 AM | 1.5 | 46 |
| | 07:27 AM | 1.3 | 40 |
| | 01:59 PM | 2.6 | 79 |
| | 10:01 PM | -0.2 | -6 |
| **29** F | 05:14 AM | 1.5 | 46 |
| | 08:01 AM | 1.3 | 40 |
| | 02:33 PM | 2.6 | 79 |
| | 10:34 PM | -0.2 | -6 |
| **30** Sa | 05:41 AM | 1.4 | 43 |
| | 08:40 AM | 1.3 | 40 |
| | 03:10 PM | 2.6 | 79 |
| | 11:08 PM | -0.1 | -3 |

Heights are referred to mean lower water which is the chart datum of sounding. All times are local. Daylight Saving Time has been used when needed. Additional tide tables are available online from NOAA at www.tidesandcurrents.noaa.gov/tide_predictions.shtml.

StationId: 8726520
Source: NOAA/NOS/CO-OPS
Station Type: Primary
Time Zone: LST_LDT
Datum: MLLW

**NOAA Tide Predictions**

# St Petersburg, Tampa Bay, FL, 2018

### Times and Heights of High and Low Waters

## July

| Day | Time | ft | cm |
|---|---|---|---|
| 1 Su | 06:07 AM | 1.5 | 46 |
|  | 09:27 AM | 1.3 | 40 |
|  | 03:51 PM | 2.5 | 76 |
|  | 11:43 PM | -0.1 | -3 |
| 2 M | 06:34 AM | 1.5 | 46 |
|  | 10:22 AM | 1.3 | 40 |
|  | 04:34 PM | 2.4 | 73 |
| 3 Tu | 12:19 AM | 0.0 | 0 |
|  | 07:06 AM | 1.6 | 49 |
|  | 11:26 AM | 1.3 | 40 |
|  | 05:24 PM | 2.2 | 67 |
| 4 W | 12:57 AM | 0.2 | 6 |
|  | 07:40 AM | 1.7 | 52 |
|  | 12:39 PM | 1.2 | 37 |
|  | 06:21 PM | 2.0 | 61 |
| 5 Th | 01:36 AM | 0.3 | 9 |
|  | 08:16 AM | 1.8 | 55 |
|  | 02:00 PM | 1.1 | 34 |
|  | 07:30 PM | 1.8 | 55 |
| 6 F | 02:17 AM | 0.5 | 15 |
|  | 08:54 AM | 2.0 | 61 |
|  | 03:22 PM | 0.9 | 27 |
|  | 08:56 PM | 1.6 | 49 |
| 7 Sa | 03:00 AM | 0.7 | 21 |
|  | 09:34 AM | 2.1 | 64 |
|  | 04:39 PM | 0.6 | 18 |
|  | 10:35 PM | 1.5 | 46 |
| 8 Su | 03:44 AM | 0.9 | 27 |
|  | 10:14 AM | 2.3 | 70 |
|  | 05:46 PM | 0.4 | 12 |
| 9 M | 12:12 AM | 1.5 | 46 |
|  | 04:28 AM | 1.1 | 34 |
|  | 10:57 AM | 2.5 | 76 |
|  | 06:46 PM | 0.1 | 3 |
| 10 Tu | 01:37 AM | 1.5 | 46 |
|  | 05:12 AM | 1.2 | 37 |
|  | 11:42 AM | 2.6 | 79 |
|  | 07:41 PM | -0.2 | -6 |
| 11 W | 02:49 AM | 1.5 | 46 |
|  | 05:56 AM | 1.3 | 40 |
|  | 12:30 PM | 2.8 | 85 |
|  | 08:33 PM | -0.4 | -12 |
| 12 Th | 03:48 AM | 1.5 | 46 |
|  | 06:40 AM | 1.4 | 43 |
|  | 01:19 PM | 2.9 | 88 |
|  | 09:23 PM | -0.5 | -15 |
| 13 F | 04:37 AM | 1.5 | 46 |
|  | 07:28 AM | 1.4 | 43 |
|  | 02:09 PM | 3.0 | 91 |
|  | 10:11 PM | -0.5 | -15 |
| 14 Sa | 05:18 AM | 1.5 | 46 |
|  | 08:21 AM | 1.3 | 40 |
|  | 03:01 PM | 2.9 | 88 |
|  | 10:57 PM | -0.4 | -12 |
| 15 Su | 05:54 AM | 1.5 | 46 |
|  | 09:21 AM | 1.3 | 40 |
|  | 03:54 PM | 2.8 | 85 |
|  | 11:41 PM | -0.2 | -6 |
| 16 M | 06:28 AM | 1.6 | 49 |
|  | 10:28 AM | 1.2 | 37 |
|  | 04:51 PM | 2.6 | 79 |
| 17 Tu | 12:23 AM | 0.0 | 0 |
|  | 07:02 AM | 1.7 | 52 |
|  | 11:44 AM | 1.1 | 34 |
|  | 05:52 PM | 2.3 | 70 |
| 18 W | 01:03 AM | 0.3 | 9 |
|  | 07:38 AM | 1.8 | 55 |
|  | 01:08 PM | 1.0 | 30 |
|  | 07:03 PM | 2.0 | 61 |
| 19 Th | 01:42 AM | 0.6 | 18 |
|  | 08:17 AM | 2.0 | 61 |
|  | 02:38 PM | 0.9 | 27 |
|  | 08:30 PM | 1.7 | 52 |
| 20 F | 02:22 AM | 0.8 | 24 |
|  | 08:59 AM | 2.1 | 64 |
|  | 04:05 PM | 0.7 | 21 |
|  | 10:15 PM | 1.5 | 46 |
| 21 Sa | 03:03 AM | 1.0 | 30 |
|  | 09:44 AM | 2.2 | 67 |
|  | 05:21 PM | 0.5 | 15 |
|  | 11:59 PM | 1.5 | 46 |
| 22 Su | 03:47 AM | 1.2 | 37 |
|  | 10:31 AM | 2.3 | 70 |
|  | 06:23 PM | 0.3 | 9 |
| 23 M | 01:24 AM | 1.5 | 46 |
|  | 04:35 AM | 1.3 | 40 |
|  | 11:16 AM | 2.4 | 73 |
|  | 07:14 PM | 0.1 | 3 |
| 24 Tu | 02:27 AM | 1.5 | 46 |
|  | 05:23 AM | 1.4 | 43 |
|  | 12:00 PM | 2.5 | 76 |
|  | 07:57 PM | 0.0 | 0 |
| 25 W | 03:14 AM | 1.6 | 49 |
|  | 06:09 AM | 1.4 | 43 |
|  | 12:41 PM | 2.5 | 76 |
|  | 08:36 PM | 0.0 | 0 |
| 26 Th | 03:49 AM | 1.6 | 49 |
|  | 06:51 AM | 1.4 | 43 |
|  | 01:19 PM | 2.6 | 79 |
|  | 09:10 PM | 0.0 | 0 |
| 27 F | 04:14 AM | 1.6 | 49 |
|  | 07:29 AM | 1.4 | 43 |
|  | 01:56 PM | 2.6 | 79 |
|  | 09:42 PM | 0.0 | 0 |
| 28 Sa | 04:33 AM | 1.6 | 49 |
|  | 08:08 AM | 1.3 | 40 |
|  | 02:32 PM | 2.6 | 79 |
|  | 10:11 PM | 0.0 | 0 |
| 29 Su | 04:49 AM | 1.6 | 49 |
|  | 08:49 AM | 1.3 | 40 |
|  | 03:08 PM | 2.6 | 79 |
|  | 10:39 PM | 0.1 | 3 |
| 30 M | 05:06 AM | 1.7 | 52 |
|  | 09:33 AM | 1.2 | 37 |
|  | 03:47 PM | 2.5 | 76 |
|  | 11:08 PM | 0.2 | 6 |
| 31 Tu | 05:26 AM | 1.7 | 52 |
|  | 10:21 AM | 1.1 | 34 |
|  | 04:29 PM | 2.4 | 73 |
|  | 11:38 PM | 0.3 | 9 |

## August

| Day | Time | ft | cm |
|---|---|---|---|
| 1 W | 05:52 AM | 1.9 | 58 |
|  | 11:15 AM | 1.0 | 30 |
|  | 05:16 PM | 2.3 | 70 |
| 2 Th | 12:09 AM | 0.5 | 15 |
|  | 06:23 AM | 2.0 | 61 |
|  | 12:15 PM | 1.0 | 30 |
|  | 06:10 PM | 2.1 | 64 |
| 3 F | 12:43 AM | 0.7 | 21 |
|  | 06:59 AM | 2.1 | 64 |
|  | 01:25 PM | 0.9 | 27 |
|  | 07:17 PM | 1.8 | 55 |
| 4 Sa | 01:20 AM | 0.9 | 27 |
|  | 07:40 AM | 2.2 | 67 |
|  | 02:43 PM | 0.7 | 21 |
|  | 08:45 PM | 1.6 | 49 |
| 5 Su | 02:01 AM | 1.1 | 34 |
|  | 08:27 AM | 2.3 | 70 |
|  | 04:06 PM | 0.5 | 15 |
|  | 10:36 PM | 1.5 | 46 |
| 6 M | 02:46 AM | 1.3 | 40 |
|  | 09:21 AM | 2.5 | 76 |
|  | 05:24 PM | 0.3 | 9 |
| 7 Tu | 12:29 AM | 1.5 | 46 |
|  | 03:40 AM | 1.4 | 43 |
|  | 10:21 AM | 2.6 | 79 |
|  | 06:31 PM | 0.1 | 3 |
| 8 W | 01:51 AM | 1.6 | 49 |
|  | 04:41 AM | 1.5 | 46 |
|  | 11:22 AM | 2.7 | 82 |
|  | 07:29 PM | -0.1 | -3 |
| 9 Th | 02:46 AM | 1.6 | 49 |
|  | 05:44 AM | 1.5 | 46 |
|  | 12:23 PM | 2.9 | 88 |
|  | 08:21 PM | -0.2 | -6 |
| 10 F | 03:25 AM | 1.6 | 49 |
|  | 06:44 AM | 1.4 | 43 |
|  | 01:20 PM | 3.0 | 91 |
|  | 09:08 PM | -0.2 | -6 |
| 11 Sa | 03:56 AM | 1.6 | 49 |
|  | 07:41 AM | 1.3 | 40 |
|  | 02:14 PM | 3.0 | 91 |
|  | 09:50 PM | -0.1 | -3 |
| 12 Su | 04:23 AM | 1.7 | 52 |
|  | 08:38 AM | 1.2 | 37 |
|  | 03:07 PM | 2.9 | 88 |
|  | 10:29 PM | 0.0 | 0 |
| 13 M | 04:48 AM | 1.8 | 55 |
|  | 09:34 AM | 1.0 | 30 |
|  | 04:00 PM | 2.7 | 82 |
|  | 11:05 PM | 0.1 | 3 |
| 14 Tu | 05:14 AM | 1.9 | 58 |
|  | 10:33 AM | 0.9 | 27 |
|  | 04:53 PM | 2.5 | 76 |
|  | 11:38 PM | 0.5 | 15 |
| 15 W | 05:43 AM | 2.0 | 61 |
|  | 11:36 AM | 0.9 | 27 |
|  | 05:50 PM | 2.2 | 67 |
| 16 Th | 12:10 AM | 0.8 | 24 |
|  | 06:15 AM | 2.1 | 64 |
|  | 12:45 PM | 0.8 | 24 |
|  | 06:57 PM | 1.9 | 58 |
| 17 F | 12:42 AM | 1.0 | 30 |
|  | 06:53 AM | 2.2 | 67 |
|  | 02:01 PM | 0.7 | 21 |
|  | 08:23 PM | 1.7 | 52 |
| 18 Sa | 01:17 AM | 1.2 | 37 |
|  | 07:38 AM | 2.3 | 70 |
|  | 03:23 PM | 0.7 | 21 |
|  | 10:15 PM | 1.6 | 49 |
| 19 Su | 01:59 AM | 1.4 | 43 |
|  | 08:33 AM | 2.3 | 70 |
|  | 04:42 PM | 0.5 | 15 |
| 20 M | 12:07 AM | 1.6 | 49 |
|  | 02:56 AM | 1.5 | 46 |
|  | 09:37 AM | 2.3 | 70 |
|  | 05:49 PM | 0.4 | 12 |
| 21 Tu | 01:21 AM | 1.7 | 52 |
|  | 04:10 AM | 1.6 | 49 |
|  | 10:44 AM | 2.4 | 73 |
|  | 06:44 PM | 0.3 | 9 |
| 22 W | 02:06 AM | 1.7 | 52 |
|  | 05:20 AM | 1.6 | 49 |
|  | 11:44 AM | 2.5 | 76 |
|  | 07:30 PM | 0.3 | 9 |
| 23 Th | 02:38 AM | 1.8 | 55 |
|  | 06:16 AM | 1.6 | 49 |
|  | 12:34 PM | 2.5 | 76 |
|  | 08:08 PM | 0.2 | 6 |
| 24 F | 03:02 AM | 1.8 | 55 |
|  | 07:00 AM | 1.4 | 43 |
|  | 01:17 PM | 2.6 | 79 |
|  | 08:42 PM | 0.2 | 6 |
| 25 Sa | 03:20 AM | 1.8 | 55 |
|  | 07:39 AM | 1.3 | 40 |
|  | 01:56 PM | 2.6 | 79 |
|  | 09:10 PM | 0.3 | 9 |
| 26 Su | 03:34 AM | 1.8 | 55 |
|  | 08:15 AM | 1.2 | 37 |
|  | 02:32 PM | 2.6 | 79 |
|  | 09:36 PM | 0.4 | 12 |
| 27 M | 03:46 AM | 1.9 | 58 |
|  | 08:52 AM | 1.1 | 34 |
|  | 03:07 PM | 2.6 | 79 |
|  | 10:01 PM | 0.5 | 15 |
| 28 Tu | 04:01 AM | 2.0 | 61 |
|  | 09:31 AM | 1.0 | 30 |
|  | 03:45 PM | 2.5 | 76 |
|  | 10:26 PM | 0.6 | 18 |
| 29 W | 04:21 AM | 2.1 | 64 |
|  | 10:13 AM | 0.8 | 24 |
|  | 04:26 PM | 2.4 | 73 |
|  | 10:52 PM | 0.7 | 21 |
| 30 Th | 04:46 AM | 2.2 | 67 |
|  | 11:00 AM | 0.8 | 24 |
|  | 05:13 PM | 2.2 | 67 |
|  | 11:20 PM | 0.9 | 27 |
| 31 F | 05:16 AM | 2.3 | 70 |
|  | 11:54 AM | 0.7 | 21 |
|  | 06:09 PM | 2.0 | 61 |
|  | 11:51 PM | 1.1 | 34 |

## September

| Day | Time | ft | cm |
|---|---|---|---|
| 1 Sa | 05:52 AM | 2.4 | 73 |
|  | 12:59 PM | 0.6 | 18 |
|  | 07:20 PM | 1.8 | 55 |
| 2 Su | 12:24 AM | 1.3 | 40 |
|  | 06:36 AM | 2.5 | 76 |
|  | 02:17 PM | 0.6 | 18 |
|  | 09:00 PM | 1.7 | 52 |
| 3 M | 01:03 AM | 1.4 | 43 |
|  | 07:31 AM | 2.5 | 76 |
|  | 03:44 PM | 0.5 | 15 |
|  | 11:13 PM | 1.6 | 49 |
| 4 Tu | 01:56 AM | 1.6 | 49 |
|  | 08:40 AM | 2.6 | 79 |
|  | 05:06 PM | 0.3 | 9 |
| 5 W | 12:51 AM | 1.7 | 52 |
|  | 03:20 AM | 1.6 | 49 |
|  | 10:00 AM | 2.6 | 79 |
|  | 06:15 PM | 0.2 | 6 |
| 6 Th | 01:40 AM | 1.8 | 55 |
|  | 04:50 AM | 1.6 | 49 |
|  | 11:19 AM | 2.7 | 82 |
|  | 07:12 PM | 0.1 | 3 |
| 7 F | 02:12 AM | 1.8 | 55 |
|  | 06:02 AM | 1.5 | 46 |
|  | 12:27 PM | 2.8 | 85 |
|  | 07:59 PM | 0.1 | 3 |
| 8 Sa | 02:38 AM | 1.8 | 55 |
|  | 07:03 AM | 1.3 | 40 |
|  | 01:27 PM | 2.9 | 88 |
|  | 08:41 PM | 0.2 | 6 |
| 9 Su | 03:01 AM | 1.9 | 58 |
|  | 07:46 AM | 1.1 | 34 |
|  | 02:21 PM | 2.8 | 85 |
|  | 09:17 PM | 0.3 | 9 |
| 10 M | 03:22 AM | 2.0 | 61 |
|  | 08:47 AM | 0.9 | 27 |
|  | 03:12 PM | 2.7 | 82 |
|  | 09:48 PM | 0.6 | 18 |
| 11 Tu | 03:43 AM | 2.1 | 64 |
|  | 09:37 AM | 0.7 | 21 |
|  | 04:02 PM | 2.5 | 76 |
|  | 10:17 PM | 0.8 | 24 |
| 12 W | 04:06 AM | 2.2 | 67 |
|  | 10:03 AM | 0.6 | 18 |
|  | 04:53 PM | 2.3 | 70 |
|  | 10:44 PM | 1.0 | 30 |
| 13 Th | 04:32 AM | 2.4 | 73 |
|  | 11:19 AM | 0.6 | 18 |
|  | 05:48 PM | 2.1 | 64 |
|  | 11:10 PM | 1.2 | 37 |
| 14 F | 05:02 AM | 2.4 | 73 |
|  | 12:16 PM | 0.5 | 15 |
|  | 06:53 PM | 1.9 | 58 |
|  | 11:38 PM | 1.4 | 43 |
| 15 Sa | 05:38 AM | 2.4 | 73 |
|  | 01:21 PM | 0.6 | 18 |
|  | 08:21 PM | 1.7 | 52 |
| 16 Su | 12:09 AM | 1.5 | 46 |
|  | 06:21 AM | 2.4 | 73 |
|  | 02:35 PM | 0.6 | 18 |
|  | 10:23 PM | 1.7 | 52 |
| 17 M | 12:53 AM | 1.6 | 49 |
|  | 07:18 AM | 2.3 | 70 |
|  | 03:54 PM | 0.6 | 18 |
| 18 Tu | 12:03 AM | 1.8 | 55 |
|  | 07:31 AM | 2.5 | 76 |
|  | 08:39 AM | 2.3 | 70 |
|  | 05:05 PM | 0.5 | 15 |
| 19 W | 12:50 AM | 1.8 | 55 |
|  | 04:09 AM | 1.7 | 52 |
|  | 10:11 AM | 2.3 | 70 |
|  | 06:03 PM | 0.5 | 15 |
| 20 Th | 01:21 AM | 1.9 | 58 |
|  | 05:26 AM | 1.6 | 49 |
|  | 11:26 AM | 2.3 | 70 |
|  | 06:49 PM | 0.4 | 12 |
| 21 F | 01:45 AM | 1.9 | 58 |
|  | 06:19 AM | 1.4 | 43 |
|  | 12:23 PM | 2.4 | 73 |
|  | 07:28 PM | 0.5 | 15 |
| 22 Sa | 02:04 AM | 2.0 | 61 |
|  | 07:01 AM | 1.3 | 40 |
|  | 01:10 PM | 2.5 | 76 |
|  | 08:00 PM | 0.5 | 15 |
| 23 Su | 02:19 AM | 2.0 | 61 |
|  | 07:38 AM | 1.1 | 34 |
|  | 01:50 PM | 2.5 | 76 |
|  | 08:27 PM | 0.6 | 18 |
| 24 M | 02:32 AM | 2.1 | 64 |
|  | 08:12 AM | 0.9 | 27 |
|  | 02:28 PM | 2.5 | 76 |
|  | 08:52 PM | 0.7 | 21 |
| 25 Tu | 02:45 AM | 2.1 | 64 |
|  | 08:46 AM | 0.8 | 24 |
|  | 03:05 PM | 2.4 | 73 |
|  | 09:15 PM | 0.8 | 24 |
| 26 W | 03:01 AM | 2.3 | 70 |
|  | 09:23 AM | 0.6 | 18 |
|  | 03:44 PM | 2.3 | 70 |
|  | 09:38 PM | 1.0 | 30 |
| 27 Th | 03:23 AM | 2.4 | 73 |
|  | 10:03 AM | 0.5 | 15 |
|  | 04:28 PM | 2.2 | 67 |
|  | 10:03 PM | 1.1 | 34 |
| 28 F | 03:49 AM | 2.5 | 76 |
|  | 10:48 AM | 0.4 | 12 |
|  | 05:18 PM | 2.1 | 64 |
|  | 10:29 PM | 1.3 | 40 |
| 29 Sa | 04:21 AM | 2.6 | 79 |
|  | 11:41 AM | 0.3 | 9 |
|  | 06:20 PM | 1.9 | 58 |
|  | 10:57 PM | 1.4 | 43 |
| 30 Su | 04:59 AM | 2.6 | 79 |
|  | 12:45 PM | 0.3 | 9 |
|  | 07:45 PM | 1.7 | 52 |
|  | 11:27 PM | 1.5 | 46 |

Heights are referred to mean lower water which is the chart datum of sounding. All times are local. Daylight Saving Time has been used when needed. Additional tide tables are available online from NOAA at www.tidesandcurrents.noaa.gov/tide_predictions.shtml.

StationId:8728690
Source:NOAA/NOS/CO-OPS
Station Type:Harmonic
Time Zone:LST/LDT
Datum:mean lower low water (MLLW) which is the chart datum of soundings

**NOAA Tide Predictions**

## APALACHICOLA, Florida, 2017

### Times and Heights of High and Low Waters

## October

| Day | Time | ft | cm | Day | Time | ft | cm |
|---|---|---|---|---|---|---|---|
| 1 Su | 02:33 AM | 1.6 | 49 | 16 M | 02:48 AM | 1.6 | 49 |
| | 07:54 AM | 1.2 | 37 | | 08:38 AM | 0.9 | 27 |
| | 12:40 PM | 1.6 | 49 | | 02:16 PM | 1.6 | 49 |
| | 08:32 PM | 0.4 | 12 | | 09:13 PM | 0.6 | 18 |
| 2 M | 03:04 AM | 1.7 | 52 | 17 Tu | 03:11 AM | 1.6 | 49 |
| | 08:41 AM | 1.1 | 34 | | 09:25 AM | 0.7 | 21 |
| | 01:50 PM | 1.7 | 52 | | 03:24 PM | 1.6 | 49 |
| | 09:12 PM | 0.5 | 15 | | 09:51 PM | 0.7 | 21 |
| 3 Tu | 03:29 AM | 1.7 | 52 | 18 W | 03:30 AM | 1.6 | 49 |
| | 09:21 AM | 0.9 | 27 | | 10:07 AM | 0.5 | 15 |
| | 02:50 PM | 1.7 | 52 | | 04:19 PM | 1.6 | 49 |
| | 09:48 PM | 0.5 | 15 | | 10:24 PM | 0.8 | 24 |
| 4 W | 03:50 AM | 1.7 | 52 | 19 Th | 03:47 AM | 1.6 | 49 |
| | 09:58 AM | 0.8 | 24 | | 10:45 AM | 0.4 | 12 |
| | 03:46 PM | 1.8 | 55 | | 05:09 PM | 1.6 | 49 |
| | 10:21 PM | 0.6 | 18 | ● | 10:52 PM | 0.9 | 27 |
| 5 Th | 04:09 AM | 1.7 | 52 | 20 F | 04:03 AM | 1.7 | 52 |
| | 10:33 AM | 0.6 | 18 | | 11:21 AM | 0.3 | 9 |
| | 04:39 PM | 1.8 | 55 | | 05:55 PM | 1.6 | 49 |
| ○ | 10:52 PM | 0.8 | 24 | | 11:16 PM | 1.1 | 34 |
| 6 F | 04:29 AM | 1.7 | 52 | 21 Sa | 04:22 AM | 1.7 | 52 |
| | 11:09 AM | 0.5 | 15 | | 11:54 AM | 0.2 | 6 |
| | 05:33 PM | 1.8 | 55 | | 06:40 PM | 1.6 | 49 |
| | 11:22 PM | 0.9 | 27 | | 11:40 PM | 1.1 | 34 |
| 7 Sa | 04:51 AM | 1.8 | 55 | 22 Su | 04:44 AM | 1.7 | 52 |
| | 11:48 AM | 0.3 | 9 | | 12:26 PM | 0.2 | 6 |
| | 06:30 PM | 1.7 | 52 | | 07:25 PM | 1.6 | 49 |
| | 11:53 PM | 1.1 | 34 | | | | |
| 8 Su | 05:16 AM | 1.8 | 55 | 23 M | 12:07 AM | 1.2 | 37 |
| | 12:31 PM | 0.2 | 6 | | 05:12 AM | 1.7 | 52 |
| | 07:32 PM | 1.7 | 52 | | 12:59 PM | 0.2 | 6 |
| | | | | | 08:14 PM | 1.5 | 46 |
| 9 M | 12:25 AM | 1.2 | 37 | 24 Tu | 12:40 AM | 1.2 | 37 |
| | 05:46 AM | 1.9 | 58 | | 05:44 AM | 1.7 | 52 |
| | 01:23 PM | 0.2 | 6 | | 01:36 PM | 0.2 | 6 |
| | 08:42 PM | 1.6 | 49 | | 09:06 PM | 1.5 | 46 |
| 10 Tu | 01:00 AM | 1.3 | 40 | 25 W | 01:23 AM | 1.3 | 40 |
| | 06:22 AM | 1.9 | 58 | | 06:22 AM | 1.7 | 52 |
| | 02:26 PM | 0.2 | 6 | | 02:20 PM | 0.3 | 9 |
| | 10:03 PM | 1.5 | 46 | | 10:03 PM | 1.5 | 46 |
| 11 W | 01:43 AM | 1.4 | 43 | 26 Th | 02:22 AM | 1.3 | 40 |
| | 07:06 AM | 1.9 | 58 | | 07:08 AM | 1.6 | 49 |
| | 03:45 PM | 0.2 | 6 | | 03:16 PM | 0.3 | 9 |
| | 11:37 PM | 1.5 | 46 | | 11:02 PM | 1.5 | 46 |
| 12 Th | 02:54 AM | 1.4 | 43 | 27 F | 03:45 AM | 1.3 | 40 |
| | 08:03 AM | 1.8 | 55 | | 08:05 AM | 1.5 | 46 |
| ◐ | 05:11 PM | 0.3 | 9 | | 04:24 PM | 0.4 | 12 |
| | | | | ◐ | 11:57 PM | 1.5 | 46 |
| 13 F | 12:57 AM | 1.5 | 46 | 28 Sa | 05:18 AM | 1.2 | 37 |
| | 04:51 AM | 1.4 | 43 | | 09:20 AM | 1.4 | 43 |
| | 09:20 AM | 1.7 | 52 | | 05:33 PM | 0.4 | 12 |
| | 06:29 PM | 0.3 | 9 | | | | |
| 14 Sa | 01:47 AM | 1.5 | 46 | 29 Su | 12:43 AM | 1.5 | 46 |
| | 06:33 AM | 1.3 | 40 | | 06:35 AM | 1.1 | 34 |
| | 11:02 AM | 1.6 | 49 | | 10:50 AM | 1.3 | 40 |
| | 07:34 PM | 0.4 | 12 | | 06:35 PM | 0.4 | 12 |
| 15 Su | 02:21 AM | 1.6 | 49 | 30 M | 01:21 AM | 1.6 | 49 |
| | 07:43 AM | 1.1 | 34 | | 07:33 AM | 0.9 | 27 |
| | 12:49 PM | 1.6 | 49 | | 12:21 PM | 1.3 | 40 |
| | 08:28 PM | 0.5 | 15 | | 07:28 PM | 0.5 | 15 |
| | | | | 31 Tu | 01:52 AM | 1.6 | 49 |
| | | | | | 08:20 AM | 0.7 | 21 |
| | | | | | 01:42 PM | 1.4 | 43 |
| | | | | | 08:16 PM | 0.6 | 18 |

## November

| Day | Time | ft | cm | Day | Time | ft | cm |
|---|---|---|---|---|---|---|---|
| 1 W | 02:18 AM | 1.6 | 49 | 16 Th | 01:24 AM | 1.5 | 46 |
| | 09:01 AM | 0.5 | 15 | | 08:57 AM | 0.0 | 0 |
| | 02:52 PM | 1.5 | 46 | | 03:43 PM | 1.3 | 40 |
| | 08:59 PM | 0.7 | 21 | | 08:43 PM | 0.9 | 27 |
| 2 Th | 02:42 AM | 1.6 | 49 | 17 F | 01:45 AM | 1.5 | 46 |
| | 09:40 AM | 0.3 | 9 | | 09:35 AM | -0.1 | -3 |
| | 03:55 PM | 1.5 | 46 | | 04:31 PM | 1.4 | 43 |
| | 09:38 PM | 0.8 | 24 | | 09:15 PM | 1.0 | 30 |
| 3 F | 03:05 AM | 1.6 | 49 | 18 Sa | 02:08 AM | 1.5 | 46 |
| | 10:18 AM | 0.1 | 3 | | 10:10 AM | -0.1 | -3 |
| | 04:55 PM | 1.6 | 49 | | 05:13 PM | 1.4 | 43 |
| | 10:16 PM | 0.9 | 27 | ● | 09:44 PM | 1.1 | 34 |
| 4 Sa | 03:30 AM | 1.7 | 52 | 19 Su | 02:33 AM | 1.6 | 49 |
| | 10:58 AM | 0.0 | 0 | | 10:42 AM | -0.2 | -6 |
| | 05:54 PM | 1.6 | 49 | | 05:52 PM | 1.4 | 43 |
| ○ | 10:52 PM | 1.1 | 34 | | 10:14 PM | 1.1 | 34 |
| 5 Su | 02:58 AM | 1.8 | 55 | 20 M | 03:01 AM | 1.6 | 49 |
| | 10:41 AM | -0.2 | -6 | | 11:13 AM | -0.2 | -6 |
| | 05:53 PM | 1.6 | 49 | | 06:30 PM | 1.4 | 43 |
| | 10:27 PM | 1.2 | 37 | | 10:46 PM | 1.1 | 34 |
| 6 M | 03:31 AM | 1.8 | 55 | 21 Tu | 03:34 AM | 1.6 | 49 |
| | 11:27 AM | -0.2 | -6 | | 11:42 AM | -0.2 | -6 |
| | 06:54 PM | 1.5 | 46 | | 07:08 PM | 1.4 | 43 |
| | 11:05 PM | 1.3 | 40 | | 11:24 PM | 1.1 | 34 |
| 7 Tu | 04:09 AM | 1.8 | 55 | 22 W | 04:12 AM | 1.5 | 46 |
| | 12:20 PM | -0.2 | -6 | | 12:13 PM | -0.1 | -3 |
| | 07:58 PM | 1.5 | 46 | | 07:48 PM | 1.4 | 43 |
| | 11:50 PM | 1.3 | 40 | | | | |
| 8 W | 04:53 AM | 1.8 | 55 | 23 Th | 12:11 AM | 1.1 | 34 |
| | 01:19 PM | -0.1 | -3 | | 04:54 AM | 1.5 | 46 |
| | 09:03 PM | 1.4 | 43 | | 12:47 PM | -0.1 | -3 |
| | | | | | 08:29 PM | 1.4 | 43 |
| 9 Th | 12:51 AM | 1.3 | 40 | 24 F | 01:09 AM | 1.1 | 34 |
| | 05:45 AM | 1.7 | 52 | | 05:42 AM | 1.4 | 43 |
| | 02:25 PM | 0.0 | 0 | | 01:28 PM | 0.0 | 0 |
| | 10:05 PM | 1.4 | 43 | | 09:10 PM | 1.4 | 43 |
| 10 F | 02:19 AM | 1.2 | 37 | 25 Sa | 02:22 AM | 1.0 | 30 |
| | 06:51 AM | 1.5 | 46 | | 06:39 AM | 1.3 | 40 |
| | 03:36 PM | 0.1 | 3 | | 02:15 PM | 0.1 | 3 |
| ◖ | 10:56 PM | 1.4 | 43 | | 09:52 PM | 1.4 | 43 |
| 11 Sa | 04:02 AM | 1.1 | 34 | 26 Su | 03:44 AM | 0.9 | 27 |
| | 08:18 AM | 1.3 | 40 | | 07:52 AM | 1.1 | 34 |
| | 04:44 PM | 0.3 | 9 | | 03:10 PM | 0.2 | 6 |
| | 11:37 PM | 1.4 | 43 | ◐ | 10:30 PM | 1.4 | 43 |
| 12 Su | 05:29 AM | 0.9 | 27 | 27 M | 05:00 AM | 0.8 | 24 |
| | 10:10 AM | 1.2 | 37 | | 09:22 AM | 1.0 | 30 |
| | 05:46 PM | 0.4 | 12 | | 04:10 PM | 0.3 | 9 |
| | | | | | 11:05 PM | 1.4 | 43 |
| 13 M | 12:10 AM | 1.4 | 43 | 28 Tu | 06:02 AM | 0.6 | 18 |
| | 06:34 AM | 0.6 | 18 | | 11:02 AM | 1.0 | 30 |
| | 12:06 PM | 1.2 | 37 | | 05:11 PM | 0.4 | 12 |
| | 06:40 PM | 0.5 | 15 | | 11:38 PM | 1.4 | 43 |
| 14 Tu | 12:38 AM | 1.4 | 43 | 29 W | 06:54 AM | 0.3 | 9 |
| | 07:28 AM | 0.4 | 12 | | 12:38 PM | 1.0 | 30 |
| | 01:38 PM | 1.3 | 40 | | 06:10 PM | 0.6 | 18 |
| | 07:27 PM | 0.7 | 21 | | | | |
| 15 W | 01:02 AM | 1.5 | 46 | 30 Th | 12:08 AM | 1.4 | 43 |
| | 08:15 AM | 0.2 | 6 | | 07:41 AM | 0.1 | 3 |
| | 02:47 PM | 1.3 | 40 | | 02:01 PM | 1.1 | 34 |
| | 08:07 PM | 0.8 | 24 | | 07:05 PM | 0.7 | 21 |

## December

| Day | Time | ft | cm | Day | Time | ft | cm |
|---|---|---|---|---|---|---|---|
| 1 F | 12:38 AM | 1.5 | 46 | 16 Sa | 12:55 AM | 1.4 | 43 |
| | 08:25 AM | -0.2 | -6 | | 09:23 AM | -0.4 | -12 |
| | 03:13 PM | 1.2 | 37 | | 04:44 PM | 1.2 | 37 |
| | 07:56 PM | 0.9 | 27 | | 08:45 PM | 0.9 | 27 |
| 2 Sa | 01:09 AM | 1.5 | 46 | 17 Su | 01:27 AM | 1.4 | 43 |
| | 09:09 AM | -0.3 | -9 | | 09:59 AM | -0.5 | -15 |
| | 04:17 PM | 1.3 | 40 | | 05:19 PM | 1.2 | 37 |
| | 08:42 PM | 1.0 | 30 | | 09:23 PM | 1.0 | 30 |
| 3 Su | 01:44 AM | 1.6 | 49 | 18 M | 02:02 AM | 1.4 | 43 |
| | 09:53 AM | -0.5 | -15 | | 10:32 AM | -0.5 | -15 |
| | 05:15 PM | 1.4 | 43 | | 05:50 PM | 1.2 | 37 |
| ○ | 09:25 PM | 1.1 | 34 | ● | 09:59 PM | 1.0 | 30 |
| 4 M | 02:22 AM | 1.6 | 49 | 19 Tu | 02:38 AM | 1.4 | 43 |
| | 10:39 AM | -0.6 | -18 | | 11:02 AM | -0.4 | -12 |
| | 06:09 PM | 1.4 | 43 | | 06:19 PM | 1.2 | 37 |
| | 10:08 PM | 1.1 | 34 | | 10:35 PM | 0.9 | 27 |
| 5 Tu | 03:05 AM | 1.7 | 52 | 20 W | 03:17 AM | 1.4 | 43 |
| | 11:27 AM | -0.6 | -18 | | 11:28 AM | -0.4 | -12 |
| | 06:59 PM | 1.3 | 40 | | 06:47 PM | 1.2 | 37 |
| | 10:54 PM | 1.1 | 34 | | 11:14 PM | 0.9 | 27 |
| 6 W | 03:52 AM | 1.6 | 49 | 21 Th | 03:58 AM | 1.3 | 40 |
| | 12:16 PM | -0.5 | -15 | | 11:54 AM | -0.4 | -12 |
| | 07:47 PM | 1.3 | 40 | | 07:14 PM | 1.2 | 37 |
| | 11:47 PM | 1.1 | 34 | | 11:57 PM | 0.8 | 24 |
| 7 Th | 04:44 AM | 1.5 | 46 | 22 F | 04:42 AM | 1.3 | 40 |
| | 01:06 PM | -0.4 | -12 | | 12:21 PM | -0.3 | -9 |
| | 08:30 PM | 1.2 | 37 | | 07:43 PM | 1.2 | 37 |
| 8 F | 12:53 AM | 1.0 | 30 | 23 Sa | 12:46 AM | 0.8 | 24 |
| | 05:43 AM | 1.4 | 43 | | 05:31 AM | 1.2 | 37 |
| | 01:58 PM | -0.2 | -6 | | 12:52 PM | -0.2 | -6 |
| | 09:10 PM | 1.2 | 37 | | 08:14 PM | 1.2 | 37 |
| 9 Sa | 02:14 AM | 0.9 | 27 | 24 Su | 01:45 AM | 0.7 | 21 |
| | 06:52 AM | 1.2 | 37 | | 06:27 AM | 1.1 | 34 |
| | 02:51 PM | 0.0 | 0 | | 01:28 PM | -0.1 | -3 |
| | 09:46 PM | 1.2 | 37 | | 08:45 PM | 1.2 | 37 |
| 10 Su | 03:43 AM | 0.7 | 21 | 25 M | 02:54 AM | 0.6 | 18 |
| | 08:19 AM | 1.0 | 30 | | 07:36 AM | 0.9 | 27 |
| | 03:46 PM | 0.2 | 6 | | 02:09 PM | 0.0 | 0 |
| ◖ | 10:20 PM | 1.2 | 37 | | 09:18 PM | 1.2 | 37 |
| 11 M | 05:05 AM | 0.5 | 15 | 26 Tu | 04:10 AM | 0.4 | 12 |
| | 10:09 AM | 0.9 | 27 | | 09:04 AM | 0.8 | 24 |
| | 04:41 PM | 0.4 | 12 | | 02:57 PM | 0.2 | 6 |
| | 10:53 PM | 1.2 | 37 | ◐ | 09:51 PM | 1.2 | 37 |
| 12 Tu | 06:14 AM | 0.2 | 6 | 27 W | 05:23 AM | 0.2 | 6 |
| | 12:14 PM | 0.9 | 27 | | 10:51 AM | 0.8 | 24 |
| | 05:35 PM | 0.6 | 18 | | 03:54 PM | 0.4 | 12 |
| | 11:24 PM | 1.3 | 40 | | 10:26 PM | 1.3 | 40 |
| 13 W | 07:11 AM | 0.0 | 0 | 28 Th | 06:26 AM | 0.0 | 0 |
| | 01:58 PM | 0.9 | 27 | | 12:46 PM | 0.8 | 24 |
| | 06:28 PM | 0.7 | 21 | | 05:00 PM | 0.6 | 18 |
| | 11:54 PM | 1.3 | 40 | | 11:03 PM | 1.3 | 40 |
| 14 Th | 08:00 AM | -0.2 | -6 | 29 F | 07:22 AM | -0.3 | -9 |
| | 03:09 PM | 1.0 | 30 | | 02:24 PM | 0.9 | 27 |
| | 07:18 PM | 0.8 | 24 | | 06:12 PM | 0.8 | 24 |
| | | | | | 11:43 PM | 1.4 | 43 |
| 15 F | 12:24 AM | 1.3 | 40 | 30 Sa | 08:14 AM | -0.5 | -15 |
| | 08:43 AM | -0.3 | -9 | | 03:38 PM | 1.1 | 34 |
| | 04:02 PM | 1.1 | 34 | | 07:19 PM | 0.9 | 27 |
| | 08:04 PM | 0.9 | 27 | | | | |
| | | | | 31 Su | 12:28 AM | 1.4 | 43 |
| | | | | | 09:03 AM | -0.6 | -18 |
| | | | | | 04:35 PM | 1.1 | 34 |
| | | | | | 08:18 PM | 1.0 | 30 |

Heights are referred to mean lower water which is the chart datum of sounding. All times are local. Daylight Saving Time has been used when needed. Additional tide tables are available online from NOAA at www.tidesandcurrents.noaa.gov/tide_predictions.shtml.

**SKIPPER'S HANDBOOK**

StationId: 8728690
Source: NOAA/NOS/CO-OPS
Station Type: Primary
Time Zone: LST_LDT
Datum: MLLW

# NOAA Tide Predictions

## Apalachicola, FL, 2018

### Times and Heights of High and Low Waters

SKIPPER'S HANDBOOK

## January

| Day | Time | Height (ft) | Height (cm) |
|---|---|---|---|
| **1** M | 01:10 AM | 1.5 | 46 |
| | 09:51 AM | -0.8 | -24 |
| | 05:32 PM | 1.2 | 37 |
| | 09:11 PM | 1.0 | 30 |
| **2** Tu ○ | 02:01 AM | 1.5 | 46 |
| | 10:38 AM | -0.8 | -24 |
| | 06:13 PM | 1.2 | 37 |
| | 09:59 PM | 1.0 | 30 |
| **3** W | 02:54 AM | 1.5 | 46 |
| | 11:23 AM | -0.8 | -24 |
| | 06:49 PM | 1.2 | 37 |
| | 10:48 PM | 0.9 | 27 |
| **4** Th | 03:49 AM | 1.5 | 46 |
| | 12:07 PM | -0.7 | -21 |
| | 07:20 PM | 1.1 | 34 |
| | 11:41 PM | 0.8 | 24 |
| **5** F | 04:45 AM | 1.4 | 43 |
| | 12:49 PM | -0.5 | -15 |
| | 07:48 PM | 1.1 | 34 |
| **6** Sa | 12:42 AM | 0.7 | 21 |
| | 05:46 AM | 1.2 | 37 |
| | 01:29 PM | -0.3 | -9 |
| | 08:15 PM | 1.1 | 34 |
| **7** Su | 01:51 AM | 0.5 | 15 |
| | 06:53 AM | 1.0 | 30 |
| | 02:07 PM | -0.1 | -3 |
| | 08:41 PM | 1.1 | 34 |
| **8** M | 03:09 AM | 0.4 | 12 |
| | 08:13 AM | 0.9 | 27 |
| | 02:45 PM | 0.2 | 6 |
| | 09:09 PM | 1.1 | 34 |
| **9** Tu | 04:29 AM | 0.2 | 6 |
| | 09:56 AM | 0.7 | 21 |
| | 03:26 PM | 0.4 | 12 |
| | 09:40 PM | 1.2 | 37 |
| **10** W | 05:42 AM | 0.0 | 0 |
| | 12:07 PM | 0.7 | 21 |
| | 04:16 PM | 0.6 | 18 |
| | 10:13 PM | 1.2 | 37 |
| **11** Th | 06:44 AM | -0.2 | -6 |
| | 12:07 PM | 0.8 | 24 |
| | 05:19 PM | 0.7 | 21 |
| | 10:51 PM | 1.2 | 37 |
| **12** F | 07:38 AM | -0.3 | -9 |
| | 03:17 PM | 0.9 | 27 |
| | 06:28 PM | 0.8 | 24 |
| | 11:32 PM | 1.2 | 37 |
| **13** Sa | 08:25 AM | -0.5 | -15 |
| | 04:01 PM | 1.0 | 30 |
| | 07:30 PM | 0.9 | 27 |
| **14** Su | 12:16 AM | 1.2 | 37 |
| | 09:07 AM | -0.5 | -15 |
| | 04:35 PM | 1.1 | 34 |
| | 08:22 PM | 0.9 | 27 |
| **15** M | 01:01 AM | 1.3 | 40 |
| | 09:44 AM | -0.6 | -18 |
| | 05:04 PM | 1.1 | 34 |
| | 09:06 PM | 0.9 | 27 |
| **16** Tu | 01:45 AM | 1.3 | 40 |
| | 10:18 AM | -0.5 | -15 |
| | 05:29 PM | 1.1 | 34 |
| | 09:44 PM | 0.8 | 24 |
| **17** W ● | 02:29 AM | 1.3 | 40 |
| | 10:47 AM | -0.5 | -15 |
| | 05:51 PM | 1.1 | 34 |
| | 10:20 PM | 0.8 | 24 |
| **18** Th | 03:12 AM | 1.3 | 40 |
| | 11:12 AM | -0.5 | -15 |
| | 06:12 PM | 1.1 | 34 |
| | 10:55 PM | 0.7 | 21 |
| **19** F | 03:55 AM | 1.3 | 40 |
| | 11:35 AM | -0.4 | -12 |
| | 06:32 PM | 1.1 | 34 |
| | 11:32 PM | 0.6 | 18 |
| **20** Sa | 04:40 AM | 1.2 | 37 |
| | 11:58 AM | -0.3 | -9 |
| | 06:54 PM | 1.1 | 34 |
| **21** Su | 12:13 AM | 0.6 | 18 |
| | 05:28 AM | 1.1 | 34 |
| | 12:25 PM | -0.2 | -6 |
| | 07:17 PM | 1.1 | 34 |
| **22** M | 01:01 AM | 0.5 | 15 |
| | 06:24 AM | 1.0 | 30 |
| | 12:55 PM | -0.1 | -3 |
| | 07:43 PM | 1.2 | 37 |
| **23** Tu | 02:00 AM | 0.3 | 9 |
| | 07:33 AM | 0.9 | 27 |
| | 01:28 PM | 0.1 | 3 |
| | 08:11 PM | 1.2 | 37 |
| **24** W ☽ | 03:12 AM | 0.2 | 6 |
| | 09:02 AM | 0.8 | 24 |
| | 02:06 PM | 0.3 | 9 |
| | 08:43 PM | 1.2 | 37 |
| **25** Th | 04:37 AM | 0.0 | 0 |
| | 11:00 AM | 0.7 | 21 |
| | 02:48 PM | 0.6 | 18 |
| | 09:20 PM | 1.3 | 40 |
| **26** F | 05:58 AM | -0.2 | -6 |
| | 01:27 PM | 0.8 | 24 |
| | 03:49 PM | 0.8 | 24 |
| | 10:04 PM | 1.3 | 40 |
| **27** Sa | 07:06 AM | -0.4 | -12 |
| | 03:11 PM | 1.0 | 30 |
| | 05:34 PM | 0.9 | 27 |
| | 10:58 PM | 1.3 | 40 |
| **28** Su | 08:05 AM | -0.6 | -18 |
| | 04:02 PM | 1.1 | 34 |
| | 07:07 PM | 1.0 | 30 |
| | 11:59 PM | 1.4 | 43 |
| **29** M | 08:57 AM | -0.7 | -21 |
| | 04:39 PM | 1.1 | 34 |
| | 08:13 PM | 1.0 | 30 |
| **30** Tu | 01:02 AM | 1.4 | 43 |
| | 09:45 AM | -0.7 | -21 |
| | 05:11 PM | 1.1 | 34 |
| | 09:07 PM | 0.9 | 27 |
| **31** W ○ | 02:05 AM | 1.5 | 46 |
| | 10:29 AM | -0.7 | -21 |
| | 05:38 PM | 1.1 | 34 |
| | 09:54 PM | 0.8 | 24 |

## February

| Day | Time | Height (ft) | Height (cm) |
|---|---|---|---|
| **1** Th | 03:04 AM | 1.5 | 46 |
| | 11:10 AM | -0.6 | -18 |
| | 06:01 PM | 1.1 | 34 |
| | 10:41 PM | 0.7 | 21 |
| **2** F | 04:00 AM | 1.4 | 43 |
| | 11:46 AM | -0.5 | -15 |
| | 06:22 PM | 1.1 | 34 |
| | 11:29 PM | 0.5 | 15 |
| **3** Sa | 04:56 AM | 1.3 | 40 |
| | 12:19 PM | -0.3 | -9 |
| | 06:42 PM | 1.1 | 34 |
| **4** Su | 12:21 AM | 0.4 | 12 |
| | 05:54 AM | 1.2 | 37 |
| | 12:49 PM | 0.0 | 0 |
| | 07:02 PM | 1.1 | 34 |
| **5** M | 01:19 AM | 0.3 | 9 |
| | 06:57 AM | 1.0 | 30 |
| | 01:17 PM | 0.2 | 6 |
| | 07:24 PM | 1.1 | 34 |
| **6** Tu | 02:24 AM | 0.2 | 6 |
| | 08:10 AM | 0.9 | 27 |
| | 01:44 PM | 0.4 | 12 |
| | 07:51 PM | 1.2 | 37 |
| **7** W ☽ | 03:38 AM | 0.1 | 3 |
| | 09:45 AM | 0.8 | 24 |
| | 02:15 PM | 0.6 | 18 |
| | 08:23 PM | 1.2 | 37 |
| **8** Th | 04:56 AM | 0.0 | 0 |
| | 11:54 AM | 0.8 | 24 |
| | 02:57 PM | 0.7 | 21 |
| | 09:02 PM | 1.2 | 37 |
| **9** F | 06:06 AM | -0.2 | -6 |
| | 01:59 PM | 0.9 | 27 |
| | 04:22 PM | 0.8 | 24 |
| | 09:51 PM | 1.2 | 37 |
| **10** Sa | 07:07 AM | -0.3 | -9 |
| | 02:53 PM | 1.0 | 30 |
| | 06:02 PM | 0.9 | 27 |
| | 10:49 PM | 1.2 | 37 |
| **11** Su | 07:58 AM | -0.3 | -9 |
| | 03:27 PM | 1.0 | 30 |
| | 07:16 PM | 0.9 | 27 |
| | 11:51 PM | 1.2 | 37 |
| **12** M | 08:42 AM | -0.4 | -12 |
| | 03:56 PM | 1.1 | 34 |
| | 08:10 PM | 0.8 | 24 |
| **13** Tu | 12:51 AM | 1.2 | 37 |
| | 09:21 AM | -0.4 | -12 |
| | 04:21 PM | 1.1 | 34 |
| | 08:54 PM | 0.8 | 24 |
| **14** W | 01:44 AM | 1.3 | 40 |
| | 09:54 AM | -0.4 | -12 |
| | 04:42 PM | 1.1 | 34 |
| | 09:31 PM | 0.7 | 21 |
| **15** Th ● | 02:32 AM | 1.3 | 40 |
| | 10:22 AM | -0.3 | -9 |
| | 05:01 PM | 1.1 | 34 |
| | 10:05 PM | 0.6 | 18 |
| **16** F | 03:17 AM | 1.3 | 40 |
| | 10:46 AM | -0.3 | -9 |
| | 05:17 PM | 1.1 | 34 |
| | 10:37 PM | 0.5 | 15 |
| **17** Sa | 04:01 AM | 1.3 | 40 |
| | 11:08 AM | -0.2 | -6 |
| | 05:34 PM | 1.2 | 37 |
| | 11:11 PM | 0.4 | 12 |
| **18** Su | 04:47 AM | 1.2 | 37 |
| | 11:31 AM | -0.1 | -3 |
| | 05:52 PM | 1.2 | 37 |
| | 11:47 PM | 0.3 | 9 |
| **19** M | 05:38 AM | 1.2 | 37 |
| | 11:56 AM | 0.1 | 3 |
| | 06:13 PM | 1.2 | 37 |
| **20** Tu | 12:29 AM | 0.2 | 6 |
| | 06:37 AM | 1.1 | 34 |
| | 12:24 PM | 0.3 | 9 |
| | 06:37 PM | 1.3 | 40 |
| **21** W | 01:21 AM | 0.1 | 3 |
| | 07:48 AM | 1.0 | 30 |
| | 12:54 PM | 0.5 | 15 |
| | 07:06 PM | 1.3 | 40 |
| **22** Th | 02:28 AM | 0.0 | 0 |
| | 09:21 AM | 0.9 | 27 |
| | 01:26 PM | 0.7 | 21 |
| | 07:40 PM | 1.4 | 43 |
| **23** F ☽ | 03:59 AM | -0.1 | -3 |
| | 11:33 AM | 0.9 | 27 |
| | 01:58 PM | 0.9 | 27 |
| | 08:24 PM | 1.4 | 43 |
| **24** Sa | 05:33 AM | -0.2 | -6 |
| | 09:21 PM | 1.4 | 43 |
| **25** Su | 06:50 AM | -0.3 | -9 |
| | 03:04 PM | 1.1 | 34 |
| | 05:48 PM | 1.1 | 34 |
| | 10:36 PM | 1.4 | 43 |
| **26** M | 07:52 AM | -0.4 | -12 |
| | 03:33 PM | 1.2 | 37 |
| | 07:16 PM | 1.0 | 30 |
| | 11:58 PM | 1.4 | 43 |
| **27** Tu | 08:44 AM | -0.5 | -15 |
| | 03:59 PM | 1.2 | 37 |
| | 08:16 PM | 0.9 | 27 |
| **28** W | 01:14 AM | 1.4 | 43 |
| | 09:30 AM | -0.4 | -12 |
| | 04:22 PM | 1.2 | 37 |
| | 09:05 PM | 0.7 | 21 |

## March

| Day | Time | Height (ft) | Height (cm) |
|---|---|---|---|
| **1** Th | 02:21 AM | 1.5 | 46 |
| | 10:11 AM | -0.3 | -9 |
| | 04:42 PM | 1.2 | 37 |
| | 09:49 PM | 0.6 | 18 |
| **2** F ○ | 03:20 AM | 1.5 | 46 |
| | 10:46 AM | -0.2 | -6 |
| | 04:59 PM | 1.2 | 37 |
| | 10:32 PM | 0.4 | 12 |
| **3** Sa | 04:15 AM | 1.4 | 43 |
| | 11:17 AM | 0.0 | 0 |
| | 05:15 PM | 1.2 | 37 |
| | 11:15 PM | 0.3 | 9 |
| **4** Su | 05:08 AM | 1.3 | 40 |
| | 11:44 AM | 0.2 | 6 |
| | 05:31 PM | 1.2 | 37 |
| | 11:59 PM | 0.2 | 6 |
| **5** M | 06:03 AM | 1.2 | 37 |
| | 12:08 PM | 0.4 | 12 |
| | 05:50 PM | 1.3 | 40 |
| **6** Tu | 12:45 AM | 0.1 | 3 |
| | 07:02 AM | 1.1 | 34 |
| | 12:32 PM | 0.5 | 15 |
| | 06:13 PM | 1.3 | 40 |
| **7** W | 01:38 AM | 0.1 | 3 |
| | 08:10 AM | 1.0 | 30 |
| | 12:58 PM | 0.7 | 21 |
| | 06:42 PM | 1.3 | 40 |
| **8** Th | 02:42 AM | 0.1 | 3 |
| | 09:33 AM | 1.0 | 30 |
| | 01:32 PM | 0.8 | 24 |
| | 07:17 PM | 1.3 | 40 |
| **9** F ☽ | 03:57 AM | 0.0 | 0 |
| | 11:18 AM | 1.0 | 30 |
| | 02:28 PM | 0.9 | 27 |
| | 08:02 PM | 1.3 | 40 |
| **10** Sa | 05:15 AM | 0.0 | 0 |
| | 12:56 PM | 1.1 | 34 |
| | 04:11 PM | 1.0 | 30 |
| | 09:00 PM | 1.3 | 40 |
| **11** Su | 07:22 AM | 0.0 | 0 |
| | 02:50 PM | 1.1 | 34 |
| | 06:53 PM | 1.0 | 30 |
| | 11:15 PM | 1.2 | 37 |
| **12** M | 08:18 AM | -0.1 | -3 |
| | 03:27 PM | 1.2 | 37 |
| | 08:03 PM | 0.9 | 27 |
| **13** Tu | 12:35 AM | 1.2 | 37 |
| | 09:05 AM | -0.1 | -3 |
| | 03:56 PM | 1.2 | 37 |
| | 08:55 PM | 0.8 | 24 |
| **14** W | 01:45 AM | 1.3 | 40 |
| | 09:44 AM | -0.1 | -3 |
| | 04:20 PM | 1.2 | 37 |
| | 09:37 PM | 0.7 | 21 |
| **15** Th | 02:44 AM | 1.3 | 40 |
| | 10:18 AM | 0.0 | 0 |
| | 04:40 PM | 1.3 | 40 |
| | 10:13 PM | 0.6 | 18 |
| **16** F | 03:35 AM | 1.4 | 43 |
| | 10:46 AM | 0.0 | 0 |
| | 04:57 PM | 1.3 | 40 |
| | 10:46 PM | 0.5 | 15 |
| **17** Sa ● | 04:23 AM | 1.4 | 43 |
| | 11:12 AM | 0.1 | 3 |
| | 05:13 PM | 1.3 | 40 |
| | 11:18 PM | 0.4 | 12 |
| **18** Su | 05:11 AM | 1.4 | 43 |
| | 11:36 AM | 0.2 | 6 |
| | 05:29 PM | 1.3 | 40 |
| | 11:50 PM | 0.2 | 6 |
| **19** M | 06:02 AM | 1.4 | 43 |
| | 12:01 PM | 0.4 | 12 |
| | 05:48 PM | 1.4 | 43 |
| **20** Tu | 12:26 AM | 0.1 | 3 |
| | 06:56 AM | 1.3 | 40 |
| | 12:24 PM | 0.6 | 18 |
| | 06:11 PM | 1.4 | 43 |
| **21** W | 01:07 AM | 0.0 | 0 |
| | 07:59 AM | 1.2 | 37 |
| | 12:57 PM | 0.7 | 21 |
| | 06:38 PM | 1.5 | 46 |
| **22** Th | 01:58 AM | 0.0 | 0 |
| | 09:15 AM | 1.2 | 37 |
| | 01:28 PM | 0.9 | 27 |
| | 07:11 PM | 1.5 | 46 |
| **23** F | 03:05 AM | -0.1 | -3 |
| | 10:52 AM | 1.1 | 34 |
| | 02:04 PM | 1.0 | 30 |
| | 07:51 PM | 1.5 | 46 |
| **24** Sa ☽ | 04:35 AM | -0.1 | -3 |
| | 08:44 PM | 1.5 | 46 |
| **25** Su | 06:09 AM | -0.1 | -3 |
| | 02:30 PM | 1.2 | 37 |
| | 05:25 PM | 1.2 | 37 |
| | 10:00 PM | 1.4 | 43 |
| **26** M | 07:26 AM | -0.1 | -3 |
| | 03:07 PM | 1.3 | 40 |
| | 07:14 PM | 1.1 | 34 |
| | 11:37 PM | 1.4 | 43 |
| **27** Tu | 08:28 AM | -0.1 | -3 |
| | 03:35 PM | 1.3 | 40 |
| | 08:23 PM | 0.9 | 27 |
| **28** W | 01:15 AM | 1.4 | 43 |
| | 09:20 AM | -0.1 | -3 |
| | 03:59 PM | 1.3 | 40 |
| | 09:15 PM | 0.7 | 21 |
| **29** Th | 02:36 AM | 1.4 | 43 |
| | 10:03 AM | 0.0 | 0 |
| | 04:19 PM | 1.3 | 40 |
| | 10:00 PM | 0.5 | 15 |
| **30** F | 03:42 AM | 1.4 | 43 |
| | 10:41 AM | 0.2 | 6 |
| | 04:35 PM | 1.3 | 40 |
| | 10:42 PM | 0.4 | 12 |
| **31** Sa ○ | 04:40 AM | 1.4 | 43 |
| | 11:13 AM | 0.3 | 9 |
| | 04:50 PM | 1.3 | 40 |
| | 11:22 PM | 0.2 | 6 |

Heights are referred to mean lower water which is the chart datum of sounding. All times are local. Daylight Saving Time has been used when needed. Additional tide tables are available online from NOAA at www.tidesandcurrents.noaa.gov/tide_predictions.shtml.

StationId: 8728690
Source: NOAA/NOS/CO-OPS
Station Type: Primary
Time Zone: LST_LDT
Datum: MLLW

**NOAA Tide Predictions**

## Apalachicola, FL, 2018

### Times and Heights of High and Low Waters

#### April

| Day | Time | ft | cm |
|---|---|---|---|
| 1 Su | 05:32 AM | 1.4 | 43 |
|  | 11:40 AM | 0.5 | 15 |
|  | 05:06 PM | 1.4 | 43 |
| 2 M | 12:00 AM | 0.1 | 3 |
|  | 06:23 AM | 1.4 | 43 |
|  | 12:05 PM | 0.7 | 21 |
|  | 05:24 PM | 1.4 | 43 |
| 3 Tu | 12:38 AM | 0.0 | 0 |
|  | 07:15 AM | 1.3 | 40 |
|  | 12:28 PM | 0.8 | 24 |
|  | 05:45 PM | 1.5 | 46 |
| 4 W | 01:17 AM | 0.0 | 0 |
|  | 08:09 AM | 1.3 | 40 |
|  | 12:55 PM | 0.9 | 27 |
|  | 06:12 PM | 1.5 | 46 |
| 5 Th | 01:59 AM | 0.0 | 0 |
|  | 09:10 AM | 1.2 | 37 |
|  | 01:29 PM | 1.0 | 30 |
|  | 06:44 PM | 1.5 | 46 |
| 6 F | 02:50 AM | 0.0 | 0 |
|  | 10:19 AM | 1.2 | 37 |
|  | 02:16 PM | 1.1 | 34 |
|  | 07:24 PM | 1.4 | 43 |
| 7 Sa | 03:53 AM | 0.1 | 3 |
|  | 11:33 AM | 1.2 | 37 |
|  | 03:30 PM | 1.1 | 34 |
|  | 08:14 PM | 1.4 | 43 |
| 8 Su | 05:08 AM | 0.1 | 3 |
|  | 12:42 PM | 1.3 | 40 |
|  | 05:11 PM | 1.1 | 34 |
|  | ◑ 09:21 PM | 1.3 | 40 |
| 9 M | 06:19 AM | 0.2 | 6 |
|  | 01:34 PM | 1.3 | 40 |
|  | 06:40 PM | 1.0 | 30 |
|  | 10:46 PM | 1.2 | 37 |
| 10 Tu | 07:19 AM | 0.2 | 6 |
|  | 02:25 PM | 1.3 | 40 |
|  | 07:45 PM | 0.9 | 27 |
| 11 W | 12:15 AM | 1.2 | 37 |
|  | 08:09 AM | 0.2 | 6 |
|  | 02:44 PM | 1.4 | 43 |
|  | 08:34 PM | 0.7 | 21 |
| 12 Th | 01:35 AM | 1.3 | 40 |
|  | 08:52 AM | 0.2 | 6 |
|  | 03:09 PM | 1.4 | 43 |
|  | 09:15 PM | 0.6 | 18 |
| 13 F | 02:41 AM | 1.3 | 40 |
|  | 09:28 AM | 0.3 | 9 |
|  | 03:29 PM | 1.4 | 43 |
|  | 09:52 PM | 0.4 | 12 |
| 14 Sa | 03:39 AM | 1.4 | 43 |
|  | 10:01 AM | 0.4 | 12 |
|  | 03:47 PM | 1.4 | 43 |
|  | 10:26 PM | 0.3 | 9 |
| 15 Su | 04:33 AM | 1.4 | 43 |
|  | 10:32 AM | 0.6 | 18 |
|  | 04:05 PM | 1.5 | 46 |
|  | 11:00 PM | 0.1 | 3 |
| 16 M | 05:27 AM | 1.4 | 43 |
|  | 11:02 AM | 0.7 | 21 |
|  | 04:25 PM | 1.5 | 46 |
|  | ● 11:35 PM | 0.0 | 0 |
| 17 Tu | 06:23 AM | 1.4 | 43 |
|  | 11:32 AM | 0.9 | 27 |
|  | 04:49 PM | 1.6 | 49 |
| 18 W | 12:13 AM | -0.1 | -3 |
|  | 07:22 AM | 1.4 | 43 |
|  | 12:03 PM | 1.0 | 30 |
|  | 05:17 PM | 1.6 | 49 |
| 19 Th | 12:58 AM | -0.2 | -6 |
|  | 08:28 AM | 1.4 | 43 |
|  | 12:37 PM | 1.1 | 34 |
|  | 05:51 PM | 1.7 | 52 |
| 20 F | 01:52 AM | -0.2 | -6 |
|  | 09:44 AM | 1.4 | 43 |
|  | 01:17 PM | 1.2 | 37 |
|  | 06:31 PM | 1.7 | 52 |
| 21 Sa | 02:58 AM | -0.1 | -3 |
|  | 11:09 AM | 1.3 | 40 |
|  | 02:17 PM | 1.3 | 40 |
|  | 07:21 PM | 1.6 | 49 |
| 22 Su | 04:18 AM | -0.1 | -3 |
|  | 12:28 PM | 1.3 | 40 |
|  | 04:03 PM | 1.3 | 40 |
|  | ◐ 08:28 PM | 1.5 | 46 |
| 23 M | 05:39 AM | 0.0 | 0 |
|  | 01:21 PM | 1.4 | 43 |
|  | 05:58 PM | 1.1 | 34 |
|  | 10:01 PM | 1.4 | 43 |
| 24 Tu | 06:50 AM | 0.1 | 3 |
|  | 01:57 PM | 1.4 | 43 |
|  | 07:19 PM | 0.9 | 27 |
|  | 11:54 PM | 1.3 | 40 |
| 25 W | 07:51 AM | 0.2 | 6 |
|  | 02:25 PM | 1.4 | 43 |
|  | 08:19 PM | 0.7 | 21 |
| 26 Th | 01:38 AM | 1.3 | 40 |
|  | 08:41 AM | 0.3 | 9 |
|  | 02:49 PM | 1.4 | 43 |
|  | 09:08 PM | 0.5 | 15 |
| 27 F | 03:01 AM | 1.3 | 40 |
|  | 09:24 AM | 0.5 | 15 |
|  | 03:08 PM | 1.4 | 43 |
|  | 09:53 PM | 0.3 | 9 |
| 28 Sa | 04:07 AM | 1.4 | 43 |
|  | 10:01 AM | 0.6 | 18 |
|  | 03:26 PM | 1.5 | 46 |
|  | 10:34 PM | 0.1 | 3 |
| 29 Su | 05:04 AM | 1.4 | 43 |
|  | 10:33 AM | 0.8 | 24 |
|  | 03:43 PM | 1.5 | 46 |
|  | 11:12 PM | 0.0 | 0 |
| 30 M | 05:55 AM | 1.4 | 43 |
|  | 11:00 AM | 0.9 | 27 |
|  | 04:02 PM | 1.5 | 46 |
|  | ○ 11:47 PM | -0.1 | -3 |

#### May

| Day | Time | ft | cm |
|---|---|---|---|
| 1 Tu | 06:43 AM | 1.4 | 43 |
|  | 11:27 AM | 1.0 | 30 |
|  | 04:25 PM | 1.6 | 49 |
| 2 W | 12:21 AM | -0.1 | -3 |
|  | 07:29 AM | 1.4 | 43 |
|  | 11:55 AM | 1.1 | 34 |
|  | 04:52 PM | 1.6 | 49 |
| 3 Th | 12:55 AM | -0.1 | -3 |
|  | 08:16 AM | 1.4 | 43 |
|  | 12:29 PM | 1.1 | 34 |
|  | 05:24 PM | 1.6 | 49 |
| 4 F | 01:31 AM | -0.1 | -3 |
|  | 09:05 AM | 1.4 | 43 |
|  | 01:12 PM | 1.2 | 37 |
|  | 06:02 PM | 1.6 | 49 |
| 5 Sa | 02:12 AM | 0.0 | 0 |
|  | 09:56 AM | 1.4 | 43 |
|  | 02:09 PM | 1.2 | 37 |
|  | 06:47 PM | 1.5 | 46 |
| 6 Su | 03:00 AM | 0.1 | 3 |
|  | 10:47 AM | 1.4 | 43 |
|  | 03:26 PM | 1.2 | 37 |
|  | 07:41 PM | 1.4 | 43 |
| 7 M | 03:57 AM | 0.1 | 3 |
|  | 11:36 AM | 1.4 | 43 |
|  | 04:55 PM | 1.1 | 34 |
|  | 08:50 PM | 1.3 | 40 |
| 8 Tu | 04:59 AM | 0.2 | 6 |
|  | 12:19 PM | 1.4 | 43 |
|  | 06:15 PM | 1.0 | 30 |
|  | ◐ 10:16 PM | 1.2 | 37 |
| 9 W | 05:59 AM | 0.3 | 9 |
|  | 12:56 PM | 1.4 | 43 |
|  | 07:18 PM | 0.8 | 24 |
|  | 11:51 PM | 1.1 | 34 |
| 10 Th | 06:53 AM | 0.4 | 12 |
|  | 01:26 PM | 1.5 | 46 |
|  | 08:08 PM | 0.6 | 18 |
| 11 F | 01:20 AM | 1.2 | 37 |
|  | 07:43 AM | 0.5 | 15 |
|  | 01:52 PM | 1.5 | 46 |
|  | 08:50 PM | 0.4 | 12 |
| 12 Sa | 02:38 AM | 1.2 | 37 |
|  | 08:28 AM | 0.6 | 18 |
|  | 02:16 PM | 1.5 | 46 |
|  | 09:30 PM | 0.2 | 6 |
| 13 Su | 03:46 AM | 1.3 | 40 |
|  | 09:10 AM | 0.8 | 24 |
|  | 02:39 PM | 1.6 | 49 |
|  | 10:07 PM | 0.0 | 0 |
| 14 M | 04:49 AM | 1.4 | 43 |
|  | 09:49 AM | 0.9 | 27 |
|  | 03:03 PM | 1.6 | 49 |
|  | 10:45 PM | -0.1 | -3 |
| 15 Tu | 05:49 AM | 1.5 | 46 |
|  | 10:26 AM | 1.1 | 34 |
|  | 03:30 PM | 1.7 | 52 |
|  | ● 11:26 PM | -0.3 | -9 |
| 16 W | 06:49 AM | 1.5 | 46 |
|  | 11:04 AM | 1.2 | 37 |
|  | 04:02 PM | 1.8 | 55 |
| 17 Th | 12:10 AM | -0.4 | -12 |
|  | 07:49 AM | 1.5 | 46 |
|  | 11:42 AM | 1.3 | 40 |
|  | 04:39 PM | 1.8 | 55 |
| 18 F | 12:58 AM | -0.4 | -12 |
|  | 08:50 AM | 1.5 | 46 |
|  | 12:26 PM | 1.3 | 40 |
|  | 05:22 PM | 1.8 | 55 |
| 19 Sa | 01:52 AM | -0.3 | -9 |
|  | 09:50 AM | 1.5 | 46 |
|  | 01:23 PM | 1.3 | 40 |
|  | 06:13 PM | 1.7 | 52 |
| 20 Su | 02:51 AM | -0.2 | -6 |
|  | 10:46 AM | 1.4 | 43 |
|  | 02:43 PM | 1.3 | 40 |
|  | 07:14 PM | 1.6 | 49 |
| 21 M | 03:55 AM | -0.1 | -3 |
|  | 11:33 AM | 1.4 | 43 |
|  | 04:22 PM | 1.2 | 37 |
|  | 08:31 PM | 1.4 | 43 |
| 22 Tu | 05:00 AM | 0.1 | 3 |
|  | 12:11 PM | 1.4 | 43 |
|  | 05:54 PM | 1.0 | 30 |
|  | ◐ 10:12 PM | 1.2 | 37 |
| 23 W | 06:02 AM | 0.3 | 9 |
|  | 12:43 PM | 1.4 | 43 |
|  | 07:07 PM | 0.7 | 21 |
| 24 Th | 12:10 AM | 1.2 | 37 |
|  | 06:58 AM | 0.5 | 15 |
|  | 01:11 PM | 1.4 | 43 |
|  | 08:06 PM | 0.5 | 15 |
| 25 F | 02:01 AM | 1.2 | 37 |
|  | 07:49 AM | 0.7 | 21 |
|  | 01:36 PM | 1.5 | 46 |
|  | 08:57 PM | 0.2 | 6 |
| 26 Sa | 03:28 AM | 1.2 | 37 |
|  | 08:33 AM | 0.8 | 24 |
|  | 01:59 PM | 1.5 | 46 |
|  | 09:42 PM | 0.0 | 0 |
| 27 Su | 04:36 AM | 1.3 | 40 |
|  | 09:13 AM | 1.0 | 30 |
|  | 02:22 PM | 1.6 | 49 |
|  | 10:24 PM | -0.1 | -3 |
| 28 M | 05:32 AM | 1.4 | 43 |
|  | 09:50 AM | 1.1 | 34 |
|  | 02:45 PM | 1.6 | 49 |
|  | 11:02 PM | -0.2 | -6 |
| 29 Tu | 06:19 AM | 1.4 | 43 |
|  | 10:23 AM | 1.2 | 37 |
|  | 03:12 PM | 1.6 | 49 |
|  | ○ 11:37 PM | -0.2 | -6 |
| 30 W | 07:00 AM | 1.4 | 43 |
|  | 10:57 AM | 1.2 | 37 |
|  | 03:42 PM | 1.7 | 52 |
| 31 Th | 12:10 AM | -0.2 | -6 |
|  | 07:37 AM | 1.4 | 43 |
|  | 11:32 AM | 1.2 | 37 |
|  | 04:16 PM | 1.6 | 49 |

#### June

| Day | Time | ft | cm |
|---|---|---|---|
| 1 F | 12:41 AM | -0.2 | -6 |
|  | 08:12 AM | 1.4 | 43 |
|  | 12:13 PM | 1.2 | 37 |
|  | 04:55 PM | 1.6 | 49 |
| 2 Sa | 01:12 AM | -0.1 | -3 |
|  | 08:47 AM | 1.4 | 43 |
|  | 01:00 PM | 1.2 | 37 |
|  | 05:37 PM | 1.6 | 49 |
| 3 Su | 01:44 AM | -0.1 | -3 |
|  | 09:22 AM | 1.5 | 46 |
|  | 01:56 PM | 1.2 | 37 |
|  | 06:25 PM | 1.5 | 46 |
| 4 M | 02:20 AM | 0.0 | 0 |
|  | 09:57 AM | 1.5 | 46 |
|  | 03:03 PM | 1.1 | 34 |
|  | 07:20 PM | 1.4 | 43 |
| 5 Tu | 03:00 AM | 0.1 | 3 |
|  | 10:33 AM | 1.5 | 46 |
|  | 04:20 PM | 1.0 | 30 |
|  | 08:27 PM | 1.2 | 37 |
| 6 W | 03:44 AM | 0.2 | 6 |
|  | 11:07 AM | 1.5 | 46 |
|  | 05:35 PM | 0.9 | 27 |
|  | ◐ 09:50 PM | 1.1 | 34 |
| 7 Th | 04:33 AM | 0.4 | 12 |
|  | 11:40 AM | 1.5 | 46 |
|  | 06:41 PM | 0.7 | 21 |
|  | 11:27 PM | 1.1 | 34 |
| 8 F | 05:27 AM | 0.5 | 15 |
|  | 12:10 PM | 1.5 | 46 |
|  | 07:36 PM | 0.5 | 15 |
| 9 Sa | 01:08 AM | 1.1 | 34 |
|  | 06:24 AM | 0.7 | 21 |
|  | 12:39 PM | 1.6 | 49 |
|  | 08:24 PM | 0.2 | 6 |
| 10 Su | 02:42 AM | 1.2 | 37 |
|  | 07:21 AM | 0.9 | 27 |
|  | 01:08 PM | 1.6 | 49 |
|  | 09:09 PM | 0.0 | 0 |
| 11 M | 04:03 AM | 1.3 | 40 |
|  | 08:15 AM | 1.1 | 34 |
|  | 01:39 PM | 1.7 | 52 |
|  | 09:53 PM | -0.2 | -6 |
| 12 Tu | 05:12 AM | 1.4 | 43 |
|  | 09:07 AM | 1.2 | 37 |
|  | 02:13 PM | 1.8 | 55 |
|  | 10:37 PM | -0.3 | -9 |
| 13 W | 06:12 AM | 1.5 | 46 |
|  | 09:55 AM | 1.3 | 40 |
|  | 02:52 PM | 1.8 | 55 |
|  | ● 11:22 PM | -0.4 | -12 |
| 14 Th | 07:07 AM | 1.5 | 46 |
|  | 10:41 AM | 1.4 | 43 |
|  | 03:35 PM | 1.9 | 58 |
| 15 F | 12:09 AM | -0.5 | -15 |
|  | 07:57 AM | 1.5 | 46 |
|  | 11:29 AM | 1.4 | 43 |
|  | 04:23 PM | 1.9 | 58 |
| 16 Sa | 12:57 AM | -0.4 | -12 |
|  | 08:42 AM | 1.5 | 46 |
|  | 12:22 PM | 1.3 | 40 |
|  | 05:16 PM | 1.8 | 55 |
| 17 Su | 01:46 AM | -0.3 | -9 |
|  | 09:21 AM | 1.5 | 46 |
|  | 01:26 PM | 1.3 | 40 |
|  | 06:15 PM | 1.7 | 52 |
| 18 M | 02:35 AM | -0.2 | -6 |
|  | 09:57 AM | 1.4 | 43 |
|  | 02:42 PM | 1.1 | 34 |
|  | 07:22 PM | 1.5 | 46 |
| 19 Tu | 03:24 AM | 0.1 | 3 |
|  | 10:29 AM | 1.4 | 43 |
|  | 04:07 PM | 1.0 | 30 |
|  | 08:41 PM | 1.3 | 40 |
| 20 W | 04:13 AM | 0.3 | 9 |
|  | 10:59 AM | 1.5 | 46 |
|  | 05:31 PM | 0.8 | 24 |
|  | ◐ 10:21 PM | 1.2 | 37 |
| 21 Th | 05:02 AM | 0.5 | 15 |
|  | 11:28 AM | 1.5 | 46 |
|  | 06:45 PM | 0.5 | 15 |
| 22 F | 12:22 AM | 1.1 | 34 |
|  | 05:52 AM | 0.7 | 21 |
|  | 11:57 AM | 1.5 | 46 |
|  | 07:48 PM | 0.3 | 9 |
| 23 Sa | 02:25 AM | 1.1 | 34 |
|  | 06:43 AM | 0.9 | 27 |
|  | 12:27 PM | 1.6 | 49 |
|  | 08:41 PM | 0.1 | 3 |
| 24 Su | 03:57 AM | 1.2 | 37 |
|  | 07:36 AM | 1.1 | 34 |
|  | 12:58 PM | 1.6 | 49 |
|  | 09:29 PM | -0.1 | -3 |
| 25 M | 05:00 AM | 1.3 | 40 |
|  | 08:27 AM | 1.2 | 37 |
|  | 01:31 PM | 1.7 | 52 |
|  | 10:11 PM | -0.2 | -6 |
| 26 Tu | 05:47 AM | 1.4 | 43 |
|  | 09:15 AM | 1.3 | 40 |
|  | 02:05 PM | 1.7 | 52 |
|  | 10:50 PM | -0.2 | -6 |
| 27 W | 06:24 AM | 1.4 | 43 |
|  | 09:59 AM | 1.3 | 40 |
|  | 02:42 PM | 1.7 | 52 |
|  | 11:26 PM | -0.2 | -6 |
| 28 Th | 06:55 AM | 1.5 | 46 |
|  | 10:40 AM | 1.3 | 40 |
|  | 03:21 PM | 1.7 | 52 |
|  | ○ 11:58 PM | -0.2 | -6 |
| 29 F | 07:21 AM | 1.5 | 46 |
|  | 11:19 AM | 1.3 | 40 |
|  | 04:01 PM | 1.7 | 52 |
| 30 Sa | 12:26 AM | -0.1 | -3 |
|  | 07:46 AM | 1.5 | 46 |
|  | 11:59 AM | 1.2 | 37 |
|  | 04:44 PM | 1.6 | 49 |

Heights are referred to mean lower water which is the chart datum of sounding. All times are local. Daylight Saving Time has been used when needed. Additional tide tables are available online from NOAA at www.tidesandcurrents.noaa.gov/tide_predictions.shtml.

SKIPPER'S HANDBOOK

StationId: 8728690
Source: NOAA/NOS/CO-OPS
Station Type: Primary
Time Zone: LST_LDT
Datum: MLLW

# NOAA Tide Predictions

## Apalachicola, FL, 2018

### Times and Heights of High and Low Waters

## July

| Day | Time | Height (ft) | Height (cm) |
|---|---|---|---|
| 1 Su | 12:52 AM | -0.1 | -3 |
|  | 08:10 AM | 1.5 | 46 |
|  | 12:42 PM | 1.2 | 37 |
|  | 05:29 PM | 1.6 | 49 |
| 2 M | 01:17 AM | 0.0 | 0 |
|  | 08:34 AM | 1.5 | 46 |
|  | 01:30 PM | 1.1 | 34 |
|  | 06:17 PM | 1.5 | 46 |
| 3 Tu | 01:44 AM | 0.1 | 3 |
|  | 09:00 AM | 1.5 | 46 |
|  | 02:26 PM | 1.0 | 30 |
|  | 07:10 PM | 1.4 | 43 |
| 4 W | 02:15 AM | 0.2 | 6 |
|  | 09:27 AM | 1.5 | 46 |
|  | 03:30 PM | 0.9 | 27 |
|  | 08:14 PM | 1.3 | 40 |
| 5 Th | 02:50 AM | 0.3 | 9 |
|  | 09:56 AM | 1.6 | 49 |
|  | 04:41 PM | 0.8 | 24 |
|  | 09:34 PM | 1.2 | 37 |
| 6 F ◑ | 03:29 AM | 0.5 | 15 |
|  | 10:27 AM | 1.6 | 49 |
|  | 05:54 PM | 0.6 | 18 |
|  | 11:14 PM | 1.1 | 34 |
| 7 Sa | 04:15 AM | 0.7 | 21 |
|  | 10:59 AM | 1.6 | 49 |
|  | 07:00 PM | 0.4 | 12 |
| 8 Su | 01:09 AM | 1.1 | 34 |
|  | 05:09 AM | 0.9 | 27 |
|  | 11:33 AM | 1.7 | 52 |
|  | 07:58 PM | 0.2 | 6 |
| 9 M | 03:02 AM | 1.2 | 37 |
|  | 06:16 AM | 1.1 | 34 |
|  | 12:12 PM | 1.7 | 52 |
|  | 08:52 PM | -0.1 | -3 |
| 10 Tu | 04:29 AM | 1.4 | 43 |
|  | 07:30 AM | 1.3 | 40 |
|  | 12:55 PM | 1.8 | 55 |
|  | 09:42 PM | -0.2 | -6 |
| 11 W | 05:29 AM | 1.5 | 46 |
|  | 08:38 AM | 1.4 | 43 |
|  | 01:43 PM | 1.9 | 58 |
|  | 10:31 PM | -0.4 | -12 |
| 12 Th | 06:17 AM | 1.6 | 49 |
|  | 09:37 AM | 1.4 | 43 |
|  | 02:35 PM | 1.9 | 58 |
|  | 11:18 PM | -0.4 | -12 |
| 13 F ● | 06:57 AM | 1.6 | 49 |
|  | 10:29 AM | 1.4 | 43 |
|  | 03:30 PM | 1.9 | 58 |
| 14 Sa | 12:03 AM | -0.4 | -12 |
|  | 07:31 AM | 1.5 | 46 |
|  | 11:21 AM | 1.3 | 40 |
|  | 04:27 PM | 1.9 | 58 |
| 15 Su | 12:47 AM | -0.3 | -9 |
|  | 08:01 AM | 1.5 | 46 |
|  | 12:15 PM | 1.2 | 37 |
|  | 05:25 PM | 1.8 | 55 |
| 16 M | 01:28 AM | -0.1 | -3 |
|  | 08:27 AM | 1.5 | 46 |
|  | 01:14 PM | 1.1 | 34 |
|  | 06:26 PM | 1.7 | 52 |
| 17 Tu | 02:07 AM | 0.1 | 3 |
|  | 08:51 AM | 1.5 | 46 |
|  | 02:21 PM | 0.9 | 27 |
|  | 07:32 PM | 1.5 | 46 |
| 18 W | 02:45 AM | 0.3 | 9 |
|  | 09:16 AM | 1.5 | 46 |
|  | 03:37 PM | 0.8 | 24 |
|  | 08:48 PM | 1.3 | 40 |
| 19 Th ◐ | 03:21 AM | 0.6 | 18 |
|  | 09:43 AM | 1.6 | 49 |
|  | 04:57 PM | 0.6 | 18 |
|  | 10:24 PM | 1.2 | 37 |
| 20 F | 03:57 AM | 0.8 | 24 |
|  | 10:13 AM | 1.6 | 49 |
|  | 06:13 PM | 0.4 | 12 |
| 21 Sa | 12:29 AM | 1.1 | 34 |
|  | 04:39 AM | 1.0 | 30 |
|  | 10:47 AM | 1.7 | 52 |
|  | 07:21 PM | 0.3 | 9 |
| 22 Su | 02:45 AM | 1.2 | 37 |
|  | 05:36 AM | 1.2 | 37 |
|  | 11:25 AM | 1.7 | 52 |
|  | 08:19 PM | 0.1 | 3 |
| 23 M | 04:08 AM | 1.3 | 40 |
|  | 06:50 AM | 1.3 | 40 |
|  | 12:09 PM | 1.7 | 52 |
|  | 09:09 PM | 0.0 | 0 |
| 24 Tu | 04:53 AM | 1.4 | 43 |
|  | 07:40 AM | 1.3 | 40 |
|  | 12:57 PM | 1.7 | 52 |
|  | 09:54 PM | -0.1 | -3 |
| 25 W | 05:27 AM | 1.5 | 46 |
|  | 08:59 AM | 1.3 | 40 |
|  | 01:46 PM | 1.7 | 52 |
|  | 10:33 PM | -0.1 | -3 |
| 26 Th | 05:55 AM | 1.5 | 46 |
|  | 09:47 AM | 1.3 | 40 |
|  | 02:33 PM | 1.7 | 52 |
|  | 11:09 PM | -0.1 | -3 |
| 27 F ○ | 06:19 AM | 1.6 | 49 |
|  | 10:29 AM | 1.3 | 40 |
|  | 03:18 PM | 1.7 | 52 |
|  | 11:39 PM | 0.0 | 0 |
| 28 Sa | 06:39 AM | 1.5 | 46 |
|  | 11:06 AM | 1.2 | 37 |
|  | 04:02 PM | 1.7 | 52 |
| 29 Su | 12:04 AM | 0.0 | 0 |
|  | 07:20 AM | 1.5 | 46 |
|  | 11:42 AM | 1.2 | 37 |
|  | 04:45 PM | 1.7 | 52 |
| 30 M | 12:26 AM | 0.1 | 3 |
|  | 07:16 AM | 1.6 | 49 |
|  | 12:19 PM | 1.1 | 34 |
|  | 05:29 PM | 1.7 | 52 |
| 31 Tu | 12:47 AM | 0.2 | 6 |
|  | 07:34 AM | 1.6 | 49 |
|  | 12:59 PM | 1.0 | 30 |
|  | 06:17 PM | 1.6 | 49 |

## August

| Day | Time | Height (ft) | Height (cm) |
|---|---|---|---|
| 1 W | 01:10 AM | 0.3 | 9 |
|  | 07:55 AM | 1.6 | 49 |
|  | 01:44 PM | 0.9 | 27 |
|  | 07:10 PM | 1.5 | 46 |
| 2 Th | 01:37 AM | 0.4 | 12 |
|  | 08:19 AM | 1.7 | 52 |
|  | 02:36 PM | 0.8 | 24 |
|  | 08:13 PM | 1.4 | 43 |
| 3 F | 02:08 AM | 0.6 | 18 |
|  | 08:46 AM | 1.7 | 52 |
|  | 03:41 PM | 0.7 | 21 |
|  | 09:33 PM | 1.3 | 40 |
| 4 Sa ◑ | 02:42 AM | 0.8 | 24 |
|  | 09:17 AM | 1.7 | 52 |
|  | 05:00 PM | 0.6 | 18 |
|  | 11:18 PM | 1.2 | 37 |
| 5 Su | 03:21 AM | 1.0 | 30 |
|  | 09:54 AM | 1.8 | 55 |
|  | 06:23 PM | 0.4 | 12 |
| 6 M | 01:30 AM | 1.3 | 40 |
|  | 04:09 AM | 1.2 | 37 |
|  | 10:37 AM | 1.8 | 55 |
|  | 07:35 PM | 0.2 | 6 |
| 7 Tu | 03:34 AM | 1.4 | 43 |
|  | 05:35 AM | 1.4 | 43 |
|  | 11:30 AM | 1.9 | 58 |
|  | 08:37 PM | 0.0 | 0 |
| 8 W | 04:35 AM | 1.6 | 49 |
|  | 07:19 AM | 1.5 | 46 |
|  | 12:30 PM | 1.9 | 58 |
|  | 09:31 PM | -0.1 | -3 |
| 9 Th | 05:14 AM | 1.6 | 49 |
|  | 08:35 AM | 1.5 | 46 |
|  | 01:35 PM | 1.9 | 58 |
|  | 10:21 PM | -0.2 | -6 |
| 10 F | 05:47 AM | 1.6 | 49 |
|  | 09:34 AM | 1.4 | 43 |
|  | 02:40 PM | 2.0 | 61 |
|  | 11:06 PM | -0.2 | -6 |
| 11 Sa ● | 06:14 AM | 1.6 | 49 |
|  | 10:25 AM | 1.3 | 40 |
|  | 11:48 PM | -0.1 | -3 |
| 12 Su | 06:38 AM | 1.6 | 49 |
|  | 11:13 AM | 1.2 | 37 |
|  | 04:40 PM | 2.0 | 61 |
| 13 M | 12:26 AM | 0.0 | 0 |
|  | 06:59 AM | 1.6 | 49 |
|  | 12:03 PM | 1.0 | 30 |
|  | 05:38 PM | 1.9 | 58 |
| 14 Tu | 01:00 AM | 0.2 | 6 |
|  | 07:18 AM | 1.6 | 49 |
|  | 12:56 PM | 0.9 | 27 |
|  | 06:37 PM | 1.7 | 52 |
| 15 W | 01:32 AM | 0.5 | 15 |
|  | 07:38 AM | 1.6 | 49 |
|  | 01:53 PM | 0.8 | 24 |
|  | 07:41 PM | 1.6 | 49 |
| 16 Th | 02:01 AM | 0.7 | 21 |
|  | 08:01 AM | 1.7 | 52 |
|  | 02:59 PM | 0.7 | 21 |
|  | 08:54 PM | 1.4 | 43 |
| 17 F | 02:29 AM | 0.9 | 27 |
|  | 08:28 AM | 1.7 | 52 |
|  | 04:13 PM | 0.6 | 18 |
|  | 10:25 PM | 1.3 | 40 |
| 18 Sa ◐ | 03:00 AM | 1.1 | 34 |
|  | 09:00 AM | 1.7 | 52 |
|  | 05:31 PM | 0.5 | 15 |
| 19 Su | 12:26 AM | 1.3 | 40 |
|  | 03:43 AM | 1.2 | 37 |
|  | 09:41 AM | 1.7 | 52 |
|  | 06:44 PM | 0.4 | 12 |
| 20 M | 02:31 AM | 1.4 | 43 |
|  | 05:00 AM | 1.4 | 43 |
|  | 10:31 AM | 1.7 | 52 |
|  | 07:48 PM | 0.3 | 9 |
| 21 Tu | 03:31 AM | 1.5 | 46 |
|  | 06:38 AM | 1.4 | 43 |
|  | 11:33 AM | 1.7 | 52 |
|  | 08:41 PM | 0.2 | 6 |
| 22 W | 04:06 AM | 1.5 | 46 |
|  | 07:54 AM | 1.4 | 43 |
|  | 12:39 PM | 1.7 | 52 |
|  | 09:27 PM | 0.2 | 6 |
| 23 Th | 04:36 AM | 1.6 | 49 |
|  | 08:51 AM | 1.3 | 40 |
|  | 01:41 PM | 1.8 | 55 |
|  | 10:07 PM | 0.2 | 6 |
| 24 F | 05:01 AM | 1.6 | 49 |
|  | 09:36 AM | 1.3 | 40 |
|  | 02:36 PM | 1.8 | 55 |
|  | 10:41 PM | 0.2 | 6 |
| 25 Sa | 05:22 AM | 1.6 | 49 |
|  | 10:15 AM | 1.2 | 37 |
|  | 03:24 PM | 1.8 | 55 |
|  | 11:10 PM | 0.2 | 6 |
| 26 Su ○ | 05:40 AM | 1.6 | 49 |
|  | 10:50 AM | 1.1 | 34 |
|  | 04:08 PM | 1.8 | 55 |
|  | 11:33 PM | 0.3 | 9 |
| 27 M | 05:55 AM | 1.6 | 49 |
|  | 11:23 AM | 1.0 | 30 |
|  | 04:51 PM | 1.8 | 55 |
|  | 11:54 PM | 0.4 | 12 |
| 28 Tu | 06:11 AM | 1.7 | 52 |
|  | 11:55 AM | 0.9 | 27 |
|  | 05:36 PM | 1.7 | 52 |
| 29 W | 12:14 AM | 0.5 | 15 |
|  | 06:28 AM | 1.7 | 52 |
|  | 12:29 PM | 0.8 | 24 |
|  | 06:24 PM | 1.7 | 52 |
| 30 Th | 12:37 AM | 0.6 | 18 |
|  | 06:48 AM | 1.7 | 52 |
|  | 01:07 PM | 0.7 | 21 |
|  | 07:19 PM | 1.6 | 49 |
| 31 F | 01:03 AM | 0.8 | 24 |
|  | 07:11 AM | 1.8 | 55 |
|  | 01:53 PM | 0.6 | 18 |
|  | 08:24 PM | 1.5 | 46 |

## September

| Day | Time | Height (ft) | Height (cm) |
|---|---|---|---|
| 1 Sa | 01:33 AM | 1.0 | 30 |
|  | 07:40 AM | 1.8 | 55 |
|  | 02:52 PM | 0.6 | 18 |
|  | 09:48 PM | 1.4 | 43 |
| 2 Su | 02:06 AM | 1.2 | 37 |
|  | 08:14 AM | 1.9 | 58 |
|  | 04:14 PM | 0.5 | 15 |
|  | 11:39 PM | 1.4 | 43 |
| 3 M | 02:44 AM | 1.3 | 40 |
|  | 08:57 AM | 1.9 | 58 |
|  | 05:51 PM | 0.4 | 12 |
| 4 Tu | 09:53 AM | 1.9 | 58 |
|  | 07:13 PM | 0.3 | 9 |
| 5 W | 03:21 AM | 1.6 | 49 |
|  | 06:01 AM | 1.5 | 46 |
|  | 11:06 AM | 1.9 | 58 |
|  | 08:19 PM | 0.2 | 6 |
| 6 Th | 03:58 AM | 1.6 | 49 |
|  | 07:38 AM | 1.5 | 46 |
|  | 12:28 PM | 1.9 | 58 |
|  | 09:15 PM | 0.1 | 3 |
| 7 F | 04:27 AM | 1.7 | 52 |
|  | 08:42 AM | 1.4 | 43 |
|  | 01:46 PM | 1.9 | 58 |
|  | 10:03 PM | 0.1 | 3 |
| 8 Sa | 04:52 AM | 1.6 | 49 |
|  | 09:34 AM | 1.2 | 37 |
|  | 02:56 PM | 2.0 | 61 |
|  | 10:45 PM | 0.2 | 6 |
| 9 Su ● | 05:13 AM | 1.6 | 49 |
|  | 10:21 AM | 1.1 | 34 |
|  | 03:59 PM | 2.0 | 61 |
|  | 11:23 PM | 0.3 | 9 |
| 10 M | 05:31 AM | 1.6 | 49 |
|  | 11:06 AM | 0.9 | 27 |
|  | 04:56 PM | 1.9 | 58 |
|  | 11:56 PM | 0.5 | 15 |
| 11 Tu | 05:48 AM | 1.6 | 49 |
|  | 11:51 AM | 0.7 | 21 |
|  | 05:52 PM | 1.9 | 58 |
| 12 W | 12:25 AM | 0.7 | 21 |
|  | 06:05 AM | 1.7 | 52 |
|  | 12:36 PM | 0.6 | 18 |
|  | 06:49 PM | 1.8 | 55 |
| 13 Th | 12:52 AM | 0.9 | 27 |
|  | 06:25 AM | 1.7 | 52 |
|  | 01:25 PM | 0.5 | 15 |
|  | 07:50 PM | 1.6 | 49 |
| 14 F | 01:18 AM | 1.1 | 34 |
|  | 06:49 AM | 1.8 | 55 |
|  | 02:19 PM | 0.5 | 15 |
|  | 08:58 PM | 1.5 | 46 |
| 15 Sa | 01:46 AM | 1.2 | 37 |
|  | 07:18 AM | 1.8 | 55 |
|  | 03:23 PM | 0.5 | 15 |
|  | 10:21 PM | 1.5 | 46 |
| 16 Su ◐ | 02:22 AM | 1.3 | 40 |
|  | 07:55 AM | 1.8 | 55 |
|  | 04:39 PM | 0.5 | 15 |
| 17 M | 12:01 AM | 1.5 | 46 |
|  | 03:22 AM | 1.4 | 43 |
|  | 08:42 AM | 1.8 | 55 |
|  | 05:56 PM | 0.5 | 15 |
| 18 Tu | 01:30 AM | 1.5 | 46 |
|  | 05:03 AM | 1.4 | 43 |
|  | 09:44 AM | 1.7 | 52 |
|  | 07:04 PM | 0.4 | 12 |
| 19 W | 02:24 AM | 1.6 | 49 |
|  | 06:38 AM | 1.4 | 43 |
|  | 11:04 AM | 1.7 | 52 |
|  | 08:00 PM | 0.4 | 12 |
| 20 Th | 03:01 AM | 1.6 | 49 |
|  | 07:46 AM | 1.3 | 40 |
|  | 12:27 PM | 1.7 | 52 |
|  | 08:48 PM | 0.4 | 12 |
| 21 F | 03:30 AM | 1.6 | 49 |
|  | 08:38 AM | 1.2 | 37 |
|  | 01:39 PM | 1.7 | 52 |
|  | 09:28 PM | 0.4 | 12 |
| 22 Sa | 03:55 AM | 1.7 | 52 |
|  | 09:20 AM | 1.1 | 34 |
|  | 02:37 PM | 1.7 | 52 |
|  | 10:02 PM | 0.5 | 15 |
| 23 Su | 04:15 AM | 1.7 | 52 |
|  | 09:58 AM | 1.0 | 30 |
|  | 03:28 PM | 1.8 | 55 |
|  | 10:30 PM | 0.5 | 15 |
| 24 M | 04:32 AM | 1.7 | 52 |
|  | 10:31 AM | 0.8 | 24 |
|  | 04:14 PM | 1.8 | 55 |
|  | 10:55 PM | 0.6 | 18 |
| 25 Tu ○ | 04:47 AM | 1.7 | 52 |
|  | 11:03 AM | 0.7 | 21 |
|  | 05:00 PM | 1.8 | 55 |
|  | 11:17 PM | 0.7 | 21 |
| 26 W | 05:03 AM | 1.7 | 52 |
|  | 11:33 AM | 0.6 | 18 |
|  | 05:48 PM | 1.7 | 52 |
|  | 11:40 PM | 0.9 | 27 |
| 27 Th | 05:22 AM | 1.8 | 55 |
|  | 12:05 PM | 0.5 | 15 |
|  | 06:39 PM | 1.7 | 52 |
| 28 F | 12:06 AM | 1.0 | 30 |
|  | 05:44 AM | 1.8 | 55 |
|  | 12:42 PM | 0.4 | 12 |
|  | 07:38 PM | 1.6 | 49 |
| 29 Sa | 12:34 AM | 1.1 | 34 |
|  | 06:11 AM | 1.9 | 58 |
|  | 01:27 PM | 0.3 | 9 |
|  | 08:47 PM | 1.6 | 49 |
| 30 Su | 01:06 AM | 1.3 | 40 |
|  | 06:43 AM | 1.9 | 58 |
|  | 02:26 PM | 0.3 | 9 |
|  | 10:13 PM | 1.5 | 46 |

Heights are referred to mean lower water which is the chart datum of sounding. All times are local. Daylight Saving Time has been used when needed. Additional tide tables are available online from NOAA at www.tidesandcurrents.noaa.gov/tide_predictions.shtml.

SKIPPER'S HANDBOOK

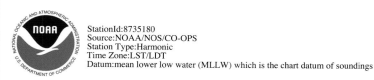

StationId:8735180
Source:NOAA/NOS/CO-OPS
Station Type:Harmonic
Time Zone:LST/LDT
Datum:mean lower low water (MLLW) which is the chart datum of soundings

**NOAA Tide Predictions**

# DAUPHIN ISLAND, Alabama, 2017

### Times and Heights of High and Low Waters

## October

| Day | Time | ft | cm | Day | Time | ft | cm |
|---|---|---|---|---|---|---|---|
| 1 Su | 07:03 AM / 05:52 PM | 1.4 / 0.5 | 43 / 15 | 16 M | 08:22 AM / 05:42 PM | 1.2 / 0.7 | 37 / 21 |
| 2 M | 08:05 AM / 06:17 PM | 1.3 / 0.6 | 40 / 18 | 17 Tu | 09:52 AM / 04:30 PM / 10:06 PM | 1.0 / 0.9 / 1.0 | 30 / 27 / 30 |
| 3 Tu | 09:11 AM / 06:26 PM | 1.3 / 0.7 | 40 / 21 | 18 W | 05:24 AM / 10:09 PM | 0.7 / 1.2 | 21 / 37 |
| 4 W | 10:28 AM / 06:04 PM / 11:32 PM | 1.1 / 0.8 / 0.9 | 34 / 24 / 27 | 19 Th ● | 07:14 AM / 10:31 PM | 0.6 / 1.3 | 18 / 40 |
| 5 Th ○ | 05:31 AM / 12:22 PM / 04:40 PM / 11:04 PM | 0.8 / 1.0 / 0.9 / 1.1 | 24 / 30 / 27 / 34 | 20 F | 08:32 AM / 11:00 PM | 0.5 / 1.4 | 15 / 43 |
| 6 F | 07:36 AM / 11:17 PM | 0.7 / 1.3 | 21 / 40 | 21 Sa | 09:35 AM / 11:31 PM | 0.4 / 1.5 | 12 / 46 |
| 7 Sa | 09:17 AM / 11:50 PM | 0.5 / 1.5 | 15 / 46 | 22 Su | 10:32 AM | 0.3 | 9 |
| 8 Su | 10:48 AM | 0.4 | 12 | 23 M | 12:05 AM / 11:26 AM | 1.6 / 0.3 | 49 / 9 |
| 9 M | 12:33 AM / 12:11 PM | 1.6 / 0.2 | 49 / 6 | 24 Tu | 12:40 AM / 12:20 PM | 1.6 / 0.2 | 49 / 6 |
| 10 Tu | 01:24 AM / 01:29 PM | 1.7 / 0.2 | 52 / 6 | 25 W | 01:19 AM / 01:12 PM | 1.6 / 0.2 | 49 / 6 |
| 11 W | 02:22 AM / 02:41 PM | 1.7 / 0.1 | 52 / 3 | 26 Th | 02:00 AM / 02:00 PM | 1.5 / 0.3 | 46 / 9 |
| 12 Th ◑ | 03:26 AM / 03:46 PM | 1.7 / 0.2 | 52 / 6 | 27 F ◐ | 02:45 AM / 02:42 PM | 1.5 / 0.3 | 46 / 9 |
| 13 F | 04:35 AM / 04:43 PM | 1.6 / 0.2 | 49 / 6 | 28 Sa | 03:32 AM / 03:17 PM | 1.4 / 0.3 | 43 / 9 |
| 14 Sa | 05:48 AM / 05:29 PM | 1.5 / 0.4 | 46 / 12 | 29 Su | 04:22 AM / 03:43 PM | 1.3 / 0.4 | 40 / 12 |
| 15 Su | 07:04 AM / 05:56 PM | 1.4 / 0.5 | 43 / 15 | 30 M | 05:21 AM / 03:56 PM | 1.2 / 0.5 | 37 / 15 |
| | | | | 31 Tu | 06:47 AM / 03:48 PM / 11:15 PM | 1.0 / 0.6 / 0.9 | 30 / 18 / 27 |

## November

| Day | Time | ft | cm | Day | Time | ft | cm |
|---|---|---|---|---|---|---|---|
| 1 W | 05:19 AM / 09:17 AM / 02:54 PM / 10:13 PM | 0.8 / 0.8 / 0.7 / 1.0 | 24 / 24 / 21 / 30 | 16 Th | 06:44 AM / 08:40 PM | 0.3 / 1.3 | 9 / 40 |
| 2 Th | 06:41 AM / 10:00 PM | 0.6 / 1.2 | 18 / 37 | 17 F | 07:25 AM / 09:06 PM | 0.1 / 1.4 | 3 / 43 |
| 3 F | 07:45 AM / 10:14 PM | 0.4 / 1.4 | 12 / 43 | 18 Sa ○ | 08:06 AM / 09:34 PM | 0.0 / 1.5 | 0 / 46 |
| 4 Sa ○ | 08:48 AM / 10:44 PM | 0.2 / 1.6 | 6 / 49 | 19 Su | 08:47 AM / 10:05 PM | 0.0 / 1.5 | 0 / 46 |
| 5 Su | 08:54 AM / 10:24 PM | 0.0 / 1.7 | 0 / 52 | 20 M | 09:30 AM / 10:37 PM | -0.1 / 1.5 | -3 / 46 |
| 6 M | 10:03 AM / 11:10 PM | -0.1 / 1.8 | -3 / 55 | 21 Tu | 10:15 AM / 11:09 PM | -0.1 / 1.4 | -3 / 43 |
| 7 Tu | 11:13 AM | -0.1 | -3 | 22 W | 10:57 AM / 11:43 PM | -0.1 / 1.4 | -3 / 43 |
| 8 W | 12:01 AM / 12:20 PM | 1.7 / -0.1 | 52 / -3 | 23 Th | 11:37 AM | -0.1 | -3 |
| 9 Th | 12:55 AM / 01:19 PM | 1.7 / 0.0 | 52 / 0 | 24 F | 12:15 AM / 12:11 PM | 1.3 / 0.0 | 40 / 0 |
| 10 F ◑ | 01:51 AM / 02:07 PM | 1.5 / 0.1 | 46 / 3 | 25 Sa | 12:45 AM / 12:38 PM | 1.2 / 0.0 | 37 / 0 |
| 11 Sa | 02:46 AM / 02:37 PM | 1.3 / 0.2 | 40 / 6 | 26 Su ◐ | 01:09 AM / 12:56 PM | 1.1 / 0.1 | 34 / 3 |
| 12 Su | 03:41 AM / 02:36 PM | 1.1 / 0.4 | 34 / 12 | 27 M | 01:09 AM / 01:00 PM / 11:12 PM | 0.9 / 0.2 / 0.8 | 27 / 6 / 24 |
| 13 M | 04:34 AM / 01:47 PM / 09:16 PM | 0.9 / 0.6 / 0.8 | 27 / 18 / 24 | 28 Tu | 12:37 PM / 09:07 PM | 0.3 / 0.8 | 9 / 24 |
| 14 Tu | 12:01 PM / 08:20 PM | 0.6 / 1.0 | 18 / 30 | 29 W | 11:07 AM / 08:16 PM | 0.4 / 0.9 | 12 / 27 |
| 15 W | 06:00 AM / 08:22 PM | 0.5 / 1.2 | 15 / 37 | 30 Th | 06:11 AM / 08:05 PM | 0.2 / 1.1 | 6 / 34 |

## December

| Day | Time | ft | cm | Day | Time | ft | cm |
|---|---|---|---|---|---|---|---|
| 1 F | 06:32 AM / 08:20 PM | 0.0 / 1.3 | 0 / 40 | 16 Sa | 07:36 AM / 08:43 PM | -0.3 / 1.2 | -9 / 37 |
| 2 Sa | 07:17 AM / 08:49 PM | -0.2 / 1.5 | -6 / 46 | 17 Su | 08:13 AM / 09:15 PM | -0.3 / 1.3 | -9 / 40 |
| 3 Su ○ | 08:12 AM / 09:28 PM | -0.3 / 1.6 | -9 / 49 | 18 M | 08:52 AM / 09:47 PM | -0.4 / 1.3 | -12 / 40 |
| 4 M | 09:14 AM / 10:13 PM | -0.4 / 1.6 | -12 / 49 | 19 Tu | 09:30 AM / 10:19 PM | -0.4 / 1.2 | -12 / 37 |
| 5 Tu | 10:17 AM / 11:01 PM | -0.5 / 1.6 | -15 / 49 | 20 W | 10:06 AM / 10:50 PM | -0.4 / 1.2 | -12 / 37 |
| 6 W | 11:18 AM / 11:49 PM | -0.5 / 1.5 | -15 / 46 | 21 Th | 10:37 AM / 11:18 PM | -0.4 / 1.1 | -12 / 34 |
| 7 Th | 12:10 PM | -0.4 | -12 | 22 F | 11:04 AM / 11:43 PM | -0.3 / 1.0 | -9 / 30 |
| 8 F | 12:36 AM / 12:50 PM | 1.3 / -0.2 | 40 / -6 | 23 Sa | 11:24 AM | -0.3 | -9 |
| 9 Sa | 01:17 AM / 01:08 PM | 1.1 / -0.1 | 34 / -3 | 24 Su | 12:01 AM / 11:35 AM / 11:54 PM | 0.9 / -0.2 / 0.7 | 27 / -6 / 21 |
| 10 Su ◑ | 01:42 AM / 12:49 PM | 0.9 / 0.1 | 27 / 3 | 25 M | 11:31 AM / 10:11 PM | -0.1 / 0.6 | -3 / 18 |
| 11 M | 12:43 AM / 11:39 AM / 08:15 PM | 0.6 / 0.3 / 0.6 | 18 / 9 / 18 | 26 Tu | 10:56 AM / 08:02 PM | 0.0 / 0.6 | 0 / 18 |
| 12 Tu | 09:35 AM / 07:25 PM | 0.2 / 0.8 | 6 / 24 | 27 W ◐ | 09:08 AM / 07:11 PM | 0.1 / 0.7 | 3 / 21 |
| 13 W | 06:49 AM / 07:28 PM | 0.1 / 1.0 | 3 / 30 | 28 Th | 06:00 AM / 07:04 PM | -0.1 / 0.9 | -3 / 27 |
| 14 Th | 06:39 AM / 07:47 PM | -0.1 / 1.1 | -3 / 34 | 29 F | 06:00 AM / 07:22 PM | -0.3 / 1.1 | -9 / 34 |
| 15 F | 07:03 AM / 08:14 PM | -0.2 / 1.2 | -6 / 37 | 30 Sa | 06:38 AM / 07:55 PM | -0.5 / 1.2 | -15 / 37 |
| | | | | 31 Su | 07:30 AM / 08:37 PM | -0.6 / 1.3 | -18 / 40 |

Heights are referred to mean lower water which is the chart datum of sounding. All times are local. Daylight Saving Time has been used when needed. Additional tide tables are available online from NOAA at www.tidesandcurrents.noaa.gov/tide_predictions.shtml.

SKIPPER'S HANDBOOK

StationId: 8735180
Source: NOAA/NOS/CO-OPS
Station Type: Primary
Time Zone: LST_LDT
Datum: MLLW

**NOAA Tide Predictions**

## Dauphin Island, AL, 2018

**Times and Heights of High and Low Waters**

### January

| Day | Time | Height (ft) | cm | Day | Time | Height (ft) | cm |
|---|---|---|---|---|---|---|---|
| 1 M | 08:22 AM / 09:19 PM | -0.8 / 1.4 | -24 / 43 | 16 Tu | 08:54 AM / 09:38 PM | -0.5 / 1.1 | -15 / 34 |
| 2 Tu ○ | 09:24 AM / 10:08 PM | -0.8 / 1.4 | -24 / 43 | 17 W ● | 09:29 AM / 10:11 PM | -0.5 / 1.0 | -15 / 30 |
| 3 W | 10:24 AM / 10:56 PM | -0.8 / 1.3 | -24 / 40 | 18 Th | 09:58 AM / 10:42 PM | -0.5 / 0.9 | -15 / 27 |
| 4 Th | 11:16 AM / 11:42 PM | -0.7 / 1.2 | -21 / 37 | 19 F | 10:21 AM / 11:10 PM | -0.5 / 0.9 | -15 / 27 |
| 5 F | 11:56 AM | -0.5 | -15 | 20 Sa | 10:37 AM / 11:33 PM | -0.4 / 0.7 | -12 / 21 |
| 6 Sa | 12:21 AM / 12:14 PM | 1.0 / -0.3 | 30 / -9 | 21 Su | 10:43 AM / 11:44 PM | -0.3 / 0.6 | -9 / 18 |
| 7 Su | 12:47 AM / 11:50 AM | 0.7 / -0.1 | 21 / -3 | 22 M | 10:29 AM / 10:19 PM | -0.1 / 0.4 | -3 / 12 |
| 8 M | 12:20 AM / 10:28 AM / 07:31 PM | 0.5 / 0.0 / 0.4 | 15 / 0 / 12 | 23 Tu | 09:35 AM / 06:24 PM | 0.0 / 0.4 | 0 / 12 |
| 9 Tu | 08:25 AM / 06:19 PM | 0.0 / 0.6 | 0 / 18 | 24 W ◑ | 07:00 AM / 05:32 PM | 0.0 / 0.5 | 0 / 15 |
| 10 W | 06:20 AM / 06:21 PM | -0.1 / 0.7 | -3 / 21 | 25 Th | 04:29 AM / 05:35 PM | -0.2 / 0.7 | -6 / 21 |
| 11 Th | 05:59 AM / 06:44 PM | -0.3 / 0.9 | -9 / 27 | 26 F | 04:46 AM / 06:04 PM | -0.4 / 0.9 | -12 / 27 |
| 12 F | 06:20 AM / 07:15 PM | -0.4 / 1.0 | -12 / 30 | 27 Sa | 05:32 AM / 06:46 PM | -0.6 / 1.1 | -18 / 34 |
| 13 Sa | 06:54 AM / 07:49 PM | -0.5 / 1.0 | -15 / 30 | 28 Su | 06:28 AM / 07:35 PM | -0.7 / 1.2 | -21 / 37 |
| 14 Su | 07:33 AM / 08:26 PM | -0.5 / 1.1 | -15 / 34 | 29 M | 07:29 AM / 08:27 PM | -0.8 / 1.3 | -24 / 40 |
| 15 M | 08:15 AM / 09:03 PM | -0.5 / 1.1 | -15 / 34 | 30 Tu | 08:32 AM / 09:19 PM | -0.8 / 1.3 | -24 / 40 |
| | | | | 31 W ○ | 09:31 AM / 10:10 PM | -0.7 / 1.2 | -21 / 37 |

### February

| Day | Time | Height (ft) | cm | Day | Time | Height (ft) | cm |
|---|---|---|---|---|---|---|---|
| 1 Th | 10:25 AM / 10:57 PM | -0.6 / 1.0 | -18 / 30 | 16 F | 09:21 AM / 10:38 PM | -0.3 / 0.8 | -9 / 24 |
| 2 F | 11:07 AM / 11:40 PM | -0.4 / 0.8 | -12 / 24 | 17 Sa | 09:33 AM / 11:13 PM | -0.2 / 0.6 | -6 / 18 |
| 3 Sa | 11:27 AM | -0.2 | -6 | 18 Su | 09:26 AM / 11:50 PM | 0.0 / 0.5 | 0 / 15 |
| 4 Su | 12:15 AM / 10:39 AM | 0.6 / 0.0 | 18 / 0 | 19 M | 08:43 AM / 04:21 PM / 07:39 PM | 0.1 / 0.3 / 0.2 | 3 / 9 / 6 |
| 5 M | 12:25 AM / 08:33 AM / 04:18 PM | 0.3 / 0.1 / 0.3 | 9 / 3 / 9 | 20 Tu | 12:27 AM / 06:51 AM / 02:47 PM | 0.3 / 0.2 / 0.4 | 9 / 6 / 12 |
| 6 Tu | 06:01 AM / 04:04 PM | 0.0 / 0.5 | 0 / 15 | 21 W | 01:28 AM / 02:56 PM | 0.1 / 0.6 | 3 / 18 |
| 7 W ◑ | 04:15 AM / 04:31 PM | -0.1 / 0.7 | -3 / 21 | 22 Th | 02:14 AM / 03:33 PM | -0.1 / 0.8 | -3 / 24 |
| 8 Th | 04:24 AM / 05:09 PM | -0.3 / 0.8 | -9 / 24 | 23 F ◐ | 03:10 AM / 04:23 PM | -0.3 / 1.0 | -9 / 30 |
| 9 F | 04:58 AM / 05:52 PM | -0.3 / 0.9 | -9 / 27 | 24 Sa | 04:11 AM / 05:21 PM | -0.5 / 1.1 | -15 / 34 |
| 10 Sa | 05:41 AM / 06:38 PM | -0.4 / 0.9 | -12 / 27 | 25 Su | 05:15 AM / 06:23 PM | -0.5 / 1.2 | -15 / 37 |
| 11 Su | 06:27 AM / 07:24 PM | -0.4 / 1.0 | -12 / 30 | 26 M | 06:20 AM / 07:24 PM | -0.6 / 1.2 | -18 / 37 |
| 12 M | 07:14 AM / 08:08 PM | -0.4 / 1.0 | -12 / 30 | 27 Tu | 07:24 AM / 08:24 PM | -0.5 / 1.2 | -15 / 37 |
| 13 Tu | 07:56 AM / 08:50 PM | -0.4 / 1.0 | -12 / 30 | 28 W | 08:26 AM / 09:21 PM | -0.5 / 1.1 | -15 / 34 |
| 14 W | 08:32 AM / 09:28 PM | -0.4 / 0.9 | -12 / 27 | | | | |
| 15 Th ● | 09:00 AM / 10:03 PM | -0.4 / 0.9 | -12 / 27 | | | | |

### March

| Day | Time | Height (ft) | cm | Day | Time | Height (ft) | cm |
|---|---|---|---|---|---|---|---|
| 1 Th | 09:25 AM / 10:16 PM | -0.3 / 0.9 | -9 / 27 | 16 F | 08:41 AM / 11:08 PM | 0.1 / 0.8 | 3 / 24 |
| 2 F ○ | 10:23 AM / 11:09 PM | -0.1 / 0.8 | -3 / 24 | 17 Sa ● | 08:37 AM | 0.2 | 6 |
| 3 Sa | 12:32 PM | 0.1 | 3 | 18 Su | 12:11 AM / 07:53 AM / 12:28 PM / 06:32 PM | 0.6 / 0.3 / 0.4 / 0.3 | 18 / 9 / 12 / 9 |
| 4 Su | 12:06 AM / 08:01 AM / 11:31 AM / 06:14 PM | 0.5 / 0.3 / 0.3 / 0.2 | 15 / 9 / 9 / 6 | 19 M | 01:56 AM / 06:00 AM / 12:23 PM / 09:12 PM | 0.5 / 0.4 / 0.6 / 0.2 | 15 / 12 / 18 / 6 |
| 5 M | 01:32 AM / 04:59 AM / 12:26 PM / 10:15 PM | 0.3 / 0.3 / 0.5 / 0.1 | 9 / 9 / 15 / 3 | 20 Tu | 12:49 PM / 11:19 PM | 0.8 / 0.0 | 24 / 0 |
| 6 Tu | 01:15 PM | 0.7 | 21 | 21 W | 01:31 PM | 0.9 | 27 |
| 7 W | 12:45 AM / 02:05 PM | 0.0 / 0.8 | 0 / 24 | 22 Th | 12:56 AM / 02:23 PM | -0.1 / 1.1 | -3 / 34 |
| 8 Th | 01:57 AM / 02:57 PM | -0.1 / 0.9 | -3 / 27 | 23 F | 02:18 AM / 03:24 PM | -0.2 / 1.2 | -6 / 37 |
| 9 F ◐ | 02:55 AM / 03:53 PM | -0.2 / 0.9 | -6 / 27 | 24 Sa ◐ | 03:32 AM / 04:32 PM | -0.3 / 1.2 | -9 / 37 |
| 10 Sa | 03:51 AM / 04:53 PM | -0.2 / 1.0 | -6 / 30 | 25 Su | 04:42 AM / 05:46 PM | -0.3 / 1.3 | -9 / 40 |
| 11 Su | 05:45 AM / 06:53 PM | -0.2 / 1.0 | -6 / 30 | 26 M | 05:49 AM / 07:00 PM | -0.3 / 1.2 | -9 / 37 |
| 12 M | 06:35 AM / 07:50 PM | -0.2 / 1.0 | -6 / 30 | 27 Tu | 06:50 AM / 08:12 PM | -0.2 / 1.2 | -6 / 37 |
| 13 Tu | 07:19 AM / 08:43 PM | -0.2 / 1.0 | -6 / 30 | 28 W | 07:47 AM / 09:21 PM | -0.1 / 1.0 | -3 / 30 |
| 14 W | 07:56 AM / 09:31 PM | -0.1 / 0.9 | -3 / 27 | 29 Th | 08:37 AM / 10:30 PM | 0.1 / 0.9 | 3 / 27 |
| 15 Th | 08:24 AM / 10:18 PM | 0.0 / 0.9 | 0 / 27 | 30 F | 02:18 PM / 11:49 PM | 0.3 / 0.7 | 9 / 21 |
| | | | | 31 Sa ○ | 06:49 AM / 10:22 AM / 05:54 PM | 0.5 / 0.5 / 0.3 | 15 / 15 / 9 |

Heights are referred to mean lower water which is the chart datum of sounding. All times are local. Daylight Saving Time has been used when needed. Additional tide tables are available online from NOAA at www.tidesandcurrents.noaa.gov/tide_predictions.shtml.

StationId: 8735180
Source: NOAA/NOS/CO-OPS
Station Type: Primary
Time Zone: LST_LDT
Datum: MLLW

**NOAA Tide Predictions**

## Dauphin Island, AL,2018

**Times and Heights of High and Low Waters**

### April

| | Time | Height (ft) | (cm) | | Time | Height (ft) | (cm) |
|---|---|---|---|---|---|---|---|
| **1** Su | 11:02 AM / 08:10 PM | 0.7 / 0.2 | 21 / 6 | **16** M ● | 10:51 AM / 08:50 PM | 1.0 / 0.1 | 30 / 3 |
| **2** M | 11:42 AM / 09:56 PM | 0.9 / 0.1 | 27 / 3 | **17** Tu | 11:20 AM / 10:08 PM | 1.2 / 0.0 | 37 / 0 |
| **3** Tu | 12:22 PM / 11:22 PM | 1.0 / 0.0 | 30 / 0 | **18** W | 11:59 AM / 11:26 PM | 1.3 / -0.2 | 40 / -6 |
| **4** W | 01:04 PM | 1.1 | 34 | **19** Th | 12:48 PM | 1.4 | 43 |
| **5** Th | 12:35 AM / 01:50 PM | 0.0 / 1.1 | 0 / 34 | **20** F | 12:43 AM / 01:43 PM | -0.2 / 1.5 | -6 / 46 |
| **6** F | 01:42 AM / 02:40 PM | 0.0 / 1.1 | 0 / 34 | **21** Sa | 01:58 AM / 02:45 PM | -0.3 / 1.4 | -9 / 43 |
| **7** Sa | 02:43 AM / 03:36 PM | 0.0 / 1.1 | 0 / 34 | **22** Su ◐ | 03:08 AM / 03:53 PM | -0.2 / 1.4 | -6 / 43 |
| **8** Su ◐ | 03:40 AM / 04:39 PM | 0.0 / 1.1 | 0 / 34 | **23** M | 04:08 AM / 05:06 PM | -0.2 / 1.3 | -6 / 40 |
| **9** M | 04:28 AM / 05:45 PM | 0.0 / 1.0 | 0 / 30 | **24** Tu | 04:59 AM / 06:24 PM | 0.0 / 1.1 | 0 / 34 |
| **10** Tu | 05:08 AM / 06:51 PM | 0.1 / 1.0 | 3 / 30 | **25** W | 05:32 AM / 07:47 PM | 0.2 / 0.9 | 6 / 27 |
| **11** W | 05:37 AM / 07:57 PM | 0.1 / 0.9 | 3 / 27 | **26** Th | 05:29 AM / 09:26 PM | 0.4 / 0.7 | 12 / 21 |
| **12** Th | 05:55 AM / 09:07 PM | 0.2 / 0.8 | 6 / 24 | **27** F | 04:20 AM / 09:57 PM / 05:13 PM | 0.5 / 0.7 / 0.4 | 15 / 21 / 12 |
| **13** F | 05:54 AM / 12:36 PM / 02:56 PM / 10:32 PM | 0.4 / 0.5 / 0.5 / 0.7 | 12 / 15 / 15 / 21 | **28** Sa | 09:50 AM / 07:03 PM | 0.9 / 0.3 | 27 / 9 |
| **14** Sa | 05:21 AM / 10:56 AM / 05:46 PM | 0.5 / 0.6 / 0.4 | 15 / 18 / 12 | **29** Su | 10:11 AM / 08:19 PM | 1.1 / 0.1 | 34 / 3 |
| **15** Su | 12:56 AM / 03:32 AM / 10:38 AM / 07:27 PM | 0.6 / 0.6 / 0.8 / 0.2 | 18 / 18 / 24 / 6 | **30** M ○ | 10:39 AM / 09:20 PM | 1.2 / 0.0 | 37 / 0 |

### May

| | Time | Height (ft) | (cm) | | Time | Height (ft) | (cm) |
|---|---|---|---|---|---|---|---|
| **1** Tu | 11:11 AM / 10:15 PM | 1.3 / 0.0 | 40 / 0 | **16** W | 10:56 AM / 10:27 PM | 1.6 / -0.3 | 49 / -9 |
| **2** W | 11:46 AM / 11:10 PM | 1.4 / -0.1 | 43 / -3 | **17** Th | 11:40 AM / 11:36 PM | 1.6 / -0.3 | 49 / -9 |
| **3** Th | 12:23 PM | 1.4 | 43 | **18** F | 12:31 PM | 1.6 | 49 |
| **4** F | 12:05 AM / 01:03 PM | -0.1 / 1.3 | -3 / 40 | **19** Sa | 12:45 AM / 01:24 PM | -0.3 / 1.6 | -9 / 49 |
| **5** Sa | 12:59 AM / 01:45 PM | 0.0 / 1.3 | 0 / 40 | **20** Su | 01:47 AM / 02:20 PM | -0.3 / 1.5 | -9 / 46 |
| **6** Su | 01:49 AM / 02:29 PM | 0.0 / 1.2 | 0 / 37 | **21** M | 02:39 AM / 03:15 PM | -0.2 / 1.3 | -6 / 40 |
| **7** M | 02:31 AM / 03:14 PM | 0.0 / 1.1 | 0 / 34 | **22** Tu ◐ | 03:15 AM / 04:08 PM | 0.0 / 1.1 | 0 / 34 |
| **8** Tu ◑ | 03:02 AM / 04:00 PM | 0.1 / 1.0 | 3 / 30 | **23** W | 03:23 AM / 04:54 PM | 0.2 / 0.8 | 6 / 24 |
| **9** W | 03:23 AM / 04:50 PM | 0.2 / 0.9 | 6 / 27 | **24** Th | 02:42 AM / 10:32 AM | 0.4 / 0.7 | 12 / 21 |
| **10** Th | 03:29 AM / 06:07 PM | 0.3 / 0.7 | 9 / 21 | **25** F | 12:51 AM / 09:07 AM / 06:51 PM | 0.5 / 0.9 / 0.3 | 15 / 27 / 9 |
| **11** F | 03:11 AM / 10:41 AM / 05:41 PM / 09:24 PM | 0.4 / 0.7 / 0.5 / 0.6 | 12 / 21 / 15 / 18 | **26** Sa | 09:03 AM / 07:30 PM | 1.1 / 0.1 | 34 / 3 |
| **12** Sa | 02:02 AM / 09:50 PM / 06:36 AM | 0.5 / 0.9 / 0.3 | 15 / 27 / 9 | **27** Su | 09:21 AM / 08:11 PM | 1.2 / 0.0 | 37 / 0 |
| **13** Su | 09:38 AM / 07:27 PM | 1.0 / 0.1 | 30 / 3 | **28** M | 09:47 AM / 08:52 PM | 1.4 / -0.1 | 43 / -3 |
| **14** M | 09:51 AM / 08:21 PM | 1.2 / 0.0 | 37 / 0 | **29** Tu ○ | 10:17 AM / 09:35 PM | 1.4 / -0.1 | 43 / -3 |
| **15** Tu ● | 10:18 AM / 09:21 PM | 1.4 / -0.2 | 43 / -6 | **30** W | 10:49 AM / 10:20 PM | 1.5 / -0.2 | 46 / -6 |
| | | | | **31** Th | 11:23 AM / 11:06 PM | 1.5 / -0.1 | 46 / -3 |

### June

| | Time | Height (ft) | (cm) | | Time | Height (ft) | (cm) |
|---|---|---|---|---|---|---|---|
| **1** F | 11:58 AM / 11:50 PM | 1.4 / -0.1 | 43 / -3 | **16** Sa | 12:25 PM | 1.6 | 49 |
| **2** Sa | 12:33 PM | 1.4 | 43 | **17** Su | 12:44 AM / 01:13 PM | -0.4 / 1.5 | -12 / 46 |
| **3** Su | 12:30 AM / 01:06 PM | -0.1 / 1.3 | -3 / 40 | **18** M | 01:29 AM / 01:57 PM | -0.2 / 1.3 | -6 / 40 |
| **4** M | 01:02 AM / 01:35 PM | 0.0 / 1.2 | 0 / 37 | **19** Tu | 01:55 AM / 02:29 PM | 0.0 / 1.0 | 0 / 30 |
| **5** Tu | 01:25 AM / 01:55 PM | 0.0 / 1.1 | 0 / 34 | **20** W ◐ | 01:45 AM / 02:04 PM | 0.2 / 0.8 | 6 / 24 |
| **6** W ◐ | 01:38 AM / 01:46 PM | 0.1 / 0.9 | 3 / 27 | **21** Th | 12:35 AM / 09:13 AM / 10:15 PM | 0.4 / 0.7 / 0.4 | 12 / 21 / 12 |
| **7** Th | 01:35 AM / 11:38 AM | 0.2 / 0.8 | 6 / 24 | **22** F | 08:04 AM / 07:19 PM | 0.9 / 0.2 | 27 / 6 |
| **8** F | 01:05 AM / 09:40 AM / 11:11 PM | 0.3 / 0.8 / 0.4 | 9 / 24 / 12 | **23** Sa | 08:04 AM / 07:16 PM | 1.1 / 0.0 | 34 / 0 |
| **9** Sa | 08:52 AM / 06:47 PM | 0.9 / 0.2 | 27 / 6 | **24** Su | 08:25 AM / 07:43 PM | 1.3 / -0.1 | 40 / -3 |
| **10** Su | 08:42 AM / 07:05 PM | 1.1 / 0.0 | 34 / 0 | **25** M | 08:53 AM / 08:19 PM | 1.4 / -0.2 | 43 / -6 |
| **11** M | 08:55 AM / 07:47 PM | 1.3 / -0.2 | 40 / -6 | **26** Tu | 09:26 AM / 08:59 PM | 1.5 / -0.2 | 46 / -6 |
| **12** Tu | 09:23 AM / 08:39 PM | 1.5 / -0.3 | 46 / -9 | **27** W | 10:00 AM / 09:41 PM | 1.5 / -0.2 | 46 / -6 |
| **13** W ● | 10:01 AM / 09:40 PM | 1.6 / -0.4 | 49 / -12 | **28** Th ○ | 10:35 AM / 10:23 PM | 1.5 / -0.2 | 46 / -6 |
| **14** Th ○ | 10:46 AM / 10:44 PM | 1.7 / -0.5 | 52 / -15 | **29** F | 11:10 AM / 11:01 PM | 1.4 / -0.2 | 43 / -6 |
| **15** F | 11:35 AM / 11:47 PM | 1.7 / -0.4 | 52 / -12 | **30** Sa | 11:43 AM / 11:32 PM | 1.4 / -0.1 | 43 / -3 |

Heights are referred to mean lower water which is the chart datum of sounding. All times are local. Daylight Saving Time has been used when needed. Additional tide tables are available online from NOAA at www.tidesandcurrents.noaa.gov/tide_predictions.shtml.

**SKIPPER'S HANDBOOK**

StationId: 8735180
Source: NOAA/NOS/CO-OPS
Station Type: Primary
Time Zone: LST_LDT
Datum: MLLW

## NOAA Tide Predictions

## Dauphin Island, AL,2018

### Times and Heights of High and Low Waters

# July

| Day | Time | ft | cm | Day | Time | ft | cm |
|---|---|---|---|---|---|---|---|
| 1 Su | 12:12 PM | 1.3 | 40 | 16 M | 12:33 AM | -0.1 | -3 |
|  | 11:56 PM | -0.1 | -3 |  | 01:05 PM | 1.3 | 40 |
| 2 M | 12:37 PM | 1.2 | 37 | 17 Tu | 12:55 AM | 0.1 | 3 |
|  |  |  |  |  | 01:36 PM | 1.0 | 30 |
| 3 Tu | 12:11 AM | 0.0 | 0 | 18 W | 12:28 AM | 0.3 | 9 |
|  | 12:52 PM | 1.1 | 34 |  | 01:21 PM | 0.8 | 24 |
|  |  |  |  |  | 10:45 PM | 0.5 | 15 |
| 4 W | 12:17 AM | 0.1 | 3 | 19 Th | 07:20 AM | 0.7 | 21 |
|  | 12:43 PM | 0.9 | 27 |  | 08:05 PM | 0.4 | 12 |
| 5 Th | 12:06 AM | 0.2 | 6 | 20 F | 06:28 AM | 1.0 | 30 |
|  | 10:44 AM | 0.8 | 24 |  | 06:13 PM | 0.3 | 9 |
|  | 11:24 PM | 0.3 | 9 |  |  |  |  |
| 6 F | 08:29 AM | 0.8 | 24 | 21 Sa | 06:42 AM | 1.2 | 37 |
|  | 09:13 PM | 0.4 | 12 |  | 06:19 PM | 0.1 | 3 |
| 7 Sa | 07:40 AM | 1.0 | 30 | 22 Su | 07:12 AM | 1.3 | 40 |
|  | 06:15 PM | 0.2 | 6 |  | 06:50 PM | 0.0 | 0 |
| 8 Su | 07:33 AM | 1.1 | 34 | 23 M | 07:48 AM | 1.4 | 43 |
|  | 06:22 PM | 0.0 | 0 |  | 07:29 PM | -0.1 | -3 |
| 9 M | 07:51 AM | 1.3 | 40 | 24 Tu | 08:27 AM | 1.5 | 46 |
|  | 07:00 PM | -0.2 | -6 |  | 08:13 PM | -0.1 | -3 |
| 10 Tu | 08:24 AM | 1.5 | 46 | 25 W | 09:08 AM | 1.5 | 46 |
|  | 07:52 PM | -0.3 | -9 |  | 08:57 PM | -0.1 | -3 |
| 11 W | 09:07 AM | 1.7 | 52 | 26 Th | 09:48 AM | 1.5 | 46 |
|  | 08:52 PM | -0.4 | -12 |  | 09:39 PM | -0.1 | -3 |
| 12 Th | 09:55 AM | 1.7 | 52 | 27 F | 10:25 AM | 1.4 | 43 |
|  | 09:54 PM | -0.4 | -12 |  | 10:14 PM | 0.0 | 0 |
| 13 F | 10:45 AM | 1.7 | 52 | 28 Sa | 11:00 AM | 1.4 | 43 |
|  | 10:55 PM | -0.4 | -12 |  | 10:40 PM | 0.0 | 0 |
| 14 Sa | 11:35 AM | 1.7 | 52 | 29 Su | 11:30 AM | 1.3 | 40 |
|  | 11:50 PM | -0.3 | -9 |  | 10:57 PM | 0.1 | 3 |
| 15 Su | 12:23 PM | 1.5 | 46 | 30 M | 11:57 AM | 1.2 | 37 |
|  |  |  |  |  | 11:04 PM | 0.2 | 6 |
|  |  |  |  | 31 Tu | 12:18 PM | 1.1 | 34 |
|  |  |  |  |  | 11:00 PM | 0.3 | 9 |

# August

| Day | Time | ft | cm | Day | Time | ft | cm |
|---|---|---|---|---|---|---|---|
| 1 W | 12:24 PM | 0.9 | 27 | 16 Th | 03:30 AM | 0.9 | 27 |
|  | 10:36 PM | 0.4 | 12 |  | 04:18 PM | 0.6 | 18 |
| 2 Th | 09:41 AM | 0.8 | 24 | 17 F | 03:59 AM | 1.1 | 34 |
|  | 09:31 PM | 0.5 | 15 |  | 03:56 PM | 0.4 | 12 |
| 3 F | 06:18 AM | 0.9 | 27 | 18 Sa | 04:41 AM | 1.3 | 40 |
|  | 06:25 PM | 0.5 | 15 |  | 04:35 PM | 0.3 | 9 |
| 4 Sa | 05:46 AM | 1.0 | 30 | 19 Su | 05:27 AM | 1.4 | 43 |
|  | 04:43 PM | 0.3 | 9 |  | 05:21 PM | 0.2 | 6 |
| 5 Su | 05:56 AM | 1.2 | 37 | 20 M | 06:17 AM | 1.5 | 46 |
|  | 05:07 PM | 0.1 | 3 |  | 06:10 PM | 0.1 | 3 |
| 6 M | 06:28 AM | 1.4 | 43 | 21 Tu | 07:09 AM | 1.5 | 46 |
|  | 05:54 PM | 0.0 | 0 |  | 07:00 PM | 0.1 | 3 |
| 7 Tu | 07:13 AM | 1.6 | 49 | 22 W | 08:00 AM | 1.5 | 46 |
|  | 06:51 PM | -0.2 | -6 |  | 07:48 PM | 0.1 | 3 |
| 8 W | 08:04 AM | 1.7 | 52 | 23 Th | 08:49 AM | 1.5 | 46 |
|  | 07:52 PM | -0.2 | -6 |  | 08:32 PM | 0.2 | 6 |
| 9 Th | 08:58 AM | 1.7 | 52 | 24 F | 09:34 AM | 1.5 | 46 |
|  | 08:56 PM | -0.2 | -6 |  | 09:06 PM | 0.2 | 6 |
| 10 F | 09:53 AM | 1.7 | 52 | 25 Sa | 10:14 AM | 1.4 | 43 |
|  | 09:57 PM | -0.2 | -6 |  | 09:30 PM | 0.3 | 9 |
| 11 Sa | 10:47 AM | 1.7 | 52 | 26 Su | 10:50 AM | 1.3 | 40 |
|  | 10:54 PM | -0.1 | -3 |  | 09:41 PM | 0.4 | 12 |
| 12 Su | 11:39 AM | 1.5 | 46 | 27 M | 11:25 AM | 1.2 | 37 |
|  | 11:43 PM | 0.1 | 3 |  | 09:37 PM | 0.5 | 15 |
| 13 M | 12:27 PM | 1.3 | 40 | 28 Tu | 12:01 PM | 1.1 | 34 |
|  |  |  |  |  | 09:12 PM | 0.6 | 18 |
| 14 Tu | 12:11 AM | 0.4 | 12 | 29 W | 12:44 PM | 0.9 | 27 |
|  | 01:11 PM | 1.1 | 34 |  | 08:15 PM | 0.7 | 21 |
|  | 11:01 PM | 0.6 | 18 |  |  |  |  |
| 15 W | 01:45 PM | 0.8 | 24 | 30 Th | 02:59 AM | 0.9 | 27 |
|  | 08:13 PM | 0.7 | 21 |  | 10:17 AM | 0.8 | 24 |
|  |  |  |  |  | 02:13 PM | 0.8 | 24 |
|  |  |  |  |  | 05:53 PM | 0.8 | 24 |
|  |  |  |  | 31 F | 02:46 AM | 1.0 | 30 |
|  |  |  |  |  | 01:18 PM | 0.6 | 18 |

# September

| Day | Time | ft | cm | Day | Time | ft | cm |
|---|---|---|---|---|---|---|---|
| 1 Sa | 03:07 AM | 1.2 | 37 | 16 Su | 03:17 AM | 1.5 | 46 |
|  | 02:24 PM | 0.4 | 12 |  | 03:21 PM | 0.3 | 9 |
| 2 Su | 03:46 AM | 1.4 | 43 | 17 M | 04:14 AM | 1.5 | 46 |
|  | 03:24 PM | 0.3 | 9 |  | 04:19 PM | 0.3 | 9 |
| 3 M | 04:37 AM | 1.5 | 46 | 18 Tu | 05:15 AM | 1.5 | 46 |
|  | 04:26 PM | 0.1 | 3 |  | 05:13 PM | 0.3 | 9 |
| 4 Tu | 05:37 AM | 1.6 | 49 | 19 W | 06:19 AM | 1.5 | 46 |
|  | 05:30 PM | 0.0 | 0 |  | 06:02 PM | 0.4 | 12 |
| 5 W | 06:42 AM | 1.7 | 52 | 20 Th | 07:20 AM | 1.5 | 46 |
|  | 06:34 PM | 0.0 | 0 |  | 06:43 PM | 0.4 | 12 |
| 6 Th | 07:47 AM | 1.7 | 52 | 21 F | 08:17 AM | 1.4 | 43 |
|  | 07:38 PM | 0.0 | 0 |  | 07:13 PM | 0.5 | 15 |
| 7 F | 08:51 AM | 1.7 | 52 | 22 Sa | 09:09 AM | 1.4 | 43 |
|  | 08:39 PM | 0.1 | 3 |  | 07:28 PM | 0.6 | 18 |
| 8 Sa | 09:53 AM | 1.6 | 49 | 23 Su | 09:58 AM | 1.3 | 40 |
|  | 09:39 PM | 0.3 | 9 |  | 07:24 PM | 0.7 | 21 |
| 9 Su | 10:54 AM | 1.5 | 46 | 24 M | 10:52 AM | 1.2 | 37 |
|  | 10:41 PM | 0.5 | 15 |  | 06:58 PM | 0.8 | 24 |
| 10 M | 11:56 AM | 1.3 | 40 | 25 Tu | 12:32 AM | 0.9 | 27 |
|  |  |  |  |  | 05:07 AM | 0.8 | 24 |
|  |  |  |  |  | 12:05 PM | 1.0 | 30 |
|  |  |  |  |  | 06:01 PM | 0.9 | 27 |
| 11 Tu | 04:10 AM | 0.7 | 21 | 26 W | 12:00 AM | 1.0 | 30 |
|  | 01:14 PM | 1.0 | 30 |  | 07:37 AM | 0.8 | 24 |
|  | 07:18 PM | 0.9 | 27 |  |  |  |  |
|  | 11:52 PM | 1.0 | 30 |  |  |  |  |
| 12 W | 08:04 AM | 0.7 | 21 | 27 Th | 12:05 AM | 1.2 | 37 |
|  |  |  |  |  | 09:31 AM | 0.6 | 18 |
| 13 Th | 12:45 AM | 1.2 | 37 | 28 F | 12:26 AM | 1.4 | 43 |
|  | 11:07 AM | 0.6 | 18 |  | 11:03 AM | 0.5 | 15 |
| 14 F | 01:34 AM | 1.3 | 40 | 29 Sa | 01:01 AM | 1.5 | 46 |
|  | 01:04 PM | 0.5 | 15 |  | 12:23 PM | 0.3 | 9 |
| 15 Sa | 02:24 AM | 1.5 | 46 | 30 Su | 01:46 AM | 1.6 | 49 |
|  | 02:19 PM | 0.4 | 12 |  | 01:37 PM | 0.2 | 6 |

Heights are referred to mean lower water which is the chart datum of sounding. All times are local. Daylight Saving Time has been used when needed. Additional tide tables are available online from NOAA at www.tidesandcurrents.noaa.gov/tide_predictions.shtml.

StationId:8760551
Source:NOAA/NOS/CO-OPS
Station Type:Harmonic
Time Zone:LST/LDT
Datum:mean lower low water (MLLW) which is the chart datum of soundings

## NOAA Tide Predictions

## SOUTH PASS, Louisiana, 2017

### Times and Heights of High and Low Waters

SKIPPER'S HANDBOOK

### October

| Day | Time | ft | cm |
|---|---|---|---|
| **1** Su | 05:44 AM | 1.6 | 49 |
| | 04:04 PM | 0.6 | 18 |
| **2** M | 07:01 AM | 1.5 | 46 |
| | 04:31 PM | 0.7 | 21 |
| **3** Tu | 08:14 AM | 1.4 | 43 |
| | 04:48 PM | 0.8 | 24 |
| | 11:31 PM | 1.0 | 30 |
| **4** W | 01:51 AM | 1.0 | 30 |
| | 09:29 AM | 1.3 | 40 |
| | 04:50 PM | 1.0 | 30 |
| | 10:13 PM | 1.1 | 34 |
| **5** Th ○ | 03:59 AM | 0.9 | 27 |
| | 11:00 AM | 1.2 | 37 |
| | 04:26 PM | 1.1 | 34 |
| | 09:52 PM | 1.3 | 40 |
| **6** F | 05:29 AM | 0.8 | 24 |
| | 09:56 PM | 1.4 | 43 |
| **7** Sa | 06:54 AM | 0.7 | 21 |
| | 10:18 PM | 1.6 | 49 |
| **8** Su | 08:21 AM | 0.5 | 15 |
| | 10:52 PM | 1.7 | 52 |
| **9** M | 09:48 AM | 0.4 | 12 |
| | 11:35 PM | 1.8 | 55 |
| **10** Tu | 11:10 AM | 0.3 | 9 |
| **11** W | 12:26 AM | 1.9 | 58 |
| | 12:24 PM | 0.3 | 9 |
| **12** Th ◐ | 01:24 AM | 1.9 | 58 |
| | 01:30 PM | 0.3 | 9 |
| **13** F | 02:33 AM | 1.8 | 55 |
| | 02:26 PM | 0.4 | 12 |
| **14** Sa | 03:58 AM | 1.7 | 52 |
| | 03:14 PM | 0.5 | 15 |
| **15** Su | 05:43 AM | 1.5 | 46 |
| | 03:49 PM | 0.7 | 21 |
| **16** M | 07:32 AM | 1.4 | 43 |
| | 04:06 PM | 0.8 | 24 |
| | 10:54 PM | 1.1 | 34 |
| **17** Tu | 02:50 AM | 1.0 | 30 |
| | 09:20 AM | 1.2 | 37 |
| | 03:51 PM | 1.0 | 30 |
| | 09:35 PM | 1.2 | 37 |
| **18** W | 04:27 AM | 0.9 | 27 |
| | 11:30 AM | 1.1 | 34 |
| | 02:38 PM | 1.1 | 34 |
| | 09:10 PM | 1.3 | 40 |
| **19** Th ● | 05:34 AM | 0.8 | 24 |
| | 09:12 PM | 1.4 | 43 |
| **20** F | 06:30 AM | 0.7 | 21 |
| | 09:28 PM | 1.6 | 49 |
| **21** Sa | 07:22 AM | 0.6 | 18 |
| | 09:50 PM | 1.6 | 49 |
| **22** Su | 08:13 AM | 0.5 | 15 |
| | 10:17 PM | 1.7 | 52 |
| **23** M | 09:06 AM | 0.5 | 15 |
| | 10:48 PM | 1.7 | 52 |
| **24** Tu | 10:03 AM | 0.4 | 12 |
| | 11:23 PM | 1.7 | 52 |
| **25** W | 11:02 AM | 0.4 | 12 |
| **26** Th | 12:02 AM | 1.7 | 52 |
| | 11:59 AM | 0.4 | 12 |
| **27** F ◐ | 12:47 AM | 1.6 | 49 |
| | 12:49 PM | 0.5 | 15 |
| **28** Sa | 01:39 AM | 1.5 | 46 |
| | 01:32 PM | 0.5 | 15 |
| **29** Su | 02:44 AM | 1.4 | 43 |
| | 02:07 PM | 0.6 | 18 |
| **30** M | 04:26 AM | 1.3 | 40 |
| | 02:31 PM | 0.7 | 21 |
| **31** Tu | 06:45 AM | 1.2 | 37 |
| | 02:42 PM | 0.8 | 24 |
| | 09:24 PM | 1.1 | 34 |

### November

| Day | Time | ft | cm |
|---|---|---|---|
| **1** W | 03:11 AM | 0.9 | 27 |
| | 09:04 AM | 1.1 | 34 |
| | 02:28 PM | 0.9 | 27 |
| | 08:42 PM | 1.2 | 37 |
| **2** Th | 04:20 AM | 0.7 | 21 |
| | 08:32 PM | 1.3 | 40 |
| **3** F | 05:22 AM | 0.5 | 15 |
| | 08:42 PM | 1.5 | 46 |
| **4** Sa ○ | 06:23 AM | 0.3 | 9 |
| | 09:08 PM | 1.7 | 52 |
| **5** Su | 06:27 AM | 0.2 | 6 |
| | 08:43 PM | 1.8 | 55 |
| **6** M | 07:34 AM | 0.1 | 3 |
| | 09:24 PM | 1.9 | 58 |
| **7** Tu | 08:43 AM | 0.0 | 0 |
| | 10:10 PM | 1.9 | 58 |
| **8** W | 09:51 AM | 0.0 | 0 |
| | 10:59 PM | 1.8 | 55 |
| **9** Th | 10:55 AM | 0.1 | 3 |
| | 11:48 PM | 1.6 | 49 |
| **10** F ◑ | 11:50 AM | 0.2 | 6 |
| **11** Sa | 12:37 AM | 1.4 | 43 |
| | 12:34 PM | 0.4 | 12 |
| **12** Su | 01:15 AM | 1.2 | 37 |
| | 12:59 PM | 0.6 | 18 |
| | 10:00 PM | 1.0 | 30 |
| **13** M | 12:50 PM | 0.7 | 21 |
| | 08:01 PM | 1.0 | 30 |
| **14** Tu | 03:20 AM | 0.7 | 21 |
| | 09:13 AM | 0.8 | 24 |
| | 11:13 AM | 0.8 | 24 |
| | 07:14 PM | 1.1 | 34 |
| **15** W | 03:59 AM | 0.5 | 15 |
| | 07:03 PM | 1.2 | 37 |
| **16** Th | 04:37 AM | 0.4 | 12 |
| | 07:12 PM | 1.4 | 43 |
| **17** F | 05:14 AM | 0.3 | 9 |
| | 07:30 PM | 1.4 | 43 |
| **18** Sa ● | 05:49 AM | 0.2 | 6 |
| | 07:53 PM | 1.5 | 46 |
| **19** Su | 06:25 AM | 0.1 | 3 |
| | 08:19 PM | 1.5 | 46 |
| **20** M | 07:04 AM | 0.1 | 3 |
| | 08:48 PM | 1.5 | 46 |
| **21** Tu | 07:45 AM | 0.1 | 3 |
| | 09:19 PM | 1.5 | 46 |
| **22** W | 08:29 AM | 0.1 | 3 |
| | 09:52 PM | 1.5 | 46 |
| **23** Th | 09:13 AM | 0.1 | 3 |
| | 10:26 PM | 1.4 | 43 |
| **24** F | 09:56 AM | 0.1 | 3 |
| | 11:00 PM | 1.3 | 40 |
| **25** Sa | 10:34 AM | 0.2 | 6 |
| | 11:30 PM | 1.2 | 37 |
| **26** Su ◑ | 11:04 AM | 0.3 | 9 |
| | 11:39 PM | 1.0 | 30 |
| **27** M | 11:22 AM | 0.4 | 12 |
| | 09:06 PM | 0.9 | 27 |
| **28** Tu | 11:20 AM | 0.5 | 15 |
| | 07:12 PM | 0.8 | 24 |
| **29** W | 03:03 AM | 0.6 | 18 |
| | 07:40 AM | 0.6 | 18 |
| | 10:07 AM | 0.6 | 18 |
| | 06:32 PM | 1.0 | 30 |
| **30** Th | 03:19 AM | 0.3 | 9 |
| | 06:26 PM | 1.1 | 34 |

### December

| Day | Time | ft | cm |
|---|---|---|---|
| **1** F | 03:59 AM | 0.1 | 3 |
| | 06:41 PM | 1.3 | 40 |
| **2** Sa | 04:47 AM | -0.1 | -3 |
| | 07:10 PM | 1.4 | 43 |
| **3** Su ○ | 05:40 AM | -0.3 | -9 |
| | 07:47 PM | 1.6 | 49 |
| **4** M | 06:36 AM | -0.4 | -12 |
| | 08:30 PM | 1.6 | 49 |
| **5** Tu | 07:34 AM | -0.5 | -15 |
| | 09:16 PM | 1.6 | 49 |
| **6** W | 08:33 AM | -0.4 | -12 |
| | 10:02 PM | 1.5 | 46 |
| **7** Th | 09:30 AM | -0.3 | -9 |
| | 10:45 PM | 1.3 | 40 |
| **8** F | 10:20 AM | -0.2 | -6 |
| | 11:19 PM | 1.1 | 34 |
| **9** Sa | 10:55 AM | 0.0 | 0 |
| | 11:16 PM | 0.8 | 24 |
| **10** Su | 11:04 AM | 0.2 | 6 |
| | 08:37 PM | 0.7 | 21 |
| **11** M ◑ | 10:09 AM | 0.4 | 12 |
| | 06:41 PM | 0.7 | 21 |
| **12** Tu | 04:00 AM | 0.3 | 9 |
| | 06:01 PM | 0.8 | 24 |
| **13** W | 03:54 AM | 0.1 | 3 |
| | 05:58 PM | 0.9 | 27 |
| **14** Th | 04:17 AM | -0.1 | -3 |
| | 06:13 PM | 1.0 | 30 |
| **15** F | 04:45 AM | -0.2 | -6 |
| | 06:36 PM | 1.1 | 34 |
| **16** Sa | 05:14 AM | -0.3 | -9 |
| | 07:03 PM | 1.2 | 37 |
| **17** Su | 05:45 AM | -0.3 | -9 |
| | 07:32 PM | 1.2 | 37 |
| **18** M ● | 06:17 AM | -0.4 | -12 |
| | 08:02 PM | 1.2 | 37 |
| **19** Tu | 06:51 AM | -0.4 | -12 |
| | 08:34 PM | 1.2 | 37 |
| **20** W | 07:25 AM | -0.4 | -12 |
| | 09:05 PM | 1.1 | 34 |
| **21** Th | 07:59 AM | -0.3 | -9 |
| | 09:37 PM | 1.1 | 34 |
| **22** F | 08:30 AM | -0.3 | -9 |
| | 10:06 PM | 1.0 | 30 |
| **23** Sa | 08:57 AM | -0.2 | -6 |
| | 10:31 PM | 0.8 | 24 |
| **24** Su | 09:17 AM | -0.1 | -3 |
| | 10:41 PM | 0.7 | 21 |
| **25** M | 09:24 AM | 0.0 | 0 |
| | 08:46 PM | 0.5 | 15 |
| **26** Tu ◑ | 09:02 AM | 0.1 | 3 |
| | 05:56 PM | 0.5 | 15 |
| **27** W | 05:43 AM | 0.1 | 3 |
| | 05:15 PM | 0.6 | 18 |
| **28** Th | 03:02 AM | -0.1 | -3 |
| | 05:14 PM | 0.8 | 24 |
| **29** F | 03:24 AM | -0.3 | -9 |
| | 05:36 PM | 1.0 | 30 |
| **30** Sa | 04:04 AM | -0.6 | -18 |
| | 06:11 PM | 1.1 | 34 |
| **31** Su | 04:51 AM | -0.7 | -21 |
| | 06:54 PM | 1.2 | 37 |

Heights are referred to mean lower water which is the chart datum of sounding. All times are local. Daylight Saving Time has been used when needed. Additional tide tables are available online from NOAA at www.tidesandcurrents.noaa.gov/tide_predictions.shtml.

StationId: 8760551
Source: NOAA/NOS/CO-OPS
Station Type: Primary
Time Zone: LST_LDT
Datum: MLLW

**NOAA Tide Predictions**

# South Pass, LA,2018

## Times and Heights of High and Low Waters

### January

| | Time | ft | cm | | Time | ft | cm |
|---|---|---|---|---|---|---|---|
| **1** M | 05:40 AM<br>07:36 PM | -0.9<br>1.3 | -27<br>40 | **16** Tu | 06:06 AM<br>07:55 PM | -0.6<br>0.9 | -18<br>27 |
| **2** Tu ○ | 06:34 AM<br>08:26 PM | -0.9<br>1.3 | -27<br>40 | **17** W ● | 06:38 AM<br>08:30 PM | -0.6<br>0.9 | -18<br>27 |
| **3** W | 07:28 AM<br>09:15 PM | -0.8<br>1.2 | -24<br>37 | **18** Th | 07:08 AM<br>09:04 PM | -0.6<br>0.8 | -18<br>24 |
| **4** Th | 08:20 AM<br>10:02 PM | -0.7<br>1.0 | -21<br>30 | **19** F | 07:34 AM<br>09:36 PM | -0.5<br>0.7 | -15<br>21 |
| **5** F | 09:05 AM<br>10:41 PM | -0.5<br>0.8 | -15<br>24 | **20** Sa | 07:54 AM<br>10:07 PM | -0.4<br>0.6 | -12<br>18 |
| **6** Sa | 09:36 AM<br>11:01 PM | -0.3<br>0.6 | -9<br>18 | **21** Su | 08:07 AM<br>10:33 PM | -0.3<br>0.5 | -9<br>15 |
| **7** Su | 09:33 AM<br>09:05 PM | -0.1<br>0.3 | -3<br>9 | **22** M | 08:05 AM<br>10:33 PM | -0.2<br>0.3 | -6<br>9 |
| **8** M ◐ | 08:13 AM<br>05:14 PM | 0.0<br>0.3 | 0<br>9 | **23** Tu | 07:30 AM<br>03:50 PM | -0.1<br>0.2 | -3<br>6 |
| **9** Tu | 04:01 AM<br>04:29 PM | 0.0<br>0.5 | 0<br>15 | **24** W ◐ | 04:53 AM<br>03:17 PM | 0.0<br>0.4 | 0<br>12 |
| **10** W | 03:16 AM<br>04:34 PM | -0.2<br>0.6 | -6<br>18 | **25** Th | 01:59 AM<br>03:30 PM | -0.2<br>0.8 | -6<br>18 |
| **11** Th | 03:33 AM<br>04:58 PM | -0.4<br>0.7 | -12<br>21 | **26** F | 02:23 AM<br>04:04 PM | -0.5<br>0.8 | -15<br>24 |
| **12** F | 03:59 AM<br>05:30 PM | -0.5<br>0.8 | -15<br>24 | **27** Sa | 03:05 AM<br>04:52 PM | -0.7<br>0.9 | -21<br>27 |
| **13** Sa | 04:29 AM<br>06:05 PM | -0.6<br>0.9 | -18<br>27 | **28** Su | 03:52 AM<br>05:46 PM | -0.9<br>1.1 | -27<br>34 |
| **14** Su | 05:01 AM<br>06:42 PM | -0.6<br>0.9 | -18<br>27 | **29** M | 04:43 AM<br>06:43 PM | -0.9<br>1.1 | -27<br>34 |
| **15** M | 05:33 AM<br>07:19 PM | -0.6<br>0.9 | -18<br>27 | **30** Tu | 05:34 AM<br>07:40 PM | -0.9<br>1.1 | -27<br>34 |
| | | | | **31** W ○ | 06:25 AM<br>08:35 PM | -0.9<br>1.0 | -27<br>30 |

### February

| | Time | ft | cm | | Time | ft | cm |
|---|---|---|---|---|---|---|---|
| **1** Th | 07:12 AM<br>09:27 PM | -0.7<br>0.9 | -21<br>27 | **16** F | 06:28 AM<br>09:11 PM | -0.3<br>0.7 | -9<br>21 |
| **2** F | 07:51 AM<br>10:16 PM | -0.5<br>0.7 | -15<br>21 | **17** Sa | 06:41 AM<br>09:51 PM | -0.2<br>0.6 | -6<br>18 |
| **3** Sa | 08:13 AM<br>10:58 PM | -0.3<br>0.4 | -9<br>12 | **18** Su | 06:42 AM<br>10:36 PM | -0.1<br>0.4 | -3<br>12 |
| **4** Su | 07:54 AM<br>11:22 PM | -0.1<br>0.2 | -3<br>6 | **19** M | 06:24 AM<br>12:45 PM<br>05:43 PM<br>11:36 PM | 0.0<br>0.2<br>0.1<br>0.2 | 0<br>6<br>3<br>6 |
| **5** M | 06:13 AM<br>01:48 PM | 0.0<br>0.3 | 0<br>9 | **20** Tu | 05:25 AM<br>12:29 PM<br>09:25 PM | 0.1<br>0.4<br>0.0 | 3<br>12<br>0 |
| **6** Tu | 01:58 AM<br>01:51 PM | -0.1<br>0.4 | -3<br>12 | **21** W | 12:43 PM<br>11:46 PM | 0.5<br>-0.2 | 15<br>-6 |
| **7** W ◖ | 01:40 AM<br>02:21 PM | -0.2<br>0.6 | -6<br>18 | **22** Th | 01:18 PM | 0.7 | 21 |
| **8** Th | 02:11 AM<br>03:03 PM | -0.4<br>0.7 | -12<br>21 | **23** F ◖ | 12:52 AM<br>02:09 PM | -0.4<br>0.9 | -12<br>27 |
| **9** F | 02:45 AM<br>03:51 PM | -0.5<br>0.7 | -15<br>21 | **24** Sa | 01:48 AM<br>03:11 PM | -0.5<br>1.0 | -15<br>30 |
| **10** Sa | 03:21 AM<br>04:43 PM | -0.5<br>0.8 | -15<br>24 | **25** Su | 02:43 AM<br>04:22 PM | -0.7<br>1.1 | -21<br>34 |
| **11** Su | 03:57 AM<br>05:35 PM | -0.6<br>0.8 | -18<br>24 | **26** M | 03:36 AM<br>05:35 PM | -0.7<br>1.1 | -21<br>34 |
| **12** M | 04:33 AM<br>06:24 PM | -0.6<br>0.8 | -18<br>24 | **27** Tu | 04:27 AM<br>06:45 PM | -0.7<br>1.1 | -21<br>34 |
| **13** Tu | 05:08 AM<br>07:10 PM | -0.6<br>0.8 | -18<br>24 | **28** W | 05:15 AM<br>07:51 PM | -0.6<br>1.0 | -18<br>30 |
| **14** W | 05:39 AM<br>07:53 PM | -0.5<br>0.8 | -15<br>24 | | | | |
| **15** Th ● | 06:07 AM<br>08:33 PM | -0.4<br>0.8 | -12<br>24 | | | | |

### March

| | Time | ft | cm | | Time | ft | cm |
|---|---|---|---|---|---|---|---|
| **1** Th | 05:58 AM<br>08:55 PM | -0.4<br>0.9 | -12<br>27 | **16** F | 06:06 AM<br>09:51 PM | 0.1<br>0.8 | 3<br>24 |
| **2** F ○ | 06:30 AM<br>09:59 PM | -0.2<br>0.7 | -6<br>21 | **17** Sa ● | 06:11 AM<br>12:07 PM<br>03:15 PM<br>10:53 PM | 0.2<br>0.3<br>0.3<br>0.7 | 6<br>9<br>9<br>21 |
| **3** Sa | 06:38 AM<br>12:16 PM<br>03:07 PM<br>11:09 PM | 0.1<br>0.2<br>0.2<br>0.5 | 3<br>6<br>6<br>15 | **18** Su | 05:57 AM<br>11:15 PM<br>05:18 PM | 0.3<br>0.5<br>0.3 | 9<br>15<br>9 |
| **4** Su | 05:54 AM<br>11:00 AM<br>11:36 PM | 0.0<br>0.4<br>0.2 | 0<br>12<br>6 | **19** M | 12:15 AM<br>05:12 AM<br>11:06 AM<br>07:01 PM | 0.5<br>0.4<br>0.6<br>0.2 | 15<br>12<br>18<br>6 |
| **5** M | 01:20 AM<br>03:22 AM<br>10:59 AM<br>08:20 PM | 0.3<br>0.3<br>0.5<br>0.0 | 9<br>9<br>15<br>0 | **20** Tu | 11:18 AM<br>08:44 PM | 0.8<br>0.1 | 24<br>3 |
| **6** Tu | 11:23 AM<br>10:29 PM | 0.7<br>-0.1 | 21<br>-3 | **21** W | 11:45 AM<br>10:26 PM | 1.0<br>-0.1 | 30<br>-3 |
| **7** W | 11:59 AM<br>11:52 PM | 0.8<br>-0.2 | 24<br>-6 | **22** Th | 12:24 PM<br>11:55 PM | 1.1<br>-0.2 | 34<br>-6 |
| **8** Th | 12:41 PM | 0.9 | 27 | **23** F | 01:13 PM | 1.2 | 37 |
| **9** F ◖ | 12:51 AM<br>01:32 PM | -0.2<br>0.9 | -6<br>27 | **24** Sa ◖ | 01:10 AM<br>02:14 PM | -0.3<br>1.3 | -9<br>40 |
| **10** Sa | 01:42 AM<br>02:32 PM | -0.3<br>0.9 | -9<br>27 | **25** Su | 02:15 AM<br>03:28 PM | -0.4<br>1.3 | -12<br>40 |
| **11** Su | 03:28 AM<br>04:43 PM | -0.3<br>0.9 | -9<br>27 | **26** M | 03:13 AM<br>04:54 PM | -0.3<br>1.2 | -9<br>37 |
| **12** M | 04:10 AM<br>05:55 PM | -0.3<br>0.9 | -9<br>27 | **27** Tu | 04:06 AM<br>06:27 PM | -0.3<br>1.1 | -9<br>34 |
| **13** Tu | 04:49 AM<br>07:02 PM | -0.2<br>0.9 | -6<br>27 | **28** W | 04:52 AM<br>07:57 PM | -0.1<br>1.0 | -3<br>30 |
| **14** W | 05:22 AM<br>08:01 PM | -0.2<br>0.9 | -6<br>27 | **29** Th | 05:28 AM<br>09:25 PM | 0.1<br>0.9 | 3<br>27 |
| **15** Th | 05:49 AM<br>08:56 PM | -0.1<br>0.8 | -3<br>24 | **30** F | 05:45 AM<br>11:34 AM<br>03:34 PM<br>10:58 PM | 0.3<br>0.5<br>0.4<br>0.7 | 9<br>15<br>12<br>21 |
| | | | | **31** Sa ○ | 05:23 AM<br>10:21 AM<br>05:26 PM | 0.5<br>0.6<br>0.3 | 15<br>18<br>9 |

Heights are referred to mean lower water which is the chart datum of sounding. All times are local. Daylight Saving Time has been used when needed. Additional tide tables are available online from NOAA at www.tidesandcurrents.noaa.gov/tide_predictions.shtml.

StationId: 8760551
Source: NOAA/NOS/CO-OPS
Station Type: Primary
Time Zone: LST_LDT
Datum: MLLW

**NOAA Tide Predictions**

## South Pass, LA,2018

**Times and Heights of High and Low Waters**

### April

| Day | Time | ft | cm | Day | Time | ft | cm |
|---|---|---|---|---|---|---|---|
| 1 Su | 01:25 AM / 03:31 AM / 10:06 AM / 06:50 PM | 0.6 / 0.6 / 0.8 / 0.2 | 18 / 18 / 24 / 6 | 16 M ● | 09:31 AM / 06:46 PM | 1.0 / 0.2 | 30 / 6 |
| 2 M | 10:19 AM / 08:05 PM | 1.0 / 0.1 | 30 / 3 | 17 Tu | 09:51 AM / 07:54 PM | 1.2 / 0.0 | 37 / 0 |
| 3 Tu | 10:44 AM / 09:15 PM | 1.1 / 0.0 | 34 / 0 | 18 W | 10:22 AM / 09:06 PM | 1.4 / -0.1 | 43 / -3 |
| 4 W | 11:15 AM / 10:23 PM | 1.2 / 0.0 | 37 / 0 | 19 Th | 11:01 AM / 10:19 PM | 1.5 / -0.2 | 46 / -6 |
| 5 Th | 11:50 AM / 11:29 PM | 1.2 / 0.0 | 37 / 0 | 20 F | 11:46 AM / 11:30 PM | 1.5 / -0.2 | 46 / -6 |
| 6 F | 12:30 PM | 1.2 | 37 | 21 Sa | 12:38 PM | 1.5 | 46 |
| 7 Sa | 12:31 PM / 01:16 PM | 0.0 / 1.2 | 0 / 37 | 22 Su ◐ | 12:38 PM / 01:35 PM | -0.2 / 1.5 | -6 / 46 |
| 8 Su ◑ | 01:28 AM / 02:11 PM | 0.0 / 1.2 | 0 / 37 | 23 M | 01:38 AM / 02:41 PM | -0.1 / 1.3 | -3 / 40 |
| 9 M | 02:19 AM / 03:21 PM | 0.0 / 1.1 | 0 / 34 | 24 Tu | 02:30 AM / 04:09 PM | 0.0 / 1.1 | 0 / 34 |
| 10 Tu | 03:02 AM / 04:48 PM | 0.1 / 1.0 | 3 / 30 | 25 W | 03:10 AM / 06:25 PM | 0.2 / 1.0 | 6 / 30 |
| 11 W | 03:37 AM / 06:24 PM | 0.2 / 1.0 | 6 / 30 | 26 Th | 03:30 AM / 10:52 AM / 03:19 PM / 09:01 PM | 0.4 / 0.7 / 0.7 / 0.8 | 12 / 21 / 21 / 24 |
| 12 Th | 04:02 AM / 07:56 PM | 0.3 / 0.9 | 9 / 27 | 27 F | 03:13 AM / 09:24 AM / 04:46 PM | 0.6 / 0.8 / 0.5 | 18 / 24 / 15 |
| 13 F | 04:14 AM / 10:48 AM / 02:49 PM / 09:30 PM | 0.4 / 0.6 / 0.6 / 0.8 | 12 / 18 / 18 / 24 | 28 Sa | 08:53 AM / 05:47 PM | 1.0 / 0.3 | 30 / 9 |
| 14 Sa | 04:05 AM / 09:45 AM / 04:24 PM / 11:25 PM | 0.6 / 0.7 / 0.5 / 0.7 | 18 / 21 / 15 / 21 | 29 Su | 08:54 AM / 06:39 PM | 1.2 / 0.2 | 37 / 6 |
| 15 Su | 03:20 AM / 09:27 AM / 05:37 PM | 0.7 / 0.9 / 0.3 | 21 / 27 / 9 | 30 M ○ | 09:10 AM / 07:26 PM | 1.3 / 0.1 | 40 / 3 |

### May

| Day | Time | ft | cm | Day | Time | ft | cm |
|---|---|---|---|---|---|---|---|
| 1 Tu | 09:34 AM / 08:11 PM | 1.4 / 0.0 | 43 / 0 | 16 W | 09:19 AM / 08:09 PM | 1.6 / -0.3 | 49 / -9 |
| 2 W | 10:02 AM / 08:57 PM | 1.4 / 0.0 | 43 / 0 | 17 Th | 09:59 AM / 09:09 PM | 1.7 / -0.3 | 52 / -9 |
| 3 Th | 10:32 AM / 09:45 PM | 1.5 / 0.0 | 46 / 0 | 18 F | 10:43 AM / 10:11 PM | 1.7 / -0.3 | 52 / -9 |
| 4 F | 11:06 AM / 10:35 PM | 1.5 / 0.0 | 46 / 0 | 19 Sa | 11:30 AM / 11:11 PM | 1.7 / -0.2 | 52 / -6 |
| 5 Sa | 11:43 AM / 11:26 PM | 1.4 / 0.0 | 43 / 0 | 20 Su | 12:16 PM | 1.5 | 46 |
| 6 Su | 12:22 PM | 1.4 | 43 | 21 M | 12:06 AM / 01:00 PM | -0.1 / 1.3 | -3 / 40 |
| 7 M | 12:15 AM / 01:03 PM | 0.1 / 1.3 | 3 / 40 | 22 Tu ◐ | 12:50 AM / 01:26 PM | 0.1 / 1.1 | 3 / 34 |
| 8 Tu ◑ | 12:57 AM / 01:45 PM | 0.2 / 1.1 | 6 / 34 | 23 W | 01:17 AM / 11:25 AM | 0.3 / 0.9 | 9 / 27 |
| 9 W | 01:30 AM / 02:28 PM | 0.3 / 1.0 | 9 / 30 | 24 Th | 01:07 AM / 08:59 AM / 05:02 PM | 0.5 / 0.9 / 0.6 | 15 / 27 / 18 |
| 10 Th | 01:49 AM / 11:16 AM | 0.4 / 0.8 | 12 / 24 | 25 F | 08:01 AM / 05:12 PM | 1.0 / 0.3 | 30 / 9 |
| 11 F | 01:48 AM / 09:08 AM / 03:56 PM / 08:56 PM | 0.5 / 0.8 / 0.6 / 0.7 | 15 / 24 / 18 / 21 | 26 Sa | 07:45 AM / 05:44 PM | 1.1 / 0.2 | 34 / 6 |
| 12 Sa | 01:07 AM / 08:23 AM / 04:41 PM | 0.7 / 0.9 / 0.4 | 21 / 27 / 12 | 27 Su | 07:54 AM / 06:19 PM | 1.3 / 0.0 | 40 / 0 |
| 13 Su | 08:12 AM / 05:28 PM | 1.1 / 0.2 | 34 / 6 | 28 M | 08:14 AM / 06:53 PM | 1.4 / -0.1 | 43 / -3 |
| 14 M | 08:22 AM / 06:18 PM | 1.3 / 0.0 | 40 / 0 | 29 Tu ○ | 08:39 AM / 07:28 PM | 1.5 / -0.1 | 46 / -3 |
| 15 Tu ● | 08:46 AM / 07:12 PM | 1.4 / -0.1 | 43 / -3 | 30 W | 09:06 AM / 08:03 PM | 1.5 / -0.2 | 46 / -6 |
| | | | | 31 Th | 09:36 AM / 08:40 PM | 1.5 / -0.2 | 46 / -6 |

### June

| Day | Time | ft | cm | Day | Time | ft | cm |
|---|---|---|---|---|---|---|---|
| 1 F | 10:07 AM / 09:19 PM | 1.5 / -0.1 | 46 / -3 | 16 Sa | 10:39 AM / 10:00 PM | 1.6 / -0.4 | 49 / -12 |
| 2 Sa | 10:40 AM / 09:58 PM | 1.4 / -0.1 | 43 / -3 | 17 Su | 11:24 AM / 10:48 PM | 1.5 / -0.2 | 46 / -6 |
| 3 Su | 11:13 AM / 10:35 PM | 1.4 / 0.0 | 43 / 0 | 18 M | 12:02 PM / 11:23 PM | 1.3 / 0.0 | 40 / 0 |
| 4 M | 11:45 AM / 11:08 PM | 1.3 / 0.1 | 40 / 3 | 19 Tu | 12:16 PM / 11:34 PM | 1.0 / 0.2 | 30 / 6 |
| 5 Tu | 12:10 PM / 11:31 PM | 1.1 / 0.2 | 34 / 6 | 20 W ◐ | 10:04 AM / 10:47 PM | 0.8 / 0.4 | 24 / 12 |
| 6 W ◑ | 12:13 PM / 11:40 PM | 1.0 / 0.3 | 30 / 9 | 21 Th | 07:31 AM / 05:41 PM | 0.8 / 0.4 | 24 / 12 |
| 7 Th | 10:09 AM / 11:23 PM | 0.8 / 0.4 | 24 / 12 | 22 F | 06:42 AM / 04:55 PM | 0.9 / 0.2 | 27 / 6 |
| 8 F | 07:59 AM / 09:12 PM | 0.8 / 0.5 | 24 / 15 | 23 Sa | 06:37 AM / 05:16 PM | 1.1 / 0.0 | 34 / 0 |
| 9 Sa | 07:15 AM / 04:39 PM | 0.9 / 0.3 | 27 / 9 | 24 Su | 06:53 AM / 05:45 PM | 1.3 / -0.1 | 40 / -3 |
| 10 Su | 07:07 AM / 05:02 PM | 1.1 / 0.1 | 34 / 3 | 25 M | 07:19 AM / 06:15 PM | 1.4 / -0.2 | 43 / -6 |
| 11 M | 07:20 AM / 05:41 PM | 1.3 / -0.2 | 40 / -6 | 26 Tu | 07:47 AM / 06:46 PM | 1.4 / -0.3 | 43 / -9 |
| 12 Tu | 07:47 AM / 06:27 PM | 1.5 / -0.3 | 46 / -9 | 27 W | 08:18 AM / 07:18 PM | 1.4 / -0.3 | 43 / -9 |
| 13 W ● | 08:24 AM / 07:18 PM | 1.6 / -0.5 | 49 / -15 | 28 Th ○ | 08:50 AM / 07:50 PM | 1.4 / -0.3 | 43 / -9 |
| 14 Th | 09:06 AM / 08:12 PM | 1.7 / -0.5 | 52 / -15 | 29 F | 09:23 AM / 08:23 PM | 1.4 / -0.2 | 43 / -6 |
| 15 F | 09:52 AM / 09:07 PM | 1.7 / -0.5 | 52 / -15 | 30 Sa | 09:55 AM / 08:54 PM | 1.4 / -0.2 | 43 / -6 |

Heights are referred to mean lower water which is the chart datum of sounding. All times are local. Daylight Saving Time has been used when needed. Additional tide tables are available online from NOAA at www.tidesandcurrents.noaa.gov/tide_predictions.shtml.

SKIPPER'S HANDBOOK

NOAA

StationId: 8760551
Source: NOAA/NOS/CO-OPS
Station Type: Primary
Time Zone: LST_LDT
Datum: MLLW

**NOAA Tide Predictions**

## South Pass, LA,2018

### Times and Heights of High and Low Waters

## July

| Day | Time | ft | cm | Day | Time | ft | cm |
|---|---|---|---|---|---|---|---|
| 1 Su | 10:27 AM | 1.3 | 40 | 16 M | 11:29 AM | 1.2 | 37 |
|  | 09:23 PM | -0.1 | -3 |  | 10:11 PM | 0.0 | 0 |
| 2 M | 10:56 AM | 1.2 | 37 | 17 Tu | 11:58 AM | 1.0 | 30 |
|  | 09:46 PM | 0.0 | 0 |  | 10:10 PM | 0.3 | 9 |
| 3 Tu | 11:20 AM | 1.1 | 34 | 18 W | 10:22 AM | 0.7 | 21 |
|  | 10:00 PM | 0.1 | 3 |  | 08:55 PM | 0.4 | 12 |
| 4 W | 11:30 AM | 0.9 | 27 | 19 Th | 05:34 AM | 0.8 | 24 |
|  | 10:00 PM | 0.2 | 6 |  | 04:35 PM | 0.4 | 12 |
| 5 Th | 10:09 AM | 0.8 | 24 | 20 F | 04:57 AM | 0.9 | 27 |
|  | 09:34 PM | 0.3 | 9 |  | 03:55 PM | 0.2 | 6 |
| 6 F | 06:43 AM | 0.8 | 24 | 21 Sa | 05:08 AM | 1.1 | 34 |
|  | 07:42 PM | 0.4 | 12 |  | 04:18 PM | 0.0 | 0 |
| 7 Sa | 05:55 AM | 0.9 | 27 | 22 Su | 05:37 AM | 1.2 | 37 |
|  | 04:15 PM | 0.2 | 6 |  | 04:49 PM | -0.1 | -3 |
| 8 Su | 05:52 AM | 1.1 | 34 | 23 M | 06:12 AM | 1.3 | 40 |
|  | 04:19 PM | 0.0 | 0 |  | 05:22 PM | -0.2 | -6 |
| 9 M | 06:12 AM | 1.3 | 40 | 24 Tu | 06:50 AM | 1.4 | 43 |
|  | 04:52 PM | -0.2 | -6 |  | 05:55 PM | -0.2 | -6 |
| 10 Tu | 06:45 AM | 1.4 | 43 | 25 W | 07:28 AM | 1.4 | 43 |
|  | 05:35 PM | -0.4 | -12 |  | 06:28 PM | -0.2 | -6 |
| 11 W | 07:28 AM | 1.6 | 49 | 26 Th | 08:06 AM | 1.4 | 43 |
|  | 06:24 PM | -0.5 | -15 |  | 07:00 PM | -0.2 | -6 |
| 12 Th | 08:16 AM | 1.7 | 52 | 27 F | 08:43 AM | 1.4 | 43 |
|  | 07:15 PM | -0.6 | -18 |  | 07:30 PM | -0.1 | -3 |
| 13 F | 09:06 AM | 1.7 | 52 | 28 Sa | 09:18 AM | 1.4 | 43 |
|  | 08:07 PM | -0.5 | -15 |  | 07:58 PM | -0.1 | -3 |
| 14 Sa | 09:57 AM | 1.6 | 49 | 29 Su | 09:51 AM | 1.3 | 40 |
|  | 08:57 PM | -0.4 | -12 |  | 08:21 PM | 0.0 | 0 |
| 15 Su | 10:45 AM | 1.5 | 46 | 30 M | 10:22 AM | 1.2 | 37 |
|  | 09:41 PM | -0.2 | -6 |  | 08:36 PM | 0.1 | 3 |
|  |  |  |  | 31 Tu | 10:51 AM | 1.1 | 34 |
|  |  |  |  |  | 08:42 PM | 0.2 | 6 |

## August

| Day | Time | ft | cm | Day | Time | ft | cm |
|---|---|---|---|---|---|---|---|
| 1 W | 11:14 AM | 1.0 | 30 | 16 Th | 02:10 AM | 0.9 | 27 |
|  | 08:32 PM | 0.4 | 12 |  | 12:44 PM | 0.6 | 18 |
| 2 Th | 11:10 AM | 0.8 | 24 | 17 F | 02:21 AM | 1.1 | 34 |
|  | 07:56 PM | 0.5 | 15 |  | 01:57 PM | 0.4 | 12 |
| 3 F | 04:17 AM | 0.8 | 24 | 18 Sa | 02:57 AM | 1.3 | 40 |
|  | 06:00 PM | 0.5 | 15 |  | 02:44 PM | 0.2 | 6 |
| 4 Sa | 03:54 AM | 1.0 | 30 | 19 Su | 03:43 AM | 1.4 | 43 |
|  | 02:57 PM | 0.3 | 9 |  | 03:26 PM | 0.1 | 3 |
| 5 Su | 04:09 AM | 1.1 | 34 | 20 M | 04:34 AM | 1.4 | 43 |
|  | 03:09 PM | 0.1 | 3 |  | 04:06 PM | 0.1 | 3 |
| 6 M | 04:43 AM | 1.3 | 40 | 21 Tu | 05:28 AM | 1.5 | 46 |
|  | 03:46 PM | -0.1 | -3 |  | 04:45 PM | 0.1 | 3 |
| 7 Tu | 05:29 AM | 1.5 | 46 | 22 W | 06:22 AM | 1.5 | 46 |
|  | 04:32 PM | -0.2 | -6 |  | 05:22 PM | 0.1 | 3 |
| 8 W | 06:22 AM | 1.6 | 49 | 23 Th | 07:12 AM | 1.5 | 46 |
|  | 05:22 PM | -0.3 | -9 |  | 05:56 PM | 0.1 | 3 |
| 9 Th | 07:20 AM | 1.7 | 52 | 24 F | 07:59 AM | 1.5 | 46 |
|  | 06:13 PM | -0.3 | -9 |  | 06:28 PM | 0.2 | 6 |
| 10 F | 08:18 AM | 1.7 | 52 | 25 Sa | 08:41 AM | 1.5 | 46 |
|  | 07:03 PM | -0.3 | -9 |  | 06:54 PM | 0.3 | 9 |
| 11 Sa | 09:15 AM | 1.6 | 49 | 26 Su | 09:21 AM | 1.4 | 43 |
|  | 07:52 PM | -0.1 | -3 |  | 07:12 PM | 0.4 | 12 |
| 12 Su | 10:11 AM | 1.5 | 46 | 27 M | 09:59 AM | 1.3 | 40 |
|  | 08:34 PM | 0.1 | 3 |  | 07:20 PM | 0.5 | 15 |
| 13 M | 11:05 AM | 1.3 | 40 | 28 Tu | 10:37 AM | 1.2 | 37 |
|  | 09:00 PM | 0.3 | 9 |  | 07:13 PM | 0.6 | 18 |
| 14 Tu | 12:00 PM | 1.1 | 34 | 29 W | 11:20 AM | 1.1 | 34 |
|  | 08:44 PM | 0.6 | 18 |  | 06:47 PM | 0.7 | 21 |
| 15 W | 03:38 AM | 0.7 | 21 | 30 Th | 01:05 AM | 0.9 | 27 |
|  | 06:25 AM | 0.7 | 21 |  | 06:41 AM | 0.8 | 24 |
|  | 01:03 PM | 0.8 | 24 |  | 12:19 PM | 0.9 | 27 |
|  | 06:53 PM | 0.7 | 21 |  | 05:45 PM | 0.8 | 24 |
|  |  |  |  | 31 F | 01:00 AM | 1.1 | 34 |
|  |  |  |  |  | 09:57 AM | 0.7 | 21 |

## September

| Day | Time | ft | cm | Day | Time | ft | cm |
|---|---|---|---|---|---|---|---|
| 1 Sa | 01:18 AM | 1.2 | 37 | 16 Su | 01:22 AM | 1.6 | 49 |
|  | 12:16 PM | 0.5 | 15 |  | 01:31 PM | 0.4 | 12 |
| 2 Su | 01:54 AM | 1.4 | 43 | 17 M | 02:16 AM | 1.6 | 49 |
|  | 01:23 PM | 0.4 | 12 |  | 02:23 PM | 0.4 | 12 |
| 3 M | 02:43 AM | 1.5 | 46 | 18 Tu | 03:18 AM | 1.6 | 49 |
|  | 02:20 PM | 0.2 | 6 |  | 03:10 PM | 0.4 | 12 |
| 4 Tu | 03:44 AM | 1.7 | 52 | 19 W | 04:30 AM | 1.6 | 49 |
|  | 03:14 PM | 0.1 | 3 |  | 03:52 PM | 0.4 | 12 |
| 5 W | 04:54 AM | 1.7 | 52 | 20 Th | 05:43 AM | 1.6 | 49 |
|  | 04:08 PM | 0.0 | 0 |  | 04:31 PM | 0.5 | 15 |
| 6 Th | 06:07 AM | 1.8 | 55 | 21 F | 06:51 AM | 1.5 | 46 |
|  | 05:00 PM | 0.0 | 0 |  | 05:03 PM | 0.6 | 18 |
| 7 F | 07:19 AM | 1.8 | 55 | 22 Sa | 07:51 AM | 1.5 | 46 |
|  | 05:50 PM | 0.1 | 3 |  | 05:28 PM | 0.7 | 21 |
| 8 Sa | 08:28 AM | 1.7 | 52 | 23 Su | 08:46 AM | 1.4 | 43 |
|  | 06:35 PM | 0.3 | 9 |  | 05:40 PM | 0.8 | 24 |
| 9 Su | 09:37 AM | 1.6 | 49 | 24 M | 09:41 AM | 1.3 | 40 |
|  | 07:12 PM | 0.5 | 15 |  | 05:36 PM | 0.9 | 27 |
|  |  |  |  |  | 11:06 PM | 1.0 | 30 |
| 10 M | 10:49 AM | 1.4 | 43 | 25 Tu | 03:34 AM | 1.0 | 30 |
|  | 07:25 PM | 0.8 | 24 |  | 10:42 AM | 1.2 | 37 |
|  |  |  |  |  | 05:10 PM | 1.0 | 30 |
|  |  |  |  |  | 10:35 PM | 1.2 | 37 |
| 11 Tu | 12:20 AM | 0.9 | 27 | 26 W | 05:17 AM | 0.9 | 27 |
|  | 04:13 AM | 0.8 | 24 |  | 12:08 PM | 1.1 | 34 |
|  | 12:15 PM | 1.2 | 37 |  | 04:11 PM | 1.1 | 34 |
|  | 06:36 PM | 1.0 | 30 |  | 10:35 PM | 1.3 | 40 |
|  | 11:17 PM | 1.1 | 34 |  |  |  |  |
| 12 W | 06:52 AM | 0.8 | 24 | 27 Th | 06:49 AM | 0.8 | 24 |
|  | 11:23 PM | 1.3 | 40 |  | 10:52 PM | 1.4 | 43 |
| 13 Th | 09:08 AM | 0.7 | 21 | 28 F | 08:24 AM | 0.7 | 21 |
|  | 11:54 PM | 1.4 | 43 |  | 11:20 PM | 1.6 | 49 |
| 14 F | 11:06 AM | 0.6 | 18 | 29 Sa | 09:59 AM | 0.6 | 18 |
|  |  |  |  |  | 11:58 PM | 1.7 | 52 |
| 15 Sa | 12:35 AM | 1.5 | 46 | 30 Su | 11:24 AM | 0.4 | 12 |
|  | 12:29 PM | 0.5 | 15 |  |  |  |  |

Heights are referred to mean lower water which is the chart datum of sounding. All times are local. Daylight Saving Time has been used when needed. Additional tide tables are available online from NOAA at www.tidesandcurrents.noaa.gov/tide_predictions.shtml.

**SKIPPER'S HANDBOOK**

SOUTHERN EDITION  **87**

StationId:8771450
Source:NOAA/NOS/CO-OPS
Station Type:Harmonic
Time Zone:LST/LDT
Datum:mean lower low water (MLLW) which is the chart datum of soundings

**NOAA Tide Predictions**

## GALVESTON, Galveston Channel,Texas,2017

### Times and Heights of High and Low Waters

## October

| Day | Time | ft | cm | Day | Time | ft | cm |
|---|---|---|---|---|---|---|---|
| 1 Su | 03:17 AM | 1.7 | 52 | 16 M | 03:11 AM | 1.7 | 52 |
| | 09:34 AM | 1.4 | 43 | | 09:20 AM | 1.1 | 34 |
| | 12:42 PM | 1.5 | 46 | | 02:27 PM | 1.6 | 49 |
| | 08:04 PM | 0.6 | 18 | | 09:09 PM | 0.7 | 21 |
| 2 M | 03:39 AM | 1.7 | 52 | 17 Tu | 03:35 AM | 1.7 | 52 |
| | 09:21 AM | 1.3 | 40 | | 09:48 AM | 1.0 | 30 |
| | 01:52 PM | 1.5 | 46 | | 03:35 PM | 1.7 | 52 |
| | 08:47 PM | 0.6 | 18 | | 09:58 PM | 0.9 | 27 |
| 3 Tu | 03:58 AM | 1.7 | 52 | 18 W | 03:56 AM | 1.6 | 49 |
| | 09:28 AM | 1.2 | 37 | | 10:15 AM | 0.8 | 24 |
| | 02:55 PM | 1.6 | 49 | | 04:35 PM | 1.7 | 52 |
| | 09:27 PM | 0.7 | 21 | | 10:40 PM | 1.0 | 30 |
| 4 W | 04:17 AM | 1.6 | 49 | 19 Th | 04:14 AM | 1.6 | 49 |
| | 09:50 AM | 1.0 | 30 | | 10:43 AM | 0.7 | 21 |
| | 03:55 PM | 1.7 | 52 | | 05:31 PM | 1.7 | 52 |
| | 10:06 PM | 0.8 | 24 | | ● 11:19 PM | 1.2 | 37 |
| 5 Th | 04:33 AM | 1.6 | 49 | 20 F | 04:30 AM | 1.6 | 49 |
| | 10:20 AM | 0.9 | 27 | | 11:11 AM | 0.5 | 15 |
| | ○ 04:56 PM | 1.7 | 52 | | 06:24 PM | 1.7 | 52 |
| | 10:47 PM | 0.9 | 27 | | 11:53 PM | 1.3 | 40 |
| 6 F | 04:50 AM | 1.6 | 49 | 21 Sa | 04:44 AM | 1.6 | 49 |
| | 10:57 AM | 0.7 | 21 | | 11:40 AM | 0.4 | 12 |
| | 05:58 PM | 1.8 | 55 | | 07:17 PM | 1.8 | 55 |
| | 11:30 PM | 1.1 | 34 | | | | |
| 7 Sa | 05:05 AM | 1.6 | 49 | 22 Su | 12:26 AM | 1.4 | 43 |
| | 11:38 AM | 0.5 | 15 | | 04:52 AM | 1.6 | 49 |
| | 07:04 PM | 1.8 | 55 | | 12:11 PM | 0.4 | 12 |
| | | | | | 08:10 PM | 1.7 | 52 |
| 8 Su | 12:14 AM | 1.3 | 40 | 23 M | 01:00 AM | 1.5 | 46 |
| | 05:19 AM | 1.6 | 49 | | 04:49 AM | 1.6 | 49 |
| | 12:24 PM | 0.3 | 9 | | 12:46 PM | 0.4 | 12 |
| | 08:15 PM | 1.9 | 58 | | 09:07 PM | 1.7 | 52 |
| 9 M | 01:04 AM | 1.5 | 46 | 24 Tu | 01:40 AM | 1.6 | 49 |
| | 05:32 AM | 1.7 | 52 | | 04:06 AM | 1.6 | 49 |
| | 01:15 PM | 0.2 | 6 | | 01:26 PM | 0.4 | 12 |
| | 09:32 PM | 1.9 | 58 | | 10:11 PM | 1.7 | 52 |
| 10 Tu | 02:03 AM | 1.6 | 49 | 25 W | 02:11 PM | 0.4 | 12 |
| | 05:38 AM | 1.7 | 52 | | 11:19 PM | 1.7 | 52 |
| | 02:13 PM | 0.2 | 6 | | | | |
| | 10:54 PM | 1.9 | 58 | | | | |
| 11 W | 03:19 PM | 0.2 | 6 | 26 Th | 03:04 PM | 0.5 | 15 |
| 12 Th | 12:14 AM | 1.9 | 58 | 27 F | 12:22 AM | 1.7 | 52 |
| | ◗ 04:34 PM | 0.3 | 9 | | ◖ 04:04 PM | 0.5 | 15 |
| 13 F | 01:19 AM | 1.9 | 58 | 28 Sa | 01:11 AM | 1.7 | 52 |
| | 05:54 PM | 0.4 | 12 | | 05:11 PM | 0.6 | 18 |
| 14 Sa | 02:07 AM | 1.8 | 55 | 29 Su | 01:45 AM | 1.7 | 52 |
| | 08:36 AM | 1.5 | 46 | | 06:16 PM | 0.7 | 21 |
| | 11:30 AM | 1.5 | 46 | | | | |
| | 07:08 PM | 0.5 | 15 | | | | |
| 15 Su | 02:43 AM | 1.8 | 55 | 30 M | 02:10 AM | 1.6 | 49 |
| | 08:55 AM | 1.3 | 40 | | 08:58 AM | 1.2 | 37 |
| | 01:08 PM | 1.6 | 49 | | 12:51 PM | 1.3 | 40 |
| | 08:14 PM | 0.6 | 18 | | 07:16 PM | 0.7 | 21 |
| | | | | 31 Tu | 02:31 AM | 1.6 | 49 |
| | | | | | 08:45 AM | 1.0 | 30 |
| | | | | | 02:08 PM | 1.4 | 43 |
| | | | | | 08:10 PM | 0.8 | 24 |

## November

| Day | Time | ft | cm | Day | Time | ft | cm |
|---|---|---|---|---|---|---|---|
| 1 W | 02:48 AM | 1.6 | 49 | 16 Th | 01:52 AM | 1.4 | 43 |
| | 08:56 AM | 0.8 | 24 | | 08:55 AM | 0.3 | 9 |
| | 03:14 PM | 1.5 | 46 | | 04:02 PM | 1.5 | 46 |
| | 09:00 PM | 0.9 | 27 | | 09:40 PM | 1.1 | 34 |
| 2 Th | 03:04 AM | 1.5 | 46 | 17 F | 02:07 AM | 1.4 | 43 |
| | 09:21 AM | 0.6 | 18 | | 09:19 AM | 0.2 | 6 |
| | 04:15 PM | 1.7 | 52 | | 04:48 PM | 1.6 | 49 |
| | 09:48 PM | 1.0 | 30 | | 10:15 PM | 1.2 | 37 |
| 3 F | 03:19 AM | 1.5 | 46 | 18 Sa | 02:20 AM | 1.4 | 43 |
| | 09:54 AM | 0.3 | 9 | | 09:44 AM | 0.1 | 3 |
| | 05:14 PM | 1.8 | 55 | | ● 05:31 PM | 1.6 | 49 |
| | 10:35 PM | 1.2 | 37 | | 10:42 PM | 1.3 | 40 |
| 4 Sa | 03:35 AM | 1.6 | 49 | 19 Su | 02:30 AM | 1.4 | 43 |
| | 10:33 AM | 0.1 | 3 | | 10:10 AM | 0.0 | 0 |
| | 06:13 PM | 1.9 | 58 | | 06:12 PM | 1.6 | 49 |
| | ○ 11:23 PM | 1.3 | 40 | | 11:04 PM | 1.3 | 40 |
| 5 Su | 02:53 AM | 1.6 | 49 | 20 M | 02:36 AM | 1.4 | 43 |
| | 10:16 AM | 0.0 | 0 | | 10:40 AM | 0.0 | 0 |
| | 06:14 PM | 1.9 | 58 | | 06:55 PM | 1.5 | 46 |
| | 11:12 PM | 1.5 | 46 | | 11:29 PM | 1.3 | 40 |
| 6 M | 03:12 AM | 1.6 | 49 | 21 Tu | 02:33 AM | 1.4 | 43 |
| | 11:04 AM | -0.1 | -3 | | 11:13 AM | 0.0 | 0 |
| | 07:18 PM | 1.9 | 58 | | 07:41 PM | 1.5 | 46 |
| 7 Tu | 12:06 AM | 1.5 | 46 | 22 W | 12:03 AM | 1.3 | 40 |
| | 03:31 AM | 1.6 | 49 | | 02:18 AM | 1.4 | 43 |
| | 11:56 AM | -0.1 | -3 | | 11:49 AM | 0.0 | 0 |
| | 08:26 PM | 1.8 | 55 | | 08:33 PM | 1.5 | 46 |
| 8 W | 01:21 AM | 1.6 | 49 | 23 Th | 12:29 PM | 0.1 | 3 |
| | 03:40 AM | 1.6 | 49 | | 09:28 PM | 1.4 | 43 |
| | 12:54 PM | -0.1 | -3 | | | | |
| | 09:36 PM | 1.8 | 55 | | | | |
| 9 Th | 01:59 AM | 0.1 | 3 | 24 F | 01:12 PM | 0.2 | 6 |
| | 10:42 PM | 1.7 | 52 | | 10:20 PM | 1.4 | 43 |
| 10 F | 03:13 PM | 0.2 | 6 | 25 Sa | 02:02 PM | 0.3 | 9 |
| | 11:36 PM | 1.7 | 52 | | 11:02 PM | 1.4 | 43 |
| 11 Sa | 06:49 AM | 1.2 | 37 | 26 Su | 02:59 PM | 0.4 | 12 |
| | 09:02 AM | 1.3 | 40 | | 11:34 PM | 1.3 | 40 |
| | 04:36 PM | 0.4 | 12 | | | | |
| 12 Su | 12:17 AM | 1.6 | 49 | 27 M | 07:48 AM | 0.9 | 27 |
| | 07:07 AM | 1.0 | 30 | | 10:05 AM | 0.9 | 27 |
| | 11:11 AM | 1.2 | 37 | | 04:05 PM | 0.5 | 15 |
| | 05:57 PM | 0.6 | 18 | | 11:57 PM | 1.3 | 40 |
| 13 M | 12:49 AM | 1.5 | 46 | 28 Tu | 07:01 AM | 0.7 | 21 |
| | 07:35 AM | 0.8 | 24 | | 12:04 PM | 1.0 | 30 |
| | 12:48 PM | 1.3 | 40 | | 05:18 PM | 0.6 | 18 |
| | 07:07 PM | 0.7 | 21 | | | | |
| 14 Tu | 01:14 AM | 1.5 | 46 | 29 W | 12:16 AM | 1.3 | 40 |
| | 08:03 AM | 0.6 | 18 | | 07:00 AM | 0.5 | 15 |
| | 02:06 PM | 1.4 | 43 | | 01:25 PM | 1.1 | 34 |
| | 08:07 PM | 0.9 | 27 | | 06:29 PM | 0.8 | 24 |
| 15 W | 01:35 AM | 1.4 | 43 | 30 Th | 12:33 AM | 1.2 | 37 |
| | 08:30 AM | 0.4 | 12 | | 07:21 AM | 0.2 | 6 |
| | 03:09 PM | 1.5 | 46 | | 02:30 PM | 1.3 | 40 |
| | 08:57 PM | 1.0 | 30 | | 07:34 PM | 0.9 | 27 |

## December

| Day | Time | ft | cm | Day | Time | ft | cm |
|---|---|---|---|---|---|---|---|
| 1 F | 12:49 AM | 1.2 | 37 | 16 Sa | 01:07 AM | 1.0 | 30 |
| | 07:53 AM | -0.1 | -3 | | 08:56 AM | -0.4 | -12 |
| | 03:28 PM | 1.4 | 43 | | 04:54 PM | 1.2 | 37 |
| | 08:32 PM | 1.0 | 30 | | 10:12 PM | 1.0 | 30 |
| 2 Sa | 01:09 AM | 1.3 | 40 | 17 Su | 01:23 AM | 1.1 | 34 |
| | 08:32 AM | -0.3 | -9 | | 09:21 AM | -0.4 | -12 |
| | 04:23 PM | 1.6 | 49 | | 05:26 PM | 1.2 | 37 |
| | 09:23 PM | 1.1 | 34 | | 10:22 PM | 1.0 | 30 |
| 3 Su | 01:33 AM | 1.3 | 40 | 18 M | 01:41 AM | 1.1 | 34 |
| | 09:15 AM | -0.5 | -15 | | 09:48 AM | -0.4 | -12 |
| | 05:17 PM | 1.6 | 49 | | 05:59 PM | 1.2 | 37 |
| | ○ 10:11 PM | 1.2 | 37 | | ● 10:30 PM | 1.0 | 30 |
| 4 M | 02:03 AM | 1.4 | 43 | 19 Tu | 02:00 AM | 1.1 | 34 |
| | 10:01 AM | -0.6 | -18 | | 10:18 AM | -0.4 | -12 |
| | 06:13 PM | 1.6 | 49 | | 06:34 PM | 1.2 | 37 |
| | 10:59 PM | 1.3 | 40 | | 10:51 PM | 1.0 | 30 |
| 5 Tu | 02:38 AM | 1.4 | 43 | 20 W | 02:16 AM | 1.0 | 30 |
| | 10:51 AM | -0.6 | -18 | | 10:50 AM | -0.4 | -12 |
| | 07:09 PM | 1.6 | 49 | | 07:13 PM | 1.1 | 34 |
| | 11:52 PM | 1.3 | 40 | | 11:26 PM | 1.0 | 30 |
| 6 W | 03:17 AM | 1.3 | 40 | 21 Th | 02:26 AM | 1.0 | 30 |
| | 11:44 AM | -0.6 | -18 | | 11:23 AM | -0.4 | -12 |
| | 08:08 PM | 1.5 | 46 | | 07:55 PM | 1.1 | 34 |
| 7 Th | 01:06 AM | 1.2 | 37 | 22 F | 12:17 AM | 0.9 | 27 |
| | 04:00 AM | 1.3 | 40 | | 02:27 AM | 0.9 | 27 |
| | 12:40 PM | -0.4 | -12 | | 11:58 AM | -0.3 | -9 |
| | 09:05 PM | 1.4 | 43 | | 08:37 PM | 1.1 | 34 |
| 8 F | 01:41 PM | -0.2 | -6 | 23 Sa | 12:36 PM | -0.2 | -6 |
| | 09:57 PM | 1.3 | 40 | | 09:16 PM | 1.0 | 30 |
| 9 Sa | 05:05 AM | 0.9 | 27 | 24 Su | 01:16 PM | 0.0 | 0 |
| | 07:17 AM | 0.9 | 27 | | 09:49 PM | 1.0 | 30 |
| | 02:50 PM | 0.1 | 3 | | | | |
| | 10:42 PM | 1.2 | 37 | | | | |
| 10 Su | 05:50 AM | 0.7 | 21 | 25 M | 02:04 PM | 0.1 | 3 |
| | 09:41 AM | 0.8 | 24 | | 10:15 PM | 0.9 | 27 |
| | 04:12 PM | 0.3 | 9 | | | | |
| | ◗ 11:18 PM | 1.2 | 37 | | | | |
| 11 M | 06:29 AM | 0.4 | 12 | 26 Tu | 05:40 AM | 0.4 | 12 |
| | 11:45 AM | 0.9 | 27 | | 10:25 AM | 0.5 | 15 |
| | 05:42 PM | 0.5 | 15 | | 03:03 PM | 0.3 | 9 |
| | 11:48 PM | 1.1 | 34 | | ◖ 10:36 PM | 0.9 | 27 |
| 12 Tu | 07:05 AM | 0.2 | 6 | 27 W | 05:42 AM | 0.2 | 6 |
| | 01:25 PM | 1.0 | 30 | | 12:17 PM | 0.7 | 21 |
| | 07:02 PM | 0.7 | 21 | | 04:21 PM | 0.5 | 15 |
| | | | | | 10:55 PM | 0.9 | 27 |
| 13 W | 12:12 AM | 1.1 | 34 | 28 Th | 06:10 AM | -0.1 | -3 |
| | 07:37 AM | 0.0 | 0 | | 01:37 PM | 0.9 | 27 |
| | 02:40 PM | 1.1 | 34 | | 05:52 PM | 0.7 | 21 |
| | 08:09 PM | 0.8 | 24 | | 11:14 PM | 0.9 | 27 |
| 14 Th | 12:32 AM | 1.0 | 30 | 29 F | 06:47 AM | -0.4 | -12 |
| | 08:06 AM | -0.2 | -6 | | 02:39 PM | 1.0 | 30 |
| | 03:35 PM | 1.2 | 37 | | 07:14 PM | 0.8 | 24 |
| | 09:04 PM | 0.9 | 27 | | 11:39 PM | 1.0 | 30 |
| 15 F | 12:50 AM | 1.0 | 30 | 30 Sa | 07:29 AM | -0.6 | -18 |
| | 08:32 AM | -0.3 | -9 | | 03:32 PM | 1.2 | 37 |
| | 04:18 PM | 1.2 | 37 | | 08:16 PM | 0.9 | 27 |
| | 09:46 PM | 0.9 | 27 | | | | |
| | | | | 31 Su | 12:14 AM | 1.0 | 30 |
| | | | | | 08:14 AM | -0.8 | -24 |
| | | | | | 04:22 PM | 1.3 | 40 |
| | | | | | 09:04 PM | 0.9 | 27 |

Heights are referred to mean lower water which is the chart datum of sounding. All times are local. Daylight Saving Time has been used when needed. Additional tide tables are available online from NOAA at www.tidesandcurrents.noaa.gov/tide_predictions.shtml.

SKIPPER'S HANDBOOK

# NOAA Tide Predictions

## Galveston Pier 21, TX, 2018

### Times and Heights of High and Low Waters

## January

| Day | Time | ft | cm | Day | Time | ft | cm |
|---|---|---|---|---|---|---|---|
| **1** M | 12:48 AM | 1.1 | 34 | **16** Tu | 01:18 AM | 0.9 | 27 |
|  | 09:01 AM | -1.0 | -30 |  | 09:32 AM | -0.7 | -21 |
|  | 05:16 PM | 1.3 | 40 |  | 05:42 PM | 0.9 | 27 |
|  | 09:58 PM | 1.0 | 30 |  | 09:47 PM | 0.8 | 24 |
| **2** Tu ○ | 01:36 AM | 1.1 | 34 | **17** W ● | 01:52 AM | 0.9 | 27 |
|  | 09:51 AM | -1.0 | -30 |  | 10:02 AM | -0.7 | -21 |
|  | 06:06 PM | 1.3 | 40 |  | 06:12 PM | 0.9 | 27 |
|  | 10:40 PM | 1.0 | 30 |  | 10:12 PM | 0.7 | 21 |
| **3** W | 02:29 AM | 1.1 | 34 | **18** Th | 02:23 AM | 0.8 | 24 |
|  | 10:43 AM | -1.0 | -30 |  | 10:33 AM | -0.6 | -18 |
|  | 06:55 PM | 1.2 | 37 |  | 06:44 PM | 0.9 | 27 |
|  | 11:30 PM | 0.9 | 27 |  | 10:48 PM | 0.7 | 21 |
| **4** Th | 03:27 AM | 1.0 | 30 | **19** F | 02:53 AM | 0.8 | 24 |
|  | 11:35 AM | -0.8 | -24 |  | 11:05 AM | -0.5 | -15 |
|  | 07:43 PM | 1.1 | 34 |  | 07:17 PM | 0.9 | 27 |
|  |  |  |  |  | 11:34 PM | 0.6 | 18 |
| **5** F | 12:36 AM | 0.8 | 24 | **20** Sa | 03:26 AM | 0.7 | 21 |
|  | 04:33 AM | 0.9 | 27 |  | 11:38 AM | -0.4 | -12 |
|  | 12:29 PM | -0.6 | -18 |  | 07:48 PM | 0.8 | 24 |
|  | 08:28 PM | 1.0 | 30 |  |  |  |  |
| **6** Sa | 02:07 AM | 0.7 | 21 | **21** Su | 12:28 AM | 0.6 | 18 |
|  | 05:59 AM | 0.8 | 24 |  | 04:14 AM | 0.6 | 18 |
|  | 01:25 PM | -0.3 | -9 |  | 12:13 PM | -0.3 | -9 |
|  | 09:09 PM | 0.9 | 27 |  | 08:15 PM | 0.8 | 24 |
| **7** Su | 03:42 AM | 0.5 | 15 | **22** M | 01:31 AM | 0.4 | 12 |
|  | 07:51 AM | 0.6 | 18 |  | 05:48 AM | 0.5 | 15 |
|  | 02:27 PM | -0.1 | -3 |  | 12:50 PM | -0.1 | -3 |
|  | 09:45 PM | 0.8 | 24 |  | 08:37 PM | 0.7 | 21 |
| **8** M ◐ | 04:51 AM | 0.2 | 6 | **23** Tu | 02:35 AM | 0.3 | 9 |
|  | 09:58 AM | 0.6 | 18 |  | 08:19 AM | 0.4 | 12 |
|  | 03:45 PM | 0.2 | 6 |  | 01:34 PM | 0.1 | 3 |
|  | 10:17 PM | 0.8 | 24 |  | 08:55 PM | 0.7 | 21 |
| **9** Tu | 05:43 AM | 0.0 | 0 | **24** W ◑ | 03:35 AM | 0.1 | 3 |
|  | 12:06 PM | 0.6 | 18 |  | 10:35 AM | 0.5 | 15 |
|  | 05:28 PM | 0.4 | 12 |  | 02:29 PM | 0.4 | 12 |
|  | 10:43 PM | 0.8 | 24 |  | 09:08 PM | 0.7 | 21 |
| **10** W | 06:25 AM | -0.2 | -6 | **25** Th | 04:30 AM | -0.2 | -6 |
|  | 01:52 PM | 0.8 | 24 |  | 12:24 PM | 0.7 | 21 |
|  | 07:05 PM | 0.6 | 18 |  | 03:51 PM | 0.6 | 18 |
|  | 11:06 PM | 0.8 | 24 |  | 09:21 PM | 0.7 | 21 |
| **11** Th | 07:02 AM | -0.4 | -12 | **26** F | 05:22 AM | -0.4 | -12 |
|  | 03:02 PM | 0.9 | 27 |  | 01:43 PM | 0.9 | 27 |
|  | 08:21 PM | 0.7 | 21 |  | 05:49 PM | 0.7 | 21 |
|  | 11:27 PM | 0.8 | 24 |  | 09:45 PM | 0.8 | 24 |
| **12** F | 07:35 AM | -0.5 | -15 | **27** Sa | 06:15 AM | -0.7 | -21 |
|  | 03:48 PM | 0.9 | 27 |  | 02:42 PM | 1.0 | 30 |
|  | 09:16 PM | 0.7 | 21 |  | 07:30 PM | 0.8 | 24 |
|  | 11:49 PM | 0.8 | 24 |  | 10:33 PM | 0.9 | 27 |
| **13** Sa | 08:05 AM | -0.6 | -18 | **28** Su | 07:08 AM | -0.9 | -27 |
|  | 04:22 PM | 1.0 | 30 |  | 03:31 PM | 1.1 | 34 |
|  | 09:49 PM | 0.8 | 24 |  | 09:07 PM | 0.9 | 27 |
|  |  |  |  |  | 11:38 PM | 0.9 | 27 |
| **14** Su | 12:14 AM | 0.8 | 24 | **29** M | 08:01 AM | -1.0 | -30 |
|  | 08:34 AM | -0.6 | -18 |  | 04:16 PM | 1.1 | 34 |
|  | 04:49 PM | 1.0 | 30 |  | 08:53 PM | 0.9 | 27 |
|  | 09:56 PM | 0.8 | 24 |  |  |  |  |
| **15** M | 12:45 AM | 0.8 | 24 | **30** Tu | 12:44 AM | 1.0 | 30 |
|  | 09:02 AM | -0.7 | -21 |  | 08:54 AM | -1.0 | -30 |
|  | 05:15 PM | 0.9 | 27 |  | 04:59 PM | 1.1 | 34 |
|  | 09:44 PM | 0.8 | 24 |  | 09:30 PM | 0.8 | 24 |
|  |  |  |  | **31** W ○ | 01:50 AM | 1.0 | 30 |
|  |  |  |  |  | 09:46 AM | -1.0 | -30 |
|  |  |  |  |  | 05:40 PM | 1.1 | 34 |
|  |  |  |  |  | 10:12 PM | 0.7 | 21 |

## February

| Day | Time | ft | cm | Day | Time | ft | cm |
|---|---|---|---|---|---|---|---|
| **1** Th | 02:54 AM | 1.0 | 30 | **16** F | 02:56 AM | 0.9 | 27 |
|  | 10:37 AM | -0.8 | -24 |  | 10:17 AM | -0.4 | -12 |
|  | 06:18 PM | 1.0 | 30 |  | 05:53 PM | 0.9 | 27 |
|  | 11:01 PM | 0.6 | 18 |  | 10:27 PM | 0.6 | 18 |
| **2** F | 04:01 AM | 1.0 | 30 | **17** Sa | 03:44 AM | 0.9 | 27 |
|  | 11:27 AM | -0.6 | -18 |  | 10:49 AM | -0.3 | -9 |
|  | 06:55 PM | 0.9 | 27 |  | 06:16 PM | 0.9 | 27 |
|  | 11:58 PM | 0.5 | 15 |  | 11:07 PM | 0.5 | 15 |
| **3** Sa | 05:14 AM | 0.8 | 24 | **18** Su | 04:41 AM | 0.8 | 24 |
|  | 12:17 PM | -0.4 | -12 |  | 11:22 AM | -0.1 | -3 |
|  | 07:28 PM | 0.8 | 24 |  | 06:36 PM | 0.8 | 24 |
|  |  |  |  |  | 11:51 PM | 0.4 | 12 |
| **4** Su | 01:04 AM | 0.3 | 9 | **19** M | 05:51 AM | 0.8 | 24 |
|  | 06:36 AM | 0.7 | 21 |  | 11:57 AM | 0.1 | 3 |
|  | 01:07 PM | -0.1 | -3 |  | 06:53 PM | 0.8 | 24 |
|  | 08:00 PM | 0.8 | 24 |  |  |  |  |
| **5** M | 02:15 AM | 0.2 | 6 | **20** Tu | 12:38 AM | 0.2 | 6 |
|  | 08:13 AM | 0.6 | 18 |  | 07:16 AM | 0.7 | 21 |
|  | 02:03 PM | 0.4 | 12 |  | 12:36 PM | 0.3 | 9 |
|  | 08:28 PM | 0.7 | 21 |  | 07:05 PM | 0.8 | 24 |
| **6** Tu | 03:26 AM | 0.0 | 0 | **21** W | 01:31 AM | 0.1 | 3 |
|  | 10:06 AM | 0.6 | 18 |  | 08:57 AM | 0.8 | 24 |
|  | 03:02 PM | 0.4 | 12 |  | 01:22 PM | 0.5 | 15 |
|  | 08:55 PM | 0.7 | 21 |  | 07:10 PM | 0.8 | 24 |
| **7** W ◐ | 04:30 AM | -0.1 | -3 | **22** Th | 02:30 AM | -0.1 | -3 |
|  | 12:09 PM | 0.7 | 21 |  | 10:43 AM | 0.9 | 27 |
|  | 05:41 PM | 0.6 | 18 |  | 02:20 PM | 0.7 | 21 |
|  | 09:19 PM | 0.7 | 21 |  | 07:08 PM | 0.9 | 27 |
| **8** Th | 05:25 AM | -0.3 | -9 | **23** F ◑ | 03:35 AM | -0.3 | -9 |
|  | 01:54 PM | 0.8 | 24 |  | 12:20 PM | 1.0 | 30 |
|  | 07:35 PM | 0.7 | 21 |  | 03:57 PM | 0.9 | 27 |
|  | 09:42 PM | 0.7 | 21 |  | 06:51 PM | 0.9 | 27 |
| **9** F | 06:13 AM | -0.4 | -12 | **24** Sa | 04:43 AM | -0.4 | -12 |
|  | 02:55 PM | 0.9 | 27 |  | 01:34 PM | 1.1 | 34 |
| **10** Sa | 06:56 AM | -0.4 | -12 | **25** Su | 05:51 AM | -0.5 | -15 |
|  | 03:33 PM | 1.0 | 30 |  | 02:29 PM | 1.2 | 37 |
|  |  |  |  |  | 07:57 PM | 1.0 | 30 |
|  |  |  |  |  | 10:12 PM | 1.0 | 30 |
| **11** Su | 07:35 AM | -0.5 | -15 | **26** M | 06:54 AM | -0.6 | -18 |
|  | 03:59 PM | 1.0 | 30 |  | 03:12 PM | 1.2 | 37 |
|  | 09:29 PM | 0.8 | 24 |  | 08:09 PM | 1.0 | 30 |
|  | 11:51 PM | 0.8 | 24 |  | 11:49 PM | 1.1 | 34 |
| **12** M | 08:11 AM | -0.5 | -15 | **27** Tu | 07:54 AM | -0.6 | -18 |
|  | 04:21 PM | 0.9 | 27 |  | 03:50 PM | 1.2 | 37 |
|  | 09:18 PM | 0.8 | 24 |  | 08:37 PM | 0.9 | 27 |
| **13** Tu | 12:41 AM | 0.9 | 27 | **28** W | 01:07 AM | 1.1 | 34 |
|  | 08:44 AM | -0.5 | -15 |  | 08:49 AM | -0.6 | -18 |
|  | 04:42 PM | 0.9 | 27 |  | 04:24 PM | 1.1 | 34 |
|  | 09:09 PM | 0.8 | 24 |  | 09:13 PM | 0.8 | 24 |
| **14** W | 01:27 AM | 0.9 | 27 |  |  |  |  |
|  | 09:16 AM | -0.5 | -15 |  |  |  |  |
|  | 05:05 PM | 0.9 | 27 |  |  |  |  |
|  | 09:22 PM | 0.7 | 21 |  |  |  |  |
| **15** Th ● | 02:11 AM | 0.9 | 27 |  |  |  |  |
|  | 09:47 AM | -0.4 | -12 |  |  |  |  |
|  | 05:29 PM | 0.9 | 27 |  |  |  |  |
|  | 09:51 PM | 0.7 | 21 |  |  |  |  |

## March

| Day | Time | ft | cm | Day | Time | ft | cm |
|---|---|---|---|---|---|---|---|
| **1** Th | 02:18 AM | 1.2 | 37 | **16** F | 03:34 AM | 1.1 | 34 |
|  | 09:41 AM | -0.5 | -15 |  | 10:28 AM | 0.1 | 3 |
|  | 04:56 PM | 1.1 | 34 |  | 05:28 PM | 1.1 | 34 |
|  | 09:54 PM | 0.6 | 18 |  | 10:31 PM | 0.7 | 21 |
| **2** F ○ | 03:25 AM | 1.2 | 37 | **17** Sa ● | 04:28 AM | 1.2 | 37 |
|  | 10:31 AM | -0.3 | -9 |  | 11:02 AM | 0.2 | 6 |
|  | 05:25 PM | 1.0 | 30 |  | 05:46 PM | 1.1 | 34 |
|  | 10:39 PM | 0.5 | 15 |  | 11:03 PM | 0.5 | 15 |
| **3** Sa | 04:33 AM | 1.1 | 34 | **18** Su | 05:24 AM | 1.2 | 37 |
|  | 11:18 AM | 0.0 | 0 |  | 11:36 AM | 0.3 | 9 |
|  | 05:52 PM | 1.0 | 30 |  | 06:02 PM | 1.1 | 34 |
|  | 11:26 PM | 0.3 | 9 |  | 11:39 PM | 0.4 | 12 |
| **4** Su | 05:42 AM | 1.1 | 34 | **19** M | 06:25 AM | 1.2 | 37 |
|  | 12:05 PM | 0.2 | 6 |  | 12:14 PM | 0.5 | 15 |
|  | 06:17 PM | 0.9 | 27 |  | 06:15 PM | 1.0 | 30 |
| **5** M | 12:15 AM | 0.2 | 6 | **20** Tu | 12:19 AM | 0.2 | 6 |
|  | 06:57 AM | 1.0 | 30 |  | 07:32 AM | 1.2 | 37 |
|  | 12:54 PM | 0.4 | 12 |  | 12:54 PM | 0.7 | 21 |
|  | 06:40 PM | 0.9 | 27 |  | 06:23 PM | 1.1 | 34 |
| **6** Tu | 01:06 AM | 0.1 | 3 | **21** W | 01:03 AM | 0.1 | 3 |
|  | 08:19 AM | 1.0 | 30 |  | 08:47 AM | 1.3 | 40 |
|  | 01:52 PM | 0.7 | 21 |  | 01:40 PM | 0.9 | 27 |
|  | 06:58 PM | 0.9 | 27 |  | 06:25 PM | 1.1 | 34 |
| **7** W | 02:00 AM | 0.0 | 0 | **22** Th | 01:53 AM | 0.1 | 3 |
|  | 09:51 AM | 1.0 | 30 |  | 10:09 AM | 1.3 | 40 |
|  | 03:42 PM | 0.8 | 24 |  | 02:34 PM | 1.1 | 34 |
|  | 07:08 PM | 0.9 | 27 |  | 06:16 PM | 1.1 | 34 |
| **8** Th | 02:59 AM | 0.0 | 0 | **23** F | 02:52 AM | -0.1 | -3 |
|  | 11:32 AM | 1.1 | 34 |  | 11:37 AM | 1.3 | 40 |
| **9** F ◐ | 04:02 AM | 0.0 | 0 | **24** Sa ◑ | 03:59 AM | -0.1 | -3 |
|  | 01:07 PM | 1.1 | 34 |  | 01:01 PM | 1.4 | 43 |
| **10** Sa | 05:07 AM | 0.0 | 0 | **25** Su | 05:15 AM | -0.1 | -3 |
|  | 02:08 PM | 1.1 | 34 |  | 02:07 PM | 1.4 | 43 |
| **11** Su | 07:06 AM | -0.1 | -3 | **26** M | 06:33 AM | -0.1 | -3 |
|  | 03:44 PM | 1.2 | 37 |  | 02:56 PM | 1.4 | 43 |
|  |  |  |  |  | 08:52 PM | 1.1 | 34 |
|  |  |  |  |  | 11:47 PM | 1.2 | 37 |
| **12** M | 07:58 AM | -0.1 | -3 | **27** Tu | 07:45 AM | -0.1 | -3 |
|  | 04:09 PM | 1.1 | 34 |  | 03:34 PM | 1.4 | 43 |
|  | 09:58 PM | 1.0 | 30 |  | 09:03 PM | 1.0 | 30 |
| **13** Tu | 12:45 AM | 1.0 | 30 | **28** W | 01:24 AM | 1.3 | 40 |
|  | 08:42 AM | -0.1 | -3 |  | 08:42 AM | 0.0 | 0 |
|  | 04:30 PM | 1.1 | 34 |  | 04:05 PM | 1.3 | 40 |
|  | 09:46 PM | 0.9 | 27 |  | 09:30 PM | 0.9 | 27 |
| **14** W | 01:47 AM | 1.1 | 34 | **29** Th | 02:42 AM | 1.3 | 40 |
|  | 09:20 AM | 0.0 | 0 |  | 09:46 AM | 0.1 | 3 |
|  | 04:49 PM | 1.1 | 34 |  | 04:32 PM | 1.3 | 40 |
|  | 09:46 PM | 0.9 | 27 |  | 10:03 PM | 0.7 | 21 |
| **15** Th | 02:42 AM | 1.1 | 34 | **30** F | 03:52 AM | 1.4 | 43 |
|  | 09:55 AM | 0.0 | 0 |  | 10:38 AM | 0.3 | 9 |
|  | 05:09 PM | 1.1 | 34 |  | 04:57 PM | 1.2 | 37 |
|  | 10:04 PM | 0.8 | 24 |  | 10:40 PM | 0.5 | 15 |
|  |  |  |  | **31** Sa ○ | 04:57 AM | 1.4 | 43 |
|  |  |  |  |  | 11:26 AM | 0.4 | 12 |
|  |  |  |  |  | 05:19 PM | 1.2 | 37 |
|  |  |  |  |  | 11:17 PM | 0.4 | 12 |

Heights are referred to mean lower water which is the chart datum of sounding. All times are local. Daylight Saving Time has been used when needed. Additional tide tables are available online from NOAA at www.tidesandcurrents.noaa.gov/tide_predictions.shtml.

SKIPPER'S HANDBOOK

StationId: 8771450
Source: NOAA/NOS/CO-OPS
Station Type: Primary
Time Zone: LST_LDT
Datum: MLLW

**NOAA Tide Predictions**

## Galveston Pier 21, TX,2018

### Times and Heights of High and Low Waters

### April

| Day | Time | ft | cm |
|---|---|---|---|
| **1** Su | 06:00 AM | 1.4 | 43 |
| | 12:13 PM | 0.6 | 18 |
| | 05:39 PM | 1.2 | 37 |
| | 11:54 PM | 0.3 | 9 |
| **2** M | 07:02 AM | 1.5 | 46 |
| | 01:01 PM | 0.8 | 24 |
| | 05:57 PM | 1.2 | 37 |
| **3** Tu | 12:32 AM | 0.2 | 6 |
| | 08:05 AM | 1.4 | 43 |
| | 01:53 PM | 1.0 | 30 |
| | 06:08 PM | 1.1 | 34 |
| **4** W | 01:11 AM | 0.1 | 3 |
| | 09:11 AM | 1.4 | 43 |
| | 03:11 PM | 1.1 | 34 |
| | 06:00 PM | 1.2 | 37 |
| **5** Th | 01:53 AM | 0.1 | 3 |
| | 10:21 AM | 1.4 | 43 |
| **6** F | 02:41 AM | 0.2 | 6 |
| | 11:36 AM | 1.4 | 43 |
| **7** Sa | 03:37 AM | 0.2 | 6 |
| | 12:51 PM | 1.4 | 43 |
| **8** Su ◐ | 04:44 AM | 0.3 | 9 |
| | 01:51 PM | 1.4 | 43 |
| **9** M | 05:57 AM | 0.3 | 9 |
| | 02:31 PM | 1.4 | 43 |
| **10** Tu | 07:03 AM | 0.3 | 9 |
| | 02:59 PM | 1.3 | 40 |
| | 09:29 PM | 1.1 | 34 |
| **11** W | 12:44 AM | 1.1 | 34 |
| | 07:59 AM | 0.4 | 12 |
| | 03:22 PM | 1.3 | 40 |
| | 09:18 PM | 1.0 | 30 |
| **12** Th | 01:56 AM | 1.2 | 37 |
| | 08:45 AM | 0.4 | 12 |
| | 03:41 PM | 1.3 | 40 |
| | 09:21 PM | 0.9 | 27 |
| **13** F | 02:59 AM | 1.3 | 40 |
| | 09:27 AM | 0.5 | 15 |
| | 03:58 PM | 1.3 | 40 |
| | 09:39 PM | 0.7 | 21 |
| **14** Sa | 03:57 AM | 1.4 | 43 |
| | 10:07 AM | 0.6 | 18 |
| | 04:14 PM | 1.3 | 40 |
| | 10:05 PM | 0.5 | 15 |
| **15** Su | 04:53 AM | 1.5 | 46 |
| | 10:48 AM | 0.7 | 21 |
| | 04:27 PM | 1.2 | 37 |
| | 10:36 PM | 0.3 | 9 |
| **16** M ● | 05:50 AM | 1.5 | 46 |
| | 11:30 AM | 0.9 | 27 |
| | 04:38 PM | 1.3 | 40 |
| | 11:12 PM | 0.2 | 6 |
| **17** Tu | 06:49 AM | 1.6 | 49 |
| | 12:15 PM | 1.1 | 34 |
| | 04:46 PM | 1.3 | 40 |
| | 11:53 PM | 0.0 | 0 |
| **18** W | 07:51 AM | 1.7 | 52 |
| | 01:04 PM | 1.2 | 37 |
| | 04:50 PM | 1.3 | 40 |
| **19** Th | 12:38 AM | -0.1 | -3 |
| | 08:57 AM | 1.7 | 52 |
| | 02:02 PM | 1.3 | 40 |
| | 04:46 PM | 1.4 | 43 |
| **20** F | 01:30 AM | -0.1 | -3 |
| | 10:08 AM | 1.7 | 52 |
| **21** Sa | 02:28 AM | -0.1 | -3 |
| | 11:22 AM | 1.6 | 49 |
| **22** Su ◐ | 03:36 AM | 0.0 | 0 |
| | 12:31 PM | 1.6 | 49 |
| **23** M ◑ | 04:54 AM | 0.1 | 3 |
| | 01:26 PM | 1.6 | 49 |
| **24** Tu | 06:18 AM | 0.2 | 6 |
| | 02:07 PM | 1.5 | 46 |
| | 08:30 PM | 1.1 | 34 |
| **25** W | 12:34 AM | 1.2 | 37 |
| | 07:36 AM | 0.4 | 12 |
| | 02:39 PM | 1.4 | 43 |
| | 08:52 PM | 0.9 | 27 |
| **26** Th | 02:06 AM | 1.3 | 40 |
| | 08:44 AM | 0.5 | 15 |
| | 03:05 PM | 1.4 | 43 |
| | 09:21 PM | 0.7 | 21 |
| **27** F | 03:21 AM | 1.4 | 43 |
| | 09:44 AM | 0.7 | 21 |
| | 03:28 PM | 1.3 | 40 |
| | 09:51 PM | 0.5 | 15 |
| **28** Sa | 04:27 AM | 1.5 | 46 |
| | 10:38 AM | 0.8 | 24 |
| | 03:48 PM | 1.3 | 40 |
| | 10:22 PM | 0.3 | 9 |
| **29** Su | 05:26 AM | 1.6 | 49 |
| | 11:28 AM | 1.0 | 30 |
| | 04:05 PM | 1.3 | 40 |
| | 10:52 PM | 0.2 | 6 |
| **30** M ○ | 06:20 AM | 1.6 | 49 |
| | 12:18 PM | 1.1 | 34 |
| | 04:18 PM | 1.3 | 40 |
| | 11:23 PM | 0.1 | 3 |

### May

| Day | Time | ft | cm |
|---|---|---|---|
| **1** Tu | 07:12 AM | 1.7 | 52 |
| | 01:11 PM | 1.2 | 37 |
| | 04:25 PM | 1.3 | 40 |
| | 11:55 PM | 0.0 | 0 |
| **2** W | 08:02 AM | 1.6 | 49 |
| **3** Th | 12:29 AM | 0.0 | 0 |
| | 08:54 AM | 1.6 | 49 |
| **4** F | 01:06 AM | 0.1 | 3 |
| | 09:48 AM | 1.6 | 49 |
| **5** Sa | 01:48 AM | 0.1 | 3 |
| | 10:46 AM | 1.5 | 46 |
| **6** Su | 02:36 AM | 0.2 | 6 |
| | 11:45 AM | 1.5 | 46 |
| **7** M | 03:31 AM | 0.3 | 9 |
| | 12:36 PM | 1.5 | 46 |
| **8** Tu ◑ | 04:35 AM | 0.4 | 12 |
| | 01:15 PM | 1.4 | 43 |
| **9** W | 05:45 AM | 0.5 | 15 |
| | 01:44 PM | 1.4 | 43 |
| | 08:52 PM | 0.9 | 27 |
| **10** Th | 12:48 AM | 1.1 | 34 |
| | 06:54 AM | 0.6 | 18 |
| | 02:06 PM | 1.3 | 40 |
| | 08:39 PM | 0.8 | 24 |
| **11** F | 02:09 AM | 1.2 | 37 |
| | 07:56 AM | 0.7 | 21 |
| | 02:24 PM | 1.3 | 40 |
| | 08:46 PM | 0.6 | 18 |
| **12** Sa | 03:15 AM | 1.3 | 40 |
| | 08:53 AM | 0.8 | 24 |
| | 02:38 PM | 1.3 | 40 |
| | 09:06 PM | 0.4 | 12 |
| **13** Su | 04:14 AM | 1.5 | 46 |
| | 09:46 AM | 1.0 | 30 |
| | 02:50 PM | 1.3 | 40 |
| | 09:35 PM | 0.1 | 3 |
| **14** M | 05:09 AM | 1.6 | 49 |
| | 10:38 AM | 1.1 | 34 |
| | 03:00 PM | 1.3 | 40 |
| | 10:10 PM | -0.1 | -3 |
| **15** Tu ● | 06:04 AM | 1.7 | 52 |
| | 11:29 AM | 1.2 | 37 |
| | 03:10 PM | 1.3 | 40 |
| | 10:50 PM | -0.2 | -6 |
| **16** W | 06:59 AM | 1.8 | 55 |
| | 12:21 PM | 1.3 | 40 |
| | 03:21 PM | 1.4 | 43 |
| | 11:34 PM | -0.3 | -9 |
| **17** Th | 07:56 AM | 1.8 | 55 |
| | 01:18 PM | 1.4 | 43 |
| | 03:32 PM | 1.4 | 43 |
| **18** F | 12:22 AM | -0.4 | -12 |
| | 08:55 AM | 1.8 | 55 |
| **19** Sa | 01:15 AM | -0.3 | -9 |
| | 09:57 AM | 1.7 | 52 |
| **20** Su | 02:14 AM | -0.2 | -6 |
| | 10:57 AM | 1.6 | 49 |
| **21** M ◑ | 03:20 AM | 0.0 | 0 |
| | 11:51 AM | 1.5 | 46 |
| **22** Tu ◐ | 04:36 AM | 0.2 | 6 |
| | 12:35 PM | 1.5 | 46 |
| | 07:36 PM | 0.9 | 27 |
| | 11:27 PM | 1.1 | 34 |
| **23** W ◑ | 06:02 AM | 0.4 | 12 |
| | 01:09 PM | 1.4 | 43 |
| | 08:02 PM | 0.7 | 21 |
| **24** Th | 01:20 AM | 1.1 | 34 |
| | 07:27 AM | 0.6 | 18 |
| | 01:37 PM | 1.3 | 40 |
| | 08:33 PM | 0.4 | 12 |
| **25** F | 02:49 AM | 1.3 | 40 |
| | 08:42 AM | 0.8 | 24 |
| | 02:00 PM | 1.3 | 40 |
| | 09:03 PM | 0.2 | 6 |
| **26** Sa | 04:01 AM | 1.4 | 43 |
| | 09:49 AM | 1.0 | 30 |
| | 02:19 PM | 1.3 | 40 |
| | 09:32 PM | 0.1 | 3 |
| **27** Su | 04:59 AM | 1.5 | 46 |
| | 10:49 AM | 1.1 | 34 |
| | 02:34 PM | 1.2 | 37 |
| | 10:00 PM | -0.1 | -3 |
| **28** M | 05:48 AM | 1.6 | 49 |
| | 11:46 AM | 1.2 | 37 |
| | 02:45 PM | 1.3 | 40 |
| | 10:28 PM | -0.2 | -6 |
| **29** Tu ○ | 06:31 AM | 1.6 | 49 |
| | 12:42 PM | 1.2 | 37 |
| | 02:48 PM | 1.3 | 40 |
| | 10:55 PM | -0.2 | -6 |
| **30** W | 07:11 AM | 1.6 | 49 |
| | 11:25 PM | -0.2 | -6 |
| **31** Th | 07:51 AM | 1.6 | 49 |
| | 11:58 PM | -0.2 | -6 |

### June

| Day | Time | ft | cm |
|---|---|---|---|
| **1** F | 08:32 AM | 1.5 | 46 |
| **2** Sa | 12:33 AM | -0.1 | -3 |
| | 09:17 AM | 1.5 | 46 |
| **3** Su | 01:11 AM | 0.0 | 0 |
| | 10:03 AM | 1.4 | 43 |
| **4** M | 01:52 AM | 0.1 | 3 |
| | 10:49 AM | 1.4 | 43 |
| **5** Tu | 02:37 AM | 0.2 | 6 |
| | 11:29 AM | 1.3 | 40 |
| **6** W ◐ | 03:27 AM | 0.3 | 9 |
| | 12:02 PM | 1.3 | 40 |
| | 08:28 PM | 0.8 | 24 |
| | 10:53 PM | 0.8 | 24 |
| **7** Th | 04:26 AM | 0.5 | 15 |
| | 12:27 PM | 1.2 | 37 |
| | 07:50 PM | 0.6 | 18 |
| **8** F | 12:58 AM | 0.9 | 27 |
| | 05:37 AM | 0.7 | 21 |
| | 12:45 PM | 1.2 | 37 |
| | 07:46 PM | 0.4 | 12 |
| **9** Sa | 02:23 AM | 1.1 | 34 |
| | 06:57 AM | 0.8 | 24 |
| | 12:59 PM | 1.2 | 37 |
| | 08:03 PM | 0.2 | 6 |
| **10** Su | 03:28 AM | 1.2 | 37 |
| | 08:17 AM | 1.0 | 30 |
| | 01:09 PM | 1.2 | 37 |
| | 08:31 PM | -0.1 | -3 |
| **11** M | 04:24 AM | 1.4 | 43 |
| | 09:28 AM | 1.1 | 34 |
| | 01:20 PM | 1.2 | 37 |
| | 09:07 PM | -0.3 | -9 |
| **12** Tu | 05:15 AM | 1.6 | 49 |
| | 10:28 AM | 1.2 | 37 |
| | 01:36 PM | 1.3 | 40 |
| | 09:48 PM | -0.5 | -15 |
| **13** W ● | 06:06 AM | 1.7 | 52 |
| | 11:19 AM | 1.3 | 40 |
| | 02:01 PM | 1.3 | 40 |
| | 10:33 PM | -0.6 | -18 |
| **14** Th | 06:57 AM | 1.7 | 52 |
| | 12:06 PM | 1.3 | 40 |
| | 02:36 PM | 1.4 | 43 |
| | 11:21 PM | -0.7 | -21 |
| **15** F | 07:49 AM | 1.7 | 52 |
| | 12:56 PM | 1.3 | 40 |
| | 03:19 PM | 1.4 | 43 |
| **16** Sa | 12:12 AM | -0.6 | -18 |
| | 08:42 AM | 1.6 | 49 |
| | 02:03 PM | 1.3 | 40 |
| | 04:09 PM | 1.3 | 40 |
| **17** Su | 01:06 AM | -0.5 | -15 |
| | 09:33 AM | 1.5 | 46 |
| **18** M | 02:04 AM | -0.2 | -6 |
| | 10:20 AM | 1.4 | 43 |
| | 05:14 PM | 1.0 | 30 |
| | 07:33 PM | 1.0 | 30 |
| **19** Tu | 03:06 AM | 0.0 | 0 |
| | 11:02 AM | 1.3 | 40 |
| | 06:05 PM | 0.7 | 21 |
| | 09:58 PM | 0.9 | 27 |
| **20** W ◐ | 04:18 AM | 0.3 | 9 |
| | 11:37 AM | 1.2 | 37 |
| | 06:48 PM | 0.5 | 15 |
| **21** Th | 12:09 AM | 0.9 | 27 |
| | 05:46 AM | 0.6 | 18 |
| | 12:07 PM | 1.2 | 37 |
| | 07:28 PM | 0.2 | 6 |
| **22** F | 02:02 AM | 1.0 | 30 |
| | 07:23 AM | 0.8 | 24 |
| | 12:32 PM | 1.2 | 37 |
| | 08:05 PM | 0.0 | 0 |
| **23** Sa | 03:28 AM | 1.2 | 37 |
| | 08:51 AM | 0.9 | 27 |
| | 12:53 PM | 1.1 | 34 |
| | 08:38 PM | -0.2 | -6 |
| **24** Su | 04:31 AM | 1.3 | 40 |
| | 10:07 AM | 1.0 | 30 |
| | 01:09 PM | 1.1 | 34 |
| | 09:09 PM | -0.3 | -9 |
| **25** M | 05:19 AM | 1.4 | 43 |
| | 11:13 AM | 1.1 | 34 |
| | 01:20 PM | 1.1 | 34 |
| | 09:37 PM | -0.3 | -9 |
| **26** Tu | 05:57 AM | 1.4 | 43 |
| | 10:05 PM | -0.4 | -12 |
| **27** W | 06:30 AM | 1.4 | 43 |
| | 10:33 PM | -0.4 | -12 |
| **28** Th ○ | 07:00 AM | 1.4 | 43 |
| | 11:03 PM | -0.4 | -12 |
| **29** F | 07:32 AM | 1.4 | 43 |
| | 11:35 PM | -0.3 | -9 |
| **30** Sa | 08:05 AM | 1.3 | 40 |

Heights are referred to mean lower water which is the chart datum of sounding. All times are local. Daylight Saving Time has been used when needed. Additional tide tables are available online from NOAA at www.tidesandcurrents.noaa.gov/tide_predictions.shtml.

**SKIPPER'S HANDBOOK**

StationId: 8771450
Source: NOAA/NOS/CO-OPS
Station Type: Primary
Time Zone: LST_LDT
Datum: MLLW

# NOAA Tide Predictions

## Galveston Pier 21, TX,2018

### Times and Heights of High and Low Waters

## July

| Day | Time | ft | cm |
|---|---|---|---|
| 1 Su | 12:09 AM | -0.2 | -6 |
|  | 08:41 AM | 1.3 | 40 |
| 2 M | 12:43 AM | -0.1 | -3 |
|  | 09:18 AM | 1.3 | 40 |
| 3 Tu | 01:18 AM | 0.0 | 0 |
|  | 09:52 AM | 1.2 | 37 |
| 4 W | 01:56 AM | 0.1 | 3 |
|  | 10:23 AM | 1.2 | 37 |
| 5 Th | 02:37 AM | 0.3 | 9 |
|  | 10:47 AM | 1.1 | 34 |
|  | 06:22 PM | 0.5 | 15 |
|  | 11:12 PM | 0.7 | 21 |
| 6 F | 03:26 AM | 0.5 | 15 |
|  | 11:05 AM | 1.1 | 34 |
|  | 06:22 PM | 0.3 | 9 |
| 7 Sa | 01:08 AM | 0.8 | 24 |
|  | 04:33 AM | 0.7 | 21 |
|  | 11:17 AM | 1.1 | 34 |
|  | 06:46 PM | 0.1 | 3 |
| 8 Su | 02:32 AM | 1.0 | 30 |
|  | 06:05 AM | 0.9 | 27 |
|  | 11:25 AM | 1.1 | 34 |
|  | 07:19 PM | -0.2 | -6 |
| 9 M | 03:33 AM | 1.2 | 37 |
|  | 07:49 AM | 1.1 | 34 |
|  | 11:35 AM | 1.2 | 37 |
|  | 07:59 PM | -0.4 | -12 |
| 10 Tu | 04:24 AM | 1.4 | 43 |
|  | 09:11 AM | 1.2 | 37 |
|  | 12:01 PM | 1.2 | 37 |
|  | 08:44 PM | -0.6 | -18 |
| 11 W | 05:11 AM | 1.5 | 46 |
|  | 10:02 AM | 1.3 | 40 |
|  | 12:48 PM | 1.3 | 40 |
|  | 09:32 PM | -0.7 | -21 |
| 12 Th | 05:58 AM | 1.6 | 49 |
|  | 10:41 AM | 1.3 | 40 |
|  | 01:46 PM | 1.3 | 40 |
|  | 10:21 PM | -0.8 | -24 |
| 13 F | 06:44 AM | 1.5 | 46 |
|  | 11:22 AM | 1.3 | 40 |
|  | 02:49 PM | 1.3 | 40 |
|  | 11:13 PM | -0.7 | -21 |
| 14 Sa | 07:28 AM | 1.5 | 46 |
|  | 12:11 PM | 1.2 | 37 |
|  | 03:57 PM | 1.3 | 40 |
| 15 Su | 12:05 AM | -0.6 | -18 |
|  | 08:11 AM | 1.4 | 43 |
|  | 01:12 PM | 1.1 | 34 |
|  | 05:12 PM | 1.2 | 37 |
| 16 M | 12:58 AM | -0.4 | -12 |
|  | 08:52 AM | 1.3 | 40 |
|  | 02:27 PM | 0.9 | 27 |
|  | 06:43 PM | 1.1 | 34 |
| 17 Tu | 01:53 AM | -0.1 | -3 |
|  | 09:29 AM | 1.2 | 37 |
|  | 03:47 PM | 0.7 | 21 |
|  | 08:31 PM | 0.9 | 27 |
| 18 W | 02:51 AM | 0.2 | 6 |
|  | 10:03 AM | 1.2 | 37 |
|  | 04:58 PM | 0.4 | 12 |
|  | 10:33 PM | 0.9 | 27 |
| 19 Th | 04:02 AM | 0.5 | 15 |
|  | 10:33 AM | 1.1 | 34 |
|  | 05:56 PM | 0.2 | 6 |
| 20 F | 12:39 AM | 1.0 | 30 |
|  | 05:43 AM | 0.8 | 24 |
|  | 11:00 AM | 1.1 | 34 |
|  | 06:46 PM | 0.0 | 0 |
| 21 Sa | 02:31 AM | 1.1 | 34 |
|  | 07:40 AM | 1.0 | 30 |
|  | 11:24 AM | 1.1 | 34 |
|  | 07:29 PM | -0.1 | -3 |
| 22 Su | 03:48 AM | 1.3 | 40 |
|  | 09:16 AM | 1.1 | 34 |
|  | 11:44 AM | 1.1 | 34 |
|  | 08:08 PM | -0.3 | -9 |
| 23 M | 04:40 AM | 1.3 | 40 |
|  | 08:43 PM | -0.3 | -9 |
| 24 Tu | 05:19 AM | 1.4 | 43 |
|  | 09:15 AM | -0.3 | -9 |
| 25 W | 05:47 AM | 1.4 | 43 |
|  | 09:46 AM | -0.3 | -9 |
| 26 Th | 06:11 AM | 1.3 | 40 |
|  | 10:16 AM | -0.3 | -9 |
| 27 F | 06:34 AM | 1.3 | 40 |
|  | 11:23 AM | 1.2 | 37 |
|  | 02:24 PM | 1.2 | 37 |
|  | 10:46 PM | -0.3 | -9 |
| 28 Sa | 06:58 AM | 1.3 | 40 |
|  | 11:32 AM | 1.1 | 34 |
|  | 03:05 PM | 1.2 | 37 |
|  | 11:16 PM | -0.2 | -6 |
| 29 Su | 07:25 AM | 1.3 | 40 |
|  | 12:05 PM | 1.1 | 34 |
|  | 03:45 PM | 1.1 | 34 |
|  | 11:47 PM | -0.1 | -3 |
| 30 M | 07:53 AM | 1.3 | 40 |
|  | 12:52 PM | 1.0 | 30 |
|  | 04:30 PM | 1.0 | 30 |
| 31 Tu | 12:18 AM | 0.0 | 0 |
|  | 08:21 AM | 1.2 | 37 |
|  | 01:45 PM | 0.9 | 27 |
|  | 05:34 PM | 0.9 | 27 |

## August

| Day | Time | ft | cm |
|---|---|---|---|
| 1 W | 12:51 AM | 0.2 | 6 |
|  | 08:46 AM | 1.2 | 37 |
|  | 02:39 PM | 0.8 | 24 |
|  | 07:16 PM | 0.9 | 27 |
| 2 Th | 01:25 AM | 0.4 | 12 |
|  | 09:06 AM | 1.2 | 37 |
|  | 03:29 PM | 0.6 | 18 |
|  | 09:21 PM | 0.8 | 24 |
| 3 F | 02:03 AM | 0.6 | 18 |
|  | 09:21 AM | 1.1 | 34 |
|  | 04:15 PM | 0.4 | 12 |
|  | 11:24 PM | 0.9 | 27 |
| 4 Sa | 02:50 AM | 0.8 | 24 |
|  | 09:28 AM | 1.1 | 34 |
|  | 05:02 PM | 0.2 | 6 |
| 5 Su | 01:11 AM | 1.1 | 34 |
|  | 03:56 AM | 1.0 | 30 |
|  | 09:27 AM | 1.2 | 37 |
|  | 05:51 PM | 0.0 | 0 |
| 6 M | 02:30 AM | 1.3 | 40 |
|  | 05:41 AM | 1.2 | 37 |
|  | 09:26 AM | 1.2 | 37 |
|  | 06:42 PM | -0.2 | -6 |
| 7 Tu | 03:26 AM | 1.4 | 43 |
|  | 07:52 AM | 1.3 | 40 |
|  | 09:59 AM | 1.3 | 40 |
|  | 07:34 PM | -0.4 | -12 |
| 8 W | 04:13 AM | 1.5 | 46 |
|  | 08:53 AM | 1.4 | 43 |
|  | 11:29 AM | 1.4 | 43 |
|  | 08:27 PM | -0.5 | -15 |
| 9 Th | 04:55 AM | 1.6 | 49 |
|  | 09:26 AM | 1.4 | 43 |
|  | 12:54 PM | 1.4 | 43 |
|  | 09:21 PM | -0.5 | -15 |
| 10 F | 05:35 AM | 1.6 | 49 |
|  | 10:03 AM | 1.3 | 40 |
|  | 02:10 PM | 1.5 | 46 |
|  | 10:14 PM | -0.5 | -15 |
| 11 Sa | 06:13 AM | 1.5 | 46 |
|  | 10:47 AM | 1.2 | 37 |
|  | 03:23 PM | 1.5 | 46 |
|  | 11:06 PM | -0.4 | -12 |
| 12 Su | 06:49 AM | 1.5 | 46 |
|  | 11:37 AM | 1.1 | 34 |
|  | 04:37 PM | 1.4 | 43 |
|  | 11:57 PM | -0.2 | -6 |
| 13 M | 07:22 AM | 1.4 | 43 |
|  | 12:35 PM | 0.9 | 27 |
|  | 05:55 PM | 1.3 | 40 |
| 14 Tu | 12:48 AM | 0.1 | 3 |
|  | 07:54 AM | 1.3 | 40 |
|  | 01:37 PM | 0.7 | 21 |
|  | 07:22 PM | 1.2 | 37 |
| 15 W | 01:41 AM | 0.4 | 12 |
|  | 08:24 AM | 1.3 | 40 |
|  | 02:44 PM | 0.5 | 15 |
|  | 08:59 PM | 1.2 | 37 |
| 16 Th | 02:39 AM | 0.7 | 21 |
|  | 08:52 AM | 1.2 | 37 |
|  | 03:50 PM | 0.4 | 12 |
|  | 10:49 PM | 1.2 | 37 |
| 17 F | 04:00 AM | 1.0 | 30 |
|  | 09:18 AM | 1.2 | 37 |
|  | 04:54 PM | 0.2 | 6 |
| 18 Sa | 12:47 AM | 1.3 | 40 |
|  | 06:19 AM | 1.1 | 34 |
|  | 09:41 AM | 1.2 | 37 |
|  | 05:52 PM | 0.1 | 3 |
| 19 Su | 02:30 AM | 1.4 | 43 |
|  | 06:45 AM | 0.0 | 0 |
| 20 M | 03:36 AM | 1.5 | 46 |
|  | 07:32 AM | 0.0 | 0 |
| 21 Tu | 04:20 AM | 1.5 | 46 |
|  | 08:15 AM | 0.0 | 0 |
| 22 W | 04:50 AM | 1.5 | 46 |
|  | 08:53 AM | 0.0 | 0 |
| 23 Th | 05:11 AM | 1.5 | 46 |
|  | 10:44 AM | 1.3 | 40 |
|  | 01:15 PM | 1.3 | 40 |
|  | 09:27 PM | 0.0 | 0 |
| 24 F | 05:29 AM | 1.4 | 43 |
|  | 10:32 AM | 1.3 | 40 |
|  | 02:08 PM | 1.4 | 43 |
|  | 09:58 PM | 0.1 | 3 |
| 25 Sa | 05:47 AM | 1.4 | 43 |
|  | 10:33 AM | 1.2 | 37 |
|  | 02:58 PM | 1.4 | 43 |
|  | 10:28 PM | 0.1 | 3 |
| 26 Su | 06:07 AM | 1.4 | 43 |
|  | 10:56 AM | 1.1 | 34 |
|  | 03:48 PM | 1.3 | 40 |
|  | 10:57 PM | 0.2 | 6 |
| 27 M | 06:28 AM | 1.4 | 43 |
|  | 11:29 AM | 1.0 | 30 |
|  | 04:40 PM | 1.3 | 40 |
|  | 11:27 PM | 0.3 | 9 |
| 28 Tu | 06:50 AM | 1.4 | 43 |
|  | 12:07 PM | 0.9 | 27 |
|  | 05:39 PM | 1.2 | 37 |
|  | 11:58 PM | 0.5 | 15 |
| 29 W | 07:09 AM | 1.4 | 43 |
|  | 12:46 PM | 0.8 | 24 |
|  | 06:49 PM | 1.2 | 37 |
| 30 Th | 12:31 AM | 0.7 | 21 |
|  | 07:25 AM | 1.4 | 43 |
|  | 01:28 PM | 0.7 | 21 |
|  | 08:11 PM | 1.2 | 37 |
| 31 F | 01:07 AM | 0.9 | 27 |
|  | 07:34 AM | 1.3 | 40 |
|  | 02:14 PM | 0.5 | 15 |
|  | 09:45 PM | 1.3 | 40 |

## September

| Day | Time | ft | cm |
|---|---|---|---|
| 1 Sa | 01:48 AM | 1.1 | 34 |
|  | 07:33 AM | 1.4 | 43 |
|  | 03:06 PM | 0.4 | 12 |
|  | 11:26 PM | 1.4 | 43 |
| 2 Su | 02:38 AM | 1.3 | 40 |
|  | 07:18 AM | 1.4 | 43 |
|  | 04:04 PM | 0.2 | 6 |
| 3 M | 01:01 AM | 1.5 | 46 |
|  | 03:54 AM | 1.4 | 43 |
|  | 06:57 AM | 1.5 | 46 |
|  | 05:07 PM | 0.1 | 3 |
| 4 Tu | 02:14 AM | 1.6 | 49 |
|  | 06:12 AM | 0.0 | 0 |
| 5 W | 03:06 AM | 1.7 | 52 |
|  | 07:16 AM | -0.1 | -3 |
| 6 Th | 03:47 AM | 1.7 | 52 |
|  | 08:46 AM | 1.5 | 46 |
|  | 11:53 AM | 1.6 | 49 |
|  | 08:16 PM | -0.1 | -3 |
| 7 F | 04:22 AM | 1.7 | 52 |
|  | 09:09 AM | 1.4 | 43 |
|  | 01:26 PM | 1.6 | 49 |
|  | 09:13 PM | 0.0 | 0 |
| 8 Sa | 04:54 AM | 1.7 | 52 |
|  | 09:46 AM | 1.3 | 40 |
|  | 02:45 PM | 1.7 | 52 |
|  | 10:07 PM | 0.1 | 3 |
| 9 Su | 05:24 AM | 1.6 | 49 |
|  | 10:29 AM | 1.1 | 34 |
|  | 03:59 PM | 1.7 | 52 |
|  | 10:58 PM | 0.2 | 6 |
| 10 M | 05:52 AM | 1.6 | 49 |
|  | 11:16 AM | 0.9 | 27 |
|  | 05:12 PM | 1.7 | 52 |
|  | 11:48 PM | 0.5 | 15 |
| 11 Tu | 06:19 AM | 1.5 | 46 |
|  | 12:04 PM | 0.8 | 24 |
|  | 06:26 PM | 1.6 | 49 |
| 12 W | 12:39 AM | 0.7 | 21 |
|  | 06:44 AM | 1.5 | 46 |
|  | 12:55 PM | 0.6 | 18 |
|  | 07:45 PM | 1.6 | 49 |
| 13 Th | 01:32 AM | 1.0 | 30 |
|  | 07:07 AM | 1.5 | 46 |
|  | 01:28 PM | 0.5 | 15 |
|  | 09:10 PM | 1.6 | 49 |
| 14 F | 02:37 AM | 1.2 | 37 |
|  | 07:26 AM | 1.4 | 43 |
|  | 02:43 PM | 0.4 | 12 |
|  | 10:44 PM | 1.6 | 49 |
| 15 Sa | 04:47 AM | 1.4 | 43 |
|  | 07:32 AM | 1.4 | 43 |
|  | 03:41 PM | 0.4 | 12 |
| 16 Su | 12:25 AM | 1.6 | 49 |
|  | 04:44 PM | 0.4 | 12 |
| 17 M | 01:56 AM | 1.7 | 52 |
|  | 05:48 PM | 0.4 | 12 |
| 18 Tu | 02:56 AM | 1.7 | 52 |
|  | 06:48 PM | 0.4 | 12 |
| 19 W | 03:32 AM | 1.7 | 52 |
|  | 07:40 PM | 0.4 | 12 |
| 20 Th | 03:55 AM | 1.7 | 52 |
|  | 10:06 AM | 1.4 | 43 |
|  | 12:25 PM | 1.5 | 46 |
|  | 08:24 PM | 0.4 | 12 |
| 21 F | 04:13 AM | 1.6 | 49 |
|  | 09:59 AM | 1.4 | 43 |
|  | 01:32 PM | 1.5 | 46 |
|  | 09:02 PM | 0.5 | 15 |
| 22 Sa | 04:29 AM | 1.6 | 49 |
|  | 09:57 AM | 1.3 | 40 |
|  | 02:31 PM | 1.5 | 46 |
|  | 09:35 PM | 0.5 | 15 |
| 23 Su | 04:45 AM | 1.6 | 49 |
|  | 10:08 AM | 1.2 | 37 |
|  | 03:26 PM | 1.6 | 49 |
|  | 10:06 PM | 0.6 | 18 |
| 24 M | 05:02 AM | 1.6 | 49 |
|  | 10:30 AM | 1.1 | 34 |
|  | 04:20 PM | 1.6 | 49 |
|  | 10:37 PM | 0.7 | 21 |
| 25 Tu | 05:19 AM | 1.6 | 49 |
|  | 10:58 AM | 0.9 | 27 |
|  | 05:16 PM | 1.6 | 49 |
|  | 11:09 PM | 0.9 | 27 |
| 26 W | 05:34 AM | 1.6 | 49 |
|  | 11:30 AM | 0.8 | 24 |
|  | 06:16 PM | 1.6 | 49 |
|  | 11:43 PM | 1.0 | 30 |
| 27 Th | 05:46 AM | 1.5 | 46 |
|  | 12:05 PM | 0.7 | 21 |
|  | 07:20 PM | 1.6 | 49 |
| 28 F | 12:20 AM | 1.2 | 37 |
|  | 05:51 AM | 1.6 | 49 |
|  | 12:45 PM | 0.5 | 15 |
|  | 08:32 PM | 1.7 | 52 |
| 29 Sa | 01:01 AM | 1.4 | 43 |
|  | 05:47 AM | 1.6 | 49 |
|  | 01:30 PM | 0.4 | 12 |
|  | 09:52 PM | 1.7 | 52 |
| 30 Su | 01:48 AM | 1.5 | 46 |
|  | 05:33 AM | 1.6 | 49 |
|  | 02:23 PM | 0.3 | 9 |
|  | 11:18 PM | 1.8 | 55 |

Heights are referred to mean lower water which is the chart datum of sounding. All times are local. Daylight Saving Time has been used when needed. Additional tide tables are available online from NOAA at www.tidesandcurrents.noaa.gov/tide_predictions.shtml.

SKIPPER'S HANDBOOK

StationId:8779750
Source:NOAA/NOS/CO-OPS
Station Type:Harmonic
Time Zone:LST/LDT
Datum:mean lower low water (MLLW) which is the chart datum of soundings

## October

| Day | Time | ft | cm | Day | Time | ft | cm |
|---|---|---|---|---|---|---|---|
| **1** Su | 02:25 AM | 2.0 | 61 | **16** M | 02:02 AM | 1.9 | 58 |
| | 06:36 PM | 0.8 | 24 | | 07:46 AM | 1.4 | 43 |
| | | | | | 12:53 PM | 1.8 | 55 |
| | | | | | 07:38 PM | 1.0 | 30 |
| **2** M | 02:42 AM | 1.9 | 58 | **17** Tu | 02:15 AM | 1.8 | 55 |
| | 08:28 AM | 1.6 | 49 | | 08:08 AM | 1.2 | 37 |
| | 11:59 AM | 1.7 | 52 | | 02:21 PM | 1.9 | 58 |
| | 07:29 PM | 0.9 | 27 | | 08:41 PM | 1.2 | 37 |
| **3** Tu | 02:55 AM | 1.9 | 58 | **18** W | 02:22 AM | 1.7 | 52 |
| | 08:31 AM | 1.5 | 46 | | 08:37 AM | 1.0 | 30 |
| | 01:24 PM | 1.7 | 52 | | 03:35 PM | 1.9 | 58 |
| | 08:20 PM | 0.9 | 27 | | 09:43 PM | 1.3 | 40 |
| **4** W | 03:06 AM | 1.8 | 55 | **19** Th ● | 02:24 AM | 1.6 | 49 |
| | 08:47 AM | 1.3 | 40 | | 09:08 AM | 0.8 | 24 |
| | 02:38 PM | 1.8 | 55 | | 04:40 PM | 2.0 | 61 |
| | 09:13 PM | 1.0 | 30 | | 10:47 PM | 1.5 | 46 |
| **5** Th ○ | 03:13 AM | 1.6 | 49 | **20** F | 02:19 AM | 1.6 | 49 |
| | 09:11 AM | 1.0 | 30 | | 09:40 AM | 0.6 | 18 |
| | 03:47 PM | 1.9 | 58 | | 05:42 PM | 2.0 | 61 |
| | 10:09 PM | 1.2 | 37 | | | | |
| **6** F | 03:17 AM | 1.6 | 49 | **21** Sa | 10:12 AM | 0.5 | 15 |
| | 09:41 AM | 0.8 | 24 | | 06:41 PM | 2.0 | 61 |
| | 04:58 PM | 1.9 | 58 | | | | |
| | 11:10 PM | 1.3 | 40 | | | | |
| **7** Sa | 03:14 AM | 1.5 | 46 | **22** Su | 10:45 AM | 0.5 | 15 |
| | 10:18 AM | 0.5 | 15 | | 07:41 PM | 2.0 | 61 |
| | 06:11 PM | 2.0 | 61 | | | | |
| **8** Su | 12:26 AM | 1.5 | 46 | **23** M | 11:19 AM | 0.5 | 15 |
| | 02:59 AM | 1.5 | 46 | | 08:43 PM | 2.0 | 61 |
| | 11:00 AM | 0.3 | 9 | | | | |
| | 07:30 PM | 2.0 | 61 | | | | |
| **9** M | 11:48 AM | 0.2 | 6 | **24** Tu | 11:56 AM | 0.5 | 15 |
| | 08:54 PM | 2.1 | 64 | | 09:47 PM | 2.0 | 61 |
| **10** Tu | 12:42 PM | 0.1 | 3 | **25** W | 12:37 PM | 0.6 | 18 |
| | 10:20 PM | 2.1 | 64 | | 10:46 PM | 2.1 | 64 |
| **11** W | 01:44 PM | 0.1 | 3 | **26** Th | 01:24 PM | 0.7 | 21 |
| | 11:36 PM | 2.2 | 67 | | 11:33 PM | 2.1 | 64 |
| **12** Th ◑ | 02:53 PM | 0.2 | 6 | **27** F ◐ | 02:18 PM | 0.8 | 24 |
| **13** F | 12:34 AM | 2.2 | 67 | **28** Sa | 12:07 AM | 2.1 | 64 |
| | 04:06 PM | 0.4 | 12 | | 03:21 PM | 0.9 | 27 |
| **14** Sa | 01:16 AM | 2.1 | 64 | **29** Su | 12:31 AM | 2.1 | 64 |
| | 05:20 PM | 0.6 | 18 | | 04:29 PM | 1.0 | 30 |
| **15** Su | 01:44 AM | 2.0 | 61 | **30** M | 12:49 AM | 2.0 | 61 |
| | 07:42 AM | 1.6 | 49 | | 07:50 AM | 1.5 | 46 |
| | 10:54 AM | 1.7 | 52 | | 10:48 AM | 1.6 | 49 |
| | 06:31 PM | 0.8 | 24 | | 05:40 PM | 1.1 | 34 |
| | | | | **31** Tu | 01:03 AM | 1.9 | 58 |
| | | | | | 07:33 AM | 1.3 | 40 |
| | | | | | 12:47 PM | 1.6 | 49 |
| | | | | | 06:50 PM | 1.2 | 37 |

## November

| Day | Time | ft | cm | Day | Time | ft | cm |
|---|---|---|---|---|---|---|---|
| **1** W | 01:13 AM | 1.8 | 55 | **16** Th | 07:15 AM | 0.5 | 15 |
| | 07:44 AM | 1.1 | 34 | | 03:24 PM | 1.9 | 58 |
| | 02:11 PM | 1.8 | 55 | | | | |
| | 08:00 PM | 1.3 | 40 | | | | |
| **2** Th | 01:19 AM | 1.7 | 52 | **17** F | 07:47 AM | 0.3 | 9 |
| | 08:07 AM | 0.8 | 24 | | 04:21 PM | 1.9 | 58 |
| | 03:22 PM | 1.9 | 58 | | | | |
| | 09:13 PM | 1.4 | 43 | | | | |
| **3** F | 01:20 AM | 1.6 | 49 | **18** Sa ● | 08:18 AM | 0.2 | 6 |
| | 08:37 AM | 0.5 | 15 | | 05:13 PM | 1.9 | 58 |
| | 04:30 PM | 2.0 | 61 | | | | |
| | 10:35 PM | 1.5 | 46 | | | | |
| **4** Sa ○ | 01:10 AM | 1.5 | 46 | **19** Su | 08:49 AM | 0.1 | 3 |
| | 09:13 AM | 0.2 | 6 | | 06:02 PM | 1.9 | 58 |
| | 05:36 PM | 2.1 | 64 | | | | |
| **5** Su | 08:54 AM | 0.0 | 0 | **20** M | 09:19 AM | 0.1 | 3 |
| | 05:44 PM | 2.2 | 67 | | 06:51 PM | 1.9 | 58 |
| **6** M | 09:40 AM | -0.2 | -6 | **21** Tu | 09:51 AM | 0.2 | 6 |
| | 06:53 PM | 2.2 | 67 | | 07:38 PM | 1.9 | 58 |
| **7** Tu | 10:30 AM | -0.2 | -6 | **22** W | 10:24 AM | 0.2 | 6 |
| | 08:01 PM | 2.2 | 67 | | 08:21 PM | 1.9 | 58 |
| **8** W | 11:24 AM | -0.1 | -3 | **23** Th | 10:59 AM | 0.3 | 9 |
| | 09:04 PM | 2.2 | 67 | | 08:57 PM | 1.9 | 58 |
| **9** Th | 12:23 PM | 0.1 | 3 | **24** F | 11:38 AM | 0.4 | 12 |
| | 09:56 PM | 2.1 | 64 | | 09:26 PM | 1.9 | 58 |
| **10** F ◑ | 01:27 PM | 0.3 | 9 | **25** Sa | 12:22 PM | 0.6 | 18 |
| | 10:34 PM | 2.0 | 61 | | 09:48 PM | 1.9 | 58 |
| **11** Sa | 02:36 PM | 0.6 | 18 | **26** Su ◐ | 01:15 PM | 0.7 | 21 |
| | 11:00 PM | 1.9 | 58 | | 10:04 PM | 1.8 | 55 |
| **12** Su | 05:48 AM | 1.4 | 43 | **27** M | 02:21 PM | 0.9 | 27 |
| | 08:47 AM | 1.4 | 43 | | 10:17 PM | 1.7 | 52 |
| | 03:50 PM | 0.9 | 27 | | | | |
| | 11:17 PM | 1.8 | 55 | | | | |
| **13** M | 05:50 AM | 1.2 | 37 | **28** Tu | 05:37 AM | 1.0 | 30 |
| | 11:19 AM | 1.5 | 46 | | 10:39 AM | 1.2 | 37 |
| | 05:07 PM | 1.1 | 34 | | 03:42 PM | 1.0 | 30 |
| | 11:28 PM | 1.7 | 52 | | 10:25 PM | 1.6 | 49 |
| **14** Tu | 06:14 AM | 0.9 | 27 | **29** W | 05:41 AM | 0.8 | 24 |
| | 01:02 PM | 1.7 | 52 | | 12:32 PM | 1.4 | 43 |
| | 06:26 PM | 1.3 | 40 | | 05:16 PM | 1.2 | 37 |
| | 11:32 PM | 1.6 | 49 | | 10:29 PM | 1.5 | 46 |
| **15** W | 06:43 AM | 0.7 | 21 | **30** Th | 06:03 AM | 0.4 | 12 |
| | 02:20 PM | 1.8 | 55 | | 01:52 PM | 1.6 | 49 |
| | 07:46 PM | 1.4 | 43 | | 06:56 PM | 1.3 | 40 |
| | 11:30 PM | 1.6 | 49 | | 10:25 PM | 1.4 | 43 |

## December

| Day | Time | ft | cm | Day | Time | ft | cm |
|---|---|---|---|---|---|---|---|
| **1** F | 06:35 AM | 0.1 | 3 | **16** Sa | 07:28 AM | -0.2 | -6 |
| | 02:58 PM | 1.7 | 52 | | 04:43 PM | 1.6 | 49 |
| **2** Sa | 07:12 AM | -0.3 | -9 | **17** Su | 08:01 AM | -0.3 | -9 |
| | 04:01 PM | 1.9 | 58 | | 05:26 PM | 1.6 | 49 |
| **3** Su ○ | 07:55 AM | -0.5 | -15 | **18** M ● | 08:32 AM | -0.3 | -9 |
| | 05:01 PM | 2.0 | 61 | | 06:07 PM | 1.6 | 49 |
| **4** M | 08:40 AM | -0.7 | -21 | **19** Tu | 09:03 AM | -0.2 | -6 |
| | 06:00 PM | 2.0 | 61 | | 06:44 PM | 1.6 | 49 |
| **5** Tu | 09:29 AM | -0.7 | -21 | **20** W | 09:32 AM | -0.2 | -6 |
| | 06:57 PM | 2.0 | 61 | | 07:17 PM | 1.6 | 49 |
| **6** W | 10:20 AM | -0.6 | -18 | **21** Th | 10:03 AM | -0.1 | -3 |
| | 07:48 PM | 1.9 | 58 | | 07:43 PM | 1.6 | 49 |
| **7** Th | 11:12 AM | -0.4 | -12 | **22** F | 10:34 AM | 0.0 | 0 |
| | 08:30 PM | 1.8 | 55 | | 08:03 PM | 1.6 | 49 |
| **8** F | 12:06 PM | -0.1 | -3 | **23** Sa | 11:09 AM | 0.1 | 3 |
| | 09:01 PM | 1.7 | 52 | | 08:19 PM | 1.5 | 46 |
| **9** Sa | 01:02 PM | 0.2 | 6 | **24** Su | 11:48 AM | 0.3 | 9 |
| | 09:23 PM | 1.6 | 49 | | 08:31 PM | 1.4 | 43 |
| **10** Su ◑ | 04:23 AM | 1.0 | 30 | **25** M | 12:34 PM | 0.4 | 12 |
| | 07:01 AM | 1.1 | 34 | | 08:40 PM | 1.3 | 40 |
| | 02:03 PM | 0.6 | 18 | | | | |
| | 09:37 PM | 1.5 | 46 | | | | |
| **11** M | 04:36 AM | 0.8 | 24 | **26** Tu ◐ | 04:15 AM | 0.7 | 21 |
| | 10:08 AM | 1.1 | 34 | | 08:35 AM | 0.8 | 24 |
| | 03:13 PM | 0.9 | 27 | | 01:33 PM | 0.7 | 21 |
| | 09:47 PM | 1.4 | 43 | | 08:45 PM | 1.2 | 37 |
| **12** Tu | 05:07 AM | 0.5 | 15 | **27** W | 04:22 AM | 0.4 | 12 |
| | 12:24 PM | 1.2 | 37 | | 11:31 AM | 0.9 | 27 |
| | 04:39 PM | 1.1 | 34 | | 03:00 PM | 0.9 | 27 |
| | 09:50 PM | 1.4 | 43 | | 08:46 PM | 1.2 | 37 |
| **13** W | 05:42 AM | 0.3 | 9 | **28** Th | 04:50 AM | 0.1 | 3 |
| | 01:56 PM | 1.4 | 43 | | 01:15 PM | 1.1 | 34 |
| | 06:25 PM | 1.3 | 40 | | 05:08 PM | 1.1 | 34 |
| | 09:43 PM | 1.3 | 40 | | 08:36 PM | 1.1 | 34 |
| **14** Th | 06:18 AM | 0.1 | 3 | **29** F | 05:26 AM | -0.3 | -9 |
| | 03:02 PM | 1.5 | 46 | | 02:24 PM | 1.3 | 40 |
| **15** F | 06:54 AM | -0.1 | -3 | **30** Sa | 06:08 AM | -0.6 | -18 |
| | 03:55 PM | 1.6 | 49 | | 03:22 PM | 1.5 | 46 |
| | | | | **31** Su | 06:54 AM | -0.9 | -27 |
| | | | | | 04:17 PM | 1.6 | 49 |

Heights are referred to mean lower water which is the chart datum of sounding. All times are local. Daylight Saving Time has been used when needed. Additional tide tables are available online from NOAA at www.tidesandcurrents.noaa.gov/tide_predictions.shtml.

SKIPPER'S HANDBOOK

StationId: 8779750
Source: NOAA/NOS/CO-OPS
Station Type: Primary
Time Zone: LST_LDT
Datum: MLLW

**NOAA Tide Predictions**

# South Padre Island, Brazos Santiago Pass, TX,2018

### Times and Heights of High and Low Waters

## January

| Day | Time | ft | cm | Day | Time | ft | cm |
|---|---|---|---|---|---|---|---|
| 1 M | 07:40 AM / 05:10 PM | -1.1 / 1.7 | -34 / 52 | 16 Tu | 08:19 AM / 06:00 PM | -0.5 / 1.3 | -15 / 40 |
| 2 Tu ○ | 08:30 AM / 06:01 PM | -1.1 / 1.7 | -34 / 52 | 17 W ● | 08:51 AM / 06:28 PM | -0.5 / 1.3 | -15 / 40 |
| 3 W | 09:21 AM / 06:44 PM | -1.0 / 1.6 | -30 / 49 | 18 Th | 09:21 AM / 06:48 PM | -0.4 / 1.3 | -12 / 40 |
| 4 Th | 10:11 AM / 07:19 PM | -0.8 / 1.5 | -24 / 46 | 19 F | 09:51 AM / 07:02 PM | -0.3 / 1.3 | -9 / 40 |
| 5 F | 11:01 AM / 07:44 PM | -0.5 / 1.4 | -15 / 43 | 20 Sa | 10:24 AM / 07:11 PM | -0.2 / 1.2 | -6 / 37 |
| 6 Sa | 11:50 AM / 08:00 PM | -0.2 / 1.3 | -6 / 40 | 21 Su | 11:00 AM / 07:16 PM | 0.0 / 1.1 | 0 / 34 |
| 7 Su | 02:14 AM / 05:24 AM / 12:40 PM / 08:10 PM | 0.8 / 0.9 / 0.2 / 1.2 | 24 / 27 / 6 / 37 | 22 M | 01:41 AM / 03:49 AM / 11:41 AM / 07:19 PM | 0.8 / 0.8 / 0.2 / 1.0 | 24 / 24 / 6 / 30 |
| 8 M ◑ | 02:54 AM / 08:07 AM / 01:32 PM / 08:16 PM | 0.5 / 0.8 / 0.5 / 1.1 | 15 / 24 / 15 / 34 | 23 Tu | 01:56 AM / 06:31 AM / 12:29 PM / 07:17 PM | 0.5 / 0.7 / 0.4 / 0.9 | 15 / 21 / 12 / 27 |
| 9 Tu | 03:39 AM / 10:59 AM / 02:36 PM / 08:15 PM | 0.3 / 0.9 / 0.8 / 1.1 | 9 / 27 / 24 / 34 | 24 W ◐ | 02:29 AM / 09:24 AM / 01:35 PM / 07:09 PM | 0.3 / 0.7 / 0.6 / 0.9 | 9 / 21 / 18 / 27 |
| 10 W | 04:24 AM / 01:15 PM / 04:24 PM / 08:03 PM | 0.0 / 1.0 / 1.0 / 1.1 | 0 / 30 / 30 / 34 | 25 Th | 03:11 AM / 11:57 AM / 03:37 PM / 06:41 PM | -0.1 / 0.9 / 0.9 / 0.9 | -3 / 27 / 27 / 27 |
| 11 Th | 05:08 AM / 02:32 PM | -0.2 / 1.2 | -6 / 37 | 26 F | 03:59 AM / 01:28 PM | -0.4 / 1.1 | -12 / 34 |
| 12 F | 05:51 AM / 03:24 PM | -0.3 / 1.3 | -9 / 40 | 27 Sa | 04:51 AM / 02:31 PM | -0.7 / 1.3 | -21 / 40 |
| 13 Sa | 06:32 AM / 04:08 PM | -0.5 / 1.3 | -15 / 40 | 28 Su | 05:45 AM / 03:25 PM | -0.9 / 1.4 | -27 / 43 |
| 14 Su | 07:10 AM / 04:49 PM | -0.5 / 1.3 | -15 / 40 | 29 M | 06:39 AM / 04:13 PM | -1.1 / 1.5 | -34 / 46 |
| 15 M | 07:46 AM / 05:27 PM | -0.5 / 1.3 | -15 / 40 | 30 Tu | 07:32 AM / 04:55 PM | -1.1 / 1.4 | -34 / 43 |
| | | | | 31 W ○ | 08:25 AM / 05:30 PM | -1.0 / 1.3 | -30 / 40 |

## February

| Day | Time | ft | cm | Day | Time | ft | cm |
|---|---|---|---|---|---|---|---|
| 1 Th | 09:16 AM / 05:55 PM / 10:30 PM | -0.8 / 1.2 / 1.0 | -24 / 37 / 30 | 16 F | 12:13 AM / 09:07 AM / 05:27 PM / 10:13 PM | 1.1 / -0.2 / 1.1 / 0.9 | 34 / -6 / 34 / 27 |
| 2 F | 01:33 AM / 10:05 AM / 06:12 PM / 11:03 PM | 1.1 / -0.6 / 1.1 / 0.8 | 34 / -18 / 34 / 24 | 17 Sa ○ | 01:29 AM / 09:41 AM / 05:33 PM / 10:33 PM | 1.0 / -0.1 / 1.1 / 0.8 | 30 / -3 / 34 / 24 |
| 3 Sa | 03:07 AM / 10:52 AM / 06:23 PM / 11:47 PM | 1.0 / -0.3 / 1.0 / 0.6 | 30 / -9 / 30 / 18 | 18 Su | 02:46 AM / 10:18 AM / 05:36 PM / 11:02 PM | 1.0 / 0.1 / 1.0 / 0.6 | 30 / 3 / 30 / 18 |
| 4 Su | 04:45 AM / 11:40 AM / 06:30 PM | 0.9 / 0.1 / 0.9 | 27 / 3 / 27 | 19 M | 04:10 AM / 11:01 AM / 05:35 PM / 11:38 PM | 0.9 / 0.2 / 0.9 / 0.4 | 27 / 6 / 27 / 12 |
| 5 M | 12:38 AM / 06:36 AM / 12:28 PM / 06:33 PM | 0.4 / 0.8 / 0.4 / 0.9 | 12 / 24 / 12 / 27 | 20 Tu | 05:50 AM / 11:51 AM / 05:30 PM | 0.9 / 0.5 / 0.8 | 27 / 15 / 24 |
| 6 Tu | 01:33 AM / 08:50 AM / 01:22 PM / 06:31 PM | 0.1 / 0.8 / 0.7 / 0.9 | 3 / 24 / 21 / 27 | 21 W | 12:23 AM / 07:50 AM / 12:57 PM / 05:14 PM | 0.1 / 0.9 / 0.7 / 0.8 | 3 / 27 / 21 / 24 |
| 7 W | 02:30 AM / 11:23 AM / 02:46 PM / 06:12 PM | 0.0 / 0.9 / 0.9 / 0.9 | 0 / 27 / 27 / 27 | 22 Th | 01:15 AM / 10:07 AM | -0.1 / 1.0 | -3 / 30 |
| 8 Th | 03:28 AM / 01:17 PM | -0.2 / 1.1 | -6 / 34 | 23 F ◐ | 02:14 AM / 12:03 PM | -0.3 / 1.2 | -9 / 37 |
| 9 F | 04:23 AM / 02:18 PM | -0.3 / 1.2 | -9 / 37 | 24 Sa | 03:19 AM / 01:18 PM | -0.5 / 1.3 | -15 / 40 |
| 10 Sa | 05:16 AM / 03:04 PM | -0.3 / 1.2 | -9 / 37 | 25 Su | 04:24 AM / 02:15 PM | -0.7 / 1.4 | -21 / 43 |
| 11 Su | 06:05 AM / 03:43 PM | -0.4 / 1.2 | -12 / 37 | 26 M | 05:28 AM / 03:00 PM | -0.7 / 1.5 | -21 / 46 |
| 12 M | 06:48 AM / 04:17 PM | -0.4 / 1.2 | -12 / 37 | 27 Tu | 06:28 AM / 03:36 PM | -0.7 / 1.4 | -21 / 43 |
| 13 Tu | 07:27 AM / 04:44 PM | -0.4 / 1.2 | -12 / 37 | 28 W | 07:25 AM / 04:02 PM / 08:34 PM / 11:54 PM | -0.6 / 1.3 / 1.1 / 1.2 | -18 / 40 / 34 / 37 |
| 14 W | 08:02 AM / 05:05 PM | -0.3 / 1.2 | -9 / 37 | | | | |
| 15 Th ● | 08:35 AM / 05:18 PM / 10:05 PM | -0.3 / 1.2 / 1.0 | -9 / 37 / 30 | | | | |

## March

| Day | Time | ft | cm | Day | Time | ft | cm |
|---|---|---|---|---|---|---|---|
| 1 Th | 08:19 AM / 04:20 PM / 08:52 PM | -0.5 / 1.2 / 0.9 | -15 / 37 / 27 | 16 F | 01:37 AM / 09:16 AM / 04:39 PM / 09:41 PM | 1.2 / 0.2 / 1.2 / 0.9 | 37 / 6 / 37 / 27 |
| 2 F ○ | 01:27 AM / 09:11 AM / 04:31 PM / 09:24 PM | 1.2 / -0.2 / 1.0 / 0.7 | 37 / -6 / 30 / 21 | 17 Sa ● | 02:45 AM / 09:56 AM / 04:43 PM / 10:03 PM | 1.2 / 0.3 / 1.1 / 0.7 | 37 / 9 / 34 / 21 |
| 3 Sa | 02:51 AM / 10:01 AM / 04:38 PM / 10:03 PM | 1.2 / 0.0 / 0.9 / 0.5 | 37 / 0 / 27 / 15 | 18 Su | 03:52 AM / 10:40 AM / 04:44 PM / 10:30 PM | 1.2 / 0.4 / 1.0 / 0.5 | 37 / 12 / 30 / 15 |
| 4 Su | 04:13 AM / 10:50 AM / 04:41 PM / 10:46 PM | 1.1 / 0.3 / 0.9 / 0.3 | 34 / 9 / 27 / 9 | 19 M | 05:04 AM / 11:30 AM / 04:41 PM / 11:04 PM | 1.2 / 0.6 / 0.9 / 0.3 | 37 / 18 / 27 / 9 |
| 5 M | 05:39 AM / 11:42 AM / 04:40 PM / 11:33 PM | 1.1 / 0.6 / 0.9 / 0.1 | 34 / 18 / 27 / 3 | 20 Tu | 06:22 AM / 12:31 PM / 04:30 PM / 11:44 PM | 1.2 / 0.7 / 0.9 / 0.0 | 37 / 21 / 27 / 0 |
| 6 Tu | 07:14 AM / 12:43 PM / 04:31 PM | 1.1 / 0.8 / 0.9 | 34 / 24 / 27 | 21 W | 07:51 AM | 1.3 | 40 |
| 7 W | 12:24 AM / 09:04 AM | 0.0 / 1.1 | 0 / 34 | 22 Th | 12:33 AM / 09:32 AM | -0.2 / 1.3 | -6 / 40 |
| 8 Th | 01:20 AM / 11:01 AM | -0.1 / 1.2 | -3 / 37 | 23 F | 01:30 AM / 11:16 AM | -0.3 / 1.4 | -9 / 43 |
| 9 F ◐ | 02:21 AM / 12:31 PM | -0.1 / 1.2 | -3 / 37 | 24 Sa ◐ | 02:35 AM / 12:41 PM | -0.4 / 1.5 | -12 / 46 |
| 10 Sa | 03:26 AM / 01:29 PM | -0.1 / 1.3 | -3 / 40 | 25 Su | 03:47 AM / 01:43 PM | -0.4 / 1.6 | -12 / 49 |
| 11 Su | 05:29 AM / 03:12 PM | 0.0 / 1.3 | 0 / 40 | 26 M | 05:00 AM / 02:29 PM | -0.4 / 1.6 | -12 / 49 |
| 12 M | 06:25 AM / 03:43 PM | 0.0 / 1.3 | 0 / 40 | 27 Tu | 06:11 AM / 03:01 PM | -0.3 / 1.5 | -9 / 46 |
| 13 Tu | 07:14 AM / 04:06 PM | 0.0 / 1.3 | 0 / 40 | 28 W | 07:16 AM / 03:22 PM / 08:28 PM | -0.1 / 1.4 / 1.0 | -3 / 43 / 30 |
| 14 W | 07:57 AM / 04:22 PM / 09:23 PM | 0.1 / 1.3 / 1.1 | 3 / 40 / 34 | 29 Th | 12:41 AM / 08:17 AM / 03:35 PM / 08:46 PM | 1.2 / 0.1 / 1.2 / 0.8 | 37 / 3 / 37 / 24 |
| 15 Th | 12:23 AM / 08:37 AM / 04:32 PM / 09:26 PM | 1.2 / 0.1 / 1.3 / 1.0 | 37 / 3 / 40 / 30 | 30 F | 02:14 AM / 09:15 AM / 03:43 PM / 09:14 PM | 1.3 / 0.3 / 1.1 / 0.6 | 40 / 9 / 34 / 18 |
| | | | | 31 Sa ○ | 03:35 AM / 10:11 AM / 03:46 PM / 09:48 PM | 1.4 / 0.5 / 1.0 / 0.4 | 43 / 15 / 30 / 12 |

Heights are referred to mean lower water which is the chart datum of sounding. All times are local. Daylight Saving Time has been used when needed. Additional tide tables are available online from NOAA at www.tidesandcurrents.noaa.gov/tide_predictions.shtml.

StationId: 8779750
Source: NOAA/NOS/CO-OPS
Station Type: Primary
Time Zone: LST_LDT
Datum: MLLW

**NOAA Tide Predictions**

## South Padre Island, Brazos Santiago Pass, TX, 2018

**Times and Heights of High and Low Waters**

### April

| Day | Time | ft | cm | | Day | Time | ft | cm |
|---|---|---|---|---|---|---|---|---|
| 1 Su | 04:49 AM | 1.4 | 43 | | 16 M ● | 04:46 AM | 1.4 | 43 |
|  | 11:08 AM | 0.7 | 21 | |  | 11:00 AM | 0.9 | 27 |
|  | 03:44 PM | 1.0 | 30 | |  | 02:39 PM | 1.0 | 30 |
|  | 10:25 PM | 0.2 | 6 | |  | 09:53 PM | 0.0 | 0 |
| 2 M | 06:02 AM | 1.4 | 43 | | 17 Tu | 05:54 AM | 1.5 | 46 |
|  | 12:10 PM | 0.9 | 27 | |  | 10:31 PM | -0.2 | -6 |
|  | 03:35 PM | 1.0 | 30 | |  |  |  |  |
|  | 11:03 PM | 0.0 | 0 | |  |  |  |  |
| 3 Tu | 07:15 AM | 1.4 | 43 | | 18 W | 07:07 AM | 1.6 | 49 |
|  | 11:44 PM | -0.1 | -3 | |  | 11:16 PM | -0.4 | -12 |
| 4 W | 08:34 AM | 1.4 | 43 | | 19 Th | 08:26 AM | 1.6 | 49 |
| 5 Th | 12:28 AM | -0.1 | -3 | | 20 F | 12:06 AM | -0.5 | -15 |
|  | 09:58 AM | 1.4 | 43 | |  | 09:47 AM | 1.7 | 52 |
| 6 F | 01:17 AM | 0.0 | 0 | | 21 Sa | 01:04 AM | -0.5 | -15 |
|  | 11:22 AM | 1.4 | 43 | |  | 11:03 AM | 1.7 | 52 |
| 7 Sa | 02:12 AM | 0.1 | 3 | | 22 Su ◐ | 02:09 AM | -0.4 | -12 |
|  | 12:31 PM | 1.5 | 46 | |  | 12:04 PM | 1.7 | 52 |
| 8 Su ◐ | 03:15 AM | 0.2 | 6 | | 23 M | 03:20 AM | -0.2 | -6 |
|  | 01:20 PM | 1.5 | 46 | |  | 12:49 PM | 1.6 | 49 |
| 9 M | 04:22 AM | 0.3 | 9 | | 24 Tu | 04:35 AM | 0.0 | 0 |
|  | 01:53 PM | 1.5 | 46 | |  | 01:18 PM | 1.5 | 46 |
| 10 Tu | 05:25 AM | 0.4 | 12 | | 25 W | 05:49 AM | 0.2 | 6 |
|  | 02:15 PM | 1.5 | 46 | |  | 01:37 PM | 1.4 | 43 |
|  |  |  |  | |  | 07:35 PM | 0.9 | 27 |
| 11 W | 06:23 AM | 0.4 | 12 | | 26 Th | 12:18 AM | 1.2 | 37 |
|  | 02:29 PM | 1.4 | 43 | |  | 07:01 AM | 0.4 | 12 |
|  | 08:27 PM | 1.1 | 34 | |  | 04:17 PM | 1.3 | 40 |
|  | 11:53 PM | 1.2 | 37 | |  | 07:51 PM | 0.7 | 21 |
| 12 Th | 07:15 AM | 0.5 | 15 | | 27 F | 02:00 AM | 1.3 | 40 |
|  | 02:38 PM | 1.4 | 43 | |  | 08:10 AM | 0.7 | 21 |
|  | 08:23 PM | 1.0 | 30 | |  | 01:51 PM | 1.2 | 37 |
|  |  |  |  | |  | 08:18 PM | 0.4 | 12 |
| 13 F | 01:21 AM | 1.2 | 37 | | 28 Sa | 03:21 AM | 1.4 | 43 |
|  | 08:06 AM | 0.6 | 18 | |  | 09:19 AM | 0.8 | 24 |
|  | 02:45 PM | 1.3 | 40 | |  | 01:50 PM | 1.1 | 34 |
|  | 08:35 PM | 0.8 | 24 | |  | 08:49 PM | 0.1 | 3 |
| 14 Sa | 02:32 AM | 1.3 | 40 | | 29 Su | 04:32 AM | 1.5 | 46 |
|  | 08:59 AM | 0.6 | 18 | |  | 10:31 AM | 1.0 | 30 |
|  | 02:48 PM | 1.2 | 37 | |  | 01:40 PM | 1.1 | 34 |
|  | 08:55 PM | 0.5 | 15 | |  | 09:23 PM | -0.1 | -3 |
| 15 Su | 03:39 AM | 1.4 | 43 | | 30 M ○ | 05:36 AM | 1.5 | 46 |
|  | 09:55 AM | 0.7 | 21 | |  | 09:57 PM | -0.2 | -6 |
|  | 02:47 PM | 1.1 | 34 | |  |  |  |  |
|  | 09:21 PM | 0.3 | 9 | |  |  |  |  |

### May

| Day | Time | ft | cm | | Day | Time | ft | cm |
|---|---|---|---|---|---|---|---|---|
| 1 Tu | 06:38 AM | 1.6 | 49 | | 16 W | 06:26 AM | 1.6 | 49 |
|  | 10:32 PM | -0.3 | -9 | |  | 10:13 PM | -0.7 | -21 |
| 2 W | 07:39 AM | 1.6 | 49 | | 17 Th | 07:32 AM | 1.7 | 52 |
|  | 11:09 PM | -0.2 | -6 | |  | 11:01 PM | -0.8 | -24 |
| 3 Th | 08:42 AM | 1.6 | 49 | | 18 F | 08:38 AM | 1.7 | 52 |
|  | 11:47 PM | -0.2 | -6 | |  | 11:53 PM | -0.8 | -24 |
| 4 F | 09:44 AM | 1.6 | 49 | | 19 Sa | 09:41 AM | 1.7 | 52 |
| 5 Sa | 12:28 AM | -0.1 | -3 | | 20 Su | 12:49 AM | -0.6 | -18 |
|  | 10:43 AM | 1.6 | 49 | |  | 10:33 AM | 1.7 | 52 |
| 6 Su | 01:14 AM | 0.1 | 3 | | 21 M | 01:49 AM | -0.4 | -12 |
|  | 11:30 AM | 1.6 | 49 | |  | 11:12 AM | 1.6 | 49 |
| 7 M | 02:04 AM | 0.2 | 6 | | 22 Tu ◐ | 02:54 AM | -0.1 | -3 |
|  | 12:03 PM | 1.5 | 46 | |  | 11:38 AM | 1.5 | 46 |
| 8 Tu ◐ | 03:02 AM | 0.4 | 12 | | 23 W | 04:05 AM | 0.2 | 6 |
|  | 12:24 PM | 1.5 | 46 | |  | 11:53 AM | 1.3 | 40 |
|  |  |  |  | |  | 06:36 PM | 0.7 | 21 |
|  |  |  |  | |  | 11:35 PM | 0.9 | 27 |
| 9 W | 04:06 AM | 0.5 | 15 | | 24 Th | 05:23 AM | 0.5 | 15 |
|  | 12:37 PM | 1.5 | 46 | |  | 12:01 PM | 1.2 | 37 |
|  | 08:05 PM | 1.0 | 30 | |  | 06:54 PM | 0.4 | 12 |
|  | 10:20 PM | 1.0 | 30 | |  |  |  |  |
| 10 Th | 05:15 AM | 0.6 | 18 | | 25 F | 01:38 AM | 1.1 | 34 |
|  | 12:46 PM | 1.4 | 43 | |  | 06:46 AM | 0.8 | 24 |
|  | 07:29 PM | 0.8 | 24 | |  | 12:02 PM | 1.1 | 34 |
|  |  |  |  | |  | 07:23 PM | 0.1 | 3 |
| 11 F | 12:38 AM | 1.1 | 34 | | 26 Sa | 03:07 AM | 1.2 | 37 |
|  | 06:25 AM | 0.7 | 21 | |  | 08:15 AM | 1.0 | 30 |
|  | 12:51 PM | 1.3 | 40 | |  | 11:56 AM | 1.1 | 34 |
|  | 07:34 PM | 0.6 | 18 | |  | 07:55 PM | -0.1 | -3 |
| 12 Sa | 02:04 AM | 1.2 | 37 | | 27 Su | 04:16 AM | 1.4 | 43 |
|  | 07:38 AM | 0.8 | 24 | |  | 08:29 AM | -0.3 | -9 |
|  | 12:53 PM | 1.1 | 34 | |  |  |  |  |
|  | 07:53 PM | 0.3 | 9 | |  |  |  |  |
| 13 Su | 03:14 AM | 1.3 | 40 | | 28 M | 05:16 AM | 1.5 | 46 |
|  | 08:55 AM | 0.9 | 27 | |  | 09:03 PM | -0.5 | -15 |
|  | 12:49 PM | 1.1 | 34 | |  |  |  |  |
|  | 08:19 PM | 0.0 | 0 | |  |  |  |  |
| 14 M | 04:19 AM | 1.4 | 43 | | 29 Tu ○ | 06:10 AM | 1.5 | 46 |
|  | 10:27 AM | 1.0 | 30 | |  | 09:37 PM | -0.5 | -15 |
|  | 12:29 PM | 1.0 | 30 | |  |  |  |  |
|  | 08:52 PM | -0.3 | -9 | |  |  |  |  |
| 15 Tu ● | 05:22 AM | 1.6 | 49 | | 30 W | 07:01 AM | 1.6 | 49 |
|  | 09:30 PM | -0.6 | -18 | |  | 10:11 PM | -0.5 | -15 |
|  |  |  |  | | 31 Th | 07:51 AM | 1.5 | 46 |
|  |  |  |  | |  | 10:45 PM | -0.5 | -15 |

### June

| Day | Time | ft | cm | | Day | Time | ft | cm |
|---|---|---|---|---|---|---|---|---|
| 1 F | 08:40 AM | 1.5 | 46 | | 16 Sa | 08:29 AM | 1.6 | 49 |
|  | 11:20 PM | -0.3 | -9 | |  | 11:46 PM | -0.9 | -27 |
| 2 Sa | 09:24 AM | 1.5 | 46 | | 17 Su | 09:12 AM | 1.5 | 46 |
|  | 11:54 PM | -0.2 | -6 | |  |  |  |  |
| 3 Su | 10:01 AM | 1.5 | 46 | | 18 M | 12:38 AM | -0.6 | -18 |
|  |  |  |  | |  | 09:43 AM | 1.4 | 43 |
| 4 M | 12:31 AM | -0.1 | -3 | | 19 Tu | 01:32 AM | -0.3 | -9 |
|  | 10:27 AM | 1.4 | 43 | |  | 10:03 AM | 1.3 | 40 |
| 5 Tu | 01:10 AM | 0.1 | 3 | | 20 W ◐ | 02:29 AM | 0.1 | 3 |
|  | 10:44 AM | 1.4 | 43 | |  | 10:15 AM | 1.1 | 34 |
|  |  |  |  | |  | 05:10 PM | 0.5 | 15 |
|  |  |  |  | |  | 10:13 PM | 0.7 | 21 |
| 6 W | 01:56 AM | 0.3 | 9 | | 21 Th ◐ | 03:34 AM | 0.4 | 12 |
|  | 10:55 AM | 1.3 | 40 | |  | 10:21 AM | 1.1 | 34 |
|  |  |  |  | |  | 05:40 PM | 0.2 | 6 |
| 7 Th | 02:51 AM | 0.4 | 12 | | 22 F | 12:53 AM | 0.9 | 27 |
|  | 11:01 AM | 1.3 | 40 | |  | 04:56 AM | 0.7 | 21 |
|  | 06:34 PM | 0.6 | 18 | |  | 10:20 AM | 1.0 | 30 |
|  | 11:12 PM | 0.8 | 24 | |  | 06:17 PM | -0.1 | -3 |
| 8 F | 04:05 AM | 0.6 | 18 | | 23 Sa | 02:41 AM | 1.1 | 34 |
|  | 11:05 AM | 1.1 | 34 | |  | 06:47 AM | 0.9 | 27 |
|  | 06:29 PM | 0.4 | 12 | |  | 10:09 AM | 1.0 | 30 |
|  |  |  |  | |  | 06:55 PM | -0.3 | -9 |
| 9 Sa | 01:20 AM | 0.9 | 27 | | 24 Su | 03:54 AM | 1.2 | 37 |
|  | 05:40 AM | 0.8 | 24 | |  | 07:34 PM | -0.5 | -15 |
|  | 11:05 AM | 1.0 | 30 | |  |  |  |  |
|  | 06:47 PM | 0.0 | 0 | |  |  |  |  |
| 10 Su | 02:42 AM | 1.1 | 34 | | 25 M | 04:49 AM | 1.3 | 40 |
|  | 07:29 AM | 0.9 | 27 | |  | 08:12 PM | -0.6 | -18 |
|  | 12:02 PM | 1.0 | 30 | |  |  |  |  |
|  | 07:16 PM | -0.3 | -9 | |  |  |  |  |
| 11 M | 03:47 AM | 1.3 | 40 | | 26 Tu | 05:37 AM | 1.4 | 43 |
|  | 07:51 PM | -0.6 | -18 | |  | 08:49 PM | -0.7 | -21 |
| 12 Tu | 04:46 AM | 1.4 | 43 | | 27 W | 06:23 AM | 1.4 | 43 |
|  | 08:32 PM | -0.9 | -27 | |  | 09:24 PM | -0.7 | -21 |
| 13 W ● | 05:44 AM | 1.5 | 46 | | 28 Th ○ | 07:06 AM | 1.4 | 43 |
|  | 09:16 PM | -1.1 | -34 | |  | 09:58 PM | -0.6 | -18 |
| 14 Th | 06:42 AM | 1.6 | 49 | | 29 F | 07:46 AM | 1.4 | 43 |
|  | 10:04 PM | -1.1 | -34 | |  | 10:30 PM | -0.5 | -15 |
| 15 F | 07:38 AM | 1.6 | 49 | | 30 Sa | 08:21 AM | 1.3 | 40 |
|  | 10:54 PM | -1.1 | -34 | |  | 11:00 PM | -0.4 | -12 |

Heights are referred to mean lower water which is the chart datum of sounding. All times are local. Daylight Saving Time has been used when needed. Additional tide tables are available online from NOAA at www.tidesandcurrents.noaa.gov/tide_predictions.shtml.

SKIPPER'S HANDBOOK

StationId: 8779750
Source: NOAA/NOS/CO-OPS
Station Type: Primary
Time Zone: LST_LDT
Datum: MLLW

**NOAA Tide Predictions**

# South Padre Island, Brazos Santiago Pass, TX, 2018

### Times and Heights of High and Low Waters

## July

| Day | Time | ft | cm |
|---|---|---|---|
| 1 Su | 08:48 AM | 1.3 | 40 |
| | 11:31 PM | -0.3 | -9 |
| 2 M | 09:05 AM | 1.3 | 40 |
| 3 Tu | 12:02 AM | -0.1 | -3 |
| | 09:16 AM | 1.3 | 40 |
| 4 W | 12:36 AM | 0.0 | 0 |
| | 09:21 AM | 1.2 | 37 |
| 5 Th | 01:16 AM | 0.2 | 6 |
| | 09:25 AM | 1.1 | 34 |
| | 04:57 PM | 0.6 | 18 |
| | 08:36 PM | 0.6 | 18 |
| 6 F | 02:05 AM | 0.4 | 12 |
| | 09:26 AM | 1.0 | 30 |
| | 05:00 PM | 0.3 | 9 |
| | 11:57 PM | 0.7 | 21 |
| 7 Sa | 03:19 AM | 0.7 | 21 |
| | 09:22 AM | 1.0 | 30 |
| | 05:26 PM | 0.0 | 0 |
| 8 Su | 01:57 AM | 0.9 | 27 |
| | 05:29 AM | 0.9 | 27 |
| | 09:07 AM | 0.9 | 27 |
| | 06:01 PM | -0.3 | -9 |
| 9 M | 03:07 AM | 1.1 | 34 |
| | 06:43 PM | -0.7 | -21 |
| 10 Tu | 04:04 AM | 1.3 | 40 |
| | 07:29 PM | -0.9 | -27 |
| 11 W | 04:58 AM | 1.5 | 46 |
| | 08:18 PM | -1.1 | -34 |
| 12 Th | 05:49 AM | 1.5 | 46 |
| | 09:08 PM | -1.2 | -37 |
| 13 F | 06:38 AM | 1.5 | 46 |
| | 09:59 PM | -1.1 | -34 |
| 14 Sa | 07:20 AM | 1.5 | 46 |
| | 10:49 PM | -0.9 | -27 |
| 15 Su | 07:53 AM | 1.4 | 43 |
| | 11:39 PM | -0.7 | -21 |
| 16 M | 08:15 AM | 1.3 | 40 |
| | 01:40 PM | 0.9 | 27 |
| | 04:00 PM | 1.0 | 30 |
| 17 Tu | 12:29 AM | -0.3 | -9 |
| | 08:30 AM | 1.1 | 34 |
| | 02:17 PM | 0.7 | 21 |
| | 06:07 PM | 0.8 | 24 |
| 18 W | 01:19 AM | 0.1 | 3 |
| | 08:38 AM | 1.0 | 30 |
| | 03:04 PM | 0.4 | 12 |
| | 08:32 PM | 0.8 | 24 |
| 19 Th | 02:11 AM | 0.4 | 12 |
| | 08:42 AM | 1.0 | 30 |
| | 03:55 PM | 0.2 | 6 |
| | 11:15 PM | 0.8 | 24 |
| 20 F | 03:14 AM | 0.7 | 21 |
| | 08:41 AM | 1.0 | 30 |
| | 04:47 PM | -0.1 | -3 |
| 21 Sa | 01:41 AM | 1.0 | 30 |
| | 04:59 AM | 1.0 | 30 |
| | 08:26 AM | 1.0 | 30 |
| | 05:37 PM | -0.3 | -9 |
| 22 Su | 03:08 AM | 1.2 | 37 |
| | 06:26 PM | -0.4 | -12 |
| 23 M | 04:04 AM | 1.3 | 40 |
| | 07:12 PM | -0.5 | -15 |
| 24 Tu | 04:50 AM | 1.3 | 40 |
| | 07:56 PM | -0.5 | -15 |
| 25 W | 05:31 AM | 1.4 | 43 |
| | 08:36 PM | -0.5 | -15 |
| 26 Th | 06:10 AM | 1.4 | 43 |
| | 09:12 PM | -0.4 | -12 |
| 27 F | 06:44 AM | 1.4 | 43 |
| | 09:45 PM | -0.4 | -12 |
| 28 Sa | 07:11 AM | 1.4 | 43 |
| | 10:15 PM | -0.3 | -9 |
| 29 Su | 07:30 AM | 1.3 | 40 |
| | 10:44 PM | -0.1 | -3 |
| 30 M | 07:40 AM | 1.3 | 40 |
| | 11:14 PM | 0.0 | 0 |
| 31 Tu | 07:45 AM | 1.2 | 37 |
| | 11:45 PM | 0.1 | 3 |

## August

| Day | Time | ft | cm |
|---|---|---|---|
| 1 W | 07:47 AM | 1.2 | 37 |
| | 01:45 PM | 0.9 | 27 |
| | 04:59 PM | 0.9 | 27 |
| 2 Th | 12:21 AM | 0.3 | 9 |
| | 07:47 AM | 1.1 | 34 |
| | 02:13 PM | 0.7 | 21 |
| | 07:08 PM | 0.8 | 24 |
| 3 F | 01:04 AM | 0.5 | 15 |
| | 07:44 AM | 1.0 | 30 |
| | 02:51 PM | 0.4 | 12 |
| | 09:45 PM | 0.9 | 27 |
| 4 Sa | 02:01 AM | 0.8 | 24 |
| | 07:36 AM | 1.0 | 30 |
| | 03:36 PM | 0.1 | 3 |
| 5 Su | 12:25 AM | 1.0 | 30 |
| | 03:45 AM | 1.0 | 30 |
| | 07:11 AM | 1.0 | 30 |
| | 04:26 PM | -0.1 | -3 |
| 6 M | 02:05 AM | 1.2 | 37 |
| | 05:21 PM | -0.4 | -12 |
| 7 Tu | 03:08 AM | 1.4 | 43 |
| | 06:16 PM | -0.6 | -18 |
| 8 W | 04:00 AM | 1.6 | 49 |
| | 07:13 PM | -0.8 | -24 |
| 9 Th | 04:47 AM | 1.6 | 49 |
| | 08:08 PM | -0.8 | -24 |
| 10 F | 05:29 AM | 1.6 | 49 |
| | 09:02 PM | -0.7 | -21 |
| 11 Sa | 06:02 AM | 1.5 | 46 |
| | 10:40 AM | 1.3 | 40 |
| | 12:44 PM | 1.4 | 43 |
| | 09:54 PM | -0.6 | -18 |
| 12 Su | 06:26 AM | 1.4 | 43 |
| | 10:50 AM | 1.2 | 37 |
| | 02:27 PM | 1.3 | 40 |
| | 10:45 PM | -0.3 | -9 |
| 13 M | 06:41 AM | 1.3 | 40 |
| | 11:22 AM | 1.0 | 30 |
| | 03:59 PM | 1.3 | 40 |
| | 11:34 PM | 0.0 | 0 |
| 14 Tu | 06:50 AM | 1.2 | 37 |
| | 12:05 PM | 0.8 | 24 |
| | 05:33 PM | 1.2 | 37 |
| 15 W | 12:24 AM | 0.3 | 9 |
| | 06:55 AM | 1.1 | 34 |
| | 12:56 PM | 0.5 | 15 |
| | 07:17 PM | 1.2 | 37 |
| 16 Th | 01:16 AM | 0.7 | 21 |
| | 06:57 AM | 1.1 | 34 |
| | 01:50 PM | 0.3 | 9 |
| | 09:19 PM | 1.2 | 37 |
| 17 F | 02:15 AM | 0.9 | 27 |
| | 06:53 AM | 1.1 | 34 |
| | 02:49 PM | 0.2 | 6 |
| | 11:37 PM | 1.2 | 37 |
| 18 Sa | 03:50 AM | 1.2 | 37 |
| | 06:29 AM | 1.2 | 37 |
| | 03:50 PM | 0.0 | 0 |
| 19 Su | 01:34 AM | 1.4 | 43 |
| | 04:52 PM | 0.0 | 0 |
| 20 M | 02:45 AM | 1.5 | 46 |
| | 05:51 PM | -0.1 | -3 |
| 21 Tu | 03:36 AM | 1.5 | 46 |
| | 06:46 PM | -0.1 | -3 |
| 22 W | 04:18 AM | 1.6 | 49 |
| | 07:35 PM | 0.0 | 0 |
| 23 Th | 04:53 AM | 1.6 | 49 |
| | 08:18 PM | 0.0 | 0 |
| 24 F | 05:21 AM | 1.6 | 49 |
| | 08:55 PM | 0.1 | 3 |
| 25 Sa | 05:41 AM | 1.5 | 46 |
| | 10:32 AM | 1.4 | 43 |
| | 12:33 PM | 1.4 | 43 |
| | 09:29 PM | 0.2 | 6 |
| 26 Su | 05:53 AM | 1.5 | 46 |
| | 10:32 AM | 1.3 | 40 |
| | 01:43 PM | 1.4 | 43 |
| | 10:00 PM | 0.3 | 9 |
| 27 M | 05:59 AM | 1.5 | 46 |
| | 10:44 AM | 1.2 | 37 |
| | 02:47 PM | 1.4 | 43 |
| | 10:32 PM | 0.4 | 12 |
| 28 Tu | 06:02 AM | 1.4 | 43 |
| | 11:05 AM | 1.1 | 34 |
| | 03:54 PM | 1.4 | 43 |
| | 11:06 PM | 0.6 | 18 |
| 29 W | 06:02 AM | 1.3 | 40 |
| | 11:31 AM | 1.0 | 30 |
| | 05:08 PM | 1.3 | 40 |
| | 11:45 PM | 0.7 | 21 |
| 30 Th | 05:59 AM | 1.3 | 40 |
| | 12:05 PM | 0.8 | 24 |
| | 06:34 PM | 1.3 | 40 |
| 31 F | 12:33 AM | 0.9 | 27 |
| | 05:53 AM | 1.2 | 37 |
| | 12:46 PM | 0.6 | 18 |
| | 08:19 PM | 1.3 | 40 |

## September

| Day | Time | ft | cm |
|---|---|---|---|
| 1 Sa | 01:36 AM | 1.1 | 34 |
| | 05:37 AM | 1.2 | 37 |
| | 01:35 PM | 0.3 | 9 |
| | 10:23 PM | 1.4 | 43 |
| 2 Su | 02:33 AM | 0.2 | 6 |
| 3 M | 12:21 AM | 1.6 | 49 |
| | 03:38 PM | 0.0 | 0 |
| 4 Tu | 01:43 AM | 1.7 | 52 |
| | 04:47 PM | -0.1 | -3 |
| 5 W | 02:42 AM | 1.9 | 58 |
| | 05:54 PM | -0.2 | -6 |
| 6 Th | 03:28 AM | 1.9 | 58 |
| | 06:58 PM | -0.2 | -6 |
| 7 F | 04:04 AM | 1.9 | 58 |
| | 07:58 PM | -0.1 | -3 |
| 8 Sa | 04:30 AM | 1.8 | 55 |
| | 09:07 AM | 1.5 | 46 |
| | 12:39 PM | 1.6 | 49 |
| | 08:55 PM | 0.1 | 3 |
| 9 Su | 04:47 AM | 1.6 | 49 |
| | 09:23 AM | 1.3 | 40 |
| | 02:15 PM | 1.7 | 52 |
| | 09:50 PM | 0.3 | 9 |
| 10 M | 04:57 AM | 1.5 | 46 |
| | 09:54 AM | 1.1 | 34 |
| | 03:41 PM | 1.7 | 52 |
| | 10:43 PM | 0.6 | 18 |
| 11 Tu | 05:02 AM | 1.4 | 43 |
| | 10:32 AM | 0.8 | 24 |
| | 05:03 PM | 1.7 | 52 |
| | 11:37 PM | 0.8 | 24 |
| 12 W | 05:03 AM | 1.3 | 40 |
| | 11:15 AM | 0.6 | 18 |
| | 06:27 PM | 1.7 | 52 |
| 13 Th | 12:34 AM | 1.1 | 34 |
| | 05:00 AM | 1.3 | 40 |
| | 12:02 PM | 0.4 | 12 |
| | 07:57 PM | 1.7 | 52 |
| 14 F | 01:44 AM | 1.3 | 40 |
| | 04:47 AM | 1.4 | 43 |
| | 12:53 PM | 0.3 | 9 |
| | 09:37 PM | 1.7 | 52 |
| 15 Sa | 01:48 PM | 0.3 | 9 |
| | 11:22 PM | 1.7 | 52 |
| 16 Su | 02:50 PM | 0.3 | 9 |
| 17 M | 12:50 AM | 1.8 | 55 |
| | 03:56 PM | 0.4 | 12 |
| 18 Tu | 01:54 AM | 1.8 | 55 |
| | 05:04 PM | 0.5 | 15 |
| 19 W | 02:40 AM | 1.9 | 58 |
| | 06:07 PM | 0.6 | 18 |
| 20 Th | 03:14 AM | 1.9 | 58 |
| | 07:01 PM | 0.6 | 18 |
| 21 F | 03:38 AM | 1.9 | 58 |
| | 07:47 PM | 0.7 | 21 |
| 22 Sa | 03:54 AM | 1.8 | 55 |
| | 09:05 AM | 1.6 | 49 |
| | 12:45 PM | 1.7 | 52 |
| | 08:28 PM | 0.8 | 24 |
| 23 Su | 04:03 AM | 1.8 | 55 |
| | 09:11 AM | 1.5 | 46 |
| | 01:54 PM | 1.7 | 52 |
| | 09:07 PM | 0.9 | 27 |
| 24 M | 04:07 AM | 1.7 | 52 |
| | 09:26 AM | 1.3 | 40 |
| | 02:56 PM | 1.7 | 52 |
| | 09:46 PM | 1.0 | 30 |
| 25 Tu | 04:08 AM | 1.6 | 49 |
| | 09:45 AM | 1.2 | 37 |
| | 03:57 PM | 1.7 | 52 |
| | 10:28 PM | 1.1 | 34 |
| 26 W | 04:07 AM | 1.5 | 46 |
| | 10:10 AM | 1.0 | 30 |
| | 05:01 PM | 1.8 | 55 |
| | 11:17 PM | 1.2 | 37 |
| 27 Th | 04:02 AM | 1.5 | 46 |
| | 10:40 AM | 0.8 | 24 |
| | 06:11 PM | 1.8 | 55 |
| 28 F | 12:17 AM | 1.3 | 40 |
| | 03:48 AM | 1.4 | 43 |
| | 11:16 AM | 0.6 | 18 |
| | 07:30 PM | 1.8 | 55 |
| 29 Sa | 12:00 PM | 0.4 | 12 |
| | 08:59 PM | 1.9 | 58 |
| 30 Su | 12:52 PM | 0.3 | 9 |
| | 10:35 PM | 2.0 | 61 |

Heights are referred to mean lower water which is the chart datum of sounding. All times are local. Daylight Saving Time has been used when needed. Additional tide tables are available online from NOAA at www.tidesandcurrents.noaa.gov/tide_predictions.shtml.

**SKIPPER'S HANDBOOK**

# Bridge Basics

Bridges have to be factors in when planning a trip. Depending on where you cruise, you may be dependent on bridge openings; a particular bridge's schedule can often decide where you tie up for the evening or when you wake up and get underway the next day. While many are high (over 65 feet), and some usually remain open (such as railroad bridges), others are restricted for different hours in specific months, closed during rush hours and/or open on the quarter-hour, half-hour or even at 20 minutes and 40 minutes past the hour. To add to the confusion, the restrictions are constantly changing. Just because a bridge opened on a certain schedule last season does not mean it is still on that same schedule. (See the Bridges & Locks section in this guide or waterwayguide.com for the most current schedules.) Changes are posted in the Coast Guard's *Local Notice to Mariners* reports, which can be found online at navcen.uscg.gov. It is also a good idea to check locally to verify bridge schedules before your transit.

Most bridges monitor VHF Channel 09, designated by the Federal Communications Commission as the "bridge tender channel." Bridges in NC and VA still answer on VHF Channel 13, as do the locks in the Okeechobee. In any waters, it is a good idea to monitor both the bridge channel and VHF Channel 16–one on your ship's radio and one on a handheld radio, if your main set doesn't have a dual-watch capability–to monitor oncoming commercial traffic and communications with the bridge tender.

When using VHF, always call bridges by name and identify your vessel by name and type (such as sailing vessel or trawler) and whether you are traveling north or south. If you are unable to raise the bridge using VHF radio, use a horn signal. (For further information, see the *Coast Pilot 4, Chapter Two: Title 33, Navigation Regulations, Part 117, Drawbridge Regulations.*) If the gates do not come down and the bridge does not open after repeated use of the radio and the horn, call the Coast Guard and ask them to call the bridge tender on the land telephone line, or you may be able to call the bridge directly. Phone numbers for many bridges are given in the following Bridges & Locks section, although some of the numbers are not for the actual bridge tender, but for a central office that manages that bridge. Some bridges are not required to open in high winds. If you encounter a bridge that won't open, it is prudent to drop the hook in a safe spot until the situation is resolved.

**Swing Bridges:**
Swing bridges have an opening section that pivots horizontally on a central hub, allowing boats to pass on one side or the other when it is open.

**Lift Bridges:**
Lift bridges normally have two towers on each end of the opening section that are equipped with cables that lift the road or railway vertically into the air.

Most bridges carry a tide board to register vertical clearance at the center of the span. (Note that in Florida waters the tide board figure–and the one noted on the chart–is generally for a point that is 5 feet toward the channel from the bridge fender.) In the case of arched bridges, center channel clearance is frequently higher than the tide gauge registers. So check your chart and the tide boards and, unless it specifically notes that vertical clearance is given "at center," you may be able to count on a little extra height at mid-channel, under the arch of the bridge. Some bridges may bear signs noting extra height at center in feet.

Because many bridges restrict their openings during morning and evening rush hours, to minimize inconvenience to vehicular traffic, you may need to plan an early start or late stop to avoid getting stuck waiting for a bridge opening.

## Pontoon Bridges:

A pontoon bridge consists of an opening section that must be floated out of the way with a cable to allow boats to pass. Do not proceed until the cables have had time to sink to the bottom.

## Bascule Bridges:

This is the most common type of opening bridge you will encounter. The opening section of a bascule bridge has one or two leaves that tilt vertically on a hinge like doors being opened skyward.

## Bridge Procedures:

■ First, decide if it is necessary to have the drawbridge opened. You will need to know your boat's clearance height above the waterline before you start. Drawbridges have "clearance gauges" that show the closed vertical clearance with changing water levels, but a bascule bridge typically has 3 to 5 feet more clearance than what is indicated on the gauge at the center of its arch at mean low tide. Bridge clearances are also shown on NOAA charts.

■ Contact the bridge tender well in advance (even if you can't see the bridge around the bend) by VHF radio or phone. Alternatively, the proper horn signal for a bridge opening is one prolonged blast (four to six seconds) and one short blast (approximately one second). Bridge operators sound this signal when ready to open the bridge, and then usually the danger signal–five short blasts–when they are closing the bridge. The operator of each vessel is required by law to signal the bridge tender for an opening, even if another vessel has already signaled. Tugs with tows and U.S. government vessels may go through bridges at any time, usually signaling with five short blasts. A restricted bridge may open in an emergency with the same signal. Keep in mind bridge tenders will not know your intentions unless you tell them.

■ If two or more vessels are in sight of one another, the bridge tender may elect to delay opening the bridge until all boats can go through together.

■ Approach at slow speed and be prepared to wait, as the bridge cannot open until the traffic gates are closed. Many ICW bridges, for example, are more than 40 years old and the aged machinery functions slowly.

■ Once the bridge is open, proceed at no-wake speed. Keep a safe distance between you and other craft, as currents and turbulence around bridge supports can be tricky.

■ There is technically no legal right-of-way (except on the Mississippi and some other inland rivers), but boats running with the current should always be given the right-of-way out of courtesy. As always, if you are not sure, let the other boat go first.

■ When making the same opening as a commercial craft, it is a good idea to contact the vessel's captain (usually on VHF Channel 13), ascertain his intentions and state yours to avoid any misunderstanding in tight quarters.

■ After passing through the bridge, maintain a no-wake speed until you are well clear and then resume normal speed.

# Locks and Locking Through

Many rivers in North America are a series of pools created by dams. When the dams also include locks, navigation is possible beyond the dam. Locks are watertight chambers with gates at each end. They raise and lower boats from one water level to the next. Many cruisers find locking through a pleasant experience and part of the adventure of boating.

## Lock Types

■ Conventional lift locks are single chambers that raise and lower boats.

■ Flight locks are a series of conventional lift locks.

■ Hydraulic lift locks have water-filled chambers supported by rams or pistons that move in opposite directions. The movement of one chamber forces the movement of the other via a connected valve. The chamber in the upper position adds sufficient water to cause it to drop, forcing the lower chamber to rise. The chambers have hinged gates fore and aft that contain the water and allow boats to enter or leave.

■ Marine railways convey boats over obstacles, usually a landmass, by containing boats in a gantry crane that moves over the land and deposits the boat on the other side of the obstruction.

River locks are usually conventional lift locks. The dam deepens water around shoals, and the lock allows vessels to bypass the dam. Conventional lift locks work by gravity alone. Water passively flows into or out of the lock. When the lock is filling, the valve at the upper end of the lock is opened, and water flows in. The downstream lock gate is closed, preventing the escape of the water. This is the time of greatest turbulence in the locks and the time of greatest vigilance for boaters. When the upper water level is reached, the upper lock gate opens to allow boats to exit or enter.

When the lock empties, both lock doors are closed, a valve on the lower end of the lock is opened, and water exits. This creates a surge of water outside the lock, but inside the lock, the water recedes like water in a tub. When the water level in the lock is the same as the lower river level, the lower lock gate opens and vessels leave.

## Locking Protocol

1. Call ahead on the VHF (Channel 13 or sound three blasts) for permission to lock through. Indicate whether you are northbound (upbound) or southbound (downbound). Your presence and communication indicate to the lock tender your desire to lock through.

2. Wait a safe distance from the lock, or find an anchorage nearby and within sight of the lock.

3. Prepare for locking by placing large fenders fore and aft and having lines ready. Fender boards are useful because they protect your fenders and provide a skid plate against the dirt and algae on the lock wall.

4. When approaching the lock, stay back to allow outbound vessels to clear the lock. Do not enter until signaled to do so. Signals vary. Look for a telephone/pull rope at the lock wall; listen for a whistle blast—one long and one short blast, or three

blasts; look for a "traffic" light–green, yellow or red. Follow directions given by the lock tender.

The order of priority is:
U.S. Military
Mail boats
Commercial passenger boats
Commercial tows
Commercial fishermen
Pleasure craft

.   When the lock tender turns on the green light or calls for you to enter, enter in the order that boats arrived at the lock. The longest waiting boat goes first, unless directed by the lock tender, who may call boats in according to size and the configuration of the lock. Do not jump the line; do not scoot in front of others; defer to faster boats so you do not have them behind you after you leave the lock.

.   When entering the lock, leave no wake, heed instruction, and respect other boaters. If they are having trouble and appear unsettled, stand by until they are secure. Listen to the directives of the lock tenders. Some lock systems require all line handlers to wear personal flotation devices (PFDs). Crew members on the bow should wear PFDs.

7.  You will be directed by the lock tender to a place along the lock wall. You will find an inset mooring pin (floating bollard), vertical cable or a rope. If there is a floating bollard, secure the boat to the pin via a center cleat by wrapping the line around the pin then back to the boat cleat. If there is a vertical cable, wrap the line around the cable, and bring it back to the boat; the loop will ride up or down the cable. If there is a drop-down line, bring the line around a cleat, and hold it. DO NOT TIE LINES! If you are asked to provide a line, throw it to the lock tender. After the lock tender has secured it, take the bitter end and wrap, but do not tie, around a cleat. Attend the bow and the stern, and adjust the line(s) as the boat rises or falls in the lock chamber.

8.  In crowded locks, move forward as far as you can to make room for others coming in behind you. Small boats may raft to bigger boats. Set adequate fenders for fending off another vessel.

9.  Inside the lock chamber, turn off engines when secure. Exhaust fumes contained in the lock chamber are an irritant to people in small, open boats. Attend the lines at all times. Be prepared for turbulence when the lock fills. Never use hands or feet to fend a boat off a lock wall. Stay alert to other boats. Be prepared to quickly cut a line if needed.

10. When the lock reaches its determined depth/height, the lock tender will loosen the line and drop it to you if you are using a line attached at the top of the lock. After receiving a whistle blast by the lock tender, recover any lines used, and prepare to exit. Leave the lock in the same order as entering. Do not rush ahead of those in front of you.

## Lock Fees

Unlike locks in other countries (including Canada), there is no fee for transiting locks managed by the Army Corps of Engineers.

# Bridges & Locks

**KEY:**

| **Statute Miles from ICW Mile 0** |
|---|
| **Vertical Clearance** |

Drawbridge clearances are vertical, in feet, when closed and at Mean High Water in tidal areas. Bridge schedules are subject to schedule changes due to repairs, maintenance, events, etc. Check Waterway Explorer at waterwayguide.com for the latest shedules or call ahead.

**FLORIDA BRIDGES MONITOR (VHF) CHANNEL 09**

## Florida's East Coast ICW

**720.7 / 5'**
**Kingsley Creek Railroad Swing Bridge:** Usually open.

**720.8 / 65'**
**Kingsley Creek (FL A1A) Twin Bridges:** Fixed

**739.2 / 65'**
**Hecksher Dr. (Sisters Creek) Bridge:** Fixed

## St. Johns River

**13.1 / 169'**
**Dames Point Bridge:** Fixed

**21.8 / 86'**
**Mathews Bridge:** Fixed

**22.8 / 135'**
**Hart–Commodore Point Bridge:** Fixed

**24.7 / 40'**
**Main Street Lift Bridge:** Opens on signal except from 7:00 a.m. to 8:30 a.m. and from 4:30 p.m. to 6:00 p.m., Mon. through Sat. (except federal holidays), when the draw need not open.

**24.8 / 75'**
**Acosta Bridge:** Fixed

**24.9 / 5'**
**FEC Railroad Bascule Bridge:** Usually open, displaying flashing green lights to indicate that vessels may pass. When a train approaches, large signs on both the upstream and downstream sides of the bridge flash "Bridge Coming Down," the lights go to flashing red, and siren signals sound. After an 8-minute delay, the draw lowers and locks if there are no vessels under the draw. The draw remains down for a period of 8 min. or while the approach track circuit is occupied. After the train has cleared, the draw opens and the lights return to flashing green.

**25.4 / 75'**
**Fuller-Warren Bridge:** Fixed

**35.1 / 65'**
**Buckman (I-295) Bridge:** Fixed

**51.4 / 45'**
**Shands Bridge:** Fixed (Note: A new fixed 65-foot vertical clearance bridge was in the planning stages at press time.)

**79.8 / 65'**
**Palatka Memorial Bridge:** Fixed

**90.2 / 7'**
**Buffalo Bluff Railroad Bascule Bridge:** Usually open.

**122.2 / 20'**
**Astor Hwy. Bascule Bridge:** Opens on signal. (Note: Open bascule overhangs channel above a height of 72 feet.)

**138.2 / 15'**
**Whitehair (SR 44) Bascule Bridge:** Opens on signal.

**156.2 / 7'**
**Port of Sanford Railway Bascule Bridge:** Usually open.

**156.3 / 45'**
**U.S. 17/U.S. 92 Bridge:** Fixed

**156.6 / 45'**
**St Johns River Veterans Memorial Twin Bridges:** Fixed

## Florida's East Coast ICW (cont.)

**742.1 / 65'**
**Wonderwood Drive Twin Bridges:** Fixed

**744.7 / 65'**
**Atlantic Beach Twin Bridges:** Fixed

**747.5 / 65'**
**McCormick (U.S. 90) Bridge:** Fixed

**749.5 / 65'**
**Butler Blvd. (Pablo Creek) Twin Bridges:** Fixed

**758.8 / 65'**
**Palm Valley (SR 210) Bridge:** Fixed

**775.8 / 65'**
**Usina (Vilano Beach) Bridge:** Fixed

**SKIPPER'S HANDBOOK**

**777.9**
**18'**

**Bridge of Lions (SR A1A):** Opens on signal, except from 7:00 a.m. to 6:00 p.m., when the draw need only open on the hour and half-hour; however, the draw need not open at 8:00 a.m., 12 noon, and 5:00 p.m. Mon. through Fri. (except federal holidays). In addition, from 7:00 a.m. to 6:00 p.m. on Sat., Sun. and federal holidays, the draw opens only on the hour and half-hour. (Note: Additional 4 feet of vertical clearance at center of bridge.) 904-824-7372

**780.3**
**65'**

**SR 312 Twin Bridges:** Fixed

**788.6**
**25'**

**Crescent Beach (SR 206) Bascule Bridge:** Opens on signal.

**803.0**
**65'**

**Hammock Dunes (Palm Coast Hwy.) Bridge:** Fixed

**810.6**
**65'**

**Flagler Beach (Moody Blvd.) Bridge:** Fixed

**816.0**
**15'**

**Bulow (L.B. Knox) Bascule Bridge:** Opens on signal.

**824.9**
**65'**

**Ormond Beach (SR 40) Bridge:** Fixed

**829.1**
**65'**

**Seabreeze Twin Bridges:** Fixed

**829.7**
**22'**

**Main Street (Daytona Beach) Bascule Bridge:** Opens on signal.

**830.1**
**65'**

**International Speedway Blvd. Bridge:** Fixed

**830.6**
**21'**

**Veterans Memorial Bascule Bridge:** Opens on signal, except from 7:45 a.m. to 8:45 a.m. and 4:45 p.m. to 5:45 p.m. Mon. through Sat. (except federal holidays), when the draw opens only at 8:15 a.m. and 5:15 p.m. Contruction underway at press time on 65-foot vertical clearance replacement bridge.

**835.5**
**65'**

**Dunlawton Ave. (Port Orange) Bridge:** Fixed

**845.0**
**24'**

**George E. Musson Memorial Bascule Bridge:** Opens on signal, except from 7:00 a.m. until 7:00 p.m. daily, when the draw opens only on the hour and half hour. (NOTE: This is a change from the 2017 schedule.)

**846.5**
**65'**

**Harris Saxon (New Smyrna) Bridge:** Fixed

**869.2**
**27'**

**Allenhurst (Haulover Canal) Bascule Bridge:** Opens on signal. 321-867-4859

**876.6**
**7'**

**NASA (Jay-Jay) Railroad Bascule Bridge:** Usually open, displaying flashing green lights to indicate that vessels may pass. When a train approaches, the lights go to flashing red, and the draw lowers and locks if there are no vessels under the draw. The draw remains down for a period of 5 min. or while the approach track circuit is occupied. After the train has cleared, the draw opens and the lights return to flashing green.

**878.9**
**65'**

**Max Brewer (Titusville) Bridge:** Fixed

**885.0**
**27'**

**NASA Causeway Twin Bascule Bridges:** Open on signal, except from 6:30 a.m. to 8:00 a.m. and 3:30 p.m. to 5:00 p.m. Mon. through Fri. (except federal holidays), when the draws need not open.

**894.0**
**65'**

**Bennett Causeway (City Point) Twin Bridges:** Fixed

**897.4**
**65'**

**Merritt Island (Cocoa) Twin Bridges:** Fixed

**909.0**
**65'**

**Pineda Causeway (Palm Shores) Twin Bridges:** Fixed

**914.4**
**65'**

**Eau Gallie Causeway (SR 518) Bridge:** Fixed

**918.2**
**65'**

**Melbourne Causeway (SR 516) Twin Bridges:** Fixed

**943.3**
**65'**

**Wabasso Bridge:** Fixed

**951.9**
**66'**

**Merrill P. Barber (Vero Beach) Bridge:** Fixed

**953.2**
**65'**

**Alma Lee Loy (17th St.) Bridge:** Fixed

**964.8**
**26'**

**North Fort Pierce (SR A1A) Bascule Bridge:** Opens on signal.

**965.8**
**65'**

**Fort Pierce (SR A1A) Bridge:** Fixed

**981.4**
**65'**

**Jensen Beach Causeway (SR 707A) Bridge:** Fixed

**984.9**
**65'**

**Ernest Lyons (SR A1A) Bridge:** Fixed

SKIPPER'S HANDBOOK

# Okeechobee Waterway (East to West)

**3.4 / 65'** — **Evans Crary (SR A1A) Bridge:** Fixed

**7.3 / 65'** — **Roosevelt (U.S. 1) Bridge:** Fixed

**7.4 / 7'** — **Florida East Coast Railroad Lift Bridge:** Usually in the fully open position, displaying flashing green lights to indicate that vessels may pass. When a train approaches, the navigation lights go to flashing red and a horn sounds four blasts, pauses, and then repeats four blasts. After an 8-min. delay, the draw lowers and locks, if there are no vessels under the draw. The draw remains down for a period of 8 min. or while the approach track circuit is occupied. After the train has cleared, the draw opens and the lights return to flashing green. Note: Only 50 feet of charted horizontal clearance.

**7.4 / 14'** — **Old Roosevelt (Dixie Hwy.) Bascule Bridge:** Opens on signal. When the adjacent railway bridge is in the closed position at the time of a scheduled opening, the draw need not open, but it must then open immediately upon opening of the railroad bridge to pass all accumulated vessels. 772-692-0321

**9.5 / 54'** — **Palm City (SR 714) Bridge:** Fixed

**10.9 / 55'** — **Indian St. (SW Martin Hwy.) Bridge:** Fixed

**14.0 / 56'** — **I-95 Twin Bridges:** Fixed

**14.5 / 55'** — **Florida Turnpike Twin Bridges:** Fixed

**15.1** — **St. Lucie Lock:** Opens 7:00 a.m. to 5:00 p.m., on request. Normally make fast on south wall. 772-287-2665

**17.1 / 56'** — **SR 76A Bridge:** Fixed

**28.1 / 55'** — **Indiantown (SR 710) Bridge:** Fixed

**28.2 / 7'** — **Seaboard (Indiantown) Railroad Swing Bridge:** Opens on signal, except from 10:00 p.m. to 6:00 a.m., when the bridge opens on signal only if at least 3-hour notice is given. 772-597-3822

**38.0 / 7'** — **Florida East Coast (Port Mayaca) Railroad Lift Bridge:** Usually in the fully open position, displaying flashing green lights to indicate that vessels may pass. When a train approaches, it will stop and a crewmember will observe the waterway for approaching vessels, which will be allowed to pass. Upon manual signal, the bridge lights will go to flashing red, and the horn will sound four blasts, pause then repeat four blasts. The draw will lower and lock, if there are no vessels under the draw. After the train has cleared, the draw will open, and the lights will return to flashing green. (Note: Vertical clearance when open is 49 feet.) The bridge is not constantly tended.

**38.8 / 55'** — **U.S. Hwys. 98 & 441 Bridge:** Fixed

**39.1** — **Port Mayaca Lock:** Opens on signal, 7:00 a.m. to 5:00 p.m. Last lockage at 4:30 p.m. Normally make fast on south wall. 561-924-2858

**60.7 / 11'** — **Torry Island (Belle Glade Dike) Swing Bridge:** Opens on signal from 7:00 a.m. to 6:00 p.m., Mon. through Thurs., and from 7:00 a.m. to 7:00 p.m., Fri. through Sun. At all other times, the draw need not be opened for the passage of vessels. Manual operation. (May not open in winds in excess of 20 mph.) 561-996-3844

**78.0** — **Moore Haven Lock:** Opens on signal, 7:00 a.m. to 5:00 p.m. Last lockage at 4:30 p.m. Normally make fast on south wall. 863-946-0414

**78.3 / 5'** — **Seaboard (Moore Haven) Railroad Swing Bridge:** Opens on signal, except from 10:00 p.m. to 6:00 a.m., when the draw need not open. (Note: Normally open. Manual operation.)

**78.4 / 55'** — **Moore Haven (U.S. 27) Twin Bridges:** Fixed

**93.5** — **Ortona Lock:** Opens on signal, 7:00 a.m. to 5:00 p.m. Last lockage at 4:30 p.m. Normally make fast on south wall. 863-675-0616

**103.0 / 28'** — **La Belle (SR 29) Bascule Bridge:** Opens on signal, except from 7:00 a.m. to 9:00 a.m. and from 4:00 p.m. to 6:00 p.m., Mon. through Fri. (except federal holidays), when the bridge need not open. The bridge will open from 10:00 p.m. to 6:00 a.m. on signal only if at least 3-hour notice is given. 863-674-4663

**108.2 / 9'** — **Fort Denaud Swing Bridge:** Opens on signal, except from 10:00 p.m. to 6:00 a.m., when the bridge will open on signal only if at least 3-hour notice is given. 863-675-2055

**116.0 / 23'** — **Alva Bascule Bridge:** Opens on signal, except from 10:00 p.m. to 6:00 a.m., when the bridge will open on signal only if at least 3-hour notice is given. 239-278-2704

SKIPPER'S HANDBOOK

**121.4** **W.P. Franklin Lock:** Opens on signal from 7:00 a.m. to 5:00 p.m. Last lockage at 4:30 p.m. Normally make fast on south wall. 239-694-5451

**126.3** **27'** **Wilson Pigott (Olga) Bascule Bridge:** Opens on signal, except from 10:00 p.m. to 6:00 a.m., when the bridge will open on signal only if at least 3-hour notice is given.

**128.9** **55'** **I-75 Bridge:** Fixed

**129.9** **5'** **SCL Railroad Lift Bridge:** Usually open. (Note: Span overhangs channel when open, resulting in a vertical clearance of 55 feet.)

**134.6** **56'** **Edison Twin Bridges:** Fixed

**135** **55'** **Caloosahatchee Bridge:** Fixed

**138.6** **55'** **Veterans Memorial (Mid-Point) Bridge:** Fixed

**142** **55'** **Cape Coral Bridge:** Fixed

# Florida's East Coast ICW (cont.)

**995.9** **21'** **Hobe Sound (SR 708) Bascule Bridge:** Opens on signal. 772-546-5234

**1004.1** **25'** **Jupiter Island (CR 707) Bascule Bridge:** Opens on signal.

**1004.8** **26'** **Jupiter (U.S. 1) Bascule Bridge:** Opens on signal.

**1006.2** **35'** **Indiantown (SR 706) Bascule Bridge:** Opens on hour and half-hour.

**1009.3** **35'** **Donald Ross Bascule Bridge:** Opens on the hour and half-hour.

**1012.6** **24'** **PGA Blvd. Bascule Bridge:** Opens on the hour and half-hour.

**1013.7** **25'** **Parker (U.S. 1) Bascule Bridge:** Opens on the quarter hour and three-quarter hour.

**1017.2** **65'** **Blue Heron Blvd. (SR A1A) Bridge:** Fixed

**1020.8** **17'** **Flagler Memorial (SR A1A) Bascule Bridge:** Opens on signal at 15 min. past the hour, except Mon. through Fri., when the draw need not open at 8:15 a.m. and 4:15 p.m. due to rush-hour traffic. (Note: New bridge under construction at press time with 21-foot closed vertical clearance. Be aware that you may have delays due to the construction and schedule may change. Check waterwayguide.com for daily updates.)

**1022.6** **21'** **Royal Park (SR 704) Bascule Bridge:** Opens on the hour and half-hour.

**1024.7** **14'** **Southern Blvd. (SR 700/80) Bascule Bridge:** Opens on the quarter and three-quarter hour. (Note: Bridge under construction at press time. The new closed vertical clearance will be 21 feet. Be aware that you may have delays due to the construction. Check waterwayguide.com for updates.)

**1028.8** **35'** **Lake Worth–Lake Ave. (SR 802) Bascule Bridge:** Opens on signal.

**1031.0** **21'** **E. Ocean Ave. (Lantana) Bascule Bridge:** Opens on the hour and half-hour.

**1035.0** **21'** **E. Ocean Ave. (Boynton Beach) Bascule Bridge:** Opens on the hour and half-hour.

**1035.8** **25'** **E. Woolbright Rd. (SE 15th St.) Bascule Bridge:** Opens on signal.

**1038.7** **9'** **George Bush Blvd. Bascule Bridge:** Opens on signal. 561-276-5948

**1039.6** **12'** **Atlantic Ave. (SR 806) Bascule Bridge:** Opens on the quarter and three-quarter hour.

**1041.0** **30'** **Linton Blvd. Bascule Bridge:** Opens on the hour and half-hour. (Note: Actual vertical clearance may be as low as 27 feet. Call ahead to verify.) 561-278-1980

**1044.9** **25'** **Spanish River Blvd. Bascule Bridge:** Opens on the hour and half-hour.

**1047.5** **19'** **Palmetto Park Bascule Bridge:** Opens on the hour and half-hour.

**23'** **Boca Raton Inlet Bascule Bridge (to ocean):** Opens on signal.

**1048.2** **9'** **Camino Real Bascule Bridge:** Opens on the hour, 20 min. past the hour and 40 min. past the hour.

**1050.0** **21'** **Hillsboro Blvd. (SR 810) Bascule Bridge:** Opens on the hour and half-hour.

**SKIPPER'S HANDBOOK**

**13'** **Hillsboro Inlet Bascule Bridge (to ocean):** Opens on signal, except from 7:00 a.m. to 6:00 p.m., the draw will open only on the hour, quarter hour, half-hour, and three-quarter hour.

**1055.0** **15'** **Pompano Beach (NE 14th Street) Bascule Bridge:** Opens on the quarter hour and three-quarter hour.

**1056.0** **15'** **Atlantic Blvd. (SR 814) Bascule Bridge:** Opens on the hour and half-hour.

**1059.0** **15'** **Commercial Blvd. (SR 870) Bascule Bridge:** Opens on the hour and half-hour.

**1060.5** **22'** **Oakland Park Blvd. Bascule Bridge:** Opens on the quarter hour and three-quarter hour.

**1062.6** **25'** **East Sunrise Blvd. (SR 838) Bascule Bridge:** Opens on the hour and half-hour. On the first weekend in May, the draw need not open from 4:00 p.m. to 6:00 p.m. on Sat. and Sun. and, on the first Sat. in May, the draw need not open from 9:45 p.m. to 10:45 p.m.

**1064.0** **24'** **East Las Olas Blvd. Bascule Bridge:** Opens on the quarter hour and three-quarter hour. On the first weekend in May, the draw need not open from 4:00 p.m. to 6:00 p.m. on Sat. and Sun. and, on the first Sat. in May, the draw need not open from 9:45 p.m. to 10:45 p.m.

## New River (North & South Forks)

**1.4** **16'** **SE 3rd Ave. Bascule Bridge:** The draw opens on signal, except from 7:30 a.m. to 9:00 a.m. and 4:30 p.m. to 6:00 p.m., Mon. through Fri. (except federal holidays), when the draw need not open.

**2.3** **21'** **Andrews Ave. Bascule Bridge:** The draw opens on signal, except from 7:30 a.m. to 9:00 a.m. and 4:30 p.m. to 6:00 p.m., Mon. through Fri. (except federal holidays), when the draw need not open. The draw need not open for inbound vessels when the draw of the Florida East Coast Railroad Bridge is in the closed position for the passage of a train.

**2.5** **4'** **Florida East Coast Railroad Lift Bridge:** Usually in the fully open position, displaying flashing green lights to indicate that vessels may pass. When a train approaches, the navigation lights go to flashing red and a horn sounds four blasts, pauses, and then repeats four blasts then the draw lowers and locks. After the train has cleared, the draw opens and the lights return to flashing green. The bridge shall not be closed more than 60 minutes combined for any 120-minute time period beginning at 12:01 a.m.

**2.7** **20'** **William H. Marshall Memorial (7th Ave.) Bascule Bridge:** The draw opens on signal, except from 7:30 a.m. to 9:00 a.m. and 4:30 p.m. to 6:00 p.m., Mon. through Fri. (except federal holidays), when the draw need not open.

**3.3** **3'** **11th Ave. Swing Bridge:** (Located on North Fork.) Opens on signal.

**0.9** **21'** **Davie Blvd. Bascule Bridge:** (Located on South Fork.) The draw opens on signal, except from 7:30 a.m. to 9:00 a.m. and 4:30 p.m. to 6:00 p.m., Mon. through Fri. (except federal holidays), when the draw need not open.

**2.0** **55'** **I-95 Twin Bridges:** (Located on South Fork.) Fixed

**2.1** **2'** **SCL Railroad Bascule Bridge:** Usually open

**4.4** **21'** **SR 84 Bascule Bridge:** Opens on signal if at least a 24 hour notice is given.

**4.5** **40'** **I-595 Bridge:** Fixed

## Florida's East Coast ICW (cont.)

**1065.9** **55'** **SE 17th St. (Brooks Memorial) Bascule Bridge:** Opens on the hour and half-hour.

**1069.4** **22'** **Dania Beach Blvd. (A1A) Bascule Bridge:** Opens on the hour and half-hour.

**1070.5** **22'** **Sheridan St. Bascule Bridge:** Opens on the quarter hour and three-quarter hour.

**1072.2** **25'** **Hollywood Beach Blvd. (SR 820) Bascule Bridge:** Opens on hour and half-hour.

**1074.0** **26'** **Hallandale Beach Blvd. (SR 858) Bascule Bridge:** Open on the quarter hour and three-quarter hour.

**1076.3** **65'** **William Lehman Causeway (SR 856) Bridge:** Fixed

**1078.0** **30'** **NE 163rd St. (Sunny Isles) Twin Bridges:** Opens on signal, except from 7:00 a.m. to 6:00 p.m. on Mon. through Fri. (except federal holidays), and from 10:00 a.m. to 6:00 p.m. on Sat., Sun., and federal holidays, when the draw need open only on the quarter hour and three-quarter hour.

**32'** **Bakers Haulover Inlet Bridge (to ocean):** Fixed

**1081.4** **16'** **Broad Causeway Bascule Bridge:** Opens on signal, except from 8:00 a.m. to 6:00 p.m., when the draw need open only on the quarter hour and three-quarter hour.

**1084.6** **25'** **West 79th St. Bascule Bridge:** Opens on signal.

**1087.2** **56'** **Julia Tuttle Causeway (I-195) Bridge:** Fixed (Note: Bridge is less than standard ICW vertical clearance.)

**1088.6** **12'** **Venetian Causeway Bascule Bridge (West):** Opens on signal, except from 7:00 a.m. to 7:00 p.m., Mon. through Fri. (except federal holidays), when the bridge need only open on the hour and half-hour.

**1088.8** **65'** **MacArthur Causeway (SR A1A) Twin Bridges:** Fixed

**1089.3** **65'** **Dodge Island Hwy. Bridge:** Fixed

**1089.4** **22'** **Dodge Island Railroad Bascule Bridge:** Usually open.

## Miami River

**23'** **Brickell Ave. Bascule Bridge:** Opens on signal, except from 7:30 a.m. to 7:00 p.m., Mon. through Fri. (except federal holidays), when the draw need only open on the hour and half-hour; however, from 7:35 a.m. to 8:59 a.m., 12:05 p.m. to 12:59 p.m. and 4:35 p.m. to 5:59 p.m., the draw need not open.

**75'** **Metro Train Bridge:** Fixed

**21'** **Miami Ave. Bascule Bridge:** Opens on signal, except from 7:30 a.m. to 7:00 p.m., Mon. through Fri. (except federal holidays), when the draw need only open on the hour and half-hour; however, from 7:35 a.m. to 8:59 a.m., 12:05 p.m. to 12:59 p.m. and 4:35 p.m. to 5:59 p.m., the draw need not open.

**75'** **SW 1st Ave. Bridge:** Fixed

**75'** **I-95 Twin Bridges:** Fixed

**18'** **SW 1st. St. Bascule Bridge:** Opens on signal, except from 7:30 a.m. to 7:00 p.m., Mon. through Fri. (except federal holidays), when the draw need only open on the hour and half-hour; however, from 7:35 a.m. to 8:59 a.m., 12:05 p.m. to 12:59 p.m. and 4:35 p.m. to 5:59 p.m., the draw need not open.

**35'** **W. Flagler St. Bascule Bridge:** Opens on signal, except from 7:30 a.m. to 7:00 p.m., Mon. through Fri. (except federal holidays), when the draw need only open on the hour and half-hour; however, from 7:35 a.m. to 8:59 a.m., 12:05 p.m. to 12:59 p.m. and 4:35 p.m. to 5:59 p.m., the draw need not open.

**12'** **NW 5th St. Bascule Bridge:** Opens on signal, except from 7:30 a.m. to 7:00 p.m., Mon. through Fri. (except federal holidays), when the draw need only open on the hour and half-hour; however, from 7:35 a.m. to 8:59 a.m., 12:05 p.m. to 12:59 p.m. and 4:35 p.m. to 5:59 p.m., the draw need not open.

**22'** **NW 12th Ave. Bascule Bridge:** Opens on signal, except from 7:30 a.m. to 7:00 p.m., Mon. through Fri. (except federal holidays), when the draw need only open on the hour and half-hour; however, from 7:35 a.m. to 8:59 a.m., 12:05 p.m. to 12:59 p.m. and 4:35 p.m. to 5:59 p.m., the draw need not open.

**75'** **Dolphin Expressway Bridge:** Fixed

**17'** **NW 17th Ave. Bascule Bridge:** Opens on signal.

**25'** **NW 22nd Ave. Bascule Bridge:** Opens on signal.

## Florida Keys

**1091.6** **65'** **William M. Powell (Rickenbacker) Causeway Bridge:** Fixed

**1126.9** **65'** **Card Sound Bridge:** Fixed

**1134.1** **65'** **Jewfish Creek (U.S. 1) Bridge:** Fixed

**1152** **15'** **Tavernier Creek Bridge:** Fixed

**1156** **27'** **Snake Creek Bascule Bridge:** Opens on signal, except from 7:00 a.m. to 6:00 p.m., when the draw need open only on the hour.

**1157** **10'** **Whale Harbor Channel Bridge:** Fixed

**1162** **7'** **Upper Matecumbe Key Bridge:** Fixed

**1162** **10'** **Teatable Key Channel Bridge:** Fixed

**1163** **27'** **Indian Key Channel Bridge:** Fixed

**1164.5** **10'** **Lignumvitae Channel Bridge:** Fixed

**1168.5** **10'** **Channel Two Bridge:** Fixed

**1170** **65'** **Channel Five Bridge:** Fixed

**1176** **23'** **Long Key Viaduct Bridge:** Fixed

**1179** **8'** **Toms Harbor Cut Bridge:** Fixed

**1180 / 7'** — **Toms Harbor Channel Bridge:** Fixed

**1188 / 13'** — **Vaca Cut Bridge:** Fixed

**1194 / 19"** — **Knight Key Channel Twin Bridges:** Fixed

**1197 / 65'** — **Seven Mile (Moser Channel) Twin Bridges:** Fixed

**1205 / 20'** — **Bahia Honda Twin Bridges:** Fixed

**1209 / 11'** — **Spanish Harbor Channel Bridge:** Fixed

**1215 / 15'** — **Little Torch Key (Pine Channel) Bridge:** Fixed

**1215 / 40'** — **Niles Channel Bridge:** Fixed

# Florida's Gulf ICW (GIWW)

**34.3 / 22'** — **Boca Grande Swing Bridge:** Opens on signal, except from 7:00 a.m. to 6:00 p.m., Mon. through Fri., when the draw opens on the hour and half-hour. On Sat., Sun. and federal holidays the draw opens every 15 min. (Note: Vessels must request an opening.)

**43.5 / 26'** — **Tom Adams (Manasota Key) Bascule Bridge:** Opens on signal.

**49.9 / 26'** — **Manasota Beach Bascule Bridge:** Opens on signal.

**54.9 / 25'** — **Tamiami Trail (Circus) Twin Bridges:** Opens on signal.

**56.6 / 30'** — **Venice Ave. Bascule Bridge:** Opens on signal, except from 7:00 a.m. to 4:30 p.m., Mon. through Fri. (except holidays), when the draw opens only at 10 min. after the hour, 30 min. after the hour and 50 min. after the hour. Between 4:35 p.m. and 5:35 p.m., the draw need not open.

**56.9 / 30'** — **KMI (Hatchett Creek) Bascule Bridge:** Opens on signal, except from 7:00 a.m. to 4:20 p.m., Mon. through Fri. (except federal holidays), when the draw opens only on the hour, 20 min. after the hour and 40 min. after the hour. Between 4:25 p.m. and 5:25 p.m., the draw need not open. On Sat., Sun. and federal holidays from 7:30 a.m. to 6:00 p.m. the draw will open only on the hour and every 15 min. thereafter.

**59.3 / 14'** — **Albee Road (Casey Key) Bascule Bridge:** Opens on signal.

**63.0 / 9'** — **Blackburn Point Swing Bridge:** Opens on signal.

**68.6 / 18'** — **Stickney Point (SR 72) Bascule Bridge:** Opens on signal, except from 6:00 a.m. to 10:00 p.m., Mon. through Fri. (except federal holidays), when the draw need open only on the hour and every 20 min. thereafter.

**71.6 / 25'** — **Siesta Drive Bascule Bridge:** Opens on signal, except from 7:00 a.m. to 6:00 p.m., Mon. through Fri., when the draw need open only on the hour and every 20 min. thereafter. On weekends and federal holidays, from 11:00 a.m. to 6:00 p.m., the draw need open only on the hour and every 20 min. thereafter.

**73.6 / 65'** — **Ringling Causeway (SR 789) Bridge:** Fixed

**23'** — **New Pass Bascule Bridge (to Gulf):** The draw need only open on the hour, 20 min. past the hour, and 40 min. past the hour from 7:00 a.m. to 6:00 p.m. From 6:00 p.m. to 7:00 a.m., the bridge will open on signal only if at least 3-hour notice is given.

**17'** — **Longboat Pass (SR 789) Bascule Bridge (to Gulf):** Opens on signal.

**87.4 / 22'** — **Cortez (SR 684) Bascule Bridge:** Opens on signal, except from 6:00 a.m. to 7:00 p.m., when the draw need only open on the hour, 20 min. after the hour, and 40 min. after the hour. From Jan. 15 to May 15, from 6:00 a.m. to 7:00 p.m., the draw need only open on the hour and half-hour.

**89.2 / 24'** — **Anna Maria Island (Manatee Ave. West) Bascule Bridge:** Opens on signal except from 6:00 a.m. to 7:00 p.m., when the draw opens on the hour, 20 min. after the hour, and 40 min. after the hour. From Jan. 15 to May 15, from 6:00 a.m. to 7:00 p.m., the draw need only open on the hour and half-hour.

**99.0 / 180'** — **Sunshine Skyway (Central Span) Bridge:** Fixed

**110.5 / 65'** — **Sunshine Skyway (Meisner) Bridge:** Fixed

**114.0 / 18'** — **Pinellas Bayway 'A' Span Bridge:** Fixed

**113.0 / 25'** — **Pinellas Bayway 'E' (SR 679) Span Bridge:** Opens on signal, except from 7:00 a.m. to 9:00 p.m., when the draw need only open on the hour and half-hour. (New bridge due to be under construction in 2018.)

## FLORIDA BRIDGES MONITOR ((VHF)) CHANNEL 09

**114.0 / 65'** — **Pinellas Bayway 'C' Span Bridge:** Fixed

**117.7 / 23'** — **Corey Causeway (SR 693) Bascule Bridge:** Opens on signal, except from 8:00 a.m. to 7:00 p.m., Mon. through Fri., and from 10:00 a.m. to 7:00 p.m., Sat., Sun. and federal holidays, the draw will open only on the hour, 20 min. after the hour and 40 min. after the hour.

**118.9 / 21'** — **Treasure Island Causeway Bascule Bridge:** Opens on signal, except from 7:00 a.m. to 7:00 p.m., Mon. through Fri., when the draw will open on the hour, 20 min. after the hour and 40 min. after the hour and on the quarter hour and three-quarter hour on Sat., Sun. and federal holidays.

**27'** — **Johns Pass Twin Bascule Bridges (to Gulf):** Opens on signal. (Note: Located 1.25 miles SW of GIWW.)

**122.8 / 25'** — **Welch Causeway (SR 699) Bascule Bridge:** Opens on signal, except from 9:30 a.m. to 6:00 p.m. on Sat., Sun. and federal holidays, when the draw opens only on the hour, 20 min. after the hour and 40 min. after the hour.

**126.0 / 20'** — **Park Blvd. (SR 248) Bascule Bridge:** Opens on signal.

**129.3 / 25'** — **Indian Rocks Beach (CR 694) Bascule Bridge:** Opens on signal.

**131.8 / 75'** — **Belleair Causeway Bridge:** Fixed

**74'** — **Clearwater Pass (SR 183) Bridge (to Gulf):** Fixed

**136.0 / 74'** — **Clearwater Memorial Causeway (SR 60) Bridge:** Fixed

**141.9 / 18'** — **Dunedin–Honeymoon Island Bascule Bridge:** Opens on signal. (Note that charted clearance is 24 feet but actual clearance is 18.)

## GIWW, East of Harvey Lock (EHL)

**361.4 / 65'** — **Apalachicola–St. George Island Bridge:** Fixed

**351.4 / 65'** — **John Gorrie Memorial (U.S. 98/319) Bridge:** Fixed

**347.0 / 11'** — **Apalachicola Railroad Swing Bridge:** Maintained in the fully open-to-navigation position and untended.

## AL, MS & LA BRIDGES MONITOR ((VHF)) CHANNEL 13

**329.3 / 65'** — **White City (SR 71) Bridge:** Fixed

**75'** — **Port St. Joe (U.S. 98) Bridge (to Gulf):** Fixed

**315.4 / 65'** — **Overstreet (SR 386) Bridge:** Fixed

**295.4 / 50'** — **Dupont (U.S. 98) Bridge:** Fixed

**284.6 / 65'** — **Hathaway (U.S. 98) Bridge:** Fixed

**271.8 / 65'** — **West Bay Creek (SR 79) Bridge:** Fixed

**250.4 / 65'** — **Clyde B. Wells (Choctawhatchee Bay) Bridge:** Fixed

**234.2 / 64'** — **Mid-Bay Bridge:** Fixed

**49'** — **Destin Twin Bridges (to Gulf):** Fixed

**223.1 / 50'** — **Brooks Memorial Bridge:** Fixed

**206.7 / 50'** — **Navarre Beach Causeway (CR 399) Bridge:** Fixed

**189.1 / 65'** — **Pensacola Beach (SR 399) Twin Bridges:** Fixed

**171.8 / 73'** — **Gulf Beach (SR 292) Bridge:** Fixed

**54'** — **Perdido Pass Channel Bridge (to Gulf):** Fixed

**158.7 / 73'** — **Foley Beach Expressway Bridge:** Fixed

**154.9 / 73'** — **Gulf Shores Parkway (Portage Creek) Twin Bridges:** Fixed

**127.8 / 83'** — **Dauphin Island (SR 163) Causeway Bridge:** Fixed

## To Lake Pontchartrain (via Rigolets)

**11'** **Rigolets Railroad Swing Bridge:** Opens on signal. Located 1 mile NW of GIWW.

**66'** **Fort Pike (The Rigolets) Hwy. Bridge:** Fixed. Located 7 miles NW of GIWW.

**73'** **I-10 Bridge:** Fixed. Located 12 miles NW of GIWW.

**13'** **U.S. 11 Hwy. Bascule Bridge:** Opens on signal. Located 13.5 miles NW of GIWW.

**4'** **Norfolk & Southern Railroad Bascule Bridge:** Usually open. Located 13.5 miles NW of GIWW. (Note: Operated remotely.)

## Leaving Lake Pontchartrain

**3.3 / 44'** **Sen. Ted Hickey (Seabrook) Bascule Bridge:** Opens on signal from 7:00 a.m. to 8:00 p.m., except from 7:00 a.m. to 8:30 a.m. and 5:00 p.m. to 6:30 p.m. Mon. through Fri., when the bridge need not open. From 8:00 p.m. to 7:00 a.m., the bridge will open on signal only if at least 2-hour notice is given.

**3.2 / 1'** **Seabrook Railroad Bridge:** Closes 10 min. before arrival of regular train and 20 min. before Amtrak. If the bridge does not automatically re-open after a train, call on VHF.

**1.6 / 50'** **Danziger (U.S. 90) Lift Bridge:** Opens on signal only if 4 hours advance notice is given. (Call 504-437-3100.)

**1.3 / 115'** **I-10 Hwy. Bridge:** Fixed

**1.2 / 0'** **Almonaster Hwy. & Railroad Bascule Bridge:** Opens on signal.

**7.5 / 0'** **Florida Ave. & Southern Railroad Lift Bridge:** Opens on signal except 6:30 a.m. to 8:30 a.m. and 3:30 p.m. to 5:45 p.m., Mon. through Fri., when bridge will not open.

**6.7 / 40'** **North Claiborne Ave. (Judge Seeber) Lift Bridge:** Opens on signal except 6:30 a.m. to 8:30 a.m. and 3:30 p.m. to 5:45 p.m., Mon. through Fri., when bridge will not open.

**6.5** **Industrial Lock:** Opens on signal. (Note that bridges on the canal are restricted.) 504-947-2606

**6.2 / 0'** **St. Claude Ave. (SR 46) Bascule Bridge:** Opens on signal, except 6:30 a.m. to 8:30 a.m. and 3:30 p.m. to 5:45 p.m., Mon. through Fri., when bridge will not open.

## Leaving Lake Pontchartrain (Algiers Alternate Route)

**0.0** **Algiers Lock:** Opens on signal. 504-394-5714

**1.0 AAR / 100'** **General de Gaulle (SR 407) Bridge:** Fixed

**3.7 AAR / 2'** **Missouri Pacific Railroad Lift Bridge:** Usually open.

**3.8 AAR / 40'** **Belle Chase Hwy. (SR 23) Lift Bridge:** Opens on signal, except from 6:00 a.m. to 8:30 a.m. and from 3:30 p.m. to 5:30 p.m., Mon. through Fri. (except federal holidays), when the draw need not open.

## GIWW, West of Harvey Lock (WHL)

**2.5 / 150'** **Crescent City Connection Bridges #1 & #2:** Fixed

**0** **Harvey Lock:** Opens on signal from 7:00 a.m. to 3:30 p.m. 504-366-4683. After hours call 504-366-5187.

**0.1 / 7'** **Union Pacific Railroad Bascule Bridge:** Opens on signal.

**0.1 / 7'** **Harvey Canal (SR 18) Bascule Bridge:** Opens on signal.

**0.8 / 95'** **West Bank Expressway Twin Bridges:** Fixed

**2.8 / 45'** **Lapalco Blvd. Bascule Bridge:** Opens on signal, except from 6:30 a.m. to 8:30 a.m. and from 3:45 p.m. to 5:45 p.m., Mon. through Fri. (except holidays), when the draw need not open.

**11.9 / 73'** **Crown Point Hwy. Bridge:** Fixed

**35.2 / 73'** **Larose Hwy. (SR 308) Bridge:** Fixed

**35.6 / 35'** **Larose-Bourg Cutoff (SR 1) Lift Bridge:** Opens on signal.

**49.8 / 0'** **Bayou Blue Pontoon Bridge:** Opens on signal. Wait until bridge is fully open before approaching. Do not proceed until underwater cables have had time to sink to the bottom.

**54.4 / 73'** **Prospect Blvd. (SR 3087) Bridge:** Fixed

**57.6 / 73'** **Park Ave. Bridge:** Fixed

**57.7 / 73'** **Main Street Bridge:** Fixed

**59.9 / 40'** **Bayou Dularge (SR 315) Bascule Bridge:** Opens on signal, except from 6:30 a.m. to 8:30 a.m., from 11:45 a.m. to 12:15 p.m., from 12:45 p.m. to 1:15 p.m. and from 4:30 p.m. to 6:00 p.m., Mon. through Fri. (except Federal holidays), when that the bridge need not open.

**93.0** **Bayou Boeuf Lock:** Opens on signal. 985-384-7626

**94.3** **Cable Ferry:** Operates from 5:30 a.m. to 10:30 p.m. Do not proceed until underwater cables have had time to sink to the bottom.

**113.0 / 73'** **North Bend (SR 317) Bridge:** Fixed

**129.7** **Cable Ferry:** Operates 24 hours a day. Do not proceed until underwater cables have had time to sink to the bottom.

**134.0 / 73'** **Cypremort (Louisa) Bascule Bridge:** Opens on signal only if 24-hour notice is given.

**163.0** **Leland Bowman Lock:** Opens on signal. 337-893-6790. After hours and on weekends call 337-893-4412.

**170.3 / 73'** **Forked Island Bridge:** Fixed

**178.4** **Cable Ferry:** Operates during daylight hours. Do not proceed until underwater cables have had time to sink to the bottom.

**219.8 / 73'** **Gibbstown (SR 27) Bridge:** Fixed

**231.5 / 0'** **Grand Lake (SR 384) Pontoon Bridge:** Opens on signal. Wait until bridge is fully open before approaching. Do not proceed until underwater cables have had time to sink to the bottom.

**238.0 / 0'** **Black Bayou (SR 384) Pontoon Bridge:** Opens on signal except 6:00 a.m. to 8:00 a.m. and 2:00 p.m. to 4:00 p.m., Mon. through Fri., when the bridge need not open. Wait until bridge is fully open before approaching. Do not proceed until underwater cables have had time to sink to the bottom.

**238.2** **Calcasieu Lock:** Opens on signal. 337-477-1482

**243.8 / 50'** **Ellender (SR 27) Lift Bridge:** Opens on signal only if at least 4-hour notice is given. 800-752-6706

**288.8 / 73'** **West Port Arthur (SR 87) Bridge:** Fixed

**319.3 / 73'** **High Island Bridge:** Fixed

**356.0 / 13'** **Pelican Island Causeway Bascule Bridge:** Opens on signal, except from 6:40 a.m. to 8:10 a.m., 12 noon to 1:00 p.m. and 4:15 p.m. to 5:15 p.m. Mon. through Fri. (except federal holidays), when the draw need not open.

**357.2 / 8'** **Galveston Causeway Railroad Bascule Bridge:** Opens on signal.

**357.3 / 73'** **Gulf Freeway (I-45) Twin Bridges:** Fixed

**393.8 / 73'** **Surfside Beach (SR 232) Bridge:** Fixed

**397.6 / 73'** **Freeport (Bryan Beach) Bridge:** Fixed

**418.0 / 0'** **Caney Creek Pontoon (Farm Road 457) Bridge:** Opens on signal. Wait until bridge is fully open before approaching. Do not proceed until underwater cables have had time to sink to the bottom.

**440.7 / 73'** **Market Street Bridge:** Fixed

**442** **Colorado River Locks (East & West Gates):** Opens on the hour. 979-863-7842 (x2005)

**533.1 / 48'** **Aransas Pass (SR 361) Bridge:** Fixed

**552.7 / 73'** **JFK Causeway Bridge:** Fixed

**665.1 / 73'** **Queen Isabella Causeway Bridge (SR 100):** Fixed

**666.0 / 0'** **Port Isabel–Long Island Pontoon Bridge:** Opens on signal, except from 5:00 a.m. to 8:00 p.m., Mon. through Fri. (excluding federal, state, and local holidays), when the draw need open only on the hour. The draw must open on signal at anytime for commercial vessels. When the draw is open for a commercial vessel, waiting pleasure craft must be passed. Wait until bridge is fully open before approaching. Do not proceed until underwater cables have had time to sink to the bottom.

**SKIPPER'S HANDBOOK**

# Skipper's Notes

# Crossing to the Bahamas

## The Gulf Stream

For vessels crossing between the Florida east coast and Bahamas, the Gulf Stream is the principal navigational consideration. It is a wide, deep and warm river of fast moving water flowing north, where sea conditions are deeply influenced by the wind. Crossing this river requires careful planning while considering the characteristics of your vessel and crew and the expected wind and weather.

The Gulf Stream current generally begins a few miles out from the Florida coast, and extends for approximately 43 nautical miles eastward. The current will gradually increase as you travel east, reaching a maximum of roughly 3.6 knots about 8 to 11 miles from the western wall. The current gradually subsides to little or no current at the eastern edge of the Stream. The average northerly speed over the 43 mile width is 2.5 knots while the average direction of flow is 1 degree True when north of Lake Worth Inlet, and about 2 degrees True south of the inlet.

The sea state in the Stream is largely a function of the prevailing ocean swell in the area combined with local wind generated waves. The National Weather Service marine forecast provides the Significant Wave Height expected for the Stream, that is, the average height of the highest one-third of the combined swells and wind waves. Be sure to check this when planning your departure. For a useful rule of thumb, south to southeast winds at 10 knots will develop 2-foot seas; 15 knots, 4- to 5-foot seas; 20 knots, 7-foot seas; and 25 knots, 9-foot seas.

For most cruising boats it is generally not advisable to cross the stream in winds higher than 15 knots. And it is never a great idea to cross in winds with any significant northerly component as winds against the current cause a very steep, choppy sea. Winds of 10 knots or less offer a relatively comfortable ride for the typical semi-displacement recreational boat 35 to 45 feet in length, provided there are no significant swells in addition to the wind waves.

In winter, the location of the Stream will sometimes be marked by mist rising from its warm waters, significantly warmer than the colder coastal water. In winter too, and whenever a northerly wind is blowing, the horizon looking toward the Stream will often look jagged or saw-toothed. Sailors observing from inshore say there are "elephants" out there–giant square topped waves are kicked up by the Gulf Stream's determination to win its way north against the wind. In bright sunlight the Gulf Stream is a deep cobalt blue in which if the sun is right, you may see light dancing in its depths. You will usually see blond colored patches of Sargasso weed drifting in its waters. Fish will often congregate near and under these patches. You can be sure you have entered the Stream when the water temperature noticeably increases over a short distance from the near shore ocean temperature. If you are navigating using GPS, you will likely see the effects of the current quickly as your course and speed over ground change significantly.

# Magnetic Heading & Time-To-Cross

| Direction (M) Distance (nm) | From | To | Top Number = Heading to Steer (Magnetic) Bottom Number = Time Between Waypoints (Hours) Based on Boat Speed (Knots) | | | | | | | | |
|---|---|---|---|---|---|---|---|---|---|---|---|
| | | | 5 kn | 6 kn | 7 kn | 8 kn | 9 kn | 10 kn | 15 kn | 20 kn | 25 kn |
| 312° 82.4 nm | West End | Fort Pierce | 296° 14.5 | 299° 12.3 | 301° 10.6 | 302° 9.4 | 303° 8.4 | 304° 7.6 | 307° 5.2 | 308° 4.0 | 309° 3.2 |
| 302° 67.5 nm | West End | Saint Lucie | 283° 12.4 | 286° 10.4 | 289° 9.0 | 290° 7.9 | 292° 7.1 | 293° 6.4 | 296° 4.3 | 297° 3.3 | 298° 2.6 |
| 282° 55.8 nm | West End | Lake Worth | 259° 11.9 | 263° 9.7 | 266° 8.2 | 268° 7.1 | 269° 6.3 | 271° 5.6 | 274° 3.7 | 276° 2.8 | 277° 2.2 |
| 101° 55.8 nm | Lake Worth | West End | 124° 12.3 | 120° 9.9 | 117° 8.4 | 115° 7.3 | 114° 6.4 | 112° 5.7 | 109° 3.8 | 107° 2.8 | 106° 2.2 |
| 65° 69.4 nm | Port Everglades | West End | 83° 12.0 | 80° 10.1 | 78° 8.8 | 76° 7.8 | 75° 7.0 | 74° 6.3 | 71° 4.3 | 70° 3.3 | 69° 2.7 |
| 111° 69.0 nm | Lake Worth | Freeport | 129° 15.6 | 126° 12.6 | 124° 10.6 | 122° 9.2 | 121° 8.1 | 120° 7.2 | 117° 4.7 | 115° 3.5 | 114° 2.8 |
| 78° 74.5 nm | Port Everglades | Freeport | 95° 13.9 | 92° 11.7 | 90° 10.0 | 88° 8.8 | 87° 7.9 | 86° 7.1 | 83° 4.8 | 82° 3.6 | 81° 2.9 |
| 258° 74.5 nm | Freeport | Port Everglades | 242° 17.6 | 245° 14.1 | 247° 11.8 | 248° 10.2 | 249° 8.9 | 250° 8.0 | 253° 5.2 | 254° 3.8 | 255° 3.1 |
| 291° 69.0 nm | Freeport | Lake Worth | 273° 13.6 | 276° 11.3 | 278° 9.6 | 280° 8.4 | 281° 7.5 | 282° 6.8 | 285° 4.5 | 287° 3.4 | 288° 2.7 |
| 336° 74.6 nm | Bimini | Lake Worth | 319° 10.7 | 322° 9.3 | 324° 8.2 | 325° 7.4 | 327° 6.7 | 327° 6.2 | 330° 4.4 | 332° 3.4 | 332° 2.7 |
| 306° 48.2 nm | Bimini | Port Everglades | 279° 8.6 | 284° 7.2 | 287° 6.2 | 289° 5.5 | 291° 4.9 | 293° 4.4 | 297° 3.0 | 299° 2.3 | 301° 1.9 |
| 281° 43.8 nm | Bimini | Miami | 251° 9.9 | 257° 7.9 | 260° 6.6 | 263° 5.7 | 265° 5.0 | 267° 4.5 | 271° 2.9 | 274° 2.2 | 275° 1.8 |
| 125° 48.2 nm | Port Everglades | Bimini | 152° 14.3 | 147° 10.8 | 144° 8.7 | 142° 7.3 | 140° 6.3 | 138° 5.6 | 134° 3.5 | 132° 2.6 | 131° 2.0 |
| 101° 43.8 nm | Miami | Bimini | 130° 10.2 | 125° 8.1 | 121° 6.7 | 118° 5.8 | 116° 5.1 | 115° 4.5 | 110° 3.0 | 108° 2.2 | 106° 1.8 |

*Corrected courses and estimated elapsed times at varying speeds under normal sea conditions*

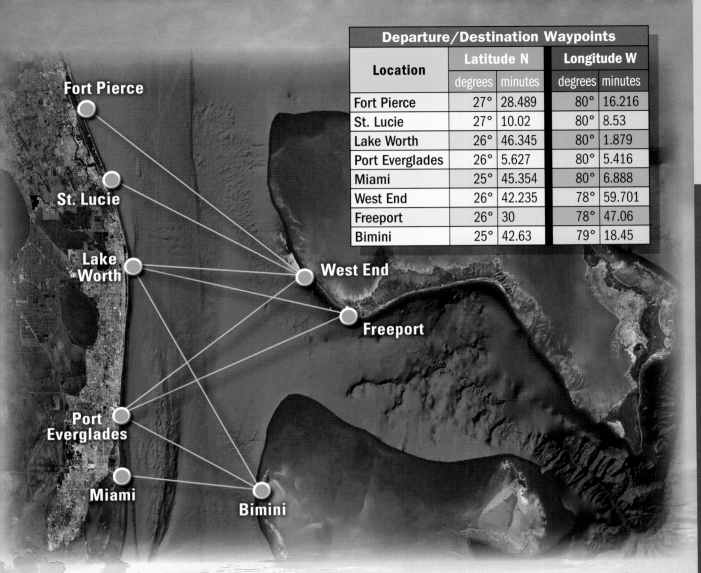

| Departure/Destination Waypoints | | | | |
|---|---|---|---|---|
| Location | Latitude N | | Longitude W | |
| | degrees | minutes | degrees | minutes |
| Fort Pierce | 27° | 28.489 | 80° | 16.216 |
| St. Lucie | 27° | 10.02 | 80° | 8.53 |
| Lake Worth | 26° | 46.345 | 80° | 1.879 |
| Port Everglades | 26° | 5.627 | 80° | 5.416 |
| Miami | 25° | 45.354 | 80° | 6.888 |
| West End | 26° | 42.235 | 78° | 59.701 |
| Freeport | 26° | 30 | 78° | 47.06 |
| Bimini | 25° | 42.63 | 79° | 18.45 |

## Planning to Cross

Crossing the Gulf Stream is like traversing a wide, moving walkway—your boat is being steadily pushed northward. The longer you spend in the Stream, the further north you will be unless you compensate for that movement. Your best strategy is to take advantage of that push, starting as far south, or upstream, of your destination as possible. To the extent that is not possible, careful planning and navigation can minimize the time it takes to cross.

NOAA weather broadcasts give daily information about the Gulf Stream, including its width, speed, distance offshore at different locations along the Florida coast, and its temperature. Many online sources also give daily, detailed maps of the Stream. But for planning, a reasonable rule of thumb is to assume the entire distance you have to run from a Florida departure to a point lying along the W 79° 15.000' line of longitude

will be subject to an average 2.5-knot, north-flowing current. For fast boats, this may have relatively little effect on your course and time to cross. But for slower boats, particularly under sail, the effect is profound and must be taken into account. There are essentially three ways to navigate this challenge:

- In the days before GPS and chartplotters, boats would compute a heading based on the average current and then steer that constant heading. The disadvantage to this approach is that it is based solely on averages, while the actual current and wind will vary from day to day and during the crossing. But it usually works because it generally gets the boat close enough to your destination that it can be recognized.

- The boat can be steered to stay pointed at the destination waypoint. This works, but is not the most efficient method and will take more time.

- For boats equipped with GPS, a chartplotter and preferably autopilot, steer to constantly keep the boat on the route from starting point to destination. The actual heading will vary constantly; adjusting to the actual current and wind drift as you move along the route. This is the most efficient way to navigate the crossing.

There are as many opinions on when to depart Florida and at what time to arrive at your Bahamian waypoint as there are vessels crossing the Gulf Stream. Night crossings are common, but they do present the additional challenge of traveling amidst the ever-growing number of freighters and cruise ships in very busy shipping lanes to and from Florida. Dawn departures provide easier travel in the shipping lanes and arrival in Bahamian waters with the sun behind you. And if you decide to continue across the banks, night passage will be in many ways easier there than in the Gulf Stream. You should consider your speed of travel, destination, and what conditions are expected when you arrive. A vessel departing for and planning to visit North Bimini will have a much different crossing schedule than one headed non-stop to Nassau. Regardless, pay attention to the weather and don't develop forward-only vision.

Be vigilant about frequent checks for other vessels to starboard, port and aft! Don't become another victim rundown by an inattentive skipper traveling on autopilot. And don't forget to file that float plan. (A number of free iOS and Android apps allow you to create a float plan and email it to participants or emergency contacts.)

## The Constant Heading Table

If you choose the constant heading approach to your passage, the Magnetic Heading and Time-to-Cross table included with the satellite graphic provides for a given boat speed, the single heading to steer and the time to cross on that heading. This data will always be an approximation but is a good estimate for your constant heading, and also a good tool for planning passage time if you will be steering to stay on a route line. The tables are based on the WGS84 datum and 2017 magnetic variation from the National Centers for Environmental Data at NOAA. The results are accurate to within one degree. The current was assumed to be the average current in the Gulf Stream, 2.5 knots. They do not consider wind drift or leeway; compensating for these for your vessel will improve accuracy.

The from/to locations correspond to the waypoints identified in the Departure/Destination Waypoints table.

They can be used regardless of your destination, but you will have to adjust your total trip plan for additional distances to be run.

For example, assume you want to leave from Lake Worth inlet and go to West End. The fourth entry in the table shows the distance traveled between these waypoints is 55.8 nautical miles at a bearing of 101 degrees magnetic. Also assume you plan to travel at 8 knots boat speed. The table shows that at 8 knots, you must steer on average 115 degrees magnetic to arrive near the destination waypoint. The time enroute will be approximately 7.3 hours between the two waypoints. So if you plan to leave your anchorage or slip early, arriving at the departure waypoint at 7 am, you should arrive at the destination waypoint at approximately 2:18 p.m. Of course you need to allow for the time required to get from there to your final overnight stop, wherever that may be. Remember that if you use GPS and remain on the route line between points, your heading will vary with the current and wind conditions, but you will average 115 degrees magnetic over that time. On the other hand, if you steer a constant 115M, you will deviate from the route line, but should end up at or very near the destination.

## Listen to the Forecast

The Gulf Stream is a relatively constant, predictable force. The weather is not. Listen to the forecasts. Believe the bad ones, and don't trust the good ones. Go to the beach if you can and look out over the ocean. What is happening out there? As stated before, the most difficult and dangerous time for any vessel to cross the Gulf Stream is when the wind is from the north, including the northeast and the northwest. Whether you are running a 180-foot motor yacht or skippering an 18-foot sailboat, northerly conditions are definitely not the ones in which to cross. Remember that the Gulf Stream is flowing north at 2.5 knots. When the wind blows from the north, it is like rubbing a cat the wrong way; all the fur kicks up and the results are the "elephants" mentioned earlier. These are high, ugly waves as closely spaced as elephants holding each other's tails in a circus parade. In those conditions, the Gulf Stream is not where you want to be.

Weather is available on the VHF NOAA weather channels, from numerous online sources, and with many weather apps. Pay close attention, plan carefully, pick your weather window and enjoy a pleasant crossing to the wonderful Bahamas.

# Inside vs. Outside Mileage

Heading north or south, many skippers mistakenly assume that they will shorten their trips by going out to sea and running down the coast. The distances shown here—both inside (red boxes) and outside (blue boxes)—demonstrate that this is not necessarily true.

While outside distances from sea buoy to sea buoy are virtually the same as the ICW distances, the mileage in and out to the buoys adds to the total distance. These differences, which may seem insignificant at first, do add up: along the coast, the total ICW mileage from the St. Marys Entrance to Government Cut is 374 nm; outside the distance is just 29 miles shorter at 345 nm (assuming you can handle the distances between the big ship inlets).

Skippers should consider the safety factor, as well. Some of the outside stretches are easy while others can be more hazardous. Watch the weather carefully; it can be uncomfortable outside despite the inside passage being calm and unaffected. Do, however, be prepared to run outside for a day if the ICW is obstructed locally by a malfunctioning bridge or severe shoaling. (The fixed Julia Tuttle Bridge at Mile 1087.2 sets the restricted vertical clearance at 56 feet. See the bridge tables for more information.)

Most importantly, prepare your boat early, plot the course in advance and only go if the forecast is good.

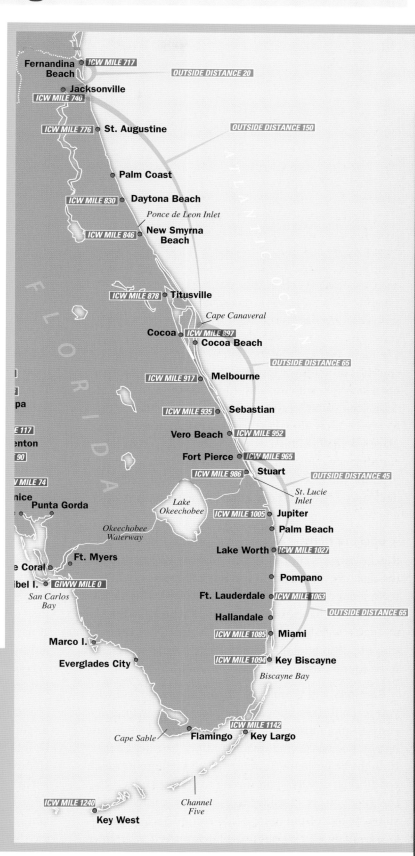

## Outside Distance to Big Ship Inlets

**St. Marys Entrance to St. Johns Entrance: 20 nm**

**St. Johns Entrance to Port Canaveral Inlet: 150 nm**

**Port Canaveral Inlet to Fort Pierce Inlet: 65 nm**

**Fort Pierce Inlet to Lake Worth Inlet: 45 nm**

**Lake Worth to Port Everglades: 40 nm**

**Port Everglades to Government Cut: 20 nm**

# Southern Inlets

For many boaters, the thought of leaving the safe confines of the Intracoastal Waterway (ICW) for the open seas is terrifying, and, for some of us, that is as it should be. While the open waters of the Atlantic can be serene, they can also turn nasty; therefore, it is no place for the unskilled or poorly prepared. Plan for every contingency while underway. If things start to go wrong, head for the next inlet and deal with the problems from dockside. There are no awards for being foolish when you are offshore.

**Offshore Runs:** Despite what you may have heard, it is not always shorter to run offshore. When you add the distances involved in leaving and returning to the ICW, you are often better off time-wise staying inside. Having said that, for those mariners who have the skills, a capable well-found vessel and the mettle to venture out into the deep blue off the coast, the beauty and challenge to be found offshore is reward enough.

**Cautions and Warnings:** If conditions are bad when you reach the sea buoy for an inlet, you may find yourself in an untenable position, being driven ashore by wind or waves and unable to find the inlet buoys. It might be far better to remain well offshore in rough conditions, possibly continuing to a better inlet, unless the inlet you are considering is a Class A inlet for big ships, or one of the more easily run inlets, such as Government Cut. Should you find yourself at an inlet

and needing direction, a call on VHF Channel 16 for local knowledge is likely to bring you a response. Sea Tow and TowBoatU.S. are two other knowledgeable sources. The Coast Guard may also be able to assist you.

**Online Resources:** Prior to your voyage, there are a number of online sources that can familiarize you with the inlets; the Waterway Guide website (waterwayguide.com) has both chart and satellite views of the inlets via the Waterway Explorer, plus cruising details from local boaters, both of which are quite useful. Obviously, this guide can give you helpful advice, particularly on what you will find inside the inlet. You will also need Coast Pilots, which can be downloaded free at nauticalcharts.noaa.gov. With inlets, it is also vital that you keep up with the *Local Notice to Mariners*, which are available online at navcen.uscg.gov/ and then click on the LNMs tab. The Tide Tables for the areas you are traveling through are also necessary and are provided in this guide and online at tidesandcurrents.noaa.gov.

Some inlets have recent U.S. Army Corps of Engineers surveys in Adobe PDF format, which can be found at saw.usace.army.mil/Missions/Navigation/HydrographicSurveys/InletsCrossings.aspx. These particular charts, when available, provide waypoint information, although it takes some patience to familiarize yourself with the format. Of particular use are the centerline waypoints and controlling depths provided within the inlet. The exact locations of all aids to navigation in the inlet are also noted. However, be advised that the markers at some inlets are moved on a regular basis and the buoys should be honored.

Check carefully the date of the survey to determine its applicability for your passage. Inlets change rapidly and even recent surveys may be inaccurate.

**Skills and Equipment:** Before you begin an offshore passage, take an honest accounting of your vessel, your crew and yourself. Is each of you up to the task? Is the vessel properly outfitted? Do you have the necessary safety equipment, charts, long distance communications gear such as single sideband radio (SSB), an Emergency Position Indicating Radio Beacon (EPIRB) and life raft? Do you and your crew have adequate experience in boating and navigation to attempt an offshore coastal passage?

Always file a float plan with a reliable person. If all your good planning goes awry, this could well be your "ace in the hole" and someone will be able to locate you if you need assistance. A sample float plan is provided in this guide.

**About the Weather:** Mother Nature is capricious and the National Weather Service is not omniscient. Sometimes a day that begins with clear skies promised by the weatherman ends in tumult, with the captain swearing he will buy a motor home—in Idaho no less—if only he can get safely into port. Check the weather using as many sources as possible. If you have access to weather routing services, they are a good option, particularly for longer offshore passages. You are seeking a weather window with enough space on each side to get you safely out and back in, with room for unexpected contingencies. Plan your trip so that you enter in daylight, with the tide, particularly if your boat is slow or underpowered. Remember that wind against tide can create short, steep waves in an inlet that can quickly make even a ship channel impassable for slower boats.

A safe offshore passage is an accomplishment. You will always remember your first one; the serenity of a calm dark night passage, the thrill of the sun rising after an endless night and the quiet confidence you feel deep inside as you bring your boat to anchor or dockside after many miles outside. Knowing that you have a convenient inlet to duck into should conditions offshore deteriorate certainly adds confidence, as well as an additional margin of safety, to your plans.

## Florida's East Coast Inlets

*Big ship inlets are denoted with the following symbol:*

## Gulf Coast Inlets

The big ship channels on the Gulf Coast are Boca Grande Channel, Tampa Bay Entrance, St. Andrew Bay Entrance, St. Joseph Bay Entrance, Pensacola Bay Entrance, Mobile Bay Entrance, and Galveston Entrance. There are several smaller channels (labeled as "Passes") that are available for smaller vessels. See Waterway Guide's Explorer for details (waterwayguide.com).

Note: All inlets require some degree of caution. Weather, depths and tides are important factors for safe navigation. Be aware that in any inlet shifting bottom conditions can result in aids to navigation being incorrectly located or nonexistent. Charts provided here are not intended to be used for navigation.

# St. Marys (Cumberland Sound) Entrance

**Sea Buoy:** No sea buoy. Steer to a waypoint of N 30° 42.630', W 81° 14.630' (2.5 nm seaward of the channel). Then steer to N 30° 42.690', W 81° 21.520' to access the center of the channel at red marker "10."

**Overview:** Big ship inlet. Most northerly of the Florida inlets located between Cumberland Island (GA) and Fort Clinch State Park.

**Navigation:** Very straightforward and well marked. From red marker "10" proceed due west into Cumberland Sound.

**Cautions and hazards:** Some shoal sections to the north of the channel inside the jetty. Current is very strong and dictates appropriate boat handling to compensate. Slower boats are well advised to time their passages for slack water or a favorable tide.

**Depth:** Refer to the most recent NOAA charts or your onboard navigation device.

**ICW connection:** ICW crosses the inlet. For either north or south, follow the banks, which remain deep outside of the channel.

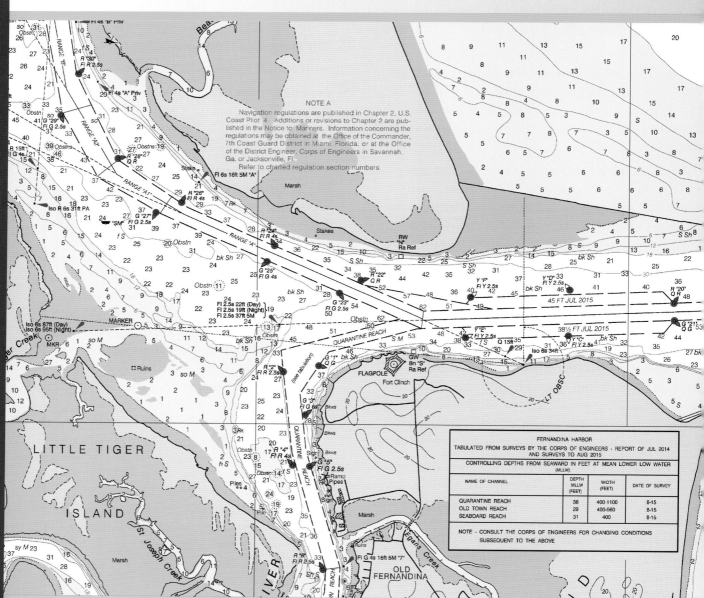

SOUTHERN INLETS

**Nearby facilities:** Fernandina Beach to the south offers full facilities at several marinas as well as an anchorage with mooring balls. Anchorage to the north (beside Cumberland Island) is managed by the National Park Service.

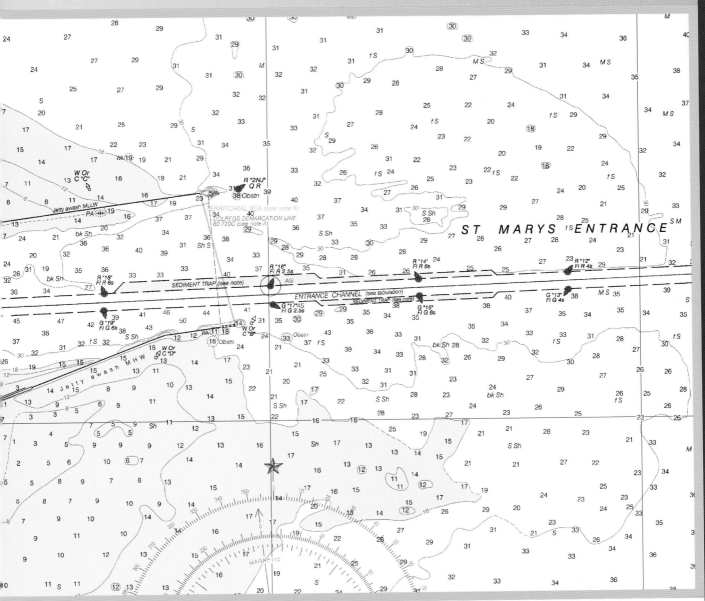

**Use Chart 11503**

# St. Johns River Entrance

**Sea Buoy:** RW sea buoy "SJ" is located at N 30° 23.600', W 81° 19.140'.

**Overview:** Big ship inlet frequented by freighters, U.S. Naval vessels and commercial fishermen, especially shrimpers, who you will see in the early morning hours. Wide, deep and trouble-free entrance. Naval Station Mayport is to the south of the entrance.

**Navigation:** Approach from the east. Ocean approach landmark is St. Johns Light, which stands 83 feet above the shore and 1 nm south of the St. Johns north jetty. Offshore waypoint is located nearly 3 nm from the jetties. Use waypoint N 30° 23.860', W 81° 22.000', which is located about halfway between flashing red buoy "4" and flashing red buoy "6" and over 0.25 nm from the jetties. Follow buoys in. Landmarks include a tower at Jacksonville Beach and a water tank (painted in a red and white checkerboard design) at the naval station.

**Cautions and hazards:** None, other than the large vessel traffic, which can be heavy at times. Slower boats are well advised to pick their tide coming in here, or settle

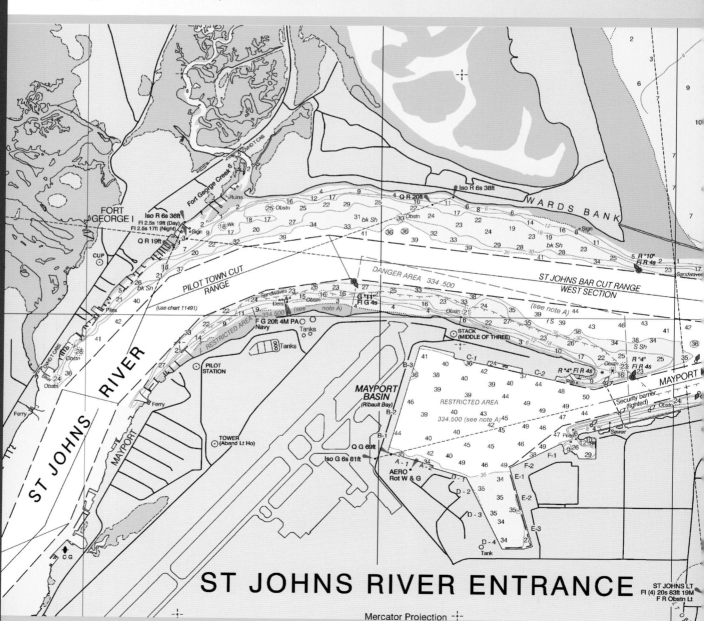

ST JOHNS RIVER ENTRANCE

Mercator Projection

SOUTHERN INLETS

own for a very long transit; the tide can run up to to 4 knots.

**Depth:** Refer to the most recent NOAA charts or your nboard navigation device.

**ICW connection:** ICW is 5 nm from the jetties. If going outh, be sure of your markers; there is an underwater etty at the south entrance to the ICW channel. The urrent here can also quickly push you out of the hannel. Caution is advised.

**Nearby facilities:** The nearest marinas are 3 nm inside he jetties in Mayport.

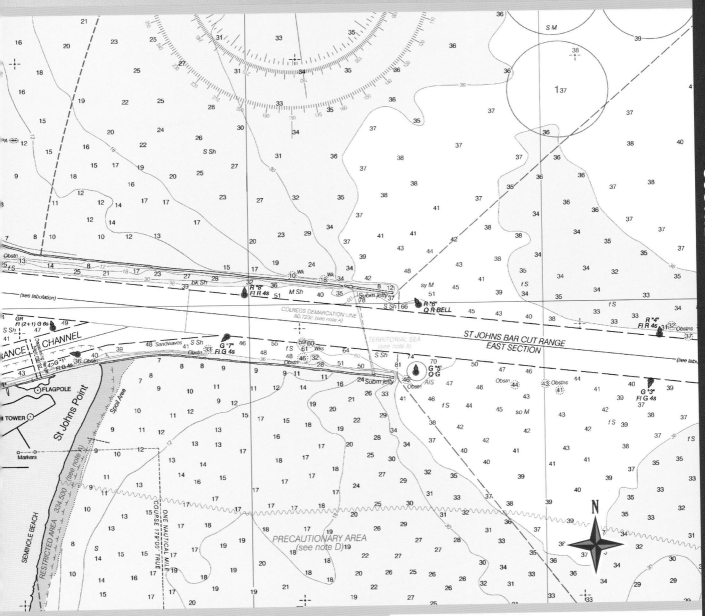

Use Chart 11490

# St. Augustine Inlet

**Sea Buoy:** RW sea buoy "STA" is east and north of N 29° 55.000', W 81°15.230'.

**Overview:** Located north of Anastasia State Park.

**Navigation:** From the sea buoy, proceed slightly south of east towards the inlet, paying close attention to the markers. You will see a tall cross ahead on shore providing an approximate range to the inlet, which will help you to orient yourself. Once past Cape Francis on the south, bear to the middle and south side of the channel as you proceed. There is a large shoal at marker "2A." If headed north once inside the inlet, note that you keep red nun buoy "60" to port, as that is part of the ICW.

**Cautions and hazards:** There is some infrequent dredging activity in this inlet, but it should be regarded as a fair weather-only inlet with no protection until well inside the inlet. There are extensive shoals with breaking water to the north and south of the inlet extending well offshore. Proceed with caution at slow speed as the temporary markers–which are frequently moved by the USCG to mark deeper water–can be very difficult to see. The currents in this inlet are very powerful and dictate appropriate boat handling skills as well as advanced local knowledge.

**Depth:** Refer to the most recent NOAA charts or your onboard navigation device.

**ICW connection:** Connects directly to the ICW. If going north, stay closest to the eastern side of the channel to avoid the marked shoal to port.

**Nearby facilities:** There are several marinas to both the north and south of the inlet, including in Salt Creek. St. Augustine provides a mooring field to the north and south of the Bridge of Lions and in Salt Creek to the south.

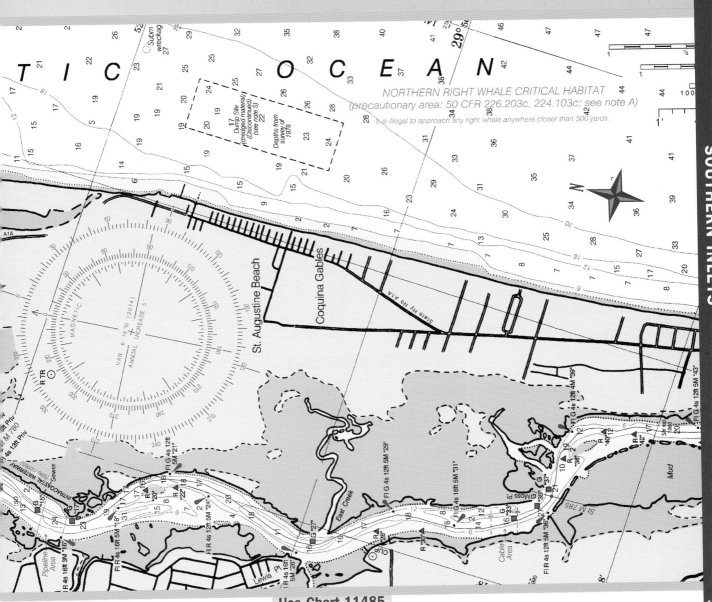

# Ponce de Leon (New Smyrna) Inlet

**Sea Buoy:** Red buoy "2" is located at N 29° 04.700', W 80° 53.700'.

**Overview:** Used extensively by locals and sport fishermen and convenient point to enter or leave the ICW between Daytona and Cape Canaveral. Sometimes referred to as New Smyrna Inlet. This is a fair weather inlet only.

**Navigation:** Coming from the offshore waypoint, the jetty on the north side of the inlet provides protection from north and northeast swells. Hold close to the jetty until inside the inlet, as there is a shoal building north and east from green buoy "7." The USCG station is located on the south channel of the inlet and will respond to calls for inlet conditions, and the local TowBoat US is up to date on local conditions. Both can be hailed on VHF Channel 16. For a live view of the inlet, visit volusia.com/explore-a-city/ponce-inlet.

**Cautions and hazards:** Seemingly constant reclamation, dredging and seawall construction, yet shoaling has been reported in the approaches both north and south of the inlet coming from the ICW. Inlet markers are continually moved by the USCG to reflect deep water. Expect substantial traffic at all hours. This is a fair weather inlet only, particularly for weather out of the south and east, which creates large swells into the inlet. Local knowledge is strongly advised before using this inlet.

**Depth:** Refer to the most recent NOAA charts or your onboard navigation device.

**ICW connection:** The inlet connects directly to the ICW with one channel leading north, another south. The north channel is not as well marked as the south channel until well inside and shows charted depths of just 7 feet.

**Nearby facilities:** There is one marina immediately to the north of the inlet in the north channel and several more in New Smyrna Beach. There are anchoring possibilities as well.

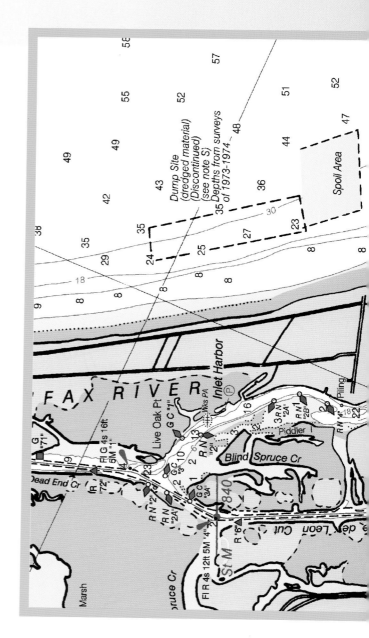

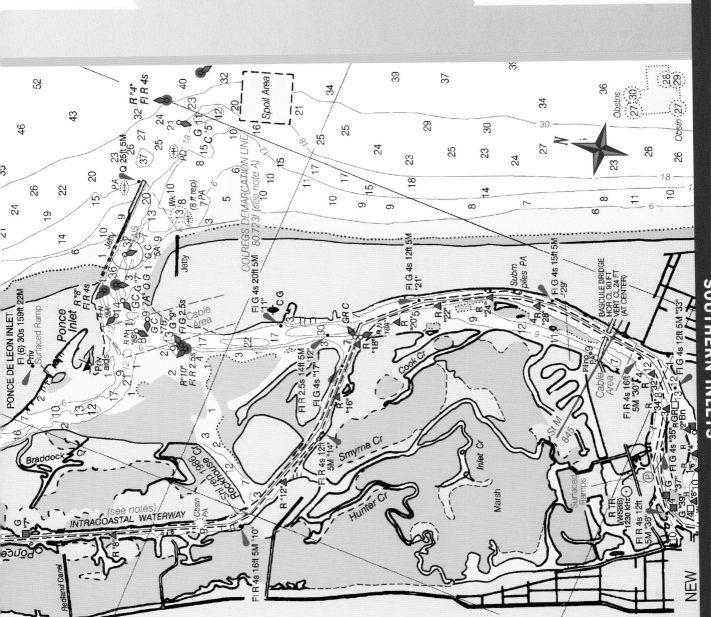

Use Chart 11485

# Port Canaveral Inlet

**Sea Buoy:** Flashing red buoy "4" (2.5 sec) is located at N 28° 22.560', W 80° 31.740'.

**Overview:** Well-marked, deep ship inlet protected from the north by the long and shallow Southeast Shoal off Cape Canaveral. The lock inside the inlet eliminates current, making this one of the easier to use inlets on the Florida coast.

**Navigation:** Southbound cruisers can make for N 28° 23.490', W 80° 33.000' after rounding red buoy "4," while northbound craft could go in much closer, at N 28° 24.570', W 80° 34.480'. The channel is well marked; simply run down the channel, turning due west at Middle Reach. Lock operating hours are 6:00 a.m. to 9:30 p.m., 365 days a year. (The observation area is open 6:00 a.m. to 9:00 p.m.) Lockage takes 20 to 30 minutes.

**Webcam:** For a live view of the port, visit portcanaveralwebcam.com.

**Cautions and hazards:** Coming from the north, the Southeast Shoal off Cape Canaveral keeps boaters several miles offshore. Stay east of W 80° 27.00' before turning in to the sea buoy after rounding red buoy "4" at N 28° 23.470', W 80° 29.100' marking the southern edge of the shoal. Note that this cuts off the offshore waypoint. From the south, cruisers can approach from within 0.5 nm of the shore in depths greater than 20 feet.

**Depth:** Refer to the most recent NOAA charts or your onboard navigation device.

**ICW connection:** Inlet is 7.5 nm from the ICW (across the Banana River).

**Nearby facilities:** There are several marinas inside the inlet, as well as a U.S. Customs office for clearing in.

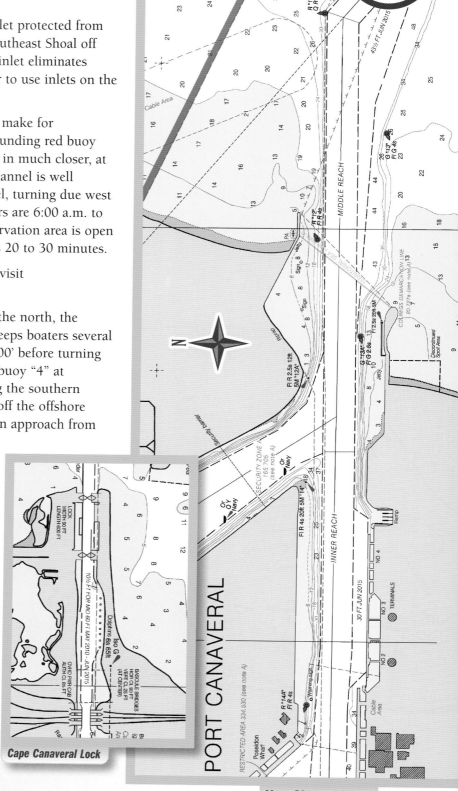

*Cape Canaveral Lock*

Use Chart 11478

# Sebastian Inlet

**Sea Buoy:** No sea buoy. Steer to waypoint N 27° 51.675', W 80° 26.500', which will place you directly east of the inlet.

**Overview:** This is the only charted inlet between Cape Canaveral and Fort Pierce and is a local knowledge, fair-weather inlet used largely by smaller recreational fishing boats. Crossed by a fixed bridge (A1A) with 37-foot vertical clearance.

**Navigation:** If you must enter, do so only from the east using the waypoint; there is an unmarked shoal blocking any approach from the south. From the waypoint, proceed due east keeping to the center of the jetties. There are no buoys and only a light at the end of the north jetty. A 3,000-foot-long by 100-foot-wide and 9-foot-deep channel provides access to the ocean, but as with all ocean inlets, a cautious approach is warranted, as shoaling is ever present and continuous.

**Webcam:** For a live view of the inlet, visit sebastianinletcam.com.

**Cautions and hazards:** Swift cross currents and the resulting shifting channel make navigation difficult without up-to-date local information. The currents in this area can also affect travel on the ICW.

**Depth:** Refer to the most recent NOAA charts or your onboard navigation device.

**ICW connection:** The inlet is 2 nm from the ICW (across the Indian River) over an area of 5- to 6-foot depths following privately maintained aids.

**Nearby facilities:** There are a few small local marinas along the west shore of the Indian River on the ICW route.

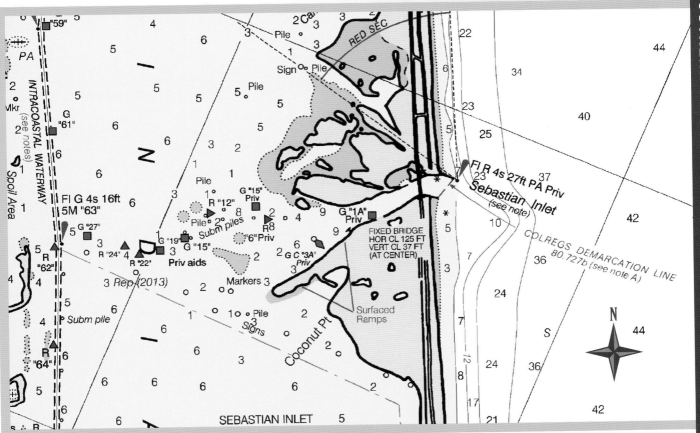

Use Chart 11472

# Fort Pierce Inlet

**Sea Buoy:** Red sea buoy "2" is located at N 27° 28.640', W 80° 15.410' (1.5 nm seaward of the channel).

**Overview:** This is a big ship inlet and one of the best and easiest inlets on Florida's east coast. Currents are strong; slower boats will want to have the tide favoring their passage. There is an inner channel and a turning basin.

**Navigation:** Above waypoint takes you 1.5 nm from the channel in deep water. Smaller craft can approach in over 20 feet to green buoy "5" and red buoy "6" at

N 27° 28.160', W 80° 16.900', which is just .2 nm from the jetties.

**Webcam:** For live view of the inlet, go to visitstlucie.com/fort-pierce-inlet-webcam.

**Cautions and hazards:** Watch for the many small fishing boats throughout the channel. Eastbound swells can create rough conditions within the inlet proper, preventing smaller boats from leaving.

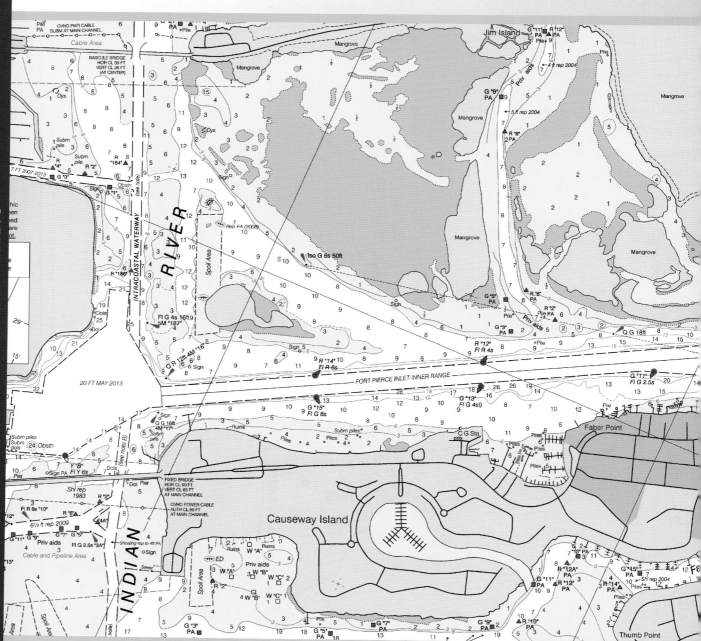

**epth:** Refer to the most recent NOAA charts or your
nboard navigation device.

**CW connection:** Connects directly to the ICW.

**earby facilities:** There are marinas in the inlet itself
nd more to the north and south of the inlet, including
epair facilities. There is an anchorage to the north of
he inlet off the ICW and to the south on the backside of
auseway Island.

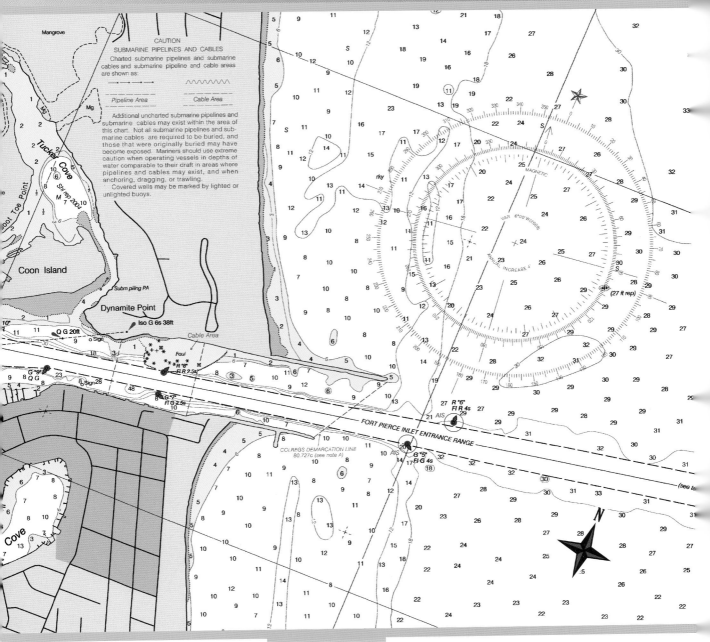

Use Chart 11475

# St. Lucie Inlet ("The Crossroads")

**Sea Buoy:** Flashing red buoy "2" (4 sec) is located at N 27° 10.000', W 80° 08.380'.

**Overview:** This marks the intersection of the Indian River, Saint Lucie, Okeechobee Waterway and ICW (hence "The Crossroads"). Used by sport fishermen, megayachts and offshore sailors.

**Navigation:** The entrance marker at N 27° 10.00', W 80° 08.380' can be used as an entrance waypoint. The jetties are visible directly west of this point.

**Webcam:** For a live view of the inlet, visit stlucieinlet. com.

**Cautions and hazards:** Conveniently located and frequently dredged but requires caution due to problematic shoaling. Jetty to the north and small breakwater to the south offer protection once inside, although protection from the south is marginal in east to southeast winds. The USCG has placed temporary markers denoting best water. Local knowledge should be obtained before using this inlet. The current can be strong.

**Depth:** Refer to the most recent NOAA charts or your onboard navigation device.

**ICW connection:** ICW is approximately 1 nm away. Due to constant shoaling, several temporary buoys have been placed between the inlet and the ICW.

**Nearby facilities:** There are several marinas and areas to anchor inside Manatee Pocket, to the west of the ICW. There is also a mooring field in Stuart beyond the fixed Evans Crary Bridge (65-foot vertical clearance). Three nautical miles to the south is Peck Lake, with deep anchorage and easy access to the Atlantic beaches via the State Park.

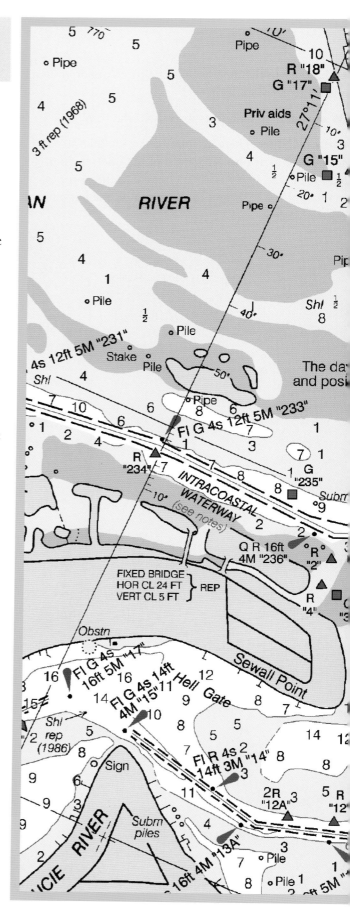

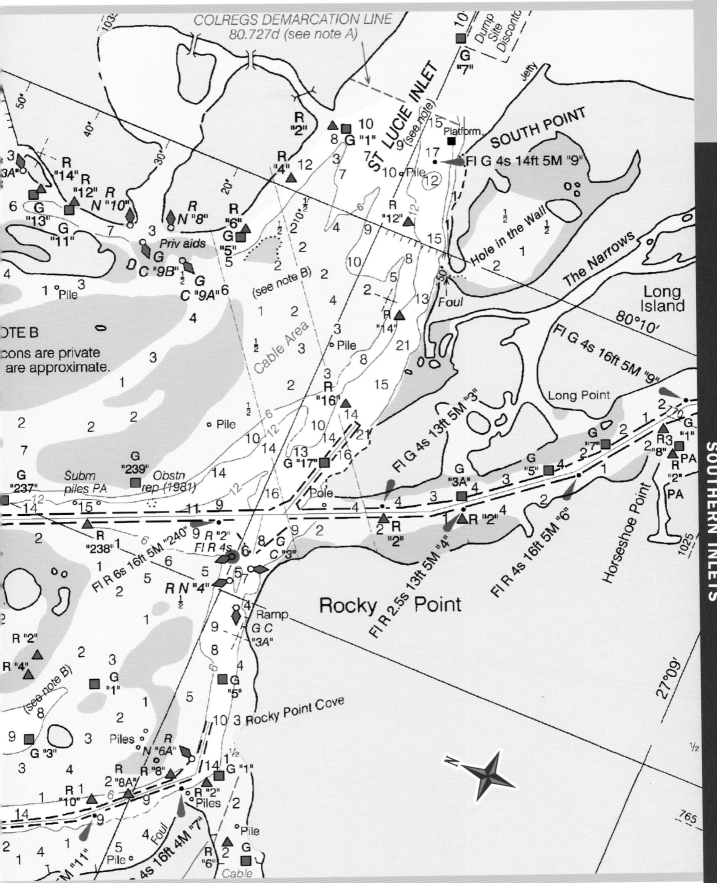

COLREGS DEMARCATION LINE
80.727d (see note A)

ST LUCIE INLET

SOUTH POINT

Dump Site Discont'd

G "7"

Platform

Fl G 4s 14ft 5M "9"

R "2"

G "1"

10

R "4"

12

R "6"

G "5"

N "8"

R "8"

Priv aids

C "9B"

C "9A"

(see note B)

Cable Area

Hole in the Wall

The Narrows

Long Island

80°10'

Fl G 4s 16ft 5M "9"

Long Point

Fl G 4s 13ft 5M "3"

R "14"

R "16"

G "17"

R "3"

R "12"

Foul

R "14"

Pile

Pole

NOTE B

cons are private
are approximate.

G "239"

Subm piles PA

Obstn rep (1981)

G "237"

R "238"

Fl R 6s 16ft 5M "240"

R "2"

Fl R 4s

G C "3"

R N "4"

Ramp

G C "3A"

Rocky Point

Fl R 2.5s 13ft 5M "4"

Fl R 4s 16ft 5M "6"

Horseshoe Point

R "2"

R "2"

G "3A"

G "5"

"7"

"8"

R3 "1"

R "2"

G "1"

PA

PA

R "2"

G "1"

G "5"

Rocky Point Cove

R "2"

R "4"

(see note B)

G "3"

R N "6A"

R "8"

R "10"

2 "8A"

G "1"

R "2"

Piles

Piles

Foul

M "11"

Fl ... 4s 16ft 4M "7"

R "6"

G

Cable

# Jupiter Inlet

**Sea Buoy:** No sea buoy. Steer to waypoint N 26° 56.620', W 80° 03.790' (0.4 nm east of the inlet).

**Overview:** Fair weather inlet only. Prone to severe shoaling and cited by the USCG as "not navigable without local knowledge."

**Navigation:** If you must enter, proceed in a westerly direction from the waypoint to the markers on the jetties. Once inside the jetties, depths increase substantially.

**Webcam:** For a live view of the inlet, visit evsjupiter.com.

**Cautions and hazards:** Severe shoaling to both the north and south of the entrance. With any swell, mariners should divert to another inlet. The inlet is considered impassable in a northeast swell of any size.

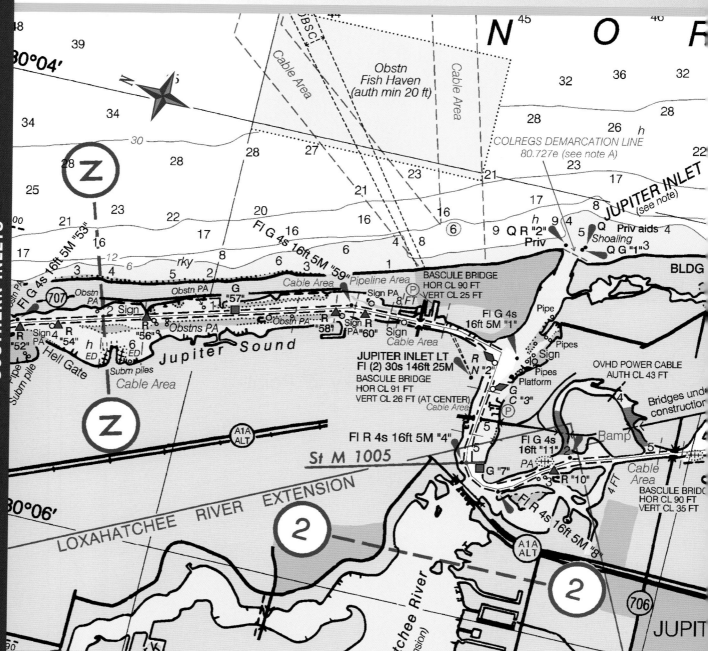

**Depth:** Refer to the most recent NOAA charts or your onboard navigation device.

**ICW connection:** Connects directly to the ICW.

**Nearby facilities:** Marinas located to the north and south of the inlet, with provisioning nearby.

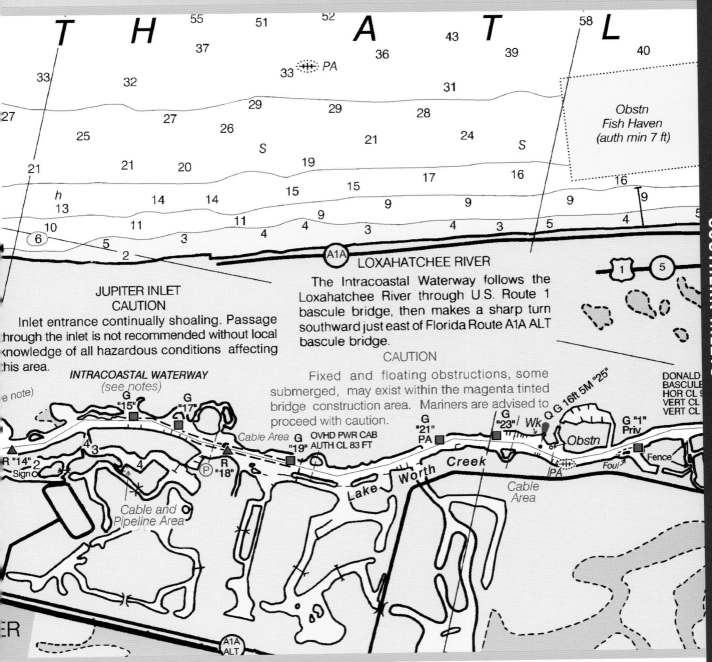

T H E      A T L

55  51  52      43  T    58  L

37              36          39              40

33          PA

33/     32          33  PA              31

27          27          29   29   28                          Obstn
        25          26          21        24        S   Fish Haven
21          21   20      19              17        16      (auth min 7 ft)

h           14   14   15   15        9    9        9    16
13          11   11    9    4    3    4    3    5    4    9
10          3    4
6       5
2                    A1A   LOXAHATCHEE RIVER                    1   5

JUPITER INLET                The Intracoastal Waterway follows the
CAUTION                Loxahatchee River through U.S. Route 1
Inlet entrance continually shoaling. Passage      bascule bridge, then makes a sharp turn
through the inlet is not recommended without local      southward just east of Florida Route A1A ALT
knowledge of all hazardous conditions affecting      bascule bridge.
this area.                        CAUTION

INTRACOASTAL WATERWAY      Fixed and floating obstructions, some    DONALD
(see note)      (see notes)      submerged, may exist within the magenta tinted    BASCULE
        G      G      bridge construction area. Mariners are advised to    HOR CL
        "15"   "17"      proceed with caution.   Q G 16ft 5M "25"   VERT CL
                                        VERT CL
                                G      G "1"
                        Cable Area G   OVHD PWR CAB   G   "23"  Wk   Priv
                        "19"   AUTH CL 83 FT   "21"          Obstn
        4 3              PA              Foul   Fence
R "14" 2                 P  R               PA
Sign      4      "18"              Lake  Worth Creek   Cable
                                        Area
        Cable and
        Pipeline Area

ER

        A1A
        ALT

Use Chart 11472

# Lake Worth (Palm Beach) Inlet

**Sea Buoy:** RW sea buoy "LW" is located at N 26° 46.360', W 80° 00.610' (1.1 nm east of the jetties).

**Overview:** Deep, easily navigable big ship inlet that is sometimes referred to as the Palm Beach Inlet. Vessels returning from the Bahamas can clear Customs and Immigration here.

**Navigation:** Straight shot from the sea buoy with no hazards of any sort. There is a long jetty to the south and a much shorter one to the north.

**Webcam:** For a live view of the inlet, visit pbcgov.com/webcams/lwi.

**Cautions and hazards:** Large commercial vessels frequently use this inlet. Further in, many small fishing boats can cause problems, particularly beside Peanut Island. Currents are strong but do not cause much difficulty in the inlet.

**Depth:** Refer to the most recent NOAA charts or your onboard navigation device.

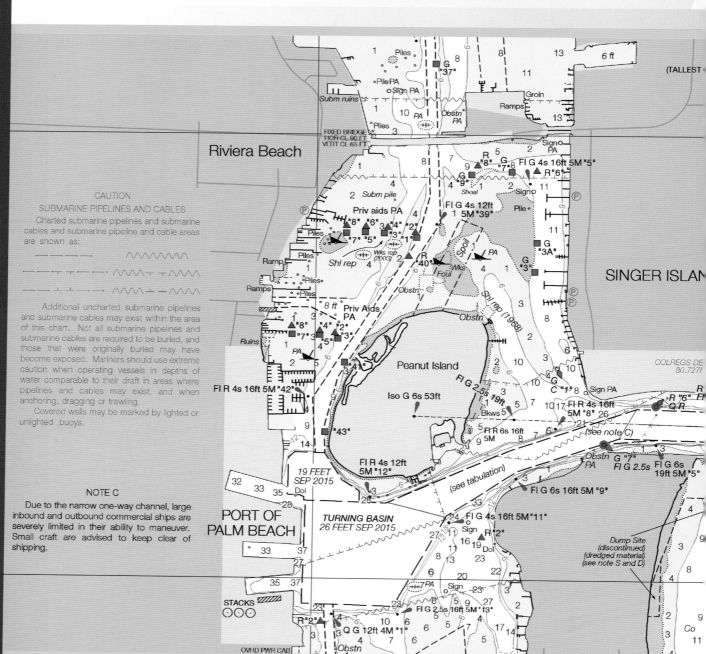

**CW connection:** Connects directly to the ICW.

**Nearby facilities:** Port caters to megayachts with numerous marinas and marine facilities. Several good anchorages also close by. No convenient dinghy dockage.

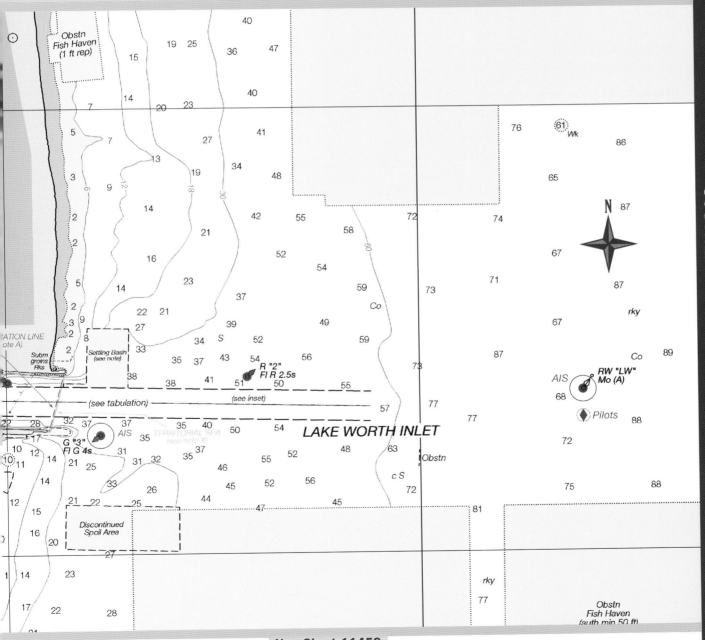

LAKE WORTH INLET

# Boca Raton Inlet

**Sea Buoy:** No sea buoy. Steer to N 26° 20.150', W 80° 04.270' and pick up the quick flashing green buoy "1" on the south jetty and quick flashing red buoy "2" on the north jetty.

**Overview:** Narrow, dredged cut located 5 nm northward of Hillsboro Inlet Light. Boca Raton Inlet (A1A) Bascule Bridge (23-foot vertical clearance) crosses the inlet and opens on signal.

**Navigation:** Tall, pink Boca Raton Resort & Club is a landmark visible from many miles offshore. The inlet's entrance has short jetties marked by private lights. Be sure to request a bridge opening upon arrival in the inlet to avoid circling in the strong current. It is strongly recommended to head south of green buoy "1" (south jetty) and approach the inlet from the south.

**Webcam:** For a live view of the inlet, visit video-monitoring.com/beachcams/bocainlet.

**Cautions and Hazards:** There is heavy traffic in the area, especially on weekends. Local knowledge is required, as shoaling outside the inlet can limit access at low tide. Depths change frequently due to shoaling and shifting sandbars, and swift-moving currents cause swells where the outflow meets the ocean. The inlet channel and markers are not charted and transit is considered dangerous. Be aware that the current usually reverses in the ICW as it passes the Boca Raton Inlet.

**Depth:** Refer to the most recent NOAA charts or your onboard navigation device.

**ICW connection:** Connects directly to the ICW.

**Nearby facilities:** Marine facilities are available on the ICW and farther south off the Hillsboro River. A small anchorage is located just south of the Palmetto Park Bridge (Mile 1047.5) at the northeastern end of Lake Boca Raton.

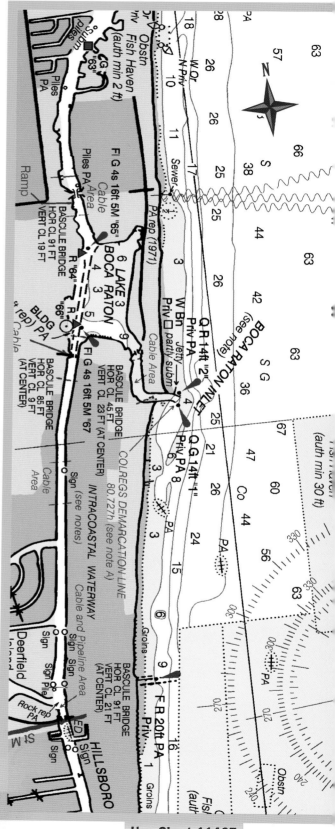

**Use Chart 11467**

# Hillsboro Inlet

**Sea Buoy:** RW sea buoy "HI" is located at N 26° 15.070', W 80° 04.630' (approximately 0.4 nm from the inlet). A course to the northwest (paying close attention to the green day marks and lighted buoys) will bring you past the jetty.

**Overview:** Frequently used and offers reliable 7-foot depths; nevertheless this inlet requires attentiveness when entering.

**Navigation:** Easily identified by 136-foot high Hillsboro Lighthouse. Hillsboro Inlet Bascule Bridge (13-foot closed vertical clearance) inside the inlet opens on signal, except from 7:00 a.m. to 6:00 p.m., the drawspans need only open only on the hour, quarter-hour, half-hour and three-quarter hour. Due to the very strong currents in this inlet, vessels should contact the bridge tender before entering the inlet.

**Webcam:** For a live view of the inlet, visit hillsborolighthouse.org/inlet-cam.

**Cautions and Hazards:** A southeast wind against a tide situation can kick up a short, vicious chop that can set an unwary boater onto the shoals to the south of the inlet. More than one vessel has been bounced onto the bottom here in the troughs. Currents to 6 knots have been reported. There is a 64-foot clearance power cable at the bridge.

**Depth:** Refer to the most recent NOAA charts or your onboard navigation device.

**ICW connection:** Connects directly to the ICW.

**Nearby facilities:** Marinas are to the north and south of the inlet, with provisioning nearby. No nearby anchorages.

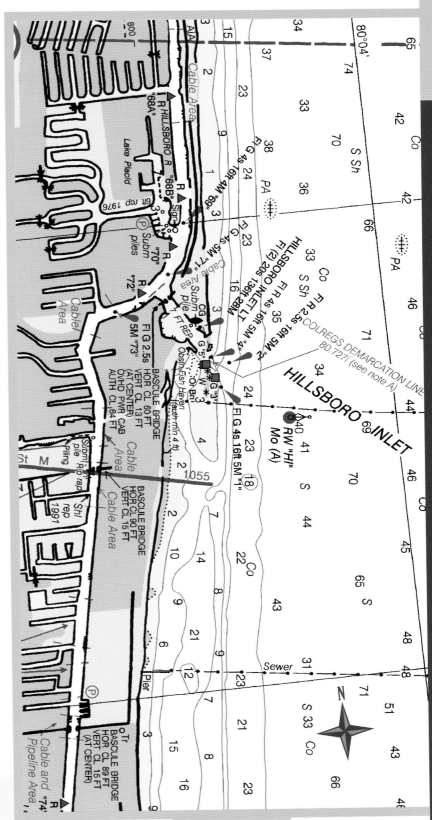

Use Chart 11467

# Port Everglades (Fort Lauderdale) Inlet

**Sea buoy:** RW sea buoy "PE" is located at N 26° 05.500', W 80° 04.790'. From the sea buoy, head due west into the cut.

**Overview:** This big ship inlet, located 9 nm south of Hillsboro Inlet, is also known as Fort Lauderdale Inlet. Wide, deep, straight and completely free of hazards; accommodates naval vessels, container ships, freighters and cruise ships. Be aware that larger vessels will often be escorted and have an enforced security perimeter.

**Navigation:** At the turning basin, swing south into the ICW, or north to the ICW and the various marinas of Fort Lauderdale.

**Webcam:** For a live view of the inlet, visit portevergladeswebcam.com. Fort Lauderdale ICW can be seen at ftlauderdalewebcam.com.

**Cautions and hazards:** Frequent large ship traffic in and out of this inlet necessitate a careful watch, particularly at night and in poor weather. The cut can get bouncy with sportfishing boats running in and out at high speeds.

**Depth:** Refer to the most recent NOAA charts or your onboard navigation device.

**ICW connection:** Connects directly to the ICW.

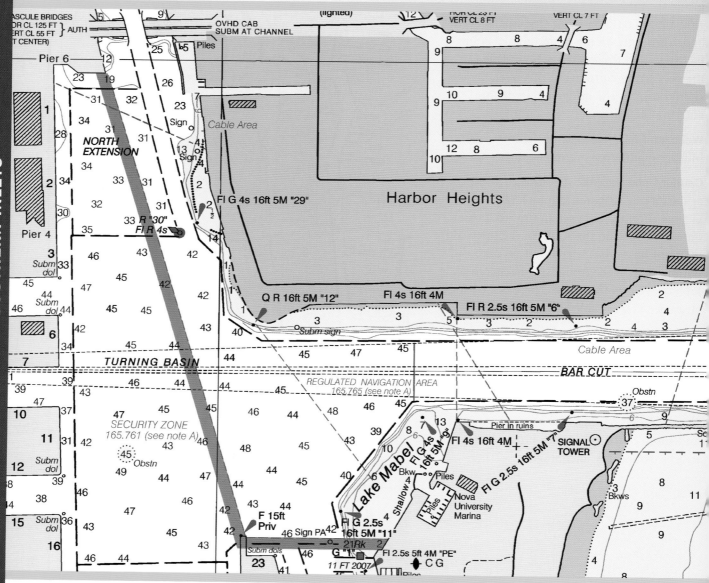

**Nearby facilities:** Several marinas are located to the north of the inlet. Some transient dockage is located in Dania Cut to the south. Las Olas Bridge mooring field is north of the inlet, in the center of town. Anchorages are available nearby, although access to shore is difficult.

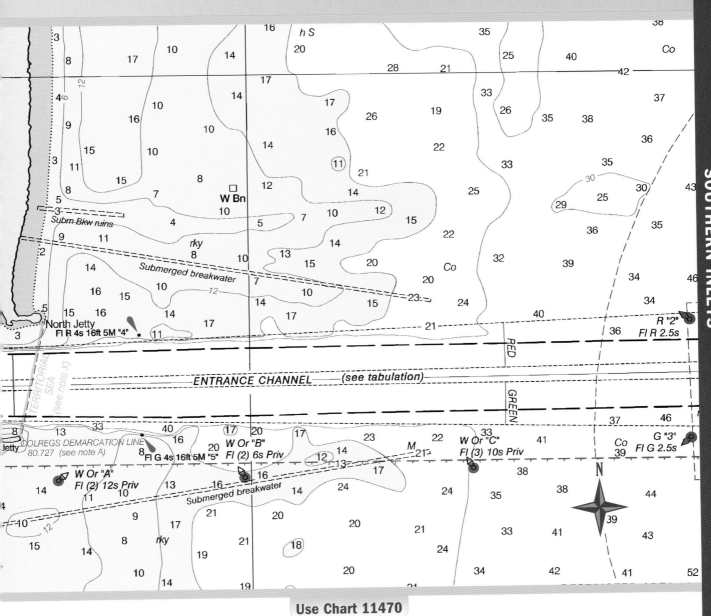

ENTRANCE CHANNEL — (see tabulation)

RED

GREEN

North Jetty
Fl R 4s 16ft 5M "4"

R "2"
Fl R 2.5s

G "3"
Fl G 2.5s

Submerged breakwater

Subm Bkw ruins

W Bn

COLREGS DEMARCATION LINE
80.727 (see note A)

Fl G 4s 16ft 5M "5"

W Or "A"
Fl (2) 12s Priv

W Or "B"
Fl (2) 6s Priv

W Or "C"
Fl (3) 10s Priv

TERRITORIAL SEA
(see note X)

Co

rky

Use Chart 11470

# Bakers Haulover (North Miami Beach) Inlet

**Sea Buoy:** No sea buoy. Steer to waypoint N 25° 54.000', W 80° 06.730'.

**Overview:** Popular and busy with local recreational fishermen and tour boats.

**Navigation:** There are no markers, other than a light on the south side of the inlet and once you have turned north, deep water is close to the shore on your port side. The inlet has a fixed bridge (A1A) with 32-foot vertical clearance.

**Cautions and hazards:** Strictly a fair-weather inlet for cruising vessels due to problems with continual ICW shoaling. Cruisers would be wise to forgo this inlet in favor of Miami's Government Cut (8 nm to the south) or Port Everglades Inlet (11.5 nm to the north). Mariners are advised to exercise extreme caution while transiting the area.

**Depth:** Refer to the most recent NOAA charts or your onboard navigation device.

**ICW connection:** Proceed due west into the inlet, turning north once inside to head for the ICW. Severe shoaling exists in the vicinity of Biscayne Bay buoy "7B" on the ICW. The shoal protrudes into the channel on the east side, which reduces the channel width by approximately half of the charted width. Biscayne Bay Buoy "7B" has been relocated by USCG to mark the best water.

**Nearby facilities:** There is a marina just to the north of the inlet.

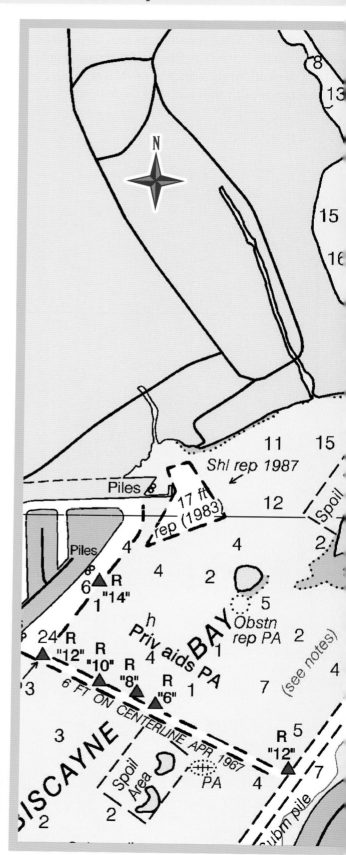

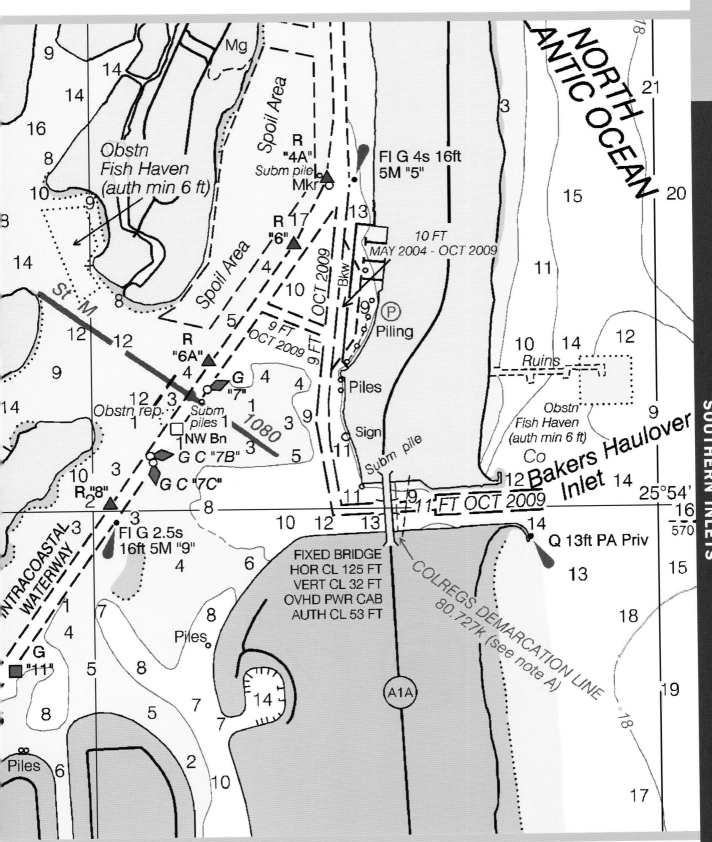

NORTH ATLANTIC OCEAN

9

14

14

16

8

10

3

14

Obstn
Fish Haven
(auth min 6 ft)

9

8

St "M"

12 12 12

9

14

10

R "8"
2

INTRACOASTAL WATERWAY

3

4

3

7

4

G "11"

5

8

14

10

2

Piles

6

Mg

Spoil Area

Spoil Area

R "4A"
Subm pile
Mkr

R "6"

Spoil Area

4

5

R "6A"
4

G "7"

Obstn rep
3

Subm piles 1

NW Bn
G C "7B"

G C "7C"

8

FI G 2.5s
16ft 5M "9"

4

7

Piles

13

FI G 4s 16ft
5M "5"

10 FT
MAY 2004 - OCT 2009

Bkw

OCT 2009

9 FT

9 FT
OCT 2009

P Piling

Piles

Sign

Subm pile

9

11

10 12 13

1080

4

4

3 9

5

11

FIXED BRIDGE
HOR CL 125 FT
VERT CL 32 FT
OVHD PWR CAB
AUTH CL 53 FT

6

8

7

14

A1A

10

3

15

21

20

11

Ruins

10 14 12

Obstn
Fish Haven
(auth min 6 ft)

Co

Bakers Haulover
Inlet 14

12

25°54'

16

570

14

Q 13ft PA Priv

13

15

18

19

17

11 FT OCT 2009

COLREGS DEMARCATION LINE
80.727k (see note A)

9

18

SOUTHERN INLETS

# Government Cut (Miami) Inlet

**Sea Buoy:** RW sea buoy "M" is located at N 25° 46.088', W 80° 04.998'.

**Overview:** This big ship inlet is wide and deep and is free of hazards. Runs between Miami Beach (to the north) and Fisher Island (to the south).

**Navigation:** In settled conditions, use the waypoint N 25° 45.400', W 80° 06.880', which brings you in to just over .5 nm from the jetties; otherwise, the sea buoy at N 25° 46.130', W 80° 04.960' is the preferable waypoint. Follow a course of 253° M inside the channel, then 299° M from green buoy "7" through the jetties. Closures are announced on VHF Channel 16. During closures, Fisherman's Channel south of Dodge Island is the alternate inlet. It is similarly free of hazards, although when entering from the ICW heading south, leave buoys "53A" and "55" well to port before turning in to the channel due to shoaling extending into the channel.

**Webcam:** For a live view of the inlet, visit portmiamiwebcam.com.

**Cautions and hazards:** A car ferry runs between Dodge Island and Fisher Island with frequent crossings. Both channels are subject to strong currents.

**Depth:** Refer to the most recent NOAA charts or your onboard navigation device.

**ICW connection:** Connects directly to the ICW.

**Nearby facilities:** There are marinas and anchorages nearby as well as provisioning opportunities.

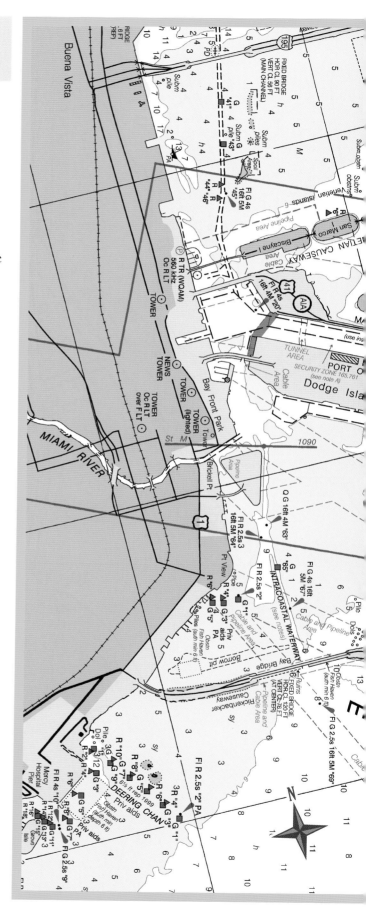

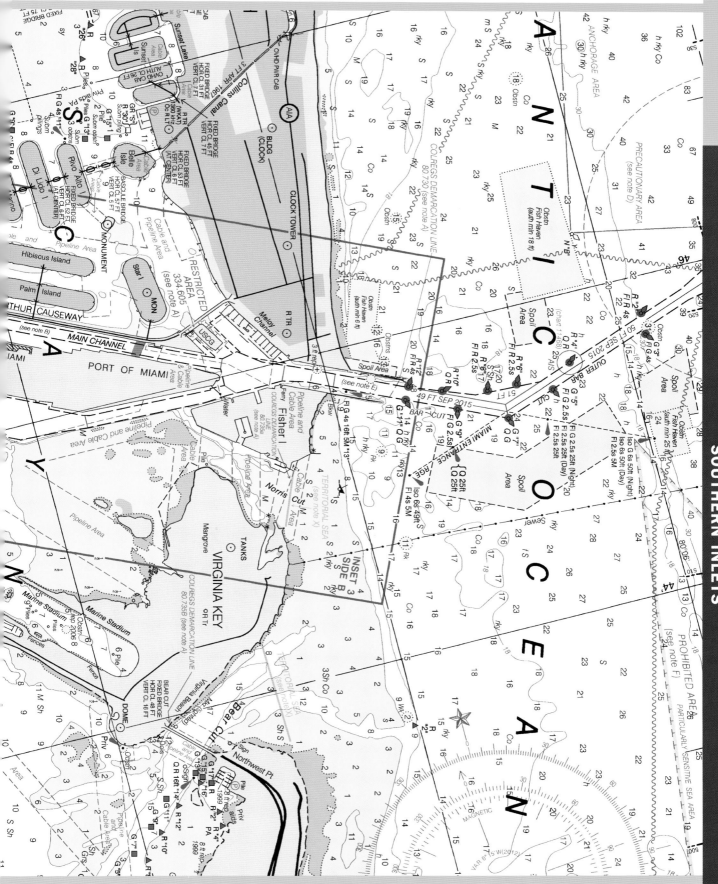

# Cape Florida (Biscayne Bay) Inlet

**Sea buoy:** Use flashing (4 sec) 37-foot Biscayne Channel Light "6M" located at N 25° 38.742', W 80° 05.373'.

**Overview:** This inlet is primarily used by cruisers heading to the islands. Located 6 nm south of Miami.

**Navigation:** Pass Biscayne Channel Light to port, then continue to entrance buoy green "1" and follow the marked channel.

**Cautions and hazards:** Local knowledge should be obtained before entering this inlet for the first time. It is a well-marked channel, but attention is required in some shallow areas (7 to 9 feet).

**Depth:** Refer to the most recent NOAA charts or your onboard navigation device.

**ICW connection:** Connects to ICW (0.5 nm).

**Nearby facilities:** There are anchorages nearby at No Name Harbor and Hurricane Harbor. No Name Harbor is part of a State Park with a restaurant, making it busy on weekends. Coconut Grove is located across the Bay and to the west and offers facilities.

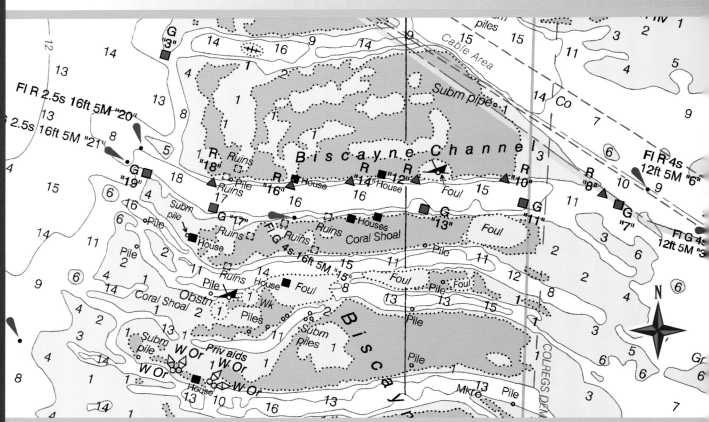

**Use Chart 11465**

# Angelfish Creek

**Sea Buoy:** No sea buoy. Steer to waypoint N 25° 19.600', W 80° 14.914'.

**Overview:** For vessels wanting to take advantage of the Gulf Stream for a transit to Bimini Island in the Bahamas, Angelfish Creek provides a more southerly approach than Miami. Be aware that the 1.8-nm-long inlet adds 14 nm to the Bahamas trip, making it 56 nm instead of 42 nm.

**Navigation:** Entering from Card Sound at flashing red buoy "14," the depths will increase quickly to 7 to 10 feet, then to over 13 feet until you approach the exit to the Atlantic. At red buoy "4" you will see three green daybeacons ahead. Favor the red side as you approach flashing red buoy "2" and proceed slowly through to the Atlantic while watching your depth. There is a cross current here; pay attention to your track so that you don't get pushed out of the channel.

**Cautions and hazards:** The channel is a fair weather proposition only, particularly from the Atlantic. The depth from the Atlantic side is approximately 4 feet at the beginning of the channel. Because of this, an ocean side approach is not recommended for cruising vessels. Vessels traveling offshore in inclement weather would be best advised to continue on to Government Cut in Miami (26 nm).

**Depth:** Refer to the most recent NOAA charts or your onboard navigation device.

**ICW connection:** Inlet leads into Card Sound, with the ICW 1.4 nm away.

**Nearby facilities:** Several anchorages are nearby.

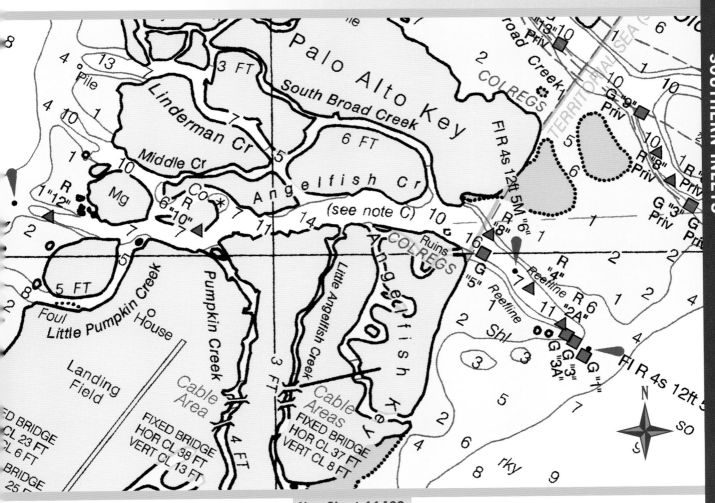

# Skipper's Notes

# Florida's Upper East Coast

- FERNANDINA BEACH TO ST. JOHNS RIVER  ■ SIDE TRIP ON THE ST. JOHNS RIVER
- ST. JOHNS RIVER TO PONCE DE LEON INLET
- NEW SMYRNA BEACH TO VERO BEACH  ■ FORT PIERCE TO ST. LUCIE RIVER  ■ OKEECHOBEE WATERWAY

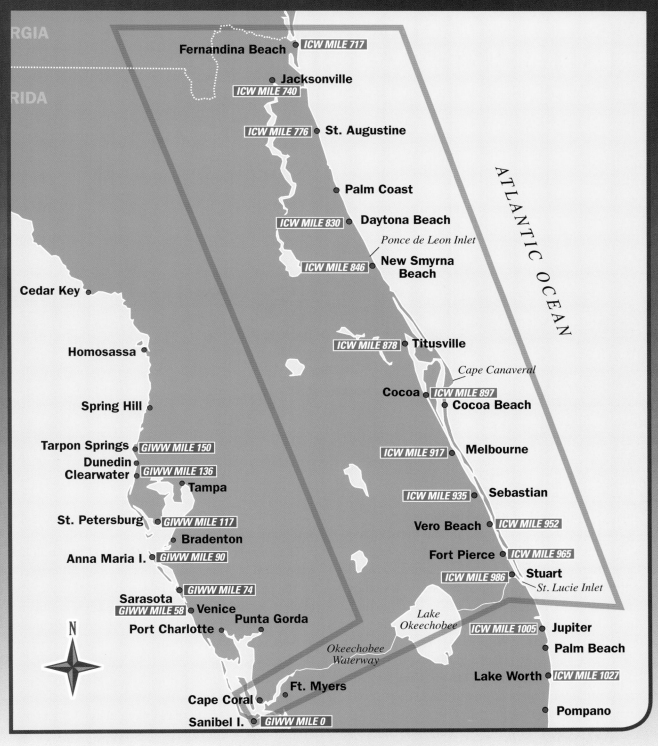

www.WaterwayGuide.com

# Florida's
## Upper East Coast

Cruising south on the Intracoastal Waterway (ICW), boaters enter Florida at Mile 714 and Fernandina Beach. A study in contrasts, the scenery slowly begins its change from nearly deserted, white-capped sounds to the confines of the busy ICW lined by beautiful homes and condominiums. As you cross Cumberland Sound and the St. Marys River, the broad expanses of the marsh-bordered Georgia ICW gives way to the narrower, more protected, and more populated Florida route. In the 375 statute miles (326 nm) to Miami, navigational aids are plentiful, and marinas and urban centers proliferate as you travel south. Below St. Lucie Inlet, the coastline becomes truly tropical, with a profusion of palm trees and exotic flowers. Here, the bustling Gold Coast comes into its own, with burgeoning development and fewer anchorages than you might wish.

The Florida ICW is well marked and easy to follow. Keep track of your position by checking off markers on the chart as you pass. Take a little extra care where inlet, river and ICW channels meet; a few moments' study of the chart ahead of time will prevent confusion in those areas where a buoy system changes direction. With a few exceptions, the ICW between Fernandina and Miami is protected from strong winds and is usually free of rough water. Tidal heights range from more than 7 feet at Fernandina to about 1.5 feet at Key West. Currents up to 4 knots may be encountered between Fernandina and Haulover Canal, especially at

Jacksonville is in northeastern Florida, where the St. John's River meets the Atlantic Ocean. A regional business center, it has many museums and cultural offerings. Championship golf courses in the area include Ponte Vedra Beach's TPC Sawgrass, headquarters of the PGA Tour.

inlets. Lesser currents up to about 2 knots occur from Haulover Canal to Miami.

U.S. Army Corps of Engineers (USACE) project depths on the ICW are 12 feet from Norfolk, VA, to Fort Pierce, FL, Mile 965; 10 feet to Miami, FL, Mile 1085; and 7 feet from Miami to Cross Bank across Florida Bay. Keep in mind that these are ideal depths, maintained as closely as possible by the U.S. Army Corps of Engineers (USACE) and the Florida Inland Navigation District (FIND). (FIND receives State funding provided by taxes on waterfront property throughout Florida; thus, Florida has more money available for waterway maintenance than states where dredging is funded only with federal money.) The controlling depth–the least water depth actually available–is what counts. Current depths are reported by the USACE and by the Coast Guard (in the *Local Notice to Mariners*) according to the latest information. The USACE and FIND schedule dredging of shoaling sections throughout the year, and what was too shallow last year may be 12 feet deep this year, and vice versa. Funds for dredging are still scarce; use caution and stay informed with the most up-to-date information at waterwayguide.com.

As boats compete for space and traffic increases along the ICW, local agencies have set up Idle-Speed/No-Wake Zones. Such speed limits protect shorelines, wildlife, shore facilities and berthed boats from wake damage and help cut down on boating accidents. Idle speed means putting the engine in gear with no increase in throttle, while taking care to maintain control of the vessel. Other areas have Slow-Speed Zones where a minimum wake is required, while others may have a limit on wake height. Read the signs. In crowded areas (such as Fort Lauderdale and Miami), especially on weekends and holidays when less experienced boaters are on the water, always slow down and keep alert. Manatee zones also have speed restrictions that are strictly enforced. Many are seasonal, and the posted signs may be difficult to read, so keep an eye out for them.

Much of Florida's eastern ICW is narrow and shoal-bordered, with scattered anchorages. As the population continues to increase, favorite anchorages become more crowded. Good anchorages are still available if you plan ahead. Using an anchor light is important and required by law, and in some places you will be ticketed for not having one on at night. Florida restrictions on anchoring are being changed on a regular basis. Before planning to anchor in an area, be sure to check to make sure you can.

The same space shortage applies to marina dockage, so you should reserve ahead or plan to arrive early at your chosen marina during the winter cruising season. Most dockmasters make every effort to find room for one more, and the friendliness of the boating community more than makes up for the crowded conditions.

See up-to-date anchorage and marina listings on the Waterway Guide Explorer at waterwayguide.com.

# DOWNLOAD

*Marinas App*

# WATERWAY GUIDE® THE CRUISING AUTHORITY

*waterwayguide.com*

# Fernandina Beach to St. Johns River

 Mile 708–Mile 740     FL: Channel 09

**CHARTS** 11489, 11490, 11491

As you cross the St. Marys River and enter the State of Florida, you will notice a change in the characteristics of the ICW. Georgia's long, open sounds and wide rivers gradually transform into a series of creeks and rivers connected by narrow land cuts, and you will see much more development. The ICW crosses several navigable inlets that no doubt attracted the early explorers. The first settlers built strategic, profitable ports along these protected inside waters. Today's cruisers use improved and connected passages that link many of these original settlements.

## ■ ST. MARYS RIVER ENTRANCE

St. Marys is a relatively easy entry and exit point, conveniently located just off the ICW. The short 20-nm offshore jump from here to the St. Johns River at Mayport (near Jacksonville) or to the inlet at St. Augustine bypasses the sometimes shallow, shifting channels at Nassau Sound. If you are on a northerly leg to St. Simons Island, you can cut out the meandering shallows found in Cumberland Sound and Jekyll Creek. Both the St. Johns and the St. Simons Inlets do involve long entry channels and strong currents to return to the ICW; be careful, and try to plan exits and entries with a slack current or fair tide. (See the Inlets section at the front of this guide for more information.)

**NAVIGATION:** Use Chart 11489. The St. Marys entrance is deep, wide, jettied and well marked, but exercise caution when going through, as there are some shoal sections to the north of the channel inside the jetties. The current in this inlet is very strong and dictates appropriate boat handling to compensate. Slower boats are well advised to time their passages for slack water or a favorable tide.

The active Kings Bay Naval Submarine Base, located in Cumberland Sound north of the junction of the St. Marys River, continues to be the reason for frequent dredging and renumbering of buoys, beginning

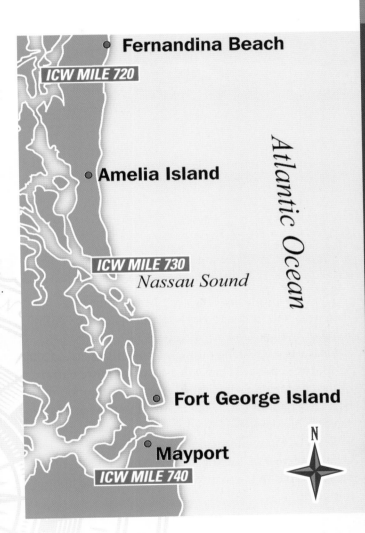

where the ICW joins the head of Cumberland Sound and continuing to the ocean inlet. The channel is consequently quite deep and wide. The St. Marys Entrance Channel buoys, offshore of the entrance, were eliminated several years ago. The buoy that formerly was "10" is now flashing red buoy "2," and every buoy in Cumberland Sound up to the head of Kings Bay was renumbered accordingly. ICW daybeacon numbering remains unchanged. Older charts may not show this change. Remember, the ICW daybeacons all have a yellow square or yellow triangle to designate them as ICW markers.

FERNANDINA BEACH TO ST. JOHNS RIVER

The ICW fronts the Kings Bay Naval Submarine Base near Mile 708, and Navy security patrols carefully monitor traffic from both directions, especially when submarines are passing through Cumberland Sound and St. Marys Entrance. They will ask you to move outside of the channel if a submarine is in the vicinity. Patrol boats respond on VHF Channel 16. The submarines travel at high speeds in open water, creating very large wakes. For more information on security zones around U.S. Naval vessels, see the "Port Security Procedures" section found in the Skipper's Handbook in the front of this guide.

## ■ FERNANDINA BEACH–ICW MILE 716

Florida's northernmost city, Fernandina Beach, is on Amelia Island east of the ICW. Although discovered in 1562 by the French explorer Jean Ribault and named Isle de Mai, it was the Spanish who ultimately settled the island in 1567. They renamed it Santa Maria, established a mission and built Fort San Fernando. In 1702, the British captured the island and gave it the name that finally stuck: Amelia, in honor of King George II's daughter.

Amelia Island has enjoyed a colorful history. In its earlier years, pirates and smugglers used it as their stronghold, and during Prohibition, rum runners continued the tradition. Eight different flags have flown over Amelia Island, among them the standard of the conquistadors and the French Huguenots, the British Union Jack and the Stars and Bars of the Confederacy. The island is the only place in the United States to have been claimed by so many governments.

The historic downtown district, next to the waterfront, has several restaurants, taverns and gift shops. The Tourist Information Center can provide a helpful map.

**NAVIGATION:** Use Chart 11489. On the Amelia River at Mile 718 past the Fernandina Beach waterfront, swing wide between red daybeacons "14" and "16" and favor the north side between red daybeacons "16" and "18" due to 6-foot depths on the magenta line between the two. Red daybeacon "18" appears to be too far to the west but head toward it to give the shoal at the bend marked by flashing green daybeacon "1" a wide berth, both above and below.

After passing flashing green daybeacon "1," swing to the east side of the channel as indicated by the magenta line on the chart. The shoal moving out from the west side is about 6 feet or less at low water, as noted by our cruising editor in spring 2017. In response to frequent roundings here, the Coast Guard has established a ermanent red marker "2" near green "3."

> Mariners are advised to exercise extreme caution when transiting this area and to favor the green side of Amelia River between flashing reen daybeacon "1" and green "3."

The Amelia River breaks off to the west of the ICW t Mile 719.8. Just southwest of the Jackson Creek entrance to the Amelia River (near Mile 720), the ICW urns south and leaves the Amelia River for Kingsley Creek. Two bridges span the ICW at Mile 720.7–the **Kingsley Creek Railroad Swing Bridge** (5-foot closed vertical clearance, normally open) and the **Kingsley Creek Twin Bridges** (65-foot fixed high-level highway bridges carrying U.S. A1A).

Although the railroad bridge is usually open, trains hauling logs to the area's two paper mills can delay your journey. The bridge gives no warning when it is going to close, and it does not have a VHF radio. If you are in this area and you hear train whistles, be aware that the bridge could close as you approach it. After passing beneath the bridges, you could see either a wide expanse of water or mud flats on either side of the channel, depending on the state of the tide.

**Dockage:** At Mile 715.3 is the entrance to Egans Creek (east of the ICW), which leads to Tiger Point Marina, the first marina you will encounter as you enter Florida from the north and Amelia Island's only natural deep water marina. Tiger Point has a full-service repair yard as well as transient slips. Diesel fuel (no gas) can be found at Port Consolidated at Mile 716.5. It is usually best to dock alongside Port Consolidated's fixed dock during higher tides. Many commercial vessels fuel up here, so there may be a wait. Transient overnight dockage is no longer permitted here.

The Fernandina Harbor Marina is located at Mile 716.7. This marina was heavily damaged from Hurricane Matthew in 2016. At press time in summer 2017, rebuilding was underway on the deep water (25 feet) floating docks. Moorings are available on a first-come, first-served basis, and there is a dinghy dock. Additional moorings are scheduled to be installed. The fuel dock is also being rebuilt. Be sure to check waterwayguide.com for the latest information.

Oyster Bay Harbour Marina off Lanceford Creek no longer accepts transients unless you are a homeowner or the guest of a homeowner. Call ahead for current information.

Amelia Island Marina, in a cove just north of the bridges to the east past green daybeacon "13," is a full-service marina (including gas and diesel) with haul-out capabilities and personalized boat service. The narrow channel leading to the marina at Mile 721 has good depths. This is a good choice in strong winds when other marinas may be too exposed, but transient space (30 slips) fills quickly in bad weather, so call ahead.

**Anchorage:** The mooring area in Fernandina Harbor is marked with yellow buoys, but anchoring is still permitted outside the marked area. Anchored boats may use the dinghy dock and showers for a modest fee. If you choose to anchor, take care that your swinging circle does not extend into the channel or the mooring area. Also make sure that you have adequate scope on your anchor for the varying depths and sometimes fast-moving current. Although it is a relatively short dinghy ride to the marina dinghy dock, the anchorage and mooring areas are open to winds, wakes and considerable tidal current.

Caution is advised, as sunken boats have been present in this area in the past, and debris may still be on the bottom. Several sunken boats have been observed outside of the channel between red daybeacons "14" and "16."

Boats have been seen anchoring off of the Amelia River, in Bells River and also in Lanceford Creek. These anchorages should be approached with caution, as the chart contours show varied depths with snags and mud banks. The tidal range is greater than 7 feet, and tidal currents run up to 2 knots here. Always display anchor lights, as commercial and other traffic can be heavy at all hours.

At Mile 719.5, entering the Amelia River and the ICW from the east, Jackson Creek provides 7-foot depths at mean low water, although its entrance is recently reported to have shoaled to 4 feet or less. Like all anchorages in the area, it has swift tidal currents. It is relatively narrow, and the north side should be favored to avoid the charted shoal.

The Amelia River breaks off to the west of the ICW at Mile 719.8 with 6-to 7-foot depths at mean low water. Although it is preferred over Jackson Creek to the north, it is also quite narrow. Enter slowly with the depth sounder on. Be sure to lay out plenty of scope due to the swift currents, but also be aware of the swing room.

**GOIN' ASHORE: FERNANDINA BEACH, FL**

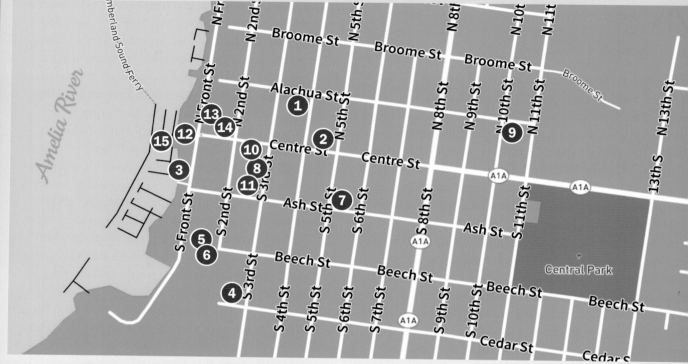

| SERVICES | |
|---|---|
| 1 | Library |
| 2 | Post Office |
| 3 | Visitor Information |

| ATTRACTIONS | |
|---|---|
| 4 | Amelia Island Museum of History |
| 5 | Maritime Museum of Amelia Island |
| 6 | Marlin & Barrel Rum Distillery |

| SHOPPING | |
|---|---|
| 7 | Amelia Island Paint & Hardware |
| 8 | Fantastic Fudge |
| 9 | Fernandina Food Mart |
| 10 | The Book Loft |

| DINING | |
|---|---|
| 11 | 29 South |
| 12 | Brett's Waterway Café |
| 13 | Marina Seafood Restaurant |
| 14 | Palace Saloon |

| MARINAS | |
|---|---|
| 15 | Fernandina Harbor Marina |

The downtown historic district, a 50-block section surrounding Centre Street, is an attractive and popular gingerbread seaport dating from the 1850s, when Florida's first cross-state railroad ran from Fernandina to Cedar Key. (The railroad tracks still run past the waterfront with occasional traffic.) The area is listed on the National Historic Register and is worth a visit.

**Attractions:** With local attractions such as Fort Clinch State Park, Cumberland Island National Seashore, Amelia Island State Park and the island itself, Fernandina makes a pleasant stopover. A good place to start is at the Welcome Center, located in an old train depot at 102 Centre St. (904-277-0717). Your next stop should be the Amelia Island Museum of History at 233 S. 3rd St., which is located in an old jail. Here you can see exhibits on the island's 4,000 years of history and local preservation efforts. Docent-led tours of all types originate here, from home tours to pub tours to even ghost tours. Call ahead for hours at 904-261-7378.

The Maritime Museum of Amelia Island is located just off the waterfront (115 S 2nd St.) with maritime history, pirate lore and marine artifacts. Highlights includes U.S. Navy memorabilia, a Soviet-era KGB diving suit, an artifact from an expedition to the *Titanic* and, of course, panish treasure. Open Tuesday through Saturday; call or hours (904-432-7086). The museum is co-located with the Marlin & Barrel Rum Distillery, which is also worth a look-see. Stop for a sampling and stay to hear bout the distilling process and the owners' use of locally ustainable organics for distilling their unique liquors.

If you have transportation, be sure to visit Florida's oldest lighthouse, Amelia Island Lighthouse, built in 1838. To register for a tour of the lighthouse (for a small ee), call 904-310-3350. It is located on Egans Creek.

**Shopping:** Be sure to try Fantastic Fudge (218 Centre St., 904-277-4801). The Book Loft (214 Centre St., 904-261-8991) offers a large selection of new and used books. Amelia Island Paint and Hardware (516 Ash St., 904-261-6604) has a large selection of hardware and paint. BuyGo Gourmet Groceries (626 S. 8th St., 904-310-9766) is a convenience store with a good selection of basic food and personal items. Winn-Dixie and Publix are about 2 miles away.

There are a surprising number of shops and restaurants in this small town. When exploring beyond the downtown Fernandina Beach area, you will need to arrange for transportation. Visit fbfl.us for more information.

**Dining:** Not far from the waterfront you will find the Palace Saloon (117 Centre St., 844-441-2444), Florida's oldest tavern. Originally named the "Ship Captain's Bar," the Palace Saloon has been a bar since 1903. (Prior to that, it was a haberdashery.) The original bar was a true "gentleman's establishment" with complimentary towels for patron's to wipe the foam from their mustaches and solid brass spittoons for those who enjoyed a good chew with their beer. Check out the original carved mahogany bar, brass cash register, hand painted wall murals, tin ceiling and inlaid tile floors. The bar is open every day from 12:00 p.m. to 2:00 a.m. Be sure to try the Pirates Punch, made from their own secret recipe. See history, specials and more at thepalacesaloon.com.

Brett's Waterway Café is located at Fernandina Harbor Marina. You can't find a better view in town (1 S. Front St., 904-261-2660). A local favorite and the oldest restaurant in town is Marina Seafood Restaurant, located just across the street from the marina (101 Centre St., 904-261-5310). 29 South gets great reviews. Find them two blocks from the waterfront (29 S. 3rd St., 904-277-7919).

# Amelia River, FL

| FERNANDINA BEACH AREA | | | Dockage | | | | | Supplies | | | Services | | | | | |
|---|---|---|---|---|---|---|---|---|---|---|---|---|---|---|---|---|
| | | | Largest Vessel Accommodated | VHF Channel Monitored | Approach / Dockside Depth (reported) | Transient Berths / Total Berths | Floating Docks | Gas / Diesel | Groceries, Ice, Marine Supplies, Snacks | Repairs: Hull, Engine, Propeller | Lift (tonnage), Crane, Rail | Laundry, Pool, Showers, Courtesy Car | Min/Max Amps | Pump-Out Station | Nearby: Grocery Store, Motel, Restaurant | |
| 1. Tiger Point Marina ⌨ WiFi 715.3 | | 904-277-2720 | 55 | 16/11 | 4/50 | 7/8 | F | – | M | HEP | L50 | 30/50 | S | – | MR |
| 2. Port Consolidated 716.5 | | 904-753-4258 | 285 | 16 | 0/13 | 50/30 | – | D | – | – | – | – | – | – | GMR |
| 3. Fernandina Harbor Marina WiFi WG 716.7 | | 904-310-3300 | 205 | 16/68 | moorings | 18/8 | F | GD | M | – | – | 30/50 | S | – | GMR |
| 4. Oyster Bay Harbour Marina ⌨ WiFi | | 904-261-4773 | 65 | – | 0/76 | 15/6 | F | – | I | – | – | 30/50 | PS | P | R |
| 5. Amelia Island Marina ⌨ WiFi WG 721 | | 904-277-4615 | 110 | 16/72 | 30/135 | 5/4 | F | GD | IMS | HEP | L50 | 30/50 | LSC | P | GMR |

⌨ Internet Access  WiFi Wireless Internet Access  WG Waterway Guide Cruising Club Partner  *(Information in the table is provided by the facilities.)*
See WaterwayGuide.com for current rates, fuel prices, web site addresses, and other up-to-the-minute information.

## ■ TO FORT GEORGE RIVER– ICW MILE 735

**NAVIGATION:** Use Chart 11489. South from the **Kingsley Creek Railroad Swing Bridge** (5-foot closed vertical clearance, normally open) and the **Kingsley Creek Twin Bridges** (65-foot fixed vertical clearance) to flashing red "14," shoaling reduces depths along the west side of the channel to 5- to 8-foot depths. In the ICW channel at green daybeacon "21" and flashing red "24," just north of the entrance to Alligator Creek, the narrow channel makes a sharp sweep to the east. Unwary skippers will find 2-foot depths outside of the channel at flashing red daybeacon "24," green daybeacon "25" and red daybeacon "26." From red daybeacon "26" to flashing red daybeacon "28," follow the magenta line on the chart and avoid the shoaling and submerged pilings to starboard.

Just past flashing red daybeacon "28" (about Mile 724), you will pass Amelia City, a small waterside hamlet tucked into a bend on the east side of the river. You will see bulkheads, some private docks and a few houses. Inside the marsh, past the bulkhead area, are more houses.

The shallowest part of the south Amelia River is between red daybeacon "34" and red daybeacon "36."

> Note that the **high-level bridges** along this stretch are unofficially considered to be among the "lowest" of the 65-foot bridges on the ICW; expect no more than 64 feet at high tide. If in doubt, check the clearance boards and go through at half tide. With the wide tidal range (7 feet), currents can be unexpectedly strong.

Although charted at 9 feet in May 2017, there was around 6 feet of water at extreme low tide. Favor the green side between red daybeacon "34" and flashing green daybeacon "37." Head toward red daybeacon "36" and follow the magenta line, rounding red daybeacon "38" and green daybeacon "39." The charted 7- to 8-foot depths are the best you will get through here.

⚠ Follow the magenta line on your chart carefully around red daybeacon "42," then favor green daybeacon "43" (to the east) rather than flashing red daybeacon "44." See the Waterway Guide Explorer at waterwayguide.com for new alerts and updates.

The charted red daybeacon at the entrance to the cut just north of Mile 730 has been renumbered as "46A," according to the 40th edition of the chart dated fall 2015. Because this is such a changeable area, remember to be on the alert for shoaling and the possibility that there may be additional aids in place when you make passage here. New charts do not have a magenta line drawn along the route across Nassau Sound. The current may be very strong, so watch your set and drift; slow boats may have to crab across. There is a fixed bridge (15-foot vertical clearance) across Nassau Sound's ocean inlet, at the southern end of Amelia Island.

The lower portion of Amelia Island is home to a large and lovely resort community, Amelia Island Plantation. No dockage is available on the premises.

**Anchorage:** As the chart clearly shows, the ICW channel hugs the Amelia Island shore just south of Amelia City. There is an anchorage just north of Mile 726 off the entrance to Alligator Creek. Enter by turning to the northeast between red daybeacon "36"

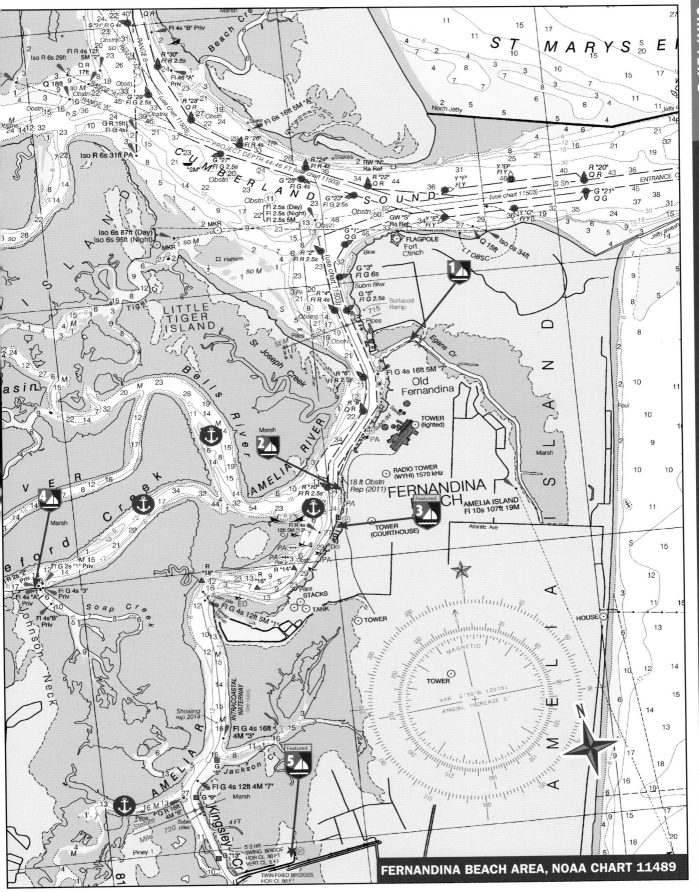

**FERNANDINA BEACH AREA, NOAA CHART 11489**

and flashing green "37." Be careful here; the entrance is shallow, carrying only 6-foot depths at low water, and then increasing to 8-foot depths off Alligator Creek. Tugboats have been observed taking a shortcut through this anchorage area at high tide. It is also possible to anchor at the mouth of Harrison Creek with 9 feet and excellent holding in mud.

## Sawpit Creek and Gunnison Cut–ICW Mile 730 to Mile 735

**NAVIGATION:** Use Chart 11489. Between ICW Miles 730 and 735, shorelines close in somewhat as the channel runs through narrow land cuts and two natural creeks. The dredging of Sawpit Creek in the past corrected the persistent shoaling in the vicinity of flashing green daybeacon "49" for a while, but it is back.

Favor the deep natural channel along the west (red) side of the ICW when rounding the bend marked by flashing green daybeacons "49" and "49A." Sawpit Creek and Gunnison Cut lead to Sisters Creek and the St. Johns River crossing. In the spring of 2017, our Cruising Editor reported 3-foot depths on the green side of the channel at mean low water, so staying to the red side is highly recommended.

**Anchorage:** At Mile 731, you will find 7 to 15 feet with excellent holding in mud behind the island between the bridge over Nassau Sound's ocean inlet and the ICW. This offers good protection but expect a strong current.

## Fort George Island–ICW Mile 735

At Mile 735 the ICW meets the Fort George River. One mile east of the ICW channel, Fort George Island makes an attractive side trip, with its Indian mounds, wildlife sanctuary and lush jungle growth.

**NAVIGATION:** Use Chart 11489. Even though some shoaling between green daybeacon "73" and flashing red daybeacon "74' is evident, if you stay toward the south shore, you should have 8 to 12 feet of water at the entrance to the George River.

**Anchorage:** Once inside the river, the water will deepen and you can enjoy a beautiful anchorage. Drop the hook in 6 to 15 feet of water with excellent holding in mud. Hug the southern shore for deeper water and be mindful of your swinging room. This is somewhat exposed to the northwest.

## Sisters Creek–St. Johns River Intersection–ICW Mile 740

South of the ICW junction with the Fort George River, the ICW route runs a straightforward path through Sisters Creek to the St. Johns River. (The ICW picks up on the other side at Pablo Creek.) As you travel along some sections of Sisters Creek, you may see the superstructures of large ships headed up or down the St. Johns River. The suspension bridge at Dames Point, at the western end of Blount Island, can be used as a landmark when you are headed south.

**NAVIGATION:** Use Chart 11489. Favor the east bank just south of flashing red "82" on Sisters Creek as shoaling has created water depths of 6 to 8 feet along the west bank. The **Hecksher Dr. (Sisters Creek) Bridge** at Mile 739.2 has 65-foot fixed vertical clearance (opened in late 2016). Expect heavy currents when passing under the bridge and approaching the St. Johns River.

Stay alert for large ships traversing the St. Johns River. Shipping traffic may be heavy. Keep in mind that large oceangoing vessels have the right of way. The pilots and captains of large vessels in this area always announce their approach and intentions at the Sisters Creek and St. Johns River intersection via Sécurité warnings. Listen on VHF Channel 16. Smaller vessels in the area should stay clear of these large vessels.

At this point, the St. Johns River is narrow compared to some of its broad expanses south of Jacksonville. Crossing can present problems to lightly powered vessels, given the strong currents (2 to 3 knots on the ebb), obstructed visibility and continuous commercial traffic. Observe markers closely until you are safely into the ICW land cut beyond the St. Johns River. This area has a clearly marked channel that should be very carefully followed. Be aware that the shipyard on the east side of the Sisters Creek entrance to the St. Johns River creates a blind spot for small boats heading into the river.

The land cut from this point southward through the Jacksonville Beach area is well marked, but at low tide the dredged channel is narrow. Follow the markers carefully to stay on the channel's centerline and be prepared to squeeze over for tugs with barges.

**Dockage:** The City of Jacksonville operates the Jim King Park and Boat Ramp at Sisters Creek. It has floating face docks on either side of the bridge and pump-out service but no overnight dockage. There is also a large boat ramp area, which causes congestion,

AMELIA ISLAND MARINA

# St. Johns River Entrance, FL

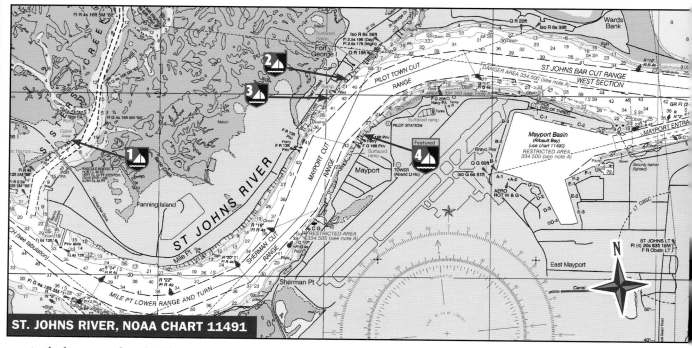

| ST. JOHNS RIVER | | Dockage | | | | | | Supplies | | Services | | | | | |
|---|---|---|---|---|---|---|---|---|---|---|---|---|---|---|---|
| | | Largest Vessel Accommodated | VHF Channel Monitored | Transient Berths / Total Berths | Approach / Dockside Depth (reported) | Floating Docks | Gas / Diesel | Groceries, Ice, Marine Supplies, Snacks | Repairs: Hull, Engine, Propeller | Lift (tonnage), Crane, Rail | Min/Max Amps | Laundry, Pool, Showers, Courtesy Car | Pump-Out Station | Nearby: Grocery Store, Motel, Restaurant | |
| 1. Jim King Park and Boat Ramp at Sisters Creek | 904-630-0839 | 40 | – | call/6 | 35/5 | F | – | – | | | | | P | – | |
| 2. Fort George Island Marina (WiFi) | 904-251-0050 | 70 | 16/68 | 5/13 | 40/25 | F | GD | IM | – | L14 | 30/50 | LS | – | R | |
| 3. St. Johns Boat Company (WiFi) | 904-251-3707 | 200 | 16 | call/5 | 41/26 | – | – | M | HEP | L100,R300 | 15/100 | – | – | R | |
| 4. Morningstar Marinas 🖥 (WiFi) | 904-246-8929 | 200 | 16/74 | 10/10 | 30/30 | F | GD | IMS | – | L6 | 30/50 | C | – | R | |

🖥 Internet Access  (WiFi) Wireless Internet Access  **WG** Waterway Guide Cruising Club Partner *(Information in the table is provided by the facilities.)*
See WaterwayGuide.com for current rates, fuel prices, web site addresses, and other up-to-the-minute information.

**ST. JOHNS RIVER, NOAA CHART 11491**

particularly on weekends. The current is strong but manageable. There is additional free overnight dockage that can handle larger cruising boats in the small creek just north of the launching area.

**Anchorage:** It is possible to anchor north of Sisters Creek Bridge at Mile 739. There is 8 to 11 feet of water with good holding in mud. It is exposed, however, to the north and wakes.

## ■ ST. JOHNS RIVER ENTRANCE

The St. Johns River entrance is one of the safest and easiest gateways from the Atlantic Ocean. Ocean freighters use it, as do military craft and fishing skiffs. Recreational boats make it a point of entry and departure for passages along the coast, coming into and leaving marinas at Mayport (2 miles upriver) and on the ICW (5 miles upriver). It is 150 nm from St. Johns Entrance to the next big ship inlet, Port Canaveral Inlet.

**NAVIGATION:** Use Charts 11489, 11490 and 11491. The ocean approach landmark is St. Johns Light, standing 83 feet above the shore, 1 mile south of the St. Johns River north jetty. The light shines from a square white tower and is easy to spot from the ocean. The St. Johns River red and white sea buoy, flashing Morse (A) "STJ," located 3 miles east of the jetties, guides boaters into the marked inlet channel.

Other landmarks include a tower at Jacksonville Beach and a water tank (painted in a red and white checkerboard design) at the Mayport Naval Air Station. Other water tanks line the beaches to the south. (See the Inlet section in the front of this guide for more information on the St. Johns River Entrance.)

MORNINGSTAR MARINAS

St. Johns River Entrance

# Mayport

**NAVIGATION:** Use Chart 11489. Inside the jetties, the St. Johns River runs unobstructed and naturally deep past the Mayport Basin, which is usually occupied by enormous naval craft. The basin is off-limits to recreational craft, except in extreme emergencies.

**Dockage:** The town of Mayport, 3 miles inside the entrance jetties on the south side of the river, is an important commercial and sportfishing center that provides dockage for cruising boats. Mayport is a good place to lay over before you start your cruise up the St. Johns River, as supplies are readily available here. On the north side of the river is Fort George Island Marina with fuel and transient dockage for vessels up to 70 feet.

St. Johns Boat Company is a full-service boatyard with a 100-ton lift and a 300-ton railway. They do not have transient slips.

On the south side of the river, Morningstar Marinas at Mayport provides fuel, transient dockage and excellent local seafood. They can accomodate vessels to 200 feet on their floating docks. A ferry runs across the St. Johns River from here to Fort George Island. You could spend hours watching the constant activity of the commercial fleet and the sportfishing boats.

A Coast Guard station is located at the south end of the Mayport waterfront, as well as a luxury residential and marina project (Fort George Harbour).

## Cruising Options

The splendid St. Johns River, which winds its way from Mayport to Sanford, is described in the following chapter. Cruisers continuing south on the ICW will find their course resuming in the following chapter, "Jacksonville to Ponce de Leon Inlet."

# Side Trip on the St. Johns River

**VHF** FL: Channel 09

**CHARTS** 11487, 11491, 11492, 11495, 11498

Southbound on the ICW, the waterway crosses the St. Johns River just west of Mile Point, about 5 miles from the St. Johns Entrance and a little over 1 mile west of Mayport. At that point, the ICW leaves Sisters Creek and enters Pablo Creek at red nun buoy "2" (Mile 740) for the run south. However, in this chapter we are going to make a turn to starboard and travel south "up" the St. Johns River.

The St. Johns River flows north for 248 miles from the heart of central Florida to the Atlantic Ocean at Mayport, meaning that if you are traveling on a southern course, you are actually going upriver. From the intersection of the St. Johns River and the ICW at ICW Mile 739.5, you may meet several types of commercial vessels—from freighters, tankers and container ships to tugs, towing barges and even cruise ships. Upriver from Jacksonville, commercial traffic consists largely of tugs and barges.

With its Atlantic Ocean access, and the St. Johns River and the ICW within easy reach, the Jacksonville area is a prime playground for boaters. The City of Jacksonville offers good restaurants, museums, a zoo, a National Football League team (the Jacksonville Jaguars) and plenty of full-service marinas.

Residential areas with private piers line the shore south of Jacksonville to the Green Cove Springs area. The trees are carefully preserved, making it difficult to see some of the houses. The river is less developed and more scenic farther south; part of the river is a wildlife sanctuary, and many skippers make this beautiful trip an annual cruise.

If you are not in a hurry while heading south in the fall or going north in the spring, stop and take a cruise south "up" the river. Unfortunately, exploring the most beautiful part of the St. Johns River is limited to boats able to pass under the Shands Bridge (45-foot fixed vertical clearance) south of Green Cove Springs at Red Bay Point, about 40 miles southwest of the ICW. There are plans to replace the old bridge with a new 65-foot span. This project was in the planning stages at press time (spring 2017), so stay tuned at waterwayguide.com for updates. Sanford on Lake Monroe is a good place to spend the winter, and many yachtsmen leave their boats there for an extended period.

The river boasts infinitely varied scenery. It is as broad in places as a great bay; it is sometimes placid, sometimes wild; with pockets of civilization scattered sparsely along its shores. Narrow and winding in other places, its subtropical vegetation and heavy stands of

One reason for the popularity of the **St. Johns River** is its fishing. The river, its lakes and its tributaries comprise what is widely known as the "Bass Capital of the World," and the evidence suggests that its reputation is well deserved. Florida requires fishing licenses for freshwater and saltwater. (Licenses are not required for those under 16 or over 65, or certified as totally and permanently disabled.)

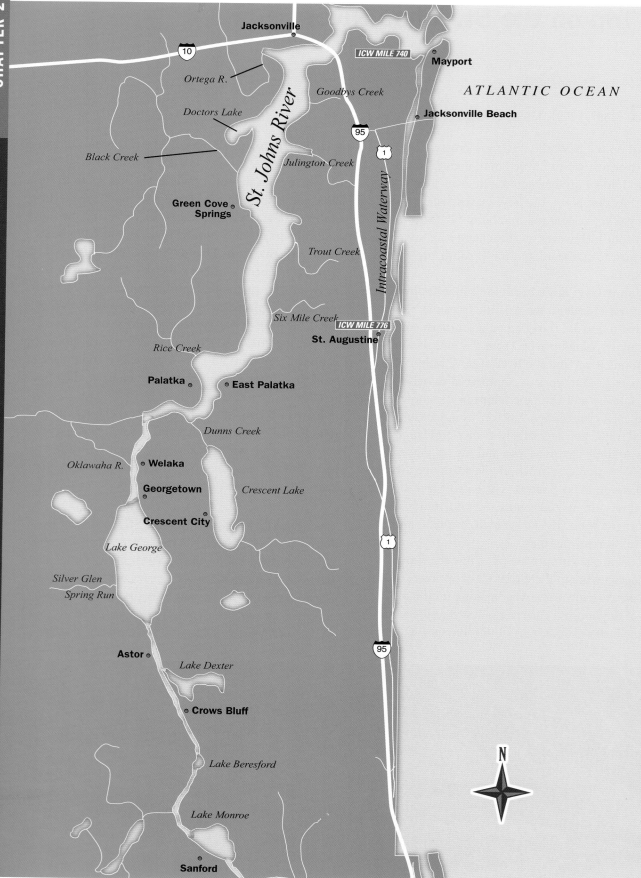

rees grow right down to the water's edge; its sloughs, creeks, oxbows and back-waters are often choked with water hyacinths. Fortunately, restraining fences and bulkheads help keep most of this floating vegetation out of the channel.

Hundreds of creeks and small rivers, deep or shoal, flow into the St. Johns River, and all have something to offer. Without a good outboard-powered dinghy, you will miss a lot in this area. The same dinghy that transports the casual fisherman upstream to discover new challenges can also enhance the cruiser's pleasure in discovering the quiet and scenic anchorages along the St. Johns River's upper reaches. Here, too, is a proliferation of bird life: osprey, turkey vultures, pelicans, anhinga, terns, cranes, herons, egrets, bald eagles, cormorants, ducks and many songbirds are visible along the river.

From November through March, the great manatees (sea cows)–which are protected by law–live along stretches of the river. There are manatee zones along all banks of the St. Johns River in Duval and Clay counties, including Doctors Lake. Shoreside development includes state parks, fish camps (both primitive and luxurious) and a few proper marinas, some large and some small. None of humanity's intrusions detract from the overall scene, but rather all blend so well that they seem like natural outgrowths of river life. The St. Johns River is a cruising ground with reliably mild winter weather, interesting towns, villages and secluded anchorages that should not be missed. The beauty is astounding and the cruising is wonderful.

## Cruising Conditions

Between Mayport and Sanford, the St. Johns River is deep and easy to cruise because the channel is maintained for commercial craft. The relatively few shoals are well marked. Overhead clearance is set by two fixed bridges (the first is the Shands Bridge at Red Bay Point which carries a 45-foot vertical clearance), but follow charts carefully and keep an eye on the depth sounder. If the chart looks doubtful, then go marker-to-marker. Several unmarked shoal spots extend toward the channel between Palatka and the Buffalo Bluff Railroad Bridge (7-foot closed vertical clearance, usually open), near Murphy Island. The Coast Guard reports that the overhead power cable just north of the Astor Highway Bridge at St. Johns River Mile 122.2 has less than the charted 50-foot clearance but we do not have an exact figure.

Snags are seldom a problem in main channels of the St. Johns River, but approach side streams and sloughs carefully. Keep an eye out for trap markers as well. These markers vary from commercially produced floats to those improvised with plastic soda bottles. Some markers are fouled with vegetation (almost impossible to see), the current pulls some under and some are black in color.

In the narrow snakelike reaches beyond Lake George, it is safest to stay in the center of the channel, although depths tend to hold close toward the riverbanks. The constant passage of fuel barges headed to and from the port of Sanford helps keep the channel clear.

The St. Johns River is used year-round by recreational craft. On weekends and holidays, especially when the weather is good, the river carries heavy traffic. You will see everything from mid-sized cruisers and small runabouts to bass boats and personal watercraft, all in a great hurry to reach their destinations. No-Wake Zones abound, especially in the Astor/Blue Springs area, where the rules are strictly enforced. Maintain only steerageway here (even sailboats producing little wake), as it is a manatee area. Be particularly observant from November through mid-April, when the manatees are in residence. Marine patrol vessels often stand by to enforce regulations.

## Dealing with River Currents

Skippers of sailboats with auxiliary power or low-powered motor cruisers should check their tidal current tables before starting upriver to Jacksonville from the ICW or Atlantic Ocean entrance. River currents meeting strong ocean tides can create tricky conditions. Be aware of the differences in tidal current times, and note that slack water does not necessarily coincide with high or low tide. The ebb in the river can run 2 to 3 knots, making for a slow passage for underpowered boats. The tidal current tables give corrections to the Shands Bridge (45-foot fixed vertical clearance) at Red Bay Point in Green Cove Springs. This location is upriver (south) of Green Cove Springs. The average maximum flood given is 0.9 knots, and the average maximum ebb is 0.6 knots. The next location is Tocoi, approximately 15 miles upriver, where the current is "weak and variable."

Current past Tocoi can be strongly influenced by the water level in the upper (southern) part of the river, as

it flows south to north. It can be strong enough to make docking across the current difficult for the unwary.

## River Tides

Tides are given in the tide tables to Welaka, 66 miles south of Jacksonville. The corrections, based on Mayport (Atlantic Ocean entrance), are all ratios that must be used as a multiplier. The spring range (full and new moon) at Mayport can exceed 5 feet and, at Palatka, is around 1.5 feet. Wind and rainfall can affect depth (and, of course, current), especially on the upper reaches. If you plan to gunkhole, it would be advisable to carry a lead line or long boat pole to supplement your depth sounder. Sounding into areas where charts may not indicate all the shoals may be advisable.

## ■ TO JACKSONVILLE

The route to Jacksonville is a big-ship channel, well marked and simple to run. It generally follows the wide, natural course of the river. For the most part, deep water prevails alongside the marked channel, there are no intricate ranges and the next light or marker ahead is always within sight. Even for slow sailboats, the trip is less than a day's travel and your efforts will be rewarded.

**NAVIGATION:** Use Chart 11491. (This chart covers the mouth of the St. Johns River on the Atlantic Ocean to the Ortega River just past downtown Jacksonville.) While currents gradually decrease upriver on the St. Johns River, the flow runs up to 3 knots at first and can be a major factor near the downtown Jacksonville bridges. Plan your trip for a fair current by calculating slack before flood and maximum flood at Mile Point (at flashing red buoy "22") on the St. Johns River to get an interval of time to arrive at the ICW crossing.

*Coast Pilot (Volume 4)* points out four critical traffic areas on the St. Johns: (1) the junction of the St. Johns River and the ICW; (2) Dames Point Turn; (3) Trout River Cut; and (4) Commodore Point. Commercial vessels must give a Sécurité call on VHF Channel 13 to avoid meeting one another at these points. Recreational boats do not need to do so—you will have enough maneuvering room to stay out of the way—but monitor VHF Channel 13 so you will know whether you will be meeting a big ship or a tug with tow.

# Dames Point–Fulton Cutoff

West of Sisters Creek and the ICW, the channel enters wide and straight Dames Point–Fulton Cutoff, dredged to eliminate a bend in the St. Johns River's natural course. The impressive high-level bridge across the St. Johns River and Mill Cove is officially named the Napoleon Bonaparte Broward Bridge but is known by locals as the **Dames Point Bridge** (169-foot fixed vertical clearance above the main channel).

Mainly a complex of wharves, warehouses and a container terminal, Blount Island (created by dredge spoil) is on the north side of the Dames Point–Fulton Cutoff channel. Although the loop behind the island is deep, three low bridges (5-, 8- and 10-foot fixed vertical clearances) prevent a complete circuit. Back River pierces Blount Island from the Dames Point–Fulton Cutoff Channel; it is entirely commercial. Recreational craft should not attempt to anchor or fish in the channel.

**Anchorage:** You may anchor off Little Marsh Island east of Blount Island and across the old St. Johns River Channel but be sure to stay clear of the channel by Blount Island. Watch for trap markers and do not interfere with the private docks along Little Marsh Island. Use this anchorage only if necessary; there is no place to go ashore here, and it is very busy with commercial traffic. You will find 7- to 10-foot depths. You can also anchor at Reed Island, located across from Blount Island, in at least 10 feet of water with good holding in mud. It is open to north and south wakes.

# Broward and Trout Rivers

The unmarked Broward River requires local knowledge and is blocked off by a wharf extending 500 yards from shore, as well as the **Route 105 Bridge** (20-foot fixed vertical clearance) crossing the entrance. Many local boats use the Trout River just 2 miles to the south, which is the waterway leading to the Jacksonville Zoo. Vessels with very shallow-drafts (or better yet, a dinghy) can reach the Jacksonville Zoo and Gardens from the Trout River.

**NAVIGATION:** Use Chart 11491. Turn off the main St. Johns River channel between flashing red buoys "64" and "66" into the Trout River and then pick up red daybeacon "2" and green daybeacon "3," which mark the Trout River Channel. The zoo's floating concrete "T" dock is located on the north bank of the Trout River, just northeast of the **Main Street (U.S. 17) Bridge** (29-foot closed vertical clearance), which is followed by

# Side Trip: Fort Caroline

About 1.7 miles west of the ICW, on the south side of the river (opposite flashing red buoy "34") at St. Johns Bluff, a national park features a recreation of French-built Fort Caroline. The French (who discovered the St. Johns River in May 1562 and called it Riviere de Mai) established North America's first Protestant settlement in 1564. They built Fort Caroline to secure their landholdings, but the Spanish, who had established St. Augustine, temporarily defeated them. Under Spanish rule it was called Fort San Mateo, but the French retook it two years later and restored its original name.

Fort Caroline is worth visiting, but the current is strong and the water, even close in, can carry 45-foot depths. It is best to rent a car in Jacksonville and drive to the fort. Do not attempt to anchor by Blount Island and then dinghy across to the fort. There is no place to land a dinghy, and the steep banks are home to rattlesnakes and water moccasins.

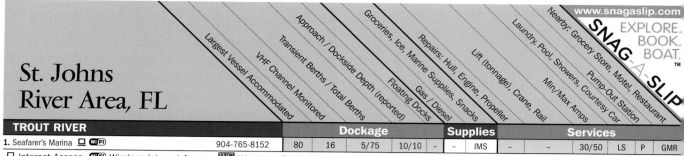

# St. Johns River Area, FL

| TROUT RIVER | | | Dockage | | | | Supplies | | Services | | | |
|---|---|---|---|---|---|---|---|---|---|---|---|---|
| 1. Seafarer's Marina 🖥 📶 | 904-765-8152 | 80 | 16 | 5/75 | 10/10 | – | – | IMS | – | – | 30/50 | LS | P | GMR |

🖥 Internet Access  📶 Wireless Internet Access  **WG** Waterway Guide Cruising Club Partner *(Information in the table is provided by the facilities.)*
See WaterwayGuide.com for current rates, fuel prices, web site addresses, and other up-to-the-minute information.

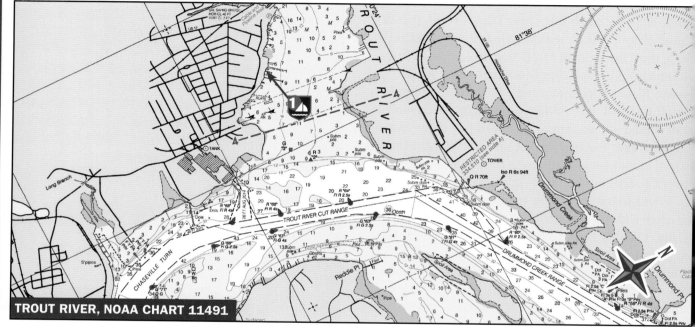

**TROUT RIVER, NOAA CHART 11491**

the **CSX Railroad Swing Bridge** (usually open). Zoo officials report the depth at the dock to be between 1 and 2 feet at low tide, and there are no plans to dredge. (For more information about the zoo, call 904-757-4463.)

**Dockage:** Seafarer's Marina is located on the Trout River with some transient space. Groceries and restaurants are nearby. It has twin daybeacons at the entrance, red "2" and green "3," central depths of 10 feet and a twin-span bridge upstream with a controlling fixed vertical clearance of 29 feet.

## The City of Jacksonville

**NAVIGATION:** Use Chart 11491. Along the St. Johns River from the ICW (between flashing red buoy "24" and flashing green buoy "25") near Mile 739.5 all the way to the Hart-Commodore Point Bridge (just past flashing green buoy "79"), the posted speed limit in the channel is 25 mph. Manatee zones are designated as Slow-Speed/Minimum-Speed Wake or Idle-Speed/No-Wake Zones

from the channel to shore. A No-Wake Zone lies from the Hart-Commodore Bridge to the Fuller-Warren (I-95) Bridge. The St. Johns River is patrolled, and speed limits are enforced.

From the ICW crossing at Mile 740, the river generally winds in an east-west direction until it broadens at Hendricks Point in South Jacksonville and turns south. At first, most of the development is on the western shore, south of the Ortega River, ranging from summer cabins and elegant homes to large commercial complexes. The heavily industrialized riverfront (with the largest deep water harbor on the southern Atlantic coast) begins just off the Trout River, back at flashing red buoy "64."

The St. Johns River runs wide and deep past the yards and wharves. About 12 miles past the high-rise Dames Point Bridge, the first of the downtown bridges appears: two high-level structures about a half-mile apart. First is the red **Matthews Bridge** (86-foot fixed vertical clearance), followed by the green **Hart-Commodore**

I-95

South Jacksonville

Jacksonville

St. Johns River

**Point Bridge** (135-foot fixed vertical clearance at center; also known as Isaiah D. Hart Bridge). Note that tugs and barges cross the river channel at all hours of the day and night, so be cautious. For more information about navigating through Jacksonville, contact the Mayport Coast Guard Operations Center, 24 hours a day, at 904-564-7500 or on VHF Channel 16. There is also a *Local Notice to Mariners* broadcast on VHF Channel 22A at 8:15 a.m. and 6:15 p.m. daily. Navigation alerts are also updated daily at waterwayguide.com.

After the Hart-Commodore Bridge, the four remaining Jacksonville bridges are less than 1 mile apart. From east to west the bridges are the unmistakable blue **Main Street Lift Bridge** (40-foot closed vertical clearance), the **Acosta Bridge** (75-foot fixed vertical clearance), the **FEC Railroad Bascule Bridge** (5-foot closed vertical clearance) and the **Fuller-Warren Bridge** (75-foot fixed vertical clearance). The Main Street Lift Bridge opens on signal, except from 7:00 a.m. to 8:30 a.m. and from 4:30 p.m. to 6:00 p.m., Monday through Saturday (except federal holidays), when the draw need not open for the passage of vessels. The railroad bridge is usually open, except when a train is expected. Trains cross relatively frequently, all at slow speed.

It is common to meet barge traffic in the area of these bridges; contact the tugboat skippers on VHF Channels 13 or 16 so they can tell you how to stay out of their way. After you pass the Fuller-Warren Bridge, the river widens. The next bridge is approximately 8 miles upriver, located past the Naval Air Station. The **Buckman (I-295) Bridge** (known locally as Three-Mile Bridge) is a twin-span high-level bridge that carries eight lanes of I-295 traffic. Its fixed vertical clearance is reported at 65 feet.

**Dockage:** The first facility you encounter when headed to Jacksonville is Arlington Marina (before the Mathews Bridge), which has transient space for vessels up to 50 feet at floating concrete docks. They also sell fuel. Next, on the north bank of the river, The City of Jacksonville operates the 75-slip Metropolitan Park Marina, located adjacent to EverBank Field (home of the Jacksonville Jaguars football team) and the tent-like pavilion of Metropolitan Park. This facility is intended for public use and does not charge for dockage except during special events such as football games and concerts. The marina has no showers or laundry facilities, but shore power is available via a kiosk on the dock (for a small fee). Water is also available at each dock. Transients may tie up here, on a space-available

CHAPTER 2

SIDE TRIP ON THE ST. JOHNS RIVER

# St. Johns River, FL

| | | Largest Vessel Accommodated | VHF Channel Monitored | Transient Berths / Total Berths | Approach / Dockside Depth (reported) | Floating Docks | Groceries, Ice, Marine Supplies, Snacks | Gas / Diesel | Repairs: Hull, Engine, Propeller | Lift (tonnage), Crane, Rail | Laundry, Pool, Showers, Courtesy Car | Min/Max Amps | Pump-Out Station | Nearby: Grocery Store, Motel, Restaurant |
|---|---|---|---|---|---|---|---|---|---|---|---|---|---|---|
| **ARLINGTON** | | | | | **Dockage** | | | **Supplies** | | | **Services** | | | |
| **1.** Arlington Marina, Inc. 🖥 WiFi | 904-743-2628 | 50 | 16/68 | 6/30 | 16/5 | F | GD | IMS | – | L30,R | 30/50 | LS | – | GR |
| **JACKSONVILLE** | | | | | | | | | | | | | | |
| **2.** Metropolitan Park Marina WG | 904-630-0839 | 80 | 72 | 78/78 | 30/15 | F | – | – | – | – | 30/50 | – | P | GMR |
| **3.** The Jacksonville Landing WiFi WG | 904-353-1188 | – | – | – | – | F | – | IS | – | – | – | – | – | R |
| **4.** River City Brewing Co. & Marina 🖥 | 904-398-7918 | 120 | 16 | 10/62 | 18/13 | F | GD | IS | – | – | 30/50 | LS | – | GMR |

🖥 Internet Access   WiFi Wireless Internet Access   WG Waterway Guide Cruising Club Partner   *(Information in the table is provided by the facilities.)*
See WaterwayGuide.com for current rates, fuel prices, web site addresses, and other up-to-the-minute information.

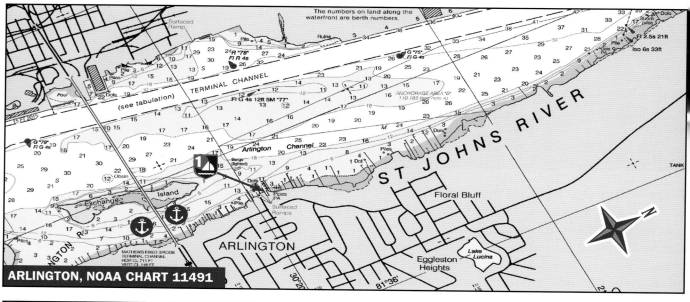

ARLINGTON, NOAA CHART 11491

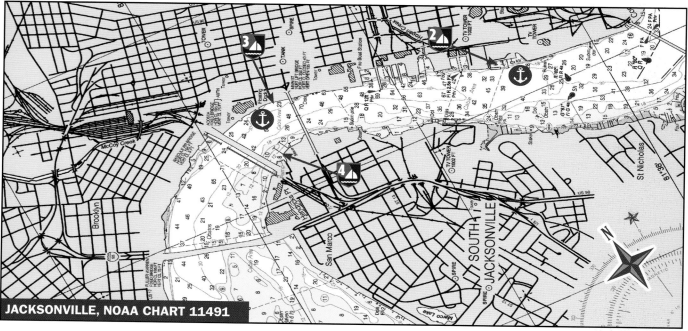

JACKSONVILLE, NOAA CHART 11491

basis, for up to 72 hours. The docks are in a park that is open only from sunrise to sunset, so when the park is closed, they lock the area and you will be unable to enter or leave. There is also a trolley for transportation. You may pick up the delightful aroma of roasting coffee, coming from the Maxwell House Coffee Co. upriver where one of their three US roasting plants is located.

The Jacksonville Landing, a festival-type marketplace located on the north waterfront, offers 72-hour complimentary dockage on a first-come, first-served basis. There is no electricity or water available, but cleats are plentiful and rafting is permitted. Recreational craft must not get in the way of the sightseeing boats or the busy water taxis. Across the river, River City Brewing Co. & Marina has dockage, gas and diesel fuel. Courtesy slips are available for guests who are dining with them.

**Anchorage:** You can anchor near the Matthews Point Bridge, between Exchange Island and the Arlington waterfront, behind the City Limits Range. Holding ground is best to the east and north of the bridge in 9 to 11 feet of water. Traffic in the main channel might jostle you here; just north of the anchorage is a dock for tugs. You may also see college rowing teams honing their skills against the swift current. With the wind out of the north, you might elect to anchor in 8 to 20 feet of water on the southern side of the Matthews Point Bridge, in the lee of Exchange Island.

# ORTEGA RIVER

The hub of Jacksonville's marine industry, the Ortega (pronounced "or-TEE-ga") River is in a residential area 3 miles southwest of the Fuller-Warren Bridge.

**NAVIGATION:** Use Chart 11491. The best way to enter the Ortega River is to head due south from the Fuller-Warren (I-95) Bridge. Heading south, delay your westward turn until you pass flashing red buoy "2" and the white daybeacon marking the shoal extending south off Winter Point. There is no light or daybeacon at the mouth of the Ortega River. With the old light missing, be sure to mind the charted obstructions and pilings north of Sadler Point. Depths here are 5 to 8 feet in the river (with shallower spots), but watch the depth sounder, and proceed slowly, especially if you have a draft of 5 feet or more. The tidal range is about 1 foot. Check for local information on depths and markers before entering the Ortega River.

For deepest water, give a wide berth to the shoal off Sadler Point, and line up for the **Ortega River Bridge** (9-foot closed vertical clearance) after you are clear of the shallow water. The bridge opens on request. Because of its low clearance in an area of high marine traffic, the bascule bridge, a 1920s-vintage classic, is the most frequently opened drawbridge in Florida (about 15,000 openings per year).

The water is relatively consistent beyond the fixed **Roosevelt Blvd. Bridge** (45-foot vertical clearance), with 5- to 8-foot depths at mean low water. A **CSX Railroad Bascule Bridge** (2-foot closed vertical clearance, opens on signal) crosses the Ortega River just past the Roosevelt Blvd. Bridge.

**Dockage:** The Ortega River (known as "Jacksonville Marina Mile") has an almost solid wall of yards, marinas and boatbuilders on the northwest bank. The Marina at Ortega Landing is the first marina to starboard when heading upstream and is part of a residential development. This 192-slip marina can accommodate boats up to 130 feet and has full cruiser amenities, including a pool. This facility is within walking distance to West Marine and shopping. They also have loaner bikes.

Next upstream is the Ortega River Marina. The marina has transient slips on floating docks. It is the closest marina to dining, shopping and provisioning. Advance reservations are required.

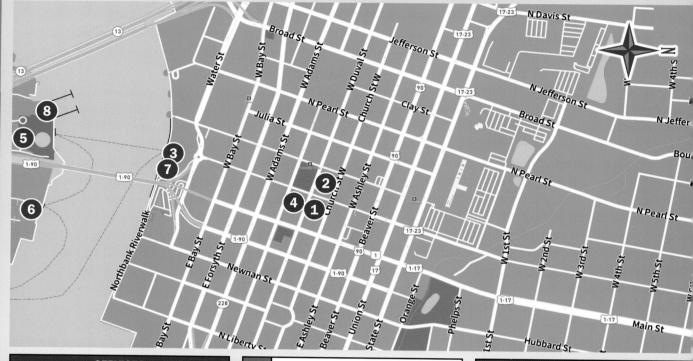

| SERVICES | |
|---|---|
| 1 | Library |
| 2 | Visitor Information |
| **ATTRACTIONS** | |
| 3 | Jacksonville Landing |
| 4 | Museum of Contemporary Art |

| | |
|---|---|
| 5 | Museum of Science and History (MOSH) |
| 6 | Southbank Riverwalk |
| 7 | USS Adams Museum |
| **SHOPPING/DINING** | |
| 3 | Jacksonville Landing |

| MARINAS | |
|---|---|
| 3 | Jacksonville Landing |
| 8 | River City Brewing Co. & Marina |

Following the Civil War, Jacksonville became a popular winter resort. Visitors arriving by steamboats and railroad enjoyed the mild winters, fine restaurants and hotels until Henry Flagler extended the railroad south to Palm Beach and then Miami in the 1890s.

In the early 1900s, Jacksonville promoted its mild climate, low labor cost and easy rail access to become the "Winter Film Capital of the World," with more than 30 studios. In the 1920s, local politicians forced the studios to go elsewhere, and Hollywood was born.

Jacksonville International Airport, 10 miles north of the city, has commercial air service to all major cities.

**Attractions:** Beyond the busy commercial area, the Jacksonville waterfront is delightful. Tranquil riverside parks and open space line the waterfront. The city's riverfront redevelopment project has included both banks of the river. On the north waterfront, Jacksonville Landing serves as a visitors center and features outdoor entertainment, a variety of dining options and more than 40 specialty shops. A state-of-the-art, interactive museum aboard the *USS Charles F. Adams* was in the planning stages at press time in spring 2017. This is part of a long-term vision for downtown Jacksonville. Stay tuned at waterwayguide.com for updates.

Across the water is the 1.25-mile wooden zigzag boardwalk known as Southbank Riverwalk. A highlight is the Friendship Fountain, a huge, circular fountain with jets of water that shoot as high as 120 feet into the air. The fountain glows with multi-colored lights at night.

The Jacksonville Maritime Museum (MOSH) is nearby and is well worth a visit, particularly if you have children aboard. The museum features interactive exhibits like he Currents of Time, which explores 12,000 years of Northeast Florida History, and the Florida Natural Center, where visitors can get up close and personal with Northeast Florida's native wildlife. MOSH is also home o the Bryan-Gooding Planetarium–the largest single-lens planetarium in the world (1025 Museum Cir., 904-396-6674).

EverBank Field, (the Gator Bowl), is also located on he north side of the river. The stadium is home to the acksonville Jaguars, the college postseason Gator Bowl Classic and the annual Georgia–Florida football game, often described as the "world's largest outdoor cocktail party."

Also on the north shore near EverBank Field and the ransient docks is Metropolitan Park (1410 Gator Bowl Blvd., 904-630-0837). This striking tent-like outdoor auditorium is a popular site for concerts and festivals.

This park also hosts the Jacksonville Fire Museum built in 1902. The Museum of Contemporary Art (333 N. Laura St.) is also on the north side of the river.

**Shopping/Dining:** Restaurants and shopping can be found on both banks of the river–at Jacksonville Landing on the north side and at Southbank Riverwalk on the south side. For provisioning, Harveys Supermarket (777 N. Market St., 904-353-6810) is located just 10 blocks north of the waterfront, and the trolley will take you to a Publix (about a 10-minute bus ride).

River City Brewing Company & Marina on the south side overlooks the river and the downtown Jacksonville skyline. They are open for lunch and dinner plus offer a Sunday brunch. The deck of the Brew House is dog friendly (under 25 pounds and on a leash) so your 4-legged crew can join you while you enjoy a Red Rooster Ale or Mad Monkey Mango Wheat (seasonal beer).

www.snagaslip.com

SNAG-A-SLIP™

EXPLORE. BOOK. BOAT.

# Ortega River, FL

| ORTEGA RIVER | | Dockage | | | | | Supplies | | Services | | | | | |
|---|---|---|---|---|---|---|---|---|---|---|---|---|---|---|
| | | Largest Vessel Accommodated | VHF Channel Monitored | Approach / Dockside Depth (reported) | Transient Berths / Total Berths | Floating Docks | Gas / Diesel | Groceries, Ice, Marine Supplies, Snacks | Repairs: Hull, Engine, Propeller | Lift (tonnage), Crane, Rail | Min/Max Amps | Laundry, Pool, Showers, Courtesy Car | Pump-Out Station | Nearby: Grocery Store, Motel, Restaurant |
| 1. The Marina at Ortega Landing 🖥 WiFi WG | 904-387-5538 | 130 | 16/08 | 20/192 | 6/6 | F | - | I | - | - | 30/100 | LPS | P | GR |
| 2. Ortega River Marina 🖥 WiFi | 904-389-1199 | 60 | 16/08 | 4/99 | 7/6 | F | - | IS | - | - | 30/50 | LPS | P | GR |
| 3. Sadler Point Marine Center 🖥 | 904-384-1383 | 50 | 16/08 | 0/65 | 6/8 | - | - | IMS | HEP | L35 | 30/50 | S | P | GR |
| 4. Huckins Yacht Corp. WiFi WG | 904-389-1125 | 80 | - | call/20 | 6/6 | F | - | M | HEP | L77 | 30/50 | - | - | GR |
| 5. Cedar Point Marina | 904-384-5577 | 80 | - | 5/24 | 12/6 | F | - | - | - | - | 30/50 | LS | - | GMR |
| 6. Lamb's Yacht Center 🖥 WiFi WG | 904-384-5577 | 120 | 16/08 | 12/240 | 8/7 | - | GD | IMS | HEP | L100, R40 | 30/100 | LS | P | GR |
| 7. Florida Yacht Club-PRIVATE | 904-387-1653 | 70 | 16/68 | call/73 | 8/6 | F | - | IS | - | - | 30/50 | PS | - | GR |

🖥 Internet Access   WiFi Wireless Internet Access   WG Waterway Guide Cruising Club Partner   *(Information in the table is provided by the facilities.)*
See WaterwayGuide.com for current rates, fuel prices, web site addresses, and other up-to-the-minute information.

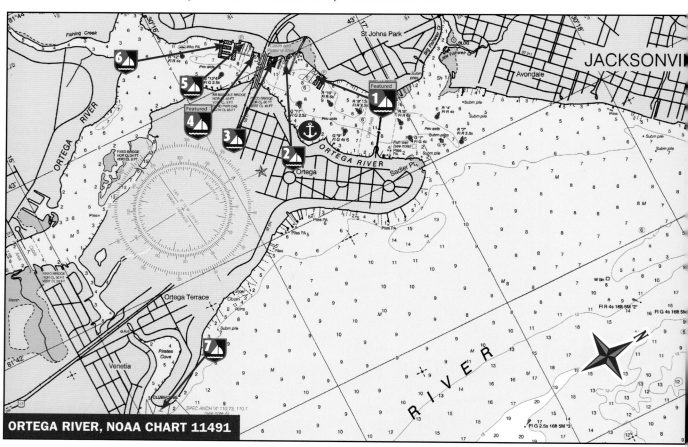

ORTEGA RIVER, NOAA CHART 11491

Just before the railroad bridge is Sadler Point Marine Center, which offers a full service and do-it-yourself boatyard with a 35-ton lift.

Immediately to starboard past the railroad bridge is Huckins Yacht Corp., known for its beautiful custom yachts. Frank Pembroke Huckins was instrumental in designing the famous PT boats of World War II. The company was originally located in what is now the Maxwell House Coffee Co. near the Jacksonville waterfront. After the war, the company moved to its present location. They offer slips, sell diesel and have 77-ton lift for large repairs.

Nearby Cedar Point Marina has dockage to 80 feet and some reserved transient space. The large full-service Lamb's Yacht Center has transient slips, all fuels and extensive repair capabilities. They are capable of hauling power cats. (Sailors Exchange, which used to be in this location, closed in 2016.)

The southwest shore is entirely residential, with private docks and wooded plots. The only problem in finding a berth here may be choosing among the yards and marinas, many of which welcome transients. All of the marinas are very convenient to Roosevelt Square, which is located four or five blocks from the waterfront. It has a large variety of shore amenities (restaurants and shops, along with a West Marine and a large Publix grocery store). Roosevelt Square also has a department store, pharmacy and loads of fast food. There is also convenient city bus service here that runs to downtown Jacksonville.

If you are planning on continuing south on the St. Johns River, this is the last place to conveniently provision the boat. Our cruising editor recommends that you provision with whatever you think you'll need until you get back into this area. There are stores along the way, but you will need ground transportation to get to most of them, which could be a problem in some of the small, out-of-the-way places you'll encounter.

**Anchorage:** A few boats can anchor, with care, in the open spaces between the various boatyards and marinas. This is a busy area, so minimizing your swinging room will be important. Keep clear of the channel and set an anchor light at night. Naturally, you should get permission from the marinas before you tie up your dinghy. A better anchorage is on the south shore between the Ortega River Bridge and the Roosevelt Blvd. Bridge (Mile 21.5) in 6 to 7 feet of water with good holding in mud.

## THE MARINA AT ORTEGA LANDING

4234 Lakeside Drive
Jacksonville, Florida 32210
904-387-5538
OrtegaLanding.com
email: Office@OrtegaLanding.com

This state-of-the-art 192-slip marina can accommodate boats up to 130' on floating Bellingham docks. The marina features a beautiful clubhouse with large, clean showers and rest rooms, laundry facilities, ice, WiFi, bicycles and is within walking distance to West Marine and shopping. Enjoy the use of our book library, cable TV and beautiful views from our clubhouse.

### APPROACH & DOCKING

Proceed up the St. John's River past downtown Jacksonville (Use chart 11491). Head due south from Fuller Warren Bridge, past flashing red "2", giving the white caution marker a wide berth (approx. 100 yards). Head west into the Ortega River leaving the green piling and floating marker approximately 50-75 feet to port. Once abeam of the floating marker, head straight for the bridge opening. Call the Ortega River Bridge on Ch. 9. Bridge opens on request 24/7. Once through the bridge, we are the first marina on the right.

### MARINA STAFF

The staff is comprised of professionals from various fields, each providing you superior service to make your stay the best possible. They will guide you in and assist with docking. Monthly theme parties and impromptu gatherings always ensure a fun experience here.

NEXT STOP

# WATERWAY® GUIDE

THE CRUISING AUTHORITY

# The Bahamas 2018

INCLUDING TURKS AND CAICOS

➤ **Updated Annually**
➤ **Marinas & Anchorages**
➤ **Goin' Ashores**

Visit waterwayguide.com

## ■ TO GREEN COVE SPRINGS

With a few exceptions, the St. Johns River seems to transform itself into a lake immediately beyond the Ortega River, with widths averaging a couple of miles or more for most of the 47 miles to Palatka. This section is great for sailing, although strong winds out of the north or south can kick up quite a chop. Deep water stretches from shore to shore, providing plenty of room for a sailor to make long, pleasant reaches.

### To the Buckman (I-295) Bridge

**NAVIGATION:** Use Chart 11492. Even when the going is tranquil, it is wise to run compass courses for each lengthy reach between the daybeacons and lights, making sure you always have a good idea of your position. This country is great for fishing and crabbing, but the bobbing floats of the commercial crabber's pots—some of which are dark and difficult to see—are numerous enough to warrant close attention.

**Dockage:** About 2 miles past the entrance to the Ortega River, at Pirates Cove on the western shore, is the Florida Yacht Club, one of the country's oldest (charted, to starboard in a protected lagoon), open only to its members and members of clubs that belong to the Florida Council of Yacht Clubs. The club may accept guests that are members of reciprocating yacht clubs, but they have to be approved ahead of time by the Board of Directors.

**Anchorage:** Beyond Goodbys Creek, on the eastern side of the river, you can anchor in Plummers Cove between Beauclerc Bluff and the Buckman Bridge, also known locally as Three Mile Bridge (65-foot fixed vertical clearance). The entrance is straightforward. Just avoid the shoal off Beauclerc Bluff, which is marked by green daybeacon "9." Go in at the approximate middle of the "entrance," dodging the pot markers that sometimes pepper both the entrance and interior. Note shoaling along the shoreline and sound your way in. This is not a cozy anchorage, but it is adequate in calm conditions or lacking any alternative. It would be wise to choose your weather carefully, as this anchorage has no protection from the west, should a thunderstorm blow through. Anchor in depths of 6 to 8 feet—the holding is good in mud. You will hear some noise from the naval air station across the river at Piney Point. Remember that all along the St. Johns River, remnants of old docks, some submerged, can be hazardous. Most of these are charted, but still warrant a close look-out.

### Doctors Lake

**NAVIGATION:** Use Chart 11492. About 2 miles south of the Buckman Bridge, on the west side of the St. Johns River, is Doctors Lake, four miles long and in many places deep (7- to 10-foot depths) almost to the banks. The lake is beautiful and protected, and its wooded shores are dotted with homes, many with their own docks.

The entrance to Doctors Lake, spanned by the **Park Ave. (Hwy. 17) Bridge** (37-foot fixed vertical clearance), is off Orange Point and marked by red daybeacon "2," which has been moved farther away from shore toward the channel. Stay clear of the shoaling on both sides of Doctors Inlet and steer toward the middle of the entrance.

**Dockage:** Doctors Lake Marina is located just inside the bridge on the south shore of Doctors Inlet with slips and gas and diesel. Eight miles of paths for walking and bicycling provide access to restaurants, laundry, pharmacies and a grocery. They only report two reserved transient slips, so call ahead for availability.

The docks at Fleming Island Marina on the south side of Doctors Inlet before the bridge are in serious disrepair and cannot be recommended by our cruising editor. The future of this facility was uncertain at press time in 2017.

**Anchorage:** If you can clear the 37-foot fixed vertical clearance bridge and decide to anchor in Doctors Lake, do so with care because the holding in some places is poor. The bottom is covered with very fine, soft silt, in which even the best of anchors will not set well.

In west through northwest winds, anchor above Peoria Point in Sugarhouse Cove; in strong northerly winds, try close in to the shore, between Macks Point and Indigo Branch; in heavy easterly weather, try the mouth of Mill Cove. In all places, be certain to power down on your hook and check it frequently. You will find 7 to 12 feet here; respect the charted submerged piling areas. Do not anchor in the middle of the lake except in an emergency; it is far too exposed.

## Julington Creek

Almost directly across the St. Johns River from Doctors Lake is Julington Creek. The fixed **Julington Creek Bridge** has 15-foot vertical clearance. That and shallow depths beyond the bridge will limit the exploration area for some.

**Dockage:** Mandarin Holiday Marina is located before the fixed bridge, while Marina at Julington Creek is located after the bridge. Both accept transients. Gas and diesel are available here as well as repairs.

**Anchorage:** Julington Creek is shoaling, so sound your way in, and check the depth of your swinging arc if you choose to anchor here. Above the opening, the creek shoals quickly to 4-foot depths or less, especially on the north side. For larger boats, Old Bull Bay at Julington Creek's mouth is a good anchorage with shelter from north through southeast winds. This attractive area is especially good for dinghy exploration. You will find 7- to 8-foot depths on a line between the points of land and 4 to 6 feet closer to the bridge South of Mandarin Point, in 11 feet of water, there is a spot for the night. It is protected from the north and northeast. This anchorage should be used in only stable weather.

## Black Creek

Black Creek empties into the St. Johns River about 3 miles north of Green Cove Springs on the western bank of the St. Johns River just north of Wilkies Point. The creek is deep, placid, unspoiled and offers a microcosm of the world's subtropical rivers. If you make

# St. Johns River, FL

| | | | Dockage | | | | Supplies | | | Services | | | | |
|---|---|---|---|---|---|---|---|---|---|---|---|---|---|---|
| | | Largest Vessel Accommodated | VHF Channel Monitored | Transient Berths / Total Berths | Approach / Dockside Depth (reported) | Floating Docks | Groceries, Ice, Marine Supplies, Snacks | Gas / Diesel | Repairs: Hull, Engine, Propeller | Lift (tonnage), Crane, Rail | Min/Max Amps | Laundry, Pool, Showers, Courtesy Car | Pump-Out Station | Nearby: Grocery Store, Motel, Restaurant |
| **DOCTORS LAKE** | | | | | | | | | | | | | | |
| 1. Fleming Island Marina ⌑ Wi-Fi | 904-269-0027 | 50 | – | 100/100 | 7/7 | F | – | IMS | HEP | L25,C | 30/30 | PS | P | GMR |
| 2. Doctors Lake Marina Wi-Fi | 904-264-0505 | 75 | – | 2/100 | 7/6 | – | GD | GIMS | HEP | | 30/50 | LS | P | GR |
| **JULINGTON CREEK** | | | | | | | | | | | | | | |
| 3. Mandarin Holiday Marina | 904-268-1036 | 50 | 16/68 | 5/150 | 6/6 | – | GD | GIMS | HEP | L15 | 30/30 | S | P | GMR |
| 4. Julington Creek Marina | 904-268-5117 | 40 | 16/09 | call/326 | 6/5 | – | G | IMS | – | L12 | 30/30 | – | P | GR |

⌑ Internet Access   Wi-Fi Wireless Internet Access   WG Waterway Guide Cruising Club Partner   *(Information in the table is provided by the facilities.)*
See WaterwayGuide.com for current rates, fuel prices, web site addresses, and other up-to-the-minute information.

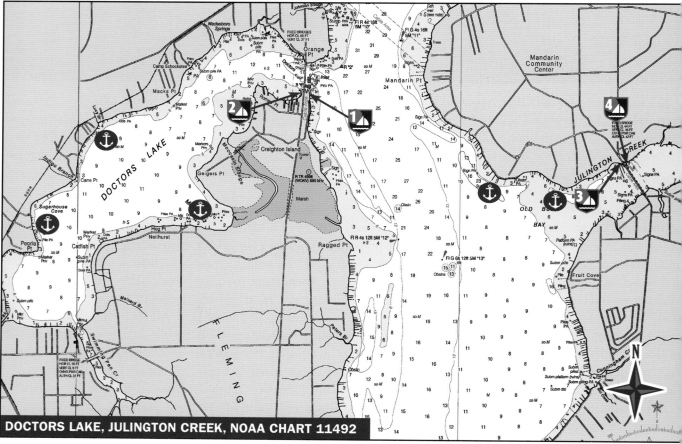

**DOCTORS LAKE, JULINGTON CREEK, NOAA CHART 11492**

the trip in late spring or summer, don't be surprised if you disturb a slumbering alligator along the banks.

The **Black Creek (US 17) Twin Bridges** at the entrance have a fixed vertical clearance of 30 feet, and upstream is another bridge with a fixed vertical clearance of 20 feet. An overhead cable with an authorized vertical clearance of 47 feet also crosses the creek about 2 miles above the first bridge. If you can get under all of these (or have your mast unstepped at a nearby marina), you can cruise upriver to the headwaters and the town of

Middleburg, which rivals St. Augustine as one of the nation's oldest settlements. A grocery store is a pleasant walk from the Middleburg waterfront, but there are no transient docks.

**Anchorage:** You can anchor in Black Creek in at least 15 feet of water with good holding in mud and all-around protection. Continuing on the St. Johns River upriver from Black Creek, both banks offer coves with safe overnight spots. Most of these are obvious on the charts. You need only select a cove on the east or west bank, depending upon the wind direction at the time of your arrival. Most of the bottom here is sticky black mud, good holding for a well-set hook. Usually a current sets with the tide as far as Lake George. South of the lake, the weak current sets downstream (northward).

## Green Cove Springs

The town of Green Cove Springs is on a very shallow, pretty cove off the St. Johns River. Here, the long piers of a World War II Navy facility jut out into the river. These piers clearly show up on the chart for the area.

Green Cove Springs took its name from the sulfur mineral spring found here. Long reputed to have medicinal qualities, the waters attracted many famous visitors in the late 1800s and early 1900s. Today, visitors will find the spring in the midst of a city park fringed with fine old homes. St. Mary's Episcopal Church, built in the late 19th century, is an elegant riverfront structure with an unusual architectural feature: fire-escape doors beneath the stained-glass windows along the sides of the building. The town is home to St. Brendan's Isle, a well-known cruiser's mail forwarding service.

**Dockage/Moorings:** Just south of Governors Creek is the Green Cove Springs City Pier with enough space for four or five boats to tie up with water available. Payment for overnight dockage should be made at the honor box on the pier. The next three facilities are in a row: Holland Marine (a boatyard that does not accept transients); Reynolds Park Yacht Center (may have transient space and also offers repairs); and Green Cove Springs Marina, which offers deep water slips on floating docks for vessels to 100 feet. If they do not have any space available at the dock, a mooring may be available; call ahead for details. Green Cove Springs is a well-protected spot for safe long-term storage. They also have on-site approved contractors for painting, mechanical, electrical repair, bottom work and canvas, as well as a marine supply store.

You won't find fuel here, but what you will find is a bank, pharmacy and several eateries within six blocks of the dock. Provisioning can be done at a supermarket located about 2 miles north of town. Home Depot, Target, Walmart, Publix and other amenities are another 12 or so miles north (transportation required).

**Anchorage:** Governors Creek, just north of the town, has a boat ramp and fishing pier. Watch for the charted overhead power lines (30-foot vertical clearances) and fixed bridges (8- and 11-foot vertical clearances heading upstream respectively) as you enter. Boats may anchor at the mouth of Governors Creek in 8 feet of water with fair holding in mud. This is open from the north through southeast.

Across the river, between Popo Point and the Shands Bridge at Orangedale (Mile 41.5) is another anchorage. Note the shoal water south of Hallowes Cove, as well as the 3-foot-deep spot northeast of flashing red daybeacon "20." Enter well southeast of flashing red daybeacon "20," avoiding the charted cable area. Protection is good only from the northeast, but holding is excellent in 7 to 10 feet of water.

# St. Johns River, FL

www.snagaslip.com

SNAG-A-SLIP

EXPLORE
BOOK
BOAT

| | | Largest Vessel Accommodated | VHF Channel Monitored | Transient Berths / Total Berths | Approach / Dockside Depth (reported) | Floating Docks | Gas / Diesel | Groceries, Ice, Marine Supplies, Snacks | Repairs: Hull, Engine, Propeller | Lift (tonnage), Crane, Rail | Min/Max Amps | Laundry, Pool, Showers, Courtesy Car | Pump-Out Station | Nearby: Grocery Store, Motel, Restaurant |
|---|---|---|---|---|---|---|---|---|---|---|---|---|---|---|
| **GREEN COVE SPRINGS** | | | | | **Dockage** | | | **Supplies** | | | **Services** | | | |
| 1. Holland Marine | 904-284-3349 | 65 | – | 0/15 | 10/10 | F | – | M | HEP | L65,C | 30/50 | – | – | GMR |
| 2. Reynolds Park Yacht Center ⌨ WiFi | 904-284-4667 | 400 | 16/68 | 10/70 | 12/6 | F | – | M | HEP | L60 | 30/200+ | LS | P | MR |
| 3. **Green Cove Springs Marina** ⌨ WiFi | **904-284-1811** | **100** | **16/68** | **5/21** | **14/11** | **F** | **–** | **IM** | **HEP** | **L30,C** | **30/50** | **LS** | **P** | **GMR** |
| **TROUT CREEK** | | | | | | | | | | | | | | |
| 4. Trout Creek Marina | 904-342-2471 | – | – | 12/13 | 7/ | F | GD | GIMS | – | – | – | 30/30 | – | G |
| **PALATKA, SAN MATEO** | | | | | | | | | | | | | | |
| 5. Crystal Cove Resort Marina WiFi | 386-325-1055 | – | – | call/45 | 5/5 | – | G | IS | HEP | – | 30/50 | PS | – | MR |
| 6. Quality Inn & Suites Riverfront ⌨ WiFi | 386-328-3481 | 100 | – | 21/21 | 25/8 | – | – | IS | – | – | 30/50 | LPS | – | GMR |
| 7. Palatka City Dock | 386-329-0100 | 50 | – | 14/14 | 9/6 | F | – | – | – | – | 30/30 | – | P | MR |
| 8. Boathouse Marina ⌨ WiFi | 386-328-2944 | 60 | 16 | 10/40 | 8/8 | – | – | IS | – | – | 30/50 | LS | P | GMR |
| 9. Gibson Dry Docks ⌨ WiFi | 386-325-5502 | 49 | – | 0/20 | 6/6 | – | – | – | HEP | L30 | 30/30 | S | – | GMR |

⌨ Internet Access  WiFi Wireless Internet Access  WG Waterway Guide Cruising Club Partner  *(Information in the table is provided by the facilities.)*
See WaterwayGuide.com for current rates, fuel prices, web site addresses, and other up-to-the-minute information.

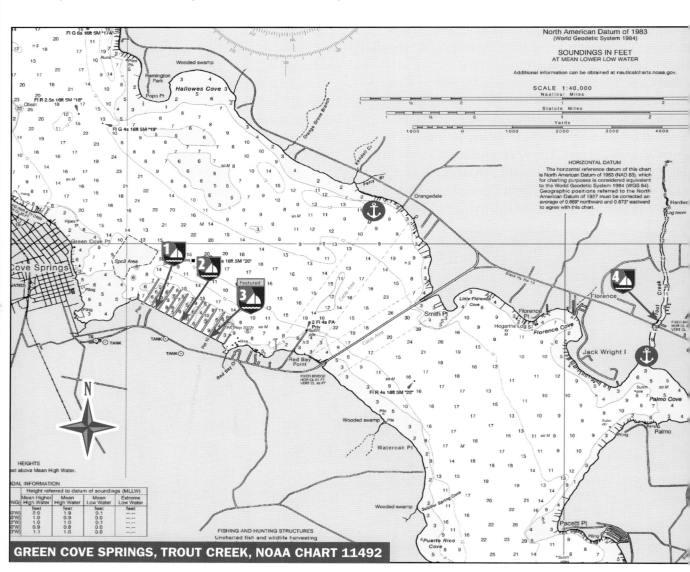

**GREEN COVE SPRINGS, TROUT CREEK, NOAA CHART 11492**

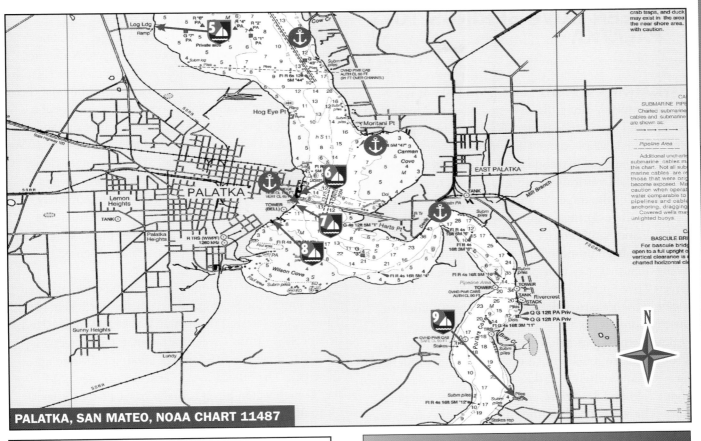

PALATKA, SAN MATEO, NOAA CHART 11487

Proud to be sponsors and members of the following organizations and associations

SSCA    AGLCA    MTOA

AIWA    MIASF

National Marine Manufacturer Association

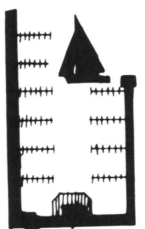

# GREEN COVE SPRINGS TO PALATKA

**NAVIGATION:** Use Charts 11487 and 11492. It is a 25-mile journey along the river's wooded and narrow banks from the Shands Bridge at Green Cove Springs to Palatka. Fish weirs (stakes) and numerous pot markers populate the river hereabouts. The **Shands Bridge** (45-foot fixed vertical clearance) that sets overhead clearance for the upper St. Johns River is located south of Green Cove Springs, running across the river between Red Bay and Smith Points. A new replacement 65-foot bridge has been proposed but there is no indication as to when that may transpire. When transiting the Green Cove Springs area, stick to the marked channel to avoid both charted shoals and possible submerged obstructions.

Beam winds, particularly from the west, can be very strong here, so remain lined up on the ranges unless you have a shallow draft. Palatka's high and low tides happen about 7.25 and 8.5 hours, respectively, after Mayport's tides. The water depth in the channels ranges from 8 to 12 feet at mean low tide. The tidal range is about 1 foot.

Heading south from Green Cove Springs, the first of six ranges starts about 8 miles past the Shands Bridge.

The river is marked from flashing red buoy "22" to flashing green buoy "31" at the first range. This one leads into the second, which takes you past Ninemile Point and leads into the third range, which passes south of Verdiere Point. Set a course eastward to the final three ranges heading southward to the massive towers of a high-tension line (60-foot vertical clearance on land, with 91-foot clearance over the channel) that crosses the river. As you proceed south, all are back ranges (look astern) except one. A power plant with twin towers is across the river from Forrester Point, approximately 4 miles north of the Palatka Bridge; it is charted and highly visible. Approaching the power plant, some of the local navigational aids may be partially obscured by bird nests.

**Anchorage:** To the south of the Shands Bridge, Trout Creek enters the St. Johns River on the north side of Palmo Cove, around the east end of Jack Wright Island, at Mile 47.2. Trout Creek is a popular anchorage, but note that there is a fixed bridge about a half-mile up the creek. The official listed vertical clearance is 14 feet at high water, but it actually has a 17-foot vertical clearance. Trout Creek is a deep and gorgeous stream, with controlling depths of 7 feet well above the bridge.

Charted depths indicate depths of at least 4 feet in Palmo Cove approaching the creek, where depths

Palmo Cove

Sixmile Creek

immediately increase to 13 to 14 feet. They go back down to 4 feet, however, just before the fixed bridge (12-foot vertical clearance).

About four miles upriver (south) from the Shands Bridge on the St. Johns River, there is a scenic cove on the west side of the river south of Bayard Point and north of another unmarked shoal northeast of Clark Creek (Mile 50). Depths are 9 to 10 feet in this cove, which is protected from the northwest and offers good holding in sandy mud. Sound your way in (charted at 3 to 6 feet entering off of St. Johns River) while dodging the pot markers that are often set here.

Four miles farther south and on the east side of the St. Johns River is Solano Cove (Mile 54.2), with 6 to 7 feet of water and good holding. It is open to the northwest through south. An excellent anchorage can also be found at Deep Creek (Mile 62.5) with all-around protection and good holding in mud.

## Palatka

Palatka retains the ambiance of an old river town. A city park along the riverfront has picnic shelters, boat ramps and restrooms, and brick-paved residential streets run beneath grand old oaks hung with Spanish moss. A long walk from the marinas south of the bridge is Ravine Gardens State Park at 1600 Twigg St. Begun in 1933, the 59-acre state park is built around natural ravines. The nature trails wander among thousands of azaleas and other ornamental plants growing near streams and ravines. There are picnic grounds and jogging trails. The park is open daily from 8:00 a.m. to sundown (386-329-3721).

**Dockage:** North of Palatka, about 1 mile west of flashing green daybeacon "41," is Crystal Cove Resort Marina. This marina's docks were destroyed in Hurricane Matthew and it was uncertain at press time (spring 2017) if they planned to rebuild. The Quality Inn & Suites Riverfront, just to the north of **Palatka Memorial Bridge** (65-foot closed vertical clearance) has berths reserved only for guests staying at the hotel.

Past the bridge to starboard is the Palatka City Dock, located in front of the clock towers. Space is available on a first-come, first-served basis for boats up to 50 feet. There is no power, water or other amenities. At Mile 77.5 is another city dock (fixed). This dock has dolphins on the outside, and it will be difficult to get off your boat here. A sign on the shore end of the dock gives the Palatka City Hall phone number and police department number. Shopping and restaurants are a few blocks away.

Boathouse Marina, south of the town dock, offers slips with full amenities. Transient dockage is available. You should head for the dock approximately midway between flashing green daybeacon "1" and flashing red daybeacon "2." Approach and dockside depths of 8 feet are reported. The town is just three blocks away. It is advisable to contact the marina in advance for reservations.

South of Palatka, just east of flashing red daybeacon "12" at San Mateo, is Gibson Dry Docks, a repair facility that allows owners to do their own work. They have a 30-ton lift but no dockage for transients.

Corky Bells' Seafood at Gator Landing is at Devils Elbow in East Palatka (across from flashing red "6"). They have a dock and will let you do some nearby shopping if you eat a meal there. Across the street are a large hardware store, a drugstore and an independent grocery store. Down the street are a fresh fruit stand and a bait shop.

**Anchorage:** You can anchor north of Palatka along the east shore near the power cables below Cow Creek at Mile 73. This has good holding in 9 to 11 feet. Carman Cove at Maritoni Point, just east of flashing green daybeacon "47," is another option. Sound your way in. The holding is good in mud and silt. Note that both anchorages are wide open to northwest through southeast winds.

There is some anchoring room south of the bridge, on the west side of the river between the bridge and the city dock. There is good depth here (12 to 15 feet) with good holding in mud and silt. Sound your way in and use an anchor light at night, making sure to stop well off the channel to clear tug and barge traffic. Stay to the north to avoid shoal areas. Avoid Wilson Cove, which is situated south of the bridge on the west side of the river. The old sawmill here was removed years ago, but the abandoned wrecks, stumps and sunken logs make passage treacherous.

Porters Cove, approximately 3.3 miles upriver from the Palatka Bridge at Mile 76.5, has good protection from the west and fair protection from the northwest and southwest. The cove, with wooded banks, is between the overhead power cables at River Crest and flashing red daybeacon "12" on the west side of the river. Sound your way in to anchor in 8- to 10-foot depths. The plentiful osprey nests here have Spanish moss woven into the usual twigs and sticks.

# ■ PALATKA TO LAKE GEORGE

Past the Palatka Memorial Bridge, the St. Johns River puts on its most beautiful face, reminiscent of the quiet, winding Waccamaw River, just north of Georgetown, SC. For 80 miles, the scenery varies, and you can enjoy an array of villages, towns and anchorages. A number of aids to navigation (which do not appear on some chart editions) mark shoals or other hazards, and bird nests change the apparent shape or obscure the numbers of some markers. All the way to Lake Monroe, osprey architecture (nest building) on the daybeacons grows more profuse, so look carefully.

Much of the area is undeveloped and excellent for bird watching. Anhingas (snakebirds) can be seen sitting on logs and drying their wings, and you may spot a bald eagle that is close enough to photograph without a telephoto lens. All types of wildlife call this home, including playful otters, lazily swimming manatees and sleepy alligators sunning along the shore. Fishing is good, but remember that you need a Florida license if you are between 16 and 65 years old. This area is the part of the St. Johns River that you should not miss. It is beautiful!

**NAVIGATION:** Use Charts 11487 and 11495. From here upriver to Welaka, about 20 miles away, the relatively narrow St. Johns River has navigational aids and adequate depths for barge traffic. Many of the boats you will encounter here are fishing skiffs and rented pontoon boats. Use caution around the rental boats, as their skippers may not be highly skilled in the arts of boathandling. Fish traps, stakes, submerged pilings and shoaling, usually along the banks, require your attention at all times, so follow the markers carefully, cruise slow and take no shortcuts. At the foot of Murphy Island is winding Dunns Creek, a wilderness stream with a controlling depth of 5 feet. It leads through 8 miles of untamed country to Crescent Lake (about 10 miles long with depths of 7 to 13 feet). The creek itself has several very sharp turns, but both Dunns Creek and Murphy Creek make for lovely gunkholing.

Once past the common mouths of Murphy and Dunns Creeks, proceed marker to marker. Two shoals extend from Murphy Island almost into the south side of the channel. The bottom here is hard sand so know your boat's position at all times. Favor the north side of the river just before and at flashing green daybeacon "23" to avoid shoaling and submerged pilings. Near green daybeacon "27," the **Buffalo Bluff Bascule Railroad Bridge** (7-foot closed vertical clearance) is normally open, but closes 20 to 30 minutes before train arrive, several times a day. The bridge tender responds on VHF Channel 09 and is usually on duty during the day. When approaching Welaka from red daybeacon "42A" to flashing red daybeacon "52," check your chart and watch the depth sounder carefully for shoals in mid-river; some are marked, but many are not.

**Dockage:** There is a free dock at Murphy Island with over 20 feet of water. It is somewhat exposed to the southwest and southeast and wakes.

**Anchorage:** Browns Landing, which is approximately 7.5 miles south of Palatka, has a good anchorage. Leave the channel between flashing red daybeacon "16" and red daybeacon "18" and head north. Holding is good in 10- to 14-foot depths. Watch for the shoal marked by red daybeacon "18." There is a dock and boat ramp located here for shore access for your four legged crewmembers.

A snug anchorage is in Murphy Creek where it crosses Dunns Creek. Enter in the middle of the Dunns Creek mouth at Rat Island between pilings and trap markers. Watch the depth sounder and proceed slowly; you should find at least 5 to 7 feet in the channel, but depths are far less outside. Murphy Creek is to starboard about a half-mile ahead and has pilings on both sides. Anchor anywhere past the pilings in 7- to 20-foot depths. Crab pots are the only signs of civilization here among the pristine wooded banks.

About 1.5 miles south of Dunns Creek on the St. Johns River, a good spot lies in the first bend of the S-turn leading to the Buffalo Bluff Railroad Bridge (a bascule bridge with 7-foot closed vertical clearance). When headed south, the half-mile sign (small, white and illegible) is between green daybeacon "25" and flashing red daybeacon "26." You must make the northwest turn before you see the bridge. You have to get closer still before you will spot the draw, on the southeast (port) side close to shore. You will find 14 to 17 feet of water and plenty of swinging room in the space between the daybeacon and the southeast shore. Keep clear of the fish traps just inshore to the south and set an anchor light.

A comfortable anchorage lies between the land and the northeast side of the most northern of the Seven Sisters Islands at Mile 88.3 past the Buffalo Bluff Railroad Bridge. Enter opposite flashing red daybeacon "28," favoring the landward side. Watch the depth sounder and stay away from the shoal area off the islet's upper tip. This anchorage is well protected and quiet, despite the houses along the northeast shore. Note the charted 6-foot spot at the entrance to this creek. The Seven Sisters area provides many anchoring possibilities; however, shore access for pets may be difficult to find.

Just before the Cross-Florida Barge Canal entrance (see sidebar) is Stokes Landing and Stokes Island. Stokes Landing features several boatyards, one of which

## Side Trip: Cross-Florida Canal

A couple of miles beyond the Buffalo Bluff Railroad Bridge (Chart 11495), the entrance to the Cross-Florida Greenway (officially named the Marjorie Harris Carr Cross Florida Greenway) is to starboard and marked by red-green "C" opposite Trout Island. A series of historic events transformed this corridor from one of the nation's largest uncompleted public works project to a 110-mile greenway. It offers hiking, biking, equestrian and paddling trails, boat ramps, fishing spots and campgrounds.

Before going through the canal, west of green daybeacon "33A," call ahead for depths and the operating hours of the Buckman Lock (386-329-3575). On the other side of the lock is Rodman Reservoir, also known as Lake Ocklawaha, created from the Ocklawaha River. Here, you will find boat ramps, camping, picnic sites and excellent fishing.

This section and a 9-mile canal on the west coast at Yankeetown were the only two portions of the Cross-Florida Barge Canal completed before public opposition, caused by environmental concerns and right-of-way problems, halted the project in 1971.

Controlling depth is reported to be 7 to 10 feet, though the chart says 12 feet. Numerous navigational aids mark the completed section of the canal from the St. Johns River to the Ocklawaha River and through the Rodman Reservoir.

Contact the Office of Greenways and Trails at 352-236-7143 for the latest canal conditions and bridge and cable clearances.

# St. Johns River, FL

| | | Largest Vessel Accommodated | VHF Channel Monitored | Transient Berths / Total Berths | Approach / Dockside Depth (reported) | Floating Docks | Groceries, Ice, Marine Supplies, Snacks | Gas / Diesel | Repairs: Hull, Engine, Propeller | Lift (tonnage), Crane, Rail | Nearby: Grocery Store, Motel, Restaurant | Laundry, Pool, Showers, Courtesy Car | Pump-Out Station | Min/Max Amps | |
|---|---|---|---|---|---|---|---|---|---|---|---|---|---|---|---|
| **WELAKA AREA** | | | | | | **Dockage** | | | **Supplies** | | | **Services** | | | |
| 1. Acosta Creek Marina WiFi | 386-467-2229 | 80 | 16/68 | 4/40 | 16/12 | – | – | M | HEP | L25 | | 30/50 | LPS | P | MR |
| 2. Welaka City Dock-Bryants Landing WiFi | 386-467-9800 | – | – | 10/10 | 15/10 | F | – | IS | – | | | | S | – | GMR |
| **GEORGETOWN** | | | | | | | | | | | | | | | |
| 3. Georgetown Marina, Lodge & RV Park ⌨ WiFi | 386-467-2002 | 70 | 16/68 | 7/7 | 12/5.5 | – | GD | IMS | – | – | | 30/50 | LS | P | M |

⌨ Internet Access   WiFi Wireless Internet Access   WG Waterway Guide Cruising Club Partner   *(Information in the table is provided by the facilities.)*
See WaterwayGuide.com for current rates, fuel prices, web site addresses, and other up-to-the-minute information.

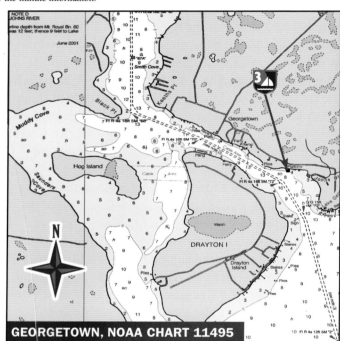

**GEORGETOWN, NOAA CHART 11495**

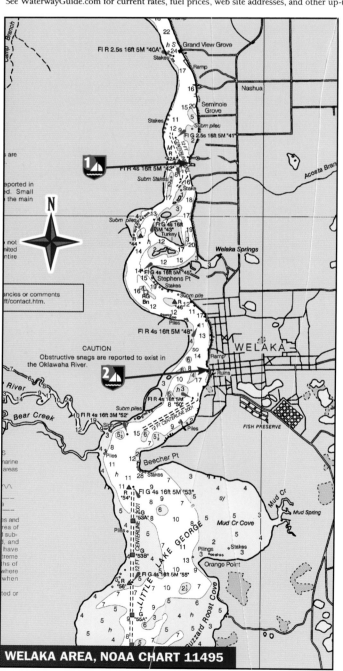

**WELAKA AREA, NOAA CHART 11495**

maintains tugs. From time to time, handsome mega-yachts are hauled for repairs here, looking out of place in the isolated, jungle-like setting. Behind Stokes Island, you will find 8- to 9-foot depths.

## Welaka

Between the Buffalo Bluff Railroad Bridge and Welaka, the early morning sun and ground fog might make it difficult to see the markers. Also, the bird nests built on the pilings obscure some marker numbers along the way. This avian architecture, from a distance, can change the shapes of triangles into squares.

Now a sleepy hamlet, Welaka was once a bustling steamboat depot for the transportation of wood, produce and tourists. Ulysses S. Grant was a passenger on the steamboat that made the trip from Welaka up the Ocklawaha River to its headwaters at Silver Springs, one of Florida's early tourist attractions. Nowadays, elegant antique steamboats rendezvous here. Welaka is also home to one of the river's upscale fishing, vacation and conference resorts, the Floridian Sports Club.

Welaka is a good stopover area about halfway up the river. There is a sign on the riverbank in front of a Welaka condominium near red daybeacon "46" that says: "Jacksonville 77, Sanford 67." This is a good place from which to visit the Welaka National Fish Hatchery and Aquarium, where striped bass are hatched and grown for reintroduction to other rivers.

**NAVIGATION:** Use Chart 11495. In this section of the St. Johns River, trap setters are about as likely to set their traps in the channel as out of it. Just south of Welaka, at flashing red daybeacon "52," the Ocklawaha River flows into the St. Johns River, carrying water that originally surfaced at Silver Springs. Follow the straight channel carefully from red daybeacon "54" to flashing red daybeacon "58" since it is narrow with shoaling on both sides.

Stay in the channel between red daybeacon "64" and flashing green daybeacon "65," as there are 3-foot depths on both sides. South of Welaka to Lake George, a good part of the channel is dredged. Pay attention to markers, watch for lateral drift and keep the depth sounder on because it is easy to get out of the channel. In spots, depths are only 2 to 3 feet on both sides.

Two ferries cross the channel in this area. The Fort Gates Ferry is about 4 miles south of Welaka; it crosses just south of the overhead power cable between Buzzards Point and Mount Royal at flashing green "61." It is the

oldest operating ferry in Florida. The second ferry is 8 miles south of Welaka, at Georgetown, south of flashing red "70." It provides the only vehicular connection between the mainland and Drayton Island. These antique ferries serve unpaved roads.

**Dockage:** Acosta Creek Marina (formerly Acosta Creek Harbor), between green daybeacon "41" and red daybeacon "42A," is built around a charming old Florida river house and offers transient and long-term dockage, as well as guest accommodations. The marina also has dry storage and is a full-service or do-it-yourself yard. Several restaurants dot the river within a couple of miles of the marina. There is a town dock in Welaka (Bryant's Landing) with good water depths but no services.

**Anchorage:** The area off flashing green daybeacon "43" is shoaling, as is the area off the islets between Turkey Island and the mainland. A shoal is also developing from a bar at flashing green daybeacon "45," as well as around the islets at the entrance. Enter approximately midway between the light and the islets; depths are charted at 12 feet or better, but watch the depth sounder carefully. Anchor inside, past the islets by Turkey Island in depths of 8 to 17 feet. Holding is good in mud, although roaring bass boats might awaken you early here.

A good secluded anchorage where, if you are lucky, you can see deer feeding on water hyacinths, is in the curve of the St. Johns River (Mile 99.5), east and behind Buzzards Point, in 13 feet of water. Entering from the west, turn off the channel halfway between flashing green daybeacon "59" and red daybeacon "60," avoiding the charted 6-foot shoal. Leaving the anchorage, follow the water's edge in 13 feet of water until a course due south brings you to flashing green daybeacon "61A," avoiding the 3-foot shoal to starboard. The anchorage is protected in northerly and easterly winds but is also prone to wakes from local fishing boats.

Another pretty spot to drop the hook is 1.5 miles south of Little Lake George in Fruitland Cove, on the St. Johns River's eastern shore. You will find good shelter here from north through east winds, and the many houses along the shore prevent any feeling of isolation. Watch the depth sounder and anchor out of the channel by flashing green daybeacon "63" in 8 to 11 feet of water. Note the cable area shown on the chart. Just past flashing green daybeacon "65" near Jenerson Point, a picture-perfect Victorian home with a matching boathouse graces the east bank of the river.

## Lake George

**NAVIGATION:** Use Chart 11495. The first of the large lakes in the St. Johns River, Lake George is 75 miles south of Jacksonville. This 10-mile-long lake is 5 miles wide with a straight, deep channel that can be rough when winds are strong up or down its length. The lake is the site of a Navy bombing range. As the charts show, the range runs parallel to the channel along three sets of pilings and encompasses much of the eastern half of the lake. The rim is marked by tall pilings, while shorter pilings mark the target area. It should be avoided.

Markers for the channel across the lake are easy to see. A range on the north end of the lake at Lake George Point leads back to the St. Johns River. A range at the south end of the lake leads through a hyacinth fence to the dredged channel across the Volusia Bar. The fence looks like a long set of bridge fenders; the channel is between the fenders, while outside it are rocks and declining depths. The area is posted as a Slow-Speed/ Manatee Zone. Shown on older charts, the Lake George South End Range Rear Light (LLNR 8780) has been permanently removed.

**Dockage:** In Georgetown on the north side of Lake George, the Georgetown Marina, Lodge and RV Park has a few transient slips, gas and diesel fuel and a pump-out station.

**Anchorage:** On the south side of Lake George, at Mile 116.5, is Zinder Point. Here you will find all-around protection in 5 to 10 feet of water. Just 2 miles south is Morrison Island which has excellent holding in mud in 5 to 6 feet of depth.

## ■ ASTOR TO HONTOON LANDING

Once through Lake George, you will enter yet another beautiful part of the river, continuing toward Lake Monroe. Much of the area is undeveloped and part of a wildlife sanctuary.

The river deepens towards Astor, about 4 miles south of Lake George. Fishing camps and waterside restaurants surround the Astor Hwy. Bascule Bridge (with 20-foot closed vertical clearance). Waterfront homeowners with docks and boat slips in the Astor area have rigged various devices—PVC pipes, float lines, fences, etc.—to keep water hyacinths from building up and choking access to the river. Without such devices, the docks become surrounded by plant life and look as if they were constructed inland.

Manatee regulations upriver from Astor are strictly enforced. From here to Lake Monroe, keep an eye out for bald eagles, anhingas, ibises, herons and egrets. In the cool months, alligators migrate south to Lake Harney, but if the winter is warm, chances are you will find many of them in the river.

**NAVIGATION:** Use Chart 11495. Astor enforces its no-wake law strictly, so be sure to slow down between the signs. The **Astor Hwy. Bascule Bridge** has a closed 20-foot vertical clearance and opens on signal. Note that the bridge span hangs over the channel when open at a height of 72 feet. The bridge monitors VHF Channels 09 and 16. The overhead power cable north of the bridge has been reported by the Coast Guard to have less than its charted 50-foot vertical clearance but an exact measurement was not provided.

Dredged cuts have eliminated many turns in the St. Johns River channel. Bars block entrance to many of the oxbows that show deep water inside. Overhanging foliage sometimes obscures daybeacons here, adding confusion to some of the cuts where the natural course of the river makes abrupt turns off the channel (with some turns actually wider than the channel itself). The markers are there, however, so go slow, pay attention and enjoy the beauty of this special place.

As the crow flies, Lake Dexter is 4 miles south of Astor and less than 20 miles from Lake Monroe. On the river, however, it is more like 30 miles through a wilderness broken only by a few convenient marinas. The route is well marked but losing concentration will put you aground quickly.

There are No-Wake Zones on both sides of the **Whitehair (SR 44) Bascule Bridge** (15-foot closed vertical clearance, opens on signal). A Manatee Zone, enforced year-round, begins just downriver of flashing green daybeacon "53" and extends all the way to flashing green daybeacon "81" south of Blue Springs. Please use common sense and common courtesy when passing through this area.

**Dockage:** The Astor Bridge Marina accepts transients and has 8-foot approach depths. They have a fuel dock with gas only. Astor Landing Campground & Marina at the north end of Lake Dexter has deep-water (17-foot) slips; call ahead for availability. For seafood, locals recommend the Blackwater Inn and the William's Landing Pub (352-759-2802), just south of the bridge on the west side. The restaurant dockage can handle vessels in the 40-foot range, but dock bow-in to get depths at your stern of 4 to 5 feet. They are closed on Mondays.

**Anchorage:** There are two unnamed loops with anchoring options. The first, between red daybeacons "30" and "32," has good holding in mud and 8 to 20 feet of depth. The second, known locally as Catfish Bend, is located between red daybeacons "36" and "38" and just north of Crows Bluff. This has good holding and

protection in up to 17 feet of water. Sound your way in. If you do not have time for the entire trip to Sanford, Crows Bluff is a good place to turn around and start back downriver (north).

An anchorage at Drigger Island at flashing green "41" is shallow (5 to 7 feet) but has excellent holding in mud and all-around protection.

## Hontoon Landing

Real wilderness lies on the Hontoon Dead River, about 3 miles from the Whitehair Bridge and just opposite the end of Beresford Peninsula. Be sure to bring along a camera and fishing gear because you may not find a prettier place, and the fishing is fantastic.

**Dockage:** St. Johns Marina & Resort and St. Johns Marina South are on opposite sides of the river and flank the Whitehair Bridge. St. Johns Marina & Resort has slips and offers repairs; St. Johns Marina South sells both gas and diesel but has no transient slips. To the south, at Hontoon Landing, Holly Bluff Marina has limited transient dockage, but nearby Hontoon Landing Resort & Marina reports 45 reserved transient slips. They both sell gas (no diesel), and you can rent a houseboat, pontoon boat or runabout at the latter.

Flashing green daybeacon "53" at the apex of the curve marks Hontoon Island State Park. The park offers picnic tables, grills, spotless showers, a nature trail and an observation tower. The park docks are on the north end of Hontoon Island, along the St. Johns' western shore next to the river's marked entrance. The dock must be approached from the south; head for the face dock. The water is reported to be 6 feet on the approach. There

# St. Johns River, FL

| Marina | Phone | Largest Vessel Accommodated | VHF Channel Monitored | Approach / Dockside Depth (reported) | Transient Berths / Total Berths | Floating Docks | Gas / Diesel | Groceries, Ice, Marine Supplies, Snacks | Repairs: Hull, Engine, Propeller | Lift (tonnage), Crane, Rail | Pump-Out Station | Laundry, Pool, Showers, Courtesy Car | Min/Max Amps | Nearby: Grocery Store, Motel, Restaurant |
|---|---|---|---|---|---|---|---|---|---|---|---|---|---|---|
| **ASTOR** | | | | **Dockage** | | | **Supplies** | | | | **Services** | | | |
| 1. Astor Bridge Marina ⌨ WiFi | 386-749-4407 | – | – | 20/70 | 8/ | – | G | IS | – | – | P | S | 30/50 | GMR |
| 2. Astor Landing Campground & Marina | 352-759-2121 | 55 | – | call/54 | 17/17 | – | – | – | – | – | P | S | 30/50 | – |
| **HONTOON LANDING AREA** | | | | | | | | | | | | | | |
| 3. St. Johns Marina & Resort ⌨ WiFi | 386-736-6601 | 70 | 16 | 12/170 | 12/10 | – | – | GIMS | HEP | L35 | P | S | 30/50 | GMR |
| 4. St. Johns Marina South | 352-589-8370 | 50 | – | call/53 | – | – | GD | IMS | E | – | – | – | 30/30 | R |
| 5. Holly Bluff Marina ⌨ WG | 386-822-9992 | – | 12 | 2/74 | 8/6 | – | G | IMS | HEP | L30 | P | LSC | 30/50 | R |
| 6. Hontoon Landing Resort & Marina ⌨ WiFi | 386-734-2474 | 60 | 88 | 45/50 | 12/6 | – | G | GIMS | | | P | LPS | 30/50 | GMR |
| 7. Hontoon Island State Park | 386-736-5309 | 50 | – | 40/40 | 17/6 | F | – | IS | | | – | S | 30/50 | M |

⌨ Internet Access   WiFi Wireless Internet Access   WG Waterway Guide Cruising Club Partner   *(Information in the table is provided by the facilities.)*
See WaterwayGuide.com for current rates, fuel prices, web site addresses, and other up-to-the-minute information.

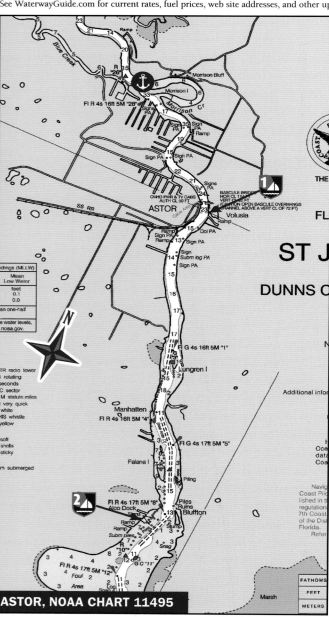

**ASTOR, NOAA CHART 11495**

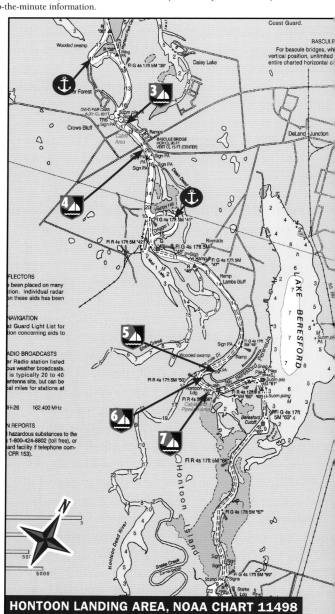

**HONTOON LANDING AREA, NOAA CHART 11498**

s water and shore power at the docks for a nominal fee. This spot is especially popular on summer weekends.

Fishermen, campers and picnickers frequently use the free pedestrian ferry, which crosses the river from the island to the mainland. The park has a leash law, ostensibly to prevent your pet from falling prey to an alligator. You will also see a lot of manatees in the area. There are signs for "Idle Speed Only" because of the number of manatees.

**Anchorage:** There is plenty of room to drop your hook for a night or two. Hontoon Dead River is a deep-water oxbow. Leave the St. Johns at red daybeacon "50" and proceed as far into the river as you like. Anchor in 10 to 15 feet with mud, silt and good holding. The protection is very good from all directions with almost no current.

Starks Landing Loop at Mile 142 (red daybeacon "70") is a little-used river loop behind the island off the western bank. Enter at the north end by flashing green daybeacon "69" and proceed slowly, as this is a manatee refuge. An area charted as having 23-foot depths may

have less than 5 feet of water. The bottom is soft mud. Our cruising editor has seen numerous boats anchored in this spot. Be sure to show an anchor light. You can dinghy to the beach just past the entrance of the springs. Sanford is only a few hours run from here, even for slow boats.

Other oxbows are at Emanuel Bend (Mile 148) and Butchers Bend at Mile 152. Emanuel Bend, a favorite anchorage for locals, is across from the Wekiva River, between green daybeacons "95" and "97." Both ends are navigable, but the south end should be avoided as it is very narrow and may be full of hyacinths and overhanging trees plus other debris on the bottom. Campers may be on the island. Depths are less than the chart indicates. At Butchers Bend, enter at either end, with 7.5-foot depths at the north entrance at flashing green daybeacon "109" and 6-foot depths at the south at green daybeacon "111." This very pretty spot is popular with locals and fishermen. Eagles, manatees and turtles like to too.

## Lake Monroe, FL

| | | Largest Vessel Accommodated | VHF Channel Monitored | Transient Berths / Total Berths | Approach / Dockside Depth (reported) | Floating Docks | Gas / Diesel | Groceries, Ice, Marine Supplies, Snacks | Repairs: Hull, Engine, Propeller | Lift (tonnage), Crane, Rail | Laundry, Pool, Showers, Courtesy Car | Pump-Out Station | Min/Max Amps | Nearby: Grocery Store, Motel, Restaurant |
|---|---|---|---|---|---|---|---|---|---|---|---|---|---|---|
| **LAKE MONROE** | | | | **Dockage** | | | **Supplies** | | **Services** | | | | | |
| 1. Boat Tree Marina 🖥 WiFi | 407-322-1610 | 70 | 16 | call/245 | 13/10 | F | G | IMS | HEP | L25 | | | 30/50 | LPS P R |
| **SANFORD AREA** | | | | | | | | | | | | | | |
| 2. Monroe Harbour Marina 🖥 WiFi | 407-322-2910 | 80 | - | 5/236 | 6/5.5 | F | G | IM | HEP | L35 | | | 30/50 | LS P GMR |
| 3. Sanford Boat Works & Marina, Inc. 🖥 | 407-322-6613 | 70 | 16 | 10/140 | 8/5 | F | GD | S | - | L25 | | | 30/50 | LPS P R |

🖥 Internet Access   WiFi Wireless Internet Access   WG Waterway Guide Cruising Club Partner  *(Information in the table is provided by the facilities.)*
See WaterwayGuide.com for current rates, fuel prices, web site addresses, and other up-to-the-minute information.

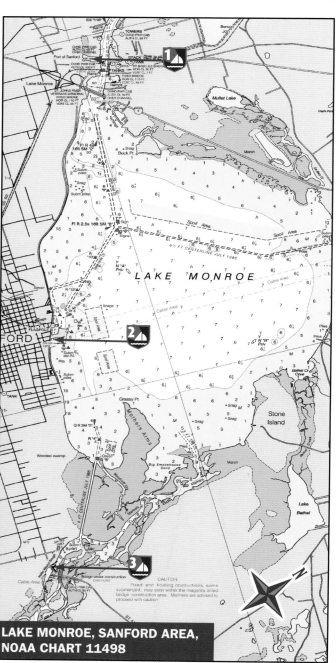

**LAKE MONROE, SANFORD AREA, NOAA CHART 11498**

## ■ LAKE MONROE

It is a 13-mile journey from Hontoon Landing to Lake Monroe. The winding river has narrow channels, land cuts, water hyacinths and snags, but there are good navigational aids. This waterway is extremely beautiful, with an abundance of birds, turtles and manatees.

Blue Springs State Park is just south of flashing green daybeacon "71." The springs are worth exploring. Hontoon Island Park and Blue Springs State Park are independent of each other, but share a common manatee area that is carefully monitored by the marine patrol. If you are moving too fast (and even auxiliary sailboats sometimes do), you could get a ticket or a warning.

**NAVIGATION:** Use Chart 11498. The river continues to meander 5 miles more from the Wekiva River to the three bridges before Lake Monroe. Just before the bridges is a power plant with multiple overhead cables crossing the river. The last two cable crossings, significantly lower than the others, have vertical clearances of 49 feet, according to the latest chart.

The first bridge before the lake is **Port of Sanford Railway Bascule Bridge**, with a 7-foot closed vertical clearance. Call the tender on VHF Channel 09 for an opening. Next is the **US 17/U.S. 92 Bridge** (45-foot fixed vertical clearance). The boat ramp immediately after this section of old bridge is very active and can generate significant congestion in the river

Soundings in **Lake Monroe** are at mean lower low water, which are typical at the end of a dry winter. Rainfall contols the depth, which usually rises almost 4 feet above the charted values after a wet summer.

channel. The **St. Johns River Veterans Memorial Twin Bridges** with 45-foot fixed vertical clearance are the last bridges before the lake.

The Lake Monroe buoyage has changed; be sure to use the latest charts. From the St. Johns River Bridge, follow the channel markers carefully to the channel junction at flashing red daybeacon "8." The channel headed toward the north leads to the power plant across the lake at Enterprise; the (unmarked) one to the southeast goes to Sanford. Stay out of the area to the northeast between the two channels; the spar buoys mark where sunken trees were placed to attract fish. Red daybeacon "10" is next, followed by junction marker "RG." Continue past "RG" to red daybeacon "10" and then to flashing green "5" at the Sanford turning basin. Monroe Harbour Marina's west entrance and the Veterans Memorial Park are here.

To reach the east entrance of the marina or to continue up the St. Johns river, turn to port to leave red daybeacon "4" and "6" to starboard but do not pass close to them, as they are on a shoal. After red daybeacon "6", the east entrance to Sanford will be abeam to starboard.

At flashing red daybeacon "96," the narrow entrance to the Wekiva River is almost totally obscured by water hyacinths. Although a boat with a 5-foot draft can be taken several miles up, the Wekiva River's entrance is tricky; explore it only with local knowledge.

**Dockage:** The Boat Tree Marina is located in the large basin on the western shore just before the bridges. The marina may offer transient dockage but call ahead to check on availability. They also sell gas and offer repairs. There is a deli on the premises.

## Sanford

At one time, Sanford was an important river port, but the only commercial traffic now is an infrequent fuel barge. Here, you enter civilization again with businesses, stores, motels and accommodations for cruising boats. Sanford, once the center of a big celery-producing area, now harvests up to four crops a year of various garden produce, including citrus fruit. The town also boasts the Riverwalk, a 2-mile paved walk or bike path that meanders along Lake Monroe through parks. It is a great way to spend a day.

**Dockage:** Sanford's municipal marina, known as Monroe Harbour Marina, is two blocks from downtown. The marina places short-term transients in either the east or west basin; you will not see the entrance to the west basin until you are almost on it. The marina does not monitor VHF Channel 16 so you need to call 407-322-2910 to get docking instructions.

From flashing green "5," run parallel to the bulkhead and the opening appears to starboard. Make a right-angle turn into the basin. Transient boats should avoid

the charted channel leading into the west basin. The entrance channel has a reported depth of 5 feet.

The marina offers a well-stocked store and a friendly staff ready to assist you. They also have a pump-out boat that comes to your slip.

Wolfy's Lakefront Bar 'n Grill (407-322-2150) is just across the street from the marina and historic Sanford has a number of good restaurants along 1st Street.

## Indian Mound Slough

A straight line at the Sanford waterfront from daymarker "6" to flashing red "2" at what locals call the "Government Cut" south of Mothers Arms will keep you in the deepest water to Indian Mound Slough. Our cruising editor found 4 feet in the dry, low-water season of spring 2017, except for a soft mud 3.5-foot shoal at "2," just as charted. Stay close to "2" and to red daybeacon "4" and head straight for green daybeacon "5." Depths of at least 5 feet have been observed from

"5" to Sanford Boat Works. Stay quite close to the right-hand shore once you have passed through the cut.

Beyond Sanford Boat Works and the **Osteen Bridge** (25-foot fixed vertical clearance), the St. Johns River system is wild, natural and unimproved, and cruising is restricted to small skiffs with shallow drafts. Numerous cattle ranches are here, and the area is excellent for bird watching.

**Dockage:** Sanford Boat Works & Marina has some transient dockage, as does Gator's Riverside Grille (407-688-9700). Call ahead to be sure there is space available for you.

## Cruising Options

From Sanford, we return you coastward to Jacksonville Beach and the ICW leg south to Daytona Beach and Ponce de Leon Inlet.

**CLEAN + DRAIN + DRY YOUR GEAR**

# St. Johns River to Ponce de Leon Inlet

**ICW** Mile 740–Mile 840

**VHF** FL: Channel 09

**CHARTS** 11485, 11489

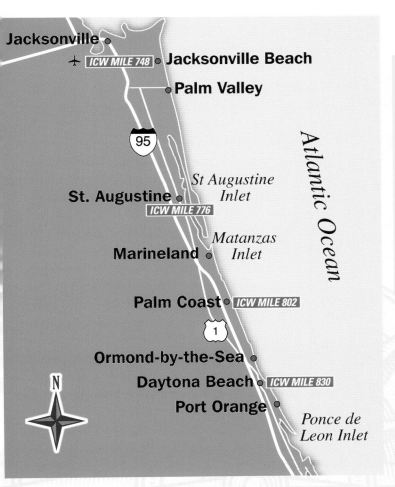

The Jacksonville Beach region is part of what Floridians call the "First Coast" because it was settled first. It vigorously competes with the Gold Coast, the Sun Coast and the Treasure Coast for developer and tourist dollars. The area begins a parade of shoreside communities such as Atlantic Beach, Neptune Beach, Jacksonville Beach and Ponte Vedra Beach.

## ■ ST. JOHNS RIVER TO ST. AUGUSTINE INLET

**NAVIGATION:** Use Chart 11489. After crossing the St. Johns River at Mile 740, the ICW continues along Pablo Creek toward Jacksonville Beach. Follow the markers carefully to stay on the narrow, dredged channel's centerline and be prepared to squeeze over for tugs with barges.

⚠ Mariners transiting in vicinity of Pablo Creek and Mile Point at Mile 740 should be wary of a shoal that is forming on the northeast side of Pablo Creek. The shoal extends from east of Pablo Creek flashing green "5" to southeast of green "7" and is encroaching to the south and west of Pablo Creek. Minimum depths of 7.5 feet have been observed. Mariners transiting this portion of Pablo Creek with draft concerns are advised to navigate with caution while passing through this area. See the Waterway Guide Explorer at waterwayguide.com for new alerts and updates.

We have received reports of a rock jetty/wall under construction at Mile 740.4 that seems to extend into the channel. Favor the west side of the channel and exercise caution.

Small boats often anchor in the land cut just beyond the river crossing on weekends and holidays. The current in the cut flows toward the St. Johns River on the ebb and can be very strong–up to 3 knots on the ebb and 2.5 knots on the flood, even without spring tides.

Eddies between red nun buoy "2" and flashing green buoy "1" at the entrance to Pablo Creek require close attention to the helm. When entering the channel, favor the green markers until you reach red daybeacon "8." This area is also a "No Wake Zone" up to the first bridge (Wonderwood Drive Bridge), which is enforced. Going slow can be difficult with the strong current.

The **Wonderwood Drive Twin Bridges** are situated at Mile 742.1, with slightly less than the charted 65 feet of vertical clearance at high tide. The 65-foot-high (also less on higher tides) **Atlantic Beach Twin Bridges** (Mile 744.7) is the gateway to the Jacksonville Beach region.

# Jacksonville Beach, FL

| JACKSONVILLE BEACH AREA | | | Dockage | | | | Supplies | | Services | | | | |
|---|---|---|---|---|---|---|---|---|---|---|---|---|---|
| | | Largest Vessel Accommodated | VHF Channel Monitored | Transient Berths / Total Berths | Approach / Dockside Depth (reported) | Floating Docks | Gas / Diesel | Groceries, Ice, Marine Supplies, Snacks | Repairs: Hull, Engine, Propeller | Lift (tonnage), Crane, Rail | Laundry, Pool, Showers, Courtesy Car | Min/Max Amps | Pump-Out Station | Nearby: Grocery Store, Motel, Restaurant |
| 1. Palm Cove Marina 🖥 WiFi WG  747.4 | 904-223-4757 | 90 | 16/69 | 25/221 | 6/6 | F | GD | GIMS | HEP | L35 | 30/50 | LPS | P | GMR |
| 2. Beach Marine WiFi  747.6 | 904-249-8200 | 125 | 16/68 | 40/350 | 6/6 | F | GD | IMS | HEP | L10 | 30/100 | LS | P | GMR |

🖥 Internet Access  WiFi Wireless Internet Access  WG Waterway Guide Cruising Club Partner *(Information in the table is provided by the facilities.)*
See WaterwayGuide.com for current rates, fuel prices, web site addresses, and other up-to-the-minute information.

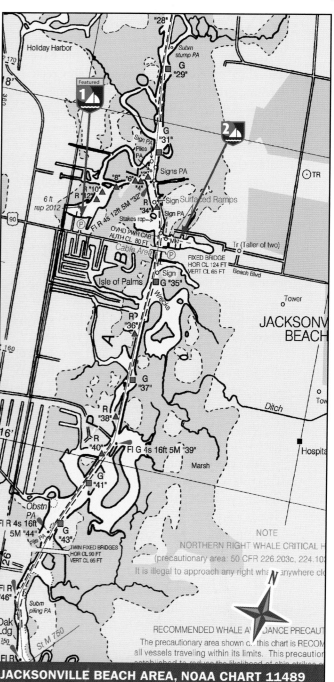

JACKSONVILLE BEACH AREA, NOAA CHART 11489

The large enclosed basin on the west side, just south of the Atlantic Beach Bridge, is a private marina for the surrounding condominium owners.

Shoaling continues on the east side of the channel at green can buoy "19," just north of the Atlantic Beach Bridges at Mile 744.7. Green can buoy "19" is sometimes difficult to locate, as often it is pulled under by the current. (Note that green can buoy "19A," shown south of the bridge on older charts, has been removed.)

After passing under the bridge, hug the west side of the channel close to the private marina, where depths should be around 15 feet. Eddies sometimes form above, under and below the bridge. The narrow, well-marked channel at the Atlantic Beach Bridges has ebb currents up to 6 knots at new and full moons, in synchrony with the St. Johns River. Attention at the helm is mandatory. It is easy to lose control here, and there is not much horizontal clearance. A number of fishermen work this area in small boats.

The *Coast Pilot* describes this area as: "On the flood, the current in the channel flows southward and at right angles to the bridge at an average velocity of 3.4 knots at strength. On the ebb, the current flows northward and sets about 15 degrees to the right of the axis of the channel at an average velocity of 5.2 knots at strength. The currents at a distance of 100 yards either side of the bridge are much weaker with practically no turbulence and give no warning of the strong current at the bridge."

Near the **McCormick (U.S. 90) Twin Bridges** (65-foot vertical clearance) at Mile 747.5 watch for strong currents, especially on the ebb (although they are not as strong as the currents through the Atlantic Beach Bridge).

**Anchorage:** On the east side of the ICW at Mile 744.2, between flashing green buoy "17" and green can buoy "19," is a wide and surprisingly deep stream. If you choose to try to anchor here, enter only from the north, with an eye out for shoaling on the south side and anchor behind the island. Leftover mooring anchors may still be on the bottom so be wary of snags and set the hook well against the swift current. This is not a great anchorage but will do in a pinch.

## Jacksonville Beach

Ponce de Leon landed here in the 1500s in his search for the Fountain of Youth, and Jacksonville Beach has been a lively resort community ever since. This popular stopover, with its beautiful beach, offers a full range of services, stores and restaurants, and makes a convenient central base for side trips to Fernandina Beach, Forts Clinch and Caroline, Kingsley Plantation or the City of Jacksonville.

The proximity of the airports at Jacksonville and Daytona makes this a fine layover and fitting-out port. Many mariners cruise south to this point in the fall, leave their boats and fly home. When the cold weather arrives up north, they return to their boats and continue their journeys southward. The renowned Mayo Clinic has an extension here (904-953-2000).

**Dockage:** North of the McCormick Twin Bridges, at flashing red "32," is a small creek on the west side leading to Lake Cusic, which is unnamed on the chart. Stay to the middle of the privately marked entrance, which has 6-foot depths at mean low water. Palm Cove Marina has competitively priced fuel (gas and diesel) and wet and dry storage. This 221-slip marina also features clean restrooms with showers, a pool, a ship store, electronics service, a 35-ton boat lift, pump-out station and transient dockage at floating docks for boats up to 90 feet. Also on site is the Marker 32 Restaurant (904-223-1534) with great views and first-class dining. Extensive shopping is just a very short walk (about a half mile) from Palm Cove Marina, including a Publix grocery/pharmacy, West Marine, Target, Walgreens Drugs and various other stores plus some fast-food eateries. Rental cars and public transportation to explore the nearby Jacksonville area are readily available.

Family-owned and -operated Beach Marine (across the bridge on the east side of the ICW) has transient slips on floating docks, gas and diesel fuel and a repair yard in a large enclosed basin. The beach is about 2 miles away, shopping is over the bridge to the west (less than a

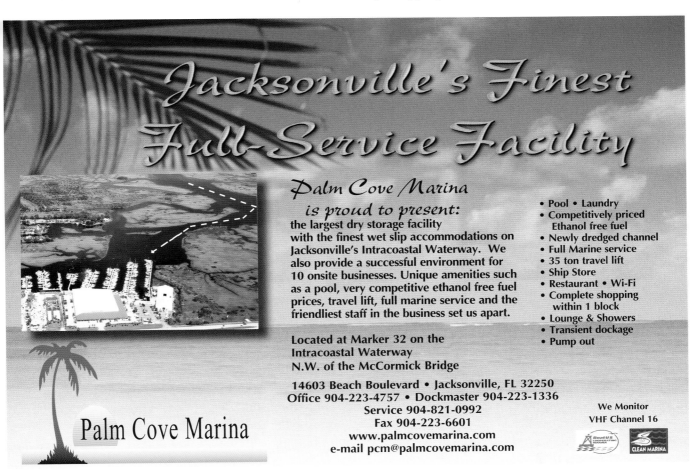

ICW

Isle of Palms

PALM COVE MARINA

U.S. 90

Jacksonville Beach

1-mile walk) and rental cars and public transportation to Jacksonville are also nearby.

## Palm Valley Cut–ICW Mile 749 to Mile 759

**NAVIGATION:** Use Chart 11489. From the McCormick Twin Bridges, the channel is well marked, and the tidal range is about 5 feet. South of the **Butler Blvd. (Pablo Creek) Twin Bridges** (65-foot fixed vertical clearance) at Mile 749.5, the route enters 10-mile-long Palm Valley Cut. There is a high-rise condominium development with a private boat basin just south of the Butler Blvd. Bridges on the west side of the ICW. The current may give your vessel a strong sideways push, and shoals are encroaching from the west side just south of Mile 750 at the intersection of Pablo and Cabbage Creeks.

Just beyond the Butler Blvd. Bridges is the straight Palm Valley Cut. The only marker in Palm Valley Cut (red daybeacon "2") is just before the bridge; stay in the middle of the channel or favor the east side if depths start to decrease suddenly. There are numerous pot markers along Palm Valley Cut that appear to be near the centerline. The deeper water is to the east of these floats.

On the east side of the ICW is the Harbour Island at Marsh Landing development, featuring home sites, new homes and private docks directly on the ICW and around a man-made harbor. Skippers, as always, are responsible for their own wakes. The narrow Palm Valley Cut is a Slow-Speed/Minimum-Wake Zone from the Marsh Landing area to just south of the Palm Valley Bridge. Proceed with appropriate caution. The east side of Palm Valley Cut is residential. Watch for debris, manatees and alligators in this popular fishing spot and mind the depth sounder.

Recent residential development is evident on parts of the western shore at the southern end, but most of it is still beautifully wild and wooded. Our cruising editor has noted that the depth through this area remains at 10 to 12 feet of water (in the center of the channel) from Mile 750 to the Palm Valley Bridge. Depths, as always, might be less at the fringes of the channel.

Near the south end of the cut, the ICW passes under the fixed 65-foot high-rise **Palm Valley (SR 210) Bridge** at Mile 758.8. Just past this bridge are the headwaters of the Tolomato River (Mile 760), which leads to St. Augustine.

# Tolomato River–ICW Mile 760 to Mile 776

**NAVIGATION:** Use Charts 11489 and 11485. At Mile 760, the ICW enters the headwaters of the Tolomato River, which flows south to meet the Matanzas River at the St. Augustine Inlet. The dredged channel between Mile 760 and Mile 765 provides a deep water route through the marshes and side waters.

The river deepens below Pine Island (just north of Mile 765), and the ICW begins to follow its natural deep channel. From Mile 765 to Mile 770, pay close attention to the chart, as shoaling extends into the channel at flashing green daybeacon "27." Give the marker a wide berth and stay toward the west bank.

Although problems have diminished recently, there is occasional shoaling near Capo Creek. Between green daybeacon "29" and red daybeacon "30" it is best to favor the east side of the channel. Above green daybeacon "33" a shoal extends toward the channel; give that marker a wide berth. South of green daybeacon "33" keep to the western side and give a wide berth to flashing red daybeacon "44" and "44A" just before Mile 770. (Chart 11485 picks up here.) Beware of the shoal that extends from flashing green daybeacon "45" below Mile 770; it juts out from the upper point of the Guana River and extends northward along the east bank.

Be alert for strong sideways currents at the junction of the Guana River and the ICW, which also may drag pot markers underwater. About 1 mile south of the Guana River on the west side, you will pass an airport. The route is well marked, wide and deep to the **Usina (Vilano Beach) Bridge** (Mile 775.8, vertical clearance of 65 feet), except for a shoal that extends into the channel at flashing green daybeacon "49." Keep a sharp eye out for this marker and the next green marker (flashing green daybeacon "51") because they both have a tendency to blend in with the buildings and docks on the eastern side of the ICW channel. There may be strong currents at an angle at the Usina Bridge, and some cruisers report that the clearance may be less than the posted 65 feet at high tide. A dredged private basin at a condominium development south of flashing red daybeacon "54" on the Tolomato River has two entrances on the east side of the river.

**Dockage:** Several restaurants with dockage for patrons are north of the Usina Bridge on the east side of the ICW. Tying up at Cap's on the Water, the popular restaurant in the vicinity of flashing green daybeacon "51," can be very rough, especially on busy summer weekends. Call the restaurant (904-824-8794) ahead of time to check on the approach and dockside depths as well as dock availability. They are closed in January and reopen in early February. Pass this area with no wake, as there are usually boats at the dock, sometimes rafted several deep.

For a little adventure, take a dinghy ride up the **Guana River** at Mile 770 to a dam about 3 miles upstream that is part of the Guana-Tolomato-Matanzas Rivers National Estuarine Research Reserve, a network of 55,000 acres of protected marsh, waters and wetlands in Flagler and St. Johns counties. Anchor your vessel at the mouth of the river, off the ICW, taking care to avoid the charted submerged piling, but do not leave it unattended. Once at the dam, the beach is just across the highway.

**Anchorage:** At Mile 765 is the entrance to the Pine Island Loop anchorage, which is a fine place to drop the hook and enjoy a pleasant evening or two. Enter just south of green daybeacon "25" and favor the north bank, as there is a shoal extending out from the south bank. Mind the depth and allow for the full range of tide in your entire swinging circle. There is a line of crab pot markers that indicates the shoal line on the southern side of the anchorage; it is deeper toward the north shore. The current is minimal and holding and protection are excellent; however, it can be very buggy when there is no wind. Shoals and submerged obstructions make the entrance north of the island between green daybeacon "21" and flashing green "23" almost impassable. The farther you anchor from the ICW, the less you will be affected by wakes of passing boats. This is a fine area to do some exploring with your dinghy. You can see alligators and a huge variety of birds and other wildlife.

## St. Augustine

**NAVIGATION:** Use Chart 11485. Use the Fernandina Beach Tide Tables. For high tide, subtract 20 minutes; for low tide, subtract 5 minutes. Between Mile 775 and Mile 780 there is continuous shoaling, as well as frequent changes to the marking system in the area. Study the chart before you get to the Usina Bridge and note that red nun buoy "58" and flashing red buoy "58A" do not appear on the most recent chart (Edition 37, dated 5/2015) and have not for a number of years, as this is such a changeable area. It may be different when you pass through.

The ICW channel south of the bridge is deceptively close to the beach (east) side as it approaches St. Augustine Inlet. Honor all markers in place south of the bridge at the time of your arrival. In spring 2017, these markers included flashing green buoy "57A," quick-flashing red buoy "60" and flashing green buoy "59," which is opposite and very close to the beach.

⚠️ There is a shoal that is bare at low tide south and west of flashing green buoy "57A" at Mile 776 that catches many unwary transient boaters each year. Favor the green side of the channel between flashing green buoys "57A and "59" and be sure to honor red buoy "60" to starboard when heading south.

After passing between flashing green buoy "59" and quick-flashing red buoy "60," the ICW channel turns sharply to the west to pass between the first set of Matanzas River markers (flashing green buoy "1" and red nun buoy "2") just inside St. Augustine Inlet. Be careful to distinguish the inlet markers from the ICW markers. Also be careful not to confuse the marked channel into Salt Run for the ICW channel. Call one of

he local towing services for advice if you are unable to sort out the numerous markers. Always remember that the ICW markers have either a yellow square or a yellow triangle.

Heading south, before you reach the **Bridge of Lions (SR A1A)** at Mile 777.9, you will see a tall white cross and then the fort Castillo de San Marcos (charted). Closer to town, the twin spires of the Catholic cathedral appear, making an interesting skyline. Beyond the inlet, on the Conch Island (east) side, the ICW channel turns sharply west, sweeps wide around Anastasia Island's northern tip and then turns up the Matanzas River and under the Bridge of Lions. This bridge, one of the most attractive on the ICW, was originally completed in 1927. The bridge has been rebuilt in recent years with the goal to improve the bridge's safety while preserving its historic value.

The Bridge of Lions opens on signal, except between 7:00 a.m. and 6:00 p.m., when the draw only opens on the hour and half-hour; however, the draw need not open at 8:00 a.m., noon or 5:00 p.m., Monday through Friday (except federal holidays). On weekends and holidays, it opens only on the hour and half-hour between 7:00 a.m. and 6:00 p.m. Although charted with 18-foot closed vertical clearance, our cruising editor has observed an additional 4 feet of clearance in the center. Be aware that the bridge sometimes closes for special events (e.g., Blessing of the Fleet, 4th of July celebrations and various 5K walk/run events). These closures are usually well publicized and reasonably short in duration.

At press time in spring 2017, the Coast Guard was considering a proposed modification to the Bridge of Lions schedule that would extend the twice an hour draw opening period from 7:00 a.m. to 9:00 p.m. daily (instead of 6:00 p.m.), and preclude the bridge draw from opening at 3:30 p.m. on weekends and federal holidays. Stay tuned for updates at waterwayguide.com.

**Dockage:** The number of berths available to transients in St. Augustine reflects its long-standing popularity as a port of call. Several elaborate marine complexes cater to cruising boats. Immediately north of the Usina Bridge on the west side of the ICW, Camachee Cove Yacht Harbor is the center of the huge Camachee Island Marina Village complex. Bulkheads and jetties on both sides of Camachee Cove's entrance help prevent shoaling and protect the outside slips. The entrance channel provides adequate depths for cruising boats of all sizes and the enclosed basin offers excellent protection.

Camachee Cove Yacht Harbor has two boater lounges, three laundry facilities and a well-stocked ship store. The complex boasts six fueling stations, and some fueling can be done from individual slips. The marina is surrounded by 20 businesses offering every imaginable service for boaters, including Camachee Yacht Yard, where trained on-site technicians can handle most any repair (50-ton lift and crane). First Mate Yacht Services is also on site offering full-service maintenance and repairs. The Kingfish Grill (904-824-2111) and Vinny's Pizza (904-342-8859) are on site as well. Downtown St. Augustine is a couple of miles away, and the marina provides two courtesy cars for exploring or provisioning.

South of the inlet, on Salt Run, is the Conch House Restaurant, Lounge, Motel and Marina. The marina has a tropical motif and full amenities. The popular Conch House Restaurant is on site, offering seafood and Caribbean fare.

Dockage is also available south of the Bridge of Lions, and these facilities are convenient to the city's many restaurants and historic attractions. The St. Augustine Municipal Marina, on the west side, offers transient dockage and convenient fuel. Consider the direction of the current when docking here. You will need to make reservations early to reserve a slip here. A little farther south, on the east side, is Fish Island Marina (Mile 779.8), which usually has some transient space available

# GOIN' ASHORE: **ST. AUGUSTINE, FL**

| SERVICES | | |
|---|---|---|
| 1 | Post Office | |
| 2 | Visitor Information | |
| **ATTRACTIONS** | | |
| 3 | Castillo de San Marcos | |
| 4 | Colonial Quarters Living History Museum | |
| 5 | Flagler College/Ponce de Leon Hotel | |

| | | |
|---|---|---|
| 6 | Lightner Museum | |
| 7 | National Greek Orthodox Shrine | |
| 8 | Pirate & Treasures Museum | |
| **DINING** | | |
| 9 | A1A Ale Works | |
| 10 | Columbia Restaurant | |
| 11 | Costa Bravo | |

| | | |
|---|---|---|
| 12 | Sangria's Wine and Tapas Piano Bar | |
| 13 | San Sebastian Winery | |
| **MARINAS** | | |
| 14 | St. Augustine Municipal Marina | |

Founded in 1565 as a Spanish military outpost, St. Augustine is the oldest continuously occupied European settlement in the United States. Traces of the city's Spanish heritage are everywhere, and a Spanish Quarter where conquistadors once strolled is recreated for the 21st-century visitor.

**Attractions:** Tourists can explore the battlements and dungeons of Castillo de San Marcos National Monument, built in 1672, and wander the narrow old streets of San Agustin Antiquo, which depict Spanish Colonial life. Walking from the old town gates across from Castillo de San Marcos, you will encounter the oldest wooden schoolhouse in the United States, the Colonial Quarter's Living History Museum and the National Greek Orthodox Shrine.

Superb examples of 19th-century Spanish Renaissance architecture can be seen here. Flagler College occupies the buildings and grounds of Henry Flagler's luxurious Ponce de Leon Hotel, built in 1888. Tours are scheduled several times a day to view the original Tiffany stained glass windows, fountains, mosaics and sculpture in the beautifully restored building, which now serves as the college offices and main dormitory. Across King Street from Flagler

College is the Lightner Museum (built by Henry Flagler, 1887). This museum of antiquities is housed within the historic Hotel Alcazar building.

Of course, Ponce De Leon's Fountain of Youth is here. It's part of a 15-acre archaeological park and there is a fee to enter the grounds ($15 at press time in 2017). The Spring House is the site of the original spring that was recorded in a 17th century Spanish land grant. It is a beautiful 60-year old coquina building. (The fountain itself is not much to look at.)

For a bit of fun, the Pirate & Treasures Museum at 12 S. Castillo Dr. is dedicated to pirate artifacts (877-467-5863). This was formerly known as the Pirate Soul Museum and was relocated from Key West.

If you happen to be in town on Palm Sunday, you can participate in the St. Augustine Blessing of the Fleet Festival, a tradition that goes back hundreds of years.

**Shopping:** The full length of St. George Street (just three blocks from the city marina) is a diner's and shopper's paradise. It is a moderate walk to reach Stewart's Market (311 Anastasia Blvd. 904-824-5637), a well-stocked small grocery store selling local fruits and vegetables, excellent meat and off-the-boat fresh shrimp and other seafood. It is well worth the walk, especially since the other stores require land transportation. Stewart's does not take credit cards or checks, however; only cash.

On Rt. 1 south just about a 1.5 miles from downtown you will find West Marine and a supermarket in the same shopping center. If you need transportation, try the Sunshine Bus Company, which operates six lines and a connector route in and around St. Augustine. Check with the marina office as to where the closest bus stop is as it changes frequently.

**Dining:** There are restaurants to suit any taste in downtown St. Augustine. One of the favorites of cruisers is A1A Ale Works (1 King St., 904-829-2977), which has a large selection of beer and serves "New World" cuisine. For more upscale dining, visit Costa Brava, located in the Casa Monica Hotel (built in 1888) across from the college at 95 Cordova St. (904-810-6810), or Columbia Restaurant (904-824-3341) at the corner of St. George and Hypolita Streets. Columbia is one of the oldest and best-regarded Cuban restaurants in Florida and has been owned and operated by the same family for 110 years. Start with the black bean soup (served over white rice) and move on to the mixto, a traditional Cuban sandwich made of ham, salami, roast pork, swiss cheese, pickle and mustard. You will dine among hundreds of hand-painted tiles and Spanish-style fountains. See menus at columbiarestaurant.com.

For something a little different, be sure to try Sangria's Wine and Tapas Piano Bar (35 Hypolita St., 904-827-1947). They have indoor and outdoor seating and live music most nights.

Don't miss a tour and wine tasting at the San Sebastian Winery (157 King St., 904-826-1594), where they produce table, sparkling and dessert wines. "The Cellar Upstairs" is a wine, jazz and blues bar located on the rooftop of the winery. Call for reservations, as the bar is only open on Friday, Saturday and Sunday.

# St. Augustine Inlet, St. Augustine, FL

| | | | Dockage | | | | Supplies | | Services | | | | | |
|---|---|---|---|---|---|---|---|---|---|---|---|---|---|---|
| | | Largest Vessel Accommodated | VHF Channel Monitored | Transient Berths / Total Berths | Approach / Dockside Depth (reported) | Floating Docks | Gas / Diesel | Groceries, Ice, Marine Supplies, Snacks | Repairs: Hull, Engine, Propeller | Lift (tonnage), Crane, Rail | Min/Max Amps | Laundry, Pool, Showers, Courtesy Car | Pump-Out Station | Nearby: Grocery Store, Motel, Restaurant |
| **TOLOMATO RIVER** | | | | | | | | | | | | | | |
| 1. Camachee Island Marina Village 🖳 WiFi WG 775 | 904-829-5676 | 155 | 16/68 | 40/260 | 6/7 | F | GD | GIMS | HEP | L50,C5 | 30/100 | LPSC | P | GMR |
| 2. Camachee Yacht Yard 775.7 | 904-823-3641 | 65 | 16 | – | – | F | GD | M | HEP | L50,C | 30/50 | LS | P | GMR |
| **SALT RUN** | | | | | | | | | | | | | | |
| 3. Conch House Marina 🖳 WiFi .65 W of 776.7 | 904-824-4347 | 200 | 16/69 | 45/194 | 6/6 | F | GD | GIMS | HEP | – | 30/100 | LPS | P | GMR |
| **MATANZAS RIVER** | | | | | | | | | | | | | | |
| 4. St. Augustine Municipal Marina 🖳 WiFi 777.7 | 904-825-1026 | 280 | 16/71 | call/100 | 20/15 | F | GD | GIMS | – | – | 30/100 | LS | P | GMR |
| 5. Fish Island Marina 779.8 | 904-471-1955 | 150 | 16 | 20/20 | 20/20 | F | D | – | – | – | 30/50 | LS | P | GMR |
| **SAN SEBASTIAN RIVER** | | | | | | | | | | | | | | |
| 6. Cat's Paw Marina | 904-829-8040 | 40 | 16 | – | – | – | GD | IMS | H | L9 | 30/30 | – | – | GR |
| 7. St. Augustine Marine Center WiFi .8 NW of 780 | 904-824-4394 | 150 | 16 | call/50 | 10/6 | F | – | IM | HEP | L110,C20 | 30/100 | S | P | MR |
| 8. Xynides Boat Yard 🖳 | 904-824-3446 | 55 | – | call/20 | 16/10 | F | – | M | HEP | L50 | – | LS | – | GMR |
| 9. Oasis Boatyard & Marina WiFi 1.2 NW of 780 | 904-824-2520 | 65 | – | call/45 | 16/16 | F | – | IMS | HEP | L50,C | 30/50 | LS | – | GMR |
| 10. St. Augustine Shipyard | 904-342-5159 | 120 | – | call/300 | – | F | GD | IMS | HEP | L | 30/30 | S | P | R |
| 11. English Landing Marina WiFi | 904-669-7363 | – | – | call/23 | 20/15 | F | – | – | – | – | 30/30 | S | – | GMR |
| 12. Rivers Edge Marina 🖳 WiFi WG 1.7 NW of 780 | 904-827-0520 | 150 | 16/72 | 15/106 | 12/10 | F | GD | IMS | EP | – | 30/100 | LS | P | GMR |
| 13. The Marine Supply & Oil Company 1.8 NW of 780 | 904-829-2271 | 200 | – | – | /12 | – | D | M | – | – | – | – | – | G |
| 14. Hidden Harbor Marina – St. Augustine 🖳 WiFi 780 | 904-829-0750 | – | 16 | 2/45 | 8/15 | F | – | – | – | – | 30/50 | LS | P | GR |

🖳 Internet Access  WiFi Wireless Internet Access  WG Waterway Guide Cruising Club Partner  *(Information in the table is provided by the facilities.)*
See WaterwayGuide.com for current rates, fuel prices, web site addresses, and other up-to-the-minute information.

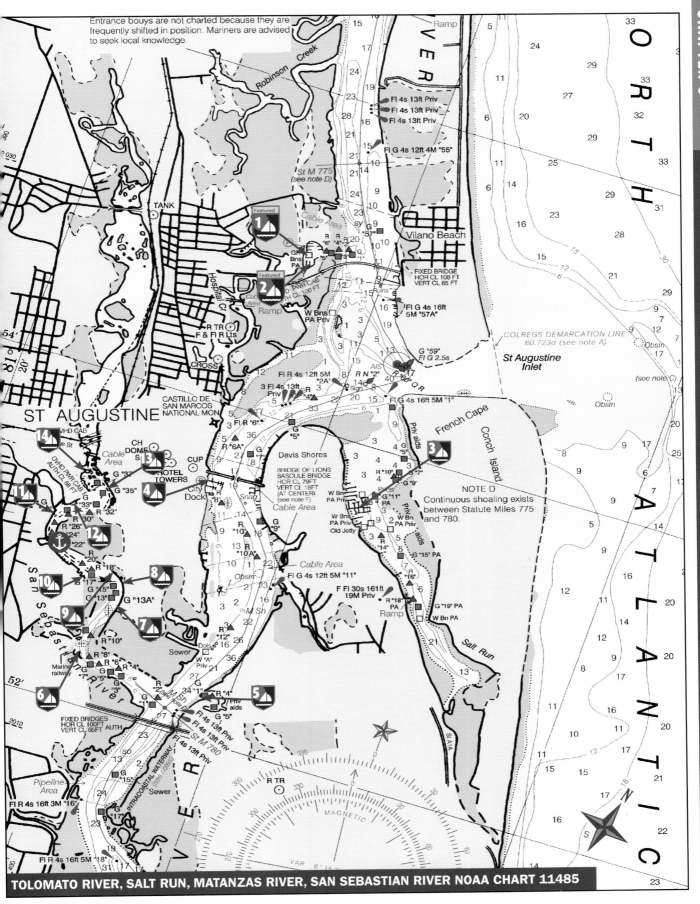

Entrance bouys are not charted because they are frequently shifted in position. Mariners are advised to seek local knowledge.

Robinson Creek

TANK

St M 775
(see note D)

Fl 4s 13ft Priv
Fl 4s 13ft Priv
Fl 4s 13ft Priv

Fl G 4s 12ft 4M "55"

Vilano Beach

FIXED BRIDGE
HOR CL 108 FT
VERT CL 65 FT

Fl G 4s 16ft
5M "57A"

COLREGS DEMARCATION LINE
80.723d (see note A)

St Augustine
Inlet

(see note C)

G "59"
Fl G 2.5s

R N "2"
AIS

Fl R 4s 12ft 5M
"2A"

3 Fl 4s 13ft
Priv

Fl G 4s 16ft 5M "1"

French Cape

ST AUGUSTINE

CASTILLO DE
SAN MARCOS
NATIONAL MON

Davis Shores

BRIDGE OF LIONS
BASCULE BRIDGE
HOR CL 79FT
VERT CL 18FT
(AT CENTER)
(see note F)
Cable Area

Conch Island

NOTE D
Continuous shoaling exists
between Statute Miles 775
and 780.

Old Jetty

Cable Area
Fl G 4s 12ft 5M "11"

F Fl 30s 161ft
19M Priv

Ramp

Salt Run

San Sebastian River

Marine
railway

Sewer

FIXED BRIDGES
HOR CL 100FT AUTH
VERT CL 65FT

Pipeline
Area

Sewer

Fl R 4s 16ft 3M "16"

Fl R 4s 16ft 5M "18"

INTRACOASTAL WATERWAY
(see note J)

St M 780

Fl 4s 13ft Priv
Fl 4s 13ft Priv
Fl 4s 13ft Priv

MAGNETIC

VAR

**TOLOMATO RIVER, SALT RUN, MATANZAS RIVER, SAN SEBASTIAN RIVER NOAA CHART 11485**

out you may want to check with them ahead of time. They also sell diesel fuel.

The San Sebastian River, which branches off the Matanzas River at Mile 780, is a better spot for provisioning and has a number of marine businesses and associated docks. You should exercise caution when docking anywhere on this river, as the current is swift. The Cat's Paw Marina is located past red day beacon "8" on the west shore of the San Sebastian River. This is a dry-storage facility with gas and diesel plus a 9-ton lift.

St. Augustine Marine Center is located near green daybeacon "13". This is a full service yard with 110-ton lift and a cat crawler capable of hauling catamarans with up to 35-foot beam. This 23-acre yard has long and short-term storage and welcomes do-it-yourself boaters. What they do not offer, however, is transient slips.

Continuing farther upriver is Xynides Boat Yard, and next door is the Oasis Boatyard & Marina. Both have a 50-ton lift, and Oasis also has a 20-ton crane. Both are strictly repair/service facilities and do not offer overnight dockage to transients.

On the other side of the river the St. Augustine Shipyard, which (as of spring 2017) is a dry-storage facility with plans for a 300-slip marina to be built in the future. This is a full-service yard with hull, engine and prop repairs.

English Landing Marina and Rivers Edge Marina are just one-half mile south of downtown St. Augustine at green daybeacons "29" and "33," respectively. The marinas are a short walk away from a supermarket and a West Marine, as well as stores offering beer, wine and spirits. Both marinas have transient slips, and Rivers Edge sells all fuels (via a fuel truck). The Marine Supply & Oil Co. is less than 2 miles away with diesel. Call for delivery options.

Hidden Harbor Marina–St. Augustine is located just before the low **King Street** fixed bridge (2-foot vertical clearance) and has limited transient dockage.

**Moorings:** The City of St. Augustine has installed a mooring field consisting of approximately 175 moorings, which are managed by the Municipal Marina. There are four different mooring fields: Salt Run has two fields (north and south) with a total of 80 moorings, while the downtown area has two different fields (Menendez with 70 moorings and San Marcos with 28 moorings). The Menendez field is south of the Bridge of Lions and San Marcos is north of the Bridge of Lions. All of the moorings have access to a free pump-out boat that operates daily between the hours of 9:00 a.m. and noon, the dinghy dock, a shuttle boat and use of all of the facilities at the marina. The moorings can accommodate vessels up to a 120 feet.

When entering the Menendez mooring field, you should enter just west of red daybeacon "8" on the ICW. Do not enter the field between daybeacons "8" and "10A" as it had shoaled and has less than 4 feet at mean low water. Shoaling to 3 feet mean low water has also been observed near and below some of the moorings. Ask the marina when you call for a mooring, and get advice on where to enter the mooring field.

The Salt Run mooring fields (Mile 777 just off the St. Augustine Inlet) can be reached by following the private channel markers of the Conch House Marina and Resort. Once past the marina, you will see the mooring fields (north and south). The two mooring areas have a total of 80 moorings. Both have a pump-out boat and dinghy dock; however, if you want to have access to the city of St. Augustine, Salt Run is a poor choice because of the distance to the city. It would be a very long dinghy

St. Augustine Inlet (Use Local Knowledge)

ICW

St. Augustine

Camachee Cove Yacht Harbor

Usina-Vilano Bridge

St. Augustine Inlet

ide and a very long walk just to get there. This area is used primarily for long-term mooring.

**Anchorage:** St. Augustine has passed an ordinance restricting anchoring outside mooring fields that essentially wiped out all previous anchorages. Specifically, no anchoring is allowed within 100 feet of mooring field boundaries, within 50 feet of maritime infrastructure, within 500 feet of shellfish areas and for no more than 30 consecutive days in any 45-day period. Fines are $100 to $500. This is a part of a pilot mooring field study in St. Augustine, Martin County, St. Petersburg, Sarasota and the Florida Keys to help alleviate issues with anchoring. The Florida Fish and Wildlife Conservation Commission was expected to complete the study by July 2017. (Results were not available at press time in spring 2017.)

In recent years, a few local and transient boats have been observed anchoring in the San Sebastian River, but this is not a good anchorage for a variety of reasons: the only deep water is directly in the narrow dredged channel, the reversing current here is very swift, and there is a sizable fleet of shrimp trawlers coming and going at all hours that use the commercial docks upriver as their base. Also, the swinging room is very limited.

## St. Augustine Inlet

When entering the St. Augustine Inlet and heading northbound on the ICW, it is important to run a sufficient distance past the tip of the beach on the north side of the inlet channel before turning into the ICW channel. (See the Inlet listing in the front of this guide for more information.) Commercial and sportfishing boats use the St. Augustine Inlet regularly; get local information but avoid this spot in rough conditions.

The inlet is frequently surveyed at around 12 to 15 feet deep at low tide at the outside bar; however, remember that this channel is subject to change at any time. Shoaling is common and the markers are frequently moved and may not be accurate, although the inlet is dredged on a regular basis.

Waves break dangerously close to the dredged channel, especially at low tide with ebb current against an onshore wind. There are nearly always breakers on the shallows on each side of the inlet, which looks intimidating even when the channel is flat calm.

Camachee Cove Yacht Harbor, and the local towing services (SeaTow and TowBoat U.S.) have updated information on possible shoaling and will be very accommodating if called for "local knowledge."

# ST. AUGUSTINE INLET TO DAYTONA BEACH

## Matanzas River to Matanzas Inlet–ICW Mile 780 to Mile 796

**NAVIGATION:** Use Chart 11485. One nautical mile south of St. Augustine on the Matanzas River at Mile 780.3, **SR 312 Twin Bridges** (65-foot fixed vertical clearance) cross the river and the current is swift here. The Matanzas River channel is deep but narrow, so follow the array of markers carefully until the dredged cut takes over south of Matanzas Inlet (closed to navigation).

About 3 miles south of the St. Augustine high-rise bridges is a beautiful, recently renovated example of Queen Anne-style architecture, near red daybeacon "28" on the west side of the ICW. Charted as "CUP" (meaning cupola), the structure is private property; do not go ashore.

Several markers along the stretch should be given a wide berth to avoid shoals. At red daybeacon "30," steer wide toward the east side of the channel to avoid the encroaching shoals from the west bank. Just north of Crescent Beach, at Mile 789, tides from St. Augustine and Matanzas inlets meet. From here, you run a dredged channel most of the next 80 miles to the Indian River.

At Crescent Beach, you will encounter the **Crescent Beach (SR 206) Bascule Bridge** (Mile 788.6, 25-foot closed vertical clearance), which opens on signal. The bridge tender is particularly helpful and accommodating. On both sides of the bridge for approximately 200 feet is a No-Wake Zone that is enforced. At Mile 792.2, shoaling extends into the channel, and red daybeacon "80" deserves a wide berth.

⚠️ A shoal has built up on the north end of Rattlesnake Island at Mile 792.2. Be sure to stay within the channel and there will be plenty of water (12 feet or more). The markers will take you very close to shore, but that is where the deep water is. Do not cut the corner! These markers are moved on a regular basis so stay in the channel.

The current between the ICW crossing of Matanzas River (Mile 792) and Marineland (Mile 796) can be strong enough to pull pot markers underwater, but it decreases as you proceed toward Palm Coast.

# Palm Coast, FL

| PALM COAST AREA | | | | Dockage | | | | | Supplies | | | Services | | | | |
|---|---|---|---|---|---|---|---|---|---|---|---|---|---|---|---|---|
| | | Largest Vessel Accommodated | VHF Channel Monitored | Transient Berths / Total Berths | Approach / Dockside Depth (reported) | Floating Docks | Gas / Diesel | Repairs: Hull, Engine, Propeller | Groceries, Ice, Marine Supplies, Snacks | Lift (tonnage), Crane, Rail | Laundry, Pool, Showers, Courtesy Car | Pump-Out Station | Nearby: Grocery Store, Motel, Restaurant | Min/Max Amps | | |
| 1. Marineland Marina 💻 📶 | 796 | 904-814-9886 | 100 | 16/68 | 20/41 | 6.5/6 | F | - | - | | - | 30/100 | LSC | P | MR |
| 2. Palm Coast Marina 💻 📶 WG | 803 | 386-446-6370 | 165 | 16/69 | 25/80 | 8/8 | - | GD | IMS | | - | 30/50 | LS | P | MR |
| 3. Marina At Hammock Beach Resort 💻 📶 | 803 | 386-597-5030 | 125 | 16/10 | 150/209 | 8/7 | F | - | GIMS | | - | 30/100 | LPS | P | GR |

💻 Internet Access  📶 Wireless Internet Access  WG Waterway Guide Cruising Club Partner *(Information in the table is provided by the facilities.)*
See WaterwayGuide.com for current rates, fuel prices, web site addresses, and other up-to-the-minute information.

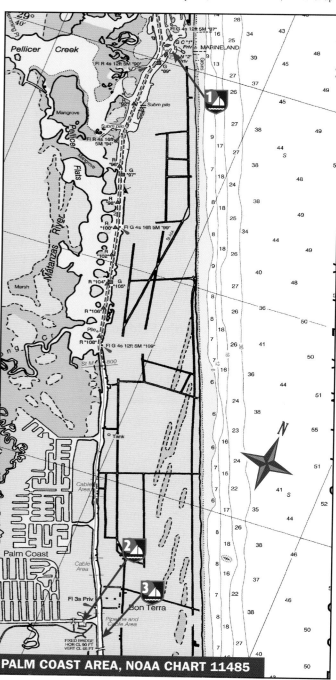

**PALM COAST AREA, NOAA CHART 11485**

**Dockage:** If you are looking to stop for the night, Marineland Marina at Mile 796 can accommodate boats under 70 feet. The marina provides direct access to the beaches and natural preserves. Marineland Dolphin Adventure offers a number of ways to interact with Atlantic bottlenose dolphins, as well as hands-on exhibits and educational programs. Current operating hours are 9:00 a.m. to 4:30 p.m. daily (except Thanksgiving and Christmas).

**Anchorage:** It is possible to drop the hook at Mile 781.2, south of flashing red "18" on the Matanzas River. The anchorage is very quiet, easy to enter and offers deep water (at least 7 feet). Tide can be up to 5 feet. Several derelict boats remain here, despite some relocations resulting from Hurricane Mathew.

An anchorage to the south at Butler Beach (Mile 786.2) offers good holding in 8 to 10 feet of water off flashing green "43"behind the spoil area. There are boat ramps nearby so this may get busy during the day.

## Side Trip: Fort Matanzas

At the north end of Rattlesnake Island (Mile 792), you will see the stark remains of Fort Matanzas, once a Spanish outpost and now a national monument. Like its larger cousin, Castillo de San Marcos in St. Augustine, this fort was built of coquina, a rock made of tiny shells. You can reach the fort via a small National Park Service ferry that runs between Anastasia Island and Rattlesnake Island. Its terminal is just north of the inlet, and it is an easy drive from St. Augustine.

**Anchorage:** You will find good holding in 8 to 10 feet of water in front of Fort Matanzas by green can "81A." To enter the anchorage, turn between cans "80A" and "80B" and stay close to the north shore. Use extra caution at low tide. This is open to the north through southeast.

## Matanzas Inlet to Palm Coast–ICW Mile 797 to Mile 803

Marshland alternates with forests along the banks of the Matanzas River here as you pass through a part of the Guana-Tolomato-Matanzas National Estuarine Research Reserve, south of Marineland Marina on the east side of the ICW. You will likely encounter kayak tour groups here during warmer weather; give them a slow, no-wake pass out of courtesy.

This cut seems eerie and almost desolate in places, so it comes as a surprise when farther down the cut on the west side several wide, rip-rapped channels appear. This is part of the community of Palm Coast, accessible via its three canals. The large planned residential community includes 6 miles of beach and ICW frontage. Across from Palm Coast on the east side of the ICW is another cleared area, Ginn Hammock Beach, with residential lots and houses, canals, a large condominium building and a large marina basin.

**NAVIGATION:** Use Chart 11485. Locals report shoaling at Mile 797, on the west side of the channel just past flashing red daybeacon "90" and additional shoaling from flashing red daybeacon "94" to red daybeacon "104." Red daybeacon "92" has been repositioned to mark deeper water. There is a fixed, high-level toll bridge, **Hammock Dunes Bridge** (Mile 803.0, 65-foot vertical clearance) just south of the entrance to the Palm Coast Marina. (This bridge is locally known as the Palm Coast Highway Bridge.)

**Dockage:** At Mile 803, a canal leads westward to the Palm Coast Marina. Once inside, favor the south side of the channel. The marina welcomes transients, and the dockmaster allows the office to serve as a mail drop. Gas and diesel fuels are available. Within walking distance

from the marina (approximately one-half mile) is the European Village, which has numerous shops and dining options. There is also an urgent care center nearby; MediQuick Walk-in Clinic is located at 6 Office Park Drive in Palm Coast (386-447-6615). No appointment is necessary.

Marina at Hammock Beach Resort is in the large dredged basin directly across the ICW from the Palm Coast Marina, where the chart shows "Bon Terra." This marina offers transients the full range of amenities available through the Club at Hammock Beach. There is also a shuttle available to transport you to a market or elsewhere. This is a large private condominium and residential community, with its own dredged basin and private slips.

## Palm Coast to Tomoka Basin–ICW Mile 804 to Mile 818

If you leave the Palm Coast area marinas on a slow boat (less than 10-knot speed) at the start of the ebb tide, you can ride the current all the way to Ponce de Leon Inlet.

As a point of interest, between Mile 804 and Mile 807, you will notice a narrow interconnecting canal on the east side of the ICW. This was part of the original ICW and gives an idea of the size of some earlier sections.

**NAVIGATION:** Use Chart 11485. For several miles south of Palm Coast Marina, condominiums with community docks and boat lifts, golf courses and private homes line both sides of the ICW. At Mile 805, on the west side of the ICW, is Grand Haven, a country club community. The west side of the ICW down to Mile 809 is currently undergoing an increase in residential development, with many docks extending out toward the ICW. Not all of the docks are in deep water, however, and boaters

should not assume that just because there is a dock that the water is deep enough. Stay in the center of the channel, especially south of the high-rise bridge at Palm Coast, near the long series of docks on the west side. If you see boats in the water at these docks, slow down out of courtesy and give them a "no-wake" pass.

Exposed rocks line both sides of the long Fox Cut from green daybeacon "1" to green daybeacon "5." Red daybeacons "2" and "4" and flashing green daybeacon "3" mark rocks that extend to the edge of the channel. A ramp, dock and launch facility have been dug out of the west side of the ICW at flashing green daybeacon "3" and red daybeacon "4." This is a Slow-Speed/No-Wake Zone. Stay to the center of the channel when passing the ramp. Rocks intermittently line the west side of the ICW close to shore at the residential construction, just south of the ramp, down to the entrance to the cement plant anchorage at Mile 809.

A dock development on the east side of the ICW, just north of the Flagler Beach Bridge, has been empty of boats since being built, and its entrance is roped off. This marina has been abandoned for a number of years, and there are prominent signs indicating "NO TRESPASSING/PRIVATE DOCKS."

The **Flagler Beach (Moody Blvd.) Bridge** (with 65-foot fixed vertical clearance) crosses the ICW at Mile 810.6. Expect shoals near the bridge along the edges of the channel. There is a busy ramp on the south side of the bridge; pass at idle speed. For the 5 miles between the Flagler Beach Bridge and the Bulow (L.B. Knox) Bridge, the channel is lined with pot markers on both sides, and some floats are in the channel itself.

At Mile 812.4, red daybeacon "20" has been moved to the bend in Smith Creek, and red daybeacon "20A" has been added at the previous location of red daybeacon "20." At Mile 814, a small, marked side channel leads to a state park and a ramp. This is the beginning of a Manatee Zone, with a 30-mph speed limit in the channel (25 mph at night), and slow speed required outside the ICW channel.

At Mile 816, expect congestion at the boat ramp at the **Bulow (L.B. Knox) Bascule Bridge**. Clearance is only 15 feet, but the bridge opens on signal. South of the bridge, the channel shoals along the east side from flashing red daybeacon "2" to flashing green daybeacon "7." The ICW enters the headwaters of the Halifax River here, which gradually widens in its reach to Daytona Beach. The channel, is straight and well marked, and

follows closely along the eastern bank and passes attractive homes. There is a negligible tidal range here.

**Anchorage:** At Mile 809, a side channel carrying less than 6-foot depths at its entrance, with 11-foot depths inside, leads west to a charted cement plant, which has been closed for some time. A Sea Ray factory that is located here generates a great deal of boat traffic at various times during the day; this activity is reported to begin early in the morning.

Enter near the center of the channel; watch the depth sounder and ease toward the north shore. Once past the un-navigable side channels, you can move back to the middle. Anchor on the south side above the side channels or past the boat factory; "No Trespassing" signs make it clear that you may not go ashore. Holding is reported to be marginal here and the swing room is very limited. There are several homes with docks on the south side at the entrance, and the north side is undergoing residential and golf course development.

## Tomoka Basin to Daytona Beach–ICW Mile 819 to Mile 829

Tomoka State Park, along the riverbanks of the Tomoka River, was once home to the Timucua Indians. Today, you can walk beneath the same ancient oaks that shaded their huts nearly 400 years ago or explore the marshes and tidal creeks by dinghy. Fishing, hiking, picnicking and bird watching are popular.

**NAVIGATION:** Use Chart 11485. For deeper-draft boats, the 5-mile-long passage from Tomoka Basin to the Ormond Beach Bridge calls for close attention to markers. Stick to the middle on this stretch because the east and west sides of the channel shoal and the water is shallow outside the channel. Depths are generally 8 feet during mean low water at mid-channel in this area, although shoaling to 4 feet has been reported at the edge of the channel near red daybeacon "20" south of the bridge. The **Ormond Beach (SR 40) Bridge** at Mile 824.9 has 65-foot fixed vertical clearance.

Just north of the Ormond Beach Bridge, the channel gradually shifts toward the middle of the river. The open water of the Halifax River here is a popular windsurfing area. On a blustery day expect to see several windsurfers crisscrossing the channel. Slow speed is required in this area for the manatee zone.

Local festivals are often held on the nearby grounds of the Casements, the former summer home of John D. Rockefeller, which now houses museum exhibits and is owned and maintained by the City of Ormond.

A high-rise condominium, visible from the ICW, has replaced the old landmark Ormond Hotel. The city has developed extensive park lands along the banks of the Halifax near the Ormond Beach Bridge. These riverfront areas are pleasant spots for walkers and picnickers, but there are no docks.

**Anchorage:** The first wide bight to the west at Mile 818.5 is—like most of the Halifax River's off-channel waters—too shallow for all but shoal-draft vessels. If you can follow the array of stakes and nudge your way in through the very shoal Tomoka Basin, the Tomoka River itself is deep quite a bit farther upstream.

Soon after the invention of the automobile, Ormond became known as the **Birthplace of Speed**. Early auto owners were searching for places where they could drive on hard surfaces. Existing roads were no more than horse trails and posed problems for the cars. The broad, smooth beach at Ormond proved to be ideal. The first timed trials were held on March 26, 1903. Replicas of the winning cars can be seen at the Birthplace of Speed Park at the beach. Late in November, Ormond Beach hosts an antique car rally, featuring a gaslight parade of old cars to commemorate its place in the birth of auto racing.

## Daytona Beach—ICW Mile 830

While the official tourist season for this northern Florida "summer resort" runs from Memorial Day to after Labor Day, Daytona Beach is popular all year long. In spring and fall, boats on the north–south run stop over, and in winter and summer, its mild climate attracts yachtsmen and tourists from other areas that are too hot or too cold. Skippers often stop at Daytona Beach either to have work done at the area's good repair yards or just to layover for a while to enjoy its many nearby attractions.

The ICW waterfront on the west side in Daytona Beach is dotted with large condominium buildings. Most conspicuous of these are the twin towers with associated docks at the complex on the north side of the Seabreeze Bridge at Mile 829.1.

**NAVIGATION:** Use Chart 11485. It's a straight 5-mile shot from Ormond Beach to the series of four bridges that welcome you to Daytona Beach: **Seabreeze Twin Bridges** (65-foot fixed vertical clearance); **Main St. (Daytona Beach) Bascule Bridge** (22-foot closed vertical clearance, opens on signal); **International Speedway Blvd. Bridge** (65-foot fixed vertical clearance); and **Veterans Memorial Bascule Bridge** (21-foot closed vertical clearance). The

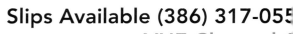

Coquina Marina    ICW

Seabreeze

Halifax Harbor Marina

Daytona Beach

Veterans Bridge at Mile 830.6 is the only bridge with restricted openings. The bridge opens on signal, except from 7:45 a.m. to 8:45 a.m., and 4:45 p.m. to 5:45 p.m., Monday through Saturday (except federal holidays), when the draw opens only at 8:15 a.m. and 5:15 p.m. Both the Veterans and Main St. Bascule Bridges respond to sound signal as well as calls on VHF Channel 09. At press time (spring 2017), construction was underway for a fixed 65-foot vertical clearance replacement bridge for the Veterans Memorial Bridge. Anticipated completion is November 2018.

**Dockage:** Marinas and yacht yards line the shore on the west side of the ICW from north of the city all the way to Ponce de Leon Inlet. Just south of the Seabreeze Twin Bridges at Mile 829 is the 61-slip Coquina Marina (formerly Sunset Harbor Yacht Club), which offers transient dockage for vessels to 90 feet and many amenities, including laundry, a pool and a tennis court. Groceries are available within 1 mile.

To the south, Suntex Marina at Daytona Beach offers transient dockage and resort-like amenities. The on-site restaurant is Caribbean Jack's (386-523-3000), which is open daily with indoor and outdoor seating. (We like the swinging glider tables on the waterfront deck.)

# Daytona Beach to Ponce de Leon Inlet, FL

www.snagaslip.com
SNAG-A-SLIP
EXPLORE. BOOK. BOAT.™

| | | Largest Vessel Accommodated | VHF Channel Monitored | Transient Berths / Total Berths | Approach / Dockside Depth (reported) | Floating Docks | Gas / Diesel | Groceries, Ice, Marine Supplies, Snacks | Repairs: Hull, Engine, Propeller | Lift (tonnage), Crane, Rail | Min/Max Amps | Laundry, Pool, Showers, Courtesy Car | Pump-Out Station | Nearby: Grocery Store, Motel, Restaurant |
|---|---|---|---|---|---|---|---|---|---|---|---|---|---|---|
| **DAYTONA BEACH** | | | | **Dockage** | | | | **Supplies** | | | **Services** | | | |
| 1. Coquina Marina (formerly Sunset Harbor Yacht Club) (WiFi) | 386-317-0555 | 90 | 16 | call/61 | 6/6 | - | - | I | - | L | 30/50 | LPS | - | GMR |
| 2. Suntex Marina at Daytona Beach ⌂ (WiFi) | 386-523-3100 | 75 | 16/79 | 10/85 | 6/6 | - | - | GIMS | - | - | 30/100 | LPS | P | GMR |
| 3. Halifax River Yacht Club ⌂ (WiFi) 830.7 | 386-255-7459 | 80 | 16/68 | 3/39 | 7/7 | F | - | IS | - | - | 30/50 | LPS | P | GMR |
| 4. Halifax Harbor Marina ⌂ (WiFi) WG 830.7 | 386-671-3601 | 100 | 16/71 | 55/550 | 8/8 | F | GD | IS | - | - | 30/100 | LS | P | MR |
| 5. Marina Point Marina ⌂ | 386-239-7166 | 55 | - | 0/16 | 8/8 | F | - | I | - | - | 30/50 | LS | - | GMR |
| 6. Daytona Marina & Boat Works (WiFi) WG 831 | 386-252-6421 | 200 | 16/72 | 91/159 | 8/8 | - | GD | IS | HEP | L55 | 30/100 | LS | P | GMR |
| **PORT ORANGE** | | | | | | | | | | | | | | |
| 7. Seven Seas Marina & Boatyard ⌂ 835.2 | 386-761-3221 | 44 | 16/72 | 10/30 | 6/9 | - | GD | IM | HEP | L35,C | 30/50 | LS | - | GMR |
| 8. Adventure Yacht Harbor ⌂ (WiFi) WG 836.8 | 386-756-2180 | 65 | 16/18 | 4/137 | 5/7 | - | GD | IMS | E | - | 30/50 | LS | P | MR |
| 9. Harbour Village Golf & Yacht Club–PRIVATE (WiFi) 839.6 | 386-316-9775 | - | 16 | call/142 | 6/10 | F | - | I | - | - | - | PS | P | GR |
| **PONCE DE LEON INLET AREA** | | | | | | | | | | | | | | |
| 10. Inlet Harbor Marina ⌂ (WiFi) | 386-767-3266 | 180 | 06 | 12/84 | 9/15 | F | GD | GI | E | L25 | 30/100 | LS | P | GR |
| 11. Sea Love Boat Works Inc. (WiFi) 1.3 SE of 839.5 | 386-761-5434 | 90 | 16/07 | 5/10 | 8/8 | F | D | IM | HEP | L70 | 30/100 | S | - | R |

⌂ Internet Access  (WiFi) Wireless Internet Access  WG Waterway Guide Cruising Club Partner  *(Information in the table is provided by the facilities.)*
See WaterwayGuide.com for current rates, fuel prices, web site addresses, and other up-to-the-minute information.

The Halifax River Yacht Club is at Mile 830.7, in a basin just south of Memorial Bridge. They have some reserved transient space on their floating docks.

The municipal Halifax Harbor Marina is in a separate enclosed basin to the south. Enter the marina through the marked entrance channel just west of ICW green daybeacon "39A." The marina boasts 550 slips on a 60-acre property park, with excellent amenities, the Marina View Restaurant & Tiki Bar (844-383-6878) and nearby shopping. They also have gas and diesel fuel, a free pump-out service and a store. The marina is convenient to downtown Daytona and the city bus stop is an easy walk away. In that same channel is Marina Point Marina, which only accepts long-term transients.

Daytona Marina & Boat Works is open 24/7 for fuel (both gas and diesel) and dockage (up to 200 feet) and offers hull engine and propeller service and repair. The gold dome you see is the on-site Chart House Restaurant (386-255-9022).

**Anchorage:** The anchorages both above and below the Seabreeze Twin Bridges were still active in 2017. The anchorage south of the bridges is deeper, but there is scattered debris on the bottom. This area is a Slow-Speed/No-Wake Zone. The anchorage north of the Seabreeze Twin Bridges shallows up quickly and is in an area with submerged cables. Signs on each shore mark the location of the cables, but the signs are difficult to pick out from the water. The sign on the western shore is just south of the twin condos. This anchorage is also at one end of a 25-mph Manatee Zone, so wakes from passing boats can be a problem. This entire anchorage area seems to be generally shoaling, but it is still handy when you arrive late in the day from St. Augustine.

The chart doesn't show it, but there is a cozy anchorage east of the ICW in the vicinity of the charted 11-foot depths at Mile 830.7. To reach this anchorage, turn east off the ICW immediately south of the Memorial Bridge. Using the yacht club's green daybeacons "3" and "5" as a back range, proceed east to within 100 to 150 feet of shore; if you stay on the range, you should find at least 6 feet of water over the bar. At this point, turn south along the shore to find a slot of water 9 to 13 feet deep about 100 feet from shore. The shoal on the channel side is less than 3 feet deep at mean low water. This protection provides fine protection from northeast to southeast winds.

Many boats also anchor in the deep-water pocket northwest of red daybeacon "44," although depths are said to be less than the 7 to 14 feet charted. Avoid the cable area if you stop here.

Locations of over 2500 anchorages and free docks
waterwayguide.com

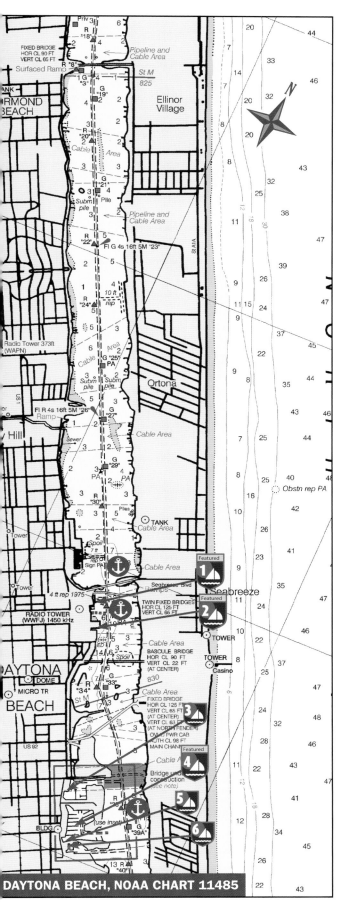

**DAYTONA BEACH, NOAA CHART 11485**

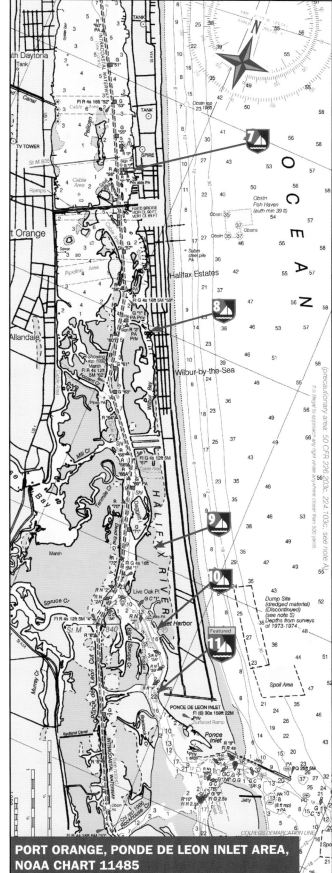

**PORT ORANGE, PONDE DE LEON INLET AREA, NOAA CHART 11485**

SEA LOVE BOAT WORKS, INC.

ICW

Ponce de Leon Inlet

## ■ DAYTONA BEACH TO PONCE DE LEON INLET

**NAVIGATION:** Use Chart 11485. Stay in the channel between Daytona and Port Orange, as there are many shoals just outside the channel. Be particularly wary of the spot between red daybeacons "42" and "44" and from "46" to "48," marked on the chart as part of a measured nautical mile course.

At Mile 835.5, about halfway between Daytona Beach and Ponce de Leon Inlet, the high-rise **Dunlawton Ave. (Port Orange) Bridge** carries state Route A1A across the ICW. It is charted with a 65-foot fixed vertical clearance but tide boards at a full-moon high tide sometimes show a center-span clearance of 63 feet. Current is swift here, and the narrow channel can be congested, especially on weekends.

Just below the Port Orange Bridge, a small mangrove island on the west side of the ICW channel is a nesting ground for pelicans, egrets and cormorants during spring. The nesting birds are prevalent above and below the Port Orange Bridge down to Ponce de Leon Inlet. If you should see any, confine your activity to watching only and do not disturb the nests.

The course south from Port Orange passes through a dredged cut that is crowded with fishermen in small outboard craft, so watch your wake. There was a shoal reported to be in the channel on the west side between red daybeacons "68" and "70" in the vicinity of Tenmile

Creek. Green daybeacon "69" has been relocated to mark the deeper water, and depths are now reported to be around 9 feet at the edge of the channel. Red daybeacon "68A" has been added here to further define the deeper water.

There is a condo with private docks on the east side of the ICW between green daybeacon "71" and red daybeacon "72." Its entrance channel is marked with a rather large red nun buoy and green can buoy, which can be confusing for ICW travelers. Do not confuse these for the floating ICW markers marking the beginning of the Ponce de Leon Cut just to the south after flashing green daybeacon "1."

⚠ This area is constantly changing. The numbering of the markers changes after marker "72" when you are going south on the ICW. Marker "1" is a permanent marker, but markers "2," "3," "2A" and "3A" are temporary and are moved on a regular basis, as are "7A" and "8A." The shoaling in this area is always on the move. Our cruising editor usually finds the deeper water by favoring the green side of this channel. As stated above, this condition is always changing so pay attention to your depth sounder. Check the Coast Guard *Local Notice to Mariners* and waterwayguide.com for updates.

**Dockage:** Seven Seas Marina & Boatyard is located above the Port Orange Bridge (east side). This marina was heavily damaged in Hurricane Matthew. The rebuilding process had begun at press time in early spring 2017. Call ahead to check on dock availability.

A short distance below the Port Orange Bridge on the east side of the ICW past flashing green daybeacon "59" is Adventure Yacht Harbor. They offer slips and sell gas and diesel. They mostly cater to sportfishing boats but are close to amenities and provisioning supplies. Look for the marked entry channel. Note that there is a tidal range here of 2.5 feet and the channel can be as low as 6.5 feet; call ahead for more exact depths.

Harbour Village Golf & Yacht Club is strictly private (their members only) and does not accept transient boats at their docks.

JACKSONVILLE BEACH TO PONCE DE LEON INLET

# GOIN' ASHORE: **DAYTONA BEACH, FL**

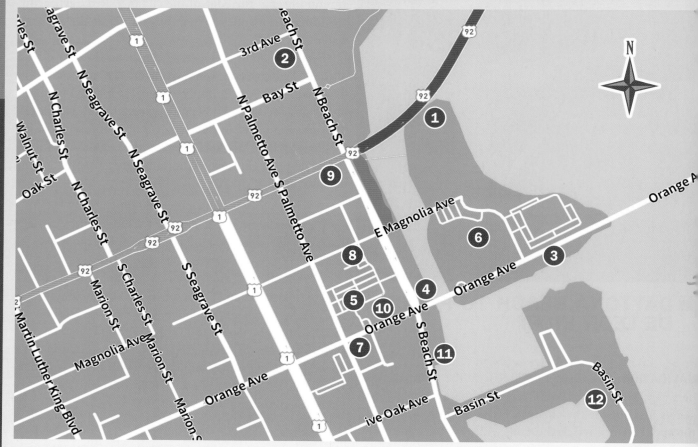

| SERVICES | |
|---|---|
| 1 | Library |
| 2 | Post Office |
| 3 | Visitor Information |
| **ATTRACTIONS** | |
| 4 | Brownie the Town Dog's Grave |
| 5 | Halifax Historical Museum |

| | |
|---|---|
| 6 | Jackie Robinson Memorial Baseball Park |
| **SHOPPING** | |
| 7 | Riverfront Shops |
| **DINING** | |
| 8 | McK's Tavern |
| 9 | Scuttlebutts Pub & Restaurant |

| | |
|---|---|
| 10 | Stavro's Pizza House |
| **MARINAS** | |
| 11 | Halifax River Yacht Club |
| 12 | Halifax Harbor Marina |

Daytona Beach's 23 miles of beach were once a proving ground for automobile engines in the early 1900s. Automobile pioneers like Louis Chevrolet and Henry Ford found the hard-packed sand, gentle slope and wide expanse of beach to be the perfect venue for auto racing. Today, the beach remains popular with motorists, although they are restricted to a leisurely 10-mph pace and must pay an access fee. Automobile racing moved inland to Daytona International Speedway in 1959 as cars became faster and crowds of spectators grew larger.

**Attractions:** The Daytona Chamber of Commerce at 126 Orange Ave. (on City Island) can get your started on your exploration. They are open weekdays from 9:00 a.m. to 5:00 p.m. (386-255-0981). O the way, you will pass the Halifax Historical Museum (252 S. Beach St., 386-255-6976), which presents Daytona Beach from a historical perspective. Another intriquing stop is the gravesite of Brownie the Town Dog who was "owned by no one but loved by all." A large, brown, short-haired stray dog, Brownie lived on Beach Street for 15 years, during which time he was nicknamed Town Dog of Daytona Beach. Locals, merchants and tourists donated funds to keep Brownie well fed and cared for until he died on Halloween in 1954. The entire city mourned the dog's passing, and 75 people attended his funeral in Riverfront Park. The Mayor gave the eulogy. Brownie's grave is located on the corner of ornage and Beach Streets, should you care to pay your respects. You can't miss it; a full-size topiary shrub dog gaurds the grave.

The Main Street Pier, Oceanfront Boardwalk and the Coquina Clock Tower are historic landmarks on the waterfront in Daytona Beach.

On the western edge of town, Daytona International Speedway (the "World Center of Racing") is where the nation's top drivers and automobiles compete in the famous 24 Hours of Daytona endurance race every January and the world-famous Daytona 500 stock car race every February. Tour the grounds or take a lap around the speedway with the Richard Petty Driving Experience. If you aren't up for the drive, ride shotgun in a two-seat authentic NASCAR stock car driven by a professional instructor at speeds in excess of 160 MPH (daytonainternationalspeedway.com).

A flea and farmers market and 20 local golf courses are available year-round. Bus tours are also available, for a variety of Central Florida excursions. Three miles west of the waterway, Daytona Beach International Airport provides scheduled service to most cities.

The area hosts many impressive events throughout the year, including Bike Week, Spring Family Beach Break, the Coke Zero 400 and Biketoberfest. The remainder of the year is peppered with a wide variety of art and music festivals, wine and chocolate walks, car shows and other delights. Minor league baseball at historic Jackie Robinson Ballpark (at Halifax Harbor) is a favorite, as is the free summer concert series at the open-air, oceanfront Daytona Beach Bandshell.

**Shopping:** Within walking distance of the marinas, the Riverfront Shops of Daytona Beach offers wide pedestrian walkways, riverfront parks and plenty of shops and restaurants. West Marine is located about 2 miles from the waterfront (1300 International Speedway Blvd., 386-255-2013). You also might find something you need at Surplus Unlimited Discount Marine (613 International Speedway Blvd., 386-252-5019). As in any city, this is an easy place to provision with numerous grocery, pharmacy and other such options.

**Dining:** There are many restaurants located in downtown Daytona along the waterfront. Caribbean Jack's (386-523-3000) at Loggerhead Marina is one of our favorites, as are Scuttlebutts Pub Restaurant (114 S. Beach St., 386-872-2939); McK's Tavern (218 S. Beach St., 386-238-3321); and Stavro's Pizza House (262 S. Beach St., 386-258-5041). The Chart House Restaurant at the Daytona Marina and Boatworks (386-255-9022) is always a fine choice.

# ■ PONCE DE LEON INLET

The Ponce de Leon Inlet area (sometimes called New Smyrna Inlet) begins north of Mile 840. Just west of the inlet, the Ponce de Leon Cut portion of the ICW is protected but subject to shoaling, especially at its north and south ends. The historic Ponce de Leon Inlet Lighthouse is open to the public (daily except Thanksgiving and Christmas) and provides a stunning panoramic view of the area.

**NAVIGATION:** Use Chart 11485. From flashing green daybeacon "1" to red daybeacon "6," on the north end of Ponce de Leon Cut, shoals are a constant problem. Our cruising editor observed 5- to 6-foot depths here at mean low water. Several buoys in this area are moved as needed and may not match what is printed on your chart. (See previous navigation alert.) Stay to the center of the channel (or closer to the green side), follow the markers and you shouldn't have any problems. The balance of the Ponce de Leon Cut up to marker "18" has 12 to 15 feet of water. Most of the cut sounded at 12 feet after the entrance at both ends.

⚠ On the south side of the Ponce de Leon Cut area of the ICW, there has, at times, been a shoal of varying depths extending across the entire ICW channel between red daybeacon "18" and floating green over red (where the older chart showed green daybeacon "19") as well as at red daybeacons "18A" and "20," so give the markers a wide berth and favor the east bank. This area is subject to change and may be marked differently when you arrive.

Ponce De Leon North Jetty Light is missing its foundation and due to Hurricane Matthew, the jetty has shifted. The area surrounding the structure is a hazard to navigation. Mariners are advised to use extreme caution while transiting the area. The next opportunity going south to leave the ICW and go offshore is the Canaveral Barge Canal at Mile 894, east to Canaveral Inlet. For additional information on the Ponce de Leon Inlet, see the Inlet section in the front of this guide. Check waterwayguide.com for daily navigational updates.

**Dockage:** Inlet Harbor Restaurant & Marina at the north end of the North Channel offers transient dockage, sells fuel and has numerous cruiser amenities. Unfortunately, the on-site restaurant was destroyed by Hurricane Matthew. Reconstruction began in spring 2017 with an anticipated completion of fall 2017.

Sea Love Marina & Boat Works, 1 mile east of Mile 840 on the North Channel of the inlet, offers transient berths, diesel fuel and almost any type of repair. Their 70-ton lift can haul boats with up to a 23-foot beam. Skills include carpentry and major wood boat repairs, painting, and propeller and shafting work. Hurricane repairs were underway at press time at the popular Down the Hatch Seafood Company located at Sea Love. It is recommended that you call ahead.

**Anchorage:** Note that all the side creeks in this area–North Channel, Spruce Creek, the unnamed side creek to the east and south of Spruce Creek, and Rockhouse Creek–are designated No-Wake Zones to protect the manatee population. All of the anchorages on these creeks have approximately 7 to 9 feet of water but are not included in the periodic dredging because they are not authorized federal channels.

Rockhouse Creek is a popular weekend anchorage and a congested small boat passage. Provisioning opportunities are nearby. The spoils island on the southeast side of Rockhouse Creek and adjacent to the ICW was scheduled to receive much of the spoil from recent dredging, which was instead used to refurbish the beach oceanside of the inlet.

## Cruising Options

For navigational information on the ICW south of the inlet, refer to the next chapter, "New Smyrna Beach to Vero Beach."

# SEA LOVE MARINA & BOAT WORKS

**CLOSEST DEEP WATER SLIPS TO THE INLET UP TO 130 FEET**
**ESCORT SERVICE TO/FROM SEA LOVE BY TOW BOAT US LOCATED ON SITE**
**TRANSIENTS WELCOME • DIESEL FUEL AVAILABLE • 30 TO 100AMP POWER**

## Sea Love Boat Works, Inc.

Located at Down The Hatch Restaurant and Deck Bar, the Area's Finest Dockside Dining

**DOWN THE HATCH**
Seafood Company
Est.-1975

Down The Hatch Restaurant
4894 Front Street
Ponce Inlet, FL 32127
386-761-4831

- Hull and Bottom Painting
- Marine Supplies and Paint
- Wood and Fiberglass Repair
- Propeller, Shaft & Rudder Repair
- Full Time Mechanics on Site
- Custom Fabrication
- On-Site Top-Side Paint Specialist
- On-Call Coast Guard Certified Welder

## LARGEST LIFT CAPACITY IN CENTRAL FLORIDA

yachtpaint.com

**70 TON TRAVELIFT • UP TO 22' BEAM**
**MONITORING VHF CHANNELS 7 & 16**
**• DIESEL FUEL**

386-761-5434 • www.sea-love-boat-works.com
Email: sealoveboatworksinc@yahoo.com
Less Than 1 Mile North of Ponce de Leon Inlet ( Daytona Beach)
4877 Front Street, Ponce Inlet, FL 32127

# New Smyrna Beach to Vero Beach

**ICW** Mile 846–Mile 952      **VHF** FL: Channel 09

**CHARTS** 11472, 11485

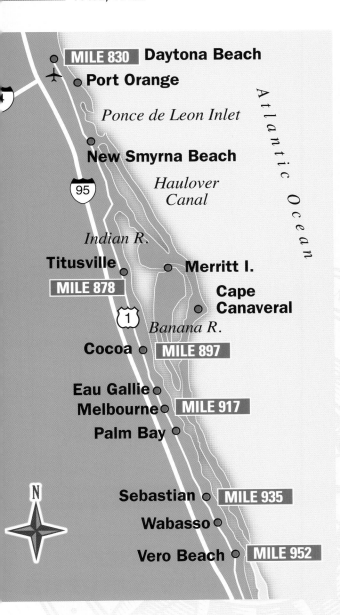

At about Mile 840, the ICW begins its departure from the Halifax River and enters the Ponce de Leon Cut north of Ponce de Leon Inlet, joining with the Indian River north just below the inlet. Strong tidal currents often run up and down the land cut and occasionally may give your vessel a sideways push.

**NAVIGATION:** Use Chart 11485. Use the Miami Harbor Entrance Tide Tables. For high tide at Ponce Inlet, add 5 minutes; for low tide, add 33 minutes. Coming in from Ponce de Leon Inlet (detailed in the previous chapter), the safest route to the ICW is the South Channel leading to New Smyrna Beach, the Indian River North and Mosquito Lagoon farther south on the ICW.

The charted floating markers for the North Channel from Ponce de Leon Inlet are on station, and the channel is always active with traffic. From the west side of North Channel to the **George E. Musson Memorial Bascule Bridge** at Coronado Beach (Mile 845.0) is a strictly enforced No-Wake Zone, as is the intersection of the ICW and the South Channel.

The George E. Musson Bridge has 24-foot closed vertical clearance and is hydraulic and relatively slow in opening; a swift-moving current complicates the approach. The bridge opens on signal, except from 7:00 a.m. to 7:00 p.m. daily, when the draw opens only on the hour and half-hour.

There is a shoal-prone area in the channel between red daybeacon "18" and the green/red floating can buoy, which has replaced green daybeacon "19,"where the chart indicates 9-foot depths. Stay as close to center channel as possible until daybeacon "20," which needs a wide berth to avoid shoals that extend into the channel from the mainland along the curved approach to the bridge.

View updated postings on
navigation and hazards alerts

**waterwayguide.com**

# New Smyrna Beach, FL

| NEW SMYRNA BEACH AREA | Phone | Largest Vessel Accommodated | VHF Channel Monitored | Transient Berths / Total Berths | Approach / Dockside Depth (reported) | Floating Docks | Gas / Diesel | Groceries, Ice, Marine Supplies, Snacks | Repairs: Hull, Engine, Propeller | Lift (tonnage), Crane, Rail | Min/Max Amps | Laundry, Pool, Showers, Courtesy Car | Pump-Out Station | Nearby: Grocery Store, Motel, Restaurant |
|---|---|---|---|---|---|---|---|---|---|---|---|---|---|---|
| **1. New Smyrna Marina dba The Fishing Store** 🖥 📶 | 386-427-4514 | 125 | 16/80 | 6/31 | 12/10 | F | GD | IMS | – | – | 30/100 | PS | – | GMR |
| 2. North Causeway Marine 846.4 | 386-427-5267 | 60 | 16 | 2/35 | 8/10 | – | GD | GIMS | HEP | L | 30/50 | – | – | GR |
| **3. New Smyrna Beach City Marina** 🖥 📶 846.5 | **386-409-2042** | 65 | 16/68 | 7/43 | 8/10 | F | – | I | – | – | 30/50 | LS | P | GMR |
| 4. Fishin' Cove Marina 846.6 | 386-428-7827 | 60 | – | 0/16 | 8/8 | F | G | IMS | HE | L | 30/50 | – | – | GMR |
| 5. Night Swan Intracoastal B & B 🖥 📶 WG 847 | 386-423-4940 | 32 | – | 3/6 | 12/9 | F | – | – | – | – | 30/30 | LS | – | GMR |
| 6. Smyrna Yacht Club 🖥 📶 847 | 386-427-4040 | 65 | 16 | 3/77 | /4 | F | – | IS | – | – | 30/50 | PS | P | R |

🖥 Internet Access  📶 Wireless Internet Access  WG Waterway Guide Cruising Club Partner *(Information in the table is provided by the facilities.)*
See WaterwayGuide.com for current rates, fuel prices, web site addresses, and other up-to-the-minute information.

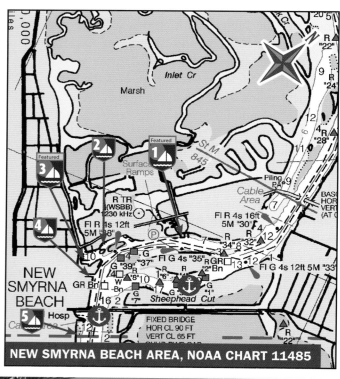

NEW SMYRNA BEACH AREA, NOAA CHART 11485

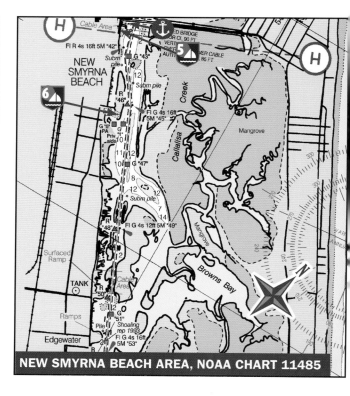

NEW SMYRNA BEACH AREA, NOAA CHART 11485

New Smyrna Beach

NEW SMYRNA BEACH CITY MARINA

New Smyrna Beach City Marina

Ponce de Leon Inlet

NEW SMYRNA MARINA DBA THE FISHING STORE

ICW

Sheepshead Cut

# NEW SMYRNA BEACH–ICW MILE 846

**NAVIGATION:** Use Chart 11485. South of the George E. Musson Bridge at Mile 845.0, continue to favor the eastern shore until the channel swings toward New Smyrna Beach. Watch for shoaling at the curve between flashing green daybeacons "33" and "35." The former shoal off flashing green daybeacon "35" has been dredged, and depths are no less than 9 feet at mean low water off red daybeacon "34." The chart will help you spot the turn to the west.

Sheephead Cut, Mile 845.5, is a more direct also marked channel between Chicken Island and Bouchelle Island; a green–red junction daybeacon indicates the eastern tip of Chicken Island. The preferred channel is the ICW route around the north side of Chicken Island. The other channel, which also has about 9-foot depths, leads through Sheephead Cut and meets the ICW and another green–red junction daybeacon at the west end of Chicken Island.

If you are considering going on the southern route around the south side of Chicken Island, stay to the center of the marked channel to avoid shoals. In the past few years before the latest dredging, there was conflicting information as to which was deeper, as both of the channels are subject to shoaling, but both routes carried adequate depths in spring 2017, according to our cruising editor.

New Smyrna Beach's harbor comes up suddenly beyond flashing red daybeacon "38," which marks the turn toward the **Harris Saxon (New Smyrna) Bridge** (Mile 846.5, 65-foot fixed vertical clearance). Do not cut corners off the ICW where green daybeacons "37" and "39" and a white "Danger" daybeacon mark a shoal; also honor green can buoy "39A," which is not shown on current charts. The ICW channel has only 10-foot depths at low tide just off the New Smyrna Yacht Club close to flashing green daybeacon "45."

The City of New Smyrna has built an attractive park at the northwest end of the bridge with a boardwalk, fishing pier and three small docking areas. Overnight docking is not allowed at the park docks. The park bulkhead takes up the entire area between the condominiums at the nearby marina and the bridge.

# GOIN' ASHORE: NEW SMYRNA BEACH, FL

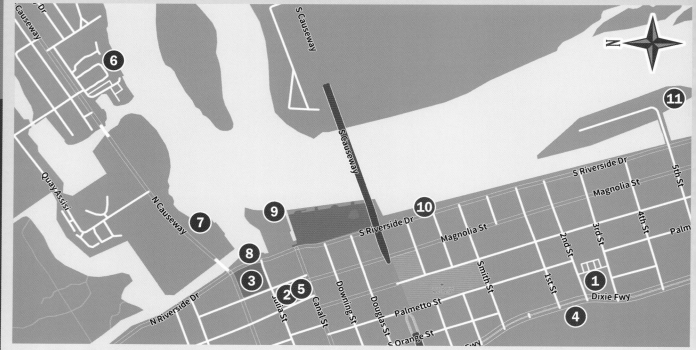

| SERVICES | |
|---|---|
| 1 | Library |
| **ATTRACTIONS** | |
| 2 | New Smyrna Museum of History |
| 3 | Old Fort Park |

| SHOPPING/DINING | |
|---|---|
| 4 | Save-A-Lot (groceries) |
| 5 | New Smyrna Brewing Company |
| **MARINAS** | |
| 6 | New Smyrna Marina |

| | |
|---|---|
| 7 | North Causeway Marine |
| 8 | New Smyrna Beach City Marina |
| 9 | Fishin' Cove Marina |
| 10 | Night Swan Intracoastal B&B |
| 11 | Smyrna Yacht Club |

The New Smyrna Sugar Mill ruins are located a few miles from the harbor. Built in the early 1800s with coquina stones (a natural limestone formed of broken shells and corals), the mill processed sugarcane into granular sugar that was shipped north. Molasses, a processing byproduct, went south for rum production.

**Attractions:** The historic Turnbull Ruins are located in Old Fort Park along Riverside Drive. The fort-like coquina ruins lead some historians to believe New Smyrna was originally the site of St. Augustine and that it could be even 500 years older than St. Augustine. Several paths and benches are scattered under a beautiful canopy of oak trees. This is the site of summer concerts and the annual Art Fiesta in February.

The Marine Discovery Center (located on the ICW at the North Causeway east of the marinas) is a nonprofit educational center that offers history and sunset tours as well as eco-tours of the New Smyrna area (386-428-4828). The nearby New Smyrna Beach Museum of History has interpretive exhibits of local culture and history (120 Sams Ave., 386-478-0052). The Atlantic Center for the Arts, a world-renowned artist-in-residence program, is based here. In addition to revolving exhibits, the Center features artist lectures, readings, demonstrations and presentations as well as workshops (atlanticcenterforthearts.org). Less than two miles away, the wide sandy beaches offer a relaxing day of sunbathing, swimming, water sports and surf fishing.

**Shopping/Dining:** There is a Save-A-Lot grocery store (720 S. Dixie Hwy., 386-847-8815) relatively close to the City Marina. The downtown area of New Smyrna Beach begins only a block away from the New Smyrna Beach City Marina where a variety of restaurants and shops line up and down the streets with local shoppers and visitors. Most of the restauarants are along Canal Street, including New Smyrna Brewing Company, with a taproom and brewery tours (386-957-3802). See more options at nsbfla.com.

**Dockage:** Located just 2.5 miles from Ponce Inlet, the New Smyrna Marina (The Fishing Store) offers transient dockage on floating docks and fuel, both gas and diesel. A fleet of offshore and inshore fishing charters and daily pontoon boat rentals are available. The on-site Outriggers Tiki Bar and Grille offers lunch, dinner and Sunday brunch. North Causeway Marine to the south has limited space reserved for transients, sells fuels and offers repairs.

At Mile 846.5, New Smyrna Beach City Marina offers slips on a first-come, first-served basis with full amenities, including cable TV, laundry and WiFi. It is close to the Canal Street Historic District, where you can find arts, history, shopping and dining. It is also across the street from the Old Fort Park historical site, which hosts a weekly Farmer's Market on Saturday. Nearby Fishin' Cove Marina generally seeks to fill its slips with full time renters and is private.

Want to get off the boat? Night Swan Intracoastal Bed and Breakfast to the south has dockage if you stay at their B&B. The Smyrna Yacht Club is beyond that, on an island west of the ICW and south of the Harris Saxon Bridge. They welcome members of clubs that are listed in the American Registry of Yacht Clubs. (They do not offer reciprocity to Florida Council of Yacht Club members.)

**Anchorage:** Sheephead Cut runs close to Chicken Island at Mile 845. There is space for three or four boats to anchor on the south side of the channel between green daybeacon "1" and just beyond green daybeacon "3" (between the markers and the condominium docks on Bouchelle Island). Show an anchor light and make sure that you will not swing into the channel or the docks at the tidal change; this is a very small, tight anchorage. The depths are 8 to 10 feet and the holding is good, but local boats use the channel at all hours.

It is possible to anchor south of the Harris Saxon bridge at Mile 847 in 12 feet of water with good holding in mud. This is, however, open to the south and passing boat wakes along with a lot of debris on the bottom.

# ■ NEW SMYRNA BEACH TO INDIAN RIVER

## ICW Mile 847 to Mile 859

**NAVIGATION:** Use Chart 11485. For about the next 10 miles, the ICW runs down a straight, dredged channel between the mainland and a jumble of small islets that support several fishing camps along with the usual Florida waterfront housing on the west side. Keep an eye out for kayaks and small fishing boats here; they frequently anchor in the channel or too close to the edge. Luckily for them, a good deal of this area is a Manatee Slow Speed, Minimum Wake Zone, from red daybeacon "64" at Mile 852.8 to green daybeacon "9A" at Mile 858.4. This is an area of frequent manatee sightings, so proceed cautiously anytime you see a circular disturbance on the surface of the water.

Staying in the center of the channel, you will see 11-foot to 14-foot depths. It shoals very quickly on the edges of the channel.

## Side Trip: Mosquito Lagoon–ICW Mile 859 to Mile 868

Mosquito Lagoon is an open, shallow expanse of water that can only be explored by dinghy or shallow-draft boat. The same conditions that make this water popular for mosquitoes and deer flies also create an ideal feeding and breeding ground for sport and commercial fish, including redfish, sea trout and mullet. Crabs, clams and shrimp thrive among the dense aquatic grass beds. Flocks of white pelicans and the small fishing boats that fill Mosquito Lagoon attest to the abundance of fresh seafood. Swimming toward a common destination, the birds herd fish together by flapping their wings on the water. Before the fish can escape, the pelicans gobble them up.

**NAVIGATION:** Use Chart 11485. Eight-foot deep spots are numerous in the channel, but depths decrease suddenly outside the channel. Shoaling has been reported between green daybeacons "25" and "29" in Mosquito Lagoon. There also is shoaling near green daybeacon "35," which is just past Mile 865.

As you reach the middle of Mosquito Lagoon, you may be able to see a large building in the distance to the south. This is the Space Shuttle hangar, or vehicle assembly building (VAB) at the Kennedy Space Center.

In clear weather, the giant VAB is visible for distances of 20 miles or more.

Stay on the green side of the channel but don't hug markers too closely, as some areas at the channel edges are shallow. Keep an eye on the depth sounder and watch your wake to avoid damaging other boats near the channel that could be fishing. Uncharted spoil banks line the outside of the dredged Mosquito Lagoon channel.

**Anchorage:** If you choose to exit the channel to anchor, seek local knowledge or do so carefully, so that if there is a spoil bank just outside the channel, you hit it at slow speed.

There are only a few places of Mosquito Lagoon deep enough for ICW travelers to anchor for the night in this stretch. Two anchoring areas are east of green daybeacon "19" at Mile 861.3 in the 6- to 7-foot deep area and southeast of red daybeacon "24" at Mile 862.8 in the 10-foot-deep charted area; however, the area of deeper water is quite small. Vessels report the best passage by entering the first anchorage from south of green daybeacon "19" and the second anchorage from north of red daybeacon "24." Be aware this anchorage is bouncy with any wind due to minimal protection and too much fetch between the anchorage and the land.

## Haulover Canal–ICW Mile 869

**NAVIGATION:** Use Chart 11485. This 1 mile-long rocky cut (with jettied entrances) provides easy passage from Mosquito Lagoon to the Indian River on the opposite side of Merritt Island. The **Allenhurst (Haulover Canal) Bascule Bridge** (27-foot closed vertical clearance) crosses the canal at Mile 869.2 and opens

In the past, the southern end of **Mosquito Lagoon** (on an imaginary line from Haulover Canal east to 3 miles out in the Atlantic Ocean) was off limits to all watercraft 72 hours before any Kennedy Space Center launches. Security boats from the Coast Guard and Kennedy Space Center patrolled these waters during this restricted time and levied fines to unauthorized boats entering this zone. This security zone did not, however, include the ICW route. All of this will probably change as the Space Center shifts to a commercial space port. As of spring 2017, no information was available about any of the above restrictions. Pay attention, ask local marinas for information and check waterwayguide.com for updates.

promptly on request. If the bridge tender does not respond to VHF Channel 09, use a horn signal (one long, one short) to request an opening or call 321-867-4859. Be aware that there are shallow areas at both entrances to the Haulover Canal.

Although the current can run swiftly here, the tidal range is minimal. Strong winds may lower or raise the river and canal levels by as much as 2 feet. The ramp on the inside of the basin (southwest of the Haulover Canal Bridge) is always busy with small fishing boats. The entire Haulover Canal is a Slow-Speed/Minimum Wake Zone, protecting the numerous (and usually visible) resident manatees that feed just below the surface. Wildlife abounds on shore, which is overgrown with vegetation. Keep a lookout for herons, egrets, alligators, manatees and small fishing boats.

On weekends, both Mosquito Lagoon and Haulover Canal are congested with small boats of every type and description. The small fishing boats often have as many as three people standing up to cast at the edge of the channel or under the bridge. Fortunately, much of the congested area is a Slow-Speed Manatee area, thus preventing wakes that could capsize these small boats.

**Anchorage:** The basin on the southwest side of the Haulover Canal Bridge is too small to even consider as an anchorage for most cruising boats, although a small boat with a shallow draft on a short scope may fit. There are reports of enough depth (8 to 10 feet) at one end of the dock for a tie up, but it is not recommended as an overnight spot.

## Indian River–ICW Mile 870 to Mile 875

**NAVIGATION:** Use Chart 11485. A straight, dredged channel extends from Haulover Canal's western mouth across the flats of the upper Indian River. This channel tends to shoal along both sides, although depths are usually well maintained in the center and in the 10-foot range. Navigate cautiously and avoid being pushed out of the channel by beam winds.

Flashing green daybeacon "1" and red daybeacon "2" are the first two aids to navigation you will encounter heading southwest out of the Haulover Canal. After reaching these markers, two huge white tanks on the Indian River's west bank line up with the less visible red markers on the channel's north side and may be used to aid in navigation. These tanks are charted as "TANK (NW OF TWO)." When steering for the tanks, keep an eye on the markers ahead and astern, watching for eeway. You do not want to stray out of the channel in this area as it shoals quickly.

Even off the marked channel, the lower Indian River is wide and deep for most of the 120 miles to the St. Lucie River and Inlet. There is 65 feet of vertical clearance at most of the fixed bridges across the Indian River but exercise care after periods of heavy rain. Observe the tide boards on the fixed high-rise bridges in the Indian River carefully, especially if your mast is close to the limit.

Several stretches allow sailboats to hoist their canvas in the right conditions and power boaters to relax, (although you should still remain watchful for shoal areas and crab trap markers). The channel is dredged from Haulover Canal to past Cocoa, but outside the channel depths vary widely and there are numerous shoals.

# ■ SPACE COAST AREA

In what has come to be known as the Space Coast Area (Mile 876 to Mile 943), the coastal topography changes from a slender barrier strip to a broad stretch of land, which forms Cape Canaveral. Inside the Cape area, the waters divide around Merritt Island, forming Indian River on the mainland side and Banana River on the east side. This section of the Indian River is a pleasure to navigate, although strong winds from the north or south may kick up an uncomfortable chop.

Watch closely for interesting sights along the banks of the river; this will add to the pleasure of the cruise. In other areas farther south, the Indian River is too wide to see much ashore.

**NAVIGATION:** Use Chart 11485. There are numerous bridges, both high span and restricted, that cross the Indian River. If a closed bridge delays your passage, you and the other waiting boats will probably have plenty of room to maneuver. You may even want to consider anchoring off the channel, as depths along the river accommodate most boats. In fall, when daylight is shorter, anchoring is preferable to entering a strange harbor at night.

## Titusville–ICW Mile 876

Titusville, (a good port from which to visit Disney World and the other theme parks in the Orlando area), is an important agricultural center for the Florida citrus industry. Its protected harbor has a well-marked entry

## The American White Pelican

A wide variety of birds inhabit the spoil islands to the north of the channel on the Indian River, so keep a close lookout for pelicans, cormorants and anhingas here. White pelicans are even more numerous here than on Mosquito Lagoon.

The American white pelican is one of the largest birds native to North America. With an overall length of 50 to 70 inches and a body weight from 11 to 20 pounds, this large bird is easily recognizable from a distance.

Unlike the brown pelican, the American white pelican does not dive for its food. Instead it catches its prey while swimming. Each bird eats more than 4 pounds of food a day. American white pelicans like to come together in groups of a dozen or more birds to feed, as they can thus cooperate and corral fish to one another. When this is not easily possible–such as in deep water where fish can escape by diving out of reach–they prefer to forage alone.

The birds will also steal food on occasion from other birds, such as Cormorants and gulls and, occasionally, a Blue Heron.

## Kennedy Space Center Visitor Complex

You will need a full day to tour the Kennedy Space Center Visitor Complex. "Must sees" include the U.S. Astronaut Hall of Fame, Astronaut Encounter (have lunch with a real astronaut), Shuttle Launch Simulator and Control Center tour. You will also want to visit the aptly named rocket garden as well as the final resting place of the Space Shuttle Atlantis. Complete your visit by visiting the inspiring tribute to America's fallen astronauts, The Astronaut Memorial.

Because the launch site itself is in a secured area, visitors must board buses for two-hour tours. The visitor complex opens daily at 9:00 a.m., closing only on Christmas Day. Admission includes a bus tour to the launch sites and two 3-D IMAX movies ($50/day). For more information, contact the Visitors Center at 866-737-5235. Purchase tickets at kennedyspacecenter.com.

For updated launch information, check the schedule at kennedyspacecenter.com.

channel that normally carries 7-foot depths. As soon as you enter the harbor, depths increase. Titusville is also the most convenient location to visit the Kennedy Space Center, an excursion that should not be missed.

**NAVIGATION:** Use Chart 11485. North of Titusville, the **NASA (Jay-Jay) Railroad Bascule Bridge** at Kennedy Space Center crosses the ICW at Mile 876.6 with a 7-foot closed vertical clearance. The bridge is normally left in the open position unless a train is approaching, which is infrequent. When a train approaches the bridge, it stops and the operator initiates a command to lower the bridge. The lights go to flashing red and the draw lowers and locks, providing scanning equipment reveals nothing under the draw. The draw remains down until a manual raise command is initiated, or will raise automatically 5 minutes after the intermediate track circuit is no longer occupied by a rail car. After the train has cleared, the draw opens and the lights return to flashing green.

About 2 miles south of the NASA Bridge, Titusville's **Max Brewer (Titusville) Bridge** with 65-foot fixed vertical clearance crosses the ICW at Mile 878.9. About 6 miles below Titusville, the **NASA Causeway Twin Bascule Bridges** (Mile 885.0, 27-foot closed vertical clearance) at Addison Point crosses the channel and has restricted hours. The bridge opens on signal, except from 6:30 a.m. to 8:00 a.m. and from 3:30 p.m. to 5:00 p.m., Monday through Friday (except federal holidays), when the draws need not open.

Stay well inside the channel between the Max Brewer Bridge and the NASA Causeway Bridges; there is shoaling to depths as shallow as 7.5 feet in spots, especially from green daybeacon "33" to south of red daybeacon "34" where the channel narrows. If you do leave the channel, proceed carefully and use your depth sounder.

At about Mile 888.5, there is a large power plant on the west side of the ICW from which power cables cross the ICW in a northeasterly direction. These cables have a charted height of 85 feet over the main channel. If you have a tall mast, be sure that you will have at least 12 feet of clearance when passing under power lines to avoid arcing.

**Dockage/Moorings:** Two marinas are located in the Titusville basin. The first is the friendly Titusville Municipal Marina, which welcomes transients on both fixed and floating docks and can accommodate boats up to 130 feet. They also have a mooring field with

18 moorings for vessels up to 60 feet. The mooring fee includes the use of the marina facilities, along with a pump-out boat that will come out to you.

The second facility in the Titusville basin is Westland Marina, with slips and an over 6-acre yard that is popular with the "do-it-yourself" boaters. They have a 30-ton lift and offer bottom painting, diesel/gas mechanic, fiberglass/gelcoat repair, and general refurbishing. Groceries, fast food, a pharmacy, a liquor store and other amenities are a short walking distance from the basin.

A few miles south on the Indian River, at green daybeacon "39," you will see a marked entrance channel leading to Kennedy Point Yacht Club & Marina (reporting 4.5 dockside depths). Call in advance for reservations. A yacht club affiliation is not required for transient dockage.

**Anchorage:** Anchoring is restricted due to the proliferation of moorings. You must stay at least 150 feet from the mooring field, so you need to be aware of your swing room. Boaters anchored nearby (outside the mooring field) may tie up at the Titusville Municipal Marina and use the dinghy dock and showers for a nominal fee.

Note that the spoil areas and shoals shown on the chart (and those not shown on the chart) seem to be expanding. At the Jay-Jay Bridge (Mile 876.6), for example, the west anchorage is shoaling at the entrance. The NASA Causeway Twin Bridges at Addison Point (Mile 885.0) and subsequent bridges that cross the Indian River can provide a better overnight anchorage from all wind directions. Simply choose the side that will be sheltered from the wind. If you leave the channel to seek out protection behind a bridge causeway, go slowly and keep an eye on your depth sounder.

Just south of Titusville, at about Mile 883 (opposite Indian River City on the mainland), you will see a large charted area of deeper water with depths of 7 to 8 feet to the east of the ICW. (This anchorage is an excellent spot to watch the space center launches.) Give the charted spoils areas a wide berth, and then sound your way over toward Merritt Island. The holding is good near red daybeacons "38" and "40", but these offer no protection from wind or choppy water. If you sound your way in far enough, wakes from channel traffic are almost entirely eliminated, although other boats moving around in the anchorage may give you a good rolling. This spot is more than a mile from the ICW.

# GOIN' ASHORE: **TITUSVILLE, FL**

| SERVICES | | |
|---|---|---|
| 1 | Visitor Information & Bike Shop | |
| **ATTRACTIONS** | | |
| 2 | American Space Museum and Space Walk of Fame | |
| 3 | North Brevard Historical Museum | |

| | | |
|---|---|---|
| 4 | Pritchard House | |
| **SHOPPING** | | |
| 5 | Downtown Art Gallery | |
| 6 | Save-A-Lot | |
| **DINING** | | |
| 7 | Playalinda Brewing Co. | |

| | | |
|---|---|---|
| 8 | Sunrise Bread Co. | |
| **MARINAS** | | |
| 9 | Titusville Marina | |
| 10 | Westland Marina | |

Titusville, FL lives up to its slogan "Gateway to Nature and Space." Kennedy Space Center is within 20 minutes of the Titusville Basin. Kennedy Space Center Visitor Complex, located at NASA's launch headquarters, is the only place on Earth where you can tour launch areas, meet a veteran astronaut, see giant rockets or train in a spaceflight simulator. (See sidebar.) For more information, visit kennedyspacecenter.com.

**Attractions:** Your first stop should be the Titusville Welcome Center at 419 S. Hopkins Ave. (321-607-6216). They have all the information you need and will gladly rent you a bike for getting around. You won't need a bike, however, to visit the Historic Pritchard House, constructed in 1891 and a fine example of Queen Anne

architecture. It is located within easy walking distance of the marina basin at 424 S. Washington Avenue. The North Brevard Historical Museum is also located within the historic downtown at 301 S. Washington Avenue. The museum displays photographs, furniture, clothing and artifacts of the early Titusville area.

Don't miss the Space Walk of Fame Museum (308 Pine Street, 321-264-0434). The items and displays have been donated by individuals, astronauts, space workers, NASA and space company contractors. On display are working consoles from Launch Pad 36A and a Model 4 Sequencer from Launch Pad 16. It is open Monday through Saturday from 10:00 a.m. to 5:00 p.m. Other places of interest (transportation required) include the American

Police Hall of Fame and Museum (6350 Horizon Drive), and the Valiant Air Command (6600 Tico Road), featuring aircraft from World War I to Desert Storm.

For the more adventuresome, the coast-to-coast connector bike trail runs through Titusville (see more at gtf.org) and kayak tours of the Indian River Lagoon are available from A Day Away Kayak Tours (321-268-2655). This is especially enjoyable during bioluminescence season. During the warm summer months, every movement in the water–from the swirl of your paddle to the ghostly glow of a slow moving manatee produces light.

There are numerous parks as well, including the Sand Point Park, Vietnam Memorial Park, Space View Park and even a special dog park for your cruising pooch.

The Merritt Island National Wildlife Refuge and Canaveral National Seashore are minutes away and provide many opportunities to enjoy natural Florida, including horseback riding, kayaking, nature walks and pristine beaches.

And, for those who love to fish, Titusville is known as the "Redfish Capitol of the World."

**Shopping:** Like all larger cities, you will have no problems provisioning here. Amenities such as groceries, pharmacies, hardware and other such shopping abounds. Save-A-Lot (groceries) is at 120 S. Hopkins Ave. The downtown area also offers a variety of outdoor-related stores.

Remember your trip with a memento from the Downtown Art Gallery. Five showrooms feature local art and photography of the Indian River Lagoon area (335 South Washington Ave., 321-268-0122).

**Dining:** The Town of Titusville appreciates and welcomes the boating public. A revitalized downtown district is within walking distance of the waterfront and offers a nice selection of dining opportunities and shops. Sunrise Bread Co. (315 South Hopkins Avenue, 321-268-1009) offers homemade bakery items, coffee and free WiFi.

If you venture out of downtown, Dixie Crossroads (1475 Garden Street, 321-268-5000) is famous for its shrimp and corn fritters, and just a few blocks south of the downtown area is Chef Larry's where exceptional low-priced meals are the norm (1111 Washington Ave., 321-368-9123). Call for hours of operation and be advised that they accept cash only.

Playalinda Brewing Company is nestled in a renovated, 100-year-old hardware store at 305 S. Washington Ave. In addition to craft beers, Playalinda offers cider, wine and non-alcoholic options, along with "brewery bites." Well-behaved dogs are always welcome at the outdoor tables in front of the brewery.

# Indian River, FL

| | | Approach / Dockside Depth | VHF Channel Monitored | Transient Berths / Total Berths | Largest Vessel Accommodated | Groceries, Ice, Marine Supplies, Snacks | Repairs: Hull, Engine, Propeller | Gas / Diesel | Floating Docks (reported) | Lift (tonnage), Crane, Rail | Laundry, Pool, Showers, Courtesy Car | Pump-Out Station | Min/Max Amps | Nearby: Grocery Store, Motel, Restaurant | | |
|---|---|---|---|---|---|---|---|---|---|---|---|---|---|---|---|---|
| **TITUSVILLE** | | | | | **Dockage** | | | | **Supplies** | | | | **Services** | | | |
| 1. Titusville Marina 🖥 📶 WG 878.3 | 321-383-5600 | 130 | 16/68 | 15/205 | 8/8 | F | GD | IMS | – | – | 30/100 | LS | P | GMR | | |
| 2. Westland Marina 🖥 📶 878.3 | 321-267-1667 | 55 | 16/71 | call/70 | 7/8 | – | | M | HEP | L30 | 30/50 | LS | P | GMR | | |
| **INDIAN RIVER CITY** | | | | | | | | | | | | | | | | |
| 3. Kennedy Point Yacht Club & Marina 🖥 📶 WG 883 | 321-383-0280 | 60 | 16/71 | 15/80 | 6/4.5 | – | – | GIS | – | – | 30/50 | LPS | P | GMR | | |

🖥 Internet Access 📶 Wireless Internet Access WG Waterway Guide Cruising Club Partner *(Information in the table is provided by the facilities.)*
See WaterwayGuide.com for current rates, fuel prices, web site addresses, and other up-to-the-minute information.

**TITUSVILLE, INDIAN RIVER CITY, NOAA CHART 11485**

## Canaveral Barge Canal–ICW Mile 894

**NAVIGATION:** Use Chart 11485. (Chart 11478 shows the route toward the ocean in detail; see the Inlet section at the front of this guide for more information on Cape Canaveral Inlet.)

At Mile 894.0 the **Bennett Causeway Twin Bridges** (also called the City Point Twin Bridges) have a 65-foot fixed vertical clearance. East of the ICW channel, just north of the bridge, look for markers indicating the entrance to the Canaveral Barge Canal, which cuts through Merritt Island to the Banana River and Canaveral Inlet, and then leads on to the Atlantic Ocean. Green daybeacons "13," "11A" (give these two wide berth due to possible shoaling) and green daybeacon "11," along with red flashing daybeacon "12," provide the transition from the ICW to the barge canal entrance. Use caution transitioning through here, it has the controlling minimum depth for the route to the Atlantic. In spring of 2017, the shallowest spot observed was about 200 yards east of beacons "11"and "12" at 7.5 to 8- feet deep (center channel with a typical river level). The canal itself is deep, 9 to 13 feet.

The 8-mile journey from the ICW to the Atlantic Ocean includes a 3-mile cut through Merritt Island with one restricted bridge, a crossing of the Banana River and passage through Canaveral Lock and then twin bascule bridges with rush-hour closures. The cut through Merritt Island is very scenic with beautiful natural flora and an abundance of marine and wildlife.

The **Christa McAuliffe Drawbridge** (Mile 1.0, 26-foot closed vertical clearance) opens on the hour and half hour from 6:00 a.m. to 10:00 p.m. daily but is closed between 6:15 a.m. and 8:15 a.m. and from 3:10 p.m. to 6:00 p.m., Monday through Friday (except federal holidays). The bridges requires a 3-hour advance notice to open between 10:00 p.m. and 5:59 a.m.

Once you have transited Merritt Island via the Barge Canal, a fairly narrow channel maintains nearly the same course for 1.25 miles across the Banana River, carrying about 10-foot depths, to the Canaveral Lock. Be careful not to stray outside the channel and as always look behind you to be sure that you are not being pushed to the side.

Hours of operation for the **Cape Canaveral Lock** (321-783-5421) are year-round from 6:00 a.m. to 9:30 p.m. It is the largest navigation lock in Florida and is designed to reduce tidal currents and prevent hurricane tides from entering the Banana River. The lift of the lock ranges from negligible to 3 to 4 feet, depending on the ocean tide stage.

Contact the lock tender on VHF Channel 13 for instructions and set your fenders in place before entering the lock. Have lines available fore and aft since they are not provided in the lock. There are synthetic rub rails with cleats spaced every 10 feet, making line control simple when locking through. The trip is worth the effort. Expect congestion around the two sets of boat ramps near the port.

East of the Cape Canaveral Lock, **State Route 401 Twin Bascule Bridges** (25-foot closed vertical clearance) at Mile 5.5 open on signal during the day, except from 6:30 a.m. to 8:00 a.m. and from 3:30 p.m. to 5:15 p.m., Monday through Friday, when they are closed (except on federal holidays). This bridge also requires a 3-hour advance notice to open between 10:00 p.m. and 5:59 a.m.

**Dockage:** The Canaveral Barge Canal contains two marinas that are considered "hurricane holes" by the locals, as the lock prevents any major tidal surge. Both have exceptionally good wind protection as well. The first (closer to the Indian River) is Harbor Square Marina, which has slips and sells diesel. Next is Harbortown Marina–Port Canaveral, conveniently located in a basin 1 mile west of the Banana River. They offer slips, long-term dry storage, a fuel station with gas and diesel, an on-site restaurant (Island Dockside Grill), a laundry and a pool. They have an area called Family Spot with grills, a fire pit, cornhole and horse shoes. They even have a fenced-in dog run area.

On the east side of the Canaveral Lock is a protected basin containing four marinas. Ocean Club Marina at Port Canaveral has floating transient slips and gas and diesel. Their 110-ton lift is wide enough for large catamarans. Nearby Port Canaveral Marine offers service, storage and sales at their 5-acre facility, and Port Canaveral Yacht Club accepts transients who are members of another yacht club. It is only a short walk from restaurants and gift shopping.

The family-owned Cape Marina is a full-service marina and boatyard with a "do-it-yourself" area. They have high-speed fuel pumps (gas and diesel) on a 150-foot dock and a complete ship store that carries everything from "bait to batteries." Relax in the poolside lounge chairs or enjoy the on-site game room.

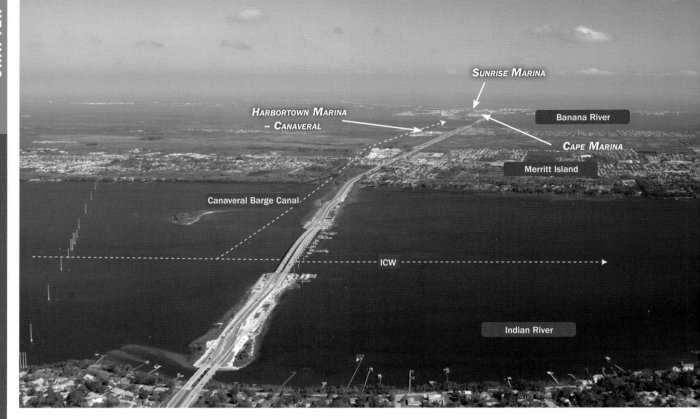

To the east is Bluepoints Marina, which sells fuel and may have transient space but there is no shore power. Call in advance for dock availability.

Sunrise Marina, closest to the inlet, welcomes transients to its floating docks. Prior reservations are required. They offer full-service repairs, gas and diesel fuel and easy ocean access. Their tackle store and gift shop caters to "fish, dive and surf."

The Cove, located near the marinas, is a waterfront dining area with numerous restaurants. At seven stories tall, Exploration Tower is an architectural landmark with interactive exhibits and observation decks, plus a cafe and gift shop. Nearby Jetty Park and Cheri Down Park are recreational areas with beaches.

**Anchorage:** At the Bennett Causeway Bridges (City Point Bridge) just south of the entrance to the Canaveral Barge Canal, you can enter on the southwest side and anchor behind the causeway in 7- to 8-foot depths with good holding. Anchorage is also possible west of the Cape Canaveral Lock, just below the spoil island (7-foot depths), or the area to the north, as long as you remain south of the overhead power lines (which denote the "No-Motor Zone").

Additionally, continuing north via the Saturn Barge Channel offers access to popular anchorage possibilities near the spoil islands just off the eastern side. Note that the previously mentioned "No-Motor Zone" signage comes close to some of these spoil islands

## Side Trip: South on the Banana River

A north–south channel intersects the Canaveral Barge Canal route to the Canaveral Lock in the Banana River near the lock. A turn here to the north at daybeacons green "13" and red "14" puts you in the Saturn Barge Channel (Chart 11478). These waters are the back yard of Kennedy Space Center and provide unique vistas.

⚠ Mariners must be aware that a Federal Manatee Sactuary with a "No-Motor Zone" (NMZ) has been established in these waters. A wandering picket of advisory signs delineates the sanctuary and it crosses about 1.75 mile up this channel near green daybeacon "17." Vessels fitted with a propeller (even stowed) are not allowed into the Sanctuary.

If heading south on the Banana River is your intention, approach flashing green daybeacon #5, then turn for the high span of the **Bennett Memorial Causeway (SR 528) Bridge** (with a fixed vertical clearance of 36 feet). Proceed with caution keeping an eye on your sounder and the chart.

# Canaveral Barge Canal & Banana River, FL

| Marina | Phone | Largest Vessel Accommodated | VHF Channel Monitored | Dockage | | | Supplies | | Services | | | | | |
|---|---|---|---|---|---|---|---|---|---|---|---|---|---|---|
| | | | | Approach / Dockside Depth (reported) | Transient Berths / Total Berths | Floating Docks | Groceries, Ice, Marine Supplies, Snacks | Gas / Diesel | Repairs: Hull, Engine, Propeller | Lift (tonnage), Crane, Rail | Min / Max Amps | Laundry, Pool, Showers, Courtesy Car | Pump-Out Station | Nearby: Grocery Store, Motel, Restaurant |
| **CANAVERAL BARGE CANAL** | | | | | | | | | | | | | | |
| 1. Harbor Square Marina [Internet][WiFi] 1.5 E of 893.6 | 321-453-2464 | 60 | 16 | 7/120 | 13/7 | – | IM | D | HP | – | 30/50 | LS | P | GMR |
| 2. Harbortown Marina–Canaveral [Internet][WiFi] 4E of 893.6 | 321-453-0160 | – | 16/10 | 50/275 | 6/6 | – | IMS | GD | HEP | L70 | 30/50 | LPS | P | GMR |
| **CAPE CANAVERAL LOCK** | | | | | | | | | | | | | | |
| 3. Ocean Club Marina at Port Canaveral [Internet][WiFi] | 321-783-9001 | 110 | 16 | 37/73 | 14/12 | F | I | GD | – | – | 30/100 | LPS | P | MR |
| 4. Port Canaveral Marine [Internet][WiFi] 0.6 E of 893.6 | 321-784-5788 | 110 | 16 | – | 15/15 | F | IMS | GD | HEP | L110,C110 | 30/100 | LPS | P | R |
| 5. Cape Marina, Port Canaveral [Internet][WiFi] 7 E of 893.6 | 321-783-8410 | 150 | 16/68 | call/115 | 12/12 | F | IMS | GD | HEP | L80 | 30/50 | LPS | P | GMR |
| 6. Port Canaveral Yacht Club [Internet][WiFi][WG] 6.9 E of 893.6 | 321-482-0167 | 60 | – | call/50 | 40/10 | F | IM | – | – | C | 30/50 | LS | P | MR |
| 7. Bluepoints Marina | 321-799-2860 | 47 | 16/10 | call/26 | 40/15 | F | IMS | GD | – | L25 | – | S | P | GMR |
| 8. Sunrise Marina | 321-783-9535 | 98 | 16 | 3/21 | 20/8 | F | IMS | GD | – | L12 | 30/50 | – | – | MR |
| **BANANA RIVER** | | | | | | | | | | | | | | |
| 9. River Palms MHP [Internet] | 321-452-8424 | 21 | – | 32/32 | 5/5 | – | – | – | – | – | 30/30 | L | – | GM- |
| 10. Banana River Marina | 321-453-7888 | 60 | – | 5/63 | 5/5 | – | M | – | – | – | 30/50 | LS | P | – |

[Internet] Internet Access [WiFi] Wireless Internet Access [WG] Waterway Guide Cruising Club Partner *(Information in the table is provided by the facilities.)*
See WaterwayGuide.com for current rates, fuel prices, web site addresses, and other up-to-the-minute information.

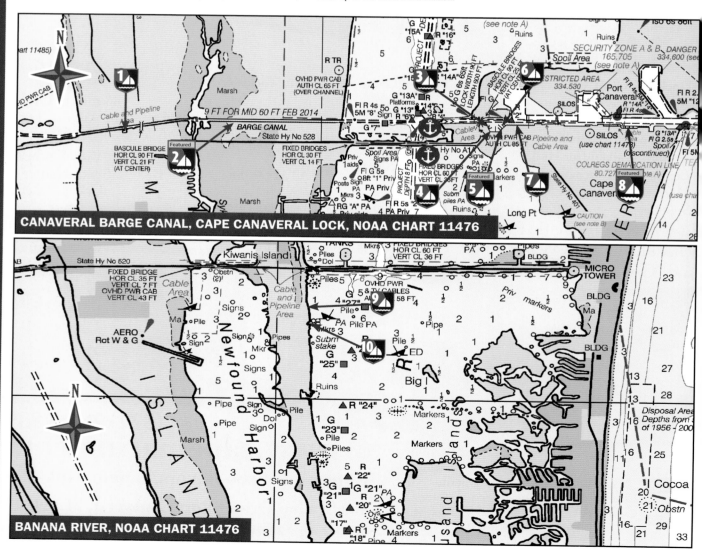

CANAVERAL BARGE CANAL, CAPE CANAVERAL LOCK, NOAA CHART 11476

BANANA RIVER, NOAA CHART 11476

NOTE: When proceeding southbound in the Banana River keep red to port. The channel begins some 18 miles south, where it branches off of the Indian River (and the ICW at Mile 914.5) at Dragon Point, near Melbourne. There are some challenges on this route and local knnowledge is desirable. See the "Eau Gallie" section for more information.

**Dockage:** South of the fixed **Willard Peebles Bridge** (36-foot vertical clearance) are two marinas: River Palms (new in 2017) and Banana River Marina. Both have some reserved transient space.

**Anchorage:** Boats that can clear the bridge can anchor in 7-foot depths in the Banana River.

## Cocoa–ICW Mile 897

**NAVIGATION:** Use Chart 11485. The **Merritt Island (Cocoa) Twin Bridges** (fixed 65-foot vertical clearances) cross the ICW at Mile 897.4 (known locally as the Cocoa Twin Bridges). Cocoa Village is on the western shore and Merritt Island is on the eastern shore. Both offer numerous cruiser amenities.

⚠ There has been the loss of two proper cruising yachts over the past few years due to encounters with the high voltage overhead cables that cross the Cocoa Yacht Basin located just south of the Merritt Island Twin Bridges at Cocoa, FL. While the cables are high at the ICW (charted at 88 feet), they progressively descend towards shore and vertical clearance is substantially reduced (charted at 38 feet). This is deceptive, and poses a serious risk for vessels operating near them, not just from physical contact but open-air arcing from the power lines to a mast. (We recommend a minimum mast-to-wire distance of 12 feet.) See the Waterway Guide Explorer at waterwayguide.com for new alerts and updates.

The Army Corps of Engineers reports continuous shoaling between flashing green daybeacon "77" and green daybeacon "81" south of the Cocoa Twin Bridges. However, as of spring 2017, this section all the way from the Twin Bridges to flashing "83" had an observed mid-channel controlling depth of 10-feet. Favor the western side of the channel but watch for pot markers. Do not attempt anchoring outside flashing green "83," due to shoaling.

**Dockage:** The City Docks in Lee Wenner Park have signage for day-only boat docks and dinghy-only docks. Additionally, the 150-foot-long T-dock welcomes cruisers with two consecutive nights of free dockage.

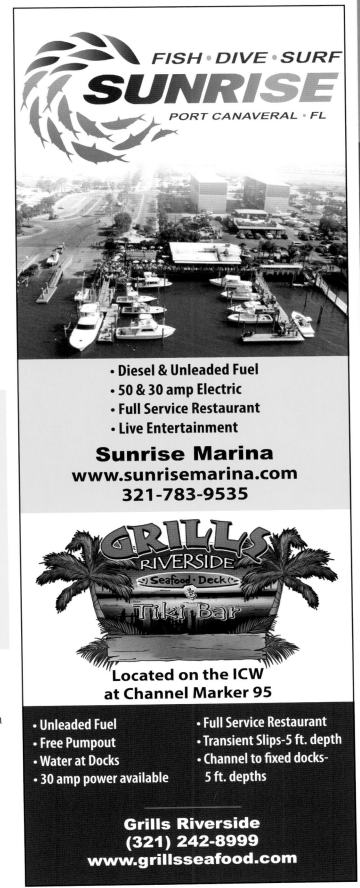

# Indian River, FL

Column headers (diagonal):
- Largest Vessel Accommodated
- VHF Channel Monitored
- Transient Berths / Total Berths
- Approach / Dockside Depth (reported)
- Floating Docks
- Groceries, Ice, Marine Supplies, Snacks
- Gas / Diesel
- Repairs: Hull, Engine, Propeller
- Lift (tonnage), Crane, Rail
- Laundry, Pool, Showers, Courtesy Car
- Min/Max Amps
- Pump-Out Station
- Nearby: Grocery Store, Motel, Restaurant

| COCOA | | | | Dockage | | | | Supplies | | | Services | | | | |
|---|---|---|---|---|---|---|---|---|---|---|---|---|---|---|---|
| 1. Cocoa Village Marina 🖥 📶 897 | 321-632-5445 | 120 | 16/68 | 24/117 | 6.5/6.5 | – | – | I | – | – | 30/100 | LS | P | GMR |

🖥 Internet Access  📶 Wireless Internet Access  WG Waterway Guide Cruising Club Partner  *(Information in the table is provided by the facilities.)*
See WaterwayGuide.com for current rates, fuel prices, web site addresses, and other up-to-the-minute information.

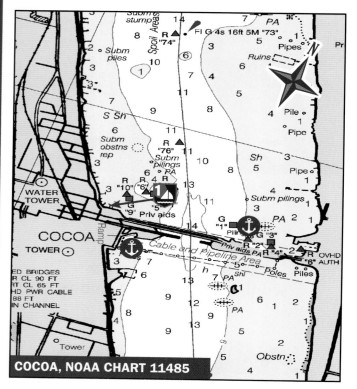

COCOA, NOAA CHART 11485

(First-come, first-served, no water or shore power.) The approach depth to the T-dock area is typically 7 feet with 5 feet dockside.

There is essentially no daily tide range that occurs from lunar tides since open passes to the ocean are far distant. However, strong currents (and some variation in level) are possible as the river responds to wind load and other factors.

The popular Cocoa Village Marina is a fully modern facility with an exceptionally friendly and helpful staff. The two-story office and clubhouse facilities are located east of the tall condominium building. A well-marked channel leads west off the ICW to the marina. It was relocated some years ago, and is now about a quarter of a mile north of the twin bridges and passes north of the marina's wave fence. Extensive dredging within the

marina ensures that most slips are at least 6 feet deep. This marina is convenient to the attractions, shops and restaurants of Historic Cocoa Village.

**Anchorage:** You can anchor west of the ICW and south of the bridges just off the town of Cocoa in Cocoa Basin. Sound your way in to a suitable depth, avoiding the charted cable and pipeline area south of the bridges. (Heed the warning signs for a submerged gas pipeline in Lee Wenner Park: It runs out from shore at the east end of the T-dock for some distance, then turns to parallel the causeway and crosses the river out to Merritt Island.)

Cocoa Basin opens out into a very popular anchorage that extends for 0.5 mile down river, along which you should find 6 to 9 feet. Lee Wenner Park is the place to come ashore here. It's located along the south causeway shoreline and offers dedicated dinghy docks as part of the dock/ramp complex. This landing puts you at the doorstep of Historic Cocoa Village and all that it offers.

On the Merritt Island (east) side of the river, north of the bridges is an anchorage that provides the closest access to provisioning. Coming easterly off the ICW and paralleling the causeway will provide about 7-foot depths all the way to the daybeacons "1" and "2" for Griffis Landing. The county park has six finger docks, a ramp and a pump-out station; however, the approach/dockside depth is only 2 to 3 feet.

A dinghy ride into this dock puts you within a 10-minute walk of West Marine, Publix, CVS, a UPS store, and other businesses along SR 520. (Add about 1 mile to the distance if you walk across the bridge or dinghy over to Merritt Island from Cocoa Village, and note the bridge walkways are narrow and exposed. If you elect to cross, use the south bridge; its walkway is noticeably wider than the north span.)

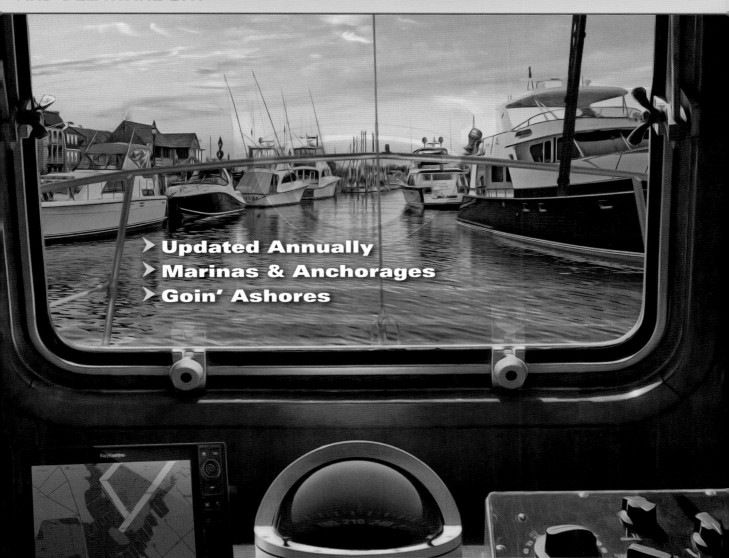

# WATERWAY GUIDE

### THE CRUISING AUTHORITY

**AT STOP**

# Chesapeake Bay 2018

**AND DELAWARE BAY**

➤ **Updated Annually**
➤ **Marinas & Anchorages**
➤ **Goin' Ashores**

**Visit waterwayguide.com**

## GOIN' ASHORE: COCOA VILLAGE, FL

| SERVICES | |
|---|---|
| 1 | Library |
| 2 | Post Office |
| 3 | Visitor Information |
| **ATTRACTIONS** | |
| 4 | Cocoa Village Playhouse |
| 5 | Cocoa Riverfront Park |

| SHOPPING | |
|---|---|
| 6 | S.F. Travis & Co. Hardware |
| 7 | Village Cycle Shoppe |
| **DINING** | |
| 8 | Crush Eleven |
| 9 | Murdock's Southern Bistro |
| 10 | Ossorio Bakery and Cafe |

| 11 | Ryan's Pizza and Pub |
|---|---|
| **MARINAS** | |
| 12 | Cocoa Village Marina |

Settlers began arriving in the Cocoa area in the mid-1800s, and the City of Cocoa was chartered in 1895. Today, on the inland side of the ICW, a water tower with three large American flags painted on it serves as a well-known, and award-winning, landmark for Cocoa. Cocoa has a riverfront district known as Historic Cocoa Village.

**Attractions:** Cocoa Main Street was formed in part to ensure the preservation of Historic Cocoa Village. With well over 100 unique shops, businesses, and restaurants the Village is dog-friendly and perfectly located for boating interests. A designated scenic drive runs through the Village as its 13-miles winds along the river's edge. With little vehicular traffic, it is very popular for biking, jogging, skating and walking. The state headquarters for the Florida Historical Society is located here and houses the Library of Florida History (425 Brevard Ave., 321-690-1971). The

Cocoa Post Office has somewhat odd hours, so call before you go (600 Florida Avenue, Ste. 101, 321-632-6846). Also in that building is the Historic Cocoa Village Association whose staff is available to provide current information for visitors on local attractions and events (600 Florida Ave, Ste. 104, 321-631-9075).

Riverfront Park, with a band shell, playground and splash fountain for the kids, along with Lee Wenner Park (primarily a boat landing and ramp facility) form the Village's shoreline for Cocoa Basin. There are dozens of sponsored events and concerts, both large and small, throughout the year in the streets and the park. Check the local calendar for specifics at VisitCocoaVillage.com. The highly acclaimed Cocoa Village Playhouse has productions throughout the year (300 Brevard Ave., 321-636-5050).

Cocoa Beach, famous for surfing, is 8 miles away and is easily accessible by bus. Ron Jon Surf Shop is the world's largest surf shop (52,000 square feet) and is Ron Jon's flagship facility. Best of all, it's open 24 hours a day, seven days a week! The shop hosts the annual 3-day Beach 'N Boards Fest in March with live music and lots of surfing. (Caution: This coincides with Spring Break for many colleges.) See more at ronjonsurfshop.com.

The Kennedy Space Center Visitor Complex (20 miles away) is a major attraction. Check the schedule for the now common launches at kennedyspacecenter.com (855-433-4210). Orlando area theme parks are about 60 miles away and accessible by rental car.

Space Coast Area Transit bus service (Route 4) goes over to Merritt Island for provision shopping or to continue out to Cocoa Beach. Contact S.C.A.T (321-633-1878) for schedules. Nearby Enterprise Rent-A-Car provides pick-up and drop-off service (1750 W King St., 321- 633-7070).

**Shopping:** Cocoa Village is renowned for a multitude of truly unique shopping opportunities: art galleries, antique shops, art studios, boutiques, and more. As you walk around, look for "Cocoa Village Loves ICW Cruisers" anchor logos in store windows. Those establishments offer some type of perk to cruisers!

S.F. Travis & Co. (circa 1885) is a multi-building, old-style hardware store with an expansive inventory. This is a "must see" but they are closed on weekends (300 Delannoy Ave., 321-636-1441). If your boat bike needs repair, Village Cycle Shoppe offers bicycle service, rentals and new/used sales at 4 Harrison St. (321-806-3917).

West Marine is just beyond the ICW bridge on Merritt Island (320 W. Merritt Island Causeway, 321-452-4661).

There are two Publix groceries (with adjacent CVS drug stores) within about 2 miles of the Village. One is on the mainland at Rockledge Square Shopping Center (1880 Rockledge Blvd., 321-639-1550). The other is across the ICW bridge at First Merritt Center (125 E. Merritt Island Causeway, 321-452-0288). The latter Publix is larger and offers many more area shops, including Merritt Square Mall (777 E. Merritt Island Causeway), which is another mile to the east. This enclosed mall features many national chains and a 16-theater cinema complex.

**Dining:** The Village offers a variety of many desirable culinary choices ranging from fine dining to seafood raw-bar, Korean-American fusion, vegan, Thai, sushi, Brazilian and others. A few of the dining establishments in the Village including fine dining at Crush 11, (11 Riverside Dr., 321-634-1100); Murdock's Southern Bistro (600 Brevard Ave., 321-633-0600) with great "southern comfort" food and live music and Ryan's Pizza and Pub (4 Harrison St., 321-634-5550) with indoor and pet-friendly outdoor dining. Check on the boat from their second-story, open-air dining and bar area that overlooks Riverfront Park and the anchorage. Finally, Ossorio Bakery and Café (316 Brevard Ave., 321-639-2423) offers free WiFi and is a popular gathering place among boaters.

# Indian River, Banana River, FL

| | | Dockage | | | | | Supplies | | Services | | | | | |
|---|---|---|---|---|---|---|---|---|---|---|---|---|---|---|
| | | Largest Vessel Accommodated | VHF Channel Monitored | Transient Berths / Total Berths | Approach / Dockside Depth (reported) | Floating Docks | Gas / Diesel | Groceries, Ice, Marine Supplies, Snacks | Repairs: Hull, Engine, Propeller | Lift (tonnage), Crane, Rail | Min/Max Amps | Laundry, Pool, Showers, Courtesy Car | Pump-Out Station | Nearby: Grocery Store, Motel, Restaurant |
| **PALM SHORES** | | | | | | | | | | | | | | |
| 1. Pineda Point Marina ⌨ 908.5 | 321-254-4199 | 60 | 16 | 0/60 | 8/8 | – | – | IMS | – | L12 | 30/50 | LPS | – | GMR |
| **2. Grills Riverside 908.5** | **321-242-8999** | – | – | **call/12** | **5/5** | – | **G** | – | – | – | **30/30** | – | **P** | **R** |
| 3. SunDance Marine Melbourne ⌨ WiFi 910.8 | 321-242-7140 | 55 | – | 2/78 | 7/5.5 | – | – | IM | E | – | 30/50 | LS | – | R |
| **INDIAN HARBOR** | | | | | | | | | | | | | | |
| 4. Telemar Bay Marina WiFi WG 1.8 E of 914.0 | 321-773-2468 | 120 | 16/68 | 20/205 | 9/8 | – | GD | IS | – | L40 | 30/50 | LS | P | GR |
| 5. Anchorage Yacht Basin ⌨ 914.5 | 321-773-3620 | 60 | – | 10/80 | 6/10 | – | G | IMS | HEP | L10,C | 30/30 | LS | P | GMR |
| **EAU GALLIE AREA** | | | | | | | | | | | | | | |
| 6. Eau Gallie Yacht Basin ⌨ WiFi 915 | 321-242-6577 | 60 | 16 | 2/60 | 8/8 | – | – | IMS | – | – | 30/50 | LS | P | GMR |
| 7. Waterline Marina ⌨ WiFi 915 | 321-254-0452 | 80 | 16/68 | 8/92 | 8/8 | – | – | – | HEP | – | 30/50 | LS | P | GR |

⌨ Internet Access    WiFi Wireless Internet Access    WG Waterway Guide Cruising Club Partner  *(Information in the table is provided by the facilities.)*
See WaterwayGuide.com for current rates, fuel prices, web site addresses, and other up-to-the-minute information.

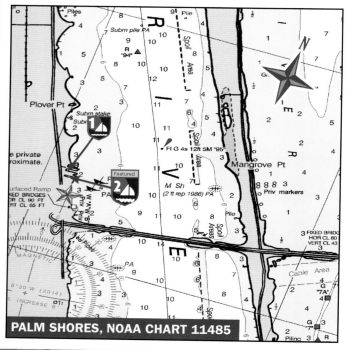

PALM SHORES, NOAA CHART 11485

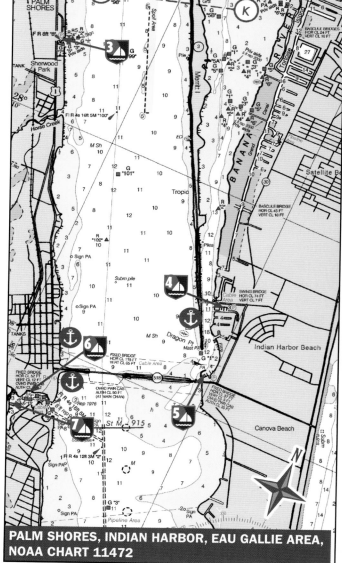

PALM SHORES, INDIAN HARBOR, EAU GALLIE AREA, NOAA CHART 11472

## Cocoa to Eau Gallie–ICW Mile 898 to Mile 914

**NAVIGATION:** Use Charts 11485 and 11472. The stretch from Cocoa to Palm Shores presents a few problems, including the ever-present pot markers that sometimes stray into the channel. At Mile 909, the **Pineda Causeway (Palm Shores) Twin Bridges** (65-foot fixed vertical clearance) cross the ICW. South of the bridges, starting about Mile 910, the channel tends to shoal. The best water can be found along the western edge. A charted spoil area extends to the south from the bridge along the east side for approximately 2.5 miles. The only craft that may have problems are sailboats attempting to tack back and forth across the river.

**Dockage:** On the west side of the ICW several full-service marinas are located above and below the Pineda Causeway Bridges. Pineda Point Marina is on the west side, north of the Pineda Causeway Bridge but is primarily a dry-stack marina.

The next facility south is a very popular dock-n-dine called Grills Riverside. The full-service restaurant will even cook your catch! They have 5-foot dockside depths; call ahead about slip availability.

SunDance Marine Melbourne has a charted, marked entry at about Mile 911. Be sure to inquire about the depths in their channel and at the docks. There are reports to our cruising editor that the channel only carries 3 to 4 feet of water which is not enough for most cruising boats.

**Anchorage:** At Mile 904.5, on the east shore of the Indian River, is "The Point." Just north is a residential stretch that provides a pleasant setting that is protected from northeast to southeast winds and good holding in 9- to 11-foot depths. Don't be alarmed if you hear the cry of peacocks on shore. (It can sound like someone yelling "help.")

The anchorage above and below the Pineda Causeway Bridge (Mile 909) on the west side of the Indian River has not been a recommended anchorage for transient boaters in the past. However, this area has recently befitted from policing and has been cleaned up, making it an acceptable anchorage. You will need to watch the depth here.

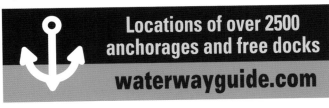

Locations of over 2500 anchorages and free docks

waterwayguide.com

## MELBOURNE AREA

On the mainland side of the ICW, two once distinct towns, Eau Gallie and Melbourne, have merged under the name of Melbourne to form a "metropolis". Each has its own harbor and facilities. Additionally, on the east side of the Indian River there are more facilities on the Banana River as well. Many skippers leave their boats in one of these areas for extended periods, catch a plane from Orlando Melbourne International Airport and then return to continue cruising.

### Eau Gallie–ICW Mile 914

**NAVIGATION:** Use Chart 11472. Eau Gallie, at Mile 914, is on the west side of the Indian River, although the chart doesn't mention it by name. A well-marked channel to the protected harbor is entered from south of the **Eau Gallie Causeway (SR 518) Bridge** at Mile 915. Just prior to ICW red flashing "2," the entry channel leads off to the west. Look for green daybeacons "1," "3," and "5" and flashing red "6" near shore. The controlling depth is reported as 6 feet, but deeper draft vessels utilize the channel. As of spring 2017, mid-channel or favoring the green provided the best water. Beware of shoaling extending to the southeast of red flashing "6."

From here, the channel bends to the northwest as it enters the headlands and continues into the harbor and the Eau Gallie River. Favor the seawalled north shoreline after you enter into this narrow passage and be alert to increased traffic at a park and launch ramp on the south side.

Across the Indian River to the east, the mouth of the Banana River is located inside Dragon Point, north of the bridge and east of the ICW. To enter, round green daybeacon "1" off Dragon Point on the north side of the entrance but keep at least 100 feet south of that daybeacon. Groundings on Dragon Point's rocky rim occur frequently. Reports are that the charted shoal building up from the bridge is well south of green daybeacon "1." It is a sandy shoal, and it would be better to ground there than on Dragon Point's rocks. If you do hit the rocks, edge off backwards; do not try to go over them! Manatees or porpoises sometimes welcome boaters to this area.

The **Mathers Swing Bridge** over the Banana River (north and on the inside of Dragon Point/Merritt Island) has 7-foot vertical clearance at mean low water. It opens

# GOIN' ASHORE: EAU GALLIE, FL

| SERVICES | |
|---|---|
| 1 | Library |
| 2 | Post Office |
| **ATTRACTIONS** | |
| 3 | Eau Gallie Square |

| | |
|---|---|
| 4 | Foosaner Art Museum |
| 5 | Intracoastal Brewing Company |
| **SHOPPING** | |
| 6 | Eau Gallie Ace Hardware |

| DINING | |
|---|---|
| 7 | Chef Mario's Café |
| 8 | Joan's Perfect Pie |
| 9 | Squid Lips |

Eau Gallie began as a small coastal town along the Indian River Lagoon in 1860. Incorporated in 1896, hardy souls settled in Eau Gallie and steamers, riverboats, and freighters plied the Indian River, transporting residents, cargo, and, in increasing numbers, tourists. Henry Flagler brought the railroad and Eau Gallie became a popular resort area and the railroad facilitated export of local products, causing Indian River Fruit to become famous nationwide and the citrus industry boomed. Eau Gallie, loosely translated as "rocky or gravel water."

**Attractions:** Eau Gallie today is a quaint, historical section that strives to retain its historical and cultural heritage while enhancing the area with new businesses and events that will grow Eau Gallie, yet preserve its distinct early Florida flavor. Historic buildings and

churches remain in and around the downtown area, some dating back to the 1920s and 30s and earlier.

The Eau Gallie Arts District (EGAD) hosts many events in the Eau Gallie Square, at the corner of Eau Gallie Blvd and Highland Ave. EGAD celebrates the First Friday of each month with a themed event featuring live entertainment in the band shell, beer and wine, arts and crafts vendors and food trucks around Eau Gallie Square, and shops and galleries are open late (5:30 to 8:30 p.m.). December's First Friday hosts Holiday Tree Lighting ceremony and an appearance by Santa. EGAD's signature events are Founders' Day, typically the first Saturday in February starting at noon, and a new event will begin in May 2017 that celebrates the waterfront. ArtWorks of Eau Gallie is a separate entity that has held the longest

running outdoor art festival in Brevard County on the weekend before Thanksgiving every year.

The Foosaner Art Museum is located in the heart of Eau Gallie at 1463 Highland Ave. It is part of Florida Institute of Technology and has studio and gallery space. In addition to art exhibits, the museum offers classes and workshops and hosts an outdoor film festival. Open Wednesday through Saturday, 10:00 a.m. to 4:00 p.m. Call 321-674-8916 for details.

Intracoastal Brewing Company has a neighborhood taproom and features a rotating menu of original brews, plus growlers to take home (652 W Eau Gallie Blvd., 321-872-7395). Our favorite activity? "Namaste for one more" yoga and beer every Sunday at 11:30 a.m. ($15 or $10 without beer).

**Shopping:** Eau Gallie Ace Hardware (590 Eau Gallie Blvd., 321-254-3261) likely has whatever you need but if not, there are many more stores and specialty shops nearby.

**Dining:** Squid Lips (1477 Pineapple Ave., 321-259-3101) offers dockside dining and Floridian flare, while Chef Mario's Café (1437 Highland Ave., 321-241-4890) is an intimate and affordable Italian café with cappuccino and gelato bars. Joan's Perfect Pie was ranked the 12th best pie shop in Florida (1478 B Highland Ave., 321-610-7953). Local restaurants will deliver dinner to your table at Intracoastal Brewing Company (see above).

Visit eaugalliearts.com for more details on entertainment, shopping and dining.

Indian River

# Indian River, FL

| | | Dockage | | | | | Supplies | | Services | | | | | |
|---|---|---|---|---|---|---|---|---|---|---|---|---|---|---|
| | | Largest Vessel Accommodated | VHF Channel Monitored | Transient Berths / Total Berths | Approach / Dockside Depth (reported) | Floating Docks | Gas / Diesel | Groceries, Ice, Marine Supplies, Snacks | Repairs: Hull, Engine, Propeller | Lift (tonnage), Crane, Rail | Min/Max Amps | Laundry, Pool, Showers, Courtesy Car | Pump-Out Station | Nearby: Grocery Store, Motel, Restaurant |
| **MELBOURNE** | | | | | | | | | | | | | | |
| 1. Melbourne Harbor Marina ⌨ 🛜 918.5 | 321-725-9054 | 130 | 16/68 | 10/85 | 8/8 | – | GD | IMS | HEP | – | 30/100 | LS | P | GMR |
| **PALM BAY** | | | | | | | | | | | | | | |
| 2. Palm Bay Marina 921.2 | 321-723-0851 | 40 | 74 | 3/60 | 3/3 | – | – | IMS | HEP | L5 | 30/30 | S | – | GMR |

⌨ Internet Access  🛜 Wireless Internet Access  WG Waterway Guide Cruising Club Partner  *(Information in the table is provided by the facilities.)*
See WaterwayGuide.com for current rates, fuel prices, web site addresses, and other up-to-the-minute information.

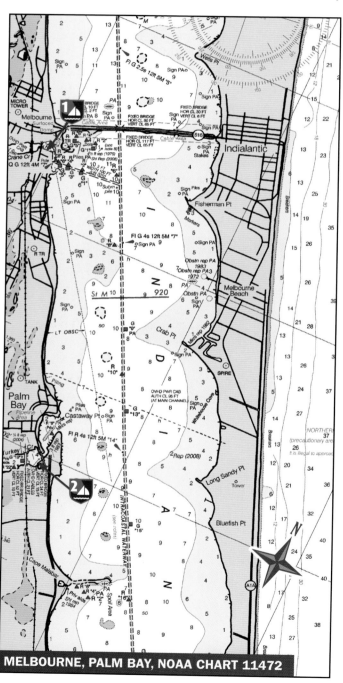

**MELBOURNE, PALM BAY, NOAA CHART 11472**

on request and monitors VHF Channel 09. However, as of summer 2017, the USCG is proposing implementing restricted openings.

The Banana River continues north up to Cape Canaveral. In about 18 miles it intersects the Canaveral Barge Canal near the Cape Canaveral Lock. This route can be tricky with distant navaids and skinny water. The controlling depth is 5 to 6 feet, but it is typically deeper. Oddly, if you follow the channel up to daybeacons red "8A" and green "9," what follows is 3-foot depths and no further course guidance. Local knowledge offers to leave the channel around red daybeacons "6B" or red "8" and sound your way cautiously west into the deeper water as shown on the chart. (This deeper water is the result of dredging for fill to extend the landmass for the runways of adjacent Partick Air Force Base.)

Note that the chart shows "Subm Piles" northwest of red daybeacon "8." Once into the deep water and around the submerged pilings, head north for 4.25 miles to pick up the marked channel at green daybeacon "11" and red daybeacon "12." Note that there is no daybeacon "10". A fixed bridge at SR 528/AIA with a vertical clearance of 36-feet establishes the air draft constraint for this route.

**Dockage:** On the east side of the Indian River in the mouth of the Banana River, two marinas are available. On the south shore, just north and east of the Eau Gallie Bridge, is Anchorage Yacht Basin. The entrance is straightforward, but you should check for current depths before entering the channel. Telemar Bay Marina is located just south of the 7-foot swing bridge and is located within (long) walking distance of shopping. They do not allow dinghy landing. If you continue east past the marina on that canal, there is a city facility with a dock called "Oars and Paddles Park," but there is "No Mooring" signage posted according to the City Managers office. You can take your dinghy all the way to the end

of the southernmost canal, by the yacht club, and walk one-half mile south to a shopping center with Publix.

Eau Gallie Yacht Basin is located on the west side of the Indian River in a basin south of the bridge and offers good protection with an easy-to-enter, well-maintained entrance. Favor the seawall to starboard as you enter, swing past the park and dock at the facilities ahead. It is a short walk from the Eau Gallie Yacht Basin through quaint streets to the historical restored downtown area of Eau Gallie, with its restaurants, shops, galleries and a farmers' market on Saturdays. Waterline Marina, associated with a condominium development, is at the head of the basin with some transient slips.

**Anchorage:** Boats anchor on either side of the Eau Gallie Causeway Bridge, depending on wind direction. This allows at least 9 feet of water but is exposed to wakes. Some vessels have been observed anchoring in the Eau Gallie Basin. There is little space outside the channel, and the holding is poor so we do not recommend it.

Between Dragon Point and the Mathers Swing Bridge on the Banana River (off the ICW), you can anchor in 10- to 18-foot depths with good holding. You will find the most room north of the bridge. No tide will worry you here, but the current must be taken into account. Depths vary with wind and rain, and wakes can be considerable (although numerous "No-Wake" signs have resulted in some improvement). Be careful not to interfere with the entrances to the yacht club or the marinas.

Recent charts show wrecks with masts on both the west and east sides of Dragon Point. There is a coquina outcropping on the west side, almost from Dragon Point to the bridge. In case the anchor or chain tangles and cannot be freed, the marina to the north by the bridge can provide a diver to help you.

In a recent change, Anchorage Yacht Basin now allows dinghy landings for cruisers between 8 am and 4pm for nearby provisioning. They require registering at the office and there is a $10 fee.

## Melbourne–ICW Mile 917

The quiet, pleasant town of Melbourne sits midway between Jacksonville Beach and Florida's Gold Coast. It is home port to the Florida Institute of Technology's big research vessels, on the port side of the harbor entrance.

## GOIN' ASHORE: MELBOURNE, FL

| SERVICES | |
|---|---|
| 1 | Post Office |
| 2 | Visitor Information |
| 3 | Downtown Yoga |
| **ATTRACTIONS** | |
| 4 | Crane Creek Promenade |
| 5 | Henegar Center for the Arts |
| 6 | Melbourne Civic Theatre |
| 7 | Strawberry Art League Gallery |
| **SHOPPING** | |
| 8 | Stebbins Hardware |
| **DINING** | |
| 9 | Chart House |
| 10 | Meg O'Malleys |
| 11 | Nomad Café |
| **MARINAS** | |
| 12 | Melbourne Harbor Marina |

Melbourne has long been a destination for cruisers transiting the ICW. For those heading south in the fall and winter, it feels like you have finally arrived in sunny Florida. For the most part, you have left the cold north winds behind you, and palm trees start becoming more the rule and not the exception.

Settlers began to arrive in the Melbourne area in the late 1800s. Peter Wright, the areas' most noted settler, used to sail regularly up and down the Indian River to deliver mail to other settlers living along the river between Titusville and Malabar. This area provided the best of both worlds to folks looking for a place to call their own–fertile land and water access.

Melbourne and its sister, Eau Gallie, grew up side-by-side, each on either side of the Indian River. They remained as individual cities until voters decided in 1969 to consolidate them into what is now the City of Melbourne.

**Attractions:** Need to stretch out after being on the boat all day? Try Downtown Yoga (532 E. New Haven Ave., 321-676-4600). Or, take a walk along the manatee and wildlife observation area at Promenade Park, located in historic downtown Melbourne along Crane Creek.

Downtown Melbourne is ripe with opportunities to engage in the arts. You can visit the Strawbridge Art League Gallery (2011 Melbourne Ct., 321-952-3070) or catch a show at either The Henegar Center for the Arts (625 E. New Haven Ave., 321-723-8698) or the Melbourne Civic Theatre (817 E. Strawbridge Ave., 321-723-6935). You can't stroll around the historic district without noticing the vibrant murals. There are currently six murals with a goal of completing 15 to 20. Subjects of existing murals include a blue bird, a sea turtle, a VW bus and a mermaid.

In April, you can find some fabulous fine art at the Melbourne Art Festival (melbournearts.org) and in the fall, there is the Downtown Melbourne Food & Wine Festival (melbournefoodandwine.com). On the second Friday of each month from 6:00 to 10:00 p.m., there is a street festival with live music, arts and crafts vendors and food called Friday Fest. The festival is located along E. New Haven Ave. between Depot Dr. and Waverly Place. To find other local events visit the Melbourne Regional Chamber at 1005 E. Strawbridge Ave. (321-724-5400) or check out DowntownMelbourne.com.

We would be remiss not to mention the BrevardZoo, even though it is aways from the downtown area off I-95 at 8225 N. Wickham Rd. (transportation required). See over 500 animals, feed giraffes or try zip-lining. Open 9:30 a.m. to 5:00 p.m. daily (321-254-9453).

**Shopping:** There are many wonderful shops and boutiques downtown selling clothes, shoes and accessories. You might, however, care more about Stebbins Hardware, where you can find home (and possibly boat) improvement items at 405 E. New Haven Ave. (321-549-9980). Melbourne Shopping Center at 1355 S. Babcock St. has a grocery store (with a pharmacy) and a bank.

**Dining:** No matter what you crave, the downtown area has a restaurant to satisfy your hunger (or thirst). The upscale Chart House Restaurant serves "seafood with style" in an intimate waterfront setting. This is a chain restaurant but doesn't feel like one. (2250 Front St., 321-729-6558). Nearby is the more relaxed Ichabods Dockside Bar & Grille with simple seafood fare at 2210 Front St. (321-952-9532).

For something altogether different, try the Nomad Café for delicious farm to table eats with an international flare (2002 S. Harbor City Blvd., 321-327-2996) or, further inland, Meg O'Malleys Irish Pub at 812 E New Haven Ave. (321-952-5510).

**NAVIGATION:** Use Chart 11472. The **Melbourne Causeway Twin (SR 516) Bridges** (both spans have 65-foot vertical clearances) cross the ICW at Mile 918.2. Melbourne's landlocked harbor is easily approached just south of the bridges. To enter the basin from the ICW, turn west at red daybeacon "6," and then follow the markers until you are close to shore. The channel turns sharply to starboard, and then leads to the enclosed basin. The harbor and channel are dredged to a controlling depth of 8 feet, although the depth is reported to be between 6 and 7 feet between red daybeacon "6" and flashing green "7." Local knowledge advises favoring the red.

**Dockage:** The Melbourne Harbor Marina is to starboard at the head of the basin mentioned above. The marina offers all types of repairs and sells fuel (both gas and diesel). The harbor is also known for a spring-time congregation of small bull sharks. They are fun to watch "finning" on the surface. Downtown Melbourne is a short walk from Melbourne Harbor Marina. Here, you will find a quaint restored historical area with shops, restaurants, antiques stores and art galleries.

At Mile 920, both Pelican Harbor Marina and Palm Bay Marina are located in a basin between two fixed bridges (15-foot and 10-foot vertical clearance). There is only approximately 3 to 4 feet of water on the approach. Palm Bay also offers some repairs.

**Anchorage:** Because of the beaches on their west sides, the spoil island accessed by heading west off the ICW just north of red daybeacon "20" at Mile 925 and the one south of it are favorite local anchoring spots. On less crowded weekdays, ICW travelers often use this area for overnight anchorage. Depths are slightly less than shown on the chart. Shoals extend westward from these islands and are usually marked with pipes or stakes.

# ■ SEBASTIAN AREA

The Sebastian area includes the town of Micco, above the Saint Sebastian River, and City of Sebastian, below the river, as well as the Sebastian Inlet.

**NAVIGATION:** Use Chart 11472. Just past Mile 925, the channel slants a bit toward the west. You will enter a dredged channel with less than 6 feet of water on both sides in most places, so stay in the middle. The spoil islands are eroding on the north side. The one nearest North Rocky Point is a pelican rookery.

The spoil islands shown on the chart west of the ICW from Melbourne down to red daybeacon "18" have receded below the surface as of spring 2017. The spoil island between red daybeacons "18" and "20" is very small with a long sandy shoal spit to its west. With frequent bends, the ICW channel passes west of Grant Farm Island (Mile 930), the only inhabited spoil island in the Indian River, which is accessible only by boat. There is a "slow-speed minimum-wake" zone from green daybeacon "37" to red daybeacon "42." From here on, proceed cautiously and be careful not to stray outside the channel, where the water may be only a few feet deep. You may have to strain to make out the markers, which seem to blend into the shoreline.

Also be alert for uncharted oyster beds and trap markers on both sides of the ICW. The lower part of Grant Farm Island is a rookery used mainly by ibis and egrets. From daybeacons "49" to "61" be sure to favor the red side of the channel in 10 feet 12 feet of depth, as opposed to 8 feet or less on the green side.

**Dockage:** Several marinas welcome cruising boats in this area. At Mile 934 is the well-regarded Sebastian River Marina & Boatyard, a full-service boatyard offering service and repairs. They have a 40-ton lift and also offer dry storage. It is in a seawall-protected basin close to a grocery store and restaurants. Sebastian Inlet Marina is just to the south with transient dockage and fuel.

Farther south at Mile 937.5, there are two entrance channels to the marinas on the west side: one on the north side of the spoil island and one to its south. Use only the southern entrance channel upon approach. Most of the northern channel has shoaled in. The northern entrance leading to Capt'n Butchers Marina and to Fins Marina is reported to carry somewhat less than the charted 6-foot depths from the ICW to the marinas. Capt'n Butchers reports 5-foot dockside depths. The southern entrance leads to Capt. Hiram's Sebastian Marina, which can be identified by its colorful rooftops. This is also a shallow (5-foot depth) channel.

**Anchorage:** Shallow-draft vessels (less than 5 feet) can anchor off Capt. Hiram's Sebastian Marina, with approximately 5-foot depths at mean low water. There are a number of permanently moored vessels here. This is close to several pubs and restaurants and can get crowded. Enter through the marked channel.

## Sebastian Inlet–ICW Mile 936

**NAVIGATION:** Use Chart 11472. Sebastian Inlet, at Mile 936, is crossed by a fixed bridge with a 37-foot vertical clearance and is used by local boats to reach the ocean. Constant shoaling necessitates careful piloting and current local knowledge. This is a local knowledge, fair-weather inlet.

Swift crosscurrents and the resulting shifting channel make navigation difficult in Sebastian Inlet, even with up-to-date local information. A 3,000-foot-long by 100-foot-wide and 9-foot-deep channel provides access to the ocean, but as with all ocean inlets, a cautious approach is warranted, as shoaling is ever present and continuous. The currents in this area can also affect travel on the ICW. See the Inlet section at the front of this guide or waterwayguide.com for more information on Sebastian Inlet.

⚠️ Private aid Sebastian Inlet Channel Daybeacon 17 is reported as destroyed. The remains of the pile is submerged and is a hazard to navigation. Mariners are advised to exercise extreme caution while transiting the area.

**Anchorage:** It is possible to anchor at Sebastian Inlet State Park near the northeast side of the inlet in 8-10 feet of water. There is only a 6-inch tide at this spot but a good current. Only anchor here on a low wind day, as it is exposed in all directions.

It is a short dinghy ride to the basin to the north side of the inlet, just after the fixed bridge, for snorkeling and swimming. Visibility for snorkeling is fair and the beach is excellent and not crowded. Great for a picnic and dog run. Park the dingy on the sand beach prior to the "lagoon." You will be joined by lots of fishermen and small boats.

## ■ VERO BEACH AREA

## Wabasso–ICW Mile 943

**NAVIGATION:** Use Chart 11472. The dredged ICW channel runs straight for 10 miles to Wabasso. At Mile 938, near red daybeacon "66A," beware of shoaling into the east side of the ICW that extends out to mid-channel. Due to a very sharp drop off from "dry land" to an observed 13-foot depth on the western side of the ICW, it is recommended you strongly favor the red

side. At Wabasso, 25 miles south of Melbourne, small wooded islands suddenly crowd the narrowing river and create a maze through which the channel twists and turns. Observe markers carefully. Expect sporadic spots of shoaling between the Sebastian area and Vero Beach. The heavily congested areas are temporarily behind you as you enter one of the Indian River's most attractive stretches.

The **Wabasso Bridge** crosses the ICW at Mile 943.3. The bridge is charted with a 65-foot fixed vertical clearance; however, 64-foot vertical clearance was observed on the tide boards by our cruising editor in spring 2017. There is a new private basin associated with a residential community on the northwest side of the Wabasso Bridge. More and more developments and private homes are springing up along the stretch between Wabasso and Vero Beach, including new condominiums.

Be on the lookout for manatees and other wildlife. Some of the islands in this area are rookeries for a variety of bird species. South of the Wabasso Bridge, on the west side of the ICW, are the docks of the Environmental Learning Center, a 64-acre habitat for birds, fish, crustaceans and mammals of many kinds. The museum here is home to a 145-gallon touch tank, plus three other aquariums, several hands-on exhibits and a life-size replica of a manatee's head, from which you can experience how a manatee eats seagrass from the lagoon floor. See details at discoverelc.org

**Dockage:** At Mile 948.5, north of Vero Beach, on the west side of the ICW, a charted, marked channel with 6-foot depths observed at the centerline leads to the docks of Suntex Marina, an elaborate development with condominiums, golf, tennis and handsome waterfront homes. The marina can accommodate transients (including catamarans) up to 75 feet with 7-foot dockside depths. They also sell fuel. You will need ground transportation to provision in this area.

**Anchorage:** Vessels have been observed anchored in a small pocket between the bridge and the Learning Center with 10 to 12-foot depths. At Mile 944.6, be alert for green can "91," marking the end of a shoal extending from the adjacent spoil island.

Shoal-draft boats, such as catamarans, have been observed at anchor behind the spoil island just south of Pine Island near Mile 946.4. The entrance to this anchorage is reported to be between that spoil island and flashing red daybeacon "112." Enter from south to find 8 feet of water. After proceeding in a northwesterly

www.snagaslip.com

SNAG-A-SLIP

EXPLORE.
BOOK.
BOAT.

# Indian River Inlet, FL

| SEBASTIAN AREA | | Dockage | | | | | | Supplies | | Services | | | | |
|---|---|---|---|---|---|---|---|---|---|---|---|---|---|---|
| | | Largest Vessel Accommodated | VHF Channel Monitored | Transient Berths / Total Berths | Approach / Dockside Depth (reported) | Floating Docks | Groceries, Ice, Marine Supplies, Snacks | Gas / Diesel | Repairs: Hull, Engine, Propeller | Lift (tonnage), Crane, Rail | Min/Max Amps | Laundry, Pool, Showers, Courtesy Car | Pump-Out Station | Nearby: Grocery Store, Motel, Restaurant |
| 1. Sebastian River Marina & Boatyard (WiFi) 934 | 772-664-3029 | 70 | 16/68 | 4/60 | 5/5 | – | GD | MS | HEP | L40 | 30/50 | S | – | GR |
| 2. Sebastian Inlet Marina ▯ (WiFi) 934.3 | 772-664-8500 | 45 | 16 | 4/250 | 5/5 | F | GD | GIMS | EP | L16 | 30/50 | S | P | GMR |
| 3. Capt'n Butchers Marina (WiFi) 937.2 | 772-589-2552 | 60 | 16 | 5/25 | 5/6 | – | GD | IS | – | – | 20/50 | L | – | GMR |
| 4. Fins Marina (WiFi) 937.5 | 772-589-4843 | 80 | 16 | 10/78 | 6/6 | – | – | I | – | – | 30/50 | S | – | GMR |
| 5. Capt. Hiram's Sebastian Marina (WiFi) 937.7 | 772-589-4345 | 50 | 16/68 | 14/46 | 5/5 | – | – | IMS | – | – | 30/50 | LPS | P | GMR |

▯ Internet Access (WiFi) Wireless Internet Access WG Waterway Guide Cruising Club Partner *(Information in the table is provided by the facilities.)*
See WaterwayGuide.com for current rates, fuel prices, web site addresses, and other up-to-the-minute information.

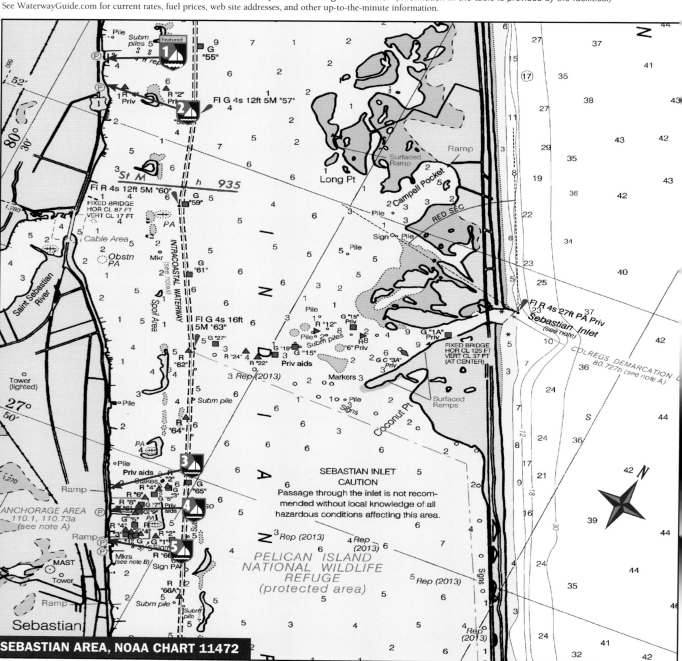

SEBASTIAN AREA, NOAA CHART 11472

# GOIN' ASHORE: VERO BEACH, FL

| SERVICES | |
|---|---|
| 1 | Post Office |
| **ATTRACTIONS** | |
| 2 | Riverside Theatre |
| 3 | Vero Beach Museum of Art |

| DINING | |
|---|---|
| 4 | Lemon Tree Restaurant |
| 5 | Mulligan's Beach House |
| 6 | Ocean Grill |
| 7 | Riverside Café |

| MARINAS | |
|---|---|
| 8 | Vero Beach City Marina |

Vero Beach is a favorite with cruisers. Many who plan to leave, don't; hence the nickname "Velcro Beach." This affluent resort community is known for its immaculate ocean and riverfront amenities. The historic downtown is part of a flourishing walkable community boasting many cultural amenities, great shopping and dining opportunities that rival Gold Coast cities to the south. Located in Indian River County, the area is known for its citrus shipped all over the world.

The Vero Beach area was first settled in the mid-1800s. The construction of Flagler's railroad in the late 1890s helped the local fishermen and farmers get products north to the East Coast. In the early 1900s, Drainage Districts were created to drain the wetlands and make them habitable. Citrus became a bumper crop, as well

as cattle ranching and timber farming. The town of Vero was planned, canals were dredged and a power plant was installed in 1918. The town continued to grow. Then a bridge was built to connect the island to the mainland in 1919 and to this day the town has been attracting tourists.

**Attractions:** The impressive Vero Beach Museum of Art (3001 Riverside Park Dr., 772-231-0707) and the Riverside Theatre (3250 Riverside Park, 772-231-6990) are within walking distance of the City Marina next to the Vero Beach Yacht Club (3601 Rio Vista Blvd., 772-231-2211). Gallery Strolls, outdoor concerts and productions and many eco-adventures await the visitor. A popular farmers market is held each Saturday morning on Ocean Dr.

**Shopping:** Within walking distance of the Vero Beach City Marina is Orchid Island Hardware, a True Value Hardware Store, at 615 Beachland Blvd. (772-231-4685). This store is well stocked and carries a limited selection of marine items. If you are in need of outboard engine parts or repairs, try Vero Marine Center (12 Royal Palm Pointe, 772-562-7922), which has a well-stocked parts department.

Village Beach Market on Hwy. A1A offers shopping and delivery services (for a fee). You would be hard pressed to not find what you need at this upscale market (772-231-2338).

On the Orchid Island side of Vero Beach there is an abundance of trendy little shops along the waterfront on Ocean Drive as well as the surrounding side streets; they are too numerous to mention here. Be sure to take your time strolling around and enjoying what the town has to offer.

One of the pluses to Vero Beach is the excellent free bus system, the GoLine (772-569-0903). The bus stops twice per hour in front of the captain's lounge at the Vero Beach City Marina. One route will take you to the Oceanside business district, with its unique shops and restaurants, and guarded beaches. Another route makes stops at major supermarkets, West Marine, liquor stores and other shops. The bus continues to a transfer station where you can connect to other routes taking you to Walmart, Target, pharmacies, a mall and a large outlet mall. All in all, it is a great service to boaters.

**Dining:** A great many dining choices await you in Vero Beach. The Riverside Café (3341 Bridge Plaza Drive, 772-234-5550) has food, music, a "Happy Hour" seven days a week and overlooks the Indian River Lagoon. This is a very popular spot for boaters and locals.

Along Ocean Dr. is the popular Lemon Tree Restaurant (3125 Ocean Dr., 772-231-0858) serving breakfast and lunch, or for oceanfront dining pleasure, try Ocean Grill (772-231-5409) or Mulligan's Beach House Bar & Grill (772-492-6744), both located in the Sexton Plaza on Ocean Dr.

Many of Vero's restaurants serve fresh local fish that you may not recognize but will never forget, including pompano, cobia, unicorn filefish, snook, fresh water crappie, or any one of 15 species of grouper. Our on-the-water cruising editors provide the locations listed here. To assist you in enjoying all Vero Beach and the surrounding area has to offer, a mobile app is available for free download from the Apple Store and through Google Play Store. Key word searches for the app are "Vero Beach," "Sebastian" and "Fellsmere." The app is usable on Apple and Android technology and incorporates an "Eat, Stay & Play" directory with comprehensive information to enhance your stay including turn-by-turn directions, integrations with Yelp and OpenTable, and a community calendar featuring major festivals and events.

# Vero Beach Area, FL

| | Largest Vessel Accommodated | VHF Channel Monitored | Approach / Dockside Depth (reported) | Transient Berths / Total Berths | Floating Docks | Gas / Diesel | Groceries, Ice, Marine Supplies, Snacks | Repairs: Hull, Engine, Propeller | Lift (tonnage), Crane, Rail | Laundry, Pool, Showers, Courtesy Car | Min/Max Amps | Nearby: Grocery Store, Motel, Restaurant | Pump-Out Station |
|---|---|---|---|---|---|---|---|---|---|---|---|---|---|
| | | | **Dockage** | | | | **Supplies** | | | **Services** | | | |
| **WABASSO** | | | | | | | | | | | | | |
| 1. Suntex Marina—Vero Beach 🖥 📶 948.5  772-770-4470 | 75 | 16/68 | 20/130 | 6/7 | – | GD | IS | – | – | 30/50 | LPS | P | GMR |
| **VERO BEACH** | | | | | | | | | | | | | |
| 2. Vero Beach City Marina 🖥 📶 952  772-231-2819 | 160 | 16/66 | 18/88 | 8/10 | F | GD | GIMS | HEP | L3 | 30/50 | LS | P | GMR |
| 3. Vero Marine Center Inc. 952  772-562-7922 | 30 | 16 | call/40 | 3/3 | – | – | M | E | L3 | 30/30 | – | – | – |

🖥 Internet Access  📶 Wireless Internet Access  **WG** Waterway Guide Cruising Club Partner  *(Information in the table is provided by the facilities.)*
See WaterwayGuide.com for current rates, fuel prices, web site addresses, and other up-to-the-minute information.

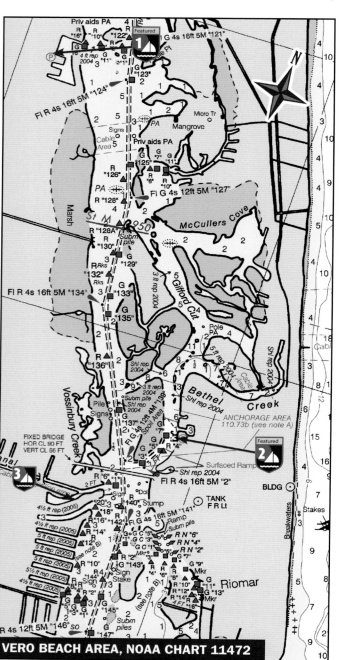

**VERO BEACH AREA, NOAA CHART 11472**

direction, anchor between the spoils island and Hole in the Wall Island. This anchorage provides protection from ICW wakes. You can dinghy ashore but beware the live oysters that may cut your inflatable and your dogs feet! This may be your last secluded anchorage when southbound.

## Vero Beach–ICW Mile 952

Just past some sizable islands, you will see Vero Beach (Mile 952), a boating center and stopover with a variety of facilities on both sides of the Indian River, above and below the **Merrill P. Barber (Vero Beach) Bridge** at Mile 951.9 (66-foot fixed vertical clearance). This is the beginning of the more densely populated areas of Florida, and the number of boats increases accordingly. Keep well inside the marked channel when passing through the bridge and maintain a firm hand on the helm, as winds and current can be strong here.

A little more than 1 mile below the Vero Beach Bridge is another high-rise bridge, the **Alma Lee Loy (17th St.) Bridge**, with a 65-foot fixed vertical clearance at Mile 953.2. Between the bridges on the west side is a power plant, which is a favorite spot for manatees to lounge. You must maintain a posted slow speed from November 15 through April 30, except when in the channel.

**NAVIGATION:** Use Chart 11472. Use the Miami Harbor Entrance Tide Tables. For high tide, add 2 hours 56 minutes; for low tide, add 3 hours 41 minutes. There is shoaling into the channel between red daybeacons "128" and "130" north of Vero Beach. Red daybeacon "128A" has been placed to help guide mariners through this area. Stay mid-channel to avoid shoals. Just north of the Vero Beach Bridge, markers to the east lead up the old ICW route past the city park to Vero Beach City Marina.

VERO BEACH CITY MARINA

ICW

Enter the harbor by turning between flashing green "139" and the bridge, and then go in parallel to the bridge until you have lined up the channel markers. Be mindful of the strong current and compensate for the set. There is shoaling off of the mangrove island to the north at the entrance so do not get too close or cut the corner while compensating for the effects of the current. Outside of the channel that leads into the marina and mooring field, you will encounter 4-foot depths or less.

As you continue south along the ICW and pass under the two bridges, stay in mid-channel as the edges of the channel shoal quickly for a mile or so south of the bridges. From north of Vero Beach at red daybeacon "120" to green daybeacon "149," the Manatee Speed Zone is enforced year-round.

**Dockage:** Vero Beach's popular north basin offers tranquility in a crowded area. No-Wake signs are posted, improving comfort. Vero Beach City Marina is situated in a park-like setting, offering transient dockage, gas and diesel fuel, laundry and a free pump-out boat twice weekly. Free bus service is available to all shopping. The ocean and beach district is only 1 mile away and is serviced by the bus system. The marina hosts a "cruisers" BYOB/appetizers party every Thursday afternoon in the north pavilion at 4:00 (weather permitting). Located just south of the marina, but still part of the same area, is a large dog park where your pet can get out and stretch its legs.

Vero Marine Center Inc. is across the ICW (on the west shore) with sales and service. The channel leading to their facility is very shallow (3 feet or less) but can be accessed by dinghy. There are several restaurants nearby.

**Moorings:** Inexpensive and well-maintained city-owned moorings are available in both the north and south basins, on either side of Vero Beach City Marina. Protection from stormy weather is very good in this basin. These moorings are very popular, and it can get quite crowded in the busy season. Each mooring is assigned by the dockmaster of the municipal marina (reservations recommended).

Be aware that even if moorings are reserved, boaters may still be expected to share them; boats traveling together are encouraged to make arrangements to raft together. Otherwise, the first boat at a mooring is asked to put out fenders and accept whatever raft is assigned. It is well protected in this area and rafting is rarely a problem. Crews of moored boats enjoy the use of showers, a comfortable lounge, laundry facilities and a picnic area. Trash disposal and use of the dinghy dock are complimentary for moored boats.

**Anchorage:** Most of the areas outside the channel and near the mangrove islands above and below Vero Beach are shallow. Boats can anchor between the little islands but need to stay clear of the moorings and watch for shoals, which can be difficult in this area. Anchored boats are not allowed use of any of the marina's facilities

## Cruising Options

Boaters proceeding south will next encounter Fort Pierce. It has a number of marine facilities, and its deep ocean inlet provides access to run outside to points south or as a gateway east to the Bahamas Islands.

# Fort Pierce to St. Lucie Inlet

 **ICW** Mile 952–Mile 988     (((**VHF**))) FL: Channel 09

**CHARTS** 11428, 11472

Once you pass Vero Beach, you are positioned midway between the upper and lower reaches of the Indian River. As the river widens, the dredged ICW channel begins to straighten out for the 13 miles south to Fort Pierce. The project depth along this stretch is 12 feet, but the actual controlling depth is 8 feet or less.

Some of the spoil islands scattered along this stretch are blanketed in the spring by nesting pelicans, cormorants, herons and egrets. Enjoy watching them, but do not disturb the nests. In winter, the area from the Vero Beach Bridge south to the high-rise 17th Street Bridge becomes a protected area for manatees. They like the warm water discharged by the neighboring power plant. You will see the plant's three stacks near the bridge on the west side. You can also keep a lookout for manatees farther south at the Fort Pierce South Bridge; this is another favorite lounging area for the gentle creatures. It's not uncommon to see several manatees entertaining people on the docks and walkways in the Fort Pierce City Marina.

## ■ FORT PIERCE AREA

### Vero Beach to Fort Pierce—ICW Mile 952 to Mile 965

**NAVIGATION:** Use Chart 11472. Use the Miami Harbor Entrance Tide Tables. For high tide, add 49 minutes; for low tide, add 1 hour 1 minute. From Vero Beach (Mile 952) to Fort Pierce (Mile 965), the ICW continues south along the Indian River. In Vero Beach, shoaling exists in spots from flashing green daybeacon "139" to red daybeacon "142," and from green daybeacon "149" to flashing green daybeacon "153," reducing water depths to 8 or 10 feet along the edges of the channel. Watch the depth sounder and stay in the middle of the channel to avoid shallow water and spoil banks outside the channel. There is also shoaling in spots from flashing green.

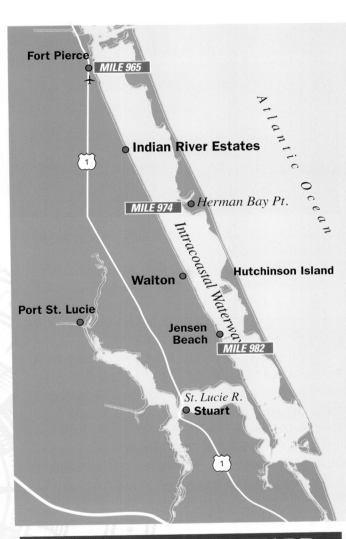

Map showing: Fort Pierce — MILE 965; Indian River Estates; MILE 974; Herman Bay Pt.; Atlantic Ocean; Intracoastal Waterway; Hutchinson Island; Walton; Port St. Lucie; Jensen Beach; MILE 982; St. Lucie R.; Stuart

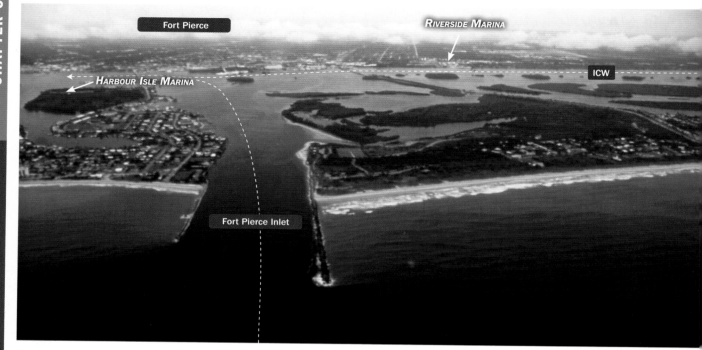

daybeacon "157" to green daybeacon "165," with depths of less than 8 feet.

From green daybeacon "155" to green daybeacon "173," the Manatee Speed Zone varies from seasonal to year-round. The zones are posted on the markers. The stretch past Harbor Branch at Mile 960 is a strictly enforced Idle-Speed/No-Wake Zone.

At Mile 964.8, the **North Fort Pierce (SR A1A) Bascule Bridge** (26-foot closed vertical clearance) opens on signal. One-half mile south of Taylor Creek (Mile 965.1) is the intersection of the ICW and Fort Pierce Inlet. Just beyond the intersection, at Mile 965.8, is the **Fort Pierce (SR A1A) Bridge** (65-foot fixed vertical clearance), sometimes referred to as South Bridge. Watch for shoaling between red daybeacon "184" and red daybeacon "186" on the eastern edge of the channel between the North Fort Pierce Bascule

Bridge and the inlet. Use caution and follow the aids to navigation closely in this area. Shoaling has also been reported on the west side of the channel just to the north of the South Bridge at the edge of the turning basin.

**Dockage:** Just north of the North Fort Pierce Bridge, on the west side, is Riverside Marina, with a large yard with some transient dockage available (call ahead). They have a 70-ton life and mechanic on site and allow do-it-yourself work in the yard.

Immediately south of the North Fort Pierce Bridge is Taylor Creek. This well-marked creek is the home of Harbortown Marina-Fort Pierce, a large full-service marina and boatyard in a tropical atmosphere. The island-themed Harbor Cove Waterfront Restaurant (772-429-5303) is located here, as is Sunnyland Canvas, specializing in marine canvas and upholstery. Also

# Indian River, FL

## FORT PIERCE AREA

| Facility | Phone | Largest Vessel Accommodated | VHF Channel Monitored | Transient Berths / Total Berths | Approach / Dockside Depth (reported) | Floating Docks | Gas / Diesel | Groceries, Ice, Marine Supplies, Snacks | Repairs: Hull, Engine, Propeller | Lift (tonnage), Crane, Rail | Min/Max Amps | Laundry, Pool, Showers, Courtesy Car | Pump-Out Station | Nearby: Grocery Store, Motel, Restaurant |
|---|---|---|---|---|---|---|---|---|---|---|---|---|---|---|
| | | **Dockage** | | | | | **Supplies** | | **Services** | | | | | |
| 1. Riverside Marina ▢ WiFi 964.1 | 772-464-5720 | 105 | 16 | 5/70 | 6/6 | – | – | M | HEP | L70 | 30/50 | S | P | GMR |
| 2. Harbortown Marina-Fort Pierce ▢ WiFi 965 | 772-466-7300 | 160 | 16/68 | 40/342 | 9/7 | F | GD | IMS | HEP | L150 | 30/100 | LPS | P | GR |
| 3. Cracker Boy Boat Works-Fort Pierce WiFi 965.1 | 772-465-7031 | – | 16/68 | – | 8/7 | – | – | M | HEP | L75,C | – | S | – | GMR |
| 4. Taylor Creek Marina 965.1 | 772-465-2663 | 40 | 68/05 | 5/600 | 8/3 | F | G | IMS | HEP | L9 | 30/30 | – | – | GMR |
| 5. Pelican Yacht Club ▢ WiFi 1 E of 965.6 | 772-464-1734 | 95 | 16 | 5/93 | 6/6 | – | GD | IMS | – | – | 30/50 | LPS | P | GR |
| 6. Fort Pierce Inlet Marina 0.8 E of 965.6 | 772-236-3675 | 90 | – | call/39 | 12/12 | – | – | – | – | – | 30/30 | LS | P | GMR |
| 7. Fort Pierce City Marina ▢ WiFi WG 966.5 | 772-464-1245 | 150 | 16/78 | 40/237 | 7/8 | F | GD | IMS | – | – | 30/50 | LS | P | GMR |
| 8. Harbour Isle Marina WG 0.8 E of 966.2 | 772-461-9049 | 120 | 16/69 | 10/63 | 9/9 | F | – | – | – | – | 30/100 | – | P | GMR |

▢ Internet Access  WiFi Wireless Internet Access  WG Waterway Guide Cruising Club Partner *(Information in the table is provided by the facilities.)*
See WaterwayGuide.com for current rates, fuel prices, web site addresses, and other up-to-the-minute information.

Harbour Isle Marina is located by the Fort Pierce Inlet and accommodates yachts to 120' in the area's best seawall enclosed and wind protected harbour. Sixty eight floating slips can be rented daily, monthly, seasonally, or annually. Luxury condos surrounding marina available for seasonal rental or purchase.

- Area's best seafood restaurants and local bars within walking distance.
- Ft. Pierce's Historic Downtown, a two minute drive away.
- Exceptional fishing area for sailfish, wahoo, dolphin, snook, redfish, trout, tarpon, lobster and blue crabs.

Harbour Isle Marina Services, LLC
805 Seaway Drive
Hutchinson Island, Florida 34949

**772-461-9049**
harbourislefl.com

## see our interactive charts

 MARINAS
 SERVICES
 ANCHORAGES
 FREE DOCK
 BRIDGES
 LOCKS
 NAV ALERTS
 FUEL

**waterwayguide.com**

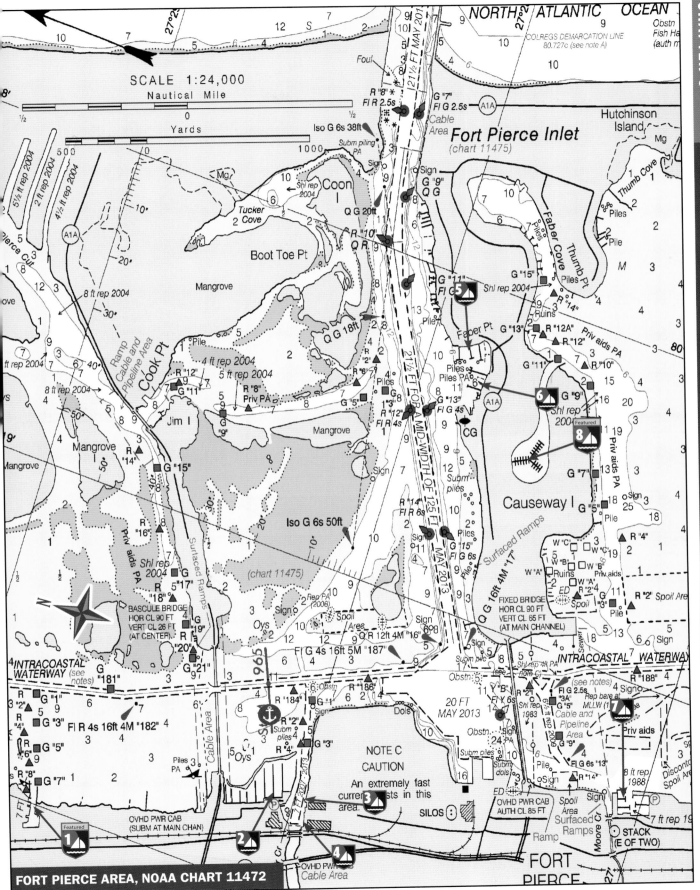

FORT PIERCE AREA, NOAA CHART 11472

## GOIN' AHORE: **FORT PIERCE, FL**

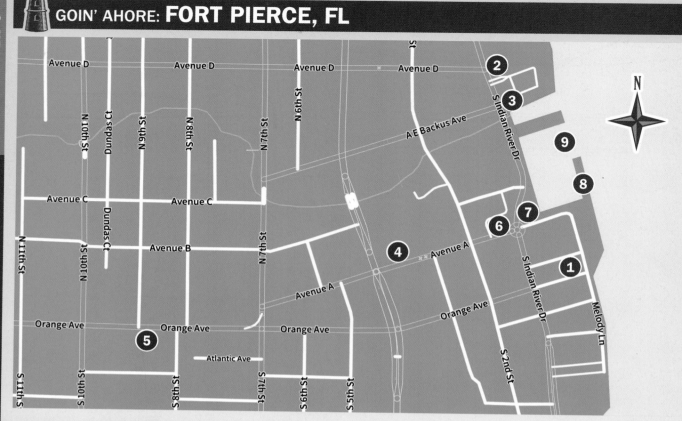

| SERVICES | |
|---|---|
| 1 | Library |
| 2 | Visitor Information |

| ATTRACTIONS | |
|---|---|
| 3 | Manatee Observations and Education Center |

| SHOPPING | |
|---|---|
| 4 | ACE Hardware |
| 5 | Papa's Meat Market |
| 6 | P.P. Cobb General Store & Deli |

| DINING | |
|---|---|
| 7 | Cobbs Landing |

| | |
|---|---|
| 8 | Original Tiki Bar & Restaurant |

| MARINAS | |
|---|---|
| 9 | Fort Pierce City Marina |

Founded as a military base during the Seminole War, Fort Pierce today is the center of the Indian River citrus industry. During World War II, its wide, gently sloping beaches provided the perfect grounds for U.S. servicemen training for amphibious assaults. Today, the beaches are still sometimes used for training Navy SEALS, but they mostly attract vacationers intent on relaxing. Within the city limits, visitors can wander through the Savannas, a large wilderness recreation project. Just north of the Fort Pierce Inlet, swimming, surfing and picnicking draw tourists and locals alike to the state recreation area.

**Attractions:** Fort Pierce has several notable attractions. A good place to start is at the Seven Gables House (Visitor Information Center) at 482 N. Indian River Dr., across the Ft. Pierce (A1A) Bridge. The

Manatee Observation and Education Center next door features hands-on exhibits and boat tours to explore the manatees, Florida's "Gentle Giants," and other sea creatures such as dolphins, pelicans and terns (772-429-6266). The on-site Vanishing Mermaid Gift Shop is worth a look.

The St. Lucie County Aquarium, featuring the Smithsonian Marine Ecosystems Exhibit, features more than 8,000 gallons of marine life. The Aquarium's six aquarium displays and touch tank accurately reflect the habitats typically found in the Indian River Lagoon, which extends 156 miles from Ponce de Leon Inlet to Jupiter. It is located across the A1A Bridge at 420 Seaway Dr. (772-462-3474).

For a look at a different type of aquatic life, the Navy SEAL Museum at 3300 N. Highway A1A (transportation

required) illustrates the training and missions of the Navy frogmen (772-595-5845).

Downtown services, such as the public library, the post office, banks, a general store, a deli, cafés, a bakery and art galleries, are all located near the City Marina.

Every Saturday (year-round), a farmers' market is held at the improved waterfront park adjacent to the marina and features fresh produce, baked goods, arts and crafts and live entertainment. Our cruising editor claims it is the best he has seen. There is also a smaller farmer's market each Wednesday.

**Shopping:** Within walking distance of the City Marina, there is an ACE Hardware (308 Avenue A,

772-461-5950); Papa's Meat Market (823 Orange Ave., 772-468-1881); P.P. Cobb General Store and Deli (100 Avenue A, 772-465-7010); and bit further, Save-a-Lot Grocery at 605 Delaware Ave. (772-467-1077). Inlet Hardware (1105 Seaway Dr., 772-468-8588) is located near Pelican Yacht Club on Causeway Island.

Publix and Winn Dixie Supermarkets and West Marine are a short cab or bus ride away. There is also a bus system, Treasure Coast Connector, which can get you around town and to a lot more shopping.

**Dining:** Harbor Cove Bar & Grill (772-429-5303) at Harbortown Marina offers casual, island-themed waterfront dining with short-term tie-up for dinghies and small boats.

The Original Tiki Bar & Restaurant is a local favorite at the Fort Pierce City Marina (772-461-0880), offering fresh seafood, great hamburgers, full bar service and live music on weekends. If you would prefer more upscale yet casual dining, try Cobb's Landing, which is also adjacent to the marina's docks (772-460-9014). There are many other restaurants scattered throughout the downtown area.

On the Edge Bar and Grill (1136 Seaway Dr., 772-882-9729) is located on Causeway Island.

located on Taylor Creek is Cracker Boy Boat Works, with a do-it-yourself repair yard, and Taylor Creek Marina, with slips and gas (no diesel). Be sure to call in advance to check on their depths as it has been reported to be extremely shallow (3 feet dockside).

**Anchorage:** You can drop the hook at Mile 961.7 at Garfield Point in 4 to 5 feet of water with excellent holding. This is open to the north. Anchor south of the channel. More convenient to For Pierce is the anchorage between the Ft. Pierce North Bridge and the Taylor Creek channel, to the west of the ICW channel off Harbortown Marina at red daybeacon "184." Depths are reported to be less than the charted 8 feet. (Depth is shallow near the bascule bridge but deeper near the entrance channel to Harbortown.) From here you can dinghy to Harbortown Marina, pay for dinghy dock, that fee may be applied towards marina services, gas or ice.

## Fort Pierce Inlet

**NAVIGATION:** Use Chart 11472. Use the Miami Harbor Entrance Tide Tables. For high tide, subtract 31 minutes; for low tide, subtract 18 minutes. The Fort Pierce Inlet is wide and deep with two stone jetties, an inner channel (30-foot depths) and a turning basin (28-foot depths). The channel is marked with ranges and buoys (both lighted and unlighted). Tidal currents in the inlet are strong, averaging 3 to 4 knots. Where the inlet channel crosses the ICW down to the Fort Pierce South Bridge (Mile 965.8), strong crosscurrents exist with a set to southward on the flood and northward on the ebb.

Note: Tidal ranges are 3 feet at the inlet jetties and 1.5 feet in the Indian River near the city marina. In the entrance channel, the large shallow area inside the north jetty is a popular weekend hangout for local boaters. In the area of South Bridge (Mile 965.8), the Idle-Speed/No-Wake Manatee Zone is poorly marked but strictly enforced.

Many cruising boats make Fort Pierce Inlet their exit or entry point for an outside run. It is 65 nm south of Cape Canaveral Inlet and 45 nm north of Lake Worth Inlet. Deep-sea fishing is a big attraction here because of the safe, deep inlet and its proximity to the Gulf Stream. See the Inlet section at the front of this guide for more information.

**Dockage:** Inside the Ft. Pierce Inlet, east of Mile 965.6, is Pelican Yacht Club, which has some reserved transient slips and sells fuel (gas and diesel). In the same basin is Fort Pierce Inlet Marina, which may have space; call ahead for slip availability.

South of the Fort Pierce (South) Bridge (65-foot fixed vertical clearance) is Fort Pierce City Marina's dredged marked entrance channel. Older charts show the former entrance farther south, but that entrance has been completely eliminated. There are now four man-made rock islands to help protect the marina entrance during storms. Consult new charts that show the relocated entrance and call the City Marina on VHF Channel 16 for information and docking and fueling instructions. They have ample transient space on their floating docks and sell fuel.

Up a marked channel just 1 mile east of Mile 965.6 is Harbour Isle Marina. Located on the south side of Causeway Island, this facility sells fuels, as well as some groceries and marine supplies. Amenities include a pool, fitness center, tennis courts, bocce ball court and outdoor kitchen.

**Anchorage:** There are several anchorage areas on the east side of the ICW south of the Fort Pierce (South) Bridge. This channel branches off the ICW at Mile 967, near red daybeacon "188." The shallowest place in this channel is at the entry where the chart shows 7- to 8-foot depths. Note that the spoil island at red daybeacon "2" on the south side of the privately marked channel was reduced to a broad shoal during hurricanes of the past few years.

The first anchorage on this channel, which runs along the south shore of Causeway Island, is south of red daybeacon "4." There is also room just south of green daybeacon "9" in the privately marked entrance channel to Faber Cove. Both of these anchorages offer at least 6 feet of water with excellent holding in mud. If the anchorage area south of green daybeacon "9" is crowded, you may want to sound around the edges with the dinghy first because the boundary of deep water is different than shown on the chart.

Beware as you round green "13" where the water becomes shallow as shown on chart. Continue on past green daybeacon "15" to Faber Cove, which is very protected and quiet with good depths of around 10 feet. In the spring of 2017 there were no anchoring restrictions for Faber Cove. This area is lined with homes so be respectful of private property. We have taken 6-foot draft boats in here. No shore access.

Causeway Island has been developed as a condominium project with its own enclosed boat basin, and the area is now not as attractive for anchoring as it once was.

<br>

## Side Trip: Hutchinson Island

Hutchinson Island stretches 22 miles between Fort Pierce Inlet and St. Lucie Inlet, on the ocean (east) side of the ICW. Visitors can reach Hutchinson Island via three long causeways that connect the mainland to the beaches. The first is the 65-foot fixed Fort Pierce (A1A) Bridge (Mile 965.8), and farther south is the 65-foot fixed Jensen Beach Causeway (SR 707A) Bridge at Mile 981.4. The third route to the beaches on Hutchinson Island is the 65-foot vertical clearance Ernest Lyons (SR A1A) Bridge at Sewalls Point at Mile 984.9. A large pier, a park, a picnic area and a playground lie on the northwest side of the Jensen Beach Causeway. Currents along this run will be affected by whichever inlet is nearer—Fort Pierce Inlet to the north or St. Lucie Inlet to the south.

## Fort Pierce to St. Lucie Inlet

Below Fort Pierce, the Indian River is deceptively wide; you will see many birds walking along the shoals outside of the channel. The ICW route, which follows the deep natural channel, continues to narrow here, so be sure to keep markers lined up ahead and astern.

**NAVIGATION:** Use Chart 11472. Shoaling to 8 feet or less may occur along this stretch, first on both sides of green daybeacon "189" in the channel and at about Mile 973.5, where private markers to Big Mud Creek head off to the east. (Do not mistake private green daybeacon "1," located in shallow water up Big Mud Creek, for an ICW marker.)

Shoaling has extended from red daybeacon "198" to the area past the overhead power cables (90-foot authorized overhead clearance at main channel) near green daybeacon "205." The shallowest depth observed by our cruising editor in spring 2017 was around 9 feet at red daybeacon "200," red daybeacon "206" and green daybeacon "207." As always, the channel shoals along the edges off to the side, so stay in the center of the channel.

At Mile 975, the St. Lucie Power Plant stands on Herman Bay Point at Big Mud Creek, on the east side of the Indian River. Here, several high-level cables cross to the mainland (with 90-foot authorized vertical clearance at channel crossing). Four nautical miles farther, on the east side at Mile 979, you should spot Nettles Island (the skinny part of the island is at Mile 977), with a trailer and marina complex built around canals. The charted

depth off the ICW here is 5 to 6 feet with shallow, unmarked spoil banks.

Other chronic shoal spots are near the **Jensen Beach (SR 707A) Causeway Bridge** (65-foot fixed vertical clearance) and just past the ICW crossing of the St. Lucie River at "The Crossroads." (Described later in this chapter in more detail.)

Martin County begins just south of Mile 980, north of the Jensen Beach Bridge. Except for hospitals, zoning restrictions allow buildings a maximum of just four stories. Local captains returning from the Bahamas are said to locate St. Lucie Inlet by merely aiming midway between the high-rise buildings of St. Lucie County to the north and Palm Beach County to the south.

The third bridge that crosses this area is the 65-foot vertical clearance **Ernest Lyons (SR A1A) Bridge** at Sewalls Point at Mile 984.9.

**Dockage:** Nettles Island Marina is located on the east side of Nettles Island. Its entrance channel leads easterly from the ICW at Mile 979.2 between flashing red daybeacon "214" and green daybeacon "215" and is marked by private green daybeacon "1." Some of the markers are difficult to see. There is a restaurant, grocery store, boutique and more on the premises.

Around the Jensen Beach Causeway Bridge, the first of the many marine facilities in and around Stuart start to appear. Thatched-roof Conchy Joe's Seafood Restaurant (772-334-1130) is located just north of the Jensen Beach Causeway on the west side of the ICW. Call for dockage availability for dinghies and boats drawing less than 2 feet. (Dockage is for dining patrons only.) Follow the well-marked channel carefully; the bottom is soft.

## Indian River, FL

| | Largest Vessel Accommodated | VHF Channel Monitored | Approach / Dockside Depth (reported) | Transient Berths / Total Berths | Floating Docks | Gas / Diesel | Groceries, Ice, Marine Supplies, Snacks | Repairs: Hull, Engine, Propeller | Lift (tonnage), Crane, Rail | Min/Max Amps | Laundry, Pool, Showers, Courtesy Car | Pump-Out Station | Nearby: Grocery Store, Motel, Restaurant |
|---|---|---|---|---|---|---|---|---|---|---|---|---|---|
| **HUTCHINSON ISLAND** | | | **Dockage** | | | **Supplies** | | **Services** | | | | | |
| 1. Nettles Island Marina 💻📶 WG 979.5 — 772-229-2811 | 115 | 16 | 10/65 | 7/10 | - | GD | GIMS | HEP | L13 | 30/100 | LS | P | GMR |
| **JENSEN BEACH** | | | | | | | | | | | | | |
| 2. Sun Dance Marine Jensen Beach/Stuart 982.2 — 772-334-1416 | 45 | 16/10 | 8/10 | 8/4 | - | G | GIMS | HEP | L8 | 30/30 | - | - | GMR |
| 3. Four Fish Inn & Marina 982.8 — 772-334-0936 | 90 | 16 | 15/35 | 8/6 | F | GD | GI | HEP | L50 | 30/50 | S | P | GMR |
| 4. Hutchinson Island Marriott Beach Resort & Marina 💻📶 772-214-7063 | 125 | 16/10 | 20/77 | 7/6 | - | GD | GIS | - | - | 30/50 | LPS | P | GMR |

💻 Internet Access   📶 Wireless Internet Access   WG Waterway Guide Cruising Club Partner *(Information in the table is provided by the facilities.)*
See WaterwayGuide.com for current rates, fuel prices, web site addresses, and other up-to-the-minute information.

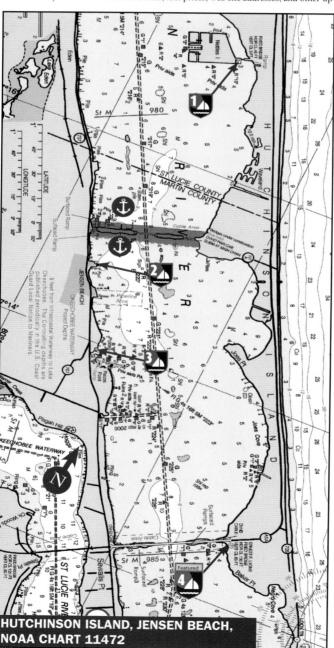

**HUTCHINSON ISLAND, JENSEN BEACH, NOAA CHART 11472**

Sun Dance Marine Jensen Beach/Stuart, is just south of the bridge on the mainland (Mile 982.2) and offers floating docks, fuel and some boat repairs. Directly to the south (at Mile 982.8) is the Four Fish Marina & Inn, situated off a marked channel with transient slips, fuel and repairs.

Located to the east of the ICW on Hutchinson Island at Mile 985, just past the Ernest Lyons Bridge (65-foot fixed vertical clearance), the Hutchinson Island Marriott Beach Resort & Marina offers short- and long-term transient dockage, a laundry and three pools, along with full use of the resort facilities, including tennis courts, a golf course, a restaurant and two tiki bars. It is just 1 mile from the beach and 2 miles from the St. Lucie Inlet, making it a very good jumping off spot for your Bahamas run.

**Anchorage:** Directly north and south of the Jensen Beach Causeway, you will find two good, although unprotected, anchorages on the west side of the ICW. Pick your anchorage according to the wind. Tidal range here is only 1 foot. The area of deep water in the north anchorage is fairly small, as there are less than the charted depths. There is a waterfront park area, as well as Conchy Joe's Seafood Restaurant (with a dinghy dock) adjacent on the northwest side of the Jensen Beach Causeway.

You will find depths of at least 7 feet in the south anchorage, but it is often crowded with boats, some of which are permanent residents. Keep clear of the charted pipeline and cable areas on both sides of the bridge. The adjacent county park (with a boat ramp) is good for dog walking. To reach the south anchorage, make your turn westward midway between red daybeacon "220" and green daybeacon "221," and then double back toward the Jensen Beach Causeway. Protection is good only in westerly to northwesterly winds and gets quite bumpy in winds from the south.

# SLIP INTO AN EXCITING ISLAND RESORT TODAY.

Pull up to our 77-slip marina and immerse yourself with unspoiled beaches, pastel sunsets and more waterfront activities than you can count. At the Hutchinson Island Marriott Beach Resort & Marina, you can spread out, dive in and truly cut loose.

Relax on more than 200 acres of lush Florida coast. Hit the links for 18 holes of challenging golf at The Ocean Club. And dive into waterfront thrills with jet skiing, kayaking, paddle boarding and much more.

Kick back and unwind at one of our two on-site tiki bars. The refreshing Sandpiper Tiki Bar serves up tasty frozen drinks, while the Latitudes Tiki Bar offers poolside bites and lively weekend entertainment. With so much to do once you dock, you'll have everything you need all in one fantastic location.

**AN UNFORGETTABLE ISLAND DESTINATION AWAITS. CALL 800.775.5936 OR VISIT MARRIOTTHUTCHINSONISLAND.COM.**

HUTCHINSON ISLAND MARRIOTT® BEACH RESORT & MARINA
555 NE OCEAN BOULEVARD, STUART, FL 34996
PHONE 800.775.5936  FAX 772.225.0003
MARINA DOCK OFFICE 772.225.6989
MARINA CELL PHONE 772.214.7063
MARRIOTTHUTCHINSONISLAND.COM

MARRIOTT RESORT
HUTCHINSON
ISLAND

Reprinted from March 2017 edition of Coastal Living

SAILS UP: THE ULTIMATE CRUISE

# Stuart to Port Canaveral

**LEG 2 of 8**

○ **START**

Cruise a fun-loving string of Florida Atlantic Coast playgrounds rich with activities worth a dropped anchor—from fishing in Stuart to strolling the sand in Vero Beach, from exploring Melbourne to surfing the break off Cocoa Beach. Get ready to find yourself dallying much longer than the easy long weekend this sunny segment of the Intracoastal Waterway inspires: It's just that much fun.

### MILE 988 + 7 nautical miles west
**GO FISH**
*Stuart*
This warm-hearted town that is neighbor to beach-blessed Hobe Sound and Jensen Beach is proud to call itself the "Sailfish Capital of the World," so soak up the fishing life (and lore), including charters out of **Port Salerno.**

### MILE 952
**BEACH AND SHOP**
*Vero Beach*
Take a free shuttle from the marina to the beach or to fun shops along the waterfront on Ocean Drive. Outdoor concerts and plays make for free year-round fun at **Riverside Park.**
**TIE UP:** Dockage rates start at $1.60 per foot per day at cruiser-friendly **Vero Beach City Marina;** covb.org.

### MILE 918
**FESTIVALS AND FOOD**
*Melbourne*
Plan to hit this town on the second Friday of each month for **Friday Fest,** a lively street festival full of food and music. Don't-miss photo opps: the historic district's vibrant murals.

### MILE 893 + 7 nautical miles east
**BEACH BAR? BINGO!**
*Port Canaveral*
For a pure Florida night, hit the beach-sand dance floor beneath palm trees and tiki torches at **Milliken's Reef.** Have a signature Beach Babe cocktail at one (or all) of Milliken's three bars.
**TIE UP:** Dockage rates are $2.25 per foot at **Cocoa Village Marina** in historic **Cocoa Village,** home to art galleries, boutiques, and fun eating.

### MILE 897 + 6 nautical miles east
**SURF'S UP**
*Cocoa Beach*
Take a day to catch your fill of waves at this surf-blessed hometown of legend Kelly Slater, with surfing and SUP lessons at **Ron Jon Surf School.**

● **END**

**NO BOAT (YET)? Treasure Coast Sailing Adventures** offers morning discovery, afternoon adventure, and romantic sunset sails on the **schooner Lily,** which is also available for private charters. *Lily* departs daily from Shepard Park in downtown Stuart.

**135 MILES SAILED**

IN 1895, JENSEN BEACH WAS THE **PINEAPPLE CAPITAL OF THE WORLD**

**52k** SQUARE FEET OF **SURFBOARD SHOPPING** AT RON JON SURF SHOP

**72.7**
AVERAGE YEAR-ROUND HIGH **TEMPERATURE** IN VERO BEACH

**AREA CODE** FOR CAPE CANAVERAL IS 321 (GET IT?)

**3,2,1**

# ■ THE CROSSROADS

At the St. Lucie Inlet, Mile 988, the intersection of the ICW and the St. Lucie River (Mile Zero on the Okeechobee Waterway route to Florida's West Coast) is locally referred to as The Crossroads. Here, you have a choice of three routes:

1. Continue down the ICW to the resort areas of southern Florida;
2. Move outside via the St. Lucie Inlet and cruise down the Atlantic Ocean; or
3. Travel along the St. Lucie River and down the South Fork through the Okeechobee Lake and Waterway to Fort Myers and Florida's West Coast.

Note that you can traverse the Okeechobee Waterway only if your draft is shallow enough to do so and you can pass under a 49-foot fixed vertical clearance bridge. (See the "Okeechobee Waterway" chapter in this guide for more information and check waterwayguide.com for the latest lake depths.)

**NAVIGATION:** Use Chart 11472. When crossing the St. Lucie River on the ICW, be careful of crosscurrents, which can result in westerly or easterly sets depending on flood or ebb tides. Allow for the crosscurrents when turning from the ICW into the St. Lucie River or vice versa. Pay close attention to all of the boat traffic in this area. You will most likely encounter numerous boats heading for the inlet to go fishing.

The 16-foot-high flashing red buoy "240" (ICW marker) at The Crossroads channel marks the beginning of the St. Lucie River and the Okeechobee Waterway westbound. Red daybeacon "2" and flashing green daybeacon "3," about .3 miles south, marks the continuation of the ICW south. You will find them past the white daybeacon on the west side of the ICW reading DANGER—SHOAL, which should be left well to starboard (red-right-returning) when southbound. This inlet is frequently dredged. There is reportedly 8 feet in the federal channel. Local knowledge should be obtained before using this inlet. See the Inlet section in the front of this guide and check waterwayguide.com for updates.

# Manatee Pocket, FL

| MANATEE POCKET | | Dockage | | | | | Supplies | | Services | | | | | |
|---|---|---|---|---|---|---|---|---|---|---|---|---|---|---|
| | | Largest Vessel Accommodated | VHF Channel Monitored | Transient Berths / Total Berths | Approach / Dockside Depth (reported) | Floating Docks | Gas / Diesel | Groceries, Ice, Marine Supplies, Snacks | Repairs: Hull, Engine, Propeller | Lift (tonnage), Crane, Rail | Min/Max Amps | Laundry, Pool, Showers, Courtesy Car | Pump-Out Station | Nearby: Grocery Store, Motel, Restaurant |
| 1. Whiticar Boat Works Inc.  1.5 | 772-287-2883 | 70 | 09 | call/15 | 6/6 | – | D | M | HEP | L75 | 15/50 | – | – | MR |
| 2. Sailfish Marina of Stuart 🖥 📶 WG .8 | **772-283-1122** | **85** | **16** | **6/55** | **12/10** | – | GD | IMS | HEP | L50 | 30/50 | LS | P | GR |
| 3. Mariner Cay Marina 🖥 📶 WG 1.1 | **772-287-2900** | 80 | 16 | 5/48 | 6/6 | – | GD | I | – | – | 30/50 | LPS | P | MR |
| 4. Pirate's Cove Resort & Marina 🖥 📶 WG 1.8 | 772-287-2500 | 100 | 68 | 10/50 | 7/6 | – | GD | GIMS | HE | – | 30/100 | LPS | P | GMR |
| 5. Hinckley Yacht Services Stuart 🖥 📶 | **772-287-0923** | **115** | **16/09** | **4/78** | **10/6.5** | F | GD | IM | HEP | L150 | 30/100 | S | P | GMR |
| 6. Stuart Corinthian Yacht Club  1.9 | 772-221-1900 | 45 | 16 | 2/25 | 8/5 | – | – | S | – | – | 50/50 | S | – | R |
| 7. A & J Boat Works  2.2 | 772-286-5339 | 60 | – | call/13 | /6 | F | – | M | HEP | L50 | 30/50 | S | – | GMR |
| 8. Manatee Marina  2.2 | 772-283-6714 | 53 | 16 | 4/40 | 7/5 | – | GD | IMS | EP | L | 30/50 | – | – | GMR |
| 9. Port Salerno Marina | 772-223-5022 | – | 16 | call/40 | 6/6 | – | – | – | – | L25 | 30/50 | – | – | R |

🖥 Internet Access  📶 Wireless Internet Access  WG Waterway Guide Cruising Club Partner  *(Information in the table is provided by the facilities.)*
See WaterwayGuide.com for current rates, fuel prices, web site addresses, and other up-to-the-minute information.

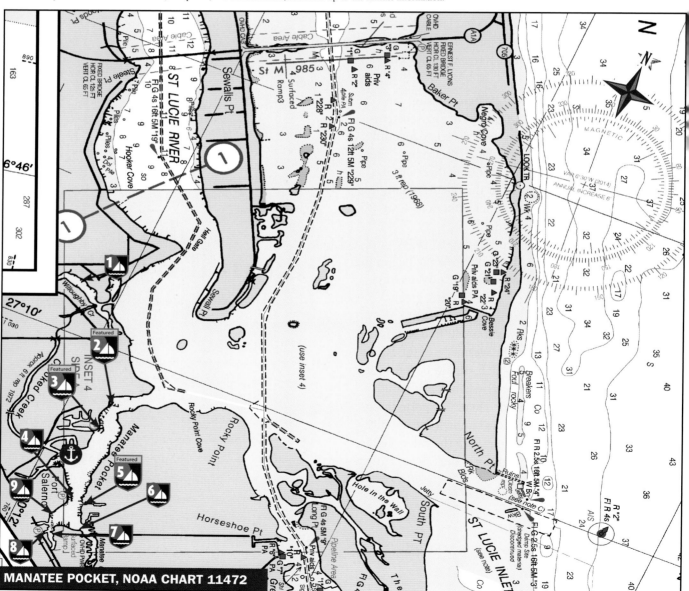

MANATEE POCKET, NOAA CHART 11472

Photo labels: ICW, St. Lucie Inlet (Use Local Knowledge), ICW, To Manatee Pocket, St. Lucie River

# ST. LUCIE RIVER

**NAVIGATION:** Use Chart 11428. For Stuart, use the Miami Harbor Entrance Tide Tables. For high tide, add 2 hours, 13 minutes; for low tide, add 3 hours, 30 minutes. From its intersection with the Atlantic ICW at Mile 987.8 and Mile Zero of the Okeechobee Waterway, the St. Lucie River heads westward before turning to the north for a few miles at Okeechobee Mile 0.5. Aids to navigation are often relocated and additional ones established to mark the best water in this area. Take time to observe all aids and do not become confused if they do not exactly match your chart.

If turning west toward Stuart and the Okeechobee Waterway, flashing red buoy "2" and green can buoy "3," southwest of flashing red "240," are the first markers in the St. Lucie River. In 2017, shoaling between 5 feet and 7 feet at mean low water was found over a bar between these two markers. More water has been observed on the green side. The nuns and cans are moved regularly to mark the deeper water. Buoy "4" has been replaced with a temporary unlit buoy and relocated to mark the best water. Always honor the markers, but especially in this area.

Be particularly alert for large wakes when traveling between The Crossroads area (where the St. Lucie River meets the ICW) and the entrance to Manatee Pocket. This short, but narrow, stretch is often crowded with powerboats speeding to or from the ocean via the St. Lucie Inlet.

Deep water in the channel starts past Manatee Pocket. Tidal range is only about a foot, but the strong current bears watching although it loses force as you proceed up the St. Lucie River.

## Manatee Pocket

Manatee Pocket is little more than .5 mile from the ICW and is often visited by cruisers traveling north and south on the ICW. Considered an all-weather anchorage, it is a delightful boating area where you can usually find dockage.

**NAVIGATION:** Use Chart 11428. There is a channel straight up the middle of Manatee Pocket of approximately 100 feet wide with a 10- to 12-foot depth. Remember, the entire Manatee Pocket is an Idle-Speed/No-Wake Zone, which also includes dinghies.

HINCKLEY YACHT
SERVICES STUART

MARINER CAY MARINA

SAILFISH MARINA
OF STUART

Manatee Pocket

Port Salerno, a small town at the head of Manatee Pocket, features several restaurants, a post office, a marine electronics store, a bank, a barbershop and a grocery store. Manatee Pocket is also home to the Chapman School of Seamanship, which offers courses and programs for recreational boaters, along with its vocational offerings in the maritime field.

**Dockage:** North of Manatee Pocket, on Willoughby Creek, is Whiticar Boat Works Inc., which sells diesel and is a repair/service facility.

The family-owned and -operated Sailfish Marina of Stuart is the first marina on the right when entering Manatee Pocket and the closest marina to the St. Lucie Inlet. They offer transient dockage, gas and diesel fuel, a well-stocked bait and tackle shop, fishing charters and a full-service boatyard.

Farther in on the right, Mariner Cay Marina accepts transients and has gas and diesel fuel, as well as restroom and laundry facilities and a pool. Their fixed docks are set in a gated community.

To the south is Pirate's Cove Resort & Marina with slips and fuel (both gas and diesel). Hinckley Yacht Services Stuart, on the opposite shore, offers fuel, repair service (150-ton lift) and transient slips. They have on-site experts in painting, fiberglass, electronics, rigging and canvas and upholstery.

At the split in the pocket is Stuart Corinthian Yacht Club (eastern branch), which will accept transients if space is available (only two reserved spots reported). Both Port Salerno Marina on the western shore and A&J Boat Works (western branch) are repair/service yards and do not accept transients. Manatee Marina has a seawall for transients, sells fuel and has an on-site restaurant.

**Anchorage:** Except in a few spots near shore, depths are a uniform 5 to 6 feet, with a soft mud bottom. Take care that your anchor sets well in the mud. The most popular anchorage is in the bay between Mariner Cay Marina and Pirate's Cove Resort & Marina. Anchoring in Manatee Pocket is limited to 72 hours and the restriction is enforced. If anyone approaches you, make sure you have a copy of Florida Statute 327.02 on board which defines "liveaboard."

Just beyond the Pirate's Cove Resort & Marina docks is a tiny waterfront pier distinguished by a sign that says, "MOORING LIMITED TO ONE HOUR." It can be used by dinghies or by craft up to about 40 feet if dinghies are not blocking the end of the pier.

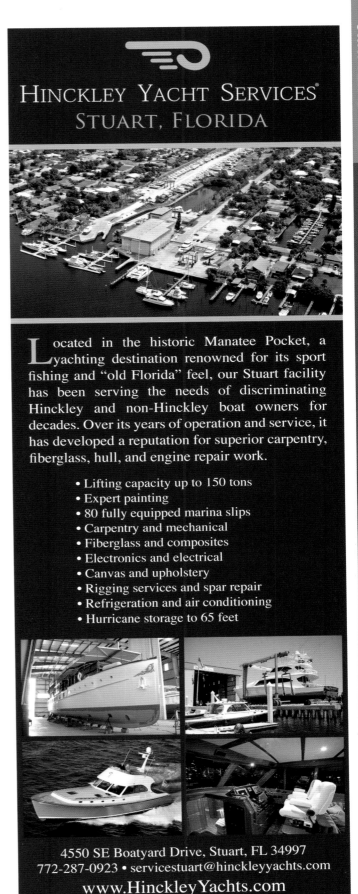

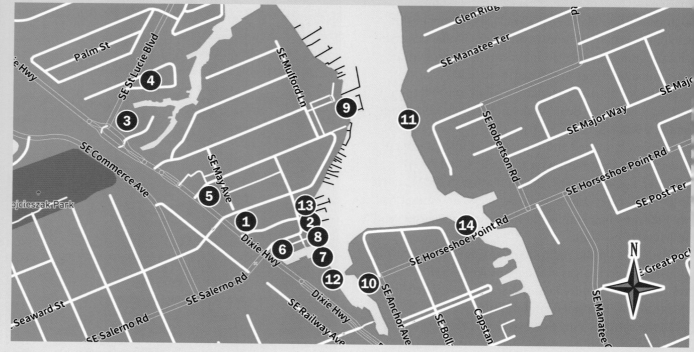

| SERVICES | |
|---|---|
| 1 | Post Office |
| **ATTRACTIONS** | |
| 2 | Fish House Art Center |
| 3 | Geoffrey C. Smith Galleries |
| **SHOPPING** | |
| 4 | Chapman School of Seamanship |

| | |
|---|---|
| 5 | Stuart Angler Bait & Tackle |
| **DINING** | |
| 6 | Manatee Island Bar and Grill |
| 7 | Shrimpers Grill & Raw Bar |
| 8 | The Twisted Tuna |
| 9 | Pirates Loft Restaurant |

| MARINAS | |
|---|---|
| 9 | Pirate's Cove Resort & Marina |
| 10 | A&J Boat Works |
| 11 | Hinckley Yacht Services Stuart |
| 12 | Manatee Marina |
| 13 | Port Salerno Marine |
| 14 | Stuart Corinthian Yacht Club |

Founded in the 1920s, Port Salerno was initially a commercial fishing village. It now has become world famous for its bill fishing tournaments. If you are in need of service, practically any marine service or specialty can be found here. Other attractions, shopping and facilities can be found in Stuart, only a short cab ride away.

The village of Port Salerno has a designated working waterfront dock area where commercial fishermen continue to work from the town docks. You can see them heading out each morning, but the village is now known for its resorts and marinas and marine repair facilities. It has all of the boat repair facilities any yacht owner might need. A visit to one of these facilities makes an interesting diversion, and the boats are magnificent.

**Attractions:** The town of Port Salerno and all its resources are easily accessed from the local marinas. While you are here you might want to visit one of the

local art galleries within easy walking distance of the town landing. The famous bronze sculptor Geoffrey Smith has a gallery in downtown Stuart that is open to the public and has a studio at 4545 SE Dixie Hwy. (772-283-8336, by appointment only). The waterfront Fish House Art Center (772-223-6303), a former working commercial fish processing facility that has been transformed into an eclectic center for working artists and crafters with studios where visitors can purchase freshly completed works of art. There is also a popular outdoor coffee, beer & wine café with live entertainment and a fantastic view of Manatee Pocket.

Sandsprit Park is a convenient landing point to take your pets ashore for some exercise. You can land at the floating piers of the ramp, or on the beach next to the launching ramps. If you have more time to explore the area in your dinghy, you will want to go to St. Lucie

Inlet State Park. This park is only accessible by boat. The entrance pier is about .75 miles south of the St. Lucie Inlet. This park is one of the very few preserved Atlantic Coast barrier islands. Whether it is beach combing, snorkeling or bird watching, this park will fascinate you.

**Shopping:** Stuart Angler Bait & Tackle is within walking distance to the marinas if you need fishing supplies or ice. Provisioning options further afield include Publix Super Market at Cove Shopping Center (5893 SE Federal Hwy, 772-287-9355) and Walmart Supercenter (4001 SE Federal Hwy., 772-288-4749). There is also a Bealle's Department Store (5803 Southeast Federal Hwy., 722-223-8205). Harbor Freight (3424 SE Federal Hwy., 772-220-9414) has a wide assortment of tools and hardware. Transportation will be required to access any of these businesses.

A light industrial park located just .75 mile from Manatee Pocket hosts a wide assortment of marine businesses. Here you will find carpentry shops, prop shops, metal fabricators, fiberglass repairs, marine electronics and hardware, and canvas shops, many of whom have moved here from locations further south. Well-known names such as Scopinich, Whiticar, Hinckley, Rupp, Jim Smith and Bonadeo call Stuart home, helping establish the Stuart area as a major boating manufacturing and service center.

Bargain hunters looking for a good used boat may want to check out Chapman School of Seamanship's collection of 75 to 100 boats donated to the school (4343 SE St. Lucie Blvd., 800-225-2841). The Chapman website (chapman.org) contains course offerings and a list of the donated boats offered for sale, plus information about the maritime library and maritime artifacts collection.

**Dining:** With Port Salerno's reputation as a commercial fishing center it is not surprising that the local eateries specialize in seafood. They are all a short walk from most marinas, and they can be accessed from the anchorage if you take your dinghy to the public pier at the town dock.

For a tropical atmosphere with outdoor dining, a dock and great views, you have many choices: Pirate's Loft Restaurant (at Pirate's Cove Resort & Marina, 772-223-5048); Shrimpers Grill & Raw Bar (4903 SE Dixie Hwy., 772-220-3287); and Manatee Island Grill (4817 SE Dixie Hwy., 772-872-7288). Many of these venues offer live music various nights throughout the week.

The largest family owned and operated waterfront restaurant in Martin County is The Twisted Tuna (772-600-7239). Lunch and dinner are served seven days a week. The restaurant is situated directly on Manatee Pocket (4290 SE Salerno Rd.) and has several outdoor waterfront dining areas that are both smoking and pet friendly. They use only local produce and bake their own breads. They offer complimentary dockage with your meal.

If you are here in late January, be sure to attend the Port Salerno Seafood Festival. Most of the fish cooked and served during the festival are caught and cleaned by the local watermen.

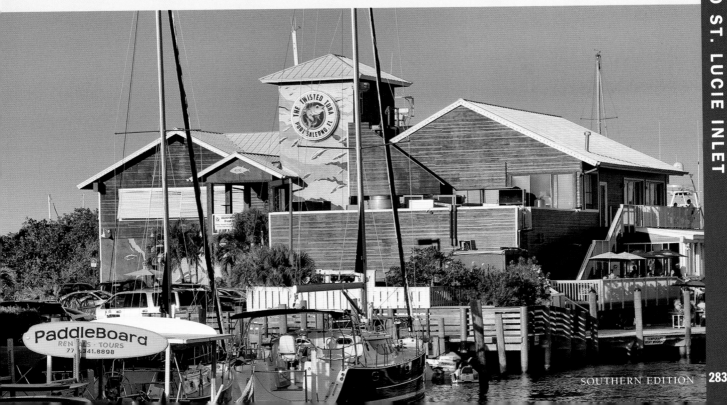

## To Stuart and the Okeechobee Waterway

Stuart, tucked back along the St. Lucie River, is barely visible, yet it is as well equipped as almost any port on the Atlantic coast and contains a sizable winter boat colony. Marine facilities and shore activities are a vital part of the community, and protection is good. Beyond that is the St. Lucie Canal and Lock, leading to the Okeechobee Waterway (described in detail in the next chapter).

**NAVIGATION:** Use Chart 11428. Where the St. Lucie River opens up and the long finger of Sewalls Point stretches downstream on the east side, the high ground is heavily wooded, with estates, both large and small, along the landscaped terrain.

The west side is equally attractive, residential and fronted by many private docks where property owners berth their vessels. Additional navigational aids, red daybeacons "6A" and "12A," were added within the last few years to better mark the shoaling along the natural channel and are not shown on older charts.

Note the shoal area shown on the chart between the ICW and the St. Lucie River's Hell Gate (at flashing green daybeacon "17"). The dredged channel splits these extensive shoals inside Sewalls Point (where tides, incidentally, run about 1 hour behind Stuart), so follow the markers carefully as you enter.

One bridge crosses the St. Lucie River along the 6 miles between Manatee Pocket and downtown Stuart. The **Evans Crary (SR A1A) Bridge** (65-foot fixed vertical clearance) at the town of Sewalls Point is also called the St. Lucie River Bridge. The channel runs just west of the highest point on the bridge.

Continuing upriver, green daybeacon "23" and flashing green daybeacon "23A," just east of the Roosevelt (U.S. 1) Bridge (also called the New Roosevelt Bridge), can be difficult to locate. Skippers should take special care to locate these markers before getting too close to the bridge.

Beyond Stuart, three bridges are clustered together within a distance of 800 feet: the **Roosevelt (U.S. 1) Bridge** (65-foot fixed vertical clearance); **Florida East Coast (FEC) Railroad Bridge** (with a 7-foot closed vertical clearance); and the **Old Roosevelt (Dixie Highway) Bascule Bridge** (with a 14-foot closed vertical clearance).

The FEC Railroad Bridge is normally open but closes automatically when a train approaches. The draw opens on signal at the Old Roosevelt Bridge, except when the adjacent FEC Railroad Bridge is in the closed position

for a scheduled opening, when the draw need not open. It must open immediately upon opening of the railroad bridge to pass all accumulated vessels. Better yet, just call and ask (772-692-0321).

To complicate matters, the FEC Railroad Bridge has a horizontal clearance (width) of only 50 feet, compared to the Old Roosevelt Bascule Bridge's horizontal clearance of 80 feet. With little in the way of a turning basin prior to the Old Roosevelt Bascule Bridge, and with marine traffic and currents running, passage through the two bridges can be tricky, especially from the wider Roosevelt to the narrower railroad bridge. Exercise care.

A turn to starboard, after passing through the old Roosevelt Bridge, takes you off the Okeechobee Waterway and up the North Fork of the St. Lucie River. This can be a very pleasant side trip if your cruising schedule allows you the time.

A turn to the south and past the **Palm City (SR 714) Bridge** (54-foot fixed vertical clearance) and the **Indian Street (SW Martin Hwy.) Bridge** (55-foot fixed vertical clearance) takes you to on a cross-Florida journey on the Okeechobee Waterway. Note that the Indian Street Bridge is also called SW Martin Highway Bridge.

**Dockage/Moorings:** Just before the New Roosevelt Bridge are Central Marine Stuart (at Mile 7) and Loggerhead Marina–Stuart (at Mile 7.2), located across the river from Stuart. Central Marine is a boat dealer and repair/service yard that does not offer transient dockage. Space is available on the floating docks at the 300-slip Loggerhead Marina for transients and long-term rentals. They also sell fuel and have a well-stocked ship store and an on-site restaurant.

Just inside Britt Point (due east of green daybeacon "5"), are three facilities: Apex Marina–Stuart, Waterway Marina and Harbor Inn & Marina. Call ahead for slip availability; Harbor Inn has slips for hotel guests only.

Located 3.7 miles northwest of the Old Roosevelt Bridge on the North Fork of the St. Lucie River is the Club Med Sandpiper Bay Marina, where transients are welcome. They offer fuel both gas and diesel, a laundry, and some supplies (including beer and wine) and can accommodate vessels to 150 feet. They also offer discounted entrance passes and memberships to the all-inclusive Club Med, which has several restaurants, bars, swimming pools, golf, a spa and water sports rentals, including jet skis, tubing, fishing, sailing, water skiing and wake boarding.

# GOIN' ASHORE: STUART, FL

| SERVICES |  |
|---|---|
| 1 | Post Office |
| **ATTRACTIONS** | |
| 2 | Arts Council of Martin County |
| 3 | Lyric Theater |
| 4 | Road to Victory Military Museum |

| SHOPPING |  |
|---|---|
| 5 | Stuart Heritage Museum |
| **SHOPPING** | |
| 6 | Downtown Stuart Shopping Center |
| **DINING** | |
| 7 | Black Marlin |
| 8 | Osceola Street Cafe |

| |  |
|---|---|
| 9 | Pelican Café |
| 10 | Riverwalk Café |
| 11 | Sailor's Return |
| **MARINAS** | |
| 12 | Sunset Bay Marina & Anchorage |

The countryside surrounding Stuart provides a little bit of everything for which Florida is noted: citrus, winter vegetables, flowers and cattle. As the Martin County seat, Stuart has most of the facilities found in an urban center, including Martin Memorial Hospital, which accepts emergency patients at its own dock (4-foot dockside depths).

The region's agricultural importance notwithstanding, the emphasis throughout the area has gradually shifted from farming to sportfishing. Although Stuart's claim to being the "Sailfish Capital of the World" is sometimes disputed by other Florida cities, no one would deny that both its outside and inside waters provide outstanding

fishing. Charter boats sail daily out of Stuart, Manatee Pocket and other nearby ports. Stuart has gained further prominence as a center of custom sportfishing boatbuilding. Several yards still build fine wooden yachts. A visit to one of these facilities makes an interesting diversion, and the boats are magnificent.

**Attractions:** Along with fishing and other water-intensive pleasures, Stuart is famed for its historic and pedestrian-friendly downtown. In historic downtown, a fountain in the shape of a sailfish marks the start of a group of unique galleries, cafés, restaurants, and shops on Flagler and Osceola Streets. One street over is the 2-mile-long wooden Riverwalk, where you can enjoy free concerts on the weekends, fishing off the pier and access to waterfront restaurants and shopping.

Start with an overview of the area at the Stuart Heritage Museum at 161 SW Flagler Street (772-220-4600). Built in 1901, the museum celebrates the town's history with more than 10,000 artifacts that stretch back to 1880, when Stuart was first settled. Located in the Stuart Feed Store, the free museum is open daily from 10:00 a.m. to 3:00 p.m. Another interesting museum is the Road to Victory Military Museum at 319 E. Stypmann Blvd. (772-334-2990). This modest museum is dedicated to those who have served in the uniformed services and includes displays including dioramas, flags, weapons and vehicles.

For performance art, the restored Lyric Theater (59 SW Flagler Ave., 772-286-7827) features shows and concerts, as well as movies and art cinema (a continuing series of art films, documentaries, independent films and hard to find international cinema). The Barn Theater at 2400 SE Ocean Blvd. (transportation required) performs comedies and musicals, year-round (772-287-4884).

At 80 SE Ocean Blvd. is the Arts Council of Martin County, which keeps an active calendar of events.

ArtsFest, held annually in February at Memorial Park, is both the biggest celebration of the arts and the largest fundraiser for the Council.

If you are visiting on a Sunday, the Stuart Green Market and Live Music event is held from 9:00 a.m. until 1:00 p.m. near City Hall.

**Shopping:** Publix Supermarket is at 746 SW Federal Hwy. (772-221-3922) for provisioning. They have groceries, a deli and bakery. Stuart Ace Hardware at 975 SE Federal Hwy. stocks tools, supplies and more. (772-287-3664). Visit forhistoricdowntownstuart.com for complete shopping suggestions in the downtown area.

**Dining:** Local favorites here include Pelican Café (351 SW Flagler Ave., 772-283-3133) and Osceola Street Café (26 SW Osceola St., 772-283-6116). Sailor's Return is a good and popular waterfront restaurant located in the Sunset Bay Marina (772-872-7250). Riverwalk Café and Oyster Bar is located at 201 SW St. Lucie Ave. (772-221-1511) in the Historic District. Reservations are highly recommended. Black Marlin (53 SW Osceola St., 772-286-3126) is also popular.

# St. Lucie River, FL

Column groups: **Dockage** (Largest Vessel Accommodated · VHF Channel Monitored · Transient Berths / Total Berths · Approach / Dockside Depth (reported) · Floating Docks) · **Supplies** (Groceries, Ice, Marine Supplies, Snacks · Gas / Diesel · Repairs: Hull, Engine, Propeller) · **Services** (Lift (tonnage), Crane, Rail · Laundry, Pool, Showers, Courtesy Car · Min / Max Amps · Pump-Out Station · Nearby: Grocery Store, Motel, Restaurant)

| Marina | Phone | Largest Vessel | VHF Monitored | Transient / Total Berths | Approach / Dockside Depth | Floating Docks | Gas / Diesel | Groceries, Ice, Marine Supplies, Snacks | Repairs | Lift, Crane, Rail | Min / Max Amps | Laundry, Pool, Showers, Car | Pump-Out | Nearby |
|---|---|---|---|---|---|---|---|---|---|---|---|---|---|---|
| **ST. LUCIE RIVER** | | | | Dockage | | | Supplies | | | Services | | | | |
| 1. Central Marine Stuart 7.0 | 772-692-2000 | 50 | – | call/20 | 6/5 | – | – | IM | HP | L50 | 30/50 | – | – | GMR |
| 2. Loggerhead Marina - Stuart [internet][wifi] 7.2 | 772-692-4000 | 90 | 16/68 | 24/300 | 8/6 | F | GD | IS | – | – | 30/100 | LPS | P | MR |
| **ST. LUCIE RIVER – NORTH FORK** | | | | | | | | | | | | | | |
| 3. Apex Marina–Stuart [wifi] 7.5 | 772-692-7577 | 120 | – | call/53 | 7/7 | – | – | M | HEP | L60 | 30/100 | – | – | R |
| 4. Waterway Marina 7.7 | 772-220-2185 | 65 | – | 51/51 | 7/6 | – | – | – | – | – | 30/50 | S | P | GMR |
| 5. Harbor Inn & Marina [internet][wifi] 7.8 | 772-692-1200 | 60 | 16/68 | /80 | 10/8 | – | – | – | – | – | 30/50 | PS | – | MR |
| 6. Sandpiper Bay Marina [wifi] | 772-335-7875 | 150 | 16/72 | 6/65 | 8/8 | – | GD | IMS | HEP | – | 30/100 | LPS | P | GMR |
| **ST. LUCIE RIVER – SOUTH FORK** | | | | | | | | | | | | | | |
| 7. Sunset Bay Marina & Anchorage [internet][wifi] 8 | 772-283-9225 | 120 | 16/69 | 60/198 | 8/8 | F | GD | GIMS | – | – | 30/50 | LS | P | GMR |
| 8. Meridian Marina & Yacht Club | 772-221-8198 | 40 | 05 | 2/2 | 6/5 | F | G | IM | HEP | L11 | 30/30 | LS | – | – |
| 9. Riverwatch Marina and Boatyard 9.6 | 772-286-3456 | 80 | 16 | 4/28 | 6/5 | F | GD | IMS | HEP | L60 | 30/50 | S | – | GMR |

[monitor icon] Internet Access  [wifi] Wireless Internet Access  WG Waterway Guide Cruising Club Partner  *(Information in the table is provided by the facilities.)*
See WaterwayGuide.com for current rates, fuel prices, web site addresses, and other up-to-the-minute information.

N 27° 14' 42.76' W 80° 18' 53.43'

Welcome

*Sandpiper Bay Marina*

sandpiperbaymarina.com

Immediately past the Old Roosevelt Bridge on the south shore, you will find the Sunset Bay Marina and Anchorage. The very modern marina offers transient slips as well as 69 moorings. The facilities ashore are top notch with a fuel dock, marine store, laundry facilities and a well-appointed captain's lounge. There is a popular restaurant on the premises called Sailor's Return (772-872-7250). It has a wonderful menu, and you can dine either inside or outside. The marina also offers loaner bikes and a shuttle van, which runs twice weekly (on Tuesday and Friday). The shuttle takes you to Publix supermarket, Harbor Freight, West Marine and Walmart.

Before reaching the Palm City Bridge (54-foot fixed vertical clearance) on the South Fork, a channel on the western shore marked by private daybeacons leads to Meridian Marina & Yacht Club. It has gasoline but limited dockage and is primarily a repair and storage facility. Across from Palm City, just south of the Palm City Bridge, a marked channel leads into Riverwatch Marina, with 6-foot depths in the approach channel and 5-foot depths in the docking basin. Transient dockage and fuel is available.

While in Stuart, the pump-out boat "M.S. Poop" will come to you. Call 772-260-8326 or use VHF Channel 16 to arrange a time to receive your free pump-out.

**Anchorage:** Boats anchor on the southwest side of Sewalls Point, at Hooker Cove in 7- to 8-foot depths. Make sure that your anchor is set; currents tend to run swiftly here. Just north of the St. Lucie River Bridge, in Hoggs Cove, protection is good from northerlies and

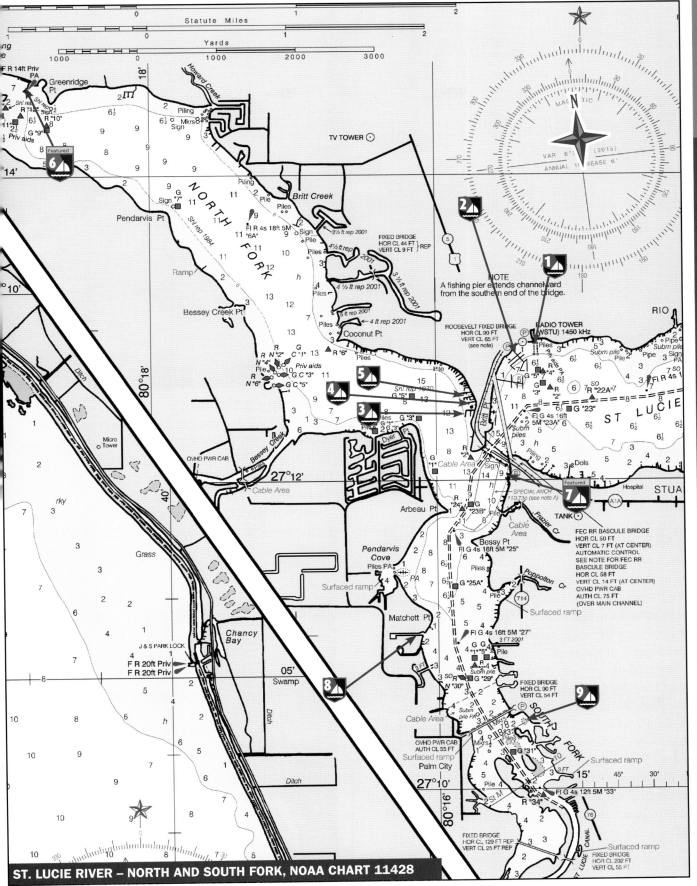

ST. LUCIE RIVER – NORTH AND SOUTH FORK, NOAA CHART 11428

SUNSET BAY MARINA &
ANCHORAGE

easterlies. Watch the charted rocky shoal off Pisgah Hill, and set the anchor in 7 to 9 feet of water. If you plan an early morning start to the east, it is better to anchor here rather than in Stuart past the Roosevelt Bridge. Here, you will have the sun in your eyes for a shorter time. The early sun can also make spotting aids to navigation difficult.

In Stuart, Riverside Pier offers free dockage for up to 4 hours with 5-to 6-foot depths. It is possible to anchor most anywhere in the North Fork but the best anchorage is up North Fork Cove, past the marinas at Britt Point. Kitching Cove, past Sandpiper Bay Marina, provides a fine anchorage in 6 to 7 feet of water. At the north end of the anchorage, take a scenic dinghy trip to the headwaters of the river.

Beyond the bridges, on the South Fork, you will find very good holding in Pendarvis Cove. There is an excellent dinghy dock just inside Fraser Creek, just a .5-mile walk from Publix, laundry, restaurants and hardware. You can tie your dinghy to the wall at Frazer Creek Park and walk the dogs. There is water at the fish cleaning station and a dumpster in the park. This anchorage has reportedly gotten more crowded recently due to boats displaced at the new mooring field in Sunset Bay.

## Cruising Options

Those wishing to continue their journey on the Okeechobee Waterway should refer to the "Okeechobee Waterway" (next chapter), which continues the cross-Florida journey from the St. Lucie Lock to Fort Myers. If you wish to return to the Atlantic ICW for the trip south, skip the next chapter and go straight to Chapter 7: "St. Lucie Inlet to Pompano Beach."

# SUNSET BAY
## MARINA & ANCHORAGE

## WELCOME HOME

- Transient and Long Term Dockage
- 69 Mooring & Dinghy Dock
- Floating & fixed docks
- 24 hour security
- Laundry & Shower Facilities
- Waterside patio with BBQ grill
- Salty's Ship Store
- Concierge Services & Shuttle Bus
- Free Wifi Marina-wide
- Pump-out facilities
- Protective Breakwater
- Boater's lounge/meeting room with HDTV & DVD
- High-speed fueling with Diesel & Non-ethanol Gas
- Pet-Friendly
- Walking distance to Downtown & Grocery Store
- Dock side lifts available up to 24k pounds
- Sailor's Return Restaurant on site 772.872.7250

sunsetbaymarinaandanchorage.com
615. SW Anchorage Way | Stuart, FL 34994
Latitude 27°12' N | Longitude 60°15' W
**772.283.9225**

# Okeechobee Waterway

 Mile 0–Mile 144    FL: Channel 09

**CHARTS** 11427, 11428

The Okeechobee Waterway (OCWW) is considered by many to be the dividing line between Central Florida and South Florida. When traveling from the north, this is where you will begin to see greater changes in the climate and vegetation.

Opened in 1937, the Okeechobee Waterway offers a chance to see rural Florida, with small towns much as they were early in the last century. The scenery varies as the passage progresses from east to west from river to canal, to lake, to canal and back to river again. On the Okeechobee Waterway, ranches and big commercial farms alternate with moss-hung wilderness, while bustling boomtowns coexist alongside sleepy villages that popped up long before Miami was built.

With its backwaters and "bywaters," its islands and coves, and its flora and fauna, the Caloosahatchee River was once the only way to get from the Gulf of Mexico to Central Florida, via small steamers and freighters. Some still consider the Caloosahatchee (76.6 miles) the most scenic part of the OCWW, thanks to the old river's

off-channel oxbows. Small cruise ships now occasionally make the trip.

For the boater, the Okeechobee Waterway and Lake Okeechobee provide quite a transition from the pace of busy coastal cities to the tranquility of Florida's heartland. The OCWW is also a tremendously efficient route from the east coast to the west coast of Florida, the only alternative being the long trek down around the Keys and up across Florida Bay. The OCWW is 154 or 165 statute miles (134 or 144 miles), from the Atlantic Ocean to the Gulf of Mexico, depending on whether you take Route 1 across Lake Okeechobee or the Rim Route (Route 2) along the lake's southern shore. Use the latter at your own risk because of debris and depth.

The OCWW can be divided into three distinct sections:

1. From Mile Zero (the intersection of the OCWW and the ICW at St. Lucie Inlet) down the South Fork of the St. Lucie River to the St. Lucie Canal to Lake Okeechobee.

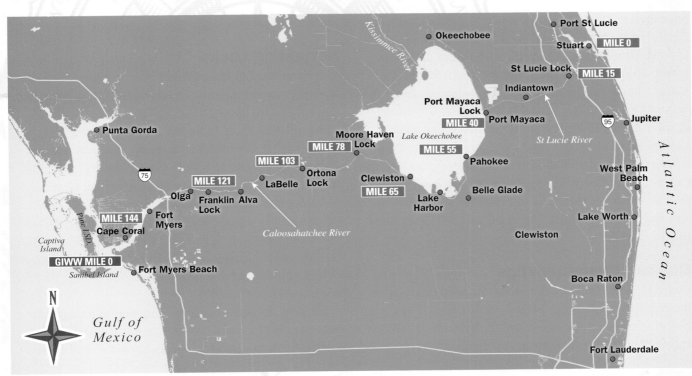

2. Lake Okeechobee itself (either the "Open-Water Route" directly across the lake, or the "Rim Route" along the lake's south shore).

3. From Clewiston through the Caloosahatchee Canal and down the Caloosahatchee River to the end of the OCWW in San Carlos Bay, at Mile Zero of the Gulf Intracoastal Waterway (GIWW) heading north.

As mentioned before, on Lake Okeechobee you have a choice of two routes for crossing. Route 1 is an open-water crossing (34 miles with 7.5-foot controlling depths in spring 2017). Route 2, which is also referred to as the Rim Route (44 miles, with 6-foot depths in spring 2017), follows the shoreline south from Port Mayaca Lock, on the eastern shore, before entering the tree-protected rim canal and running past Clewiston to the City of Moore Haven. If your boat has a very shallow draft (4 feet or less), you can try Route 2 but be aware of the challenges. It is our suggestion that you call the Army Corps of Engineers in Clewiston (863-983-8101) to get the latest information about the lake and the different routes. The good news? There's no tide in the lake.

## Cruising Characteristics

Chart 11428 covers the area from the intersection with the Atlantic ICW to Fort Myers, while Chart 11427 continues down the Caloosahatchee River to the GIWW and the Gulf of Mexico. From that point, cruisers have the option of moving north on the GIWW to the Sun Coast, outside in the Gulf to the Big Bend or the Panhandle, or south to southwest Florida and the Keys.

Note that much of Chart 11428 is at a scale of 1:80,000, which is different from the charts adjoining at either end, 11472 and 11427, both of which are at 1:40,000, or the usual ICW scale. Chart 11428 has two insets at its eastern end and one where it reaches Lake Okeechobee, plus an extension at its western end; all of these are at various larger scales.

## Navigating Locks

The water level in Lake Okeechobee is higher than anywhere on the Atlantic Ocean or Gulf ICW. Whether you are headed east or west, you ascend through the locks to Lake Okeechobee and then descend after you leave. The OCWW has five modern, spacious and well-handled locks and more than 20 bridges, ranging from electronic controlled to hand operated. Normally, locks operate between 7:00 a.m. and 5:00 p.m.. Check in advance for current lock-through instructions. Visit the Waterway Guide Explorer (waterwayguide.com) for detailed information on locks before you go. Please note that the lockage schedule varies depending on lake levels.

Locking through is simple compared to procedures necessary in the northeastern U.S. canal systems. Lock personnel furnish all necessary lines, and regular boat fenders will suffice when locking through. Allow approximately 15 minutes once inside a lock. The OCWW locks are easier to transit when you are the only boat locking through, and the lock attendant will give you the windward dock line first when winds are strong. Gusty winds can set up a surge in the locks, so use caution. The attendant also might warn you that you could be locking through with a manatee or an alligator.

Also, note that the Army Corps of Engineers requires boat operators to turn off radar units during lockage to avoid exposing lock personnel to possible radiation risks. It is recommended, however, that engines be left running.

When you reach the mooring dolphins and the sign Arrival Point before each lock, contact the lockmaster on VHF Channel 13. Give your vessel's name and direction and request lockage. At that time, they will inform you of the current lockage status and estimate your wait time. It could be as long as 45 minutes to an hour in the unusual case where they have just started locking through from your side. The lockmaster will also instruct you "port-to" or "starboard-to," indicating which side of the lock to steer to and how to arrange your fenders; the lockmaster will then indicate for you to enter when the traffic light is green.

If you receive no response on VHF, sound two long and two short blasts. (Clewiston Lock is used to leave the waterway and reach the facilities at Clewiston and Roland Martin Marina & Resort; it is the only lock without a VHF radio.) At each lock, for the smallest of craft, there is a pull-cord hanging down by a sign marking its location. The green light is your signal to enter the lock. The lockmaster will then hand or drop down to you (depending on the water level), a bow line and a stern line, or the lines will be hanging down from the top of the lock's sidewall, and you will have to steer to them and pick them up. (Keep a boathook handy.) Remember that the first boat into the lock should be the first boat out of the lock. Don't get too anxious.

Be prepared for moderate turbulence as water rushes in or out of the lock. Two people can safely handle a small or medium-sized boat, but an extra pair of hands is always useful on large boats. Single-handing through the locks is not safe and is strongly discouraged.

Check when you are doing your pre-cruise planning, and recheck again at the first lock to make sure the entire OCWW is open. Maintenance on the locks is normally conducted each summer, and through-passage from the East Coast to the Gulf Coast may not

be possible for as long as several months. During such times, Lake Okeechobee may be accessible from one side or the other, but not both. During a drought, lockage may be restricted depending on water supply. Call the Army Corps of Engineers at Clewiston (863-983-8101) for information or go to saj.usace.army.mil and select "Coastal Navigation" and then "Navigation Projects and Studies." Closures are usually well publicized and, as always, waterwayguide.com is a very good source.

## Depths and Clearances

The depth of water in Lake Okeechobee can vary widely as a result of rainfall onto the drainage area to the north and the lake itself. As a result of an ongoing drought, the level fell to a record low of 3.36 feet in mid-2007–the lowest level ever recorded. The Army Corps of Engineers and the South Florida Water Management District manage the level of the lake. There are a variety of ecological, environmental and economic reasons for various levels, and some of them conflict with others.

The depths charted in Lake Okeechobee are based on a datum of 12.56 feet. If skippers know the lake level, they can determine the difference between the datum and the current level and modify the charted depths accordingly. Depths in the sections between dams on either side of the lake vary slightly with lake level changes, but the differences are seldom enough to affect navigation.

The Florida East Coast (Port Mayaca) Railroad Lift Bridge, Mile 38.0, sets the 49-foot controlling vertical clearance (when open) of the OCWW. If you have any questions about clearance, call the Army Corps of Engineers at Clewiston (863-983-8101). Sailboaters can have their mast unstepped at Stuart, or wait and have it done at the Indiantown Marina, which is closer to the Port Mayaca Bridge.

## Navigating the Okeechobee Waterway

With the exception of a lake crossing in imperfect weather, passage along the OCWW is easy, piloting is simple and navigational aids are adequate for daytime running. Aids to navigation are numbered in several sequences from east to west all the way across; even-numbered red aids are on the starboard side (as they are southbound along the Atlantic ICW). Conversely, leave red aids to port eastbound on the OCWW, as you would when northbound on the ICW. Yellow squares and triangles are shown on daybeacons and buoys.

Nighttime navigation is not recommended as shoals and deadheads (partially submerged objects) are obscured. Fortunately, ample facilities and occasional anchorages make after-dark travel unnecessary. Some of the bridges operate daily from 6:00 a.m. to 10:00 p.m. and require a minimum of 3 hours notice to open at other times. Phone numbers are posted on each bridge; calls are best made during normal office hours. You can use adjacent dolphins for tie-ups. Make note that tying up to the dolphins can be tricky, and the dolphins are there for commercial boats and tugs with barges to use in case of any delays. They have priority.

Currents are not a problem on the OCWW, except for the turbulence that occurs when locks are opened. Average tides at the mouth of the St. Lucie River are 1.1 feet; 1.3 feet at Fort Myers; and 2.4 feet at Punta Rassa (at the western end of the waterway) near Mile Zero of the GIWW heading north.

## Dockage & Anchorage

Reservations are recommended at marinas on the OCWW. Anchoring in approach areas to some of the locks is also possible, and the lockmasters can provide local knowledge concerning depths and conditions.

In the last few years, many boats cruising the OCWW have found anchoring limits are being enforced by the Army Corps of Engineers. Officers have been instructed to enforce a "one-night-only" policy for anchoring. You may anchor for 24 hours, but the following day your vessel needs to show one day's travel distance before anchoring again. This applies to the OCWW between the St. Lucie Lock and the W. R. Franklin Lock, including all of Lake Okeechobee (OCWW Miles 15 to 121.4).

The ordinance does not allow for weather delays, rest days or maintenance needs, although it does make an exception "in case of emergency." The necessity for that exception would be up to a Park Ranger. The penalties associated with a citation are not outlined in the *Local Notice to Mariners*; however, we have heard reports of $100 per day fines.

If your vessel is left unattended at anchor for more than 24 hours, it is subject to impoundment, according to the Notice. Meanwhile, expect to be asked to "move along" after anchoring along the OCWW; officers are telling boaters that they must continue down the OCWW or find a marina or other facility or risk a citation and fine. For updates on this somewhat contentious issue, stay tuned to navigation updates at waterwayguide.com

## Weather

Central Florida weather is generally mild. In winter, the prevailing wind is north to northeast, as opposed to summer, when wind is normally east to southeast, with very little rain except when cold fronts from the north pass through. Summer days are calm in the mornings, with occasional patchy fog; winds pick up at about 10:00 a.m. Afternoons often bring showers and thunderstorms, particularly late in the day, so it is a good idea to plan on getting in early. Hurricanes do occur in season–June through November–as well as other times.

Since Lake Okeechobee is the second largest freshwater lake located wholly in the continental United States (Lake Michigan is the largest), it can get nasty. You should know the forecast before you leave port. The continuous NOAA marine weather comes from West Palm Beach and Fort Myers on VHF Channel WX-3 and from Belle Glade on WX-2. In the last few years, weather has gotten substantially easier because of cell phones and tablets. There are also many very reliable apps.

## ■ ST. LUCIE CANAL

**NAVIGATION:** Use Chart 11428. The OCWW departs the South Fork of the St. Lucie River near this point and continues as the start of the St. Lucie Canal with the St. Lucie Lock at Mile 15 of the OCWW. Check for local information regarding the OCWW if you plan to proceed through any of the locks. In 2017, the lake levels provided channel depths across the lake of approximately 7.5 to 8.5 feet.

Route 2 was open in spring 2017. However, it is always a good idea to call the Army Corps of Engineers in Clewiston (863-983-8101) for the latest conditions. The water depths there are reported by our cruising editor to be 6.5 to 7.5 feet. The shallowest water on Route 2 is right at the beginning of the route when heading west. After about 1.5 miles, the water gets deeper (10-plus feet), but the Army Corps of Engineers warned that those who take this route do so at their own risk.

On Route 1 (heading west) the depth is shallowest just after leaving the Port Mayaca Lock for about one-half

# St. Lucie Canal, FL

| | | Largest Vessel Accommodated | VHF Channel Monitored | Transient Berths / Total Berths | Approach / Dockside Depth (reported) | Floating Docks | Gas / Diesel | Groceries, Ice, Marine Supplies, Snacks | Repairs: Hull, Engine, Propeller | Lift (tonnage), Crane, Rail | Min/Max Amps | Laundry, Pool, Showers, Courtesy Car | Pump-Out Station | Nearby: Grocery Store, Motel, Restaurant |
|---|---|---|---|---|---|---|---|---|---|---|---|---|---|---|
| **ST. LUCIE CANAL** | | | | **Dockage** | | | **Supplies** | | **Services** | | | | | |
| 1. American Custom Yachts Inc. WiFi 14.5 | 772-221-9100 | 135 | 16/68 | 6/25 | 8/8 | – | GD | M | HEP | L150,C | 50/100 | S | – | MR |
| 2. River Forest Yachting Center - Stuart WiFi 16 | 772-287-4131 | 150 | 16 | – | 10/9 | – | – | – | HEP | L66 | 30/100 | S | P | – |
| **INDIANTOWN** | | | | | | | | | | | | | | |
| 3. Indiantown Marina 🖳 WiFi 29 | 772-597-2455 | 120 | 16 | 10/34 | 8/8 | F | GD | GIMS | HEP | L50,C | 30/50 | LS | P | GMR |

🖳 Internet Access  WiFi Wireless Internet Access  **WG** Waterway Guide Cruising Club Partner  *(Information in the table is provided by the facilities.)*
See WaterwayGuide.com for current rates, fuel prices, web site addresses, and other up-to-the-minute information.

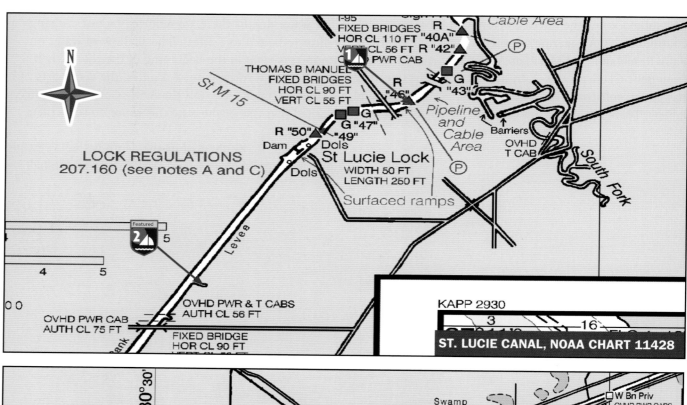

ST. LUCIE CANAL, NOAA CHART 11428

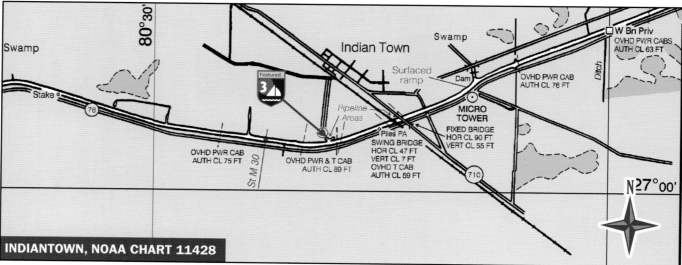

INDIANTOWN, NOAA CHART 11428

mile, then you will encounter 10 to 14 feet across the Lake. At daybeacon "9" approaching Clewiston, the depth will come up to 8 feet and remain there until you turn into the channel heading toward Moore Haven.

You can find navigation and lock schedule information at saj.usace.army.mil. Conditions can change, especially if tropical storms or hurricanes pass over Lake Okeechobee.

The canal carrying the OCWW up to Lake Okeechobee itself is deep and easy to traverse. You will pass under the **Indian St. (SW Martin Hwy.) Bridge** (55-foot fixed vertical clearance) at Mile 10.9, the **I-95 Twin Bridges** (56-foot fixed vertical clearance) at Mile 14 and the **Florida Turnpike Twin Bridges** (55-foot fixed vertical clearance) at Mile 14.5.

**Dockage:** American Custom Yachts, a full-service boatyard and custom builder, is located on the south shore between the bridges. It has limited space for transients and specializes in repairs or other services.

River Forest Yachting Center is located west of the St. Lucie Lock and offers transient dockage as well as a full range of on-site repair, maintenance and installation services. Be sure to call well in advance for availability of transient dockage. They have two freshwater locations with climate-controlled indoor storage buildings for 200 vessels from 20 to 90 feet. The marina offers a members-only Hurricane Club to offer boat owners safe harbor during hurricane conditions in both Stuart and LaBelle.

## St. Lucie Lock–OCWW Mile 15.1

**NAVIGATION:** Use Chart 11428. The **St. Lucie Lock** at Mile 15.1 operates on request from 7:00 a.m. to 5:00 p.m. (Last lockage is at 4:30 p.m.) Radio ahead or call the lock (772-287-2665) prior to your departure for current schedules. Waterway Guide also lists important updates to navigation at waterwayguide.com.

This first lock of the system lifts you approximately 13 feet. When approaching the No-Wake Zone entrance area, check the light system. If the light is red and a call on VHF Channel 13 or 16 does not get a response, give two long and then two short blasts, then wait well downstream in the standby area to avoid the discharge from the dam and lock. Many boats arrive at the lower side of this lock and then turn around and go back without locking through, so the lockmaster does not assume, even if he sees you arrive, that you wish to lock through. You must call him via VHF or horn.

On each side of each lock, there is a sign marked "Arrival Point." Enter slowly on the green signal and be prepared to accept lines fore and aft from the lockmaster. As the water level rises, maintain your position with care. Remember that the Army Corps of Engineers requires boat operators to turn off radar units during lockage to avoid exposing lock personnel to possible radiation risks. It is recommended, however, that engines be left running. Additional information may be obtained from the lockmaster for the route ahead.

A note of caution: The OCWW plays host not only to many varieties of fish but also to manatees (an endangered species), alligators and turtles of all sizes. The manatees frequently are "locked through," so take extra care if they are reported in the area.

**Dockage:** Immediately west of the St. Lucie Lock is a group of 8 slips for boats up to 35 feet, offering picnic and playground areas and nature trails. Four of the slips are first-come, first-served, and advance reservations can be made for the other four slips with the Army Corps of Engineers (877-444-6777). Reservations must be made at least 72 hours before arrival. Stays are limited to 2 weeks. If you do stay at these slips, be sure to go to the Visitor Center just east of the lock for interesting and instructive exhibits.

**Anchorage:** Directly across the OCWW from the Army Corps of Engineers slips at Mile 15, at the entrance to a narrow bay, is a quiet overnight anchorage for one boat with 8 foot depths and good holding in mud.

## Indiantown–OCWW Mile 29

The small community of Indiantown, less than 1 mile north of the river, has a post office, medical center, markets, banks and casual restaurants. Indiantown has lots of citrus groves and near the river is Owens Grove, selling excellent fruit and fresh-squeezed juices. It has a small gift shop, a muster of freely roaming peacocks and the historic Cracker House, a Florida pioneer farm home that can be toured. It is also the home of Payson Park, a premiere horse racing facility.

The Seminole Country Inn and Restaurant (15885 SW Warfield Blvd.) was built in 1925 by S. Davis Warfield, a railroad executive, and was used by his niece, Wallis Warfield Simpson, on her honeymoon with the Duke of Windsor, explaining why Main Street in Indiantown is named Warfield Boulevard. If you want to eat at the Seminole Inn, you need to make arrangements ahead of time. They are open for lunch on Monday through Saturday, dinner on Saturday evenings only, and brunch is served on Sundays. Reservations are definitely required (772-597-3777). You will need some form of land transportation to get there, but it is worth the effort.

**NAVIGATION:** Use Chart 11428. Approaching Indiantown from the east, you will first pass under the fixed **SR 76A Bridge** (56-foot vertical clearance) at Mile 17.1, then the **Indiantown (SR 710) Bridge** (55-foot vertical clearance) at Mile 28.1. At Mile 28.2 is the **Seaboard (Indiantown) Railroad Swing Bridge** with a 7-foot closed vertical clearance. The operator may anticipate you, but if it is closed, call on VHF Channel 09. If a train is approaching, you may be delayed, as the train always has the right-of-way. The bridge opens on signal between 6:00 a.m. and 10:00 p.m. and requires a 3-hour notice to open between 10:00 p.m. and 6:00 a.m. (772-597-3822). Less than 1 mile east of these bridges, on the north side of the canal, is a park with a boat ramp and a posted No-Wake Zone.

**Dockage:** A short distance beyond the railroad bridge in Indiantown is Indiantown Marina. For those intending to cross Lake Okeechobee via the direct route, this is the last marina until Clewiston, which is 35 miles

away. Indiantown Marina is a well-protected hurricane hole offering transient slips as well as long-term boat storage. They have a do-it-yourself and full service boat yard and sell all fuels. The staff is very accommodating and friendly. Skippers planning to overnight here should call ahead for availability.

## Port Mayaca–OCWW Mile 38

**NAVIGATION:** Use Chart 11428. At Mile 38.0, the **Florida East Coast (Port Mayaca) Railroad Lift Bridge** (49-foot open vertical clearance) sets the controlling overhead clearance for the OCWW. Elsewhere, at least 54 feet of overhead clearance can be carried. The bridge has 7-foot closed vertical clearance but is usually open.

Be sure to stay south of red daybeacon "52," as a ledge of rocks and submerged pilings runs from the marker to the northern bank of the canal. The **U.S. Hwy. 98 & 441 Bridge** (Mile 38.8) has a 55-foot fixed vertical clearance, and the **Port Mayaca Lock** is just a short distance ahead, serving as the entrance to the lake. Mooring dolphins provide the only place to make fast before reaching the lock, but they may be in use by barges.

At certain water levels, the Port Mayaca Lock is open at both ends, and on the flashing (or steady) green (or yellow) light, you may proceed through cautiously. You should contact the lockmaster on VHF Channel 16 or 13 before entering or if you have any questions. Eastbound boats may experience some difficulty with adverse winds and resulting seas. Under these conditions, entering the lock and making fast can be tricky. Until the lock is closed, waves tend to ricochet from wall to wall. Heading westbound is considerably easier, but if the winds are brisk, be prepared for a choppy exit. Operating hours are 7:00 a.m. to 5:00 p.m. with a last lock opening at 4:30 p.m. (561-924-2858).

**Anchorage:** Be warned that anchoring beyond the lock is precarious. A layover elsewhere would be a better plan. The mooring dolphins before the lock are a possibility for tie-up if not occupied by barges.

It might be possible to anchor in the mouth of the Port Mayaca Overflow Canal at OCWW Mile 36.6. You will find 7 feet of water here and all-around protection; however, there is only room for one to two boats here.

# ■ CROSSING LAKE OKEECHOBEE

Originally the headwaters of the Everglades, which author Marjorie Stoneman Douglas called "the river of grass," Lake Okeechobee is now the centerpiece of South Florida's water resource system. The lake is completely enclosed by an impressive levee system, officially named the Herbert Hoover Dike. The dike's construction began during the Hoover administration as a result of two disastrous hurricanes in the 1920s, when the lake was literally blown out of its banks.

Lake Okeechobee is the second-largest freshwater lake located wholly in the continental United States (after Lake Michigan). Likened to a saucer full of water, Lake Okeechobee is shallow, with normal depths from 7 to 11 feet, depending on the season and annual rainfall; in periods of prolonged drought, it has fallen to below 8 feet. For up-to-date information on lake depths, call the Army Corps of Engineers office in Clewiston at 863-983-8101. Also check waterwayguide.com for regular updates. During periods of strong winds, the lake becomes choppy and turbulent with short, hard seas typical of shallow water.

Bass fishermen and their specialized boats frequent the known "holes" and wrecks of the lake. Pan fishermen are along the edges, in drainage canal entrances, near the locks and in the crannies of the many spoil islands along the southern rim. Seasonal tournaments bring out hordes of amateurs and professionals.

Be sure you have all needed provisions with you before you start the trek across the lake, as you will have few options once on the lake (on either route).

## Route 1: The Open Water Route–OCWW Mile 40 to Mile 65

The Open Water Route is normally an enjoyable run, and Clewiston (at Mile 65) is a worthwhile stopover point. The controlling depth for Route 1 by specific lake level can be determined by subtracting 6.06 feet from the published lake level. If the lake level and season are right, expect to see hundreds of beautiful white pelicans bunched together on the half-dozen offshore spoil islands that line the Clewiston approach channel. Unlike brown pelicans, which plunge-dive from high above the water for their meals, white pelicans scoop up fish by merely submerging their heads and necks while swimming.

# Lake Okeechobee— Rim Route, FL

www.snagaslip.com
SNAG-A-SLIP
EXPLORE. BOOK. BOAT.™

| | | | Dockage | | | | | Supplies | | Services | | | | |
|---|---|---|---|---|---|---|---|---|---|---|---|---|---|---|
| | | Largest Vessel Accommodated | VHF Channel Monitored | Transient Berths / Total Berths | Approach / Dockside Depth (reported) | Floating Docks | Gas / Diesel | Groceries, Ice, Marine Supplies, Snacks | Repairs: Hull, Engine, Propeller | Lift (tonnage), Crane, Rail | Laundry, Pool, Showers, Courtesy Car | Min/Max Amps | Pump-Out Station | Nearby: Grocery Store, Motel, Restaurant |
| **PAHOKEE** | | | | | | | | | | | | | | |
| 1. Pahokee Marina and Campground (WiFi) 50.5 | 561-924-7832 | 70 | 16 | call/100 | 5/8 | F | – | GIS | – | – | 30/50 | LPS | P | GMR |
| **CLEWISTON** | | | | | | | | | | | | | | |
| 2. Roland and Mary Ann Martins Marina & Resort (internet)(WiFi) | 800-473-6766 | 130 | 16/68 | 12/15 | 8/7 | F | GD | IMS | EP | – | 30/50 | LPS | P | GMR |

☐ Internet Access (WiFi) Wireless Internet Access (WG) Waterway Guide Cruising Club Partner *(Information in the table is provided by the facilities.)*
See WaterwayGuide.com for current rates, fuel prices, web site addresses, and other up-to-the-minute information.

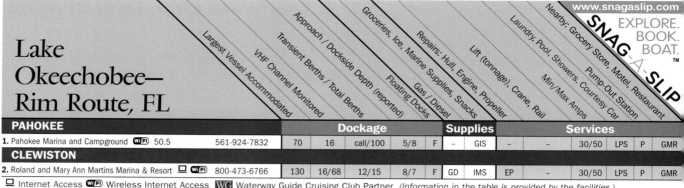

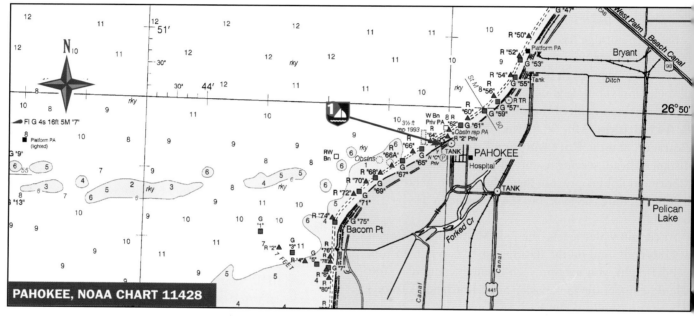

PAHOKEE, NOAA CHART 11428

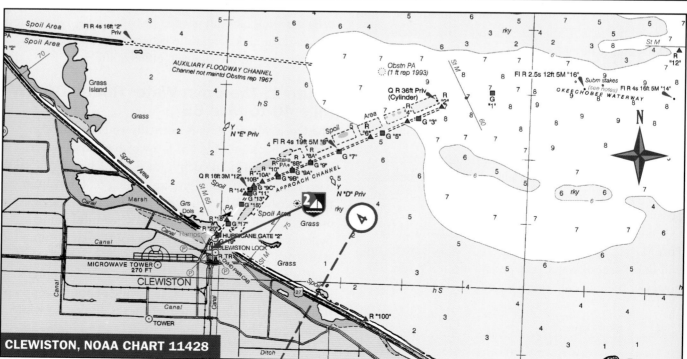

CLEWISTON, NOAA CHART 11428

**NAVIGATION:** Use Chart 11428. Crossing the southern portion of Lake Okeechobee, this 25-mile-long passage departs from the Port Mayaca channel in a southwesterly direction. The first run of 15 miles has just one aid to navigation, flashing red daybeacon "6," which is located about 7 miles out to help you compensate for a slight magnetic anomaly in this area, which might affect your compass. About 3 miles out from the Port Mayaca Lock, there is a visible wreck to starboard. Do not be led off course. Your GPS chartplotter or radar could be useful on this stretch if visibility is compromised.

As you approach flashing green daybeacon "7" on the eastern edge of Rocky Reef, note what appears to be a cluster of markers and the remains of a platform. Sort things out beforehand and follow the chart's magenta line carefully. After clearing the cut through the reef, stick to the charted course. The apparent shortcut due west, an auxiliary floodway channel, is shoaled in and obstructed with large boulders (particularly noticeable at low lake levels). This cut should not be attempted by cruising boats.

Entering the Clewiston approach channel, marked by a private concrete cylinder and numerous lights and daybeacons, is simple. Westbound, green daybeacon "1" is difficult to spot. If the water level is low or the winds are brisk, pay strict attention to course keeping; this is where the controlling depth for Route 1 applies. The channel is lined on both sides with rocks and spoil areas here. Exercise special care in the area between red daybeacons "4" and "6." This is another area in which the use of your GPS chartplotter will come in handy.

Close in to Clewiston, be aware that fishnets and traps are a way of life here, and their small markers are sometimes difficult to see. Some of the fishermen in high-speed bass boats or skiffs also add to the

annoyance, but Clewiston, which bills itself as the "Sweetest Town in America" (due to its role in sugarcane production) is a real pleasure to visit.

Directly before reaching the Clewiston Lock, the channel makes a hard 90-degree turn to the northwest. There are no nearby channel markers on this northwesterly stretch, and a sign on the levee pointing to Moore Haven is difficult to read. The intersection can be confusing, but don't go through the lock unless you wish to visit Clewiston.

The **Clewiston Lock** is not technically part of the OCWW and is not equipped with a VHF radio, but if lake levels are not unusual, the lock is left open. If the traffic light is green, proceed through. If you wish passage and the lockmaster does not wave to you, use two long and two short blasts of your horn or whistle. The Army Corps of Engineers in Clewiston (863-983-8101) has more information on scheduled maintenance and lock operations.

On an eastbound trip from Clewiston, heading toward Indiantown, the Port Mayaca entrance markers may be hard to pick out. On the charted course, power company stacks are clearly visible at the port from many miles

out, and a heading directly toward them will bring you almost directly to the channel entrance. Previously taken GPS readings will simplify matters.

## Route 2: The Rim Route–OCWW Mile 40 to Mile 75

At the time of publication (spring 2017), the Rim Route was open (with a depth of just over 5.2 feet), but the Army Corps of Engineers warned that boaters use this route at their own risk. While the channel is marked, there are submerged obstructions and uncharted shoals with which to contend.

**NAVIGATION:** Use Chart 11428. If you are not pressed for time, or if the lake crossing is questionable due to weather, the Rim Route (10 miles longer), can be an interesting alternative, if the water level allows it. While open to Lake Okeechobee for about 15 miles, the exposure is from west through north. Unless winds are from this quadrant (and in the small craft advisory category), this part of the passage should be a pleasant one.

From Mile 55 on to Clewiston, where it joins the previously described route (referred to as Route 1), and farther to the Caloosahatchee Canal entrance, the course stays between the mainland levees surrounding Lake Okeechobee and the regular and spoil islands lining the rim. Depths vary according to lake levels and wind conditions; the controlling depth for this route can be determined by subtracting 8.66 feet from the official lake level. The shallowest stretch is the easternmost 4 miles; depths increase significantly beyond that.

Other than Pahokee and Clewiston, the only stopping points along the way are Slim's Fish Camp at Torry Island (which can only accommodate very small boats with shallow draft) and possibly pilings or dolphins.

## Pahokee–OCWW Mile 50.6

**NAVIGATION:** Use Chart 11428. The local harbor can be reached from red entrance daybeacon "2," which is opposite red channel daybeacon "62." If the wind is strong from the northwest or north, waves from Lake Okeechobee will be reflected back from the breakwater and, when combined with the incoming waves, can result in an uncomfortable, or even dangerous, situation for boats in the channel as they pass the breakwater. Near red daybeacon "78," Mile 54, there is a charted, straight, well-marked channel that leads out through the

shallows bordering the Rim Route to the "deep" water of the lake.

**Dockage:** The City of Pahokee owns a marina that can accommodate cruising boats that can navigate the shallow approach depths. When the lake water levels fall below 12.5 feet the water depths in the marina entrance become extremely shallow, less than 6 feet. Vessels that draw greater than 4 feet should exercise extreme caution until water levels rise. The city also manages the KOA campground that is located immediately next to the marina. The marina is a nice facility, but it is quite a hike to markets or restaurants. (The town of Pahokee is five very long blocks away.)

## Torry Island/Belle Glade–OCWW Mile 60.7

This section of the OCWW from Mile 55 to Mile 75.7 (Clewiston) has always been one of the more interesting stretches on the trip; however, hyacinths and water lettuce grow in profusion, sometimes even clogging the channel. If you must pass through them, do it slowly. Should you clog your prop and rudder, back down and then push ahead. Occasionally, the Rim Route will be closed to navigation because of vegetation in the water. These closures will be announced in the *Local Notice to Mariners*. Waterway Guide also lists important updates to navigation at waterwayguide.com.

The **Torry Island (Belle Glade Dike) Swing Bridge** has only an 11-foot closed vertical clearance at normal lake levels. The fixed span just west of the swing span has a vertical clearance of 13 feet, which may be an advantage if you only require 12 feet of clearance. This bridge is hand-operated, and it takes awhile for the operator to get in place to open the span, so be sure to call ahead on VHF Channel 09 and give the operator an estimate as to the time of your arrival. Hours are from 7:00 a.m. to 6:00 p.m. Monday through Thursday, and 7:00 a.m. to 7:00 p.m. Friday through Sunday (fishing days). The bridge remains closed at night. It also need not open if winds are in excess of 20 mph. Call 561-996-3844 for details.

**Dockage:** Slim's Fish Camp and Marina at Torry Island has some provisions and very limited dockage for small boats. The water is extremely shallow (in the 2- to 3-foot range). You can probably find a way to get into the town area proper (nearly 2 miles distant), where you will find a community golf course, a small airfield and numerous stores.

Courtesy of U.S. Army Corps of Engineers.

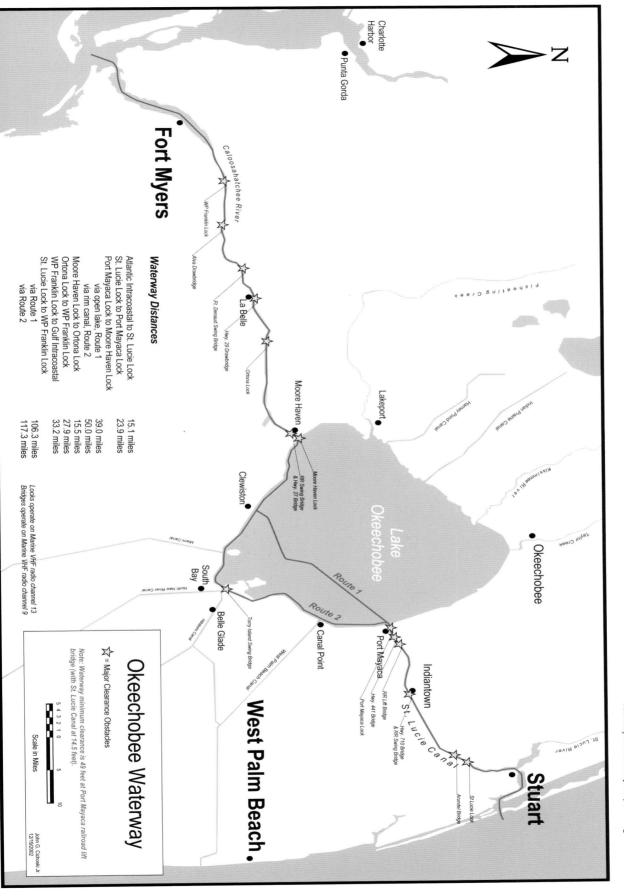

### Waterway Distances

| | |
|---|---|
| Atlantic Intracoastal to St. Lucie Lock | 15.1 miles |
| St. Lucie Lock to Port Mayaca Lock | 23.9 miles |
| Port Mayaca Lock to Moore Haven Lock | |
| via open lake, Route 1 | 39.0 miles |
| via rim canal, Route 2 | 50.0 miles |
| Moore Haven Lock to Ortona Lock | 15.5 miles |
| Ortona Lock to WP Franklin Lock | 27.9 miles |
| WP Franklin Lock to Gulf Intracoastal | 33.2 miles |
| St. Lucie Lock to WP Franklin Lock | |
| via Route 1 | 106.3 miles |
| via Route 2 | 117.3 miles |

*Locks operate on Marine VHF radio channel 13*
*Bridges operate on Marine VHF radio channel 9*

## Okeechobee Waterway

☆ = Major Clearance Obstacles

*Note: Waterway minimum clearance is 49 feet at Port Mayaca railroad lift bridge (with St. Lucie Canal at 14.5 feet).*

Scale in Miles

John G. Cichoski Jr.
12/19/2002

**Anchorage:** Some anchoring room is west of the Torry Island Swing Bridge if you want an early start, but note that early risers also include many small-boat fishermen who rarely show concern for anchored craft. There is also a town dock at Point Chosen but overnight dockage is not allowed. A better bet is to anchor behind the spoil and natural islands in the lee of Kreamer Island. In fact, this protected stretch extending to Torry Island is considered the best area on the route for a secure anchorage. The west side of Hurricane Gate 4, outside the immediate channel, is also a recommended anchorage. The "gate" is normally closed.

## Belle Glade to Clewiston–OCWW Mile 60.7 to Mile 75.7

From Belle Glade, the OCWW first heads south for several miles, and then angles northwest past such communities as Bean City and Lake Harbor. A road parallels the OCWW most of the way, but you will not see it since it is behind the ubiquitous levee.

Hurricane Gate 3 at about Mile 67 is usually closed. There are markers along the way: Red daybeacon "94" is at Mile 70, and the channel is narrow and straightforward. As you approach Clewiston (Mile 75.7),

be alert for small fishing boats anchored off and in the channel.

**Anchorage:** Where the OCWW turns westward at Mile 62.5, there is a charted small lagoon (South Bay Basin) on the lake side of the channel; this can be a fair-weather anchorage for several boats. Leave the OCWW just west of launch ramp and head north into the kidney-shaped basin shown on your NOAA chart. Anchor across from the boat ramp in 8 feet with good holding in mud. Islands, both natural and spoil, offer protection from winds off the lake along this route, although if the water level is high, it can get a bit unpleasant but not dangerous. You may be joined by up to 10 boats, lots of birds and bugs!

## Clewiston to Caloosahatchee Canal– OCWW Mile 75.8 to Mile 78

From Clewiston to Moore Haven and the entrance to the Caloosahatchee Canal, Mile 78, the OCWW is fairly wide and deep. Speeds obtainable on Lake Okeechobee by the fast boats are frequently matched along this route. Small-boat fishermen anchor or drift-fish in the cuts and channel, and wakes are a potential annoyance.

The variety of growth ranges from grass to scattered clumps of bamboo, melaluka and cypress, plus a few small trees with a crown of lobulated leaves and melon-like fruit. This last is the female papaya with edible fruit. If it is a sunny day, have your camera ready because this canal is probably one of the best places to see alligators sunning themselves on shore.

**NAVIGATION:** Use Chart 11428. Route 1 (open-water route) joins Route 2 (Rim Route) at Clewiston, a point about halfway between Stuart and Fort Myers. Mileage from this point on is based on the lesser "cross-lake" figure of Mile 65; the rim mileage of 75.7 stops here. A hurricane gate and the 50 feet wide by 60 feet long **Clewiston Lock**, operated by a contractor for the South Florida Water Management District (SFWMD), allow access through the levee into Clewiston Harbor. This lock is not equipped with a VHF radio, so contact with the lockmaster must be made visually (waving is the method of choice) or by whistle signals, two long and two short. As mentioned before, if the lake is at normal levels, the lock is usually left open and clear for traffic; watch the traffic light to see if it is green or red.

After entering the lock, grab a couple of the lines hanging from the top of the chamber and hold on. Lock personnel may help with the lines, but the change in water level as the lock opens and closes usually will not cause excessive turbulence. The schedule calls for an open lock if the water level is low, and the Clewiston Lock is often open for direct passage. Otherwise, the hours are: 7:00 a.m. to 5:00 p.m. NOAA Weather is on WX2/Belle Glade.

**Dockage:** Roland and Mary Martin's Marina & Resort is a popular spot for transients and boat clubs to spend a weekend or more, particularly bass fishing groups. They sell gas and diesel fuel and have a popular tiki bar and restaurant. Also, if you want some time off of the boat, the marina has rooms to rent. Reservations are a must. The main street of this town of more than 7,000 is only 3 blocks away and includes a small grocery store one-half mile from the marina and a pharmacy is 1.5 miles away. The famous Clewiston Inn Motor Lodge (108 Royal Palm Ave., 863-983-8151), owned and operated by the U.S. Sugar Corporation, offers lodging to visitors. You may want to call a taxi, although it is a comfortable walk there.

**Anchorage:** Several mooring dolphins on the channel's edge northwest of Clewiston can be used for making fast.

# Caloosahatchee Canal & River, FL

| | Facility / Phone | | Dockage | | | | | Supplies | | Services | | | | | |
|---|---|---|---|---|---|---|---|---|---|---|---|---|---|---|---|
| | | | Largest Vessel Accommodated | VHF Channel Monitored | Transient Berths / Total Berths | Approach / Dockside Depth (reported) | Floating Docks | Groceries, Ice, Marine Supplies, Snacks | Gas / Diesel | Repairs: Hull, Engine, Propeller | Lift (tonnage), Crane, Rail | Laundry, Pool, Showers, Courtesy Car | Pump-Out Station | Min/Max Amps | Nearby: Grocery Store, Motel, Restaurant |
| **MOORE HAVEN AREA** | | | | | | | | | | | | | | | |
| 1. | Moore Haven City Docks 78.4 | 863-946-0711 | – | – | – | 6/6 | – | – | – | | | S | – | 30/50 | GMR |
| 2. | River House Marina [Internet][WiFi] 78.5 | 863-946-0466 | – | 16/68 | 10/10 | 5/5 | – | I | – | | | PS | – | 30/50 | GMR |
| 3. | The Glades Marina [Internet][WiFi] 89 | 863-673-5653 | 90 | 16 | 8/26 | 12/8 | F | IS | – | | | LPS | P | 30/50 | MR |
| 4. | Glades Boat Storage, Inc. [Internet][WG] | 863-983-3040 | – | 16/68 | – | – | | | | | L40 | LS | – | | – |
| **LA BELLE AREA** | | | | | | | | | | | | | | | |
| 5. | **River Forest Yachting Center - LaBelle** [WiFi] 92.8 | **863-612-0003** | 150 | 16 | 20/20 | 9/8 | F | – | – | HEP | L82 | S | P | 30/100 | – |
| 6. | Port LaBelle Marina [WiFi] 100 | 863-675-2261 | 70 | – | 2/100 | 6/6 | F | I | GD | | | LS | P | 30/30 | MR |

[icon] Internet Access  [WiFi] Wireless Internet Access  [WG] Waterway Guide Cruising Club Partner *(Information in the table is provided by the facilities.)*
See WaterwayGuide.com for current rates, fuel prices, web site addresses, and other up-to-the-minute information.

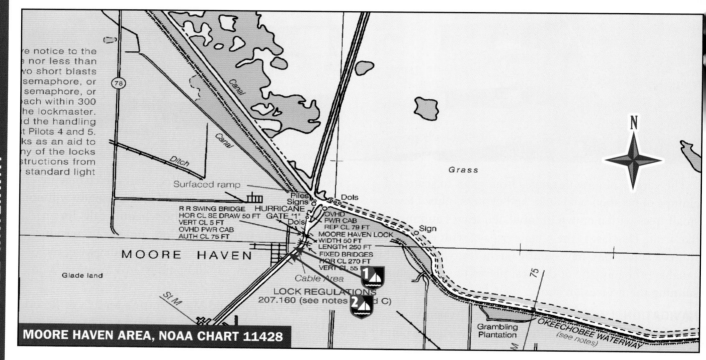

MOORE HAVEN AREA, NOAA CHART 11428

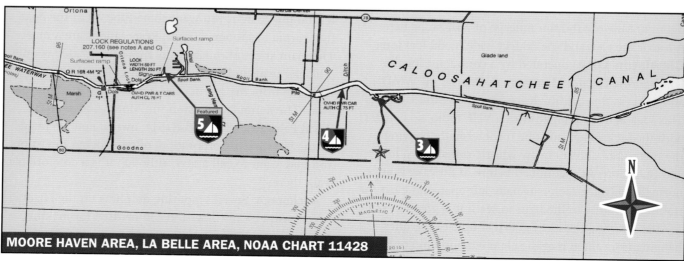

MOORE HAVEN AREA, LA BELLE AREA, NOAA CHART 11428

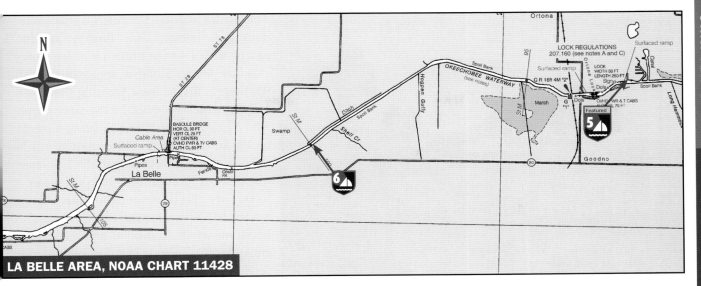

**LA BELLE AREA, NOAA CHART 11428**

# ■ CALOOSAHATCHEE CANAL

**NAVIGATION:** Use Chart 11428. The entrance to the **Moore Haven Lock** (Mile 78) is directly to port and easy to see and negotiate. The rim canal continues on well up the west side of Lake Okeechobee and provides some sheltered anchoring areas (again with limited swinging room and shallow water). Several facilities for small fishing boats are along the way, and at times, fishing activity is intense.

As noted previously, hyacinths and water lettuce can clog the channel, as well as your prop and rudder here. Stay well back from the lock until the green light comes on and enter carefully. Information about conditions farther on can usually be obtained from the lockmaster (863-946-0414). Remember, you are now being lowered with the water level, so do not tie off your bow or stern lines and be prepared for some surge as you drop. Wait for the gates to open completely before releasing the lines and then proceed slowly out of the lock. The lock operates from 7:00 a.m. to 5:00 p.m. with a last lock opening at 4:30 p.m.

## Moore Haven–OCWW Mile 78

Because it is in a protected canal, the Moore Haven Lock is even easier to pass through than the St. Lucie Lock, with equally capable lock tenders. It has smooth walls that do not catch rails and fenders as the old timbered walls did for many years. However, if Hurricane Gate 1 is in use during discharge of high water, turbulence on the "down" side of the lock can be considerable.

Immediately beyond the Moore Haven Lock are two bridges. The first, the **Seaboard (Moore Haven) Railroad Swing Bridge** (Mile 78.3, 5-foot closed vertical clearance), is usually open; if closed, it opens on signal, except from 10:00 p.m. to 6:00 a.m., when it will not open. Signal before you leave the lock. The bridge is hand-operated, and the delay can be considerable. Use the eastern draw. The **Moore Haven (U.S. 27) Twin Bridges** has a fixed vertical clearance charted at 55 feet, but there are no clearance gauges or a fendering system.

**Dockage:** On the west side of the Caloosahatchee Canal (where the OCWW runs nearly north to south), the City of Moore Haven has provided alongside dockage for 3 or 4 (depending on size) visiting yachts. Normally, space is available, but during peak travel seasons, the early bird scores. The dock has a substantial rub rail on the outside of the pilings; fenders will be needed, of course, to protect your boat from black marks. Use minimum space for tie-up so that the next boat will have room. Dockage fees may be paid at City Hall across the street, or to the dockmaster who calls in the early evening (and is a good source of local information). Showers are available behind City Hall during regular operating hours. You can get a key from the dockmaster.

The post office, a Dollar General (with some limited groceries), a few small restaurants, a liquor store and other convenience stores are nearby on U.S. Route 27. The public library, with free WiFi, is across the street from the wharf, next to City Hall.

Just beyond the City Dock is the River House Marina with slips. Dockage fees are collected on the "honor system." In the morning, you will find an envelope on your deck, or where your power cord is plugged in, with

information on the dockage rate. Put cash or a check in the envelope and deposit it in the marked locked box near the gate that allows access to the dock. At the far edge of these docks, there is an overhead telephone or television cable (not a power line) crossing; clearance seems quite adequate, but specific height is not charted or known.

**Anchorage:** If you arrive at the east side of the Moore Haven Lock late in the day and would prefer not to lock through until morning, you can proceed on past the turn into the lock and anchor in the canal, or you can make fast for the night between the mooring dolphins located on the lake side of the OCWW, just before the canal turns into the lock. If you plan to anchor, mind the overhead power cable (reported to have only an 18-foot vertical clearance) that crosses the creek to the north.

## Lake Hicpochee–OCWW Mile 82.5

**NAVIGATION:** Use Chart 11428. Early morning fog and mist sometime curtail an early departure, but normally the Caloosahatchee Canal is straightforward, wide and deep, with no surprises. At about Mile 82.5, the channel passes through shallow Lake Hicpochee, where again you may encounter small fishing boats anchored along the shore. Watch your wake as a matter of both prudence and courtesy.

**Dockage:** Just past Lake Hicpochee and the bend in the Caloosahatchee Canal, on the south bank is

The Glades Marina. The basin is small and dockage is limited. Glades Boat Storage, Inc. is nearby with a 40-ton lift (no transient space).

A little farther along, at approximately Mile 93, there is River Forest Yachting Center–LaBelle, which is owned by the same people who own the River Forest Yachting Center on the St. Lucie River. This facility is just like the one on the eastern side of the lake, except it is twice as large (at over 100,000 square feet). They also boast an 82-ton lift. This marina has been constructed to withstand hurricane winds. Transients are welcome with amenities that include showers and pump-out service. Be sure to call in advance for dockage availability.

**Anchorage:** At Mile 92.5, just before Turkey Creek, there is a narrow canal that leads into Lollipop Lake anchorage. It is small, but if you go all the way into the lake, you will find ample room for anchoring in very protected water. The water in the canal is 8- to 9-feet deep, and our cruising editor reports that it is much deeper (30-plus feet) once inside the basin. There is a lot of wildlife

to see; you will be joined by eagles, osprey and owls to name a few. This is a nice out-of-the-way spot to spend an evening on the hook.

## Ortona Lock–OCWW Mile 93.5

Before you get to Ortona Lock, several small canals lead off to the north into the Turkey Creek community. Most of its residents are boaters, and their docks usually are full of cruising boats of all descriptions.

**NAVIGATION:** Use Chart 11428. Like the Moore Haven Lock, Ortona Lock's smooth concrete walls are a vast improvement over timbered sides that invariably catch fenders and rub rails. Tie-up dolphins are located outside both ends of the locks; boats normally make fast to the south wall. The **Ortona Lock** operates the same way as the others; again, be prepared for some surge as the water is let out. The change in level varies, but 8 to 10 feet is normal depending on lake level. The lock operates from 7:00 a.m. to 5:00 p.m. with a last lock opening at 4:30 p.m. (863-946-0414).

**Dockage:** At Mile 100, an entry channel leads off to the south into the Port LaBelle Marina, with two reserved transient slips, fuel and some other amenities. Just east of the marina, there is another cove (known to some cruisers as Tranquility Cove) that is an extension of the marina.

At approximately Mile 100.5, there is a free dock that two boats can tie-up to. It is located on the south river bank and is 40-feet long with cleats. Shore access is difficult, but there are reports that a plank has been laid out for access. There is nothing in the surrounding area except farm land, but it might provide a walking area for your pets if you can get ashore.

## La Belle–OCWW Mile 103

This quiet old river town of La Belle dates back to the early 1800s. The Swamp Cabbage Festival (863-675-0154) is held in La Belle during the last full weekend in February. Swamp cabbage, also known as hearts of palm, is the growing part of the sable palm. (Another local delicacy is alligator.) La Belle is also known as the "Honey Capital." The Harold P. Curtis Honey Company (355 N. Bridge St., 863-675-2187) is located near the beginning of the business district on the south side of the bridge. The company maintains about 1,000 beehives and will permit you to sample different types of honey.

The **La Belle (SR 29) Bascule Bridge** (Mile 103.0, 28-foot closed vertical clearance) opens on signal, except from 7:00 a.m. to 9:00 a.m. and 4:00 p.m. to 6:00

p.m., Monday through Friday (except federal holidays), when the bridge need not open. The bridge will open on signal between 10:00 p.m. and 6:00 a.m. if at least a 3-hout notice is given. Call 866-335-9696 for an opening during these hours.

**Dockage:** Just beyond the bridge, La Belle City Dock on the south side has free dockage with a 3-day limit, after which you must leave and not return for at least 8 days. These docks are usually full on the weekends and are on a first-come, first-served basis. They have mooring posts, making it more difficult to off-board for smaller boats. They are also exposed to the wake of passing boats.

South along Bridge Street (within four blocks) are a library, hardware store, bank, coin laundry and post office. A park is across the highway at the foot of the bridge. A Save-A-Lot at 71 S Lee St. (863-675-8080) is within walking distance for your provisioning needs. There is a Dollar General Market (50 N. Bridge St., 863-674-0786) on the way. A number of fast food restaurants are nearby as well.

To the west of the Town Dock is a Hendry County Boat Ramp with a pier for small boats. The municipal Bob Mason Town Park on the same side of the canal offers day dockage. (No overnight docking.)

# Caloosahatchee River, FL

### OLGA

| | | Dockage | | | | | Supplies | | Services | | | | | |
|---|---|---|---|---|---|---|---|---|---|---|---|---|---|---|
| | | Largest Vessel Accommodated | VHF Channel Monitored | Transient Berths / Total Berths | Approach / Dockside Depth (reported) | Floating Docks | Gas / Diesel | Groceries, Ice, Marine Supplies, Snacks | Repairs: Hull, Engine, Propeller | Lift (tonnage), Crane, Rail | Min/Max Amps | Laundry, Pool, Showers, Courtesy Car | Pump-Out Station | Nearby: Grocery Store, Motel, Restaurant |
| 1. W.P. Franklin Campground-Boat-In Docks  122 | 239-694-8770 | 40 | – | 8/8 | – | – | – | – | – | – | 30/50 | LS | – | – |
| 2. Calusa Jacks Marina 💻 WiFi  124.2 | 239-694-2708 | 200 | 16/68 | 3/15 | 23/8 | – | GD | IMS | HEP | L10 | 30/50 | S | – | GMR |
| **3. Owl Creek Boat Works  125.5** | **239-543-2100** | **125** | **–** | **6/48** | **7/7** | **–** | **–** | **M** | **HEP** | **L150** | **50/50** | **S** | **–** | **GMR** |
| 4. Sweetwater Landing Marina  126 | 239-694-3850 | 200 | 16 | 10/65 | 9/5 | – | G | IMS | HEP | L18 | 30/50 | LPS | P | GMR |

💻 Internet Access   WiFi Wireless Internet Access   **WG** Waterway Guide Cruising Club Partner *(Information in the table is provided by the facilities.)*
See WaterwayGuide.com for current rates, fuel prices, web site addresses, and other up-to-the-minute information.

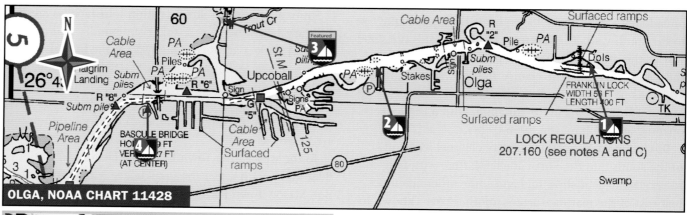

OLGA, NOAA CHART 11428

## ■ CALOOSAHATCHEE RIVER

The Calusa Indians used this river as a highway. So did early settlers to Fort Myers. Today, powerboats and sailboats traverse the 67-mile-long Caloosahatchee River, which is an important link the OCWW. The river is wide enough to accommodate everyone, including the abundant wildlife. The Caloosahatchee River and its meandering tributaries are bordered by lush, towering leather ferns, stately oaks dripping with moss and verdant vegetation along every shore.

### La Belle to Franklin Lock–OCWW Mile 103 to Mile 121

These are the scenic headwaters of the Caloosahatchee River, once a major transportation artery in the settling of Florida. Today, you will rarely encounter tugs and barges, as over-land trucking has diminished the commercial importance of the river.

**NAVIGATION:** Use Chart 11428. Where the Caloosahatchee River once wandered, it is now a series of straight sections punctuated by gentle turns and numerous intriguing oxbows and streams. Still a beautiful waterway, the water runs quite deep to the banks. Swinging room on the river, even at its widest points, is limited and anchoring is not recommended unless you can keep your vessel from swinging into the channel. Some of the oxbows are deep enough if you feel adventurous, but snags or shoals and even low-hanging power cables are prevalent. At about Mile 106.6, well out from the northern bank, red daybeacon "2" marks a shoal.

Two bridges cross this section of the Caloosahatchee River. The **Fort Denaud Swing Bridge**, at Mile 108.2, has a 9-foot closed vertical clearance. The bridge opens on request, and arrows indicate which side of the draw to use. It is closed from 10:00 p.m. until 6:00 a.m. and requires a 3-hour notice to open during those hours; call 863-675-2055. The **Alva Bascule Bridge**, at Mile 116, has a 23-foot charted closed vertical clearance and likewise opens on signal. Use VHF Channel 09 (same restrictions as Fort Denaud Bridge; call 239-278-2704).

**Anchorage:** Boats are not permitted to anchor on the north side of the Caloosahatchee River in the wide spot across from the entrance to the former Rialto Harbor Docks. However, you may be able to anchor in nearby Hickey Creek behind the unnamed island. Here you will find all-around protection from wakes in 7 feet of water. Be aware that this anchorage has poor holding in mud; check your holding!

## W.P. Franklin Lock–OCWW Mile 121.4

The final lock on the Okeechobee Waterway is at Olga. The **W.P. Franklin Lock** normally operates on request from 7:00 a.m. to 5:00 p.m. daily. (Last lockage at 4:30 p.m.) Enter on the green light, and remember not to tie off your lines tightly, as the level will drop about 3 feet. Wait until the lock is fully open before casting off and exit slowly. Sometimes eastbound boats are waiting nearby to enter. Please note that low water levels in Lake Okeechobee may result in lock schedule changes at the W.P. Franklin. Be sure to call in advance to check schedules (239-694-5451).

**Dockage:** Immediately east of the lock and dam, on the north shore, is a small, but attractive Army Corps of Engineers marina (W.P. Franklin Campground-Boat-in Docks) that can accommodate boats not more than about 45 feet long. Reservations must be made at least 72 hours before arrival (877-444-6777) and only 4 of the 8 slips can be reserved. The other 4 are on a first-come, first-served basis.

**Anchorage:** A protected anchorage is just below the Franklin Lock, next to the Army Corps of Engineers campground, with ample room and 10-foot depths.

## Franklin Lock to Fort Myers–OCWW Mile 121.5 to Mile 135

**NAVIGATION:** Use Chart 11428. Use the St. Petersburg Tide Tables. For high tide, add 1 hour 56 minutes; for low tide, add 2 hours 23 minutes.

⚠️ The Caloosahatchee River has many aids to navigation, beginning with red daybeacon "2" just downriver from the W. P. Franklin Lock. Although this is a navigable river coming in from the Gulf of Mexico, it is not marked with the conventional "red-right-returning" system with numbers increasing as one proceeds inland. The daybeacons, lights, and such are a continuing part of the Okeechobee Waterway system; numbers increase as you cruise westward, and the "reds" are on your right side even though you are going downriver. This can be confusing if you do not understand the system.

From here to Fort Myers, you have several bridges to consider. The first, **Wilson Pigott (Olga) Bascule Bridge** at Mile 126.3, has a 27-foot closed vertical clearance. The bridge opens on signal, except between 10:00 p.m. and 6:00 a.m., when it requires at least a 3-hour notice to open. Call 866-335-9696.

At Mile 127.5, the scale of Chart 11428 changes to 1:40,000 for its final section, an inset marked "Fort Myers Extension." A Manatee Speed Zone here is strictly enforced; specific restrictions vary in the channel and outside, and also during different seasons. Beginning at Mile 128, signs near the overhead power cables, and the large power plant adjacent, mark the zone. Manatees can be found all along the OCWW, but as usual, they seem to congregate most often near the warm water outflows of power plants.

The **I-75 Bridge** crosses the OCWW at Mile 128.9 with a 55-foot fixed vertical clearance. At Mile 129.9 the **SCL Railroad Lift Bridge** at Beautiful Island is normally open unless a train is due. The closed vertical clearance is only 5 feet, so signal or call, and then hold well off until the train has passed and the bridge is fully opened. (Note that the overhang is 55 feet when the bridge is open.) Beautiful Island lives up to its name, but do not get in too close due to depth concerns. There are some areas, particularly on the south side, where you can leave the channel, but do so very cautiously after examining your chart.

**Dockage:** At Mile 124.2 Calusa Jacks Marina has transient space and sells gas and diesel and offers some repairs.

Approaching Mile 125.5, just before the Olga Bascule Bridge, a channel leads off to the north and the Owl Creek Boat Works, a full-service yard with a covered freshwater storage area. They have 3 lifts for hauling up to 150 tons and can handle all types of repairs. They have been around since 1953.

A little farther on is Sweetwater Landing, a full-service marina that accepts transients, has gas available and offers some repairs. If you need to re-step a mast, this is a good time to do so (although it can be done in Fort Myers).

**Anchorage:** Because the Caloosahatchee River is more than a mile wide, it can get rough in nasty weather, so anchoring, although possible, could be unpleasant. Across from flashing green "13," at Mile 128, is the last good anchorage before Fort Myers. Locally known as Power Plant Slough, the western channel is reached by entering southwest of the manatee sign, about halfway between the sign and shore. Continuing in, the deepest water (8-foot plus depths) is about 100 feet off the western shore. The eastern channel of the slough is narrower, shallow and more difficult to follow.

Manatees love it here too, so be mindful that you are likely sharing this space.

## Fort Myers–OCWW Mile 135

While Fort Myers is not actually the western end of the OCWW, most cruisers consider it to be. Like most of Florida, the city boasts a growing population, especially if you include the Cape Coral area, which is across the river on the north shore.

**Dockage/Moorings:** Before the **Edison Twin Bridges** (56-foot fixed vertical clearance) at Mile 134 in North Fort Myers (on the north bank of the river) is Prosperity Pointe Marina, which may have transient space. Be cautious when approaching their shallow entrance channel. They also report 5-foot dockside depths; call the marina in advance for depth information.

On the north bank, south of the **Caloosahatchee Bridge** (55-foot fixed vertical clearance) at Mile 135 is Marinatown Yacht Harbour. The flashing green daybeacon "1" and red daybeacon "2" for the beginning of the well-marked channel to Hancock Creek are beside the Caloosahatchee River flashing red daybeacon "52." The marina is around the first bend above green daybeacon "25." Within Hancock Creek, there is 5 to 7 feet at mean low water. In the section of the channel that parallels the shore, between green daybeacons "17" and "21," the channel carries only 4 to 4.5 feet at mean low water with a soft mud bottom. Marinatown Yacht Harbour has plenty of transient space on their docks, but you should still call in advance for reservations. From the marina it is a relatively short walk to a CVS, large liquor store, several banks and a number of other stores, including a grocery.

# Caloosahatchee, FL

| FORT MYERS AREA | Phone | Largest Vessel Accommodated | VHF Channel Monitored | Transient Berths / Total Berths | Approach / Dockside Depth (reported) | Floating Docks | Gas / Diesel | Groceries, Ice, Marine Supplies, Snacks | Repairs: Hull, Engine, Propeller | Lift (tonnage), Crane, Rail | Min/Max Amps | Laundry, Pool, Showers, Courtesy Car | Pump-Out Station | Nearby: Grocery Store, Motel, Restaurant |
| --- | --- | --- | --- | --- | --- | --- | --- | --- | --- | --- | --- | --- | --- | --- |
| | | | | **Dockage** | | | **Supplies** | | **Services** | | | | | |
| 1. Prosperity Pointe Marina [WiFi][WG] 134 | 239-995-2155 | 56 | 16/06 | 10/53 | 6/5 | F | – | IS | – | – | 30/50 | LS | P | GMR |
| 2. Marinatown Yacht Harbour [□][WiFi] 135 | 239-997-7711 | 68 | – | 40/135 | 6/5 | – | – | IS | EP | – | 30/100 | LPS | P | GMR |
| 3. City of Fort Myers Yacht Basin [□][WiFi][WG] 134.5 | 239-321-7080 | 300 | 16/68 | 25/241 | 10/7 | – | GD | GIMS | – | – | 30/100 | LS | P | GMR |
| 4. Legacy Harbour Marina [□][WiFi] 135 | 239-461-0775 | 120 | 16/12 | 10/131 | 7/7 | F | – | I | – | – | 30/50 | LPS | P | GMR |
| 5. The Marina at Edison Ford [□][WiFi] | 239-895-7703 | 80 | 16/73 | 25/45 | 7/5 | – | – | IS | – | – | 30/50 | LS | P | GR |

□ Internet Access  WiFi Wireless Internet Access  WG Waterway Guide Cruising Club Partner *(Information in the table is provided by the facilities.)*
See WaterwayGuide.com for current rates, fuel prices, web site addresses, and other up-to-the-minute information.

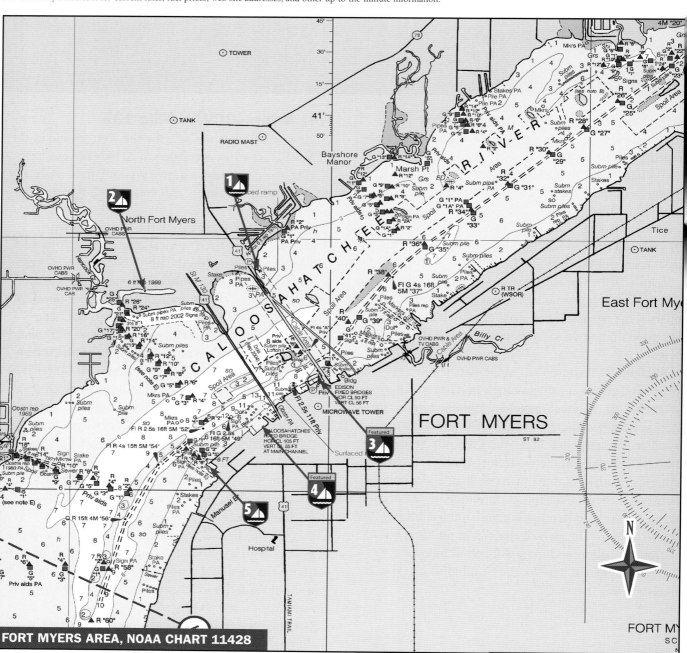

FORT MYERS AREA, NOAA CHART 11428

The City of Fort Myers Yacht Basin, situated on the south shore of the Caloosahatchee River between the western-most span of the Edison Twin Bridges and the Caloosahatchee River Bridge, is within walking distance of supplies. The full-service facility can accommodate vessels both large and small, but reserve your slip ahead to make sure space is available when you arrive. They also sell fuel. Across the river are 10 moorings administered by the City Yacht Basin; access across the shallows is by a marked channel. These are available to liveaboards on smaller sailboats.

Legacy Harbour Marina's entrance is on the east side of the marina. Look for the piling with a white marina flag by the OCWW. Turn at that piling, leaving it to starboard and head for the south shore. You will be headed toward a restaurant with a green roof (Joe's Crab Shack). Make a right into the marina basin. Legacy Harbour Marina has concrete floating docks that can accommodate vessels up to 120 feet. One of the largest floating breakwaters in the Gulf of Mexico protects the marina from the wakes of the river traffic. The marina has cable TV, laundry, air-conditioned showers, metered-at-the-slip electric, WiFi and an in-slip pump-out station. A well-equipped and very pleasant boaters' lounge is available in the harbormaster's building. Adjacent to the marina is a hotel with well-appointed waterfront suites and standard hotel rooms (reservations recommended). Grocery, shops and restaurants are within walking distance in the Historic Downtown River District.

The family-owned and -operated Marina at Edison Ford is located about 1 mile beyond the Caloosahatchee River Bridge. The marina maintains a well-marked channel on the south shore. A restaurant is on site, as is a coin-operated laundry. It is only a short walk to groceries and plenty of shopping and dining.

## Cape Coral–OCWW Mile 142

Cape Coral was born when the Rosen family purchased 103 square miles of swampland known as Redfish Point. At 114 square miles, it is now the second largest city in Florida. The canals of Cape Coral total more mileage than those of Venice, Italy.

**NAVIGATION:** Use Charts 11428 and 11427. Southwest of Fort Myers, the Caloosahatchee River continues somewhat circuitously for another 15 miles. At Mile 138.6 is the **Veterans Memorial (Mid-Point) Bridge**, with a 55-foot fixed vertical clearance. At Mile 142, the OCWW passes under the **Cape Coral Twin Bridges** (charted at 55 feet, but do not count on more than 54 feet of fixed vertical clearance).

⚠ Frequent groundings occur in the Caloosahatchee River west of Cape Coral. Be sure to use front and rear ranges. See the Waterway Guide Explorer at waterwayguide.com for new alerts and updates.

This is a boating-oriented area, and the traffic is reminiscent of downtown Fort Lauderdale. Exercise some care in transiting the remaining miles of the OCWW. Numerous shoal areas are outside the channel.

**Dockage:** Between flashing red daybeacons "70" and "72" on the south side of the river, a marked channel near shore leads into the private The Landings Marina, with gasoline and diesel fuel but no transient dockage. MarineMax Fort Myers is nearby, on a channel off Deep Lagoon, with slips, fuel and repairs. Reservations are required.

Near quick-flashing green daybeacon "73," a well-marked channel leads southward to the Gulf Harbour Marina, a full-service facility that welcomes transients. East of flashing green daybeacon "85," a marked channel (starting with green daybeacon "1") leads southward to the St. Charles Yacht Club, a member of the Florida Council of Yacht Clubs that recognizes reciprocity.

At Redfish Point (on the north shore), the municipal Cape Coral Yacht Basin offers daily, monthly and annual rentals on a first-come, first-served basis. It is located north of red daybeacon "78" off a marked channel. Individuals who rent slips in the marina have access to amenities within the nearby Yacht Club Community Park, including a public beach, tennis courts, a pool and a restaurant (Boat House Tiki Bar & Grill).

At red daybeacon "92," a channel leads behind Cattle Dock Point to the north, where markers guide you into the well-appointed Tarpon Point Marina. The resort-style facilities include a pool, a fuel dock with both gas and diesel and access to boutique shopping at the nearby resort. They can accommodate vessels to 120 feet. Once again, reservations are a must.

Located just past Cattle Dock Point and Tarpon Point, signs will guide you to a small lock that provides access to the Cape Harbour Marina. The marina offers transient dockage in a condominium setting. A laundry, pool and competitive fuel pricing make this a popular stop.

**Anchorage:** At red daybeacon "84A," there is a well-marked channel off to starboard that will lead you into Bimini Basin. You need to stay in this channel, and make a 90-degree turn to port when you get to green daybeacon "25." Then keep the red markers on your

## Meet the Burrowing Owl

Cape Coral is home to Florida's largest population of Burrowing Owls. One of Florida's smallest owls, the Burrowing Owl averages 9 inches in height with a wingspan of 21 inches. It lives in open, treeless areas and spends most of its time on the ground, where its sandy brown plumage provides camouflage from potential predators. While it lacks the ear tufts of the more familiar woodland owls, it has distinctive bright yellow eyes and a white chin. It also has unusually long legs for additional height from its ground-level perch.

Aptly named, the owls either create new or make use of abandoned burrows to live in and nest. They are active both during day and night, and their nesting season starts mid-February and extends to mid-July. The owls first showed up in Cape Coral when the land was clear-cut for development. The sandy soil provides a suitable habitat for the owls.

If you don't understand what all the fuss is about, read the book *Hoot* by Carl Hiaasen. Visit capecoralburrowingowls.com for more information or to book a tour.

# GOIN' ASHORE: FORT MYERS, FL

| | SERVICES | | | |
|---|---|---|---|---|
| 1 | Library | | 10 | Firestone Grille, Martini Bar & Sky Lounge |
| 2 | Post Office | | 11 | Fords Garage |
| 3 | Visitor Information | | 12 | Los Cabo's Cantina |
| | **ATTRACTIONS** | | 13 | United Ale House |
| 4 | Burroughs Home & Garden | | | **MARINAS** |
| 5 | Edison's Estate | | 14 | City of Fort Myers Yacht Basin |
| 6 | Henry Ford Estate | | 15 | Legacy Harbour Marina |
| | **SHOPPING** | | 16 | The Marina at Edison Ford |
| 7 | Franklin Shops | | | |
| 8 | Publix | | | |
| | **DINING** | | | |
| 9 | Bennett's Fresh Roast | | | |

Fort Myers is named for a fort established during the Seminole Indian War of 1841. The fort briefly saw action as a union fort during the Civil War. The town remained a small but important winter resort until the Tamaimi trail bridged the Caloosahatchee in 1924. This sparked the first real estate boom and the town grew rapidly. It became the winter home of Thomas Alva Edison in 1884 and remained so for almost 50 years. In 1911, Henry Ford purchased property adjacent to Edison and lived there for several winters.

**Attractions:** The side-by-side Edison and Ford Winter Estates are open to the public (239-334-7419). Edison's 14-acre riverfront estate is situated along McGregor Boulevard, which is lined for 15 miles with 2,000 royal palms (the reason Fort Myers is known as the "City of Palms"). When enjoying the gardens, visitors should note the tropical plants given to Edison by friends. The immense Australian fig tree was tiny when Henry Ford sent it, and the 400-foot banyan (a gift from Harvey Firestone) was only 2 inches in diameter when planted. There is a laboratory where Edison created several of his many inventions, and both homes have been restored to their original grandeur. The grounds are spectacular.

This is a must-see tour when visiting Fort Myers. The stately Burroughs Home at 2505 First St. (239-337-0706) overlooks the Edison Bridge. Built in 1901, this Georgian Revival Mansion offers guided tours (Tuesday through Thursday at 11:00 a.m., reservation required). Contact tera@burroughshome.com or call 239-337-9505 for a reservation.

Strolling through the downtown area and all its shops and restaurants is a great way to spend an afternoon or evening. Just seeing how the 20th century buildings have been refurbished is well worth the time.

Art lovers are sure to find events of interest throughout the year, with the premier event being Art Fest Fort Meyers, held along the waterfront in early February each year. Theatre fans will find the plays, shows, and performances at the Florida Repertory Company at the Arcade, located right on the waterfront, to be greatly entertaining. On the first Friday of each month all year long, the city sponsors an Art Walk in the downtown River District area. It's very popular and well attended. Also, each Thursday morning from 7:00 a.m. to 1:00 p.m., there is a farmers market located at Centennial Park (Heitman and First Streets).

Nature lovers will find plenty to do; whether you are a bird lover or a manatee watcher, opportunities to experience the local flora and fauna abound in the Fort Meyers area.

**Shopping:** There are several boutiques and gift shopping opportunities downtown. For provisioning, a Publix Market is at First Street Village at 2160 McGregor Blvd. The Franklin Shops at 2200 First St. (239-333-3130) are close to the marinas. Being a small city, all sorts of big name shops are within a short cab ride from the waterfront.

**Dining:** There are several dining options within easy walking distance from the waterfront. Ford's Garage (2207 First St., 239-332-3673) is one of the most popular for lunch or dinner. They specialize in hamburgers and beer, with over 100 types of beer of the latter from which to choose. Cabo's Cantina & Tequila Bar (2226 First St., 239-332-2226) is an outstanding choice if you are interested in a great Mexican meal in a lively atmosphere. Next door is United Ale House (2236 First St., 239-362-1831), a London pub for beer and grub. For fantastic views, visit Firestone Grille, Martini Bar & Sky Lounge (2224 Bay St., 239-334-3473) with four floors of food and fun.

Start your day at Bennett's Fresh Roast at 2011 Bayside Pkwy. with house-roasted coffee and donuts made on-site (239-332-0077).

# Caloosahatchee River, FL

www.snagaslip.com
SNAG-A-SLIP
EXPLORE. BOOK. BOAT.™

| CAPE CORAL AREA | | Largest Vessel Accommodated | VHF Channel Monitored | Transient Berths / Total Berths | Approach / Dockside Depth (reported) | Floating Docks | Gas / Diesel | Groceries, Ice, Marine Supplies, Snacks | Repairs: Hull, Engine, Propeller | Lift (tonnage), Crane, Rail | Laundry, Pool, Showers, Courtesy Car | Min/Max Amps | Pump-Out Station | Nearby: Grocery Store, Motel, Restaurant |
|---|---|---|---|---|---|---|---|---|---|---|---|---|---|---|
| | | | | **Dockage** | | | **Supplies** | | **Services** | | | | | |
| **1.** The Landings Marina-PRIVATE 142.5 | 239-481-7181 | 60 | 16 | call/193 | 5/ | – | GD | GIMS | HEP | – | – | S | – | GR |
| **2.** MarineMax Fort Meyers at Deep Lagoon 💻 WiFi 143 | 239-481-8200 | 90 | 16 | call/75 | 6/6 | F | GD | IM | HEP | L75 | 30/100 | S | P | GR |
| **3.** Gulf Harbour Marina 💻 WiFi WG 143.5 | 239-437-0881 | 101 | 16/11 | 10/186 | 6/5 | F | GD | I | – | – | 30/50 | LS | P | GMR |
| **4.** St. Charles Yacht Club WiFi 146 | 239-466-4935 | 78 | 16/68 | call/65 | 5/5 | – | GD | – | – | – | 50/50 | LPS | P | R |
| **5.** Cape Coral Yacht Basin 💻 WiFi 144 | 239-574-0809 | 50 | 16/78 | 4/89 | 5/5 | – | GD | IMS | EP | – | 30/50 | LPS | P | GMR |
| **6.** Tarpon Point Marina 💻 WiFi 147 | **239-549-4900** | **120** | **16/18** | **15/225** | **7/8** | **F** | **GD** | **GIMS** | – | – | **30/100** | **PS** | **P** | **GR** |
| **7.** Cape Harbour Marina WiFi 147 | 239-945-4330 | 60 | 16 | 16/76 | 6/6 | – | GD | IS | – | L11 | 30/50 | LPS | P | GMR |

💻 Internet Access   WiFi Wireless Internet Access   WG Waterway Guide Cruising Club Partner   *(Information in the table is provided by the facilities.)*
See WaterwayGuide.com for current rates, fuel prices, web site addresses, and other up-to-the-minute information.

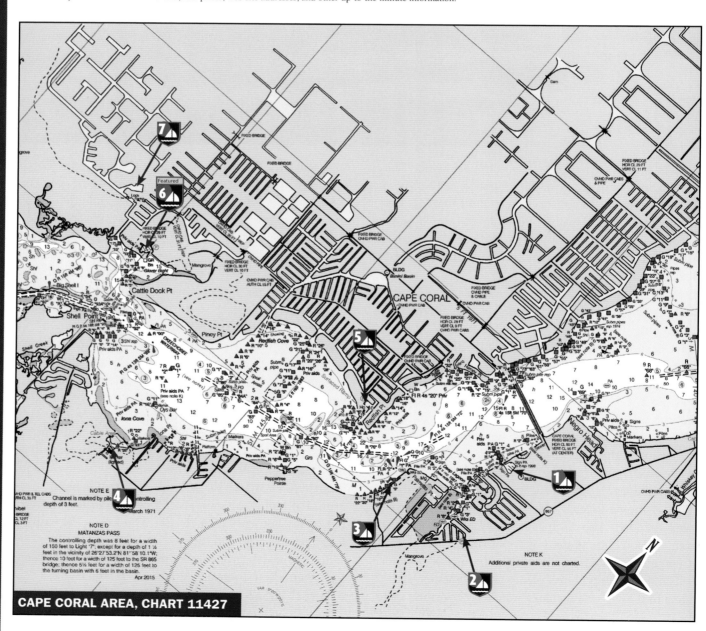

**CAPE CORAL AREA, CHART 11427**

TARPON POINT MARINA

239-549-4900

port side (we know that this is different, but it is very important) until you come to the canal that will lead you into the anchorage. It is well protected and is a handy spot to get to a couple of supermarkets and West Marine, plus a very large hardware store, as well as a variety of other services. There is also a dinghy dock at the park. You can anchor in 10 feet of water for up to 30 days.

Glover Bight, just behind Cattle Dock Point at Mile 147, is another excellent, all-weather anchorage. You will find good protection from all points with 10 to 12 feet of good holding in mud. There is also a restaurant and tiki bar at the water's edge along with a number of boutique shops.

## Cruising Options

In the following chapter, Waterway Guide returns to the ICW traveling south with "St. Lucie Inlet to Pompano Beach."

# CLEAN + DRAIN + DRY YOUR GEAR

# Florida's Lower East Coast

■ ST. LUCIE INLET TO POMPANO BEACH
■ FORT LAUDERDALE TO HOLLYWOOD ■ MIAMI & BISCAYNE BAY

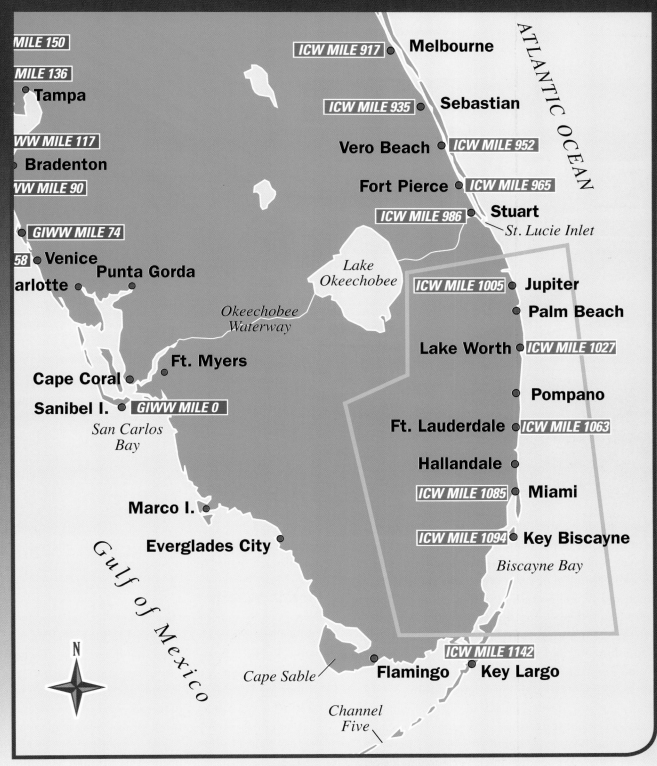

MILE 150

MILE 136

Tampa

WW MILE 117

Bradenton

VW MILE 90

GIWW MILE 74

58 Venice

Punta Gorda

arlotte

Cape Coral

Ft. Myers

Sanibel I.    GIWW MILE 0

San Carlos
Bay

Marco I.

Everglades City

*Gulf of Mexico*

N

*Cape Sable*

Flamingo

*Channel
Five*

ICW MILE 917    Melbourne

ICW MILE 935    Sebastian

Vero Beach    ICW MILE 952

Fort Pierce    ICW MILE 965

ICW MILE 986    Stuart
*St. Lucie Inlet*

*Lake
Okeechobee*

*Okeechobee
Waterway*

ICW MILE 1005    Jupiter

Palm Beach

Lake Worth    ICW MILE 1027

Pompano

Ft. Lauderdale    ICW MILE 1063

Hallandale

ICW MILE 1085    Miami

ICW MILE 1094    Key Biscayne

*Biscayne Bay*

ICW MILE 1142
Key Largo

*ATLANTIC OCEAN*

www.WaterwayGuide.com

# Florida's Lower East Coast

Once you leave the Crossroads, you will notice an increase in population—both on and off the water—as well as an increase in boat and home size. Large estates with manicured lawns line the waterways in Hobe and Jupiter Sounds, and they get more opulent in Palm Beach. The "water highway" widens at Lake Worth and continues past Boynton and Delray Beaches. Upscale shopping and art galleries define the Boca Raton area, and Pompano Beach offers harness racing and poker tournaments in addition to great fishing.

More than 300 miles of mostly navigable inland waterways carve through the Fort Lauderdale area, making it the "Venice of America." It is well known as a yachting center and boating amenities and services are readily available. There is also access to the Everglades National Park and the alligators, colorful birds and other wildlife that makes its home there.

## Florida Weather

Before you assume every day is paradise, it's good to know a bit more about southern Florida's weather patterns. The primary factors that determine the weather patterns of warm, humid summers and mild, cool winters are latitude and inland lakes. The heat can be life-threatening; in fact, more people die from excessive heat here than from lightning strikes. This is notable because Florida is known as the thunderstorm capital of the U.S. These typically occur June through September

*The east bascule drawbridge on the Venetian Causeway, connecting Miami and Miami Beach, through the Venetian Islands*

in the afternoons and early evenings. There is also the possibility of tornadoes in April, May and June, which ushers in the Atlantic hurricane season. That begins June 1 and ends November 30, with the highest storm probability from August through October. In short, be aware that it's not always sunny in "the Sunshine State!"

## Manatees

West Indian manatees, also known as sea cows, are enormous aquatic mammals. The average adult male is about 10 feet long and weighs around 1,000 pounds. Manatees live in shallow, slow-moving waters, such as quiet rivers, peaceful saltwater bays, and calm coastal canals from spring to fall. In the winter, they search for warmer waters, heading to inland springs or even the

heated outflow of power plants. Since manatees usually travel together in a long line with their bodies mostly submerged, they can resemble drifting coconuts. Also look for concentric circles in the water, a signal that manatees are about to surface.

Manatees are protected by the Marine Mammal Protection Act of 1972, the Federal Endangered Species Act of 1973 and the Florida Manatee Sanctuary Act of 1978. Many manatees are wounded and killed by watercraft and their propellers. Because of this, there are Manatee Zones posted along the waterways with restricted, no-wake speed limits. Some are seasonal (winter months) while others are year-round. Pay attention to these signs or risk fines.

# DOWNLOAD

*Marinas App*

WATERWAY GUIDE® THE CRUISING AUTHORITY

waterwayguide.com

# St. Lucie Inlet to Pompano Beach

 Mile 986–Mile 1057     FL: Channel 09

**CHARTS** 11467, 11472

Manatee speed zones occur with increasing frequency south of St. Lucie Inlet. From green daybeacon "13" to green daybeacon "15" you will encounter a Manatee Zone for approximately 1 mile. If you pay attention, you we see a lot of manatees swimming around.

Most commonly, speed zones in the ICW channel will be 25 mph; outside the channel, speed zones will read "Slow-Speed/Minimum-Wake to Shore." Be alert, however, to whether the posted speed zone includes or excludes the channel and if it is seasonal. See the Inlet Section at the front of this guide for more information.

## ■ ST. LUCIE INLET TO JUPITER INLET

**NAVIGATION:** Use Chart 11472. On the east side of the ICW, the incoming St. Lucie Inlet markers end with green daybeacon "17" near the junction with the ICW. (Leave those to port as you continue south on the ICW.) The first aid to navigation on the southbound continuation of the ICW is a daybeacon with white dayboards, reading DANGER—SHOAL, which should be left well to starboard (red-right-returning) when southbound. This is followed by red daybeacon "2" and flashing green daybeacon "3."

### St. Lucie State Park–ICW Mile 990

When entering Great Pocket past Horseshoe Point, watch for shoaling and use caution in the area. Long docks and piers are on both sides of Great Pocket that are not shown on the chart.

A bit of wilderness is preserved just south of the inlet in the St. Lucie Inlet State Park and adjoining Reed Wilderness Seashore Wildlife Refuge at the north end of Jupiter Island at Mile 990.

**Dockage:** A small floating dock and a long pier with slips for smaller boats are near the north end of the park. Depths here average 4 feet. Tie off carefully and use fenders, as powerboats often pass without slowing,

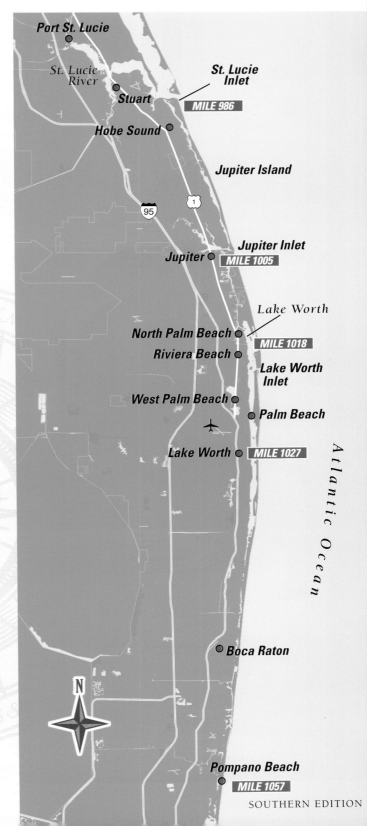

causing heavy wakes. A small charge is collected on the honor system for use of the park, which is accessible only by boat. From the dock, an elevated wooden walkway with restrooms and picnic pavilions at either end cuts through the mangrove swamp to the ocean about a .5 mile away. You may swim, fish or beach comb at the beautiful ocean beach. Dogs are allowed on the walkway but not on the beach.

## Peck Lake–ICW Mile 991

Low dunes, uninhabited beaches and sparkling ocean waters may beckon, and dredging of the lake and lake access has made anchoring in Peck Lake less of a challenge than in the past. Peck Lake, east of the ICW channel, has depths of 6 to 12 feet, from the ICW to close to shore.

**NAVIGATION:** Use Chart 11472. There is an additional posted Manatee Zone from green daybeacon "21" in Peck Lake to the Hobe Sound (SR 708) Bascule Bridge (Mile 995.9), which includes areas both outside and inside the channel. North of green daybeacon "21," the Manatee Zone does not include the ICW channel and has a 25-mph speed limit in the channel only. This speed limit goes past the Peck Lake anchorage, at flashing green "19," which is very close to the ICW channel and can be subject to large wakes, although some boaters are usually courteous enough to slow for the anchored boats here. Some Manatee Speed Zones are seasonal (winter months), while others are year-round. Assume that restrictions are year-round if no specific dates appear on the sign.

**Dockage:** On the west side of the ICW, just across from Peck Lake, is Loblolly Marina. Do not be scared off by the two "Private" signs; transient and long-term dockage is available in this residential community in a very protected and pretty basin. Loblolly boasts "No bridges, no wakes, no worries." The marina is surrounded by lush mangroves and is adjacent to the Hobe Sound Wildlife Refuge. They offer complete marine services as well as full cruiser amenities, including both gas and diesel.

**Anchorage:** Deep water for entrance to Peck Lake is located close to flashing green "19," on the south side. Take it slowly, and head in on a course of 060 toward the "Danger" sign. There is more depth than charted here and room for half a dozen boats. There is the possibility of debris on the bottom, so exercise caution when choosing an anchoring spot. Even though it is well protected on all sides, you will still encounter wakes

from some passing boats. The anchorage is often busy during the week and becomes even more crowded on weekends.

Once anchored, a dinghy ride to shore brings you to within a short distance over the dunes to a beautiful, unspoiled ocean beach. The park is for daytime use only, and the portion north of the crossover path is closed in the spring and early summer months to protect nesting Least Terns (*sterna antillarum*, the smallest of the American terns). South of this path, the beach is available for walking and swimming. When temperatures are above 60 degrees, with little or no wind, sand gnats (commonly called "no-see-ums") can be a problem.

A platform structure, apparently for collecting weather data, has been erected in Peck Lake just off the beach.

## Hobe Sound–ICW Mile 996

The Jove Indians, whose name the Spanish pronounced "Ho-bay," gave Hobe Sound its name. A highly exclusive area, sometimes compared with Palm Beach, Hobe Sound shows off many of its grand mansions and manicured lawns along the eastern shore of the channel. The Hobe Sound National Wildlife Refuge dominates the western shore of the sound at about Mile 997, and its natural wilderness contrasts strikingly with the sculptured lawns on the eastern shore.

**NAVIGATION:** Use Chart 11472. At the northern end of Hobe Sound, the **Hobe Sound (SR 708) Bascule Bridge** crosses the ICW at Mile 995.9. The bridge has a closed vertical clearance of 21 feet at center and opens on signal. Both sides of the well-marked channel through Hobe Sound have good depths, but do not stray too far and give points a wide berth.

Hobe Sound is heavily populated with both Slow-Speed/Minimum-Wake and Idle-Speed/No-Wake Zones to protect the manatees. Manatees frequent the area from November through March, so keep them in mind as you transit the sound. Much of the ICW channel itself is exempt from these speed restrictions, but check posted warnings to be certain. In one area, for example, signs on daybeacons cite different speed restrictions for craft larger and smaller than 35 feet.

**Dockage:** At Mile 1002, both Blowing Rocks Marina and Jupiter Pointe Club & Marina sell fuel and have limited transient space. Call ahead for availability. Groceries and restaurants are about 1.5 miles away.

To the south is Black Pearl Marina and Gilbane Boatworks. This is a repair/service facility that does not

# Hobe Sound, Jupiter Inlet Area, FL

| | | Largest Vessel Accommodated | VHF Channel Monitored | Transient Berths / Total Berths | Approach / Dockside Depth (reported) | Floating Docks | Gas / Diesel | Groceries, Ice, Marine Supplies, Snacks | Repairs: Hull, Engine, Propeller | Lift (tonnage), Crane, Rail | Min/Max Amps | Laundry, Pool, Showers, Courtesy Car | Pump-Out Station | Nearby: Grocery Store, Motel, Restaurant |
|---|---|---|---|---|---|---|---|---|---|---|---|---|---|---|
| **PECK LAKE** | | | | **Dockage** | | | | **Supplies** | | | **Services** | | | |
| 1. Loblolly Marina ☐ WiFi WG 992.2 | 772-546-3136 | 110 | 16/10 | 5/74 | 7/7 | – | – | I | – | – | 30/100 | LS | – | – |
| **N. JUPITER AREA** | | | | | | | | | | | | | | |
| 2. Blowing Rocks Marina ☐ WiFi 1002.2 | 561-746-3312 | 70 | 16 | 2/60 | 6/5 | F | GD | IMS | HEP | L10 | 30/50 | S | P | GMR |
| 3. Jupiter Pointe Club & Marina 1002.8 | 561-746-2600 | 55 | 16 | – | 5/5 | F | GD | IS | HEP | L | 30/50 | P | P | GMR |
| 4. Black Pearl Marina and Gilbane Boatworks | 561-744-2223 | – | – | call/58 | 8/8 | – | – | IMS | H | – | 30/30 | S | – | GMR |
| **JUPITER AREA** | | | | | | | | | | | | | | |
| 5. JIB Yacht Club Marina ☐ WiFi 1004.2 | 561-746-4300 | 70 | 16 | 4/40 | 8/8 | – | GD | IMS | – | – | 30/50 | PS | P | GMR |
| 6. Jupiter Yacht Club & Marina–PRIVATE 1006.5 | 561-741-3407 | 65 | – | call/79 | 5/5 | – | – | – | – | – | 30/50 | – | – | GMR |
| 7. Suntex Marina at Jupiter WG 1006.8 | 561-747-8980 | 100 | 16 | call/31 | 7/6 | F | G | IMS | EP | – | 30/50 | LPS | P | GMR |
| 8. Admirals Cove Marina ☐ WiFi 1007.8 | 561-745-5930 | 170 | 16/10 | 5/65 | 11/10 | F | GD | GIMS | HEP | – | 50/100 | LPS | P | GMR |
| 9. The Bluffs Marina WiFi 1008 | 561-627-6688 | 130 | 16 | call/102 | – | F | GD | – | – | L | 50/100 | S | – | R |
| 10. Loggerhead Marina–Palm Beach Gardens ☐ WiFi | 561-627-6358 | 120 | 16/10 | 10/136 | 8/8 | – | GD | IMS | – | – | 30/100 | S | P | GMR |

☐ Internet Access  WiFi Wireless Internet Access  WG Waterway Guide Cruising Club Partner  *(Information in the table is provided by the facilities.)*
See WaterwayGuide.com for current rates, fuel prices, web site addresses, and other up-to-the-minute information.

offer transient dockage. There is a Publix Supermarket about one-half mile south of Black Pearl.

**Anchorage:** Because there is a 25-mph speed limit in the Hobe Sound channel, almost all anchorages here are susceptible to annoying boat wakes. In easterly winds, craft drawing less than 5 feet will find an attractive anchorage just off the western shore of Harbor Island. Sound your way in and set the hook well. There are numerous anchorages west of the ICW channel between red daybeacon "38" and green daybeacon "49" north of Mile 999. (See details on the Waterway Explorer at waterwayguide.com.) Follow your chart carefully. In the daytime, passing vessels and water skiers may throw some wake your way, but nights are generally peaceful. Do not be surprised by a routine boarding from local marine police and be sure to show an anchor light.

## ■ JUPITER INLET TO LAKE WORTH

The ICW leads into Jupiter Sound at Mile 1002, where the estates of Hobe Sound give way to only slightly more modest homes. Nearby spoil areas and shoals demand careful attention; stay in the channel! Jupiter Inlet marks the confluence of Jupiter Sound to the north, Lake Worth Creek to the south and Loxahatchee River to the west. The inlet is known for its red brick lighthouse and aquamarine-colored waters.

**NAVIGATION:** Use Chart 11472. Use the Miami Harbor Entrance Tide Tables. For high tide, subtract 10 minutes; for low tide, subtract 9 minutes. A submerged obstruction lies north of flashing green daybeacon "53," but off the channel. Several small marinas and dry storage facilities are on the western shore of Jupiter Sound. The **Jupiter Island (CR 707) Bascule Bridge** (hail it as the "707 Bridge") at Mile 1004.1 has a 25-foot closed vertical clearance and opens on signal. If your vessel is lightly powered, do not get caught by the swift current here while waiting for the bridge. Contact the bridge tender prior to your arrival and allow for the set of the current.

Jupiter Inlet fights a constant battle with shifting sand. A short jetty protects the inlet entrance from the north, and a steel barricade extends halfway into the inlet from the south bank. The mouth of the inlet has strong currents, eddies, turbulence and breaking seas over sandbars that extend from the south side of the inlet offshore towards the northeast.

Jupiter Inlet has a mean tidal range of 2.5 feet. Despite constant dredging, the inlet is cited by the Coast Guard as "not navigable without current local knowledge." The inlet channel is unsafe for all but small boats with local knowledge and very shallow draft. If you are tempted to try and run the inlet, be sure to refer to the Jupiter

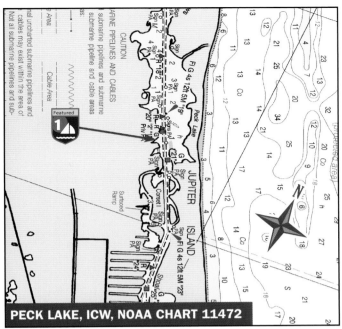

**PECK LAKE, ICW, NOAA CHART 11472**

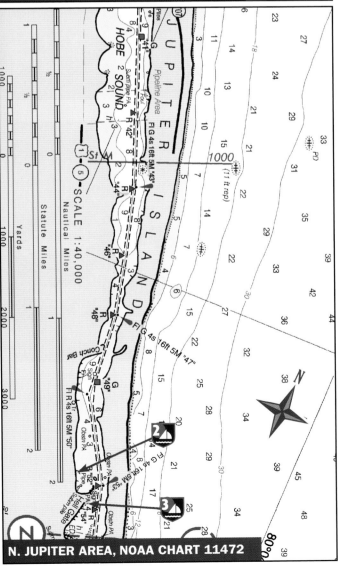

**N. JUPITER AREA, NOAA CHART 11472**

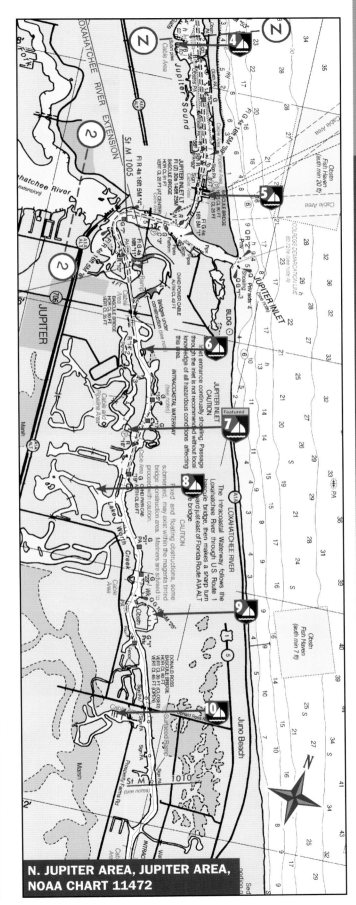

**N. JUPITER AREA, JUPITER AREA, NOAA CHART 11472**

Peck Lake

LOBLOLLY MARINA

**Location:** situated at Loblolly, a distinguished private residential community on the west shore of Peck's Lake at Hobe Sound between Palm Beach and Stuart, Florida; forty minutes north of Palm Beach International Airport.

**Convenience:** close by Stuart offers complete marine services; the St. Lucie Inlet is only 3 bridgeless miles north for access in minutes to some of the world's greatest game fishing, cruising, and sailing waters.

LOBLOLLY MARINA

**Facilities:** secure, safe, and able to accommodate craft up to 110 feet in length. Surge protected 30, 50 and 100 amp electrical service, telephone, and softened water. Restrooms, showers, wireless internet service, and laundry facilities. We also offer a private beach shuttle to the adjacent Hobe Sound National Wildlife Refuge and over 3 miles of dedicated bike paths. Complimentary bicycles available. A limited number of slips are available to transients and on an annual or seasonal basis.

7407 S.E. Hill Terrace, Hobe Sound, Florida 33455     Telephone (772) 546-3136 • marina@loblollyinfo.com

**A Limited Number of Marina Memberships Are Available.**

We monitor Channel 16 • ICW MM 992.2

Jupiter Inlet (Use local knowledge)

Atlantic Ocean

Inlet District Commission site at jupiterinletdistrict.org (561-746-2223). They have a live web cam that reports current weather and sea conditions and allows you to observe the inlet conditions at any time. Additional information on Jupiter Inlet is provided in the Inlet section at the front of this guide.

**Dockage:** The JIB Yacht Club Marina is just south of the Jupiter Island Bridge on the east side of the ICW and offers gas and diesel fuel and some transient dockage.

**Anchorage:** Jupiter Sound, which is protected from boat wakes by a nearly continuous spoil bank, is just south of red daybeacon "54" at Mile 1002. This crowded anchorage is hard to enter and exit due to a proliferation of private moorings and derelict boats and is not a recommended anchorage. White spherical buoys mark the northern entrance, which carries 6.5-foot depths. The former southern entrance has shoaled badly. On warm days you will have plenty of company. Small powerboats will pull right up on the spoil bank.

## ICW Mile 1004 to Mile 1011

**NAVIGATION:** Use Chart 11472. Use the Miami Harbor Entrance Tide Tables. For high tide, add 28 minutes; for low tide add, 1 hour and 5 minutes. At Mile 1004, at the intersection of the ICW and Jupiter Inlet, the route south begins a sharp reverse S-curve, first to starboard (west) into the Jupiter Inlet/Loxahatchee River, then under the **Jupiter (U.S. 1) Bascule Bridge**, then to port (south) out of the Loxahatchee into Lake Worth Creek. The Jupiter Island Bridge at Mile 1004.8 has 26-foot closed vertical clearance and opens on signal.

There has been consistent shoaling over the years at red nun buoy "2" at the turn into Jupiter Inlet (Mile 1004). Give red nun buoy "2" a wide berth as the shoal extends well off the point. Always follow the buoys, watch inlet currents and make the final turn to port cautiously. You will not see the opening southbound into Lake Worth Creek until you are almost on it, and boats coming from the south will not be visible until after you have begun the final swing.

The route appears to dead end in a false lead created by the **Old Dixie Highway Bridge** (SR Alternate A1A Bridge), which has a 25-foot fixed vertical clearance, and the **Loxahatchee Railroad Bridge** that follows (4-foot closed vertical clearance, normally open except during train traffic), both crossing the Loxahatchee River.

The **Loxahatchee River**, Florida's only designated wild and scenic river, is shallow beyond the bridges. It is virtually unnavigable for craft drawing more than 3.5 or 4 feet and for any craft requiring overhead clearance greater than 25 feet, but it is definitely worth exploring, if possible. It is marked by private aids to navigation. You may be able to dock at the Jupiter marinas and investigate by dinghy. Several miles of the Loxahatchee River's main northwest fork border the 11,500-acre Jonathan Dickinson State Park, which offers great freshwater and saltwater fishing, canoeing, hiking, bicycling, along with picnicking, camping and guided tours of the Loxahatchee.

The ICW, however, continues past green daybeacon "7," where the channel bustles with boats of all sizes, and the shore gleams with one-story condominiums and houses set among beautifully manicured lawns. Do not let your eye stray too far from mid-channel and check the depth and boat speed frequently. This patrolled stretch is a marked Idle-Speed/No-Wake Zone, channel included. Much of the length below Mile 1007 does not have speed restrictions.

The **Indiantown (SR 706) Bascule Bridge** (35-foot closed vertical clearance) crosses the ICW at Mile 1006.2 and has restricted openings. The bridge opens on the hour and half-hour 24 hours a day, 7 days a week. This is an enforced No-Wake Zone. The **Donald Ross Bascule Bridge** (35-foot closed vertical clearance) at Mile 1009.3 opens on the hour and half-hour.

**Dockage:** The Jupiter Yacht Club & Marina, on the east side at Mile 1006.5, is a private club. A little farther south on the west side at Mile 1006.8 is Suntex Marina at Jupiter, offering dry storage and wet slips. They offer gas and pump-out service and have a tiki bar.

At Mile 1007.8, Admirals Cove Marina offers slips and resort-style amenities. They can accommodate boats up to 130 feet and the marina is considered a natural weather refuge for yachts. The Bluffs Marina, at Mile 1008 is primarily a dockominium marina with limited transient slips.

Loggerhead Marina–Palm Beach Gardens, at Mile 1009, is just south of the Donald Ross Bridge in a well-protected basin off the ICW. Loggerhead can accommodate transient boats up to 120 feet and has pump-out service at each slip. They also sell fuel and some supplies and offer easy access to restaurants, shopping, golf, tennis and other social activities.

**Anchorage:** The shallow anchorage north of the Indiantown Bridge on the east side of the ICW is full of small boats permanently moored, along with a public boat ramp and a floating hot dog stand on weekends.

# ■ LAKE WORTH (PALM BEACH) AREA

A concentration of marinas offering all kinds of services and repairs is located on the ICW stretch from just north of the PGA Boulevard Bridge in North Palm Beach to Palm Beach. All are convenient to the area's famous shopping, from The Gardens Mall in Palm Beach Gardens to Worth Avenue in Palm Beach.

## North Palm Beach–ICW Mile 1012 to Mile 1016

**NAVIGATION:** Use Chart 11472. At Mile 1012.6, the **PGA Blvd. Bascule Bridge** and the **Parker (U.S. 1) Bascule Bridge** are about 1 mile apart and both have restricted openings. The PGA Blvd. Bridge (24-foot closed vertical clearance) opens on the hour and half-hour, while the Parker Bridge at Mile 1013.7 (25-foot closed vertical clearance) opens at 15 and 45 minutes past the hour.

The well-developed area in the 1 mile or so between the PGA Blvd. and Parker Bridges, and including the North Palm Beach Waterway (a canal splitting off to the west of the ICW), is a well-justified Slow-Speed/Minimum-Wake Zone. The No-Wake Zone continues to the opening into Lake Worth at Mile 1014.2.

The PGA Bridge area is restaurant junction for boaters. Just north of the bridge on the east bank is Seasons 52 Restaurant (561-625-5852). Just south of the bridge on the west bank is Waterway Café (561-694-1700) featuring salads and seafood items. Traffic can be congested from boats docking at these restaurants.

At Mile 1014, just past the Parker Bridge (U.S. 1), the ICW enters the open waters of Lake Worth proper. The lake is long and broad, but shallow, except for the ICW channel. Do not confuse the ICW markers leading south with those splitting off to the east and then north to hospitable Old Port Cove Marina and the extreme upper end of Lake Worth (and then to Little Lake Worth, a separate body of water). Lining both shores of

Lake Worth are boating-oriented towns and cities with marinas that include all the resort amenities.

Some of Lake Worth is a Manatee Zone with Slow-Speed/Minimum-Wake restriction, but with a few exceptions, most of the ICW channel is exempt from these restrictions and enjoys a 25-mph speed limit. Limited stretches of Idle-Speed/No-Wake Zones appear at bridges and adjacent to marinas. Carefully observe restricted speed limits, where they prevail. Lake Worth is crowded with boats, marinas and private docks, so damage from wakes can be severe.

**Dockage:** North of the PGA Bridge, Ways Boatyard and Seminole Marine Maintenance both offer haulout and repairs. Seminole has some transient space. Next is the Soverel Harbour Marina, which welcomes transients. It is a well-known "hurricane hole" and is close to dining, shopping and entertainment. Gas and diesel fuel are available next door at PGA Marina, along with some transient dockage.

Just south of the Parker Bridge (U.S. 1) to starboard is the North Palm Beach Marina. It is located in a secluded, sheltered keyhole-shaped harbor and can accommodate vessels to 150 feet. The marina features hardwood decked floating docks, a fully stocked ships store, fuel and pump-outs at every slip.

A short distance farther south, at green daybeacon "27," turn to port to enter Lake Worth and you will see Old Port Cove Marina on your port side, which has floating docks and a convenient fuel dock with pump-out facilities. On-site amenities include Sandpiper's Cove Restaurant & Bar, Captain's Lounge, fitness room and indoor laundry facilities. A West Marine and Publix are nearby. To reach Old Port Cove Marina, turn off the ICW to the east after entering Lake Worth proper, following the private green daybeacons, then head north around the Old Port Cove townhouses and condominiums. You will spot the entrance off to port shortly after passing green daybeacon "7." Hail Old Port Cove Marina on VHF Channel 16 to be directed to a slip.

**Anchorage:** Some cruisers have reported adequate depths for anchoring in the lagoons off the North Palm Beach Waterway. They are reached by turning to starboard at the bend just before Parker Bridge. The canal is charted at 7 feet with 6-foot depths in the first basin and 8 feet in the second, both of which will be to starboard. This is a very fine residential community.

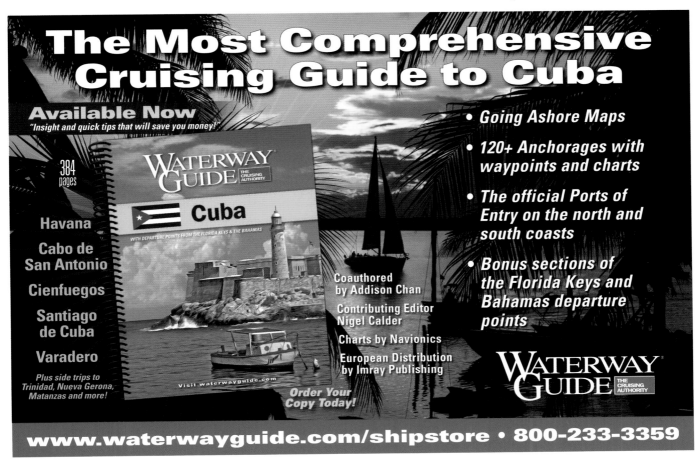

## Popular Peanut Island

Peanut Island was originally created in 1918 as a result of material excavated when the Lake Worth Inlet was created. Originally called Inlet Island, Peanut Island amounted to only 10 acres. Today, as a result of continued maintenance dredging of the inlet and the ICW, Peanut Island comprises approximately 80 acres.

Peanut Island is very popular with small powerboaters who anchor around its perimeter and party in the shallow, sandy-bottom water that extends out into the ICW. (There's even a pizza boat you can reach only by water.)

Swimming areas, kayaking lagoons and terrific snorkeling are among the draws of Peanut Island, which is a public park. There are paved walkways with scenic outlooks. Island facilities include picnic shelters and restrooms, and a dredged boat basin on its northwest side for dinghy tie-up.

The former Coast Guard Station and JFK Bomb Shelter on the south side of Peanut Island are part of the Palm Beach Maritime Museum and open for tours. The shelter, about 1,500 square feet in all, was abandoned after JFK's assassination in 1963 and was close to ruin when the Palm Beach Maritime Museum took over in the 1990s.

Water taxi service is available from Palm Beach Water Taxi (561-683-8294) and Peanut Island Shuttle Boat (561-723-2028). Call the water taxi on VHF Channel 16.

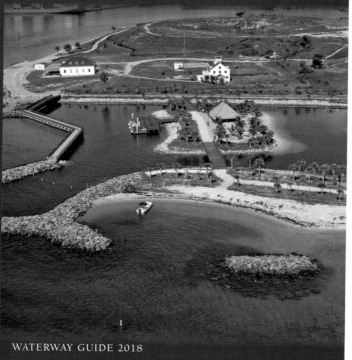

In the past, anchoring required a permit, but that is not presently required with the passage of Florida Statute 327.02; however, landing is not permitted.

Another anchorage is located at the north end of Lake Worth in Turtle Cove. Just after clearing the Parker Bridge and passing North Palm Beach Marina to starboard, enter Lake Worth and immediately turn off the ICW to port. Follow the green and red daybeacons off to the east, then north around Old Port Cove Marina, and follow the daybeacons to the extreme (northern) head of Lake Worth. You can drop the hook in 9- to 14-foot depths and have plenty of swinging room. You will find a handy place to land the dinghy at the east abutment of the A1A Bridge (8-foot fixed vertical clearance) over the cut between Lake Worth and Little Lake Worth.

This area is in a residential neighborhood and is only a small patch of sand. Cruisers tie up their dinghies to anything that will hold them. Be mindful of private property. Groceries, marine supplies and extensive shopping areas are nearby. There is a West Marine Superstore within a 20-minute walk from the dinghy landing. Boaters who anchor on the east side of Old Port Cove in Lake Worth are not bothered by restrictions on anchoring.

## Riviera Beach Area–ICW Mile 1016 to Mile 1018

**NAVIGATION:** Use Chart 11472. Lake Worth is broad in the first stretch leading to the **Blue Heron Blvd. (SR A1A) Bridge** at Mile 1017.2. Riviera Beach is on the ocean (east side) of the ICW.

⚠️ The Blue Heron Boulevard Bridge has a charted clearance of 65 feet but actual clearance has been reported to be as low as 60 feet; check the tide boards mounted on the fender system to be sure.

The channel is narrow, but a 25-mph speed limit holds, with Slow-Speed/Minimum-Wake outside the channel to shore. A Slow-Speed/Minimum-Wake Zone was established in the ICW channel in the past, in the vicinity of the Lake Park Harbor Marina south to Blue Heron Bridge. In a strong crosswind, watch the set of your course.

Just through the bridge, you must make a decision. Directly ahead is Peanut Island. If you plan to continue south on the ICW, you will alter course to starboard, following the ICW around Peanut Island on the west side. (See sidebar.) If you plan to utilize Lake Worth Inlet, there are two channels.

After you pass under the Blue Heron Bridge, you can turn to port in a marked channel and reach the inlet. Be sure to stay to the north "red" side of the channel as that is where you will find the deeper water. There are marinas on the east side of this channel so watch your wake.

**Dockage:** Above the Blue Heron Blvd. Bridge at Mile 1016.2 is Lake Park Harbor Marina with slips and fuel. They can accommodate vessels to 80 feet on both floating and fixed docks. Here you will receive personalized service from a knowledgeable staff. (And they are dog friendly too!)

The Suntex Marina at Riviera Beach is on the west side just above the bridge (Mile 1017). It's easy to spot its two towers and huge dry storage facility. The marina offer slips with club-type amenities as well as hurricane-rated (140 mph winds) dry storage. This location is convenient to waterfront restaurants, shopping, golf, beaches, tennis and nightlife.

South of the Blue Heron Blvd. Bridge, marine facilities are abundant on both shores, north and south of Lake Worth Inlet. On the mainland western shore, beginning at Riviera Beach, are repair yards capable of handling boats of any size. New Port Cove Marine Center has a state-of-the-art dry stack storage system, 49 in-water slips for vessels up to 80 feet, fuel with high-speed pumps and engine repair services. They also have a fully stocked marine store and complimentary WiFi.

The next facility heading south, opposite Peanut Island, is Rybovich Marine Center. Their in-house tug fleet can escort you to their floating dry dock space for any service or refit.

Continuing south is the Riviera Beach City Marina (Mile 1018), which offers dockage to 150 feet plus catamaran slips. They boast floating concrete and Brazilian hardwood docks and pump-out service at every slip. The municipal marina is adjacent to Cracker Boy Boat Works–Riviera Beach, which has repair services and do-it-yourself facilities.

On the eastern shore, the resort area of Singer Island is crowded with houses, motels, docks and restaurants. There is a strong current at all the marinas on Singer Island, so exercise care while docking. The 54-slip Cannonsport Marina is the northernmost facility on Singer Island. It caters to sportfishing vessels, but transients are welcome, and they sell both gas and diesel fuel. They are "an intimate marina that's big on service."

# Lake Worth, FL

www.snagaslip.com
**SNAG-A-SLIP**
EXPLORE. BOOK. BOAT.™

| | Phone | Largest Vessel Accommodated | VHF Channel Monitored | Transient Berths / Total Berths | Approach / Dockside Depth (reported) | Floating Docks | Gas / Diesel | Groceries, Ice, Marine Supplies, Snacks | Repairs: Hull, Engine, Propeller | Lift (tonnage), Crane, Rail | Min/Max Amps | Laundry, Pool, Showers, Courtesy Car | Pump-Out Station | Nearby: Grocery Store, Motel, Restaurant |
|---|---|---|---|---|---|---|---|---|---|---|---|---|---|---|
| **NORTH PALM BEACH** | | | | | | | | | | | | | | |
| 1. Ways Boatyard 1012 | 561-622-8550 | 80 | 16 | call/10 | 10/5 | – | – | MS | HEP | L70,C,R | 30/50 | S | – | GMR |
| 2. Seminole Marine Maintenance 1011.9 | 561-622-7600 | 100 | – | 9/9 | 6/6 | – | – | GIMS | HEP | L100,C | 50/100 | S | – | GMR |
| 3. Soverel Harbour Marina 🖳 (WiFi) 1011.9 | 561-691-9554 | 100 | 16/8 | 10/146 | 12/8 | F | GD | GIMS | – | – | 30/50 | LS | P | GMR |
| 4. PGA Marina 1011.9 | 561-626-0200 | 90 | 16 | 5/30 | 8/8 | F | GD | GIMS | HEP | L35 | 30/50 | – | – | GMR |
| 5. North Palm Beach Marina (WiFi) WG 1013.7 | 561-626-4919 | 150 | 16/08 | 10/107 | 10/8 | F | GD | IMS | E | – | 30/100 | LS | P | GMR |
| 6. Old Port Cove Marina 🖳 (WiFi) WG 1014 | 561-626-1760 | 200 | 16/08 | 5/202 | 8/15 | F | D | GIS | EP | – | 30/200+ | LPS | P | GMR |
| **RIVIERA BEACH** | | | | | | | | | | | | | | |
| 7. Lake Park Harbor Marina (WiFi) WG 1016.2 | 561-881-3353 | 80 | 16/08 | 10/112 | 6/5.5 | F | GD | I | – | – | 30/50 | LS | P | GMR |
| 8. Suntex Marina at Riviera Beach 1017 | 561-840-6868 | 47 | – | call/300 | 6/6 | – | GD | IMS | – | – | 30/50 | – | P | G |
| 9. New Port Cove Marine Center 🖳 (WiFi) WG 1017.4 | 561-844-2504 | 80 | 16/08 | 10/49 | 5/5 | F | GD | IMS | HEP | – | 30/50 | LS | P | GMR |
| 10. Rybovich Marine Center 🖳 (WiFi) 1017.8 | 561-863-4126 | 250 | 16/65 | 4/9 | 13/13 | F | – | IMS | HEP | L150 | 30/100 | PS | – | GR |
| 11. Riviera Beach City Marina 🖳 (WiFi) 1018 | 561-842-7806 | 150 | 16/11 | 70/140 | 8/7 | F | GD | IMS | – | – | 30/200+ | LS | P | GR |
| 12. Cracker Boy Boat Works-Riviera Beach (WiFi) 1018.1 | 561-845-0357 | 110 | 16/11 | – | 19/19 | – | – | IM | HEP | L150,C | 30/100 | S | – | GMR |
| **SINGER ISLAND** | | | | | | | | | | | | | | |
| 13. Cannonsport Marina 🖳 (WiFi) | 800-627-8328 | 130 | 16/11 | 54/54 | 10/8 | – | GD | GIMS | – | – | 30/100 | LPS | P | GMR |
| 14. Buccaneer Marina 1017.6 | 561-842-1620 | 85 | 16/68 | call/16 | 12/12 | – | GD | IS | – | – | 30/50 | LPS | P | GMR |
| 15. Sailfish Marina Resort 🖳 (WiFi) 1017.7 | 561-844-1724 | 110 | 16/68 | 40/94 | 8/8 | F | GD | GIMS | – | – | 30/200+ | LPS | – | GMR |

🖳 Internet Access  (WiFi) Wireless Internet Access  WG Waterway Guide Cruising Club Partner  *(Information in the table is provided by the facilities.)*
See WaterwayGuide.com for current rates, fuel prices, web site addresses, and other up-to-the-minute information.

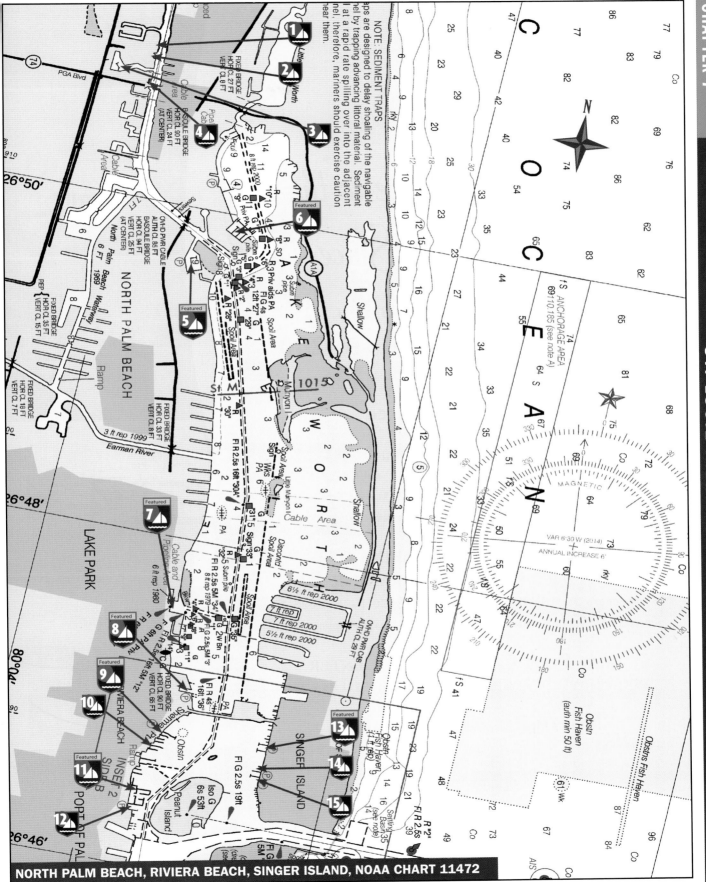

NOTE: SEDIMENT TRAPS

...aps are designed to delay shoaling of the navigable
...nel by trapping advancing littoral material. Sediment
...l at a rapid rate spilling over into the adjacent
...nel, therefore, mariners should exercise caution
...ear them.

**NORTH PALM BEACH, RIVIERA BEACH, SINGER ISLAND, NOAA CHART 11472**

Cannonsport Marina
Singer Island
Lake worth Inlet
Riviera Beach City Marina
JCW
Peanut Island
ICW

## Clean Marinas Program

The Florida Clean Marina Programs are designed to bring awareness to marine facilities and boaters regarding environmentally friendly practices intended to protect and preserve Florida's natural environment. Marinas, boatyards and marine retailers receive clean designations by demonstrating a commitment implementing and maintaining a host of best management practices.

The Florida Clean Boater Program, in turn, encourages boaters to use the designated clean marinas, boatyards and marine retailers. Boaters are also encouraged to adopt their own environmentally friendly efforts such as practicing proper trash management, using bilge socks and fueling collars and recycling.

Visit dep.state.fl.us/cleanmarina for more information and to sign the clean boater pledge.

*Source: Florida Dept. of Environmental Protection*

# Lake Worth, FL

| | Marina | | Phone | Largest Vessel Accommodated | VHF Channel Monitored | Approach / Dockside Depth (reported) | Transient Berths / Total Berths | Floating Docks | Gas / Diesel | Groceries, Ice, Marine Supplies, Snacks | Repairs: Hull, Engine, Propeller | Lift (tonnage), Crane, Rail | Min/Max Amps | Laundry, Pool, Showers, Courtesy Car | Pump-Out Station | Nearby: Grocery Store, Motel, Restaurant |
|---|---|---|---|---|---|---|---|---|---|---|---|---|---|---|---|---|
| | | | | **Dockage** | | | | | **Supplies** | | | **Services** | | | | |
| **WEST PALM BEACH** | | | | | | | | | | | | | | | | |
| 1. | Rybovich Marina ⬜ WiFi | 1019.5 | 561-840-8308 | 330 | 16/65 | 20/60 | 18/18 | F | GD | IMS | HEP | L660 | 30/200+ | PS | P | GMR |
| 2. | Palm Beach Yacht Club & Marina WiFi | 1022.9 | 561-655-8711 | 150 | 16/68 | 5/47 | 13/13 | – | GD | IM | – | L15 | 30/100 | LS | – | GR |
| 3. | Palm Harbor Marina ⬜ WiFi | 1022 | 800-435-8051 | 250 | 16/68 | 25/200 | 11/11 | F | GD | GIS | – | – | 30/200+ | LS | P | GMR |
| **PALM BEACH** | | | | | | | | | | | | | | | | |
| 4. | Palm Beach Town Docks ⬜ WiFi | 1024.5 | 561-838-5463 | 262 | 16/69 | 83/83 | 9/12 | – | – | I | – | – | 50/100 | S | P | GMR |

⬜ Internet Access  WiFi Wireless Internet Access  WG Waterway Guide Cruising Club Partner  *(Information in the table is provided by the facilities.)*
See WaterwayGuide.com for current rates, fuel prices, web site addresses, and other up-to-the-minute information.

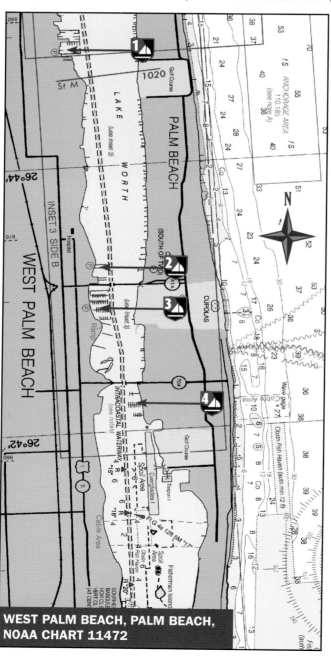

**WEST PALM BEACH, PALM BEACH, NOAA CHART 11472**

Buccaneer Marina at Mile 1017.6 has slips and fuel, as does Sailfish Marina Resort, located just inside Lake Worth Inlet on Singer Island. Giant "jacks," a type of schooling fish, patrol the docks at Sailfish Marina. During the afternoon, while fishermen clean their catch, the school waits patiently for leftovers at the cleaning tables. It is quite a spectacle and worth watching.

## Lake Worth Inlet–ICW Mile 1018

Wide, well-marked and jettied, Lake Worth Inlet (also known as Palm Beach Inlet) boasts a deep straightforward big ship channel that is one of the easiest to enter on the Atlantic coast. The meandering Gulf Stream is closer here than at any point in the United States (sometimes as close as 1 mile offshore, but usually out about 8 to 12 miles), and both commercial and recreational craft give the inlet heavy use. Its location, approximately midway between two other easy-to-navigate inlets–Fort Pierce Inlet (45 nm north) and Ft. Lauderdale (Port Everglades) Inlet (40 nm south)–makes it popular with boaters who prefer to travel offshore.

Lake Worth is a favorite point of departure for boats bound to and from the Bahamas Islands. Operators of small pleasure vessels arriving in the United States from a foreign port are required to report their arrival to Customs and Border Patrol (CBP) immediately by calling 800-432-1216 or 800-451-0393. CBP has designated specific reporting locations within the Field Offices that are staffed during boating season for pleasure boats to report their arrival and be inspected by CBP. For more details and exceptions, see the Skippers Handbook located at the front of this guide.

Some shoaling lies close in on the north side of the entrance channel, but it is frequently dredged. For additional details on Lake Worth Inlet, see the Inlet section at the front of this guide. About 1 mile west, inside the Lake Worth Inlet, the Port of Palm Beach handles commercial cargo, ranging from construction supplies to seafood, to tropical fruit and cruise ships.

**NAVIGATION:** Use Chart 11472. Use the Miami Harbor Entrance Tide Tables. For high tide, subtract 21 minutes; for low tide, add 4 minutes. To access the ocean, continue on the ICW around Peanut Island and pick up the official Lake Worth Inlet channel and follow it to the ocean. It is deep and well marked.

The Coast Guard establishes fixed and moving security zones at the Port of Palm Beach for the protection of passenger vessels (cruise ships), vessels carrying cargoes of a particular hazard and vessels carrying hazardous gases. A moving security zone activates when such a vessel passes red and white buoy "LW" when entering the port and becomes a fixed zone when the ship is docked. These zones cover the waters within 100 yards all around the subject vessels, and no craft can enter without prior permission. Patrol craft may be contacted on VHF Channel 16 for the status of these security zones.

**Anchorage:** There are several anchorages in the vicinity of Lake Worth Inlet. Anchor lights should be used in all Lake Worth anchorages. When entering any of the following anchorages pay strict attention to your depthsounder as there are several areas of shallow water. Anchorages include:

- Just northeast of the Blue Heron Boulevard Bridge in 8- to 13-foot depths over the "Discontinued Spoil Area." There are a number of derelict boats and a few sunken ones here. Beware of wreckage on the bottom.
- Just southeast of the turning basin marked by flashing green daybeacons "11" and "13" in 9 to 13 feet of water; avoid the "cable area" shown on the chart. This area is subject to tidal currents from the inlet, so observe proximity of other anchored vessels and their anchor set.
- One-half nautical mile south of the inlet along the east shore of Lake Worth, just southwest of Palm Beach at red daybeacon "6." Avoid the charted spoil and cable areas here. There are numerous permanently moored vessels in this area. Depths are 8 to 12 feet.

## West Palm Beach–ICW Mile 1018 to Mile 1023

South of the inlet and Peanut Island, Lake Worth is open, the ICW channel is well marked and maintained, and patches of deep water appear along the eastern Palm Beach shore. Palm Beach remains a winter ocean resort of elegance and charm. Across Lake Worth from Palm Beach, the West Palm Beach shore is given over to marinas, boatyards and yachting amenities.

In other places, any one of these would be outstanding in size, quality of work and service; here, though, mariners can be overwhelmed by the choices. Not all the services available are confined to the waterfront. A phone call or a short walk can put you in touch with just about every known kind of boat specialist—sailmakers, electronic sales and services, boat designers, boat maintenance and cleaning and diving services. Supplies of all kinds are close at hand.

Downtown West Palm Beach and City Place, an upscale outdoor mall surrounding an open-air plaza, are near the marinas. City Place has live entertainment, shopping, theaters, restaurants, groceries and art galleries; this is a festive commercial and cultural district. A free trolley runs from Clematis Street in West Palm Beach to City Place.

West Palm is the home of the Palm Beach International Boat Show, held in March. The event includes hundreds of boats from inflatables to megayachts, plus tents full of the latest electronics and accessories, seminars and fishing clinics for kids.

**Dockage:** Just before Mile 1020, privately maintained green daybeacon "1" marks the entrance to Rybovich Marina, which is a megayacht service facility with a 660-ton lift. They can accommodate vessels to 330 feet and also sell fuel, both gas and diesel.

North of the Flagler Memorial Bridge at Mile 1022.9 is Palm Beach Yacht Club & Marina with slips and fuel. Just south of the bridge, also on the West Palm Beach side, is Palm Harbor Marina, which has transient berths and sells both gas and diesel.

## Palm Beach–ICW Mile 1018 to Mile 1028

Palm Beach's famous Worth Avenue deserves a visit, with its collection of boutiques, jewelers, art galleries, restaurants and antiques stores. Grand old hotels such as the Brazilian Court and the Breakers have been renovated and still set the standard for this historically significant resort. One pleasant way to see Palm Beach is to have lunch or dinner at one of the numerous fine restaurants, then, have a leisurely stroll around town to take in the sights.

**NAVIGATION:** Use Chart 11472. At Mile 1021.8, you will come to **Flagler Memorial (SR A1A) Bascule Bridge**. At press time in spring 2017, the 21-foot closed vertical clearance bridge was under construction (replacing one with 17 feet of clearance). The bridge opens at 15 minutes past the hour, except Monday through Friday, when it does not open at 8:15 a.m. and 4:15 p.m. due to rush-hour traffic. As with all other Palm Beach County bridges, openings are restricted 24 hours a day, seven days a week, year-round. Be aware that there could still be construction equipment in the area and delays due to construction. The **Royal Park (SR 704) Bascule Bridge** at Mile 1022.6 has a 21-foot closed vertical clearance and opens on the hour and half-hour.

One final bridge connects the mainland and Palm Beach in this area. The **Southern Blvd. (SR 700/80) Bridge** (Mile 1024.7, 14-foot closed vertical clearance) opens at 15 and 45 minutes past the hour daily, 24 hours a day. Construction of a replacement 21-foot bascule bridge was under construction at press time in spring 2017. The project is planned to be completed sometime in late 2020. Be aware that you could experience delays due to the construction.

Note that when the President of the United States is visiting Mar-a-Lago, Flagler Memorial and Royal Park Bridges will be on an hourly schedule, Monday through Friday (excluding federal holidays). Flagler Memorial Bridge will be allowed to open at 2:15 p.m., 3:15 p.m., 4:15 p.m. and 5:15 p.m., while the Royal Park (Middle) Bridge will be allowed to open at 2:30 p.m., 3:30 p.m., 4:30 p.m. and 5:30 p.m. The Southern Boulevard Bridge will remain closed until the motorcade passes. These restrictions also apply to tug and barge traffic.

**Dockage:** The Palm Beach Town Docks offer complimentary dockage not to exceed 4 hours during the daytime hours of 8:00 a.m. to 5:00 p.m. There is no complimentary dockage offered after 5:00 p.m. and a minimum charge is assessed for overnight stays, regardless of boat length.

## South of Palm Beach

Lake Worth may be wide in this area, but south of Palm Beach, the water is shallow outside the ICW channel. Small islands (many of them originating as dredge spoil banks) break the open expanses and are overgrown with foliage. Estates border a large portion of the eastern shore, and tall condominiums appear with increasing frequency on both banks.

Small water-oriented communities, with many amenities for yachtsmen, are located all along Lake Worth. The first of these, the town of Lake Worth, has small shops, restaurants and art galleries. A large municipal beach and a 1,000-foot-long fishing pier provide recreational opportunities. The **Lake Worth-Lake Avenue Bridge** (35-foot closed vertical clearance) is at Mile 1028.8 and opens on signal. A public launch ramp on the mainland near the western end of this bridge has piers that can serve as dinghy landings.

Continuing south over the next 30 miles, the ICW alters its configuration and becomes a narrow land cut in the vicinity of Boynton Beach. Lined with residences and spanned by numerous bridges, the ICW truly looks like a water highway here. Two small, shallow lakes, Wyman and Boca Raton, and a brief stretch of the Hillsboro River are the only naturally formed bodies of water along this route. Even though the Atlantic Ocean is barely one-half mile away in places, you will find it hard to see among the proliferation of houses, motels, high-rise apartments and condominiums that line the route.

# LANTANA TO DELRAY BEACH

Lake Worth ends just north of the E. Ocean Avenue (Lantana) Bascule Bridge. The ICW becomes a canal, with concrete bulkheads lining its borders. Along this stretch, town follows town, and beautiful homes surrounded by subtropical growth add to the view.

Traveling south from Lake Worth, keep an eye out for the many Slow-Speed/Minimum-Wake Zones. They increase with greater frequency the closer you get to Fort Lauderdale. Be ready to call on VHF Channel 09 or whistle signal (two blasts: one prolonged, one short) for the opening of many of the 28 bridges that span the channel between Lake Worth and Government Cut at Miami Beach. Schedule a little extra time to allow for restricted openings, occasional bridge malfunctions and No-Wake Zones.

## Lantana to Boynton Beach–ICW Mile 1031 to Mile 1038

**NAVIGATION:** Use Chart 11467. Lantana is the next mainland town on Lake Worth. The **E. Ocean Avenue (Lantana) Bascule Bridge** at Mile 1031 (21-foot closed vertical clearance) connects Lantana on the mainland with Hypoluxo Island and South Palm Beach on the ocean side. The bridge has scheduled openings on the hour and half-hour. South of the Lantana Bridge, the route enters the Boynton Inlet approach area. Four miles to the south of the Lantana Bridge is the **E. Ocean Avenue (Boynton Beach) Bridge** with 21-foot closed vertical clearance, which opens on the hour and half-hour. The **E. Woolbright Rd. (SE 15th St.) Bridge** crosses the ICW at Mile 1035.8 (with 25-foot closed vertical clearance, opens on signal). Bridge restrictions apply 24 hours a day, 7 days a week.

Beginning with red daybeacon "52, there is some shoaling both on the western shore and the eastern shore until your reach green daybeacon "53." Stay in the center of the channel. There is also some shoaling in spots along the channel just south of Lake Roger to the north side of Lake Wyman and again in the channel on the south side of Lake Wyman.

**Dockage:** North of the Lantana Bridge, on the west side, is Suntex Marina at Lantana (Mile 1030.2), with wet and dry storage and slips up to 100 feet. They also sell gas and diesel fuel, offer repairs and have a

www.snagaslip.com
SNAG-A-SLIP™
EXPLORE. BOOK. BOAT.

# Boynton Inlet Area, FL

| LANTANA | | Dockage | | | | | Supplies | | Services | | | | | |
|---|---|---|---|---|---|---|---|---|---|---|---|---|---|---|
| | Phone | Largest Vessel Accommodated | VHF Channel Monitored | Transient Berths / Total Berths | Approach / Dockside Depth (reported) | Floating Docks | Gas / Diesel | Groceries, Ice, Marine Supplies, Snacks | Repairs: Hull, Engine, Propeller | Lift (tonnage), Crane, Rail | Min/Max Amps | Laundry, Pool, Showers, Courtesy Car | Pump-Out Station | Nearby: Grocery Store, Motel, Restaurant |
| 1. Suntex Marina at Lantana ☐ WiFi | 561-582-4422 | 100 | 16 | 25/83 | 6/8 | – | G | IMS | EP | L8 | 30/50 | S | – | GR |
| 2. Murrelle Marine WiFi 1030.4 | 561-582-3213 | 55 | 16 | 2/36 | 4.5/5 | – | – | IMS | HEP | L50,C | 30/50 | S | – | R |
| 3. Suntex Marina at South Lantana ☐ WiFi 1030.5 | 561-721-3888 | 120 | 16 | 12/80 | 5/7 | – | G | IMS | – | – | 30/50 | PS | – | GR |
| **BOYNTON BEACH** | | | | | | | | | | | | | | |
| 4. Palm Beach Yacht Center WiFi 1032.7 | 561-588-9911 | 80 | 16 | 10/100 | 6/6 | – | GD | IMS | HEP | L80 | 30/50 | S | P | GMR |
| 5. Gateway Marina 1033.1 | 561-588-1211 | 35 | 68 | 2/211 | 6/6 | F | G | IMS | HEP | L10 | – | – | – | GMR |
| 6. Boynton Harbor Marina 1035 | 561-735-7955 | 40 | 16/11 | 4/23 | 12/6 | – | GD | IMS | – | – | 50/100 | – | – | GMR |

☐ Internet Access  WiFi Wireless Internet Access  WG Waterway Guide Cruising Club Partner *(Information in the table is provided by the facilities.)*
See WaterwayGuide.com for current rates, fuel prices, web site addresses, and other up-to-the-minute information.

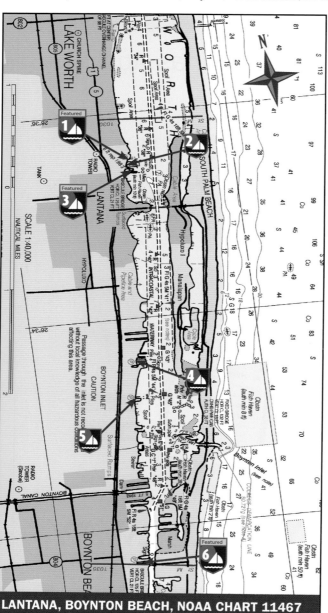

LANTANA, BOYNTON BEACH, NOAA CHART 11467

well-stocked ship store. To the south is Suntex Marina at South Lantana, which has transient dockage, including catamaran slips. This location is convenient to groceries and restaurants. Located between the two Loggerhead facilities is Murrelle Marine, offering repairs (50-ton lift). Call ahead for slip availability.

On the west side of the ICW, two repair yards with transient dockage are co-located in a basin. The approach is marked and has depths to 6 feet. Palm Beach Yacht Center (Mile 1032.7) offers slips, fuel and repairs (with 80-ton lift). Gateway Marina is primarily a "dry stack" marina and has no shore power but water is available at the dock.

In Boynton Beach, Boynton Harbor Marina at Mile 1035 sells gas and diesel and may have a slip on a face dock with 10 feet of water at dockside. They offer a multitude of water activities including fishing charters, drift fishing, scuba diving charters, jet-ski rentals, boat rentals and waterfront dining. A shopping center and supermarket are within walking distance of the waterfront.

**Anchorage:** Just to the south and west of the Lantana Bridge is a good anchorage with 6- to 8-foot depths and room for many boats. Anchoring here is limited to 18 hours. Commercial fishing boats operate from a nearby pier, and Old Key Lime House Waterfront Grill & Bar is nearby (at 300 E. Ocean Ave.) with daily specials, happy hour (during the week) and live music (except Mondays). They claim to be Florida's oldest waterfront restaurant (561-582-1889).

# Boynton Inlet–ICW Mile 1034

**NAVIGATION:** Use Chart 11467. Boynton Inlet, also known as South Lake Worth Inlet, is popular with local fishermen, but it is narrow, shallow and crossed by the fixed **Boynton Inlet Bridge** with an 18-foot vertical clearance. The Coast Guard does not recommend passage through the inlet without complete local knowledge of all the hazardous conditions that exist. A seawall helps stabilize Boynton Inlet's shoreline, but currents run swiftly, and bad tidal rips develop in strong easterly winds. See the Inlet section in the front of this guide for more information on Boynton Inlet.

The ICW, where it passes Boynton Inlet, is narrow and shallow, inside and outside the channel. Shoaling in the ICW channel where the inlet current crosses the channel is a continuing problem, reducing depths in the vicinity of red nun buoy "46." This area both north and south of red nun buoy "46" has not been dredged in recent years, so check locally for information on depths and/or marking before you pass through. The shoaling seems to be worse on the western edge of the channel. It is about 7 feet or less; stay to the green side. Watch your course carefully and do not be confused by the green buoys (quite large) marking a channel leading in to the western shore. Follow the ICW channel markers carefully, as groundings are frequent here, usually resulting from the current at Boynton Inlet pushing vessels out of the channel.

Remember, all ICW markers have either a yellow triangle for the red markers or a yellow square for the green markers.

# Delray Beach–ICW Mile 1039 to Mile 1044

Delray Beach is a first-class resort destination and a diverse, vibrant, community situated on the Atlantic Ocean between Boca Raton and West Palm Beach. The area has diverse restaurants, a great art museum housed in a 1913 schoolhouse (The Cornell) and the quirky Silverball Museum, which is dedicated to the preservation of the vintage arcade. In this arcade you pay by the hour ($10), not with tokens or quarters, and play as much as you want in that hour. Games include favorites such as Pac-Man (and, of course, Ms. Pac-Man), Asteroids, Frogger, Space Invaders and more pinball machines than we have room to name. This is a great rainy-day diversion.

# Hillsboro River, FL

| | Largest Vessel Accommodated | VHF Channel Monitored | Transient Berths / Total Berths | Approach / Dockside Depth (reported) | Floating Docks | Gas / Diesel | Groceries, Ice, Marine Supplies, Snacks | Repairs: Hull, Engine, Propeller | Lift (tonnage), Crane, Rail | Min / Max Amps | Laundry, Pool, Showers, Courtesy Car | Pump-Out Station | Nearby: Grocery Store, Motel, Restaurant |
|---|---|---|---|---|---|---|---|---|---|---|---|---|---|
| | | | **Dockage** | | | **Supplies** | | **Services** | | | | | |
| **DELRAY BEACH** | | | | | | | | | | | | | |
| 1. Marina Delray  1038   561-276-7666 | – | 16 | 1/9 | 5/5 | – | GD | IM | HE | L | 30/50 | PS | – | R |
| 2. The Seagate Yacht Club 🖥 WiFi 1039.8   561-272-2700 | 130 | 16 | 6/44 | 6.5/6.5 | – | D | IS | – | – | 30/100 | LPS | – | GMR |
| 3. Delray Beach City Marina  1039.8   561-243-7250 | 55 | – | call/24 | /10 | – | – | I | – | – | 30/50 | LS | P | GR |
| 4. Delray Harbor Club Marina WiFi WG 1040.5   561-276-0376 | 200 | 16/08 | 7/44 | 8/8 | F | GD | IMS | HEP | L80 | 30/100 | PS | – | GR |
| **BOCA RATON** | | | | | | | | | | | | | |
| 5. Boca Raton Resort & Club 🖥 1048.2   561-447-3474 | 170 | 16 | 32/32 | 12/10 | – | – | GIS | – | – | 50/100 | LPS | – | GMR |
| **DEERFIELD BEACH** | | | | | | | | | | | | | |
| 6. Two Georges at the Cove Waterfront Restaurant and Marina 954-427-9747 | 65 | 16/09 | 5/31 | 7/7 | – | GD | GIMS | – | – | 30/50 | – | – | GMR |
| **HILLSBORO INLET AREA** | | | | | | | | | | | | | |
| 7. Lighthouse Point Yacht and Racquet Club 🖥 WiFi   954-942-6688 | 100 | 16/68 | 5/76 | 10/8 | – | GD | I | – | – | 30/100 | LPS | P | GR |
| 8. Lighthouse Point Marina Inc. 🖥 WiFi 1053.7   954-941-0227 | 80 | 16 | 10/100 | 7/7 | – | GD | IMS | – | – | 30/50 | LPS | P | GR |
| 9. Yacht Management Marina 🖥 WiFi WG   954-941-6447 | 130 | 16 | 5/24 | 12/5 | – | – | – | HEP | L | 30/50 | L | P | GMR |
| 10. Merritt's Boat & Engine Works 1054.8   954-941-5207 | 100 | – | – | 10/8 | – | – | MS | HEP | L100 | 30/30 | – | – | MR |
| 11. Aquamarina Hidden Harbour 🖥 WiFi 1054.8   954-941-0498 | 43 | – | 3/3 | – | F | GD | IMS | HEP | L75 | 30/30 | – | P | R |
| 12. Sands Harbor Resort & Marina 🖥 WiFi 1056.2   954-942-9100 | 100 | 16/10 | 30/50 | 10/10 | – | GD | GIMS | HEP | L80 | 30/100 | LPS | P | GMR |

🖥 Internet Access  WiFi Wireless Internet Access  WG Waterway Guide Cruising Club Partner  *(Information in the table is provided by the facilities.)*
See WaterwayGuide.com for current rates, fuel prices, web site addresses, and other up-to-the-minute information.

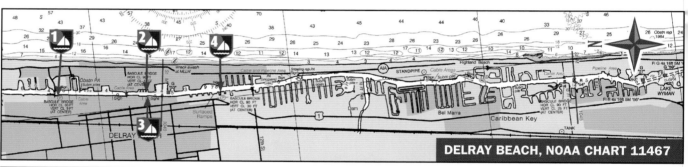

DELRAY BEACH, NOAA CHART 11467

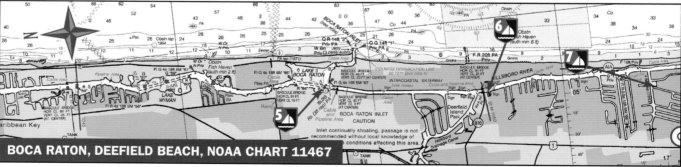

BOCA RATON, DEEFIELD BEACH, NOAA CHART 11467

HILLSBORO INLET AREA, NOAA CHART 11467

**NAVIGATION:** Use Chart 11467. Use the Miami Harbor Entrance Tide Tables. For high tide, add 1 hour 24 minutes; for low tide, add 2 hours 7 minutes. From Delray Beach south to Fort Lauderdale, smaller boats, and those bothered by the constant buffeting of the irregular, choppy sea caused by wakes, might consider traveling on weekdays when traffic is lighter. Wakes on this narrow channel retain their energy between opposing cement bulkheads, bouncing back and forth for some time after the passing of the craft that caused them. If the weather permits, you may just want to make the outside run from Lake Worth South to avoid the numerous bridges and boat wakes.

The first Delray Beach bridge you will encounter is the **George Bush Blvd. Bascule Bridge** (Mile 1038.7, 9-foot closed vertical clearance). This bridge opens on signal at all times. The second bridge in Delray Beach is the **Atlantic Ave. (SR 806) Bascule Bridge** (Mile 1039.6, 12-foot closed vertical clearance), which opens at 15 and 45 minutes past the hour. The **Linton Blvd. Bascule Bridge** (Mile 1041.0, charted 30-foot closed vertical clearance) opens on the hour and half-hour at all times. (Call ahead to verify as our cruising editors have observed an actual clearance of 27 feet: 561-278-1980.)

Approximately 0.6 miles south of this bridge, at Mile 1041.7, steer well clear of the white buoy marked "Rocks" well out from the western shore of the ICW.

**Dockage:** Boating amenities at Delray Beach range from municipal slips (usually full of long-term rentals with a reported 5-year waiting list) to restaurants with their own dockage and full-service marinas and repair shops. Just north of the Atlantic Avenue Bridge is a city park complex (lawn bowling, shuffleboard, etc.) on the mainland side of the ICW. At one time, complimentary daytime dockage was available at the park (2-hour limit, no overnight docking) but this dock was closed for repairs in 2016 and in 2017 with no anticipated opening date. (Note that a sign advises 4-foot depth at mean low water.)

Just south of the George Bush Blvd. Bridge is the small (9-slip) Marina Delray with only 1 reserved transient slip and 5 foot approach and dockside depths. Continuing south, past the Atlantic Ave. Bridge, are the Seagate Yacht Club and Delray Beach Municipal Marina, both with transient space. The Seagate Yacht Club also sells diesel fuel. To the south is Delray Harbor Club Marina. This full-service marina has slips, fuel and an 80-ton lift.

**Anchorage:** At about Mile 1042, the round basin to the west of the ICW, known locally as Pelican Harbor, is a 24-hour only anchorage (by order of the town of Delray Beach). The basin has 5-foot depths at the entrance and 6-foot depths inside. Poor holding has been reported due to a very soft bottom.

Boca Raton Inlet

# ■ BOCA RATON AREA

**NAVIGATION:** Use Chart 11467. Use the Miami Harbor Entrance Tide Tables. For high tide, add 23 minutes; for low tide, add 1 hour 7 minutes. The **Spanish River Blvd. Bascule Bridge** at Mile 1044.9 has 25-foot closed vertical clearance and opens on the hour and half-hour, 24 hours a day. About 1 mile to the south, the ICW crosses broad, shallow Lake Wyman through a narrow, well-marked channel favoring the eastern shore. If you stray from the channel, unmarked shoals call for extra caution. Be on the lookout for water skiers and swimmers in the water.

About 5 miles south of Delray Beach, the ICW route leads into Lake Boca Raton through a cut lined with beautiful homes. Before entering the lake, the ICW passes under **Palmetto Park Bascule Bridge** (19-foot closed vertical clearance) at Mile 1047.5. The bridge opens on the hour and half-hour. This bridge crosses a narrow opening through which strong currents stream. If your vessel is lightly powered, when running with the current be sure to avoid being carried into the bridge or being carried by eddies into the concrete walls and

docks along the sides. During weekends and particularly in season, many small boats mill around the boat ramp next to the southwestern bridge abutment at Silver Palm Park, adding to the confusion. This is usually a very busy area and extra caution should be taken.

The ICW next passes through Lake Boca Raton on its western side and continues south through the **Camino Real Bridge** (Mile 1048.2, 9-foot closed vertical clearance). It opens on the hour, and at 20 and 40 minutes past the hour 24 hours daily. This is the only restricted bridge in Palm Beach County that opens more than twice an hour, attesting to the large number of boats passing through. This is also the southernmost bridge in Palm Beach County.

When heading south through the Palmetto Park and Camino Real bridges, keep in mind that the current usually reverses in the ICW as it passes the Boca Raton Inlet. It is nothing even a lightly powered vessel can't handle, but be aware of it, particularly on an incoming tide. The Camino Real Bridge can be quite busy, particularly on weekends in season.

The ICW channel through Lake Boca Raton is an Idle-Speed/No-Wake Zone, and the local marine police make a point to strictly enforce it. It is busy with tour boats and water taxis ferrying passengers between the Boca Raton Resort & Club and its private beach.

**Dockage:** The Boca Raton Resort & Club is located at Mile 1048.2 on Lake Boca Raton. The pink hotel is a local landmark and offers dockage with a 50-foot minimum charge. Nearby is Waterstone Resort & Marina, which may have transient space for daytime use only; no overnight docking is allowed.

**Anchorage:** Just south of the Palmetto Park Bridge (Mile 1047.5), a small anchorage is located at the northeastern end of Lake Boca Raton. Enter north of flashing green "65," and anchor in 8-foot depths north and east of the charted shoal areas. An unmarked channel runs through the anchorage area and along the eastern shore to the Boca Raton Inlet. There is heavy traffic in the area, especially on weekends.

## Boca Raton Inlet–ICW Mile 1048

The Boca Raton Inlet is not recommended for passage without local knowledge. The tall, pink Boca Raton Resort & Club is a landmark visible from many miles offshore. The inlet's entrance has short jetties marked by private lights, and depths change due to shoaling and shifting sandbars. The inlet channel and markers are not charted and transit is considered dangerous. The **Boca Inlet Bascule Bridge** (23-foot closed vertical clearance) crosses the inlet and opens on signal. See the Inlet section in the front of this guide for more information on Boca Raton Inlet.

## ■ DEERFIELD BEACH TO POMPANO BEACH

### Deerfield Beach to Hillsboro Inlet–ICW Mile 1048 to Mile 1053

**NAVIGATION:** Use Chart 11467. The ICW leaves Lake Boca Raton through the Camino Real Bridge at Mile 1048.2, as described earlier. It then enters another straight section with many canals, followed at Mile 1050 by the Hillsboro River with its many bridges and speed restrictions.

Manatee Zones and Boating Safety Zones are frequent and often overlap. Where they do, the more restrictive limitation applies. Some are seasonal (November 15 through March 31), some are year-round, some are weekends only, some are for the full width of the water, and some are more restrictive within a specified distance from the shore. The official signs are well placed and repeated at intervals, and some vary in only small details. You must keep a sharp lookout and read each sign carefully. The speed and wake limits are enforced by state, county and municipal police boats.

Deerfield Beach is the next city, closely followed by the Lighthouse Point area, Hillsboro Inlet and Pompano Beach proper. A maze of manmade canals shoots off the ICW in all directions, and from here southward, virtually all land routes end up at the water.

Hillsboro Inlet

The area now known as Boca Raton is shown on old Spanish navigational maps charts as Boca de Ratones, meaning "mouth of the harbor of the hidden rocks." It appears that the name was originally applied to Biscayne Bay near Miami Beach, but early mapmakers moved the name to the present location. The construction of the Florida East Coast Canal (today's ICW) and the Florida East Coast Railway in the 1890s brought pioneers and farmers to the area. In 1925, eccentric architect Addison Mizner was hired to design a world-class resort community. His exclusive hotel, known as the Cloister Inn, was completed in 1926, and remains a landmark as the Boca Raton Resort and Club. The ICW route through Lake Boca Raton hugs the western shore and passes within view of the resort Mizner designed and built, and the many other buildings that mimic his Mediterranean revival design.

**Attractions:** Want some culture? This is the place! The Boca Raton Museum of Art has more than 4,000 works ranging from pre-Columbian to the modern masters, as well as traveling exhibits (501 Plaza Real, 561-392-2500). The Boca Raton Historical Society and Museum (71 N. Federal Highway, 561-395-6766) is located in the historic "Old Town Hall" and offers a wide range of

exhibits and lecture series. The Wick Theatre & Costume Museum (7901 N. Federal Highway, 561 995-2333) produces current Broadway hits, musicals and revivals. In the north end of Downtown Boca, the Mizner Park Amphitheater is a public venue of community events and concerts. This is part of Mizner Park, a unique mixed-use development of shops, restaurants, a movie theater, offices, residences and public spaces.

**Shopping/Dining:** For provisioning, there's a Trader Joe's at 855 S. Federal Hwy. and a Publix Super Market at 1001 S. Federal Hwy. These are within walking distance to Boca Raton Resort. At 75 SE 3rd St. is the small, family-owned 4th Generation Organic Market & Cafe (561-314-1341), which is open daily from 9:00 a.m. to 9:00 p.m. This organic food store sells produce, groceries and prepared dishes you can bring back to the boat to enjoy.

"Downtown Boca" along Federal Highway and East Palmetto Park Road features upscale shopping, restaurants, art galleries, events and festivals with something for everyone. Just south of Palmetto Road is Royal Palm Place, another center in downtown with dining, shopping and living. There are too many shopping and dining options to list here. Visit delraybeach.com or mydelraybeach.com for a complete listing.

Near Deerfield Beach, the Hillsboro Drainage Canal enters the ICW from the west at Mile 1049.9. During times of high flow from the canal, strong currents exist in the ICW about 100 yards from the **Hillsboro Blvd. (SR 810) Bascule Bridge** at Mile 1050.0. The bridge (21-foot closed vertical clearance) opens on the hour and half-hour at all times. Southbound boats approaching the bridge should not proceed past the canal until the bridge is fully open and should maintain adequate headway to avoid being pushed into the east bridge fender by the canal crosscurrents. From the bridge to Mile 1052 (south of red daybeacon "68") shoaling exists along the edges of the channel.

All ICW bridges in Broward County are on schedules 24 hours a day, 7 days a week, year-round, except during the annual Air and Sea Show the first weekend in May (East Las Olas Blvd. and East Sunrise Blvd. will be the only bridges affected). Other special events that may require deviations from schedules are announced in the *Local Notice to Mariners* and on the Waterway Guide Explorer at waterwayguide.com.

**Dockage:** Deerfield Island Park is on the west side of the ICW with picnic areas and nature walks. A short distance up the Hillsboro Drainage Canal, the park boat dock can accommodate dinghies and small runabouts up to about 16 feet. Marina One is located .6 mile to the north on the canal. It is a boat storage facility with fuel (no overnight dockage).

Back on the ICW, Two Georges at the Cove Waterfront Restaurant and Marina is just south of the Hillsboro Blvd. Bridge. They might have transient dockage with a 7-foot-deep approach and offer gas and diesel fuel. Call ahead for reservations.

## Hillsboro Inlet–ICW Mile 1053

**NAVIGATION:** Use Chart 11467. Use the Miami Harbor Entrance Tide Tables. For high tide at Hillsboro Inlet Coast Guard Station, subtract 16 minutes; for low tide, add 3 minutes. Just south of Hillsboro Inlet, the ICW swings wide around a projecting point that builds out from the eastern shore. South from the inlet, for the next 1.5 miles shoaling occurs in spots along the edges of the channel.

The speed limit is Slow-Speed/Minimum-Wake to just before the next bridge, where an Idle-Speed/No-Wake Zone begins. Beyond that bridge, a sign lists the complex speed restrictions that prevail for the next 2.5 miles.

At Hillsboro Inlet, the 136-foot-tall lighthouse for which the area is named has one of the most powerful beacons on the coast (visible from 28 miles at sea). The fast-operating **Hillsboro Inlet Bridge** (13-foot closed vertical clearance), spanning the inlet approach from the ICW, opens on signal, except from 7:00 a.m. to 6:00 p.m., when it need only open on the hour and at 15, 30 and 45 minutes past the hour. (Note that this bridge is not on the ICW proper.) If you are planning on using the Hillsboro Inlet, be sure to get up-to-date information regarding the status of the bridge. The current runs swiftly beneath the bridge. Wait for the bridge to open completely before you start your passage.

Although Hillsboro Inlet's shoals shift rapidly, dredging is frequent, and local boats and the large fleet of charter fishing and head boats heavily travel the passage here. The outer channel was dredged to 20-foot depths, which resulted in controlling depths seaward from the jetties of 15 feet, and 8 feet from the jetties to the bridge. Swells and/or tidal rip on the ebb against an easterly wind will decrease the available depth from 8 feet.

Under good weather conditions, boats with 5-foot drafts or less can run the inlet safely by observing the constant flow of local boats going in and out. With any swell from the east, passage becomes hazardous. Local

Pompano Beach

reports indicate to proceed all the way to the red-and-white sea buoy "HI" before turning south, to avoid shoals. A rock jetty extends southeast from the north side of the inlet and is submerged at the outer end. It is wise to seek local knowledge before running this inlet. See the Inlet section at front of this guide for more information on Hillsboro Inlet.

**Dockage:** Lighthouse Point Yacht and Racquet Club (Mile 1052.2) and Lighthouse Point Marina (Mile 1053.7) have transient slips and sell fuel (both gas and diesel). Just past the Hillsboro Inlet is Yacht Management Marina, which may have space for you. Call ahead for docking availability and details.

## Hillsboro Inlet to Pompano Beach–ICW Mile 1053 to Mile 1056

Pompano Beach means "fishing." Even its name was inspired by one of the more popular species found in its waters. When some native folks served a group of surveyors who were mapping the area the local game fish, they wrote the name of the pompano fish on their map, and the name has stuck to the spot ever since.

In April, the Pompano Beach Seafood Festival brings together arts and crafts, non-stop live entertainment and great seafood. During the summer, "Music Under the Stars" sponsors a variety of free concerts throughout the city.

**NAVIGATION:** Use Chart 11467. Two bascule bridges cross the ICW in Pompano Beach, both with 15-foot closed vertical clearance. The northernmost, the **Pompano Beach (NE 14th St.) Bridge** (15-foot fixed vertical clearance) crosses the ICW at Mile 1055. The bridge opens at 15 and 45 minutes past the hour. The **Atlantic Blvd. (SR 814) Bridge** at Mile 1056 opens on the hour and half-hour. Both bridges monitor VHF Channel 09.

**Dockage:** Pompano Beach has abundant boating services on protected side canals or in enclosed basins along the ICW. Almost anything the yachtsman might want in the way of service, supplies, convenience or outright luxury is available in the immediate area.

Just north of the Pompano Beach Bridge, Merritt's Boat & Engine Works is a major yacht yard. Transient dockage is not available, but they offer all types of repairs and have a 100-ton lift. Nearby Aquamarina Hidden Harbour also does repair work and sells fuel but does not have transient dockage. Just before the Atlantic Boulevard Bridge, the Sands Harbor Resort & Marina is part of a large resort complex and provides transient dockage and fuel.

**Anchorage:** Anchoring in Lake Santa Barbara (approximately Mile 1057.0) on the west side of the ICW is still possible. The local marine police do not encourage it, but cannot forbid it. (Refer them to Florida Statute 327.02.) Remember to always stay apprised of the current Florida anchoring laws. They are challenged almost every year in the state legislature. Wakes from ICW traffic make this an uncomfortable anchorage and charted depths of 5 to 6 feet are not reliable.

Anchoring is also possible in Lettuce Lake on the east side of the ICW (7- to 12-foot depths) but not recommended, as the lake (actually just a wide spot in the ICW) is exposed to heavy and fast ICW traffic and holding is notoriously poor in very soft mud.

## Cruising Options

Ahead to the south lies a true yachting center, Fort Lauderdale, the Venice of America, detailed in the next chapter. Check our *Waterway Guide Bahamas* edition for headings from either Hillsboro Inlet or Port Everglades Inlet that will take you to Grand Bahama or Bimini.

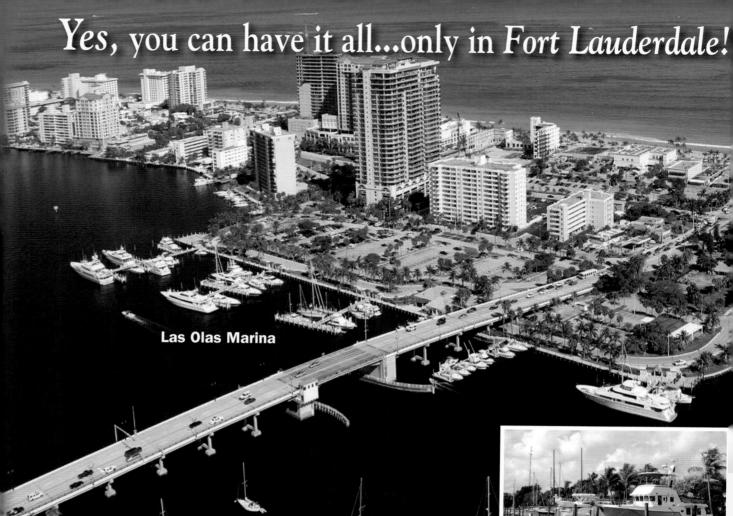
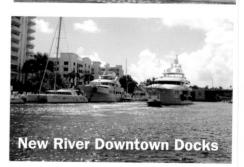

# Fort Lauderdale to Hollywood

 ICW Mile 1059–Mile 1073   ((VHF)) FL: Channel 09

**CHARTS** 11466, 11467, 11469, 11470

Nearly 300 miles of canals, channels and waterways wind through the Fort Lauderdale area, and at least half are navigable by virtually any size recreational craft. Often referred to as the "Yachting Capital of the World," the city lies about halfway between the Palm Beaches and Miami. With the Atlantic Ocean surf to the east and the traffic-laden ICW running north and south, the city is conspicuously water-oriented. The New River and its tributaries cut through the center of town and artificial side canals run almost everywhere.

Well known as a yachting center, Fort Lauderdale harbors more recreational boats than any other port in Florida. Not surprisingly, the marine industry–marinas, boatyards and builders, yacht and charter brokers and marine services–ranks second only to tourism.

Although the entire city of Fort Lauderdale has the look of a huge yachting center, most boating amenities and services are concentrated in three main areas: the main ICW channel, the New River and the Dania Cut-off Canal. Jostling each other for room is a collection of marinas, yacht services, sailmakers, boatyards, sales organizations, dinghy manufacturers, marine supply stores and other useful facilities.

## ■ FORT LAUDERDALE AREA

### Lauderdale-by-the-Sea to New River Sound–ICW Mile 1059 to Mile 1064

Fort Lauderdale is an important commercial harbor. The straight, deep inlet at Port Everglades forms an excellent big-ship terminal and commercial port, handling millions of tons of ocean cargo each year. The cruise ship terminals in the port often accommodate cruise ships, tankers, freighters and military vessels.

**NAVIGATION:** Use Charts 11467 and 11470. Use the Miami Harbor Entrance Tide Tables. For high tide at Bahia Mar, subtract 5 minutes; for low tide, add 33 minutes. For the 8 miles from Pompano Beach to Port

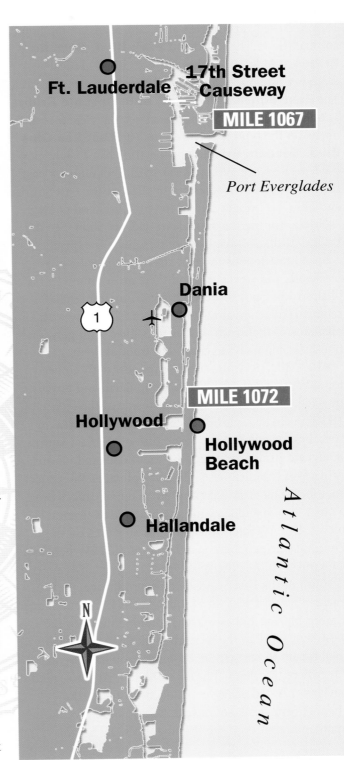

Everglades, the boater faces five bridges, scores of canals and rows of homes, small and large, on both sides of the ICW. For all practical purposes, the Fort Lauderdale area begins at Mile 1059, 2 miles south of Pompano, just past Lauderdale-by-the-Sea.

Between Mile 1059 and Mile 1064 are four bridges, all with restricted schedules. The first, the **Commercial Blvd. (SR 870) Bascule Bridge** at Mile 1059.0 has 15-foot closed vertical clearance and opens on the hour and half-hour. The **Oakland Park Blvd. Bascule Bridge** at Mile 1060.5 has 22-foot closed vertical clearance and opens at 15 and 45 minutes past the hour. The **East Sunrise Blvd. (SR 838) Bascule Bridge** at Mile 1062.6 has 25-foot closed vertical clearance and opens on the hour and half-hour. The **East Las Olas Blvd. Bascule Bridge** at Mile 1064 has 25-foot closed vertical clearance and opens at 15 and 45 minutes past the hour. Special closures are in effect at the East Sunrise and Las Olas bridges during the first weekend of May each year during the annual Air and Sea Show. See the Bridges listings in the front of this guide for specifics.

Speed restrictions in open stretches differ for weekends and weekdays, and there are a number of short Idle-Speed/No-Wake Zones. In one 3-mile segment, there are almost 60 side canals, many with offshoots of their own, and each is lined with gorgeous houses, some with large boats in front of them.

After Mile 1059, the ICW is straight (with no need for aids to navigation), densely populated and heavily traveled. To the east, on the ocean side of the ICW, 180-acre Hugh Taylor Birch State Recreation Area stretches for one-quarter mile north of the East Sunrise Boulevard Bridge, opposite the yacht club and marina. A pleasant, wooded oasis, the park provides the perfect spot for a sailor's holiday and offers rental canoes on a quiet lagoon and a swimming beach for a tropical picnic. Unfortunately, the park has no docks on the ICW. Local marine police frequently patrol the ICW here and vigorously enforce the speed limit.

South of the East Sunrise Boulevard Bridge, the channel zigzags past Coral Ridge Yacht Club and Sunrise Harbor Marina and associated condominiums to the west. Stay close to the western bank until you reach the first aid to navigation, flashing green daybeacon "3," where the channel heads southeast. At the second navigation aid, flashing green daybeacon "5," the channel turns back southwest. Be careful to give the mainland point opposite flashing green daybeacon "5" a

wide berth. Before you make your turn, be sure to locate the next marker, flashing red daybeacon "8."

An Idle-Speed/No-Wake Zone begins north of flashing red daybeacon "8," north of the East Las Olas Boulevard Bridge.

**Dockage:** Numerous restaurants just above and below the Oakland Park Boulevard Bridge have docks for their customers. Chart House Restaurant (954-561-4800) and Shooters Waterfront (954-566-2855) are among them. On weekends, several of the livelier drinking and dining spots on the east side have boats rafted out into the ICW, six or more deep.

Just north of the East Sunrise Boulevard Bridge (Mile 1062.6) are the Coral Ridge Yacht Club (private) and the Sunrise Harbor Marina, which caters to megayachts (up to 200 feet). Amenities at the upscale Sunrise Harbor include a controlled-access garage, 24-hour valet parking, concierge service, Club Room, climate-controlled wine room, business center, health and fitness center, spa, tennis courts and two heated pools.

There is an area of privately rented slips about .5 miles north of the East Las Olas Bridge at Mile 1063.5. To reach the long-term dockage areas at Isle of Venice and Hendricks Isle, turn west off of the ICW at Middle River between flashing green daybeacons "3" and "5." These canals are the last three straight north–south canals in the Nurmi Isles section. Hendricks Isle is the westernmost large isle; Isle of Venice is the next one east. Many properties rent slips on these two islands. Most are long-term rentals, but some properties rent slips on a daily basis. The various docks are different sizes, provide different shoreside amenities and are priced accordingly. The best way to find a slip here is to stop elsewhere temporarily, and then visit the area to check slip availability. During the winter season, slips here may be hard to find.

All liveaboard docks here are equipped with a direct pump-out hose to each slip, which must be hooked up to each vessel's holding-tank deck fitting. "Y" valves must be locked, and flow-through treatment devices cannot be used. With new condominium development in this area, there is considerably less liveaboard dockage space than in the past.

**Anchorage:** Florida legislation passed in 2016 bans overnight anchoring in the Middle River at Mile 1063.4. It is illegal to anchor at any time during the period between one-half hour after sunset and one-half hour before sunrise.

Lake Sylvia is your best bet now for anchoring in this area. To reach the anchorage, head east past the southwestern corner of Bahia Mar Marina, cut well inside flashing green daybeacon "13," then hug the eastern sea wall when approaching the entrance channel into the lake. There is a 5-foot shoal that is building in the center of the channel so go slow until you enter the lake. You will pass a large condominium building and private residences with docks as you head south. Stay close to the docks on the east side until about two-thirds of the way into the entrance channel, then move into the middle of the channel and enter the lake. The last stretch of the entrance, where you head into the middle of the canal,

# Fort Lauderdale, FL

| FORT LAUDERDALE AREA | | Dockage | | | | | Supplies | | Services | | | | | |
|---|---|---|---|---|---|---|---|---|---|---|---|---|---|---|
| | | Largest Vessel Accommodated | VHF Channel Monitored | Transient Berths / Total Berths | Approach / Dockside Depth (reported) | Floating Docks | Gas / Diesel | Groceries, Ice, Marine Supplies, Snacks | Repairs: Hull, Engine, Propeller | Lift (tonnage), Crane, Rail | Min/Max Amps | Laundry, Pool, Showers, Courtesy Car | Pump-Out Station | Nearby: Grocery Store, Motel, Restaurant |
| 1. Coral Ridge Yacht Club – PRIVATE [WiFi] 1062.3 | 954-566-7886 | 100 | – | 3/58 | 10/8 | – | – | – | – | – | 30/50 | PS | P | GR |
| 2. Sunrise Harbor Marina ☐ [WiFi] 1062.3 | 954-667-6720 | 200 | 16/11 | call/22 | 10/8.5 | F | – | – | – | – | 50/200+ | P | – | GMR |
| 3. Las Olas Marina ☐ [WiFi] 1063.4 | 954-828-7200 | 200 | 16 | 60/60 | 10/10 | F | – | I | – | – | 30/200+ | LS | – | GMR |
| 4. Hall of Fame Marina ☐ [WiFi] 1063.8 | 954-764-3975 | 150 | 16/08 | 40/40 | 9/9 | – | – | IM | – | – | 30/200+ | LPS | P | GMR |
| 5. Bahia Mar Yachting Center ☐ [WiFi] [WG] | 954-627-6309 | 250 | 16/68 | 150/240 | 16/16 | F | GD | GIMS | – | – | 30/200+ | LPS | P | GMR |
| 6. Lauderdale Yacht Club 1066.0 | 954-527-2209 | – | 16/69 | 5/64 | 5/5 | – | – | IS | – | – | 30/30 | PS | – | R |
| 7. Lauderdale Marina/15th Street Fisheries ☐ [WiFi] 1066.2 | 954-523-8507 | 165 | 16 | 10/60 | 10/10 | F | GD | IMS | HEP | L35 | 50/200+ | S | P | GMR |
| 8. Hilton Fort Lauderdale Marina [WiFi] 1066.5 | 954-463-4000 | 300 | 16/71 | 33/33 | 20/10 | – | – | IS | – | – | 30/50 | LPS | P | GMR |
| 9. Marina Boathouse of Fort Lauderdale ☐ [WiFi] | 954-343-2470 | 200 | – | 10/10 | 14/12 | – | GD | – | E | – | 50/100 | L | P | GMR |
| 10. Cable Marine East 1066.4 | 954-462-2822 | 120 | 16/09 | call/12 | 20/15 | – | – | M | HEP | L40 | 50/50 | – | – | GMR |
| 11. Hyatt Regency Pier Sixty-Six Marina ☐ [WiFi] | 954-728-3578 | 350 | 16 | 127/127 | 16/17 | – | GD | GIMS | – | – | 30/200+ | LPS | – | GMR |
| 12. The Sails Marina [WiFi] 1067 | 954-525-3484 | 500 | 16 | 15/20 | 45/24 | F | GD | GIMS | – | – | 30/200+ | LPS | – | GMR |

☐ Internet Access  [WiFi] Wireless Internet Access  [WG] Waterway Guide Cruising Club Partner *(Information in the table is provided by the facilities.* See WaterwayGuide.com for current rates, fuel prices, web site addresses, and other up-to-the-minute information.)

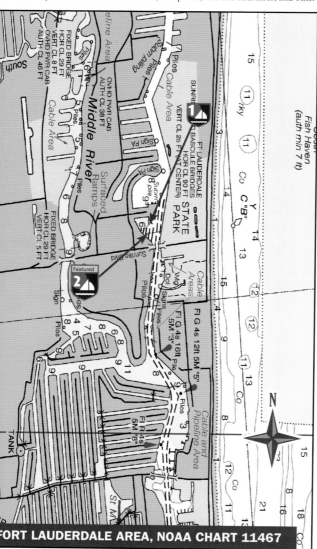

**FORT LAUDERDALE AREA, NOAA CHART 11467**

has an uneven bottom and is about 7 feet deep at mean low water. Luxurious homes surround the anchorage. On weekends, Lake Sylvia is full of local boats, many rafted for the night. It is frequented by water skiers.

There is not a dinghy landing in Lake Sylvia, but there is a space to land approximately 1 mile from the anchorage at Southport Raw Bar (954-525-2526). They will allow you to leave your dinghy for a $10 fee, which will be returned to you if you eat or drink at the restaurant. To reach the restaurant, go into the farthest side channel in the lake, run west to the ICW and cross over to the channel that is occupied by the boathouse-covered slips. Go to the very end of the channel. There is a supermarket, liquor store and several other stores just a short walk away.

It is imperative that you stay up-to-date on the anchoring restrictions in these waters. The Florida State Legislature was considering restrictions on Lake Sylvia at press time in spring 2017. Check waterwayguide.com for updates.

## East Las Olas Blvd. Bridge to Port Everglades–ICW Mile 1064 to Mile 1066

Between the East Las Olas Blvd. Bridge and the SE 7th St. Bridge there is a concentration of marinas close to the bridges. Canals branch off in all directions, lined by spectacular homes with yachts docked in their back yards. Many of these residences have been "remodeled" or expanded in size numerous times. Multimillion-dollar

**FORT LAUDERDALE AREA, NOAA CHART 11467**

homes are often torn down here to make room for even more expensive homes.

Ashore, the Fort Lauderdale oceanfront between Bahia Mar and Sunrise Blvd. is limited to one-way northbound traffic and features bike trails, sidewalks and landscaping, all creating an attractive setting. Beach Place, an oceanfront multilevel shopping and entertainment complex with a Marriott resort, is drawing crowds, as are the numerous restaurants and nightclubs both north and south of Las Olas Boulevard. A large number of high-rise luxury condominium resorts, quite conspicuous from offshore, line the strip between

Sunrise and Las Olas Blvds. Many of these offer upscale shopping and dining experiences on their lower floors.

**NAVIGATION:** Use Chart 11470. Between the Las Olas and SE 17th St. bridges, and farther south beyond the Dania Beach Boulevard Bridge, there are nearly continuous Slow-Speed/Idle-Speed Zones.

The **SE 17th St. (A1A) Bascule Bridge** at Mile 1065.9 (also known as Brooks Memorial Bridge) has a vertical clearance of 55 feet and opens on the hour and half-hour as needed. Vessels waiting on the south side for bridge openings should stay clear of the turning

LAS OLAS MARINA

NEW RIVER/
DOWNTOWN DOCKING

COOLEY'S LANDING
MARINA

basin and cruise ship berths, as well as any government patrol boats. To the south, Port Everglades is a major cruise ship port, and traffic is heavy in the area. If approaching from the south, the ICW channel may be difficult to pick out along the east side of the turning basin.

Marine Police boats are active in the vicinity of the Lauderdale Marina and the SE 17th St. Bridge. It is necessary to maintain the slowest possible speed through this area to avoid a warning or ticket. Do not be tempted to speed up to make the bridge.

**Dockage/Moorings:** Although jam-packed with permanent year-round or seasonal boats, most marinas reserve some space for transients, so the visiting cruiser is almost certain to find a berth at one place or another. At the height of the season, you must reserve a berth in advance of arrival.

The first concentration of marine facilities southbound begins at the Las Olas Bridge on the eastern side of the ICW. (The western side is residential except for the small anchorage and mooring area just south of the bridge.) Going south, the marinas that appear are: Las Olas Marina (with slips north and south of the bridge); Hall of Fame Marina; and the large (240-slip) Bahia Mar Beach Resort and Yachting Center.

The municipal Las Olas Marina has slips on floating docks with an array of amenities, including a comfort station with clean rest rooms, showers and a laundromat. This facility is just steps from the beach.

Hall of Fame to the south offers slips and full amenities, including a pool, laundry service, beach access and three adjacent restaurants. They can accommodate a wide variety of craft, with plenty of slips for year-round tenants and visitors.

Bahia Mar Yachting Center has dockage to 250 feet and sells gas and diesel (high-speed fueling) and some supplies. The property features a Doubletree Hilton, complete with restaurants, shops, swimming pool and tennis and directly across the street from a sand beach. Bahia Mar is also the home to the world-renowned Fort Lauderdale International Boat Show.

The Las Olas mooring area at Mile 1064 contains 10 city-owned moorings, which are available on a first-come, first-served basis. The city dockmaster, whose office stands by on VHF Channels 09 and 16, will come by to collect fees. Phone ahead at 954-828-7200 for more information about availability. Any one vessel may rent moorings for no more than 30 days during a calendar year. White and orange buoys have been placed along the south boundary of the moorings. All landing of dinghies is done at the Las Olas Marina on the opposite (east) side of the ICW from the anchorage. Showers, laundry and trash disposal are available there for moored boats.

The second concentration of marinas begins just north of the SE 17th St. Bridge. Heading south on the west side of the ICW, the Lauderdale Yacht Club has a narrow marked entrance channel through shallows. You must belong to a yacht club to dock here. (Call ahead for availability.) Next on the western side is the Lauderdale Marina/15th Street Fisheries offering berths and some repairs. (They have a 35-ton lift on site.) The marina also sells all fuels. Boaters should try to come in against the current, take up as short a space as possible and fuel up quickly. There is often a line of boats waiting, especially on weekends. TowBoat U.S. boats are based here.

The Hilton Fort Lauderdale Marina can accommodate megayachts up to 300 feet with 10-foot dockside depths. This facility is at the head of a channel that leads to Marina Boathouse of Fort Lauderdale and Cable Marine East. Both facilities offer some repairs (Cable Marine East has a 40-ton lift) and may have transient space. Marina Boathouse also sells fuel. On the east side of the ICW, the Hyatt Regency Pier Sixty-Six Marina has dockage for vessels to 350 feet and offers resort amenities and fuel.

Just south of the SE 17th St. Bridge is The Sails Marina with slips to 500 feet, plus repairs and fuel.

**Anchorage:** A cove along the west shore, immediately south of the East Las Olas Bridge, offers the only designated anchorage area within Fort Lauderdale's city limits. Unfortunately, it is also the mooring area, and you must stay at least 500 feet from the moorings, leaving little room for anchoring. Boats anchored on the outside close to the channel are subject to the current's effect. Anchored vessels are requested not to block access to the docks at private residences adjacent to the Las Olas mooring area.

Water taxis stand by on VHF Channel 68 and will pick up or drop off passengers at locations throughout Fort Lauderdale, along both the ICW and the New River. A pass provides the passenger with unlimited stops and rides for the whole day. Details on fares, routes and stops are at watertaxi.com (954-467-6677).

View updated postings on navigation and hazards alerts

waterwayguide.com

# GOIN' ASHORE: FORT LAUDERDALE (PORT EVERGLADES), FL

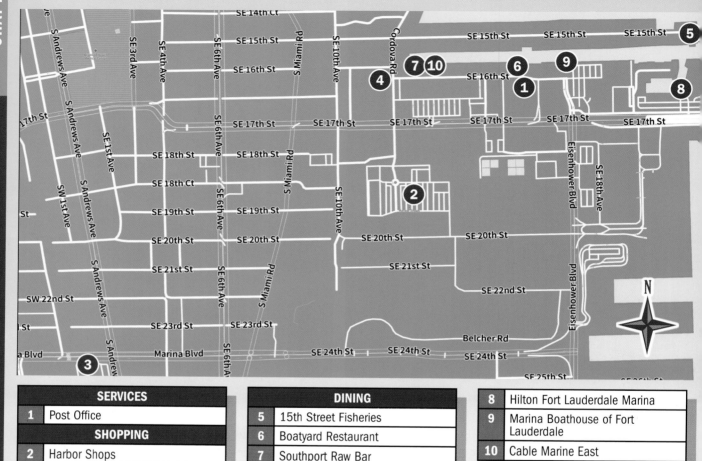

| SERVICES | |
|---|---|
| 1 | Post Office |
| **SHOPPING** | |
| 2 | Harbor Shops |
| 3 | West Marine |
| 4 | Winn Dixie |

| DINING | |
|---|---|
| 5 | 15th Street Fisheries |
| 6 | Boatyard Restaurant |
| 7 | Southport Raw Bar |
| **MARINAS** | |
| 5 | Lauderdale Marina |

| | |
|---|---|
| 8 | Hilton Fort Lauderdale Marina |
| 9 | Marina Boathouse of Fort Lauderdale |
| 10 | Cable Marine East |

Fort Lauderdale is known for its beaches and boating canals. Some skippers travel only on weekdays to avoid the heavy weekend traffic between Pompano Beach and Miami. However, there isn't another harbor like Fort Lauderdale, and it would be a shame to miss it.

**Shopping/Dining:** Skippers can tie up at on-the-water restaurants and shopping centers for shoreside dining, shopping or strolling. Most shopping and services line the 15th Street Canal, the first canal on the west side of the ICW just north of the SE 17th St. Bridge. The canal runs parallel to the busy shopping strip along SE 17th Street. The 15th Street Fisheries Restaurant (954-763-2777) at the Lauderdale Marina and the Boatyard Restaurant (954-525-7400) on the south side of the canal are popular eateries in this area. The Southport Raw Bar (954-525-2526) at the west end of the canal is a popular spot to visit by dinghy. The Harbor Shops shopping center on the south side of SE 17th Street is where Bluewater

Books and Charts, Publix, Total Wine & More and various other shops and restaurants are located. There are also a hardware store, a Winn-Dixie and several dive shops nearby.

A relatively short land-taxi ride away from the marinas is a West Marine store. The "superstore" at 2401 S. Andrews Ave. (954-400-5323) is the largest West Marine in the country. Boat Owners Warehouse, located a few blocks west of South Federal Highway on SR 84, offers competitive prices, knowledgeable help and special ordering from an extensive network of local marine suppliers (954-522-7998). Sailorman at 350 SE 24th St. (954-216-7295) sells new and used boating equipment. You can buy, sell, trade or consign marine gear there. They specialize in hard to find items, marine surplus, scratch n' dent and used marine merchandise See more shopping and dining options at fortlauderdale.gov/visitors.

# SIDE TRIP: NEW RIVER

The gently curving, meandering New River bisects the heart of Fort Lauderdale and serves as another major yacht service area. The New River is Fort Lauderdale's yachting center, with some of the finest facilities for building, repair, haul-out and storage on the entire East Coast. Even if you don't need anything, it is worth taking a trip–by boat, dinghy or one of the regularly scheduled sightseeing craft–just to see the contrast of the old and new Fort Lauderdale. In the past several years, there has been major construction of high-rise condominiums and apartment buildings near the river.

**NAVIGATION:** Use Chart 11470. Use the Miami Harbor Entrance Tide Tables. For high tide at the Andrews Ave. Bridge, add 15 minutes; for low tide, add 51 minutes. Entrance to the New River depends on the direction you travel. The mouth is forked, and its two openings merge obliquely with the ICW at two different points. Check your chart carefully.

Heading south, the route to the New River follows the ICW around a sharp turn to the west past flashing red daybeacon "16." Just beyond, the channel splits. Care should be taken when you pass red and green junction daybeacon "A." To go up the New River, leave the marker to port; to continue down the ICW channel, leave it to starboard. The water is very shallow immediately behind this daybeacon, and boats going up the New River frequently run aground by passing it on the wrong side. Leave it to port and, heading west, watch for daybeacons "1" through "4." There is a white-and-orange DANGER daybeacon marking a charted shoal, as well as one marking a shoal on the opposite side of the ICW from the New River entrance.

When traveling the southern approach to the New River, watch the chart closely, and sort out the confusing transposition of buoys and colors before trying the entrance. Once inside the river's mouth, the buoy pattern is easy to follow.

Depending on the tide, small boats with less than 10 feet of overhead clearance and drawing less than 2 feet can make the full circuit of the **New River, South New River Canal and the Dania Cut-off Canal** and rejoin the ICW just south of Port Everglades. The entire trip is 11.7 miles.

If heading north, the ICW is basically a straight line from the SE 17th St. Bridge to flashing red daybeacon "20," where the ICW channel starts a turn to the east, but a secondary channel continues northward to the mouth of the New River. If bound for the New River from the ICW heading north, vessels should leave flashing red daybeacon "20" to starboard. After passing the light, favor the bulkhead-lined western shore just opposite red daybeacon "2" until you have made the turn into the river's buoy system. Aids to navigation on the New River route, after passing red and green junction daybeacon "A" or flashing red daybeacon "20," follow the normal red-right-returning rule for the river itself. (River aids to navigation do not have the yellow squares or triangles of ICW aids.)

## Bridges

The strong tidal current should be considered when transiting the New River, because there is always congestion, especially at the bridges and along the Las Olas Riverfront dining and entertainment area.

- **SE 3rd Ave. Bascule Bridge** (16-foot closed vertical clearance): Opens on signal, except from 7:30 a.m. to 9:00 a.m., and from 4:30 p.m. to 6:00 p.m., Monday through Friday (except federal holidays), when the draw need not open.
- **Andrews Ave. Bascule Bridge** (21-foot closed vertical clearance): Opens on signal, except from 7:30 a.m. to 9:00 a.m., and from 4:30 p.m. to 6:00 p.m., Monday through Friday (except federal holidays), when the draw need not open. The bridge will not open if the FEC Railroad Bridge is closed.
- **FEC Railroad Bascule Bridge** (4-foot closed vertical clearance): Usually open unless train approaching. Remotely operated.
- **William H. Marshall (7th Ave.) Memorial Bascule Bridge** (20-foot closed vertical clearance): The draw opens on signal except from 7:30 a.m. to 9:00 a.m., and from 4:30 p.m. to 6:00 p.m., Monday through Friday (except federal holidays), when the draw need not open.

The New River forks beyond the William H. Marshall Memorial Bridge into the North Fork and the South Fork of the New River. The North Fork is residential and has only one bridge (**11th Ave. Swing Bridge**) with 3-foot closed vertical clearance and a hand-operated swing. The South Fork is residential for a distance but becomes commercial where it makes a sharp turn to the

# New River, FL

| NEW RIVER | | Largest Vessel Accommodated | VHF Channel Monitored | Transient Berths / Total Berths | Approach / Dockside Depth (reported) | Floating Docks | Gas / Diesel | Groceries, Ice, Marine Supplies, Snacks | Repairs: Hull, Engine, Propeller | Lift (tonnage), Crane, Rail | Min/Max Amps | Laundry, Pool, Showers, Courtesy Car | Pump-Out Station | Nearby: Grocery Store, Motel, Restaurant |
|---|---|---|---|---|---|---|---|---|---|---|---|---|---|---|
| | | **Dockage** | | | | | **Supplies** | | **Services** | | | | | |
| 1. New River Downtown Docks | 954-828-5423 | 170 | 16/09 | 90/100 | 15/8 | – | – | GM | – | – | 30/100 | L | P | GR |
| 2. Riverfront Marina | 954-527-1829 | 40 | 16 | – | 10/6 | – | G | GIMS | HEP | L7.5 | 30/30 | P | – | GMR |
| 3. Cooley's Landing Marina 🖳 📶 | 954-828-4626 | 50 | 09 | call/30 | 10/6 | – | – | GIM | – | – | 30/50 | LS | P | GMR |
| **NEW RIVER – SOUTH FORK** | | | | | | | | | | | | | | |
| 4. Lauderdale Marine Center 🖳 | 954-713-0333 | 200 | 16 | 99/198 | 10/12 | F | – | IMS | HEP | L300,C | 30/100 | LS | P | GMR |
| 5. Fort Lauderdale Boatyard and Marina | 954-895-8360 | 200 | – | – | 8/8 | – | – | M | HEP | L70,C | – | – | – | – |
| 6. Marina Mile Yachting Center 🖳 📶 | 954-583-0053 | 150 | – | 10/35 | 12/10 | F | – | – | HEP | L70,C25 | 50/100 | – | – | GMR |
| 7. Marina Bay Marina Resort 🖳 📶 WG | 954-791-7600 | 150 | – | 10/168 | 12/45 | F | – | – | – | – | 30/200+ | LPS | – | GMR |
| 8. Yacht Haven Park & Marina 📶 | 954-583-2322 | 130 | – | – | 10/6 | – | – | I | – | – | 30/100 | LPS | – | MR |
| 9. Cable Marine West Yard 📶 | 954-587-4000 | 120 | 16 | call/75 | 12/12 | – | – | M | HEP | L100 | 50/50 | – | – | GMR |
| 10. Rolly Marine Service Inc. 🖳 📶 | 954-583-5300 | 150 | – | – | 9/9 | – | – | IM | HEP | L200,C40 | 50/100 | S | – | – |
| 11. Billfish Marina 🖳 | 954-587-6226 | 130 | 16 | 45/45 | 14/9 | F | – | – | HEP | L70 | 30/100 | S | – | GMR |
| 12. Yacht Management South Florida 🖳 📶 | 954-941-6447 | 140 | 16 | 5/25 | 13/7 | F | D | GM | HEP | L80 | 50/50 | – | P | GMR |
| 13. Bradford Marine Inc. 🖳 📶 | 954-791-3800 | 180 | 78 | 60/105 | 10/8 | F | – | – | HEP | L300 | 20/100 | S | – | GMR |
| 14. Roscioli Yachting Center 🖳 📶 | 954-581-9200 | 140 | – | 75/75 | 10/10 | – | – | MS | HEP | L250 | 30/200+ | LS | P | GMR |
| 15. Aquamarina Marina Road Boat Yard | 954-793-4214 | 65 | – | call/4 | – | – | – | – | HEP | L30 | 30/30 | – | – | MR |
| **DANIA CUT-OFF CANAL EXTENSION** | | | | | | | | | | | | | | |
| 16. Anglers Avenue Marine Center | 954-962-8702 | 70 | – | call/65 | 8/8 | – | – | IM | HEP | L30 | 30/30 | S | – | GMR |
| 17. Sundance Marine WG | 954-964-4444 | – | – | – | – | F | – | I | – | L10 | 30/30 | S | – | GMR |
| 18. Thunderboat Marine Service Center-Dania Beach | 954-924-9444 | 44 | – | call/60 | 5/5 | F | G | I | HEP | L10 | – | – | S | GMR |
| 19. Cozy Cove Marina 🖳 | 954-921-8800 | 100 | – | call/59 | – | F | – | MS | HEP | L30 | 30/30 | – | – | GR |

🖳 Internet Access  📶 Wireless Internet Access  WG Waterway Guide Cruising Club Partner
See WaterwayGuide.com for current rates, fuel prices, web site addresses, and other up-to-the-minute information.

west at Pier 17 and River Bend Marina. Several bridges cross the South Fork:

- **Davie Blvd. Bridge** (21-foot closed vertical clearance): Opens on signal, except Monday through Friday from 7:30 a.m. to 9:00 a.m., and from 4:30 p.m. to 6:00 p.m. (except federal holidays), when the draw need not open.
- **I-95 Twin Bridges** (55-foot fixed vertical clearance): There is also a fixed 55-foot vertical clearance railroad bridge for Tri-Rail passenger trains running alongside the I-95 Twin Bridges.
- **SCL Railroad Bascule Bridge** (2-foot closed vertical clearance): Open except when trains are approaching.
- **SR 84 Bridge** (21-foot closed vertical clearance): Span opens only with 24-hour advance notice. This unmanned bridge is one of the few in Fort Lauderdale not equipped with a VHF radio. Call the bridge at 954-776-4300.
- **I-595 Bridge** (40-foot fixed vertical clearance)

## New River (North Fork)

Just beyond its mouth, the New River wanders lazily through a short stretch edged by fine lawns and some of the area's older, grander and more gracious homes. Entering the commercial area, you pass over south Florida's only traffic tunnel, which carries U.S. Highway 1 beneath the river. This area was Fort Lauderdale's original business district and its first boating center. Long before World War II, the wooded riverbanks were lined with docks, much as they are today.

Spanning the north and south banks of the New River is the Riverwalk Park, a waterfront park in the heart of downtown with lush tropical landscaping and winding brick walkways linking attractions, restaurants and shops. Most cruisers thoroughly enjoy this stretch of river dockage. Water traffic is heavy on weekends, and extra fendering is desirable, although wake action is not nearly as noticeable as might be expected. The variety of watercraft is seemingly endless, and the sights and sounds of this traffic are fascinating. Las Olas Boulevard offers excellent restaurants, gourmet food shops, fashionable boutiques and specialty shops.

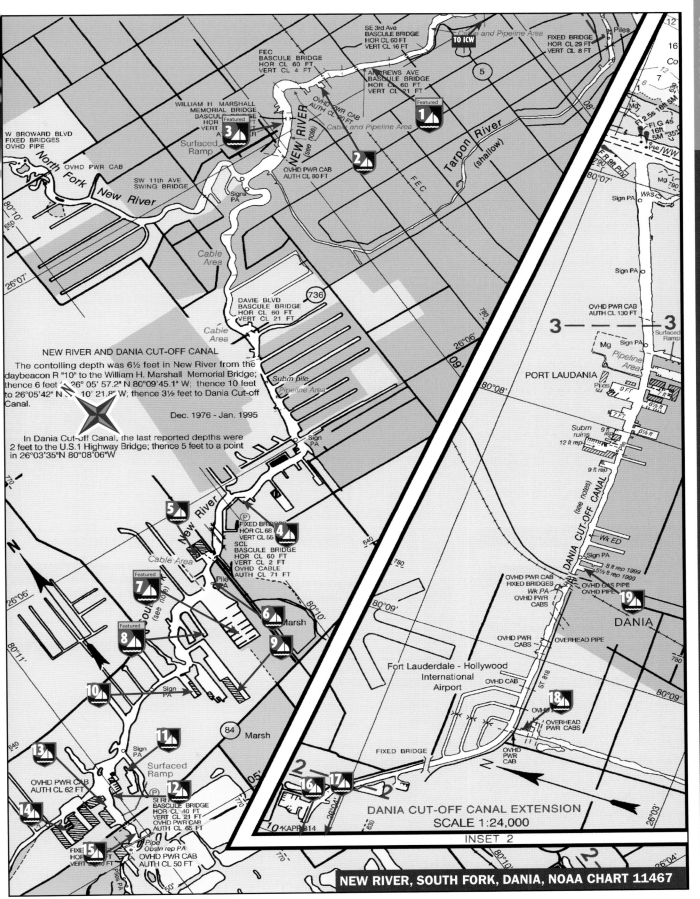

SE 3rd Ave
BASCULE BRIDGE
HOR CL 60 FT
VERT CL 16 FT

Cable and Pipeline Area
TO ICW

FIXED BRIDGE
HOR CL 29 FT
VERT CL 8 FT

Piles

FEC
BASCULE BRIDGE
HOR CL 60 FT
VERT CL 4 FT

ANDREWS AVE
BASCULE BRIDGE
HOR CL 60 FT
VERT CL 21 FT

WILLIAM H. MARSHALL
MEMORIAL BRIDGE
BASCULE
HOR
VERT
AT

Featured

NEW RIVER

OVHD PWR CAB
AUTH CL 80 FT

Cable and Pipeline Area

Tarpon River
(shallow)

FEC

Featured
**1**

**2**

Surfaced
Ramp

**3**

W BROWARD BLVD
FIXED BRIDGES
OVHD PIPE

OVHD PWR CAB

SW 11th AVE
SWING BRIDGE

OVHD PWR CAB
AUTH CL 80 FT

North Fork New River

Sign
PA

Cable
Area

DAVIE BLVD
BASCULE BRIDGE
HOR CL 60 FT
VERT CL 21 FT

736

26°06'

Cable
Area

OVHD PWR CAB
AUTH CL 130 FT

3 — — — 3

Surfaced
Ramp

Sign PA

Mg

Pipeline
Area

PORT LAUDANIA

Piles

NEW RIVER AND DANIA CUT-OFF CANAL

The contolling depth was 6½ feet in New River from the daybeacon R "10" to the William H. Marshall  Memorial Bridge; thence 6 feet to 26° 05' 57.2" N 80°09'45.1" W; thence 10 feet to 26°05'42" N 80° 10' 21.8" W; thence 3½ feet to Dania Cut-off Canal.

Dec. 1976 - Jan. 1995

In Dania Cut-off Canal, the last reported depths were 2 feet to the U.S.1 Highway Bridge; thence 5 feet to a point in 26°03'35"N 80°08'06"W

Subm pile
Pipeline Area

Sign
PA

Submr ruins
12 ft rep

9 ft rep

DANIA CUT-OFF CANAL

Wk ED

Sign PA

8 ft rep 1999
5½ ft rep 1999

OVHD GAS PIPE
OVHD PIPE

**19**

DANIA

N

New River

**5**

Cable Area

Featured
**7**

Featured
**8**

FIXED BRIDGE
HOR CL 68
VERT CL 55
SCL
BASCULE BRIDGE
HOR CL 60 FT
VERT CL 2 FT
OVHD CABLE
AUTH CL 71 FT

**4**

Pile
PA

Marsh

**6**

**9**

OVHD PWR CAB
FIXED BRIDGES
Wk PA
OVHD PWR
CABS

OVHD PWR
CABS

OVERHEAD PIPE

**10**

Sign
PA

**11**

Sign
PA

Surfaced
Ramp

**13**

OVHD PWR CAB
AUTH CL 62 FT

**12**

St Rt
BASCULE BRIDGE
HOR CL 40 FT
VERT CL 21 FT
OVHD PWR CAB
AUTH CL 65 FT

**14**

Pipe
Obstn rep PA
OVHD PWR CAB
AUTH CL 50 FT

**15**

FIXED
HOR
VERT

Fort Lauderdale - Hollywood
International
Airport

OVHD PWR
CABS

OVHD CAB

**18**

OVHD
OVERHEAD
PWR CABS

FIXED BRIDGE

OVHD
PWR
CAB

84    Marsh

2

**16**

**17**

2

2

DANIA CUT-OFF CANAL EXTENSION
SCALE 1:24,000

INSET 2

KAPR 814

# GOIN' ASHORE: FORT LAUDERDALE (NEW RIVER), FL

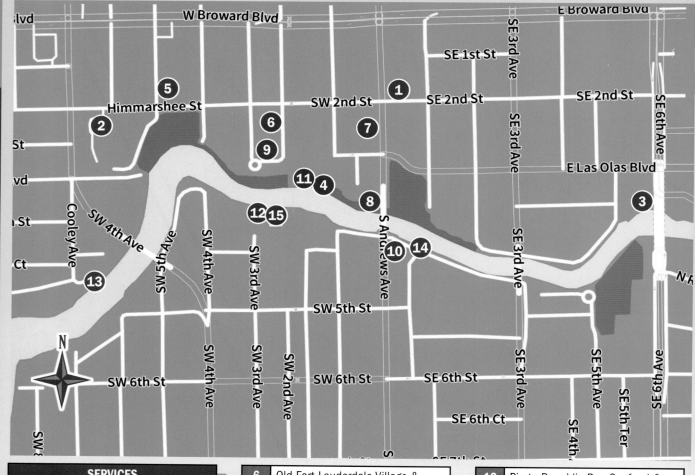

| SERVICES | | 6 | Old Fort Lauderdale Village & Museum | | 12 | Pirate Republic Bar, Seafood & Grill |
|---|---|---|---|---|---|---|
| 1 | Library | 7 | Riverwalk | | **MARINAS** | |
| **ATTRACTIONS** | | **SHOPPING/DINING** | | | 13 | Cooley's Landing Marina |
| 2 | Broward Center for the Performing Arts | 8 | Briny's Riverfront Pub | | 14 | New River Diwntown Docks |
| 3 | Historic Stranahan House Museum | 9 | Himmarshee Historic District | | 15 | Riverfront Marina |
| 4 | History Museum Fort Lauderdale | 10 | DownTowner | | | |
| 5 | Museum of Discovery and Science | 11 | Las Olas Riverfront | | | |

The New River area of Fort Lauderdale is an important destination port on the ICW and has many onshore attractions and superb boating amenities. Spanning the north and south banks of the river is the Riverwalk Park, a waterfront park in the heart of downtown. The lush tropical landscape and winding walkways link attractions, restaurants and shops and is the epicenter for special events, including a Jazz Brunch, held the first Sunday of every month in the Bubier Park area of Riverwalk.

**Attractions:** Coming up the New River you will pass the historic Stranahan House, which looks a bit out of place among the high-rise buildings that flank it. The two-story structure was originally a 1901 trading post that was later converted to a residence. It is open for tours daily at 335 SE 6th Ave. (954-524-4736). You will have to "hoof it" as there is no dockage here.

The Broward Center for the Performing Arts is a commanding presence at the heart of historic Sailboat Bend. Located at 201 SW 5th Ave., the center is home of the Florida Grand Opera and also hosts ballet and dance

performances, music, theater, family entertainment and more (954-462-0222). The downtown district is also home to the Museum of Discovery and Science (401 SW 2nd St., 954-467-6637). Hands-on exhibits and an IMAX 3D Theater are the big draws here. There is a long floating dock available to the public, for day use only, in front of the Museum of Discovery and Science. You can tie up your boat and walk a very short distance to all of the museums and attractions.

Continuing our museum tour, the History Museum Fort Lauderdale is housed in Broward County's oldest standing hotel at 231 SW 2nd Ave.(954-463-4431) and at Old Fort Lauderdale Village & Museum are several more historic buildings, including an inn, a schoolhouse and a library (219 SW 2nd Ave., 954- 463-4431).

The Sun Trolley offers inexpensive ($1.00 in exact change for each trip or you can purchase an all-day pass for $3.00) transportation around the downtown area and to the beach (every 10 minutes on weekends) as well as several other routes for similar fares (or free to the Tri-Rail). Information is available at 954-761-3543 and at suntrolley.com.

Adventuresome travelers can take the shuttle bus to the Tri-Rail Terminal just west of I-95 off Broward Boulevard, three miles from the New River dockage area. The Tri-Rail (800-874-7245) makes connections to towns with marinas from West Palm Beach to Miami. The city bus terminal, located near the river, provides excellent transportation anywhere in Broward County. Rental car agencies with competitive rates are also conveniently located.

**Shopping/Dining:** For convenient provisioning, Publix supermarket/pharmacy (601 S. Andrews Ave.) is just a short walk or bike ride away from the New River Downtown Marina.

The Himmarshee Historic District, inland and adjacent to this area, features numerous restaurants and shops in a restored historical setting. Nightly live entertainment at the gazebo, a 23-screen cinema with new releases, restaurants ranging from casual to fine cuisine and extraordinary martini bars are all part of this festive riverfront.

On the north side of the New River, just east of the FEC Railroad Bridge, is a large shopping and entertainment complex, Las Olas Riverfront, with a dazzling array of shops and restaurants. (Visit lasolasboulevard.com for a map and details.)

For riverfront dining, try the historic DownTowner (10 S. New River Dr., 954-463-9800) or Briny's Irish Pub (305 S. Andrews Ave., 954-376-4742), which is accessible by water taxi. The Pirate Republic Bar, Seafood & Grill, located across the river from the Broward Center, can accommodate vessels to 100 feet on their docks (first come, first served) if you dine with them (400 SW 3rd Ave., 954-761-3500).

**NAVIGATION:** Use Chart 11470. A Slow-Speed/Minimum-Wake Zone is in effect along the New River between the ICW and Tarpon Bend, where the Tarpon River branches off to the south. The last New River marker, red daybeacon "12," marks a hard shoal extending into the channel at Tarpon Bend. Deep-draft vessels should not hug this too closely as they make the hard turn around it. The bottom is a rock ledge. After red daybeacon "12," keep to the middle of the river. Minimum depths are around 8 feet, but there are plans to dredge it to accommodate the megayachts needing to get to the facilities upriver. Above Tarpon Bend, the New River is an Idle-Speed/No-Wake Zone.

Beyond the William H. Marshall Memorial Bridge (20-foot closed vertical clearance), the river branches, and the principal channel takes the South Fork into another opulent residential section. The water is brown and murky, tinted by the Everglades' cypress swamps and drains into an inland link in the river. Floating water hyacinths, coconuts and other debris appear frequently. Occasionally, you will spot the broad back of a manatee or the bulging eyes of an alligator. Another Idle-Speed/No-Wake Zone on the New River extends about 500 yards on either side of the I-95 Twin Bridges.

**Dockage:** At the New River Downtown Docks, the city offers dockage along the river available on a first-come, first-served basis or by reservation a few days in advance. The docks (actually a seawall) are located in the heart of downtown, beginning a short distance upriver from the SE 3rd Ave. Bridge and extending intermittently to the William H. Marshall (7th Avenue) Bridge at Cooley's Landing. This facility offers ample deep water dockage, two pump-out stations and grassy picnic areas. On the same side of the river, just above the FEC Railroad Bridge, is the Riverfront Marina, which sells gas but does not offer transient dockage. There is a Publix supermarket just two blocks south of the bridge on Andrews Ave.

Cooley's Landing Marina, also city owned, is located on the north bank and is situated next to the Arts and Science District. The marina has slips and sells some supplies. The city dockmaster's office is on the south bank, just east of the Andrews Ave. Bridge and next door to the DownTowner (954-463-9800). The Himmarshee Historic District's shops and restaurants, as well as Las Olas Riverfront are within walking distance.

## New River (South Fork)

**NAVIGATION:** Use Chart 11467. A 2-mile stretch of yacht yards, service shops and freshwater storage begins less than 1 mile above the Davie Blvd. Bridge, on the New River's South Fork. The channel accommodates deep-draft vessels to the storage and yacht-repair yards up to the I-95 Twin Bridges (55-foot fixed vertical clearance). You may encounter strong currents near the twin bridges and around the nearby railroad bridges; turning room is limited. Extra caution is needed here.

The South New River Canal continues to the southwest. Although narrow, it holds good depths, but a 50-foot-high cable south of the boatyards limits vertical clearance here. This is as far as most cruising boats go. The South New River Canal passes under the SR 84 Bridge (21-foot closed vertical clearance) and the I-595 Bridge (40-foot fixed vertical clearance) before joining the Dania Cut-off Canal, located 2 miles south.

**Dockage:** Most of the facilities on the South Fork of the New River offer repairs. For details on each facility, see the "New River" marina table in this chapter.

On the north side of the I-95 Twin Bridges is the full-service Lauderdale Marine Center, followed by the Fort Lauderdale Boatyard and Marina, located just south of the bridge on the north shore. Marina Mile Yachting Center is located directly across the river on the southern shore. Next is Marina Bay Marina Resort, which offers "country club style" amenities, including an expansive activity center with a resort pool, fitness and tennis facilities, private theater, racquetball court, sauna and spa and complete Captain's Lounge.

Nearby Yacht Haven Park & Marina is a combination RV park and marina. It is located in a gated 20-acre, park-like setting. Cable Marine West is in a basin to the south (call for slip availability), followed by Rolly Marine Service (repair yard; no transient space).

The next group of marinas are about one-half mile south. Billfish Marina is first, followed by Yacht Management South Florida, Bradford Marine and Aquamarina Marina Road Boat Yard (on the South Fork New River Canal with repairs only.) Roscioli Yachting Center rounds out the options. All of these facilities offer varying levels of repairs, sales and service.

## Dania Cut-Off Canal Extension

**NAVIGATION:** Use Chart 11467 (New River Extension and Dania Cut-Off Canal Extension insets). Chart 11467 notes that in the Dania Cut-Off Canal, the latest reported depths were 2 feet west of the U.S. 1 Highway Bridge. This passage along the canal is surrounded by wilderness and swamp, has a 2-foot controlling depth and is suited for small-boat exploration only. East of this junction is a water-control gate that rises like a guillotine to allow vessels with less than 10-foot vertical clearance to pass beneath. Various fixed bridges have limited vertical clearances that are not shown on the chart, but 10 feet is the controlling height west of Dania. For this reason, the Dania Cut-Off Canal is typically entered from the ICW, proceeding to the west. There are several large yards at Port Laudania, where small freighters and cargo ships

MARINA BAY
MARINA RESORT

dock. We cover the dockage at the east end of the Dania Cut-Off Canal in the Dania Beach section of this chapter.

**Dockage:** The route proceeds eastward past several marinas, including Anglers Avenue Marine Center, Sundance Marine and Cozy Cove Marina. These all offer repairs and storage, but have no transient space. Thunderboat Marine Service Center-Dania Beach sells gas and also offers repairs.

# ■ PORT EVERGLADES TO HOLLYWOOD

## Port Everglades–ICW Mile 1066 to Mile 1069

Port Everglades is a modern deepwater harbor and the third of Fort Lauderdale's important boating areas. Ashore, expensive waterfront homes overlook the endless stream of cruise ships, recreational craft, tankers, freighters and warships constantly parading through the inlet. Nearly 150 warships, both domestic and foreign, visit the port every year. Port Everglades is now off limits to private vehicular traffic, with police guards at each entrance.

⚠️ Keep clear of large-vessel traffic in the busy inlets, especially Port Everglades, Government Cut and Lake Worth. The Coast Guard establishes a moving security zone for the protection of passenger vessels (cruise ships), vessels carrying cargoes of particular hazard and vessels carrying liquefied hazardous gas, when such a vessel passes buoy "PE" to enter the port. Approaching closer than 100 yards to such a vessel is prohibited without prior permission.

When such vessels are docked in the port, boat traffic may still proceed along the ICW, provided that they stay to the east of law enforcement craft and cruise ship tenders being used to mark the transit lane. When such vessels are not docked, boats may use the ICW without restriction. Occasionally, all traffic may be halted temporarily while ships are docking or undocking. Patrol craft may be contacted on VHF Channel 16 for the status of these security zones.

The Coast Guard has also established a Slow-Speed Zone in the Port Everglades Entrance Channel from the outer end of the jetties to the turning basin and ICW. The Coast Guard strictly enforces this Slow-Speed Zone.

**NAVIGATION:** Use Charts 11470 and 11467. When approaching the port from offshore, the RACON sea buoy will be your best offshore waypoint. However, the

ICW

Port Everglades Inlet

air traffic into and out of the Fort Lauderdale airport will give you a visual aid from miles out to sea. The entire port area has deep water, with the exception of the northeastern corner outside the marked ICW channel. Deepwater docking extends to the south along the ICW to the Dania Cut-Off Canal. At the point where the ICW crosses the ship channel, keep the inlet and ICW buoys sorted out in your mind. Remember that ICW markers have a yellow triangle or square above the numerals.

Vessels southbound on the ICW follow the arrow-straight course on the chart across the turning basin into the channel leading south from the southeastern corner where the Fort Lauderdale Coast Guard Station is located. After passing close to the Coast Guard Station, be careful to avoid the mangroves and partially submerged rocks outside of the channel on the eastern side of the ICW, while keeping the required distance from the cruise ships usually berthed on the mainland side and paying close attention to the Slow-Speed/Minimum-Wake Zones.

## Port Everglades Inlet

One of the best and safest big ship inlets in Florida, Port Everglades Inlet (also called Fort Lauderdale Inlet) is well marked with flashing buoys along the entrance channel. Currents average .7 knots with a tidal range

of 3.1 feet in the turning basin. See the Inlets listing in the front of this guide for more information. The port and inlet may be crowded with both commercial and recreational traffic.

The inlet is a popular take-off point for cruisers heading to and from the Bahamas, fishermen heading out to the nearby Gulf Stream and skippers cruising north and south along the coast to escape the bridges and speed restrictions. It is also popular with ICW boaters hankering for different scenery.

Broward County has placed buoys at locations of interest in the offshore waters of Broward County for **divers and snorkelers.** To protect the coral from damage caused by anchoring, the buoys should be used as moorings. Buoy locations are:

Pompano Drop-Off: N 26° 13.034'/W 80° 05.028'
Hall of Fame: N 26° 11.581'/W 80° 05.00'
Anglin's Ledge: N 26° 11.338'/W 80° 05.246'
Oakland Ridges: N 26° 09.276'/W 80° 05.072'
The Caves: N 26° 07.631'/W 80° 05.354'
Barracuda Reef: N 26° 04.575'/W 80° 05.505'
Broward County mooring buoys are maintained by the Natural Resources Planning and Management Division. For more information or to report a problem concerning the buoys, call 954-519-1270.

Vessels with mast heights over 56 feet that are headed south of Miami's Julia Tuttle Causeway Bridge (Mile 1087.2, 56-foot fixed vertical clearance) have no choice but to go outside at Port Everglades. These vessels can then rejoin the ICW via Miami's Government Cut at Dodge Island. (See sidebar: "The Outside Run to Miami.")

## Dania Beach–ICW Mile 1069 to Mile 1070

Named for its early Danish settlers, the city of Dania Beach was once the "Tomato Capital of the World." Visitors today can enjoy the beach, the 800-foot-long fishing pier and a remarkable collection of antiques shops. The Dania Marine Flea Market is billed as the largest marine flea market in the world. It is held annually in March. Check online at daniamarinefleamarket.com for general information, dates and location, as it moves from year to year. Both commercial vendors and private sellers show their wares. Just about anything for a boat can be found at the event. If you love garage sales, this is the largest one of all and is worth visiting if you are passing through in March.

## The Outside Run to Miami

In ordinary weather, the outside run—north or south—is easy, safe and pleasant. Proceeding out the wide, straight channel at Port Everglades Inlet, you will find good depths in waters that are reportedly clear of obstruction out beyond the jetties and inlet buoys. On the south side, the good water extends well inshore, so many boaters turn south just beyond flashing green buoy "5." On the north side, however, a submerged breakwater and a large spoil area parallel the ship channel can obstruct navigation. The local small craft that often run along the beach inside the spoil area (which sometimes surfaces at low tide) follow a hazardous course. Those aboard larger boats should stay clear of this area by standing offshore past the jetty and flashing red buoy "2."

Southbound boats can travel safely within a quarter to a half-mile of the beach, outside the breakers, all the way to Miami. This route keeps you inshore of the Gulf Stream, with its approximately 2-knot northerly set. Going north, stand out to sea to take advantage of the free push. Boats equipped with GPS will easily recognize the Gulf Stream by the increase in speed over the bottom or a sudden tendency to drift off course to the north.

The NOAA Weather Stations (Miami, WX-1, serves this area) broadcast the location of the inshore edge of the Gulf Stream from 4:00 p.m. to 8:00 p.m. on Mon., Wed. and Fri., and from 4:00 a.m. to 8:00 a.m. on Tues., Thurs. and Sat. in the fall and winter. NOAA Weather does not give Gulf Stream hazards and locations in periods of warm weather because satellite photographs do not adequately distinguish between water and air temperatures.

The western edge of the Gulf Stream ranges from as close as 1 nm offshore to more than 10 nm; the width of the Gulf Stream is also stated in the WX broadcasts. The Gulf Stream really moves water. A sailboat can travel along at a good clip going south in the stream and stay in the same place all day. Sometimes southbound boats are lucky enough to find a counter-current running close to the shoreline.

# Hollywood Beach, FL

| DANIA CUT-OFF CANAL | | | Largest Vessel Accommodated | VHF Channel Monitored | Transient Berths / Total Berths | Approach / Dockside Depth (reported) | Floating Docks | Groceries, Ice, Marine Supplies, Snacks | Gas / Diesel | Repairs: Hull, Engine, Propeller | Lift (tonnage), Crane, Rail | Laundry, Pool, Showers, Courtesy Car | Min/Max Amps | Pump-Out Station | Nearby: Grocery Store, Motel, Restaurant |
|---|---|---|---|---|---|---|---|---|---|---|---|---|---|---|---|
| | | | **Dockage** | | | | | **Supplies** | | | **Services** | | | | |
| 1. Dania Beach Marina (WiFi) 954-924-3796 | | – | 16 | call/92 | 4/4 | F | – | IS | – | – | 30/50 | LS | P | MR | |
| 2. Harbour Towne Marina ⌨ 1 W of 1068.6 | **954-926-0300** | 200 | 16/11 | 35/165 | 17/7 | – | GD | GIMS | HEP | L100 | 30/200+ | LS | P | | GMR |
| 3. Sun Power Diesel & Marine 1 W of 1068.6 | 954-237-2200 | 100 | – | 2/13 | 20/10 | F | – | IMS | E | R | 50/50 | – | – | | GMR |
| 4. Playboy Marine Center (WiFi) 1 W of 1068.6 | **954-920-0533** | 86 | 16 | 3/3 | 17/15 | – | – | IM | – | L88,C18 | 30/50 | S | – | | GMR |
| 5. Royale Palm Yacht Basin (WiFi) 1 W of 1068.6 | 954-923-5900 | 80 | 78 | 30/60 | 7/7 | – | – | – | HEP | L70 | 30/50 | LS | – | | GMR |
| 6. Derecktor Shipyards ⌨ (WiFi) 1 W of 1068.6 | 954-920-5756 | 210 | – | 1/49 | 14/14 | F | – | – | HEP | L900,C35 | 30/200+ | S | – | | GMR |
| 7. Marine Max East Florida Yacht Center 1 W of 1068.6 | 954-926-0308 | 112 | 16/71 | call/11 | 6/6 | – | – | M | HEP | L90 | 30/50 | – | – | | GMR |
| **HOLLYWOOD BEACH AREA** | | | | | | | | | | | | | | | |
| 8. Hollywood Marina (WiFi) 1072.1 | 954-921-3035 | 115 | 16/68 | 5/55 | 6/7 | – | GD | IS | – | – | 30/50 | LS | P | | GMR |
| 9. Suntex Marina at Hollywood ⌨ (WiFi) 1072.5 | **954-457-8557** | 120 | 16 | 15/190 | 15/8 | – | GD | GIS | – | – | 30/100 | LPS | P | | GMR |

⌨ Internet Access   (WiFi) Wireless Internet Access   **WG** Waterway Guide Cruising Club Partner *(Information in the table is provided by the facilities.)*
See WaterwayGuide.com for current rates, fuel prices, web site addresses, and other up-to-the-minute information.

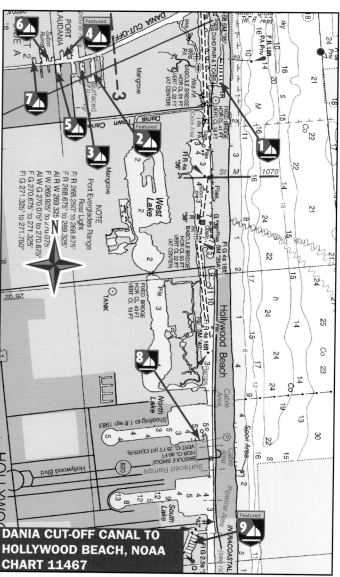

**DANIA CUT-OFF CANAL TO HOLLYWOOD BEACH, NOAA CHART 11467**

**NAVIGATION:** Use Chart 11467. The area from Port Everglades Inlet to the next bridge south along the ICW is a manatee protection Slow-Speed/Minimum-Wake Zone. Take special care opposite the power plant, where the warm discharge water frequently attracts manatees. The area is well marked with signs, and speed limitations are rigidly enforced, especially during weekends and the winter season.

Leaving Port Everglades, observe the buoys and, if in doubt, favor the mainland. The eastern side is shallow and marshy with rocks outside the channel. The expanding port complex now extends to the Dania Cut-Off Canal south of the inlet at Mile 1069.4.

The Dania Cut-Off Canal area is a busy marine service center. Businesses here include well-equipped yards, modern marinas, boatbuilders and marine service specialists.

In addition to good protection, the canal offers a rare treat for this part of the coast: There are no bridges on the ICW between the canal and Port Everglades so boats berthed on the canal have unimpeded access to the inlet and ocean. Moreover, it is the nearest dockage to the Fort Lauderdale–Hollywood International Airport for those arriving and departing by air.

The Dania Cut-Off Canal is an interesting waterway to explore. Consult the New River text earlier in this chapter for the North and South Forks to the Dania Cut-Off Canal. When approaching the canal from either direction along the ICW, keep a sharp lookout for high-speed traffic swinging out of the canal into the ICW.

**Dockage:** Dania Beach Marina, just off the ICW on the east side behind an 18-foot vertical clearance fixed bridge, offers transient dockage but reports 4-foot dockside depths; call ahead.

On the Dania Cut-Off Canal, Harbour Towne Marina has over 20 waterside businesses located on the property and is able to provide a wide range of services and amenities for professional captains as well as the weekend boater. They offer wet and dry storage, can accommodate transient vessels to 200 feet, sell fuel and offer repairs. Sun Power Diesel & Marine is in the next basin to the west, with limited transient space.

Playboy Marine Center is a "Do-It-Yourself" boatyard but has highly qualified technicians should you decide to seek professional services. Each visiting boat receives a clean, spacious work space equipped with its own water connection plus electrical hook-ups. They also provide (at no charge) ladders and sturdy scaffolding for ease of access to elevated work areas. Their 88-ton lift can handle sail or power boats to 80 feet in length (with a maximum beam of 21 feet).

Royale Palm Yacht Basin has dockage and offers repairs. Marine Max East Florida Yacht Center is primarily a repair/service facility, as is Derecktor Shipyard, which has a 900-ton lift and a 35-ton crane.

## Hollywood–ICW Mile 1073

South of Dania Beach is an area that has become almost a suburb of Fort Lauderdale and Miami. Hollywood Beach's proximity to Fort Lauderdale makes it a fine alternative when berths are hard to find.

Just a short walk from the Hollywood Municipal Marina, across the Hollywood Blvd. Bridge, is beautiful Hollywood Beach and Oceanwalk, a 2-mile-long, brick-lined pedestrian promenade with lots of outdoor dining options. A few miles west (a 45-minute walk) on U.S. 1 in downtown Hollywood you will find extensive shopping and a historic, recreated old town with a new family-oriented park in the center of Hollywood Circle.

**NAVIGATION:** Use Chart 11467. The **Dania Beach Blvd. (A1A) Bascule Bridge** (Mile 1069.4) has 22-foot vertical clearance and opens on the hour and half hour. South of Dania Beach, the ICW cuts through several broad natural areas where the water is spread thinly, and the dredged channel is narrow. Pay careful attention to navigational markers and your depth sounder. The **Sheridan St. Bascule Bridge** (Mile 1070.5, 22-foot closed vertical clearance), which opens at 15 and 45 minutes past the hour, has a dogleg approach. The

channel cuts across from the east close to the western shore before passing under the bridge. Be sure not to stray out of the charted, marked channel. Shoaling near green daybeacon "39" leaves depths at about 6 feet. Stay clear of the submerged pilings along the east shore at flashing green "39A."

The speed limit within the ICW channel is 25 mph (with a Slow-Speed/Minimum-Wake Zone buffer within 50 feet of shore) until reaching an Idle-Speed/No-Wake Zone about one-quarter mile south of the Sheridan Street Bridge, then continues past the next bridge, the **Hollywood Beach Blvd. (SR 820) Bascule Bridge** (Mile 1072.2, 25-foot closed vertical clearance), which opens on the hour and half-hour. Farther south, Slow-Speed/Minimum-Wake Zones will alternate with 25-mph limits within the ICW channel and more Idle-Speed/No-Wake Zones. Watch carefully for regulatory signs and read them carefully. In some areas, the ICW channel is exempt; in others, different speeds apply on weekends and/or seasonally, and other restrictions may apply.

**Dockage:** South of the Sheridan Street Bridge, the eastern shore is lined with casual restaurants complete with tie-up locations on the bulkhead for dining customers. The municipal Hollywood Marina lies at the southeast corner of North Lake (Mile 1072.1) and maintains slips for transients plus sells gas and diesel fuel. Call ahead if you wish to dock here. Controlling depths in the middle of North Lake at large are reportedly as little as 1.5 to 2.5 feet. If docking at Hollywood Marina, stay close to the docks and follow the contour of the docks; minimum depth alongside is reportedly 7 feet at mean low water.

At red daybeacon "42," just south of the Hollywood Boulevard Bridge, Suntex Marina at Hollywood offers a wealth of amenities. In addition to the conventional water and shore power, the facility offers slip-side cable TV, a vacuum pump-out system for each slip and a lounge with Internet access, TV and daily newspapers. Complimentary bicycles are also available and the Hollywood Beach boardwalk is just minutes away.

**Anchorage:** Near the Sheridan Street Bridge, anchorages are available both north and south of the bridge along the east shore. The little cove with the beach at the north anchorage is within the boundaries of a park where anchoring is prohibited. Therefore, be sure you drop your anchor a bit north of the cove for 7-foot depths. On the south side, there is a snug anchorage for one or two boats north of the line of docks along the edge of the ICW in 9- to 11-foot depths.

A short distance south of the Hollywood Boulevard Bridge is South Lake. Although the chart still shows depths of 4 and 5 feet, dredging has increased controlling depths to 28 feet and as much as 40 feet; investigate with caution. There is room for a number of boats and the holding is good, but you may be rolled by the wake of passing boats on the ICW.

## Cruising Options

Next the *Waterway Guide* takes you to the Greater Miami Area, including North Miami, Miami Beach, the Miami River, Key Biscayne, Coconut Grove and Coral Gables.

# Miami & Biscayne Bay

**ICW**  Mile 1074–Mile 1106

**VHF**  FL: Channel 09

**CHARTS**  11465, 11467

Miami today is a top global city. It is a uniquely multicultural region with a large and diverse Hispanic population; the global headquarters for major multinationals, international trade, banking and tourism; and the cruise capital of the world. Year-round outdoor sports, theater and an abundance of hotels, restaurants and nightclubs provide visitors with a kaleidoscope of opportunities for entertainment and the shoreside facilities are excellent.

Our coverage of the Greater Miami area includes from the mainland to Miami Beach, Government Cut and the islands of Biscayne Bay, all of which could be considered part of the Florida Keys, but in reality are normally considered part of the approach to the Keys. Boca Chita is considered the official start of the Florida Keys by water and Key Largo by land. Visiting boaters may call the Marine Council at 305-569-1672 for information on the local marine and tourism industry.

## ■ NORTH MIAMI BEACH AREA

### Hallandale to Bakers Haulover Inlet– ICW Mile 1074 to Mile 1080

South of Hollywood, the channel is well marked, relatively straight and bordered by high-rise condominium buildings leading through this growing suburban area to North Miami and Greater Miami.

**NAVIGATION:** Use Chart 11467. The **Hallandale Beach Blvd. (SR 858) Bascule Bridge** at Mile 1074.0 (26-foot closed vertical clearance) opens at 15 and 45 minutes past the hour. At this point to south of Sunny Isles, boaters must comply with the Idle-Speed/No-Wake (minimum steerage) and Slow Speed/Minimum-Wake (5 knots) signs (except for one brief passage in the middle of Dumfoundling Bay, where signs indicate a 25-mph speed limit in the channel).

North Miami

95

Little River

Buena Vista

1

MILE 1080
Broad Causeway

Biscayne Pt.

JFK Causeway (79th St.)

Julia Tuttle Causeway

MILE 1087

195

Sunset I.

Venetian Causeway

Miami Beach

MacArthur Causeway

Miami

Rickenbacker Causeway

Virginia Key

Coconut Grove

MILE 1096

Key Biscayne

*Biscayne Bay*

N

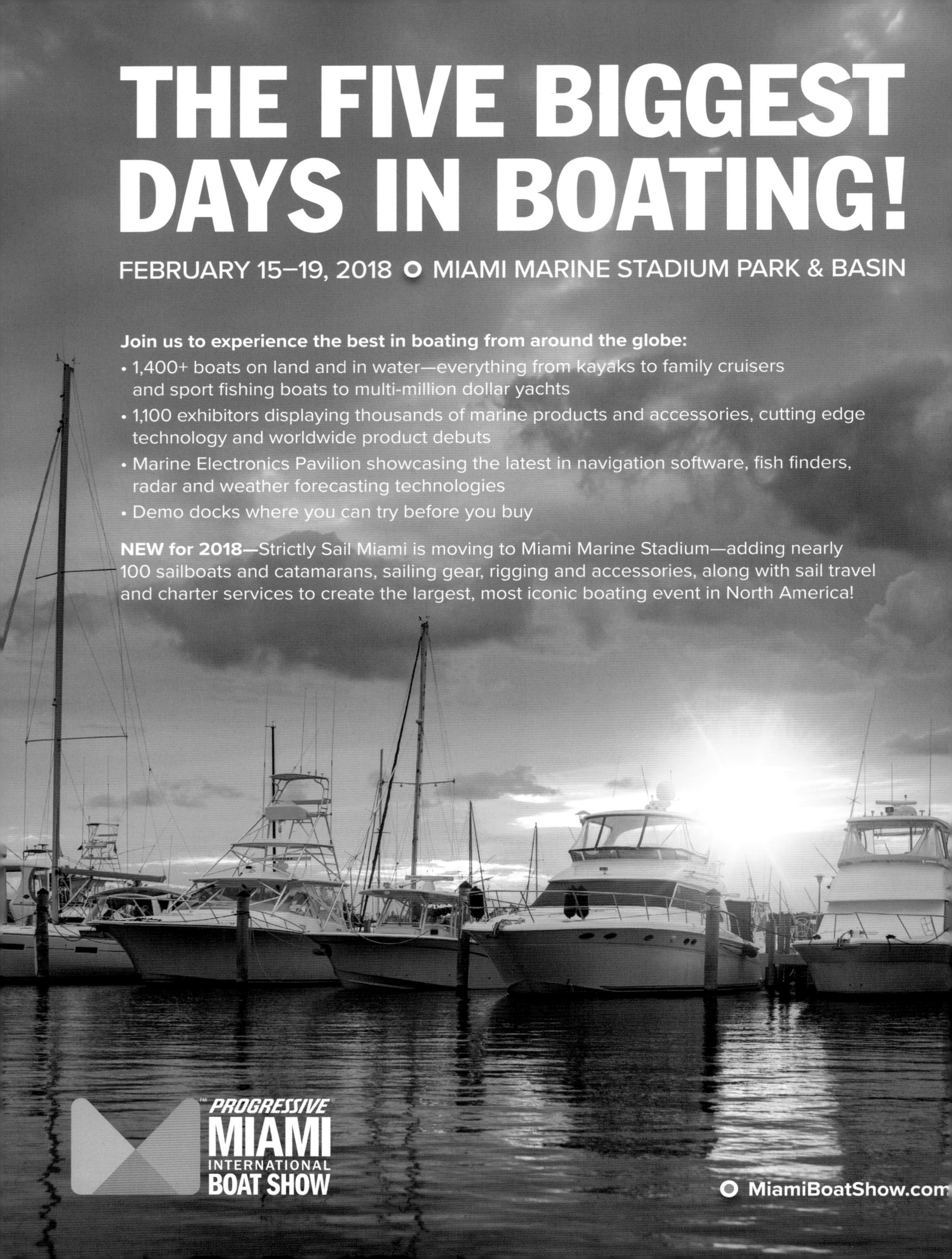

# THE FIVE BIGGEST DAYS IN BOATING!

**FEBRUARY 15–19, 2018** ◉ MIAMI MARINE STADIUM PARK & BASIN

**Join us to experience the best in boating from around the globe:**

- 1,400+ boats on land and in water—everything from kayaks to family cruisers and sport fishing boats to multi-million dollar yachts
- 1,100 exhibitors displaying thousands of marine products and accessories, cutting edge technology and worldwide product debuts
- Marine Electronics Pavilion showcasing the latest in navigation software, fish finders, radar and weather forecasting technologies
- Demo docks where you can try before you buy

**NEW for 2018**—Strictly Sail Miami is moving to Miami Marine Stadium—adding nearly 100 sailboats and catamarans, sailing gear, rigging and accessories, along with sail travel and charter services to create the largest, most iconic boating event in North America!

PROGRESSIVE
MIAMI
INTERNATIONAL
BOAT SHOW

◉ MiamiBoatShow.com

The fixed **William Lehman Causeway (SR 856) Bridge** crosses the ICW at Mile 1076.3 with a 65-foot vertical clearance. South of Golden Beach, the ICW is especially well marked as it enters the Miami area. Dumfoundling Bay is a broad, open and generally shallow body of water with a few deeper patches along its eastern shore. (There is no anchorage room here; it is all a cable crossing area.) At Dumfoundling Bay's southern end, the marked route crosses over to the western shore. To the north of the Maule Lake entrance, there is a shoal marked by a privately maintained white daybeacon; give it a wide berth.

From Dumfoundling Bay, the ICW enters Biscayne Creek, home of the community of Sunny Isles (on the eastern shore). At Mile 1078.0, the **NE 163rd St. (Sunny Isles) Twin Bridges**, with a 30-foot charted closed vertical clearance, links that community to the mainland. The bridge opens on signal, except from 7:00 a.m. to 6:00 p.m., Monday through Friday (except federal holidays) and from 10:00 a.m. to 6:00 p.m., on weekends and federal holidays, when the draw need only open at 15 and 45 minutes past the hour.

**Dockage:** The Hallandale Beach City Marina is located at Mile 1074 on the west side of the ICW in the canal just north of the Hallandale Beach Blvd. Bridge. The marina has just three reserved transient slips. Be aware that there is a fixed bridge (**Three Islands Blvd. Bridge**) with 17-foot vertical clearance prior to reaching the marina. Call the marina for more approach details.

The Suntex Marina at Aventura located across from Golden Beach accept transients in their large, protected harbor. They can accommodate vessels up to 120 feet and have numerous amenities including waterfront dining and great shopping (including groceries) adjacent to the property.

To the south, at Mile 1075.5, Turnberry Isle Marina Yacht Club is a world-class hotel marina offering full amenities, including WiFi, laundry facilities and a dockside pool. Complimentary shuttle service is available between the marina, Turnberry Isle Miami Resort, the beach access and Aventura Mall. The marina also offers personalized dockside service.

Past the William Lehman Causeway Bridge on the western shore is Aquamarine Hi Lift on a canal cut at Mile 1077.3. They sell gas and offer some repairs.

Just to the south, a straight, narrow and deep canal cuts westward off the ICW to Maule Lake and Williams Island Marina, which offers full resort amenities and dockage in a well-protected harbor. Nestled on

## Offshore Run from Miami

Coming up on the outside from the south, northbound boats that want to enter inshore waters can take either Cape Florida Channel or Biscayne Channel, once they have passed Fowey Rocks Light, or they can continue on to Government Cut. The Miami GPS Differential Beacon (nominal range 75 miles) is located on Virginia Key near the west end of the fixed bridge across Bear Cut.

Coming down along the ocean side of Key Biscayne, southbound boats should stand offshore on the run from Miami. Take a heading due south from the entrance buoys off Government Cut's Outer Bar Cut to pick up Biscayne Channel Light (better known locally as Bug Light), the 37-foot-high spidery pipe structure (flashing white every four seconds) marking the seaward entrance of Cape Florida and Biscayne Channels. Coming in at flashing red daybeacon "6," you have a choice of two channels leading to Biscayne Bay. Depths in the shared entrance channel to the Cape Florida Channel and the Biscayne Channel are charted at 7 feet at mean low water over the bar.

From the sea, the right-hand, northern fork is the Cape Florida Channel leading past the prominent lighthouse and the lovely palm-fringed beach. The chart clearly identifies the deep-water passage along the curving shoreline, indicating also the two shoal spots situated between .1 and .2 mile southwest of the shore. Hug the shore along the curving concrete bulkhead of the park property to clear the charted shoals, marked by green daybeacon "1." At the inner end, bear off to leave red daybeacon "2" and flashing red daybeacon "4" to starboard. From the outside, this is the easiest route to No Name Harbor, the area's most popular jump-off point for mariners awaiting favorable weather for a Bahamas passage.

The southern route, which is better marked and deeper than the unmarked Cape Florida Channel, is known as Biscayne Channel. It is wide, straight, well marked and easy to run. Depths in the channel range from 11 to 16 feet. Even so, the entrance depth from the ocean sometimes limits the channel. At its western end, the channel produces good fishing during flood tide.

84 lush acres, Williams Island offers an amenities-rich experience; you can go to the spa or gym, play tennis at one of the 16 courts or have a dip in one of the multiple pools. Afterwards, enjoy fine dining, an inviting cafe or the pool and bar grill.

Marina Palms Yacht Club is in a condominium complex in Maule Lake that has slips, along with gas and diesel fuel. They offer a full range of activities from jet skiing to kayaking and snorkeling. Reservations should be made in advance.

**Anchorage:** It is possible to anchor in Maule Lake west of red daybeacon "54" in 8 to 20 feet of water. Even though this provides all-around protection, the holding is just fair due to the mud and rock bottom.

## Bakers Haulover Inlet—ICW Mile 1080

When you observe that the tidal current is speeding up along the ICW route, you are nearing Bakers Haulover Inlet. Northernmost of Miami's entrances from the Atlantic Ocean, Bakers Haulover Inlet is heavily used by fishermen and local boats.

**NAVIGATION:** Use Chart 11467. Coming in from the Atlantic, Bakers Haulover Inlet is marked by a quick-flashing white light on the south jetty and is spanned by the **Bakers Haulover Inlet Bridge** (32-foot fixed vertical clearance). Jetties are short here, and currents are strong (2.0 to 3.0 knots). The inlet can

become especially nasty when wind and current oppose. Because of this, it is best to head just 8.3 miles south to Government Cut, a clear, well-marked inlet of choice.

If you are determined to use this inlet, turn to port out of the ICW at red daybeacon "4A" and take a bearing on the entrance to the inlet, a straight shot. The shoaling problem on the ICW channel west of Bakers Haulover Inlet, Mile 1080, south of red daybeacon "6A," is legendary. Periodically it is dredged, and like clockwork, it fills back in.

Follow buoys "7," "7A," "7B" and "7C" even if it appears that they are leading you to one side of the normal channel. If the sun is at the proper angle, you can see the path through the shoal area.

⚠ Severe shoaling exists in the vicinity of Biscayne Bay Buoy "7B." The shoal protrudes into the channel on the east side, which reduces the channel width by approximately half of the charted width. Shoal depths of 3.5 to 4 feet at mean low water were reported at press time in spring 2017. Buoy "7B" has been relocated to mark the best water. Watch for a strong set to the west with flood tide and to the east with the ebb. See the Waterway Guide Explorer at waterwayguide.com for news and navigational updates.

There is a Slow-Speed/Minimum-Wake restriction along this entire area. See the Inlet section at the front

## Marina

Berths within Protected Harbour
10 foot Deep-Water Approach
Monitored VHF Channel 16
106 Yacht Berths | Max 160 Ft/8 Ft Draft
Parallel Docking for Larger Yachts
Three Phase Electric Dockage
North Marina Slips with Pump Out
Wi Fi Internet & Cable
24 Hour Monitored Security
Complimentary Club Membership

## Marina Office

Staffed with over 30 years of Experience
Richly appointed Lobby & Reception
Fully Equipped Business Center
Spacious Conference Room
Boaters Lounge with Smart TV
Top-of-the-line Laundry Facility
Modern Showers & Lockers
Convenient Fitness Center

## Club Amenities

27,000 Sq. Ft. Spa & Fitness Center
    with personalized programs
16 Hard & HAR-TRU Courts and Tennis
    Center with Pro Shop
Fully Refurbished Island Club
Three Dining Venues
    Island Club Prime | Fine Dining
    The Cafe | Overlooking Tennis
    Pool Bar & Grille | Informal Open Air

Welcome to Williams Island, The Florida Riviera, nestled on 84 acres in Aventura, Florida, mid-way between Miami and Fort Lauderdale. Close to both airports and seaports. Williams Island offers an exclusive, private way of life to those accustomed to the finest of things at one of South Florida's most prestigious addresses. This magnificent Marina worthy of those in its sister Rivieras enjoys a protected harbour with berth's up to 160 feet and depths of 10 feet approaching the marina and 8 feet within the marina itself, plus a Marine Basin area to help assure a calm, restful environment. Our 106 berths are as comfortable and convenient for our boaters as they are for their vessels.

Marina guests will be treated to an amenity-rich lifestyle that encompasses an all-new Marina office with richly appointed conveniences, and complimentary Williams Island Club membership. Williams Island Club Amenities include a newly renovated Spa and Fitness Center. The Grand Slam-inspired Tennis Center with 16 tennis courts is expertly staffed. Exquisite fine dining at the Island Club Prime, an inviting Cafe overlooking Center Court, and the Pool Bar & Grille offer relaxed pool side tropical favorites. Entertainment and Social events are offered in the recently refurbished Island Club.

The Marina is conveniently open daily from 9 am to 6 pm.

4100 Island Boulevard, Aventura, Florida 33160 | 305.937.7813 office | 305.936.5713 fax

# Hallandale & North Miami Beach, FL

www.snagaslip.com
SNAG-A-SLIP — EXPLORE. BOOK. BOAT.™

| | Phone | Largest Vessel Accommodated | VHF Channel Monitored | Transient Berths / Total Berths | Approach / Dockside Depth (reported) | Floating Docks | Gas / Diesel | Groceries, Ice, Marine Supplies, Snacks | Repairs: Hull, Engine, Propeller | Lift (tonnage), Crane, Rail | Min/Max Amps | Laundry, Pool, Showers, Courtesy Car | Pump-Out Station | Nearby: Grocery Store, Motel, Restaurant |
|---|---|---|---|---|---|---|---|---|---|---|---|---|---|---|
| | | | | **Dockage** | | | **Supplies** | | **Services** | | | | | |
| **HALLANDALE** | | | | | | | | | | | | | | |
| 1. Hallandale Beach City Marina (WiFi) | 954-457-1653 | 60 | – | 3/26 | – | – | – | – | – | – | – | S | P | GMR |
| 2. Suntex Marina at Aventura 💻(WiFi) 1075.2 | 305-935-4295 | 120 | 16/68 | 12/99 | 20/10 | – | – | GI | – | – | 30/100 | – | P | GMR |
| 3. Turnberry Isle Marina Yacht Club 💻(WiFi)(WG) 1075.5 | 305-933-6934 | 180 | 16/68 | 30/117 | 30/20 | F | – | I | – | – | 30/100 | LPS | P | GMR |
| **NORTH MIAMI BEACH** | | | | | | | | | | | | | | |
| 4. Aquamarina Hi Lift 1077.3 | 305-931-2550 | 40 | – | call/9 | – | F | G | IMS | HEP | L | 30/30 | – | – | R |
| 5. Williams Island Marina 💻(WiFi) 1076.6 | 305-937-7813 | 160 | 16/10 | 15/106 | 10/8 | F | GD | IS | – | – | 30/100 | LPS | P | GMR |
| 6. Marina Palms Yacht Club (WiFi) | 786-707-2629 | 100 | 16 | 12/112 | /9 | F | GD | IS | – | – | 30/200+ | – | P | GR |
| **BAKERS HAULOVER INLET AREA** | | | | | | | | | | | | | | |
| 7. Bill Bird Marina at Haulover Park (WiFi) 1079.7 | 305-947-3525 | 90 | – | call/150 | 8/8.5 | F | GD | IMS | – | – | 30/100 | LS | P | GMR |
| 8. Bal Harbour Yacht Club – PRIVATE (WiFi) | 305-865-6048 | 140 | – | call/35 | 8/8 | – | GD | – | – | – | – | – | – | – |
| 9. Keystone Point Marina 1.3 W of 1080.8 | 305-940-6236 | 110 | 16/09 | 10/26 | 8/8 | F | GD | IMS | HEP | L | 30/50 | – | P | GMR |

💻 Internet Access  (WiFi) Wireless Internet Access  (WG) Waterway Guide Cruising Club Partner *(Information in the table is provided by the facilities.)*
See WaterwayGuide.com for current rates, fuel prices, web site addresses, and other up-to-the-minute information.

of this guide for more information on Bakers Haulover Inlet.

**Dockage:** North of the inlet on the east side of the ICW is Bill Bird Marina at Haulover Park with slips on floating docks, along with both gas and diesel. Bal Harbour Yacht Club to the south in a basin off Indian Creek is private and does not accept transients for dockage or fuel.

On the mainland opposite Bakers Haulover Inlet is the start of North Miami. Here, in protected New Arch Creek, are a number of boating amenities, repair yards and stores that are eager to serve transient mariners, including Keystone Point Marina. There is a well-marked approach channel leading west from ICW red daybeacon "12." The marina is usually full so call in advance to check on the availability of a slip. Keystone is locally known for their very competitive fuel pricing.

**Anchorage:** One of the finest overnight anchorages along this section of the ICW is the basin across the ICW from Bakers Haulover Inlet at Mile 1080. The only drawback is its entrance. According to cruiser reports, at high tide you should turn northwest off the ICW, approximately 75 feet north of red daybeacon "6A," and then slowly head directly toward the large, green, rounded roof of the Florida International University athletic building (approximately 305 degrees magnetic). To pass safely between the 3-foot-deep bar to port and the 4-foot-deep spoil area to the north, use the large-scale inset on side B of Chart 11467. If you encounter depths of less than 8 feet within the first couple of hundred feet, you are beginning to stray out

of the channel. Once you pass over the bar (soft mud and sand), you will find good depths of 8 to 12 feet. Inside this virtually undeveloped deepwater basin are serene anchorages protected from all wind directions. The bottom is quite soft (there may be debris in some places); make sure that your anchor is set well. Visiting boaters are not permitted ashore on the University's property.

## Bakers Haulover Inlet to Government Cut: ICW Mile 1080 to Mile 1090

A variety of routes wait south of Broad Causeway Bridge. While threading between markers, passing under or through various bridges and causeways, the mariner can opt to stay with the ICW to Miami and the Keys, or leave the ICW, via any of several routes, to explore Miami Beach.

**NAVIGATION:** Use Chart 11467. Use the Miami Harbor Entrance Tide Tables. For high tide at Baker's Haulover Inlet, add 57 minutes; for low tide, add 1 hour 37 minutes. The upper bay is extremely shallow, and the ICW cuts diagonally across it from northeast to southwest down to the 79th Street JFK Causeway. The channel is narrow but well marked, favoring the eastern shore until it passes under Broad Causeway. The **Broad Causeway Bridge** (Mile 1081.3, 16-foot closed vertical clearance) is the first of five restricted Miami spans. The span opens at 15 and 45 minutes past the hour, year-round, between 8:00 a.m. and 6:00 p.m.

Continuing south from Broad Causeway, follow your chart carefully. The channel runs diagonally across

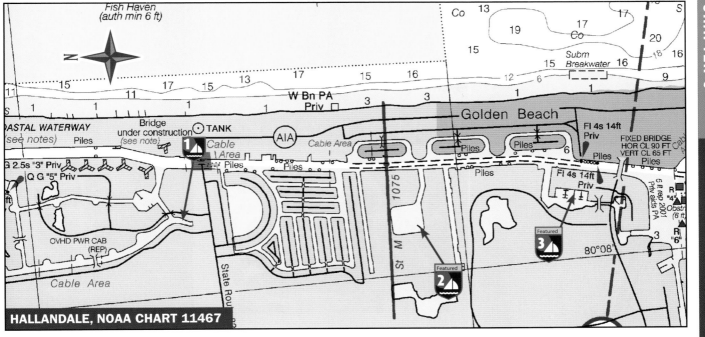

**HALLANDALE, NOAA CHART 11467**

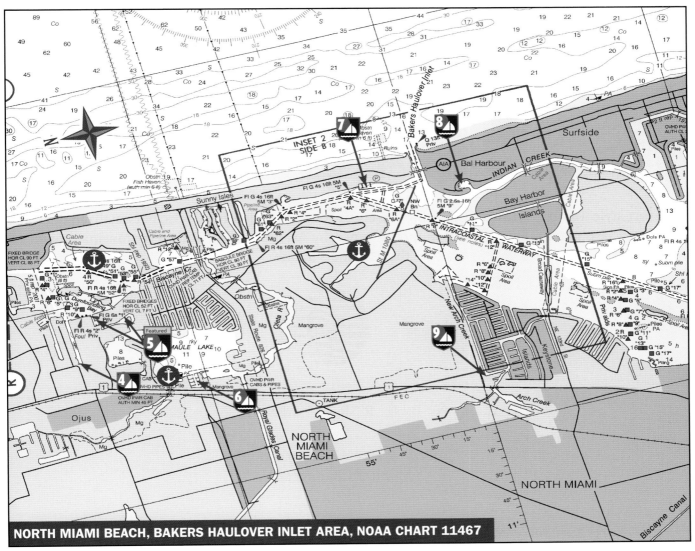

**NORTH MIAMI BEACH, BAKERS HAULOVER INLET AREA, NOAA CHART 11467**

## ALL THE ESSENTIALS IN ONE MARINA

Resort-style marina features 68 slips for vessels up to 180 feet, floating docks, personalized dockside service, access to tennis courts, and shopping at nearby Aventura Mall. Turnberry Marina provides all the essentials in one.

## T U R N B E R R Y   M A R I N A

N25° 57.450' W080° 07.660'
Monitor Channel 68

19735 Turnberry Way, Aventura, FL 33180 | P. 305.933.6934| dcastillo@turnberry.com

Biscayne Bay to the western shore and the west span of the **West 79th St. (JFK) Bridge** at Mile 1084.6 (25-foot closed vertical clearance, opens on signal). Be sure to indicate that you want the "western" span when calling the bridge on VHF Channel 09; there is another span of the 79th Street Causeway to the east.

To the south of the **East 79th Street Bascule Bridge** (25-foot vertical clearance, opens on signal), the Indian Creek is a narrow body of water that splits off Miami Beach proper and the beach. It skirts down across the road from many of the lavish hotels in Miami Beach's Bar Harbor area. Favor the eastern shore in Indian Creek; shoaling occurs along parts of the western bank of the creek.

Just south of the West 79th Street Bridge on the western shore is the marked entrance to Little River, which has facilities with various services for transients. South of Little River, the ICW—now narrow and surrounded by shoals—continues relatively straight to the **Julia Tuttle Causeway (I-95) Bridge** at Mile 1087.2.

⚠ The Julia Tuttle Bridge (56-foot fixed vertical clearance) sets the limiting overhead clearance for the inside passage from Fort Lauderdale to Miami. A few extra feet may be gained at low tide, but study the tide gauge before starting through because there is only a 2-foot tidal range.

The next pair of bridges are only a short distance apart. The **Venetian Causeway Bascule Bridge (West)**, at Mile 1088.6, has a 12-foot closed vertical clearance and opens on signal, except from 7:00 a.m. to 7:00 p.m., Monday through Friday, when the draw need only open on the hour and half hour. The **MacArthur Causeway (A1A) Twin Bridges** at Mile 1088.8 have a 65-foot fixed vertical clearance.

Although well marked, it is wise to take particular care navigating the ICW at the MacArthur Causeway, as the markers here can be confusing. Just north of the causeway, channel markers lead off from the ICW to enter the Main Ship Channel of Government Cut. (No small-boat traffic is allowed when the cruise ships are in, and marine police diligently patrol the entrance.) Once through the MacArthur Causeway Twin Bridge, markers indicate the route southeast to Fishermans Channel, south of Dodge Island.

Dodge Island railway and highway bridges cross the ICW at Mile 1089.3. The fixed **Dodge Island Hwy. Bridge** has a 65-foot vertical clearance, while the **Dodge Island Railroad Bascule Bridge** has a 22-foot closed vertical clearance; however, the railroad bridge is usually in the open position unless a train is approaching. Once you pass these bridges, you can access Fishermans Channel, the alternate route east to reach Government Cut (as well as Miami Beach Marina) when the Main Ship Channel is closed.

# Upper Biscayne Bay, FL

| | | Largest Vessel Accommodated | VHF Channel Monitored | Transient Berths / Total Berths | Approach / Dockside Depth (reported) | Floating Docks | Gas / Diesel | Groceries, Ice, Marine Supplies, Snacks | Repairs: Hull, Engine, Propeller | Lift (tonnage), Crane, Rail | Min/Max Amps | Laundry, Pool, Showers, Courtesy Car | Pump-Out Station | Nearby: Grocery Store, Motel, Restaurant |
|---|---|---|---|---|---|---|---|---|---|---|---|---|---|---|
| | | | | Dockage | | | Supplies | | Services | | | | | |
| **TREASURE ISLAND AREA** | | | | | | | | | | | | | | |
| 1. Grandview Palace Yacht Club 1.5 E of 1083.8 | 305-300-6828 | 120 | 16/68 | call/118 | 8/8 | – | G | GIMS | – | – | 50/50 | LPS | P | GMR |
| 2. Gator Harbor West Marina 2 E of 1084.8 | 305-754-2200 | 45 | – | call/20 | 6/6 | – | – | – | – | – | 30/100 | S | – | GMR |
| 3. Pelican Harbor Marina 1084.8 | 305-754-9330 | 50 | 16/68 | 10/112 | 6/6 | – | GD | I | – | – | 30/50 | LS | P | GMR |
| 4. North Beach Marina 1084.8 | 305-758-8888 | 43 | – | call/6 | – | – | – | GIMS | HEP | L9 | 30/30 | – | – | GR |
| **INDIAN CREEK** | | | | | | | | | | | | | | |
| 5. Miami Beach Resort ⌨ WiFi | 305-532-3600 | 200 | 16/09 | 20/20 | 7/7 | – | – | IS | – | – | 30/50 | LPS | – | MR |
| 6. Fontainebleau Marina | 305-538-2022 | 140 | – | 4/23 | 7/7 | – | – | IS | – | – | 30/100 | PS | – | GMR |
| **MIAMI BEACH** | | | | | | | | | | | | | | |
| 7. Sunset Harbour Yacht Club ⌨ WiFi 2 E of 1088 | 305-398-6800 | 210 | 16/11 | call/125 | 8/8 | – | D | IS | – | – | 30/100 | LPS | P | GMR |
| 8. Miami Beach Marina ⌨ WiFi 1089 3 E of 1089 | 305-673-6000 | 250 | 16/68 | 100/400 | 13/12 | F | GD | GIMS | – | – | 30/100 | LPS | P | GMR |
| 9. One Island Park - Miami Beach (IGY) WiFi 1089 | 754-701-4020 | 800 | 16/11 | call/8 | /40 | – | GD | – | – | – | 100/200+ | – | P | GMR |
| **GOVERNMENT CUT** | | | | | | | | | | | | | | |
| 10. Sea Isle Marina & Yachting Center WiFi 1089 | 305-377-3625 | 132 | 16/11 | call/220 | 13/10 | – | GD | GIMS | – | – | 30/100 | LS | P | GMR |
| 11. Island Gardens Deep Harbour Marina WiFi | 305-531-3747 | 550 | 16/71 | call/50 | 13/22 | F | GD | IMS | – | – | 50/200+ | LSC | P | MR |
| 12. Miami Yacht Club ⌨ WiFi 1089 | 305-377-9877 | 40 | – | 2/40 | 6/6 | F | – | IMS | – | L2 | 30/30 | PS | – | GR |

⌨ Internet Access  WiFi Wireless Internet Access  WG Waterway Guide Cruising Club Partner *(Information in the table is provided by the facilities.)*
See WaterwayGuide.com for current rates, fuel prices, web site addresses, and other up-to-the-minute information.

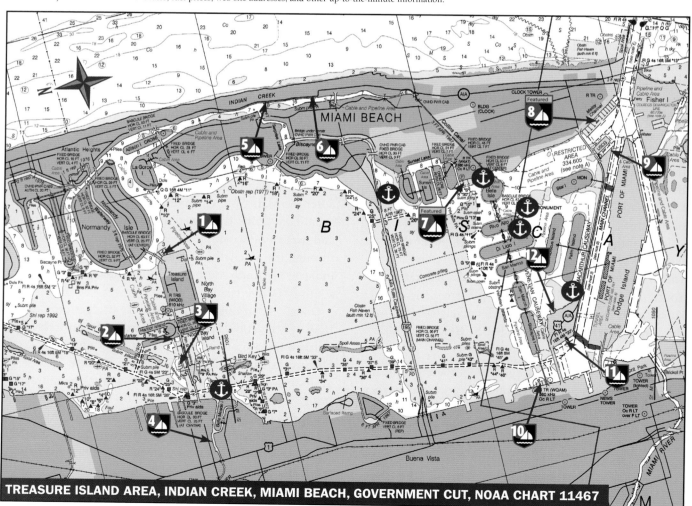

**TREASURE ISLAND AREA, INDIAN CREEK, MIAMI BEACH, GOVERNMENT CUT, NOAA CHART 11467**

SUNSET HARBOUR
YACHT CLUB

**Dockage/Moorings:** Grandview Palace Yacht Club is 1.5 miles east of the ICW at Mile 1083.8, before the 79th St. Bridge (East) between Treasure Island and Normandy Isle. Call in advance for slip availability. They also sell gas (no diesel). On the north side of the 79th Street Causeway are two facilities: Gator Harbor West Marina and the municipal Pelican Harbor Marina. Both have transient slips (call ahead) and Pelican Harbor sells fuel.

Miami-Dade County Parks and Recreation Department has a mooring field and dinghy dock at Pelican Harbor Marina. There are 27 moorings for boats up to 35-feet long. There is a dinghy dock. Farther south of the 79th Street Causeway on a marked channel of the Little River is North Beach Marina. They do not accept overnight transients, only long-term (6-month or longer) stays.

Nearby Indian Creek is chock-full of hotel and condominium docks, such as Miami Beach Resort and Fontainebleau Marina. These marinas provide easy access to the bustling Collins Avenue.

**Anchorage:** It is possible to anchor near the NE 79th Street Bridge at North Bay Island (south side) in 6 to 8 feet with good holding in mud. This is open to the south through west and wakes. There is a 7-day anchoring limit.

You can drop the hook in 8 to 9 feet of water with excellent holding and protection from all but the west at the Tuttle Causeway Bight, south of the east span of the bridge. (Due to increased usage, this anchorage has recently expanded and spilled over into Biscayne Bay on the other side of the channel.) Anchoring here is limited to 7 days; this ordinance is enforced. (See Anchoring Update at the end of this chapter.)

## ■ SIDE TRIP: MIAMI BEACH

Whether you take the ICW or the well-marked Miami Beach Channel to Miami Beach, be sure to allow ample time for sightseeing once you get there. Essentially a creation of the tourism industry, Miami Beach and its islands are mostly manmade. Its hip, vibrant image thrives in the Art Deco District, with its numerous hotels and acclaimed restaurants, as well as the trendy South Beach area. So many people in the entertainment industry have moved here that it has been dubbed "Hollywood East."

Some of the world's most flamboyant hotels and residences grace the 9 miles of beach here, where visitors will find spectacular water views and thousands of graceful coconut palms. If you travel with a pet aboard, you will find that virtually all the sidewalk restaurants are extremely pet-friendly.

**NAVIGATION:** Use Chart 11467. A major commercial and recreational port, Greater Miami bustles with activity on land and water. Study your charts carefully before attempting to transit this busy and sometimes confusing area. The routes between the ICW and the Miami Beach Channel, each paralleling one or another of the causeways that connect the mainland to the ocean islands, are all readily apparent on the chart. While most are safe, they still call for close attention to the chart, buoys and depth sounder. These are described in detail below. Visit the Waterway Guide Explorer at waterwayguide.com for more information.

# Sunset Harbour Yacht Club

Sunset Harbour Yacht Club offers a unique equity club membership program where owners and shareholders share a piece of the prime waterfront real estate in Miami Beach. In addition, to their berths and a gated covered parking space, new buyers are granted membership privileges including private access to the equity members lounge, use of a private fitness centre, heated Olympic-size pool, high power electrical service, fresh water, phone, extremely fast internet, digital satellite TV and a personal dock box.

## LOCAL POINTS OF INTEREST

- Ocean Drive and South Beach 1 mile away with Bal Harbour shoppes
- Le Gorce Golf Course, The Forge and Nobu Restaurant
- Art Basel International Art Show
- Annual Miami International Boat Show
- Located In Sunset Harbour Shops with 17 restaurants, 10 retail shops, 4 salons, 6 fitness/spa just across the street

*Slip into South Beach*

*Slide into the lifestyle*

## TECHNICAL SERVICES

Extremely fast hard wire internet and Wifi
Private gym
Olympic-size heated pool
In-slip fueling and pump-out
24-hour security with CCTV and access control
Private equity membership clubhouse
Assigned private parking space
Up to 480v 3 phase 200 amps

## BERTHING DETAILS:

125 slips ranging in size from 40' up to 310'
8 slips over 120 feet
Controlling draft at Mean Low Tide is 8 feet

Sunset Harbour Yacht Club

dmason@sunsetharbouryc.com

305-398-6800

www.sunsetharbouryc.com

1928 Sunset Harbour Dr.
Miami Beach, Fl 33139
USA

## Did You Know?

Sunset Harbour Yacht Club is Miami Beach's only private yacht club that sells equity memberships with berths in perpetuity. The values of these berths have more than doubled in the past four years.

MIAMI BEACH MARINA

**Dockage:** You will find many excellent, expensive marinas with substantial amenities. You will also find less fancy but somewhat more economical ones. For dockage information, visiting boaters may also call the Marine Council at 786-586-4688 for information on the Miami-Dade marine and tourism industry.

The Miami Beach Channel leads directly to Sunset Harbour Yacht Club on Biscayne Bay, which offers slips for lease or sale. Membership privileges including use of private fitness center, heated Olympic-size pool, high power electrical service, fresh water, phone, Internet digital satellite TV and a personal dock box. Transient space is available but be sure to call ahead to check availability. The marina also sells diesel.

A major supermarket, drugstore, post office and a city bus stop are less than 3 blocks from Sunset Harbour. The Lincoln Road Mall, a pedestrian-only street mall on 16th Street, has numerous art galleries, shops, restaurants and theaters, all within easy walking distance, as is the Miami Beach Convention Center, principal location of the Miami International Boat Show.

Farther south on Meloy Channel (the southern end of Miami Beach Channel), just opposite the Coast Guard base, the 400-slip Miami Beach Marina can accommodate vessels up to 250 feet and sells fuel. There is a dive shop on site as well as boat and jet ski rentals. The famous Art Deco District is nearby with shopping and the night life of trendy South Beach. A well-known restaurant, Monty's Sunset (305-672-1148) is on site and offers excellent food and service, both in a swimming pool/raw bar setting and upstairs in a fine food restaurant. A Brazilian steakhouse is also on site.

**Anchorage:** You can anchor just off the Sunset Harbour Channel (privately maintained daybeacons and lights) on the northeast side of Belle Isle in 7 to 11 feet. Wakes from passing vessels, particularly on weekends, can be disturbing. There is a 7-day anchoring limit here.

Good anchorages lie west and south of the small island with the Flagler Monument (south of the eastern span of the Venetian Causeway). Approach these via the Miami Beach Channel or the cross-bay route south of the Venetian Causeway (on the northern side of the entrance channel with 6-foot depths). It is also possible to anchor on the east side of Watson Island (7 to 8 feet). Remember that all of the anchorages in the Miami area are limited to 7 days. (See Anchoring Update at the end of this chapter.)

As of spring 2017 there are only a couple of places to land your dinghy to go ashore: the Marine Patrol dock and the City-owned dinghy dock up the Collins Canal. Markets and other shopping and restaurants are available at both locations. It is our suggestion that you check with locals or the Marine Patrol (305-673-7959) before using either of the docks.

## Crossover: Broad Causeway

**NAVIGATION:** Use Chart 11467. The northernmost crossover to Miami Beach appears just below Broad Causeway Bridge. The relatively well-marked channel (called the Miami Beach Channel) actually runs south along the eastern coast of Biscayne Bay (the western shore of Miami Beach) all the way to Government Cut. Land for homes was created by pumping sand up from Biscayne Bay's bottom and depositing it behind bulkheads. As a consequence, minimum depths of 6 to 7 feet lie almost anywhere near the shore, except where indicated on the chart. The open bay outside the ICW channel, on the other hand, has depths of only 1 to 3 feet.

At green daybeacon "15," south of the Broad Causeway Bridge, bear a bit east of south off the ICW toward flashing red daybeacon "2" (leave it to starboard), which then leads to the short, marked channel at the tip of Biscayne Point. When passing through the narrow channel marked by green daybeacons "3" and "5" to port and red daybeacons "4" and "6" to starboard, steer for red daybeacon "8" at the western tip of Normandy Isle. Here, you will come upon deep water but do not try to circumnavigate the island unless you use a dinghy. The fixed **71st Street Bridge** with a 5-foot vertical clearance connects the island to the ocean beach.

## Crossover: East 79th Street Causeway

**NAVIGATION:** Use Chart 11467. At the East 79th Street Causeway (the second crossover) connecting Normandy and Treasure Islands, this route meets the second crossover. The bridge has 25-foot closed vertical clearance and opens on signal. (Be sure to include "east" in your call for an opening.) Going south on the Miami Beach Channel, you can leave the route at red daybeacon "10" south of Normandy Isle and go east to the beginning of Indian Creek. Be sure to stay within the charted deep water and enter between La Gorce Island and Normandy Isle.

From this point, head south on the eastern side of Allison Island through the **63rd Street Bascule Bridge**, which connects Allison Island with the beach island. This bridge has 11-foot vertical clearance and opens on signal, except from 7:00 a.m. to 7:00 p.m., Monday through Friday (except federal holidays), when the draw need only open on the hour and half-hour. From 7:10 a.m. to 9:55 a.m. and 4:05 p.m. to 6:59 p.m., Monday through Friday (except federal holidays),

the draw need not open for the passage of vessels. In February of each year during the period 7 days prior to the City of Miami Beach Yacht and Brokerage Show and the 4 days following the show, from 10:00 a.m. to 4:00 p.m., the bridge need not open except for 10 minutes at the top of the hour. Make sure to check waterwayguide.com for schedule changes.

If you are continuing down the Miami Beach Channel, steer south between flashing green daybeacon "11" to port and red daybeacon "12" to starboard to the next eastern terminus of the third crossover, the Julia Tuttle Causeway (East), which is not recommended without local knowledge.

⚠️ Shoaling has been reported at the eastern end of Treasure Island, between the island and red daybeacon "8" off Normandy Isle. Give a good wide berth to the daybeacon, and you will find the best water along the Treasure Island shore.

Even at dead low water, depths of at least 8 feet are available near and at the East 79th Street Causeway Bridge.

## Crossover: Julia Tuttle Causeway

**NAVIGATION:** Use Chart 11467. This east-west crossover is not recommended without local knowledge. Leaving the ICW at green daybeacon "39," a channel parallels the north side of the Julia Tuttle Causeway. The channel runs just north of a few 2- to 3-foot-deep shoal areas along the causeway. The only aid to navigation identifying the channel is green daybeacon "25" marking the 35-foot vertical clearance fixed Julia Tuttle Causeway (East) over the Miami Bridge Channel on the eastern shore of Biscayne Bay.

## Crossover: Venetian Causeway (North and South)

**NAVIGATION:** Use Chart 11467. The next two crossings between the ICW and Miami Beach are north and south of the Venetian Causeway. Both routes are safe and easy, with the one on the north being slightly deeper. To cross to the north of the Venetian Causeway, turn east from the ICW at flashing green daybeacon "49." The channel is relatively well marked, though some daybeacons may be missing. This causeway jumps over a series of small islands to Belle Isle, the oldest island in Biscayne Bay and the closest to Miami Beach. The two cross-routes skirt the islands' northern and southern extremities.

## Crossover: MacArthur Causeway East

**NAVIGATION:** Use Chart 11467. The final cross-bay passage is along the main ship channel to the end of the MacArthur Causeway. The southernmost approach to Miami Beach is spanned by the 35-foot fixed **MacArthur Causeway East Bridge** near the U.S. Coast Guard base at the inner end of Government Cut at Meloy Channel.

## ■ GOVERNMENT CUT & FISHERMANS CHANNEL

**NAVIGATION:** Use Chart 11467. Use the Miami Harbor Entrance Tide Tables. A Class A big ship inlet, Government Cut (Miami Inlet) is wide, deep and free of hazards. It runs between Miami Beach (to the north) and Fisher Island (to the south). An alternate to Government Cut, Fishermans Channel is used by cruisers when Government Cut is closed for security reasons. Watch for frequent dredging operations in this area. Through the short passage from the west end of this channel to the ICW, controlling depth is about 10 feet at mean low water, but make sure you identify the markers carefully.

Biscayne Bay pilots report that recent dredging in and around the Port of Miami has affected currents in the harbor. Both flood and ebb are stronger than published predictions. If outward bound, just follow the buoys.

See the Inlet section at the front of this guide for more information on Miami Inlet.

Whenever there are cruise ships at the docks, Fishermans Channel must be used. Closures are announced on VHF Channel 16. It is similarly free of hazards, although when entering from the ICW heading south, one should leave green daybeacons "53A" and "55" well to port before turning in to the channel due to shoaling extending into the channel. The channel is wide with depths of 22 feet from the end of Lummus Island to the west end of Dodge Island.

There is a car ferry that runs between Dodge Island and Fisher Island, with frequent crossings. You must pay attention in this area and always give the ferry the right of way.

**Dockage:** Sea Isle Marina & Yachting Center, located in the heart of Downtown Miami, is home to the annual Miami International Boat Show. They may have slips and sell fuel. Island Gardens Deep Harbour Marina is on the west side of Watson Island, while the Miami Yacht Club is on the east side. Both have limited transient space, so be sure to call in advance. Island Gardens also sells gas and diesel.

**Anchorage:** Long-passage cruisers sometimes follow Fishermans Channel as far as Fisher Island and anchor off its southern side off the western tip, clear of traffic, in order to get an early start at the Atlantic. The holding is good here and you should have 12 feet of water or more.

# MIANI RIVER

One of Miami's principal boating-service areas is along the Miami River, which flows out of the Everglades to divide the city. The Miami River extends 4 miles between its mouth, at Mile 1090 on the ICW, and the head of navigation at 36th Street. This river has mostly repair facilities. Boating services along its banks include custom builders, yacht brokers and boat dealers, sales and service agents, propeller specialists and sailmakers. Along with these are completely equipped haul-out, repair and storage yards.

**NAVIGATION:** Use Chart 11467. South of the Dodge Island bridges, the ICW runs south in deep water for about .5 mile to the mouth of the Miami River on the west bank, between Bay Front Park and Claughton Island. Favor the starboard (western) shore all the way past Bay Front Park, and then execute a sharp turn to starboard into the river's mouth. Give green daybeacons "1" and "3" (the river's only markers) a wide berth and favor the starboard side upon entry. Shoals extend off the north side of Claughton Island and are at the side of the marked channel.

Miami River's controlling depth is 14 feet at mean low water up to the Northwest 27th Avenue Bridge and then 9 feet up to the 36th Street Dam. Boats proceeding upriver should lower outriggers and antennas for bridge clearance. If land traffic is heavy (and it usually is), bridge tenders will enforce the law.

The stated controlling depths hold on Miami River's more important side branches, South Fork (3 miles from the river's mouth) and Tamiami Canal (1 mile farther on). Both shoot obliquely off to the southwest and, like the main river, each has its own series of boatyards and marine installations. Tamiami Canal, a drainage ditch that parallels the Tamiami Trail to the northwest almost completely across Florida, is navigable for 6-foot draft vessels (8 feet at high tide) as far as a low limiting fixed bridge over Northwest 37th Avenue.

In addition to the vast array of recreational craft and amenities to serve them, the Miami River carries considerable commercial traffic. Tugs working in pairs maneuver to place the big oceangoing vessels that line the last mile or so of the river. Give these ships plenty of room.

## Miami River Bridges

A dozen bridges cross the Miami River and, except for two fixed bridges (with vertical clearances of 75 feet), all have restricted openings. They remain closed year-round from 7:35 a.m. to 9:00 a.m., and from 4:45 p.m. to 6:00 p.m. weekdays (except federal holidays), except the Brickell Bridge and Miami Ave. Bridge, which close at 4:35 p.m.

Most Miami River clearance gauges show the clearance at the fenders instead of the center of the span; there may be a sign indicating the additional clearance available at the center.

Closed vertical clearances for the other bridges in sequence up the Miami River (with type of bridge) are:

**Brickell Avenue Bridge** (23 foot clearance)
**Metro Train Bridge** (75 foot fixed clearance)
**Miami Ave. Bascule Bridge** (21 foot clearance)
**SW 1st Ave. Bridge** (75 foot fixed clearance)
**SW 2nd Ave. Bascule Bridge** (11 foot clearance)
**I-95 Twin Bridges** (75 foot fixed clearance)
**SW 1st St. Bascule Bridge** (18 foot clearance)
**West Flagler St. Bascule Bridge** (35 foot clearance)
**NW 5th St. Bascule Bridge** (12 foot clearance)
**NW 12th Ave. Bascule Bridge** (22 foot clearance)
**Dolphin Expressway Bridge** (75 foot fixed clearance)
**NW 17th Ave. Bascule Bridge** (17 foot clearance)
**NW 22nd Ave. Bascule Bridge** (25 foot clearance)
**NW 27th Ave. Bascule Bridge** (21 foot clearance)
**Railroad Bascule Bridge** (6 foot clearance)

There is one fixed bridge (8-foot vertical clearance) over the South Fork, and a swing bridge (erroneously charted as bascule), with 6-foot vertical clearance crossing the Tamiami Canal.

Whenever a big event takes place at Orange Bowl Stadium, home of the University of Miami Hurricanes football team, extra closures are usually imposed. If you plan to go upriver, check ahead of time for bridge restrictions. All closures for the regularly scheduled events at the Orange Bowl, from August through January, are posted online in the *Local Notice to Mariners* starting in late July; they are repeated a week or two before the event dates. These closures usually last only about two hours. Bridge schedules are always subject to change. Stay tuned for updates on the Waterway Guide Explorer at waterwayguide.com.

**Dockage:** Miamarina at Bayside is south of the Dodge Island bridges at Bayfront Park and may have transient space; call ahead. Epic Marina is at the mouth of the Miami River, across the river from Brickell Point, before

# Miami Harbor & Miami River, FL

| | Phone | Dockage — Largest Vessel Accommodated | VHF Channel Monitored | Transient Berths / Total Berths | Approach / Dockside Depth (reported) | Floating Docks | Supplies — Groceries, Ice, Marine Supplies, Snacks | Gas / Diesel | Services — Repairs: Hull, Engine, Propeller | Lift (tonnage), Crane, Rail | Min/Max Amps | Laundry, Pool, Showers, Courtesy Car | Pump-Out Station | Nearby: Grocery Store, Motel, Restaurant |
|---|---|---|---|---|---|---|---|---|---|---|---|---|---|---|
| **MIAMI HARBOR** | | | | | | | | | | | | | | |
| 1. Miamarina at Bayside [WiFi] 1089.5 | 305-960-5180 | 165 | 16/18 | 26/130 | 14/10 | F | IS | – | – | – | 30/100 | LS | P | GMR |
| **2. Epic Marina ⌨ [WiFi] 1090** | **305-400-6711** | **325** | **16/68** | **20/20** | **17/15** | **–** | **–** | **–** | **–** | **–** | **20/200+** | **PS** | **P** | **GMR** |
| **MIAMI RIVER** | | | | | | | | | | | | | | |
| 3. 5th Street Marina ⌨ | 305-324-2040 | 240 | – | – | 15/13 | – | – | – | HEP | L100 | 50/100 | – | P | – |
| 4. Norseman Shipbuilding Corp. ⌨ | 305-545-6815 | 90 | – | call/25 | 15/10 | – | – | – | HEP | L100,C | 50/50 | – | – | – |
| 5. Anchor Marine of Miami | 305-545-6348 | 50 | – | – | – | – | M | GD | EP | L15 | 30/30 | – | – | G |
| 6. RMK Merrill-Stevens [WiFi] [WG] | 305-324-5211 | 250 | – | 10/20 | 16/15 | – | M | GD | HEP | L70,C30,R500 | 30/100 | S | P | GMR |
| 7. Hurricane Cove Marina & Boatyard | 305-324-8004 | 85 | – | call/150 | 12/10 | – | M | GD | HEP | L80 | 30/30 | – | – | GMR |
| 8. River Cove Marina | 305-545-5001 | 60 | – | call/72 | 12/10 | – | M | – | – | L14 | 30/30 | S | P | GMR |
| 9. Austral International Marina [WiFi] [WG] | 305-325-0177 | 40 | – | 5/35 | 6/6 | – | M | – | HEP | L20,C18 | 30/50 | S | – | G |
| 10. Brisas del Rio Marina | 305-392-1487 | – | – | – | 15/15 | – | – | – | HEP | – | 30/50 | – | – | GR |
| 11. Jones Superyacht Miami Inc . [WiFi] | 305-635-0891 | 300 | – | call/11 | 15/15 | – | MS | – | HEP | L950 | 50/200+ | – | – | – |

⌨ Internet Access  [WiFi] Wireless Internet Access  [WG] Waterway Guide Cruising Club Partner  *(Information in the table is provided by the facilities.)*
See WaterwayGuide.com for current rates, fuel prices, web site addresses, and other up-to-the-minute information.

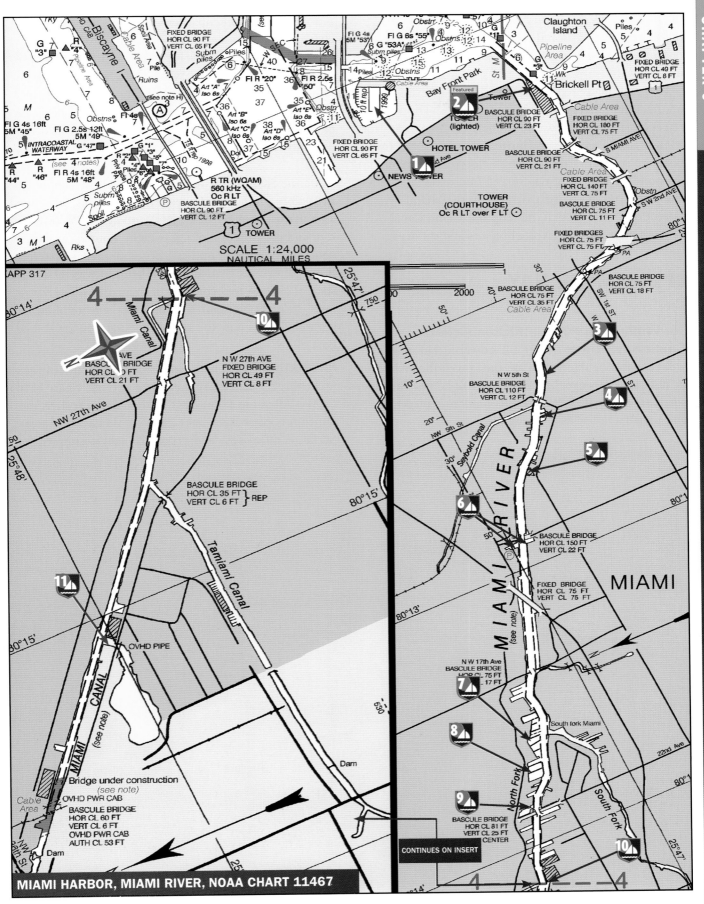

the bridge. This is a luxury destination directly on the Miami River with full amenities and two on-site restaurants. They can accommodate yachts over 300 feet in deep water slips.

There are many repair facilities for the cruising boater on the Miami River but few transient slips. The 5th Street Marina has a seawall for dockage. Anchor Marine, RMK Merrill-Stevens and Hurricane Cove Marina & Boatyard sell both gas and diesel. Norseman Shipbuilding Corp., River Cove Marina, Austral International Marina and Brisas del Rio Marina are also on the Miami River. Jones Boat Yard Inc. is located up the Miami Canal. All of these offer varying levels of repairs and services.

## ■ BISCAYNE BAY

The **William M. Powell (Rickenbacker) Causeway Bridge** (65-foot fixed vertical clearance) will probably be referred to as "the Powell/Rickenbacker" or just "Rickenbacker" for some time to come. The older structure is dwarfed alongside its modern replacement and remains in use as a fishing pier.

South of the Rickenbacker Causeway, Biscayne Bay changes character, becoming broad, relatively deep (average 10 feet) and lovely. Sailing regattas are held in these waters nearly every weekend, while fishing, swimming, water skiing and cruising are everyday, year-round activities. Cruisers will find this part of Biscayne Bay especially inviting. The deep, open water makes a pleasant change from the narrow confines of much of the ICW.

Marine Stadium on Virginia Key was originally built in 1963 to promote powerboat racing. It was considered a modernist icon because of its cantilevered, fold-plate roof and construction of lightweight, poured-in-place concrete, popular in mid-century stadiums. At 326 feet in length (longer than a football field), it was the longest span of cantilevered concrete in the world when it was built. Its eight big slanted columns are anchored in the ground. This is now the site of the Miami International Boat Show.

**NAVIGATION:** Use Chart 11467. Cruising south of the Rickenbacker Causeway is easier if you use Chart 11465 (ICW—Miami to Elliot Key). Although the scale is the same on both charts, Chart 11465 covers a larger area (as far as Elliot Key) and makes navigation simpler.

Bear Cut is on the southeast side of Virginia Key, between it and Key Biscayne. It is unmarked at its northeastern end, except for red daybeacon "2," which provides an outlet to the ocean for smaller boats that can pass under the **Bear Cut Bridge** (16-foot fixed vertical clearance).

Skippers southbound along the main ICW channel should follow the chart closely and take time to sort out the buoys. On the ICW east of the mouth of the Miami River, several channels (described earlier), all with their own markers, meet and intersect. There are a couple of different marker numbering sequences; steer toward green daybeacon "59" and then make your turn to follow the ICW channel. Slow down, and take your time picking out the navigational aids for your particular course.

ICW markers all have either a small yellow square on the green or a small yellow triangle on the red. Normal channel markers are just green or red.

**Dockage:** Rickenbacker Marina is located in the Marine Stadium with limited reserved dockage for transients. There are restaurants and shopping within walking distance. Marine Stadium Marina has no wet slips, only dry storage. Both of these facilities sell gas.

Just south of the Rickenbacker Causeway, on the mainland side, is an emergency dock belonging to Mercy Hospital (305-285-2768). It has depths of 4 feet at mean low water and 6 feet at high tide and provides a telephone, restricted to emergency use only.

**Anchorage:** You can anchor at the Marine Stadium for 24 hours only. The anchoring is good in 8 to 12 feet with a mud and sand bottom. There are signs that indicate no dinghy landing and our cruising editor said that they were being enforced.

Anchoring is also possible on the southeast side of Virginia Key in at least 7 feet with good holding in sandy mud. Drop the hook outside the basin north of the Miami Seaquarium.

## Key Biscayne–ICW Mile 1094

Key Biscayne, site of southern Florida's first town, was founded in 1839. It was also headquarters for a band of renegades who lured ships onto the reefs and "salvaged" their cargo. Today, the key is made up of two parks: The northern end is taken up by Dade County's Crandon Park, while the southern is home to Bill Baggs Cape Florida State Park. Crandon Park occupies the northern end of Key Biscayne at Mile 1094. This county park boasts a marina (Crandon Park Marina), boat ramp,

two miles of ocean beach and excellent picnic grounds; nearby is the International Tennis Center and an excellent golf course. Bus service is available to the city.

**Dockage:** The Crandon Park Marina complex includes gas and diesel fuel. (Note that the showers are cold water only.) It is best approached from Biscayne Bay by a privately marked natural channel that leads northeastward from the shoal light (flashing white, four seconds) off West Point. The marina also has moorings available to sailboats only in its protected cove with easy access to marina amenities. If you have to do any type of shopping, you will need to arrange for ground transportation, as there are no shops or other restaurants for 2 to 3 miles.

**Anchorage:** Two of the most popular harbors among boaters waiting for favorable weather to cross over to the Bahamas are Hurricane Harbor, near the southwest corner of Key Biscayne, and No Name Harbor, around the point from Hurricane Harbor and in the Bill Baggs State Park. Hurricane Harbor does not have shore access. Here you will find 5 to 13 feet with excellent holding and some exposure to the northwest. When the wind is out of the east, another option is to simply anchor in the lee of the west side of Key Biscayne, just north of Hurricane Harbor's entrance in 8 to 13 feet (exposed west to southwest).

Your best bet is No Name Harbor, which has shore access and a fee for overnight anchoring. The bottom is hard mud in 11 to 12 feet of water, and holding is good with wind protection from all directions except due west (and that is actually not too bad). At the head of No Name Harbor, the Boaters' Grill (305-361-0080) offers a menu of appetizers, light meals, deli take-out, along with beer and wine. Also available are clean restrooms, inexpensive showers and a laundry (although not always operational). Cleats along the seawall make going ashore much simpler. There are no fenders along the raw concrete seawall, so you should rig your own fenders in advance.

A pump-out station is located on the southern side of the harbor, near the entrance, but it is not always working. There is no seawall protection here either, so rig your own fenders in advance. There is a small fee for daily tie-ups ($8), but overnight stays along the wall are prohibited. In 2017, overnight anchorage (and use of the facilities) was available for $20. Envelopes are provided for depositing the fees in an honor box ashore. There is room for about 25 boats. The weekdays are great, the weekends are very crowded.

# Key Biscayne, FL

| KEY BISCAYNE AREA | | | Dockage | | | | | Supplies | | Services | | | | | |
|---|---|---|---|---|---|---|---|---|---|---|---|---|---|---|---|
| | | | Largest Vessel Accommodated | VHF Channel Monitored | Transient Berths / Total Berths | Approach / Dockside Depth (reported) | Floating Docks | Gas / Diesel | Groceries, Ice, Marine Supplies, Snacks | Repairs: Hull, Engine, Propeller | Lift (tonnage), Crane, Rail | Pump-Out Station | Laundry, Pool, Showers, Courtesy Car | Min/Max Amps | Nearby: Grocery Store, Motel, Restaurant |
| 1. Rickenbacker Marina Inc. 🖥 📶 1091.5 | | 305-361-1900 | 100 | 16 | 2/200 | 8/9 | – | G | IMS | HEP | L | | 30/50 | S | P | R |
| 2. Marine Stadium Marina 1091.5 | | 305-960-5140 | 43 | 16/83 | – | 8/10 | – | G | GI | HEP | L9 | | – | – | – | GMR |
| 3. Crandon Park Marina 1094 | | 305-361-1281 | 80 | 16/68 | 10/294 | 6/5 | F | GD | GIMS | – | – | | – | LS | P | GMR |

🖥 Internet Access  📶 Wireless Internet Access  **WG** Waterway Guide Cruising Club Partner  *(Information in the table is provided by the facilities.)*
See WaterwayGuide.com for current rates, fuel prices, web site addresses, and other up-to-the-minute information.

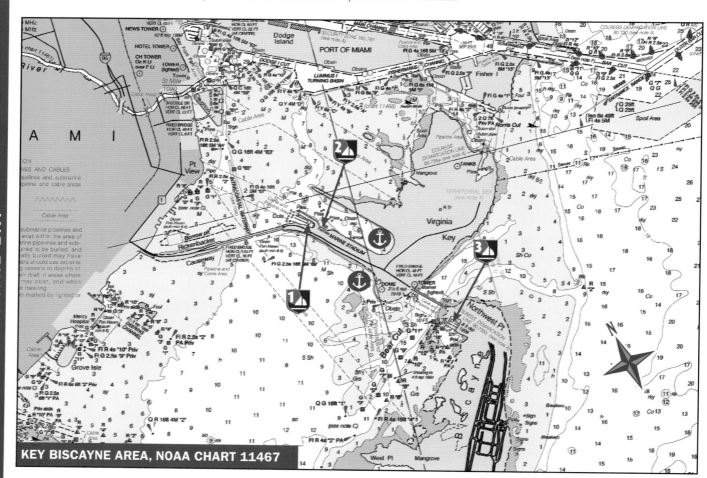

KEY BISCAYNE AREA, NOAA CHART 11467

see our interactive charts

MARINAS

SERVICES

ANCHORAGES

FREE DOCK

BRIDGES

LOCKS

NAV ALERTS

FUEL

waterwayguide.com

# Coconut Grove Area–ICW Mile 1095

Across Biscayne Bay from Bear Cut is Dinner Key, the major center of boating activity for the southern sector of Biscayne Bay, which is served by a 1.5-mile-long, well-marked channel on the western mainland shore. It was once a seaplane base–first for the enormous Pan American clippers flying to the Caribbean and South America and later for the U.S. Coast Guard.

**Dockage:** Palmeiras Beach Club at Grove Isle at Mile 1093 offers docking with resort-style amenities. One nautical mile south is the Coral Reef Yacht Club, which uses the same entrance channel from Biscayne Bay as the marina. Members of other yacht clubs may be able to arrange brief transient dockage; call ahead before reaching the club. Next, still heading south, are Prime Marina Miami, Grove Harbour Marina and Dinner Key Marina. All have very limited transient space, and fuel is only available at Grove Harbour Marina. Most of the private marinas and yacht clubs in the area offer reciprocal agreements for members of other recognized yacht clubs. Be sure to call ahead because space may be tight.

**Moorings:** Dinner Key Marina offers a mooring field with 225 mooring balls. Call the marina for your mooring assignment. Included in the cost of the mooring are pump-out service and a dinghy dock next door at the launching ramp. A water taxi will take you into the marina, which is very close to the attractions of Coconut Grove. You can also come in to take on water. Trash pickup and recycling are available as well. This is a popular spot to wait for favorable weather to cross to the Bahamas.

For your provisioning needs, The Fresh Market (2640 S. Bayshore Dr.) is just one block away from the marina area. Dinner Key's location puts boaters within walking distance of the popular Coconut Grove area with its galleries and cafes.

**Anchorage:** Anchoring is still possible outside of the mooring field to the north (on the opposite side of the channel) and to the east in 7 to 8 feet of water. This is open and exposed to the east through southeast. The anchorage is usually crowded so look carefully before dropping your hook.

## Bill Baggs State Park

At the southern end of Key Biscayne is Bill Baggs Cape Florida State Park, named after the late Miami newspaper editor who championed the fight to designate this area a state park. With more than 1 mile of ocean beach, the park is set in a wilderness of tropical growth. There are bike paths and running trails in a beautiful tropical setting here; this is a great place to get off the boat and stretch your legs but will require a walk or bike from Hurricane or No Name Harbors. Don't forget your camera; there are numerous opportunities for beautiful shots.

The oldest structure in Miami-Dade County is the 95-foot-high Cape Florida Lighthouse. The original light was built in 1825 and has survived numerous hurricanes, an 1836 Seminole Indian attack that resulted in a fire, and the harsh effects of the environment. Refurbished that same year, its replacement was in service until 1878, when Fowey Rocks Light took over in a position 5 miles offshore, which enabled it to better guide deep-draft ships that had to stand far out to sea. The original structure was restored to its authentic 1855 condition and is now maintained and charted as a private aid to navigation, flashing a white beam that is visible 7 nm out to sea.

# GOIN' ASHORE: COCONUT GROVE, FL

| SERVICES | |
|---|---|
| 1 | Library |
| 2 | Post Office |
| 3 | Visitor Information |
| **ATTRACTIONS** | |
| 3 | Miami City Hall (original PanAm terminal) |

| SHOPPING | |
|---|---|
| 4 | CocoWalk |
| 5 | Fresh Market |
| **DINING** | |
| 6 | Grove Bay Grill |

| MARINAS | |
|---|---|
| 7 | Coral Reef Yacht Club |
| 8 | Dinner Key Marina |
| 9 | Grove Harbour Marina |
| 10 | Prime Marina Miami |

Part of the City of Miami, Coconut Grove is known to locals as "The Grove." It is one of the hippest, most energetic and most inviting corners of South Florida. Unlike the rest of Miami, low-key and restful Coconut Grove preserves much of the ambiance of traditional Florida. All the usual daily necessities—laundries, supermarkets, restaurants, post office, library, bank, drugstores—are only a short distance from the marinas, as are art galleries, antiques and gift shops, boutiques and craft shops catering to tourists.

Coconut Grove was once a seaplane base for the enormous Pan American clippers flying to the Caribbean and South America. Known as the "Air Gateway between the Americas," the Pan Am Seaplane Base and Terminal Building at Dinner Key linked the United States with Latin America. The inaugural flight from Dinner Key to Panama took place on December 1, 1930. The original Pan Am complex was designed to look like an airplane when viewed from above: Pan Am Drive and Circle were designed to be the body of the plane; the Terminal Building the cockpit, and the hanger buildings representing the wings. (See more at coconutgrovevillagecouncil.com/history.) The original building now serves as Miami City Hall, where you can pick up visitor information.

The giant, 3.5 ton revolving world globe once located in the lobby of the Pan Am terminal greeted visitors to the old Miami Museum of Science for 55 years. The museum relocated to the Patricia and Phillip Frost Museum of Science in the Grove at 3280 S. Miami Ave. in 2017. This hands-on facility offers exhibits on weather and technology, a planetarium and wildlife centers. Call 305-646-4200 for details. On the Bay at 3251 S. Miami Ave. is Vizcaya Museum & Gardens, housed in a 1914 mansion with 34 period decorated rooms and 10 acres of formal gardens with sculptures and grottos (305-250-9133).

Many special events are held here throughout the year, although the most special might be the annual Coconut Grove Arts Festival, scheduled each February to occur during President's Day weekend. The three-day event is one of Florida's most vibrant outdoor art festivals, highlighting works of hundreds of artists.

For years, the U.S. Sailing Winter Sail Training Center has been at Coconut Grove's Kennedy Park. Equipped with a 40-foot-wide ramp and a pair of 2-ton capacity hoists, as well as good weather and good winds virtually all winter long, the Center proves invaluable to those training for the Olympics and for the various one-design classes holding mid-winter regattas here.

**Shopping:** The Grove is home to CocoWalk, a popular shopping and dining district. First Flight Out is located here, featuring a collection of Pan Am merchandise, luggage, travel apparel, aviation collectibles and gifts.

For provisioning, a Fresh Market is conveniently located near the marinas at 2640 S. Bayshore Dr.

**Dining:** There are numerous places in which to dine, from simple fare to the more elegant. The Grove Bay Grille (3381 Pan American Dr., 305-285-1366) is the closest, with a great waterfront view and a bar-type menu. It's popular with the locals and always busy.

Next to Prime Marina Miami is Monte's Raw Bar, a funky bayside hangout with drinks, a raw bar, live music and weeknight happy hour (2550 S. Bayshore Dr., 305-856-3992). For great pizza or other Italian dishes, try Spartico at the Mayfair Hotel & Spa (3000 Florida Ave., 305-779-5100).

# Biscayne Bay West Shore, FL

| COCONUT GROVE AREA | Phone | Largest Vessel Accommodated | VHF Channel Monitored | Transient Berths / Total Berths | Approach / Dockside Depth (reported) | Floating Docks | Gas / Diesel | Groceries, Ice, Marine Supplies, Snacks | Repairs: Hull, Engine, Propeller | Lift (tonnage), Crane, Rail | Min/Max Amps | Laundry, Pool, Showers, Courtesy Car | Pump-Out Station | Nearby: Grocery Store, Motel, Restaurant |
|---|---|---|---|---|---|---|---|---|---|---|---|---|---|---|
| | | | | Dockage | | | Supplies | | | Services | | | | |
| 1. Palmeiras Beach Club at Grove Isle ▢ 1093 | 305-858-8300 | 120 | 16 | 85/85 | 8/12 | F | - | IS | EP | - | 30/100 | PS | P | MR |
| 2. Coral Reef Yacht Club 1094 | 305-858-1733 | 65 | 71 | call/104 | 7/7 | F | - | IS | - | C | 30/100 | PS | P | GMR |
| 3. Prime Marina Miami WiFi 1094 | 305-854-7997 | 100 | 16/68 | call/114 | 5/6 | F | - | I | - | L20 | 30/100 | LS | P | GMR |
| 4. Grove Harbour Marina ▢ 1094 | 305-854-6444 | 150 | - | call/58 | 18/8 | F | GD | GI | HP | L90 | 30/100 | - | P | GMR |
| 5. Dinner Key Marina ▢ 1095 | 305-329-4755 | 110 | 16/68 | 50/582 | 8/7 | F | - | IS | - | - | 30/100 | LS | P | GMR |
| 6. Matheson Hammock Marina 3.6 W of 1098 | 305-665-5475 | 55 | - | call/243 | 5.5/5 | F | GD | IS | - | - | 30/50 | PS | P | R |
| **HOMESTEAD AREA** | | | | | | | | | | | | | | |
| **7. Suntx Marnas at South Miami 1106** | **305-258-3500** | **38** | **16/08** | **1 /299** | **5/9** | **F** | **GD** | **IMS** | **HEP** | **L** | **30/30** | **-** | **-** | **GR** |
| 8. Black Point Park & Marina 1106 | 305-258-4092 | 55 | 16/09 | 20/200 | 4.9/5.5 | F | GD | IMS | - | L | 30/50 | - | P | GMR |
| 9. Herbert Hoover Marina at Homestead Bayfront Park WiFi | 305-230-3033 | 50 | 16/72 | 174/174 | 3.5/5 | - | GD | GIMS | - | L | 30/50 | PS | P | GMR |

▢ Internet Access  WiFi Wireless Internet Access  WG Waterway Guide Cruising Club Partner *(Information in the table is provided by the facilities.)*
See WaterwayGuide.com for current rates, fuel prices, web site addresses, and other up-to-the-minute information.

## Coral Gables–ICW Mile 1096

**NAVIGATION:** Use Charts 11467 and 11465. Located directly south of Coconut Grove, Coral Gables has its own waterway with a well-marked entrance and a 5-foot controlling depth at mean low water. Since bridges on both branches of this waterway are fixed (most offer about a 12-foot vertical clearance), you will likely have to explore by dinghy. The canals interconnect, wind through residential sections and finally exit to the bay just north of Coral Gables' wide Tahiti Beach.

**Dockage:** About 4 miles south of Coconut Grove is Matheson Hammock Park, a county park, beach and marina (Matheson Hammock Marina). It is one of South Florida's few remaining natural areas, with native forest and a lagoon-type atoll beach. This marina has slips for transients, a sandy beach and other amenities, including fuel.

Farther south, in the Homestead Area, is Suntex Marina at South Miami, which provides dry storage as well as transient dockage (call ahead), a Captain's Lounge with coffee and popcorn and a well-stocked ship store. They also have diesel and gas and have an on-site restaurant (The Ocean Grill, 305-258-3918), which has live bands on weekends.

Located in the same protected basin is Black Point Park & Marina with transient dockage, bike trails and fishing as well as gas and diesel fuel. Continuing south is Herbert Hoover Marina at Homestead Bayfront Park offering transient dockage and fuel. It is in a beautiful tropical setting with a natural atoll pool and a pristine beach. Approach depths, however, are reported as 3.5 feet; call ahead for actual depths.

## Cruising Options

Cruisers are now in an ideal position to head east to the Bahamas or continue south into the fabled Florida Keys. The run north, outside from Government Cut, is spectacular and offers the best available view of the Miami Beach skyline. The run south from Government Cut offers some interesting coastline as well, leading past Virginia Key and Key Biscayne to the next entry from the ocean at Cape Florida. At Key Biscayne's southern end is the restored Cape Florida Lighthouse.

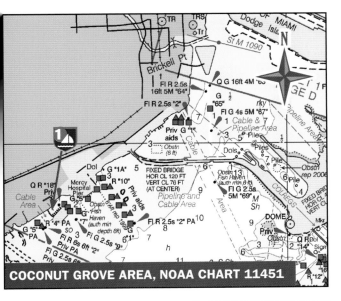

**COCONUT GROVE AREA, NOAA CHART 11451**

**COCONUT GROVE AREA, NOAA CHART 11451**

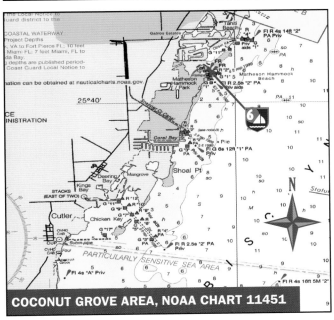

**COCONUT GROVE AREA, NOAA CHART 11451**

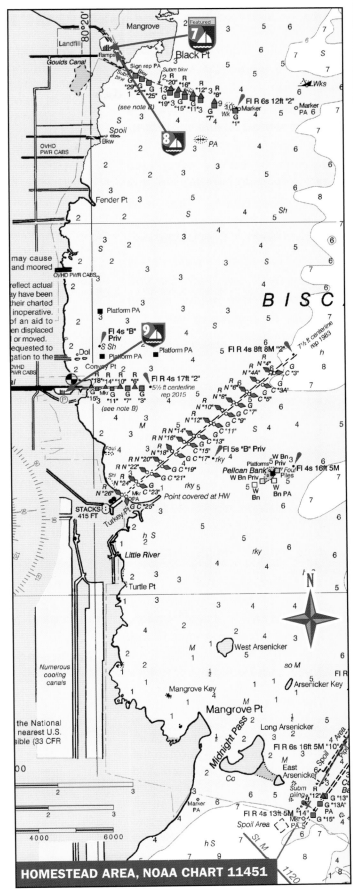

**HOMESTEAD AREA, NOAA CHART 11451**

# Anchoring Update

*Effective July 1, 2017 the Florida legislature approved House Bill 7043 that codifies anchoring regulations in the state. Following the completion of pilot programs that provided insight into the multitude of issues associated with vessels anchoring in the state's waterways, the new regulations offer clear guidance and specific requirements for boaters, localities, public safety agencies and law enforcement. The areas listed below remain off-limits to anchoring with the exceptions listed:*

- The section of Middle River lying between Northeast 21st Court and the ICW in Broward County.

- Sunset Lake in Miami-Dade County. (The City of Miami Beach also recently passed an amendment to an ordinance which now makes it unlawful to tie a dinghy to the canal wall to visit the city, leaving only limited dinghy access.)

- The sections of Biscayne Bay in Miami-Dade County lying between Rivo Alto Island and Di Lido Island, San Marino Island and San Marco Island, and San Marco Island and Biscayne Island.

### There are exceptions:

- If the vessel suffers a mechanical failure that poses an unreasonable risk of harm to the vessel or the persons onboard unless the vessel anchors. The vessel may anchor for three business days or until the vessel is repaired, whichever occurs first.

- If imminent or existing weather conditions in the vicinity of the vessel pose an unreasonable risk of harm to the vessel or the persons onboard unless the vessel anchors. The vessel may anchor until weather conditions no longer pose such risk. During a hurricane or tropical storm, weather conditions are deemed to no longer pose an unreasonable risk of harm when the hurricane or tropical storm warning affecting the area has expired.

- During events described in s.327.48 or other special events, including, but not limited to, public music performances, local government waterfront activities, or fireworks displays. A vessel may anchor for the lesser of the duration of the special event or three days.

- Vessels owned or operated by a governmental entity for law enforcement, firefighting, military, or rescue purposes.

- Construction or dredging vessels on an active job site.

- Vessels actively engaged in commercial fishing.

- Vessels engaged in recreational fishing if the persons onboard are actively tending hook and line fishing gear or nets.

The bill provides that citations will result in a mandatory court appearance and a $50 civil penalty. Those failing to show up for court may be found guilty of a misdemeanor of the second degree, with more severe penalties.

### The Bottom Line:

House Bill 7043 effectively prevents cities, towns, counties or other municipal entities from passing laws or ordinances preventing boaters from anchoring. HB 7043 now provides specific language related to where vessels may anchor in proximity to marinas, docks, boatyards, mooring fields, superyacht repair facilities and other vessels. If you have any question about your location, check the regulations. This new measure also provides clear guidance on derelict vessels and regulations for proving that your vessel's holding tanks are pumped out regularly.

**Anchoring Ban Areas** ■

# The Florida Keys

■ FLORIDA UPPER KEYS    ■ FLORIDA LOWER KEYS

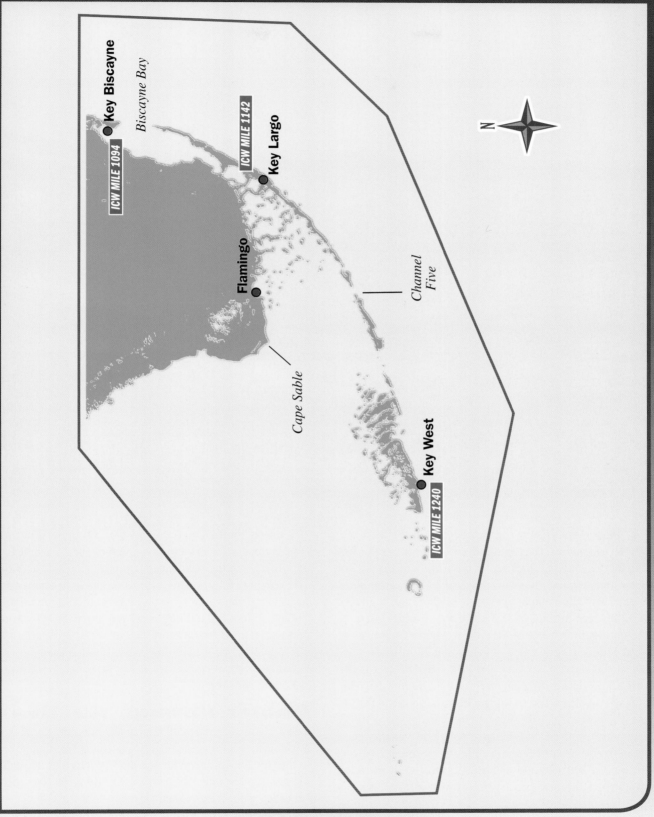

Key Biscayne

*Biscayne Bay*

ICW MILE 1094

ICW MILE 1142

Key Largo

Flamingo

*Channel Five*

*Cape Sable*

Key West

ICW MILE 1240

N

www.WaterwayGuide.com

The old Bahia Honda Rail Bridge in the lower Florida Keys that connected Bahia Honda Key with Spanish Harbor Key. After a new Bahia Honda Bridge was opened in 1972, two spans of the old bridge were removed to accommodate boat traffic.

# The Flor

Extending in a sweeping southwesterly curve from Miami and the mainland, the Florida Keys offer the cruising mariner an environment unlike any other waterway area. In many ways, the Keys resemble the islands of the Bahamas, except for the main highway and 42 bridges (a total of 18.94 miles of bridges) that tie them together. West of Marathon, Moser Channel, (Seven Mile) Bridge–which is actually 6.77 miles–is the longest, the Harris Gap Channel Bridge at 108 feet is the shortest and the Jewfish Creek Bridge is the newest. The highway runs from the tip of the Florida peninsula to Key West, the nation's southernmost city. Farther west, the Marquesas and the Dry Tortugas provide the challenge of remote and unconnected islands, accessible only by water or air. Tourism and fishing support the numerous communities lining U.S. 1 South, known as the Overseas Highway.

With outstanding natural and artificial underwater reefs, fishermen, snorkelers and divers have found a tropical paradise along the southeastern (ocean side) of the Keys. The northern and northwestern sides are a fisherman's heaven and the gateway to the Everglades National Park.

Cayo Hueso (Island of Bones) was discovered by Ponce de Leon, named Las Martines and claimed by Spain in 1513. In 1815 Don Juan de Estrada granted the land (now known as Key West) to Juan Pablo Salas for meritorious service to the crown.

## Routes through the Keys

Below Miami, two different, but equally interesting, routes are available for the cruise along the Keys to Key West and beyond to the Dry Tortugas. One follows the ICW "inside" through Florida Bay. The other, deeper passage, which traverses the "outside," is the Hawk Channel route.

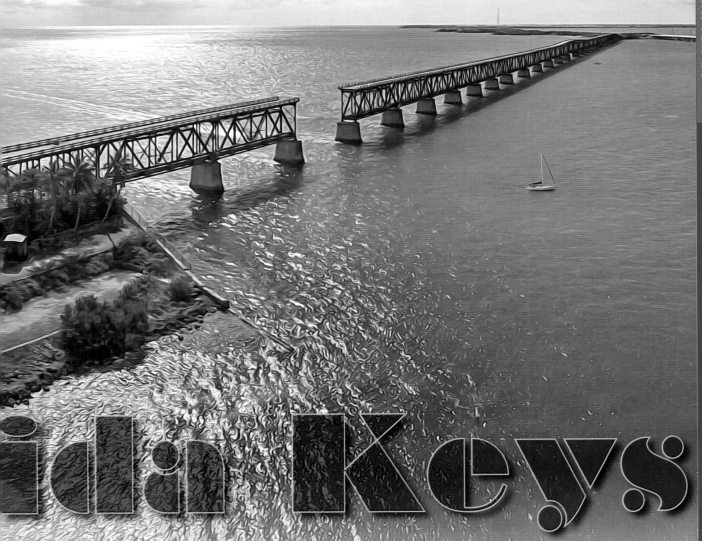

# ICW to Florida Bay

The well-marked but shallow ICW channel down to Florida Bay, northwest and north of the main chain of islands, is well protected in all but the worst weather.

While a hard chop built up from strong winds can provide a wet ride, most cruising boats should experience no difficulties making this passage. Because of numerous shallow areas and the possibility that a strong northerly can literally blow the water out, pay strict attention to navigational aids and the course of the charted magenta line. Better yet, pay more attention to the weather you expect to encounter. If it is going to be bad, stay put. Many boats will leave "tracks" somewhere along this route. This is usually just stirred-up, powdery sand. Should you go aground, it is generally not too difficult to regain deeper water unless, of course, you plow your way in at fairly high speed. There are towing services available; both the Coast Guard and its Auxiliary monitor VHF Channel 16 and

have stations along the way. They are not permitted to tow except in a life-threatening situation, but they can provide assistance, such as contacting a commercial towing service (e.g., BoatUS or SeaTow) should you have trouble making direct contact.

Be advised that if you run aground in the Keys and hit coral heads, coral reefs or sea grass beds, you could be levied a large fine for your transgression. And that is in addition to what it costs to get your boat out of trouble and repaired. Take care not to damage this fragile ecosystem.

# Hawk Channel Offshore

The deepest and most viable route for vessels with a draft of 5 feet or more is Hawk Channel, running from Miami to Key West. Not "officially" part of the ICW, it lies southeast and south of the Keys, taking the form of a somewhat protected "channel" running between the line of Keys and the Florida Reef (actually a series of reefs paralleling the islands).

With a controlling depth of 9 feet at mean low water, and in the lee of the Keys themselves, it is generally rather well protected from winter northerlies and affords even more protection the farther down the Keys you go. In ordinary weather, it is a pleasant sail or an easy run for the entire length of the Keys.

The prevailing southeasterly winds can provide a nice boost for a long reach under sail. With numerous breaks in the outer reef, however, it can offer its share of rough water should the wind be strong from the southern or southwestern quarter.

During the winter season (November through April), lobster or crab pots marked by floats of all descriptions are found along both routes. Most ICW cruisers should be prepared to dive to check and clear their own props. As for navigation, GPS and radar are both extremely useful, but a reliable compass and an accurate depth sounder are just as necessary. An autopilot has its place, particularly along the Hawk Channel route, but you still must watch for and dodge the crab pots, as well as other vessels.

## To Florida's West Coast

Two routes are available to leave the ICW and traverse Florida Bay westward for Cape Sable and points north along Florida's west coast. The first begins at ICW Mile 1173, north of Long Key and skirting shoals on and surrounding Old Dan Bank (use Charts 11449 and 11452). The so-called "Yacht Channel" is well marked and protected. However, it abounds in charted, but otherwise unmarked, shoal patches of 5 to 6 feet in depth (less in a significant blow from the north and less still for vessels straying even marginally off course). This route is not recommended for boats drawing over 4 feet or for travel in poor light.

A second route begins just west of ICW Mile 1190, due north of Vaca Key (City of Marathon). Deeper-footed vessels will need to look out for shoals surrounding Rachel Bank to begin a course of 003 degrees magnetic in 7- to 11-foot depths direct to flashing red daybeacon "2," located 2.2 miles south of East Cape Sable.

**Note:** The best-marked route to the north consists of six markers along Moser Channel between the bridge and Bullard Bank. Older chart editions do not show these markers. When traveling in this area, be sure to use the latest charts available The charts would be the 36th edition of Chart 11442 and the 17th edition of Chart 11449. As both of these charts are older, be sure to check online for the latest updates. At Bullard Bank, you can head directly to the aforementioned flashing red daybeacon "2" off East Cape Sable. At lighted daybeacon "2," there is well-marked and relatively straightforward access either easterly to Flamingo, in the heart of Everglades National Park, or northwesterly, roughly paralleling the Three Nautical Mile Line (the outer limit of the U.S. territorial sea) along the west coast to visit Little Shark River or the Thousand Islands.

Please consider what your final destination is before you pick a route to use. If you have a vessel big enough to cruise along offshore, then heading for East Cape is just adding extra miles to your trip. Basically, if the weather is right, and you are seriously heading north from the Seven Mile Bridge (over Moser Channel), you may not want to go anywhere near the tip of Florida. In that case, we suggest that you consider a course of 337 degrees magnetic and a distance of 136 miles that will bring you in proximity of land up around Boca Grande Channel. Please be aware that there are several shallow (4 to 5 feet) areas that need to be avoided. Study the charts for the course you plan to use.

## Connections Between the Inside and Outside Route

There are only three major routes between the ICW and Hawk Channel. The first, the Cape Florida/Biscayne Channels at ICW Mile 1096, is the northern crossover from Biscayne Bay to the Atlantic. The others–Channel Five at ICW Mile 1170 and Moser Channel at ICW Mile 1195–are under bridges with 65-foot vertical clearances along U.S. Route 1. Several other channels with mixed limitations exist but are not recommended. For detail, see the Inlet section in the front of this guide.

## Prevailing Winds

A mariner needs to be particularly aware of the winds while navigating in the Keys. There are, for example, a number of marinas located along the "top" of the Keys; by that, we mean the Florida Bay side. These marinas will have higher water readings when the wind blows out of the north and lower depths when the wind is southeasterly. For marinas on the Hawk Channel side of the Keys, the opposite is true. If you considers the water that embraces the Keys to be a moveable entity, no matter which side, then you will allow for it being where you want it to be or not where you want it to be and make allowances. If it is windy, and you are not sure how the depths are going to play out for you, stay put.

# Florida Upper Keys

 ICW  Mile 1094–Mile 1197     FL: Channel 09

**CHARTS**  11449, 11451, 11453, 11463, 11464, 11465, 11467, 11468

If continuing further on to Key West, there are three options: crossing over to Hawk Channel in the Atlantic at either Cape Florida Channel/Biscayne Channel, Channel Five or Moser Channel (outside route), or going through Big Spanish Channel, southwest of Marathon, into Florida Bay and running down the northern edge of the remaining keys on the ICW (inside route). For boats that draw over 4.5 feet, cruising through the keys will require you to stay on the ocean side of the Keys, in Hawk Channel.

If winds are blowing from the north or northeast at more than 10 to 15 knots, Hawk Channel (outside route), on the south and sheltered side of the Keys, will be the more comfortable route heading southwest, as the westerly curve of the keys can provide more protection. The route through Big Spanish Channel (inside route) involves navigating shifting shoals and will take a bit longer, but in southerly or southeasterly winds, it will be the more protected route heading southwest.

The Keys are unique in that there are many different, distinct areas requiring a great variety of charts. We will refer to charts with their appropriate titles and the most current edition numbers for a given cruising area. We

then refer to the proper chart by number only when discussing specific locations within that area.

A word to the wise: There are no marine facilities on the Florida Bay side (inside route) between Big Spanish Channel and Key West. Also, when you are in the Florida Keys, your travel is totally weather dependent. There is plenty of good weather here and a lot to enjoy. Waiting for good travel weather is smart boating, especially in the Keys.

## ■ UPPER KEYS: INSIDE (ICW) ROUTE

For boats that draw no more than 4.5 feet and that can take the occasional short, hard chop of shallow water, the inside (ICW) route provides a relatively protected and interesting passage to Islamorada, Marathon, Bahia Honda and beyond to Key West. This route is clearly marked; however, the daybeacons in certain stretches are often far apart. It is essential to pay attention to your course as you do not have to drift too far out of the channel to find yourself hard aground. This inside route

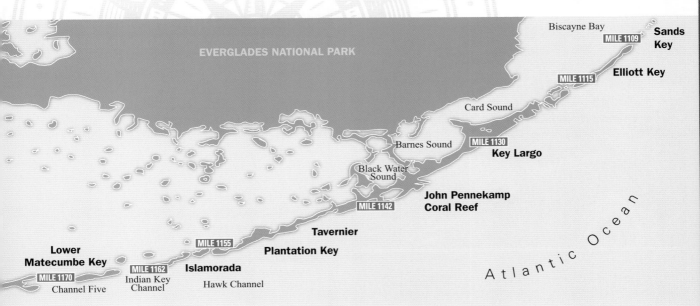

has a wide variety of marinas and shore facilities, plus a variety of anchorages for different wind and weather conditions. Be aware that some of the northern keys are privately owned.

## Key Biscayne Area

**NAVIGATION:** Use Charts 11467 and 11451. Heading south, after passing beneath the **William M. Powell (Rickenbacker) Causeway Bridge** (65-foot fixed vertical clearance) at Mile 1091.6, you pass Virginia Key to the east. Immediately following is Key Biscayne (described in the previous chapter). Here, you enter lower Biscayne Bay and Biscayne National Park. Up to 8 miles wide and about 28 miles long, lower Biscayne Bay is a cleaner, different body of water than all the other bays along this coast.

Just below Key Biscayne to the east, you will see the remaining houses of Stiltsville, an eclectic group of homes on stilts that now belong to the National Park Service. Stiltsville has a colorful history that dates back to the 1930s. The remaining structures are visible along the reef. To the west lies Dinner Key (Mile 1094) with a cluster of friendly marine services, including yacht

clubs, marinas, a boatyard, restaurants and a mooring field. (Detailed in the previous chapter.)

## Biscayne National Park–ICW Mile 1108 to Mile 1120

**NAVIGATION:** Use Charts 11451 and 11463. After a straight run for approximately 14 miles, the ICW route passes through the well marked, but narrow channel at Featherbed Bank (Mile 1108). Biscayne National Park boundary flashing yellow light "C" lies exactly on the ICW route and serves as a helpful intermediate checkpoint on this long run. East of the ICW channel near Mile 1107 is a side channel marked by daybeacons and lights, with 6-foot controlling depths. It runs past several small islands and past Boca Chita Key, then close in to Sands and Elliott Keys. Be aware that both channels are prone to shoaling and spots can be very shallow.

Elliott Key, about 3 miles east of ICW Mile 1113, is part of Biscayne National Park and, as such, is open to the public. During summer months with prevailing winds from the southeast, Elliott Key plays host to hundreds of boats. Graced with a hardwood jungle and a shell-laden ocean beach, Elliott Key is the largest of the 25 keys encompassed by Biscayne National Park. Campsites and picnic grounds are available through the park rangers at the visitor center. Pets must be on an attended leash that is no longer than 6 feet in length. Be sure to bring lots of bug spray because you will encounter mosquitoes and no-see-ums. Visitors are requested not to feed the wildlife. The rest of the

## Distances
### Inside Route: ICW (Miles from Miami)

| LOCATION | STATUTE MILES | NAUTICAL MILES |
|---|---|---|
| Miami (Mile 1090) | 0 | 0 |
| Angelfish | 30 | 26.1 |
| Jewfish Creek | 43 | 37.4 |
| Tavernier | 60 | 52.1 |
| Islamorada | 69 | 60.0 |
| Channel Five | 80 | 69.5 |
| Marathon (Sisters Creek) | 102 | 88.6 |
| Moser Channel | 107 | 93.0 |
| Harbor Key Bank Light | 128 | 111.2 |
| Northwest Channel | 147 | 127.7 |
| Key West | 154 | 133.8 |

*(Moser Channel to Key West via Hawk Channel is 40 statute miles.)*

181,500-acre park (including much of Biscayne Bay) includes portions of the ocean reef and numerous shipwreck sites.

**Dockage:** Showers and restrooms are located in a building a short distance from the boat basin at Elliott Key and have only non-potable water; drinking-quality water is available from a faucet there, but not at the slips.

To the north is tiny Boca Chita Key. Here, the National Park Service operates a facility for cruising boats. A channel with at least 4-foot depths begins one-half mile north of Sands Key Light (flashing green daybeacon "3") and runs straight in toward the middle of Boca Chita Key. The channel is marked with three pairs of daybeacons. Alongside dockage for 25 to 30 craft is available but there is neither drinking water nor showers, although there are restrooms ashore. Boats with pets onboard are not permitted to dock, even if the animal remains on the boat.

Dockage is available at Elliot Key for boats up to about 26 feet at the park center, midway down the key. There are slips for 60 small craft and two dinghy landings. An automated machine collects dockage fees at Elliot Key (half price for holders of National Park Service or Golden Access passes); it is sort of a "reverse ATM" that accepts coins and bills up to $20. There is no

approach channel to the boat basin, and depths may be as little as 2 feet; cruising craft habitually join the crowd by anchoring well offshore. You will have to stay about one-half mile offshore and keep an eye out for storm systems during the summer. During the winter, far fewer boats will visit this beautiful island because frequent northerlies make anchoring here risky and downright uncomfortable. Biscayne National Park prohibits all personal watercraft ("jet skis").

**Anchorage:** Ragged Keys at Mile 1106 has 7 to 8 feet of water with good holding in grass and mud. This is exposed northwest through southwest.

The inner anchorage at Sands Key (Mile 1108) has excellent holding in 7 to 8 feet and all-around protection, but for shoal draft boats the approach can be a little tricky (4-foot depths), and you might have to wait for high tide to either enter or exit. There are a few rocks but you should find a place to drop your hook. If you can't manage the inner anchorage, you can anchor outside on the west side of Sands Key in 5 to 6 feet with good holding in grass and mud. This is exposed, however, north through southwest.

It is possible to anchor off Coon Point on the northwest side of Elliot Key in 4 to 6 feet of water with good holding. This is exposed north through southwest. At the southeastern end of Elliott Key is

Caesar Creek (southeast of Mile 1116), with a shallow entrance marked by Park Service buoys. Caesar Creek winds around tiny Adams Key (7- to 12-foot depths and facilities ashore for day use only) and has a southern spur leading to an anchorage between Rubicon and Reid Keys; it then meanders past Elliott Key and out toward Hawk Channel. It is a pretty passage, but not for cruising-sized boats because of the depth; there is only about 3 feet of water entering the anchoring area. After you get in, however, you should have up to 12 feet. Following the park markers, boats with less than a 4-foot draft can reach Hawk Channel. For more information, visit nps.gov/bisc or call 305-230-1144.

## Card Sound–ICW Mile 1120

**NAVIGATION:** Use Charts 11451 and 11463. After traversing Featherbed Bank and altering course to approximately 192 degrees magnetic for about 7 miles, you will find flashing red daybeacon "8." At this point, you will alter course to about 221 degrees magnetic (just to the west of Rubicon Keys and Caesar Creek) for the straight, 2.6-mile, well marked, but narrow channel run through 3- and 4-foot shoals to the pass through Cutter Bank and into Card Sound (at about Mile 1119).

Once in Card Sound, you will pass numerous fishing channels between the adjacent keys to the east. One is Angelfish Creek, heavily used for passage between the ICW and Hawk Channel. Angelfish Creek is a fair weather proposition only, particularly from the Atlantic. The depth from the Atlantic side is approximately 4 feet at the beginning of the channel. It is similar on the Bay side. (For more information on Angelfish Creek, see the Inlet section in the front of this guide.)

**Dockage:** On Key Largo, the Ocean Reef Club (305-367-2611) once welcomed transients, but now has a "members and sponsored guests only" policy.

**Anchorage:** Just past Mile 1120, the entrance to Angelfish Creek from Card Sound is a well-known rendezvous and anchoring spot under the lee of small Pumpkin Key. Here you will find good holding in rock and mud in 7 to 9 feet of water. Little Pumpkin Creek is another locals spot and can get busy on weekends. Also popular with locals as a hurricane hole, ICW cruisers frequently congregate here, some waiting to cross the Gulf Stream to the Bahamas by exiting the bays via Angelfish Creek and others just to enjoy a quiet stop en route. Drop the anchor in 5 to 13 feet with excellent holding in grass and mud. (No shore access.)

The southernmost anchorage in Card Sound is at Jew Point, about 1.5 miles east of the mouth of Steamboat Creek (Mile 1125). There is 7 to 9 feet of water with good holding in grass and mud.

# Upper Keys, FL

| | | Dockage | | | | | Supplies | | Services | | | | | |
|---|---|---|---|---|---|---|---|---|---|---|---|---|---|---|
| | | Largest Vessel Accommodated | VHF Channel Monitored | Transient Berths / Total Berths | Approach / Dockside Depth (reported) | Floating Docks | Gas / Diesel | Groceries, Ice, Marine Supplies, Snacks | Repairs: Hull, Engine, Propeller | Lift (tonnage), Crane, Rail | Min/Max Amps | Laundry, Pool, Showers, Courtesy Car | Pump-Out Station | Nearby: Grocery Store, Motel, Restaurant |
| **KEY LARGO AREA: INSIDE ROUTE** | | | | | | | | | | | | | | |
| 1. Manatee Bay Marine Inc.  3.4 NW of 1131.5 | 305-451-3332 | 50 | 16/72 | call/45 | 4.5/5 | F | – | M | HEP | L60,C50 | 30/30 | S | P | R |
| 2. Gilbert's Resort and Marina [WiFi] 1134 | 305-451-1133 | 105 | 16 | 10/50 | 6/15 | – | GD | IMS | – | – | 30/50 | LPS | P | GMR |
| 3. Anchorage Resort & Yacht Club [WiFi] 1134 | 305-451-0500 | 180 | 16/09 | 6/20 | 6/8 | – | – | I | – | – | 30/50 | LPS | – | MR |
| 4. The Marina Club at BlackWater Sound [Int][WiFi] | 305-453-0081 | 40 | 16 | – | 4/4 | F | G | GIMS | HEP | L | 30/50 | S | – | GMR |
| **KEY LARGO AREA: OUTSIDE ROUTE** | | | | | | | | | | | | | | |
| 5. Garden Cove Marina [Int][WiFi] | 305-451-4694 | 45 | 16/78 | 6/14 | 4/14 | – | G | IM | EP | L10,R2 | 30/30 | S | – | GMR |
| 6. John Pennekamp Coral Reef State Park | 305-451-6325 | 50 | 16 | 9/9 | – | – | – | – | – | – | 30/30 | S | P | – |
| 7. Key Largo Harbor Marina [WiFi] 1.7 E of 1141.3 | 305-451-0045 | 65 | 16 | – | 4/10 | – | GD | IM | HEP | L80,C | 30/50 | LS | – | G |
| 8. Ocean Divers | 305-451-1113 | 50 | 16 | – | 5/20 | – | GD | – | – | – | – | – | – | GR |
| 9. Marina del Mar Resort and Marina [Int][WiFi] | 305-453-7171 | 60 | 16 | 50/77 | 4.5/18 | – | – | GI | – | – | 30/50 | LPS | P | GMR |
| 10. Pilot House Marina [Int][WiFi] | 305-747-4359 | 85 | 16 | 25/55 | 4.5/10 | F | GD | IMS | HEP | L20 | 30/100 | LPS | P | GMR |
| **PLANTATION KEY AREA: INSIDE ROUTE** | | | | | | | | | | | | | | |
| 11. Mangrove Marina [WiFi] 1.3 S of 1150.0 | 305-852-8380 | 50 | – | call/111 | 5/5 | – | GD | IM | – | L7 | 30/50 | LS | P | GMR |
| 12. Tavernier Creek Marina 1.4 SE of 1151.7 | 305-852-5854 | 36 | – | call/21 | 5/5 | – | G | GIMS | HEP | L10 | 30/30 | S | – | GMR |
| 13. Plantation Yacht Harbor Marina [Int][WiFi] | 305-852-2381 | 80 | 16/10 | 7/85 | 5/5 | – | GD | I | – | – | 30/100 | LPS | P | MR |
| 14. Smuggler's Cove Marina [Int][WiFi] 1157 | 305-664-5564 | 60 | 79 | 10/33 | 5/6 | – | GD | GIMS | HEP | L8 | 30/50 | PSC | – | GMR |
| **PLANTATION KEY AREA: OUTSIDE ROUTE** | | | | | | | | | | | | | | |
| 15. Curtis Marine Inc. [WiFi] 1.3 SE of 1149.7 | 305-852-5218 | 60 | – | 1/20 | 4.5/14 | – | – | M | – | – | 30/50 | LS | – | GMR |
| 16. Blue Waters Marina [WiFi] 1.3 SE of 1149.7 | 305-853-5604 | 60 | – | call/20 | 4.5/20 | – | – | I | – | – | 30/50 | LS | – | GMR |
| 17. Treasure Harbor Marine [Int][WiFi] | 800-FLA-BOAT | 50 | 16/09 | 5/23 | 4/7 | F | D | – | – | – | 30/50 | LS | – | MR |
| 18. Snake Creek Marina [Int][WiFi] | 305-396-7724 | 40 | 09 | 10/20 | 3.5/3.5 | F | G | IS | HE | L9 | 30/50 | S | P | MR |

⌨ Internet Access  [WiFi] Wireless Internet Access  [WG] Waterway Guide Cruising Club Partner  (Information in the table is provided by the facilities.)
See WaterwayGuide.com for current rates, fuel prices, web site addresses, and other up-to-the-minute information.

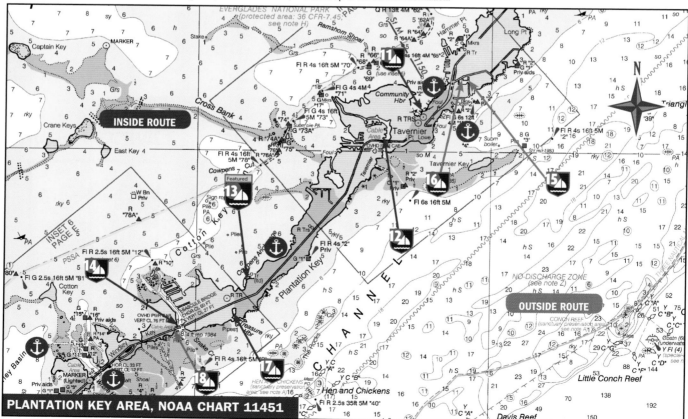

PLANTATION KEY AREA, NOAA CHART 11451

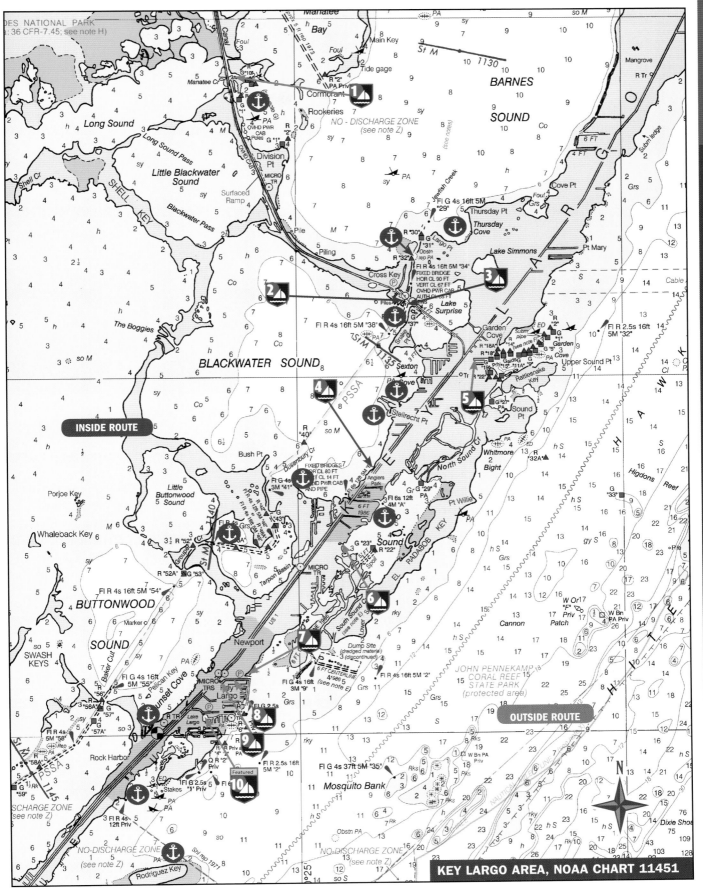

KEY LARGO AREA, NOAA CHART 11451

## Barnes Sound–ICW Mile 1126

**NAVIGATION:** Use Charts 11451 and 11463. From Cutter Bank Pass set a course of 233 degrees magnetic for about 4.7 miles to flashing green daybeacon "17," which leads to the pass through Card Bank to Little Card Sound (Mile 1125). The **Card Sound Bridge** (65-foot fixed vertical clearance bridge) at Mile 1126.9 serves as the next landmark. This is the first of two highway bridges leading to the Keys from the mainland.

The channel under the bridge is marked and dredged, but it shallows rapidly upon entering Barnes Sound, so follow your markers closely. Once you are through the channel to flashing red daybeacon "26" in Barnes Sound, good depths (6 to 8 feet) run the straight 4.5 miles or so to the end of Barnes Sound and the Jewfish Creek channel leading to Blackwater Sound. Depending on wind direction, the chop can build and Barnes Sound can get sloppy.

During the winter season, you will likely encounter commercial stone crabbing or lobster boats, in addition to the usual menagerie of sportfishermen and ICW cruisers.

**Dockage:** Inside Manatee Bay, where Manatee Creek was dead-ended by construction of the Overseas Highway (U.S. Route 1) decades ago, Manatee Bay Marine operates a working yard. The facility normally reserves dockage for repair customers. Transients looking for dockage in this laid-back and out-of-the-way location may find it at one of the three smaller marinas just east of Manatee Bay Marine.

**Anchorage:** There are 5-foot depths in Manatee Creek with good holding in mud. This is open to the north. At the northeast end of Barnes Sound, near Steamboat Creek is a fairly protected cove with 7 to 9 feet of water. It offers protection from the north through east only. (It is more protected inside where there is just 4 to 5 feet of water.) At Mile 1132.8, boats anchor in Thursday Cove with excellent holding and protection from all but the north and west. Be sure to have plenty of bug spray at all times of the year!

## Jewfish Creek–ICW Mile 1134

At about Mile 1133, you enter the well-marked, deep Jewfish Channel. From here on, you really are in the Keys. Key Largo lies to the east and offers many sites of historical, geological and romantic interest in its 30-mile length. Some sites are close to the marinas, but if this is a first visit, it is best to arrange for land transportation. Private watercraft are rented locally, so be prepared to navigate carefully and defensively here. The local radio station in this area is WCTH-FM 100.3, offering up-to-date local weather information and music.

**NAVIGATION:** Use Charts 11451 and 11463. Jewfish Creek itself is a favorite fishing spot and small boats often congregate in the area. The numerous anchored or slow-trolling small fishing boats occupying this narrow channel require a close watch and a fast hand on the throttle to slow to Idle-Speed/No-Wake. The route leads to the **Jewfish Creek (U.S. 1) Bridge** at Mile 1134.1 (65-foot fixed vertical clearance).

**Dockage:** Immediately south of the bridge, on the western side, is the well-known Gilbert's Resort and Marina, with a long wooden wharf along the channel for easy access to the gasoline and diesel pumps. Their lively tiki bar has music nightly. On the east side of the channel, the Anchorage Resort & Yacht Club also has slips for transients.

**Anchorage:** It is possible to anchor in Jewfish Creek at the junction with Cross Key Creek at red daybeacon "32." Space is limited but there is 8 feet of water and all-around protection. Boats are often seen anchoring just to the south of the Jewfish Creek Bridge near green daybeacon "37." Charted depths outside of the channel in the immediate vicinity are 6 to 8 feet. Our cruising editors have always found this area to be full of local boats with very limited room to anchor on the east side of the channel. However, there is room to anchor on the west side, just pay attention to your depth sounder. This anchorage is exposed to wakes and winds from any westerly quadrant and promises to be very buggy.

## Blackwater Sound–ICW Mile 1135

**NAVIGATION:** Use Charts 11451 and 11464. Leaving Jewfish Creek at flashing red daybeacon "38" and setting a course of 224 degrees magnetic will take you the 2.6 miles to the entrance to Dusenbury Creek and Tarpon Basin (Mile 1139). In Blackwater Sound to the west lies the Everglades National Park with its vast expanses of water and mangrove forests. All of the keys within the park are restricted from landings except where specifically designated and charted by park authorities. The fishing on the expansive shallow flats here is outstanding, but catch and licensing regulations are in effect here and enforcement is strict.

**Dockage:** The Marina Club at Blackwater Sound is located just north of a dredged canal, which leads to Largo Sound on the ocean side. This facility is storage only (no transients), sells gas and offers repairs.

**Anchorage:** There are numerous anchorages on the eastern side of Blackwater Sound. Sexton Cove at the northeast end (Mile 1135) has 6 to 7 feet of water and

a grassy bottom with fair holding. (Lake Surprise to the north is not a viable anchorage, despite its size, unless you can traverse the 3-foot-deep entrance channel.)

To the south, you can snug up to the south of Stellrecht Point in 6 to 7 feet of water with good holding in grass and mud. At the southeast end of Blackwater Sound, you can drop the hook in 6 to 7 feet with good holding and protection from the south.

## Buttonwood Sound–ICW Mile 1140

**NAVIGATION:** Use Charts 11451 and 11464. Buttonwood Sound (Mile 1141) starts the area of 5-foot controlling depths along the ICW. Deeper water is sometimes inexplicably found to either side of the channel. Nevertheless, adhere strictly to the marked channel on the chart unless you maintain constant watch of your depth sounder or you have obtained local knowledge. Pay close attention to your exact location in relation to ICW markers, both forward and astern. Groundings are frequent for unwary boaters. Although the normal 1-foot tidal range may not warrant concern, strong winds can create considerable alterations in depth, making the water difficult to read, and may blow a boat just enough off course to make a difference.

From Blackwater Sound, the ICW snakes through mangrove-lined Dusenbury Creek (Mile 1138), where roseate spoonbills occasionally can be seen. The birds look for food by making sweeping motions with their flat bills. They are pink in color and rather pretty. Tarpon Basin is next; if you draw more than 3 feet, pay close attention to channel markers, and take it slowly. Our cruising editor draws 4 feet and found plenty of depth when in the channel.

Pay particular attention to red daybeacon "42" through flashing red daybeacon "48" and hug them closely while making the hard turn to starboard. The water here is clear most of the time, so keep your head up, out of the cockpit. Although charts show 5 to 6-foot depths, depth sounders may register 2.5- to 3-foot depths in certain spots just off the channel. At flashing red "48," steer directly for red daybeacon "48A" and then on to flashing red daybeacon "50."

Narrow Grouper Creek is marked by red daybeacon "52" and exits between green daybeacon "53" and red daybeacon "52A." Flashing red daybeacon "54" leads into Buttonwood Sound. Quite often fast boats will travel through this area at high speeds with no regard for other boats. Caution should be taken if this occurs.

PLANTATION YACHT
HARBOR MARINA

**Anchorage:** In Buttonwood Sound, to the south of Baker Cut, you will find the Upper Keys Sailing Club. This is a private sailing club, but if you get permission, you may be able to stop here for a short time and wander down to town, which isn't more than a half-mile walk. Nearby is a liquor store, some good restaurants and several stores including a Publix supermarket.

To the east of Baker Cut lies Sunset Cove. If you turn to port between daybeacons red "54" and green "55" and proceed towards the beach, you can anchor in 4 to 6 feet with good holding. Snook's Bayside Restaurant and Bar (305-453-5004) is located here. They have an excellent "happy hour" and great food. The anchorage is exposed to the north and west and is shallow (5 feet), but it is a very flat bottom with almost no tide. You will not be alone; there are always numerous boats anchored here.

You can anchor by Butternut Key (Mile 1146) in 5 to 6 feet of water with fair holding. This will provide some protection from the northeast.

## Pigeon Key to Cowpens Cut– ICW Mile 1149 to Mile 1155

**NAVIGATION:** Use Charts 11451 and 11464. Leaving Buttonwood Sound, the ICW continues its shallow course through a well-marked, but narrow channel (Baker Cut) into Florida Bay at Mile 1144. Shoal spots lie on either side of the channel. After you pass Pigeon Key and swing to starboard to avoid a little (unnamed) island that will be to your right, you will pass red daybeacon "64A" to starboard. Paying careful attention

to your chart and your depth sounder, you can head south from here to a little bay with private markers. The water depths just off the channel are 6 feet, and then shallow to 4 feet as you get closer to shore.

The area just beyond Cowpens Cut can be confusing when you arrive at flashing red daybeacon "78" (Mile 1153.7). It appears as if the ICW ends here; the yellow squares and triangles no longer appear on aids to navigation, and the daybeacons and lights appear in a different section of the *Light List* published by NOAA (navcen.uscg.gov). On the other hand, NOAA considers the ICW to continue on to Key West. The magenta line continues on charts, and the mileage continues to increase. Coverage in the *Coast Pilot* chapter on the ICW also continues to Key West.

**Dockage:** Mangrove Marina is a popular marina and transient slips must be reserved in advance. Call Mangrove Marina for specific navigation. The depth on the approach is 5 feet with 5 feet also at dockside. If you are in need of supplies, there is a shopping center with a supermarket close by. In the area labeled "Community Hbr" on the chart is the Old Tavernier Restaurant and Tavern (90311 Overseas Hwy., 305-852-6012) with an active local crowd. This Italian and Greek restaurant is open for dinner only.

If you get chased out of the little bay by northerly conditions, you could always go into Tavernier Creek and access the shopping center from there. Tavernier Creek is deep, but the limiting factors are the fixed **Tavernier Creek Bridge** with a vertical clearance of

15 feet and the very strong current that runs through here. Tavernier Creek Marina, north of the bridge, is primarily a dry-stack marina that sells gas only.

**Anchorage:** Anchor at red daybeacon "48A" at Tarpon Basin but be aware that holding is just fair due to the grassy bottom. If you drop a hook here, be sure to seek local knowledge about the mangrove tunnels that you can explore from the comfort of your dinghy.

Good dinghy docks and picnic tables can be found in the Nelson Government Center Park, behind the Monroe County Nelson Government Center in Tarpon Basin. Cruisers can use the restrooms in the Government Center during office hours. The park is .7 miles east of the Trade Winds Plaza Shopping Center, which has a very good Publix and a large Kmart, and .8 miles west of a West Marine. There are several restaurants and other shopping within 1 mile of the dinghy dock.

The Cowpens anchorage at Mile 1155 has 5 to 6 feet of water with good holding in grass and mud. This anchorage is open and exposed to the west.

## Plantation Key Area–ICW Mile 1156

**NAVIGATION:** Use Charts 11451 and 11464. Cowpens Cut through Cross Bank (at Mile 1153) leads into the Plantation Key area. (Cowpens was named for the pens used to hold manatees, which were once used for food.)

At Mile 1156, Snake Creek leads off to the southeast. Its channel is marked with flashing red daybeacon "12" at the northern end; note that the aids here are numbered from the ocean side. The **Snake Creek Bascule Bridge** has 27-foot closed vertical clearance and opens on signal, except from 7:00 a.m. to 6:00 p.m., when it will only open on the hour. The Snake Creek channel provides very shallow access to Hawk Channel on the ocean side. The channel on the ocean side of the bridge has shoaled, and the passage is not recommended. Coast Guard Station Islamorada may be able to provide depth information.

⚠️ From Cotton Key at ICW red daybeacon "80" (Mile 1158) to Steamboat Channel, the ICW passes through what is perhaps the shallowest part of the entire route. Remember, touching a sandy bottom at slow speeds is rarely dangerous but, at high speeds, can do considerable damage to your props.

Marker floats for lobster and stone crab traps fill the channel and surrounding water in season so be careful about fouling your propeller shaft. During the off-season (May 15 to October 15), all traps and floats are supposed

www.snagaslip.com

SNAG-A-SLIP™

EXPLORE.
BOOK.
BOAT.

# Upper Keys, FL

| MATECUMBE KEYS: INSIDE ROUTE | Largest Vessel Accommodated | VHF Channel Monitored | Transient Berths / Total Berths | Approach / Dockside Depth (reported) | Floating Docks | Gas / Diesel | Groceries, Ice, Marine Supplies, Snacks | Repairs: Hull, Engine, Propeller | Lift (tonnage), Crane, Rail | Min/Max Amps | Laundry, Pool, Showers, Courtesy Car | Pump-Out Station | Nearby: Grocery Store, Motel, Restaurant |
|---|---|---|---|---|---|---|---|---|---|---|---|---|---|
| | | | **Dockage** | | | | **Supplies** | | | **Services** | | | |
| 1. Islamorada Yacht Basin Lorelei Restaurant 🖳 (WiFi) 1160.2  305-664-2692 | 45 | 16 | 3/15 | 4.5/4.5 | – | – | I | – | – | 30/50 | LS | P | GMR |
| 2. Coral Bay Marina (WiFi) 1160.2  305-664-3111 | 62 | 16 | 10/35 | 5/6 | – | – | M | HEP | L50 | 50/50 | LS | P | GMR |
| 3. Caribee Boat Sales & Marina 1160.2  305-664-3431 | 32 | – | – | 5.5/5.5 | – | G | IM | HEP | L | 30/30 | – | – | GMR |
| 4. World Wide Sportsman/Bayside Marina  305-664-3398 | 40 | 16/68 | 20/43 | 3/4 | – | GD | IMS | – | – | 30/50 | S | P | GMR |
| 5. Islamorada Marina 1161.0  305-664-8884 | 50 | – | 2/18 | 8/4.5 | F | GD | I | HEP | L10 | 30/50 | S | – | GMR |
| 6. Angler House Marina  305-664-5247 | 45 | – | – | 8/4 | – | GD | I | – | – | 30/50 | S | – | GMR |
| **MATECUMBE KEYS: OUTSIDE ROUTE** | | | | | | | | | | | | | |
| 7. Islamorada Resort Co. ~ Post Card Inn Marina at Holiday Isle 🖳 (WiFi)  305-664-2321 | 110 | 16/73 | 19/56 | 4.5/8 | – | GD | IMS | – | – | 30/50 | P | P | MR |
| 8. Whale Harbor Marina  305-664-4511 | – | – | call/22 | 5/6 | – | – | IS | – | – | 30/30 | S | – | GMR |
| 9. La Siesta Resort & Marina (WiFi)  305-250-0755 | 45 | – | 5/20 | 3.5/6 | – | G | I | – | – | 30/50 | LPS | – | GMR |
| 10. Bud'n Mary's Fishing Marina 1162.1  305-664-2461 | 45 | 77 | 10/35 | 4.5/4.5 | – | GD | GIM | HP | L | 30/50 | – | – | GMR |
| 11. Caloosa Cove Marina & Resort (WiFi) 1169.5  305-664-4455 | 70 | 16 | 5/32 | 5/4 | – | GD | GIMS | E | L6 | 30/50 | LS | – | GMR |

🖳 Internet Access  (WiFi) Wireless Internet Access  WG Waterway Guide Cruising Club Partner  *(Information in the table is provided by the facilities.)*
See WaterwayGuide.com for current rates, fuel prices, web site addresses, and other up-to-the-minute information.

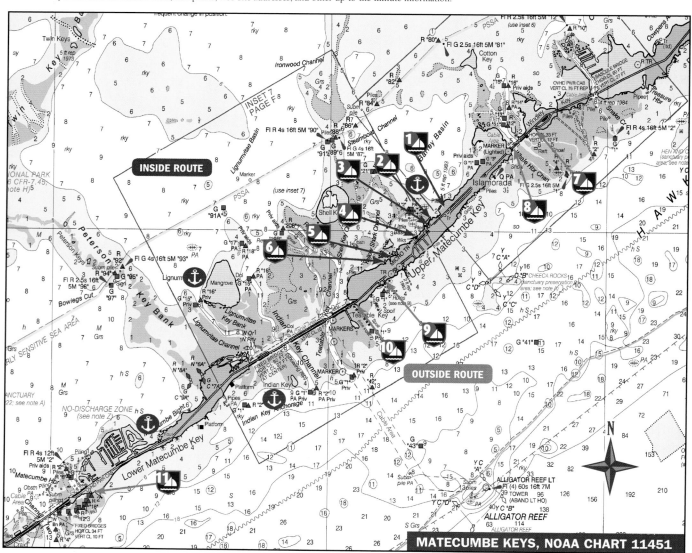

INSIDE ROUTE

OUTSIDE ROUTE

MATECUMBE KEYS, NOAA CHART 11451

to be removed. Navigation is much simpler then, but some stray traps do remain, requiring a sharp lookout.

**Dockage:** Plantation Yacht Harbor Marina offers protection from all but hurricane-force winds. If westbound from flashing red daybeacon "78," continue toward red daybeacon "78A" for 1 mile, then alter course to about 150 degrees magnetic and continue about 1 nm toward shore. You will spot a red and white horizontally striped lighthouse at the end of the marina's breakwater. Leave it to starboard, make a sharp starboard turn around the lighthouse and move up the marked channel to the marina.

The village of Islamorada owns the 42-acre park in which Plantation Yacht Harbor Marina is located. In addition to the slips and the regular cruiser amenities, it has a soccer pitch, tennis courts, a swimming pool, a dog park, basketball courts, a saltwater swimming beach, a baseball diamond and a place to jog. Good restaurants are nearby.

South of Plantation Yacht Harbor Marina is Smuggler's Cove Marina, with slips, hotel rooms and all fuels.

**Anchorage:** You can anchor in 5 to 6 feet south of Cotton Key at Mile 1158 in Barley Basin. This provides protection from the east through southeast with excellent holding in at least 5 feet of water.

## Islamorada, Upper Matecumbe Key– ICW Mile 1160

The village of Islamorada stretches 18.2 miles, from the Channel Two Bridge at Keys Mile Marker (MM) 72.8 to the Tavernier Creek Bridge at Keys Mile Marker 91. Note that the highway Mile Markers (or MM) do not correspond to the waterway statute miles. Also, addresses are given as "bay side" or "ocean side," depending on which side of Overseas Highway (U.S. 1) they fall.

**NAVIGATION:** Use Charts 11451 and 11464. Use the Miami Harbor Entrance Tide Tables. For high tide, add 2 hours 45 minutes; for low tide, add 4 hours. Plantation Key and Upper Matecumbe Key are separated by tiny Windley Key and then Whale Harbor Channel. Islamorada is located on Upper Matecumbe Key, the third largest island in the Keys. The village of Islamorada (Spanish for "Purple Island") may be reached on a southeasterly course from red daybeacon "84" prior to entering Steamboat Channel.

**Dockage:** At Mile 1160.2, Islamorada Yacht Basin & Lorelei Restaurant has 4.5- foot approach and dockside depths and has three spaces reserved for transients. To the south, a set of white stakes mark the entrance to Coral Bay Marina, which has a 50-ton lift and on-site mechanics. Caribee Boat Sales & Marina is nearby with gas (no transient slips). Farther south are Worldwide Sportsman/Bayside Marina, Islamorada Marina and Angler House Marina. All three offer transient slips and various amenities, including fuel.

**Anchorage:** From red daybeacon "84," steering a course of 150 degrees magnetic and keeping your eye dead ahead on the charted tall radio tower, you will pass through a local anchorage area offshore from Lorelei's Restaurant and Cabana Bar. There is a tight, well-protected yacht basin (4-foot controlling depth at mean low water) beside the casual outdoor bar and restaurant, which is a magnet for locals, cruisers and land-based tourists and the place to be at sunset.

Dinghies from anchored boats are welcome at the Lorelei Dinghy Dock (for a fee if not dining with them), at The Worldwide Sportsman and at the Morada Bay Beach Café's small boat dock. The Coral Bay Marina does not have a dinghy dock; when the office is open dinghies can, with permission and space permitting, tie up in front of the office for an hour or two.

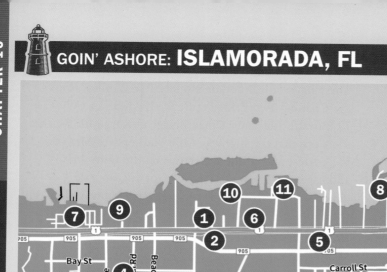

| SERVICES | |
|---|---|
| 1 | Library |
| **ATTRACTIONS** | |
| 2 | Hurricane Monument |
| 3 | Keys History & Discovery Center |
| 4 | Redbone Gallery |
| **SHOPPING** | |
| 5 | Hooked on Books |

| | |
|---|---|
| 6 | Trading Post Market and Deli |
| 7 | Worldwide Sportsman |
| **DINING** | |
| 7 | Islamorada Fish Company Restaurant and Seafood Market/ Zane Grey Long Key Lounge |
| 8 | Lorelei Restaurant and Cabana Bar |
| 9 | Morada Bay Beach Cafe |

| MARINAS | |
|---|---|
| 7 | World Wide Sportsman/Bayside Marina |
| 8 | Islamorada Yacht Basin |
| 10 | Caribee Boat Sales & Marina |
| 11 | Coral Bay Marina |

Islamorada is made up of four islands. The first one you would come to from the north is Plantation Key, then Windley Key, Upper Matecumbe Key and Lower Matecumbe Key. Indian Key and Lignum Vitae are islands just off the highway only accessible by boat and belong to the State of Florida. They are now state parks.

**Attractions:** The Islamorada Chamber of Commerce and Visitors Center is located at MM 87 (305-664-4503) and is a perfect first stop for information about the area. Another good stop is the Keys History & Discovery Center, located on the property of the Islander Resort (MM 82). Here you can see a model of Indian Key the way it looked in 1840, a "legends of the line" fishing exhibit and numerous historical photos of the area. Open Thursday through Sunday from 9:00 a.m. to 5:00 p.m. (305-922-2237).

The Matecumbe Historical Trust has a self-guided tour brochure that can be downloaded from their web site

at MatecumbeHistoricalTrust.com. There are markers on historic sites throughout the islands of Islamorada, including many located by the water. One to look for is the 1935 Hurricane Memorial, located at MM 81.5, across from the library. It was dedicated November 14, 1937 as The Florida Keys Memorial and memorializes the World War-I veterans and civilians who perished in the 1935 hurricane.

The Redbone Gallery at 200 Morada Way at MM 81.5 specializes in fine original angling and island art. The Gallery is run by a fund raising organization supporting a cure for Cystic Fibrosis. Portions of all original art sales benefit The Cystic Fibrosis Foundation. Unique paintings, sculptures and jewelry (much of which is related to saltwater fishing) are among their offerings (305-664-2002).

Along U.S. Route 1 (Overseas Highway), you will find paved pedestrian/bike paths that make walking and biking on the Key pleasant, easy and safe. On foot or by bicycle, Upper Matecumbe Key is a manageable 4.8 miles.

**Shopping:** For provisions, the 24-hour Trading Post Market and Deli (305-664-2571) at MM 81.8 is a small, well-stocked supermarket and deli. (The nearest full-size supermarket is the Winn Dixie in Tavernier at MM 92. As for boating supplies, if you can't find what you need at Worldwide Sportsman at MM 81.5 on the Bay side (305-664-4615), check Caribee Boat Sales (305-664-3431), located next to the Trading Post at MM 81.5 (also Bay side), which has a marine supply store, complete with a Parts Department.

Just for fun, at MM 81.9 on the ocean side is Hooked on Books (305-517-2602), a small, independent book seller with an excellent collection of books about the Keys, the Everglades and Florida.

**Dining:** The Islamorada Restaurant and Bakery (also known as "Bob's Bunz") is at MM 81.6 for breakfast and lunch (305-664-8363). There are several excellent restaurants at the top of the Keys, including Wahoo's Bar and Grill (305-664-9888) at the Whale Harbor Inn on Upper Matecombe Key. At MM 82 on the Bay side (at the large mermaid sign) is the Lorelei Restaurant and Cabana Bar (305-664-2692) with good food (breakfast, lunch and dinner), reputedly the best happy hour on the Key, live entertainment seven nights a week and, for boaters, a marina and dinghy dock–the place to be at sunset, when it is crowded and alive.

In the same area is Morada Bay Beach Café at MM 81.6 (305-664-0604), which offers Mediterranean cuisine and a small boat/dinghy dock on the Little Basin (Bay side).

Adjacent to the Worldwide Sportsman (owned by Bass Pro Shop) at MM 81.5 is the excellent Islamorada Fish Company Restaurant and Seafood Market (305-664-9271). Be sure to check out the tarpon swimming in the pen alongside the dock. Zane Grey Long Key Lounge (305-664-4615) is located upstairs in the Worldwide Sportsman building. Visit the Islamorada Visitors Center at MM 87; they can provide more options.

## Lignumvitae Basin–ICW Mile 1161 to Mile 1165

At just 18 feet above sea level, Lignumvitae Key is the highest of the Keys; it is named for one of the hardest woods in the world, "the tree of life." A visit to the Lignumvitae State Botanical Site is worthwhile. Rangers conduct tours at 10:00 a.m. and 2:00 p.m. except on Tuesdays and Wednesdays, when the site is closed. As a historical aside, Indian Key was the first county seat of Dade County. Now Indian Key doesn't have a soul living on it.

**NAVIGATION:** Use Charts 11451 and 11464. Lying between Steamboat Channel (Mile 1161) and Bowlegs Cut (Mile 1165), Lignumvitae Basin offers good depths for substantial keels and fair-weather anchorages in the lees of Shell Key and Lignumvitae Key to the south. These two keys, bordered by the three navigable channels between Upper and Lower Matecumbe keys and historic Indian Key (at the south end of Indian Key Channel), are all now a part of the Lignumvitae Key Management Area.

All channels in the management area are well marked, but only **Indian Key Channel Bridge** offers significant fixed vertical clearance (27 feet). **Teatable Key Channel Bridge** has just 10 feet of fixed vertical clearance, the same as **Lignumvitae Channel Bridge**. The shallow turtle-grass flats in this area are clearly marked. The flats are all closed to boats with internal combustion engines (gas or diesel, inboard or outboard). State law enforcement officers police the area,

and violators (particularly those who have damaged the grass with their props) are subject to stiff fines.

**Dockage/Moorings:** Indian Key has small boat docks, and the pier at Lignumvitae Key can accommodate medium-size cruising craft (4-foot depths) at both locations, although no docking is permitted after 5:00 p.m., and pets are not allowed ashore. One mooring (complimentary for up to 1 week) may be available at Shell Key. The mooring pick-up line was reported to be in poor condition at press time (spring 2017).

**Anchorage:** Matecumbe Bight in Lower Matecumbe offers 6 to 7 feet with excellent holding in mud. Anchoring near Shell Key is problematic due to the abundance of closely spaced crab trap floats.

## To Channel Five–ICW Mile 1170

Leaving Bowlegs Cut through Peterson Key Bank at Mile 1165, cruisers have the option of continuing on the ICW inside, or crossing over to the Hawk Channel (ocean) passage outside, which is discussed later in this chapter.

**NAVIGATION:** Use Charts 11451 and 11449. Hawk Channel is reached through the second major crossover point: deep, well-marked Channel Five, crossed by the fixed **Channel Five Bridge** with a 65-foot vertical clearance. To reach Channel Five from green daybeacon "97" (near Mile 1165), steer about 210 degrees on a course to the south-southwest for 5 miles. This will bring you to a point just north of the bridge.

In 2017 the Coast Guard reported that there was at least 8 feet of depth in the marked Channel Five, but out of the channel it shallows very quickly. The channel

itself is sparsely marked. There are a couple of marks south of the Channel Five Bridge–red daybeacon "4," flashing red daybeacon "2" and green daybeacon "1." After passing under the bridge, take those marks in the order given if heading for Hawk Channel. There is a prominent shoal to port south of the bridge. The red aids mark its westernmost edge. There are no marks indicating the best water to the north of the bridge. Pay attention! Heading straight for the center span should keep you out of trouble.

From the bridge, if you are heading south, plot your course southwesterly to flashing red daybeacon "44" which, when left to starboard, puts you into Hawk Channel. At that point, alter course westerly to 247 degrees magnetic.

To continue on the ICW inside from Mile 1165 and Bowlegs Cut, steer a course of 246 degrees magnetic to flashing green daybeacon "1," about 6 miles west, just north of Old Dan Bank.

## Long Key to Moser Channel–ICW Mile 1168 to Mile 1196

Long Key is the home of Long Key State Park (305-664-4815), a 300-acre wild area with a campground, numerous picnic tables and grills.

**NAVIGATION:** Use Charts 11449, 11451 and 11453. The ICW passes west of Old Dan Bank on a course of 246 degrees magnetic for about 5 miles in good depths to Channel Key Pass, the passage between the shoals of Channel Key Bank (Mile 1179). **Long Key Viaduct Bridge** (23-foot fixed vertical clearance) lies to the southeast at Mile 1176 before passing through Channel Key Pass. Power boaters with local knowledge frequently use it en route to Duck Key and the marina at Hawk's Cay Resort on the Hawk Channel (i.e., ocean side).

Grassy Key Bank (Mile 1182) projects northerly from long, low Grassy Key. At this point, if you plan to stop at one of the marinas on the Bay side of Marathon, you can take the shortcut. Plot a course between Bamboo Key and the shoal to its northwest. Skirt Stirrup Key and then take a bearing on Rachel Key, passing between Rachel Key and the marked shoal on Rachel Bank. Thereafter, you should have depths of at least 7 feet until quite close to shore.

At this point, you can pick from among the marinas on the north shore of Marathon, or (if you have sufficient clearance to pass under the 19-foot fixed vertical clearance of the channel) follow on around Knight Key and south through the **Knight Key**

**Channel Bridge** (Mile 1194) to find flashing green daybeacon "1," marking the entrance to the channel to Boot Key Harbor, between Knight Key and Boot Key.

Our cruising editor suggests that cruising boats follow the ICW to Moser Channel and then enter Boot Key Harbor going west to east. Cruisers with deep-draft vessels (up to 8 feet) will want to overlook the shortcut and remain on the ICW route.

**Dockage:** There have been some turnovers in the yacht docking business in Marathon, but names and facilities have not changed much. The marinas that line the western entrance to Boot Key Harbor are all intact. As conditions change with the seasonal hurricanes, you can get up-to-date information on all the marinas in the Marathon area by visiting the Waterway Guide Explorer at waterwayguide.com.

At Mile 1193, Blackfin Resort and Marina has slips and good (8-foot) approach depths. Those with drafts of less than 5 feet may want to try the nearby Banana Bay Resort Marina. It has been reported to us that this small marina has a great seasonal community of boaters. Restaurants, grocery stores and a Home Depot are all within easy walking distance. Nearby Keys Boat Works offers repairs and has a 50-ton lift (no transient slips).

# Middle Keys, FL

| | | Dockage | | | | | Supplies | | Services | | | | | |
|---|---|---|---|---|---|---|---|---|---|---|---|---|---|---|
| | | Largest Vessel Accommodated | VHF Channel Monitored | Transient Berths / Total Berths | Approach / Dockside Depth (reported) | Floating Docks | Gas / Diesel | Groceries, Ice, Marine Supplies, Snacks | Repairs: Hull, Engine, Propeller | Lift (tonnage), Crane, Rail | Min/Max Amps | Laundry, Pool, Showers, Courtesy Car | Pump-Out Station | Nearby: Grocery Store, Motel, Restaurant |
| **DUCK KEY: OUTSIDE ROUTE** | | | | | | | | | | | | | | |
| 1. Hawks Cay Resort Marina ▯ WiFi WG 1180 | 888-974-8469 | 110 | 16/10 | 52/85 | 5/5 | – | GD | GIMS | – | – | 30/50 | LPS | P | GMR |
| **MARATHON AREA: INSIDE ROUTE** | | | | | | | | | | | | | | |
| 2. Blackfin Resort and Marina WiFi | 305-743-2393 | 40 | – | 20/27 | 8/10 | – | – | I | – | – | 30/30 | LPS | P | GMR |
| 3. Banana Bay Resort & Marina WiFi 1193 | 305-743-3500 | 60 | 16 | 34/34 | 5/7 | – | – | IS | – | – | 30/50 | LPS | P | GMR |
| 4. Keys Boat Works | 305-743-5583 | 67 | – | – | 5/7 | – | – | M | HEP | L50,C | 30/30 | S | – | MR |
| 5. Faro Blanco Resort & Yacht Club WiFi | 305-743-9018 | 130 | 16/09 | 74/74 | 7.5/9 | – | GD | IMS | – | – | 30/100 | LPSC | P | GMR |
| 6. Capt. Pip's Marina & Hideaway | 305-743-4403 | – | 16 | – | 5/5 | – | – | IS | – | – | – | S | – | GMR |
| **MARATHON AREA: OUTSIDE ROUTE** | | | | | | | | | | | | | | |
| 7. Driftwood Marina & Storage 1187.3 | 305-289-0432 | 60 | – | – | 4/18 | F | – | M | HP | L60 | – | – | – | GMR |
| 8. Outta The Blue Marina 1187.3 | 305-289-0285 | 48 | – | 5/10 | 8/12 | – | – | IM | HEP | L60 | 30/30 | S | P | GMR |
| 9. White Marlin Marina WiFi | 305-481-6721 | 80 | – | 27/27 | 6.5/12 | – | – | I | – | – | 20/50 | LS | – | MR |
| 10. Shelter Bay Marine | 305-743-7008 | 38 | – | call/20 | 8/12 | F | GD | M | HEP | L | – | – | – | GMR |
| 11. Key Colony Beach Marina WiFi 1187.0 | 305-289-1310 | 120 | 16 | 8/35 | 12/8 | – | GD | IMS | – | – | 30/100 | – | P | GMR |
| 12. Skipjack Resort & Marina ▯ WiFi | 305-289-7662 | 65 | 16 | 10/54 | 10/15 | – | – | I | – | – | 30/50 | LPS | P | GMR |
| 13. Sombrero Marina Dockside WiFi 1192.0 | 305-743-5663 | 85 | 16 | 20/57 | 7/9 | – | – | IS | – | – | 30/50 | LS | P | GMR |
| 14. Boot Key Harbor City Marina ▯ WiFi 1193 | 305-289-8877 | 60 | 16 | 12/12 | 10/20 | F | – | IS | – | – | 30/50 | LS | P | GMR |
| 15. Marathon Boat Yard Marine Center ▯ WiFi 1193 | 305-743-6341 | 80 | 16 | 5/20 | 8/20 | F | – | IM | HEP | L75 | 30/50 | LSC | P | GMR |
| 16. Burdines Waterfront Marina 1193 | 305-743-5317 | 120 | 16 | 21/21 | 10/7 | F | GD | GIMS | – | – | 30/50 | LS | P | GMR |
| 17. Pancho's Marina and Fuel Dock WiFi 1193 | 305-743-2281 | 90 | 16 | 3/20 | 8/6.5 | – | GD | GIMS | – | – | 30/50 | LS | P | GMR |
| 18. Marathon Marina & Resort ▯ WiFi WG 1193 | 305-743-6575 | 130 | 16/10 | 60/118 | 9/11 | F | GD | IMS | HEP | L75 | 30/100 | LPS | P | MR |

▯ Internet Access   WiFi Wireless Internet Access   WG Waterway Guide Cruising Club Partner   (*Information in the table is provided by the facilities.*)
See WaterwayGuide.com for current rates, fuel prices, web site addresses, and other up-to-the-minute information.

Florida Bay

HAWKS CAY RESORT MARINA

Hawk Channel

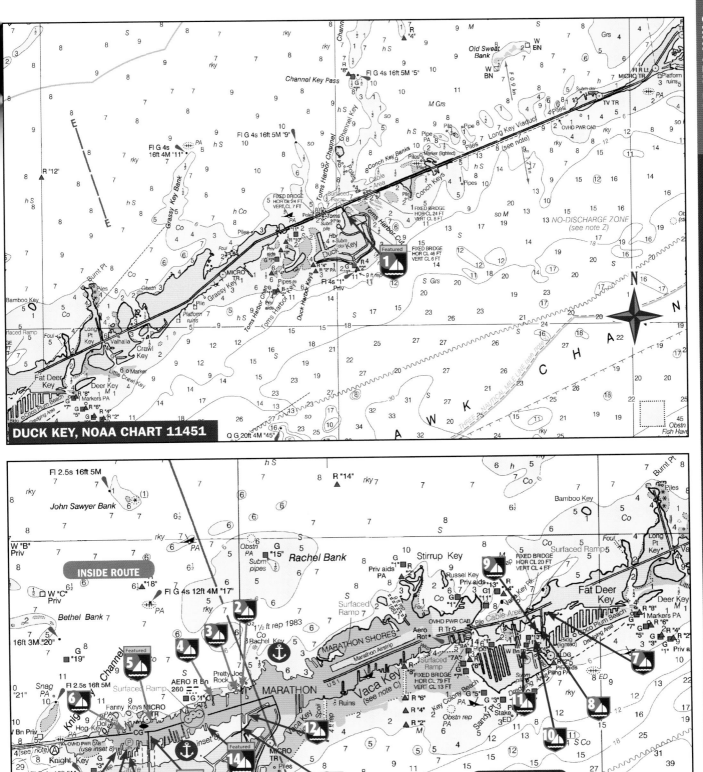

DUCK KEY, NOAA CHART 11451

MARATHON AREA, NOAA CHART 11451

Marathon Marina & Resort

Marathon Boat Yard Marine Center

Faro Blanco Resort & Yacht Club

Boot Key Harbor City Marina

Boot Key Harbor

Pilot House Marina

Faro Blanco Resort & Yacht Club has state-of-the-art facilities and world-class amenities including fuel, pump-out service, 24-hour security, marine concierge services, WiFi, a marine store, pool and fitness center and first-class room accommodations on site.

Capt. Pip's Marina & Hideaway is before the Seven Mile Bridge. Dockage is reserved for charter boats.

## Boot Key Harbor

**NAVIGATION:** Use Chart 11453. The preferred access to the south side of Vaca Key and Boot Key Harbor, is through the fixed **Seven Mile (Moser Channel) Bridge** at Mile 1197. Over Moser Channel the arch of the Seven Mile Bridge has a 65-foot fixed vertical clearance. Here, about 1 mile west of Pigeon Key, the channel is deep and well marked. Once under the bridge and past Moser Channel red daybeacon "2," you should turn east and head to the red daybeacon "2" at the entrance to Boot Key Harbor.

Although frequently used by small power boaters, Knight Key Channel Bridge at Mile 1194 has a 19-foot minimum fixed vertical clearance, in two of the spans and is not well marked. Currents run swiftly with either tide, and the monofilament lines of numerous anglers dangle from the old bridge. If you do choose this route, once through to the ocean side, keep well clear of the shoal extending west of Knight Key. This is not the preferred route for cruising-size boats.

## ■ UPPER KEYS: OUTSIDE (HAWK CHANNEL) ROUTE

For boats that draw over 4.5 feet, cruising through the keys will require you to stay on the ocean side of the Keys, in Hawk Channel. For deep draft vessels this is the only route, save for an ocean leg bucking the Gulf Stream outside of the reefs. In westerly through northerly winds of 15 knots or more, Hawk Channel may provide a more protected passage along the Keys than the ICW route.

Access to Hawk Channel from Miami and Miami Beach is through Government Cut. From just below Miami in Biscayne Bay, the Florida Channel/Biscayne Channel (treated as one) provides a more protected route. In winter, northerlies frequently become northeasters (20 knots or more) for several days and give Hawk Channel a lumpy, irregular following sea. It only abates where the Keys bend to the west.

Well-found and appropriately crewed sailboats will get a great sleigh ride. Powerboats, depending on size, may find it a wet and uncomfortable passage. Obviously, knowledgeable skippers with larger boats equipped with stabilizers and autopilots should not have difficulties.

Hawk Channel is relatively wide; nevertheless, navigation should be precise because the aids to navigation are frequently far apart and difficult to spot. Compass courses should be the rule, as well as following prudent piloting practices. GPS will be extremely useful in this passage, particularly during times of poor visibility.

You should take a cautious attitude when planning daily runs and plan to complete each day's run well before dark. As in the Bahamas, night passages are not recommended. Fortunately, both anchorages and marinas can be found at reasonable intervals throughout the Keys.

In heavy easterly weather, beam seas are the rule, amplified by current and counter-current in the stretches abeam the numerous gaps in the Florida reef. Sailboats might like this weather, but powerboats may wish to sit it out or move inside to the ICW.

When winds slacken and veer to the southeast and south, conditions quiet down. With slack winds, sailboats may motorsail or make short close-hauled runs. Powerboats may still roll, but the journey will be generally enjoyable.

## Distances
### Outside Route: Hawk Channel
### (Miles from Miami)

| LOCATION | STATUTE MILES | NAUTICAL MILES |
|---|---|---|
| Miami (Government Cut) | 0 | 0 |
| Miami (Cape Florida) | 8 | 6.9 |
| Fowey Rocks Light | 14 | 12.0 |
| Angelfish Creek | 28 | 24.0 |
| South Sound Creek | 51 | 44.0 |
| Tavernier | 63 | 54.7 |
| Islamorada | 70 | 60.8 |
| Channel Five | 82 | 71.0 |
| Duck Key | 92 | 79.9 |
| Marathon (Sisters Creek) | 102 | 88.6 |
| Moser Channel | 109 | 94.7 |
| Key West | 151 | 131.0 |

*(Moser Channel to Key West via Hawk Channel is 40 statute miles.)*

## Biscayne Bay to Lower Matecumbe Key

**NAVIGATION:** Use Charts 11451, 11463, 11465 and 11468. (The charts listed provide different perspectives on the navigation routes discussed.) To enter Hawk Channel from Miami you will depart through Government Cut, or if you are in the Coconut Grove area you will depart through the more southerly openings of the Cape Florida Channel/Biscayne Channel. If you are departing from the Miami area, remember that when there are cruise ships docked at the Port of Miami the main channel is closed to recreational boats. This restriction is strictly enforced. You will access the cut through channel on the south side of Dodge Island and Fisher Island.

As you exit Government Cut, you must go seaward through Outer Bar Cut past the spoil areas. Or, if you are familiar with the area, cut between the range markers just south of the jetty. Either way, bear in mind there is a 3-foot shoal area extending out from Cape Florida. Keep red daybeacon "2," outside of Bear Cut just past Virginia Key, well off to starboard. You might do well to set a southeasterly course to pass about 1 mile inside Fowey Rocks Light (flashing white every 10 seconds) and the red daybeacon "2" and green daybeacon "3" marking the start of Hawk Channel. The channel markers, as with the ICW, generally follow red-right-southbound. Some variation has crept in with recent storms and channel changes, so navigate carefully using the latest charts. (The latest edition of Chart 11451 is the 36th from January 2017.)

The route from the Coconut Grove area gives a choice of the Cape Florida or Biscayne Channels. Both of these converge at 12-foot flashing red daybeacon "6" south of Cape Florida's lighthouse. Vessels using Biscayne Channel from the west must pass between the two daybeacons (green daybeacon "7" and red daybeacon "8") just before flashing red daybeacon "6." The cluster of houses amidst the reefs south of Biscayne Channel is Stiltsville, whose landmark homes are part of Biscayne National Park. When going to seaward in either channel, remember that green markers are to starboard until you reach green flashing daybeacon "1."

From here to Hawk Channel, between red daybeacon "2" and green daybeacon "3," at ICW Mile 1098 west

Unlike on the ICW, NOAA charts show no magenta line or mile markers on **Hawk Channel**. All mile indications here refer to approximate comparable ICW mile markers.

of Fowey Rocks, swing well east of the shoals south of Biscayne Channel green flashing daybeacon "1," red flashing daybeacon "2" and the flashing white light on a 37-foot skeleton tower. From this point to Channel Five is approximately 74 miles.

Slower boats may want to plan short runs between anchorages or marine facilities along the way. If you are sightseeing, you may want to do the same. To the west, as you pass Fowey Rocks Light, you will see the first of the small keys projecting above the ancient reef between the ocean and Biscayne Bay. About 3 miles on, the Ragged Keys appear, followed closely by Boca Chita, Sands and Elliott Keys. At Bowles Bank Light (flashing red "8"), the channel bends to the south-southwest as the westward curve of the Florida Keys commences.

## Caesar Creek

**NAVIGATION:** Use Charts 11451 and 11463. At the southwest end of Elliott Key, Caesar Creek is the first crossover to the ICW. It is open to shallow-draft vessels only due to the shallows on the western end of the cut. The channel is well marked, but narrow and bounded by 1- to 2-foot depths at low tide; use extreme caution when transiting this area. Try to obtain local knowledge before using this as a crossover.

Caesar Creek also provides a tight little anchorage at its western end. Flashing red daybeacon "20" is at the entrance to the Park Service's marked channel. The channel is charted with at least 7 feet at mean low water and has a low point of 4 feet on the Bay side. Pay attention to the wind direction as it will affect depths. Enter in the early morning when the water is easy to read.

## Angelfish Creek

**NAVIGATION:** Use Charts 11451 and 11463. Local skippers use well-marked Angelfish Creek, about 3 nm south of Caesar Creek, to cross over from ocean to the Bay and back. There are shoals at both the east and west ends but for boats that draw 5 feet or less, it is fairly simple. If you draw over 5 feet, you can use the channel on a rising tide. The tidal range in this area is approximately 1 foot. Stay well out until the channel markers line up before you enter. Just inside the entrance from Hawk Channel is a rocky ledge with 5-foot depths at low water.

Keep dead center in Angelfish Creek at low tide and maintain enough speed to prevent leeway. Do not enter if another boat is coming out; you need to stay on the centerline. Once inside, the controlling 5-foot depth creates no problem, and you can often find deeper water. Depths of 7-foot-plus along this passage are the rule rather than the exception. Side creeks offer anchorages, but the bottom is rocky and currents are strong. For more details, see the Inlet section at the front of this guide.

**Dockage:** South of the ocean-side entrance to Angelfish Creek is the private Ocean Reef Club. It accepts only members and sponsored guests. Other facilities along the Hawk Channel side cater to transients, although many are oriented primarily to charters and sport fishermen. Average approach depths are 5 feet or less to many of these privately marked channels. Be sure to call ahead for channel depths.

A little over 10 nm to the south, Garden Cove Marina's well-marked channel begins at red daybeacon "32." Turn to starboard and sound your way into their channel. The approach depth is around 4 feet. There is plenty of water once you get into their basin, where you will find slips, gas and some repairs.

## John Pennekamp Coral Reef State Park

The John Pennekamp Coral Reef State Park offers glass-bottom boat tours, Scuba gear rentals and instruction, boat rentals, a campground and a visitor's center with a 30,000-gallon saltwater aquarium. There are 50 miles of natural mangrove trails to explore via kayak or paddleboard, and the underwater park contains 178 square miles of coral reef, sea grass beds, mangrove swamps and the larger of two living reefs that lie in Florida waters. Tropical fish live around the coral, and there are shipwrecks, making an underwater paradise for divers and snorkelers. Only hook-and-line fishing is permitted here.

**NAVIGATION:** Use Charts 11451 and 11463. At green daybeacon "23," you cross the northwest boundary of the State Park. To reach the park's land attractions by boat, enter through South Sound Creek on the southwest side of Largo Sound, about midway down Key Largo and less than 2 miles to the north of Mosquito Bank flashing green daybeacon "35." Flashing red daybeacon "2" marks the entrance. The channel carries 6-foot depths, but 5-foot depths have been reported in Largo Sound.

Dive and sightseeing boats use this channel frequently, so be prepared to move, but not too far, because 3-foot depths have been reported out of the channel. Because of the narrow channel and blind turns, commercial vessels make a Sécurité call on VHF Channel 16 before entering it. Listen for such calls and make your own if appropriate.

Vessels with drafts of 4 feet or less and overhead clearances of 14 feet or less can cross over from Largo Sound to Blackwater Sound via a rock cut that connects the southernmost corner of Blackwater Sound with the western shore of Largo Sound. (The shallowest water lies at the beginning and end of the cut.) If you cannot get your big boat through here, it makes a great dinghy trip. Bear in mind that a strong current runs through here.

**Dockage/Moorings:** The John Pennekamp Coral Reef State Park's marina offers nine full-service slips. It is highly recommended to call the dockmaster on VHF Channel 16 to check availability and the current depths.

Although overnight anchoring is prohibited in Largo Sound, about a dozen white mooring balls are located in the southwest corner of the sound, near the park headquarters. Simply tie up to an empty one and dinghy over to the dockmaster's office (in the dive center) to check in.

## Key Largo to Tavernier Key

**NAVIGATION:** Use Charts 11451 and 11463. To the south of John Pennekamp State Park is Port Largo Canal with more dockage options. Make your approach to the canal starting at green daybeacon "7" on a northeasterly course and watch your depth as the approach is only around 5 feet. Continue a short distance down the Hawk Channel to marker "8" and turn to starboard to enter the canal leading to Lake Largo and the Pilot House Marina.

**Dockage:** Key Largo Harbor Marina on Port Largo Canal offers slips, fuel and repairs (with an 80-ton lift). A bit farther into the canal is Marina del Mar Resort and Marina, also offering dockage and some amenities. On the same canal is Ocean Divers, a charter company that offers fuel.

The secure Pilot House Marina on Lake Largo is a full-service facility with slips on floating docks, fuel and repairs. There is a restaurant on the premises with a glass-floored Tiki Bar where you can watch the sea life swim by.

About 7 nm south at Long Point, you will find two additional marinas–Curtis Marine, Inc. and Blue Waters Marina. There is a channel leading to both, but it is very shallow (4.5 foot reported depths). It is strongly recommended that you call ahead for the latest information and slip availability as well as the current depth of their channel.

**Anchorage:** Only a short distance (2 nm) from the entrance of Largo Canal you will find Rodriguez Key, a favorite anchorage. Be aware of which way the wind will be blowing, as it is fairly open. Depths behind Rodriguez Key average 7 to 8 feet, and the holding is good over grass and sand.

About 1 mile north of Rodriguez Key is the Rock Harbor anchorage with 5 to 6 feet of water and good holding in sand and grass. There are several small marinas and a boat ramp in and around Rock Harbor where you might land in your dinghy. Several restaurants and a Publix Market are a short cab ride away. Straight out from the anchorage is Molasses Reef for easy snorkeling. This is a good stop for boats preparing to cross to the Bahamas or heading on to Marathon. (See more at "Crossing the Gulf Stream" in the Inlet section of this guide.)

## Tavernier Key to Lower Matecumbe Key

**NAVIGATION:** Use Charts 11451 and 11464. Below Rodriguez Key, Hawk Channel leads from the charted Triangles, marked by green daybeacon "39" (equivalent to about ICW Mile 1150) west of Molasses Reef, about 9 miles southwest to Hen and Chickens flashing red daybeacon "40." The unmarked shoal known as "The Rocks," with depths of 3 feet at mean low water, lies northwest of flashing red daybeacon "40." Take care in navigating as these rocks have created problems for daydreaming sailors.

Snake Creek (ICW Mile 1157), at the east end of Windley Key, is a limited crossover to the ICW that leads off to the northwest below "The Rocks." The marked channel is reportedly shallow, with 4-foot depths or less at the entrance, even though small boats and the Coast Guard use it. Windley Key is home to Windley Key Fossil Reef Geological State Park, which has self-guided trails, including one along an 8-foot high quarry wall.

At the western end of Windley Key is Whale Harbor Channel, a privately marked and maintained channel that leads into a basin with 5-foot approach depths just before the **Whale Harbor Channel Bridge** (10-foot fixed vertical clearance).

Next is tiny and picturesque Teatable Key (ICW Mile 1163). Once a navy base and now a private island, it lies on the Hawk Channel side of the southwest end of Upper Matecumbe Key. Between Teatable and Indian Keys lie two channels to the Bay side: Teatable Key Channel and Indian Key Channel. The fixed Teatable Key Channel Bridge with a 10-foot vertical clearance limits access to Teatable Key Channel. Indian Key Channel is also a simple run all the way to ICW Mile 1163 northwest of the Lignumvitae Key State Botanical Site. This would be considered a major crossover if it were not for the 27-foot fixed vertical clearance Indian Key Channel Bridge.

Lower Matecumbe Key is the midpoint in the run from Fowey Rocks to Key West. At its western tip, Channel Two, with the 10-foot fixed vertical clearance bridge (**Channel Two Bridge**) is a restricted crossover.

**Dockage:** Treasure Harbor Marine is in a protected harbor on the ocean side. They welcome transients, as well as short- and long-term boaters. Nearby Snake Creek Marina (to the west of Snake Creek Bridge) has 3.5-foot approach depths and sells gas and offers some repairs.

At the north end of the Whale Harbor Channel Bridge, Post Card Marina at Holiday Isle offers sportfishing activities, and there are motel rooms, restaurants and many bars ashore. (Their tiki bar is one of our favorites!) A nearby sandbar is a gathering spot for locals on the weekends. At the south end of the Whale Harbor Channel Bridge is Whale Harbor Marina, which may have slips; call ahead.

Less than 4 nm to the west is a privately marked channel that leads to La Siesta Resort & Marina. Before entering this channel, you would be well advised to call for instructions due to reported 3.5-foot depths.

> The reception of weather information in the Middle Keys has improved with the establishment of a transmitter on **Teatable Key** on Channel WX-5 (162.450 MHz). The local radio station is WCTH-FM 100.3. On TV, Channel 17 is the NOAA Channel, repeating the same weather reports available on VHF weather channels.

Behind Teatable Key to the east, a privately maintained channel (controlling depth 4.5 feet) leads to Bud n' Mary's Fishing Marina, one of the oldest and most active sportfishing/charter centers in the Florida Keys. Rental skiffs and guided fishing charters are available, as well as transient dockage. Call ahead for reservations. There are a number of retail shops, art galleries and restaurants to the north of the marina.

Caloosa Cove Marina & Resort is located at Lower Matecumbe Key with slips and sells both gas and diesel fuel. Approach depths of 4.5 feet were observed by our cruising editor in spring 2017.

**Anchorage:** You can anchor in the harbor at Tavernier Key in 4 to 7 feet with good holding in sand and grass.

In calm conditions or with light winds from the west through to the north-northeast, it is possible for vessels drawing up to 5 feet to anchor on the sand off the Whale Harbor Inn (Mile 1158). This is not a particularly good or a recommended anchorage, but if you do anchor here, you and your dinghy are welcome at the Whale Harbor Inn. Whale Harbor Channel continues under the 10-foot fixed Whale Harbor Channel Bridge to the ICW side.

The designated Indian Key anchorage has at least 7 feet of water with good holding in sand and grass. This anchorage is open and exposed to the south through southwest.

# ◼ MIDDLE KEYS: OUTSIDE (HAWK CHANNEL) ROUTE

## Long Key to Marathon

**NAVIGATION:** Use Charts 11449, 11451 and 11453. Opposite Channel Five in Hawk Channel, at flashing red daybeacon "44," your course to Vaca Key and the City of Marathon is relatively clear in the range of 247 to 258 degrees magnetic to East Washerwomen Shoal at flashing green daybeacon "49." To the west of Duck Key (NOAA Chart 11453) you will find Grassy, Crawl, Little Crawl, Deer and Fat Deer Keys. Fat Deer Key is fronted by Coco Plum Beach, which is well marked by a 14-story-high condominium tower, an excellent landmark from Hawk Channel (and the highest building in all of the Florida Keys).

On Hawk Channel, abeam of Channel Five, it is about 10 nm to Hawk's Cay Resort on Duck Key. Heading south in Hawk Channel, at flashing red daybeacon "44,"

Boot Key Harbor City Marina is a modest community of liveaboards, ranging from year-round residents to transient loopers to cruisers from all over the world. With the City Park located just next door, you can enjoy bocce ball, tennis, basketball, or one of the several events hosted there throughout the year...and walk back to your boat when you're done. We hope to welcome you soon!

## Boot Key Harbor City Marina
(305) 289-8877
VHF Channel 16 for Dock or Mooring Assignment
www.cityofmarathonmarina.com

MARATHON MARINA & RESORT
MARATHON BOAT YARD MARINE CENTER
BOOT KEY HARBOR CITY MARINA

follow a heading of about 255 degrees magnetic to the 8 entry daybeacons that guide you into the Duck Key moat.

**Dockage:** Once inside the channel entrance, turn to the right and, at Idle Speed/No Wake, enjoy the deep water on your way to the marina at Hawk's Cay Resort. The area in front of the dolphin and seal pens has shoaled somewhat; call ahead for exact depths. If your assigned slip lies across the marina, skirt the slips clockwise and avoid the center shoals. A swift crosscurrent can test your docking skills; check with the marina staff and use caution. Hawks Cay Marina features 85 boat slips, can accommodate vessels up to 110 feet in length and offers boat in/boat out service and dockage for resort guests who wish to trailer their boat to the Keys. All overnight boaters have access to Hawks Cay's pools, restaurants and attractions.

To the south on Fat Deer Key, Driftwood Marina & Storage has repair (with a 60-ton lift) and storage facilities in a protected basin with a dredged channel (reported 4-foot approach depths).

Bonefish Towers lie at the eastern edge of the deep channel leading to the Key Colony Beach Basin. In the basin are several facilities, including Outta the Blue Marina, White Marlin Marina, Shelter Bay Marine and Key Colony Beach Marina. Here you can find slips, repairs and fuel; see the marina table for details.

This location puts you in the heart of the city of Key Colony Beach. Shops, restaurants, hotels and some of the Keys' best ocean beaches are within walking distance. Within a short cab ride are restaurants regarded as among the best in the middle keys. Some are situated on nearby Grassy Key. The five-star Hideaway Café is tucked within the Rainbow Bend Resort and provides courtesy transportation (305-289-1554). They are open daily, serving until 11:00 p.m. The Key Colony Inn is just down the street from the marina and has great seafood and Italian dishes (305-743-0100).

**Anchorage:** The protected Long Key Bight (west of the Channel 5 Bridge) has 4- to 6-foot depths with good holding in sand and grass.

## Marathon Area

**NAVIGATION:** Use Charts 11451 and 11453. Continuing west in Hawk Channel past Key Colony Beach, Vaca Key lies off to starboard. The closest gateway to it and the community of Marathon lies where Vaca Key and Boot Key Harbor meet at Sister Creek, just northwest of East Washerwoman Shoal, marked by flashing green

daybeacon "49." The creek entrance, with 5-foot mean low water depths, is marked by flashing red daybeacon "2." Boot Key Harbor, one of the best and most heavily populated harbors in the Keys, lies just beyond the head of the creek.

 There are overhead cables in this area with 65-foot clearance.

Sister Creek is lined on one side with residential developments, docks and canals. Skippers of vessels with drafts over 5 feet will need to enter Boot Key Harbor via the east–west channel between Boot Key and Vaca Key.

Boot Key Channel is approached from Hawk Channel (heading west) by a turn due north once Sombrero Key Light is directly abeam to port. Four nautical miles north of Sombrero Key, you will find the channel's entry markers, flashing green daybeacon "1" and red daybeacon "2," situated just south of Knight Key. These are supplemented by additional daybeacons leading to an abundance of marine facilities along Boot Key Channel and in the harbor beyond. Strictly observe the posted "SLOW-SPEED/MINIMUM-WAKE ZONE" in this busy area. This channel carries 7 feet at mean low water.

**Dockage/Moorings:** A turn to starboard (coming from Hawk Channel) when entering Boot Key channel will take you to Skipjack Resort & Marina, at the end of Boot Key Harbor. The nearby Sombrero Marina Dockside also offers slips, along with useful services geared toward the liveaboard population of Boot Key. Dockage is available by the day, week, month or year, although some slips are available for sale.

The friendly Boot Key Harbor City Marina manages 211 moorings for boats up to 45 feet and 15 moorings for boats to 60 feet, as well as slips and a designated anchorage. They do not take reservations, but if you appear in person, you can go on a waiting list if they are full. The mooring rates are on a daily, weekly or monthly basis and include showers and weekly pump-out service, plus they provide a large dinghy dock adjacent to their facility. More information is available from ci.marathon. fl.us (search "Marathon moorings").

The marina is located next to a beautiful park and sports complex and is minutes from Sombrero Reef, an internationally renowned diving and snorkeling venue. (Photo-op! Create Instagram snapshots at the natural coral limestone arch.) Provisions and repairs are all available within 1 mile of the marina, and public bus service connects to Key West and the mainland.

# GOIN' ASHORE: **MARATHON, FL**

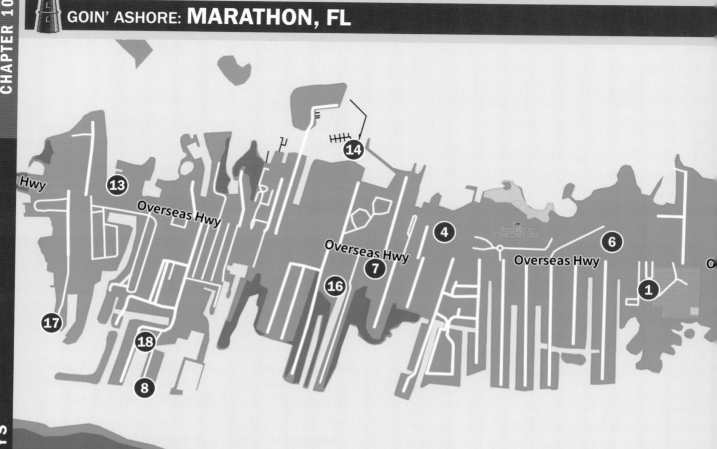

| SERVICES | | |
|---|---|---|
| 1 | Library | |
| 2 | Post Office | |
| **ATTRACTIONS** | | |
| 3 | Crane Point Museum & Nature Center | |
| 4 | Turtle Hospital | |
| **SHOPPING** | | |
| 5 | Publix | |

| | | |
|---|---|---|
| 6 | Seamark Electronics | |
| 7 | West Marine | |
| **DINING** | | |
| 8 | Burdines Waterfront | |
| 9 | Keys Fisheries Restaurants | |
| **MARINAS** | | |
| 8 | Burdines Waterfront Marina | |

| | |
|---|---|
| 10 | Banana Bay Resort & Marina |
| 11 | Blackfin Resort and Marina |
| 12 | Boot Key Harbor City Marina |
| 13 | Capt. Pip's Marina & Hideaway |
| 14 | Faro Blanco Resort & Yacht Club |
| 15 | Keys Boat Works |

| | |
|---|---|
| 16 | Marathon Boat Yard Marine Center |
| 17 | Marathon Marina & Resort |
| 18 | Pancho's Marina and Fuel Dock |
| 19 | Skipjack Resort & Marina |
| 20 | Sombrero Marina Dockside |

The islands of Marathon boast some of the best boating and fishing activities anywhere, plus waterfront restaurants, kayaking and paddleboarding, and access to world-class diving and snorkeling. A bike ride on Sombrero Beach Road leads to one of the finest public beaches in the Keys.

**Attractions:** For diversions ashore, consider the Crane Point Museums & Nature Center. The Natural History Museum's nature trails wind through a tropical palm forest, canopied with thatch palms and loaded with trees and shrubs native to the area. The longer (.5-mile) trail leads to the Crane House, surrounded by exotic specimen trees and open to the Gulf of Mexico with spectacular views. The complex has a natural history museum, marine touch tanks and a bird rescue center (5550 Overseas Hwy., 305-743-3900).

There are lots of opportunities nearby for interacting with the local marina life. The Turtle Hospital is located in a 1940s-era motel at 2396 Overseas Hwy. The hospital is dedicated to the rehabilitation of endangered sea turtles and offers 90-minute guided tours with proceeds directly benefiting the program. At the end of each program guests are invited to feed the permanent residents. Call for hours and fees (305-743-2552). At the north end of Marathon is the

Florida Keys Aquarium Encounters at 11710 Overseas Hwy (305-407-3262), an interactive place to see sharks, stingrays, bonefish, barracuda, turtles and more. For interactive dolphin encounters, swimming with the dolphins, dolphin demonstrations and more, visit the Dolphin Research Center, located on Grassy Key (7 miles east of Marathon), a not-for-profit organization that provides education about dolphins (305-289-1121).

**Shopping:** Provisioning possibilities abound, most clustered along U.S. Route 1 within walking distance of the inner harbor boat basin and Sombrero Beach Road. Just west of Sombrero Beach Road, you will find a Publix Supermarket, pharmacy, bank (with ATM) and Post Office. Also nearby is Marathon Liquor & Deli (MM 50), with a huge selection of beers, wines and liquor and perhaps the best gourmet deli selection in the Keys. Seamark Electronics at 2994 Overseas Hwy. (305-743-6633) provides commercial and recreational boating equipment.

East of Sombrero Beach Road are fast food restaurants, a Kmart, a Winn-Dixie supermarket and the Marathon Airport (MM 52). Several national car rental services operate from the airport.

**Dining:** Located at the foot of the Seven Mile Bridge is one of the best places to see the sunsets: Sunset Grille and Raw Bar (305-396-7235). For a unique Lobster Reuben sandwich, eat at the Keys Fisheries Restaurant (305-743-4353). Burdines Waterfront is another very popular waterfront restaurant with docking for dining patrons (305-743-5317).

Continuing to work "outward" from Boot Key Harbor, immediately before the remnants of the Boot Key Bridge, you will see the entry channel to the very well protected Marathon Boat Yard Marine Center. The full-service boatyard has a 75-ton lift and a paint tent. They have earned a "Clean Boat Yard" designation and are known for quality workmanship. Boaters will also have access to their service team of certified technicians and master craftsmen. A large West Marine is next door. Marine supplies are also available at Home Depot (with boating supplies) and the local NAPA auto parts store, which stocks a large variety of marine engine parts.

Pancho's Marina and Fuel Dock are next to Burdine's Waterfront Marina. Both offer gas and diesel fuel and the store at Burdine's stocks a professional fishing tackle inventory. The Chiki Tiki Bar and Grille (305-743-9204) on site here is one of our cruising editors' favorites for a simple menu with good food and a great view.

Marathon Marina & Resort has deep-water slips, as well as a great restaurant, Lazy Days South (305-289-0839), with a great happy hour and spectacular sunset views. Another dining option is a one-half mile stroll to the end of Knight Key. Here, you will find the 7-Mile Grill (305-743-4481) close to the old trestle bridge. It is open 7 days a week for breakfast, lunch and dinner. Breakfast here, on a warm winter's day, is not to be missed.

**Anchorage:** Finding a place to anchor in Boot Key Harbor can be a challenge from Thanksgiving through March. You can anchor on the south side of the western approach channel, either on the west side of the bridge or on the east side. For a fee, you can have dinghy tie-up privileges (nearest to complete shopping), a bike rack, message services and water at Sombrero Marina Dockside.

You can also anchor outside of the harbor in the lee of Boot Key in 8 to 9 feet on a line between red daybeacon "2" and Sombrero Key Light. Shoal-draft vessels can work their way closer to shore in the charted 5-foot area. This anchorage is comfortable in northeast through southeast winds, but you will want to move around to the north side of Marathon for any strong winds out of the south or southwest.

Boot Key Harbor City Marina has pump-out facilities and a pump-out boat. They will provide pump-out services for $5 either at their dock or at your anchored boat in Boot Key Harbor or in Sister Creek.

About 4 miles out from the Knight Key Channel Bridge, look for the bog tower. Pick up a mooring ball on the outside (deep side) and snorkel the beautiful Sombrero Reef.

## Cruising Options

From here, we will continue to the Lower Keys, where the pace will pick up the closer you get to the "Conch Republic" (Key West), an extremely walkable and exceedingly fun place to visit. Hold on to your hats...

# Florida Lower Keys

 **ICW** Mile 1197–Mile 1243    ((**VHF**)) FL: Channel 09

**CHARTS** 11438, 11439, 11441, 11442, 11445, 11447, 11448, 11451

If you are continuing on to Key West from Marathon, the ICW will take you through Big Spanish Channel into Florida Bay and running down the northern edge of the western keys. If winds are blowing from the north or northeast at more than 10 to 15 knots, Hawk Channel, on the south and sheltered side of the Keys, will provide more protection. The route through Big Spanish Channel will take a bit longer to traverse, but in southerly or southeasterly winds, it will be the more protected route. There are no marine facilities on the Florida Bay side between Big Spanish Channel and Key West. Also, when you are in the Florida Keys, your travel is totally weather dependent. There is plenty of good weather here and a lot to enjoy. Waiting for good travel weather is a smart boating decision, especially in the Keys.

## ■ LOWER KEYS: INSIDE (ICW) ROUTE

**NAVIGATION:** Use Charts 11445, 11448, 11451 and 11453. The famous Seven Mile (Moser Channel) Twin Bridges begins its passage to Key West at the western end of Vaca Key, immediately crossing Knight Key Channel. Though frequently used by skiffs and center consoles, the passage through the spans at **Knight Key Channel Twin Bridges** (19-foot fixed vertical clearance) is not well marked. Currents run swiftly with either tide, and the monofilament lines of numerous anglers dangle in profusion from the old bridge above for about half the distance into Knight Key Channel from shore. If you do choose this route, once through to the ocean side, keep well clear of the shoal extending west of Knight Key.

The preferred passage is Moser Channel (Mile 1197), the primary passageway and the last major crossover to the inside route from Hawk Channel. (The next crossover at Bahia Honda Channel has twin bridges with 20-foot fixed vertical clearance.) Over Moser Channel, the arch of the **Seven Mile (Moser Channel) Twin Bridges** have a 65-foot fixed vertical clearance. Here, about 1 mile west of Pigeon Key, the channel is deep and well marked, and as you head into Florida Bay set a course towards red daybeacon "24" and rejoin the ICW.

The ICW route to Key West from Bethel Bank continues past Bahia Honda into the National Key Deer Wildlife Refuge. The route, shown best on Chart 11448, then bends north just past green daybeacon "29" at about Mile 1204, steering a course of about 300 degrees magnetic. At this point, you are in the well-marked Big Spanish Channel route to the Gulf and then to Key West via the Northwest Channel. Markers have been changed and added to this area, requiring use of only the most recent chart editions (Edition 15, Jan. 2017).

# Lower Keys, FL

| | | Largest Vessel Accommodated | VHF Channel Monitored | Transient Berths / Total Berths | Approach / Dockside Depth (reported) | Floating Docks | Groceries, Ice, Marine Supplies, Snacks | Gas / Diesel | Repairs: Hull, Engine, Propeller | Lift (tonnage), Crane, Rail | Laundry, Pool, Showers, Courtesy Car | Nearby: Grocery Store, Motel, Restaurant | Pump-Out Station | Min/Max Amps | | | |
|---|---|---|---|---|---|---|---|---|---|---|---|---|---|---|---|---|---|
| **BAHIA HONDA KEY AREA** | | | | **Dockage** | | | | **Supplies** | | | **Services** | | | | | | |
| 1. Sunshine Key RV Resort & Marina 🖥 WiFi | 305-872-2217 | 50 | /16 | 14/172 | /5 | F | GD | GIMS | – | – | 30/50 | LPS | P | GMR |
| 2. Bahia Honda State Park & Marina WiFi 1205 | 305-872-3210 | 50 | 16/10 | 19/19 | 3.5/4.5 | – | – | GIS | – | – | 30/30 | S | P | GMR |
| **NEWFOUND HARBOR AREA** | | | | | | | | | | | | | | | | | |
| 3. Little Palm Island Resort | 305-872-2524 | 120 | 16/09 | 14/14 | 6/6 | – | GD | IS | – | – | 30/50 | PS | – | MR |
| 4. Dolphin Marina & Cottages WG 1215 | 305-872-2685 | 50 | 16/09 | call/5 | 4/10 | – | GD | IS | – | – | 30/50 | S | P | GMR |

🖥 Internet Access  WiFi Wireless Internet Access  WG Waterway Guide Cruising Club Partner  *(Information in the table is provided by the facilities.)*
See WaterwayGuide.com for current rates, fuel prices, web site addresses, and other up-to-the-minute information.

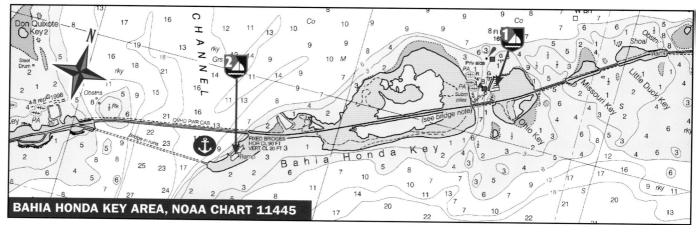

**BAHIA HONDA KEY AREA, NOAA CHART 11445**

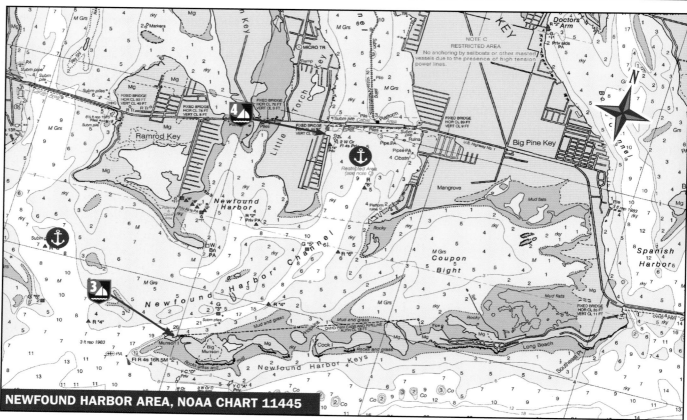

**NEWFOUND HARBOR AREA, NOAA CHART 11445**

On the ICW, prior to reaching Seven Mile Bridge, at Bethel Bank (Mile 1194), you will note a split in the chart's magenta track, which is clearly shown on Chart 11451. The southern route leads closer to Moser Channel, and then continues west past Little Money Key and the massive RV resort on Ohio Key. It then bends southward, following the northern shore of Bahia Honda Key, leading to the Bahia Honda Twin Bridges (20-foot fixed vertical clearance) at Mile 1205, the last possible crossover from the ICW to Hawk Channel. If you are cruising the Florida Keys in a boat that can get under a bridge with 20-foot vertical clearance, you have a few more options than most.

The other ICW route continues on a more northerly route to Big Spanish Channel heading for Florida Bay, the Gulf of Mexico and the Northwest Channel to Key West.

Head for red daybeacon "32" south of Little Pine Key, being sure to regard red daybeacon "26" at Mile 1200. Turn northwest and proceed about 8 miles to red daybeacon "42" leaving all navigational aids to the correct side. (You are returning to Florida Bay so red navigational aids are to be passed to starboard.) As you pass red daybeacon "42" at Cudjoe Key and head for green daybeacon "43" the channel shoals to 5 feet for about .5 mile. At this point, the channel deepens again to 10 feet. The channel is deep but narrow for the next quarter mile; follow the marks and be aware of a

submerged pile near green daybeacon "49." Bear north at red daybeacon "52" and in 2.5 miles you will turn to port at green daybeacon "57" for the 28-mile run to Key West.

Just 8 miles west from green daybeacon "57" is Cudjoe Channel with 7 feet of water with a deeper channel cutting back to the southeast through the flats. This might be a nice place to hang out when the weather is good and forecasted to stay that way. You are off the beaten track, but close enough to it to get underway again with no trouble. The fishing in the deeper channel could be great. There really aren't a lot of places to anchor when traveling from Florida Bay to Key West. It is a very shallow bank (4 to 4.5 feet) with mangrove islands most of the way along the ICW route.

At this point, you should shift to Chart 11442. From Harbor Key Bank Light, a course of 250 degrees magnetic will carry you to flashing green bell buoy "1," marking the Northwest Channel to Key West (N 24° 38.880'/W 081° 53.960'). In navigating to the marker, be sure to avoid low keys about 2 nm offshore in depths up to 26 feet. Without current local knowledge, the Calda Channel and various other shortcuts are not recommended.

**Dockage:** On tiny Ohio Key, the Sunshine Key RV Resort & Marina might have transient space, although they primarily cater to small, trailerable boats.

# LOWER KEYS: OUTSIDE (HAWK CHANNEL) ROUTE

## Bahia Honda to Sugarloaf Key

**NAVIGATION:** Use Chart 11445. You will see the Seven Mile Bridge as you head southwest, once you pass Sombrero Key Light to port. The old Bahia Honda Bridge (Mile 1207), at Bahia Honda Key's western end, is a national historic monument that is slowly disintegrating into the water. The bridge has a section removed so that sailboats can pass through to the cove between the old bridge and the newer **Bahia Honda Twin Bridges** (20-foot fixed vertical clearance). Do not make your approach from the southeast; stay west of the little island one-half mile off the tip of Bahia Honda Key to avoid the shifting sand shoals. There is plenty of water (9-plus feet mean low water), but be aware of the currents under the bridge.

**Dockage:** Transients can find dockage in the well-protected boat basin at the Bahia Honda State Park & Marina (entrance from the north side of Bahia Honda). There is plenty of water in the harbor, but the entrance is shallow (controlling depth of 3.5 feet mean low water with an average tidal range of a little over 1 foot; favor the east side of the channel on entry).

Little Palm Island Resort, a secluded and very luxurious resort on Little Palm Island (westernmost of the Newfound Harbor Keys and called Little Munson on some charts), is located at the mouth of Newfound Harbor Channel, off to starboard as you enter the channel. It is accessible only by boat or seaplane.

The resort's restaurant is open to visiting mariners (305-872-2551). We recommend that visiting mariners dress appropriately—collared shirt for the men as a minimum with slacks and slacks or a dress for women. Sunday brunch is served from 11:00 a.m. to 2:30 p.m. Dockage is complimentary while dining, or you can anchor to the northeast dinghy in. Reservations are required; children under 16 years of age are not allowed

On the west side of Pine Channel, the canal nearest the Overseas Highway leads directly to Dolphin Marina & Cottages, with a controlling depth of 4 feet at mean low water. Both gasoline and diesel fuel are available here. Dolphin Marina is the departure point for the Little Palm Island ferry service.

**Anchorage:** Anchor off the Bahia Honda State Park and go ashore to enjoy two of the nicest beaches in the Keys. The palm-rimmed Calusa Beach on the western edge is sheltered and roped off for swimming and snorkeling. A park concession stand is nearby. Mile-long Sandspur Beach across the road looks out on Hawk Channel. Bring shoes or aqua socks to hike one of the three nature trails, including one that winds along the shore of a tidal lagoon; you will see tropical plants and beautiful birds here. The old Bahia Honda Key Bridge is a great place for spotting rays and the occasional shark.

Continuing west past Bahia Honda Key, you will see the Newfound Harbor Keys, about 4.5 miles due north of the superb diving sites of Looe Key National Marine Sanctuary (an excellent snorkeling site). The relatively well-marked and well-protected Newfound Harbor Channel has become an increasingly popular anchorage area with depths of up to 10 feet (mean low water) in sand and grass. On entry, give flashing red daybeacon "2" a wide berth to starboard to avoid shoaling that extends about 75 yards west of this mark.

With some ingenuity, you may be able to locate a dinghy landing on Big Pine Key near the east end of the **Little Torch Key (Pine Channel) Bridge** (15-foot fixed vertical clearance). This may mean just tying to a mangrove tree. From here, complete provisioning is possible about 1 mile east at the island's full-sized Winn-Dixie store. If you can locate transportation (and decent directions), No Name Pub (305-872-9115), just west of the bridge crossing Bogie Channel on Big Pine Key, is a funky and unique classic, considered a Florida Keys landmark since 1935. The ceilings are covered with thousands of fluttering dollar bills but the pizza is the main event, and folks drive miles for it. There is good reason….It is fantastic!

About 2 nm to the west, Niles Channel (crossed by the fixed 40-foot vertical clearance **Niles Channel Bridge**) offers a reasonably well-protected anchorage between Ramrod Key and Summerland Key. Anchor between red daybeacons "4" and "6" in 7 to 10 feet of water. Be careful to avoid a couple of 2- and 3-foot shoals here. The area is also not well protected from southerlies.

Farther west, before Loggerhead Keys and due north of flashing red daybeacon "50A," a marked shoal-draft channel with the entrance marked by green daybeacon "1" leads to sheltered, though relatively shallow Kemp Channel, between Cudjoe and Summerland Keys. This

channel only carries 4 to 5 feet at best. Be sure to watch your depthsounder.

Saddlebunch Harbor, about 10 nm to the south, has fair holding in 7 to 8 feet with a grassy and mud bottom. It offers no protection from the south.

## Boca Chica Key to Key West

**NAVIGATION:** Use Charts 11441, 11442 and 11445. Hawk Channel narrows past the marked and lighted Ninefoot Shoal (Mile 1224) and passes safely north of West Washerwoman Shoal to Key West. From the western end of Sugarloaf, the Saddlebunch Keys extend for about 3 miles to the start of the Boca Chica Key complex. Here, about 2 miles past flashing red daybeacon "56," the deep, well-marked Boca Chica Channel (Mile 1235) leads into the basin and mooring area of the Boca Chica Naval Air Station. This facility is open to retired and active-duty members of the armed forces. Rental moorings, ice, showers and limited snacks are available.

**Dockage:** Immediately west of Boca Chica Channel is an unnamed, but charted channel leading into Stock Island. Several boat builders, boat storage and fishing docks are here. Provisioning from this location, however, requires ground transportation.

The first marina you will encounter on Stock Island is Florida Marina Clubs–Key West Harbor, which has transient slips and fuel, both gas and diesel. The on-site restaurant here offers Cuban- and Caribbean- inspired cuisine accompanied by incredible views of the Atlantic Ocean. Nearby Oceanside Marina Key West has slips and all fuels and Accurate Marine Electronics (305-432-8252) is located on site. You will also find Prop Doc of Key West (305-292-0012) and Key West Sail & Canvas (305-393-3862) on Stock Island. A little farther west on Stock Island is Robbie's of Key West LLC. Traditionally, Robbie's is heavily involved in the repair and refurbishing of large, commercial vessels, as well as megayachts, and has a 125-ton lift and 50-ton crane.

Stock Island Marina Village can accommodate vessels up to 300 feet and sells fuel. With 220 slips and state-of-the-art floating docks, every type of boat can be accomodated. Every reservation includes dockage, water, pump-out and other amenities There is a restaurant on the premises, the Shrimp Road Grille (305-928-0662), which serves breakfast, lunch and dinner.

The Hogfish Bar and Grill (305-293-4041) is a unique open-air restaurant and bar that is famous for its hogfish sandwich, cold beer, local flavor and entertainment. Hogfish has an "old Florida" laid-back style and is a local favorite, as well as with the *Waterway Guide* staff.

## ■ KEY WEST

Key West is the sunny, end-of-the-line destination for tourists and travelers of all descriptions. Lots of them come down U.S. 1. Thousands more make their way via cruise ships that dock at the Key West waterfront. Casual sailing duds substitute for more formal attire almost anywhere on this island. Jimmy Buffett tunes, smoke from handmade cigars and frangipani blossoms fill the air; tourist shops and raucous bars are juxtaposed to what are surely some of the finest open-air restaurants and most tastefully preserved period architecture in America.

Key West is difficult to categorize. It is a unique and irresistible magnet to yachtsmen, long-distance cruisers and sportfishermen. For them, Key West offers amenities and attractions of virtually every level and description.

**NAVIGATION:** Use Charts 11441 and 11447. Past Stock Island, the towers and radar domes of Key West International Airport appear to starboard, along with many waterfront hotels and condominiums. At Whitehead Spit (Mile 1241), the southwesterly tip of Key West, you can cut inside, leaving to port flashing red daybeacon "12," which marks the eastern side of the Main Ship Channel from the ocean. Turn sharply to starboard, steering for flashing green daybeacon "13," leaving it to port as you turn northwestward up the well-buoyed Main Ship Channel.

The entrance to Key West from the Atlantic Ocean side is relatively straightforward, yet the abundance of buoys in the area can confuse a first-time visitor, particularly at night. We strongly recommend that first-timers do not attempt a night passage, particularly

MAIN SHIP CHANNEL

MALLORY SQUARE

OLD TOWNE AREA

PIER HOUSE

GALLEON RESORT
AND MARINA

HYATT HOTEL
& RESTAURANT

MARKER 24

ENTRANCE

RED MARKER 4

# Key West's Luxurious Resort Marina

## The Galleon MARINA

The Galleon's breakwater shielded floating docks have been engineered for maximum protection and security (24 hrs.) for your vessel. The Galleon provides Old Towne Key West's finest accommodations for yachts up to 150 ft. Guests not staying on board may find luxurious two bedroom, two bath suites with complete kitchens at the dockside Galleon Resort . . . all near the exciting nightlife of famous Olde Towne Key West. A full watersports program . . . small boat and jet skis, as well as mopeds and bicycles. Our Harbourmaster is on duty 24 hours, 7 days a week monitoring channel 16. Plenty of fresh water at no extra charge, 50 amp electricity, cable TV, telephones and 9 ft. of water dockside. A warm welcome awaits you!

Marina guests enjoy the pool, fitness center, sauna, outdoor spa, sundecks and the harbor view tiki bar.

619 Front Street, Key West, FL 33040. For additional information call Toll free: 1-800-6MARINA or 305-292-1292

www.galleonmarinakeywest.com

# Stock Island, Key West, FL

| STOCK ISLAND | Phone | Largest Vessel Accommodated | VHF Channel Monitored | Transient Berths / Total Berths | Approach / Dockside Depth (reported) | Floating Docks | Gas / Diesel | Groceries, Ice, Marine Supplies, Snacks | Repairs: Hull, Engine, Propeller | Lift (tonnage), Crane, Rail | Min/Max Amps | Laundry, Pool, Showers, Courtesy Car | Pump-Out Station | Nearby: Grocery Store, Motel, Restaurant |
|---|---|---|---|---|---|---|---|---|---|---|---|---|---|---|
| 1. Florida Marina Clubs-Key West Harbour □ WiFi | 305-292-3121 | 110 | 16/11 | 20/100 | 8/10 | F | GD | IMS | HEP | – | 30/100 | LPS | P | GMR |
| 2. Oceanside Marina Key West □ WiFi 1237 | 305-294-4676 | 140 | 16/78 | 3/111 | 20/12 | – | GD | GIMS | EP | L11 | 30/50 | LS | P | GMR |
| 3. Robbie's of Key West LLC WiFi 1237 | 305-294-1124 | 400 | – | – | /15 | F | – | GI | HEP | L125,C50 | 30/100 | S | – | GMR |
| 4. Stock Island Marina Village □ WiFi WG | 305-294-2288 | 300 | 16/10 | 125/215 | 15/20 | F | GD | GIS | – | – | 30/200+ | LPS | P | GMR |
| 5. Sunset Marina Key West □ WiFi 1239 | 305-296-7101 | 120 | 16 | 25/120 | 6/9 | F | GD | GIMS | P | – | 30/100 | LS | P | GMR |
| **KEY WEST** | | | | | | | | | | | | | | |
| 6. Margaritaville Resort & Marina □ WiFi 1243 | 305-294-4000 | 160 | 16 | 25/37 | 37/14 | F | – | IS | – | – | 15/100 | LPS | P | GMR |
| 7. Galleon Marina WiFi 1243 | 305-292-1292 | 150 | 16 | 80/91 | 12/9 | F | – | GIMS | – | – | 30/100 | LPS | P | GMR |
| 8. A & B Marina □ WiFi 1243 | 305-294-2535 | 190 | 16/10 | 40/50 | 14/12 | F | D | GIMS | – | – | 30/100 | LS | P | GMR |
| 9. Key West Bight Marina □ WiFi 1243 | 305-809-3984 | 140 | 16/17 | 33/145 | 20/12 | – | GD | GIMS | – | – | 30/100 | LPS | P | GMR |
| 10. Conch Harbor Marina □ WiFi 1243 | 305-294-2933 | 195 | 16 | 20/40 | 30/9 | – | GD | IMS | – | – | 30/100 | LPS | P | GMR |
| 11. Spencer's Boat Yard 1243 | 305-296-8826 | 45 | – | – | 4/6 | – | – | M | HEP | L25 | 30/50 | – | P | GMR |
| 12. Garrison Bight Marina 1243 | 305-294-3093 | 40 | – | 10/280 | 4/6 | – | G | GIMS | EP | L | – | – | – | GMR |
| 13. City Marina at Garrison Bight WiFi 1243 | 305-809-3981 | 70 | 16 | 30/245 | 7/6 | F | – | I | – | – | 30/50 | LS | P | GMR |
| 14. Key West Yacht Club WiFi 1243 | 305-896-0426 | 58 | 16 | 3/67 | 6/9 | – | – | IS | – | – | 30/50 | S | – | MR |

□ Internet Access   WiFi Wireless Internet Access   WG Waterway Guide Cruising Club Partner *(Information in the table is provided by the facilities.)*

See WaterwayGuide.com for current rates, fuel prices, web site addresses, and other up-to-the-minute information.

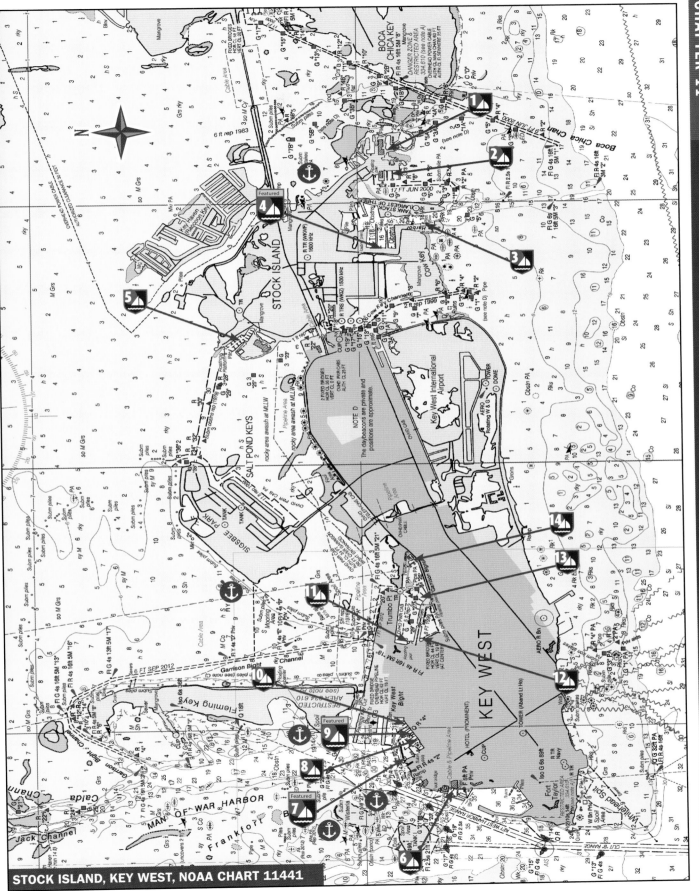

STOCK ISLAND, KEY WEST, NOAA CHART 11441

## The Conch Republic

On April 23, 1982, the U.S. Border Patrol established a military-style roadblock on U.S. 1 at Florida City. The Border Patrol stopped all northbound highway traffic at a place motorists know as The Last Chance Saloon and searched for illegal aliens and drugs. The ensuing well-publicized traffic jam–traffic stretched back for 19 miles–supposedly stymied the Key's tourism industry.

This spurred a movement in which citizens of the Keys (called "Conchs") elected to secede from the Upper 48. With tongue in cheek, but with a serious gleam in their eyes, they selected a flag, designated their boundaries and became the "Conch Republic." They proclaimed their independence, declared war on the United States and then immediately surrendered, applying for foreign aid. The roadblock was discontinued after several days, and the economy was saved.

Today, the tradition of the Conch Republic revolution continues with a yearly celebration in April and appointment of various Conch Ambassadors. To many Key West locals, both natives and transplants alike, the event symbolizes both the intense individualism of the island's people and the keen sense of humor that they enjoy.

through the Northwest Channel Entrance from the Gulf of Mexico.

The Main Ship Channel guides the deepest-draft commercial vessels in from the Atlantic Ocean on a well-marked path leading just west of north from lighted red-and-white whistle buoy "KW" on a range to the prominent (and lighted) red-and-white water tank on the western end of the island. The channel takes an abrupt dogleg to the northwest at quick flashing red buoy "8," and then another dogleg (about 1 mile farther), this time to the north, between flashing green buoy "9" and quick flashing red buoy "12." Entrance for boats southbound on Hawk Channel should be made at the first elbow in the Main Ship Channel.

The Northwest Channel (shown best on Chart 11441, Edition 41) begins at flashing green bell buoy "1." At this point, steer a course for red nun buoy "2," leaving it to starboard and continuing between quick-flashing green buoy "3" to port and red nun buoy "4" to starboard. Both are located to bring you safely inside between two submerged jetties, east and west. (The eastern jetty is awash at high tide.) Then, continue on down the well-marked channel to the Main Ship Channel at flashing green buoy "19." Continuing on Chart 11447, a sharp turn to the northeast here will bring you to flashing red buoy "24" and the Key West Bight. Again, only highly experienced navigators should attempt this channel at night.

Take the well-marked channel around the north end of Fleming Key to access Garrison Bight. Note that the chart depicts 50-foot-high power lines at the opening of Garrison Bight, but the yacht club and others there claim it is closer to 60 feet of vertical clearance. If vertical clearance is a consideration, call ahead, wait for low tide and then make your own decision.

**Dockage:** The Margaritaville Report & Marina (formerly the Westin Key West) is located just off the main channel to starboard as you enter the harbor. Access to the marina may be limited because cruise ships dock on the outside pier. If the wind and waves are up, you may want the greater protection of docking opportunities within Key West Bight.

To reach Key West Bight, continue in the Main Ship Channel until just before flashing red buoy "24," then turn right, heading to flashing red buoy "2" and quick flashing red buoy "4" to starboard at the end of the seawall. The spacious floating docks (finger piers port and starboard) of the Galleon Marina lie immediately to starboard on rounding the seawall. Adjacent to the

Historic Seaport Harbor Walk, which extends all the way to the restaurants and shops on the southeast side of the Bight, the Galleon Marina is a popular spot. Reservations are recommended far in advance during high season, and especially for regatta weeks and Fantasy Fest. Take advantage of all of the resort amenities including pool, private beach, sauna, and exercise room. The marina is breakwater shielded and provides specially engineered docks for maximum protection. They also have bicycle, moped and Jet Ski rentals on site. A & B Marina is nearby with transient slips and diesel.

On the south side is the Historic Seaport at Key West Bight (a.k.a. Key West Bight Marina), identified by the Chevron sign at the easily accessible fuel dock, as well as the cluster of schooners available for harbor cruises. The marina can accommodate deep-draft boats (up to 10-foot drafts) in its transient slips.

There are several good restauarants in this immediate area, connected by the Harbor Walk. (See "Goin' Ashore.") Key West Marine Hardware is within easy walking distance at 818 Caroline Street (305-294-3425) and has a complete selection of marine paint and hardware.

At the southeast end of the inner harbor, Conch Harbor Marina is dead ahead as you enter the Bight, rounding flashing red daybeacon "4" at the end of the breakwater, and easily identified by the large TEXACO sign (both gasoline and diesel fuel available). Most slips are reserved well in advance and reservations must be made via a faxed form.

A bit farther afield, Spencer's Boat Yard in Garrison Bight has a 25-ton lift and repair capabilities (no transient slips). This is the only lift in Key West proper; the others are out on Stock Island (described previously in this chapter). Additional transient dockage may be available at Garrison Bight Marina, which is primarily used by local small-boat fishermen, many of them utilizing the marina's ample dry storage capability. (Note 4-foot approach depths.) Also in this inner harbor is City Marina at Garrison Bight, which has dockage on both sides of the 19-foot vertical clearance fixed **Garrison Bight Bridge**. Limited transient slips are also available at the Key West Yacht Club at the east end of Garrison Bight.

Key West is a federal No-Discharge Zone, meaning no waste, even that which has been treated, should be discharged overboard. A pump-out service for boats on moorings, anchored or in marinas is provided by City Marina Pump-Out (305-809-3981 or VHF Channel 16), with service available Monday through Saturday 8:00 a.m. to 4:00 p.m. Check our Waterway Guide Explorer at waterwayguide.com for updates.

At the tip of Stock Island, Sunset Marina Key West (on the Bay side) is an oasis offering transients slips in a resort atmosphere. It is a short walk from here to The Key West Golf Club, a public golf course. Between the west side of Stock Island and the east side of Key West on Cow Key Channel, Hurricane Hole Restaurant and Marina (305-294-0200) has slips for dining patrons, serving excellent conch and calamari dishes. This is a short walk across Route 1 or, if conditions permit, you can dinghy the short distance. Fresh catches of tuna, wahoo, grouper and mahi-mahi are served alongside traditional non-seafood meals. .

**FLORIDA LOWER KEYS**

| SERVICES | |
|---|---|
| 1 | Library |
| 2 | Post Office |
| 3 | Visitors Center |
| **ATTRACTIONS** | |
| 4 | Conch Tour Train |
| 5 | Ernest Hemmingway House |
| 6 | Key West Aquarium |
| 7 | Key West Butterfly & Nature Conservatory |
| 8 | Key West Lighthouse |
| 9 | Key West Memorial Sculpture Garden |
| 10 | Key West Shipwreck Museum |
| 11 | Mallory Square |

| | |
|---|---|
| 12 | Mel Fisher Maritime Museum |
| 13 | Southernmost Point |
| 14 | Tennesee Williams House |
| 15 | Truman Little White House |
| **SHOPPING** | |
| 16 | Ace Hardware |
| 17 | Fausto's Food Palace |
| 18 | Key West Marine Hardware |
| 19 | West Marine |
| **DINING** | |
| 20 | Blue Heaven |
| 21 | El Siboney |
| 22 | Harbor Walk |

| | |
|---|---|
| 23 | Kelly's Caribbean Bar, Grill & Brewery |
| 24 | Louie's Backyard |
| 25 | Pepe's Café |
| **MARINAS** | |
| 26 | A&B Marina |
| 27 | City Marina at Garrison Bight |
| 28 | Conch Harbor Marina |
| 29 | Galleon Marina |
| 30 | Garrison Bight Marina |
| 31 | Key West Bight Marina |
| 32 | Key West Yacht Club |
| 33 | Margaritaville Resort & Marina |
| 34 | Spencer's Boat Yard |

In the past three decades, the City of Key West has undergone a noticeable transformation from a tiny tourist and fishing curiosity into a luxurious, moneyed resort. Nowhere is this more evident than in the aggressive but controlled development of quality hotels, Key West-styled condominiums, proudly restored wooden homes, historic sites and inventive new restaurants.

Within an easy walk from the major marinas and public dinghy landing, Old Town serves up a savory variety of provisioning and dining possibilities, along with shops, watering holes, dives and other local color. Pick up a free Key West map before you start out, available at most marinas and many shops. Except for the resort hotels and strip malls on along U.S. Route 1, architecture is largely "Conch Island" style and worthy of a serious walking tour.

**Attractions:** Tourist attractions abound (all with fees), and include the Ernest Hemingway House at 907 Whitehead St. (305-294-1136), Tennessee Williams House at 1431 Duncan St. and President Harry S. Truman Little White House at 111 Front St. (305-294-9911). There are numerous other historic structures here and not enough space to list them all. Other popular tourist stops are the Mel Fisher Maritime Museum (200 Greene St., 305-294-2633); Key West Butterfly & Nature Conservatory (1316 Duval St., 305-296-2988); and the Key West Shipwreck Museum (305-292-8990) and Key West Aquarium (305-296-2051), which–in true Key

West style–both claim 1 Whitehead St. as their address when they are actually located across the street from one another. Another option is the tourist-laden, but highly informative, Conch Tour Train, which boards at the corner of Duval and Front Streets (305-294-5161). It's one of the oldest attractions, entertaining visitors to Key West since 1958.

There is an amazing amount of free entertainment as well. The sunset celebration at Mallory Square is always a draw, whether it is your first or 100th visit to Key West. Spread between the area behind the Westin Resort and the old square, you will find many evenings' worth of sunset entertainment. Wander through the crowd and enjoy performances of trained cats that leap through hoops of fire, acrobatic musicians, pig acts, mimes, contortionists, sword swallowers, bicycle tricksters and

other oddities. There are always tempting concoctions (such as chocolate-dipped cheesecake) to snack on while waiting for the sunset.

On your way to or from Mallory Square, don't miss the Key West Historic Memorial Sculpture Garden on the corner of Wall Street and Tifts Alley. Bronze busts of the island's historic figures portray a colorful and intriguing past. The tour is financed entirely by individual memorials etched in the bricks of the garden walkway (more than $700,000 worth).

Be sure to take the obligatory photo at the popular Southernmost Point in the Continental United States. This multi-striped buoy at the end of Whitehead Street is just "90 Miles to Cuba." Another good photo-op is from the top of the Key West Lighthouse (88 steps), located across the street from the Hemingway House, at 938 Whitehead Street (305-294-0012).

**Shopping:** Within a block of Harbor Walk, Key West Marine Hardware (818 Caroline St., 305-294-3519) is an unusually well-stocked chandlery. West Marine at 951 Caroline St. (305-296-0953) has the usual selection of supplies in a large facility, but the fact that it is close to Key West Bight makes it extremely handy. You may also

find what you need at the Ace Hardware (1101 Eaton St., 305-296-9091).

Fausto's Food Palace (522 Fleming St., 305-296-5663) is a great place to do some provisioning. They not only have a wonderful meat and seafood selection but also a full grocery department, as well as beer, wine and prepared foods.

**Dining:** The restaurant selection in Key West rivals that of any major American port city. Local residents from as far away as Key Largo will travel the full length of the Overseas Highway for lunch in Key West in preference to a shorter run to Miami. One such draw is Louie's Backyard, which is actually a backyard that is right on the Atlantic Ocean (700 Waddell Ave.). Indoor and spectacular outdoor seating is arranged in a series of terrace levels, descending to the sea. Louie's is widely regarded as having the best and most innovative cuisine in the Florida Keys; prices are high, but customers come away satisfied. Reservations are advised (305-294-1061).

The Harbor Walk connects virtually all marine facilities, restaurants, bars, shops and an excellent market that cluster around Key West Bight. Just across the Harbor Walk, the Half Shell Raw Bar (305-294-7496) has seafood selections in tempting variety. Situated between the A&B and Galleon Marinas is Alonzo's Oyster Bar (305-294-5880). Located across the Bight, Turtle Kraals (305-294-2640) is famous for its colorful seafood preparations, Floribbean-style and its tower bar. Bahamian or blues music fills the air here nightly. The nearby A&B Lobster House serves up Florida's famous crustacean and plenty of steak (305-294-5880, reservations definitely recommended). The next stop along the Harbor Walk is the Conch Republic Seafood Company (305-294-4403), famous for its Baked Oysters Callaloo and featuring indoor and outdoor dining.

Close to the inner harbor, the oldest restaurant in Key West is Pepe's Café (806 Caroline St., 305-294-7192, no reservations accepted). Pepe's was established in 1909 and has served everyone from Ernest Hemingway and Harry Truman to Carl Hiaasen and Bob Dylan.

Kelly's Caribbean Bar, Grill & Brewery (301 Whitehead St., 305-293-8484) serves delicious beef, poultry and seafood at reasonable prices. Kelly McGillis of "Top Gun" fame founded it, and it serves as the regatta headquarters for Key West Race Week.

For a complete change of pace, try Blue Heaven (729 Thomas St., 305-296-8666), open Mon. through Sat. for lunch and dinner, and only for brunch on Sundays; limited reservations for dinner. Most of the seating is outside under a tropical canopy. For seriously authentic and inexpensive Cuban cuisine, El Siboney (900 Catherine St., 305-296-4184) is consistently recommended as the place to go.

We would be remiss to not mention the active bar scene in Key West. Up on the corner of Greene and Duval, Sloppy Joe's Bar has been in the same location since 1937. Capt. Tony's Saloon is just around the corner, as is The Hog's Breath Saloon, a biker favorite, which serves the saloon's own medium-weight beer on tap, along with lunch and dinner daily. Nearby, at 505 Front St., is the Island Dogs Bar with a slogan of "Come as you are." Margaritaville at 500 Duval St. is awash in Jimmy Buffett memorabilia, and you can buy the famed cocktail along with Buffett clothing, CDs and other items. This is but a sampling of the purported 650 or so bars on the 4-mile-long and 2-mile-wide island!

For more options, visit fla-keys.com/keywest.

## The Elusive Green Flash

Some say it brings luck; others believe it's a bad omen. Everyone can agree, however, that the green flash is not an everyday occurrence.

The green flash refers to the elusive (and often tiny) flash of green sometime seen at the beginning of a sunrise or end of a sunset, just above the disk of the sun. It is called a "flash" because it last only one to two seconds. It is caused by the refraction of the sun's rays at the horizon, or the Earth's atmosphere acting as a prism.

The momentary change in color is dependent on weather, latitude and season. The green flash is best seen after a cold front, when the water temperature is warmer than the air. A clear sky and flat horizon are essential. Because of this, your best bet for witnessing a green flash are in Hawaii, the Caribbean and Florida.

Key West, as the southernmost point in the U.S., is a great place to see the phenomena, but it can also be seen along the Gulf Coast. Seaman are most likely to see the green flash because they have the clearest view of the horizon. Remember: It is not safe to look directly at the sun until it is close to the horizon.

**Moorings:** The City of Key West has a mooring field east of Fleming Key with daily and monthly rates. Key West City Marina at Garrison Bight administers these. For reservations call 305-809-3981. To the west of Fleming Key (north of the Key West Historic Harbor) is a second mooring field that is free.

**Anchorage:** If you are short on money, and time spent going to and from your boat is not a consideration, Key West abounds with anchorage possibilities, although many locations afford only modest protection from fast-shifting winds and swift currents. The holding southwest of Wisteria Island (known locally as Christmas Tree Island), for example, is poor. The exposure from north through east can be a problem in unsettled weather.

A better choice is just west of Fleming Key, but the reversing current is particularly strong here, making careful watches during the first turn of the tide a virtual necessity. Remember to take into consideration the number of anchors, swinging radius and windage of surrounding vessels. Fresh winds against the tides regularly make for some interesting float patterns; keep an eye out for other vessels that may wander too close to your vessel. You will find 7 to 10 feet here.

Both the Wisteria Island and Fleming Key anchorages are relatively close to Old Town and the Key West Bight Marina dinghy dock. Just inside the breakwater protecting the Bight, turn to starboard in front of the Chevron sign, pass the first dock, and then turn to port toward the Waterfront Market. Turn again to port as you approach the seawall. The dinghy dock is located immediately in front of Turtle Kraals Restaurant. The fee for tying up your dinghy is payable to the Key West Bight Marina. For those who prefer to anchor, dinghy dockage is available (up to 13 feet).

An alternative to the first two anchorages is in the area just to the north of the mooring field and Sigsbee Park. There are good depths of 7 to 10 feet and good holding. Make sure you are outside of the mooring field buoys. From here, you can access the second dinghy dock at Garrison Bight and pay your fee to the Garrison Bight Marina. (Remember to bring your pump-out receipt.) This anchorage is exposed to the north, but has much less current and boat wakes than the others. Even in

> If you wish to come into town from an anchorage, you must have **proof of recent pump-out service** before you can tie up your dinghy...and the marinas really do check! This rule is true for all of Key West.

strong northerly winds, the shallow water between here and the Gulf cuts down most of the swells, just leaving you with wind waves. Note in a strong northerly a significant chop can build up. Some cruisers have been unable to dinghy back to this anchorage under some conditions; be sure to monitor the weather when you do go ashore.

If you decide to explore the wonders of the water, you can take a leisurely 6-mile-long boat ride southeast of Key West to Sand Key. Mariners should be aware that the U.S. Coast Guard extinguished Sand Key Light because it was structurally compromised. A temporary light has been established in its place. Exercise caution when transiting this area. At Sand Key, you can secure your boat to one of 21 mooring balls made available at this natural shallow reef. If no mooring buoy is available and you are outside a no-anchor zone; you may anchor in sand (but not on the coral).

# ■ SIDE TRIP: DRY TORTUGAS

Seventy nautical miles from the nearest settlement in Key West, the Dry Tortugas are the westernmost of the Florida Keys, the most remote and, in some respects, the most fascinating and beautiful. The Marquesas Keys lie in the path to the Tortugas, only 24 nm west of Key West. They make an excellent stop to break up the trip to the Dry Tortugas. Other than the Marquesas, there are no intermediate anchorages and no facilities or supplies of any kind.

Because of erratic, and sometimes severe, weather in the area (unpredicted fronts packing high winds are not that unusual), passage to the Dry Tortugas requires planning for the unexpected and packing everything–water, food, fuels, clothing and all other supplies–for a trip of substantially longer duration than anticipated. Schedules are not recommended. Weekend trippers, Caribbean-bound cruisers and fishermen alike frequently find themselves holed up for a week or more in the modestly protected harbor off Garden Key in persistent 25- to 35-knot winds attending stalled fronts in the Gulf of Mexico or off the Cuban coast.

If weather conditions are less than ideal, a trip to the Dry Tortugas should be postponed. In all conditions, boats bound for the Dry Tortugas should be equipped, at a minimum, with a VHF radio, depth sounder and GPS unit. Careful checking with NOAA radio forecasts

before and during such a trip is essential for your safety. Once at Garden Key, the National Park Service posts daily NOAA weather reports at its docks. Before departure from Key West, skippers should also check with the Coast Guard for the current *Local Notice to Mariners*, available online at navcen.uscg.gov. In addition to changes in aids to navigation in the area, you should check on any military operations in the restricted area west of the Marquesas Keys. The Coast Guard can be reached on VHF Channels 16 and 22A in Key West. With careful preparation, a voyage to the Dry Tortugas can be most rewarding.

**NAVIGATION:** Use Charts 11441 and 11447. One route to the Dry Tortugas runs south of the Marquesas and the other to the north. The southern route, via West Channel, then west past Man Key and then Boca Grande Key, permits easy access to the best anchorage in the Marquesas. Check your charts for shoal areas and stay clear of both keys.

Approach the Mooney Harbor Key from the southeast. The northern route, via the Northwest Channel, leads out past Harbor Key Bank and then to the west. You can switch channels if you change your mind and head through the north-south Boca Grande Channel, approximately 2 nm west of Boca Grande Key and

identified by green daybeacon "1" to the north and red daybeacon "2" to the south.

**Anchorage:** If you choose to take the southern route, stop off and anchor to the west of Boca Grande Key near green daybeacon "17" in 10 to 16 feet at mean low water. Choose your location based on wind direction.

## The Marquesas
An interesting stopover with a fairly well-sheltered lagoon, the Marquesas are made up of numerous small keys arranged in the shape of a South Seas atoll. Chart 11439 shows Mooney Harbor as having room for several boats, but that is deceiving. Use binoculars to locate a suitable entrance. If you have a shoal-draft boat, a high tide and an overhead sun, then you might want to try it; otherwise, forget it!

Some promising-looking entrances might be between the two large islands to the southeast marked "mangrove" on the chart. Two other potential entrances on the south side to the west of Mooney Harbor Key might provide enough depth. A third possibility exists on the western side of the atoll. Only very shoal-draft vessels should attempt entry, and be prepared to get yourself off the bottom if you run aground. You are likely out of VHF range for assistance here.

**FLORIDA LOWER KEYS**

First charted by Spanish explorer Ponce de Leon and named for the turtles gathering there, the Dry Tortugas became U.S. territory in 1821 with the purchase of Florida from Spain. Situated on the rim of the Gulf Stream at the pivot point of trade routes to the Mississippi River and Gulf Coast, the Dry Tortugas were quickly recognized for their navigational and strategic importance. Garden Key soon became the site of a substantial lighthouse. A quarter-century later, construction began on a mighty fortress there. But the technologies of seamanship and national defense changed before the fort was completed. Chief among them was the invention and use of rifled cannon shot, which went through the sides of masonry forts like they were made of cookie dough.

Today, the eerie presence of massive, but never-finished Fort Jefferson still dominates Garden Key, but its importance is historical. The working lighthouse, long since moved to Loggerhead Key to the west, also appears as a sentinel from the past. Contemporary value of this island group is found in its pristine natural beauty, including the unpolluted clarity of its waters and sparkling live reef systems, and the raucous wonder of thousands of nesting seabirds.

In 1992, the entire area, bound by an elliptical circuit of 10 large yellow buoys, was dedicated as the Dry Tortugas National Park. Touring Fort Jefferson on your own is an option, but you will learn much more if you take one of the ranger-guided tours. The rangers share many interesting and unusual facts that will enhance your visit and understanding of life at the fort. The largest of the forts of last century's American coastal defense perimeter (8-foot-thick brick walls, standing 50 feet high to support three gun tiers and surrounding a 17-acre quad), it is also one of the most well preserved.

On arrival at the Dry Tortugas, you must first check in at the National Park Service Visitor Center in Fort Jefferson (fortjefferson.com, 888-382-7864). You will receive a copy of the park's brochure with maps and regulations and the latest weather report. The Park Service has restrooms at its docks and beach space for dinghy landings. The park is a No-Discharge Zone and, time permitting, park rangers may check your vessel's Y-valve. There are picnic tables, a few charcoal grills and a beautiful sandy beach at the fort's south end. Everything you require must be brought with you, and all trash must be carted back to your boat. Visit drytortugas.com for more information on this fascinating area.

**Anchorage:** If you need to stop here, try to figure out the winds and then anchor in the lee of the Marquesas. An anchorage on the southwestern side of the atoll is comfortable in winds from an easterly quadrant. Depths of 8 to 13 feet can be found fairly close to shore. Shallow draft boats can snug up due west of Mooney Harbor Key in at least 4 feet of water with exposure from the south. You will find excellent holding here.

Enjoy a dinghy ride through the maze of passages in the atoll, but do not go ashore. This is a marine sanctuary and signs on the shore prohibit you from landing. This area is known for the famous Spanish treasure ship, the *Atocha*, which sank just to the west of the Marquesas in the Quick Sands. Many boat captains from Key West bring their clients here to bonefish or angle for tarpon.

## The Marquesas to Dry Tortugas

Heading west from either the anchorage or the lagoon, after clearing the shoals to the west of the Marquesas, use Halfmoon Shoal and Rebecca Shoal Light as waypoints. Mind your depth sounder as you leave the shallows east of the light. On the northern route, the same suggestion applies, but you do have some markers along the shallows south of your course. The marker on the western edge of New Grounds Shoal (flashing four seconds, 19 feet high) can also serve as a waypoint before passing Rebecca Shoal. From the light, you pass over deep water. As you approach the eastern edge of the Dry Tortugas, you can pick out Bush Key and Garden Key with Fort Jefferson dominating the island landscape.

A cruiser essential in the clear water of the Keys is a **"Lookie Bucket"** or an underwater viewer. Bascially, it is a bucket with a clear plastic bottom. When placed on top of the water, it acts like a snorkeling mask allowing you to see what is underwater.

The approach for long-distance cruisers from the north is best made due south on the meridian W 082° 52.00, passing immediately abeam of lighted boundary buoy "I" (yellow) to a point about .one-quarter mile east of the red and green daybeacon at Middle Ground. From there, head to red daybeacon "6" and the Northwest Channel. Skip the eastern channel, as you cannot count on it. Vessels approaching from the south are advised to use Southwest Channel east of Loggerhead Key and marked initially by green can buoy "1." At red daybeacon "6," Garden Key's southerly entry channel requires an abrupt turn to starboard to follow the closely spaced markers on both sides of the deep channel into the anchorage.

A solid isthmus between Bush Key and Garden Key was observed in spring 2017. The latest corrected chart (Edition 14 of 11438, dated January 2017) indicated the presence of the isthmus. We would suggest that you buy print-on-demand charts if you are interested in the latest information on the channels in and out of the Garden Key anchorage beside Fort Jefferson.

**Anchorage:** Best anchorage is found in front (to the east) of the deteriorated steamship docks at Garden Key's southern end. There is variable holding here in 15 to 20 feet of water. Be careful; outside the channel, charted depths are about 1 foot. It is best to search out a sandy spot, and then make sure your anchor is set well and securely buried with either a "lookie bucket" or an anchor dive. In this relatively confined and exposed area, there are nearly always at least half a dozen boats, often more than twice that number during a blow. Park regulations restrict overnight anchoring to within 1 mile of Garden Key. During nesting season, you may want to anchor away from Bush Key to avoid the nighttime noise of the sooty terns.

Prior to making the passage, you should carefully the latest weekly *Local Notice to Mariners* from the Coast Guard, available online at navcen.uscg.gov/lnm for changes to navigation aids. Also check the interactive Waterway Guide Explorer at waterwayguide.com for the latest navigational updates.

## Cruising Options

Next up is the eclectic West Coast of Florida, where you the alligators, fish camps and seagrass of the Everglades give way to the face-paced urban life of the Tampa Bay area to the north.

# Anchoring in the Keys

Carry a couple types of anchors on board with you, as no one anchor will fit every situation. Be prepared for 180-degree swings and strong tidal flows, both of which are common in these anchorages.

The Bahamian Moor was used with early types of anchors–the types that did not hold well when twisted or tripped. With the advent of newer-style anchors and the technology to analyze load and force on objects, experts learned that when two anchors are set, the strain on each anchor is at times actually increased. Therefore, it is better to use one anchor, not two, in most anchoring situations. The current philosophy on anchoring is never use two anchors when one will do. However, if you find yourself in a situation where nothing but two anchors will do, such as a crowded anchorage where everyone is already on two anchors, the easiest solution is to set your first anchor and either dinghy out your second anchor, or drop back to put down the second anchor and then position yourself between them. Remember that current and tidal flow always win over wind for sailboats, where as wind will generally have a  stronger influence on powerboats..

There is no perfect anchor, but most anchorages require a burying-type anchor such as a plow or a spade. When the bottom gets grassy, when hard marl or coral lie under a shallow layer of powdery sand or when coral and rock line an area, then a good, solid, hooking anchor or kedge is best.

Mileage indicated here is in statute miles, and no effort has been made to tell you how far off the channel the anchorage is located. You should be able to find these spots easily on your chart. Each of these anchorages has been visited or observed by a *Waterway Guide* contributor. There are other places, though, where a prudent boater can anchor. Let us know how these anchorages are, or if you find other good ones. Visit us online at waterwayguide.com to submit information.

## ICW ROUTE

**Ragged Keys (Mile 1106).** East of the ICW, 7-foot approach, 8 feet to shoal west of Keys. Holding fair to good in grassy mud. Limited protection from northeast through southeast.

**Sands Key (Mile 1108).** East of the ICW, 6-foot approach, 5 feet in area west of northern portion of the key. Holding fair to good in grassy mud. Protected from south to northeast.

**Elliott Key (Mile 1109 to Mile 1114).** East of the ICW, 5-foot approach, 5 feet to shoal anywhere along west side of the key. Holding fair to good depending on rocky to grassy mud bottom. Protection from northeast through southeast.

**Caesar Creek (Mile 1115).** East of the ICW, anchorage open to both routes. Four-foot approach from ICW; 12 feet in best area between Rubicon and Reid keys. Holding good; mud and some grass. Well protected.

**Angelfish Creek (Mile 1120).** East of the ICW, anchorage open to both routes. Five-foot approach from both ends. Anchorage in side creeks north of channel is 5 feet deep. Holding mixed: some rocky areas, some hard. Strong currents. Well protected.

**Pumpkin Key (Mile 1122).** East of the ICW, 9-foot approach, 7 feet to shoal anywhere in lee of key depending on winds. Holding fair to good in grassy mud with some rocks.

**Steamboat Creek in Card Sound (Mile 1125).** East of the ICW, 9-foot approach, 7 feet to shoal north and in mouth of creek off Jew Point. Holding good in grassy mud. Protection only from southwest to east.

**Manatee Bay in Barnes Sound (Mile 1132).** West of the ICW, 5-foot approach and 5 feet to shoal in area near marked channel leading into Manatee Creek. Holding good in hard bottom. Protection fair to good except in strong winds from north to northwest.

**Sexton Cove (Mile 1135).** East of the ICW, 7-foot approach, 6-foot depth to shoaling close in. Holding fair in grass and hard bottom with some rocks. Protection from northwest through southeast.

**Stellrecht Point (Mile 1136).** Southeast of the ICW, 7-foot approach, 6 feet to shoal just south of the point. Holding fair to good in grassy mud. Protected from north through southwest.

**Sunset Cove, Buttonwood Sound (Mile 1142).** Southeast of the ICW, 5-foot approach, 4 feet or less close in, 5 feet near Pelican Key and near Upper Keys Sailing Club docks. Holding fair to good. Protection from east through south and to west. From the north, close in to the key.

**Butternut Key (Mile 1146).** Northwest of the ICW, 6-foot approach, 5 feet near eastern Butternut Key just north of marker "60." Holding fair in soft bottom. Protection only from northwest to north.

**Tavernier Community Harbor (Mile 1150).** South of the ICW, 5-foot approach, 5 feet outside basin, 4 feet inside. Holding poor to fair in dense, grassy bottom. Protection fair to good in all but strongest north winds.

**Cowpens (Mile 1155).** Southeast of the ICW, 5-foot approach and depth. Numerous spots to anchor in Cowpens anchorage area. Fair to good holding in soft bottom, some grass. Protection from east through west, depending on exact anchoring spot.

**Upper Matecumbe Key (Mile 1160).** South of the ICW, 6-foot approach and 5 feet in the anchorage off of the restaurant/bar. Protection from south and southeast. Holding fair in soft bottom.

**Lignumvitae Key (Mile 1164).** Southeast of the ICW, 7-foot approach to either side of key. DO NOT ANCHOR; use the heavy moorings provided. Protection is dependent on being in the lee of the key.

**Long Key Bight (Mile 1170).** On ocean side of Channel Five Bridge, 9-foot approach, shoaling to 5 feet at center. Anchor as far in as draft allows. Holding good, some grass. Protection good from all but east winds.

**Rachel Key (Mile 1190).** Southwest of the ICW, south of Rachel Bank, 7-foot approach, 5 feet in area southwest of Rachel Key and southeast of charted shoal. Holding fair to good in sand and grass. Protection fair to good depending on exact anchorage.

**Boot Key Harbor (Mile 1195).** East of the ICW, accessible through Knights Key Channel or Moser Channel, then east to Boot Key Channel. See details in anchorages for Hawk Channel route.

**Bahia Honda area (Mile 1205).** Southwest of the ICW in charted cove, 7-foot approach, 7 feet to shoal inside 6-foot line. Holding fair in grassy mud. Protection from east through southwest only. You can, with care, anchor just outside the park basin in 8 feet if you can get under the 20-foot clearance at the bridge.

**Key West (Chart 11447).** Anchorages in the Key West area are limited. However, enterprising yachtsmen are continually finding new ones. The best accepted one is Wisteria Island at Mile 1245. It is the northernmost of the two small islands off Key West Bight. Anchorage is north or east, as south of the island the holding is poor. Seven-foot-depth approach, with 7 feet to shoal near shore. West of Fleming Key is another alternative. Note: The anchorage is adjacent and contiguous to the harbor and is exposed to the wash and wake of passing vessels. Holding is good in fairly hard bottom. Protection from east and south, with shoals providing wave reduction from the north. Or proceed around the north end of Fleming Key and anchor north of the mooring field and off of Sigsbee Park.

## HAWK CHANNEL ROUTE

*(Mileage in statute miles from Government Cut, parallel to ICW Mile 1090.)*

**Caesar Creek (Mile 1118).** Anchorage open to both routes. Seven-foot approach from Hawk Channel, 4 feet from ICW. Anchorage best between Rubicon and Reid keys. Twelve-foot depth, holding good. Well protected.

**Angelfish Creek (Mile 1122).** Anchorage open to both routes. Five-foot approach from both channels. Anchorage in side creeks north of channel. Five-foot depth, holding mixed, some hard and some rocky areas. Strong currents, well protected.

**Largo Sound (Mile 1141).** Five-foot approach, some 5-foot depths near the channel, but 3 feet is the norm. Holding fair, some grass, well protected.

**Rodriguez Key (Mile 1145).** Seven-foot approach, 7 feet or less close in. Anchor in lee as required for protection. Holding good. Note wrecks north of key and shoal to the west.

**Rock Harbor (Mile 1144).** Seven-foot approach, anchor as close in as draft will permit. Protection from north to northeast. Mandalay Restaurant (cash only) has a dinghy beach.

**Tavernier Key (Mile 1150).** Six-foot approach, less close in. Anchor in Tavernier Harbor area. Holding good. Some protection from northwest to north, southwest through south.

**Whale Harbor (Mile 1158).** Five-foot approach, 5 feet in anchorage. Anchor in lee relative of keys to north and to small key to southwest near marker "5A." Holding fair, some grass. Protection fair northwest through east. Note shoals.

**Indian Key (Mile 1165).** Seven-foot approach, 7 feet or less at anchorage close in. Anchor on southeast side of key in lee. Holding good in sand and sea grass. Protection fair from northwest through northeast.

**Long Key Bight (Mile 1172).** Nine-foot approach, shoaling to 5 feet in center. You can anchor as far in as draft allows. Holding good in some sea grass. Good protection from all but due east.

**Boot Key Harbor (Mile 1193).** Five-foot approach from Sister Creek, 7-foot approach from Boot Key Channel. Eleven feet to shoaling near head of harbor. Holding good. Good protection for 360 degrees except in severe east-northeast winds. Little room to anchor outside of mooring field.

**Bahia Honda Key (Mile 1207).** Ten-foot approach, 9 feet or less close in between bridges. Holding fair to good. Fair to good protection.

**Newfound Harbor (Mile 1215).** Seven-foot approach, 9 feet or less close in toward highway bridge. Holding good. Fair to good protection in all but worst southerly winds.

**Niles Channel (Mile 1215).** Seven-foot approach, depths of 7 to 21 feet in sand and grass. Holding fair to good in mud and grass. Fair to good protection in all but worst winds from the south.

**Saddlebunch Harbor (Mile 1228).** Five-foot approach through narrow channel between Saddlebunch Keys and Pelican Key. Anchor in 7 to 8 feet of water just inside. Holding fair. Buoy your anchor. Fair to good protection.

**Key West (Mile 1241).** See ICW route.

# Florida's West Coast

■ **FLAMINGO TO FORT MYERS BEACH**
■ **SAN CARLOS BAY TO SARASOTA**   ■ **ANNA MARIA ISLAND TO TARPON SPRINGS**

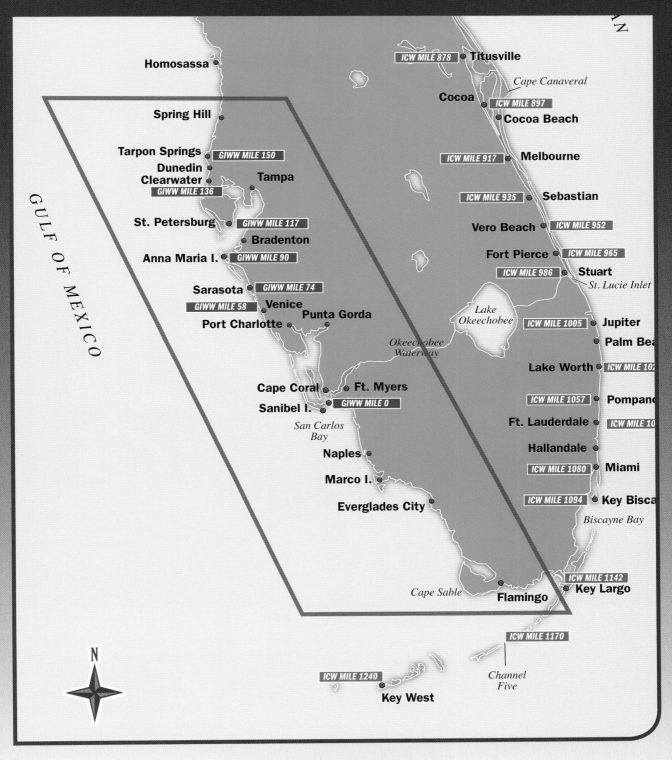

Homosassa

Spring Hill

Tarpon Springs  `GIWW MILE 150`
Dunedin
Clearwater       Tampa
`GIWW MILE 136`

St. Petersburg  `GIWW MILE 117`
Bradenton
Anna Maria I.  `GIWW MILE 90`

Sarasota  `GIWW MILE 74`
`GIWW MILE 58`  Venice
Port Charlotte  Punta Gorda

*GULF OF MEXICO*

Cape Coral  Ft. Myers
Sanibel I.  `GIWW MILE 0`
*San Carlos Bay*

Naples

Marco I.

Everglades City

*Cape Sable*  Flamingo

Titusville  `ICW MILE 878`
*Cape Canaveral*
Cocoa  `ICW MILE 897`
Cocoa Beach

Melbourne  `ICW MILE 917`

Sebastian  `ICW MILE 935`

Vero Beach  `ICW MILE 952`

Fort Pierce  `ICW MILE 965`
Stuart  `ICW MILE 986`
*St. Lucie Inlet*

*Lake Okeechobee*

Jupiter  `ICW MILE 1005`
Palm Bea

*Okeechobee Waterway*

Lake Worth  `ICW MILE 102`

`ICW MILE 1057`  Pompano

Ft. Lauderdale  `ICW MILE 10`

Hallandale

`ICW MILE 1080`  Miami

`ICW MILE 1094`  Key Bisca
*Biscayne Bay*

`ICW MILE 1142`  Key Largo

`ICW MILE 1170`
*Channel Five*

`ICW MILE 1240`
Key West

N

www.WaterwayGuide.com

# Florida's West Coast

Zoologically and geographically, Florida's lower west coast differs substantially from the east. The lower east coast is crowded with people and cultures and, except for the Keys, represents a mega-city stretching from Biscayne Bay to Palm Beach. The cruising, too, is entirely different. The sophistication, glamour and luxury so prevalent on the east coast comes in more measured doses on the west coast. The pace is slower, the atmosphere more relaxed and the amenities more limited and spaced farther apart, but the cruising is superb. From the swampy wilderness of the Everglades to the long sweep of Sanibel and Captiva Islands, from picturesque fishing villages to the bustling big-city ports in Tampa Bay to the quaint, restaurant-laden Greek sponge center of Tarpon Springs, Florida's southwestern waters have much to offer.

The Ringling Museum of Art is the State art museum of Florida and is located in Sarasota. It was established in 1927 as the legacy of Mable and John Ringling for the people of Florida.

The lower half of the coast is alternately wild and developed. At the bottom of the peninsula, the Ten Thousand Islands guard the swampland of the Everglades. Up the coast, the shoreline develops into sandy beach backed by a solid wall of pine and tropical hardwood jungle.

At San Carlos Bay, the tropical barrier islands emerge. Deep water moves in closer toward shore, and resort communities begin to appear. The Gulf Intracoastal Waterway (GIWW) begins at Mile Zero at the mouth of the Caloosahatchee River, where the Okeechobee Waterway ends (or begins, depending on the direction you are traveling).

Now the west coast begins to somewhat resemble the east, with increased boat traffic, houses, marinas and shore activity. From as far south as Naples up the coast to Clearwater, the mangroves increasingly give way to extensive shoreside development.

## Cruising Conditions

Cruising waters through much of the lower half of Florida's west coast are protected. The GIWW–which is for the most part either a dredged channel behind barrier islands or a passage shielded from the Gulf of Mexico–begins at the mouth of the Caloosahatchee River and runs 150 statute miles north to Anclote Keys through a narrow channel. Outside the marked route, shoals are everywhere, similar to the ICW on Florida's east coast.

Though they might seem worse to the inexperienced, most tidal currents are less than 2 knots here. At 1 to 3 feet, the tidal range is relatively small, and water depths tend to be governed more by wind than by tide. When winds blow from the northeast, the water is driven out of the bays, while strong winds from the southeast and southwest push water in. Under northeast wind conditions, there is generally less water in the bays than the chart shows. Be especially wary when a spring low tide combines with a fresh northeast breeze.

From time to time, your skill at navigating a compass course will be tested as you follow the course offshore into the Gulf proper. The occasionally capricious weather may surprise you with a severe and sudden storm. Be prepared with the latest charts and weather advisories, and make sure your boat and equipment are in top shape.

## Florida's West Coast: The Gulf Intracoastal Waterway (GIWW)

Florida's west coast waterway provides the same type of protection from inclement weather as the Atlantic ICW and, like its East Coast counterpart, the GIWW varies in nature with location. In some areas, the GIWW is serpentine with many sharp bends and turns; in other places, it runs in open straightaways. No matter its course, the GIWW still requires navigational vigilance, so keep the following precautions in mind:

- Look astern as often as ahead and keep markers lined up fore and aft to maintain your course in-channel.

- Stay to mid-channel as often as possible and be alert to side currents that may cause lightly powered vessels to drift off course and out of the channel.

- Slow down in any area where shoaling is likely, especially if your boat draws more than 3 feet. West coast bottoms tend to commonly consist of soft mud or sand. Grounding at slow speed will do less damage than running full-tilt onto a shoal.

# Flamingo to Fort Myers Beach

**VHF** FL: Channel 09

**CHARTS** 11427, 11429, 11430, 11431, 11432, 11451

The wild and undeveloped Everglades swampland, beginning at Flamingo, provides a glimpse into nature that is both amazing and educational. Heading north toward the desolate Ten Thousand Islands, cruisers will continue to wonder if they are still in Florida, but it is this very diversity that makes cruising the west coast of Florida such a draw for the adventuresome.

For approximately 130 miles from Flamingo to Fort Myers Beach, the cruising skipper first travels off Cape Sable's East, Middle and Northwest Capes, along the edge of the wild, primitive and beautiful Ten Thousand Islands region, and then through the impromptu continuation of the ICW behind the green mangrove curtain from the Ten Thousand Islands region to the Goodland/Marco Island area. At that point, the cruising skipper has the choice of moving offshore at Marco Island or following the winding 8-mile stretch of the ICW from Marco Island to Naples and finally out to the Gulf of Mexico. From there, the skipper runs the shoreline to San Carlos Bay and the official start, Mile Zero, of the Gulf Intracoastal Waterway (GIWW) at its juncture with the Okeechobee Waterway, crossing Florida to the east.

## ▉ FLAMINGO TO TEN THOUSAND ISLANDS

**NAVIGATION:** Use Chart 11451. The combination of Hurricanes Katrina and Wilma set Flamingo back substantially as the unique overnight stopover it had become. The Flamingo Marina is open; however, the facilities remain limited. The channel into the marina has been dredged but is still shallow (approximately 3.5 to 4 feet at mean low water). Boats drawing more than 3 feet should be extremely cautious. Before you venture into Flamingo, we suggest that you call ahead for up-to-date information and conditions. Taking it slow and easy is recommended when exploring this area.

**Where Am I?** Flamingo to Fort Myers is 120 miles but you may notice that no mile markers are referred to in this chapter. That's because there is no "Intracoastal Waterway" in this area, and therefore no mile markers. The Gulf Intracoastal Waterway (GIWW) begins to the north, in San Carlos Bay, where the Okeechobee Waterway ends (or begins, depending on the direction you are traveling).

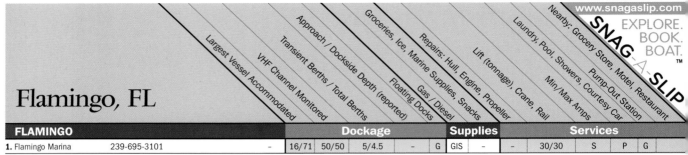

# Flamingo, FL

| FLAMINGO | | Largest Vessel Accommodated | VHF Channel Monitored | Transient Berths / Total Berths | Approach / Dockside Depth (reported) | Dockage | | | Supplies | Services | | | | | |
|---|---|---|---|---|---|---|---|---|---|---|---|---|---|---|---|
| | | | | | | Floating Docks | Gas / Diesel | Repairs: Hull, Engine, Propeller | Groceries, Ice, Marine Supplies, Snacks | Lift (tonnage), Crane, Rail | Min/Max Amps | Laundry, Pool, Showers, Courtesy Car | Pump-Out Station | Nearby: Grocery Store, Motel, Restaurant | |
| **1.** Flamingo Marina | 239-695-3101 | – | 16/71 | 50/50 | 5/4.5 | – | G | | GIS | – | – | 30/30 | S | P | G |

🖥 Internet Access 📶 Wireless Internet Access 🆆🅶 Waterway Guide Cruising Club Partner *(Information in the table is provided by the facilities.)*
See WaterwayGuide.com for current rates, fuel prices, web site addresses, and other up-to-the-minute information.

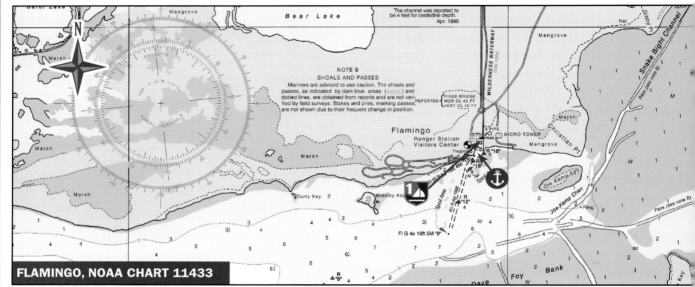

**FLAMINGO, NOAA CHART 11433**

The key to reaching Flamingo, either for a daytime visit or an anchorage, is locating flashing red daybeacon "2," which is 1.95 nm on a course of 178 degrees magnetic from East Cape, on Cape Sable. The approaches to flashing red daybeacon "2" are either from the Keys, via Yacht Passage, directly from Key West across Florida Bay (both covered in the previous "Florida Keys" section), or from the north, skirting the edges of Everglades National Park on the west coast of Florida. (For activity schedules, trail guides, a backcountry trip planner, natural history and more, visit the home page of the Everglades National Park website at nps.gov/ever or call 305-247-7700.)

To reach Flamingo, you will travel approximately 8 miles east-by-northeast from flashing red daybeacon "2," passing four markers to flashing green daybeacon "9," which starts off the marked entry to Flamingo proper. You will then turn north-northeast for a little over 1 mile in the narrow but well-marked channel to the Flamingo basin. Follow the markers carefully; depths outside the channel are 1 to 2 feet at mean low water. Play the tides if your draft is over 3 feet; the chart

shows 4.5 feet in the entry channel, but the date of the sounding data is quite old.

**Dockage:** Controlling depths are 4.5 feet inside the basin at Flamingo with a soft muddy bottom. Flamingo Marina has berths and sells gas. If you need shore power and/or water, be sure to specify that, as not all slips have those amenities. The showers may not be operational (and there is no hot water).

**Anchorage:** It is possible to anchor in Flamingo Basin in 4 to 5 feet of water with good holding in mud. This provides all-around protection.

## North from East Cape Sable

**NAVIGATION:** Use Charts 11429, 11431 and 11451. From Flamingo, retrace your entry route and round East Cape Sable heading north. You will encounter thousands of lobster and crab pot markers if you leave the marked boundaries of Everglades National Park.

Pay close attention to your chart and the depth sounder. Enter the appropriate waypoints into your GPS, and plot your course around Middle and Northwest Capes inside the park boundaries. If you are planning to head for Cape Romano, Marco Island or Naples, set your course to remain well offshore. Remember to stay well south of the finger shoals, about 12 miles below Cape Romano. This entire area is riddled with shoals and spots of very shallow water (2 to 3 feet). Your depth sounder and your chartplotter will be your friend.

Remember the weather caveat for this area. The winter season's stronger winds and frontal storms arrive with ample warning from the northwest through north and finally the northeast. When you clear the East Cape, if the winds are strong from the northwest, seas can increase rapidly. The farther out into the Gulf of Mexico you go, the worse it will get. A closer-to-shore, but slower route will provide many rewards.

Heading toward Cape Romano and its long shoals, your exposure is from the entire northern sector. "Holing up" in a blow is recommended. Even in the summer, squall lines and even high winds from the prevailing southeasterlies can stir things up. NOAA weather reports on VHF Channel WX2 or WX3 should keep you informed so you can make the passage safely.

**Anchorage:** If the winds are light and the weather pleasant, you can anchor off the beach between East and Middle Capes and dinghy ashore. There is 6 to 8 feet of water here with good holding in sand and grass. This is open northwest through south. The area provides excellent beach combing opportunities, and you will have little competition as few people anchor here. Be aware, however, that there is no cell service...whatsoever.

The Middle Cape Canal just north of Middle Cape is reported to be a good fishing spot, but you will need a freshwater license if you intend to dip the rod in Lake Ingraham.

# ◼ TEN THOUSAND ISLANDS

Passing Cape Sable .4 nm offshore and then paralleling the coast inside the occasional Everglades National Park markers brings you into the Ten Thousand Islands. This area stretches for about 56 nm to Cape Romano. Primitive, remote and uninhabited, these islands form the coastline of the Everglades National Park.

## Little Shark River

**NAVIGATION:** Use Charts 11431 and 11432. About 6 miles above the Northwest Cape, pick up the marked

entrance to the Little Shark River off the point just south of Ponce de Leon Bay.

Little Shark River is a gateway to the inner regions of the Everglades National Park and can provide access to the Everglades Wilderness Waterway connecting Flamingo and Everglades City. This route is not recommended for vessels requiring more than 18 feet of clearance nor those that have high cabins and/or windscreens because of the narrow channels and over-hanging foliage in some areas. However, if you are looking to wait out nasty northerly weather, getting a hook down in Little Shark River and out of the waves is good for anyone. The water is deep (10 to 15 feet), and the scenery is beautiful. Mariners have been waiting out bad weather here for many years.

Marked channels lead into coffee-colored wide and shallow bays, or up narrow rivers through and past hundreds of islands and winding waterways. Remember, navigating this type of course requires knowing where you are at all times; it is easy to get lost. Don't rely on a cell phone to call for any assistance; there is no signal in this area.

**Anchorage:** Many cruising boats anchor in the first mile or so of the Little Shark River, which is protected by a 60-foot-high mangrove forest. It has been reported to us that the anchorage at the mouth of the river has shoaled in with mud/shell from the charted depth of 12 feet to 4 feet at mean low water. Since the bottom is so soft, you can slowly feel your way to anchor. There is a strong current, so make sure your anchor is well set. Boats have been seen anchored along the river near the south shore.

If your boat is not screened in, keep plenty of bug repellent handy. (On second thought, keep some handy even if you do have screens.) Those with keen eyes can spot alligators along the banks or in the water. At night, a flashlight shone into the wilderness will usually reveal dozens of little red eyes that belong to alligators. This is a definite "no swimming" area!

The pelicans work this area quite often and are fun to watch. A crab line dropped overboard and carefully hauled in will supply the galley with a magnificent meal. Fishing is good, but licenses are required and limits must be carefully observed. Leave the area as you found it. There are no shoreside facilities in this area.

## Everglades City

Everglades City's history, dating back more than 1,000 years to the age of the coastal mound dwellers, was

# Everglades Harbor, Gullivan Bay, FL

| | | Largest Vessel Accommodated | VHF Channel Monitored | Approach / Dockside Depth (reported) | Transient Berths / Total Berths | Floating Docks | Gas / Diesel | Groceries, Ice, Marine Supplies, Snacks | Repairs: Hull, Engine, Propeller | Lift (tonnage), Crane, Rail | Nearby: Grocery Store, Motel, Restaurant | Laundry, Pool, Showers, Courtesy Car | Pump-Out Station | Min/Max Amps |
|---|---|---|---|---|---|---|---|---|---|---|---|---|---|---|
| **EVERGLADES CITY** | | | | **Dockage** | | | | **Supplies** | | | **Services** | | | |
| 1. Everglades Rod & Gun Club 💻 | 239-695-2101 | 100 | 16 | 17/17 | 5.5/6 | – | – | IS | – | – | 50/50 | PS | – | GMR |
| 2. Everglades Isle Marina 📶 | 239-695-2600 | 60 | – | call/100 | – | F | G | I | – | – | 20/100 | LPS | P | GMR |
| **GULLIVAN BAY** | | | | | | | | | | | | | | |
| 3. Port of the Islands Marina 💻 📶 | 239-389-0367 | 65 | 16 | 20/140 | 5/6 | F | G | GIMS | – | – | 30/50 | LPS | P | GMR |
| 4. Walker's Coon Key Marina | 239-394-2797 | 60 | 16 | 5/40 | 8/6 | F | GD | IMS | HEP | L35 | 30/30 | – | – | GMR |
| 5. Calusa Island Marina 📶 | 239-394-3668 | 70 | 16/05 | 25/84 | 5/6 | F | GD | IMS | HEP | L50 | 30/50 | LS | P | MR |

💻 Internet Access   📶 Wireless Internet Access   **WG** Waterway Guide Cruising Club Partner   *(Information in the table is provided by the facilities.)*
See WaterwayGuide.com for current rates, fuel prices, web site addresses, and other up-to-the-minute information.

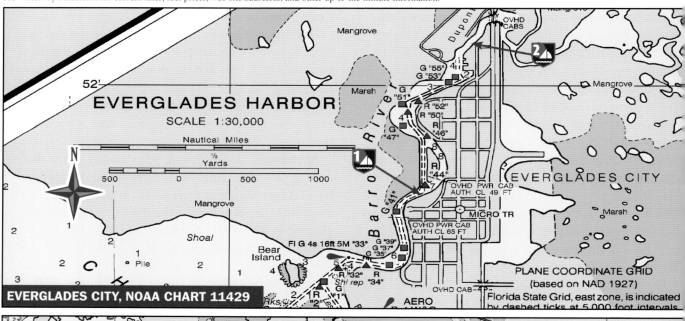

EVERGLADES CITY, NOAA CHART 11429

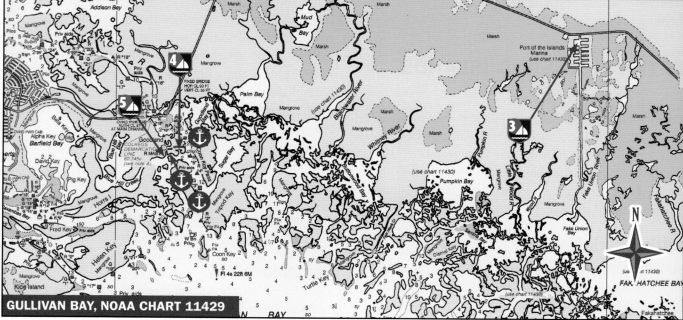

GULLIVAN BAY, NOAA CHART 11429

Everglades City

based on trade, fishing and shellfishing. With the arrival of early settlers, it gradually evolved into a shipping port for produce and seafood. Seafood is still a major economic factor in the area but is following the decline of the produce market.

Unique to Everglades City is the Rod and Gun Club. Once a rambling, private, wood frame home, it is now a delightful hotel right on the Barron River, and it is worthy (if you have the time) of a trip all the way in from Indian Key just to see it, dine here and maybe stay overnight. You will be in touch with another era entirely. Lots of people whose names you may recognize have been here: Presidents Roosevelt, Truman, Eisenhower, Hoover and Nixon, as well as actors John Wayne, Burt Reynolds, Sally Field, Sean Connery, Danny Glover and Joe Pesci. Novelist Ernest Hemingway was a frequent guest here as well.

Everglades City has the basics: a very limited market, a museum, a hardware store and a post office. There are also good restaurants, including Camellia Street Grill (202 Camellia St. W., 239-695-2003) with creative southern cuisine and City Seafood (702 Begonia St., 239-695-4700), which specializes in fresh Gulf seafood. Triad Seafood is a small, family-owned restaurant at the waters edge (401 W. School Dr.), which also has a fresh seafood market (239-695-0722). The city is the northern terminus of the Everglades Wilderness Waterway and offers water-based tours of all types, including airboats, kayaks, canoes and swamp buggies.

**NAVIGATION:** Use Charts 11429 and 11430. North of the Little Shark River, it is advisable to follow the markers out and farther offshore to transit the wide and shallow mouth of Ponce de Leon Bay. Prudence would indicate staying outside the Three Nautical Mile Line. For about 33 nm, only channels among the islands break the coast. Some are deep enough to attract shoal-draft boats and increasing numbers of skippers seeking more remote anchorages and good fishing.

Since heavy insecticide spraying has been virtually eliminated in the Everglades National Park, **mosquitoes** have become almost as important a consideration as weather. They swarm continually in warm weather. If you plan to anchor in this area, opt for spots that garner what breeze there is and keep plenty of bug spray on hand.

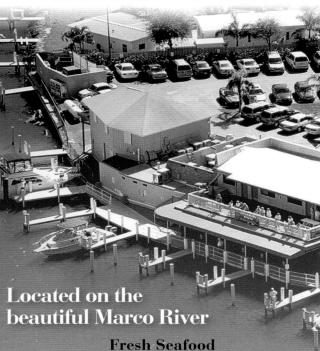

These unmarked channels require careful, experienced navigation. A remote ranger station can be spotted on the north shore of one channel, but no other sign of civilization will be evident beyond Everglades National Park boundary signs until you reach a mark offshore of Everglades City. At this point, you find the 16-foot-high flashing white light "IK," about 3.5 nm off flashing green daybeacon "1" at Indian Key, which leads into the marked channel to Everglades City. Flashing green daybeacon "1" is difficult to pick out from offshore; try using GPS coordinates to guide you in.

Between the flashing red daybeacon "22" and the red daybeacon "30," where the channel crosses the Chokoloskee Bay, there is a strong lateral current from the south during the ebb and to the north during the flood. The channel is deep but narrow, and you need to watch the marks ahead and behind as it is easy to drift into 2 to 3 feet of water and out of the channel.

In Everglades City, between the red daybeacons "44" and "46" the marked channel cuts off a natural bend in the river. Depths at the bend are charted at 7 to 8 feet but it has shoaled to less than 4 feet at mean low water. Be sure to stick to the marked channel.

Seven miles west (as the crow flies) of Everglades City is the shallow Faka Union River, home of the Port of the Islands Marina. After exiting Indian Key Pass (the entry you followed into Everglades City from the Gulf), turn northwest to find green daybeacon "3" off Gomez Point at the tip of Panther Key. This marks the entrance to the 5-mile-long mangrove-fringed channel on the Faka Union River to the marina.

Most of the passes and waterways in this area, other than Indian Key Pass, have numerous sandbars and shoals. The small-boat operator can be a good source of information for side trips and excursions off the main channels.

**Dockage:** Up the Barron River, The Everglades Rod and Gun Club, built by the late Barron G. Collier, has dockage with limited facilities. Water is available but is not potable. The old clubhouse is well worth a visit, and a bike ride to nearby Chokoloskee Island is a good diversion. The general store and post office is out of another age entirely. One-half nautical mile further up the Barron River is Everglades Isle Marina. The marina is situated in a "Class A" motor home facility and sells gas. Call ahead for approach and dockside depths.

Those desiring the amenities of a full-service resort in a primeval setting will find it at Port of the Islands Marina,

# Marco Island, FL

| GOODLAND TO MARCO ISLAND | Phone | Largest Vessel Accommodated | VHF Channel Monitored | Approach / Dockside Depth (reported) | Transient Berths / Total Berths | Floating Docks | Groceries, Ice, Marine Supplies, Snacks | Gas / Diesel | Repairs: Hull, Engine, Propeller | Lift (tonnage), Crane, Rail | Min/Max Amps | Laundry, Pool, Showers, Courtesy Car | Pump-Out Station | Nearby: Grocery Store, Motel, Restaurant |
|---|---|---|---|---|---|---|---|---|---|---|---|---|---|---|
| 1. Pelican Bend Restaurant & Marina | 239-394-3452 | 60 | 16/14 | 3/18 | 5/7 | – | IS | GD | – | – | 30/30 | – | – | R |
| 2. The Tarpon Club Marina | 239-417-6802 | 36 | 16 | call/140 | 4/5 | F | M | G | – | – | 50/50 | – | – | R |
| 3. Snook Inn | 239-394-3313 | 60 | – | 10/20 | 15/6 | – | S | – | – | – | – | – | – | GMR |
| 4. Marina at Factory Bay ⌨ 📶 | 239-389-2929 | 107 | 16/06 | call/72 | 12/10 | F | I | – | – | – | 30/100 | LS | P | GMR |
| 5. Rose Marina ⌨ 📶 | 239-394-2502 | 160 | 09 | 20/109 | 7/8 | F | GIMS | GD | HEP | L75 | 30/100 | LS | P | GMR |
| 6. Walker's Hideaway Marina of Marco Island 📶 | 239-394-9333 | – | – | – | – | – | IMS | G | HEP | L,C | – | C | – | GM |
| 7. Marco Island Marina ⌨ 📶 | 239-642-2531 | 110 | 16/14 | 25/121 | 7/6.5 | F | I | – | – | – | 30/100 | LPS | P | GMR |
| 8. Esplanade Marina ⌨ | 239-394-6333 | 60 | 16/11 | 11/77 | 6/6 | F | IS | – | – | – | 50/50 | LS | P | GMR |

⌨ Internet Access  📶 Wireless Internet Access  **WG** Waterway Guide Cruising Club Partner *(Information in the table is provided by the facilities.)*
See WaterwayGuide.com for current rates, fuel prices, web site addresses, and other up-to-the-minute information.

## see our interactive charts

 MARINAS   SERVICES   ANCHORAGES   FREE DOCK   BRIDGES   LOCKS   NAV ALERTS   FUEL

# waterwayguide.com

GOODLAND TO MARCO ISLAND, NOAA CHART 11430

located at the head of the Faka Union River. The channel to the marina is well marked by daybeacons, beginning with green daybeacon "3" and red daybeacon "4." Controlling depths in the channel are 3 feet at mean low water, so you may have to wait for tides to pass through. Tides in this area are from 1 to 3 feet. Call ahead on VHF Channel 16 to verify available space and for advice on tide and channel conditions.

**Anchorage:** If you do not want to go all the way to Everglades City and would rather drop the hook, you can do so behind New Turkey Key (Mile 75). Depths are 3 to 6 feet so only shallow draft boats will find refuge here. You can also anchor shortly after entering Indian Key Pass, just northwest of flashing green "7" in Russell Pass where you will have at least 7-foot depths at mean low water. For more wind protection, you can proceed farther up Russell Pass to where it opens up to starboard and find 7- to 8-foot depths. Make sure you avoid the uncharted pocket to starboard or you could find yourself on the bottom at low tide. Make sure you set your anchor well as the currents in this area are strong.

# ■ TO MARCO ISLAND

Two routes are available to travel from the Ten Thousand Islands area to Marco Island and beyond: the Inland Passage and the Outside Passage.

## Inland Passage: The Thousand Islands to Goodland

Situated on a small peninsula of a large island and marsh complex, the village of Goodland is a laid-back fishing village with good but unpretentious restaurants, fishing supplies and some very limited groceries.

**NAVIGATION:** Use Chart 11430. If your draft is 4 feet or less and height above water is less than 55 feet, you may save some time by taking the inside and protected route to Marco Island. Vessels with slightly deeper drafts may take this route if they have the flexibility to schedule their trip at high tide.

The route begins about 6 miles west of Faka Union Bay at the head of Gullivan Bay off Coon Key where Coon Key Light, a 22-foot-high flashing white light, marks the entrance to Coon Key Pass. Stay well east of the light (400 to 500 yards) and head north up the east side of Coon Key to pick up red daybeacon "2" (on the west side of Tripod Key), and then through well-marked Coon Key

Pass (heading north, leave red markers to starboard) to the village of Goodland, which is east of Marco Island. The route is a bit lean in spots, but fortunately, the bottom is reported to be soft mud. Local boats frequently use this passage (some at high speed), so ask for latest channel conditions, and then make your own decision. The fixed 55-foot Goodland Bridge sets the vertical clearance for the rest of this route.

**Dockage:** Walker's Coon Key Marina does not accept transients, but they do have a fuel dock with gas and diesel and offer repairs. The Calusa Island Marina (west of Coon Key Pass red daybeacon "6") welcomes transients to its docks and sells fuel. They also have a boatyard with repair facilities.

While in the area, be sure to experience Stan's Idle Hour Seafood Restaurant (239-394-3041). This waterfront seafood fixture has a festive vibe, lots of outdoor seating and frequent live music. The Old Marco Lodge Crab House (239-642-7227), with panoramic views, and Marker 8.5 (239-394-8818) are two more good restaurants in the area. There is also a local fish market that sells to the public.

**Anchorage:** Panther Key at Mile 56.5 has 7 to 10 feet of water with good holding in soft mud. At Tripod Key (Mile 53), you can anchor at the intersection of Sugar Bay at Coon Key Pass in 5 feet. You can also anchor at Blue Hill Creek (to port at red daybeacon "6") in 7 to 10 feet of water, or across the channel from green daybeacon "7" in 8- to 10-foot depths and dinghy to town. There are 4-foot mean low water approach depths here; pay close attention to your instruments and stay in deep water.

## Inland Passage: Goodland to Marco Island

**NAVIGATION:** Use Chart 11430. This section of the ICW and the Big Marco River requires considerable care, even for those who have traveled it before. Local knowledge, which is available at Goodland or over the VHF radio, can help. Markers are moved when necessary to reflect shifting shoals and may not be exactly where the chart shows them. Many prefer a rising tide for obvious reasons.

After you have passed Goodland, you may notice that daybeacon "8" is missing. At red daybeacon "10," you will need to make a sharp turn to starboard, staying close to the marker, and very soon you will make a turn to port to pass under the **Goodland Bridge** (55-foot fixed vertical clearance). Our cruising editor

draws 4 feet and did not have a problem on a rising tide. Maintain a close watch on the depth sounder, and use a pre-set alarm, if available. It is also a good idea to study your charts and GPS carefully after you have gathered some local knowledge. It is very doable; just pay close attention to your depth sounder and charts. Also, make sure that your charts are as up to date as possible.

After passing under the Goodland Bridge, you will find deeper water for a short time. Just beyond daybeacon "16," there is a very shallow area when approaching daybeacon "18." Once past "18," the water deepens again. When you pass green daybeacon "25," make sure you do not head straight for the bridge open span. You will need to veer to port and head for daybeacon "26." Don't be fooled by what the smaller boats are doing because it gets extremely shallow if you go straight. It looks as though you are going completely off track because daybeacon "26" is almost to shore on the west side of the river. Leave red daybeacon "26" to starboard and run parallel to the **Marco Island Bridge** (55-foot fixed vertical clearance) a short distance until you can turn to port through the center passage span.

As you pass under the bridge, to the east is a string of small islands that are bird sanctuaries for thousands of pelicans, egrets and cormorants. Be sure to have the binoculars and camera handy.

⚠️ Just past the Marco Island Bridge, the daybeacons change sides; now you will have green to starboard and red to port until you reach the Gulf of Mexico. In short, where the ICW crosses the Big Marco River channel, the markers are somewhat confusing. Pay attention and sort them out for the route you are taking.

If you plan to continue into the Gulf, be aware that Coconut Island was totally obliterated by Hurricane Wilma, but it is a visible sand bar. The area is well marked, so just pay close attention to the markers. Big Marco Pass is too shallow for passage. Capri Pass is marked and tricky but usually quite passable.

## Outside Passage: To Marco Island

**NAVIGATION:** Use Chart 11429. To reach Marco Island from Everglades City, or farther south outside in the Gulf, you must pass outside the shoals of Cape Romano and well offshore of the Cape itself. Charts record isolated depths of as little as 1 and 3 feet mean low water as far out as the Three Nautical Mile Line. Your course should take you at least 3 to 4 miles west of

Cape Romano if coming from the south or north. Use your GPS and enter a good standoff waypoint south of the finger shoals. If using radar, Cape Romano will be prominently displayed as you run offshore to avoid it.

The shoals extend out from Big Marco Pass and the southern end of Marco Island. If you are heading south, or if you are approaching Capri Pass from the south, make sure you chart a course to 16-foot-high flashing red buoy "2" and the 16-foot flashing white light to stay clear of the shoaling near Big Marco Pass. As mentioned above, the charted Coconut Island is no longer visible. However, it lies just under the surface, so pay attention when you get to red daybeacon "6" and continue into the pass with caution. There is plenty of room, but it does get busy on weekends.

**Dockage:** If you continue on the Isle of Capri Pass, you will find the Pelican Bend Restaurant & Marina, which has slips and sells fuel. The Tarpon Club South is located on Tarpon Bay, accessible from the Big Marco River, and has slips and sells gas.

The Snook Inn, a landmark for more than 30 years, offers dockage for patrons and waterfront dining inside or out at the tiki bar. They have live entertainment 7 days a week and offer daily specials. Snook Inn can accommodate vessels up to 60 feet. (They also offer free transportation from other marinas.)

The Marina at Factory Bay is the closest and deepest marina upon entering Capri Pass heading up the Big Marco River past Collier Bay. Bear to starboard past flashing red daybeacon "14" and the Snook Inn Restaurant; the Marina at Factory Bay is just around the corner. Hail the dockmaster for assistance tying up and to arrange a long-term or transient stay.

**LOOK UP!** You may come across the Air Force communication towers in the lower Gulf, between Cape Romano and the Dry Tortugas, and in the upper Gulf near Apalachicola. Military pilots practice dogfights high up in the sky in the general area of the towers. The planes carry transponders, and the signals from the planes are recorded by the towers and sent back to a central location. The airspeed, attitude and altitude of the planes are constantly monitored so when the pilots get back to base, they can replay the dogfight to see how the mission went and how they can improve. If you are near these towers, be aware that sometimes the jets break the sound barrier, creating a sonic boom. The fishing around these accidental fish havens, by the way, is reportedly spectacular.

The full-service Rose Marina is in the southwestern corner of Factory Bay and may be hailed on VHF Channel 16 for reservations and directions. Their highly qualified team of technicians can haul vessels up to 70 feet and offer as array of services. Their floating and fixed docks can accommodate a variety of vessels, including catamarans.

If you are looking for quiet surroundings, Marco Island Marina, on the south side next to the Marco Island Bridge, is a very nice stop. The well-marked entrance is approximately 3 miles from Capri Pass, past the stanchion of power lines, and has 7-foot approach depths. They have the usual amenities, plus free weather reports, free tide charts, WiFi, cable TV and taxi service. They also have an excellent slip-side pump-out facility. Stay here and you will receive a guest card for the full-service restaurant at the adjacent yacht club. From the facility, a walk of less than 1 mile leads to a Publix, a Walgreen's Pharmacy and other shopping amenities.

Esplanade Marina is tucked inside Smokehouse Bay, which is tricky to get into, but once inside, is well protected (360 degrees). When entering the channel, just past daybeacon "12," turn to starboard and enter a shallow but well-marked pass into Smokehouse Bay. Esplanade Marina has 6-foot approach and dockside depths alongside their floating docks. Each slip has water, shore power, pump-out service, and a dock box, as well as cable TV. There are numerous restaurants, markets and West Marine just a short walk away.

**Anchorage:** Protected anchorages and good holding are available in both Smokehouse Bay and Factory Bay. Once you work your way into the channel in Smokehouse Bay, proceed to daybeacon "7" and then enter the anchorage. There is 10 feet of water here and very good holding. Grocery shopping is easily accessed by going through the low bridge at the end of the anchorage, then to port to the convenient dinghy dock that is located beside the Winn-Dixie Supermarket. Before dropping the hook, be sure to know what the current Florida anchoring restrictions are. This is one of the areas that has been, in the past, under scrutiny.

Factory Bay also has good holding with 10 to 12 feet of water. A sand bar splits the bay, but there is plenty of water around the edge. Anchor in the southeast side by red daybeacons "2" and "4" for good protection. You can also anchor in Capri Pass to the northwest of flashing green daybeacon "15" in 10 to 12 feet.

# ■ TO NAPLES

## Inside Passage: To Naples

**NAVIGATION:** Use Chart 11430. From Capri Pass to just past Little Marco Island on the ICW route, the channel shown on the chart bears the following warning: "This area is subject to continual change." There are spots, particularly at daybeacon "30A," where the water gets very shallow. Pay strict attention to the channels and don't stray. This is a very pretty pass and shouldn't be missed if your draft allows. Our cruising editors' boat draws 4 feet, and they have never had any problems.

About halfway along (red daybeacon "46"), you pass Rookery Bay, a major wildlife sanctuary and will likely encounter local fishing boats. The Gordon River used to be a "no wake" zone from Gordon Pass to the Route 41 Bridge (fixed vertical clearance of 10 feet). The "no wake" zone now extends from flashing red "34" (south of the Naples Yacht Club) to the bridge and is frequently ignored by "weekend warriors."

Whether you are returning from a trip south or just starting out, Naples is a good place to pick up or discharge crew. The airport (or a rental car) is a quick cab ride away.

## Outside Passage: To Naples

**NAVIGATION:** Use Chart 11430. If you choose to go outside for this 8.2-mile-long stretch, it is a fairly straightforward passage along the face of Marco Island to the well marked, but slightly tricky channel entrance to Gordon Pass.

A rock jetty on the south side of Gordon Pass extends 100 yards into the Gulf of Mexico. Favor the south side of the channel along the jetty. With onshore winds and outgoing tide, it can be challenging for slow or underpowered vessels. Once inside, do not run green daybeacons "7" to "7A" as a straight line. Take it wide to the right to avoid the shoal off the northern spit (visible at low tide).

⚠️ There is dangerous shoaling from Gordon Pass Channel daybeacon "1" to Naples Bay Channel Light "20." There are currently no plans by the Army Corps of Engineers to maintain the federal project channel depth of 12 feet. Check the Waterway Guide Explorer (waterwayguide.com) for news and updates.

# Naples Bay, FL

| NAPLES | | Dockage | | | | | | Supplies | Services | | | | | |
|---|---|---|---|---|---|---|---|---|---|---|---|---|---|---|
| | | Largest Vessel Accommodated | VHF Channel Monitored | Transient Berths / Total Berths | Approach / Dockside Depth (reported) | Floating Docks | Gas / Diesel | Groceries, Ice, Marine Supplies, Snacks | Repairs: Hull, Engine, Propeller | Lift (tonnage), Crane, Rail | Min/Max Amps | Laundry, Pool, Showers, Courtesy Car | Pump-Out Station | Nearby: Grocery Store, Motel, Restaurant |
| 1. Hamilton Harbor Yacht Club | 239-775-0506 | 60 | 16 | call/36 | 7/7 | F | GD | IMS | - | L27 | - | - | P | R |
| 2. South Pointe Yacht Club and Marina | 239-774-0518 | 72 | 16/12 | call/72 | 5/5 | - | - | S | - | - | - | PS | - | R |
| 3. Royal Yacht Services | 239-775-0117 | 60 | 16 | call/12 | - | - | - | M | HEP | L60 | - | - | - | - |
| 4. Naples Yacht Club 💻 WiFi | 239-262-7301 | 130 | 16/09 | 5/88 | 8/6 | F | GD | I | - | - | 30/200+ | PS | P | GR |
| 5. Naples City Dock | 239-213-3070 | 120 | 16/14 | 10/84 | 9/9 | - | GD | IS | - | - | 30/100 | LS | P | GMR |
| 6. Olde Naples Seaport WiFi | 239-643-0042 | 100 | 16 | 10/30 | 8/7 | F | - | I | HEP | - | 30/50 | LS | P | GMR |
| 7. Naples Boat Club Marina WiFi WG | 239-430-4994 | 110 | 16/14 | 20/47 | 8/8 | F | GD | GIMS | HEP | L70, C70 | 30/100 | LPS | P | GMR |
| 8. MarineMax Naples Yacht Center | 239-262-1000 | 65 | 16 | - | 6/6 | - | - | M | HEP | L70 | 50/50 | - | - | MR |
| 9. Naples Sailing & Yacht Club WiFi | 239-774-0424 | 65 | 16/68 | 7/75 | 6/4 | F | GD | I | - | - | 30/100 | PS | - | MR |
| 10. Marina at Naples Bay Resort 💻 WiFi WG | 239-530-5134 | 90 | 16/68 | call/97 | 5.5/5.5 | F | G | GIS | - | - | 30/50 | LPS | P | GMR |
| 11. Walker's Hideaway Marina of Naples WiFi | 239-213-1441 | - | - | call/25 | - | F | GD | IMS | HEP | L | - | PS | - | GMR |

💻 Internet Access  WiFi Wireless Internet Access  WG Waterway Guide Cruising Club Partner  *(Information in the table is provided by the facilities.)*
See WaterwayGuide.com for current rates, fuel prices, web site addresses, and other up-to-the-minute information.

## City of Naples

Naples is known for high-end shopping, sophisticated dining and an abundance of golf courses. The Naples Pier is a popular fishing and dolphin-spotting destination, and the miles of fine white "sugar" sand and calm waters make the beaches here especially desirable.

**Dockage/Moorings:** Dock space is usually available at Naples' numerous marinas, but local marina operators recommend calling ahead for slip or mooring reservations, particularly during the peak periods (holidays and weekends). Hamilton Harbor Yacht Club and South Pointe Yacht Club and Marina are both convenient to Gordon Pass, are to starboard as you turn north for Naples. Call ahead to check on slip availability. Hamilton Harbor sells gas.

Royal Yacht services is located up Haldeman Creek after flashing red "24." The charted depths are just 2 to 3 feet; call ahead for approach and dockside depths.

Farther north, after flashing red daybeacon "32" is Naples Yacht Club, with slips and fuel. Naples City Dock, beginning just to the west of green daybeacon "35" and extending to the north, has slips and also controls a total of 12 moorings in two well-protected coves. Rental of the moorings includes use of a public bathhouse and laundry facilities. If you rent a mooring, it is mandatory that you receive a (free) pump out before picking up the mooring and every four days thereafter. The floating dinghy dock is on the same side of the pier as the mooring field. Note that this facility was temporarily closed at press time in spring 2017. Call ahead.

If you continue north on the Gordon River (beware of the shoal 200 feet northwest of red daybeacon "36"), the next marina on the west bank is Olde Naples Seaport, a private "dockominium." When owners are away, the dockmaster rents slips to last-minute transients. In a convenient location on Naples Bay at red daybeacon "40" is the full-service Naples Boat Club Marina with transient slips, a fuel dock (both gas and diesel) and repairs. Marine Max Naples Yacht Center to the north also offers repairs.

At the south end of the island in the Gordon River (before the 5th Ave. Bridge) is Naples Sailing & Yacht Club, which offers reciprocity to members of other recognized yacht clubs. Note that they report 4-foot approach and dockside depths. The Marina at Naples Bay Resort, on the east side of the river, has slips and gas; call ahead. On the north side of the 5th Ave. Bridge is Walker's Hideaway Marina of Naples. Call ahead for slip availability, approach depths and bridge clearance.

**Anchorage:** Anchorage areas abound, but you will need to be careful where you go off the marked channel, as it becomes very shallow. After entering Gordon Pass, turn north between red daybeacons "10" and "12." A charted bar with 4-foot depths crosses the entrance. Enter the first canal to starboard and anchor in a well-protected cove in 9-foot depths among beautiful homes. There is no place to land a dinghy.

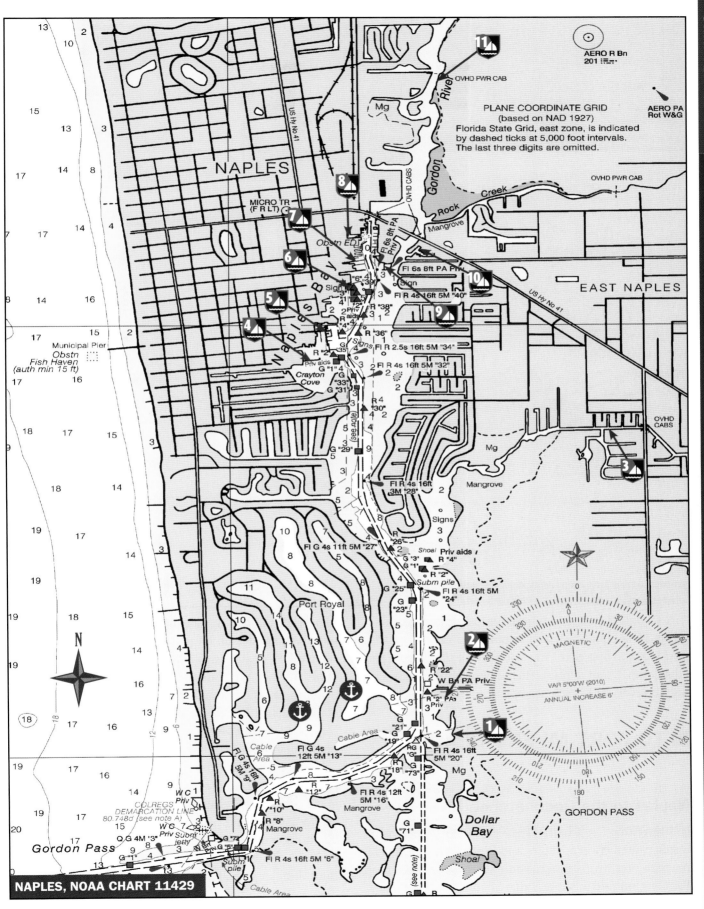

NAPLES, NOAA CHART 11429

# Cocohatchee River, FL

| WIGGINS PASS | | | Dockage | | | | Supplies | | Services | | | | |
|---|---|---|---|---|---|---|---|---|---|---|---|---|---|
| | | | VHF Channel Monitored | Transient Berths / Total Berths | Approach / Dockside Depth (reported) | Floating Docks | Gas / Diesel | Groceries, Ice, Marine Supplies, Snacks | Repairs: Hull, Engine, Propeller | Lift (tonnage), Crane, Rail | Laundry, Pool, Showers, Courtesy Car | Min/Max Amps | Pump-Out Station | Nearby: Grocery Store, Motel, Restaurant |
| 1. Pelican Isle Yacht Club 🖥 | 239-566-1606 | 55 | 16/68 | 3/190 | 5/4.5 | F | GD | IS | – | – | 30/50 | LPS | P | GMR |
| 2. Cocohatchee River Park Marina | 239-514-3752 | 30 | 16 | 15/39 | 6/6 | – | GD | IMS | – | – | 30/50 | – | P | MR |

🖥 Internet Access  📶 Wireless Internet Access  **WG** Waterway Guide Cruising Club Partner  *(Information in the table is provided by the facilities.)*
See WaterwayGuide.com for current rates, fuel prices, web site addresses, and other up-to-the-minute information.

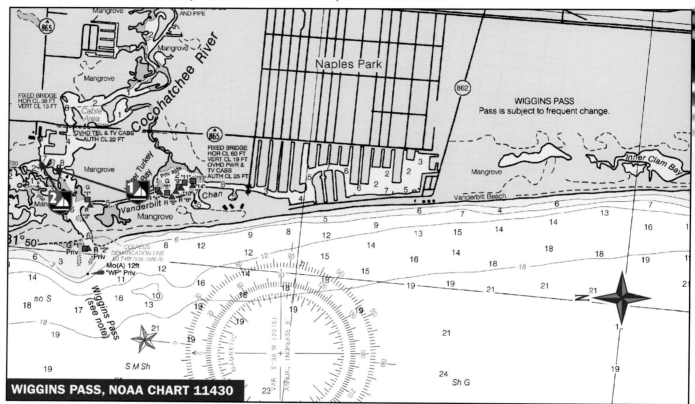

WIGGINS PASS, NOAA CHART 11430

A second option is to proceed into Gordon Pass to green daybeacon "21," turn to port, and then again to port into the first cove. You will be well protected from all sides in 7-foot depths. There is no shore access here but you may find beach access just east of red "22."

## ■ TO FORT MYERS BEACH

### Naples to the Cocohatchee River

**NAVIGATION:** Use Charts 11427 and 11430. There is no inside route between Naples and Fort Myers Beach, so to reach Fort Myers Beach, you must either exit Gordon Pass or continue offshore if that is how you came from

Marco Island. Plan to stay about 2 nm off the beach. In good weather, which locals say is almost always the case, the Gulf of Mexico is calm and easy to transit. In winter months, when the winds are often out of the northwest or north, it can get rough. If the winds are northwest at more than 12 knots, you may want to wait it out in Naples. Pick your weather correctly, and it should be no problem.

If you are hugging the coastline about 1 nm offshore, you should note where the shoal projects out on the north side of Big Carlos Pass. If you are trying to reach Estero Bay and Fort Myers Beach, you can enter here if you know the present location of the channel or can find a lead-in boat to follow. Although charts indicate controlling depths of 4 to 6 feet, the channel reportedly carries about 8 feet of water. Although constantly shifting, it reportedly follows the contour of Lovers Key on approach from the south. It is best to call ahead to nearby Estero Bay Boat Tours (VHF Channel 79) for an update on directions and controlling depths.

Daybeacons lead from Wiggins Pass for a distance of just under one-half mile into the Cocohatchee River. Wiggins Pass admits vessels drawing 4 feet or less.

⚠️ Shoaling has been reported in Wiggins Pass between Safe Water Light "WP" and Wiggins Pass daybeacon "12." Mariners are advised to exercise extreme caution while transiting the area.

**Dockage:** Once through Wiggins Pass, controlling channel depths to the marina are 4 to 5 feet. Pelican Isle Yacht Club, located just inside Wiggins Pass, may have transient dockage and sells fuel. Directly across from Pelican Isle is Cocohatchee River Park Marina, which has slips (for boats 30 feet or smaller) and offers fuel.

**Anchorage:** About 5.7 miles north of Gordon Pass, narrow Doctors Pass has, at times, served as a harbor of refuge. The area is marked and frequently dredged. Favor the center of Doctors Pass. Once inside, Moorings Bay has 6 feet of water with good holding and all around protection. There are no services for transients.

## Big Carlos Pass (Inside Route)

**NAVIGATION:** Use Chart 11427. Once you are past Big Carlos Pass (dredged in May 2017), the inside route north to Fort Myers Beach is well marked from Big Carlos Pass along the northeast side of Estero Island to Matanzas Pass and the north side of Fort Myers Beach.

Once you pass under the **Big Carlos Pass Bascule Bridge** (23-foot closed vertical clearance, closed from 7:00 p.m. to 8:00 a.m. daily), daybeacons guide your passage either north or south through the natural and historic beauty of Estero Bay. From there, it is a matter of carefully watching the many markers blazing the trail to Matanzas Pass and the facilities along the northern shore of Fort Myers Beach. It is very shallow in spots and a 5- to 5.5-foot draft vessel might have problems. Traveling at high tide would be wise.

**Dockage:** After passing Big Carlos Pass, the first marina you encounter will be Waterside at Bay Beach Marina, which is private. Fish Tale Marina is located a little farther up Estero Island in a channel behind Coon Key with slips and gas. (Call ahead.)

Approximately halfway along Estero Island you will find Snook Bight Yacht Club & Marina. Away from the hustle and bustle of the harbor area, Snook Bight offers

# Fort Myers Beach, FL

| BIG CARLOS PASS | | Largest Vessel Accommodated | VHF Channel Monitored | Transient Berths / Total Berths | Approach / Dockside Depth (reported) | Floating Docks | Groceries, Ice, Marine Supplies, Snacks | Gas / Diesel | Repairs: Hull, Engine, Propeller | Lift (tonnage), Crane, Rail | Min/Max Amps | Laundry, Pool, Showers, Courtesy Car | Pump-Out Station | Nearby: Grocery Store, Motel, Restaurant |
|---|---|---|---|---|---|---|---|---|---|---|---|---|---|---|
| | | **Dockage** | | | | | **Supplies** | | **Services** | | | | | |
| 1. Waterside at Bay Beach Marina – PRIVATE [WiFi] | 239-765-6400 | 60 | – | 0/42 | 10/8 | F | – | – | – | – | 50/50 | PS | P | GMR |
| 2. Fish Tale Marina [WiFi] | 239-463-3600 | 80 | 77 | call/100 | 4/8 | F | G | IMS | HEP | L37 | 30/50 | LS | P | GMR |
| 3. Snook Bight Yacht Club & Marina ☐ [WiFi] | **239-765-4371** | **70** | **16/72** | **21/74** | **6.5/6.5** | **F** | **GD** | **GIMS** | **HEP** | **L30** | **30/50** | **LPS** | **P** | **GR** |
| **ESTERO ISLAND** | | | | | | | | | | | | | | |
| 4. Pink Shell Beach Resort and Marina ☐ [WiFi] | **239-463-8620** | 120 | 16/12 | 30/41 | 15/8.5 | F | – | IMS | HEP | – | 30/100 | LPS | P | MR |
| 5. Moss Marina ☐ [WiFi] | 239-765-6677 | 180 | 16/14 | 35/40 | – | F | GD | IMS | E | L | 30/50 | LS | P | GR |
| 6. Matanzas Inn Bayside Resort and Marina ☐ [WiFi] | **239-463-9258** | 60 | 16 | 16/16 | 12/8 | – | – | – | – | – | 30/50 | LPS | P | GMR |
| 7. Fort Myers Beach City Mooring Field | **239-463-9258** | 70 MOORING BALLS MANAGED BY MATANZAS INN RESORT & MARINA | | | | | | | | | | | | GMR |
| 8. Gulf Star Marina ☐ | 239-463-9552 | 55 | 16/07 | 20/20 | 17/8 | – | G | IM | H | L9 | 30/50 | LPS | P | GMR |
| 9. Olsen Marine Service Inc. | 239-463-6750 | 55 | 16 | – | 6/6 | – | – | M | HEP | L37,C | 50/50 | S | – | GMR |
| 10. Gulf Marine Ways & Supply | 239-463-6166 | 130 | – | call/2 | 10/10 | – | – | IMS | HEP | L150,C | 50/50 | – | – | GMR |
| 11. Ballard Oil Company [WiFi] | 239-463-7677 | – | – | FUEL DOCK | – | – | D | – | – | – | – | – | – | – |
| 12. Salty Sam's Marina ☐ [WiFi] | 239-463-7333 | 225 | 16/17 | 50/130 | 14/12 | F | GD | IMS | HEP | L13 | 30/100 | LS | P | GMR |

☐ Internet Access  [WiFi] Wireless Internet Access  [WG] Waterway Guide Cruising Club Partner  *(Information in the table is provided by the facilities.)*
See WaterwayGuide.com for current rates, fuel prices, web site addresses, and other up-to-the-minute information.

everything a boater could ask for in a marina, including an on-site service center, plenty of indoor, covered storage, waterfront dining (The Bayfront Bistro with daily happy hours) and a well-stocked ship store. They also offer boats, kayaks and paddleboards for rent so you can explore the waters of Estero Bay up close. A Publix supermarket is right next door.

## San Carlos Bay (Outside Route)

**NAVIGATION:** Use Chart 11427. Controlling depths in the marked channel from New Pass to Big Carlos Pass are reported to be 4 feet mean low water with a 2.5-foot tidal range. New Pass is unmarked and impassable to the Gulf of Mexico. Shoal markers warn of 2-foot mean low water depths. Keep a close watch for the numerous traps set for Atlantic blue crabs.

From Big Carlos Pass, chart a course for the Morse (A) 16-foot-high marker "SC." From that point, you should be able to pick out 16-foot flashing red buoy "2" approximately 1 mile to the north-northwest. (Be careful. Shoals move around here a bit.) From that point, you should be able to pick out the well-marked entrance channel leading off from San Carlos Bay into Matanzas Pass, making a 90-degree turn to starboard behind the northwestern hook of Estero Island.

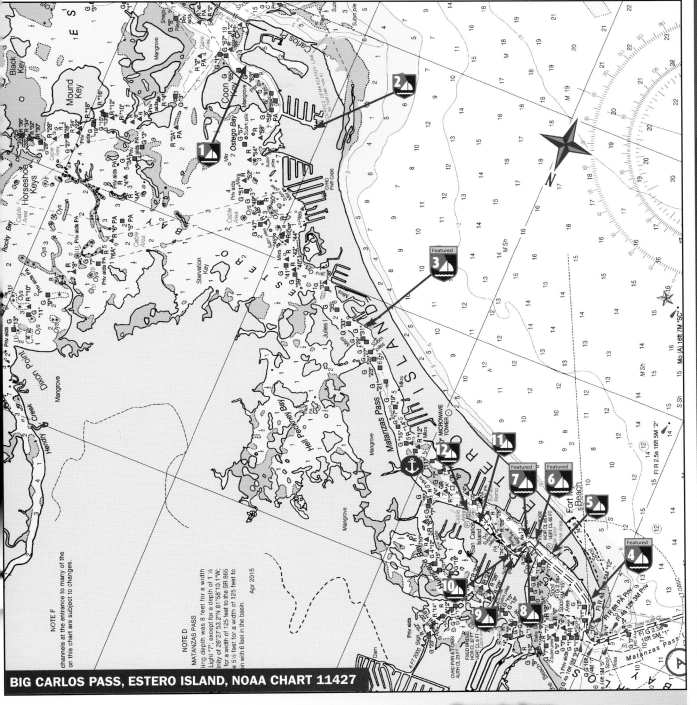

**BIG CARLOS PASS, ESTERO ISLAND, NOAA CHART 11427**

NOTE F
channels at the entrance to many of the
on this chart are subject to changes.

NOTE D
MATANZAS PASS
ling depth was 8 feet for a width
Light "7"; except for a depth of 1 ½
inity of 26°27′53.2″N 81°58′10.1″W;
for a width of 125 feet to the SR 865
e 5 ½ feet for a width of 125 feet to
sin with 6 feet in the basin.
Apr 2015

**MATANZAS INN BAYSIDE RESORT AND MARINA**

**FORT MYERS BEACH CITY MOORING FIELD**

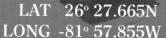

Currents are sometimes swift, depending on the tide, and an endless stream of fishing boats of all sizes utilize the channel that runs between Estero Island and San Carlos Island. About 2 miles after you enter the channel you will pass under the **Fort Myers Beach (Matanzas Pass) Bridge** (65-foot fixed vertical clearance).

**Dockage/Moorings:** Heading south after entering Matanzas Pass, the first marina you will find is the full-service Pink Shell Beach Resort and Marina, which is set on 12 lush acres. The marina can accommodate vessels up to 120 feet on floating docks. Guests at the marina are welcome to the resort's numerous amenities, including the pool and beach club, a fitness center and water sport rentals. (Be sure to ask about their grocery service.) As always, call in advance for reservations.

Moss Marina's complex of white buildings is highly visible to starboard, adjacent to daybeacon "17." Transient berths are available, but make advance reservations, particularly during the winter months. They also have multiple fueling stations.

Soon after you pass under the Fort Myers Beach Bridge on the south shore is Matanzas Inn Bayside Resort and Marina with 70 mooring balls for boats up to 60 feet in length. They also have slips for rent. They provide restrooms/showers and a dinghy dock for those who rent a mooring, and a pump-out boat is available.

The on-site restaurant, Matanzas on the Bay, serves up seafood and pizza, delicious drinks and nightly entertainment.

On the north shore is Gulf Star Marina, which accepts transients and has a fuel dock (gas only). Olsen Marine Service offers some repairs and may have slips; call ahead. Gulf Marine Ways & Supply is close by with a 150-ton lift, and a little farther up the channel is Ballard Oil Company, a fuel dock with diesel fuel at great prices. At the end of the harbor (beyond the shrimp fleet) is Salty Sam's Marina, where you can get gas and diesel fuel or tie up for a bite at the Parrot Key Caribbean Grill and Bootleggers Waterfront Grill. Overnight slips are also available.

**Anchorage:** You can drop the hook in 5 to 7 feet east of red daybeacon "4" in Matanzas Pass, on the north side of the unnamed island. Boats also anchor east of the bridge in the south channel (not in the northern Matanzas Pass channel).

## Cruising Options

Fort Myers Beach is a pivotal location for vessels making passages farther north up the west coast of Florida or south along the coast to Flamingo and the Keys. Or you can pick up the Okeechobee Waterway and cruise all the way to its east coast terminus at the ICW in Stuart. This is a genuine nautical crossroads.

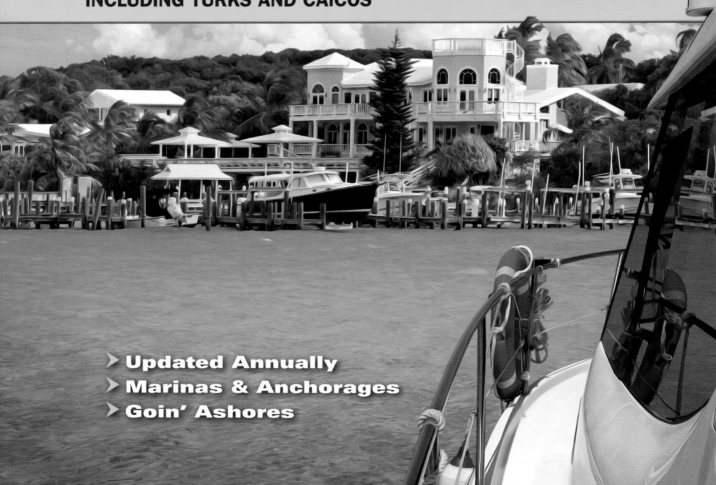

NEXT STOP

# WATERWAY® GUIDE
## THE CRUISING AUTHORITY

# The Bahamas 2018
## INCLUDING TURKS AND CAICOS

> Updated Annually
> Marinas & Anchorages
> Goin' Ashores

Visit waterwayguide.com

# San Carlos Bay to Sarasota

 GIWW Mile 0–Mile 87

(VHF) FL: Channel 09

**CHARTS** 11425, 11426, 11427

With its popular coastal barrier islands–Sanibel, Captiva, North Captiva, Cayo Costa, Gasparilla Island, Little Gasparilla Island, Don Pedro Key and Manasota Key–fertile fishing grounds and one of Florida's great bodies of water (Charlotte Harbor), the 60-mile-long stretch from San Carlos Bay to Sarasota Bay and Sarasota itself is a mariner's paradise. The almost-tropical climate is kept comfortable by Gulf breezes much of the year, although some summer days can get very hot.

Traveling north from Fort Myers Beach, a skipper can choose between two passages from San Carlos Bay: outside up the Gulf of Mexico or inside along the Gulf Intracoastal Waterway (GIWW). Unless you must hurry to meet a deadline and are in a powerboat that can hit high double numbers, we suggest you take the protected and infinitely more interesting GIWW route inside.

The U.S. Army Corps of Engineers' project depth for the length of the 150-mile-long GIWW is purported to be 9 feet, but do not count on having that much water. Keep an eye on the depths here, especially in winter when northerly winds push the water out of bays and channels. Even under optimum conditions, in certain spots (noted in the text) shoaling is so chronic that boats must slow down and gently ease their way through.

Going north on the GIWW, leave red daybeacons to starboard, green to port. As with the Atlantic ICW, GIWW channel markers are green or red with small yellow triangles on red markers and squares on green markers (and an occasional yellow stripe), in addition to the numbers and/or letters. Another way to remember this is that the red marks delineate the mainland side of the GIWW channel.

A number of bridges cross the GIWW. Some open on signal; others are restricted. See the Skipper's Handbook section in the front of

this guide for bridge schedules, but to stay on the safe side, verify information locally or with the Coast Guard. Remember that Florida bridge tenders are required to monitor VHF Channel 09.

## ■ TO CHARLOTTE HARBOR: INSIDE (GIWW) ROUTE

### Fort Myers Beach to Punta Rassa

**NAVIGATION:** Use Chart 11426 or 11427. If you come out of the Okeechobee Waterway here, you will transition to the GIWW at Shell Point. There is not so much as a bump to delineate the transition. To reach the GIWW from Fort Myers Beach, head west from Matanzas Pass. If your vessel's overhead clearance requirements are no more than 26 feet above the water, you can use the fixed span "C" of the **Sanibel Causeway Blvd. "C" Span**; if not, you will have to go through span "A" (70-foot fixed vertical clearance) on the Punta Rassa side of the bay. If you plan on transiting span "C" from Matanzas Pass, set a course of 265 degrees magnetic from flashing green daybeacon "1" when leaving the Matanzas Pass channel to flashing red daybeacon "2" on the Sanibel Island side of the entrance to San Carlos Bay, a distance of about 2.75 nm.

To reach the high span ("A") of the Sanibel Causeway from flashing green daybeacon "1" at Matanzas Pass, steer a course of 282 degrees magnetic to flashing red daybeacon "6," indicating the start of the channel to the Caloosahatchee River and the Okeechobee Waterway. Follow the channel from flashing red daybeacon "6," through the bridge and then to flashing red daybeacon "14," leaving it to starboard. Shortly past that red lighted aid, watch for the green daybeacon "1" to the southwest and flashing green daybeacon "101" to the northeast, which mark the end of the Okeechobee Waterway and the beginning of the GIWW (Mile 0). Turn to port, and carefully follow the well-marked channel southwest until you reach the junction of the GIWW and the main channel coming into San Carlos Bay from the Gulf (via the fixed 26-foot "C" span of the Sanibel Causeway).

Once under the "C" span and about 2.5 nm up the well-marked channel, you will pick out quick flashing green daybeacon "11" of the GIWW channel. Just past flashing red daybeacon "14" (to starboard) off to the northeast, you will spot quick-flashing green daybeacon "101," which marks Mile Zero, the official beginning of the GIWW–heading generally westward before turning northwest–and the official end of the Okeechobee Waterway coming in from the east. At this junction, boats from Florida's east coast, the Keys and the southwest coast all meet. (See the "Okeechobee Waterway" chapter of this guide for coverage of the passage to and from Florida's east coast.)

**Dockage:** Just north of the eastern end of the fixed bridge (span "A") west of Punta Rassa, you may find a berth at Port Sanibel Marina, which also sells gas and diesel. (The nearby Sanibel Harbour Yacht Club is private.)

**Anchorage:** Vessels have been seen anchoring between span "A" and the GIWW in a couple of different places. One is in the deeper water slot between Kitchel Key and Fisherman Key in 7 to 11 feet and the other is just north of Punta Rassa Cove in 8- to 13-foot depths. Both places are fairly exposed but will suffice during settled weather for those who want to make an early start in the morning through the Okeechobee—outside heading south, or heading north on the inside in the GIWW.

## Punta Rassa to Charlotte Harbor

Liberally dotted with small islands and protected from the open Gulf by a string of barrier islands, Pine Island Sound runs about 15 miles to the mouth of Charlotte Harbor at Boca Grande Pass. Many of the small islands in the sound are part of the Pine Island National Wildlife Refuge, closed to all public access to protect the wildlife. Along this stretch, you will see many ospreys tending their large nests.

**NAVIGATION:** Use Chart 11427. Sailors in auxiliary-powered sailboats know the "Miserable Mile" well. Here, the tide sweeps in and out directly across the arrow-straight channel, and strong crosscurrents are likely. Allow for the set, and line up markers fore and aft. The channel is well marked and easy to follow. Be especially careful crossing south of Matlacha Pass (pronounced Mat-la-shay). The channel cuts off to the northwest just past flashing green daybeacon "5" (when headed west). Do not stray too far to the west into 2- to 3-foot depths at mean low water. Around that same green daybeacons "5" and green daybeacon "9," the currents are very strong and the channel, running through shoals, is prone to silting. One nautical mile farther west, near where the channel bends to the northwest south of Pine Island, the problem worsens. Northerly winds tend to build up silt in the area.

The channel runs a jagged course, often at an angle to the swift current, through pools of relatively deep water interspersed with great shallow bays. Exercise caution. Stay to mid-channel, take navigational aids in order, and do not try any shortcuts. In Pine Island Sound, between flashing green daybeacon "23" and red daybeacon "24" at about Mile 8, power lines cross the channel with a charted vertical clearance of 95 feet at the main channel.

Matlacha Pass (Chart 11426) carries a marked, but shallow, crooked channel north between Pine Island and the mainland to Charlotte Harbor. Controlling depth is about 3 feet, and a 32-foot-high power cable and the **Matlacha Pass Bascule Bridge** (restricted schedule, with a 9-foot closed vertical clearance) cross the pass. This passage is not recommended, but can be safely explored from the northern entrance.

**Anchorage:** At the southern tip of Pine Island sits St. James City, the central point for fishing on the lower sound. Fishing camps and small boat marinas abound here, along with shallow water and numerous private

markers that can be confusing to the stranger. You can anchor south of town by the mangroves in 8 to 9 feet of water and dinghy to shore. There are several waterside "Tiki-type" restaurants if you dinghy up the residential canals, and each one brings its own flavor to the area.

To the north, Chino Island in Pine Island Sound offers protection from easterly and northerly winds with good holding. Leave the GIWW at flashing green daybeacon "23," and you will find 7- to 8-foot depths almost to the shore. You may receive a few wakes from vessels traveling the GIWW and locals who use this area for fishing and a shortcut to nearby canals.

A number of anchorages are located off the Pine Island Sound to both the north and south, where deeper water is indicated, and in the deep pockets of Matlacha Pass to the north. It may be possible to anchor southeast of the bridge. Restaurants are within dinghy range.

## ◼ TO CHARLOTTE HARBOR: OUTSIDE (GULF) ROUTE

**NAVIGATION:** Use Charts 11425, 11426 and 11427. Mariners running the Gulf of Mexico need only to choose their weather and go. The only complications along this route are the shoals and bars that extend out from many areas of the shoreline and form an integral part of virtually every pass and inlet on Florida's West Coast. Be sure you are standing sufficiently offshore to clear them, which may make the trip somewhat longer than cutting up Pine Island Sound. Staying 3 to 4 nm off the coastline should get the job done.

To head north on the outside, head south down the marked channel that goes underneath Sanibel Causeway Bridge. Once far enough south of the bridge, at the San Carlos Bay Morse (A) marker "SC," it is safe to turn west, but keep a sharp eye on your course and track, as there are well-charted shoals to starboard.

Note the shoal area south of Sanibel where depths of 1 to 2 feet are reported. Once clear of the southern shore of Sanibel, lay a course west of the Boca Grande flashing

# San Carlos Bay, FL

| | | Largest Vessel Accommodated | VHF Channel Monitored | Approach / Dockside Depth (reported) | Transient Berths / Total Berths | Groceries, Ice, Marine Supplies, Snacks | Gas / Diesel | Floating Docks | Repairs: Hull, Engine, Propeller | Lift (tonnage), Crane, Rail | Laundry, Pool, Showers, Courtesy Car | Min/Max Amps | Pump-Out Station | Nearby: Grocery Store, Motel, Restaurant |
|---|---|---|---|---|---|---|---|---|---|---|---|---|---|---|
| **PUNTA RASSA** | | | | **Dockage** | | | | | **Supplies** | | **Services** | | | |
| 1. Sanibel Harbour Yacht Club–PRIVATE | 239-333-4200 | 50 | 16 | 0/4 | – | – | G | S | – | – | – | S | – | MR |
| 2. Port Sanibel Marina WiFi | 239-437-1660 | 65 | 16/68 | 10/104 | 5/5 | – | GD | IMS | – | L35 | 30/50 | LS | P | R |
| **SANIBEL ISLAND** | | | | | | | | | | | | | | |
| 3. Sanibel Marina 🖥 WiFi | **239-472-2723** | 120 | 16 | 15/65 | 6/6 | – | GD | IMS | EP | – | 50/50 | LS | P | R |

🖥 Internet Access  WiFi Wireless Internet Access  WG Waterway Guide Cruising Club Partner  *(Information in the table is provided by the facilities.)*
See WaterwayGuide.com for current rates, fuel prices, web site addresses, and other up-to-the-minute information.

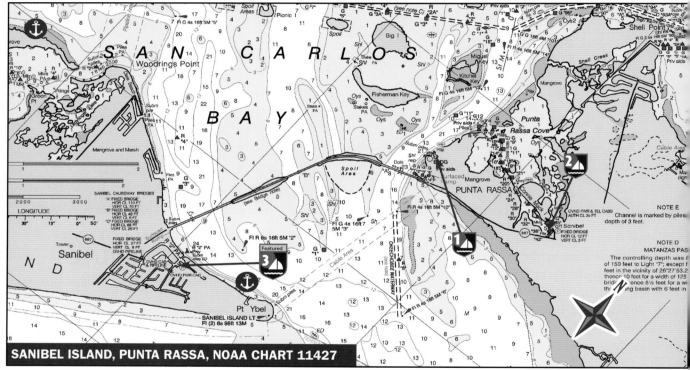

**SANIBEL ISLAND, PUNTA RASSA, NOAA CHART 11427**

red bell buoy "2" (roughly 4.5 nm outside the entrance to Charlotte Harbor; GPS coordinates: N 026° 39.846'/W 082° 19.565'). You might find it convenient at this point to enter a target waypoint just offshore of your target destination. No matter where you choose to stop, you can always keep that waypoint to check distance to your final destination. Just make sure that waypoint keeps you far enough offshore to avoid shoal areas.

If you definitely plan to visit Sarasota, you may want to move inside at some point, and Venice is a good choice if you are heading north due to a clean, well-marked inlet. Using the two passes closest to Sarasota (New Pass and Big Sarasota Pass) to enter Sarasota Bay definitely requires local knowledge.

A line of barrier islands, including Sanibel, Captiva, North Captiva and Cayo Costa, separate Pine Island Sound from the Gulf of Mexico. Together, the islands form a shallow crescent lying at an angle to the currents. That accident of shape and location causes what are said to be the world's most prolific shell deposits and the resultant "Sanibel stoop" of the island's visitors. More than 300 varieties of shells have been found on these beaches. A Sanibel Island law prohibits collectors from taking live shells, living starfish and sand dollars. The best shelling is at low tide after a storm, when winds and waves have washed a new supply up on the beaches. Sanibel Island can have as many as four tides a day. In March, the annual Shell Show attracts collectors from all over the world.

# Sanibel Marina

## Gramma Dot's Ireland Yacht Sales
### "Dedicated to Yachting Excellence"

Facilities for transient mariners on Sanibel and Captiva Islands range from rather simple overnight stops, to full-service marinas and resorts. Be careful making your approach, however. The sandy bottom is always shifting. You are best advised to enter these basins at half-tide or better and to call ahead for the latest local information.

## Sanibel Island

The 6,354-acre J.N. "Ding" Darling National Wildlife Refuge takes up much of 12-mile-long Sanibel Island, mainly along the northern (Pine Island Sound) side. The refuge also serves as headquarters for several small wildlife refuges on nearby islands. During the nesting season, mariners are asked not to land on these rookery islands. If pelicans are frightened off their nests by human intruders, they leave their eggs exposed to fish crows. The refuge offers nature walks, canoe trips, a wildlife drive and an interpretive center. Even the most casual visitor here will inevitably see numerous Florida alligators, anhinga ("snakebirds"), roseate spoonbills, snowy egrets, wood storks, turkey vultures and great blue herons. Pink flamingos are seen quite often as well. The park is open daily and hours are 10:00 a.m. to 4:00 p.m. For more information, call 239-472-1100.

Sanibel Island has miles of bicycle paths (rental bikes are readily available from numerous sources) for easy access to all parts of the island. Heading southeast from the marina, you will come to the historic Sanibel Lighthouse at Point Ybel (circa 1884), the Lighthouse Beach Park and a fishing pier. Heading northwest from the marina, the tree-lined main thoroughfare, Periwinkle Way, takes you to the Sanibel Historical Village and Museum (239-472-4648), which showcases the island's history with pioneer-vintage island residents and 1920s versions of a general store, post office and tearoom. The Bailey-Matthews Shell Museum (239-395-2233) houses shells from around the world, as well as special Florida exhibits.

The only public landing on the island, other than dropping the hook and landing by dinghy, is at Sanibel Marina. If you want to explore the island by land, you will need to obtain permission to tie up your dinghy at the marina.

**NAVIGATION:** Use Chart 11427. Plot a course for flashing red daybeacon "2" south of span "C" of the Sanibel Causeway and about .5 nm due east of the coast of Sanibel. A little less than 1 nm to the northwest-by-west, you will see red daybeacon "2" marking the

entrance to the channel to Sanibel Marina. Enter the channel, take a sharp turn to port, then to starboard, avoid the obvious shoal to port and you will arrive at Sanibel Marina's fuel dock.

**Dockage:** A snug harbor is available at the full-service Sanibel Marina, the only marina on the island. The marina monitors VHF Channel 16 and has transient slips for vessels up to 120 feet in an unhurried, palm-fringed setting. They have all the usual amenities, plus laundry, fuel (gas and diesel) and fishing tackle. There is a ship store on site with a large inventory of boat necessities and clothing. The award-winning Gramma Dot's Seaside Saloon (239-472-2723) is on site at Sanibel Marina. They serve seafood, chowder, gourmet burgers, specialty salads and famous desserts seven days a week at lunch and dinner.

West of the marina, and within walking distance, is Huxter's Market & Deli (239-472-2151), a complete deli with some fruits and vegetables, as well as an excellent beer, liquor and wine selection. Depending on direction, it is .5 miles to either one of the world's most famous shelling beaches or two supermarkets. Thanks to a reverse osmosis water-treatment system, Sanibel Island has some of the best water in the area.

**Anchorage:** J.N. "Ding" Darling National Wildlife Refuge offers an excellent anchorage possibility during settled weather in the cove due south of flashing red daybeacon "16" (situated south of York Island). Holding is excellent in sand and mud close to Sanibel Island's mangrove shoreline in 5 to 6 feet of water. It's a very scenic anchorage and a great spot to explore.

You can anchor with good protection in San Carlos Bay. When you enter from the Gulf of Mexico, proceed to flashing red "6" northeast of Port Ybel and turn toward the fixed bridge to port (span "C") on the Sanibel Island side of the Punta Rassa-Sanibel Causeway. Good holding is also available past the fishing pier on Sanibel Island, although the tidal current may call for a Bahamian moor.

## Captiva Island

**NAVIGATION:** Use Chart 11427. Just to the north of Sanibel is Captiva Island, about 6 miles long and separated from Sanibel Island by Blind Pass, which is crossed by a 7-foot fixed vertical clearance bridge. Heading north up Pine Island Sound at red daybeacon "38," a course of about 215 degrees magnetic brings you back through shoal water to the little village of Captiva, where transients will find marinas and amenities.

'TWEEN WATERS INN & MARINA

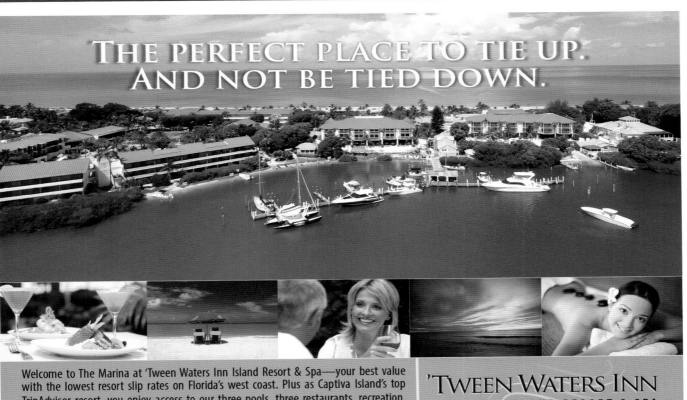

# Pine Island Sound, FL

| | | Dockage | | | | | | Supplies | | Services | | | | | |
|---|---|---|---|---|---|---|---|---|---|---|---|---|---|---|---|
| | Phone | Largest Vessel Accommodated | VHF Channel Monitored | Transient Berths / Total Berths | Approach / Dockside Depth (reported) | Floating Docks | Gas / Diesel | Groceries, Ice, Marine Supplies, Snacks | Repairs: Hull, Engine, Propeller | Lift (tonnage), Crane, Rail | Min/Max Amps | Laundry, Pool, Showers, Courtesy Car | Pump-Out Station | Nearby: Grocery Store, Motel, Restaurant |
| **CAPTIVA ISLAND** | | | | | | | | | | | | | | |
| 1. 'Tween Waters Inn & Marina 11.0 | 239-472-5161 | 100 | 16/72 | 41/41 | 6/6 | – | GD | GIMS | – | – | 30/50 | LPS | P | GMR |
| 2. Jensen's Twin Palm Cottages and Marina 🖥 📶 12 | 239-472-5800 | 25 | 16/14 | call/20 | 5/5 | – | G | IMS | – | – | – | S | – | GMR |
| 3. McCarthy's Marina | 239-472-5200 | – | 16 | call/19 | 5/5 | – | – | IS | – | – | – | S | – | GMR |
| 4. South Seas Island Resort & Marina 🖥 📶 13.6 | 888-777-3625 | 120 | 16 | – | 6/6 | – | GD | GIMS | – | – | 30/100 | LPS | P | GMR |
| **PINE ISLAND AREA** | | | | | | | | | | | | | | |
| 5. Useppa Island Club 🖥 📶 22 | 239-283-1061 | 110 | 16 | call/50 | 10/10 | – | – | IS | – | – | 30/100 | LPS | – | MR |
| 6. Cabbage Key Inn 📶 21.4 | 239-283-2278 | 85 | 16 | 23/25 | 8/6 | – | – | IS | – | – | 30/50 | LS | – | MR |
| 7. Pineland Marina 🖥 | 239-283-3593 | 38 | 16 | 4/30 | 5/7 | – | GD | IMS | HEP | L | – | – | – | MR |
| 8. Four Winds Marina 🖥 📶 6 NE of 19 | 239-283-0250 | 40 | 16/14 | call/89 | 3.5/4 | F | G | IM | HEP | L5 | 30/50 | PS | – | MR |
| 9. Jug Creek Marina | 239-283-3331 | 30 | 16/12 | 35/35 | /3 | – | GD | IMS | – | L20 | 30/50 | S | – | GMR |

🖥 Internet Access  📶 Wireless Internet Access  **WG** Waterway Guide Cruising Club Partner  *(Information in the table is provided by the facilities.)*
See WaterwayGuide.com for current rates, fuel prices, web site addresses, and other up-to-the-minute information.

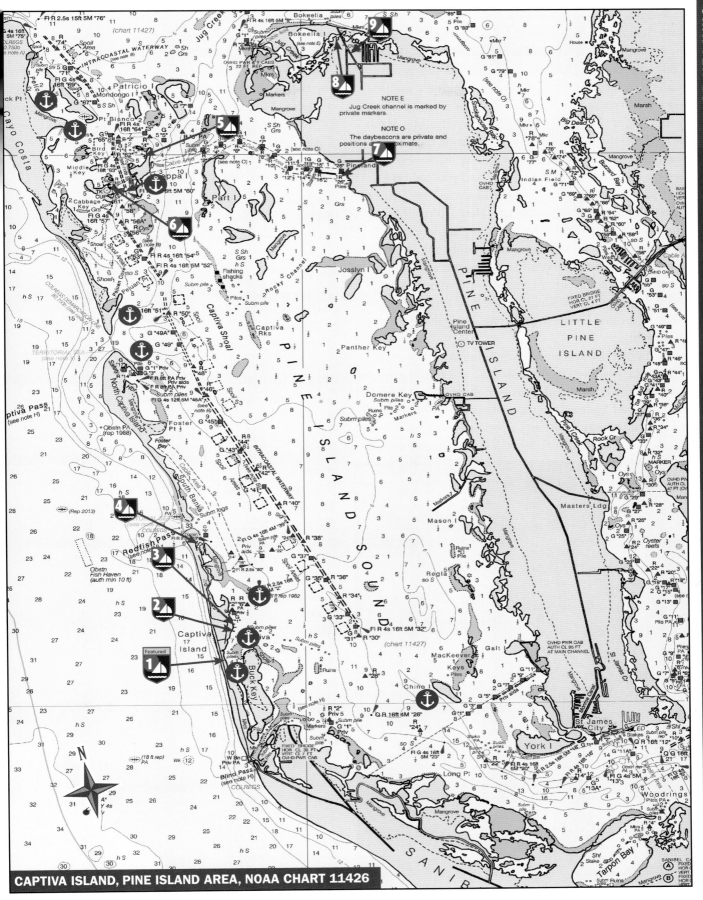

CAPTIVA ISLAND, PINE ISLAND AREA, NOAA CHART 11426

Redfish Pass, recommended only with local knowledge, has gained some depth and width with past hurricane activity. Reasonably well marked, this channel has been recently changed and remarked with mean low water depths of 8 to 13 feet. Boaters routinely use this pass and have reported ample water for cruising boats.

**Dockage:** Honor the red markers (controlling depth is 6.5 feet) to reach 'Tween Waters Marina tucked in behind Buck Key. To reach this marina, turn west at red daybeacon "38" of the GIWW and proceed on a course of 215 degrees magnetic (for about one-quarter of a mile) to locate their channel. Here, you will find the 'Tween Waters Inn. The resort is complete, but unpretentious with beach access, a pool complex, tennis courts and lively pub-style bar (with entertainment on weekends). Farther up the channel is Jensen's Twin Palm Cottages and Marina, followed by McCarthy's Marina, located before Redfish Pass. Call ahead for slip availability.

A channel marked with daybeacons leads from the GIWW between red daybeacon "38" and flashing green daybeacon "39" to South Seas Island Resort & Marina. The channel leading into the marina is well marked. All vessels must announce entry upon arrival at the entrance marker on VHF Channel 16. A call to the South Seas

Island Resort's harbormaster (VHF Channel 16) for local conditions and guidance is highly recommended.

**Anchorage:** One anchorage is still available near 'Tween Waters Marina at green daybeacon "21"; however the marina does not offer dinghy docking privileges to anchored boats. Another anchorage area is located north of 'Tween Waters at green daybeacon "17" off the Green Flash Restaurant (239-472-3337) dock.

## North Captiva Island

**NAVIGATION:** Use Chart 11427. Shifting, shoaling Redfish Pass divides Captiva Island from North Captiva Island. This pass should only be used with current local knowledge. If you choose to exit or enter the Gulf of Mexico here, call the South Seas Island Resort Marina for advice. Remember that currents are strong in this area and shoaling persists.

Although used by fishermen with local knowledge, Captiva Pass–between North Captiva Island and Cayo Costa–is unmarked and subject to change. North Captiva Island is accessible only by boat. There are many private and rental homes here and a few restaurants in the Safety Harbor area. Stilt houses guard the entrance. Boca Grande Pass, a good exit to the Gulf of Mexico, is only 6 miles away to the north and is the preferred pass to use.

A marked channel runs north from Captiva Pass across the GIWW toward Charlotte Harbor, but do not use it as a shortcut unless yours is a very shallow-draft boat. This channel depth shoals in its upper reaches to about 5 feet. In the rest of the channel, depths run 7 to 13 feet with occasional spots for anchoring. The channel leads to Pineland, where there is a small marina with 3-foot controlling depths that services North Captiva Island.

**Anchorage:** Off the southeast tip of Cayo Costa, an anchorage is within a dinghy-pull of the beaches at both North Captiva Island and Cayo Costa in 9 and 10 feet, respectively.

## Useppa Island

**NAVIGATION:** Use Chart 11427. Opposite Cayo Costa, north of the GIWW at about flashing red daybeacon "60," is the private island of Useppa. This lovely, 100-acre island stands 37 feet above the water due to the numerous shell mounds here. The dunes are covered with more than 200 varieties of tropical trees, plants and flowers.

Legend claims the pirate José Gaspar kept a Spanish noblewoman prisoner here, and the island's name is a derivation of her name, Joseffa de Mayorga. A small museum on Useppa Island, open for a few hours a day, presents the history of the island and surrounding area in wonderful detail. It is a must stop for all visitors.

**Dockage:** Accessible only by water, Useppa Island Club has been established as a private club that has preserved the authentic flavor of the past. They do not accept transients; you must be a member or a guest of a member. All vessels must announce entry upon arrival at entrance marker on VHF Channel 16. Barron Collier first built the cottages here in 1912 for his tarpon-fishing friends; his mansion now serves as the clubhouse and restaurant.

**Anchorage:** A large, popular anchorage is available off the GIWW between flashing red daybeacon "60" and red daybeacon "62" near the west side of Useppa Island. This anchorage can sometimes be uncomfortable from wakes of passing boats, especially on weekends, but the scenery is beautiful. It is also somewhat exposed to wind, so caution should be used when anchoring. The advantages of this anchorage far outnumber the disadvantages. Cabbage Key, across the GIWW channel to the west, is a short dinghy ride away and definitely worth the effort.

## Cabbage Key

**NAVIGATION:** Use Chart 11427. Just west of the GIWW channel at Mile 21, Cabbage Key lies in the lee of Cayo Costa. This delightful and unspoiled island (accessible only by boat) offers ample opportunity for observing nature in all its forms. For bird and nature enthusiasts, a bird watching and nature walk should not be missed here. It is best begun at the top of the inn's walk-up water tower for an overview of the island. Easily

A great side trip by dinghy gives you access to the front beach by way of **The Tunnel**. If you are anchored northeast of flashing red "60," proceed south around Cabbage Key to Murdock Bayou. Go almost to the end of Murdock Bayou, and you will see a small, open area in the mangroves on the west side. There is enough room to tie a couple of dinghies to the mangroves. Walk through the tunnel of mangroves to the path that leads to the beach. (Watch for alligators.) It is a great place to picnic and enjoy the white sandy beach. In north winds, depths through The Tunnel and Murdock Bayou may be too shallow even for dinghies.

followed trails traverse Cabbage Key's connected shell mounds, revealing representative varieties of subtropical trees, shrubs, plants and bird life. Nesting ospreys are abundant, as are telltale signs of the Florida gopher tortoise.

**Dockage:** Reached by the privately-marked entry channel just west of green daybeacon "61" is the classic old Florida island retreat, the Cabbage Key Inn. This special inn (with cottages and rooms available) is the former home of the son of Mary Roberts Rinehart, the famous mystery novelist. The marina is tucked into the foot of the 38-foot-high Indian shell mound upon which sits the Cabbage Key Restaurant and Inn.

For years, visiting fishermen, passing to and from local tarpon-fishing hot spots, have taken rest and refreshment in the bar here. The story goes that to guarantee a cold beer on their return, they started the tradition of posting signed dollar bills on the Old House Bar walls. The accumulated currency has piled up dollars deep over every square inch of wall and ceiling space, now adding up to more than $50,000. In addition to the expensive décor, the fresh shrimp, grouper and mahi-mahi are prepared to order. Also, their burgers are unmatched.

## Cayo Costa

**NAVIGATION:** Use Chart 11427. Spanish fishermen from Havana gave 6-mile-long Cayo Costa its name (translated as "Coastal Key"). Located at the north end of Pine Island Sound on the south side of Boca Grande Pass, this almost-uninhabited island (home to a swine of feral pigs) is accessible only by boat.

Both Punta Blanca Island and Cayo Costa are part of the Cayo Costa State Park (941-964-0375). The park headquarters are located on Cayo Costa, just inside Pelican Pass. Here you will find daytime dockage for small boats (25 feet and under) and some overnight dockage (no hookups). The park extends to the Gulf side of the island where there are not only beautiful beaches, but also cabins and camping. Transportation across the island is by foot, tram or rental bike. The beaches on the Gulf side are very popular shelling beaches.

**Anchorage:** At Mile 22.5, at the southern tip of Punta Blanca Island, is a slice of deep water that provides an attractive anchorage. The adventurous skipper can take up to a 6-foot draft vessel completely around the point where there is an exceptionally cozy anchorage. The downside of the equation is that this anchorage has poor ventilation and is best in winter months.

# Charlotte Harbor, FL

| PUNTA GORDA AREA | | Dockage | | | | | Supplies | | Services | | | | | |
|---|---|---|---|---|---|---|---|---|---|---|---|---|---|---|
| | Phone | Largest Vessel Accommodated | VHF Channel Monitored | Transient Berths / Total Berths | Approach / Dockside Depth (reported) | Floating Docks | Gas / Diesel | Groceries, Ice, Marine Supplies, Snacks | Repairs: Hull, Engine, Propeller | Lift (tonnage), Crane, Rail | Min/Max Amps | Laundry, Pool, Showers, Courtesy Car | Pump-Out Station | Nearby: Grocery Store, Motel, Restaurant |
| 1. Burnt Store Marina 💻 WiFi WG | 941-637-0083 | 100 | 16/14 | 30/525 | 7/6 | F | GD | GIMS | E | L8 | 30/100 | LPS | P | GR |
| 2. Safe Cove Boat Storage 💻 WG | 941-697-9900 | 65 | 63 | call/15 | 6/7 | – | GD | M | HEP | L35 | 30/30 | LS | P | – |
| 3. Charlotte Harbor Boat Storage WiFi | 941-828-0216 | 55 | – | – | – | – | – | I | HEP | L30,C | – | LS | – | – |
| 4. Fishermen's Village Marina 💻 WiFi WG | 941-575-3000 | 100 | 16/12 | call/111 | 7/5 | – | GD | IS | – | – | 30/100 | LPS | P | GMR |
| 5. Laishley Park Municipal Marina 💻 WiFi WG | 941-575-0142 | 80 | 16/19 | 20/94 | 7/7 | F | – | IS | – | – | 30/50 | LS | P | MR |
| 6. Punta Gorda Marina | 941-639-2750 | 60 | – | – | 5/5 | – | – | – | HEP | L30, C5 | – | – | – | – |
| 7. Charlotte Harbor Yacht Club WiFi | 941-629-5131 | 60 | 16/68 | 4/18 | 4/6 | – | GD | IM | – | – | 30/50 | S | P | GMR |

💻 Internet Access   WiFi Wireless Internet Access   WG Waterway Guide Cruising Club Partner  *(Information in the table is provided by the facilities.)*
See WaterwayGuide.com for current rates, fuel prices, web site addresses, and other up-to-the-minute information.

At Mile 25, at the northern end of Punta Blanca Island (between Punta Blanca and Cayo Costa), is Pelican Pass and Pelican Bay. Although the Pelican Pass entrance may at first appear a bit dicey, the anchorage beyond is well worth the effort. With caution, a little help from the tide and a reliable depth sounder, boats drawing up to 5 feet can normally get through Pelican Pass into Pelican Bay.

To reach the anchorage from red daybeacon "74," travel southwest toward the tip of the beach on Cayo Costa. Stay to within about 75 feet of the sand beach, and just past the little sign in the water, turn slightly to port (east) and follow the beach up into Pelican Bay. You will find 5 to 6 feet of water in the pass. When inside Pelican Bay, pay attention to your depth sounder as there are several very shallow areas. You can anchor in 7 to 8 feet with plenty of swinging room and really good holding. This is a very popular anchorage so it can get crowded on weekends.

If feeling adventuresome, take your dinghy and look for the unmarked small but deep creek that opens into a small lake of about 200 yards in diameter. The depth in the creek is more than adequate for dinghies. There is a small dock on the lake that was once used for loading supplies on the island. You can land your dinghy there and explore. It is very pretty and worth the effort! This is one of the best anchorages on the west coast of Florida and should not be missed.

## Pine Island

**Dockage:** At the northwestern end of Pine Island is Wilson Cut, which leads to Pineland Marina. Call ahead for approach depths. Before the Boca Grande Pass, on the north end of Pine Island is the small settlement of Bokeelia on Bokeelia Island. Bokeelia Island is home to Four Winds Marina with slips and gas, as well as the smaller 35-slip Jug Creek Marina, which sells all fuels and accepts limited transients. Be sure to call in advance for depth information as this area is very shallow.

# ■ CHARLOTTE HARBOR

About 60 miles southeast of Tampa Bay, Charlotte Harbor is a wide, elbow-shaped bay carrying 9-foot depths to Punta Gorda at the mouth of the Peace River. Stretching 20 miles long and 10 miles wide, Charlotte Harbor offers a lot for the cruising boater.

Charlotte Harbor is formed by the confluence of the Peace and Myakka Rivers. Tidal range averages 2 feet, but winds from the west reportedly can increase water levels as much as 5 feet. The open sweep and relatively uniform depths of water in Charlotte Harbor provide a welcome change from the narrow, shoal-bordered GIWW. The high sandbars that protect the shoreline limit opportunities for gunkholing, but both the Peace and Myakka Rivers compensate for that weakness by offering opportunities for scenic dinghy trips.

It is a good place for daysailing and has variable winds. Yacht clubs in the area are involved year-round in sailboat racing and offer privileges to members of reciprocating clubs. When entering any marina in Charlotte Harbor be sure to stay inside the well-marked channels; the water can be very shallow outside of them.

When you leave Boca Grande for the northward push to Sarasota, or farther to Tampa Bay, you can choose

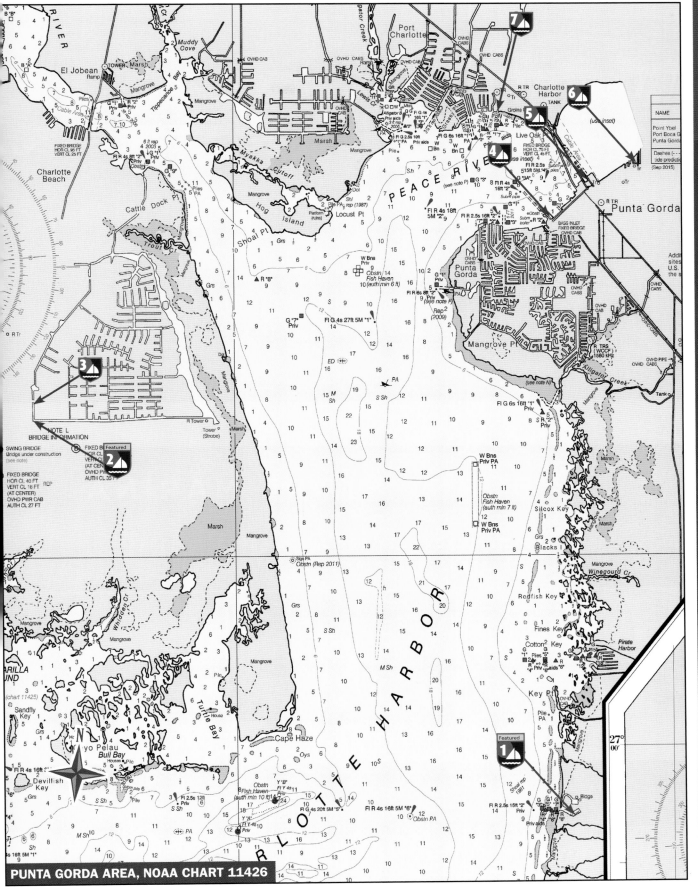

**PUNTA GORDA AREA, NOAA CHART 11426**

.o go outside to run north up the Gulf of Mexico or continue on the GIWW.

**Dockage:** Opposite Boca Grande Channel, and midway up the eastern shore of Charlotte Harbor, the large Burnt Store Marina is a very popular stop. Flashing red daybeacon "6" leads off the approach from Charlotte Harbor and is then followed by flashing red daybeacon "2" and a series of daybeacons into the protected harbor. Amenities include gas and diesel fuel, groceries and Cass Cay Restaurant & Bar (941-347-7148). Taxis are available for the relatively lengthy ride to Punta Gorda for extensive provisioning.

## Side Trip: North on the Myakka River

Myakka State Park, in the upper reaches of the Myakka River, preserves a wilderness reminiscent of the Everglades. This is home to large alligators, feral hogs, eagles, deer, rattlesnakes even the very rare Florida panther.

**NAVIGATION:** Use Chart 11427. Wandering through dense woodland, the Myakka River runs from the northwest from Myakka Lake to Charlotte Harbor. Boats drawing 3 feet or less and armed with local knowledge can travel about 17 miles up the Myakka River. Three nautical miles up the river the **SR 776 Bridge** with 25-foot fixed vertical clearance limits overhead clearance; the railroad bridge just beyond is open and abandoned.

At the mouth of the Myakka River, past green daybeacon "9" on the south shore of the river, is a set of daybeacons that lead to an automated lock and the Santa Cruz Waterway, which has 6.5-foot depths.

**Dockage:** A series of canals (6-mile long) lead to Placida Harbor where there are a few marine facilities, including Safe Cove Inc. and Charlotte Harbor Boat Storage. Safe Cove is primarily a dry storgae facility but may have room for you; Call ahead. They allow do-it-yourself or you can choose from the full range of services they offer.

**Anchorage:** Protected anchorages lie between the bridge and green daybeacon "9" in the river and Tippecanoe Bay. Here you will find 5 to 7 feet of water.

## Punta Gorda, Peace River

**NAVIGATION:** Use Chart 11427. The Peace River enters Charlotte Harbor from the northeast. It is very shallow (7 to 8 feet) and marked for only about 6 miles, but its channel is navigable to the town of Hull, 15 miles upriver. Offering 3-foot depths, this stretch calls for

local knowledge, and the snags and heavy growths of hyacinths in the upper river require caution as well. Two 45-foot fixed vertical clearance bridges (Tamiami Trial Twin Bridges and I-75 Bridge) and a 12-foot fixed vertical clearance bridge cross the Peace River. If you can get under the lower bridge, there is a lot of adventure ahead. You need to be resourceful for this out-of-the-comfort-zone kind of travel, but you will come back with some colorful stories.

At the foot of the Tamiami Trail Twin Bridges on the southern shore of the Peace River is Punta Gorda. This is a charming boating community made up of 60 miles of canals that meander through its neighborhoods and lead to Charlotte Harbor. The city has a historic district with 157 significant historical residential and commercial structures along its brick-lined streets. Its designation as a Florida Main Street Community has resulted in many new or renovated amenities now available to boaters. Along the Punta Gorda coastline of Charlotte Harbor is Harborwalk, a scenic pedestrian- and bicycle-friendly river walk lined with palm trees, brick pavers and park amenities.

**Dockage/Moorings:** Fishermen's Village Marina is located on upper Charlotte Harbor with no bridges or other restrictions to the Gulf of Mexico and is within walking distance of Historic Punta Gorda. This is a very popular spot for transients to spend the winter and spring months. The marina has courtesy docks for day-trippers and a long dinghy dock. A Publix supermarket/pharmacy is located approximately 1.5 miles away.

Laishley Park Municipal Marina has floating concrete slips and a mooring field. Be sure to call in advance for availability. They also have a day-use only dock. The marina is situated in Laishley Park, which hosts many festivals and activities throughout the year, including the nationally broadcast ESPN Redfish Tournament each spring. In the park is the 16,000-square foot Laishley

Crab House restaurant (941-205-5566), which offers an assortment of seafood and steaks.

Farther along is the Punta Gorda Marina, which is strictly a repair/storage facility. (No transient dockage.) At the north end of the Peace River at Port Charlotte is Charlotte Harbor Yacht Club, which recognizes reciprocity from other clubs. Call ahead for availability.

## ■ TO SARASOTA: OUTSIDE (GULF) ROUTE

**NAVIGATION:** Use Chart 11425. From Boca Grande Pass, local knowledge permits use of the shortcut route (known locally as "The Swash Channel"), primarily of value to shoal-draft boats (5-foot draft or less). The channel leads to deep water well inshore of the end of the big-ship route, the main ship channel. To follow The Swash Channel around the tip of Gasparilla Island, you should proceed west in Boca Grande Pass until you reach the end of the dilapidated commercial pier, bearing 340 degrees magnetic. Pass the old concrete pier about 50 to 100 feet out in 8- to 9-foot depths (mean low water), avoiding the long shoal that runs off to the south-southeast. Once clear of the shoal, you will find 10- to 11-foot depths at mean low water.

Note, however, that if you are returning to Charlotte Harbor from the Gulf of Mexico in a brisk northwesterly with an outgoing tide, the longest way around is the shortest way home. Under such conditions, Boca Grande Pass can appear reasonably docile until you are almost next to the piers, then you can be in breaking waves before you know it. (The waves break away from you and are hard to recognize.) It is wise to avoid The Swash Channel in such conditions because there is no "wiggle room" there. Current local knowledge is advisable.

The more prudent, safer approach, particularly if the water is rough, is to enter via the ship channel. The shoals along the ship channel, particularly on the northwest side, need to be monitored carefully as the charted channel runs very close to them. If entering Boca Grande Channel when coming from the north, take care to come all of the way to green buoy "3" and red nun buoy "4" to avoid the shoal entirely. You will be at about the Three Nautical Mile line and can then turn safely toward the northeast. Deeper water lies to the south side of the channel if you need to get out of the way of commercial vessels. Inexperienced skippers have lost their vessels on these shoals, so take heed.

## Gulf Inlets

- **Boca Grande Pass (Inlet):** Well marked, deep and straightforward. If you follow the charts, you shouldn't have any problems.
- **Gasparilla Pass:** Not well marked and plagued with shoaling. Should NOT be attempted by cruising vessels.
- **Stump Pass:** The Coast Guard does not maintain marks in this pass and it should NOT be attempted.
- **Venice Inlet:** Well maintained, well marked and with plenty of depth. Leads to the town of Venice. After passing the jetties, be aware of a "No-Wake Zone," which is strictly enforced.
- **Midnight Pass:** Closed. The popular public beach is approachable by dinghy only. The pass itself shoaled in many years ago.
- **Big Sarasota Pass:** Follow the charted marks. Has reasonably good depths for most cruising boats. Be sure to call for local information. Towing services are really good about giving information, as is the Sarasota Yacht Club. Go to sarasotayachtclub.org on a mobile device and choose "Big Pass." The Yacht Club updates the information for the pass on a regular basis.
- **New Pass:** For the adventurous only; shallow and not recommended for boats with more than 3 or 4 feet of draft. Not marked by the Coast Guard. There is also a bascule bridge (23-foot closed vertical clearance) to contend with at the opening of the pass. Call one of the towing services for local knowledge before attempting this pass.
- **Longboat Pass:** Well marked and has good depths (10 to 15 feet) but has a 17-foot closed vertical clearance bascule bridge (opens on request). A call to a towboat captain for local knowledge is wise.
- **Passage Key Inlet:** Follow the charts closely and stay in deep water. Not marked, so be aware that there could be hazards. Should only be attempted with local knowledge.
- **Southwest Channel:** Well marked, deep and is an easy way to go. This is the inlet into Tampa Bay. It carries a lot of commercial traffic, so stay alert and pay attention. Remember, tonnage rules!

# ■ TO SARASOTA: INSIDE (GIWW) ROUTE

The inside route from Charlotte Harbor to Sarasota Bay is well marked and not too heavily congested with manatee or boating safety areas. The 25-mph speed zone in the GIWW channel (Slow-Speed/Minimum-Wake within a specified distance from the shore) is more the rule than the exception. Pay close attention to posted signs in these slow-speed restriction areas.

## Gasparilla Island (Boca Grande)– GIWW Mile 28 to Mile 34

The waters around Boca Grande Pass are one of the world's great tarpon fishing grounds. Boca Grande, on the south end of Gasparilla Island, located about halfway between Fort Myers and Tampa, makes a good stop. In a bygone era, Boca Grande was a winter resort and fishing retreat for Northern socialites and tycoons. For the most part, the gracious old homes they once occupied have been faithfully maintained, preserving the elegance of the past. Those in the entertainment business seem to favor the Gasparilla Inn for its privacy and good manners as well as the absolutely charming atmosphere. This is a wonderful stop and shouldn't be missed if time permits.

**NAVIGATION:** Use Chart 11425. Use the St. Petersburg Tide Tables. For high tide, subtract 1 hour 12 minutes; for low tide, subtract 1 hour 56 minutes. The Boca Grande Channel, one of the primary inlets from the Gulf, runs between Cayo Costa and Gasparilla Island, forming the entrance to Charlotte Harbor. Easy to navigate, deep, well marked and lighted, it is one of the primary, important passes on the stretch between Naples and Tampa.

To cross Boca Grande Channel from the GIWW inside, coming from the south, leave flashing red daybeacon "76" to starboard off the northeast point of Cayo Costa. Take a bearing of about 350 degrees magnetic to cross the channel and pick up flashing green daybeacon "1" off the eastern shore of Gasparilla Island. The channel carries 10 to 12 feet of water and is well marked.

The landlocked Boca Grande yacht basin (not a business, but a designation on some charts), located about a quarter of the way up Gasparilla Island when you are headed north, offers secure berths, limited anchorage and a full range of amenities for visiting boaters. Sixteen-foot flashing green daybeacon "1" must

# GOIN' ASHORE: BOCA GRANDE, FL

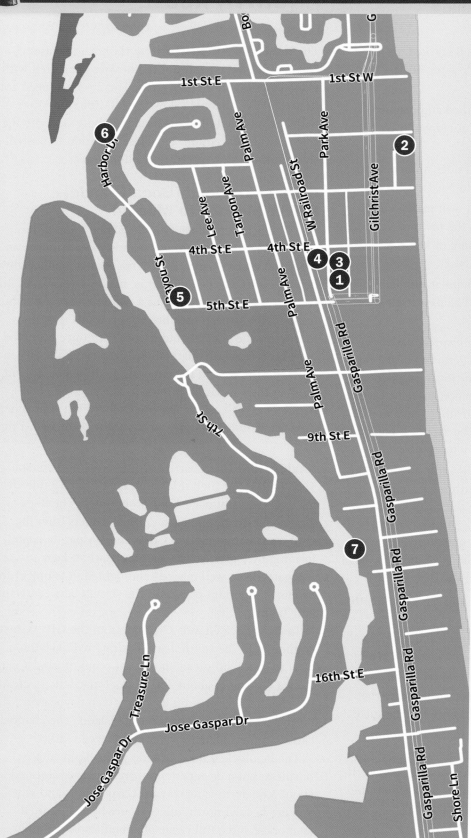

| SERVICES | |
|---|---|
| 1 | Visitor Information |
| **ATTRACTIONS** | |
| 2 | Boca Grande Art Center |
| **SHOPPING** | |
| 3 | Hudson's Grocery |
| 4 | Railway Depot |
| **DINING** | |
| 4 | Loose Caboose Restauarant |
| 5 | Pink Elephant/The Gasparilla Inn & Club |
| **MARINAS** | |
| 5 | The Gasparilla Inn & Club |
| 6 | Boca Grande Marina |
| 7 | The Innlet on the Waterfront |

The restored and upscale old Florida town of Boca Grande is at the south end of Gasparilla Island. It is a charming place, with some of the feel of old Key West in the 1950s and 1960s, before the tourist boom. As a point of interest, "Boca Grande" means "big mouth" in Spanish, referring to the deep Boca Grande Pass, one of Florida's deepest natural inlets.

**Attractions:** One of Gasparilla Island's prime attractions is the community bike path, which runs almost the entire length of this 7-mile island, from the lighthouse at Boca Grande Pass to the Courtyard near Gasparilla Pass at the northern end of the island. Another popular way to tour Boca Grande is by golf cart at Kappy's Market & Deli at 5800 Gasparilla Rd (941-964-2506). Make a reservation for a cart well in advance, as Kappy's

only has a few available. There are more available in the town, but it is a cab ride to get there. The beautiful vistas and accessible beaches along the way make this trek–whether by foot, bike or golf cart–well worth the effort.

The Boca Grande Chamber of Commerce at 471 Park Ave. (941-964-0568) can make sure you hit all the main attractions. The Boca Grande Art Center "BGAC" was founded in 1986 by a small group of talented artists in search of a venue to show their art works to residents and visitors. Located at 236 Banyan St., the BGAC offers exhibits and classes.

Boca Grande's most famous landmark is the Boca Grande Lighthouse at the south end that was built in 1890 to mark the entrance to Charlotte Harbor. It is open to the public 10:00 a.m. to 4:00 p.m. daily from November through April, and Wednesday through Sunday from May through October (880 Belcher Rd., 941-964-0375). The lighthouse is closed in August and all major holidays. And no tour of the island is complete without a walk along Banyan Street, south of the depot.

**Shopping:** Hudson's Grocery (441 Park Ave., 941-964-2621) sells fresh produce, meat, fish, cheese and wine (closed on Sundays). The old railway depot in the center of town has been converted into a mini-mall with a variety of shops. Nearby are two banks, a hardware store, a health center, the post office (on Fourth Street), various boutiques and a bookstore.

**Dining:** The Gasparilla Inn & Club is home to the popular Pink Elephant (491 Bayou Ave., 941-964-4540), where lunch and dinner menus focus on imaginative regional cuisine, seafood and steaks. Other dining options at the Club include the upscale main dining room or the more relaxed Beach Club. A four-course, traditional heritage experience dinner is served in the evening from 6:30 p.m. to 9:00 p.m. in the main dining room, while the Beach Club serves beverages poolside or on their own beach, as well as hosting delightful daily luncheons.

The well-regarded Loose Caboose Restaurant is located in the historic train depot. Lunch and dinner are served seasonally and include menu items such as southern fried green tomato and crab cake combo, fresh grouper sandwich and seafood pot pie (433 4th St. W., 941-964-0440).

www.snagaslip.com
**SNAG-A-SLIP**
EXPLORE. BOOK. BOAT.™

# Gasparilla Sound, FL

| BOCA GRANDE AREA | Largest Vessel Accommodated | VHF Channel Monitored | Transient Berths / Total Berths | Approach / Dockside Depth (reported) | Floating Docks | Gas / Diesel | Groceries, Ice, Marine Supplies, Snacks | Repairs: Hull, Engine, Propeller | Lift (tonnage), Crane, Rail | Min/Max Amps | Laundry, Pool, Showers, Courtesy Car | Pump-Out Station | Nearby: Grocery Store, Motel, Restaurant |
|---|---|---|---|---|---|---|---|---|---|---|---|---|---|
| | | | Dockage | | | Supplies | | Services | | | | | |
| 1. Boca Grande Marina ⌨ WiFi 28.5 — 941-964-2100 | 150 | 16/14 | 15/20 | – | – | GD | GIMS | – | – | 30/50 | LS | P | GMR |
| 2. The Gasparilla Inn & Club 29.5 — 941-964-4620 | 50 | – | call/24 | 6/4.5 | F | GD | IM | EP | L | 50/50 | S | – | GMR |
| 3. The Innlet On The Waterfront WiFi 29.5 — 941-964-4600 | 35 | – | call/23 | 6/5 | – | – | IS | – | – | 30/30 | PS | – | GR |
| 4. Uncle Henry's Marina WiFi 32.8 — 941-964-0154 | 90 | 16/14 | 40/58 | 6/9 | – | GD | GI | – | – | 30/50 | LS | P | GMR |
| 5. Gasparilla Marina ⌨ WiFi — 941-697-2280 | 100 | 16/14 | 10/225 | 7/6 | F | GD | GIMS | HEP | L70 | 30/100 | LS | P | GR |

⌨ Internet Access  WiFi Wireless Internet Access  WG Waterway Guide Cruising Club Partner  *(Information in the table is provided by the facilities.)*
See WaterwayGuide.com for current rates, fuel prices, web site addresses, and other up-to-the-minute information.

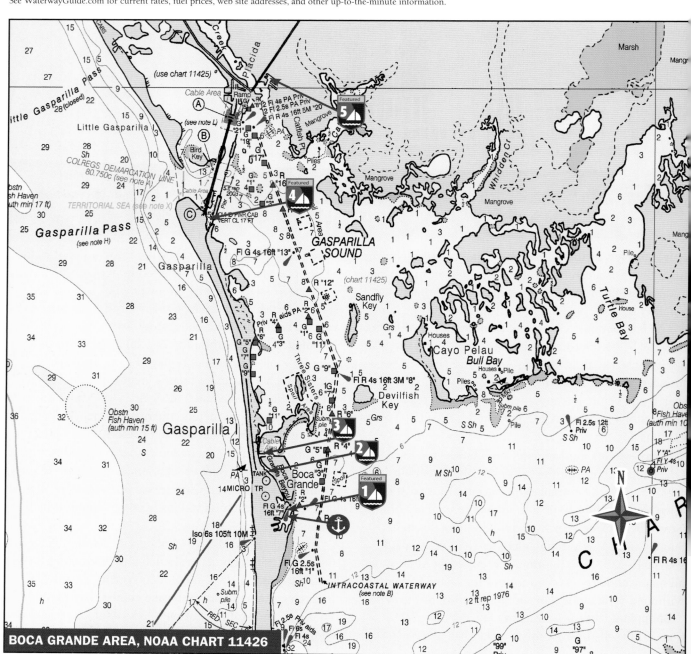

**BOCA GRANDE AREA, NOAA CHART 11426**

Gasparilla Marina

GIWW

Uncle Henry's Marina

Little Gasparilla Island

Gasparilla Island

Gulf of Mexico

be kept to port, then turn west at red daybeacon "2" and pick up the channel markers into the harbor. The channel carries 7 to 9 feet of water. On entering the Boca Grande Bayou, flashing green daybeacon "7" should be given a wide berth because of the encroaching sandbar. Controlling depths are 6 feet mean low water in Boca Grande Bayou.

**Dockage:** Boca Grande Marina, located one-half mile from downtown and inside the yacht basin, has slips with dockage rate options (with or without shore power) and water hookups. Guests also enjoy friendly dockside assistance, a well-stocked ship store and two on-site restaurants and bars. Miller's Dockside Bar & Grill offers casual dining (inside or out), while Eagle Grille offers a more upscale menu with outstanding views. Both restaurants have the same phone number for reservations (941-964-8000).

At both the Gasparilla Inn & Club and The Innlet on the Waterfront, you must make a room reservation to dock. You cannot stay aboard your vessel at night.

**Anchorage:** You can drop the hook in the small basin before the fixed 13-foot fixed vertical clearance bridge. The anchoring in Boca Grande is very tight. You need to drop your anchor, back down on it and then tie off on the mangroves with a stern line to stop your swing.

## Little Gasparilla Island–GIWW Mile 35 to Mile 40

**NAVIGATION:** Use Chart 11425. Those running north on the GIWW will find the bays beginning to narrow somewhat. Shores are closer and more developed, and you should watch the markers carefully.

The channel from Boca Grande and Charlotte Harbor winds sufficiently to maintain interest. Channel depths average 7 to 11 feet at mean low water, although depths are extremely shallow outside the marked channel where the birds are often able to walk in the shallows.

When moving up the GIWW from the south and traversing Gasparilla Sound near the town of Placida at green daybeacon "19," the waterway channel doglegs to port.

Pass through the permanently opened railway bridge just past green daybeacon "21," then leave green daybeacon "1" to port before approaching the **Boca Grande Swing Bridge** at GIWW Mile 34.3. The 22-foot closed vertical clearance swing bridge opens on signal, except 7:00 a.m. to 6:00 p.m., Monday through Friday, when the draw need only open on the hour and half-hour. Saturdays, Sundays, and federal holidays, the draw opens every 15 minutes. Vessels must request an opening. (Note that our cruising editor reported an actual 23-foot vertical clearance.) Be sure to check the Coast Guard *Local Notice to Mariners* or the Waterway Guide Explorer at waterwayguide.com for schedule changes, or use VHF Channel 09 to get in touch with the bridge tender.

When approaching from the Gulf, Gasparilla Pass is not recommended. This is an access used by local fishermen with a lot of local knowledge and very shallow-draft boats. The area around the pass is riddled with charted 2- to 3-foot spots, and the entire north side of the pass has a 1-foot bar on its border. Use Boca Grande Pass instead.

**Dockage:** Arriving at this northern tip of Gasparilla Island, along the GIWW from the south, transients can find dockage at Uncle Henry's Marina. This is a quiet, peaceful marina with all of the usual cruiser amenities plus fuel. They offer daily, monthy and annual rentals. Kappy's Market and Deli (941-964-2506) is nearby for groceries and golf cart rentals. Entrance to the marina is on your port side just after passing the open railroad bridge and before reaching the Boca Grande Swing

# Lemon Bay, FL

| CAPE HAZE TO ENGLEWOOD | | Largest Vessel Accommodated | VHF Channel Monitored | Transient Berths / Total Berths | Approach / Dockside Depth (reported) | Gas / Diesel | Floating Docks | Groceries, Ice, Marine Supplies, Snacks | Repairs: Hull, Engine, Propeller | Lift (tonnage), Crane, Rail | Min/Max Amps | Laundry, Pool, Showers, Courtesy Car | Nearby: Grocery Store, Motel, Restaurant, Pump-Out Station |
|---|---|---|---|---|---|---|---|---|---|---|---|---|---|
| | | | | **Dockage** | | | | **Supplies** | | **Services** | | | |
| 1. Aquamarina Palm Harbour 🖥 📶 38.5 | 941-697-4356 | 65 | 16/14 | 27/90 | 7/6 | – | GD | IM | HEP | L50 | 30/50 | LPS | P | GMR |
| 2. Cape Haze Marina 🖥 WG 39 | 941-698-1110 | 70 | 71 | 4/105 | 6/9 | F | GD | I | HEP | L14 | 30/50 | LPS | – | GR |
| 3. Stump Pass Marina 40.8 | 941-697-4300 | 50 | 66 | call/300 | 4.5/4 | – | GD | GIMS | HEP | L | 30/50 | – | – | GMR |
| 4. Skip's Placida Marina | 941-460-8157 | 25 | 71 | call/80 | 3/4 | – | G | IMS | HEP | L | – | – | – | GMR |
| 5. Harbor at Lemon Bay–PRIVATE | 941-475-7100 | 50 | 08 | 0/15 | 6/6 | F | GD | I | HEP | L20 | 30/50 | S | – | G |
| 6. Royal Palm Marina 🖥 📶 45.8 | 941-475-6882 | 100 | 16/14 | 20/160 | 5/9 | – | GD | GIMS | HEP | L50 | 30/50 | S | P | GMR |

🖥 Internet Access  📶 Wireless Internet Access  WG Waterway Guide Cruising Club Partner  *(Information in the table is provided by the facilities.)*
See WaterwayGuide.com for current rates, fuel prices, web site addresses, and other up-to-the-minute information.

- Transients Welcome
- Quick & Easy Gulf Access
- Heated Pool & Spa, Gas Grills
- Free Laundry Facilities
- New 30/50 Amp Pedestals
- New Surveillance Cameras
- 224 Fully Enclosed Dry Racks
- Inside Hurricane Reservations
- 50-Ton Travelift
- Platinum Mercury Dealership
- ValvTect Gas and Diesel

941-697-4356

Monitoring VHF 16
www.ilovemymarina.com
Dockmaster@ilovemymarina.com

VALVTECT
MERCURY
CLEAN MARINA

## Royal Palm Marina
### Englewood, Florida

Royal Palm Marina
SNOOK'S BAYSIDE BAR & GRILL
Englewood, FL

(941) 475-6882

779 W. Wentworth
Englewood, FL 34223

All your boating needs are covered! Royal Palm Marina offers a Full Service marina with dry and wet boat storage, transient dockage, supplies, bait, and full service from mast to motor. In addition, Royal Palm Marina has new and used boats, trailers, and motors, and can consign your vessel as well.

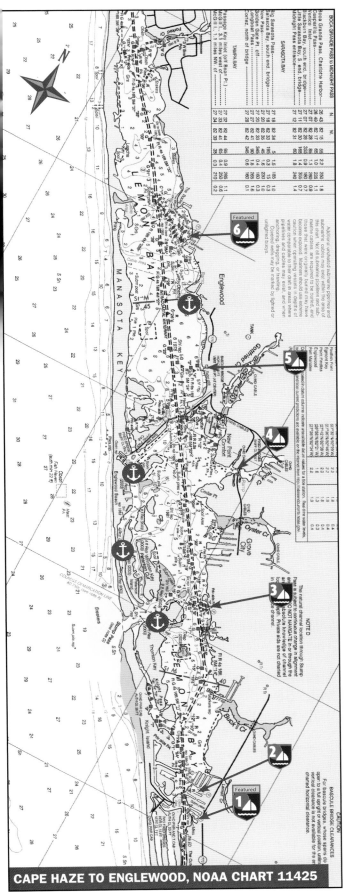

CAPE HAZE TO ENGLEWOOD, NOAA CHART 11425

Bridge. Uncle Henry's Marina leads off to port at green daybeacon "1." The entrance has 6 to 7 feet of depth mean low water and a 1.5- to 2-foot tidal range. With a wind out of the north, depths will be less. Pay attention to the tide tables; deep-draft vessels should call Uncle Henry's for a current report. There has been some silting along both sides of this access passage, so honor all markers and stay as close to center channel as possible.

At flashing red daybeacon "20," a channel leads off to starboard (east) past the mouth of Coral Creek to the 225-slip Gasparilla Marina, the largest marina in the area with deep water slips in an enclosed basin. The marina has a fuel dock, well-stocked ship store and hurricane-rated storage buildings and offers waterfront dining and live entertainment at Waterside Grill (breakfast, lunch and dinner). They also provide service and repairs (70-ton lift).

**Anchorage:** Anchorage is limited around Gasparilla Island and any available space is often filled with local boats on permanent moorings. At Mile 36, Cape Haze offers a nice, quiet anchorage northeast of red daybeacon "30" in 9-foot depths surrounded by private homes. Set your anchor carefully as the bottom is soft mud. This is a pleasant anchorage with more protection from the GIWW than is evident from the chart.

## Lemon Bay–GIWW Mile 40 to Mile 50

**NAVIGATION:** Use Chart 11425. Beyond Placida Harbor, the GIWW turns south and threads through a series of small islands to a narrow 2.25-mile straight stretch called The Cutoff, leading into Lemon Bay. At green daybeacon "7" toward the end of The Cutoff, watch for the car ferry that crosses the waterway.

Once into Lemon Bay, the GIWW swings to the northeast shore (starboard going north) and opens up for a 7.5-mile narrow straightaway through shallow water to the end of the bay. Shortly after green daybeacon "17A," daybeacons will indicate a channel turning off to port, leading to Stump Pass, which opens to the Gulf. Stump Pass is not navigable without very current local knowledge. The marks are all private and not maintained by the Coast Guard. It is very shallow (less than 4 feet) and not recommended. At GIWW Mile 43.5 is the **Tom Adams (Manasota Key) Bascule Bridge** (26-foot closed vertical clearance), which opens on signal.

At Mile 49.9 is the **Manasota Beach Bascule Bridge** (26-foot closed vertical clearance). This bridge also opens on signal. Past Lemon Bay, at Mile 53, the

GIWW becomes a long, high-banked land cut, which runs through a corner of the Venice Municipal Airport. Watch for water-soaked debris in the cut; there is little tidal flushing action to move it out, and it can be a nuisance.

At GIWW Mile 54.9 the **Tamiami Trail (Circus) Twin Bridges** (25-foot vertical clearance) opens on signal. This is followed by the **Venice Ave. Bascule Bridge** at Mile 56.6 (30-foot vertical clearance), which opens on signal, except from 7:00 a.m. and 4:30 p.m., Monday through Friday, when it opens at 10, 30 and 50 minutes past the hour. (Note that it does not open between 4:35 p.m. and 5:35 p.m.).

**Dockage:** Marinas in Lemon Bay tend to be small, unpretentious and friendly but are geared to handle cruising boats. Two marinas are located near Mile 38 before the GIWW enters Lemon Bay at Englewood Beach or at Englewood on the mainland shore. The sheltered Aquamarina Palm Harbour (formerly Palm Island Marina), located on the mainland side near green daybeacon "7," is a boutique, resort style marina with full amenities. The marina features dry stack storage for up to 40 feet and wet slips up to 65 feet. Johnny Leverock's Seafood House (941-698-6900) is in the marina basin.

From Leverock's restaurant, take the water taxi across the GIWW to Rum Bay Restaurant (941-697-0566) on Knight Island and visit the white sandy beach. If your timing is good, you will arrive during one of the barbecues and enjoy the tangy ribs and sunset entertainment. Just to the north is the Cape Haze Marina

with a narrow, dredged channel. The friendly marina has transient dockage in a protected basin just off the ICW.

At green daybeacon "17A," right at the entrance to the Stump Pass Channel and just off the GIWW at Mile 40.8, is the large, full-service Stump Pass Marina with overnight dockage and some boat repair services. A towering rustic lighthouse identifies the marina. Just before the Tom Adams Bascule Bridge is Skip's Placida Marina, which sells gas and may have transient space for smaller shallow-draft boats. North of the bridge at about Mile 43.5 is Harbor at Lemon Bay, which is private.

Royal Palm Marina is tucked away at Mile 45.8 and has "old Florida charm." They offer transient dockage, a well-stocked ship store, rental boats, the on-site Snook's Bayside Bar & Grill with panoramic views and a waterfront Tiki bar. The restaurant is open daily for lunch and dinner (941-475-6882).

**Anchorage:** Anchorages in the area include one at the north end of Thornton Key (Mile 40.9) and one on the south side of Peterson Island (mile 43.3). Both offer good holding and protection.

At Mile 43.5, on the west side of the GIWW, is a large, quiet anchorage with 7- to 10-foot depths mean low water at Englewood Beach. The anchorage is reached by heading southwest between lighted red daybeacon "22" and the Tom Adams Bascule Bridge. Buildings around the anchorage help to protect visiting yachts from buffeting winds. If you continue south, hugging the mangroves, you will be sheltered from all directions. Watch depths closely. You can dinghy to a nearby dock and restaurant. You can tie up your dinghy, but you will be required to have either a drink or a meal. A convenience store and souvenir shop, dive shops, restaurants and the beach are across the street.

To the north is an anchorage with 6 feet and excellent holding at Mile 44.5 east of red daybeacon "26."

## Manasota to Venice–GIWW Mile 50 to Mile 58

Warm Mineral Springs is located 12 miles south of Venice. Known as Florida's Fountain of Youth, its waters are 87 degrees year-round. Call 941-426-1692 for details.

About 15 miles south of Sarasota, Venice is one of Florida's younger towns. Around a central green, and amidst the ambiance of a small Florida town, are shops of all varieties, from clothing stores to drug and food stores, plus numerous restaurants. As you can imagine, there are several good Italian restaurants here as well. You shouldn't leave Venice feeling hungry.

From the marinas, it is a short walk to one of the widest and loveliest beaches on Florida's west coast. Fossilized sharks' teeth–either gray or black and with a triangular shape–are abundant here.

**NAVIGATION:** Use Chart 11425. Entering Venice waters, the first bridge is the **KMI (Hatchett Creek) Bascule Bridge** at GIWW Mile 56.9 has 30-foot closed vertical clearance and restricted openings year-round. It opens on signal, except from 7:00 a.m. to 4:20 p.m., Monday through Friday (except federal holiday), when the draw need only open on the hour and at 20 and 40 minutes past the hour (except between 4:25 p.m. and 5:25 p.m. when it is closed). On weekends and holidays, it opens from 7:30 a.m. to 6:00 p.m. on the hour and at 15, 30 and 45 minutes past the hour. Call ahead on VHF Channel 09.

After leaving the land cut, the GIWW runs through Roberts Bay. Lightly powered vessels should be cautious of the strong currents flowing in and out of Venice Inlet, which cross the route and create some navigational challenges. Shoaling is a recurrent condition, although the Army Corps of Engineers advises that 9-foot depths are maintained in Venice Inlet. The inlet is jettied and easily navigable (9-foot depths), except when strong westerly winds oppose an ebbing tide.

**Dockage:** Fisherman's Wharf Marina at GIWW Mile 57 has been serving the boating community in Venice since 1949. With deep water slips located directly on the GIWW, they offer all amenities and floating docks for monthly and yearly rentals as well as overnight stays. Their Bait Shack offers live and frozen bait, snacks, beer, tackle and ice. There is outstanding waterfront dining here at Dockside Waterfront Grill at Marker 4, which is accessible by land or sea (941-218-6418). Fisherman's Wharf is just a short walk from quaint downtown Venice, which offers shopping, a theater, and a variety of dining options. Marine supplies are available at Mile 55.1 at MarineMax of Venice, with a well-stocked ship store but no transient slips.

At Mile 58, between quick-flashing green daybeacon "13" and red daybeacon "14," a privately marked channel leads west toward the private Venice Yacht Club (with reciprocal privileges for members of the Florida Yacht Council only). Located just opposite the Venice Yacht Club docks is a small city dock at Higel Marine Park (941-316-1172) that five or six boats could tie up

# Venice Inlet, FL

| | | Dockage | | | | | | Supplies | | | Services | | | |
|---|---|---|---|---|---|---|---|---|---|---|---|---|---|---|
| **VENICE AREA** | | Largest Vessel Accommodated | VHF Channel Monitored | Transient Berths / Total Berths | Approach / Dockside Depth (reported) | Floating Docks | Gas / Diesel | Groceries, Ice, Marine Supplies, Snacks | Repairs: Hull, Engine, Propeller | Lift (tonnage), Crane, Rail | Min / Max Amps | Laundry, Pool, Showers, Courtesy Car | Pump-Out Station | Nearby: Grocery Store, Motel, Restaurant |
| 1. MarineMax of Venice 55.1 | 941-485-3388 | 68 | 16/72 | call/60 | 12/9 | – | GD | IMS | HEP | L | 30/50 | LS | P | GMR |
| **2. Fisherman's Wharf Marina of Venice** 🖥 Wi-Fi | **941-486-0500** | **120** | **16/71** | **call/47** | **8/7** | **F** | **GD** | **IMS** | **E** | **–** | **30/100** | **S** | **P** | **GR** |
| 3. Venice Yacht Club 57.5 | 941-483-3625 | 100 | 16 | 3/67 | 10/10 | – | GD | I | – | – | 30/50 | LPS | P | GMR |
| **4. Crow's Nest Marina & Restaurant** 🖥 Wi-Fi 58 | **941-484-7661** | **140** | **16** | **24/34** | **12/12** | **–** | **GD** | **IS** | **–** | **–** | **30/50** | **LS** | **P** | **GMR** |
| **CASEY KEY** | | | | | | | | | | | | | | |
| 5. Gulf Harbor Marina 59 | 941-488-7734 | 45 | 16 | – | 10/6 | – | GD | IMS | HEP | L | 30/30 | – | – | GMR |
| 6. Escape at Casey Key Resort & Marina | 941-882-4654 | 50 | – | call/15 | 10/ | – | – | – | – | – | 30/30 | LPS | – | GMR |

🖥 Internet Access   Wi-Fi Wireless Internet Access   WG Waterway Guide Cruising Club Partner *(Information in the table is provided by the facilities.)*

See WaterwayGuide.com for current rates, fuel prices, web site addresses, and other up-to-the-minute information.

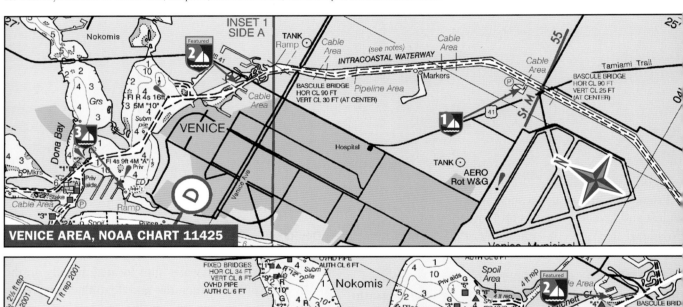

VENICE AREA, NOAA CHART 11425

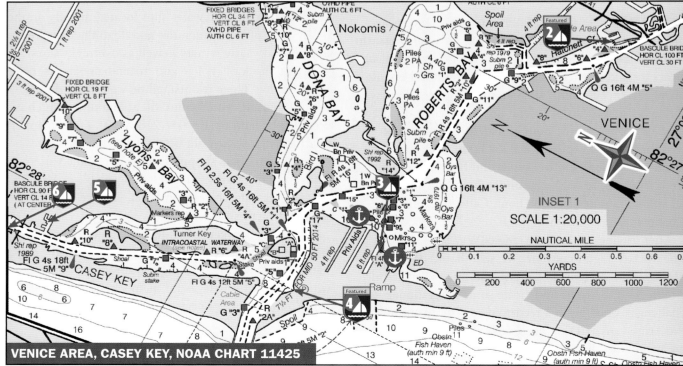

VENICE AREA, CASEY KEY, NOAA CHART 11425

to for the day, but you must vacate the dock between midnight and 6:00 a.m.

Conveniently situated inside the inlet, the Crow's Nest Marina & Restaurant can accommodate deep-draft boats with slips up to 140-feet and offers the usual cruiser amenities plus fuel, a laundry and the very popular on-site Crow's Nest Restaurant and Tavern (941-484-9551). The restaurant serves a full range of moderately priced entrees, with fine foods upstairs and a tavern atmosphere downstairs. Courtesy bikes are available for the 1.5-mile ride to town (well worth the ride).

**Anchorage:** You can drop the hook at red daybeacon "14" with good holding in 6 feet of water with a sand bottom. This is somewhat exposed to the north and east and to GIWW wakes.

## Venice to Casey Key—GIWW Mile 58 to Mile 65

**NAVIGATION:** Use Chart 11425. North of Venice, the GIWW continues its sheltered path behind Casey Key through the **Albee Road (Casey Key) Bascule Bridge** (14-foot closed vertical clearance) at Mile 59.3 to the **Blackburn Point Swing Bridge** (9-foot closed vertical clearance) at Mile 63 in Osprey. Both bridges open on signal. Boaters who require an opening

at the Albee Road Bridge should radio ahead on VHF Channel 09 before entering the channel. Passage through both bridges is on an angle in tight quarters (51-foot horizontal clearance), and little maneuvering room is available on either side of the bridge, so, use caution.

Blackburn Bay, outside the GIWW at Mile 60, is very shallow and has only limited tie-ups. Proceed with caution and definitely do not attempt transiting this area at night. The course crosses Little Sarasota Bay, the approach to Sarasota.

Always a prime source of waterway shoaling, Midnight Pass, at Mile 65, which separates Casey Key from Siesta Key, has been closed for years by the action of nature. Despite continuing attention, the GIWW channel both north and south of the inlet tends to silt in at some point. Keep an eye on your depth sounder throughout this area. Overall, the channel is well marked and maintained and, if you keep to the middle of the channel, you should encounter no problems.

**Dockage:** Gulf Harbor Marina at Mile 59, past Lyons Bay and red daybeacon "10," sells fuel but has no transient dockage. It is a storage facility. On the north side of the Albee Road Bridge is Escape at Casey Key Resort & Marina. Slips are reserved for guests staying at the resort.

FISHERMAN'S WHARF
MARINA OF VENICE

GIWW

Venice

CROW'S NEST MARINA
& RESTAURANT

Casey Key

Gulf of Mexico

(941) 484-9551 | www.crowsnest-venice.com

*Prime location just inside the inlet with direct access to the Gulf!*

BEST OF VENICE

FIRST PLACE

*Award Winning Restaurant!*

THE CROW'S NEST
MARINA RESTAURANT

OVERNIGHT DOCKAGE

FUEL & STORE

## Little Sarasota Bay, FL

| SIESTA KEY | Largest Vessel Accommodated | VHF Channel Monitored | Transient Berths / Total Berths | Approach / Dockside Depth (reported) | Floating Docks | Gas / Diesel | Repairs: Hull, Engine, Propeller | Groceries, Ice, Marine Supplies, Snacks | Lift (tonnage), Crane, Rail | Min/Max Amps | Laundry, Pool, Showers, Courtesy Car | Pump-Out Station | Nearby: Grocery Store, Motel, Restaurant |
|---|---|---|---|---|---|---|---|---|---|---|---|---|---|
| | | | **Dockage** | | | | **Supplies** | | | **Services** | | | |
| 1. Bayfront Excursions 🖳 WiFi 66   941-349-9449 | 50 | – | call/25 | 5/5 | – | GD | IMS | HEP | L70 | 30/50 | S | P | R |
| 2. Hidden Harbor Marina Boat Storage Sales & Service   941-927-4800 | 40 | – | call/16 | 6/6 | F | G | IMS | HEP | L | 30/30 | S | – | R |

🖳 Internet Access   WiFi Wireless Internet Access   WG Waterway Guide Cruising Club Partner   *(Information in the table is provided by the facilities.)*
See WaterwayGuide.com for current rates, fuel prices, web site addresses, and other up-to-the-minute information.

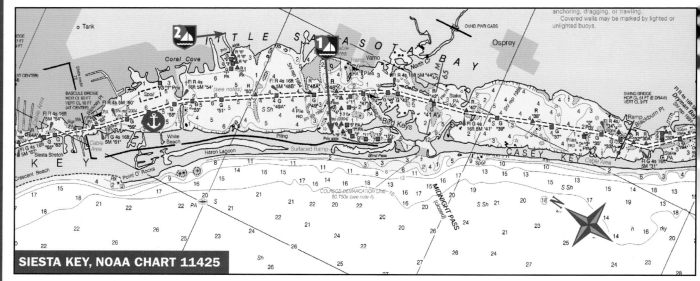

SIESTA KEY, NOAA CHART 11425

## Siesta Key–GIWW Mile 65 to Mile 72

Writers and artists congregate on the slender, heavily wooded Siesta Key, which boasts large private estates and deluxe condos with their own docks. A favorite among people from all over the world, Siesta Beach's sand is soft and cool. The beach facilities include picnic areas, restrooms, concession stands, a playground, trails and tennis and volleyball courts.

**Dockage:** Bayfront Excursions at Mile 66 is mainly a paddleboard and watercraft rental operation. They also sell fuel and offer storage and repairs. Across Little Sarasota Bay is the protected channel of Hidden Harbor Marina Boat Storage Sales & Service, which is primarily a storage and launching site that also offers repairs. They also sell gas.

There are several small marinas along this stretch of the GIWW that cater to "day boats" such as center consoles and pontoon boats. Marinas with facilities and slips to handle transient cruisers are largely located in Venice and in Sarasota Bay.

**Anchorage:** You can anchor at White Beach at Mile 67.4 west of green daybeacon "55" in 5 to 6 feet of water with good holding. This is somewhat exposed to wakes from passing boats. There is another anchorage west of green daybeacon "79" at Mile 71. Here you will find good holding in 5 to 6 feet of water.

## ■ SARASOTA AREA

At Siesta Key, off to port heading north after clearing Little Sarasota Bay, the Sarasota area officially begins and then continues for about 15 miles. The passage starts with a well-marked stretch through the shoals of Roberts Bay and ends with the exit through Longboat Key Pass to the north of Sarasota Bay. This section of the GIWW traverses a sophisticated, fast-growing region and is a popular layover spot for cruising boats.

As such, facilities are plentiful, ranging from fishing camps to marina resorts, and all manner of boating needs and repairs can be handled here. As the mainland's ocal point for a cluster of offshore island resorts (linked o it by causeways), Sarasota acts as the hub of an mportant agricultural and cattle-ranching district but is most proud of its cultural image.

**NAVIGATION:** Use Chart 11425. Use the St. Petersburg Tide Tables. For high tide, subtract 1 hour 38 minutes; for low tide, subtract 58 minutes. Behind Siesta Key, the narrow, dredged GIWW runs up the center of Little Sarasota Bay until the bay narrows to the north. At the **Stickney Point (SR 72) Bascule Bridge** at GIWW Mile 68.6 the route moves over to the western shore, then swings out into the middle again at Roberts Bay. The bridge has charted 18-foot closed vertical clearance but as much as 20 feet has been observed. The bridge opens on signal, except from 6:00 a.m. to 10:00 p.m., Monday through Friday (except federal holidays), when the draw opens on the hour and every 20 minutes thereafter.

At the northern end of Siesta Key at GIWW Mile 71.6 is the **Siesta Drive Bridge** (25-foot closed vertical clearance). The bridge opens on signal, except from 7:00 a.m. to 6:00 p.m., Monday through Friday (except federal holidays), when the draw opens on the hour and every 20 minutes thereafter. On Saturdays, Sundays and federal holidays, from 11:00 a.m. to 6:00 p.m., the draw opens on the hour and every 20 minutes thereafter.

After traversing Roberts Bay, the GIWW widens amidst a variety of marine facilities and then passes under the **Ringling Causeway (SR 684) Bridge** at Mile 73.6, with a fixed vertical clearance of 65 feet. From flashing green daybeacon "13" north of the causeway and opposite New Pass Bridge to the west, Sarasota Bay opens up, both in width and–in certain areas–in depth. Ringling Causeway at Mile 73.6 crosses three Sarasota Bay keys (Bird, Coon and St. Armands) to link Lido Key to the mainland. The bridge span between Bird and Coon keys is fixed, with only a 10-foot vertical clearance.

Farther north from the Ringling Causeway, Longboat Key shields Sarasota Bay from the Gulf of Mexico and opens wide with central controlling depths of 7 to 12 feet mean low water. The low purple building on the east side of Sarasota Bay, just north of the causeway, is the Van Wezel (pronounced Vann WAY-zull) Theatre of Performing Arts. At about Mile 77, also on the east side, you can see the coral-colored mansion of John Ringling (of circus fame).

In this area, the GIWW runs a straight line down the middle of Sarasota Bay, with markers along this stretch spaced about 2 miles apart. At flashing green daybeacon "17" (near the midpoint of Longboat Key, at Mile 80), the route turns sharply west, Sarasota Bay narrows, and you must observe all aids to navigation very carefully. Along this stretch, the GIWW follows a dredged path through shoal water (1- and 2-foot depths outside the channel).

Near the northern end of Longboat Key and Sister Keys, watch for strong crosscurrents to and from Longboat Pass.

**Dockage/Moorings:** Many of Sarasota's marine facilities are on the mainland near the Ringling Causeway, in Whittaker Bayou and clustered around New Pass. Repairs and service are readily available.

Field Club is located on the east shore just to the south of the Siesta Drive Bridge with fuel. They only accommodate members of the Florida Council of Yacht Clubs (FCYC) for dockage.

Tucked in behind Island Park, Marina Jack is at the doorstep to downtown Sarasota. Renting a mooring from them entitles you to pump-out service (at your boat) and the use of their facilities, along with a dinghy dock.

South of the Ringling Causeway before Lido Key are Bird Key Yacht Club and Sarasota Yacht Club, both of which may have transient space for reciprocating yacht club members only. Be sure to call ahead. Gas and diesel fuel are available from the two facilities.

# GOIN' ASHORE: SARASOTA, FL

| SERVICES | | |
|---|---|---|
| 1 | Visitor Information | |
| **ATTRACTIONS** | | |
| 2 | Florida Studio Theatre | |
| 3 | Sarasota Opera House | |

| | | |
|---|---|---|
| 4 | Surrender Statue | |
| **SHOPPING** | | |
| 5 | Publix | |
| 6 | Whole Foods | |

| DINING | | |
|---|---|---|
| 7 | Marina Jack | |
| 8 | O'Leary's Tiki Bar & Grill | |
| **MARINAS** | | |
| 7 | Marina Jack | |

In 1929, John Ringling chose Sarasota as winter headquarters for his "Greatest Show on Earth" circus, and even though the circus has moved on, the Ringling legacy is very much alive here.

**Attractions:** The Ringling Museum at 5401 Bay Shore Rd. (941-359-5700) is a Renaissance-style palace that the circus king built to house his art collection. In addition to the 31 galleries of art, the Ringling includes a 66-acre bayfront garden, the Ringling's 56-room mansion (off site) and a circus museum where a large collection of circus memorabilia—from ancient Roman relics to contemporary carnival props—is on display. Next to his museum, Ringling reconstructed an 18th-century Italian theater with stones, brought piece by piece from Asolo, Italy. Throughout the year, visitors can see plays and operas in the playhouse built for Queen Catherine. For additional musical/theatrical entertainment, the Florida Studio Theater at 1241 N. Palm Ave. (941-366-9000)

and the Sarasota Opera House at 61 N. Pineapple Ave. (941-328-1300) are to the south of Ringling and just a block apart.

Music lovers will especially enjoy Sarasota during the Sarasota Music Festival in the spring. On par with Tanglewood in the Berkshires, the festival is held annually in June. Concerts, lectures and seminars are open to the public. For program information, contact the Sarasota Convention and Visitors Bureau at 941-957-1877. Other musical events are held every weekend, as well as a jazz festival at City Island Park.

And speaking of City Island Park...Mote Marine Science Aquarium (1600 Ken Thompson Pkwy., 941-388-4441) and Save Our Seabirds, Inc. (1708 Ken Thompson Pkwy., 941-388-3010) are interesting stops there. Sarasota's efficient bus system can get you there and around town at bargain prices. On the way to City Island, you will pass Unconditional Surrender, one in a

series of sculptures replicating an iconic photo taken of a sailor and nurse kissing in Times Square at the end of World War II.

For more ideas of things to see and do, visit the Sarasota County Visitor Information Center at 1710 Main St. (941-706-1253).

**Shopping:** There is a Publix at 2031 Bay St. (941-366-4089) and a Whole Foods at 1451 1st St. (941-316-4700). There is also shopping on Main Street within just a couple of blocks of the waterfront.

**Dining:** Many excellent restaurants are within walking distance of the dinghy beach. Give them a try. You won't be disappointed. If you're in the mooring field, dinghy down the channel and tie up at The Old Salty Dog (1601 Ken Thompson Pkwy., 941-388-4311), a pleasant beer and burger place directly across from Mote Marine.

If you are staying in Marina Jack, you can take in their seafood spot with an outdoor raw bar patio, upstairs dining room, piano bar and expansive water views. Or, take a nice stroll and visit O'Leary's Tiki Bar & Grill (5 Bayfront Dr., 941-953-7505), with casual food and drinks in an open-air, tropical-themed joint on the beach.

# Sarasota Bay, FL

The table columns, left to right, are grouped as **Dockage** | **Supplies** | **Services** with the following headings: Largest Vessel Accommodated · VHF Channel Monitored · Approach / Dockside Depth (reported) · Transient Berths / Total Berths · Floating Docks · Groceries, Ice, Marine Supplies, Snacks · Gas / Diesel · Repairs: Hull, Engine, Propeller · Lift (tonnage), Crane, Rail · Laundry, Pool, Showers, Courtesy Car · Pump-Out Station · Min/Max Amps · Nearby: Grocery Store, Motel, Restaurant

| | Name | Phone | Largest Vessel | VHF | Transient / Total Berths | Approach / Dockside Depth | Floating Docks | Gas / Diesel | Groceries, Ice, Marine Supplies, Snacks | Repairs (Hull/Engine/Prop) | Lift/Crane/Rail | Min/Max Amps | Laundry, Pool, Showers, Courtesy Car | Pump-Out | Nearby |
|---|---|---|---|---|---|---|---|---|---|---|---|---|---|---|---|
| **SARASOTA** | | | | | | | | | | | | | | | |
| 1 | Field Club | 941-924-1201 | – | 16/68 | – | 5/5 | – | GD | S | – | – | 30/30 | PS | – | GR |
| 2 | **Marina Jack** 🖥️ 📶 73.5 | **941-955-9488 x1** | 228 | 16/71 | 25/316 | 8/8 | F | GD | IMS | HEP | – | 30/100 | LS | P | GMR |
| 3 | Bird Key Yacht Club 🖥️ 📶 | 941-953-4455 | 50 | 16 | call/42 | 12/8 | – | GD | IMS | – | – | 30/50 | PS | P | R |
| 4 | Sarasota Yacht Club 🖥️ 📶 | 941-365-4191 | 120 | 16/68 | 3/113 | 16/10 | – | GD | IS | – | – | 30/50 | LPS | P | MR |
| 5 | Hyatt Regency Sarasota 🖥️ 📶 | 941-812-4063 | 60 | – | 32/32 | 8/8 | F | – | IS | – | – | 30/50 | LPS | P | GMR |
| 6 | Sarasota Sailing Squadron | 941-388-2355 | – | – | – | 10/9 | – | – | – | – | – | 30/30 | LS | – | MR |
| 7 | Marine Max Sarasota | 941-388-4411 | – | – | – | 10/6 | – | GD | IMS | – | L | – | – | – | R |
| 8 | Longboat Key Club Moorings 📶 WG  2.5 NW of 76 | 800-858-0836 | 145 | 16/08 | 30/287 | 8/20 | – | GD | IMS | HEP | – | 30/100 | LPS | P | GMR |
| 9 | The Dock on the Bay 🖥️ 📶  2 SW of 80.5 | 941-383-3716 | 45 | – | 6/20 | 7/5 | – | – | – | – | – | 30/30 | LPS | P | GMR |
| 10 | Ramada Sarasota 🖥️ 📶  1.5 N of 78.5 | 941-358-1000 | 70 | 16 | 78/78 | 4/6 | F | GD | IS | EP | – | 30/50 | LPS | P | GMR |
| 11 | Sara Bay Marina 📶  1.5 N of 78.5 | 941-359-0390 | 50 | 16/74 | 20/60 | 4/4 | F | – | IM | EP | L8 | 30/50 | LPS | P | GMR |
| **LONGBOAT PASS** | | | | | | | | | | | | | | | |
| 12 | Cannons Marina 83.5 | 941-383-1311 | – | – | – | 5/5 | – | G | IMS | HEP | – | – | – | – | – |

🖥️ Internet Access   📶 Wireless Internet Access   WG Waterway Guide Cruising Club Partner   *(Information in the table is provided by the facilities.)*

See WaterwayGuide.com for current rates, fuel prices, web site addresses, and other up-to-the-minute information.

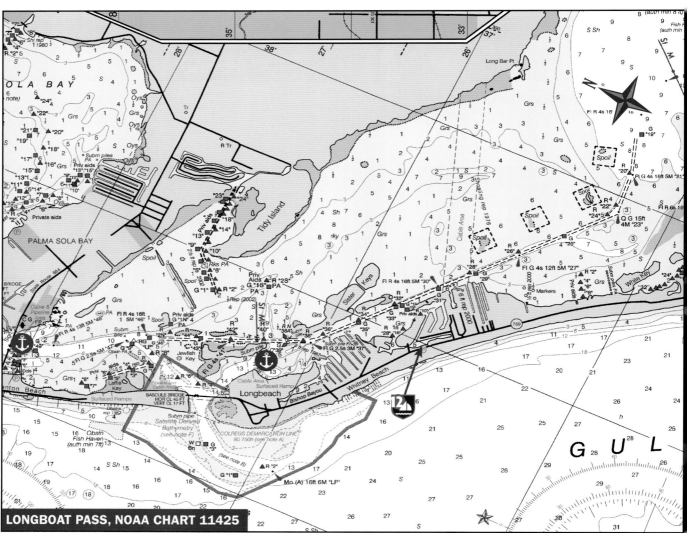

LONGBOAT PASS, NOAA CHART 11425

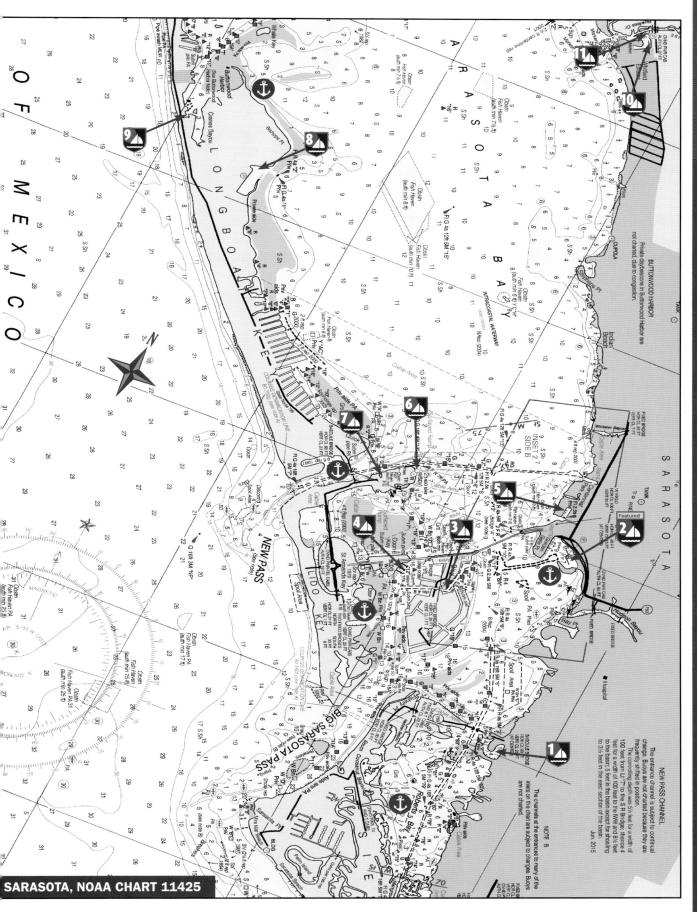

SARASOTA, NOAA CHART 11425

Hyatt Regency Sarasota is north of the Ringling Causeway Bridge and to the east (Sarasota side) with resort amenities and facilities for hotel guests only. To the north, on Lido Key, are Sarasota Sailing Squadron and MarineMax Sarasota. Both have fuel but no transient slips.

To get farther away from the crowd, take a mooring at the Resort at Longboat Key Club. To reach its channel, steer 255 degrees true from flashing green daybeacon "15." On this course, point toward the one farthest south of the three high-rise condominiums, where you will encounter the privately maintained entrance channel to the facility. Located adjacent to the marina are a Publix supermarket and a CVS Pharmacy. The Dock on the Bay is also on Longboat Key in the Buttonwood Harbor area and may have transient space for you.

At red daybeacon "16" in Sarasota Bay, steering a course of 038 degrees magnetic for 1.5 nm will bring you to the entrance markers to the Ramada Sarasota, which has a long seawall for tie ups and an on-site restaurant. Head towards the house with a white roof and chimney, take a hard left and hug the right shoreline. This facility shares an entrance with Sara Bay Marina, which offers ample amenities, including lodging and a restaurant. Be aware that there is only 3 to 4 feet of water on the approach near low tide.

At Longboat Pass, Cannons Marina (Mile 83.5) offers no transient dockage. It is a sales/service facility.

**Anchorage:** Many transient and local boats anchor in Sarasota Bay. What used to be the main anchorage (south and west of Marina Jack on the outside of Island Park) is now the mooring field. You can still anchor here, but you must be at least 150 feet outside and away from any of the moorings. You will be exposed to weather coming out of the north and west.

There is a dinghy beach on the eastern side of Island Park near O'Leary's Sailing School, but that part of the beach is primarily for the sailing school and your dinghy might be removed by the city. O'Leary's charges a nominal fee for dinghy dockage. At the newspaper boxes near O'Leary's, pick up a Sarasota Visitors Guide, which includes a map of Sarasota's attractions and shopping centers. They also sell block ice here.

Privately owned Bickell's Bayou is offered for transient cruiser use and is located on the north (mainland) side of the Ringling Causeway Bridge. Be sure to anchor only in the area exposed to the west and not in the rest of basin. The access channel has a controlling depth of about 6 feet mean low water. Approach from the GIWW directly eastward towards the basin where you will find 9-foot depths at mean low water. Please leave enough space in the central channel for other boats to access the rest of the basin. Shallow-draft vessels should leave the deeper areas for those with deeper keels. There is no shore access here; please do not trespass on private land.

Other anchorages are between Otter and Lido Key (at least 6 feet with good holding in sand and mud with all-around protection), and also in the cove to port coming into New Pass from the Gulf, before the **New Pass Bridge**. The bridge has closed vertical clearance of

23 feet and a restricted schedule. The draw opens on signal, except from 7:00 a.m. to 6:00 p.m., when the draw only opens on the hour, 20 minutes past the hour, and 40 minutes past the hour. From 6:00 p.m. to 7:00 a.m., the draw will open on signal only if at least 3 hour notice is given to the bridge tender (on VHF Channel 9). Anchor by green daybeacon "9" here in 6 to 9 feet of water with excellent holding in sand and mud.

Closer to the north end of Longboat Key at Mile 78.4 there is an anchorage west of green daybeacon "15" where you will find 7 to 11 feet of water with good holding in sand and mud. Just before red daybeacon "40" to the north, a good anchorage in 13-foot depths lies behind the tip of Longboat Key just off Longbeach.

The Mar Vista Dockside Restaurant (941-383-2391) is within dinghy range of this anchorage with good food and patio seating. You can also take your dinghy across the Longboat Pass Inlet, secure it to the dock next to the city boat ramp, and then catch a free trolley into Bradenton Beach. Here, you will find the quaint old Florida feel, with shopping, shoreside restaurants and beaches. You can reach the Whitney Beach Plaza by taking the dinghy almost all the way down Bishop Bayou and tying up to the cement wall on the left side. The plaza offers a grocery, liquor store, post office, and the Bayou Tavern (941-312-4975) with pizza, pasta and typical Italian entrees, plus views of the canal.

## Cruising Options

Continuing north, cruisers next encounter Anna Maria Island and the popular Tampa-St. Petersburg area. Beyond that Clearwater and its famous resort beaches beckon.

# WATERWAY EXPLORER
# RATINGS & REVIEWS

***Waterway Explorer* has ratings and reviews. See what others say about Marinas, Anchorages, Bridges/Locks and Navigation Alerts!**

**1. Marathon Boat Yard Marine Center**
☆☆☆☆☆

Max Length: 80
Total/Transient Slips: 20/5
Approach/Dockside Depth: 8.0/20.0
Fuel...
Repairs: Hull / Eng...

**No stars indicate that this marina is awaiting a review**

**2. Faro Blanco Res... Club**
☆☆☆☆☆

**Max Length:** 130
**Total/Transient Slips:** 74/0
**Approach/Dockside De...**
**Fuel:** Diesel/Gas
**Pumpout:** Yes

Max Length...
Total/Transient Slips: 20/3
Approach/Dockside Depth: 8.0/8.0
Fuel: Diesel/Gas
Pumpout: Yes
Repairs: No

**Yellow stars indicate the rating that this marina got from reviewers**

## Faro Blanco Resort & Yacht Club

**Mile Marker:** between markers 17 and 18

**Marathon, FL 33050**

**Phone:** (305) 743-9018

**Hailing Channel:** 16

☑ Compare to other marinas in the area

✎ ☆☆☆☆☆
1 Boater Review

✎ Suggest Updates

↩ Complete Marina Listing

***Be the first to review and rate – or add your comments to the list!***

- **Fill out the review form and post your rating**
- **No log in required**
- **No private information shared**

***Waterway Guide staff and editors validate and verify postings and content to ensure accuracy***

## Reviews: Faro Blanco Resort & Yacht Club

These are observations from the boating community. Waterway Guide information is verified regularly and all efforts will be made to validate any ... here. Thank you for taking the time to share comments abou... ...ience.

Back to the Waterway Explorer

**Faro Blanco Resort & Yacht Club**

1990 Overseas Highway
Marathon, FL 33050
Florida Bay between markers 17 and 18  48
**Lat / Lon :** N 24° 42.693' / W 081° 06.309'
**Hours:** 7:00 am to 7:00pm
**Contact:** Alain Giudice
**VHF Monitored:** 16
**VHF Working:** 9
**Phone:** (305) 743-9018
**Email:** srudek@faroblancomarina.com
**Website:** faroblancoresort.com

☆☆☆☆☆ (1)
5.00 out of 5 stars

**Review for Faro Blanco Resort & Yacht Club**

**Reviewed by:** Ed, *Adonia*, on Jun 29, 2016
**Boat Type:** Power
**LOA:** 61'
**Draft:** 4.5'

**Rating:** ☆☆☆☆☆

Faro Blanco is a wonderful facility. We were there in May 2016 for the Marlow Marine Cruising Club 20th rendezvous. The staff members were on top of their game. Hospitality, facilities and ambiance are top notch. The docks and slips are all new and no expense has been spared. The Hyatt is also new. Plan on visiting this icon of the Keys. It's a great facility.

View location on the Waterway Guide Explorer

**Name** *(Displayed)*

| |
|---|

**Email** *(Not Displayed)*

Email

**Vessel Name** Display? ☐

Vessel Name

**LOA (ft)**   **Draft (ft):**   **Boat Type:**

Sail   Power

**Rating:**
★★★★★

**Comments:**

Type review here. How was the service? Amenities? Ambience? Ease of docking?

☑ Yes, sign me up for the Cruisers' Weekly Update.

Submit   Review Policies

# Anna Maria Island to Tarpon Springs

 **GIWW** Mile 88–Mile 150  **VHF** FL: Channel 09

**CHARTS** 11411, 11415, 11416, 11425

Lovely Anna Maria Island is noted for its white sandy beaches, good tarpon fishing and premium restaurants. Just north of Longboat Key, which is separated by **Longboat Pass (SR 789) Bascule Bridge**, the island lies between Sarasota Bay on the south, Anna Maria Sound (separating the island from the mainland at the towns of Cortez and Bradenton) and Tampa Bay on the north. Cruisers can reach Tampa Bay and points north either directly from the Gulf of Mexico or via the inside GIWW route from Sarasota Bay.

## ■ SARASOTA TO ANNA MARIA ISLAND

**NAVIGATION:** Use Chart 11425. Traveling north from Sarasota Bay, there is no "quick" route north by going out into the Gulf of Mexico at Longboat Pass. Just stay on the inside. Even with a couple of bascule bridges that will have to open, you will save time and fuel. The inside route will bring you out in Tampa Bay at red daybeacon "68." Anna Maria Island is the barrier island that has been on your port side, heading north, since Longboat Pass.

Two bascule bridges cross the GIWW on this stretch before reaching Tampa Bay: the **Cortez (SR 684) Bridge** (Mile 87.4, 22-foot closed vertical clearance) and the **Anna Maria Island (Manatee Ave. West) Bridge** (Mile 89.2, 24-foot closed vertical clearance). Both have year-round restrictions: Open on signal, except from May 16 to January 14, from 6:00 a.m. to 7:00 p.m., when the draws open on the hour and every 20 minutes thereafter. From January 15 to May 15, from 6:00 a.m. to 7:00 p.m., the draws open on the hour and half-hour. If you have questions, call the bridge tenders on VHF Channel 09.

The GIWW channel cuts through shoals in much of Anna Maria Sound and at red daybeacon "52," starts swinging toward Perico Island just south of the Anna Maria Bridge. A back range at Mile 90 helps you stay in

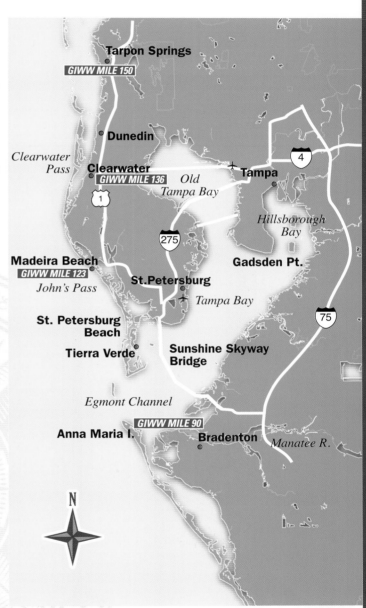

the center of the channel until you reach the sand bar charted as "The Bulkhead," which is marked by flashing red "64" at Mile 92. After leaving red daybeacon "68," the water is deep, and you can head into Tampa Bay, go up the Manatee River to the east, or turn due west for about one-half mile to pick up green daybeacon "1." Leave it to port and head in to the channel through Key Royale Bar to Bimini Bay on Anna Maria Island.

# Anna Maria Sound, FL

| BRADENTON BEACH AREA | Phone | Largest Vessel Accommodated | VHF Channel Monitored | Approach / Dockside Depth (reported) | Transient Berths / Total Berths | Floating Docks | Gas / Diesel | Groceries, Ice, Marine Supplies, Snacks | Repairs: Hull, Engine, Propeller | Lift (tonnage), Crane, Rail | Min/Max Amps | Laundry, Pool, Showers, Courtesy Car | Pump-Out Station | Nearby: Grocery Store, Motel, Restaurant |
|---|---|---|---|---|---|---|---|---|---|---|---|---|---|---|
| | | **Dockage** | | | | | **Supplies** | | **Services** | | | | | |
| 1. Yacht Solutions @ Cortez Cove Marina WiFi | 941-761-4554 | 70 | – | call/35 | 7/7 | – | – | M | HEP | L65 | 30/50 | S | – | GMR |
| 2. Bradenton Beach Marina 🖵 WiFi 87.2 | 941-778-2288 | 65 | 16/07 | 15/40 | 6/4 | – | GD | GIM | HEP | L77 | 30/50 | LS | P | GMR |
| 3. Seafood Shack Marina, Bar & Grill 🖵 WiFi 87.4 | 941-807-1801 | 120 | 16/68 | 62/68 | 14/12 | – | – | I | – | – | 30/50 | S | – | R |
| 4. Cove Sound Moorings | 941-795-4852 | 50 | 09 | call/57 | – | – | – | – | – | – | 30/30 | S | – | R |
| **ANNA MARIA ISLAND** | | | | | | | | | | | | | | |
| 5. Waterline Marina Resort & Beach Club WiFi | 844-863-9443 | – | – | call/50 | 5/4 | – | – | – | – | – | | PS | – | MR |
| 6. Galati Yacht Basin WiFi 1 W of 91.8 | 941-778-0755 | 105 | 16/68 | 12/60 | 7/7 | F | GD | IMS | HEP | L75 | 50/50 | LS | P | GMR |

🖵 Internet Access  WiFi Wireless Internet Access  WG Waterway Guide Cruising Club Partner  *(Information in the table is provided by the facilities.)*
See WaterwayGuide.com for current rates, fuel prices, web site addresses, and other up-to-the-minute information.

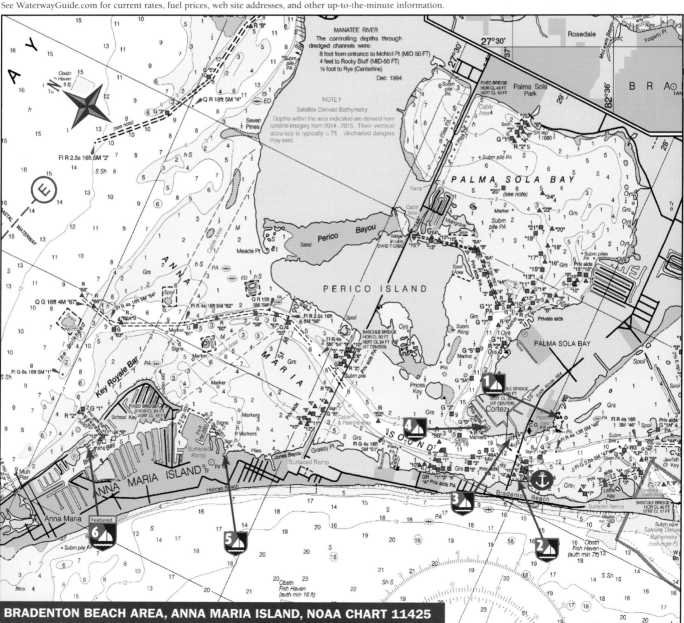

**BRADENTON BEACH AREA, ANNA MARIA ISLAND, NOAA CHART 11425**

**Dockage:** South of the Cortez Bridge, on the mainland side of the west coast ICW at Mile 87 is Yacht Solutions @ Cortez Cove Marina, which has a lift and offer repairs. (Call ahead for slip availability.) To the west of the ICW on the south side of the Cortez Bridge is the Bradenton Beach Marina, which permits do-it-yourself work, sells fuel and has transient slips.

Shortly after flashing red daybeacon "48" and the Cortez Bridge, on the eastern shore is the Seafood Shack Marina, Bar & Grill a popular restaurant and marina with transient slips (for short-term stays of one to two nights). The bar and grill serves sandwiches, fried clams and the like. The helpful dockmaster answers on VHF Channel 16. A Winn-Dixie supermarket (941-795-4638) is several miles to the east at 75th Street.

Also on the mainland side is Cove Sound Moorings, a facility geared more towards longer-term (one month or more) stays. Cortez Market, within walking distance, is just up the road, along with a post office and laundry. Several fish markets are located near the Cortez Coast Guard Station.

At press time, Waterline Marina Resort & Beach Club on Anna Maria Island was scheduled to open in fall 2017. It is advertised as "a modern resort with Old Florida authenticity." Slips, an on-site restaurant and bar, resort pool and beach access are planned in a resort atmosphere.

To the northwest on Anna Maria Island, Galati Yacht Basin, in Bimini Bay, offers slips and services, including fuel (both gas and diesel) and a ship store with an excellent parts department. If you are coming in for the first time, it is easy to get confused by the marina markers. To enter the basin, go out of Anna Maria Sound northbound past quick flashing green daybeacon "67," hang a sharp left heading west for a little more than a one-half mile to flashing green daybeacon "1," and on your left you will see the markers to Bimini Bay, which are privately maintained. The Beachhouse Restaurant (941-779-2222) is at the southern end of Anna Maria Island and offers Gulf-front dining.

**Anchorage:** It is possible to anchor on the west side of the Cortez Bridge in 4 to 8 feet. Stay out of the channel.

### Side Trip: Egmont Key

Square in the middle of the entrance to Tampa Bay at Mile 95 lies Egmont Key, 3 miles off the tip of Anna Maria Island. The island is a bird sanctuary, and you will also see a lot of gopher tortoises, which are on

the endangered species list. Unfettered wandering is discouraged.

**Anchorage:** Egmont Key is a popular daytime anchorage that gets crowded on the weekends in the summer. You can anchor close to shore on the southeast end of the island and dinghy in. As an overnight anchorage, the waters on the east side off Egmont may be uncomfortable when an evening breeze kicks in and creates a lee shore. The bottom is hard sand with good holding.

# ■ TAMPA BAY

One of the great natural harbors of the world, Tampa Bay extends about 25 miles north to south and about 10 miles east to west. It has two important cities (Tampa and St. Petersburg) and several large rivers that meander in from the east and north. Fringing the west side of the coast and extending northward is a pencil-thin chain of barrier islands with resort communities famous for their Gulf beaches.

Tampa Bay comprises three vast bodies of water—Tampa Bay proper, Old Tampa Bay to the northeast

and Hillsborough Bay to the northwest—providing excellent cruising. Lower Tampa Bay opens to the Gulf of Mexico, but enjoys the protection of barrier islands. Old Tampa Bay reaches northwest from Tampa Bay to the shoal water around Safety Harbor and Mobbly Bay. Hillsborough Bay branches off to the northeast between Interbay Peninsula and the mainland, to serve the city of Tampa, Ybor City and Davis Islands, with their extensive shipping and industrial areas.

From the open mouth of Tampa Bay, St. Petersburg lies due north, with metropolitan Tampa to the northeast. Each dominates one of the two big peninsulas that pierce the bay.

Pinellas, to the west, extends about 45 miles from the southern edge of St. Petersburg almost to Tarpon Springs. MacDill Air Force Base occupies the southern tip of Interbay, the second peninsula (about 3 miles wide and 10 miles long).

For the cruising skipper, Tampa Bay is a welcome change from the confines of the GIWW. Here, there are some 300 square miles of cruising waters, Gulf fishing, interesting ports, pleasant anchorages, good yacht facilities and superb sailing.

If you are entering Tampa Bay from outside the U.S., St. Petersburg has a U.S. Customs office at the St. Pete/Clearwater International Airport (727-453-7800). (There is also one in nearby Tampa.) Additionally, you can also use the U.S. Customs Local Boater Option and clear with a phone call (cbp.gov). For more information on Customs procedures, consult the Skippers Handbook at the front of this guide.

Two airports serve this area: Tampa International (919-870-8700) and St. Pete/Clearwater (727-453-7800). Super Shuttle services (727-571-4220) are available and run 24 hours a day seven days a week.

**NAVIGATION:** Use Charts 11425 and 11415. After crossing The Bulkhead at red daybeacon "68, the mariner faces about 4.5 miles of open water across lower Tampa Bay to the continuation of the GIWW on the north side of the bay after crossing the main shipping channel. Commercial shipping traffic has the right-of-way, so be careful. Accidents (big ones) can and have happened here. With its long fetch, this stretch can kick up an uncomfortable chop. Flashing red buoy "70," near Mile 95, is a useful checkpoint on this open-water run.

On clear days, the high-level **Sunshine Skyway Bridge**, the span of which forms a 15-mile-long highway across lower Tampa Bay, is clearly visible

from The Bulkhead. The span is 425 feet high at the top of the two cable towers. At a charted fixed vertical clearance of 175 feet at the center, it has 25 more feet of vertical clearance than the previous bridge (closed in 1987) and is located 1,000 feet farther east. Small manmade islands—called dolphins—flank the 12 columns that support the Sunshine Skyway Bridge nearest the shipping channel. Their function is to deflect ships that might wander out of the channel. Half of the old southbound span, damaged when struck in 1980, remains on both sides as fishing piers.

## City of Bradenton

The Manatee River's main city, Bradenton, is a popular layover port for those who want to explore the river and other waters. The protected marina basin has good depths and includes slips for liveaboards and weekenders alike.

**NAVIGATION:** Use Charts 11415 and 11425. Use the St. Petersburg Tide Tables. For high tide, subtract 1 hour 24 minutes; for low tide, subtract 55 minutes. From the exit at The Bulkhead in Anna Maria Sound, a sharp turn to the east, around red daybeacon "68," leads to the mouth of the lovely Manatee River, one of Tampa Bay's finest cruising and gunkholing areas. The almost-tropical

Manatee River has a well-marked, deep channel (8-foot depths), interesting side streams to explore by dinghy and friendly towns to visit. The entrance channel threads through shoals, but a series of ranges are strategically placed to keep the mariner from finding those shoals.

If you plan to enter the Manatee River, head for flashing red daybeacon "2" northeast of The Bulkhead. When traveling in from the north, be aware of the shoal that is north of quick-flashing red daybeacon "4," stay close to the buoy but inside the channel. Follow the markers closely until you are past DeSoto Point, marked by flashing red daybeacon "12," where there is ample water. Continuing up the river, be aware of flashing red daybeacon "14" and green daybeacon "15," as there are shoals growing in and around the markers. Give them a wide berth.

At Bradenton, three bridges cross the Manatee River within 1 mile of each other. The first is has 41-foot fixed vertical clearance; the second is a railway bridge (5-foot closed vertical clearance) that is usually open, except from 11:00 a.m. to 1:00 p.m.; and the third has 40-foot fixed vertical clearance. The upper Manatee River, east of these three bridges, offers some cruising options and holds depths of 10 feet or better to the I-75 Bridge at Ellenton (40-foot fixed vertical clearance). After that,

## Manatee River, FL

| PALMETTO AREA | | Largest Vessel Accommodated | VHF Channel Monitored | Transient Berths / Total Berths | Approach / Dockside Depth (reported) | Floating Docks | Groceries, Ice, Marine Supplies, Snacks | Gas / Diesel | Repairs: Hull, Engine, Propeller | Lift (tonnage), Crane, Rail | Laundry, Pool, Showers, Courtesy Car | Min/Max Amps | Pump-Out Station | Nearby: Grocery Store, Motel, Restaurant |
|---|---|---|---|---|---|---|---|---|---|---|---|---|---|---|
| | | | | **Dockage** | | | | **Supplies** | | | **Services** | | | |
| **1.** Snead Island Boat Works Inc. | 941-722-2400 | 65 | – | 8/75 | 8/8 | – | – | M | HEP | L70 | 30/50 | S | – | – |
| **2.** Bradenton Yacht Club WiFi | 941-722-5936 | 185 | 16/68 | 8/52 | – | – | GD | IS | – | – | 30/50 | PS | P | R |
| **3.** Marlow Marine Sales, Inc. | 941-729-3370 | 97 | – | – | 5/5 | – | – | M | HEP | L | – | – | – | R |
| **4.** Cut's Edge Harbor Marina | 941-729-4878 | 60 | – | call/36 | – | – | – | M | HEP | L40 | 30/30 | – | – | – |
| **5.** Tropic Isles Marina | 941-729-8128 | 40 | – | call/15 | 5/5 | – | G | IS | – | – | 30/30 | P | – | – |
| **6.** Regatta Pointe Marina 🖥 WiFi WG | 941-729-6021 | 120 | 16/71 | 75/350 | 10/10 | – | GD | IMS | – | – | 30/100 | LPS | P | GMR |
| **7.** Twin Dolphin Marina 🖥 WiFi WG | 941-747-8300 | 80 | 16/72 | 25/225 | 12/9 | F | GD | GI | – | – | 30/50 | LPS | P | GMR |
| **8.** Tarpon Pointe Marina | 941-745-1199 | 38 | – | – | 13/5 | – | GD | M | HEP | L9 | – | – | – | – |
| **9.** Riviera Dunes Marina 🖥 WiFi WG | **941-981-5330** | 120 | 16/68 | 10/218 | 9/18 | F | GD | I | – | – | 30/100 | LPS | P | GMR |

🖥 Internet Access  WiFi Wireless Internet Access  WG Waterway Guide Cruising Club Partner  *(Information in the table is provided by the facilities.)*
See WaterwayGuide.com for current rates, fuel prices, web site addresses, and other up-to-the-minute information.

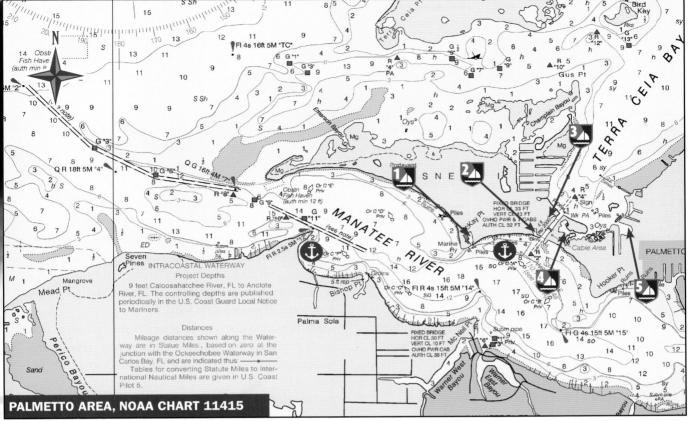

PALMETTO AREA, NOAA CHART 11415

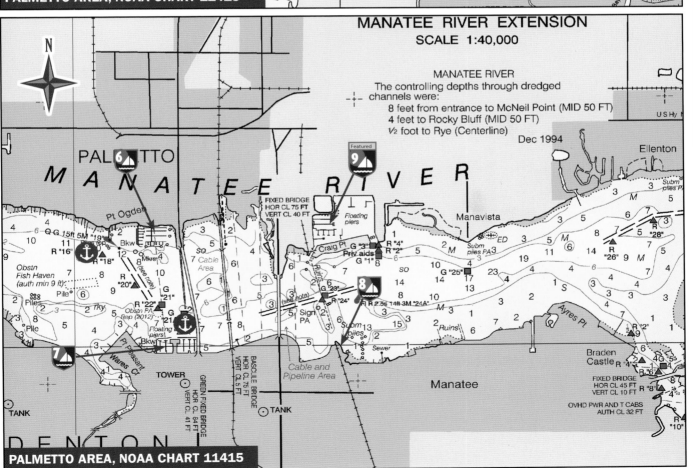

MANATEE RIVER EXTENSION
SCALE 1:40,000

MANATEE RIVER
The controlling depths through dredged channels were:
8 feet from entrance to McNeil Point (MID 50 FT)
4 feet to Rocky Bluff (MID 50 FT)
½ foot to Rye (Centerline)
Dec 1994

PALMETTO AREA, NOAA CHART 11415

depths shallow considerably and venturing farther is not recommended. Two nautical miles beyond the last of the bridges, the Braden River opens to starboard. A lush and scenic stream with plenty of wildlife, it is unmarked and full of shoals, but nonetheless offers some fine gunkholing by dinghy.

**Dockage:** Snead Island Boat Works, Inc., located on the north bank of the river, opposite red flashing daybeacon "14," is locally renowned for their repair service. At the Bradenton Yacht Club, east of McKay Point (northeast of red daybeacon "14") membership in a reciprocal yacht club is required.

Between Snead Island and Palmetto, a land cut beside the Bradenton Yacht Club leads into Terra Ceia Bay. This entrance offers channel depths of about 5 feet and a fixed bridge with a 13-foot vertical clearance. In this area you will find Marlow Marine Sales, Inc.; Cut's Edge Harbor Marina; and Tropic Isles Marina. Repairs an fuel is available, however, the approach to all of these marinas is very shallow (4 to 5 feet), and they cater to small boats only.

Conveniently located on the Manatee River, west of the Hwy 41 Bridge, is the well-equipped and well-appointed Regatta Pointe Marina, which accommodates transient guests and sells fuel.

Directly across the river, Twin Dolphin Marina is close to downtown Bradenton attractions and offers transient dockage at floating docks. The marina is at green daybeacon "21" and red daybeacon "22." Twin Dolphin Marina has a single-opening entrance configuration through its breakwaters; sound your horn going in or coming out. From red daybeacon "22" to daybeacon "41," there is an Idle-Speed/No-Wake Zone between the channel and the south shoreline. If you are staying at the Twin Dolphin Marina, a must-stop is at the Pier 22 restaurant (941-748-8087), which features jumbo lobster tails along with many other menu choices including Lobster Thermidor. You won't be disappointed.

Farther east, after the three bridges, on the south side of the Manatee River, is Tarpon Pointe Marina, which may have slips and sells fuel.

On the opposite (north) shore is the full-service and lively Riviera Dunes Marina offering fuel, repairs and resort amenities. The on-site Blu Mangrove Grill (941-479-7827), is popular for its wide selection of seafood and smoked American BBQ menu choices. Riverfront dining with outdoor seating and live music make this

worthwhile stop. On Seventh Street, you will find a Winn-Dixie Supermarket and Pharmacy (515 Seventh St. West, 941-722-1954) and bank with an ATM.

**Anchorage:** Follow the channel past flashing red daybeacon "12," then turn west into the cove behind DeSoto Point, being mindful of the charted shoal in the center of the cove. You can land your dinghy on shore to visit the DeSoto National Memorial. (See more at nps.gov/deso.) DeSoto Point offers a good anchorage, regardless of the shoal. There is still plenty of room for several boats to anchor. It is protected except from the east and carries 9 to 10 feet of water.

There is a second anchorage across the river at McKay Point, which is located east of Snead Island Boat Works. Depths range from 6 to 9 feet, but protection is good only from north winds.

Farther upriver, boats anchor just west of the bridge on either the Bradenton (near red daybeacon "22") or Palmetto (east of red daybeacon "18") side with good holding in mud.

## Bradenton to Tampa

**NAVIGATION:** Use Chart 11415 and 11416. Use the St. Petersburg Tide Tables. For high tide at Davis Island, add 3 minutes; for low tide, add 32 minutes. To get to Tampa from The Bulkhead, at the exit of Anna Maria Sound, set a course of 022 degrees magnetic for flashing red buoy "70" well out in Tampa Bay at GIWW Mile 95 (marked on chart). Continue on the same heading until you pick up quick-flashing red buoy "26" at Mullet Key Channel, the big-ship route up Tampa Bay. Go under the center spans of the Sunshine Skyway Bridge, and you may follow the big-ship channel the 20 to 25 miles all the way northeast to the City of Tampa.

**Dockage:** Located on the eastern side of Tampa Bay (north of the Little Manatee River) the Village Marina at Little Harbor offers dockage with full amenities and multiple restaurants. Antigua Cove at Little Harbor Marina has transient slips, sells fuel and offers repairs, and to the south, near the mouth of the Manatee River, Shell Point Marina may have space and sells gas; call ahead.

Land's End Marina at Apollo Beach is approached on a southeasterly course from the Cut "C" Channel range light. They have gas and diesel, some transient slips and a restaurant on site. Apollo Beach Marina is approached from the north via the Big Bend Channel. This facility is usually full with long-term rentals so be sure to call first for transient availability.

# Hillsboro Bay, Tampa Bay, FL

| | | Largest Vessel Accommodated | VHF Channel Monitored | Transient Berths / Total Berths | Approach / Dockside Depth (reported) | Floating Docks | Groceries, Ice, Marine Supplies, Snacks | Gas / Diesel | Repairs: Hull, Engine, Propeller | Lift (tonnage), Crane, Rail | Min/Max Amps | Laundry, Pool, Showers, Courtesy Car | Pump-Out Station | Nearby: Grocery Store, Motel, Restaurant |
|---|---|---|---|---|---|---|---|---|---|---|---|---|---|---|
| **LITTLE MANATEE RIVER** | | | | **Dockage** | | | | **Supplies** | | **Services** | | | | |
| 1. Village Marina at Little Harbor 🖥 📶 | 813-645-2288 | 65 | 16/72 | 20/112 | 6/10 | – | GD | IMS | EP | – | 30/50 | LPS | – | MR |
| 2. Antiqua Cove at Little Harbor 🖥 📶 | 813-645-2288 | 65 | 16/72 | 20/105 | 6/10 | F | GD | IMS | HEP | L12 | 30/50 | PS | P | MR |
| 3. Shell Point Marina 🖥 📶 | 813-645-1313 | 60 | – | 2/40 | 6/9 | – | G | – | HEP | L35 | 30/30 | S | P | – |
| **APOLLO BEACH** | | | | | | | | | | | | | | |
| 4. Lands End Marina 📶 | 813-645-5594 | 100 | – | call/105 | 10/10 | – | GD | IM | HEP | L5 | 30/50 | LS | P | R |
| 5. Appollo Beach Marina | 813-645-0720 | – | – | call/12 | 8/5 | – | – | – | – | L | 30/30 | S | – | R |
| **TAMPA AREA** | | | | | | | | | | | | | | |
| 6. Tampa Yacht & Country Club – PRIVATE | 813-831-1611 | 65 | 68 | 5/81 | 10/4 | F | GD | GIMS | – | – | 30/50 | PS | – | GMR |
| 7. Davis Island Yacht Club – PRIVATE | 813-251-1158 | 55 | – | call/114 | 10/8 | F | – | IMS | – | R | 30/30 | PS | – | R |
| 8. Marjorie Park Yacht Basin | 813-259-1604 | 90 | 16 | 19/51 | 21/9 | F | GD | GIMS | – | – | 50/50 | LPS | P | GR |
| 9. The Westin Tampa Harbour Island 🖥 📶 | 813-229-5000 | 60 | – | 2/2 | /6 | – | – | IS | – | – | 30/50 | LPS | – | MR |
| 10. Tampa Convention Center Transient Docks 🖥 📶 | 813-402-9352 | 160 | 16/68 | 27/27 | 19/19 | F | – | IS | – | – | 30/50 | – | – | GMR |
| 11. Marriott Tampa Waterside Hotel & Marina 🖥 📶 | 813-314-1006 | 60 | 16/9 | 32/32 | 19/19 | F | – | IS | – | – | 30/50 | LPS | – | GMR |

🖥 Internet Access  📶 Wireless Internet Access  **WG** Waterway Guide Cruising Club Partner  *(Information in the table is provided by the facilities.)*
See WaterwayGuide.com for current rates, fuel prices, web site addresses, and other up-to-the-minute information.

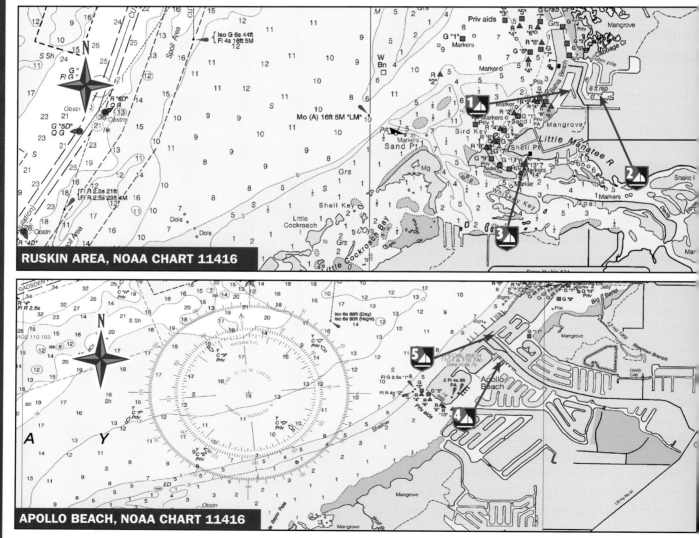

**RUSKIN AREA, NOAA CHART 11416**

**APOLLO BEACH, NOAA CHART 11416**

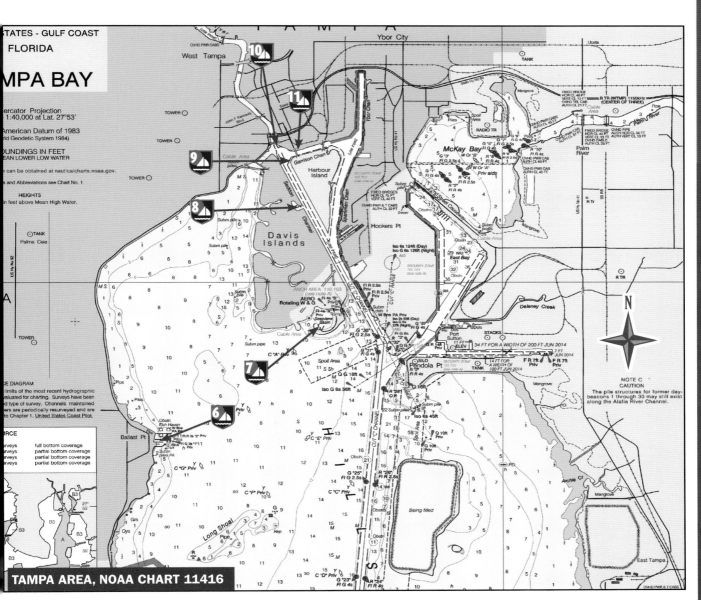

TAMPA AREA, NOAA CHART 11416

# Old Tampa Bay, FL

| PORT TAMPA AREA | | Largest Vessel Accommodated | VHF Channel Monitored | Transient Berths / Total Berths | Approach / Dockside Depth (reported) | Floating Docks | Gas / Diesel | Groceries, Ice, Marine Supplies, Snacks | Repairs: Hull, Engine, Propeller | Lift (tonnage), Crane, Rail | Laundry, Pool, Showers, Courtesy Car | Pump-Out Station | Min/Max Amps | Nearby: Grocery Store, Motel, Restaurant |
|---|---|---|---|---|---|---|---|---|---|---|---|---|---|---|
| 1. Florida Marina Clubs – Tampa Harbour [WiFi] | 813-831-1200 | 80 | 16 | /48 | 25/12 | F | GD | IMS | HEP | L15 | 30/50 | L | P | GMR |
| 2. Westshore Yacht Club [🖥] | 813-805-6871 | 150 | 16/71 | /149 | 25/8 | F | – | IS | – | – | 30/100 | PS | P | GMR |

🖥 Internet Access   [WiFi] Wireless Internet Access   [WG] Waterway Guide Cruising Club Partner  *(Information in the table is provided by the facilities.)*
See WaterwayGuide.com for current rates, fuel prices, web site addresses, and other up-to-the-minute information.

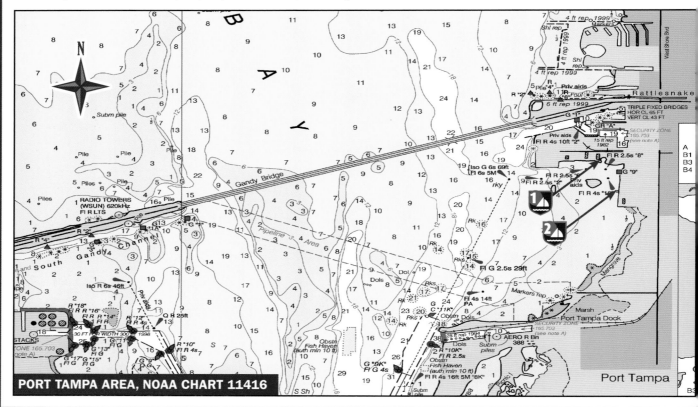

PORT TAMPA AREA, NOAA CHART 11416

At the end of Davis Islands in Hillsborough Bay to the north is a park that offers a small beach area, off-leash area for dogs, picnic area, canoe launch and boat ramps. Davis Islands Park is adjacent to the Davis Island Yacht Club (private, no transients) and Davis Island Seaplane Basin. Tampa Yacht & Country Club across Hillsboro Bay at Ballast Point is also private.

## City of Tampa

**Dockage:** Nearly all of the dockage at Harbour Island, which is in downtown Tampa, is private. A few restaurants are located in the Harbor Island complex and at the hotel. Marjorie Park Yacht Basin, on the channel between Harbor and Davis Islands is a full-service facility, with slips, all fuels and easy access to mass transit. The Westin Tampa Harbour Island has limited transient space, while the Tampa Convention Center has 27 reserved transient slips but no shore power or water. This facility is very convenient to the sights, sounds and activities of Downtown Tampa and Ybor City. Tampa Marriott Waterside Hotel & Marina may have transient slips on their floating docks, but call well in advance to check availability.

## Old Tampa Bay

**Dockage:** On the opposite side of Interbay Pennisula from the City of Tampa is Old Tampa Bay, which is crossed by three bridges. Just south of the fixed **Gandy Twin Bridges** (43-foot vertical clearance) is Florida Marina Clubs–Tampa Harbor with slips and some repairs. To the south, on the same side (east), is Westshore Yacht Club, part of a condominium complex that has transient slips on floating docks for vessels up to 150 feet. Guests have access to the waterfront Bay Club with a spa, fitness center, tropical pool deck, tiki bar and ship store.

## City of St. Petersburg

Facilities of one kind or another line all sides of the peninsula in St. Petersburg (often called St. Pete by locals). Boaters heading up Tampa Bay reach those at the south end first, but there are also facilities downtown on the east side of the peninsula and in Boca Ciega Bay on the west side.

**NAVIGATION:** Use Charts 11411, 11415 and 11416. Use St. Petersburg Tide Tables. Two routes, both clearly marked on Chart 11416, lead from Anna Maria Sound

# GOIN' ASHORE: ST. PETERSBURG, FL

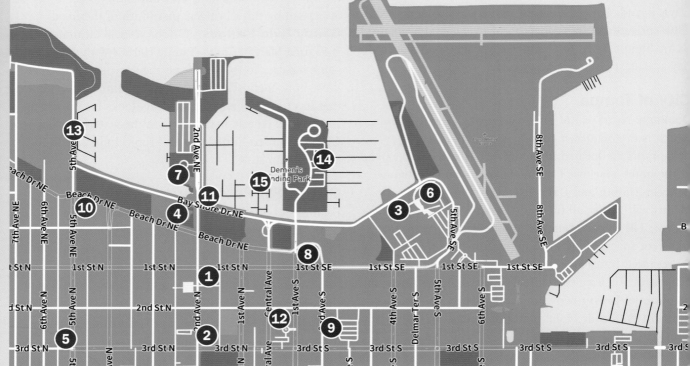

| | SERVICES |
|---|---|
| 1 | Visitor Information |
| | **ATTRACTIONS** |
| 2 | American Stage Theatre Company |
| 3 | Mahaffey Theater |
| 4 | Museum of Fine Arts |
| 5 | Palladium Theater |
| 6 | Salvador Dali Museum |

| | |
|---|---|
| 7 | Saint Petersburg Museum of History |
| | **SHOPPING** |
| 8 | Al Lang Stadium (farmers market) |
| 9 | Publix |
| | **DINING** |
| 10 | 400 Beach Seafood & Tap House |
| 11 | Fresco's Waterfront Bistro |

| | |
|---|---|
| 12 | The Mill Restaurant |
| | **MARINAS** |
| 13 | Renaissance Vinoy Resort Marina |
| 14 | St. Petersburg Municipal Marina |
| 15 | St. Petersburg Yacht Club |

Known as the "Sunshine City" because of its climate and great weather, St. Petersburg boasts a large variety of activities from professional sporting events, to performing and visual arts, to shopping and dining. The City has the largest public waterfront park system of any U.S. city. St. Petersburg is an easy city to negotiate by foot or public transportation.

**Attractions:** The downtown "Looper" trolley (loopertrolley.com, 727-821-5166) stops at many of the tourist spots and downtown locations, every 15 minutes, for a minimal charge. The public bus service (PSTA) (727-540-1800) also can get you around the rest of the city and most lines run through downtown near Williams Park.

Hopefully, you will choose to get off the boat and enjoy some of the area's entertainment venues. You won't be at a loss for things to do. There are year-round plays at American Stage Theater Company (3rd St. N., 727-823-7529) and performing arts concerts by the symphony and traveling Broadway plays at the Mahaffey Theater (400 1st St. S, 727-892-5767). The Museum of Fine Arts is at 255 Beach Dr. NE with antiquities and modern art (727-896-2667) and the Saint Petersburg Museum of History is nearby at 335 2nd Ave NE (727-894-1052) with exhibits and artifacts. The grand Palladium Theater is at 253 5th Ave. N. in a circa-1925 former church. This performing arts center hosts plays and films. Call for details (727-822-3590).

Perhaps the most well-known museum in the area is the Salvador Dali Museum (1 Dali Blvd., 727-823-3767), where a large collection of the artist's works can be seen. Here you will find displays of paintings, sculpture, holograms and art glass. The collection spans Salvador Dali's entire career (1904-1989) and is the largest collection of the artist's works outside of Europe. The hulking modern concrete building itself is a work of art, as are the fantastical gardens around back, compete with a hedge maze and melting clock benches. There is also a museum shop and a cafe.

The famous St. Petersburg Pier has been completely closed down and removed in preparation for a new enhanced facility. For up-to-date information, research newstpetepier.com. Visit the city's website for maps and a calendar of upcoming events (discoverdowntown.com).

**Shopping:** Great boat provisioning can be had at a weekly Saturday farmers market in the Al Lang Stadium parking lot (1st Ave. and 1st St. S.) from October through May from 9:00 a.m. to 2:00 p.m.

A Publix grocery store (250 3rd St. S, 727-822-1125) is about one-half mile from the Municipal Marina. The closest West Marine is at 2010 Tyrone Blvd. N (727-342-8001). You will need transportation.

**Dining:** The Mill Restaurant offers an innovative menu with a Southern spin at 200 Central Ave. #100 (727-317-3930). The popular 400 Beach Seafood & Tap House offers indoor or outdoor dining on Beach Drive (727-896-2400). They offer lunch and dinner daily, plus an early bird special (3:00 p.m. to 6:00 p.m.), a Sunday brunch buffet, and extensive liquor, beer and wine options.

Fresco's Waterfront Bistro is a laid-back spot with "dockside drinks and fine cuisine" and featuring bay views. Located at the foot of the pier (300 2nd Ave. NE, (727-894-4429).

As in all larger cities, there are many dining options—many more than we could list here—both indoors or at sidewalk cafes. See visitstpeteclearwater.com for suggestions.

# Tampa Bay, FL

| ST. PETERSBURG AREA | | Dockage | | | | | Supplies | | Services | | | | | |
|---|---|---|---|---|---|---|---|---|---|---|---|---|---|---|
| | | Largest Vessel Accommodated | VHF Channel Monitored | Approach / Dockside Depth (reported) | Transient Berths / Total Berths | Floating Docks | Groceries, Ice, Marine Supplies, Snacks | Gas / Diesel | Repairs: Hull, Engine, Propeller | Lift (tonnage), Crane, Rail | Laundry, Pool, Showers, Courtesy Car | Min/Max Amps | Pump-Out Station | Nearby: Grocery Store, Motel, Restaurant |
| 1. Renaissance Vinoy Resort Marina ▫ WiFi | 727-824-8022 | 130 | 16/68 | 22/74 | 12/12 | – | – | IS | – | – | 30/100 | LPS | P | GMR |
| 2. St. Petersburg Municipal Marina ▫ | 727-893-7329 | 125 | 16/68 | call/650 | 12/12 | – | GD | IMS | – | – | 30/100 | LS | P | GR |
| 3. St. Petersburg Yacht Club | 727-822-3227 | 150 | 16/69 | 13/80 | 10/14 | – | GD | IS | – | – | 50/100 | PS | P | MR |
| 4. Harborage Marina at Bayboro ▫ WiFi | 727-821-6347 | 200 | 16/68 | 15/340 | 24/12 | F | GD | IS | – | – | 30/200+ | LPS | P | GMR |
| 5. Sailor's Wharf Yacht Yard ▫ WG | 727-823-1155 | 80 | – | 1/23 | 10/9 | F | – | M | HEP | L75,C2 | 30/50 | S | – | GMR |
| 6. Embree Marine | 727-896-0671 | 70 | – | – | 7/7 | – | – | M | HEP | L55 | 30/50 | – | – | GMR |
| 7. Salt Creek Marina ▫ WiFi | 727-895-4481 | 72 | – | call/12 | 10/9 | – | – | M | HEP | L50 | 30/50 | S | – | GMR |

▫ Internet Access  WiFi Wireless Internet Access  WG Waterway Guide Cruising Club Partner  *(Information in the table is provided by the facilities.)*
See WaterwayGuide.com for current rates, fuel prices, web site addresses, and other up-to-the-minute information.

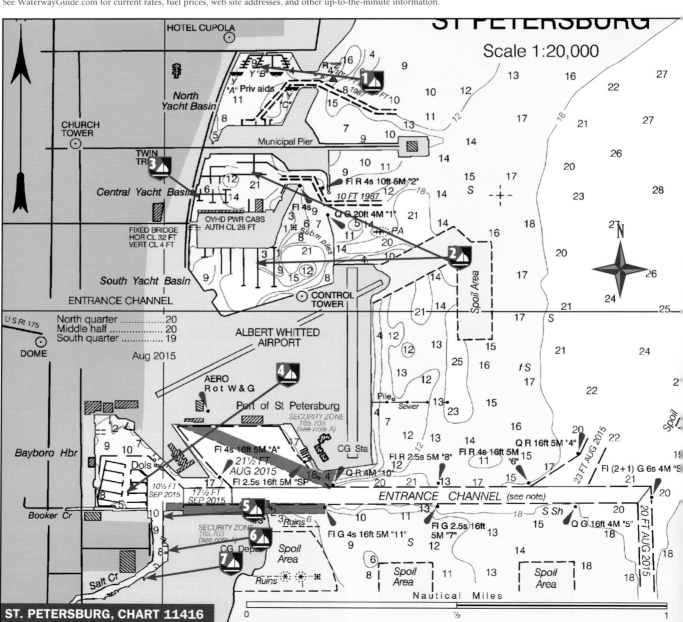

ST. PETERSBURG, CHART 11416

to St. Petersburg. Starting from The Bulkhead, as you would if going to Tampa, set a course of 022 degrees magnetic for flashing red "70" well out in Tampa Bay at Mile 95. Continue on the same heading until you pick up quick-flashing red buoy "26" at Mullet Key Channel, the big-ship route up Tampa Bay.

The GIWW follows Mullet Key Channel eastward through the Sunshine Skyway Bridge, then turns north, (to port) at quick-flashing green buoy "5A" and quick-flashing red buoy "6A" at about Mile 102, leaving the main channel to Tampa for the well-marked route to St. Petersburg.

At green daybeacon "13A," you meet the GIWW: Here, turn to starboard and follow the GIWW eastward under the 65-foot fixed vertical clearance bridge, which is locally known as the **Meisner Bridge**, until it converges with the northbound channel to St. Petersburg. St. Petersburg is located on a peninsula, so water is everywhere, but unfortunately for boaters, much of it isn't very deep. Watching your charts is critical to avoid the shoals, which are often difficult to see. Unless you know the waters, stay in the well-marked channels

to avoid bumping the sandy bottom. Also, keep an eye out for large ships heading to the ports of Manatee and Tampa.

Be advised that if you are trying to avoid easterly winds out in Tampa Bay, you will have them right on your nose when you turn to starboard at green daybeacon "13A." It is several miles to the northbound channel.

If you are coming up the channel to St. Pete from Tampa Bay, you can turn to port at flashing green daybeacon "S" to get into Bayboro Harbor and the Port of St. Petersburg. Coast Guard ships and cruise ships come in here, so the water is deep.

**Dockage:** The Renaissance Vinoy Resort Marina, near the big pink historic Vinoy Hotel, is a Marriott property offering resort amenities and deep water slips. In downtown St. Petersburg, the large (650-slip) St. Petersburg Municipal Marina offers transient facilities with all amenities, including gas and diesel. Nearby is the St. Petersburg Yacht Club, where membership in a reciprocal yacht club is required.

The Harborage Marina at Bayboro is around the bend from downtown but close to a trolley stop so you can get around if needed. The marina offers all fuels and slips. To the south, at the end of the entrance channel, are Sailor's Wharf Yacht Yard and Embree Marine. Both of these are strictly repair facilities (no transient slips). There might be limited space available at nearby Salt Creek Marina, but call in advance.

**Moorings:** Anchoring in the north basin, which is known as Vinoy Basin, has been eliminated. There are 13 moorings, which are managed by the St. Petersburg Municipal Marina (727-893-7927), in 14 to 16 feet of water. You should call ahead of your arrival to make sure that a mooring will be available. There is a handy dinghy dock nearby and great access to the city.

# ■ BOCA CIEGA BAY

The GIWW runs from Tampa Bay to Anclote Key, at the mouth of the Anclote River leading to Tarpon Springs. There it ends and picks back up at Carrabelle, past the Big Bend or Nature Coast territory. From Carrabelle, it runs west all the way to Brownsville, TX, with an Army Corps of Engineers project depth of 12 feet.

There are six bridges in the Pinellas Bayway Span Bridge system with only two of them coming into play with the GIWW. **Pinellas Bayway "C" Span** is a 65-foot fixed bridge, but **Pinellas Bayway "E" Bascule Bridge** has a 25-foot vertical clearance and a restricted schedule. There are plans for a new 65-foot vertical clearance fixed bridge to be completed in 2021. Be aware that there could be some activity in the area related to this construction. Check the *Local Notice to Mariners.*

The Pinellas Bayway "E' span opens on signal, except from 9:00 a.m. to 7:00 p.m., when it need only open on the hour and half-hour. Call ahead on your VHF radio to get the latest information. (Call "Structure Echo," so there will be no confusion about which one you are calling.) For more information, see the Bridges & Locks section at the front of this guide.

Two routes reach boating facilities on the west side of the Pinellas Peninsula. Those who can clear **Pinellas Bayway "A" Span** (with 18-foot fixed vertical clearance) can use the shortcut past Cats Point off the straight-line extension of the Sunshine Skyway Channel. Otherwise, follow the GIWW channel through the

Pinellas Bayway Spans "E" and "C." At the northern end of the GIWW, approaching Clearwater, the waterway tends to narrow and bridges and shoaling become more frequent. Boats with significant draft should be very cautious.

From Tampa Bay to Clearwater, any one of three inlets affords easy access from the GIWW to and from the Gulf of Mexico (in good weather and daylight):

- **North Channel** (just north of Tampa Bay): Well marked and leads from the Gulf to Pass-a-Grille Channel
- **Johns Pass**: Located about 6.5 nm north of North Channel. Connects with the GIWW between Mitchell and Sunshine beaches and is crossed by the twin **Johns Pass Bascule Bridges.** The closed vertical clearance is 27 feet at the center of the channel and the horizontal width has been expanded from 60 to 100 feet. The bridges open on request. This inlet tends to shoal rapidly. Calling for local knowledge from one of the tow services would be wise. Even though it is marked, it is shallow.
- **Clearwater Pass:** Located about 13 nm north of Johns Pass. Leads right into the heart of Clearwater proper. The 74-foot fixed vertical clearance **Clearwater Pass (SR 183) Bridge** spans the pass. This is the preferred channel unless you have solid local knowledge for the others.

## Pass-a-Grille Channel

**NAVIGATION:** Use Chart 11411. At the start, the GIWW is a well-marked, dredged channel winding through shallows inside the barrier islands. From Pass-a-Grille Channel, it meanders northward inside the barrier islands referred to as the Holiday Isles: St. Petersburg Beach, Treasure Island and Sand Key. It threads around a maze of manmade islets pierced by canals.

The route begins where the main GIWW channel intersects Pass-a-Grille Channel near Mile 114. If you explore Pass-a-Grille Channel, watch for shoaling and keep clear of the north side. See the Bridges and Locks section at the front of this guide for the opening times for the **Corey Causeway (SR 693) Bascule Bridge** (23-foot vertical clearance), **Treasure Island Causeway Bascule Bridge** (21-foot vertical clearance) and the **Welch Causeway (SR 699) Bridge** (at Madeira Beach, 25-foot vertical clearance). While openings are usually prompt, delays can occur. Some opening schedules change every few months due to local pressure. When approaching bridges in

this section, bide your time and leave ample room for maneuvering while waiting. Call ahead on VHF Channel 09 if you are in doubt of the opening schedule and check the Waterway Guide Explorer at waterwayguide.com for updates.

⚠ At GIWW Mile 114.5, just north of the Pinellas Bayway Bridges is a shoal spot that sometimes catches the unwary. It is well marked, but do not be confused by the markers for the beginning of a side channel to Gulfport on the mainland. Red daybeacon "2," flashing red daybeacon "26" and red daybeacon "26A" lead past the shoal.

**Dockage:** Marine services run the gamut from small fishing camps and motel and restaurant docks to large, elegant marina complexes. You should contact these facilities ahead of time in to be sure they can accomodate you.

On the back side of Maximo Point is Magnuson Hotel Marina Cove, north of the Sunshine Skyway Bridge. Turn north at green daybeacon "13" to reach the marina. The marina welcomes transients up to 55 feet.

Suntex Marina at St. Petersburg is located in Frenchman Creek at Maximo Pt. They can accommodate vessels up to 60 feet and provide Category 4 hurricane-rated dry storage. Additionally, they have a captain's lounge, ship store, all fuels plus easy access to restaurants, shopping and activities.

Just North of Cats Point is Maximo Marina, which has slips, sells fuel, offers repairs. Two blocks from Maximo Marina is a shopping center with a large, well-stocked West Marine, a grocery store, a post office and a few restaurants.

To reach Gulfport and its boating facilities, turn to starboard at red daybeacon "2" at GIWW Mile 114.5. The red flashing light marks a shoal. (See Navigation Alert in yellow box.) Gulfport Municipal Marina is located here with a full complement of transient facilities in its well-protected basin. It offers pump-out service, fuel (gas and diesel), marine supplies, bait and tackle and there is a restaurant nearby.

Other marinas in this area include Pasadena Yacht & Country Club, MarineMax St. Petersburg, Pasadena Marina, Tierra Verde Marina Resort, Tierra Verde Marina,

# Boca Ciega Bay, FL

| BOCA CIEGA BAY AREA | | Largest Vessel Accommodated | VHF Channel Monitored | Transient Berths / Total Berths | Approach / Dockside Depth (reported) | Floating Docks | Gas / Diesel | Groceries, Ice, Marine Supplies, Snacks | Repairs: Hull, Engine, Propeller | Lift (tonnage), Crane, Rail | Min/Max Amps | Laundry, Pool, Showers, Courtesy Car | Pump-Out Station | Nearby: Grocery Store, Motel, Restaurant |
|---|---|---|---|---|---|---|---|---|---|---|---|---|---|---|
| | | **Dockage** | | | | | | **Supplies** | | **Services** | | | | |
| 1. Magnuson Hotel Marina Cove WiFi 110.3 | 727-867-1151 | 55 | 16 | 32/32 | 5/8 | - | - | IS | - | - | 50/50 | LPS | - | GMR |
| **2. Suntex Marina at St. Petersburg ☐ WiFi** | **727-867-2600** | 60 | 16 | 143/143 | 5/5 | F | GD | GIMS | HEP | L | 30/50 | LPS | P | GMR |
| 3. Maximo Marina (IGY) 1.5 NE of 115 | 727-867-1102 | 110 | 6/16 | call/220 | 8/8 | F | GD | IMS | HEP | L50,C | 30/50 | LS | P | GMR |
| **4. Gulfport Municipal Marina ☐ WiFi 1.5 NE of 115** | **727-893-1071** | 45 | 16/68 | 10/250 | 7/6 | F | GD | IMS | P | - | 30/50 | S | P | GR |
| 5. Pasadena Yacht & Country Club ☐ WiFi 116.5 | 727-381-7922 | 70 | 16/69 | 6/82 | 10/6 | - | - | IS | - | - | 30/100 | PS | P | GMR |
| 6. MarineMax St. Petersburg WiFi | 727-343-6520 | 75 | - | call/130 | - | F | - | IM | HEP | L80 | 30/50 | S | P | GMR |
| 7. Pasadena Marina WiFi 116 | 727-343-4500 | 56 | - | 1/125 | 6/6 | - | - | I | - | - | 30/50 | LPS | P | GMR |
| 8. Tierra Verde Marina Resort ☐ 113 | 727-867-0400 | 120 | 16/71 | 20/107 | 12/12 | F | GD | GIMS | HEP | L12 | 30/50 | LPS | P | GMR |
| 9. Tierra Verde Marina 113 | 727-866-0255 | 60 | 16 | 10/64 | 20/15 | F | GD | GIMS | HEP | L10 | 30/50 | - | P | GR |
| 10. The Pass-A-Grille Marina ☐ WiFi 113.8 | 727-360-0100 | 50 | 16 | 5/20 | 20/15 | F | GD | IMS | HEP | L | 30/100 | - | - | GMR |
| 11. Isla Del Sol Yacht Club Marina ☐ WiFi 114.5 | 727-906-4752 | 65 | 16/68 | 3/74 | 20/6 | - | - | I | - | L | 30/50 | LPS | P | R |
| 12. Blind Pass Marina ☐ 118.5 | 727-360-4281 | 55 | 16/69 | 4/110 | - | F | - | IS | - | L10 | 30/50 | LS | P | GR |
| 13. John's Pass Marina WiFi 1 S of 121.4 | 727-367-3835 | 75 | 16 | 15/34 | 10/5 | F | GD | IMS | - | - | 30/50 | S | - | MR |
| 14. Madeira Bay Docks, Inc. ☐ WiFi 1 S of 121.4 | 727-639-2862 | 80 | - | 3/44 | 8/10 | F | - | GIS | HEP | L77 | 30/50 | LPS | P | GMR |
| 15. Snug Harbor Inn 1 S of 121.4 | 727-395-9256 | 50 | - | 6/6 | 6/5 | - | - | - | HEP | L35 | - | PS | - | GMR |
| 16. Madeira Beach Municipal Marina ☐ 122.2 | 727-399-2631 | 100 | 16/68 | 6/80 | 6/11 | F | GD | IMS | HEP | - | 30/50 | LS | P | GMR |
| 17. Bay Pines Marina WiFi 1.5 NE of 120.5 | 727-392-4922 | 50 | 16 | call/60 | 5/7 | F | G | IMS | E | L | 30/50 | - | P | R |

☐ Internet Access WiFi Wireless Internet Access WG Waterway Guide Cruising Club Partner *(Information in the table is provided by the facilities.)*
See WaterwayGuide.com for current rates, fuel prices, web site addresses, and other up-to-the-minute information.

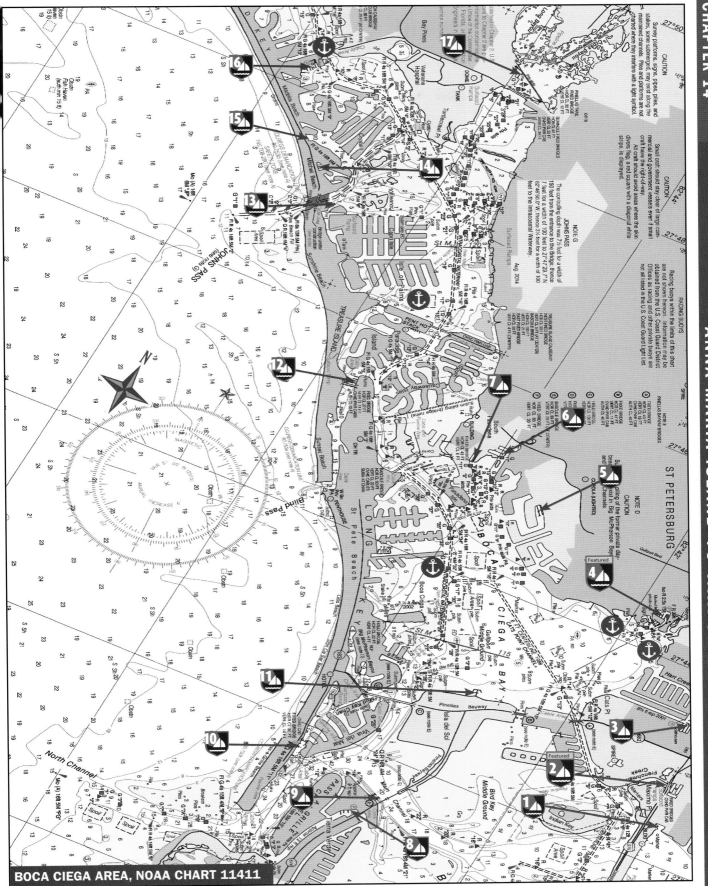

**BOCA CIEGA AREA, NOAA CHART 11411**

GULFPORT MUNICIPAL MARINA

The Pass-A-Grille Marina, Isla Del Sol Yacht Club Marina and Blind Pass Marina. You need to call ahead for transient dockage availability. See "Boca Ciega Bay" marina table in this chapter for details on dockage, amenities, fuel and repairs.

From Johns Pass at Mile 121 north to Sand Key are full-service municipal marinas and facilities on both shores, including John's Pass Marina, Madeira Bay Docks, Snug Harbor Inn, and Madeira Beach Municipal Marina. Refer to the marina table and chart for details. There are also motels and on-the-water restaurants with dockage. To the northeast of Turtlecrawl Point, between two fixed bridges (32-foot vertical clearance on first bridge) is Bay Pines Marina with slips and gas.

**Anchorage:** When traveling the GIWW along its western leg beginning at Mile 104, you can anchor at the northeast corner of Boca Ciega Bay at Maximo Point West just east of the Sunshine Skyway Causeway. The area is exposed to winds from the southeast and the wakes of passing vessels, but can serve in a pinch. Depths are 9 to 12 feet. You can also anchor on the east side of the bridge in 7 to 9 feet outside Magnuson Hotel Marina Cove.

A number of anchorages can be found in Boca Ciega Bay just north of Mile 115. Proceed west between green daybeacon "31" and red daybeacon "30" from flashing red daybeacon "32," then anchor where the chart shows 7- to 8-foot depths. Proceed between the last two No-Wake markers to find the best depths. Or, proceed east at red daybeacon "32" in Cats Point Channel and anchor anywhere you can find sufficient depth and wind protection between Cats Point and Gulfport. Depths in the area are generally 7 to 10 feet, with 5 to 6 closer to shore.

Across Boca Ciega Bay at Gulfport are two anchorages, one near the municipal marina in 5 to 7 feet and the other to the northwest in 6 to 10 feet. These offer protection from all but southern blows.

Just north of the Treasure Island Bridge at green daybeacon "17," turn west, and stay north of the charted spoil area for a well-protected anchorage. Mean low water depths around the spoil are roughly 4 to 6 feet, and the bottom is sand. Highly visible west of the GIWW on St. Pete Beach is the renovated Don CeSar Hotel, a longtime landmark for mariners. Finally, you can anchor north of the Welch Causeway Bascule Bridge (Mile 122.1) in 7 feet of water with good holding.

## The Narrows–GIWW Mile 126

Nine nautical miles south of Clearwater, the GIWW enters the well-named Narrows, a deep, but narrow channel, connecting Boca Ciega Bay to Clearwater Harbor, which is comparatively broad and open. **Park Blvd. (SR 248) Bridge** at Mile 126.0 has a 20-foot closed vertical clearance and opens on request.

**Dockage:** South of Conch Key green daybeacon "27A" are two restaurants and a deli with docks, including the Pub Waterfront Restaurant (727-595-3172), located on the west side of The Narrows near red daybeacon "26." However, the docks are only available while dining; no overnight dockage is permitted. Indian Springs Marina at GIWW Mile 29 has a 30-ton lift and sells gas; call for slip availability.

The **Indian Rocks Beach (CR 694) Bascule Bridge** at Mile 129.3 has a 25-foot closed vertical clearance and opens on request. Near the bridge is the Holiday Inn Harbourside Marina, offering gas and transient slips, plus a pool, tiki bar and restaurant. On the beach side of the waterway just at red daybeacon "32" are the new Indian Beach public docks. Call 727-595-2517 for information regarding these docks. These are free day-use docks only with no overnight stays allowed. Be careful when approaching these docks. It is very shallow, and we would advise only small shallow-draft boats attempt docking here. Largo Intercoastal Marina is at Mile 129.6 with gas and some slips.

# The Narrows/ Clearwater Harbor, FL

| | | Dockage | | | | | | Supplies | | | Services | | | |
|---|---|---|---|---|---|---|---|---|---|---|---|---|---|---|
| | Phone | Largest Vessel Accommodated | VHF Channel Monitored | Transient Berths / Total Berths | Approach / Dockside Depth (reported) | Floating Docks | Gas / Diesel | Groceries, Ice, Marine Supplies, Snacks | Repairs: Hull, Engine, Propeller | Lift (tonnage), Crane, Rail | Min/Max Amps | Laundry, Pool, Showers, Courtesy Car | Pump-Out Station | Nearby: Grocery Store, Motel, Restaurant |
| **INDIAN SHORES** | | | | | | | | | | | | | | |
| 1. Indian Springs Marina 129 | 727-595-2956 | 40 | – | call/48 | 4.5/4.5 | F | G | IM | HP | L30 | 30/30 | – | – | GMR |
| 2. Holiday Inn Harbourside Marina 🖥 📶 129.4 | 727-517-3652 | 70 | 16 | 50/50 | 8/6 | F | – | IMS | HEP | | 30/50 | LPS | – | GMR |
| 3. Largo Intercoastal Marina 129.6 | 727-595-3592 | 35 | – | 3/381 | 4/4 | F | G | IMS | HEP | L | 50/50 | S | P | GMR |
| **CLEARWATER BEACH AREA** | | | | | | | | | | | | | | |
| 4. Clearwater Municipal Marinas (Clearwater Harbor Marina) 📶 727-562-4981 | | 125 | 16/68 | 12/126 | 7/7 | F | – | I | – | – | 30/50 | LS | P | GR |
| 5. Chart House Marina 📶 136 | 727-449-8007 | – | – | 26/26 | 7/7 | | – | – | | | 30/30 | LPS | – | GMR |
| 6. Clearwater Yacht Club 🖥 📶 136 | 727-447-6000 | 70 | 16/71 | 6/42 | 7/7 | | – | IS | | | 30/50 | PS | – | MR |
| 7. Clearwater Municipal Marinas (Clearwater Beach Marina) 📶 727-462-6954 | | 125 | 16/68 | 23/207 | 7/12 | F | GD | GIS | | | 30/100 | LS | P | GMR |

🖥 Internet Access  📶 Wireless Internet Access  [WG] Waterway Guide Cruising Club Partner *(Information in the table is provided by the facilities.)*
See WaterwayGuide.com for current rates, fuel prices, web site addresses, and other up-to-the-minute information.

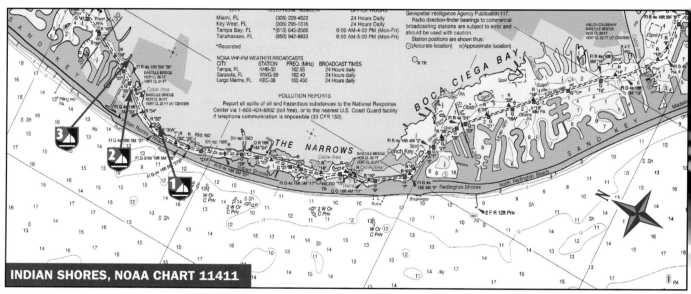

INDIAN SHORES, NOAA CHART 11411

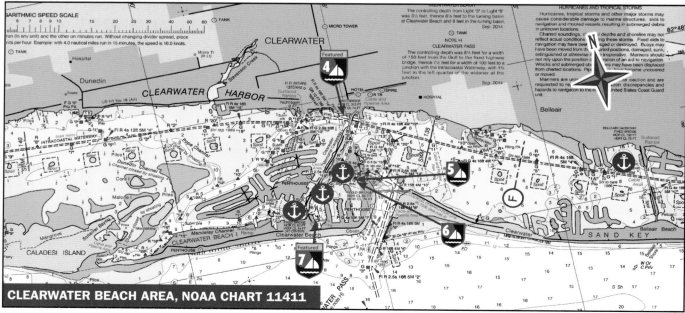

CLEARWATER BEACH AREA, NOAA CHART 11411

CLEARWATER BEACH MARINA

CLEARWATER HARBOR MARINA

# Clearwater Harbor, FL

| DUNEDIN AREA | | Dockage | | | | | Supplies | | | Services | | | | |
|---|---|---|---|---|---|---|---|---|---|---|---|---|---|---|
| | | Largest Vessel Accommodated | VHF Channel Monitored | Transient Berths / Total Berths | Approach / Dockside Depth (reported) | Floating Docks | Groceries, Ice, Marine Supplies, Snacks | Gas / Diesel | Repairs: Hull, Engine, Propeller | Lift (tonnage), Crane, Rail | Nearby: Grocery Store, Motel, Restaurant | Laundry, Pool, Showers, Courtesy Car | Pump-Out Station | Min/Max Amps |
| 1. Dunedin Municipal Marina 139 | 727-298-3030 | 70 | 16 | 9/194 | 5/4.5 | – | – | – | – | – | 30/50 | S | P | GMR |
| 2. Marker 1 Marina 🖥 WiFi .5 E of 141.5 | 727-733-9324 | 78 | 16/14 | 10/150 | 6/6 | – | GD | IMS | HEP | – | 30/50 | LPS | P | GMR |
| 3. Caladesi Island State Park Marina | 727-469-5918 | – | – | call/108 | 4/4 | F | – | IS | – | – | 30/30 | S | – | – |

🖥 Internet Access   WiFi Wireless Internet Access   WG Waterway Guide Cruising Club Partner   *(Information in the table is provided by the facilities.)*
See WaterwayGuide.com for current rates, fuel prices, web site addresses, and other up-to-the-minute information.

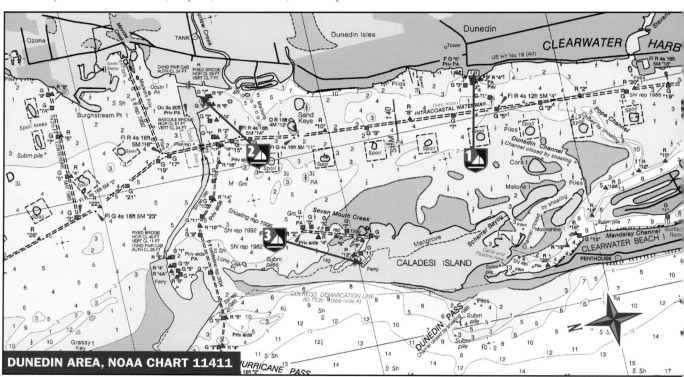

DUNEDIN AREA, NOAA CHART 11411

# ■ CLEARWATER HARBOR

Although divided by the GIWW channel, Clearwater and Clearwater Beach constitute one very boat-minded community. The seat of Pinellas County and one of Florida's fastest-growing resort cities, Clearwater extends across the upper end of the Pinellas Peninsula.

Boaters are finding it an increasingly important port of call, both as a base of operations from which to enjoy the nearby resort attractions and also as a layover stop. The yacht services and elegant marinas here are mostly deepwater and capable of handling the largest boats that travel the GIWW. Marinas and repair installations are busy, but transient berths are generally available.

**NAVIGATION:** Use Chart 11411. The best access to Clearwater from the Gulf of Mexico is through Clearwater Pass, just south of Clearwater. The 74-foot fixed vertical clearance **Clearwater Memorial Causeway (SR 60) Bridge** crosses Clearwater Pass at GIWW Mile 136. This is one of the west coast's better daytime passes, and it is easy to use in good weather. North of the causeway, the channel has shoaled; proceed with caution.

From Clearwater Pass, once you are in the channel just after passing flashing red daybeacon "8" and passing under the bridge, you will spot quick-flashing red daybeacon "10," then flashing red daybeacon "14" as you follow the channel. At flashing red daybeacon "14," turn to port into the channel marked by red daybeacon "2" (leave it to starboard) and green daybeacon "3." A well-marked channel will take you to green daybeacon "9," where you will turn to port into the channel leading in from the GIWW to the Clearwater Municipal Marina.

For more docking choices, after passing flashing red daybeacon "12," look for green daybeacon "1" just short of the Clearwater Causeway. Turn to port, and then follow the well-marked channel parallel to the causeway to green daybeacon "9," where that channel merges with the one coming in from Clearwater Pass. At this point, you can continue on to the marina of your choice.

**Dockage:** Approaching from the GIWW channel, the Clearwater Municipal Marinas (Clearwater Harbor Marina, on the mainland side) is at green daybeacon "11." A sizable charter boat fleet is berthed here, as well as tour and fishing boats of all sizes. The marina takes reservations and the helpful marina staff can usually accommodate transients. The "Jolly Trolley" (clearwaterjolleytrolley.com) stops in front of the marina complex and provides a convenient ride to the grocery store. "Sunsets at Pier 60," a daily celebration similar to Key West's Mallory Square, includes music, entertainment, food and crafts for sale.

Clearwater's largest concentration of marinas is on the beach side between the Clearwater Pass and Clearwater Causeway. They can be approached either via a clearly marked and easy-to-navigate channel off the Clearwater Pass entrance channel, if you are coming from the Gulf of Mexico, or by a channel from the GIWW, if you are traveling by the inside route. Facilities located between Clearwater Pass and the Causeway include Chart House Marina, Clearwater Yacht Club and the municipal Clearwater Beach Marina (on the beach end of the bridge). All have some transient space and the municipal marina sells fuel, both gas and diesel, plus some groceries. Adjacent to the municipal marina is The Bait House Tackle and Tavern (727-446-8134), featuring cold beer, fresh bait and outstanding tackle. At the other end of the parking lot is Crabby's Dockside (727-210-1313) with a noteworthy happy hour from 11:00 a.m. to 7:00 p.m. The Island Way Grill (20 Island Way, 727-461-6617) and Bobby's Bistro and Wine Bar (447 Mandalay Ave., 727-446-9463) are close by as well.

**Anchorage:** There are more anchoring choices in Clearwater Harbor than in Boca Ciega Bay, beginning with Belleair at GIWW Mile 131.9. On the northern side of the **Belleair Causeway Bridge** (75-foot fixed vertical clearamce) you will find 7 to 8 feet with good holding in sand.

At Clearwater Beach, Clearwater Yacht Club has an anchorage with 6 to 9 feet of water. You can also anchor on either side of the west side of the **Causeway Blvd. (SR 60) Bridge** (14-foot fixed vertical clearance).

## Dunedin Pass Area

Dunedin (Mile 139) is home to several beaches, including Dunedin Causeway, Honeymoon Island, and Caladesi Island State Park (accessible only by boat), which is consistently rated among the best beaches in the world. The island has trails and quiet beaches and is definitely worth the effort to get there.

Dunedin is one of the few open waterfront communities from Sarasota to Cedar Key where buildings do not completely obscure the view of the waterway and the Gulf of Mexico beyond from the highway. There is also a lack of large commercial signage to obscure the view and no franchise restaurants or chain retail stores.

The Pinellas Trail, a 39-mile-long (63 km) bicycle and pedestrian trail that traverses all of Pinellas County, bisects downtown Dunedin. A large portion of the trail lies on the former roadbed of the Orange Belt Railway, the first railroad in Pinellas County, which arrived in 1888.

# St. Joseph Sound, FL

| PALM HARBOR AREA | | Largest Vessel Accommodated | VHF Channel Monitored | Transient Berths / Total Berths | Approach / Dockside Depth (reported) | Floating Docks | Gas / Diesel | Groceries, Ice, Marine Supplies, Snacks | Repairs: Hull, Engine, Propeller | Lift (tonnage), Crane, Rail | Min/Max Amps | Laundry, Pool, Showers, Courtesy Car | Pump-Out Station | Nearby: Grocery Store, Motel, Restaurant |
|---|---|---|---|---|---|---|---|---|---|---|---|---|---|---|
| **1.** Island Harbor Marina | 727-784-3014 | 30 | – | call/43 | 5/5 | F | – | – | EP | L | – | S | – | GMR |
| **2.** Home Port Marina **WiFi** | 727-784-1443 | 42 | – | call/187 | 5/5 | – | GD | IMS | HEP | L | 30/30 | LPS | P | GMR |
| **3.** George's Marina | 727-784-3798 | 40 | – | call/11 | /5 | – | – | IS | HEP | L10 | – | – | – | GMR |
| **4.** Ozona Fish Camp 💻 **WiFi** | 727-614-8041 | 32 | 68 | – | – | – | G | IMS | – | – | 30/30 | – | P | GMR |

💻 Internet Access  **WiFi** Wireless Internet Access  **WG** Waterway Guide Cruising Club Partner *(Information in the table is provided by the facilities.)*
See WaterwayGuide.com for current rates, fuel prices, web site addresses, and other up-to-the-minute information.

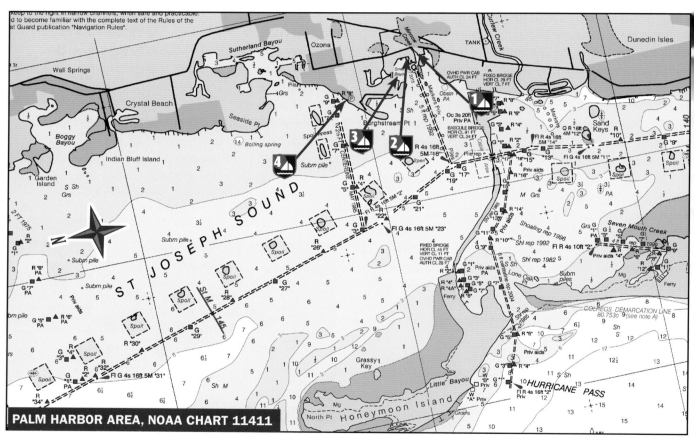

**PALM HARBOR AREA, NOAA CHART 11411**

**Dockage:** The Dunedin Municipal Marina has transient docks and is within walking distance to Dunedin's restaurants and shopping. The Bon Appetit Restaurant and Bar is next to the municipal marina and has docks for mariners who want to dine ashore (727-733-2151). Marker 1 Marina, immediately south of the **Dunedin-Honeymoon Island Bridge** (opens on signal) offers transient dockage and gas and diesel fuel. (Note that although the Dunedin-Honeymoon Island Bridge has a charted clearance of 24-feet when closed, our cruising editor observed and verified that it is actually a clearance of 18 feet.)

There are 90 slips in the wonderfully isolated Caldesi Island State Park. To get to Caldesi Island, turn west just south of the Dunedin Bridge (green daybeacon "17") and then follow the Honeymoon Island Channel to a separate buoyed channel into Seven Mouth Creek. Only three slips here are wider than 11 feet; however, there are three "T" docks for larger boats. Average depths on the approach and dockside are reported at 4 feet, so you need to travel at high tide, go slowly and obtain up-to-date local knowledge. Call 727-469-5918 for reservations.

# ST. JOSEPH SOUND

About 3 miles north of Clearwater, the barrier islands fall away and the GIWW enters unprotected St. Joseph Sound and the approach to Anclote Key. After this final stretch on the GIWW, boaters continuing north beyond Anclote Key and the Anclote River have two choices. They may cross the open Gulf of Mexico for about 140 nm to Carrabelle, or they can follow a series of several markers relatively close in-shore around the Big Bend section of Florida for about 160 or 165 miles to Carrabelle.

**Anchorage:** A popular anchorage in St. Joseph Sound is Three Rooker Bar, a narrow C-shaped island located between Honeymoon Island and Anclote Key, about 2.5 miles offshore from Tarpon Springs. Three Rooker's white sand beaches line the north and seaward sides of the island and offer some of the best shelling and beachcombing. The bay side of the island's shallow water teems with fish and birds. It is a well-protected anchorage from all but east winds. Enter around the north end of the bar, dropping anchor in the crescent near the beach in 4- to 8-foot depths over a soft mud bottom. Use the depth sounder and line-of-sight navigation, avoiding the white sand bars that run out from the beach. On holiday weekends, this normally placid anchorage becomes a maelstrom of activity, with jet skis, small outboards and a floating hamburger stand all vying for space.

## Palm Harbor Area

**NAVIGATION:** Use Chart 11411. North of the Dunedin-Honeymoon Island Bridge (24-foot vertical clearance, opens on demand), turn east at green daybeacon "17" and follow the privately marked channel into Palm Harbor, which is shown on the chart as Smith Bayou.

**Dockage:** To reach Island Harbor Marina and Home Port Marina, head up the channel toward the large dry stack buildings. Call for slip availability. Ozona Blue Gulfside Grill (727-789-4540) is at Home Port Marina. George's Marina is on the northeast side of the harbor and may have transient space as well. Ozona Fish Camp has a marked channel to the north and they sell gas and may have transient dockage for smaller boats (up to 32 feet).

## Side Trip: Tarpon Springs

Tarpon Springs is still the "Sponge Capital of the World" and has managed to diversify without losing its old-time flavor. While a large shrimp fleet and a lively boat-building industry make their homes in Tarpon Springs, colorful spongers still ply the waters as well. You will find Greek restaurants galore along the picturesque sponge docks.

**NAVIGATION:** Use Chart 11411. A range helps you through the big offshore shoal around the entrance to the Anclote River. (If you cannot see the onshore light, locate quick-flashing green daybeacon "1.") Channel markers are no more than three-quarters of a mile apart. For help in orienting, you will see a tall, strobe-lighted power plant chimney on the north side of the Anclote River entrance, visible from 22 nm at sea on a clear day. The chimney, illuminated by flashing lights at night, is plotted on Chart 11411 ("STACK") and mentioned in the *U.S. Coast Pilot*.

Respect the shoal south of Anclote Key. When entering the GIWW south of Anclote Key, or entering the Anclote River, give flashing green daybeacon "7" near Mile 150 its due respect. Older charts may not show the extension of the shoal southward. When traveling in this area, it is important to keep your charts current and your depthsounder on.

⚠️ Severe shoaling has been observed in the Anclote River in the vicinity of Anclote River turning basin daybeacons "51" and "53" at Tarpon Springs. Mariners are advised to use extreme caution while transiting the area.

Take it easy going upriver the 3 miles to Tarpon Springs and observe the posted Idle-Speed/No-Wake Zone. There are many boats at slips in the river, and your wake can cause serious damage. Also, commercial fishing and sponging boats use the channel. The Cut C range's eastern mark is partially obscured by trees. Favor the southern side of the channel to avoid the shoal.

**Dockage:** You will pass several dry-stack marinas that may have space for transients. Just as you enter the river, on the northeast side (to port) is Anclote Village Marina. With some transient slips available, and "high and dry" storage for small boats, the marina offers a convenient stopping place if you do not have the time to go upriver.

Opposite green daybeacon "39" on the northeast side (to port entering the river), Port Tarpon Marina has a convenient fuel dock with gas and diesel just off the

www.snagaslip.com

SNAG-A-SLIP™

EXPLORE. BOOK. BOAT.

# Anclote River, FL

| TARPON SPRINGS AREA | Phone | Largest Vessel Accommodated | VHF Channel Monitored | Transient Berths / Total Berths | Approach / Dockside Depth (reported) | Floating Docks | Gas / Diesel | Groceries, Ice, Marine Supplies, Snacks | Repairs: Hull, Engine, Propeller | Lift (tonnage), Crane, Rail | Min/Max Amps | Laundry, Pool, Showers, Courtesy Car | Pump-Out Station | Nearby: Grocery Store, Motel, Restaurant |
|---|---|---|---|---|---|---|---|---|---|---|---|---|---|---|
| | | | | **Dockage** | | | **Supplies** | | **Services** | | | | | |
| 1. Anclote Village Marina (WiFi) (WG) | 727-937-9737 | 55 | – | 2/20 | 5/7 | F | GD | IMS | E | L10 | 30/50 | – | – | R |
| 2. Port Tarpon Marina ☐ (WiFi) | 727-937-2200 | 75 | 16 | 10/58 | 9/9 | F | GD | IMS | HEP | L50 | 50/100 | S | – | R |
| 3. Anclote Harbors Marina (WiFi) | 727-934-7616 | 45 | 16 | 4/30 | 9/6 | F | G | I | HEP | L | 50/50 | LS | – | GMR |
| 4. Anclote Isles Marina ☐ (WiFi) (WG) | 727-939-0100 | 65 | 16 | 10/70 | 8/6 | – | – | GIMS | – | – | 30/100 | S | P | GMR |
| 5. Belle Harbour Marina ☐ (WiFi) (WG) | 727-943-8489 | 50 | 16/68 | 3/18 | 6/5 | F | G | IM | HEP | L7 | 30/50 | LS | P | GMR |
| 6. Tarpon Landing Marina | 727-937-1100 | 65 | – | 5/50 | 5/6 | – | GD | IM | HEP | – | 30/50 | – | P | GR |
| 7. Tarpon Springs Yacht Club | 727-934-2136 | 60 | – | call/18 | – | – | – | – | – | – | – | S | – | R |
| 8. City of Tarpon Springs Municipal Marina | 727-937-9165 | 50 | 16 | 6/21 | 11/10 | – | – | IS | – | – | 30/50 | S | – | GMR |
| 9. River Energy-The New F & Y Inc. | 727-937-4351 | 200 | 01 | – | 12/12 | – | D | M | – | – | 50/50 | – | – | GMR |
| 10. Gulf Marine Ways | 727-937-4401 | 85 | – | – | 10/10 | – | – | IM | HEP | R | 50/50 | – | – | GR |
| 11. Turtle Cove Marina (WiFi) | 727-934-2202 | 50 | 16/72 | 10/56 | 5/6 | F | GD | IMS | HEP | L12 | 30/50 | LPS | P | GMR |

☐ Internet Access   (WiFi) Wireless Internet Access   (WG) Waterway Guide Cruising Club Partner   *(Information in the table is provided by the facilities.)*
See WaterwayGuide.com for current rates, fuel prices, web site addresses, and other up-to-the-minute information.

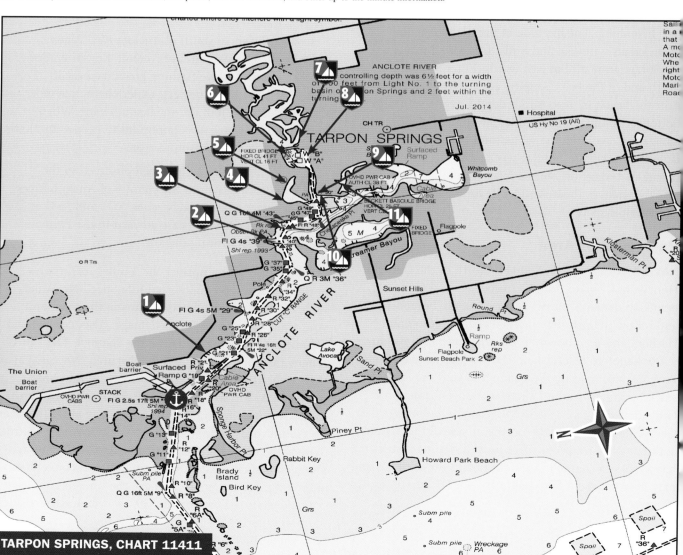

**TARPON SPRINGS, CHART 11411**

iver channel, a limited number of transient slips and an on-site restaurant. Next door, Anclote Harbors Marina welcomes cruising boats up to 45 feet. To the east, Anclote Isles Marina and Belle Harbour Marina have dockage.

Staying at any of the marinas on the north side of the river means you will need to arrange for transportation if you wish to get to the sponge docks and restaurants, most of which are on the south side of the river. The exception is Tarpon Landing Marina, from which sponge docks and Greek restaurants are a short walk across the fixed **SR 19 Alternate Hwy. Bridge** to the south side of the river. As evening approaches, the sounds of live music and laughter can be heard from Capt'n Jack's restaurant and bar at the head of the slips (727-944-3346).

At the end of the navigable portion of the river, to starboard, right next to the sponge docks and the Sponge Museum is the City of Tarpon Springs Municipal Marina. It retains an old-time flavor and offers transient slips; reservations are a must. Its location at the east end of the sponge docks is ideal for exploring Tarpon Springs, with its sponge-diving trips, aquarium and many excellent Greek restaurants. The nearby Tarpon Springs Yacht Club welcomes members of reciprocating yacht clubs.

On the south side of the river are River Energy (the New F&Y Inc.) and Gulf Marine Ways; both are repair and service facilities. Turtle Cove Marina is a full-service facility with fuel and other amenities.

**Anchorage:** An anchorage with 6-foot depths is located by the river's entrance east of green daybeacon "17" and just beyond the stack. There is a nearby park with a boat ramp and restrooms. Up the river in Tarpon Springs, some boats anchor in front of the city marina, but shoaling and traffic may be a problem, and it is not recommended. It is also possible to anchor at Anclote Key (Mile 151) in 8 to 10 feet with excellent holding and protection from the west.

## Cruising Options

Tarpon Springs on the Anclote River marks the end of the Florida GIWW at Mile 150. (The GIWW picks back up in Carrabelle, FL, where mileages are measured east and west of Harvey Lock, LA, notated as EHL or WHL.) Beyond, from Anclote Key at the mouth of the Anclote River, lie the intriguing Big Bend (or Nature Coast) and the Florida Panhandle.

# GOIN' ASHORE: TARPON SPRINGS, FL

| SERVICES | |
|---|---|
| 1 | Library |
| 2 | Visitor Information |
| **ATTRACTIONS** | |
| 3 | Historic Tarpon Springs |
| 4 | Splash Museum |
| 5 | Sponge Docks |
| 6 | Sponge Factory |

| | |
|---|---|
| 7 | Tarpon Springs Heritage Museum |
| **SHOPPING** | |
| 8 | Sav-A-Lot |
| **DINING** | |
| 9 | Captain Jack's Waterfront Bar & Grille |
| 10 | Rusty Bellies Waterfront Grill |
| 11 | ShrimpWrecked Restaurant & Dockside Bar |

| MARINAS | |
|---|---|
| 2 | City of Tarpon Springs Municipal Marina |
| 10 | Gulf Marine Ways |
| 12 | Anclote Isles Marina |
| 13 | Belle Harbour Marina |
| 14 | Tarpon Landing Marina |
| 15 | Tarpon Springs Yacht Club |
| 16 | Turtle Cove Marina |

In reality, there are two Tarpon Springs. Both are intimately interrelated and well worth a visit. The sponge docks, the unbroken string of Greek restaurants and charming shops along Dodecanese Boulevard and the marinas are one aspect, while the other (historic downtown Tarpon Springs) is a charming complement to the docks. Be sure to stop at the Visitors Center at the City Marina (100 Dodecanese Blvd., 727-934-2952) to pick up a map of the area.

**Attractions:** A casual walk along the Dodecanese Boulevard waterfront brings to mind Europe more so than Florida. Many of the boutiques and restaurants are housed in former sponge warehouses. Your tour should include the Sponge Factory (15 Dodecanese Blvd., 727-938-5366), where a brief movie tells the story of the original Greek sponge divers who made Tarpon Springs the "Sponge Capital of the World" and left an indelible mark on the city. Included in the theater is a museum, featuring sponge-diving exhibitions and exhibits of authentic sponging ships of bygone years; a 90-foot "mother" ship and a 38-foot diving boat. You can also buy from a broad range of sponges of all sizes, shapes and types. You can then take an hour-long trip on an authentic sponge boat and watch a diver go through his paces.

The second Tarpon Springs, Historic Tarpon Springs, is a 10-minute cab ride from the sponge docks or you can catch a ride on the city trolley or municipal bus; both have stops close by the city marina. This is an unusual and charming area, well worth the cruiser's stop.

For cruisers with dogs on board, a 10-minute walk from either marina leads to a dog park, with two separate fenced-in play areas, where the dogs can romp without leashes. Adjacent to the dog park is a Children's Splash Park with restrooms and a picnic pavilion, a children's play area, a fitness park with 10 pieces of outdoor equipment (under sail shades) and a lawn for yoga, etc.

From November to early spring, you will find manatees that make their home in the shallow Spring Bayou close to downtown. Craig Park offers a great vantage point for observing these gentle giants. It only takes a short dinghy ride to get to the Bayou, but it becomes a non-motorized area so you will need to row in and around the bayou to view the manatees.

While at Craig Park, why not stop in the Tarpon Springs Heritage Museum? The facility has two separate wings: The History Wing contains an exhibit about the Greek community of Tarpon Springs, as well as a collection of Native American archaeological artifacts from local excavations, while the ecology wing features large-scale murals of Tarpon Springs by artist Christopher Still. Visitors also can view a 16-minute documentary about the local sponge industry (727-937-0686).

**Shopping:** Dodecanese Blvd. and Athens St. on the Sponge Docks have hundreds of gift shops offering clothing, jewelry, sponges, souvenirs, and more. You will also find bakeries and a small convenience store on Athens St. There is a Save-A-Lot downtown (780 S. Pinellas Ave., 727-934-0446), but to the east (near Rt. 19) is a Publix and Walmart plus other shopping.

**Dining:** No visit is complete without sampling the Greek food on Dodecanese Boulevard. When you have worked up an appetite from a hard day of sightseeing, stop in at one of the many authentic restaurants lining the main street. If you do not go for the flaming saganaki (cheese appetizer) or the broiled octopus, their generous-sized Greek salads and hearty lamb dishes are particularly noteworthy (and available at too many restaurants to name here). After dinner or at snack time, sample some of the pastries sold at the bakeries inside each of the restaurants, especially the baklava.

For outdoor deck dining and entertainment, visit Captain Jack's Waterfront Bar & Grille (21 Oscar Hill Rd., 727-944-3346) at Tarpon Landing Marina. Rusty Bellies Waterfront Grill (937 Dodecanese Blvd., 727-934-4047) is a restaurant and seafood market that serves seafood fresh off the boats. Visit rustybellies.com for details. ShrimpWrecked Restaurant & Dockside Bar (210 Dodecanese Blvd., 727-943-9879, next to the City Marina) offers expansive outdoor dining and a Tiki bar. There are also Italian, Cuban, and Asian restaurants nearby. After dinner, you can catch a show, listen to live music or take in some belly dancing!

**Marinas**   **Services**   **Anchorages**   **Bridges & Locks**   **Nav Alerts**   **Fuel**

# 6 Waterway Explorer provides different icons that overlay on the maps as modes

## Modes

**Info Pane with details**

*Plan your time on the water with Explorer*

# www.waterwayguide.com

# Florida's Upper Gulf Coast

■ THE BIG BEND: ANCLOTE KEY TO CARRABELLE
■ THE PANHANDLE: APALACHICOLA TO PENSACOLA

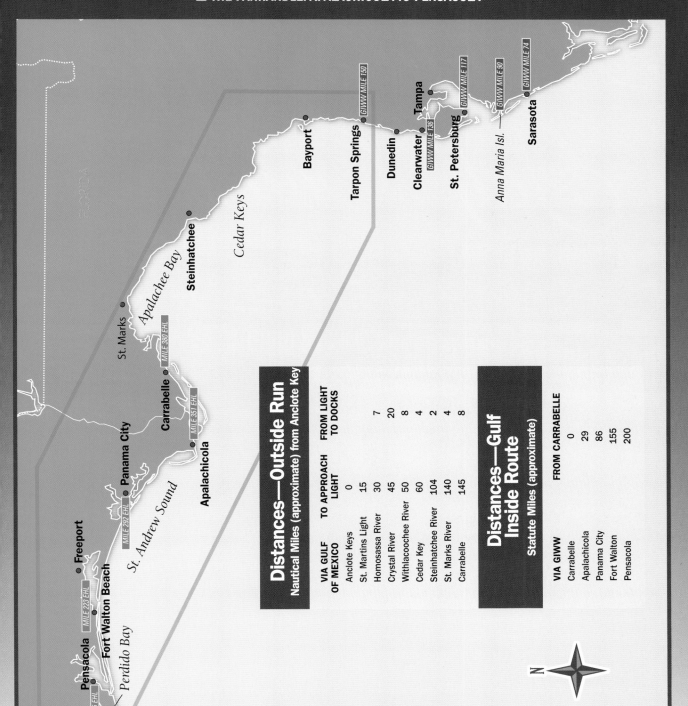

**FLORIDA'S UPPER GULF COAST**

## Distances—Outside Run
**Nautical Miles (approximate) from Anclote Key**

| VIA GULF OF MEXICO | TO APPROACH LIGHT | FROM LIGHT TO DOCKS |
|---|---|---|
| Anclote Keys | 0 | |
| St. Martins Light | 15 | 7 |
| Homosassa River | 30 | 20 |
| Crystal River | 45 | 8 |
| Withlacoochee River | 50 | 4 |
| Cedar Key | 60 | 2 |
| Steinhatchee River | 104 | 4 |
| St. Marks River | 140 | 8 |
| Carrabelle | 145 | |

## Distances—Gulf Inside Route
**Statute Miles (approximate)**

| VIA GIWW | FROM CARRABELLE |
|---|---|
| Carrabelle | 0 |
| Apalachicola | 29 |
| Panama City | 86 |
| Fort Walton | 155 |
| Pensacola | 200 |

www.WaterwayGuide.com

# Florida's Upper Gulf Coast

F

Florida's Upper Gulf Coast stretches from the Anclote Keys on the eastern end to Pensacola and Perdido Bay on the west. It offers two distinct cruising regions: the fascinating swampy marshland and wilderness of the Big Bend/Nature Coast and the stretches of blazing white sand beaches, spiked by high-rise condominiums, of the dazzling coastline that is Florida's Panhandle.

Skippers visiting Florida's Upper Gulf Coast for the first time find a very different kind of cruising, first from the Anclote Keys to Carrabelle across the Big Bend, then into the true Florida Panhandle, from Apalachicola to Pensacola and the Alabama line. The first part of this 350-nm stretch, known as the Big Bend area (but officially called Florida's Nature Coast), has no protected inside route. Mariners must make the trip across the open Gulf of Mexico. For the second half, from Carrabelle on to Florida's Panhandle, you can travel the Gulf Intracoastal Waterway (GIWW) or continue outside in the Gulf of Mexico.

## Weather

You will feel the effects of the higher latitude of this region. The Upper Gulf Coast of Florida is the only coastal section of the state that experiences a noticeable winter. For example, whereas "The Season" in South Florida runs generally from November to April, "The Season" in the Upper Gulf Coast, depending on the marine facility and location, may

run from Memorial Day to Labor Day. It gets chilly in the winter, but it is still possible to enjoy these uncrowded, clear waters, award-winning beaches and boating-oriented communities.

## Tides

Along the panhandle of Florida, a rather unique change occurs to tides. West of St. George Sound/Apalachicola Bay, there are only 2 tides per 24 hours (one high and one low), while east of this demarcation, the tides are the normal 4 per 24 hours (2 highs, and 2 lows).

## The Coastal Cruiser

Along the west coast shore of the Big Bend/Nature Coast, from Anclote Key almost to Carrabelle, the Gulf of Mexico is relatively shallow and the coastline low and indistinct. If you are running along the shore, keep a close eye on the depth sounder and tide charts and the little buoys for crab pots and lobster traps. This is a fine sailing area, but boats with deep drafts should be wary of the shoals.

Skippers with time to spare and a taste for exploring an area not yet swarming with cruising tourists shouldn't ignore the rivers of the "Lonesome Leg." But remember, only an able, shallow-draft boat with a reliable depth sounder should attempt to cruise in this territory.

The long rivers offer splendid gunkholing and excellent fishing, but go in carefully and follow the approach and channel markers. Since many of these streams are loaded with weeds, be sure you have got strainers on all seawater intakes. This is brown pelican country. They have a tendency to deface buoy numbers, and a pelican perched on a can buoy will, from a distance, change the outline to that of a nun buoy. Get in the habit of checking floating marks carefully.

## Offshore Crossing: To St. George Island

If you don't plan to cruise the Big Bend area, running the 130- to 140-nm rhumb line directly from Tarpon Springs or Clearwater to the St. George Island East Pass entrance buoy to Carrabelle can save a lot of time, but only an able boat enjoying good weather should attempt this passage. Many cruisers prefer to follow a route closer to the coastline. There used to be markers, called the Big Bend markers, which provided an inside route closer to the coastline. These were discontinued, but there are channel entrance markers that can be used to run a course closer to shore.

Before setting out, make sure your boat is seaworthy and your engine sound. Know your compass error. Be sure you are using the latest charts. There have been numerous changes to the navigation aids in recent years. Along the route, plot your courses carefully and stick to them. The land is low lying and it can be a long stretch between the navigation aids as you traverse this coastline. Always track your position, by dead reckoning and GPS. There are some remote sections of this coast and even though you are not far off shore, you may be far from help. A registered Emergency Position Indicating Radio Beacon (EPIRB) is an excellent addition to your safety equipment.

Those choosing the direct route, particularly in the Big Bend area, should leave a float plan with a friend or relative. If trouble occurs, rescue units will arrive much faster if they know your route. Unless you are very experienced, run only in daylight. It is particularly important to have daylight while you are within 20 nm or so of the Florida coast, as the crab pots can be very thick. Keep an eye to the sky and watch for changes in the weather. NOAA weather radio or local commercial AM or FM radio stations and satellite weather services, such as XM Weather, should be monitored regularly for the latest information.

## Inside Route: Carrabelle to Pensacola

You can travel outside in the Gulf of Mexico by following the coastline all the way to Pensacola. The more interesting GIWW route connects big bays and sounds that are protected by narrow, wooded barrier islands. From Carrabelle to Pensacola, there are 200 statute miles of inside cruising with occasional passes to the Gulf of Mexico. Fixed bridge heights of 50 feet will prevent most sailboats from using some of the inside route.

On the east, the Florida Panhandle extends north beyond Carrabelle and inland to Tallahassee, the state capital. To the west, the Panhandle extends to Pensacola, once an outpost of the Spanish colony of New Orleans, and later the capital of British West Florida during the American Revolution. Midway along the route is Panama City, a well-equipped sportfishing and boating center surrounded by pure white beaches. Other worthwhile stops include Apalachicola, Port St. Joe, Destin and Fort Walton Beach. A fixed 49-foot bridge at Destin to the Gulf will dictate whether or not you can access the inner route to Fort Walton.

# The Big Bend: Anclote Key to Carrabelle

**VHF** FL: Channel 09

**CHARTS** 1114A, 11401, 11404, 11405, 11406, 11407, 11408, 11409

Floridians call it "The Big Bend." The State government and local Chambers of Commerce call it "The Nature Coast." For boaters, it is the longest open water unprotected passage for the 3,000 miles between Newport, RI, and Port Isabel, TX. It is a common topic of conversation between boaters in and near this region. For cruisers with the time, the right boat and the ability this is the area for those interested in lovely, and often isolated, wilderness grounds. Most cruising is done in the rivers entering the Gulf of Mexico, and there is no inside waterway or protected route to take. Fishing and hunting are the name of the game here. But sharpen up your navigation skills and cruise carefully. You may be a long and expensive distance from commercial assistance if you make a mistake.

North of Anclote Key and Tarpon Springs, as far as Carrabelle to the west, the coastline presents cruising skippers with a very different kind of Florida cruising. Shoaling normally extends so far out that cruisers are basically in open, although shallow, Gulf of Mexico waters. These are fishermen's waters, both fresh and saltwater. The entrance channels can be shallow and tricky but they are loaded with fish of all types.

Most of the coast is low and marshy. The countryside is still undeveloped, even primitive in spots, and any place you put in will offer fascinating and unique side trips with their own navigational challenges.

The Coast Guard station on the Withlacoochee River at Yankeetown, about 17 miles southeast of Cedar Key, covers this area and monitors VHF Channel 16. This station also operates and maintains three vessels for emergency search and rescue. In addition to VHF, the station can be reached by telephone at 352-447-6900.

## ■ EXPLORING THE BIG BEND

This section is uniquely different and purposefully prepared and included in this chapter to underline the care and caution warranted for navigating the Big Bend waters of Florida. You don't have to be apprehensive about sailing these waters. There are no reports of monsters (although there is an occasional black bear), and the vast majority of cruisers discover worthwhile experiences and fond memories; however, you must be attentive and responsible in all of your preparations.

There are still some old salts who remember when navigation consisted of a good timepiece, knot log, paper

# Little Pine Island Bay, FL

| HERNANDO BEACH | | Largest Vessel Accommodated | VHF Channel Monitored | Transient Berths / Total Berths | Approach / Dockside Depth (reported) | Floating Docks | Gas / Diesel | Groceries, Ice, Marine Supplies, Snacks | Repairs: Hull, Engine, Propeller | Lift (tonnage), Crane, Rail | Min/Max Amps | Laundry, Pool, Showers, Courtesy Car | Pump-Out Station | Nearby: Grocery Store, Motel, Restaurant |
|---|---|---|---|---|---|---|---|---|---|---|---|---|---|---|
| **1.** Hernando Beach Marina | 352-596-2952 | 40 | – | call/31 | 4/4 | F | GD | IMS | HEP | L30 | 30/30 | S | – | GMR |
| **2.** Blue Pelican Marina | 352-610-9999 | 30 | – | 4/4 | 4/4 | F | G | IMS | HEP | L10 | – | S | – | GMR |

◻ Internet Access  📶 Wireless Internet Access  **WG** Waterway Guide Cruising Club Partner  *(Information in the table is provided by the facilities.)*
See WaterwayGuide.com for current rates, fuel prices, web site addresses, and other up-to-the-minute information.

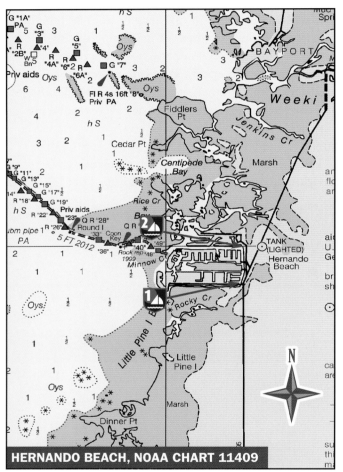

**HERNANDO BEACH, NOAA CHART 11409**

charts, sextant, reduction tables, tide tables, divider, parallel ruler and plotter. Then there was a time when radio direction finders were giving way to something new called Loran. Locally, the Big Bend is referred to as, "Old Florida." Don't discount the value of good paper charts with penciled rhumb lines that include course and distance. (You probably can leave the sextant at home.)

When sailing in difficult waters for which you have little knowledge and past experience, it may be safer to be farther out than nearer to land. Nevertheless, it is possible to safely make the Big Bend Passage and never lose sight of land.

The navigation sections in this chapter will provide information and options to help along each route as cruising boat crews and captains pick their way through the shallow depths of the Gulf of Mexico and into the unpredictable depths of the narrow channels and rivers. Considering the nature of these waters, it is not possible to guarantee total accuracy. Navigational information about shoals, location of river channels, aids to navigation and water depths are ever changing. On the land, marinas, facilities, restaurants, etc. come and go. Check the Waterway Guide Explorer for the most up-to-date information.

## A Choice of Two Routes

Your trip through the Big Bend starts with one of two choices regarding your route:

1. Travel an outside route in deeper water for whatever time it takes to reach your western destination. Without extensive local knowledge, plan your arrival for daylight. Weather will be a serious consideration. You need a boat capable of the offshore passage, a captain and crew with the ability and confidence to make the voyage.

2. Travel an inside route closer to shore and find safe harbor before dark. Chart a careful course and do not travel after sunset. These are shallow waters. Know where you are going to go, how you are going to get there, and the condition of the water all along the route...before you leave the dock! There are reefs in the Big Bend. Many are oyster bars, and some are littered with rocks. Channel and river depths can be difficult. It is advisable to call ahead and ask for local knowledge if you can.

**NAVIGATION:** Use Chart 1114A. Let's start by drawing course lines. Most of your cruising will be in Gulf waters, so all distances are measured in nautical miles (nm). All routes will start from Anclote Key flashing buoy red "2" at

## Routes

1. **Outside route from Anclote Key:** From Anclote Key red "2" draw a rhumb line (one line) all the way to East Pass flashing red "2" at N 29°44.541'/W 84°39'199'. The distance is 130 nm at a course of 313 degrees magnetic.

2. **Outside route from Clearwater Beach:** From the west end of Clearwater Pass 20-foot flashing green "1" draw a rhumb line at N 27°58.27'/W 82°50.84' to East Pass red "2." This course will take you 142.5 nm on a course of 323 degrees magnetic to East Pass flashing red "2."

3. **Inside route:** You will need to establish a series of courses for an inside route. Start at Anclote Key red "2" just as above, then:

A. Draw a rhumb line to St Martins Outer Shoal Lighted Buoy red "10" at N 28°25.864'/W 82°55.076'. The distance is 11 nm on a course of 354 degrees magnetic.

B. Draw a rhumb line from red "10" to St. Martin Keys Lighted Buoy red "2" at N 28°47.542'/W 82°58.571' (13 nm west of Homosasssa). The distance is 21.4 nm on a course of 350 degrees magnetic.

C. Draw a rhumb line from St. Martin Keys Red "2" to Cross Florida Barge Canal Light red "2" at N 28°55.430'/W 83°11.735'. The distance is 14 nm on a course of 303 degrees magnetic.

D. Draw a rhumb line from Barge Canal red "2" to the Ochlockonee Shoal Lighted Buoy red "24" at N 29°51.485'/W 84°10.318'. The distance is 76 nm at a course of 322 degrees magnetic.

E. Draw a rhumb line from Ochlockonee Light red "24" to East Pass flashing red "2" at N 29°44.541'/W 84°39.199'. The distance is 26 nm on a course of 254 degrees magnetic.

Chart your course as you navigate. It is unlikely that your compass course will be exactly as those above. Keep a constant eye on your depth. Watch your time. These are difficult waters to navigate at night.

28°15.089'/W 82°52.896'. Its location is 2.6 nm at 290 degrees from the north end of Anclote Key, or .6 nm at 277 degrees from red "4."

⚠ Red daybeacon "2" was reported to be missing in 2016. The steel piling may be present and it is reported to be marked by a TRLB flashing green "4M." No reports were available at the time of this writing in 2017 that red daybeacon "2" has been replaced. Approach this area with caution or consider using Anclote Key red daybeacon "4" as your starting point.

Along both direct offshore routes you will be as much as 45 nm from land. Channel entrances to find shelter from weather are probably too far away and, in inclement weather, too dangerous to navigate. Waiting for an agreeable weather window will make a big difference in the comfort and safety of your trip along this course. The average cruising boat may want to wait for winds that are less than 10 knots with sea conditions less than 4 feet. Westerly winds are the least desirable. If winds are blowing greater than 15 knots wait 24 hours after they fall below 10 knots before you depart.

You can plot a course closer to shore by using entrance buoys to the various river channels. The caveat here is to make sure when plotting the course that your bearing does not carry you over shoals your vessel cannot negotiate. If weather is fair and winds are no more than 10 to 15 knots from the east, northeast or southeast, seas should be less than 4 feet.

For vessels traveling by day, along an inside route, consider the following as possible ports for shelter before the sun goes down. Do not attempt to enter these channels after the sun goes down. All distances are total daily nautical miles from point of departure to an anchorage or marina at the end of each day.

### Daily distance of approximately 50 nm:
1. Anclote Key to Hernando Beach–25 nm
2. Hernando Beach to Crystal River–50 nm
3. Crystal River to Yankeetown–30 nm
4. Yankeetown to Suwannee River–50 nm
5. Suwannee to Steinhatchee–40 nm
6. Steinhatchee to St. Marks–60 nm
7. St. Marks to East Pass–40 nm

(Note that it is possible to go directly from Hernando Beach to Yankeetown, a distance of 50 nm. The channel is shallow and it can take more time to find deep water and work your way in to the Withlacoochee River.)

### Daily distance of approximately 60 nm:
1. Anclote Key to Crystal River–55 nm
2. Crystal River to Suwannee River–55 nm
3. Suwannee River to Steinhatchee–40 nm
4. Steinhatchee to St. Marks–60 nm
5. St. Marks to East Pass–45 nm

### Alternate Route:
1. Anclote Key to Yankeetown–55 nm
2. Yankeetown to Suwannee–50 nm
3. Suwannee River to Steinhatchee–40 nm
4. Steinhatchee to East Pass–70 nm

### Daily distance of approximately 80 nm:
1. Anclote to Suwannee River–75 nm
2. Suwannee River to Steinhatchee–40 nm
3. Steinhatchee to East Pass–70 nm

(Note that it is possible to go directly from Suwannee to East Pass, a distance of 90 nm.)

# ANCLOTE KEYS TO HOMOSASSA RIVER

...................................................................

**NAVIGATION:** Use Chart 11409. St Martins Reef runs along the coast north from Anclote Key for some 40 nm. The shoals of this reef extend over 10 nm offshore. St. Martin Outer Shoal Light 16-foot red daybeacon "10" marks the outer limit of the shallow water. Many of the rocks and shoals are identified by private markers. Cruisers without local knowledge should approach the coast with care, and deep draft vessels should stand out in deeper waters. Smaller boats with drafts of 3 to 4 feet can usually follow the coast and find smooth water by keeping about 7 nm offshore.

## Hernando Beach

Hernando Beach is a reachable stop between Anclote and Crystal River and is an easy daylight passage with a good weather window. It is a small community, but restaurants are within walking distance and Hernando Beach Marina has a small ship store.

**NAVIGATION:** Use Chart 11409. Travel the distance from Anclote Key red "2" to St Martin Outer Shoal "10," 11 nm at 350 degrees magnetic. From Outer Shoal red "10" set a course of 60 degrees magnetic for 8.5 nm to the private Oc flashing 14-foot marker. Then, go 3.5 nm at 58 degrees magnetic to a point where you can turn toward the Hernando Beach Channel. The channel entrance is 1 nm at 142 degrees magnetic. Controlling channel depth is reported as 4 feet; however, mariners with local knowledge say it is common for boats with drafts of 5 feet to use the channel.

**Dockage:** Hernando Beach Marina is the only marina here with transient slips; however, be aware that their widest slip is 14 feet. Blue Pelican Marina is primarily a dry stack facility and may not have transient space; call ahead for slip availability and to verify that shoaling is not a problem in this well-marked channel.

## Homosassa River

The Homosassa River is a comparatively narrow and shallow waterway with winding channels and unforgiving oyster bars and rock beds, but it supplies some great fishing for both salt and freshwater species. The village of Homosassa is an attractive fishing center

## Swim with the Manatees

Crystal River is Florida's second largest system of natural springs, with a daily flow of about 3 million cubic yards of water, at a constant temperature of 72 degrees. When the water temperature drops in the Gulf of Mexico, manatees move to the warmer waters of the Crystal River. This area may host Florida's largest population of manatees.

Do not leave this area without checking out the spectacular caverns nearby. You can look down from King's Bay and see springs 60 feet under the surface. This is the only place where you can legally swim with manatees in the wild in the U.S. (during designated times). Be respectful of the manatees and remember that <u>you</u> are in <u>their</u> waters.

We recommend going with a local guide who can take you to the manatee "hot spots" and who will also educate you about them, giving you a more full experience and a greater understanding of these gentle creatures.

Another option is to board a free bus tour to Three Sisters Spring during the Florida Manatee Festival, held the third weekend in January in downtown Crystal River. Tours run continuously during the Festival. Manatee boat tours are also available for a nominal charge to take you out into Kings Bay and other favorite hangouts of the manatees.

# Crystal River, Homosassa River, FL

| | | Largest Vessel Accommodated | VHF Channel Monitored | Transient Berths / Total Berths | Approach / Dockside Depth (reported) | Floating Docks | Gas / Diesel | Repairs: Hull, Engine, Propeller | Groceries, Ice, Marine Supplies, Snacks | Lift (tonnage), Crane, Rail | Min/Max Amps | Laundry, Pool, Showers, Courtesy Car | Pump-Out Station | Nearby: Grocery Store, Motel, Restaurant |
|---|---|---|---|---|---|---|---|---|---|---|---|---|---|---|
| **HOMOSASSA** | | | | | **Dockage** | | | **Supplies** | | | **Services** | | | |
| **1.** MacRae's of Homosassa 📶 | 352-628-2602 | 35 | 16/68 | call/10 | 6/3 | F | G | | IMS | P | – | 30/30 | LS | – | GMR |
| **CRYSTAL RIVER** | | | | | | | | | | | | | | |
| **2.** Twin Rivers Marina 🖥 📶 | 352-795-3552 | 60 | 16 | 6/53 | 5/8 | F | GD | | IMS | HEP | L35 | 30/50 | – | – | GR |
| **3.** Pete's Pier Inc. 🖥 | 352-795-3302 | 80 | 68 | 4/120 | 8/8 | – | GD | | IS | – | L | 30/50 | S | P | MR |

🖥 Internet Access    📶 Wireless Internet Access    **WG** Waterway Guide Cruising Club Partner   *(Information in the table is provided by the facilities.)*
See WaterwayGuide.com for current rates, fuel prices, web site addresses, and other up-to-the-minute information.

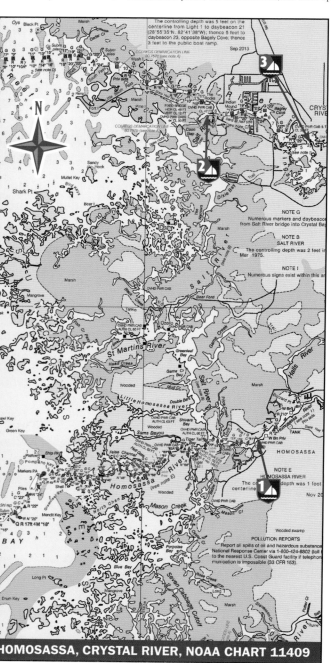

**HOMOSASSA, CRYSTAL RIVER, NOAA CHART 11409**

that grows more popular each year; more than 20 fishing guides operate year-round. Fishermen should remember that the river qualifies as freshwater, so a fishing license is required.

**NAVIGATION:** Use Chart 11409. The channel into the Homosassa River is narrow and shallow. The route twists and turns its way to the fishing village of Homosassa, about 4 miles upriver. It may be best described as treacherous for mariners without local knowledge piloting boats with drafts greater than 4 feet. Boats with drafts greater than 4 feet should not attempt this channel at low tide. Be aware that you may encounter many fast moving small fishing boats.

Travel the distance from Anclote Key red "2" to St Martin Outer Shoal "10," 11 nm at 350 degrees magnetic. From Outer Shoal red "10" set a course of 18 degrees magnetic for 16.5 nm to Homosassa Bay entrance lighted buoy red "2" at N 28°41.435'/
W 82°48.641'. Keep a close eye on your depth. Avoid the shoals to starboard just before and at red buoy "2."

⚠️ From this point through the river entrance, depths are reported from 3.5 to 7 feet at mean low water. Local mariners report depths of 3 feet at what they call "Hells Gate," a very narrow passage close the entrance of the marked channel. Proceed with great care. The channel and the river twist and turn and are very narrow. Currents can be strong. The slightest deviation could result in an encounter with rocks in the shoals.

**Dockage:** MacRae's of Homosassa has slips, sells gas and has a hotel, bait house (for anglers) and a riverfront tiki bar. They report 3-foot dockside depths, so call ahead if that is a concern.

# CRYSTAL RIVER TO CEDAR KEY

## Crystal River

Crystal River and Crystal Bay are located 45 nm north of Anclote River and 23 nm southeast of Cedar Key. A marked channel leads from the Gulf through Crystal Bay and the Crystal River 6 nm to Kings Bay and the Town of Crystal River.

**NAVIGATION:** Use Chart 11409. Travel the distance from Anclote Key red daybeacon "2" to St. Martin Outer Shoal "10," 11 nm at 350 degrees magnetic. From Outer Shoal red "10" continue on a course of 353 degrees magnetic for 21.4 nm to St. Martin Keys red daybeacon "2." As local channels and rivers go, Crystal River is navigable, and King's Bay is worth the trip. From red buoy "2" through the channel and the river, depths are posted from 5 to 8 feet at mean low water. Local mariners say the depth is 6 to 9 feet. During periods of north winds, depths can drop dramatically. There is a posted 25 mph speed limit.

King's Bay, at the head of Crystal River, is a designated Slow- and Idle-Speed Zone all along the river because of the manatee population.

**Dockage:** Transient slips, gas and diesel can be found at two marinas. At the junction of the Salt and Crystal Rivers, you will find the full-service Twin Rivers Marina. Use caution approaching the marina on the Salt River, and check your height; the charted overhead power cables have a 47-foot vertical clearance. This is the only complete full-service boatyard in Crystal River. Water depth to the marina and dockside is at least 6 feet.

Pete's Pier Inc. is located in the City of Crystal River at Kings Bay. They have some transient slips reserved and sell fuel. This is the only transient marina near downtown Crystal River. A grocery store, fish market, liquor store and a laundry are all about 1 mile from the waterfront. You can get a bite to eat at Crackers Bar and Grill (352-795-3999), which has a fun tiki hut with live entertainment on the weekends. (Transportation required.) There is a dock for small boats at the restaurant.

**Anchorage:** You can anchor anywhere in the wide part of Kings Bay before Pete's Pier. East of Pete's toward the docks at the Cracker's Restaurant is a smaller lagoon

# Withlacoochee River, FL

| YANKEETOWN | | Largest Vessel Accommodated | VHF Channel Monitored | Approach / Dockside Depth (reported) | Transient Berths / Total Berths | Floating Docks | Gas / Diesel | Repairs: Hull, Engine, Propeller | Groceries, Ice, Marine Supplies, Snacks | Lift (tonnage), Crane, Rail | Laundry, Pool, Showers, Courtesy Car | Pump-Out Station | Min/Max Amps | Nearby: Grocery Store, Motel, Restaurant |
|---|---|---|---|---|---|---|---|---|---|---|---|---|---|---|
| | | | | **Dockage** | | | | **Supplies** | | | **Services** | | | |
| 1. Yankeetown Marina | | 352-447-2529 | 50 | 16 | 1/50 | 6/6 | – | – | GIMS | – | – | 50/50 | – | GMR |
| 2. B's Marina & Campground 🖥 📶 | | 352-447-5888 | 60 | – | 3/12 | 12/12 | – | GD | I | – | – | 30/30 | LS | GMR |
| 3. Riverside Marina & Cottages 📶 | | 352-447-2980 | 60 | – | 3/15 | 25/6 | – | – | – | – | – | 30/30 | LS | GMR |

🖥 Internet Access  📶 Wireless Internet Access  **WG** Waterway Guide Cruising Club Partner  *(Information in the table is provided by the facilities.)*
See WaterwayGuide.com for current rates, fuel prices, web site addresses, and other up-to-the-minute information.

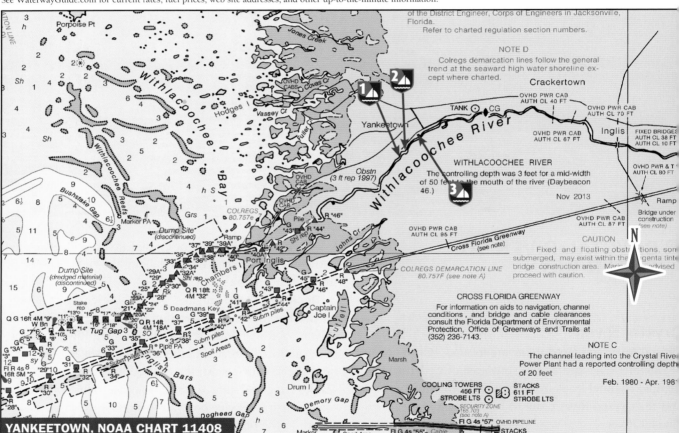

**YANKEETOWN, NOAA CHART 11408**

with depths of 4 feet or less. Kings Bay has very good holding and protection with plenty of room to swing. From here you can kayak or dinghy to the springs or to town.

## Withlacoochee River

There are two Withlacoochee Rivers in Florida. The other river flows from Georgia and empties into the Suwannee River. Big Bend's Withlacoochee River empties into the Gulf of Mexico 17 nm southeast of Cedar Keys. Yankeetown is the primary boating community on the river. It is a very small fishing and winter resort 3 nm above the mouth. The river is navigable for 8 miles

upstream where it intersects with a bridge with a fixed clearance of 10 feet. This is a navigable channel and river. The river itself is worth the trip to Yankeetown.

**NAVIGATION:** Use Charts 11408 and 11409. You need to work your way through the well-marked confusion of the Cross Florida Barge Canal into the channel for the Withlacoochee River. Back on your inside course through the Big Bend, leave St. Martin Keys red daybeacon "2" on a course of 3 degrees magnetic. Travel with a watchful eye on the depth sounder for 8 miles to the Florida Power Corporation red "4" at N 28°55.512'/W 82°58.004' W. The Cross Florida Barge

Canal runs in an easterly direction. Follow the canal to green "17" where a channel will branch of to the right and a channel will go slightly left or straight. Take the channel straight ahead and leave green daybeacon "19" to port.

At green daybeacon "23" leave the Barge Canal to the port on a course of 36 degrees magnetic for 0.5 mile to the marked Withlacoochee River Entrance channel. Stay in the channel. Rocks can be encountered on both sides. From green daybeacon "3" it is about 8 miles to Yankeetown. Controlling depths for the channel, canal and river are reported to be 5 plus feet at mean low water. The Withlacoochee definitely fits the bill for those wanting to take the path less traveled.

**Dockage:** This is a great place to visit, but do not expect high end docks or amenities. It is a remote location. Yankeetown Marina (6-foot approach depths), was under new management at press time in spring 2017, and there are plans for improvements. B's Cypress Marina and Campground is farther upriver and has some transient space and sells gas. They can make arrangements for delivery of diesel. Riverside Marina and Cottages does not have transient slips. You can tie alongside their dock if you are dining in the restaurant.

**Anchorage:** Sailboats have been seen anchoring near the Hwy. 19 Bridge on the cross Florida Greenway.

## Cedar Key

The Cedar Keys are a group of low sandy islets covered with mangrove trees. The outermost islet is Seahorse Key, where the white tower of an abandoned lighthouse stands on its south side. The lighthouse is visible from offshore.

Cedar Key is a small town on Way Key, located roughly one-third of the way between Anclote Key and Carrabelle. Named for the stand of cedar trees that once grew here, today the island is all logged out, and the town subsists on fishing, both commercial and sport, with tourism playing an increasingly important role. Cedar Key is the top U.S. producer of farm-raised clams.

**NAVIGATION:** Use Chart 11408. Resume your course for this route at St. Martin Keys red buoy "2." Leave St. Martin Keys buoy "2" on a course of 341 degrees magnetic, and travel for 17 nm to Cedar Key main channel lighted green "1." The approach to Cedar Key begins with 16-foot flashing green "1" (N 29°04.000'/ W 083°04.500') at the start of the charted Main Ship Channel. Depths in the Main Ship Channel are at least 7 feet, but you must follow the well-marked channel carefully. Study an up-to-date chart in detail before you enter, and you should have no difficulty. Use the inset on Chart 11408, or obtain a print-on-demand

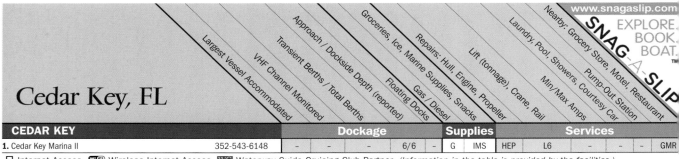

# Cedar Key, FL

| CEDAR KEY | | Dockage | | | | | | Supplies | | Services | | | | | |
|---|---|---|---|---|---|---|---|---|---|---|---|---|---|---|---|
| | | Largest Vessel Accommodated | VHF Channel Monitored | Approach / Dockside Depth (reported) | Transient Berths / Total Berths | Floating Docks | Gas / Diesel | Groceries, Ice, Marine Supplies, Snacks | Repairs: Hull, Engine, Propeller | Lift (tonnage), Crane, Rail | Laundry, Pool, Showers, Courtesy Car | Min/Max Amps | Pump-Out Station | Nearby: Grocery Store, Motel, Restaurant | |
| 1. Cedar Key Marina II | 352-543-6148 | – | – | – | 6/6 | – | G | IMS | HEP | L6 | – | – | – | GMR | |

💻 Internet Access  📶 Wireless Internet Access  🆆🅶 Waterway Guide Cruising Club Partner  *(Information in the table is provided by the facilities.)*
See WaterwayGuide.com for current rates, fuel prices, web site addresses, and other up-to-the-minute information.

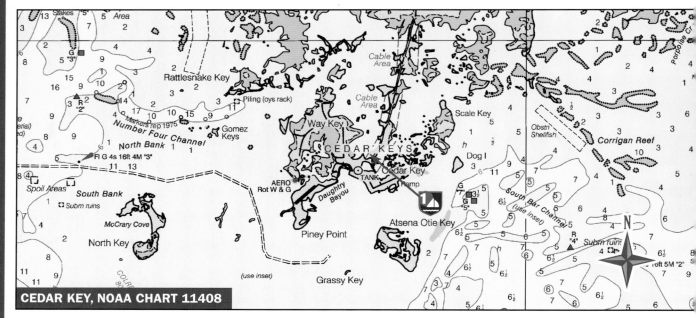

CEDAR KEY, NOAA CHART 11408

updated chart online. Check Waterway Guide Explorer (waterwayguide.com) for navigational updates.

Southwest from Seahorse Key, Seahorse Reef extends for 11 nm. This is a dangerous shoal with little depth. The outer end of the reef is marked by Seahorse Reef Light (N 28°58.310'/W 83°09.130'), with a height of 31 feet. The shoal between red daybeacons "10" and "12" is building out into the channel. When transiting this area, give red daybeacon "12" a wide berth, favoring the Seahorse Key side of the channel to port.

Be careful: Legions of unwary visitors seeking a shortcut have been grounded by the S-curve in the winding channel. Also, pay close attention at the junction of Ship and Northwest Channels, just past Grassy Key. Sorting out the maze of shoals and lights demands serious concentration. Go slowly, attempt no shortcuts and be aware of the currents.

When leaving northbound, take Northwest Channel, which leaves the Main Ship Channel at quick-flashing red "30" about 1 nm from the town dock, off Grassy Key. Do not attempt Northwest Channel on a low tide if your draft exceeds 4 feet or during darkness or rough water conditions. Shoaling is particularly acute between green daybeacon "17A" and flashing red "18," and also between flashing green "19" and red daybeacon "20." Prominent marks in the Town of Cedar Key are a radio tower and 140-foot municipal water tank.

**Dockage:** There are no marinas with transient slips at Cedar Key. Cedar Key Marina II provides small boat dockage and dry storage. Boats used to tie to the fishing pier, but since it has been rebuilt as a concrete structure it is no longer possible or allowed.

**Anchorage:** Anchorage, with depths around 8 feet, can be found on the north side of Atsena Otie Key. Feel your way in cautiously. The island is part of the Cedar Keys National Wildlife Refuge. The "cut" between the two halves of the island provides a great place to paddle a kayak. If you decide to go ashore, don't miss the 19th century cemetery and ruins of the once-thriving village.

Another alternative is to anchor just southwest of the fishing pier (out of the channel) in 8 to 14 feet, and then dinghy in under the bridge to the small-boat docking area in the basin. Because of the strong tidal current in the anchorage, you may want to use a two-anchor Bahamian moor. You can also find anchorage just north of the small boat basin and the restaurants on Dock St.

These are exposed anchorages with little protection. You should only anchor here in fair weather. This is not cruising boat territory.

## Leaping Sturgeons!

The Suwannee River appears to support the largest viable population of Gulf sturgeon, according to the Florida Fish and Wildlife Conservation Commission (FWC). Biologists estimate the annual population at 10,000 to 14,000 fish, averaging approximately 40 pounds each. Adult fish spend 8 to 9 months each year in the river spawning and three to four of the coolest months in Gulf waters.

The sturgeon can be hazardous to boaters, as they tend to leap unexpectedly straight up and out of the water, turning sideways and landing with a loud noise. Much like deer hit by cars, jumping sturgeon are sometimes struck by boats. A large sturgeon can weigh more than 100 pounds, so impact with a fast-moving boat can cause serious injury to both boat passengers and the sturgeon alike. Numerous people have been injured in accidental collisions with the jumping sturgeon on the Suwannee River.

Sturgeon are generally observed jumping during the summer and fall months (May-October). Jumping occurs most frequently in mid-summer (May-early August) when sturgeon are fasting. Researchers have determined that the sturgeon jump to communicate with other fish and to gulp air to fill their swim bladders. This allows the sturgeon to maintain neutral buoyancy. Sturgeon can leap more than 7 feet out of the water.

In 2006, FWC officials initiated a public awareness campaign to alert boaters to the risks of jumping sturgeon and recommended that boaters slow down to reduce the risk of impact and to have more reaction time if a jumping sturgeon is encountered. And boaters are always encouraged to wear their life jackets at all times while on the water. To report sturgeon collisions, call 888-404-FWCC (3922).

# Suwannee River, FL

| SUWANNEE | Largest Vessel Accommodated | VHF Channel Monitored | Transient Berths / Total Berths | Approach / Dockside Depth (reported) | Floating Docks | Gas / Diesel | Groceries, Ice, Marine Supplies, Snacks | Repairs: Hull, Engine, Propeller | Lift (tonnage), Crane, Rail | Min/Max Amps | Laundry, Pool, Showers, Courtesy Car | Pump-Out Station | Nearby: Grocery Store, Motel, Restaurant |
|---|---|---|---|---|---|---|---|---|---|---|---|---|---|
| | | | **Dockage** | | | | **Supplies** | | | **Services** | | | |
| **1.** Gateway Marina (formerly Miller's Marina of Suwannee, Inc.) 🖥 📶 352-542-7349 | 70 | 16/17 | 10/200 | 10/6 | F | GD | GIMS | HEP | L5,C40 | 30/30 | L | P | GMR |
| **2.** Suwannee Marina Inc. 352-542-9150 | 38 | 16 | /47 | 7/7 | F | G | GIMS | EP | – | – | – | – | GR |

🖥 Internet Access  📶 Wireless Internet Access  WG Waterway Guide Cruising Club Partner  *(Information in the table is provided by the facilities.)*
See WaterwayGuide.com for current rates, fuel prices, web site addresses, and other up-to-the-minute information.

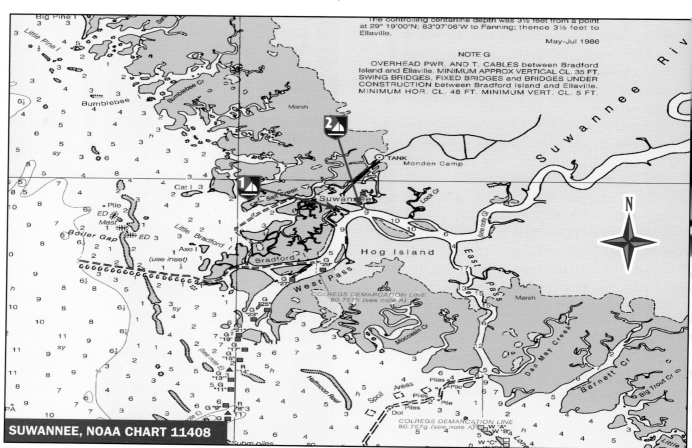

SUWANNEE, NOAA CHART 11408

# ■ SUWANNEE AND STEINHATCHEE RIVERS

It is just over 100 statute miles from Cedar Keys to the town of St. Marks. Anchoring near the mouth of the St. Marks River cuts about 10 statute miles off this leg. Another good stopover is Steinhatchee about 45 nm from Cedar Keys.

## Suwannee River

This part of Old Florida is the inspiration for Stephen Foster's Suwannee River from "Old Folks at Home,"
Florida's official state song. The river meanders about 280 miles before reaching the Gulf of Mexico. It originates in Georgia's Okefenokee Swamp. This is indeed Old Florida and you won't find much here but the beauty of the river and the 70 plus springs that feed millions of gallons of water into it every day.

On approach from the Gulf of Mexico there are three passes/channels into the Suwannee that can be confusing. Approaching from the south you will pass Derrick Key Gap at the south end of Suwannee Reef and Suwannee Sound. This is where you will find East Pass, the first of the three channels. Depths in East Pass are

about 2 feet. You may see small fishing boats using the Pass, but it is doubtful you will be tempted to enter.

The second is West Pass, sometimes referred to as Alligator Pass by locals. It is the first marked channel and you may see small boats coming and going in West Pass. At high tide it should carry depths of 4 feet or more, but it is not recommended for a cruising boat.

The third channel you will encounter is the Main Pass, often referred to as Wadley Pass. It is the northern most of the three channels. Depths are posted at a controlling depth of 3 feet. Our cruising editor passed through the channel in March of 2017 at low tide and never saw depths less than 5 feet. If a north wind is blowing and a winter front is coming through depths can drop considerably.

**NAVIGATION:** Use Chart 11407. Starting at daybeacon green "1" at the entrance of the Crystal River Channel, travel 2 nm on a course of 269 degrees magnetic. Then, on a course of 281 degrees magnetic for 20 nm to the 31 foot tower, flashing "7M" at Sea Horse Reef. Make sure you leave this tower/marker to the east. Soon after you leave Crystal River and travel on a course of 281 degrees you will cross the Florida Barge Canal. Be mindful to avoid the markers as you cross the canal. From Sea Horse Reef, travel on a course of 352 degrees magnetic for 20 nm. Then, 68 degrees magnetic for 0.5 nm to the entrance channel for the Main/Wadley Pass to the Suwannee River. Along the route from Sea Horse Reef, in 16 nm, you will pass daybeacon flashing red "2"

marking the entrance to West Pass. Do not enter West Pass, even though there are markers for the channel. This is not recommended for cruising vessels. The total distance from the Crystal River Channel entrance to the Main/Wadley channel entrance is 42 nm.

Follow the channel markers in to the Suwanee River. The average cruising boat should be able to enter the river and travel the 34 miles or so upriver to Fanning, where you will encounter the 34-foot Hwy 19 Bridge. Depths in the river average 15 feet. Be wary and mindful of the unmarked shoal, Jack's Reef, about 13 miles above the river entrance, 3.7 miles north of Fowlers Bluff. The reef occupies about two thirds of the east bank with depths as shallow as one foot. Stay close to the west bank where you will find depths of more than 10 feet. The location of Jack's Reef is identified on some charts.

**Dockage:** Gateway Marina (formerly Miller's Marine) has slips and fuel, plus offers repairs. Significant renovations were underway at Gateway Marina at press time in spring 2017. At low tide the channel depth to Gateway was 4.5 feet. Suwannee Marina Inc. sells gas and has slips. You can tie up at Salt Creek Restaurant at the town of Suwannee (north of Barbree Island) if you plan to dine there.

**Anchorage:** You can anchor in many places along the Suwannee River. North of Hog Island carries at least 5 feet and excellent holding in mud. Salt Creek, adjacent to the town of Suwannee, has 5 feet of water with good holding in mud. These both provide all-around

# Steinhatchee River, FL

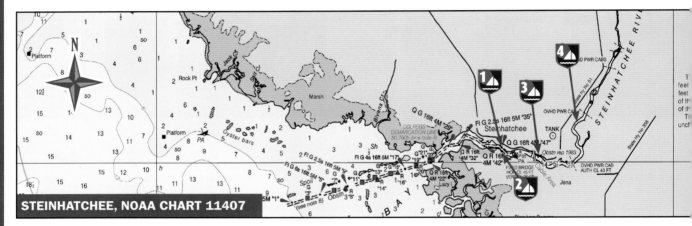

| STEINHATCHEE | | Dockage | | | | Supplies | | Services | | | | | |
|---|---|---|---|---|---|---|---|---|---|---|---|---|---|
| | | Largest Vessel Accommodated | VHF Channel Monitored | Transient Berths / Total Berths | Approach / Dockside Depth (reported) | Floating Docks | Gas / Diesel | Groceries, Ice, Marine Supplies, Snacks | Repairs: Hull, Engine, Propeller | Lift (tonnage), Crane, Rail | Laundry, Pool, Showers, Courtesy Car | Min/Max Amps | Nearby: Grocery Store, Motel, Restaurant | Pump-Out Station |
| 1. Sea Hag Marina 💻 📶 | 352-498-3008 | 45 | 09 | 6/20 | 5/8 | F | GD | IMS | HEP | L7 | 30/50 | LSP | – | GMR |
| 2. Good Times Motel & Marina 💻 📶 WG | 352-498-8088 | 45 | 09 | 3/50 | 9/9 | F | GD | GIMS | – | – | 30/30 | S | – | GMR |
| 3. River Haven Marina & Motel 💻 📶 | 352-498-0709 | 70 | 10 | 4/51 | 3.5/10 | F | GD | GI | HEP | L15,C | 30/50 | LS | P | GMR |
| 4. Steinhatchee Landing Resort | 352-498-3513 | 28 | – | 12/12 | 8/5 | F | – | S | – | – | 30/30 | LPS | – | GM |

💻 Internet Access  📶 Wireless Internet Access  **WG** Waterway Guide Cruising Club Partner  *(Information in the table is provided by the facilities.)*
See WaterwayGuide.com for current rates, fuel prices, web site addresses, and other up-to-the-minute information.

**STEINHATCHEE, NOAA CHART 11407**

protection. A trip to Manatee Springs and the State Park dock is well worth the 25-mile trip up river. You can anchor in the river and enjoy all the park has to offer.

## Steinhatchee River

The interesting fishing village of Steinhatchee (pronounced "STEEN-hatchee") supports several seafood plants. Found about 4 nm from flashing green "1," which marks the entrance to the Steinhatchee River, Steinhatchee's dock space is limited, but locals try their best to make room for everyone.

**NAVIGATION:** Use Chart 11407. From the inside route penciled through the Big Bend leave the Cross Florida Barge Canal red buoy "2" on a course of 335 degrees magnetic. Stay on this course for 40 nm, until you are standing out from Bull Cove. At Bull Cove keep a distance from shore of about 6 nm. Keep a close eye on the depth to make sure you avoid shoals that extend as far as 4 nm from the coast. From Bull Cove change course to 17 degrees magnetic and run 7.5 nm to Steinhatchee River light green "1" at N 29°39.357'/ W 83°27.347'. Flashing green "1" marks the entrance to the channel for Steinhatchee River. Controlling depth

is 5 feet at mean low water. The channel is narrow in places, but depths of 6 plus feet are common. This is on of the more accessible ports of call along Florida's Big Bend.

**Dockage:** There is one marina with transient slips before the bridge. Sea Hag is the most prominent marin in Steinhatchee and should be able to handle boats with a draft of 6 feet or more dockside, although they report 5-foot approach depths; call ahead. They sell gas and diesel and offer repairs. Good Times Motel & Marina ha limited transient space (three slips) and sells fuel. River Haven Marina & Motel has transient slips. They are not set up for large boats (over 36 feet) and are located past a 25-foot fixed vertical clearance bridge. Call for availability, directions and updated knowledge about water depths. Steinhatchee Landing Resort has transient space on floating docks and 5-foot dockside depths.

**Anchorage:** An anchorage is located on the outside of the bend, several hundred feet beyond red daybeacon "36," in 6- to 7-foot depths. The holding is soupy, but protection from all directions is excellent. Anchorage is also available just above Sea Hag Marina after daybeacon red "48."

# ST. MARKS

Four rivers flow into the eastern Apalachee Bay: St. Marks, Aucilla, Econfina and Fenholloway. Residential and commercial development is minimal along this part of the coast. This is truly a part of "old Florida," spared from human infringement and very beautiful.

From Cedar Key it is 83 miles to the St. Marks River. Cape St. George is 54 miles to the northeast. The town of St. Marks is 5.5 miles above the river entrance. Barge traffic is prevalent in the river.

Wakulla Springs is less than 10 miles away. This immense freshwater spring reaches a maximum depth of 185 feet, and more than 600,000 gallons flow from the spring every minute, literally creating the Wakulla River.

**NAVIGATION:** Use Charts 11406, 11407, 11408 and 11405. A good reference for a route to St. Marks is to begin at the Cross Florida Barge Canal Approach lighted red "2" located 4 nm southwest of the Seahorse Reef Light. From Barge Canal red "2" set a course of 322

degrees magnetic for 76 nm to Ochlockonee Shoal lighted buoy red "24." From Ochlockonee Shoal Light red "24" it is 9.5 nm on a course of 3 degrees magnetic to the red and white "SM" buoy at the entrance of the St. Marks Channel.

St. Marks is easily accessible from Steinhatchee. From 30-foot flashing green "1," marking the entrance to the Steinhatchee River Channel, set a course of 273 degrees magnetic for 9 nm to the yellow special purpose buoy at Steinhatchee Reef at N 29°39.893'/W 83°37.823'. Depths at the reef are charted at 15 feet. From Steinhatchee Reef your course is 306 degrees magnetic for 36 nm to the red and white Morse (A) buoy "SM" marking the entrance to the St. Marks River.

Well before arriving at Morse (A) buoy "SM," you will see the 82-foot-high St. Marks Lighthouse (no longer lighted) on shore but do not shortcut this leg. The well-marked entry channel twists and turns through a maze of shoals. Daylight passage should present no problems but avoid going in at night. The single orange range marker is used in conjunction with the St. Marks Lighthouse; lining both up will keep you in mid-channel from flashing green "1" to the first dogleg at green can buoy "3A."

St. Marks has a straightforward channel and river. Both are wide, well-marked and carry enough depth (six feet plus) to accommodate almost any cruising boat.

**Dockage:** Up the St. Marks River, you will find St. Marks Yacht Club, Shields Marina and Riverside Marina. The yacht club has just one reserved transient slip on their flowing dock. Shields Marina is a friendly, full-service marina that welcomes visitors but reports just two reserved slips. Two restaurants and a small grocery store are within easy walking distance. Riverside Marina sells gas and reports just one transient slip. A call ahead is essential here, based on the minimal number of reserved transient slips.

**Anchorage:** About 1 mile above the marinas, around the first bend, the St. Marks River offers an anchorage completely different from the usual Gulf Coast beaches. Tropical plants line both riverbanks, wildlife abounds and you can anchor in complete solitude. Be sure to install your screens and apply plenty of insect repellent. You should have minimum 9-foot depths.

# St. Marks River to Carrabelle River, FL

| | | Largest Vessel Accommodated | VHF Channel Monitored | Approach / Dockside Depth (reported) | Transient Berths / Total Berths | Floating Docks | Gas / Diesel | Groceries, Ice, Marine Supplies, Snacks | Repairs: Hull, Engine, Propeller | Lift (tonnage), Crane, Rail | Laundry, Pool, Showers, Courtesy Car | Min/Max Amps | Pump-Out Station | Nearby: Grocery Store, Motel, Restaurant |
|---|---|---|---|---|---|---|---|---|---|---|---|---|---|---|
| **ST. MARKS** | | | | **Dockage** | | | | **Supplies** | | | **Services** | | | |
| **1.** St. Marks Yacht Club | 850-925-6606 | 50 | – | 1/25 | 7/7 | F | – | – | – | – | 50/50 | LPS | – | GMR |
| **2.** Shields Marina | 850-925-6158 | 60 | 16 | 2/100 | 12/10 | – | GD | GIMS | EP | L | 50/50 | LS | P | GMR |
| **3.** Riverside Marina | 850-925-6157 | 60 | 06 | 1/55 | 12/8 | F | G | GIM | H | C | 30/50 | S | P | GMR |
| **ALLIGATOR HARBOR** | | | | | | | | | | | | | | |
| **4.** Alligator Point Marina | 850-349-2511 | 45 | 16 | 3/45 | 4/5 | F | GD | IMS | – | – | 30/50 | S | – | R |
| **CARRABELLE** | | | | | | | | | | | | | | |
| **5.** Carrabelle Boat Club | 850-697-5500 | – | – | call/18 | – | – | – | IS | – | L | – | S | – | MR |
| **6.** The Moorings of Carrabelle 🖥 📶 380 EHL | 850-697-2800 | 150 | 16/68 | 15/150 | 15/9 | – | GD | IMS | – | – | 30/50 | LPS | P | GMR |
| **7.** C-Quarters Marina 🖥 📶 380 EHL | 850-697-8400 | 100 | 16/18 | 30/67 | 12/9 | – | GD | IMS | EP | – | 30/50 | LS | P | GMR |
| **8.** MS Dockside Marina | 850-697-3337 | 65 | 16 | call/22 | 16/19 | F | – | IM | HEP | L60 | 30/50 | – | – | R |

🖥 Internet Access  📶 Wireless Internet Access  **WG** Waterway Guide Cruising Club Partner  *(Information in the table is provided by the facilities.)*
See WaterwayGuide.com for current rates, fuel prices, web site addresses, and other up-to-the-minute information.

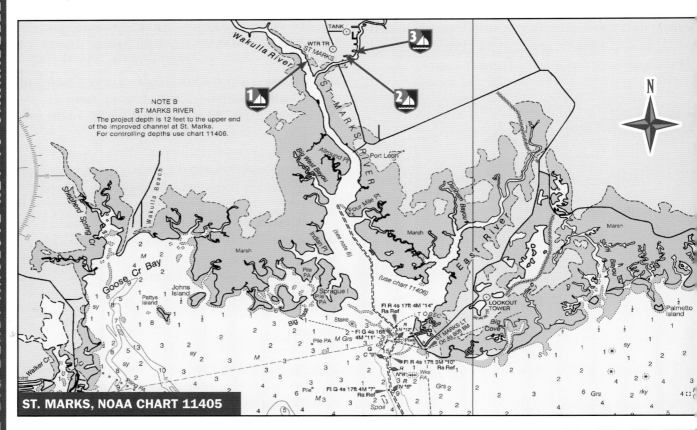

NOTE B
ST MARKS RIVER
The project depth is 12 feet to the upper end
of the improved channel at St. Marks.
For controlling depths use chart 11406.

**ST. MARKS, NOAA CHART 11405**

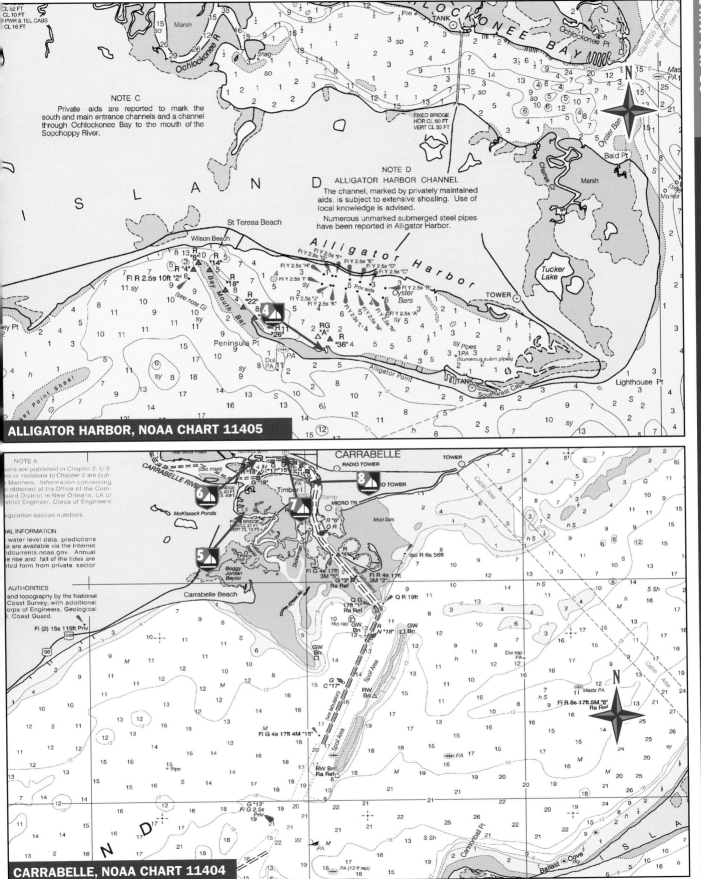

**ALLIGATOR HARBOR, NOAA CHART 11405**

NOTE C

Private aids are reported to mark the south and main entrance channels and a channel through Ochlockonee Bay to the mouth of the Sopchoppy River.

NOTE D

ALLIGATOR HARBOR CHANNEL

The channel, marked by privately maintained aids, is subject to extensive shoaling. Use of local knowledge is advised.

Numerous unmarked submerged steel pipes have been reported in Alligator Harbor.

**CARRABELLE, NOAA CHART 11404**

NOTE A

ions are published in Chapter 2. U.S. ns or revisions to Chapter 2 are pub- Mariners. Information concerning obtained at the Office of the Com- uard District in New Orleans, LA or strict Engineer, Corps of Engineers.

egulation section numbers.

AL INFORMATION

water level data, predictions a are available via the Internet ndcurrents.noaa.gov. Annual e rise and fall of the tides are ted form from private sector

AUTHORITIES

and topography by the National Coast Survey, with additional orps of Engineers, Geological . Coast Guard.

## Alligator Point

**NAVIGATION:** Use Chart 11405. To reach Alligator Point, take your departure from flashing red bell buoy "26" south of South Shoal. From there, take a course of 312 degrees magnetic to flashing green "1" at the northeast end of Dog Island Reef. At this point, you can alter course to 350 degrees magnetic. After just more than 3 nm, you will pick up red flashing "2," marking the entrance to Alligator Harbor. Follow the daybeacons all the way to the marina.

**Dockage:** Watch your depth. Charted shoals at the entrance are marked at 3 to 5 feet. The Alligator Point Marina is primarily for small fishing boats, but transient slips are available. End of the World Oasis (an on-site Tiki hut) will cook your catch on site (850-349-9792).

To port of red "12," at **East Pass**, the GIWW begins again at Mile 375 EHL (east of the Harvey Lock) and proceeds in a westerly direction to New Orleans and Mile 0 at the Harvey Lock. West of Harvey Lock distances are referred to as WHL to Brownsville, TX and the border of Mexico at Mile 682 WHL.

## ■ CARRABELLE

East Pass into St. George Sound marks the end of the trek across Florida's Big Bend. Once again cruising boats, with a vertical clearance of less than 50 feet, can choose to travel the GIWW or go offshore in the Gulf of Mexico. To the west is the port city of Apalachicola, and to the east is the port city of Carrabelle. Carrabelle is the closest to East Pass. It is an excellent stop for boats looking for a place to rest after crossing The Big Bend.

**NAVIGATION:** Use Charts 11401, 11404 and 11405. If you are traveling west, this is the last leg of your trip along an inside passage for Florida's Big Bend. The inside route penciled on your chart runs from Ochlockonee Shoal Light red daybeacon "24" to the East Pass entrance to St. George Sound and on to Carrabelle.

For the cruising boaters coming from St. Marks, your transit begins at the red and white "SM" entrance buoy for the St. Marks River. From the "SM" buoy, travel on a course of 183 degrees magnetic for 9.5 nm to Ochlockonee Shoal lighted red "24" at N 29°51.50'/ W 84°10.30'. From Shoal Light "24" travel a course of 250 degrees magnetic for 9.3 nm to flashing red "26" at N 29°47.50'/W 84°20.00'. From red "26" change course to 265 degrees magnetic for 17 nm to flashing red "2" at

N 29°44.50'/W 84°39.20', marking the entrance to East Pass and St. George Sound.

East Pass, one of the better Florida west coast passes, leads 5 nm through St. George Sound to the Carrabelle River. Follow the marked channel through East Pass and make a turn to starboard at red "12." Stay in the channel to Carrabelle.

**Dockage:** One mile north of the GIWW on the Carrabelle River, three marinas offer transient dockage (Carrabelle Boat Club is private). The full-service Moorings of Carrabelle has slips and fuel plus provides complimentary bicycles. C-Quarters Marina also has slips and fuel and bicycles can be rented just across the street. MS Dockside Marina has slips and amenities and offers repairs (with a 60-ton lift). C-Quarters is closest to what the city has to offer, but bicycles allow you to access everything in the small downtown area of Carrabelle from the other local marinas.

**Anchorage:** You can anchor in the main river in 5 feet of water south of green marker "17." Be sure not to block the channel.

## Side Trip: Dog Island Anchorage

Due south of the Carrabelle River is Dog Island with numerous anchoring possibilities. Just inside the hook of the west end of Dog Island, you can anchor at Shipping Cove, an excellent spot in deep water (charted at 17 to 20 feet). A small embayment at the east end of Dog Island can provide limited shelter. Tyson Harbor at the northeast end of Dog Island also offers protection from all but northwest winds. The 6-foot-plus channel leading to the small ferry dock is narrow, but well-marked. Stay in the center, and watch for the abruptly shoaling edges.

The island's hospitable owners allow cruising mariners to explore the beaches but please stay off private docks and property. A portion of the island is a bird breeding and nesting area, posted with "Keep Out" signs. Please honor them. (The posted section does not include the beach.)

## Cruising Options

At this point, we will leave the Big Bend area and enter the Florida Panhandle area. You will need to decide if you want to travel outside in the Gulf of Mexico by following the coastline all the way to Pensacola or take the GIWW route (200 statute miles). Fixed bridge heights of 50 feet will prevent most sailboats from using some of the inside route.

THE BIG BEND: ANCLOTE KEY TO CARRABELLE

| SERVICES | |
|---|---|
| 1 | Post Office |
| 2 | Library |
| 3 | Visitor Information |
| **ATTRACTIONS** | |
| 4 | Camp Gordon Johnston WWII Museum |
| 5 | Carabelle History Museum |
| 6 | World's Smallest Police Station |

| SHOPPING | |
|---|---|
| 7 | Carabelle Medical Pharmacy |
| 8 | Ganders Gulf Supply Hardware |
| 9 | Gulfside IGA Plus |
| 10 | Millender & Son Seafood |
| **DINING** | |
| 11 | Fathon's Steam Room & Raw Bar |

| | |
|---|---|
| 12 | Harry's Bar & Package/Marine Street Grill |
| 13 | The Fisherman's Wife |
| **MARINAS** | |
| 14 | C-Quarters Marina |
| 15 | MS Dockside Marina |
| 16 | The Moorings of Carabelle |

Carrabelle is a small, quiet town known for relaxing, boating, fishing, hunting, friendly people and white sand beaches. The eastern panhandle area of Florida is largely undeveloped and unspoiled. Ecotourism has become the most popular aspect of the area; experienced "green guides" conduct tours (usually requiring advance reservations). This is a good way to explore the area's rich and diverse mixture of plants, flowers, wildlife, butterflies and birds. Land and water adventure tours are also available for hiking, kayaking, off-road trails, fishing and sightseeing.

**Attractions:** Carrabelle claims to be home to the World's Smallest Police Station. Located on US 98 at the corner of CR 67, the phone booth-sized police station has an interesting history. In the early 1960s policemen made phone calls from a pay phone located on the outside of the station to get around a regulation regarding making unauthorized long distance calls from a police phone. When the telephone company decided to replace its worn out phone booth in front

of Burda's Pharmacy with a new one, they placed the police phone in the old booth. A replica of the booth is on display across the street from the Visitor Center at 105 St. James Avenue. The tiny police station has been featured in multiple television shows and one movie (about nearby Tate's Hell State Forest).

Other colorful history can be uncovered at the Carrabelle History Museum at 106 SE Ave B. (850-697-2141) and at the Camp Gordon Johnston WWII Museum, the largest WWII museum in the State of Florida (1001 Gray Ave., 850-697-8575).

Most attractions are within walking/cycling distance or you can pre-arrange a shuttle for your visit. You will need transportation, for example, to visit the Crooked River Lighthouse & Keeper's House Museum at 1975 Hwy 98 W. (850-697-2732).

**Shopping:** Grocery and convenience stores, hardware and marine supplies, a post office, a package store, a public library and a bank with 24-hour ATM are conveniently located within 1 mile of the marinas. The Carrabelle Medical Pharmacy also contains a gift shop. There are several other gift and antiques shops with a unique beachside flavor, to browse and shop.

For provisioning, a Gulfside IGA Plus is convenient to the marinas at 812 Ave. A N. (850-697-2710). If you want to prepare fresh seafood on the boat, the go to is Millender & Sons Seafood (607 Ave. B S., 850-697-3301).

**Dining:** Harry's Bar & Package has been in continuous operation in a historic waterfront building since 1942. Located at 306 Marine St. (850-697-9982), this is a true "locals" spot with a ton of character. Outside is the Marine Street Grill (850-646-3088) in a New Orleans-style courtyard where you can have a burger and a beer or wings and wine...Your choice!

Fathom's Steam Room and Raw Bar at 201 St. James Ave. (850-697-9712) is not fancy but has good seafood and entertainment (open March through November). The Fisherman's Wife at 201 8th St. W. (850-697-4533) offers seafood and burger baskets.

You will find variety in menu choices in Carrabelle, and local seafood is generally available. It's a good idea to call ahead for hours and days of operation for the restaurants. Also, keep in mind that the pace is slower here than in some areas. Your patience will pay off when your seafood is fresh from the Gulf and made to order.

See carrabelle.org or call 850-697-2585 for more information on the area.

# WATERWAY EXPLORER
# RATINGS & REVIEWS

**Waterway Explorer** has ratings and reviews. See what others say about Marinas, Anchorages, Bridges/Locks and Navigation Alerts!

### 1. Marathon Boat Yard Marine Center
☆☆☆☆☆

**Max Length:** 80
**Total/Transient Slips:** 20/5
**Approach/Dockside Depth:** 8.0/20.0
**Fuel:** ...
**Repairs:** Hull / Eng...

No stars indicate that this marina is awaiting a review

### 2. Faro Blanco Res... Club
☆☆☆☆☆

**Max Length:** 130
**Total/Transient Slips:** 74/0
**Approach/Dockside De...**
**Fuel:** Diesel/Gas
**Pumpout:** Yes

**Max Length:**
**Total/Transient Slips:** 20/3
**Approach/Dockside Depth:** 8.0/8.0
**Fuel:** Diesel/Gas
**Pumpout:** Yes
**Repairs:** No

Yellow stars indicate the rating that this marina got from reviewers

## Faro Blanco Resort & Yacht Club

**Mile Marker:** between markers 17 and 18

**Marathon, FL 33050**

**Phone:** (305) 743-9018

**Hailing Channel:** 16

☑ Compare to other marinas in the area

✎ ☆☆☆☆☆
1 Boater Review

✎ Suggest Updates

↩ Complete Marina Listing

*Be the first to review and rate – or add your comments to the list!*

- # Fill out the review form and post your rating
- # No log in required
- # No private information shared

☆☆☆☆☆

*Waterway Guide staff and editors validate and verify postings and content to ensure accuracy*

## Reviews: Faro Blanco Resort & Yacht Club

These are observations from the boating community. Waterway Guide information is verified regularly and all efforts will be made to validate any comments about... ...here. Thank you for taking the time to share comments about... ...ience.

Back to the Waterway Explorer

**Faro Blanco Resort & Yacht Club**

1990 Overseas Highway
Marathon, FL 33050
Florida Bay between markers 17 and 18 48

**Lat / Lon:** N 24° 42.693' / W 081° 06.309'
**Hours:** 7:00 am to 7:00pm
**Contact:** Alain Giudice
**VHF Monitored:** 16
**VHF Working:** 9
**Phone:** (305) 743-9018
**Email:** srudek@faroblancomarina.com
**Website:** faroblancoresort.com

☆☆☆☆☆ (1)
5.00 out of 5 stars

**Review for Faro Blanco Resort & Yacht Club**

**Reviewed by:** Ed, *Adonia*, on Jun 29, 2016
**Boat Type:** Power
**LOA:** 61'
**Draft:** 4.5'
**Rating:** ☆☆☆☆☆

Faro Blanco is a wonderful facility. We were there in May 2016 for the Marlow Marine Cruising Club 20th rendezvous. The staff members were on top of their game. Hospitality, facilities and ambiance are top notch. The docks and slips are all new and no expense has been spared. The Hyatt is also new. Plan on visiting this icon of the Keys. It's a great facility.

View location on the Waterway Guide Explorer

### Name *(Displayed)*
|

### Email *(Not Displayed)*
Email

### Vessel Name  Display? ☐
Vessel Name

### LOA (ft):   Draft (ft):   Boat Type:
Sail  Power

### Rating:
☆☆☆☆☆

### Comments:
Type review here. How was the service? Amenities? Ambience? Ease of docking?

☑ Yes, sign me up for the Cruisers' Weekly Update.

Submit   Review Policies

# The Panhandle: Apalachicola to Pensacola

 **GIWW** Mile 375 EHL-Mile 170 EHL   **VHF** FL: Channel 09

**CHARTS** 11378, 11385, 11389, 11390, 11391, 11393, 11401, 11402, 11404

The Panhandle is a strip of land in northwest Florida that runs some 200 miles and is 50 to 100 miles wide. Geographically its location is roughly from Apalachicola to Pensacola. Sometimes this region is referred to as the Emerald Coast, describing the beaches and resorts spanning from Port St. Joe to Pensacola.

The typical cruising boat approaches the Florida Panhandle from the west or the southeast. Cruisers from as far as Texas and southbound Loopers exiting the Tombigbee River into Mobile Bay will reach The Panhandle from the west. Boaters who skirt the shores of Florida's Big Bend or make the 140- to 170-nm run offshore from Anclote Key or Clearwater will approach from the southeast.

Depending on the amount of time you have, your personal inclination for offshore or inland cruising and the forecasted weather, you can take either the outside route or the inside route (if you have a vertical clearance less than 50 feet) all the way along the Florida Panhandle from Carrabelle to Pensacola and Perdido Bay.

This part of the GIWW is much more intriguing and enjoyable than many segments of the ICW. It meanders along for a couple of hundred miles, sometimes along the barrier island beaches and sometimes inland through the woods and marshlands. Real estate development is not as dense. You can enjoy the cypress- and hardwood-lined banks of the waterway, state parks, national seashore, secluded anchorages or a good marina at the end of each day.

The region is rich with cypress and hardwood trees, sugar white beaches, clear natural springs, clear blue waters and abundant seafood. Fish the ageless Steinhatchee, explore the wilderness of St. Vincent Island, enjoy the history of Apalachicola, the beach and nightlife of Panama City Beach and the rich history and culture of Pensacola. The pace of life here is slow. Embrace the laid-back southern style that is all mixed in a magnificent blueprint that makes the Florida Panhandle a great place to hang out for a while.

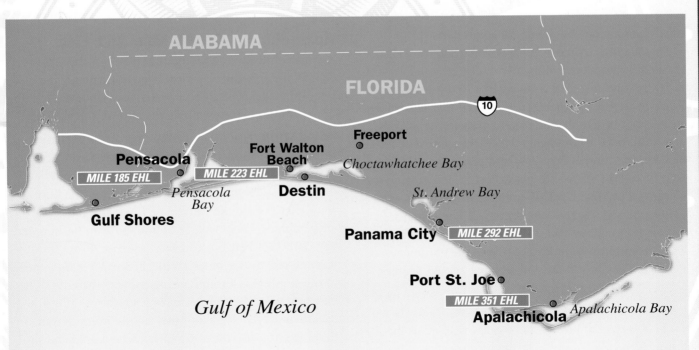

# ■ OFFSHORE TO PENSACOLA

For the cruising boat that reaches St. George Sound (and has a vertical clearance of less than 50 feet), it is difficult to recommend an offshore passage to Pensacola. The GIWW distance from Mile 375 EHL to Mile 180 in Pensacola Bay is 195 statute miles through an enjoyable, low-stress section of the GIWW.

Boats with vertical clearance greater than 45 feet may not be able to follow the route on the GIWW due to three bridges, spaced conveniently between offshore inlets, with fixed clearances of 50 feet. The offshore passage from East Pass must go around the shoals that extend from Cape St. George and Cape San Blas. The offshore distance from Mile 375 EHL to the entrance at Pensacola Bay is 158 nm (182 statute miles).

From the flashing red "2" at the end of East Pass, set a course of about 230 degrees magnetic for 25 nm to avoid the shoals at Cape St. George and Cape San Blas. Then, for Pensacola, set a course of about 295 degrees magnetic for 130 nm (for a total distance of 155 nm).

There are two inlets that will allow you to break the trip into two days to enjoy this part of the Emerald Coast. The well-marked inlet at St. Andrews Bay will be a total distance of 80 nm from East Pass. The front range of the inlet is missing so only the back range remains, acting as a 35-foot green marker. There are two sets of red and green nuns and cans marking shoals inside the inlet that may not be shown on your charts.

The channel at Destin is passable but not as well marked. It has a controlling depth of 6 feet and a width of 50 feet and is a total distance of 120 nm from East Pass. From this channel, you can reach marinas before the 49-foot bridge that blocks the pass to the GIWW.

An alternate, recommended offshore route is to enter St. George Sound at East Pass and proceed along the GIWW to Port St. Joe. To reach Port St. Joe, turn to the southwest at Mile 328 EHL at the Gulf County Canal. (There are signs at this intersection.). The distance to Port St. Joe from Mile 375 EHL is 52 statute miles. The offshore run from Port St. Joe to the entrance at Pensacola Bay is 100 nm) on a course of 283 degrees.

⚠ This area of the Gulf is used extensively by the U.S. Air Force. Along the entire route you will be passing by and over areas marked as missile testing, unexploded ordnance and fish havens. Check the *Local Notice to Mariners* and the Waterway Guide Explorer at waterwayguide.com for updates.

As mentioned in the introduction to this Upper Gulf Coast section, along the **panhandle of Florida**, a rather unique change occurs to tides. West of St George's Sound/ Apalachicola Bay, there are only 2 tides per 24 hours-one high and one low-while east of this demarcation, the tides are the normal 4 per 24 hours-2 highs, and 2 lows.

# ■ CARRABELLE TO APALACHICOLA

The segment of the GIWW from East Pass to Pensacola covers 195 statute miles of relatively pleasant inside cruising. There is very little white-knuckle cruising here. The GIWW passage along the Florida Panhandle ranges in ambiance from lovely and lonesome, narrow channels winding through swamp and bayou areas to "Northern" settings of deciduous trees and modern housing, connecting big, clear bays, bayous and sounds. Narrow barrier islands protect the entire passage.

Depths range from 10 to 12 feet but shoaling is possible, so be sure to keep an eye on your depth sounder. There are three bridges with a fixed vertical clearance of 50 feet: DuPont Bridge in East Bay (Mile 295.4 EHL), Brooks Memorial Bridge at Fort Walton Beach (Mile 223 EHL) and Navarre Beach Bridge (Mile 206.6 EHL).

## Apalachicola–GIWW Mile 351 EHL
A worthwhile layover along this stretch of the GIWW is Apalachicola, with its quaint, village-like atmosphere, excellent local oysters and unique shopping opportunities within walking distance of the marinas.

**NAVIGATION:** Use Chart 11404. It is a pleasant trip through the Sound and Apalachicola Bay to the unique and beautiful City of Apalachicola. If you go into Carrabelle, you will have to come back out the same way. After exiting the Carrabelle River and retracing your course into St. George Sound, pick up flashing red "2" (Mile 374 EHL) just inside East Pass. From there, flashing red "6" becomes visible, about 2.5 statute miles to the southwest. From flashing red "6," the GIWW is clearly marked as it jogs south by southwest at quick flashing red "20" for about two statute miles to quick-flashing red "28" (Mile 365 EHL), where it resumes its southwest direction. From that point, it is a straight shot southwest for about 9.3 statute miles under the fixed

**Apalachicola–St. George Island Bridge** at Mile 361.4 EHL (65-foot vertical clearance) over Apalachicola Bay at Bulkhead Shoal (red nun buoy "48"). Watch your depths carefully in the area of Bulkhead Shoal where the oyster beds come right to the edge of the channel. The channel is especially narrow on the east side of the bridge, so keep an eye on the markers ahead and behind to keep from crabbing into the shallows. The bridge is the boundary of demarcation between St. George Sound and Apalachicola Bay.

After traversing much of Apalachicola Bay, at quick-flashing red "76," make a 90-degree turn to starboard, and follow the GIWW about 3.5 statute miles to red nun buoy "24," marking the entrance to the Apalachicola River and the town of Apalachicola.

**Dockage:** After passing red nun buoy "24," and just south of the fixed **John Gorrie Memorial (U.S. 98/319) Bridge** at Mile 351.4 EHL (65-foot vertical clearance), is the easily sighted Apalachicola municipal marina (Battery Park Marina). A few transient slips are available on the outboard end. This facility is open to wakes left by passing boaters transiting the GIWW, so be sure to use ample spring lines and fenders. Dockage north of the bridge includes Apalachicola Marina, Inc., which has dockage with 12-foot dockside depths and full amenities, including gas and diesel. A supermarket, drug store and restaurants are within easy walking distance. Close by is the Apalachicola River Inn complex, featuring guest rooms and transient slips.

Most of the other transient facilities are located farther north, along with various fuel docks, a boatyard and a waterfront hotel with ample dock space. Facilities include Water Street Hotel and Marina and J.V. Gander Distributors, Inc., which sells marine fuel. Take care while docking, as the Apalachicola River can have a strong current depending on tidal flow.

If you want to get away from GIWW traffic, Scipio (the "c" is silent) Creek Marina is a popular stopover for cruisers. It has less tidal current than facilities located directly on the Apalachicola River. The marina is located to the northwest of the river at green-red can "A." Motels, restaurants and provisions are within a three-block walk, and the marina has a riverfront restaurant.

**Anchorage:** It is possible to anchor in Apalachicola, just north of the John Gorrie Memorial Bridge. Here you will find 9 to 12 feet of water with good holding. You will be exposed to wakes; be sure to anchor well out of the channel. There are also anchorages at Shell Point on St. George Island in 7 to 10 feet of water.

# GOIN' ASHORE: APALACHICOLA, FL

| SERVICES | |
|---|---|
| 1 | Post Office |
| 2 | Library |
| 3 | Visitor Information |

| ATTRACTIONS | |
|---|---|
| 4 | Apalachicola Maritime Museum |
| 5 | Battery Park |
| 6 | John Gorrie State Museum |
| 7 | Veterans Memorial Park |

| SHOPPING | |
|---|---|
| 8 | Bowery Art Gallery |
| 9 | Down Town Books and Purl |
| 10 | Forgotten Coast Books |
| 11 | On the Waterfront |
| 12 | Tin Shed |

| DINING | |
|---|---|
| 13 | Caroline's River Dining/Boss Oyster |

| | |
|---|---|
| 14 | Gibson Inn |
| 15 | Papa Joe's Oyster Bar & Grill |

| MARINAS | |
|---|---|
| 13 | Apalachicola River Inn |
| 16 | Apalachicola Marina, Inc. |
| 17 | Battery Park Marina |
| 18 | J.V. Gander Distributors, Inc. |
| 19 | Scipio Creek Marina |
| 20 | Water Street Hotel & Marina |

While taking a rest from the rigors of the sea, a walk around the quaint town of Apalachicola as the shadows fall and the heat subsides will be like a time-travel trip to yesteryear. Many of the preserved historic buildings and homes are in Victorian style, and a number of the restored antebellum houses have been turned into picturesque bed and breakfasts. As an interesting side note, several of the larger houses in Apalachicola were originally built in

Port St. Joe (40 miles to the west) but were moved after a Yellow Fever outbreak in the 1800s. Annual features include the Seafood Festival, held during the first week of November at Battery Park, and the Antique Boat Show held on the waterfront in April.

**Attractions:** A visit to the John Gorrie State Museum might be in order, located just two blocks from the municipal pier at 42 6th St. He doesn't get much recognition for his discovery today, but in the 1830s Dr. John Gorrie invented a machine that made ice. A replica of the mechanical refrigerator is on diplay for which he was granted the first U.S. patent in 1851. While Dr. Gorrie's invention was originally designed to help yellow fever patients, it changed the world by making southern climes more habitable.

Another interesting museum is the Apalachicola Maritime Museum located at 103 Water St. (850-653-2500). They sponsor many local events, including educational tours, kayaking, a wooden boat school, a maritime library and exhibits. The Veterans Memorial Park is close by at 18 Seventh St. (850-653-8990). The park features a bronze sculpture cast from the same molds used to craft the Three Servicemen Statue at the Vietnam Veteran's Memorial in Washington, DC.

**Shopping:** The Tin Shed near the marinas boasts "the most comprehensive maritime collection east of the Mississippi." Several art galleries have opened in recent years, thanks to the influx of artists and tourists to this riverside town. Bowery Art Gallery (149 Commerce St., (850-653-2425) and On the Waterfront (117 Market St., (850-653-9699) are particularly noteworthy.

There is a quaint bookstore as well. Down Town Books and Purl (67 Commerce St., 850-653-1290) offers a very wide selection of books that should pique the interest of everyone. They also sell exquisite yarns, games and diversions. Forgotten Coast Books is a gem for browsing. They feature regional literature from old and new Florida and the south, with special editions of classic and modern authors as well as travel, hiking and water guides. They are located at 236A Water Street (850 653-2080).

**Dining:** The fully-restored and expanded Gibson Inn (51 Ave. C, 850-653-2191), just a block from the municipal pier, is an early 1900s "cracker" style structure. Florida cracker homes are characterized by metal roofs, raised floors, large porch areas (often wrapping around the entire home) and straight central hallways from the front to the back of the home (sometimes called "dog trot" or "shotgun" hallways). The Inn offers lodging, a bar and one of the many area restaurants that specialize in seafood, especially the renowned local Apalachicola oysters brought fresh from the bay's shell beds. Papa Joe's Oyster Bar & Grill (301-B Market St., 850-653-1189) has some of these oysters and also great seafood.

Happy hour at the various bistros draws an interesting hodgepodge of oystermen, artists and, naturally, cruisers. Locals and transients keep an eye on the weather fronts via the Weather Channel, which is usually on at the Apalachicola River Inn (123 Water St., 850-653-8139). Caroline's River Dining and Boss Oyster are both located at the Inn. Boss Oyster has a more casual atmosphere with charm and character, serving oysters prepared a whopping 17 different ways.

# Apalachicola River, FL

| APALACHICOLA | | Largest Vessel Accommodated | VHF Channel Monitored | Transient Berths / Total Berths | Approach / Dockside Depth (reported) | Floating Docks | Gas / Diesel | Groceries, Ice, Marine Supplies, Snacks | Repairs: Hull, Engine, Propeller | Lift (tonnage), Crane, Rail | Laundry, Pool, Showers, Courtesy Car | Min/Max Amps | Pump-Out Station | Nearby: Grocery Store, Motel, Restaurant |
|---|---|---|---|---|---|---|---|---|---|---|---|---|---|---|
| | | **Dockage** | | | | | **Supplies** | | **Services** | | | | | |
| 1. Battery Park Marina 351 EHL | 850-653-9319 | 50 | – | 15/ | 6/5 | – | – | G | – | – | 50/50 | – | P | GR |
| 2. Apalachicola Marina, Inc. WIFI 351 EHL | **850-653-9521** | **100** | 16/09 | 3/6 | 15/12 | – | GD | IM | – | – | 30/50 | S | – | GMR |
| 3. Apalachicola River Inn 351 EHL | 850-653-8139 | 90 | 16 | 17/17 | 6/6 | – | – | I | – | – | 50/50 | S | – | GMR |
| 4. Water Street Hotel and Marina ⌑ WIFI WG 351 EHL | 850-653-3700 | 55 | 16 | 20/20 | 12/8 | F | – | GIMS | – | – | 50/50 | PS | – | GMR |
| 5. J.V. Gander Distributors, Inc. 351 EHL | 850-653-8889 | 150 | – | – | 9/9 | – | GD | GIMS | – | – | – | – | – | GMR |
| 6. Scipio Creek Marina WIFI 351 EHL | 850-653-8030 | 100 | 16 | 6/14 | 12/10 | – | GD | IMS | HEP | L | 30/50 | LS | P | GMR |

⌑ Internet Access  WIFI Wireless Internet Access  WG Waterway Guide Cruising Club Partner  *(Information in the table is provided by the facilities.)*
See WaterwayGuide.com for current rates, fuel prices, web site addresses, and other up-to-the-minute information.

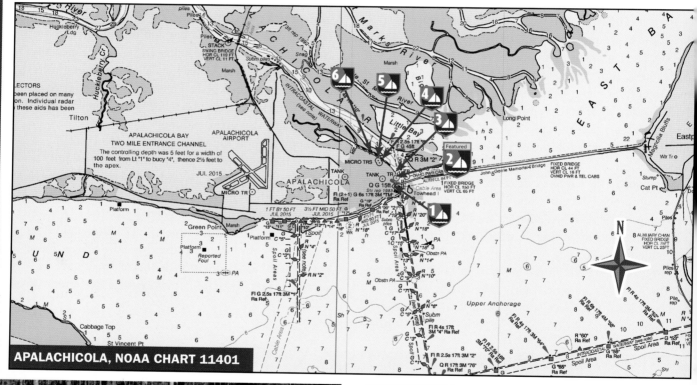

APALACHICOLA, NOAA CHART 11401

## Side Trip: St. Marks Island

Boaters seeking a side trip can follow the Apalachicola River upstream through a few miles of heavily wooded swampland to the St. Marks, East and Brothers Rivers, also from red daybeacon "30." There is ample depth of water here for smaller vessels. (Controlling depths of 9 and 10 feet are available to St. Marks Island on the St. Marks River.)

The really adventurous can navigate the river up to the Jim Woodruff Dam at Chattahoochee, but be advised to obtain local knowledge and be sure of your source before setting out. A grounding up here requiring commercial assistance will take a large amount of money, especially if you don't have unlimited towing.

# ■ APALACHICOLA TO PANAMA CITY

### Apalachicola to White City—GIWW Mile 351 to Mile 329 EHL

The GIWW leaves Apalachicola Bay and the Gulf of Mexico at Mile 350 EHL, and then winds along on the scenic Apalachicola River, undulating generally northwest to the **Apalachicola Railroad Swing Bridge** at Mile 347.0 EHL (11-foot closed vertical clearance, usually open). Keep a sharp eye out for tree limbs and other floating debris. Night passages are not recommended.

**NAVIGATION:** Use Charts 11393, 11401 and 11402. From the mouth of the Apalachicola River, the GIWW is well marked. Past red daybeacon "30," the Apalachicola River turns north, and the GIWW continues along the Jackson River (named for Stonewall Jackson when he was governor of the territory) to Lake Wimico at Mile 340 EHL.

You will soon take a hairpin turn to the south past flashing green "9," just west of Mile 345 EHL, and about 1 mile later, take a sharp curve to the west and proceed to Lake Wimico at Mile 340 EHL and green daybeacon "3" and red daybeacon "4." The course for the straight shot across the lake is about 310 degrees magnetic. Follow the daybeacons carefully as the spoil areas are close to the narrow channel.

At flashing green "15," enter Searcy Creek at the end of Lake Wimico (Mile 335 EHL). Follow the well-marked channel from here about 6 miles to the **White City (SR 71) Bridge** (65-foot fixed vertical clearance) at Mile 329.3 EHL. The waterway is relatively wide, relatively deep and there is little to intrude on an enjoyable view from all sides as you traverse swamp country (described on the charts as "impenetrable," "cypress" and "low swampy area").

**Dockage:** There is a free dock at White City with restrooms in the adjacent park. Tie up to either the seawall or floating dock. There is a convenience store with minimal supplies 1 mile north on the highway. The bulkhead is subject to wakes from GIWW traffic.

At White City, **Central Standard Time** meets Eastern Standard Time, so you gain an hour heading west (turn your clocks back) or lose an hour heading east.

# St. Joseph Bay, FL

| | | Approach / Dockside Depth (reported) | Transient Berths / Total Berths | VHF Channel Monitored | Largest Vessel Accommodated | | Groceries, Ice, Marine Supplies, Snacks | Floating Docks | Gas / Diesel | Repairs: Hull, Engine, Propeller | Lift (tonnage), Crane, Rail | | Laundry, Pool, Showers, Courtesy Car | Pump-Out Station | Min/Max Amps | | Nearby: Grocery Store, Motel, Restaurant |
|---|---|---|---|---|---|---|---|---|---|---|---|---|---|---|---|---|---|
| **PORT ST. JOE** | | | | **Dockage** | | | | **Supplies** | | | | **Services** | | | | |
| 1. Port St. Joe Marina 🖥 WiFi | 850-227-9393 | 120 | 16/10 | 25/114 | 15/7 | – | GD | | IMS | – | – | 30/50 | | LS | – | GMR |
| **MEXICO BEACH** | | | | | | | | | | | | | | | | |
| 2. Mexico Beach Marina 🖥 WiFi | 850-648-8900 | – | 16/11 | 10/34 | /6 | – | G | | IMS | HEP | L7 | 30/30 | | – | – | GMR |

🖥 Internet Access  WiFi Wireless Internet Access  WG Waterway Guide Cruising Club Partner  *(Information in the table is provided by the facilities.)*
See WaterwayGuide.com for current rates, fuel prices, web site addresses, and other up-to-the-minute information.

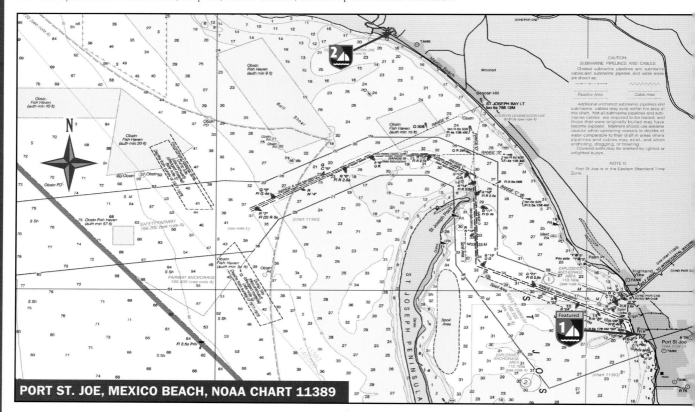

**PORT ST. JOE, MEXICO BEACH, NOAA CHART 11389**

**Anchorage:** Just after the Jackson River splits off from the Apalachicola, at Saul Creek (head northeast at Mile 345 EHL between green "7" and red "8"), an excellent protected anchorage in 8 feet of water is located at the junction of Saul Creek and the Saul Creek Cutoff. Depths exceed 30 feet in much of this lovely creek; for optimum holding, use your depth sounder to find an appropriate depth to set the hook. Alligator sightings are not unusual here and birds are abundant. After exiting Lake Wimico into Searcy Creek, the chart indicates shoal in the oxbow, but the oxbow around the island at Mile 334 EHL normally carries 10 feet of water or better and provides an excellent secluded anchorage.

## White City to Panama City: Gulf County Canal Route

**NAVIGATION:** Use Charts 11389, 11393 and 11401. About 1.5 statute miles from White City on the GIWW, at about Mile 328 EHL, the Gulf County Canal cuts off 90 degrees south and extends 5 miles southwest from the waterway to Port St. Joe on St. Joseph Bay. The controlling depth is 12 feet, and there is a 75-foot

> Port St. Joe, which is southwest of White City, is on **Eastern Time**. You will have to switch your watch back and forth a bit if you don't continue on in the GIWW and, instead, come out into St. Joseph Bay.

xed **Port St. Joe (U.S. 98) Bridge** near the exit
o St. Joseph Bay. Exiting into St. Joseph Bay, if you are
eading for the pass to the Gulf of Mexico, the channel
om Port St. Joe to the Gulf is clearly marked. You will
ave been coming southwestward on the canal. When
ou intersect the ship channel, you will turn to the
orthwest and later, north to get around St. Joseph Point
t the tip of St. Joseph Peninsula and out of St. Joseph
ay. You will be doing this incrementally, with the last
traight run to the southwest until you get into the Gulf
f Mexico and 30-plus feet of water.

To get to the entrance buoy (RW "SA") off Panama
City, steer northwest. The distance is 21 miles. The "SA"
tands for either St. Andrew or St. Andrews, depending
n whether you are looking at a chart or listening to
he locals; it is best to be flexible. Dead ahead, to the
ortheast across the bay, you will spot the Panama City
Municipal Marina.

**Dockage:** Port St. Joe can be a convenient stopover
oint, regardless of the direction you are traveling.
o reach Port St. Joe Marina, follow the deep, well-
arked channel into the harbor. The marina welcomes
ransients, has a well-stocked ship store, sells gas and
iesel and is home to the popular open-air Dockside

Café. Nearby Bluewater Outriggers sells clothing and
equipment for anglers and other outdoor enthusiasts
(850-229-1100). There is also a Piggly Wiggly
supermarket next door to Bluewater with an ATM, a
CVS pharmacy and several fast food establishments just
a short walk from the marina. Mexico Beach Marina to
the north and west also has slips and sells gas. There's
not much to do in Mexico Beach, and there isn't even
a stoplight. This is a place to slow down and enjoy the
white sandy beach.

## White City to Panama City—GIWW Mile 329 to Mile 290 EHL

**NAVIGATION:** Use Charts 11390, 11391 and 11393.
From White City, the GIWW continues to run clean,
relatively wide and deep, with no need for navigational
aids. At about Mile 318 EHL, it becomes the South
Prong of Wetappo Creek and continues beneath
**Overstreet (SR 386) Bridge** at Mile 315.4 EHL
(65-foot fixed vertical clearance) to about Mile 314 EHL,
where it joins the North Prong and becomes Wetappo
Creek.

At that point, aids to navigation appear again, starting with green daybeacon "1" at about Mile 313 EHL and continuing down the Wetappo Creek and into Big Cove. At that same green daybeacon "1," eastbound vessels need to stay alert, as the channel bends southeast here and the small bay to starboard can be confused with the GIWW.

During strong southerlies, the narrow channel leading west to the sharp turn at Mile 310 EHL (quick-flashing red "28") can pose serious difficulties to barge traffic. If meeting a tow along this stretch, be sure to coordinate on VHF Channel 13 to clarify your intentions. As a matter of practical concern, if you have your VHF radio cycling between Channel 16 and Channel 13 on this section of the GIWW, you will be in great shape.

The GIWW channel runs southwest from Raffield Island, and turns west at red "44" to Murray Point. Near Mile 306 EHL, favor the southwestern side of the channel to avoid oyster reefs on the northeast side (generally marked with "Danger" signs).

On this part of your journey, you will be passing a bay that leads to Sandy Creek just past Mile 310 EHL. You will pass Raffield Island on your port side (at 3 feet mean sea level). From there, the GIWW into East Bay winds through well-marked, but relatively narrow channels. Watch your markers carefully in this area, as some very shoal water can be found out of the channel. For example, at red daybeacon "38" off Piney Point (Mile 300.75), there is a 4-foot-deep shoal charted just northeast of the channel.

Just past Long Point is the **Dupont (U.S. 98) Bridge** at Mile 295.4 (50-foot fixed vertical clearance).

From here to Panama City, the GIWW runs through relatively deep water (25 to 35 and even 40 feet).

⚠ Study the chart carefully for the run up East Bay to Panama City. Starting with flashing green "29" (Mile 294.2 EHL) off Parker Bayou flashing green "29" should be left to starboard because the GIWW buoy system gives way to the Panama City buoy system (red-right-returning from the Gulf). This can be confusing, as red buoys are now on your port si as you travel west, switching back to red on the right with flashing red buoy "6" off Buena Vista Point west o Panama City.

**Anchorage:** Between White City and Panama City or the GIWW, a pleasant, protected overnight anchorage is located at Wetappo Creek (Mile 314.5). Just around the first bend of the creek (North Prong), you can safel anchor over a soft mud bottom in about 10 feet of water. Because of the current, a Bahamian moor might be appropriate here, preferably on the side of the river by the marshlands. Walker Bayou (Mile 307.5 EHL), Murray Bayou (Mile 305.7 EHL) and California Bayou (Mile 302 EHL) are also options. For boats with shallov draft, Laird Bayou (Mile 299.5 EHL) provides ample protection from north winds in 6 to 8 feet of water wit plenty of room to swing. This anchorage is northeast of the GIWW, across from Cedar Point in East Bay. One cove over is Callaway Bayou–Sun Point with good holding in 8 feet of water and all-around protection.

# Panama City–GIWW Mile 290 EHL

Panama City boasts a large year-round charter fishing fleet, party boats, fishing piers, diving and surf fishing. Gulf fishing has greatly improved in the area, thanks to conservation efforts, and inshore light-tackle catch-and-release fishing on the bay has become very popular. Snapper, grouper and scamp are plentiful, and offshore fishing is considered magnificent. Boaters can also enjoy the area's sparkling white sugar sand beaches, rated as some of the finest in the country.

**NAVIGATION:** Use Chart 11389 and 11390. Shell Island, the barrier island forming the southern side of the main pass from the Gulf of Mexico into St. Andrew Bay, provides shelter for Panama City, which is a major harbor for transient yachts. The cut itself is considered one of the best deep-water channels on the Gulf Coast.

St. Andrew Bay, one of Florida's finest bays and home to Panama City, is deep and almost landlocked. It is a good hurricane hole for larger vessels, but cruising boats should, if possible, seek shelter in a more protected bayou. The Bay's exit to the Gulf of Mexico is a land cut through St. Andrews Park that has a rock jetty and is well marked. The Navy operates a lab on the west end of the bay and south of the **Hathaway (U.S. 98) Bridge** at Mile 284.6 EHL (65-foot fixed vertical clearance); you will frequently see helicopters, hovercraft and some esoteric "special ops" equipment here.

⚠️ Under no circumstances should cruisers attempt to navigate the entrance to St. Andrew Bay at the eastern tip of Shell Island, labeled "Lands End" on the chart. It is unmarked and, with the bottom continually shifting, is considered unsafe. Rest assured that the boats fishing or anchored in this area arrived from St. Andrew Bay, not the Gulf.

**Dockage:** Panama City is probably the best-equipped harbor north of Tampa and St. Petersburg, and berths are usually available except on holiday weekends. It is a good idea, particularly during the season, to call ahead and reserve a berth. There are facilities throughout the area, beginning from the east at Watson Bayou (due north of flashing green buoy "25") and extending west to flashing red "14" off Dyers Point.

Pier 98 at Pitts Bayou sells fuel and may have space for you; call ahead. Directly northeast of the pass from the Gulf, and due north of Redfish Point and quick-flashing green buoy "17" (Mile 290.5 EHL) are the office, ship's store and fuel dock of Panama City Marina.

The marina's transient docks are to the east of the fuel dock. Other amenities at the municipal marina include a pump-out station, clean showers and laundry facilities, a ship store and gift shop and WiFi. The marina is one block from downtown Panama City, with several fine restaurants, a post office and a variety of services. Unique local and traveling exhibits are on display at the nearby Visual Arts Center. Banks, delis, bookstores, the public library, theaters and performing arts centers all lie within a perimeter of about 10 blocks from the marina. Marine parts are available here as well, but you will need transportation to get to West Marine. Consult local boaters for the best places to get repairs. Virtually all of the boatyards and several of the marinas have fallen prey to condominium development.

Moving westward up the GIWW, Buena Vista Point is one-half mile north of flashing red buoy "6." Once primarily a workboat marina, St. Andrews Marina now welcomes transients on their floating docks and fuel service is available 24 hours a day, 7 days a week. Nearby is Uncle Ernie's Bayfront Grill & Brew House (1151 Bayview Ave., 850-763-8427), a historic home with home-brewed beer and lighted docks and St. Andrews Coffee House & Bistro (1006 Beck Ave., 850-215-0669). The townies reportedly eat at nearby Captain's Table Fish House Restaurant (1110 Beck Ave., 850-767-9933) or you can try The Shrimp Boat Restaurant (1201 Beck Ave, 850-785-8706).

Continuing west on the GIWW, just south of the Hathaway Bridge is the deep-water Sun Harbor Marina, where deep-water transient berths for vessels up to 55 feet are available. They sell all fuels, have a well-stocked ship store and there is popular on-site restaurant, Shipyard Grill. Sun Harbor Marina is known as the home of the *Columbia*, a 141-foot replica of a 1923 Gloucester fishing schooner.

**Anchorage:** Along this stretch of the GIWW, from the Dupont Bridge to Panama City, virtually any cove well away from the channel offers good anchorage. Pitts and Parker Bayous are viable anchorages. Pearl Bayou used to be a nice anchorage, but it is said to be full of crab pots. It could, however, be considered as a hurricane hole.

Watson Bayou before a 9-foot fixed bridge offers 360-degree protection and good holding in 8 to 10 feet. It is a short walk to the store from a landing near the bridge. Farther west of Watson Bayou, on the southern side of the GIWW (near flashing red "20"), Redfish Point and Smack Bayou offer protection from southerly

# St. Andrew Bay, FL

| | | Largest Vessel Accommodated | VHF Channel Monitored | Approach / Dockside Depth (reported) | Transient Berths / Total Berths | Floating Docks | Gas / Diesel | Groceries, Ice, Marine Supplies, Snacks | Repairs: Hull, Engine, Propeller | Lift (tonnage), Crane, Rail | Min/Max Amps | Laundry, Pool, Showers, Courtesy Car | Pump-Out Station | Nearby: Grocery Store, Motel, Restaurant |
|---|---|---|---|---|---|---|---|---|---|---|---|---|---|---|
| | | | | **Dockage** | | | **Supplies** | | **Services** | | | | | |
| **PANAMA CITY** | | | | | | | | | | | | | | |
| 1. Pier 98 Marina (WiFi) | 850-874-8723 | 66 | – | call/10 | 12/12 | – | GD | GIM | – | – | 30/50 | S | P | GMR |
| 2. Panama City Marina 🖥 (WiFi) WG 290 EHL | 850-872-7272 | 110 | 16/12 | 20/240 | 10/10 | – | GD | GIMS | – | – | 30/100 | LS | P | GMR |
| **BUENA VISTA POINT** | | | | | | | | | | | | | | |
| 3. St. Andrews Marina 🖥 287 EHL | 850-872-7240 | 200 | 16/10 | 15/102 | 15/8 | F | GD | IMS | – | – | 30/50 | LS | P | GMR |
| 4. Sun Harbor Marina 🖥 (WiFi) 285 EHL | 850-785-0551 | 55 | 16 | 6/96 | 12/12 | – | GD | IMS | – | – | 30/50 | LS | P | GR |
| **GRAND LAGOON** | | | | | | | | | | | | | | |
| 5. Bay Point Marina 🖥 (WiFi) 280 EHL | 850-235-6911 | 120 | 16/78 | 20/180 | 6/7 | – | GD | I | EP | – | 30/200+ | LPS | P | GMR |
| 6. Lighthouse Marina (WiFi) 280 EHL | 850-625-2728 | 70 | 16/68 | 20/50 | 8/8 | – | GD | IMS | HEP | L55 | 30/50 | LSC | – | GMR |
| 7. Treasure Island Marina 280 EHL | 850-234-6533 | 70 | 16 | 6/85 | 8/6 | – | GD | GIMS | HEP | L35 | 30/50 | S | – | GMR |
| 8. Pirates Cove Marina (WiFi) 280 EHL | 850-234-3939 | 60 | 16/68 | 25/400 | 6/8 | – | GD | I | HEP | L12 | 30/50 | LPSC | – | GMR |
| **NORTH BAY** | | | | | | | | | | | | | | |
| 9. Miller Marine 🖥 (WiFi) | 850-265-6768 | – | – | – | – | – | – | M | HEP | L88 | – | C | – | GR |

🖥 Internet Access  (WiFi) Wireless Internet Access  WG Waterway Guide Cruising Club Partner  *(Information in the table is provided by the facilities.)*

See WaterwayGuide.com for current rates, fuel prices, web site addresses, and other up-to-the-minute information.

Panama City Marina

St. Andrews Marina

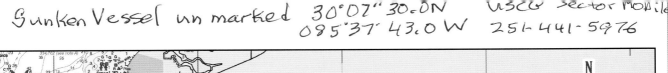

Sunken Vessel unmarked 30°07"30.0N 085°37'43.0 W    USCG Sector Mobile 251-441-5976

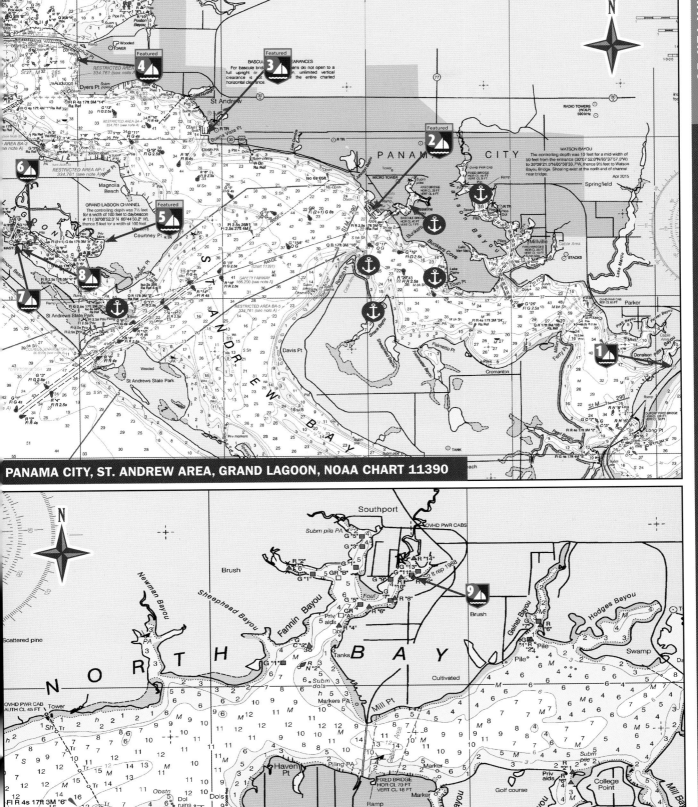

**PANAMA CITY, ST. ANDREW AREA, GRAND LAGOON, NOAA CHART 11390**

**SOUTHPORT, NOAA CHART 11390**

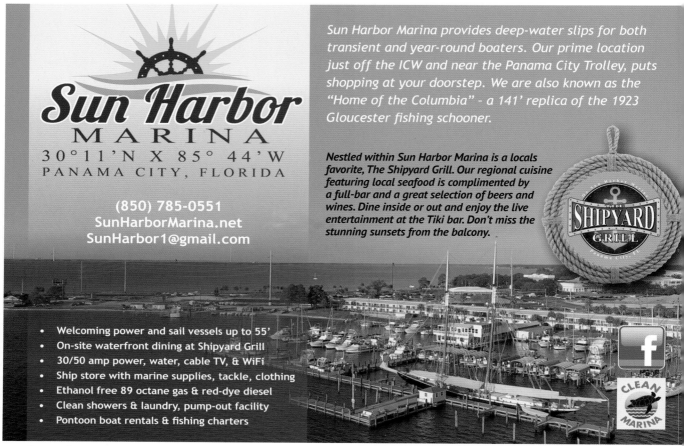

winds. Bunkers Cove is across the water if you need northerly protection.

West of Watson Bayou, and just east of Panama City Marina, you will find some anchoring room and restaurants ashore in Massalina Bayou. The drawbridge at the entrance (7-foot closed vertical clearance) opens on demand 24 hours a day. If you are hungry, tie up at Bayou Joe's (112 E. 3rd Ct., 850-763-6442). They serve breakfast, lunch and dinner daily, featuring southern-style breakfast and fried seafood platters.

Shell Island has some excellent anchorages off the beach, over a hard sand-and-shell bottom. If boat wakes from the channel bother you, head farther east on the island. Be wary of the charted sandbars between Davis Point and Shell Island. If your depth sounder shows less than 7-foot depths, you are in the wrong place. You are either too close to the island or too far north over the Camel Humps.

## Side Trip: Grand Lagoon at Panama City Beach

NAVIGATION: Use Charts 11390 and 11391. Grand Lagoon, immediately inside and west of St. Andrews Inlet, off St. Andrew Bay, offers an interesting side trip and some superior hospitality. Follow the marked channel and this trip should not provide too many challenges.

Dockage: At flashing green "5," a well-marked channel leads to Bay Point Marina off to starboard. The full-service marina is a very impressive facility in the sheltered Marriott Hotel complex. Marina guests can explore the resort on complimentary bicycles and take advantage of the resort's waterfront dining, the only Nicklaus-designed golf course in Northwest Florida, a spa, clay tennis courts and more. The tradition of flying weather flags is still honored there, and cruisers are definitely welcome.

Lighthouse Marina, Treasure Island Marina and Pirates Cove Marina are about 1 mile farther into Grand Lagoon. All have some transient space reserved, sell fuel and offer repairs. Past the Hathaway Bridge, on North Bay is Miller Marine, which is a repair facility with an 88-ton lift (no transient slips).

Anchorage: The anchorage at Grand Lagoon has 10 to 13 feet of water with good holding in sand. It is open and exposed, however, to the southeast and wakes. Note that jets flying overhead (often early in the morning) is pretty typical of the entire area.

## PANAMA CITY TO FORT WALTON BEACH

rom Panama City, westbound cruisers will find about 2 miles of relatively trouble-free transit through West ay, then about 16.5 miles of transit through a land cut nown to some as the "Grand Canyon," ending up in hoctawhatchee Bay, about 30 miles long and 3 to miles wide.

**AVIGATION:** Use Charts 11385 and 11390. When estbound from Panama City and approaching the athaway Bridge at Mile 284.6 EHL (65-foot fixed ertical clearance), stay well to port of flashing red 4" off Dyers Point (Bird Island), as shoaling off the nall island reaches into the marked channel. Beyond athaway Bridge, the GIWW opens up. Heading north ast the shoals at Shell Point (keep flashing green "5" ell to port). From there, the GIWW curves northwest rough West Bay, cuts under the **West Bay Creek R 79) Bridge** at Mile 271.8 EHL (65-foot fixed ertical clearance) and then enters the relatively narrow nannel of West Bay Creek, the start of the land cut nown as the "Grand Canyon." For purposes of careful navigation, however, you may assume that you are in narrow circumstances at quick-flashing green "15."

While in the "Grand Canyon," watch aids to navigation and your course carefully, as shoal water with depths of 2 to 4 feet runs very close to either side of the channel. The narrow channel persists past green daybeacon "39," and then aids to navigation cease, as they are not needed. The channel here runs relatively wide and deep. This situation continues for about 16.5 statute miles to Mile 254.5 EHL, entering Choctawhatchee Bay.

In the event of strong crosswinds, make it a point to check with any tows (VHF Channel 13) in the channel east of the **Clyde B. Wells (Choctawhatchee Bay) Bridge** at Mile 250.4 EHL (65-foot fixed vertical clearance), as the narrow channel may require coordinated meeting or passing. Barges, especially empties, are exceptionally difficult to handle for towboat operators in heavy wind and current.

While the cut is frequently dredged to 10.5-foot depths, shoaling is chronic, so hold to the center except when passing and realize that hugging the shore while passing will likely run you aground in soft mud. Also, use particular caution when transiting after strong winds or heavy rain, as large pine trees frequently break away from the nearly vertical banks. From time to time, when high winds are expected on Choctawhatchee Bay, be prepared to find westbound barges waiting inside the "Grand Canyon" at about Mile 254 EHL for better conditions. Cautious mariners might follow suit. Tying up to a commercial barge here is entirely possible, if you make a proper approach to the towboat's skipper.

**Anchorage:** Burnt Mill Creek at Mile 277. 7 EHL in West Bay has 7 to 9 feet of water. If you need it, you can find anchorage in 7 feet of water over good holding ground in the lee of the causeway on either side of the Choctawhatchee Bay Bridge.

## Choctawhatchee Bay–GIWW Mile 253.5 EHL

**NAVIGATION:** Use Chart 11385. As you travel into Choctawhatchee Bay from the east, the water deepens from about 9 feet to 38 feet but is generally shallow along its southern shore. Be cautious passing Tucker Bayou (Mile 254 EHL), as it sometimes shoals to 3-foot depths or less at its mouth.

The route is closely pegged with markers for the first 5 to 6 nm, but as the bay broadens and deepens, buoys thin out. Markers are used mainly to indicate shallows to the south, and these should be given a wide berth due to the possibility of shoaling. There is room to roam on this big open bay, but be aware that it can get rough in hard easterly or westerly blows because of the 20-mile east–west fetch. The approach to the 64-foot fixed vertical clearance **Mid-Bay Bridge** (Mile 234.2 EHL) is well marked from both east and west.

**Dockage:** In La Grange Bayou, off the north side of the Choctawhatchee Bay, are two marinas with limited services: Fisherman's Boatyard (repairs only) and Freeport Marina and Yacht Club (slips and gas).

Near the center of the long Choctawhatchee Bay, south of Mile 239 EHL in Horseshoe Bayou, is the full-service Sandestin's Baytowne Marina, part of a large resort community that stretches from the bay to the beach. The gated community offers marina guests all resort amenities. A small ferry runs between the marina and the Village of Baytowne Wharf, or you can take a walk on the boardwalk built over the marshland. The Village of Baytowne Wharf has many charming shops and boutiques, restaurants, nightclubs, art galleries and other facilities.

To approach Baytowne Marina, head south once you are clear of Four Mile Point and line up for flashing green "1" and flashing red "2" at the beginning of the entrance to the facility. Be careful to avoid the shoal depths when approaching shore to the east.

Located at the southeastern foot of the Mid-Bay Bridge is Legendary Marina, which offers dockage with amenities and sells fuel; call ahead for details.

To the northwest of flashing red "58," after passing under the Mid-Bay Bridge, at a distance of a little more than 3 miles, you will find flashing green "1," and that means you are on course for Rocky Bayou. Ward Cove is to starboard as you approach Rocky Bayou on the north side of Choctawhatchee Bay. Locate flashing red "2" and green daybeacon "1," which mark the entrance to Ward Cove and Bluewater Bay Marina. Bluewater Bay is a full resort complex with an outstanding ship store and an excellent restaurant and oyster bar. Nearby Boggy Bayou is home to North Light Yacht Club, which may have transient space. Both facilities sell fuel.

**Anchorage:** Rocky Bayou on the north shore provides a scenic anchorage. To enter Rocky Bayou, follow the directions above for Bluewater Bay Marina, pass Ward Cove to starboard and turn right into Rocky Bayou. Be aware of the 20-foot fixed vertical clearance bridge shortly after turning to starboard. Alternatively, anchor before the bridge in the cove east of Nelson Point.

You can also anchor in Boggy Bayou to the west, either at Toms Bayou with 13-foot depths or Niceville, by North Light Yacht Club, in 11 to 12 feet of water.

For an anchorage on the south side of the bay, a turn to the south at Mile 230 EHL will bring you to a marked entry to Joes Bayou, a 360-degree protected anchorage, with a soft mud bottom and depths of 10 feet or more.

## Destin–GIWW Mile 227 EHL

A major sportfishing and recreational center on northwest Florida's "Miracle Strip," Destin is renowned for its sparkling beaches, crystal-clear waters and seaside resort activities, which attract thousands of tourists and boaters year-round. This is possible because the Gulf Coast's temperatures are relatively moderate from October through March. The average air temperature is 67.3 degrees maximum, with a minimum average of 52.2 degrees. Winter visitors throng from the north by both boat and car for respite from the chill and snow. Destin lies just north and east of the Choctawhatchee Bay entrance on the barrier peninsula sheltering

Choctawhatchee Bay on the south. Full-service marinas, waterfront hotels and restaurants abound.

Destin sponsors a bill-fishing tournament each year, while the month of October is mainly devoted to the more than 50-year-old Deep Sea Fishing Rodeo. Big game fish that ply the Loop Current that circulates clockwise in the Gulf of Mexico are the reason, and the current comes relatively close to shore near Destin. The rodeo draws thousands of expectant anglers who search the offshore waters, inshore bays and bayous for prize-winning fish, worth thousands of dollars. Scuba divers get their chance for fun and games at the annual Destin Underwater Easter Egg Hunt in April. Great food and friendly people add to the attraction of these events.

**NAVIGATION:** Use Chart 11385. The main docking area in Destin is immediately south and east of the twin fixed bridges over the Choctawhatchee Bay entrance from the Gulf (south of the GIWW). The charted vertical bridge clearance at the **Destin Twin Bridges** is 49 feet, but there have been reports that 48 feet is closer to reality, so sailors should use caution if their vessel's mast height is more than 48 feet.

⚠️ If entering the pass from the Gulf, care should be taken when crossing the bar if there is a swell running. Also note that buoys are not charted in the Choctawhatchee Bay entrance channel, as constant shoaling necessitates frequent relocation. This is a pass that needs to be negotiated in flat water, daylight, with good visibility and during reasonable tides. (Refer to Tide Tables in front of this guide.)

To enter the main Destin Harbor, commonly known as Old Pass Lagoon, from Choctawhatchee Bay to the north, turn sharply to port (east) after passing under the bridges. The channel into the large harbor is narrow, but well-marked with daybeacons. It runs between the mainland to the north and the protective sandbar to the south.

Many facilities line the northern shore of the harbor. The pristine beaches and dunes of Santa Rosa Island are located across the peninsula on the Gulf side. Because of the substantial development along the beach, you will have to search for a spot with public access.

**Dockage:** Along the north shore of the harbor are Destin Marina, Harborwalk Marina and Destin Fishermen's Co-op. Many locally popular eating establishments also offer dockage along with everything from snacks to gourmet meals. Destin Marina (northeast side of the twin Destin Bridges) has only 8 slips and no amenities; however, the marina is within walking distance of downtown.

Fuel and limited transient dockage (two reserved slips) is available at Harborwalk Marina, located southeast of the bridge and on the north side of Destin Harbor. This facility gets high marks from cruisers for the friendly and helpful staff. They have a ship store and gift shop on site. Their web cams are pretty fun too; check them out on the marina's web site. Restaurants and provisions are within walking distance of the marina.

Destin Fisherman's Co-op is located on the north side of the harbor and can accommodate vessels to 100 feet and sells fuel. Farther in Destin Harbor is Dockside Watersports, which does not offer transient space.

Many restaurants lacking dockage welcome customers coming ashore in their dinghies. You can have a great time just dinghy-hopping from one bistro to the next.

# Destin to Fort Walton Beach, FL

| Facility | Phone | Largest Vessel Accommodated | VHF Channel Monitored | Transient Berths / Total Berths | Approach / Dockside Depth (reported) | Floating Docks | Gas / Diesel | Groceries, Ice, Marine Supplies, Snacks | Repairs: Hull, Engine, Propeller | Lift (tonnage), Crane, Rail | Min/Max Amps | Laundry, Pool, Showers, Courtesy Car | Pump-Out Station | Nearby: Grocery Store, Motel, Restaurant |
|---|---|---|---|---|---|---|---|---|---|---|---|---|---|---|
| **LA GRANGE BAYOU** | | | | Dockage | | | | Supplies | | Services | | | | |
| 1. Fisherman's Boatyard | 850-835-4848 | – | – | – | – | – | – | – | HP | L88 | – | – | – | – |
| 2. Freeport Marina and Yacht Club (WiFi) | 850-835-2035 | 55 | 09/16 | 8/38 | 15/10 | – | G | IMS | – | – | 30/30 | S | P | GR |
| **HORSESHOE BAY** | | | | | | | | | | | | | | |
| 3. Sandestin's Baytowne Marina □ (WiFi) 240 EHL | 850-267-7773 | 130 | 16/10 | 20/113 | 8/7 | – | GD | GIS | HEP | – | 30/100 | LPS | P | GMR |
| **MORENO POINT** | | | | | | | | | | | | | | |
| 4. Legendary Marine 234 EHL | 850-337-8200 | 50 | 16 | call/350 | 8/ | F | GD | GIMS | HEP | L | 30/50 | S | P | GMR |
| **WARDS COVE** | | | | | | | | | | | | | | |
| 5. Bluewater Bay Marina □ (WiFi) 232 EHL | 850-897-2821 | 110 | 16 | 10/120 | 8/8 | – | GD | GIMS | HE | – | 30/50 | LPSC | P | GMR |
| 6. North Light Yacht Club (WiFi) | 850-678-2350 | 65 | 16 | 10/55 | 15/8 | – | GD | IMS | HEP | L | 50/50 | LPS | P | GMR |
| **DESTIN** | | | | | | | | | | | | | | |
| 7. Destin Marina | 850-837-2470 | 30 | – | 8/10 | 6/6 | – | GD | GIMS | – | – | – | – | – | GMR |
| 8. HarborWalk Marina □ (WiFi) 230 EHL | 850-650-2400 | 85 | 16 | 2/52 | 10/6 | F | GD | GIMS | – | – | 30/50 | – | P | GMR |
| 9. Destin Fisherman's Co-op 230 EHL | 850-654-4999 | 100 | – | call/40 | 8/8 | – | GD | IM | HEP | L88 | 30/30 | – | – | MR |
| 10. Dockside Watersports | 850-428-3313 | – | – | – | 10/8 | – | – | IS | – | – | – | – | – | GMR |
| **FORT WALTON BEACH** | | | | | | | | | | | | | | |
| 11. Shalimar Yacht Basin □ 225 EHL | 850-651-0510 | 125 | 16 | 6/134 | 32/8 | – | GD | IMS | HEP | L35 | 30/50 | LSC | P | GMR |
| 12. Brooks Bridge Bait & Tackle Inc. 223 EHL | 850-243-5721 | 130 | 16 | – | 8/8 | – | GD | IS | – | – | – | – | P | GMR |
| 13. Ft. Walton Beach Landing Dock 223 EHL | 850-833-9504 | 50 | – | 6/ | 6/ | – | – | – | – | – | 30/30 | – | P | GMR |
| 14. Legendary Marine's Fort Walton Beach | 850-244-1099 | 40 | – | 10/15 | 30/5 | – | – | M | HEP | – | 30/50 | – | P | GMR |
| 15. Emerald Coast Boatyard | 850-244-2722 | – | – | – | 9/7 | – | – | – | HEP | L75,C20 | 30/50 | – | – | GMR |
| 16. Fort Walton Beach Yacht Basin 222 EHL | 850-244-5725 | 50 | 16 | 4/94 | 9/7 | – | G | I | – | – | 30/50 | S | P | GMR |

□ Internet Access  (WiFi) Wireless Internet Access  **WG** Waterway Guide Cruising Club Partner  *(Information in the table is provided by the facilities.)*
See WaterwayGuide.com for current rates, fuel prices, web site addresses, and other up-to-the-minute information.

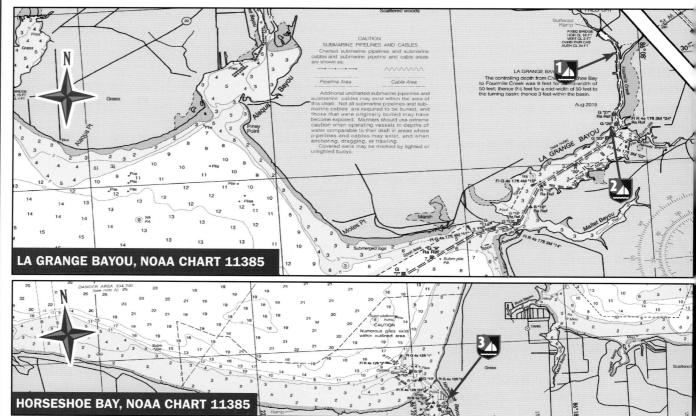

CAUTION
SUBMARINE PIPELINES AND CABLES
Charted submarine pipelines and submarine cables and submarine pipeline and cable areas are shown as:

Pipeline Area        Cable Area

Additional uncharted submarine pipelines and submarine cables may exist within the area of this chart. Not all submarine pipelines and submarine cables are required to be buried, and those that were originally buried may have become exposed. Mariners should use extreme caution when operating vessels in depths of water comparable to their draft in areas where pipelines and cables may exist, and when anchoring, dragging, or trawling.
Covered wells may be marked by lighted or unlighted buoys.

LA GRANGE BAY
The controlling depth from Choctawhatchee Bay to Fourmile Creek was 9 feet for a mid-width of 50 feet; thence 9½ feet for a mid-width of 50 feet to the turning basin; thence 3 feet within the basin.
Aug 2015

**LA GRANGE BAYOU, NOAA CHART 11385**

**HORSESHOE BAY, NOAA CHART 11385**

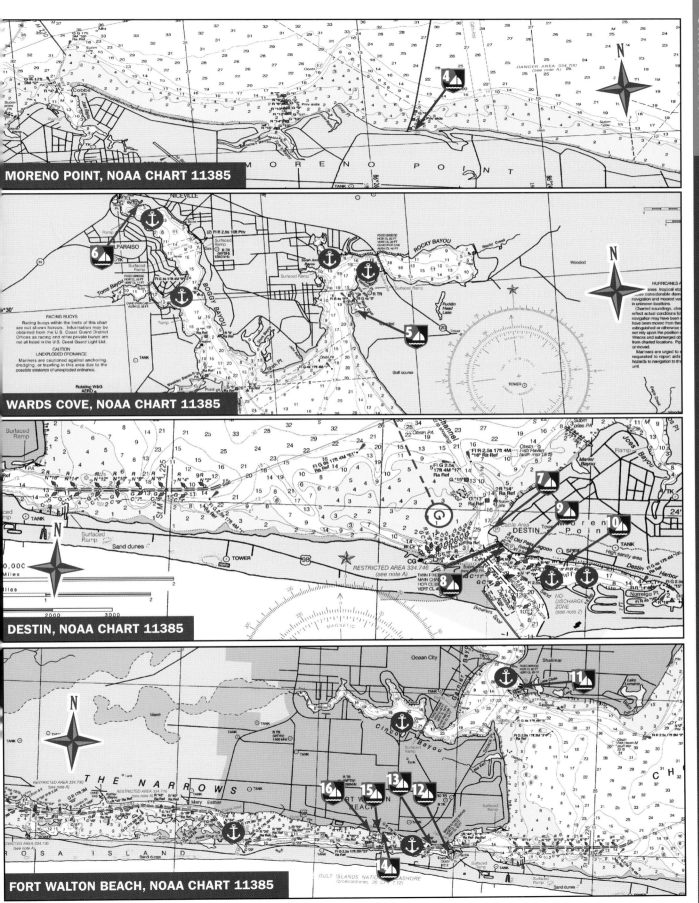

MORENO POINT, NOAA CHART 11385

WARDS COVE, NOAA CHART 11385

DESTIN, NOAA CHART 11385

FORT WALTON BEACH, NOAA CHART 11385

For a first-class meal, tie up at the Marina Café Yacht Club or dinghy to the beach. Others to explore include the Boathouse Oyster Bar (288 Harbor Blvd. East, 850-837-3645) with outdoor music; Harry T's (46 Harbor Blvd., 850-654-4800) with excellent cuisine and bands; and McGuire's Irish Pub and Brewery (33 Harbor Blvd., 850-433-6789), the legendary Pensacola bistro, which now has a Destin counterpart just across the road near the bridge. Florida law requires that a dinghy carry a life jacket (with whistle attached) for every passenger. If you don't want a flashing blue light from a law enforcement boat from the Florida Fish and Wildlife Conservation Commission (FWC) approaching you, make certain you pay attention to this decree. It is actively enforced and not negotiable.

**Anchorage:** Destin Harbor provides excellent anchorage with no surge, and wakes are strictly controlled. Note that the harbor is a No-Discharge Zone. Inside, the channel splits to avoid a shoal down the center and then converges past the shoal. You can anchor on the southwest side of the harbor or just off Harbor Docks Restaurant to the east. A municipal water taxi service is available during the summer months.

## Fort Walton Beach–GIWW Mile 224 EHL

Fort Walton Beach combines the many charms of a major seaside resort and is well worth a cruising layover. Besides the swimming and snorkeling in crystal-clear water (locals swear you can see a quarter on the bottom at 30 feet), the area is an angler's delight.

Fort Walton Beach has been and continues to be an Air Force town. The linchpin is Eglin Air Force Base, a military facility that's larger than the entire state of Rhode Island. At Mary Esther, you will be close to the north–south runway at Hurlburt Field, so look for planes coming and going.

This captivating town is a shopper's bonanza with its many antiques stores, novelty shops, boutiques, upscale dress shops and bookstores. Golf and tennis facilities abound, and there is an eclectic variety of restaurants and nightclubs.

**Dockage:** Transient space may be found on the eastern shore of the entrance to Garnier Bayou, approximately 2 miles northwest of Mile 225 EHL on the GIWW. A well-marked channel entrance with a tall cylindrical water tower serves as a beacon to the Shalimar Yacht Basin, a full-service repair facility with slips and fuel. This area has comprehensive cruiser amenities and services. While Cinco and Garnier Bayou offer a number of marine facilities, the 19-foot fixed vertical clearance **Elgin Parkway Bridge** limits access to both.

At Mile 225 EHL, the GIWW narrows down considerably, and you will come across a series of floating marks that will get that point across to you quite well. On the west side of the **Brooks Memorial Bridge** (50-feet fixed vertical clearance), Brooks Bridge Bait & Tackle offers pump-out service at their dock or they can also come to you. They also sell fuel but do not have transient slips.

Fort Walton Beach offers a free pump-out station at a city park about a block west of Brooks Bridge, on the north side, where you can also stay overnight after obtaining approval by calling the city manager's office at 850-833-9500. Depth at the dock's T-Head is 6 feet, but it is considerably shallower near the shore. From the GIWW make your turn toward the Ft. Walton Beach Landing Dock, on the north shore, between red "6" and red "8."

On the southern shore, Legendary Marine's Fort Walton Beach may have transient space and they offer repairs. Nearby Emerald Coast Boatyard has a 75-ton lift and offers repairs but no transient slips. Fort Walton Beach Yacht Basin sells gas and has some transient space reserved. Call ahead for slip availability in this area and refer to the marina table in this chapter for more details.

# ■ FORT WALTON BEACH TO PERDIDO BAY

### The Narrows and Santa Rosa Sound– GIWW Mile 223 to Mile 189 EHL

From the southwestern terminus of Choctawhatchee Bay, west of Fort Walton Beach, the GIWW enters a section known as The Narrows. This waterway, which is actually the eastern end of Santa Rosa Sound, is appropriately named. Although well-marked, the channel twists back and forth through shallows for about 6 statute miles before it widens somewhat as it approaches Santa Rosa Sound proper.

As the GIWW winds through Santa Rosa Sound to Pensacola Bay, you will see an abundance of attractive homes along the mainland side, with beach communities dotting the barrier side. Santa Rosa Sound, which is almost as narrow as The Narrows has numerous coves and good anchorages along its shores. However, check your depths, and remember the effect of the wind on tides, as the anchorages could be somewhat more shallow than charted.

Pensacola Bay, west of Deer and Fair Points, has always been considered one of Florida's largest and safest harbors. It has served as a heavy weather refuge for commercial and naval ships, as well as for smaller craft.

**NAVIGATION:** Use Charts 11378 and 11385. At Mile 206.7 EHL, the **Navarre Beach Causeway (CR 399) Bridge** has a charted fixed vertical clearance

of 50 feet but may have only a 48-foot fixed vertical clearance due to tide conditions. East of the bridge, between flashing green "87" and quick-flashing red "88," is a shoal into the channel, so favor the green (south) side.

While transiting The Narrows, monitor VHF Channel 16 and Channel 13 for barge traffic to avoid a "squeeze" when meeting with an oncoming barge. "Passing one whistle" means that you both agree to alter course to starboard and pass port-side to port-side. "Two whistles" means that you are altering course to port and will pass starboard-to-starboard. If you are clever enough to ask the skipper of the tow what is best for him, you will get extreme cooperation. Remember, barges are not maneuverable like your pleasure craft, so give the barge traffic the benefit of the doubt.

At Mile 205 EHL, the GIWW emerges from shoal territory into Santa Rosa Sound. Though the GIWW does move through some shoal areas in Santa Rosa Sound (5- and 6-foot depths at mean low water), for the most part it carries respectable depths of 13 to 17 feet.

⚠ On your westward journey near Mile 200 EHL, note that red daybeacon "124" (between flashing green lights "123" and "125") marks a shoal encroaching into the channel. Some charts do not show this marker. At this point, you should switch to Chart 11378 for your approach to the Pensacola Beach Twin Bridges .

**Anchorage:** Anchorages abound in The Narrows. Mary Esther at Mile 219.7 EHL has at least 4 feet of water and good holding. On Santa Rosa Island, there are viable anchorages at Mile 217.4 EHL (green daybeacon "51"); Mile 215 EHL (green daybeacon "69"); and Mile 213.9 EHL at Manatee Point (red daybeacon "74A"). On the

**Did You Know?** You can thank the Apalachicola River, 130 miles east of Ft. Walton Beach, for the fine, white of sand found here. The quartz–sand combination, delivered to the Gulf from the Appalachian mountains via the river, was deposited along the shores when Santa Rosa Island began to extend like an arm from Destin. This extension continues today as these small, white grains of quartz sand move to the west before reaching their final destination at the Pensacola Pass. The sand here is so fine that it actually "squeaks" underfoot.

# Pensacola Bay, FL

| | | Dockage | | | | | Supplies | | Services | | | | | |
|---|---|---|---|---|---|---|---|---|---|---|---|---|---|---|
| | | Largest Vessel Accommodated | VHF Channel Monitored | Transient Berths / Total Berths | Approach / Dockside Depth (reported) | Floating Docks | Gas / Diesel | Groceries, Ice, Marine Supplies, Snacks | Repairs: Hull, Engine, Propeller | Lift (tonnage), Crane, Rail | Min/Max Amps | Laundry, Pool, Showers, Courtesy Car | Pump-Out Station | Nearby: Grocery Store, Motel, Restaurant |
| **PENSACOLA BEACH** | | | | | | | | | | | | | | |
| 1. Santa Rosa Yacht & Boat Club 🖥 WiFi 189 EHL | 850-934-1005 | 70 | 16 | 5/40 | 8/8 | – | GD | I | – | – | 30/100 | LS | P | GMR |
| 2. Pensacola Beach Marina 🖥 WiFi 189 EHL | 850-931-2030 x4 | 100 | 16 | 4/30 | – | – | GD | GIS | – | – | 30/50 | S | P | GMR |
| 3. Sabine Marina 🖥 WiFi 189 EHL | 850-932-1904 | 57 | 16 | 5/64 | 9/8 | – | – | IS | – | – | 30/50 | LS | P | GMR |
| **SAYVILLE HARBOR** | | | | | | | | | | | | | | |
| 4. Palafox Pier Yacht Harbor WiFi 186 EHL | 850-432-9620 | 175 | 16/09 | 10/88 | 20/13 | F | GD | I | – | – | 30/50 | LS | P | R |
| 5. Baylen Slips Marina WiFi | 850-432-9620 | 55 | 16/09 | call/24 | 20/13 | F | GD | I | – | – | 30/50 | LS | P | R |
| **PENSACOLA AREA** | | | | | | | | | | | | | | |
| 6. Pensacola Yacht Club 🖥 185 EHL | 850-433-8804 | 100 | 16 | call/58 | 8/8 | – | GD | I | – | – | 30/50 | LPS | P | MR |
| 7. MarineMax Pensacola at Bahia Mar WiFi 185 EHL | 850-477-1112 | 50 | 16/09 | 6/60 | 6/4 | F | GD | IMS | HEP | L50 | 30/30 | LS | P | GR |
| 8. Yacht Harbor Marina 🖥 WiFi 185 EHL | 850-455-4552 | 65 | 16 | 8/52 | 9/6.5 | F | – | I | – | – | 30/50 | S | P | GMR |
| 9. Palm Harbor Marina 🖥 WiFi | 850-455-4552 | 70 | – | 10/64 | 9/6.5 | F | – | I | – | – | 30/50 | S | P | GMR |
| 10. Pelican's Perch Marina & Boatyard WiFi 185 EHL | 850-453-3471 | 50 | – | call/55 | 15/6 | F | – | MS | HEP | L50,C | 30/50 | S | – | – |
| 11. Bell Marine Service 185 EHL | 850-455-7639 | 48 | – | call/20 | 5/6 | – | – | M | E | – | 30/30 | – | – | G |
| 12. Island Cove Marina 🖥 WiFi 185 EHL | 850-455-4552 | 75 | – | 6/94 | 7/6 | – | – | IMS | – | – | 30/50 | S | P | GMR |
| 13. Pensacola Shipyard Marina & Boatyard WiFi 185 EHL | 850-439-1451 | 100 | – | 4/52 | 18/7 | F | – | MS | HE | L110,C14 | 30/100 | LS | P | – |

🖥 Internet Access  WiFi Wireless Internet Access  WG Waterway Guide Cruising Club Partner  *(Information in the table is provided by the facilities.)*
See WaterwayGuide.com for current rates, fuel prices, web site addresses, and other up-to-the-minute information.

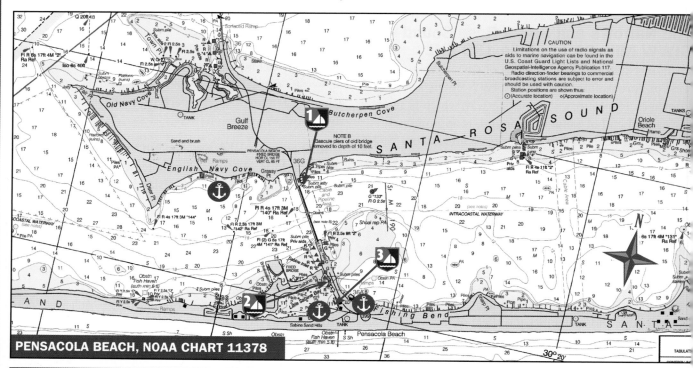

PENSACOLA BEACH, NOAA CHART 11378

## see our interactive charts

 MARINAS
 SERVICES
 ANCHORAGES
 FREE DOCK
 BRIDGES
 LOCKS
 NAV ALERTS
 FUEL

## waterwayguide.com

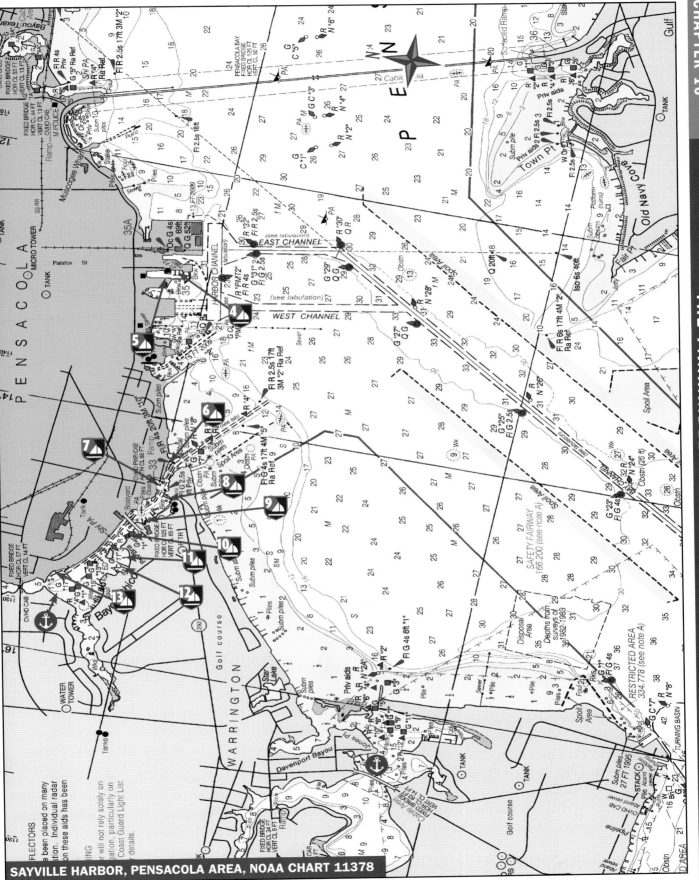

SAYVILLE HARBOR, PENSACOLA AREA, NOAA CHART 11378

# Perdido Key, FL

| PERDIDO KEY | | | Dockage | | | | | Supplies | | Services | | | | | | |
|---|---|---|---|---|---|---|---|---|---|---|---|---|---|---|---|---|
| | | | Largest Vessel Accommodated | VHF Channel Monitored | Approach / Dockside Depth (reported) | Transient Berths / Total Berths | Floating Docks | Gas / Diesel | Groceries, Ice, Marine Supplies, Snacks | Repairs: Hull, Engine, Propeller | Lift (tonnage), Crane, Rail | Min/Max Amps | Laundry, Pool, Showers, Courtesy Car | Pump-Out Station | Nearby: Grocery Store, Motel, Restaurant |
| 1. Perdido Key Oyster Bar Restaurant & Marina, LLC 💻 | 850-492-5600 | | 150 | 16 | 20/50 | 10/12 | - | GD | IS | - | - | 30/50 | - | - | R |
| 2. A & M Perdido Resort & Marina (WiFi) | 850-492-7304 | | - | - | call/24 | - | | - | - | - | - | - | LPS | P | M |
| 3. Holiday Harbor Marina & Grill 💻 (WiFi) WG | 172 EHL | 850-492-0555 | 125 | 16/14 | 2/48 | 7/7 | - | GD | GIMS | EP | L12 | 30/50 | LS | P | GR |

💻 Internet Access (WiFi) Wireless Internet Access WG Waterway Guide Cruising Club Partner *(Information in the table is provided by the facilities.)*
See WaterwayGuide.com for current rates, fuel prices, web site addresses, and other up-to-the-minute information.

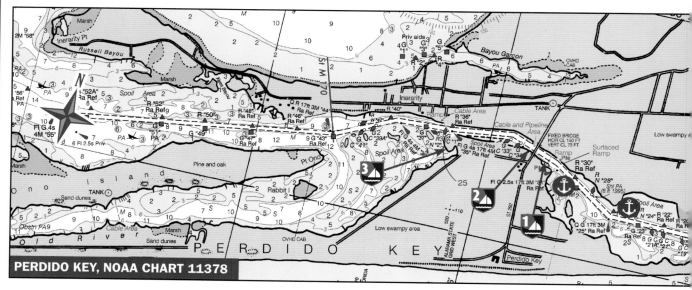

PERDIDO KEY, NOAA CHART 11378

north shore at Mile 208.6, you can drop the hook at Lower Pritchard Long Point in 9 foot depths.

You can also anchor on either side of the Navarre Bridge (Mile 206.7 EHL) at green daybeacon "89" or at "93" on the south shore or on the north shore, just east of the bridge.

## Pensacola Bay–GIWW Mile 189 to Mile 179 EHL

Keep within all channel markers if you are entering the bay from the Gulf of Mexico. This good all-weather passage is subject to shoaling, which is almost always well marked. A principal mark for the entrance is the 171-foot conical brick Pensacola Light. Currents can be significant in this channel, especially at the 90-degree turn into the Bay. The Pensacola Coast Guard Station is 1 mile east of Pensacola Light.

Pensacola Bay is relatively narrow (3 statute miles) and stretches in an east–west direction for about 22 statute miles. On its west side, Escambia Bay and East Bay extend some 10 statute miles north. Pensacola Bay carries depths of 20 to 50 feet, but the bays to the north run 9 to 12 feet with more extensive shoals as you go north.

⚠ For westbound skippers, as you enter Pensacola Bay, note that after passing flashing green "145" (at about Mile 184.2 EHL) the buoys shift to that of the Pensacola Ship Channel (red-right-returning for vessels inbound from the Gulf to Pensacola). Thus, traveling the GIWW from this point, all the way across Pensacola Bay to the Pensacola Landcut and re-entering the GIWW at about Mile 179.5 EHL, you should leave red markers to port and green to starboard. (These markers carry the appropriate small yellow triangles and squares indicating their dual role as GIWW route markers.)

The City of Pensacola lies about 5 statute miles north of the GIWW. The **Pensacola Beach Twin Bridges** (65-foot fixed vertical clearance) span the GIWW at Mile 189.1 EHL.

**Dockage:** Immediately east of the Pensacola Beach Twin Bridges at Mile 190 EHL, on the north side of Santa Rosa Sound is the Santa Rosa Yacht & Boat Club, offering transient dockage and fuel. Just past the bridges, if you turn south and parallel the bridges, you will see channel markers for Little Sabine Bay. Pensacola Beach Marina is the first marina on the port side after entering Little Sabine Bay. It provides dockage, fuel, restaurants and a grocery store. Just to the south in Little Sabine Bay is Sabine Marina, which may also have transient space.

The Palafox Pier Yacht Harbor facility is 6 miles northeast of the GIWW, on the west side of the Commercial Port of Pensacola. The slips are on floating piers with deep water. The marina is home to Jaco's Bayfront Bar and Grille (850-432-5226) and is within walking distance of downtown. Nearby Baylen Slips Marina may also have transient space on their floating docks.

The popular Fish House Restaurant (600 S. Barracks St., 850-470-0003) is on the western edge of Seville Harbor. The Fish House has deck dining and an outdoor bar, as well as inside dining. When the weather is right, this is the place to be. Check out the award-winning wine list. Next door, and under the same ownership, is the Atlas Oyster House (850-437-1961) featuring Apalachicola oysters. The latter is the more casual of the two. There are literally hundreds of "best" spots to eat within the city, but just a few blocks up Palafox Street from Palafox Pier you can find any number of restaurant choices.

One nautical mile southwest of the Port of Pensacola is a channel running northwest to Bayou Chico (Mile 185 EHL), which has a yacht club, full-service boatyards with facilities to handle most repairs and a number of full-service marinas. The 65-foot fixed vertical clearance **Bayou Chico (Barrancus Ave.) Bridge** crosses Bayou Chico. Before the bridge to starboard are Pensacola Yacht Club and the MarineMax Pensacola at Bahia Mar. Both sell fuel. There are restaurants nearby plus a bed-and-breakfast. To port before the bridge are Yacht Harbor Marina and Palm Harbor Marina. Both have slips on floating docks.

Beyond the Bayou Chico high-rise bridge on the port side, full-service repairs and transient dockage is available at Pelican's Perch Marina & Boatyard. Past Pelican's Perch are Bell Marine Service and Island Cove Marina, which has a barbecue area and a community kitchen. Call ahead for slip availability.

A little farther up Bayou Chico is the Pensacola Shipyard Marina & Boatyard, a full-service facility with a 110-ton lift and a 14-ton crane, plus mechanical, fiberglass, carpentry, electrical systems and painting services.

**Anchorage:** At Pensacola Beach, to the east of the bridge, Quiet Water Beach Pier is a free dock. If the dock is full, you can anchor nearby in 7 to 11 feet. It is also possible to anchor in Little Sabine Bay in 5 to 11 feet of water. On the north shore of Santa Rosa Sound, English Navy Cove carries 11 to 15 feet. In Bayou Chico, you can anchor north of the marinas in 9 to 11 feet with good holding in mud and all-around protection. Bayou Grande at Jones Point (Mile 183 EHL) has 9-foot depths and offers good protection from wind and wakes.

## Big Lagoon to Perdido Bay–GIWW Mile 179 to Mile 172 EHL

Continue west from Pensacola Bay into the GIWW. The intersection is about 1 statute mile from the exit into the Gulf of Mexico. It is a run of about 8 to 10 miles from Fort McRee at Pensacola's Gulf entrance to the Alabama line at about Mile 170 EHL. Ahead on the GIWW are some fabulous anchorages, great waterfront restaurants and fine repair facilities.

**NAVIGATION:** Use Chart 11378. Traffic here can get confusing, because the markers change to red-right-returning for vessels inbound from the Gulf to Pensacola, to GIWW red on the north or land side, green on the south or Gulf side. Charts are handy in these areas.

After flashing green buoy "15," in the middle of the Caucus Channel between Forts Pickens and Barrancas, head west-southwest to green can "1" (leave to port) and flashing red daybeacon "2" (leave to starboard) to transit the short and narrow, but well-marked passage known locally as the Pensacola Land Cut (about Mile 178 to Mile 179 EHL) leading to Big Lagoon.

Be careful not to confuse green can buoy "1" with green can buoy "13" just to its south, which is a marker for the Caucus Channel. You can also line up the range markers to get to the land cut, which leads into Big Lagoon. As you enter, keep an eye out for shoaling caused by strong tidal currents through the Caucus Channel. The shallows are easily seen on sunny days, but if it is overcast, they will be harder to make out, so stay to the center except to pass. If you see a barge entering the pass, wait. There is not much room in there.

**Anchorage:** There is a great anchorage in 10 to 13 feet in Big Lagoon at GIWW Mile 178.4 EHL. This is adjacent to Fort McRee, so expect to see planes flying overhead. Dinghy to the beaches on the Bay or Gulf side. This anchorage is somewhat exposed to the west.

Redfish Point is a good anchorage south of the GIWW that is well protected in most weather. Turn south before flashing red "10," which marks a very shallow shoal; you can anchor as close to shore as your draft permits in hard sand. You can also turn north at red "10" to access Trout Point with 11 feet and good holding.

If you continue to flashing green "15" and double back toward the beach on Perdido Key, you will find 12-foot depths. For a bit of shore side recreation, you can swim or dinghy to the beach. The Gulf beach is a short walk across the dunes, which are part of the Gulf Coast Island National Seashore Park. This is a favorite weekend getaway for locals, but there is a bothersome chop during a northerly.

You can anchor before the bridge at Siguenza Cove (Mile 172 EHL) in 5 to 7 feet. This is somewhat exposed to the east and wakes.

## Perdido Bay–GIWW Mile 172 to Mile 170 EHL

From Big Lagoon, it is a short trip to Perdido Bay, down the middle of which runs the state line separating Florida from Alabama. Perdido Bay offers a variety of enticements for the cruising yachtsman.

**NAVIGATION:** Use Chart 11378. Leaving either the anchorage or the marinas, as you approach the left turn at the west end of Big Lagoon, be careful not to shortcut the channel, as flashing red "12" is well up in the cove and hard to see. The area southeast of green can buoy "11" is shallow (you will realize this when you see pelicans walking on the bar) so favor the center of the channel to avoid joining the many who have run aground here. Follow the markers because this entire area is surrounded by shoal water. After a turn at

flashing red "16" and green daybeacon "15," you will se the Gulf Beach Bridge at Mile 171.8 EHL with a 73-foot fixed vertical clearance.

After flashing green "35," enter the open but shoaled area between Perdido Key (FL) and Ono Island (AL, Mile 170 EHL). The GIWW is well marked as it extend along the northern side of Ono Island and Innerarity Peninsula. From there at flashing green "57," the GIWW swings north into Perdido Bay. At this stage, the last of Florida, Innerarity Point, is now north of you, and the first part of Alabama, Ono Island, is now to the south. (Contrary to popular belief, not all of Alabama is west o Florida.)

**Dockage:** Immediately before the bridge on your left is the Perdido Key Oyster Bar Restaurant & Marina. The marina has transient slips and fuel. The Oyster Bar Restaurant (850-492-5600) offers both inside and outdoor accommodations, with oysters and a full-fare, excellent seafood menu. Call ahead for reservations.

Just after the bridge is A&M Perdido Resort, an RV resort with condos and a marina. Call ahead for slip availability (850-492-7304).

If you are in need of repairs or a break, just one-half mile west of the bridge and immediately past flashing green "35," you can turn south (to port if westbound) and follow the private markers a short distance to Holiday Harbor Marina & Grill. The marina offers transient dockage, gas and diesel and boat work/repairs. They are either the last marina in Florida heading west, or the first marina in Florida heading east, depending on your perspective.

**Anchorage:** On the western side of Perdido Bay there are anchorages at Soldier and Palmetto Creeks, which offer protection from the north and good holding in mu

## Cruising Options

You are now cruising the waters of Alabama's Gulf Coas on the way to the Mississippi, Louisiana and Texas coasts.

# Gulf Coast

■ PERDIDO BAY TO LOUISIANA   ■ LAKE PONTCHARTRAIN & NEW ORLEANS
■ NEW ORLEANS TO THE TEXAS BORDER   ■ THE TEXAS BORDER TO FREEPORT, TX   ■ FREEPORT TO BROWNSVILLE, TX

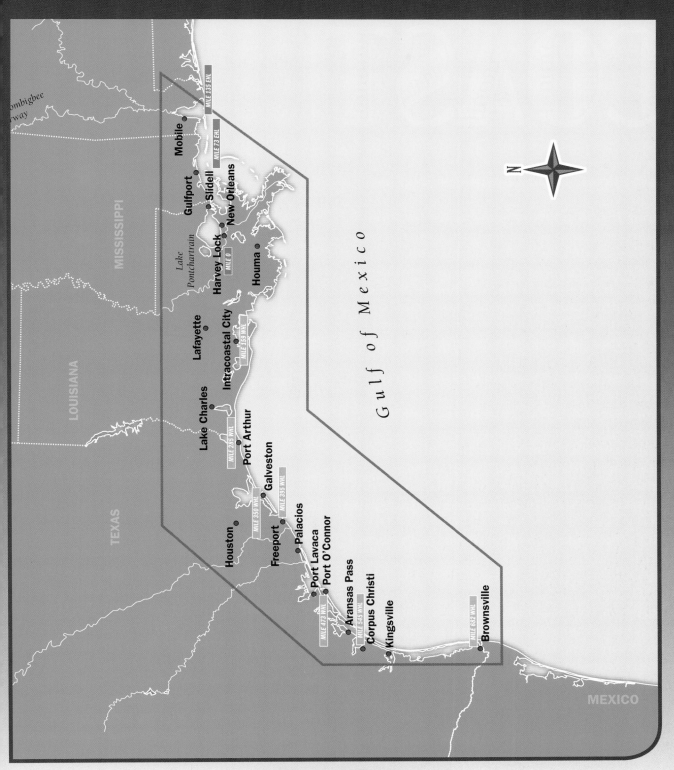

# GULF COAST

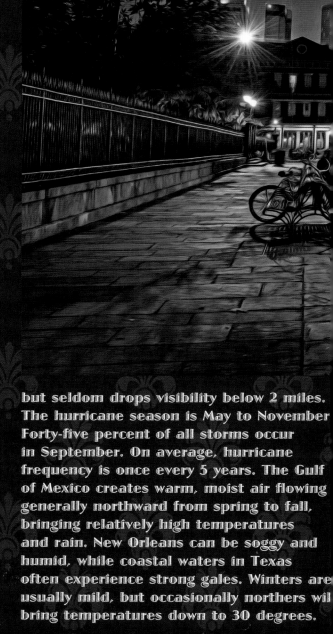

The area west from Florida along the Gulf Coast historically has been described as the playground of the South. The region is known for its miles of pure white beaches, scenic landscapes and historic towns. This trip can challenge your boating skills. Expect to encounter a variety of conditions, ranging from open water on Mobile Bay and Mississippi Sound to narrow, sometimes cramped, canals and waterways. Lagoons and bayous often alternate with long and sometimes tedious land cuts. The route runs past historic Southern cities rich in antebellum history, as well as those, such as Mobile and Biloxi, that have come to represent the New South.

The protected route, the Gulf Intracoastal Waterway (GIWW), arcs 870 miles from Pensacola to the Rio Grande. Distances are measured in statute miles east and west of Harvey Lock at New Orleans (given as EHL and WHL). The route is well marked and charted, with well-maintained depths.

## Weather

A word on the weather: Summers are hot but tolerable; otherwise, this is an exceptional area from April through November. The area is semi-tropical and influenced heavily by the Gulf of Mexico. Summers are warm and humid while winters are cool and mild. Occasionally cold air pushes far enough south to bring cold spells that can drop temperatures below freezing. Fog is prevalent in winter and spring, but seldom drops visibility below 2 miles. The hurricane season is May to November. Forty-five percent of all storms occur in September. On average, hurricane frequency is once every 5 years. The Gulf of Mexico creates warm, moist air flowing generally northward from spring to fall, bringing relatively high temperatures and rain. New Orleans can be soggy and humid, while coastal waters in Texas often experience strong gales. Winters are usually mild, but occasionally northers will bring temperatures down to 30 degrees.

Fog is an occasional problem in the
Mississippi Delta region westward to the
mid Texas coast in springtime. In these
cases, be especially cautious of the
commercial traffic that is more frequent in
this area than in other parts of the
Gulf Coast.

## Tides
Tides are semi-diurnal west of the
Mississippi Delta but are mostly diurnal
(with one high and one low each day)
eastward to Port St. Joe. They are easily
affected by winds and pressure. Prolonged

northerlies drop tides while southerlies
raise them. Generally, the range is 1 to
2 feet. Local tidal currents are usually
weak–less than 2 knots–except near
shoals, through certain cuts and at harbor
entrances.

## Commercial Traffic
Many commercial ships run offshore in the
Gulf of Mexico, heading from port to port or
serving offshore oil rigs. Gulf Coast waters
are also worked intensively by large fishing
and shrimping fleets, as well as by the ever-
present sportfishermen running in and out

is often crowded with tugs and barges.

Commercial craft expect yachts to stay clear. Barge rigs can be enormous, exceeding 1,000 feet in length in some cases. Vessels of this size must swing wide in turns and need up to a quarter mile to stop. Moreover, they usually travel together. The recreational boat must give way under all circumstances. On the other hand, most of the professional captains working these waters are valuable sources of information, and normally happy to help visiting boaters.

It is hard to overestimate the importance of VHF radio. Contact with towboats makes the journey easier. Call captains to find out when it is safe to pass, what traffic lies ahead and the best way to pass. Know the whistle signals; you will be told to pass on one whistle, two whistles or not at all. Call towboats on VHF Channels 13 or 16. In areas with heavy commercial traffic, you may want to leave your VHF on Channel 13. AIS is also useful along this coast.

In many areas of the Gulf Coast, marinas and fuel stops are scarce and often hold irregular hours. Keep a sizable reserve in your tanks and call ahead to fuel docks as soon as you are in range. Because the GIWW was once strictly a commercial waterway, many facilities remain geared to commercial vessels. In Louisiana and Texas a cell phone is a necessity, as many facilities geared to pleasure craft no longer monitor the VHF.

## Distances—GIWW
### Statute Miles (approximate)

#### East of Harvey Lock

| LOCATION | MILES |
|---|---|
| Pensacola | 185 |
| Mobile Bay Channel | 134* |
| Dauphin Island | 128 |
| Pascagoula | 104* |
| Biloxi | 88* |
| Gulfport | 73* |
| Pass Christian | 65* |
| Rigolets | 34 |
| New Orleans West End | 11 |

#### West of Harvey Lock

| LOCATION | MILES |
|---|---|
| Houma | 58 |
| Morgan City | 95 |
| Intracoastal City | 160 |
| Calcasieu River | 241 |
| Sabine River | 266 |
| Port Arthur | 282 |
| Galveston | 354 |
| Freeport | 395 |
| Port O'Connor | 474 |
| Aransas Pass | 533 |
| Corpus Christi | 542 |
| Port Mansfield | 632 |
| Port Isabel | 667 |
| Port Brownsville | 684 |

* Distance to junction of GIWW and Ship Channel

# Perdido Bay to Louisiana

GIWW  Mile 170 EHL–Mile 40 EHL    (((VHF)))  AL, MS & LA: Channel 13

**CHARTS**  11367, 11371, 11372, 11373, 11374, 11375, 11376, 11378

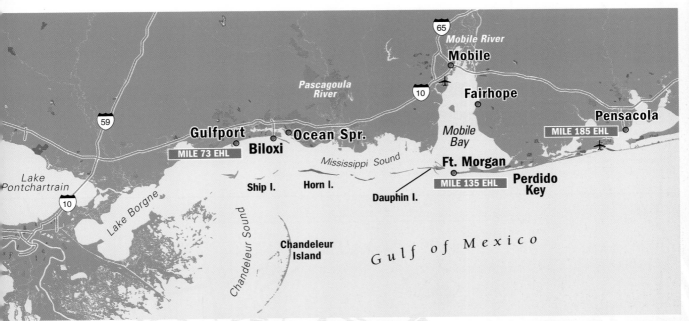

West of the Pensacola Inlet you will enter the GIWW, pass Sherman Cove to the north, and enter Big Lagoon. You will begin to notice that the waters are not as clear and as you continue west, they become cloudy to murky. As you approach Mobile Bay you are entering a vast delta basin fed by many rivers. These rivers feed into the Bay and spread across the area to comprise the second largest drainage basin in the United States, with the largest being the Mississippi River Delta. The hundreds of GIWW miles west are an adventure with a rich history, scenic beauty, and endless opportunities to entice the cruising boater.

Along this stretch of the GIWW, you cross into Alabama waters. The waterway route from the Alabama border, Mile 170 EHL to Mile 160 EHL is a wonderland of excellent protected anchorages, including Perdido Bay, Terry Cove, Cotton Bayou, Soldier Creek, Roberts Bayou, Ingram Bayou and Wolf Bay. Check your charts, and pick any one of these places for a pleasant, protected overnight stop.

There are also plenty of marinas in the area, along with repair facilities, restaurants and other amenities. Until you get to Mobile Bay, the only water-accessible town is Orange Beach, AL, named for the orange groves that once were plentiful there.

## ■ ORANGE BEACH

At Mile 170 EHL, heading west on the GIWW, the tip of private Ono Island appears to port as you cruise the straight westward line of the GIWW to the entrance to Perdido Bay. At flashing green "57," turn north to explore Perdido Bay or southwest to explore Bayou St. John.

**NAVIGATION:** Use Chart 11378. From flashing green "57" on the GIWW, there is a marked channel extending from the GIWW through Bayou St. John to Perdido Pass to the Gulf of Mexico. The Pass has a 9-foot controlling depth (mean low water) and the **Perdido Pass Channel Bridge** has a 54-foot fixed vertical clearance. This Pass is a popular well-marked gateway to and from the Gulf of Mexico.

A number of restaurants and marinas are located in the bays and bayous on the way to Perdido Pass. To visit here, turn southwest off the GIWW at flashing green

# Perdido Key, FL to Bon Secour Bay, AL

| | | Largest Vessel Accommodated | VHF Channel Monitored | Transient Berths / Total Berths | Approach / Dockside Depth (reported) | Floating Docks | Groceries, Ice, Marine Supplies, Snacks | Gas / Diesel | Repairs: Hull, Engine, Propeller | Lift (tonnage), Crane, Rail | Min/Max Amps | Laundry, Pool, Showers, Courtesy Car | Pump-Out Station | Nearby: Grocery Store, Motel, Restaurant |
|---|---|---|---|---|---|---|---|---|---|---|---|---|---|---|
| | | **Dockage** | | | | | **Supplies** | | **Services** | | | | | |
| **ORANGE BEACH AREA** | | | | | | | | | | | | | | |
| 1. SanRoc Cay Marina WiFi 167 EHL | 251-981-5423 | 150 | 16 | 75/75 | 5/5 | - | GD | GIMS | - | - | 50/50 | S | P | GMR |
| 2. Zeke's Landing Marina 163 EHL | 251-981-4044 | 100 | 69 | 4/50 | 7/7 | - | GD | GIMS | - | L | 50/50 | LS | P | GMR |
| 3. Saunders Yachtworks □ WiFi 163 EHL | 251-981-3700 | 75 | - | 0/1 | 6/6 | - | - | IMS | HEP | L60,C6 | 30/50 | LS | P | GMR |
| 4. Orange Beach Marina □ WiFi 163 EHL | 251-981-4207 | 130 | 16/69 | 30/161 | 9/8 | - | GD | GIMS | HEP | L60 | 30/100 | LSC | P | GMR |
| 5. Sportsman Marina □ WiFi 163 EHL | 251-981-6247 | 140 | 19 | 25/100 | 12/8 | - | GD | GIMS | HEP | L15 | 30/100 | LS | P | GR |
| **ARNICA BAY** | | | | | | | | | | | | | | |
| 6. Bear Point Harbor WiFi 165 EHL | 251-981-2327 | 50 | 16 | 5/83 | 12/8 | - | GD | IS | - | - | 30/50 | LS | P | R |
| **ELBERTA** | | | | | | | | | | | | | | |
| 7. Barber Marina □ WiFi 163 EHL | 251-987-2628 | 125 | 16 | 30/155 | 12/12 | F | GD | GIMS | HEP | L110 | 30/200+ | LSC | P | G |
| 8. Pirates Cove Marina & Restaurant 165 EHL | 251-987-1224 | 65 | - | 16/16 | 10/10 | - | - | I | - | - | 30/30 | LS | P | R |

□ Internet Access  WiFi Wireless Internet Access  WG Waterway Guide Cruising Club Partner  *(Information in the table is provided by the facilities.)*
See WaterwayGuide.com for current rates, fuel prices, web site addresses, and other up-to-the-minute information.

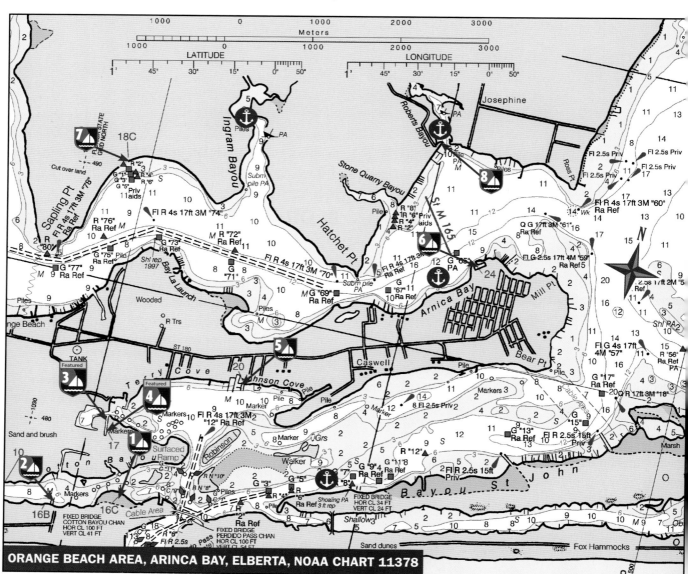

**ORANGE BEACH AREA, ARINCA BAY, ELBERTA, NOAA CHART 11378**

# *Experience*
## ORANGE BEACH MARINA

Home of the

**Haven or Heaven**
Enjoy the experience.

---

**Relax**. Every need is met at our beautifully secluded, secure location with covered and open slips available. Enjoy on site waterfront dining and shopping as your yacht gets all the attention it needs with on site service and repair. Located just minutes from the Gulf of Mexico at Perdido Pass and the Intercoastal Waterway.

Selected as one of the Top 25 US Marinas

**TENANT AMENITIES**
Outstanding Marina Staff
2 Restaurants On Site
24 Hr Security
6 Bay Fuel Dock
Free Wi-Fi & Cable TV
Upscale Dock Store
Courtesy Cars & Ample Parking
Dockage to 130'
Covered Grilling & Picnic Areas
Laundry Center
Private Showers & Restrooms

**ON SITE SERVICES**
Fisher's at Orange Beach Marina
        Upstairs & Dockside
Saunders Yachtworks
Bluewater Yacht Sales
Coldwell Banker Seaside Realty
Orange Beach Marina Water Sports
Mobile Big Game Fishing Club
Boat Washing & Detailing Service
Inshore & Offshore Charters

**NEARBY**
White Sand Beaches
Commercial & Private Airports
Walking, Biking & Nature Trails
Shopping & Outlet Centers
Grocery & Drug Stores
Golf Courses - 6 within 20 Minutes

---

27075 Marina Road • Orange Beach, AL • 251.981.4207 • OrangeBeachMarina.com

"57," then head for green daybeacon "17." Note that at the beginning of this channel, there are several private markers to a small cut into Ono Island to the south, which you should not follow. Also, remember, if you are approaching from the east as you enter Bayou St. John, you are no longer on the GIWW and are encountering the buoy system from Perdido Pass Inlet from the Gulf (red-right-returning). Leave green to starboard (e.g., leave green daybeacon "17" to starboard and quick-flashing red "18" to port).

If you want to explore marinas and facilities in Cotton Bayou, Terry Cove or Johnson Cove, turn to starboard at green daybeacon "1," before the Perdido Pass Channel Bridge and parallel the bridge running west, on the bridge's north side. At the western end of the bridge there are two channels: one that goes farther west into Cotton Bayou, and the other going north from red daybeacon "8" and green daybeacon "9." This will take you into the body of water holding both Terry Cove and Johnson Cove.

If you choose to enter Cotton Bayou, be careful of shoal water. Downtown Orange Beach amenities can be reached from the bayou. You will see the marked

channel just past both green daybeacon "1" (which once marked the channel leading back northeast to Perdido Bay and the GIWW) and red daybeacon "8" to starboard, returning to Johnson Cove from the Gulf. There is a moderate current here as you pass the inlet, so be careful. Boaters with deep-draft vessels should use caution in Cotton Bayou; keep an eye on your depth sounder. There are generally 6-foot depths here during normal tides.

**Dockage:** On the south side of Cotton Bayou, SanRoc Cay Marina can accommodate transient vessels and sell fuel. Zeke's Landing Marina primarily handles charter fishing boats; however, gas and diesel fuel are available here, along with marine supplies and groceries.

Either from Cotton Bayou or Perdido Pass, if you are heading up to Terry Cove for Saunders Yachtworks or Orange Beach Marina or to Johnson Cove for Sportsman Marina, north of red daybeacon "10" (leave to starboard) and green daybeacon "11" (leave to port), you will pass a boat ramp on the west headland (port side). Just past this boat ramp is flashing red "12" to starboard.

For Orange Beach Marina, look due west (about 50 to 200 yards) to see green daybeacon "1" and red daybeacon "2." This marked channel curves southward and then westward along private docks and residences. Follow them, keeping red to starboard, and at the very end you will see Orange Beach Marina's private channel, running due south. The full-service Orange Beach Marina has plenty of transient dockage in a secluded and fully protected harbor. They offer all the usual amenities, plus two restaurants (the upscale Fisher's Upstairs and the more casual Fisher's Dockside) and a full-service boatyard, Saunders Yachtworks. Saunders is equipped with a 60-ton lift and handles repairs from minor to extensive.

Located on the north shore of Johnson Cove or eastern end of Terry Cove, Sportsman Marina is easy to reach. At flashing red "12" in Johnson Cove, carefully proceed north by northeast, but give flashing red "12" a wide berth to avoid shoals lying east of the marker. They have slips and sell fuel.

**Anchorage:** There is an anchorage at Bayou St. John at Mile 167 EHL with 7 to 8 feet of water and excellent holding in sand. (Somewhat exposed to the west.)

## ■ BEAR POINT TO BON SECOUR BAY

There are even more "must-see" spots off the GIWW, particularly for gunkholers. Many cruisers have a problem when they visit this bountiful area; they do not want to leave. Some who plan to stay for a week or so can only tear themselves away after several weeks. Some stay permanently.

**NAVIGATION:** Use Chart 11378. Reversing course toward the GIWW, as you leave Bayou St. John, you can safely cut across from green daybeacon "17" (which will now be on your port side) to GIWW flashing red "58" (leave to starboard, as you are back on the GIWW westbound) at Mile 166 EHL.

The channel around Mill Point is well marked, but it is narrow and shallow on the edges; a sharp watch is required. Once in Arnica Bay, the channel opens up–particularly to starboard–before it closes down again off Hatchett Point at flashing red "68." From flashing red "68" to red daybeacon "90," the GIWW is relatively open through Bay La Launch, past Sapling Point

and through the straight shot across Wolf Bay to red daybeacon "90" at the entrance to Portage Creek.

From here (Mile 160 EHL) the GIWW is bordered by land to Oyster Bay at Mile 152.5 EHL. Along this route you will pass under **Foley Beach Expressway Bridge** at Mile 158.7 EHL, which has a fixed vertical clearance of 73 feet. The next and last bridges along this route are the **Gulf Shores Parkway (Portage Creek) Twin Bridges** at Mile 154.9 EHL with a fixed vertical clearance of 73 feet.

A tugboat crew-change station and supply store is east of the Gulf Shores Parkway Twin Bridges. There is an Idle-Speed/No-Wake Zone along this stretch. Shrimp boats and barges sometimes tie up to both banks east of the bridge to wait out inclement weather.

**Dockage:** Most of the marinas in the Orange Beach/Bear Point area (and there are several small ones not listed here) welcome transients. These and the facilities at Gulf Shores, AL, are the last recreational boat marinas located on or near the GIWW east of New Orleans. Full-service marinas at Mobile and Fairhope, AL; Biloxi and Gulfport, MS; and Slidell, LA, all require side trips of up to 20 miles from the GIWW proper.

Curving around the green buoys off Bear Point into Arnica Bay, you will soon find Bear Point Harbor south of green daybeacon "65" at Mile 165 EHL. This has traditionally been a favorite stopover for cruising boats. Both gas and diesel are available.

Barber Marina is located north off the GIWW (Mile 163 EHL) at red daybeacon "74." This marina can accommodate boats on floating docks and sells fuel. Nearby (at Mile 165 EHL) Pirates Cove Marina & Restaurant may have transient space. You will see the entrance to the marina docks and boatyard off to port as you approach the narrow cut into Roberts Bayou.

At this point, activity increases on the GIWW. Heading west, just past the Foley Beach Bridge, is The Wharf Marina at Mile 158.8 EHL. In addition to floating slips, a variety of restaurants, shopping centers and condominiums are here. Saunders Yachtworks is located at GIWW Mile 155.5 EHL. They have a 165-ton lift and can accommodate boats up to 130 feet.

The protected Homeport Marina is located at Mile 155.0 EHL just under the Gulf Shores Parkway Twin Bridges with plenty of room for transients at its floating docks, along with gas and diesel fuel. LuLu's restaurant, operated by Lucy Buffett (Jimmy's sister), is located on site. There is a 120-foot-long dock in front of the restaurant where you can tie up if you are stopping

# GOIN' ASHORE: ORANGE BEACH, AL

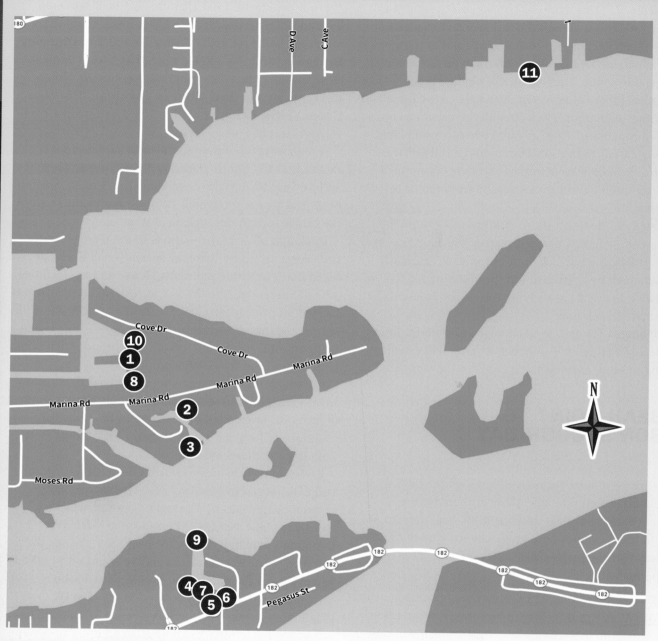

| DINING (North Shore) | | |
|---|---|---|
| 1 | Fisher's Dockside | |
| 2 | Sassy Bass Caribbean Grille | |
| 3 | Tacky Jacks | |
| **DINING (South Shore)** | | |
| 4 | Cafe Grazie | |

| | | |
|---|---|---|
| 5 | Fiddlefish | |
| 6 | Gulf Shores Steamer | |
| 7 | Louisiana Lagniappe | |
| **MARINAS** | | |
| 8 | Orange Beach Marina | |
| 9 | SanRoc Cay Marina | |

| | | |
|---|---|---|
| 10 | Saunders Yachtworks | |
| 11 | Sportsman Marina | |

Spanish Explorer Carlos Sequenza was looking for a permanent base when he stumbled upon Perdido Bay, which means "lost" in Spanish. Presumably Perdido Bay was named "lost" because of its narrow entrance. Pirates reportedly once favored the bay and the many coves and bayous in the area because they made good hiding places. Citizens using picks and shovels opened the Perdido Pass Inlet from the Gulf in Orange Beach proper in 1906.

**Attractions:** The 222-acre Wharf Resort contains a full-service marina on the GIWW, condominiums, several restaurants, a variety of specialty and retail shops, a 10,000-seat amphitheater, a movie theater and a record-height (112-foot) Ferris wheel.

**Special Events:** Coastal Alabama Business Chamber coordinates the annual Shrimp Festival on the second weekend in October, drawing more than 200,000 people to Pleasure Island at the Gulf Shores Beach Boardwalk for four days of entertainment, savory foods and numerous booths featuring arts and crafts of all kinds (mygulfcoastchamber.com).

**Shopping:** The beachside communities of Gulf Shores and Orange Beach have numerous restaurants, nightclubs and shopping. For provisioning, there is a Publix at 25771 Perdido Beach Blvd., convenient to Cotton Bayou. There is a Winn-Dixie and Walmart nearby as well. A West Marine is located at 24369 Canal Rd. (transportation required). Close by at 25472 Canal Rd. is Orange Beach Auto Marine with boating supplies and needs. OBA Canvas at 4161 Orange Beach Blvd. can handle all your canvas needs

**Dining:** Orange Beach, long known as the "Fishing Capital of Alabama," has a large charter fleet and boasts a variety of restaurants offering everything from Cajun cuisine to seafood specialties. For the sake of space (and your convenience), we have chosen to concentrate on options near the marinas. Fisher's Dockside at the Orange Beach Marina offers casual dockside dining downstairs or more upscale fare upstairs (251-891-7308). Two waterside restaurants of note on the north shore in Cotton Bayou are Sassy Bass Caribbean Grille (27212 Marina Rd., 251-981-1910) and Tacky Jacks Grill and Tavern (27206 Safe Harbor Dr., 251-981-4144).

Several restaurants are at SanRoc Cay Marina (27767 Perdido Beach Blvd.) on the south shore, including the upscale Louisiana Lagniappe (251-981-2258) and the more casual Italian Café Grazie (251-981-7278). Nearby Fiddlefish (251-923-3474) is a seafood cafe of note, as is Gulf Shores Steamer (251-948-6344), located right next door. One mile down Perdido Beach Boulevard to the west of Cotton Bayou (not on the water) is Hazel's Seafood Restaurant (251-981-4628), a favorite for tourists and locals. Its varied cuisine includes breakfast, lunch and dinner buffets or a full-service menu.

The town's popular and famous Flora-Bama Lounge, Package and Oyster Bar (251-980-5118) is at the Alabama/Florida line and is known affectionately as the "Ultimate Dive." The establishment always has live music from local and visiting bands in various parts of the bar playing a variety of music. Visit their web site at florabama.com for a complete schedule.

On Portage Creek in Gulf Shores is LuLu's at Homeport Marina (251-967-5858). Tacky Jack's Gulfport (251-948-8881) is just across the waterway, alongside Acme Oyster House (251-424-1783).

Also not to be missed is the cheeseburger at Pirates Cove (251-987-1224), north of Bear Point Marina at the end of Orange Beach, just across Amica Bay. It is rumored to be the home of the original "cheeseburger in paradise." Anchor just off the restaurant and dinghy in. Call ahead for dockside depths before bringing a cruising vessel to the docks.

# Oyster Bay Area, AL

| GULF SHORES | | | Largest Vessel Accommodated / VHF Channel Monitored | Transient Berths / Total Berths | Approach / Dockside Depth (reported) | Groceries, Ice, Marine Supplies, Snacks / Floating Docks | Gas / Diesel | Repairs: Hull, Engine, Propeller | Lift (tonnage), Crane, Rail | Laundry, Pool, Showers, Pump-Out Station | Min/Max Amps | Nearby: Grocery Store, Motel, Restaurant, Courtesy Car |
|---|---|---|---|---|---|---|---|---|---|---|---|---|
| | | | **Dockage** | | | | **Supplies** | | **Services** | | | |
| 1. The Wharf Marina 🖥 WiFi WG | 158.8 EHL | 251-224-1900 | 150 | 16/68 | 30/210 | 10/10 F | GD | GIMS | EP | – | 30/200+ LPS | P | GMR |
| 2. Saunders Yachtworks 🖥 WiFi | 155.5 EHL | 251-981-3700 | 130 | – | call/14 | 10/8 – | – | IM | HEP | L165, C6 | 30/200+ – | P | GMR |
| 3. Homeport Marina 🖥 WiFi WG | 155 EHL | 251-968-4528 | 115 | 16 | 10/77 | 10/8 F | GD | GIS | – | – | 30/100 LS | P | GMR |

🖥 Internet Access   WiFi Wireless Internet Access   WG Waterway Guide Cruising Club Partner *(Information in the table is provided by the facilities.)*
See WaterwayGuide.com for current rates, fuel prices, web site addresses, and other up-to-the-minute information.

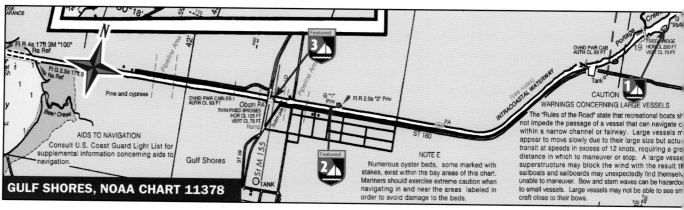

**GULF SHORES, NOAA CHART 11378**

NOTE E
Numerous oyster beds, some marked with stakes, exist within the bay areas of this chart. Mariners should exercise extreme caution when navigating in and near the areas labeled in order to avoid damage to the beds.

AIDS TO NAVIGATION
Consult U.S. Coast Guard Light List for supplemental information concerning aids to navigation.

WARNINGS CONCERNING LARGE VESSELS
The "Rules of the Road" state that recreational boats sh[...] not impede the passage of a vessel that can navigate [...] within a narrow channel or fairway. Large vessels m[...] appear to move slowly due to their large size but actua[...] transit at speeds in excess of 12 knots, requiring a gre[...] distance in which to maneuver or stop. A large vesse[...] superstructure may block the wind with the result th[...] sailboats and sailboards may unexpectedly find themselv[...] unable to maneuver. Bow and stern waves can be hazardo[...] to small vessels. Large vessels may not be able to see sm[...] craft close to their bows.

o eat. The daily "countdown to sunset" is not to be missed. Call 251-967-5858 to check availability.

**Anchorage:** You can anchor just to the west of Bear Point Marina and dinghy in. This is open and exposed to the north and west as well as wakes. Almost due north from Bear Point Marina, on the other side of Arnica Bay, is Roberts Bayou, commonly known both to cruisers and locals as "Pirates Cove." There is a narrow entrance with private markers leading to the bayou. While the narrow entrance may seem intimidating, a local sailing charter boat, the 50-foot former world cruiser *Daedelus* often transits the channel under sail. There is a spot at the mouth of Roberts Bayou and the end of the entrance channel that narrows to one boat width, so plan ahead. Roberts Bayou is a popular anchorage for cruisers and locals, with about 8 feet of water and good holding ground. As in any anchorage that is or might be crowded, it is a good idea to buoy your anchor with a trip line, not only so someone will not drop their hook over your rode, but to prevent snarling and tangling in tight quarters.

An idyllic location for cruisers and locals alike is Ingram Bayou (Mile 164 EHL, due north of red daybeacon "72") about 1.5 miles west on the GIWW from Roberts Bayou. Turn right at red daybeacon "72," and then go straight into Ingram Bayou, right down the center. There is shoaling on either side of this excellent, all-weather anchorage, but 9-foot depths hold most of the way in. Larger boats can find 8-foot depths just past the sharp bend to the left at the head of Ingram Bayou. This is one of our cruising editor's favorite spots. Once inside, you will be surrounded by total greenery and quiet (except on a busy weekend), and there is usually a breeze to keep most of the bugs away.

There are also plenty of places to anchor in 5- to 8-foot depths at Wolf Bay, including in Graham Bayou and at Wolf Bay Lodge. This is a busy thoroughfare, so anchor appropriately.

## Bon Secour Bay–GIWW Mile 151 EHL

Bon Secour lies at the southeasterly reaches of Mobile Bay. Moving west on the GIWW, enter Bon Secour Bay at the 17 foot green "103" and red "104." The next daybeacon will be the 17 foot red marker "2" marking the entrance of a well-marked channel north into the Bon Secour River.

The GIWW tracks west across lower Mobile Bay and crosses the Main Ship Channel at flashing red buoy "26" on the channel (Mile 133.75 EHL). This is where the cruising sailor with plenty of time might be tempted to change course, head north and sample some of the breezy bay's delights.

# Bon Secour Bay to Mobile Bay, AL

www.snagaslip.com
SNAG-A-SLIP
EXPLORE BOOK BOAT

| | | Largest Vessel Accommodated | VHF Channel Monitored | Transient Berths / Total Berths | Approach / Dockside Depth (reported) | Floating Docks | Gas / Diesel | Groceries, Ice, Marine Supplies, Snacks | Repairs: Hull, Engine, Propeller | Lift (tonnage), Crane, Rail | Min/Max Amps | Laundry, Pool, Showers, Courtesy Car | Pump-Out Station | Nearby: Grocery Store, Motel, Restaurant |
|---|---|---|---|---|---|---|---|---|---|---|---|---|---|---|
| | | **Dockage** | | | | | **Supplies** | | **Services** | | | | | |
| **GULF SHORES AREA** | | | | | | | | | | | | | | |
| 1. Gulf Shores Marina 135 EHL | 251-540-2628 | 70 | 16 | 6/70 | 4/4 | – | GD | GIMS | – | L10 | 30/30 | S | P | GR |
| **DAUPHIN ISLAND** | | | | | | | | | | | | | | |
| 2. Dauphin Island Marina (WiFi) 127.8 EHL | 251-861-2201 | 60 | 16 | 5/90 | 6/6 | – | GD | IMS | – | L5 | 30/50 | LPS | P | GMR |

🖥 Internet Access   (WiFi) Wireless Internet Access   **WG** Waterway Guide Cruising Club Partner   *(Information in the table is provided by the facilities.)*
See WaterwayGuide.com for current rates, fuel prices, web site addresses, and other up-to-the-minute information.

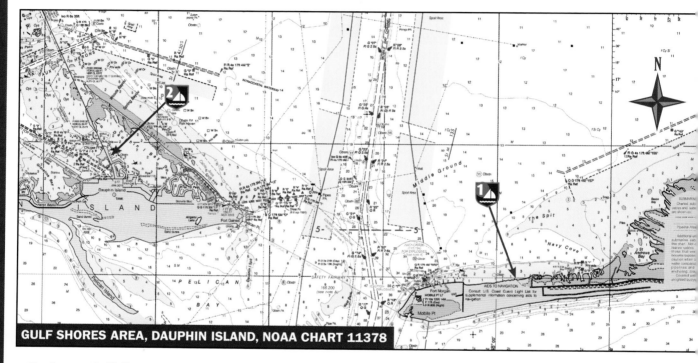

**GULF SHORES AREA, DAUPHIN ISLAND, NOAA CHART 11378**

**Dockage:** Gulf Shores Marina, located near Fort Morgan at the southeastern end of Mobile Bay (Mile 135 EHL), offers transient dockage, dry storage, a fuel dock and an on-site restaurant, Tacky Jacks 2 (251-968-8341).

**Anchorage:** Located south of flashing green "135" in Bon Secour Bay is the Edith Hammock anchorage. There is a cut through the spoil area at flashing green "123." Watch your chart and take care to avoid the fish haven and submerged pilings as you head toward the water tower. Anchor in sand in 7 to 9 feet of water. You are protected from the southwest through southeast, and exposed to northerly winds. Holding is good. You can also anchor up the Bon Secour River by daybeacon red "38" in 4 to 7 feet with good holding in mud.

## Dauphin Island–GIWW Mile 130 EHL

On the west side of the entrance to Mobile Bay, Dauphin Island, with its long sandy spit to the west, is the first of the barrier islands running from Mobile Bay to New Orleans. Of the many recreational and boating centers in the Mobile area, Dauphin Island is the closest to the GIWW. The island is a pleasant and interesting stopover, with a sizable marina, anchorages along the entire length of the island and excellent beaches.

Dauphin Island is home to Fort Gaines, once a Confederate stronghold used to defend the east entrance to Mobile Bay. Now a historic site and museum, it can be explored daily (except Thanksgiving and Christmas). Every year, Fort Gaines hosts a variety of theme weekends, such as Civil War reenactments. For details visit dauphinisland.org or call 251-861-3607.

The island is also home to Dauphin Island Sea Lab, Alabama's marine education and research center. The lab operates the Estuarium, an extensive public aquarium, displaying features of coastal Alabama's ecosystems: the Delta, Mobile Bay and the Gulf of Mexico. For more information, call 251-861-2141 or visit disl.org.

**NAVIGATION:** Use Chart 11378. It is possible to enter Dauphin Island Bay via two channels. The first channel, for boats heading west across Mobile Bay, Middle Ground, is on the east side of the island by Fort Gains at Pelican Point. This entrance is referred to locally as "Billy Goat Hole." Move west through the channel in the spoil areas at flashing green "25" and flashing red "26." Local knowledge suggests that depth over the spoils is about 10 feet. Turn south to the well-marked channel through Billy Goat Hole. You will pass a Coast Guard Station and ferry dock just inside the entry. Depths are charted at 4.5 feet mean low water.

The second channel is Aux Heron's Channel, 1.6 miles west of the **Dauphin Island Causeway Bridge** (fixed 83-foot vertical clearance) at Mile 127.8 EHL. Entrance via this second channel is limited by a fixed bridge (**Dauphin Island Bridge**) with a 25-foot vertical clearance. At red "22" in the Aux Heron's Channel, leave the GIWW on a southeast course and pick up flashing green "1" marking the entrance to a channel to Bayou Aloe. Proceed on a southeast course past the 17-foot flashing red "2" and green boy "3." The next marker should be flashing green "1," leading into a privately marked channel to Chugae Point and the clearly visible Dauphin Island Bridge. Depths are charted at 4.5 feet mean low water.

**Dockage:** The only marina here, Dauphin Island Marina, is a full-service facility welcoming transients. It would be prudent to call ahead for reservations and the latest information on markers and water depths. Motels and restaurants are a short walk from the marina. This marina also has good access to a post office, a bank and groceries.

**Anchorage:** Dauphin Island has many fine anchorages protected from southerly winds but not from the north. Hurricane Rita broke through the middle of Dauphin Island, leaving a breach in the island. Keep this in mind when deciding where to anchor.

If you need someplace close to the channel entrance on the east side of the island, you can anchor in Billy Goat Hole. With a draft less than 5 feet you can travel 400 to 500 feet then go east to the beach at Billy Goat Hole. To make sure you stay away from service boats and the ferry, put you bow on the beach and carry an anchor to shore. A deeper anchorage (6 to 9 feet) is Confederate Pass on the eastern end. This is well protected and marked and is within dinghy distance of a restaurant; however, it is usually occupied by commercial boats.

Other options are Bayou Aloe with good holding in sand (very shallow), and near green daybeacon "27" at the west end of the island in 7 to 9 feet. On the south side of the island you can find a quiet anchorage in Pelican Bay. Leave the main ship channel at green "15" and navigate past the shoals at Pelican Island, which has become more of a peninsula, then into the smaller bay/lagoon where you should find depths of 10 to 12 foot with good holding.

# ■ MOBILE BAY

Mobile Bay sits on the northern Gulf Coast, 40 miles west of Pensacola and 90 miles northeast of South Pass at the Mississippi River. It is the approach to the City of Mobile and to the Alabama and Tombigbee Rivers. The Bay has depths of 7 to 12 feet outside the dredged channels. The Gulf approach to the Bay is 3 miles wide and is bordered by Mobile Point on the east and Pelican Point on the west. Stay in the dredged channel to avoid shoals that extend 4 miles south (into the Gulf) on both sides.

High rise condominiums are prominent along the shoreline and can be seen on approach. West of the entrance is a chain of low wooded islands for 50 nm. The black conical tower that is Sand Island Light is the most prominent landmark near the entrance at 131 feet. On the east side of the entrance, the pentagon-shaped walls of Fort Morgan at Mobile Point are clearly visible. To the west of the entrance, a spherical, elevated tank two miles west of Fort Gains on the east end of Dauphin Island at Pelican Point is clearly visible.

Mobile Bay is shallow and with its long fetch running south to north it can build substantial waves. In 15-knot winds it will be rough. Winds at greater speeds will and have made the bay dangerous.

The best way to cover cruising in Mobile Bay is through a literary "tale of two shores."

# GOIN' ASHORE: DAUPHIN ISLAND, AL

On Dauphin Island, less is more. The little island in the southwest tip of Alabama is well known and much loved for being less congested than other Gulf Coast resorts. It's also noted for its breathtaking sunsets, pristine beaches, walking and biking trails, bird sanctuaries, charter fishing boats, ferry across Mobile Bay, outdoor recreation and historic sites. Truth is, Dauphin Island is awash in history. Long before Europeans arrived in 1699, Native Americans came and went on the island; and long before modern-day folks were opening oysters on the island, the Indians were steaming and roasting them and then discarding the shells at a site now called Indian Shell Mound Park, which is on the National Register of Historic Places.

**Attractions:** When you visit Dauphin Island, you can golf; rent bicycles, kayaks, canoes and stand-up paddle boards; take a nature tour, a dolphin watch boat ride, a lighthouse cruise or a sunset cruise; and visit the Island Heritage and Art Gallery, which features high-quality paintings, pottery, woodworking, jewelry and other items produced by local artists.

In addition, visitors won't want to miss historic Fort Gaines, built in the early 19th century and a key coastal fortification in the Civil War's Battle of Mobile Bay. Besides cannons, artifacts and regular blacksmithing demonstrations, the fort annually hosts re-enactors from throughout the Southeast who fire weapons and re-create living conditions at the fort during that August 1864 conflict.

Birds and birders love the island, too. Dauphin Island is home to a 137-acre Audubon Bird Sanctuary, which draws bird-watchers from all over the country, especially during the annual fall and spring migrations.

The National Audubon Society calls the island "globally important" for birds, and it has been voted the "Birdiest Small Coastal City in America" several years in a row.

Dauphin Island holds a special place in the hearts of fishermen and boaters, who love the fact that it is surrounded by water: The Mississippi Sound is on the north side, the Gulf of Mexico is on the south, and there are small bays, inlets and bayous all over the 14-mile-long island. Boaters will find easy access to marinas as well as to public and private boat launches.

Fishermen converge on the island each July for the three-day Alabama Deep Sea Fishing Rodeo, which is nearing its 85th anniversary. Sailors come for the annual Dauphin Island Sailboat Regatta, held in April and billed as the largest one-day point-to-point regatta in the United States.

**Shopping/Dining:** Locally owned boutiques, restaurants and gift shops dot the island, adding to its old-fashioned, charming atmosphere.

Regardless of the time of year, when tourists and island residents are ready to relax, Dauphin Island restaurants offer them fresh, locally caught seafood and other specialties. And as the day draws to an end, diners and other folks across the island can look to the west, knowing that as the "Sunset Capital of Alabama," Dauphin Island is the perfect place to watch Mother Nature paint the sky in spectacular shades of scarlet, orange, yellow and copper.

Want to learn more about this unique beach community? Go todauphinislandchamber.com andtownofdauphinisland.org, and follow the Town of Dauphin and Friends of Dauphin Island pages on Facebook.

## Mobile Bay: Eastern Shore

The allure of the east is its quaint attractive communities. There are fewer facilities and they are more widely spaced. Marinas are mostly self-contained, resort-type facilities.

**NAVIGATION:** Chart 11376, 11378. Westbound on the GIWW you will enter the Mobile Bay area via Bon Secour Bay. You can cruise north into Mobile Bay by leaving the GIWW and navigating through the open waters of the bay, or continue east and turn north when you enter the Main Ship Channel.

The Ship Channel provides a well-defined, well-marked route to follow north. You can leave the channel almost anywhere. It is bordered by spoils, but local boaters say the depth over the spoils is usually about 10 feet. You may choose to leave the GIWW for a shorter route, but be aware that this requires navigating the more open shallower waters of the Bay. Eastbound cruisers will almost surely choose the Main Ship Channel, which is a shorter route to the north and east.

For the north route in the bay, leave the GIWW at Mile 145 EHL, at green "129," on a course of 337 degrees magnetic. Continue for 10 statute miles

to the 30-foot red "2" at Mullet Point. Continue on a course of 337 degrees magnetic for another 7.25 statute miles to the 37-foot "4" at Great Point Clear. Leave the charted shoals to the east (starboard). From this point, head northwest if you are going to the marina at the Grand Hotel Marriott Resort.

If you are continuing on a northerly route, turn to starboard on a course of 142 degrees magnetic. The Town of Fairhope is 4 miles farther on this course, then 1 mile to the east. To reach the marinas at Fly Creek, continue a course of 142 degrees magnetic for 1 mile, then turn east for 1 mile. If you want to continue a northerly trek in the Bay, it is best to go west to the Ship Channel.

## Fairhope

The Fairhope Municipal Pier is in Fairhope Park at the end of Fairhope Avenue and is a short walk into town. It is the only place where a boat can tie up within walking distance of the historic town.

**Dockage:** To get to the Grand Hotel Marriott Resort & Spa, use the charted Point Clear approach and follow the daybeacons that line the entrance channel. The depth

# Mobile Bay to Dauphin Island, AL

www.snagaslip.com

SNAG-A-SLIP

EXPLORE. BOOK. BOAT.™

| | | Largest Vessel Accommodated | VHF Channel Monitored | Transient Berths / Total Berths | Approach / Dockside Depth (reported) | Floating Docks | Gas / Diesel | Groceries, Ice, Marine Supplies, Snacks | Repairs: Hull, Engine, Propeller | Lift (tonnage), Crane, Rail | Min/Max Amps | Laundry, Pool, Showers, Courtesy Car | Pump-Out Station | Nearby: Grocery Store, Motel, Restaurant |
|---|---|---|---|---|---|---|---|---|---|---|---|---|---|---|
| **FAIRHOPE AREA** | | | | | | | | | | | | | | |
| 1. Grand Hotel Marriott Resort & Spa 🖥 WiFi | 251-928-9201 | 115 | 16 | 34/34 | 6/5 | - | GD | GIMS | - | - | 30/50 | PS | P | GMR |
| 2. Eastern Shore Marine Inc. 🖥 WiFi 134 EHL | 251-928-1283 | 80 | 16/68 | 12/65 | 8/7 | - | GD | IM | HEP | L35,C15 | 30/50 | LSC | P | GR |
| 3. Fly Creek Marina 🖥 WiFi | 251-928-4868 | 36 | 16 | 10/50 | 9/6 | - | GD | I | - | - | 30/50 | LS | P | MR |
| **DOG RIVER AREA** | | | | | | | | | | | | | | |
| 4. Fowl River Marina | 251-973-2670 | 50 | 16 | 3/60 | 5/5 | F | GD | GIMS | - | - | 50/50 | S | P | GR |
| 5. Beachcomber Marina | 251-443-8000 | 65 | - | 15/96 | 9/16 | - | - | - | HEP | L40 | 30/30 | - | - | R |
| 6. Grand Mariner Marina & Mariner Restaurant 🖥 WiFi | 251-525-8395 | 200 | 16/68 | 20/100 | 15/12 | - | GD | IMS | - | L35 | 30/50 | LSC | P | R |
| 7. Turner Marine Supply Inc. 🖥 WiFi WG | 251-476-1444 | 100 | 16 | 40/150 | 8/7 | - | - | M | HEP | L55,C2 | 30/50 | LSC | - | R |
| 8. Dog River Marina and Boat Works Inc. 🖥 WiFi | 251-471-5449 | 200 | 16 | 50/100 | 8/10 | - | GD | I | HEP | L70 | 30/100 | LSC | P | - |
| 9. River Yacht Basin Marina WiFi | 251-776-4435 | 70 | - | 10/72 | 6/6 | - | - | - | - | - | 30/50 | LS | - | GR |

🖥 Internet Access  WiFi Wireless Internet Access  WG Waterway Guide Cruising Club Partner  *(Information in the table is provided by the facilities.)*
See WaterwayGuide.com for current rates, fuel prices, web site addresses, and other up-to-the-minute information.

in the channel and in the harbor is at least 7 feet. Gas and diesel fuel are available here as well as dockage for vessels to 115 feet.

Stay to the south side of the channel (starboard) as you enter Fly Creek. Eastern Shore Marine, Inc. is on the north side of the channel (to port on entering the channel). The marina has covered and open slips, as well as a fuel dock, and they are a full-service repair facility. The approach and dockside depths are 8 feet at mean low water.

Fly Creek Marina is located further up Fly Creek, at the town of Seacliff. Follow the Fly Creek Channel from Mobile Bay, holding to the south side until you are inside the breakwater; it is the second facility just past the private Fairhope Yacht Club's docks. This marina, similar to other eastern shore marinas, is heavily populated by sailboats. It is a tidy, clean marina in a lovely wooded area.

## Mobile Bay: Western Shore

On the western shore of Mobile Bay, boaters will find facilities that are work-a-day marinas with good basic services but fewer frills. Other facilities, however, are within convenient reach to downtown Mobile, either by rental car or marina courtesy car.

The City of Mobile is a metropolis with an recently expanded and updated commercial waterfront, and since the completion of the Tennessee-Tombigbee Waterway in 1985, heavy barge traffic has greatly increased in the area, especially on the northern end near the mouth of the Mobile River. There is also a cruise ship terminal, which increases waterfront traffic.

**NAVIGATION:** Use Chart 11376. All cruising boats visiting the west shore will want to move north in the large ship channel. Boats heading west across Bon Secour Bay can leave the GIWW at the 17-foot green "147." Set a course of 298 degrees magnetic for 6.5 miles to a cut through the spoil into the ship channel. Follow the same course through the cut for 1.5 miles and enter the ship channel at the 17-foot flashing red "34." Boats coming from the east through Pass Aux Heron can leave the GIWW at red nun "10" and green can "9" after passing under the Dauphin Island Causeway Bridge. Set a course of 61 degrees magnetic for 5 miles to the cut entering the ship channel. Follow the same course for 1.5 miles and enter the ship channel at the 17-foot flashing green "33."

Moving north in the ship channel for 8 miles, you will come to a cut in the spoil just before 17-foot green "49." To access the facilities on the western shore at Fowl River, exit the ship channel before green "49" on a course of 275 degrees magnetic for 4.3 miles to the channel entry at green "1" and red "2."

Further north (2.7 miles) in the ship channel you will pass the Hollinger Island and Theodore Ship Channel, opposite the 17-foot red "54." The channel leads to an industrial complex with no facilities for cruising boats.

Continuing north past the 17-foot green "63" and red "64" for 5 miles where you will intersect the channel to Dog River to the west. Enter the channel between green

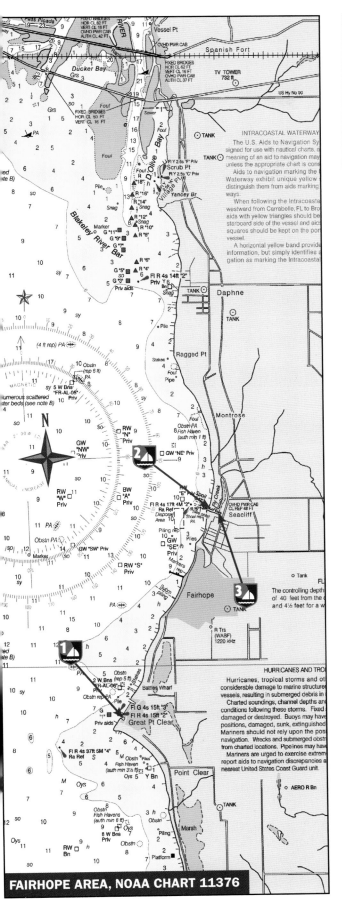

**FAIRHOPE AREA, NOAA CHART 11376**

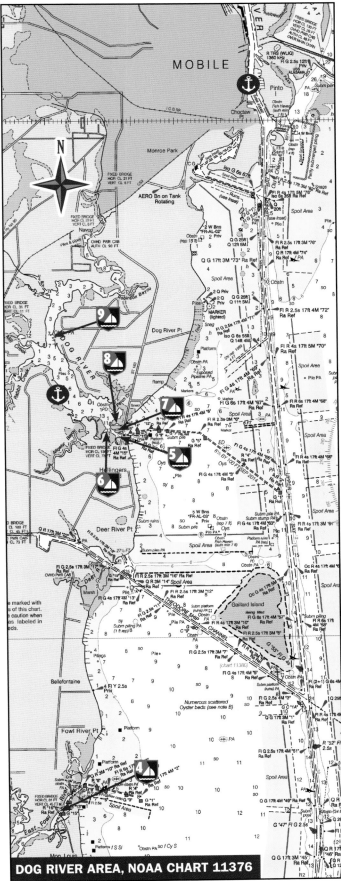

**DOG RIVER AREA, NOAA CHART 11376**

# GOIN' ASHORE: **FAIRHOPE, AL**

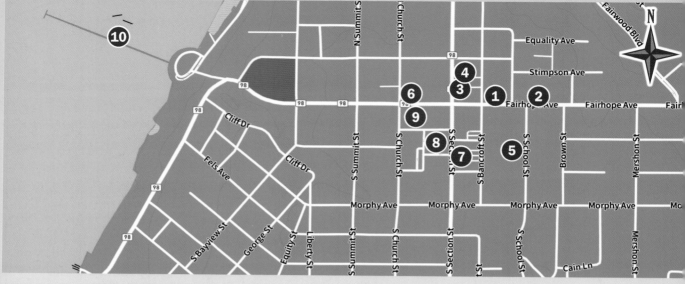

| SERVICES | |
|---|---|
| 1 | Library |
| 2 | Post Office |
| 3 | Visitor Information |
| **ATTRACTIONS** | |
| 4 | Fairhope Museum of History |

| | |
|---|---|
| 5 | Marietta Johnson Museum |
| **SHOPPING** | |
| 6 | Fairhope True Value Hardware |
| 7 | Greer's Market |
| **DINING** | |
| 8 | Panini Pete's Cafe & Bakeshoppe |

| | |
|---|---|
| 9 | Pinzone's Italian |
| 10 | Shucks on the Pier |

In 1894 a group of 28 Populist reformers led by E.B. Gaston landed on the eastern shore of Mobile Bay to establish a Single Tax Colony, as prescribed by noted economist Henry George (1839-1897). Their mission was to: "establish and conduct a model community or colony, free from all forms of private monopoly, and to secure to its members therein equality of opportunity, the full reward of individual efforts, and the benefits of co-operation in matters of general concern."

Incorporated as the Fairhope Industrial Association, the group purchased a large tract of land and then leased it back to individuals, charging an annual rent (the Single Tax) in return for municipal services. They retained the bluff and the best waterfront property for the use and enjoyment of the community. As new people moved in, services expanded and the model community thrived. The Fairhope Single Tax Corporation, a non-profit entity, owns 4,200 acres. Homeowners and merchants still lease parcels of land from the Corporation. The Corporation pays all state and local taxes from the rent and manages a fund to make community improvements.

Land use planning continues through green areas for public use. The Corporation has also taken an active role in developing the museum, rebuilding the library, and contributing to major hospital improvements.

There is much to intrigue and delight visiting cruisers to Mobile Bay's eastern shore. The people who began the initial experimental community were a freethinking, intellectual group. Fairhope continues to attract artists, philosophers, musicians, and writers. The town boasts independent bookstores and hardware stores in the thriving downtown district. Unique art galleries, shops and restaurants abound.

**Attractions:** The Fairhope Municipal Pier is a gathering place where townspeople and visitors meet, picnic, fish, stroll the pier, and enjoy the sunsets. There are benches for watching Mobile Bay, and walking paths for walking and running. The Fairhope Welcome Center, located at 20 North Section Street, is your resource for maps, brochures and restaurant and lodging guides for the Fairhope area (251-928-5095).

The Marietta Johnson Museum is housed in the Bell Building at 10 S. School Street. Marietta Johnson, a

eader in the Progressive Education Movement, founded Fairhope's first school, the School for Organic Education in 1907. The fascinating story of this visionary educator and author and her school that boasted "no tests, no grades, no shoes" is told at this delightful museum. For more information call 251-990-8601.

The Fairhope Museum of History features permanent displays highlighting the unique history of Fairhope. The museum is located at 24 North Section Street (251-929-1471) in a Spanish Mission Revival structure originally built in 1928 as the city's first municipal building and rehabilitated in 2007 for the museum (with the help of the Single Tax Corporation).

There is a Dog Park at 701 Volanta Ave. that caters to free spirits of your canine pals. Watering stations are provided, as are waste bag and collection stations. For cruisers interested in touring by bicycle, there is a designated bike route from the *USS Alabama Battleship Memorial Park* south through Daphne and Fairhope and ends at Point Clear. For detailed information, visit thetrailblazers.org

**Special Events:** Each February Fairhope celebrates Mardi Gras with colorful parades and related festival events (fairhopemardigras.com). In mid-March cruisers can enjoy the three-day Annual Arts & Crafts Festival featuring several hundred artists from across the nation. There is live entertainment and unique cuisine throughout the show. This prestigious juried art exhibition draws over 200,000 visitors each year (fairhopeartsandcraftsfestival.com).

An Art Walk featuring art exhibits and musical entertainment is held the first Friday of every month in downtown Fairhope. Between 20 and 30 venues are open between 6:00 p.m. and 8:00 p.m. for the Art Walk.

**Shopping:** It is easy to provision in Fairhope. A Publix Supermarket is within 1 mile of Fly Creek Marina and Eastern Shore Marina, both located on Fly Creek. Greer's Market at 75 S. Section St. sells quality meat and produce and has a deli counter. The summer and fall Farmers' Markets are held on Thursday afternoons on Bancroft Street, behind the Fairhope Public Library. The downtown shopping area features a hardware store (Fairhope True Value), art galleries, gift shops, boutiques, a locally owned bookstore (Page & Pallette), antiques and collectibles shops and a bicycle shop.

**Dining:** There is a smörgåsbord of options for dining in Fairhope. These are well worth the trip ashore, but a vehicle or the desire to pedal long distances and possibly uphill is recommended. Check your marina for a courtesy car.

On the municipal pier you can tie up and enjoy seafood served over the water at Shucks on the Pier (251-421-8021). For those seeking Italian food, try Pinzone's Italian at 18 Laurel Ave. (251-990-5535). Panini Pete's Cafe & Bakeshoppe at 42 1/2 S. Section St. comes highly recommended (251-929-0122), as does Sunset Pointe at Fly Creek Marina, which has the same owner. Sunset Pointe offers vivid sunsets along with your meal.

"1" and red "2." Stay in the channel on a heading of about 305 degrees magnetic for 2.5 miles to green "5." Channel depths are charted at 6.5 feet. Turn to the left at green "5" and follow the channel for 2 miles to the **Dauphin Island Parkway (Dog River) Bridge**. The bridge has a 73-foot fixed vertical clearance. Several marinas can be found just under the bridge.

**Dockage:** Working clockwise around Mobile Bay from the southwest corner, Fowl River Marina appears first. The channel into Fowl River is well marked. The marina is located .5 miles upriver on the north side at red daybeacon "16," before the 45-foot fixed vertical clearance **East Fowl River Bridge**. The on-site Pelican Reef Restaurant is open daily and serves fresh seafood straight from its own boats.

There is a cluster of four marinas on Dog River to the north on the western shore of Mobile Bay, roughly two-thirds of the way up the Ship Channel from the pass entering Mobile Bay. Two marinas are on each side of the river within 100 yards of the Dauphin Island (Dog River) Parkway Bridge. Beachcomber Marina is the first marina to port (south) after the bridge. They have slips and a 40-ton lift for repairs.

The large Grand Mariner Marina & Mariner Restaurant is the second marina to port after passing under the bridge, heading upriver. This full-service marina has a fantastic restaurant. Turner Marine Supply Inc. is about 150 yards past the bridge to starboard with slips and repairs (55-ton lift). Full-service Dog River Marina & Boat Works Inc. is to starboard (north). They have a very complete West Marine store on the premises as well as a 70-ton lift. Farther upriver is River Yacht Basin Marina, which may have space for you. If you plan to transit north up the Tennessee-Tombigbee Waterway, see Waterway Guide's Great Lakes edition.

**Anchorage:** There is room to anchor up the East Fowl River in 6 to 8 feet if you can fit under the 45-foot fixed East Fowl River Bridge. Dog River offers a good anchorage near River Yacht Basin Marina. Anchor according to wind direction.

There is a free dock at the Mobile Convention Center. Call 251-208-2165 for details. There are several more anchorages north of Mobile. See waterwayguide.com for details.

# ■ MISSISSIPPI SOUND

West of Mobile Bay, the GIWW opens up to the Mississippi Sound, a bay-like expanse of water between the mainland and a string of barrier islands known as the Gulf Islands National Seashore. This open stretch of waterway extends from east to west for 85 statute miles. The width of the sound is 10 to 12 miles. This long stretch and significant width, when combined with a 15-knot wind, will result in considerable chop. When the winds blow over 15 knots, consider staying in a safe harbor or looking for shelter if you find yourself underway in these conditions. Wait for fair weather and the Sound can be a very enjoyable and rewarding cruising area worth exploring in detail. Sunrise over the beaches of Horn Island has been heralded as truly spectacular.

Shoreside facilities in this area are limited. The number and quality of destinations is growing, however, due to both the popularity of the area as well as the ongoing rebuilding effort from past hurricanes.

Anchorage is often available in the lee of the Gulf Islands during warm weather months when a south wind prevails. Pleasure boaters should keep in mind that traveling west from this point will increase the frequency of encounters with commercial vessels, most often towboats. Give these vessels a wide berth, particularly in shallower waters and narrow channels. As suggested earlier, it is advisable to monitor both VHF Channels 13 and 16. Additionally, AIS is used extensively on the GIWW.

Gulf inlets (usually referred to in these waters as "passes") are not all trustworthy. Only the three inlets at Pascagoula, Biloxi and Gulfport provide reliable access to the Gulf of Mexico.

## Pass Aux Heron to Pascagoula– GIWW Mile 125 EHL to 104 EHL

Pascagoula is primarily a commercial shipping port. The harbor, located about 9 miles north of Horn Island Pass is one of the important deep water ports on the Gulf Coast. The city, which is located at the mouth of the Pascagoula River, is home to many large industries, which will contribute to commercial ship traffic.

Steeped in a past with French Louisiana influence, the area was settled in the 1700s by French and French Canadians. After the Louisiana Purchase, a militia group took control of the city and raised the American flag. In

870 a railroad route that ran directly through the city
as completed. The railroad–combined with the deep
ater port–ensured the economic success of the city.

AVIGATION: Use Charts 11367, 11372, 11373, 11374,
1375. From Mobile Bay, the GIWW passes through
ass Aux Herons Channel and then enters Mississippi
ound. When leaving the channel at Mile 124 EHL, most
narkers are lighted and elevated, although some are as
nany as 4 miles apart. Pay close attention to compass
eadings and position fixes on the long run between
narkers. The next 70 or more miles are a long and only
artially protected passageway. Natural depths of 12 to
8 feet are found throughout the Sound, and a channel
rom Mobile Bay to New Orleans is regularly dredged.

Stay in the channel to GIWW Mile 118.5 EHL at
7-foot flashing red "40" and green "41." The next
hannel marker is 17-foot green "5" at GIWW Mile 114
EHL at a distance of 4.5 statute miles on a course of
bout 255 degrees magnetic. Chart your course to stay
n or close to the GIWW channel through the rest of the
ound.

It is 10.5 miles from the large ship channel at Horn
sland Pass to Pascagoula. North in the Pascagoula
Channel you will encounter a Y at red buoy"36." To port
s the route to Pascagoula; to starboard is Bayou Casotte.

**Dockage:** Pascagoula Inner Harbor Marina is at Lake
Yazoo and has limited space. They report 3-foot dockside
depths, so call ahead. Also off of the Pascagoula River to
the north and west is the Mary Walker Marina, catering
mostly to sportfishermen, but welcoming to transients of
all kinds.

**Anchorage:** It is possible to anchor in Lake Yazoo in
5 feet of water with all-around protection. Another
option is north of the **CSX Railroad (Pascalouga-
Singing River) Swing Bridge** (8-foot vertical
clearance, opens on request) and the **US 90
(Pascagoula-Singing River) Bridge** (80-foot fixed
vertical clearance), where you will find 8 to 15 feet of
depth on the Pascagoula River.

## Pascagoula to Biloxi Bay–GIWW Mile 104 EHL to Mile 87.5 EHL

Biloxi is a city on a peninsula jutting east into
Mississippi Sound. The port is accessible from the Gulf
through Dog Keys Pass and Little Dog Keys Pass and
from the GIWW, which passes through Mississippi
Sound about 6 miles south of the city. It is an important
sportfishing and resort area with a large commercial
seafood industry. Keesler Air Force Base and a large

veteran's hospital are at the west end of the city. The
waterfront on the sound is protected by Deer Island, and
the harbor in Back Bay of Biloxi is landlocked.

**NAVIGATION:** Use Charts 11372, 11373 and 11374.
Cross the Pascagoula Channel at green buoy "29" and
red "30." Continue west in the Mississippi Sound and
the next GIWW mark will be flashing green "1" in 4.4
miles. From here continue for 2 miles to 17-foot red "2"
and 17-foot green "3." Turn to starboard (north) on a
course of about 320 degrees magnetic for 2.5 miles to
17-foot flashing green "5." The GIWW makes this turn
to the north to avoid the shoals at Middle Ground, and
will shoal slightly (8 to 12 feet) until you reach green
"5." Continue west for 9 miles to Biloxi Bay Channel.

At Mile 87.5 EHL, follow the Biloxi Ship Channel
into Biloxi Bay, and turn to port at green daybeacon
"35" and quick-flashing red "26." Do not drift outside
the channel, as the water depth is as low as 2 to 4 feet
on the edges with an oyster shell bottom. Deer Island
is south of the channel. Heading west-southwest, the
channel opens up to the Biloxi waterfront and many
marine facilities at red daybeacon "26."

Eastbound cruisers can return to the GIWW along
the Biloxi Ship Channel as described above. Westbound
cruisers can save some time by continuing along the

# Biloxi Bay, MS to St. Louis Bay, MS

www.snagaslip.com
SNAG-A-SLIP
EXPLORE · BOOK · BOAT

| | | Largest Vessel Accommodated | VHF Channel Monitored | Transient Berths / Total Berths (Dockage) | Approach / Dockside Depth (reported) | Floating Docks | Gas / Diesel (Supplies) | Groceries, Ice, Marine Supplies, Snacks | Repairs: Hull, Engine, Propeller (Services) | Lift (tonnage), Crane, Rail | Min/Max Amps | Laundry, Pool, Showers, Courtesy Car | Pump-Out Station | Nearby: Grocery Store, Motel, Restaurant |
|---|---|---|---|---|---|---|---|---|---|---|---|---|---|---|
| **PASCAGOULA AREA** | | | | | | | | | | | | | | |
| 1. | Pascagoula Inner Harbor Marina · 228-938-6627 | 40 | – | 1/60 | 7/3 | – | – | – | – | – | 30/50 | – | P | – |
| 2. | Mary Walker Marina WIFI · 228-497-3141 | 50 | – | 6/150 | 6/5 | – | GD | GIMS | – | – | 30/50 | LS | P | GMR |
| **BILOXI AREA** | | | | | | | | | | | | | | |
| 3. | Biloxi Small Craft Harbor · 228-436-4062 | 50 | 16 | call/124 | – | – | GD | IMS | – | – | 30/50 | S | P | GMR |
| 4. | Biloxi Schooner Pier Complex ☐ WIFI 88 EHL · 228-435-6320 | – | – | 6/27 | 10/ | F | – | I | – | – | 30/50 | – | P | GMR |
| 5. | Point Cadet Marina 88 EHL · 228-436-9312 | 100 | 16 | 20/246 | 12/10 | F | GD | IMS | – | – | 30/50 | LS | P | MR |
| 6. | Biloxi Boardwalk Marina WIFI WG · 228-432-2628 | 60 | 16/11 | 25/72 | 6/5.5 | – | GD | GIMS | HEP | L19 | 30/50 | S | P | GMR |
| **GULFPORT** | | | | | | | | | | | | | | |
| 7. | Gulfport Municipal Marina WIFI · 228-867-8721 | 140 | 16/68 | 50/327 | 12/11 | – | GD | IMS | – | – | 30/100 | LS | P | GMR |
| 8. | Long Beach Harbor WIFI · 228-863-4795 | 65 | 16/08 | 20/213 | 8/8 | – | GD | GIMS | – | – | 30/100 | LS | P | GMR |
| **BAY ST. LOUIS** | | | | | | | | | | | | | | |
| 9. | Pass Christian East Harbor Expansion · 228-452-5128 | 70 | – | 21/164 | 10/10 | – | GD | I | – | – | 30/50 | – | P | R |
| 10. | Pass Christian Harbor · 228-452-5128 | 100 | – | 20/370 | 10/10 | – | GD | IMS | – | – | 30/50 | – | P | R |
| 11. | Bay St. Louis Municipal Harbor ☐ WIFI 55 EHL · 228-467-4226 | 110 | 16 | 13/160 | 8/8 | – | GD | I | E | – | 30/100 | S | P | GMR |
| 12. | Bay Marina & R.V. Park WIFI 55 EHL · 228-466-4970 | 50 | 16 | 10/75 | 5/5 | – | GD | IMS | – | – | 30/50 | LS | P | GMR |

☐ Internet Access   WIFI Wireless Internet Access   WG Waterway Guide Cruising Club Partner   *(Information in the table is provided by the facilities.)*
See WaterwayGuide.com for current rates, fuel prices, web site addresses, and other up-to-the-minute information.

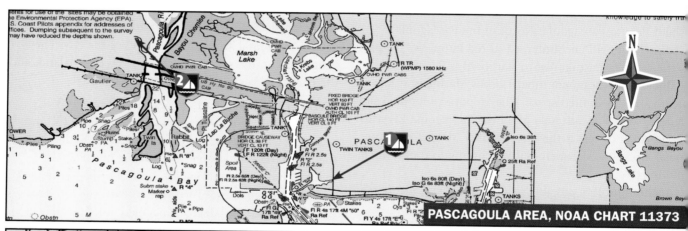

PASCAGOULA AREA, NOAA CHART 11373

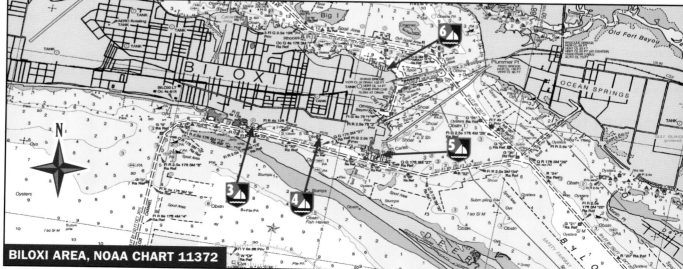

BILOXI AREA, NOAA CHART 11372

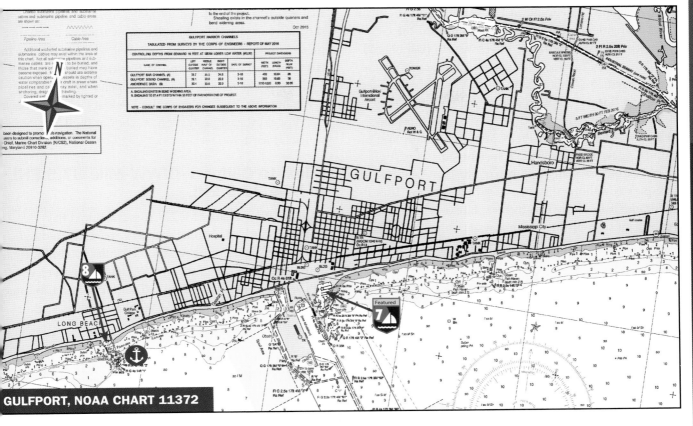

**GULFPORT, NOAA CHART 11372**

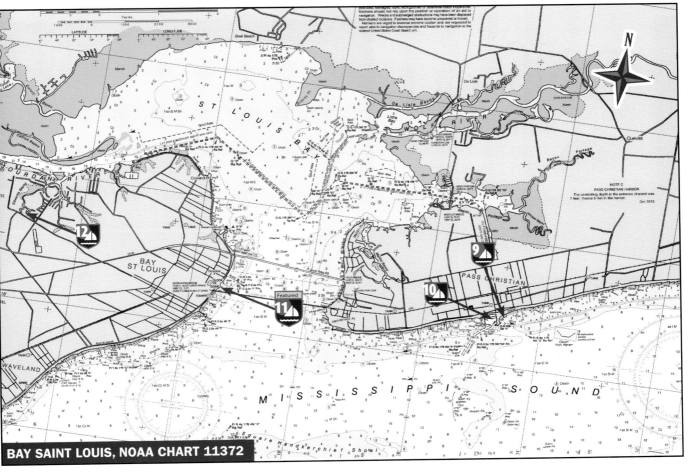

**BAY SAINT LOUIS, NOAA CHART 11372**

Biloxi Channel extending east to west along the city and then changing direction to the south toward the GIWW. From the Biloxi waterfront, travel west to flashing red "12," and then turn south to green daybeacon "5" and flashing red "6." This section of the channel is 150 feet wide and 6 feet deep with a soft mud bottom.

**Dockage:** Biloxi Small Craft Harbor has slips and sells fuel. The Schooner Pier Complex, .5 mile west of Point Cadet, includes some transient slips as part of the Maritime & Seafood Industry Museum facility. This complex is walking distance to several casinos. It is also the home base of the two historic Biloxi Schooners, replicas of turn-of-the-century oyster ships that make daily sails around Mississippi Sound.

The Point Cadet Marina, at the eastern tip of Biloxi, offers transient berths and sells fuel. After passing under the railroad bridge you will see Biloxi Boardwalk Marina, which has slips and fuel and offers repairs.

## Back Bay of Biloxi

**NAVIGATION:** Use Chart 11372. The Biloxi Ship Channel continues north into Back Bay of Biloxi. Three bridges cross the channel. The first is the **Biloxi Bay (U.S.**

**90) Bridge** with a fixed 95-foot vertical clearance; the second is an abandoned bridge (now used as a fishing pier) with channel sections removed, and the third is the **Biloxi Bay (CSX Railroad) Swing Bridge** with a 14-foot closed vertical clearance (opens on signal).

**Anchorage:** You can drop the hook anywhere in Back Bay. For northeast protection, anchor at Big Lake in deep water (at least 14 feet).

## Biloxi to Gulfport–GIWW Mile 87.5 EHL to Mile 72.5 EHL

**NAVIGATION:** Chart 11372. Cross the Biloxi Bay Channel south of channel markers green "1" and red "2." Set a course to the west for 15 miles to Gulfport Sound Channel. The first GIWW channel marker you will see is 17-foot red "2" in 5.5 statute miles. Continue west 5.5 miles to 17-foot red "4" then 4 miles to the Gulfport Sound Channel.

## City of Gulfport

Gulfport, the seat of Harrison County, is a seaport and tourist center. It is one of Mississippi's most successful commercial ports. For the cruising boater Gulfport

eatures casinos, restaurants, museums and the ferry to hip Island; all near marinas. Take a bus or taxis to the nall and outlet stores on Interstate 49, about 3.5 miles orth of the harbor.

**NAVIGATION:** Use Chart 11372. At Mile 73 EHL, travel iorthwest for 6 miles until you reach Gulfport. Pass etween flashing green "43" and flashing red "44," and hen travel along Gulfport Shipping Channel to flashing ed "62." From here, follow the channel markers into the Gulfport Small Craft Harbor, just east of the Mississippi State Port.

**Dockage:** The friendly Gulfport Municipal Marina s deep-water marina that can accommodate vessels ip to 140 feet. This modern facility offers easy access no bridges to negotiate) and all amenities, including howers, laundry, security, wide fairways and full-ength finger piers. They offer a 24-hour fuel dock and beautiful white sand beach right on the gulf. There s only one tidal cycle per day here with a very small idal range of just over 1 foot. Casinos and downtown estaurants are within walking distance. Long Beach Harbor is about 3 statute miles to the west of Gulfport. The marina there may have transient space for you and sells all fuels.

**Anchorage:** Drop the hook north of Long Beach Harbor in 8 to 9 feet of water with excellent holding in soft mud. Keep in mind that this is exposed to the south.

# GULFPORT TO LOUISIANA

### To Lake Ponchartrain–GIWW Mile 72.5 EHL to Mile 40 EHL

**NAVIGATION:** Use Charts 11367, 11371 and 11372. From the Gulfport Channel the GIWW follows a route west for 7.5 miles to GIWW Mile 65 EHL, at flashing green "1." Here it makes a southerly turn to about 225 degrees magnetic and passes through 17-foot WR"2" and 17-foot green "3." Channel markers begin to get closer together, but are still at distances of 1 mile or more. In 7.5 miles, at GIWW Mile 58 EHL you enter the well-marked Marianne Channel at 17-foot red "14." At 17-foot "1," GIWW Mile 54 EHL, turn west into Grand Island Channel. Grand Island Channel ends at GIWW Mile 48 EHL at 17-foot "15."

Turn south to a course of about 255 degrees magnetic and make way through St. Joe Pass. The channel

## Communicating With Barges

In virtually any marked channel, common courtesy, as well as safety, urges you to communicate with tows when you plan to pass.

A common problem is that tugs often do not have their names on their transom, or anywhere a trailing vessel can identify a hailing name. In those cases, hail the tug on VHF Channel 13 and identify it by the direction, east or west, and the approximate mile marker or other identifying feature of the ICW where you plan to pass and identify yourself.

Remember, the tug has a much better view ahead and experience with predicting and identifying a safe course. An Automatic Identification System (AIS) linked in with your chartplotter is very handy in the GIWW, as it helps you see towboats pushing barges before they suddenly appear. If you have an AIS device equipped with a transponder, the tow captains can see you well before you meet.

# GOIN' ASHORE: BILOXI, MS

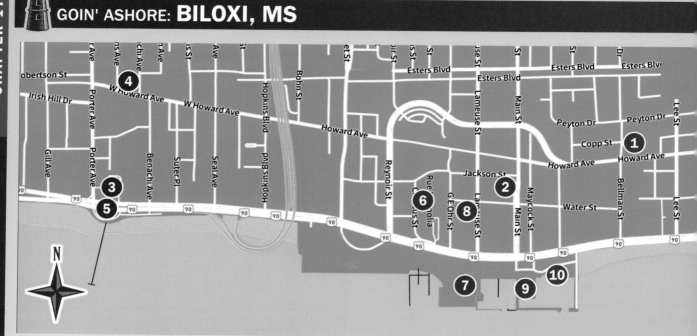

| SERVICES | |
|---|---|
| 1 | Library |
| 2 | Post Office |
| 3 | Visitor Information |
| **ATTRACTIONS** | |
| 4 | Biloxi Fire Museum |

| | |
|---|---|
| 5 | Biloxi Lighthouse |
| 6 | Mardi Gras Museum |
| **DINING** | |
| 7 | Ben & Jerrys |
| 8 | Half Shell Oyster House |
| 9 | McElroys Harbor House |

| MARINA | |
|---|---|
| 10 | Biloxi Small Craft Harbor |

Originally inhabited by American Indians known as Biloxis ("first people"), the French first occupied and governed Biloxi in 1699. In 1763, the French ceded its territory east of the Mississippi River to the English, who controlled the territory until 1779. Spain took over soon after and governed the Mississippi coast until 1810. During a revolution against the Spaniards, the Anglo-Americans took control of Biloxi, which then became part of the short-lived Republic of West Florida. Most of the early settlers planted crops, built boats, raised cattle and lived a fairly peaceful co-existence with the native Indians.

From 1815 to 1850, Biloxi slowly evolved from an undeveloped area into a summertime resort community for affluent Southerners. In 1969, Hurricane Camille devastated the Mississippi coastline and destroyed much of Biloxi. Years of rebuilding followed, and in 1992, the State of Mississippi legalized dockside gaming. Since Biloxi was already a popular waterfront vacation spot, major casinos were built, and the local economy exploded.

**Attractions:** The Mississippi resort coast begins at Biloxi Bay. Ocean Springs is on the eastern shore, with Biloxi to the west. Ocean Springs is noted for its art galleries, which line the streets, several museums, boutique shops, restaurants and outside cafes, a few of which are walking distance from the marina.

Across the ship channel from Ocean Springs is Biloxi, a world-class vacation destination with Las Vegas-style gambling resorts, restaurants, continuous nightlife and entertainment of all types. These amenities are within walking distance of several full-service marinas.

Biloxi is one of the largest processors of shrimp and oysters in the world. Testaments to its fishing history are found in the Maritime and Seafood Industry Museum located at 115 E. 1st St. with special exhibits such as boatbuilding, net making, sail making and marine blacksmithing.

A good place to start is the Visitors Center at 1050 Beach Blvd., which is open 7 days a week from 8:00 a.m. until 5:00 p.m. (except Thanksgiving Day, Christmas Day, Easter and Fat Tuesday). The two-story structure is modeled after the Dantzler House, which was destroyed in 2005 by Hurricane Katrina. The house alone is worth a visit to see the two-story porches, grand staircase, floor-to-ceiling windows and a great view of the beach. There is a 67-seat movie theater on site with continuous showings of the 10-minute film *We Are Biloxi*.

The Visitor Center sits in the shadow of the landmark Biloxi Lighthouse, which holds the title of being the only lighthouse in the U.S. to stand in the middle of a four-lane highway. The 1848 cast-iron lighthouse was one of the few structures to survive Hurricane Katrina unscathed and is likely the most photographed landmark on the Mississippi Gulf Coast. Tours of the Lighthouse are offered every morning at 9:00, 9:15 and 9:30 a.m. (weather permitting) for a small fee.

Museum staff members can direct you on a walking tour of 17 historic sites (dating back to 1699), including Biloxi's Main Street District and the museums, shops and restaurants that wind through the city. A trolley travels along the tree-lined streets of Biloxi and makes many stops along the way.

One popular stop is the Ohr-O'Keefe Museum of Art (386 Beach Blvd., 228-374-5547), which houses a permanent collection of pottery by George E. Ohr, the "Mad Potter of Biloxi." The museum has rotating exhibitions; visit.georgeohr.org for details.

A treat for history buffs is Beauvoir, the Jefferson Davis Home & Presidential Library at 2244 Beach Blvd. The estate includes a library, antebellum home, Confederate museum and veteran's cemetery on 50 landscaped acres fronting the Gulf of Mexico. It is open daily 9:00 a.m. to 5:00 p.m.; there is an admission fee. Call 228-388-4400, or visit beauvoir.org for details.

Although not as well known as the above museums, the Biloxi Fire Museum at 1046 Howard Ave. is worth a visit. It is housed in a historic 1937 fire house and features historic photographs as well as antique fire equipment that documents the history of the Biloxi Fire Department, which dates back more than 120 years.

Another fun and informative stop is the Mardi Gras Museum at 119 Rue Magnolia, where you can ogle the elaborate costumes and props and read all about the history of Mardi Gras.

Of course, casinos are open 24 hours a day, 7 days a week and offer excellent entertainment, as well as a variety of dining experiences. The Coast Transit Authority operates the Casino Hopper, a shuttle bus that makes a continuous loop around the Biloxi casinos for a fare of $1.50 per person.

A post office and a library are located downtown. For complete information, visit gulfcoast.org.

**Shopping:** Reaching the local West Marine will require transportation. It is located at Shoppes at Popps Ferry Shopping Center on Pass Rd. A Winn Dixie grocery store and Walgreens drug store are nearby.

**Dining:** Biloxi Casinos offer a wide variety of dining options. At Biloxi Small Craft Harbor is the family-owned McElroys Harbor House Seafood, open for breakfast, lunch and dinner. Our cruising editor recommends Half Shell Oyster House located two blocks from the Biloxi Small Craft Harbor at 125 Lameuse St. There is a Ben & Jerry's nearby for an after-dinner treat.

www.snagaslip.com

SNAG-A-SLIP

EXPLORE BOOK BOAT.

# Mississippi River, LA

| | | Dockage | | | | | Supplies | | Services | | | | |
|---|---|---|---|---|---|---|---|---|---|---|---|---|---|
| | | Largest Vessel Accommodated | VHF Channel Monitored | Transient Berths / Total Berths | Approach / Dockside Depth (reported) | Floating Docks | Gas / Diesel | Groceries, Ice, Marine Supplies, Snacks | Repairs: Hull, Engine, Propeller | Lift (tonnage), Crane, Rail | Min/Max Amps | Laundry, Pool, Showers, Courtesy Car | Pump-Out Station | Nearby: Grocery Store, Motel, Restaurant |
| **VENICE** | | | | | | | | | | | | | | |
| 1. Cypress Cove Marina & Lodge ⌨ | 504-534-9289 | 120 | 16 | 40/107 | 8/10 | F | GD | GIMS | HEP | L | 50/50 | LPS | P | GMR |
| 2. Venice Marina ⌨ | 504-534-9357 | 100 | 16 | 30/120 | 10/8 | F | GD | GIMS | – | C | 50/50 | L | – | GMR |
| **PORT EADS** | | | | | | | | | | | | | | |
| 3. Port Eads Marina | 504-308-1602 | – | – | 30/60 | – | – | GD | I | – | – | 30/30 | S | – | MR |

⌨ Internet Access  📶 Wireless Internet Access  WG Waterway Guide Cruising Club Partner  *(Information in the table is provided by the facilities.)*
See WaterwayGuide.com for current rates, fuel prices, web site addresses, and other up-to-the-minute information.

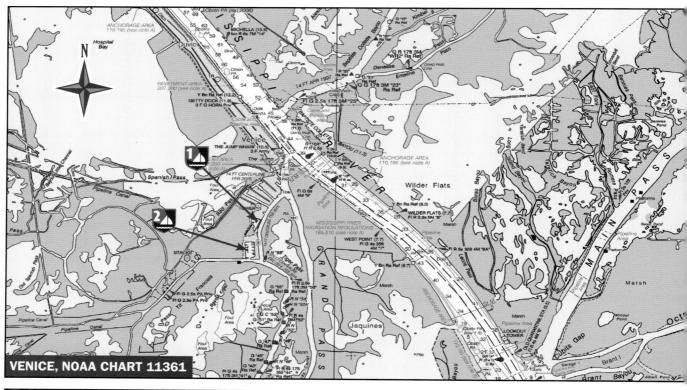

VENICE, NOAA CHART 11361

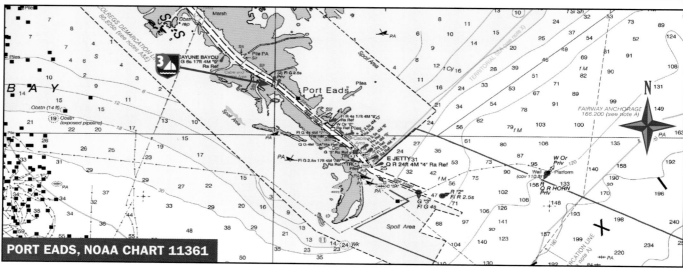

PORT EADS, NOAA CHART 11361

through St. Joe Pass is wide and has good depths along the GIWW. The next GIWW marker you will see is daybeacon red "2" at Mile 45 EHL. St. Joe Pass leads to Lake Borgne and the Louisiana State Line. The state line is marked by the entrance to the Pearl River and then GIWW Mile 40 EHL. Avoid the charted obstruction north of the GIWW at the Pearl River.

## Bay St. Louis–North of GIWW Mile 55 EHL

At the western entrance to St. Louis Bay, the town of Bay St. Louis is the last of the Mississippi coastal resorts. In Bay St. Louis, visiting shallow-draft vessels will find many suitable anchorages and fine fishing.

The John C. Stennis Space Center (where NASA does research work) offers free tours, but you will need ground transportation to get there. It is well worth the trip for those who are interested in the technical side of space travel. Visit nasa.gov/centers/stennis for more information.

**NAVIGATION:** Use Chart 11372. From GIWW Mile 54 EHL, at the junction of Marianne Channel and the Grand Island Channel, travel 5 miles north to flashing red "2" (west side of Square Handkerchief Shoal) and

then 2.5 miles to the **Bay St. Louis Railway Swing Bridge** (13-foot closed vertical clearance), which opens on signal. This is followed by the **Bay St. Louis (US 90) Highway Bridge** (85-foot vertical clearance).

Bayou Caddy, located along the shoreline just a few miles west of Bay St. Louis, is mostly a commercial fishing port. Carefully follow the 50-foot-wide channel (5.5-foot depths) into the bayou, which itself has 6-foot depths. The atmosphere is very friendly toward visiting pleasure boaters. Many interesting hours can be spent watching the commercial and private fishermen as they come and go.

Heron Bay, just northwest of Lighthouse Point and north of flashing green "3," may look like a good anchorage or fishing hole, but note its shallow depths. The many fishing boats you see are of the Lafitte skiff type, which draw less than 2 feet.

**Dockage:** Bay St. Louis Municipal Harbor is conveniently located between the bridges and offers transient slips for vessels up to 110 feet with full amenities (including free WiFi). They also sell gas and diesel fuel. Groceries and restaurants are nearby. Courtesy transportation to nearby casinos is also available. Bay Marina & R.V. Park is located just west of the casino on the Jourdan River. They have transient slips and fuel.

There are two marked channels leading to the Pass Christian Harbor, located about 4 miles east of Bay St. Louis. The eastern channel reportedly has better depths. Pass Christian Harbor & the East Harbor Expansion both have slips and sell fuel. Water and pump-out service are available at each slip. The fun, open-air Shaggy's Harbor Bar & Grill (228-452-9939) is located near the marina (and is highly recommended by our managing editor.) Also close by is a gas station with a well-stocked convenience store.

**Anchorage:** There are no viable anchorages in Bay St. Louis due to the shallow depths.

## Pearl River–GIWW Mile 40 EHL

**NAVIGATION:** Use Chart 11367. The Pearl River can be entered from the GIWW just east of Mile 40. The entrance marks start with flashing green "1," which also serves as a borderline between Mississippi and Louisiana. Pearl River extends past the **Rigolets Railway Swing Bridge** (11-foot closed vertical clearance), which opens on signal, and the 66-foot fixed vertical clearance **Fort Pike (The Rigolets) Hwy. Bridge**. The river depth is a reported 12 feet. Little Lake and East Pass, which divert from the Pearl River at quick-flashing green "21," return to the Rigolets and are covered in the next chapter.

**Anchorage:** The Pearl River offers many anchorage opportunities, but you need to choose carefully. Old Pearl River branches into two different Middle Rivers and provides numerous quiet, isolated anchorages and scenic cruising. At the intersection of the Pearl River and East Pass, it is possible to anchor in 8 feet of water with all-around protection.

# ■ OFFSHORE PASSAGES

This is a good region for the cruising sailor wanting some time offshore in the Gulf of Mexico. With fair weather and a well-found boat, you can choose several offshore passages. All passages should be during daylight hours unless you have significant local knowledge and experience in this area. It is 41 nm from Pensacola to the Main Ship Channel at Mobile Bay. Mobile Bay Main Ship Channel to Horn Pass is 25 nm, and from Horn Pass to Ship Island Pass it is 21 nm.

Note: These distances are measured from jetty to jetty and do not include miles in the bay and channel to the end of the jetties. Take these distances into consideration to make sure you reach a safe anchorage or marina before nightfall. Plan your trip according to your boat, your ability, tides, currents and weather.

## Offshore: Mississippi Sound to Venice, Louisiana

For those wishing to bypass New Orleans an offshore route from Mobile Bay or the Mississippi Sound to Venice may be a viable option. For access to the Mississippi River and then Venice you must pass through Baptiste Collette Channel. Your point of departure will determine if you will travel east or west of the Chandeleur and Breton Islands.

If your route is to the east of the islands make your entrance to Breton Sound through one of two locations. North of Breton Islands the old cut for The Mississippi

Gulf Outlet is still marked on charts. You can use that cut to enter Breton Sound. The Mississippi Gulf Outlet, 20 nm to the northwest across Breton Sound, was permanently closed in 2009. The second option is to travel south of Breton Island past West Point, before heading west into Breton Sound. Be aware that shoals extend for 3 nm southwest of West Point. Chart your course with great care to avoid the shallow waters in this area. This is a lonely place to run aground; dangerous in inclement weather.

If your route is to the west of the Islands, enter Chandeleur Sound south of Ship Island Pass. Follow the sparsely marked channel through Chandeleur Sound and Breton Sound to the entrance of Baptiste Collette.

Look for the entrance markers of the Baptiste Collette Bayou, markers "1" and "2," which will lead in a southwesterly direction to the Mississippi River. The Bayou is well marked and has good depths due to its primary use as a channel for commercial traffic. This route is strewn with oil platforms and wrecks and should only be attempted with good daylight and the latest charts and navigational equipment. Once you fuel up in Venice, you can head back offshore through Tiger Pass.

Baptist Collette and Tiger Passes appear to be much wider than charted. Recent storms and erosion have damaged the marshes. Stay in the channel at all times. Oil rig service and crew boats also use these channels. They do not slow down and their wakes are huge. Pay attention to shipping traffic while negotiating the passes.

**Dockage:** There are two marinas located in Tiger Pass, at the City of Venice. Cypress Cove Marina & Lodge is a full-service marina with gas and diesel, lodging and a restaurant. Nearby Venice Marina is a full-service facility with gas, diesel and a bar and grill. At the southern end of South Pass, Port Eads Marina offers transient slips and fuel, along with a restaurant and lodging.

## Cruising Options

Our coverage continues in the next chapter back on the GIWW at Mile 34 EHL and into Lake Pontchartrain and then to New Orleans

# OFFSHORE PASSES

## Southwest Pass to Freeport

**NAVIGATION:** Charts 411, 1116A, 11330, 11366 and 1321. On a straight rum line of 270 degrees it is 07 nm from the end of the Southwest Pass to Freeport. Leaving from Venice, it is about 35 nm to the Gulf of Mexico through the Southwest Pass. In 28 nm after leaving Southwest Pass you will cross an anchorage area and Safety Fairway. The prominent mark is a privately maintained 213-foot flashing Horn/Racon "NM-3." Sixty nautical miles from Southwest Pass is a shoal with depths as shallow as 20 feet. It is marked with privately maintained buoys. Leave this shoal area to the north. Approximately 110 nm after leaving Southwest Pass, you will enter an area of oil platforms that will continue for many miles. Many will be visible at one time, so keep a close watch. Freeport is just 200 nm to the west.

## Venice and Tiger Pass

**NAVIGATION:** Chart 11361. You can travel to the Gulf of Mexico from Venice in Tiger Pass. The distance from Venice to the Gulf is 12 statute miles. The channel is well marked with depths reported at 10 feet, but you will need to seek out local knowledge before you begin this trip.

## Barataria Waterway at Grand Isle

**NAVIGATION:** Chart 11361 and 11364. From the Southwest Pass the Barataria Inlet is 34 nm on a course of 311 degrees. From Grand Isle the town of Lafitte is 34 statute miles north. Depths at the inlet and in the Barataria Waterway can be as shallow as 5 feet.

## Atchafalaya River

**NAVIGATION:** Chart 11351, 11356, 11357, 11358 and 11361. From the Southwest Pass the entrance to the Atchafalaya River is about 115 nm, on a course of 274 degrees to Whiskey Point, then 284 degrees to the Atchafalaya Inlet RW "A." From the Atchafalaya Inlet to Freeport the distance is 195 nm at 265 degrees. The Lower Atchafalaya entrance is marked by bell buoy, RW "A" in a water depth of 65 feet. From RW "A" it is 21 nm to shore on a course of 38 degrees. The trip north in the river leads to Morgan City in 40 statute miles. The channel is deep and well marked.

## Vermillion Bay Southwest Pass and Intracoastal City

**NAVIGATION:** Chart 11351, and 11349. From the Atchafalaya Inlet it is 35 nm on a course of 304 degrees to the inlet at the Vermillion Bay Southwest Pass. From Vermillion Bay Southwest Pass it is 170 nm on a course of 270 degrees to Freeport. The channel from the Vermillion Bay Southwest Pass is well marked all the way to Intracoastal City, a distance of 17 nm. Depths offshore are 5 to 9 feet upon approach. When approaching from offshore, this Pass is difficult to see until you are close to shore and the water shallows to 7 feet. Local knowledge is very helpful when approaching this Pass. Plan your approach and entry to Vermillion Bay carefully.

## Freshwater Bayou Canal

**NAVIGATION:** Chart 11349 and 11350. From Vermilion Bay Southwest Pass, it is 11 nm on a course of 264 degrees to the Freshwater Bayou Canal. The Pass is well marked, but approach with care and caution. It is difficult to see on an offshore approach. Depths are 10 feet at a 17-foot red "2" marking the entrance of the channel. From red "2" it is 5.4 nm to shore. Local knowledge is helpful for this approach. Freshwater Bayou Canal is navigable north to the Intracoastal Waterway close to Intracoastal City. From the channel entrance the GIWW is about 25 nm north. Freshwater Bayou Lock is 1.3 miles north of the entrance. The lock is open and operational, so attempt to contact the Lockmaster on VHF Channel 14 before passing through.

## Mermentau River Navigation Canal

**NAVIGATION:** Chart 11349, 11344 and 11348. From Freshwater Bayou Canal it is 38 nm on a course of 289 degrees to the Mermentau River Navigation Canal. Don't go without local knowledge. This is not a good Pass for a cruising boat unless you have an emergency and need to reach a sheltered port. It is difficult to see and close to shore. The channel entrance is marked by red "2" in 15-foot depths, 1.4 nm from shore. Short jetties protect the entrance, but shoals are an ever-shifting and difficult problem. The channel does reach the GIWW through a circuitous route that takes you through Lower Mud Lake, Upper Mud Lake, Grand Lake and many winding channels.

# Calcasieu Pass

**NAVIGATION:** Chart 1116A, 1117A, 11330, 11339, 11341, 11323 and 11321. Calcasieu Pass is the only deep-water channel west of the Mississippi and east of Sabine Pass. The small town of Cameron is immediately inside the Pass. There are no boating facilities, fuel or services. From here the Calcasieu River travels north 23 miles to the GIWW, 35 miles to Lake Charles and then continues north for many miles. It is a well-marked Pass with jetties that extend from the shoreline approximately 1 nm. Commercial ships and tankers travel it. It is wide and deep all the way to Lake Charles.

Calcasieu Pass is 210 nm from the Southwest Pass at the Mississippi River. Follow a course of 272 degrees for 70 nm to Whiskey Pass, then 284 degrees for 135 nm to Calcasieu Pass.

The distance to Freeport is 110 nm on a course of 247 degrees. On the route from Calcasieu Pass to Freeport you will travel past the two deep-water ports at Sabine Pass and Galveston. Sabine Pass is 21 nm from Calcasieu Pass and leads to Sabine Lake and Port Arthur. Galveston is 70 nm from Sabine Pass and takes you into the extremely busy area of Galveston Island, Galveston Bay and the Houston Ship Channel.

# Lake Pontchartrain & New Orleans

 **GIWW** Mile 33 EHL–Mile 0 (Harvey Lock)    LA: Channel 13

**CHARTS** 11340, 11361, 11364, 11367, 11368, 11369

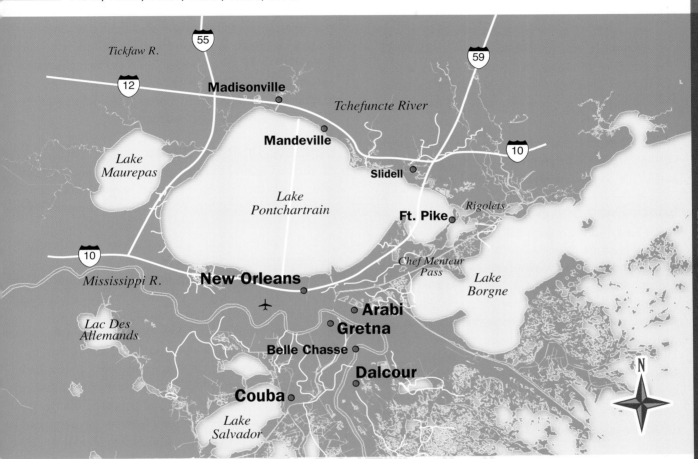

Welcome to the Big Easy. It is an understatement to say you have arrived at a unique and interesting cruising destination. Just passing through these waterways is a notable encounter. Stop and stay for a while and discover memorable experiences in New Orleans, the vast and substantial waterway of canals, lakes, rivers and the small communities along their shores. Quiet places to relax can be found along the north shore of Lake Pontchartrain and most of Lake Maurepas. The unique beauty and tranquility is an allure that has drawn many cruising boats into making this area their permanent home. When you are looking for more festive activities, there is someplace, everywhere and you can "live large."

## ■ FROM THE GULF TO THE MISSISSIPPI RIVER

**NAVIGATION:** Use Charts 11340, 11361, 11364 and 11367. South of New Orleans the Mississippi River empties into the Gulf of Mexico. This part of the Mississippi River Delta is made up of four navigable channels that lead from the River to the Gulf of Mexico, which is sometimes referred as "Birds Foot Delta" because it is shaped like the foot of a bird with toes extending into the Gulf of Mexico. Distances in the river are measured by statute mile. They are often referred to by origin at the "Head of Pass" or "Above Head of Pass" (AHP). The River and the Delta and its tributaries make up the largest network of navigable waters in the

A Word on **VHF Channels**: At Mile 14 EHL the VHF frequency for commercial vessels changes from VHF Channel 16 to VHF Channel 13. East of Mile 14 EHL, VHF Channel 16 is the frequency for commercial vessels. West of Mile 14 EHL, VHF Channel 13 remains the commercial frequency for the GIWW to the Galveston Causeway Bridge, Mile 357.2 WHL, where it changes back to VHF Channel 16. Due to the high volume of commercial traffic in this area, recreational boaters should monitor the same frequency as commercial traffic.

world. Currents in the area of these entrances can be considerable. The complexity of this area makes navigation a very serious and detailed responsibility.

## South Pass and Southwest Pass

South Pass and the Southwest Pass are the two primary offshore routes to the Mississippi River. From Tampa Bay to the South Pass entrance is approximately 350 nm. From Southwest Pass to the Galveston Bay entrance is approximately 280 nm. Plan passage times to include the long distances that can be encountered after you reach these offshore entrances. The red and white "SW" whistle buoy for the Southwest Pass is 1.5 nm south of the jetty entrance. It is 20 nm from the "SW" buoy to Mile 0, where the Southwest Pass and the South Pass come together in the Mississippi River and 94 nm from Mile 0 to New Orleans. There are no charted bridges or overhead cables until you are in New Orleans at Mile 95.9 when you will encounter the **Crescent City Connection Bridges** with their fixed clearance of 150 feet.

Pass Loutre and Main Pass on the east side of the river have shoaled considerably and are not recommended for cruising boats. Basically, if you are offshore and coming from the east, enter the Mississippi River at South Pass.

## Tiger Pass

On the west side of the Delta, Tiger Pass is 15 nm north of the Southwest Pass. From the jetties it is approximately 10 nm northeast to Venice along the Tiger Pass route. Depth in Tiger Pass is charted to be 5.5 feet. There are no charted bridges or overhead cables along this route.

## Empire Waterway

The Empire Waterway offers passage from the Gulf of Mexico to the Mississippi River 11 nm northwest of Tiger Pass. The channel is not surveyed and is reported to carry depths of 5.5 feet, and there are no charted bridges or overhead cables along this route until you reach the City of Empire. Empire is approximately 10 nm north of the channel entrance. There are no facilities here. The Empire Waterway enters the city through a floodgate. Shortly after the floodgate are a fixed bridge (53-foot fixed vertical clearance) and a swing bridge (3-foot closed clearance, opens on signal). To enter the Mississippi River you have to transit the Empire Lock. Contact the lockmaster on VHF Channel 9 or 14 for instructions.

## Baptiste Collette Bayou

On the east side of the Delta there is only one navigable inlet, other than the main channel of South Pass. A channel through Baptiste Collette Bayou connects Brenton Sound to the Mississippi River just above the City of Venice. The channel in Baptiste Collette is well marked and has been dredged for barge traffic, so it is wide and carries depths up to 12 feet. From Brenton Sound, enter the channel through a well-marked jetty. Most cruising boats will have traveled from the Mississippi Sound through Ship Island Pass, then south past the Chandeleur Island, through Chandeleur Sound and then Brenton Sound. Others can arrive from routes that carried them along the coast line of Florida, Alabama and Mississippi, then south through the sounds to Baptiste Collette. It is possible to enter Brenton Sound from an offshore passage by traveling northwest from a point where you would be approaching South Pass.

Note: Brenton and Chandeleur Sounds should not be considered protected waters or inland bays. Check weather and sea conditions and plan your trip as if you are making an offshore passage.

The Gulf Outlet Canal to the northeast is closed to navigation (blocked by rocks).

# ENTERING NEW ORLEANS

At Mile 35 EHL westbound vessels must decide if they are going to proceed to New Orleans by passing through the Rigolets (pronounced "rig-o-lees") and crossing Lake Pontchartrain or by continuing west in the GIWW and arriving in New Orleans at the Inner Harbor Navigation Canal. The distance is about the same. Conditions in Lake Pontchartrain will contribute to the decision. Planning, preparation and paper charts are important to a safe and comfortable passage in this area.

The GIWW route to New Orleans (Route 1) is the preferred route if proceeding west on the GIWW or if the weather in Lake Pontchartrain is dubious. The most popular route (Route 2) is to depart the GIWW to the north at Mile 35 EHL (East of Harvey Lock), enter the Rigolets and follow this passage to Lake Pontchartrain. The Rigolets, from the French word "rigolet," meaning "little canal," is not hard to traverse. At times, strong currents can be a problem. The distance from the GIWW to the marinas at West End, New Orleans is 35 miles, with other marinas along the route and on the north side of Lake Pontchartrain.

## Route 1: GIWW Westbound

**NAVIGATION:** Use Chart 11367. The GIWW route starts at Catfish Point at Mile 34 EHL. Pass between flashing green "25" and quick flashing red "26." Follow the markers, and stay well inside the channel for the first one-half mile, as shoaling is prevalent here. The channel carries good depths from Mile 34 EHL to Mile 26 EHL.

At Mile 26 EHL you will cross Chef Menteur Pass. It is a deep-water pass that goes south into Lake Bornge, and north into Lake Pontchartrain. Immediately north of the GIWW on the Pass are two swing bridges, both with closed clearances of 10 feet. It will be difficult to enter Lake Pontchartrain from this pass with a draft of more than 4 feet.

Located near the west end of the Chef Menteur Bridge (closed to auto traffic since Hurricane Katrina) are the brick remains historic Fort Macomb. The fort was built between 1820 and 1828 and was manned by both Confederate and Union troops during the Civil War. Inconspicuously hidden behind the crumbling fort is an older marina containing only covered sheds. It has a narrow, shallow entry flanking the crumbling brick

## About Vessel Traffic Services

When entering the Mississippi River from any direction consider contacting the Lower Mississippi River (LMR), Vessel Traffic Services (VTS) on VHF Channel 11 or 12. They will want to know the name, type, location, and destination of your boat. They may have a picture of your boat from your point of entry to the river, so don't be surprised if they call you by the boat's name. This is especially true if traveling south of Algiers Point. The proper VHF channel depends on location. Channel 12 is used from Mile 109 to 86. Channel 11 is used from Mile 86 to 12 miles offshore of Southwest Pass. The primary purpose is to manage commercial traffic.

The Vessel Traffic Center is located in a high-rise office building in the New Orleans Central Business District. VTS LMR is a component of the Waterway Division of USCG Sector New Orleans. VTS LMR manages vessel traffic on one of the most hazardous waterways in the U.S. due to the complexity of the marine traffic and the powerful currents of the Mississippi River. The VTS provides advisory and navigational assistance services at all times in these areas of responsibility.

When the river reaches high water levels of 8 feet in New Orleans, the VTS controls traffic at the Algiers Point Special Area (Mile 93.5 to Mile 95). VTS LMR is a unique Coast Guard Vessel Traffic Service because it maintains advisory service and direct control of vessel traffic with a workforce of highly trained and experienced civilian Coast Guard personnel with the assistance of pilot advisors.

More information is available online at homeport.uscg.mil. Select Vessel Traffic Services in the shaded area to the right.

# Lake Pontchartrain, LA

| | | Largest Vessel Accommodated | VHF Channel Monitored | Transient Berths / Total Berths | Approach / Dockside Depth (reported) | Floating Docks | Groceries, Ice, Marine Supplies, Snacks | Gas / Diesel | Repairs: Hull, Engine, Propeller | Lift (tonnage), Crane, Rail | Min/Max Amps | Laundry, Pool, Showers, Courtesy Car | Pump-Out Station | Nearby: Grocery Store, Motel, Restaurant |
|---|---|---|---|---|---|---|---|---|---|---|---|---|---|---|
| **THE RIGOLETS** | | | | **Dockage** | | | **Supplies** | | | **Services** | | | | |
| 1. The Rigolets Marina | 985-641-8088 | 60 | – | – | /7 | | GD | GIS | – | – | 30/50 | S | – | G |
| 2. Pelican Pointe Marina | 504-460-6101 | 50 | – | call/26 | – | – | GD | IS | – | L35 | 30/30 | – | – | – |
| 3. Island Marina Lake Catherine (WiFi) | 504-662-5741 | 60 | 16 | call/52 | 6/6 | | GD | IMS | HEP | L60 | 30/30 | S | P | GM |
| **LAKE PONTCHARTRAIN (NORTHEAST SHORE)** | | | | | | | | | | | | | | |
| 4. Oak Harbor Marina | 985-641-1044 | 110 | 16 | 3/96 | 8/12 | – | – | – | – | – | 30/50 | LS | – | GMR |
| 5. The Dock Slidell | 985-645-3625 | 90 | – | – | – | – | GD | IS | – | L12 | – | S | – | GMR |

□ Internet Access  (WiFi) Wireless Internet Access  WG Waterway Guide Cruising Club Partner  *(Information in the table is provided by the facilities.)*
See WaterwayGuide.com for current rates, fuel prices, web site addresses, and other up-to-the-minute information.

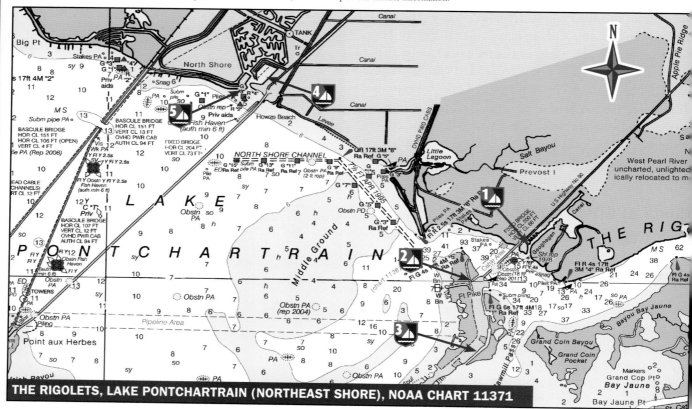

**THE RIGOLETS, LAKE PONTCHARTRAIN (NORTHEAST SHORE), NOAA CHART 11371**

walls. There is no on-site management, and no transient facilities are available.

As you continue east in the GIWW stay in the center of the channel up to Mile 19 EHL due to shallow depths along both banks. When entering the Michaud shipping area at Mile 15 EHL, be aware of large commercial vessels, water turbulence in the narrow waterways and the East Closure Sector Gate (originally named Lake Borne Surge Barrier. You can try to contact them on VHF Channel 14, but the floodgates may not have a full-time attendant. The high-rise **Paris Road Bridge** (referred to by commercial vessels as the Route 47 Bridge) at

Mile 13 has a 137-foot fixed vertical clearance. When reporting their position in this area, commercial boats may also say they are at Michaud Slip.

The merging of the GIWW at Mile 2 EHL with the Inner Harbor Navigational Canal and passage through the Industrial Locks is covered later in this chapter.

## Route 2: The Rigolets (GIWW Mile 35 EHL)

This route is deep and wide but plagued with strong currents. Use extra caution around the Rigolets Railroad Swing Bridge and the Fort Pike (The Rigolets) Hwy.

Bridge. Fishing is popular in the Rigolets at the trestles of both bridges and at the mouth of the Pass where its deep water meets the shallow lake. Cruisers should slow down and proceed at no-wake speeds as a courtesy to the fishermen.

Near Sawmill Pass along I-90 is Fort Pike. The large stonework fort was built in the early 1800s, after the Battle of New Orleans, to protect the Lake Pontchartrain approach to the city. Seek local knowledge to determine current depths in the approach channel to the small marinas in the area.

**NAVIGATION:** Use Chart 11367, 11369. Entering the Rigolets at Mile 35, you pass under two bridges. The first is the **Rigolets Railroad Swing Bridge**, which has a closed clearance of 11 feet and is usually open. If not, call ahead on VHF Channel 13 for an opening. When addressing the railroad bridge operator for an opening, use the name "CSX Rigolets Railroad Bridge" to prevent confusion with other nearby bridges. About 6 miles to the west, the fixed **Fort Pike (The Rigolets) Hwy. Bridge** (carrying I-90) has a 66-foot vertical clearance. Passage through the bridge brings you to the 17-foot-high Rigolets flashing green "5," which is about 90 feet from the abandoned West Rigolets Lighthouse. The

lighthouse was built in 1854 and moved to its present location after storm damage in 1869. The entrance to Lake Pontchartrain is marked by flashing red "6."

**Dockage:** The Rigolets Marina is on the north side of the Rigolets Channel one-quarter mile up the charted Geoghegan Canal. Pelican Pointe Marina is on the south side of the Rigolets up the charted Fort Pike Canal. Island Marina Lake Catherine is to on the Fort Pike Canal. All of these caters mostly to fisherman and sell fuel.

**Anchorage:** Whether heading on to New Orleans via the GIWW or Lake Pontchartrain, overnight anchorage can be found in the oxbow behind Catfish Pt. (at Rabbit Island) or in the Blind Rigolets on the side closest to the GIWW. When anchoring in the oxbow, the northern side has better anchoring depths at 14- to 16-feet. The anchorage in the Blind Rigolets is a comfortable overnight anchorage in 15-foot depths with the occasional rumble from a passing train. A third anchorage is to the north at West Mouth on the north side of Hog Island where you will find 8 to 15 feet with a mud bottom.

# LAKE PONTCHARTRAIN

Lake Pontchartrain is an almost ideal body of water for boating. The oval-shaped lake is nearly 40 miles from east to west and 24 miles from New Orleans to the north shore. It is consistently 10 to 12 feet deep, and the tidal range is normally less than 1 foot. Lake Pontchartrain deserves a high level of respect when storm winds blow. Keep a sharp eye out for numerous crab traps that seem to be randomly scattered across the lake; usually indicated by a small round white buoy.

Lake Pontchartrain is not a true lake. It is an estuary connected to the Gulf of Mexico via the Rigolets Straight and Chef Menteur Pass into Lake Borgne. It receives fresh water from the Tangipahoa, Tchefunct, Tickfaw, Amite and Bogue Falaya rivers, and from Bayou Lacombe and Bayou Chinchuba. This area makes up one of the largest wetlands along the Gulf Coast of North America. Efforts to preserve Lake Pontchartrain and its ecology have had positive effects. Dredging for commercial shell from the lake bottom and drilling for oil and gas were discontinued many years ago.

The high-level Lake Pontchartrain Causeway Bridge first opened in 1969 amid much publicity as the longest bridge in the world (nearly 24 miles). A twin bridge system, the Causeway connects the south shore at Metairie to the north shore at Lewisburg.

New Orleans dominates the southern shore. The small towns of Mandeville and Madisonville are prominent features of the north shore.

NAVIGATION: Use Chart 11369. The shallow area in the eastern part of the lake is named Middle Ground. Travel northwest past green daymarks "3" through "9" in the 7-foot-deep channel. After a westerly turn and a 1.5-mile run, you will pass under the **Pte. Aux Herbes (I-10) Bridge** (73-foot fixed vertical clearance), followed by the **U.S. Hwy. 11 Bascule Bridge** (13-foot closed vertical clearance) and the **Norfolk & Southern Railroad Bascule Bridge** (4-foot closed vertical clearance). Both open on signal. When addressing the railroad bridge for an opening, use the name "NS Highway 11 Bridge."

Once you are west of the highway and railroad bridges, you have a choice of heading southwest to New Orleans or northwest around the northern rim of Lake Pontchartrain. There are no buoyed channels in Lake Pontchartrain.

**Dockage:** The Oak Harbor Marina entrance is located on the northeast shore between the high-rise Pte. Aux Herbes Bridge and the U.S. 11 Highway Bascule Bridge in Slidell, LA. A limited number of slips are allocated for transient boaters. Gas and diesel are available across the basin at The Dock at Slidell.

# LAKE PONTCHARTRAIN: NORTH SHORE

The North Shore of St. Tammany Parish (22 miles north of New Orleans) offers everything from quaint bed and breakfast inns to antiques stores, fine restaurants and must-see swamp tours, which is the best way to see the nature estuary. One of the most pristine swamps in America is Honey Island. Pirates such as Jean Lafitte, who captured Spanish merchant ships in the Gulf of Mexico, took refuge from the authorities at Honey Island. Legends of buried treasure persist wherever Jean Lafitte came ashore.

While the North Shore may be only 22 miles from New Orleans, it is worlds apart; a much more relaxed area with the feel of the country. Many visiting boaters are attracted to the North Shore's peacefulness with ready access to central New Orleans and its cuisine and nightlife.

NAVIGATION: Use Chart 11369. You can stay within 5 miles of the coast of Lake Pontchartrain for most of the lake's shoreline. You have to find places to pass under the **Lake Pontchartrain Causeway Bridge** that will accommodate the height and draft your vessel. The South Pass Span has 50-foot fixed vertical clearance, while the North Pass Span is bascule and has 42-foot closed vertical clearance. The North Pass opens on signal with at least 3-hour notice, except from 5:30 a.m. to 9:30 a.m. and from 3:00 p.m. until 7:00 p.m., Monday through Friday (except Federal holidays), when the draw need not be open for the passage of vessels. Be aware of the overhead cables on the east side of the lake. A GPS with coverage of the lake is very helpful.

## Mandeville

This town on Bayou Castine is the sister port to Madisonville (on the Tchefuncta River) in terms of ambiance, amenities and popularity. Its shoreline and streets are landscaped with majestic oak, magnolia and

sycamore trees, which augment the Southern charm and blend in with an array of fine dining houses and pubs.

**Dockage:** Northshore Marine Sales & Services Inc. has a full-service boatyard on Bayou Castine with engine and hull repair and transient dockage. A restaurant, groceries and a motel are nearby. Prieto Marina LLC sits along Bayou Castine, approximately 2 miles east of the Causeway. Green daymark "1" and flashing red "2" are located at the entrance to Bayou Castine. Transients at Prieto Marina tie up along the bulkhead. Colbert Cove Marina and Heron's Way Marina are located further up the Bayou. These marinas are adjacent to the Fontainebleau State Park and the Tammany Trace Bike Trail.

## Lewisburg

The Lewisburg Harbor is located in the northeast corner of Lake Pontchartrain at the foot of the Lake Pontchartrain Causeway Bridge. The harbor entrance has about 10-foot depths.

**Dockage:** Lake Pontchartrain Harbor Marina has a dredged channel and docks that can accommodate boats up to 60 feet in length. Gas and diesel are available. Sailing classes and sailboat rentals are also in place.

Groceries, a restaurant and a motel are within 15-minute walking distance, as is a West Marine store.

## Madisonville

The Tchefuncta ("cha-funk-ta") River, 4 miles west of Lewisburg and 8 miles northwest of the Lake Pontchartrain Causeway, is Lake Pontchartrain's most popular weekend destination. This beautiful deep river has clean water, great anchorages, golf, tennis, country clubs, residential areas, marinas and miles of undeveloped shores. It is also a popular waterway for crabbers, so watch for crab pot floats.

The welcome mat is always out for pleasure boaters at Madisonville (1.5 miles up the Tchefuncta River), where dockage is usually available either north or south of the **Highway 22 Swing Bridge** (1-foot closed vertical clearance, opens on signal) on the west side. The docks become crowded with small boats during the shrimp season, and the town stays lively on weekends, so sleeping may be a challenge. A grocery store, post office, a local maritime museum and other shops and services are within walking distance. The town is famous for its Wooden Boat Festival (woodenboatfest.org) held every October.

www.snagaslip.com

SNAG-A-SLIP

EXPLORE
BOOK
BOAT

# Lake Pontchartrain North Shore, LA

| | | Largest Vessel Accommodated | VHF Channel Monitored | Transient Berths / Total Berths | Approach / Dockside Depth (reported) | Floating Docks | Gas / Diesel | Groceries, Ice, Marine Supplies, Snacks | Repairs: Hull, Engine, Propeller | Lift (tonnage), Crane, Rail | Min/Max Amps | Laundry, Pool, Showers, Courtesy Car | Pump-Out Station | Nearby: Grocery Store, Motel, Restaurant |
|---|---|---|---|---|---|---|---|---|---|---|---|---|---|---|
| | | **Dockage** | | | | | **Supplies** | | **Services** | | | | | |
| **MANDEVILLE** | | | | | | | | | | | | | | |
| 1. Northshore Marine Sales & Services Inc. | 985-626-7847 | 48 | – | 2/11 | 10/9 | – | – | M | HEP | L15 | 50/50 | S | P | R |
| 2. Prieto Marina LLC | 985-626-9670 | 58 | – | call/153 | 10/9 | – | – | – | – | – | 20/30 | S | – | R |
| 3. Colbert Cove Marina | 985-626-1156 | 66 | – | call/200 | /7 | – | – | I | – | – | 30/30 | S | – | R |
| 4. Heron's Way Marina | 985-626-4287 | 65 | – | call/48 | /7 | – | – | I | – | – | 30/30 | S | – | R |
| **LEWISBERG** | | | | | | | | | | | | | | |
| 5. Lake Pontchartrain Harbor Marina (WIFI) (WG) | 985-626-1517 | 60 | 16 | call/90 | 5.6/8 | – | GD | – | – | – | 50/50 | LS | P | GMR |
| **MADISONVILLE** | | | | | | | | | | | | | | |
| 6. Marina del Ray (internet) (WIFI) | 985-845-4474 | 200 | 16 | 100/1000 | 10/8 | F | GD | GIMS | HEP | – | 30/100 | LPS | P | GMR |
| 7. Salty's Marina | 985-845-8485 | – | 16 | 5/100 | 40/12 | F | – | IS | – | – | 30/30 | – | – | GR |
| 8. Bent Marine North Shore Service Center | 985-845-7398 | 50 | – | 6/12 | 15/8 | – | – | M | HEP | L35 | – | – | – | GR |
| 9. Hidden Harbor Marina | 985-845-7656 | 45 | – | call/35 | 18/12 | – | – | MS | HEP | L | 30/30 | – | – | GR |
| 10. Marina Beau Chene (internet) | 985-845-3454 | 60 | – | call/153 | 20/8 | – | G | – | – | – | 30/50 | LS | P | |

🖵 Internet Access  (WIFI) Wireless Internet Access  (WG) Waterway Guide Cruising Club Partner  *(Information in the table is provided by the facilities.)*
See WaterwayGuide.com for current rates, fuel prices, web site addresses, and other up-to-the-minute information.

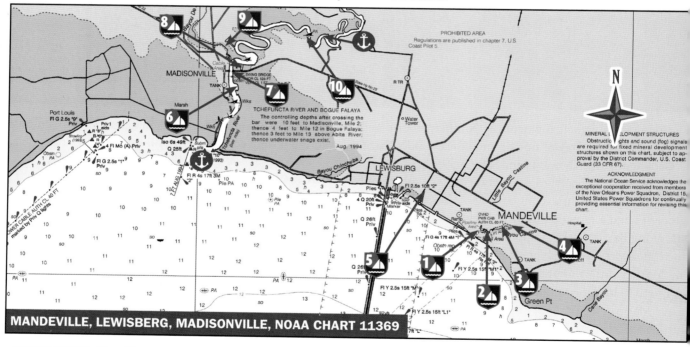

**MANDEVILLE, LEWISBERG, MADISONVILLE, NOAA CHART 11369**

**NAVIGATION:** Use Chart 11369. The entrance to the Tchefuncta River from Lake Pontchartrain is well marked, but take care to enter properly. Follow the marked channel (7-foot depths) north from flashing red "2" toward the old lighthouse, and then turn to the east and use red daymarks "6," "8" and "10" to the river entrance. Keep the red daymarks to starboard, as cutting across the doglegged entrance has caused many vessels to go hard aground. The 40-foot-high Tchefuncta River Lighthouse, built in 1838, is still in service, although it is now automated. A black vertical stripe makes it easy to see as a daytime range mark. At the Tchefuncta River entrance, a heavily used launch ramp is on the west bank. The river depth is 10 feet from the entrance upstream for several miles, and then decreases to 4 feet. A No-Wake Zone extends northward from the southern tip of Marina Del Ray.

Six miles from the mouth the I-12 Bridge (the direct route from the Mississippi Gulf Coast to Baton Rouge and I-10 West) crosses the river. Cruising and anchorage are limited north of the bridge, as river depths decline rapidly.

**Dockage:** On the west side of the river the Madisonville City Dock/bulkhead is just south of the Highway 22 Swing Bridge. Boats are free to tie to the bulkhead and enjoy all that the city has to offer, all within easy walking distance. On the east side of the Tchefuncta River just south of the Highway 22 Swing Bridge is Marina Del Ray, which has transient dockage and fuel. A large swimming pool is located in a barge between the marina and the river.

Around the bend to the east in a basin on the south bank, is the small but popular Salty's Marina. This friendly marina stays full most of the time with regular rentals but will try to make room for transients in temporarily empty slips. Bent Marine North Shore Service Center is located right in downtown Madisonville and can accommodate your hauling and service needs with their 35-ton lift.

North of the Highway 22 Swing Bridge on Bayou DeZaire is Hidden Harbor Marina with slips and repairs. Farther north on the curvy Tchefuncta River, Marina Beau Chene is in a country club community with homes, golf courses and tennis courts. Transient dockage is available; it is probably one of best hurricane holes in the Lake Pontchartrain area. Transients must call ahead and make a reservation.

**Anchorage:** A very popular anchorage is just past the beach to the east upon entering the river. Upriver is a small state park, a multitude of great anchorage spots, country clubs and residential areas ranging from cottages to southern mansions.

# ◼ LAKE MAUREPAS

**NAVIGATION:** Use Chart 11369. On the western shore of Lake Pontchartrain, Pass Manchac provides a 7-mile-long entrance into Lake Maurepas. The north and south entrances to the pass from Lake Pontchartrain are well marked with lighted platforms and buoys. Vessels with more than 3-foot drafts prefer the south channel, which has 6.5-foot depths. Follow flashing green "1" to green daymarks "3" and "5," and then to flashing green "7." From here, steer east into Pass Manchac (23-foot minimum depths). An abandoned lighthouse marks what was once the north bank, but it is now a shoal area protected by rocks.

Watch your wake while traveling the 7 miles to the bridges at the western end of Pass Manchac. As you pass the houses with small boats moored to their docks, be aware of the small skiffs and fishing trawlers anchored in Pass Manchac. Trawlers use the currents to usher the catch into their nets.

The entrance to Lake Maurepas from Pass Manchac is marked by two bridges and one overhead cable. The overhead cable has a vertical clearance of 64 feet. The first bridge is the **Canadian National/Illinois Central Railroad Bridge**. It has a closed vertical clearance of 10 feet, and an open clearance of 56 feet. The bridge is automated and only closes when a train is passing. The bridge is monitored remotely. If needed, there is a phone number on the bridge. The second bridge is the **I-55/U.S. 51 Bridge** with a 50-foot fixed clearance. On the north bank is a boat landing and a well-known seafood restaurant, Middendorf's, which is famous for its catfish dinners.

The 4-mile-long northwest run across the shoreline from flashing red "6" will bring you to the mouth of the Tickfaw River. The channel to the river entrance has 5-foot depths. Stumps on the east side and shallow water to the west require a straight-in entrance from the lake. Flashing green "1" guides you into the river toward green daymark "3." Often referred to as "Bikini Beach," the sandy and shallow shoreline on the west side is popular with swimmers and sunbathers. Once inside the Tickfaw River, depths increase to a controlled depth of 12 feet, with observed depths of 25 feet or more.

Dinghies and jet skis are plentiful on the Tickfaw River, and it is also a favorite destination for high-performance powerboats, so be alert. Officials patrol the river for "BWIs" (intoxicated boaters), as weekend traffic from Baton Rouge and New Orleans can get rowdy. On the first Saturday of every May, this area hosts the Tickfaw 200, one of the largest powerboat poker runs in Louisiana.

**Dockage:** Upriver, within a couple of miles, are various small marinas including Sun Buns, Tin Lizzy's and the Prop Stop. At the 7-mile point, just before the highway bridge near Springfield, is the Tickfaw Marina, and just beyond the bridge on the Blood River are Warsaw Marina and Vacajun Marina. Fuel is available at the Tickfaw Marina, and all three offer limited transient dockage. Nearby Blood River Landing is private, but may have dockage. Call ahead for slip availability.

**Anchorage:** An anchorage can be found near almost every bend. Boats sometimes anchor south of the Tickfaw River–Rome Ferry Bridge with all-around protection in at least 6 feet of water.

# Lake Maurepas, LA

| TICKFAW RIVER | | Largest Vessel Accommodated | VHF Channel Monitored | Transient Berths / Total Berths | Approach / Dockside Depth (reported) | Floating Docks | Gas / Diesel | Repairs: Hull, Engine, Propeller | Groceries, Ice, Marine Supplies, Snacks | Lift (tonnage), Crane, Rail | Laundry, Pool, Showers, Courtesy Car | Min/Max Amps | Nearby: Grocery Store, Motel, Restaurant | Pump-Out Station |
|---|---|---|---|---|---|---|---|---|---|---|---|---|---|---|
| | | | | **Dockage** | | | | **Supplies** | | | **Services** | | | |
| **1.** Tickfaw Marina | 225-695-3340 | 60 | – | call/80 | 10/2 | – | GD | | GIMS | – | – | 30/50 | S | P | GMR |
| **2.** Warsaw Marina | 225-294-3000 | 50 | – | 2/35 | 12/12 | – | – | | GIS | – | – | 30/50 | S | – | GR |
| **3.** Vacajun Marina | 225-294-3105 | 55 | – | – | 10/6 | – | – | | I | – | – | 30/30 | S | – | R |
| **4.** Blood River Landing | 225-294-3876 | 60 | – | 2/30 | 10/6 | – | – | | – | E | – | 30/50 | LS | – | GR |

⌨ Internet Access 📶 Wireless Internet Access **WG** Waterway Guide Cruising Club Partner *(Information in the table is provided by the facilities.)*
See WaterwayGuide.com for current rates, fuel prices, web site addresses, and other up-to-the-minute information.

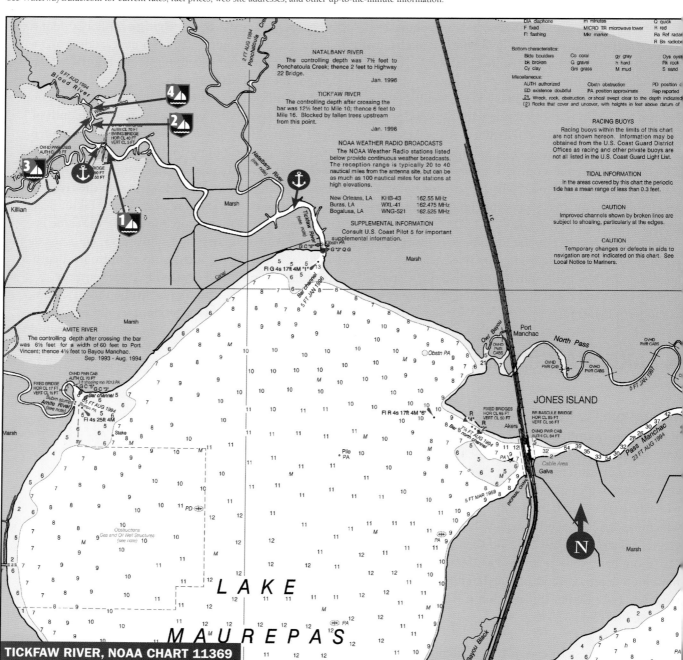

**TICKFAW RIVER, NOAA CHART 11369**

# NEW ORLEANS

"The Big Easy" offers the cruising yachtsman a wide and varied choice of activities. There are so many events, tourist sights, hotels, motels and restaurants that Waterway Guide's humble attempt at a "Goin' Ashore" section to help cruisers enjoy their visit to New Orleans barely scratches the surface of the magnificent city. Whether you stay a few days or a few weeks, your visit to New Orleans will be a memory maker.

**NAVIGATION:** Use Chart 11369. From the Rigolets to New Orleans, head southwest for 10 miles after clearing the U.S. 11 Hwy. Bascule Bridge and Norfolk & Southern Railroad Bridge (13- and 4-foot closed vertical clearances, respectively), and you should spot the New Orleans Lakefront Airport runway lights, some 4 miles away. Be careful of crab-trap floats strewn through the lake. If going to the South Shore Harbor Marina, you will keep the runway lights to starboard to enter the harbor at the east side of the airport.

If you are heading back to the GIWW via the Inner Harbor Navigational Canal (which most locals refer to as the Industrial Canal) leave the runway lights to port, and then turn to the south. The Industrial Canal is described toward the end of this chapter.

**Dockage:** The East Basin, which is just east of the Lakefront Airport and the Inner Harbor Navigation Canal, is home to South Shore Harbor Marina. Situated next door to Lakewood Airport, South Shore is not within walking distance to shoreside amenities. Less than 1 mile south of the Senator Ted Hickey Bridge, on the west side of the Inner Harbor Canal is Seabrook Harbor, home of The Marina at Pontchartrain Landing and Seabrook Harbor/Seabrook Marine. Seabrook Marine has a fuel dock (gas and diesel) and a full-service boat repair facility on the property. Pontchartrain Landing offers shuttle service to the French Quarter.

The passage to the other marinas and facilities, at what is known as West End, is another 5 miles west of the runway light structures, which extend more than a 0.5 mile into Lake Pontchartrain from the airport itself. Follow the lighted buoys at the entrance to the harbor. Follow flashing green "1" and flashing red "2" into the canal basin. The Coast Guard lighthouse (west of the airport) marks the entry into the twin basins of West End, the home of Schubert's Marina, Southern Yacht Club, New Orleans Yacht Club, M.G. Mayer Yacht Services and Orleans Marina. Call ahead for availability. Schubert's and M.G. Mayer Yacht Services have full-service boatyards and offer repairs. Markets and other shopping is only a block away from M.G. Mayer. A bus stop is conveniently located at the corner.

A large park with acres of landscaped waterfront along Lakeshore Drive separates the two basins.

# Lake Pontchartrain, South Shore, LA

| NEW ORLEANS | | Largest Vessel Accommodated | VHF Channel Monitored | Transient Berths / Total Berths | Approach / Dockside Depth | Floating Docks | Gas / Diesel | Groceries, Ice, Marine Supplies, Snacks | Repairs: Hull, Engine, Propeller | Lift (tonnage), Crane, Rail | Min/Max Amps | Laundry, Pool, Showers, Courtesy Car | Pump-Out Station | Nearby: Grocery Store, Motel, Restaurant |
|---|---|---|---|---|---|---|---|---|---|---|---|---|---|---|
| | | **Dockage** | | | | | | **Supplies** | | **Services** | | | | |
| 1. South Shore Harbor Marina | 504-245-3152 | 150 | 16 | 8/479 | 8/10 | - | GD | - | - | - | 30/100 | S | P | GR |
| 2. The Marina at Pontchartrain Landing (WiFi) | 504-286-8157 | - | - | call/40 | 25/15 | - | - | GIS | - | - | 20/100 | LPS | - | GMR |
| 3. Seabrook Harbor/Seabrook Marine 🖥 (WiFi) | 504-283-9801 | 120 | - | 12/33 | 25/15 | F | GD | IMS | HEP | L77,C20 | 30/50 | LSC | P | GMR |
| 4. Schubert's Marine 🖥 | 504-282-8136 | 80 | 16 | - | 10/10 | - | GD | IMS | HEP | C65 | 50/50 | - | - | GMR |
| 5. Southern Yacht Club | 504-288-4200 | - | 68 | call/150 | 8/8 | - | - | IS | - | - | 30/30 | PS | - | GMR |
| 6. New Orleans Yacht Club | 504-283-2581 | 60 | - | call/150 | 8/8 | F | - | IS | - | L3 | 30/30 | S | - | GMR |
| 7. M.G. Mayer Yacht Services (WiFi) | 504-282-1700 | 90 | - | call/6 | 8/8 | F | - | GIM | HEP | C35 | 30/50 | S | - | GR |
| 8. Orleans Marina 🖥 | 504-288-2351 | 110 | 16 | 15/353 | 8/10 | - | - | GM | - | - | 30/100 | LS | P | GMR |

🖥 Internet Access  (WiFi) Wireless Internet Access  WG Waterway Guide Cruising Club Partner  *(Information in the table is provided by the facilities.)*
See WaterwayGuide.com for current rates, fuel prices, web site addresses, and other up-to-the-minute information.

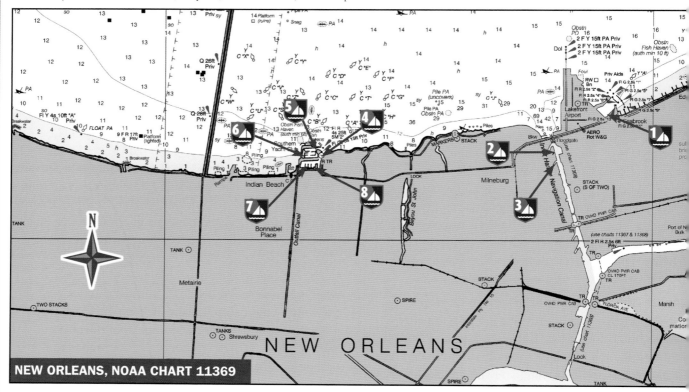

NEW ORLEANS, NOAA CHART 11369

New Orleans is also known as the "Big Easy" due to its "laissez-faire" nature and laid-back, easy style of living. It is a city of streetcars, courtyards, iron balconies and delectable cuisine. With Mardi Gras, Jazz Fest and other world-class special events drawing people from near and far, the excitement of the city is contagious.

The fire of 1788, started by gas lamps in New Orleans, crumbled the city into a smoky pile of rubble, leaving only 20 percent of the original structures erect. New Orleans rebuilt itself into the strong community that it is today. St. Charles streetcars (some electric) still travel the city past Creole cottages and shotgun houses. The city lives in a time warp, still unique and yet not totally discovered.

**Special Events:** New Orleans is full of interesting attractions to please your personal tastes. If you enjoy a good party with great music, food, parades and entertainment of all types, Mardi Gras (also called "Fat Tuesday") is an event to behold. Mardi Gras is always scheduled 47 days before Easter and celebrations are concentrated for about two weeks. Usually there is one major parade daily (weather permitting) and on some days there may be several large parades. The largest and most elaborate parades take place the last five days of the Mardi Gras season.

The New Orleans Jazz & Heritage Festival held at the end of April is a two-weekend, seven-day music festival featuring world-famous musicians in all genres. The New Orleans Wine and Food Experience is held Memorial Day weekend. The Satchmo Summer Fest honoring Louis "Satchmo" Armstrong occurs in early August and features the "music of the man who spread the language of jazz around the world." Music, theater and film festivals are held here year-round; a complete listing can be seen at neworleansonline.com.

**Attractions:** You don't want to rush in this wonderful city. A city tour is a good place to start, before exploring the French Quarter, Riverwalk, the Garden District and the famous cemeteries. Jackson Square is the perfect place to gather historical facts and watch people.

For history buffs, the National World War II Museum at 945 Magazine St. relives the war with interactive exhibits and a chilling audio/video presentation. The 31,000-square-foot Campaigns of Courage pavilion employs digital technology, personal stories and iconic artifacts to explore the experience of the average American fighting the war.

The popular Audubon Aquarium of the Americas and IMAX Theater is on the waterfront at 1 Canal Street. The Audubon Butterfly Garden and Insectarium is at 423 Canal Street. Both offer a nice break from the hustle and bustle of the streets.

French Quarter cemetery walking tours of the macabre are offered all around town. Another popular tour is

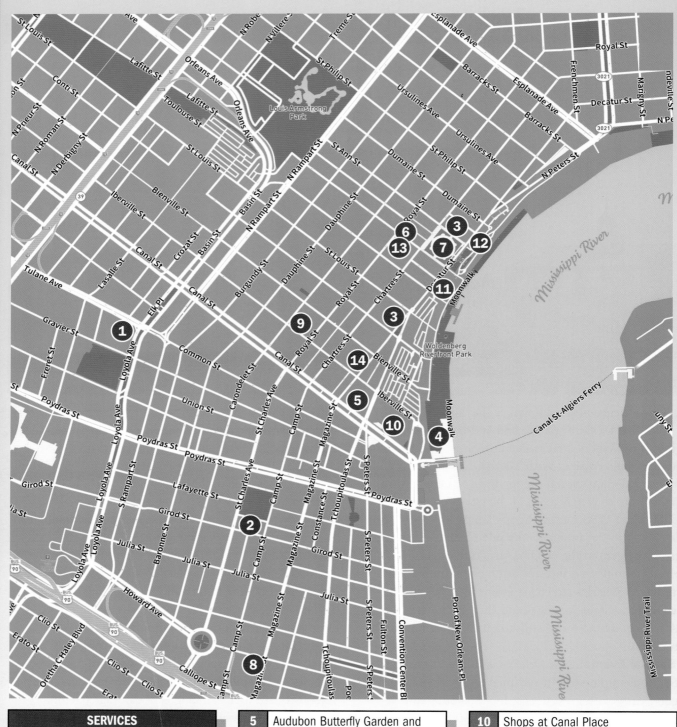

| SERVICES | |
|---|---|
| 1 | Library |
| 2 | Post Office |
| 3 | Visitor Information |
| **ATTRACTIONS** | |
| 4 | Audubon Aquarium |

| | |
|---|---|
| 5 | Audubon Butterfly Garden and Insectarium |
| 6 | Forever New Orleans |
| 7 | Jackson Square |
| 8 | National WW II Museum |
| **SHOPPING** | |
| 9 | Cigar Factory of New Orleans |

| | |
|---|---|
| 10 | Shops at Canal Place |
| 11 | Shops at Jax Brewery |
| **DINING** | |
| 12 | Café Du Monde |
| 13 | Gumbo Shop |
| 14 | House of Blues |

e Monde Creole at Forever New Orleans Shop at 622 oyal Street. This tour relives five generations of one ew Orleans family through the journal of Laura Locoul, Creole woman and plantation mistress. For tour nformation, visit mondecreole.com. Architectural tours f New Orleans are available through the Preservation esource Center (923 Tchoupitoulas St., 504-581-7032). hese tours are arranged by appointment with 24-hour otice.

**Shopping:** There is a West Marine Store on Harrison venue, 10 blocks south of the Orleans Marina. A hopping center just east of the marinas offers a upermarket, bank with ATM, drugstore, mail service enter and other businesses. Groceries can be delivered o your boat (for a fee) from Robért Fresh Market (504- 82-3428, robertfreshmarket.com). Just place your rocery order by 5:00 p.m., then select your delivery me and locations for the following day.

RTA bus service to the downtown area and the rench Quarter is available from the marinas. Maps and chedules are available at norta.com. Single or multi-day asses for streetcars and buses are available online or at ocal hotels, grocery stores, banks and retailers. Cabs and ar services are also very easy to catch from any location  this busy tourist city.

When uptown, go to Magazine Street and St. Charles venue to find an array of shops from trendy boutiques  CD warehouses that buy, trade and sell, to wine cellars nd tattoo parlors. The wildly popular French Quarter ffers 0.66 square miles (12 x 6 blocks) of shopping and ining. Royal Street is one of the more popular shopping treets with a variety of antique stores and art galleries. imilarly, Decatur Street and North Peter Street both ave some boutiques as well as national brand stores.

At Cigar Factory New Orleans (206 Bourbon St.), you an explore the on-site museum and watch cigar-making emos before choosing your own hand-rolled cigar.

Serious shoppers will enjoy the exclusive Shops at anal Place, which features such names as Tiffany & ompany, Saks Fifth Avenue, Armani, and Michael Kors. here is also a movie theater. Located at 333 Canal St. At 00 Decatur St., Jax Brewery on the riverfront has four oors of stores, restaurants, and bars and houses the JAX eer Museum.

**Dining:** Dining opportunities are endless. Several estaurants are within walking distance of the marinas long the east bank of the New Basin Canal and the est side of the harbors. The cuisine is excellent, arying from fine to casual dining, including New

Orleans cuisine, local seafood, Italian, Chinese and some of the best steaks from Texas. Day docks at some of the waterfront restaurants are popular, but subject to shoaling, wind, waves and "party boat" wakes. You can eat (and drink) just about anything, anywhere, anytime in this city. Just walk around and see what suits your fancy.

Since the 1860s, Café Du Monde (800 Decatur St.), open 24 hours a day, has been the city's original French market coffee stand. Hot beignets, coffee and iced coffee are their specialties. The Gumbo Shop has a sampler of different New Orleans specialties (630 Saint Peter St.) and is open 11:00 a.m. to 11:00 p.m. daily, with a moderate price range. Another landmark is Landry's Restaurant, located at the south shore at the mouth of the New Basin Canal. Boaters are welcome to tie up at the Landry's bulkhead while dining. You can eat (and drink) just about anything, anywhere, anytime in this city. Just walk around and see what suits your fancy.

New Orleans is a city that doesn't sleep. Jazz clubs abound, and nightclubs go from upscale to funky. The House of Blues (225 Decatur St., 504-310-4999) was opened by original Blues Brother Dan Aykroyd, Aerosmith and others. The club offers live music and a restaurant. See houseofblues.com for details. For more options, visit bigeasy.com.

# ■ LOCKING OUT OF NEW ORLEANS

Remember that when entering the Mississippi River from any direction consider contacting the Lower Mississippi River (LMR), Vessel Traffic Services (VTS). For this section use VHF Channel 12. They will want to know the name, type, location, and destination of your vessel.

The Inner Harbor Navigational Canal, referred to locally as the Industrial Canal, is the route from Lake Pontchartrain to the Mississippi River. Time your trip with the morning and evening bridge curfews in mind. The bridges on this route open and close at different times in the morning and afternoon to accommodate traffic.

Note that the **bridges** (VHF Channel 13) and the **locks** (VHF Channel 14) typically use separate radio channels. It is the responsibility of the boater to independently coordinate all lock and bridge crossings.

**NAVIGATION:** Use Chart 11369. Heading south, you will leave Lake Pontchartrain and enter the Inner Harbor Navigation Channel. When entering the Inner Harbor Navigational Canal you will pass under the Seabrook Bridge, which has been renamed the **Sen. Ted Hickey (Seabrook) Bridge**. This is a lift bridge with a 44-foot closed vertical clearance. It opens on signal from 7:00 a.m. to 8:00 p.m., except from 7:00 a.m. to 8:30 a.m. and from 5:00 p.m. to 6:30 p.m., when it may not open due to rush-hour traffic. After 8:00 p.m., at least a 2-hour notice is required. Contact the bridge on VHF Channel 13 or 16 if you need a greater vertical clearance. Immediately after the Ted Hickey Bridge is the **Seabrook Railroad Bascule Bridge**. The bridge is usually open unless a train is approaching. It has a 1-foot vertical clearance when closed. Contact the Seabrook Railroad Bridge on VHF Channel 13.

The next bridge traveling south is the **Danzinger (U.S. 90/Chef Menteur Hwy.) Lift Bridge**, with a charted 50-foot closed vertical clearance. (Note: Four-hour advanced notice is required for an opening at the Danzinger Bridge.)

The **I-10 Highway Bridge** (115-foot fixed vertical clearance) is just before the **Alamonaster Highway & Railroad Bridge**, which is usually open (no vertical clearance when closed).

The Inner Harbor Navigational Canal merges with the GIWW at Mile 2 EHL at the turning basin and continues toward the Mississippi River on what is commonly called the Industrial Canal. The Industrial Canal narrows to the dual-purpose **Florida Ave. & Southern Railroad Bascule Bridge** with a closed clearance of 0 feet. It opens on signal, except between 6:30 a.m. and 8:30 a.m. and between 3:30 p.m. and 6:45 p.m. Monday through Friday, when the bridge need not open. The last bridge before the Industrial Locks is the **North Claiborne Ave. (Judge Seeber) Lift Bridge**, more commonly known as the Claiborne Avenue Lift Bridge. The bridge has a closed vertical clearance of 40 feet.

## The Industrial Lock

The Industrial Lock is 5 miles down the Mississippi from the Harvey Canal (GIWW Mile 0) on the Mississippi River. It was built between 1918 and 1923 and measures 626 feet long by 75 feet wide. In 2016 it underwent extensive repairs and was closed for an extended period. NOAA Chart 11369 gives a good presentation of the three locks–Harvey, Algiers and Industrial–and the distance/directions between them. A Coast Guard station is on the west side of the Industrial Lock. Be aware that the Coast Guard occasionally conducts safety and documentation checks here. When locking through, the lockmaster will often direct you to hold position at "the dolphins," which are the large semi-circular structures that extend outward along each side of the canal. Do not attempt to tie up to the dolphins or any structure near the lock. Engines must be in idle, ready to make a move at any moment to maneuver through traffic.

**NAVIGATION:** Use Chart 11367, 11368 and 11369. Contact the lockmaster on VHF Channel 14 while you are between the Florida Avenue and Southern Railway and the Claiborne Avenue bridges. Have your boat name and registration number available along with the length, beam and draft of your vessel. The lockmaster will inform you of the traffic lineup and provide instructions for entering the lock. You may want to have fenders on both sides of the boat with ample line (at least 30 feet) fore and aft. A dock pole is handy for keeping the boat away from the muddy concrete sidewalls of the chamber. Boats less than 40 feet usually use one breast line.

Once inside, the lockmaster may ask for one crewmember wearing a personal flotation device (loosely enforced) to stand ready on the bow with a line. The line should be about 30 feet in length with a loop tied in one end. You may be asked to pass the looped end an attendant on top of the wall. Make one turn with ne other end around a mid-ship cleat, pull it taught, nd secure by hand. Remember, the boats elevation will e going up or down, so tend the line at all times and on't pull the line taught and secure it to a cleat. you nust be able to tighten or loosen the line when the boats evation changes. A secured line on a boat that is going o drop 8 feet will have serious consequences.

You may be asked to "float the chamber," which means ou will hold your boat, by power, in the middle of ne lock. You may be instructed to tie side by side with nother vessel. The most unlikely and untenable position to line up in any fashion behind a large tow vessel. lined up behind a tow vessel use a bow and stern ne. Then, after you have changed elevation, consider king two turns on a cleat, so you can handle the prop ash from the tow ahead. "Red Flag" tows, carrying azardous cargo, fly red flags on their barges and display blue light at night. Regulations prohibit passenger and leasure craft from sharing the lock with a "Red Flag" w.

The usual lift at the lock is 3 to 6 feet, but during ringtime, floods can be over 10 feet. Tie-up procedures ary, and many times securing to the hip of a tug or arge is better than the normal wall position.

On the south side of the Industrial Lock, the t. Claude Ave. Bascule Bridge monitors the pening of the locks; however, you must contact the ridge (VHF Channel 13) and ask for an opening. It pens on signal, except between 6:30 a.m. and 8:30 a.m. nd between 3:30 p.m. and 6:45 p.m., Monday through riday, when the bridge need not open. Once in the ver, you are required to check in with the Gretna Light

traffic service on VHF Channel 67 until you reach the next lock out point. Monitor VHF Channel 67 at all times while in the river.

## ■ TO THE MISSISSIPPI RIVER

A decision about which westward route to take should be made before entering the Mississippi River. The choices are the Algiers Lock (Route 1) or the Harvey Lock (Route 2). Overall, the Algiers Lock is a longer route and will have much more commercial traffic than Harvey Lock; however, the Algiers Lock is 4 miles downriver and the Harvey Lock is 5 miles upriver. Mississippi River currents are strong enough at times to make the Algiers Alternative Route (AAR) the first choice, in spite of the heavy commercial traffic and occasional delays while waiting in the canal before the lock, or in the open river.

### Route 1: Algiers Lock

**NAVIGATION:** Use Chart 11367. The Algiers Alternate Route has three bridges. The first, a mile downstream from the Algiers Lock, is the 100-foot fixed vertical clearance **General de Gaulle (SR 407) Bridge.** Next, 3.5 miles farther downstream, is the **Missouri Pacific Railroad Bridge** (100-foot clearance when raised, usually open), which is followed by the **Belle Chasse Hwy. (SR 23) Lift Bridge** with a 40-foot closed vertical clearance. Openings are restricted during traffic rush hours from 6:00 a.m. to 8:30 a.m. and from

## GIWW Mile 0: Harvey Lock

If you have gotten this far, you know the Intracoastal Waterway (ICW) is a commercial and recreational boater's highway. Its length runs for some 3,000 miles to Florida and around the Gulf of Mexico to Brownsville, TX, on the Border of Mexico. (Distances on the ICW are measured in statute miles, while "outside" or offshore passages are measured in nautical miles.)

The ICW encompasses two main waterways: the Atlantic ICW and the Gulf ICW (GIWW). Within the GIWW are two additional subcategories—East of Harvey Lock and West of Harvey Lock, referring to Harvey Lock on the Mississippi River (Mile 0). To clarify, the waterways are divided as follows:

- Atlantic ICW: Mile 0 (Norfolk, VA) to Mile 1240 (Key West, FL).
- Gulf ICW (GIWW): Mile 0 (San Carlos Bay/Okeechobee Waterway) to Mile 150 (Anclote Key, FL).
- GIWW EHL: Mile 375 (St. George Sound) to Mile 0 (Harvey Lock).
- GIWW WHL: Mile 0 (Harvey Lock) to Mile 682 (Brownsville, TX)

Note: In case you were counting, there really are technically three "Mile 0" designations on the ICW—one on the ICW and two on the GIWW.

3:30 p.m. to 5:30 p.m., Monday through Friday (except federal holidays).

The Algiers Alternate Route rejoins the GIWW at Barataria Bayou. There are no amenities for pleasure boats until reaching Lafitte and the Barataria Waterway.

## Route 2: Harvey Lock

One reason to take the Harvey Lock route is the trip upriver itself. Along this route you will enjoy the full view of New Orleans: the French Quarter at Jackson Square and St. Louis Cathedral (the oldest active cathedral in the U.S.), the red brick Pontalbo apartment on either side of Jackson Square (the oldest apartment buildings in the U.S.), the French Market, the Moon Walk (scenic boardwalk) and much more. Canal Street, where ferries still cross the river to the "west bank," downtown high-rise buildings and miles of wharves lined with oceangoing freighters and passenger cruise ships add to the scenery. You will also pass the site of the 1984 World's Fair, now called Riverwalk.

The Harvey Lock/Harvey Canal route is generally the preferred route for pleasure vessels. This is because the Harvey Lock is much shorter (415 feet long) than the Algiers Lock (760 feet long). Also, the Harvey Canal is narrower and more congested than the wider, straighter Alternate Route, so there is much less breaking of tows and barge handling than on the Alternate Route and at the Algiers Lock.

⚠️ On rare occasions there is a small control vessel directing pleasure craft and some smaller commercial vessels to the Harvey Lock, leaving no option to take the alternate Algiers Lock route.

**NAVIGATION:** Use Chart 11367. The Harvey Canal and Lock are 5 miles upriver. The Canal Street ferry crosses the Mississippi River north of Algiers Point.

Usually you will experience only short delays before locking through. When it is necessary to wait in the river, stay close to the bank on either side to stay out of the mainstream currents and traffic.

## Cruising Options

Harvey Lock represents Mile 0 on the GIWW. We will now start referring to miles west of Harvey Lock (WHL) through Louisiana and Texas to the Mexico border.

# New Orleans to the Texas Border

 Mile 0 (Harvey Lock)–Mile 265 WHL (TX Border)      LA: Channel 13

**CHARTS**  11311, 11339, 11342, 11343, 11345, 11347, 11348, 11349, 11350, 11351, 11352, 11354, 11355, 11365, 11367

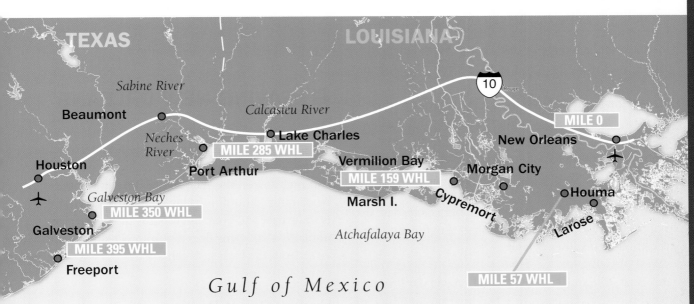

The western portion of the GIWW begins at the Harvey Lock. Mileage is denoted as WHL, or West of Harvey Lock on the Mississippi River at Mile 0. This is an area where Acadians from Nova Scotia began settling in 1755, and in recent years, fishermen from Asia. It is common to hear commercial skippers on the VHF channels converse in English, French or a mixture of both, as well as Vietnamese. Many cruising boats pass by Mile 0 at the Harvey Lock that separates the GIWW from the Mississippi River. From here west, the waterways offer great diversity and interest for hundreds of miles worthy of exploration.

The GIWW trip from New Orleans to Freeport is just over 400 statute miles. It is a rewarding voyage and New Orleans is a good place to start. Louisiana is a historic picturesque landscape with a laid-back life style. It is well worth the time and experience to know these waters and the people who live here. Just steps from a boat dock you can find resort style living at hotels and casinos where you can relax and enjoy swimming, eating, gambling, shows, dancing and more.

Louisiana waterways retain much of the flavor of the past, when they were commercial ditches providing a primary means of transporting goods and people to and from the Mississippi River at New Orleans. The Harvey Canal was originally a private enterprise dug by hand in the early 1720s from the Mississippi River to the Barataria Waterway. Goods for New Orleans had to be unloaded on the Harvey Canal side, moved over the levee and then loaded in boats on the river. The lock was completed in 1934.

From the Mississippi River through the Harvey Lock on to the west is an area of great complexity in terms of navigation, commercial traffic, and the many bayous and rivers that cross the GIWW, some of which are navigable to the Gulf of Mexico. Careful preparation and planning is essential for Louisiana waters.

Commercial traffic is prominent on the waterways, and in harbors, facilities and services. A cruising boat will encounter large tugs and tows. Other commercial traffic will include shrimp boats, oyster trawlers, supply vessels, crew boats and shallow water drilling barges. VHF radio is the accepted communication medium.

You can get valuable information readily if you request advice from commercial captains. Yield the right-of-way to commercial vessels. When meeting, crossing or overtaking a vessel, you should call the vessel (on VHF Channel 13) by name if possible, and request instructions for safe passage. If you are putting up a big wake, slow down, or ask the captain if it will be a problem for them.

Always use anchoring information with caution. A beautiful inlet may have been deep with good holding a short time ago but could have shoaled, or be occupied by an abandoned barge or drilling rig. Many inlets to drilling sites that were great spots to drop the hook are now barricaded at the entrance, or to shallow.

It is a long quiet stretch from Lake Charles to the upper coast of Texas. Soon after you cross the Texas border you are in Port Arthur, where you can enter Sabine Lake and find boater-friendly marinas. Then you begin another long quiet stretch to Galveston. The Galveston–Clear Lake area is a vacation destination where the pace of life is faster and more active. The list of opportunity and activity is endless. Anything and everything is readily available.

West of Galveston the Texas waterway is quiet and more sparsely populated. It is a reasonable day trip to Freeport and Surfside Beach where marinas and fuel are readily and easily available.

From New Orleans to Freeport marinas, fuel stops, marine stores, provisions and restaurants are available, but spaced far apart, so study the charts and plan for each day's run. Anchorages can be spaced far apart, but they are available and often in a quiet isolated sanctuary. There are many twists and turns along this stretch of the GIWW and you will encounter a significant amount of commercial traffic.

All locks west of the Harvey Canal are designed to prevent saltwater intrusion into the marshlands and to assist in flood control; they were not designed for changing from one elevation to another. The exception is Bayou Boeuf, located at Mile 93.3 WHL. It is capable of raising and lowering traffic but only during times of extreme flooding. A majority of the time Bayou Boeuf operates the same as a floodgate. The lockmaster at all of the locks are normally only needed for traffic control through the open lock. Call the lockmaster on

Note that all **locks** between New Orleans and Lake Charles use VHF Channel 14.

VHF Channel 14 to receive instructions and permission to proceed through the lock. It is a good idea to check the *Local Notice to Mariners*, or call ahead for possible closures.

The Southwest Pass in the northern Gulf of Mexico leads into the Mississippi River then on to New Orleans 92 statute miles north. Offshore from the Southwest Pass to Freeport is a distance of just over 300 nm. Along the coast between Southwest Pass and Freeport, there are multiple jetties and inlets each with its unique conditions, challenges and opportunities. Offshore passe are discussed later in this chapter.

# ■ LEAVING NEW ORLEANS

There are two routes to the Barataria Waterway: the Harvey Canal (the preferred lock for pleasure craft) and the Algiers Alternate Route (primarily used by commercial traffic). This section of the GIWW is industrial and commercial. It is mostly straight, unmarked and runs deep up to the channel banks. Stay away from the banks, which are littered with wrecks and cypress stumps.

## Harvey Canal Route

**NAVIGATION:** Use Chart 11367. Crew members are required to wear PFDs at **Harvey Lock**, even though the requirement does not seem to be enforced. Car and boat traffic will impact wait time. Have fenders in place on both sides of the boat and ample line fore and aft. The lines will be looped around bollards built into the walls of the lock. Boats less than 40 feet usually use one breast line, while larger vessels usually use a fore and aft line. If an attendant is on duty, he may ask for a line with a loop in the end to tie to his line and secure on top of the lock. The line should be at least 30 feet in length. All locks between New Orleans and Lake Charles use VHF Channel 14. Call the lockmaster on VHF Channel 14 for instructions before entering the lock. Contact by phone: Monday through Friday, 7:00 a.m. to 3:30 p.m. at 504-366-4683. At all other times, call 504-366-5187. Lock updates and status can be checked at the web site for the Army Corp of Engineers (New Orleans District).

On the west end of the lock are overhead cables with a height of 90 feet. The **Harvey Canal (SR 18) Bascule Bridge** and **Union Pacific Railroad Bascule Bridge**, both with a 7-foot clearance and located on the rest side of the lock, should go up automatically when the west lock gate opens. You will pass under two more sets of power cables with heights exceeding 120 feet. At Mile 0.8 WHL the Harvey Canal travels under the fixed **West Bank Expressway Twin Bridges** with a 95-foot vertical clearance. At Mile 2.8 WHL you will encounter the **Lapalco Blvd. Bascule Bridge** with a closed vertical clearance of 45 feet. The Lapalco Bridge opens on signal, except from 6:30 a.m. to 8:30 a.m. and 3:45 p.m. to 5:45 p.m., Monday through Friday (except holidays), when the draw need not open. At Mile 6.3 WHL the Harvey Lock joins the Algiers Channel at the flashing red "2+1" light to the south. From there you continue west in the GIWW heading into Bayou Barataria.

**Dockage:** There are no marinas along this stretch of the waterway. On the south side of the Harvey Canal it is possible to tie along the bulkhead of the Boomtown Casino at Mile 4.6 WHL. Water depth along the dock, in front of the parking lot, is at least 5 feet, and approach depths are up to 12 feet. It is an old poorly maintained bulkhead that can be hazardous to a boats hull, and it can be difficult to find something on which to tie a line. Supply boats use the bulkhead as a location for crew changes and re-supply. There is no one to call in advance, but there is usually plenty of space available. The casino is within easy walking distance.

**Anchorage:** At Mile 4.4 WHL, immediately east of Boomtown Casino, are two manmade lagoons (i.e., mud pits). The westerly of the two is used by the casino and is not accessible to cruising boats. The other is devoid of all development and can accommodate about four boats at anchor. There is almost always room. Depths average 7 feet, but proceed with caution to avoid unwanted encounters with unknown shoals. The bottom is very soft mud and protection is good. The Harvey Lock is easily accessible from here. An emergency-only anchorage is available at Hero Canal (Mile 7 WHL) in 7-foot depths. This area is heavy with tow traffic.

## Algiers Alternate Route

Westbound pleasure boats may be forced to use the **Algiers Lock** during times of high water generating too much downstream current. On this route you will pass under three power cables with clearances from 117 feet to 126 feet. You will encounter one fixed bridge and two lift bridges on the Algiers route. Heading west, the first is the **General de Gaulle (SR 407) Bridge** with a fixed clearance of 100 feet. The second is the **Missouri Pacific Railroad Bridge** (usually open)

# Barataria Waterway, LA

| | | Largest Vessel Accommodated | VHF Channel Monitored | Transient Berths / Total Berths | Approach / Dockside Depth (reported) | Floating Docks | Gas / Diesel | Groceries, Ice, Marine Supplies, Snacks | Repairs: Hull, Engine, Propeller | Lift (tonnage), Crane, Rail | Min/Max Amps | Laundry, Pool, Showers, Courtesy Car | Pump-Out Station | Nearby: Grocery Store, Motel, Restaurant |
|---|---|---|---|---|---|---|---|---|---|---|---|---|---|---|
| | | **Dockage** | | | | | **Supplies** | | **Services** | | | | | |
| **LAFITTE** | | | | | | | | | | | | | | |
| 1. Joe's Landing | 504-689-4304 | - | - | call/8 | - | - | G | IS | - | - | - | - | - | R |
| 2. Seaway Marina Lafitte  15 WHL | 504-689-3148 | 60 | 71 | 5/150 | 10/8 | - | GD | GIMS | HEP | L20,R | 30/30 | - | - | GMR |
| 3. Team Lafitte Harbor Marina  15 WHL | 504-689-2013 | 52 | 80 | 4/52 | 7/6 | - | GD | GIMS | - | L8,C | 30/50 | LS | - | GMR |
| **BARATARIA PASS** | | | | | | | | | | | | | | |
| 4. Nautical Pointe Marina–PRIVATE 🖥 | 985-693-7892 | - | - | - | - | - | - | IMS | HEP | - | 30/30 | - | - | GMR |
| 5. Sand Dollar Marina | 985-787-2500 | 65 | - | call/56 | - | F | D | IMS | - | L5 | 30/30 | - | P | GMR |
| 6. Hurricane Hole Marina 🖥 WIFI | 985-441-9903 | - | - | 2/60 | 10/10 | - | GD | IMS | - | - | 30/200+ | PS | - | GMR |

🖥 Internet Access  WIFI Wireless Internet Access  WG Waterway Guide Cruising Club Partner  (Information in the table is provided by the facilities.)
See WaterwayGuide.com for current rates, fuel prices, web site addresses, and other up-to-the-minute information.

with a closed clearance of 2 feet. The third is the **Belle Chase Hwy. (SR 23) Lift Bridge** with a closed clearance of 40 feet. The Belle Chase bridge opens on signal, except from 6:00 a.m. to 8:30 a.m. and from 3:30 p.m. to 5:30 p.m., Monday through Friday (except federal holidays), when the draw need not open.

One-half mile south of the intersection of the Harvey and Algiers channels the large imposing West Closure Complex (WCC) extends into the GIWW. The one billion dollar WCC project was completed in 2013 as a part of the New Orleans Drainage System to protect against damage from tropical storm events. It is made up of a 225-foot floodgate, the world's largest pump station, floodwalls and earthen levy. The gates are usually open and may not have an attending lockmaster. (No contact phone number is available.)

## ■ BARATARIA WATERWAY TO THE GULF (SOUTH)

In the picturesque area from the town of Crown Point to Lafitte (Mile 10 WHL to Mile 15 WHL), homes, businesses and parks line the waterway. Most have boat docks and/or ramps. The town of Lafitte is named after Jean Lafitte, the most infamous pirate of the Gulf Coast. Legend has it that many of his treasures are buried along the Barataria Waterway. Pirates no longer use this passage to the Gulf of Mexico, but cruisers and fishermen enjoy its scenic bays, bayous and marshland.

**NAVIGATION:** Use Charts 11365 and 11367. Heading south from the GIWW in Lafitte at Mile 15 WHL the Barataria Waterway is a 35-mile trip through scenic bayou country to Grand Isle on the Gulf of Mexico. The waterway offers a well-earned respite after maneuvering through the Mississippi River locks and the New Orleans waterfront. The channel is well marked by lighted fixed markers as it meanders through the Barataria Waterway. Controlling depth for the waterway appears to be 5 feet. The **Crown Point Highway Bridge** crosses the GIWW at Mile 11.9 WHL with a 73-foot fixed vertical clearance. **Kerner (SR 302) Swing Bridge** opens on signal at Mile 35.7 WHL (with 7-foot closed vertical clearance).

**Dockage:** There are few marina facilities. All marinas are very limited in dockage, fuel and supplies. It is highly advisable to call ahead and make plans before you begin this trip. A few miles from the GIWW are Joe's Landing, Seaway Marina Lafitte and Team Lafitte Harbor Marina. All three have limited overnight dockage. Joe's Landing sells gas; Seaway and Team Lafitte Harbor sell gas and diesel and offer some repairs.

Heading south, the remaining 28 miles of the Barataria Waterway lead through scenic and less-developed bayou country, ending at Grand Isle, Louisiana's offshore fishing capital and the entrance to the Gulf of Mexico. The Sand Dollar Marina on Grand Isle offers diesel and has a motel, restaurant and groceries. Nearby Nautical Pointe is private (no transient slips). Hurricane Hole Marina at the west end of Grand Isle (by Caminada Pass) sells fuel and may have space for you.

**Anchorage:** There are two anchoring possibilities before the Kerner Swing Bridge: Bonne Isle and Lafitte (Mile 14.9 WHL), where you will find 8 to 11 feet. In Lafitte, it is possible to anchor just southwest of the airboat docks. Boat traffic dies down at night.

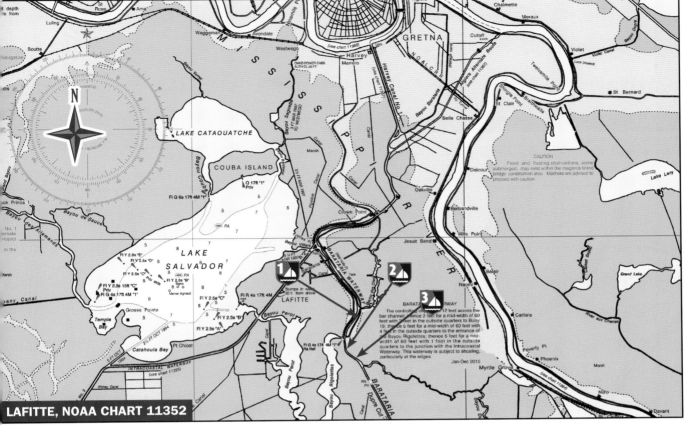

**LAFITTE, NOAA CHART 11352**

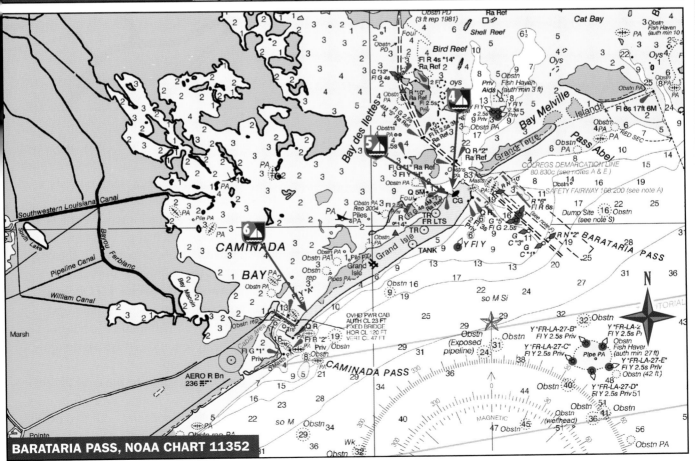

**BARATARIA PASS, NOAA CHART 11352**

# GIWW, LA

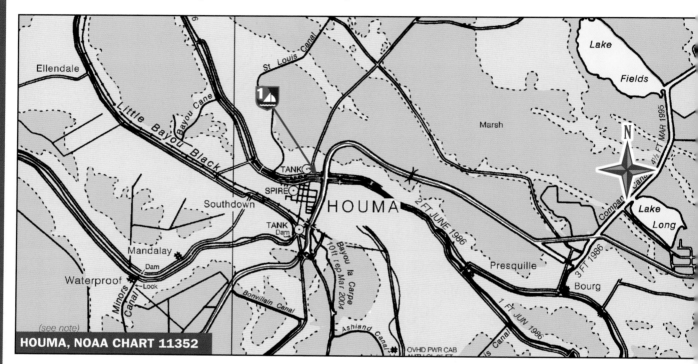

| HOUMA | | | | | | Dockage | | | | Supplies | | | | Services | | | |
|---|---|---|---|---|---|---|---|---|---|---|---|---|---|---|---|---|---|
| | Largest Vessel Accommodated | VHF Channel Monitored | Transient Berths / Total Berths | Approach / Dockside Depth (reported) | Floating Docks | Groceries, Ice, Marine Supplies, Snacks | Gas / Diesel | Repairs: Hull, Engine, Propeller | Lift (tonnage), Crane, Rail | Laundry, Pool, Showers, Courtesy Car | Min/Max Amps | Pump-Out Station | Nearby: Grocery Store, Motel, Restaurant | | | | |
| 1. Downtown Marina of Houma  60 WHL | | 985-873-6408 | 140 | – | 5/5 | 7/5 | – | – | – | – | – | 30/50 | – | P | GMR |

⌑ Internet Access  **WiFi** Wireless Internet Access  **WG** Waterway Guide Cruising Club Partner  *(Information in the table is provided by the facilities.)*
See WaterwayGuide.com for current rates, fuel prices, web site addresses, and other up-to-the-minute information.

**HOUMA, NOAA CHART 11352**

## ◼ BARATARIA WATERWAY TO HOUMA (WEST)

**NAVIGATION:** Use Charts 11355 and 11365. In the warmer months, hyacinths may be so thick on this waterway that they impede the passage of pleasure vessels. Large clusters sometimes hang on hidden debris. At Mile 20 WHL, leave red daybeacons "2" and "4" to the north and be sure to stay in the channel near Lake Salvador.

### Larose—GIWW Mile 35 WHL

The picturesque Acadian town of Larose straddles the intersection at Bayou Lafourche (pronounced "Lafoosh"). At Mile 35 WHL you cross under the **Larose Highway (SR 308) Bridge** with a 73-foot fixed vertical clearance. Small shipyards are located at both ends of town, while fishing trawlers and pleasure boats border the banks on both the GIWW and Bayou Lafourche. There is a No-Wake Zone in the area of the shipyards for about 2 miles where small rafts are used for work platforms. Overnight dockage is scarce.

The Bayou Lafourche Channel intersects the GIWW at Mile 35.5 WHL. There are many restaurants and grocery stores located in close proximity to the channel. Immediately south of the channel is a floodgate followed by the **Bayou Lafourche Lift Bridge** with a closed vertical clearance of 2 feet and open clearance of 73 feet. Bayou Lafourche is navigable north to Thibodeaux (pronounced "Tib-ah-dough") and south 35 miles to the Gulf of Mexico, but there are many obstacles. Going south to the Gulf of Mexico you will encounter one fixed bridge, four lift bridges, two pontoon bridges, two floodgates, and two overhead power cables with uncharted heights.

West of Larose at Mile 35.6 is the **Larose-Bourg Cutoff (SR 1) Lift Bridge** with a closed vertical clearance of 35 feet (opens on signal). Continuing west on the Larose-Bourg Cutoff is the **Bayou Blue Pontoon Bridge** at GIWW Mile 49.8 WHL. This bridge is difficult to see until you are close to it. A pontoon bridge is not a swing bridge (no vertical clearance) and can best be described as a barge that is pulled out of your way by cables, which hover just under the water where they cannot be seen. The bridge opens on signal–one long blast followed by a short blast, or contact on VHF Channel 13. Be sure to allow time for the cables to sink to the bottom before proceeding.

At Mile 48.8 WHL you cross the Bourg Canal. Tow captains and local boaters refer to it as the "49er." Even though this is a heavy commercial area, no fuel or other conveniences are available for pleasure craft.

At Mile 54.4 you will encounter the **Prospect Blvd. Bridge** with a fixed 73-foot vertical clearance. The GIWW then makes a turn to the south and enters Houma. The entire 10-mile-long section from Mile 52 WHL to Mile 62 WHL should be considered a "No-Wake" area.

## Houma–GIWW Mile 57 WHL

Houma was named for the Houma ("red") Indians who settled there in the early 18th century. It is a pleasant mid-size city where cruising boaters are welcome; however, most shoreside amenities are not within walking distance.

**NAVIGATION:** Use Chart 11355. The **Park Avenue Bridge** at Mile 57.6 and **Main Street Bridge** at Mile 57.7 WHL both have 73-foot fixed vertical clearances.

At Mile 59.5 WHL, the Houma Navigational Canal goes south from the GIWW to Cat Island Pass at the Gulf of Mexico, near the picturesque cities of Cocodrie and Chauvin. The waterway makes a 45-degree turn to the west and many skippers have inadvertently wandered southward into the wide-open canal. If you are approaching a swing bridge, instead of a bascule bridge, you are in the wrong channel.

The last bridge going west is on the west side of Houma at Mile 59.9 WHL. The **Bayou DuLarge (SR 315) Bascule Bridge** (40-foot closed vertical clearance) opens on signal, except from 6:30 a.m. to 8:30 a.m., 11:45 a.m. to 12:15 p.m., 12:45 p.m. to

1:15 p.m. and 4:30 p.m. to 6:00 p.m., Monday through Friday, when the draw need not open.

No marinas or fuel docks are located between Houma and the next major stop, Morgan City (approximately 40 miles); plan your trip accordingly.

**Dockage:** The Downtown Marina of Houma, at Mile 57.6 WHL below the Park Avenue and Main Street Bridges, is a small marina that is mostly for transient boats. The marina is located in a small park immediately off the GIWW between the two bridges and is easy to see. Boats can tie up within feet of the GIWW at the bulkhead or take a slip just inside the marina (5-foot dockside depths). This marina is equipped with shore power, fresh water and pump-out facilities but no restrooms or fuel. The dockmaster must be contacted by phone to come to the marina and unlock the power box. Access to slips is on a first-come, first-serve basis. The landscaped park offers a great place to relax or exercise and also includes a message board for local information.

Access to fuel in Houma is a challenge. With prior arrangement, gas or diesel fuel may be available at Retif Oil located at the intersection of the Houma Canal, on the north side of the GIWW. No transient slips are available at Retif. It is recommended that transiting boaters take on fuel prior to reaching Houma.

The area is proud of the centuries-old recipes passed down through the generations and claims some of the best gumbo, ètoufèes and creole dishes around. There are several restaurants of various "flavors" west of the marina in the Main Street area. Free wireless Internet access is available at the Coffee Zone, also on Main Street. A West Marine sits on the west side of town, but is not within walking distance. Friendly cabbies will come take you to Walmart or other stores for provisioning. The excellent web site houmatravel.com details attractions, dining, lodging and events in the area.

# ■ HOUMA TO MORGAN CITY

The most scenic section on the Louisiana GIWW is probably the area from Houma to Morgan City. Majestic cypress trees line the banks. Their knee-like roots protrude from the water surface to breathe, and Spanish moss hangs from tree branches. Keep a lookout for eagles.

**NAVIGATION:** Use Chart 11355. Beware of submerged pilings from Mile 65 WHL to 75 WHL. Stay close to the middle of the channel. At Mile 74 WHL, submerged pilings are along the northern half of the channel with Lake Hackberry to the north. During the summer, water hyacinths may cover the GIWW. Floating debris may be submerged underneath the hyacinths, so be careful.

From Mile 76 WHL through Mile 80 WHL the GIWW cuts through Lake Cocodrie. The lake is very shallow but the GIWW is well marked. The waterway becomes part of Bayou Cocodrie then Bayou Black east of Morgan City.

Westbound between Mile 84 WHL and Morgan City, the GIWW and the contiguous waterways can be confusing and very busy. The splendor and beauty of the Atchafalaya (discussed below) is replaced with a conspicuous display of commercial and industrial activity. At Mile 84 WHL you enter Bayou Black. The Bayou Black Channel goes to the north (starboard). Continue west in the GIWW.

**Anchorage:** Shallow-draft boast can anchor at Bay Wallace at Mile 80.4 WHL in 5 to 6 feet. A better-known anchorage is at Bayou Black, just east of Mile 84 WHL. This is also a designated mooring area for large barges waiting for dock space and many times they arrive during the night. Your best bet is to proceed well past the first bend, beyond the pipes lining the bayou. Show a bright anchor light and for added safety you may want a stern line to the trees ashore. The bayou is wider than the chart would have you believe and depths are 11 feet or better.

## Bayou Boeuf Lock–GIWW Mile 93 WHL

**NAVIGATION:** Use Charts 11354 and 11355. Contact the Bayou Boeuf (pronounced "buff") Lock on VHF Channel 14 or by phone at 985-384-7202 or 985-384-7626. If the locks are closed for repairs, Bayou Chene at Mile 85 WHL is the bypass route. During times of flooding, **Bayou Boeuf Lock** can close at both ends

nd change a vessel's elevation. Most of the time it operates the same as a water intrusion floodgate.

If the lock is changing elevation be prepared with fenders and lines. Bayou Boeuf Lock has timbered walls. The timbers are horizontal and cleats are far apart, so tying can be difficult. Ample lines should be in place fore and aft. Vessels less than 40 feet should be able to tie with one line amidships. Tie fenders vertically. The lines and fenders will not be used if the lockmaster directs you to "float the chamber." The Bayou Boeuf Locks have a depth over the sill of 13 feet, a width of 75 feet and a length of 1,150 feet.

When leaving the locks, check in with Berwick Traffic on VHF Channel 11. They will request your name, type of vessel and destination, and then will give you instructions, traffic information and the checkpoints where you should make location reports between the locks and Mile 102 WHL, the western limit of Berwick Traffic for pleasure boats.

⚠️ Just past the Bayou Boeuf Lock (at Mile 94.3 WHL) is a cable ferry that is difficult to spot. They might blow one horn when ferry starts crossing & one horn as all clear signal. Make sure the cable is clear before proceeding.

## Alternate Route: Bayou Chene—GIWW Mile 85 WHL

Mile 85 WHL marks the east intersection of the GIWW and Bayou Chene. The GIWW continues west (starboard), while the Bayou Chene Channel turns to the south (or port if you are westbound). The Bayou Chene Channel is navigable to Morgan City, but it adds 10 miles to the trip. The Bayou Chene route takes you through the delta of the Atchafalaya and some of the most pristine and beautiful swamplands in the state. The channel is 150-feet wide with depths of 10 to 15 feet.

**NAVIGATION:** Use Charts 11351, 11352, 11354 and 11355. The Bayou Chene Channel is only recommended as a bypass route if the locks at Bayou Boeuf are closed, or if you want to avoid the extended no-wake zone in Morgan City. The channel is mostly unmarked for the first miles until you reach green marker "15." Proceed along the Big Horn Bayou to green can buoy "1," at the Atchafalaya River. When entering the river make sure you keep green can "1" to the north (starboard) to avoid shallow water on the east side of the riverbank. Steer north upstream and follow the river through Sweet Bay Lake. The Atchafalaya River is well marked, wide and deep up to the GIWW at Mile 98 WHL. Currents during the spring months may warrant consideration if you are in a low-powered vessel.

## Morgan City–GIWW Mile 95 WHL

Morgan City is where the railroads for New Orleans, Opelousas, and Great Western came together. It was incorporated as Brashear City in 1860, the family name for the plantation upon which it was built. It was a hub where freight and passengers from rail and steamboats came together to continue on to Galveston, Houston, and other Texas ports. In later years it was renamed in honor of the railroad president, Charles Morgan.

Morgan City is homeport to more than a thousand fishing boats and what may be an equal number of workboats. It has a unique waterfront with a concrete seawall to keep out the floodwaters. The downtown city marina is hard to miss: Morgan City is spelled out in huge letters on the wall.

**NAVIGATION:** Use Charts 11354 and 11355. From Mile 85 to Mile 102 WHL, the GIWW is mostly a No-Wake Zone. Along this route, between Mile 93 WHL and Mile 102 WHL, you are operating within the boundaries of Berwick Traffic Control. Recreational boats are not required to contact them but can communicate with them on VHF Channel 11 to inform them of their intended route and provide requested information. More information is available at homeport.uscg.mil. Select Vessel Traffic Services in the shaded area to the right.

At Mile 95 WHL, turn north out of the GIWW into Berwick Bay. In about .25 mile you will encounter the **Southern Pacific Railroad Lift Bridge**. It is usually open and has an open vertical clearance of 73 feet (4-foot closed vertical clearance). The railroad bridge can be contacted on VHF Channel 13. If there is no answer try VHF Channel 11. The bridge lowers for trains many times day and night and can be lowered as much as 20 minutes before the train comes into view. A horn signal (four blasts) is clearly audible before the bridge is lowered. This area is headquarters for Berwick Traffic Control.

Immediately north of the railroad bridge are two highway bridges. The first is the **U.S. 90 Hwy. Bridge**, with a fixed vertical clearance of 73 feet. Next is the **Long Allan Bridge** with a fixed vertical clearance of 50 feet. During spring floods currents in the river can be over three knots.

**Dockage:** After you pass under the Southern Pacific Railroad Bridge, the Morgan City Public Dock is located just before the Highway 90 Bridge on the east side of Berwick Bay. The city bulkhead is currently not available for docking. The entire bulkhead and road alongside the

bulkhead have been demolished and a new bulkhead is currently under construction with no clear completion date.

Fuel is available for boats with vertical heights less than the 50-foot clearance of the Long Allan Bridge. Rio Fuel, primarily a commercial dock, is located north, up river, just past the US Highway 90 and Long Allan Bridges, on the east (Morgan City) side of the river. If you go under the middle span of the bridges, travel past Rio Fuel, then turn towards shore. About 100 yards from shore you can turn back to the Rio Fuel Dock. North of the bridges a shoal runs between the channel and Rio Fuel. The preferred route is to go under the bridge span on the Morgan City side of the river where you should find depths of about 15 feet to the fuel dock. You can call Rio Fuel at 985-384-8090.

Behind the seawall on the Morgan City side of the river are marine-oriented businesses, a post office, banks, grocery, hardware stores and other shopping. Morgan City has a historic downtown Main Street with a variety of shops, restaurants and museums. Download the Cajun Coast Travel Guide app for walking tour, history and more.

## Berwick–GIWW Mile 95 WHL

Berwick, with its little red lighthouse, is a small town in St. Mary Parish with a population of about 5,000. It is directly across the waterway from Morgan City and ideally located on waterways, highways and rail lines that support a significant economy that includes industry, oil, gas, fishing and other commercial businesses. The area also includes the 800,000-acre Atchafalaya Basin. It is one of the nation's largest natural water systems. It offers excellent recreational activity with a large population of bald eagles and black bear.

**Dockage:** The Berwick Town Docks are on the west side of the river directly across from Morgan City. It is clearly marked by 6-foot tall white letters, "Berwick." The letters are lighted at night. Approach depths should be at least 12 feet, and depth alongside the bulkhead should be more than 6 feet.

There is no water, electricity or other amenities, but dockage is free. Space is available for many boats and there is almost always room for at least one more. It is a nice place to stop but is noisy because of the trains and traffic on the bridges. Local fisherman may pass within feet of the bulkhead with little regard for their wakes. A grocery store and restaurant are within walking distance.

During extreme floodwater conditions (usually April and May) docks may be submerged and the floodgates closed. You can call ahead for local conditions at 985-384-8858 (day) or 985-384-7710 (night).

Beebee's Seafood Restaurant is the only shoreside amenity within walking distance. Beebee's is located at the base of the I-90 Bridge at 102 Bowman Street.

## Side Trip: North to the Mississippi

**NAVIGATION:** Use Chart 11354. Bayou Boeuf and the Lakeside Route to Port Allen join the GIWW at Mile 87 WHL. This provides access to Lake Palourde, a shallow pleasure boat area, and then north to the Mississippi River.

Continue north in Berwick Bay past the Morgan City waterfront until you see red "2" in the middle of the channel, just before Drews Island. You will be facing three channels: Atchafalaya Channel to the left, Flat Lake immediately right and the Morgan City Port Allen Channel farthest right. Take the Morgan City Port Allen Channel (mile markers denoted "MP"). The distance is approximately 55 miles. Port Allen lies just across the Mississippi River from downtown Baton Rouge (covered in previous chapter.) There are no facilities for recreational vessels.

## Side Trip: South to the Gulf

**NAVIGATION:** Use Chart 11354. South to the Gulf of Mexico can be initiated from three locations: Bayou Chene at Mile 85 WHL, Bayou Shaffer at Mile 94.5 WHL and the Atchafalaya River at Mile 95.5 WHL. All three of the routes take you through some of the most beautiful swamplands in the state. All three routes come together in the Lower Atchafalaya at Horseshoe Channel. Distance to the Gulf of Mexico, from the GIWW, is approximately 40 nm.

## ■ MORGAN CITY TO INTRACOASTAL CITY

The GIWW at the Atchafalaya River (Mile 98 WHL) extends westward to the Vermilion River and Intracoastal City (Mile 160 WHL). The waterway is mostly straight, has no locks, and presents just one cable ferry and one swing bridge. Along this route limited dockage is available and no fuel. Enjoy the pleasant scenery and watch for commercial traffic.

**NAVIGATION:** Use Charts 11350 and 11355. Remember that along this route, between Mile 93 WHL and Mile 102 WHL, you are operating within the boundaries of Berwick Traffic Control. Recreational boats are not required to contact them, but can communicate with them on VHF Channel 11 to inform them of their intended route and provide requested information.

South from Berwick Bay and Morgan City, the GIWW follows the Lower Atchafalaya River for 3 miles, and then turns to the southwest on Little Wax Bayou at flashing green "A," quick-flashing red "2" and quick-flashing green "1." One-half mile after you make the turn into the GIWW you will pass Mile 99 WHL, which is referred to locally as "The 99." At GIWW Mile 108 WHL, the route crosses Wax Lake Outlet, a deep drainage ditch from Bayou Teche and the Atchafalaya Basin. Strong currents, especially after heavy storms, can make towboat transit a "hair-raising" experience. Wait for oncoming tows to cross before proceeding.

Take care as you cross the swift north to south currents, which cause a few accidents each year. Low power is a handicap at this point. Heavy debris becomes more plentiful during high water periods. An estimated 40 percent of the flow from the Atchafalaya River is diverted through the Wax Lake Outlet Canal, representing roughly 12 percent of the Mississippi River's flow.

The town of North Bend at Bayou Sale (pronounced "sall-e") is a small commercial town with no transient services. The **North Bend (SR 317) Bridge** at Mile 113.0 WHL has a 73-foot fixed vertical clearance.

The first entrance into West Cote Blanche Bay and Vermilion Bay is through The Jaws just east of Mile 122.5 WHL, where the Charenton Drainage and Navigation Canal crosses the GIWW. Charenton Canal is the choice route north to scenic Bayou Teche. The area in the proximity of Mud Lake (Mile 121 WHL to Mile 122 WHL between flashing green "9" and flashing green "11") is subject to shoaling just before the bend at the canal. Do not attempt to enter Mud Lake due to shoaling and submerged pilings.

If you are traveling west through **West Cote Blanche Bay** and **Vermilion Bay**, use Charts 11349 and 11351. This is the same distance and a much more open route to the Gulf of Mexico at Southwest Pass or back to the GIWW via Four Mile Cut that is a dredged extension of the Vermilion River. Chart GPS coordinates before taking this route.

At Mile 129.7 WHL, a cable ferry operates (24 hours a day) across the waterway. Cables may be at or near the water surface. After the ferry captain gives you a visual or horn signal, proceed cautiously at low speed. You can notify the ferry by sounding one long blast and one short.

The 73-foot vertical clearance, fixed **Cypremort (Louisa) Bascule Bridge** is west of the ferry at Mile 134.0 WHL. This is the midway point between New Orleans and the Texas border. The area has become congested with loading platforms on both banks. Towboats with barges also use this area to make crew changes.

At Mile 137 WHL is the Weeks Island Terminal where workers are usually busy loading barges. At night the run is difficult and confusing due to the great number of lights, some moving and some stationary. Just past Mile 137 WHL the south bank is washed out, and at Mile 138 WHL Weeks Bayou empties into Weeks Bay, creating swift currents during the tide changes and in southwesterly winds.

Rising 171 feet above the marsh to starboard, the huge salt dome of Weeks Island is the largest salt mine operation in Louisiana and the source of heavy barge traffic. Such a salt dome is actually a huge mound of salt that has risen from the ground over thousands of years. Other salt domes can be found on Avery, Jefferson and Cote Blanche Islands. Salt domes such as this usually cover huge deposits of oil and gas.

Between Mile 137 WHL and Mile 140 WHL are many pipeline crossings, wellheads and storage tanks in side canals. They are protected by a limestone wall and idle barges. The area from Weeks Island to Intracoastal City is low marshland. If it is windy be prepared for signals from tows indicating how they want you to pass.

**Dockage:** At the intersection of the Atchafalaya River, Little Wax Bayou and the GIWW, the Parish of St. Mary has a boating facility on the northwest corner that is most commonly referred to as Berwick Landing. It has docks and power stations. Controlling water depths are reported to be 4 feet. Cruising boats have docked here for the night; however, there does not appear to be anyone to contact, and we have been told the Parish does not encourage overnight docking.

**Anchorage:** Just north of the GIWW on the Charenton Canal (Mile 123 WHL) is a comfortable, overnight anchorage in 9 feet at mean low water. Proceed about 2 miles from the GIWW and anchor on the starboard side of the canal. You will have plenty of water close to shore to help keep you out of the way of commercial traffic. A shallower anchorage is at the Franklin Canal (Mile 120 WHL) where you will find 4 feet at mean low water.

# tracoastal City–GIWW Mile 160 WHL

e Vermilion River crossing at Mile 159 WHL is a
avy commercial area for petroleum and fishing.
eavy wake action is the norm here, and pleasure craft
em to lose all claims to right-of-way, so all eyes are
eded on watch.

**AVIGATION:** Use Charts 11349 and 11350. To the
uth is the Four Mile Cutoff, which diverts the original
erbed from the GIWW to Vermilion Bay and the
uthwest Pass onward to the Gulf of Mexico. To the
rth on the Vermilion River (shown on the chart as
e Vermilion River Extension), the interesting cities
Abbeville and Lafayette are located beyond the
mmercial area. The route is navigable to Lafayette, but
ere are no transient facilities.

**Dockage:** One mile west of the Vermilion River
ossing, on the north side of the GIWW at Mile 160
HL is a commercial facility that tries in every way to
commodate transient pleasure boats. Although it is
Texaco dealer, it is named the Shell Morgan Landing,
c., which is a combination of family names. Dockage
r vessels is first-come, first-serve, whether you are a
-footer needing 30 gallons of fuel, or a larger vessel
eding 300 gallons; the fuel pumps for recreational
aters are located next to the red office building. (Note
at the fuel dock closes at 6:00 p.m.) Use your fenders
he dock is draped with huge black tires) and approach
ith caution, keeping an eye on any commercial traffic
wakes. The Maxie Pierce Grocery Store, located just
st of Shell Morgan Landing is within easy walking
stance. It has all of the provisions needed for the
ansient boater. Sandwiches and salads are available
the store until 1:00 p.m. every day. Young's Grocery
about 1.5 miles from the dock. When you leave the
arina turn right on Highway 333, or call them (337-
93-3854) to request a ride. They may be willing to pick
u up and bring you back to the boat.

Danny Richard (pronounced "Ree-shard") Marina, on
e Vermilion River just north of the GIWW often has
ansient accommodations but no fuel; call ahead for
etails.

**Note:** The next "official" fuel stop is in the Lake
harles area almost 100 miles away. The exception is at
ile 193 WHL where Martin's Landing (337-785-3440),
commercial facility, offers diesel fuel but only to larger
leasure vessels.

## Side Trip: Avery Island

If you can navigate to Avery Island it is an interesting
side trip. Avery Island is home to the world famous
TABASCO® Pepper Sauce factory. In addition to
touring the visitor center and the pepper sauce
factory, you can see how TABASCO® Sauce is
aged in white oak barrels and shipped all over the
world. You can also visit Avery Island's 170-acre
Jungle Gardens and see, if in season, a variety of
azaleas, camellias and bamboo and, amidst it all, a
centuries-old Buddha statue. The McIlhenny family
created "Bird City" in a pond on the site in the late
1800s to help save the snowy egret from extinction
by plume hunters (gathering feathers for fashionable
hats). Today, the Jungle Garden is home to thousands
of these and other water birds.

Try to arrive at the day docks (call ahead for
reservations) before 1:00 p.m. There is a small general
store and deli that serves lunch. The security guard
at the entrance gate can direct you to the visitor's
center. Visit tabasco.com/avery-island or call 800-634-
9599 for more information or to arrange a visit.

NAVIGATION: Use Chart 11350. Approximately 6 miles
north of the GIWW at Mile 146 WHL, Bayou Petite
Anse (pronounced "pet-E-onz") winds its way to Avery
Island. Approximately 3 miles to the north of the
GIWW is a fork in the channel. Bayou Petite Anse and
Avery Island are to the right. The channel to the left
leads to Delcambre and North Pier Marina, 6 more
miles to the north. This area is not charted on the
GIWW chart. Channel depths in both channels should
be about 9 feet. Watch your depth carefully in Bayou
Petite Anse after you make the right turn at the fork
and approach Avery Island.

Dockage/Anchorage: Dockage (but no power) is
available at the public dock at the head of the bayou,
next to the boat launch. Do not tie to the private pier
across from the launch adjacent to the security shack.

Ten miles north of Mile 146 WHL on the GIWW
is the Port of Delcambre's North Pier Marina. This
marina offers slips and numerous amenities, including
free grocery delivery. Gas and diesel are available at
Leblanc's Oil.

You can anchor in Bayou Petite Anse, in Avery
Canal or just off the dock at Avery Island.

# GIWW, Lake Charles, LA

www.snagaslip.co

| | Largest Vessel Accommodated | VHF Channel Monitored | Approach / Dockside Depth (reported) | Transient Berths / Total Berths | Groceries, Ice, Marine Supplies, Snacks | Gas / Diesel | Floating Docks | Repairs: Hull, Engine, Propeller | Lift (tonnage), Crane, Rail | Laundry, Pool, Showers, Courtesy Car | Min/Max Amps | Pump-Out Station | Nearby: Grocery Store, Motel, Restaurant |
|---|---|---|---|---|---|---|---|---|---|---|---|---|---|
| **DELCAMBRE** | | | **Dockage** | | | **Supplies** | | | **Services** | | | | |
| 1. North Pier Marina, Louisiana (WiFi) | 800-884-6120 | 70 | – | 6/31 | 11/6 | F | GD | – | HEP | – | 30/50 | S | P |
| **INTRACOASTAL CITY AREA** | | | | | | | | | | | | | |
| 2. Danny Richard Marina  159.2 WHL | 337-893-2157 | 65 | – | – | 8/5 | – | – | GI | HP | – | 30/30 | – | – |
| 3. Shell Morgan Landing Inc. (🖳) (WiFi) 160 WHL | 337-893-1211 | 200 | 13 | 2/2 | 7/5 | – | GD | IMS | – | C35 | 50/50 | S | – |

🖳 Internet Access  (WiFi) Wireless Internet Access  **WG** Waterway Guide Cruising Club Partner  *(Information in the table is provided by the facilities.)*
See WaterwayGuide.com for current rates, fuel prices, web site addresses, and other up-to-the-minute information.

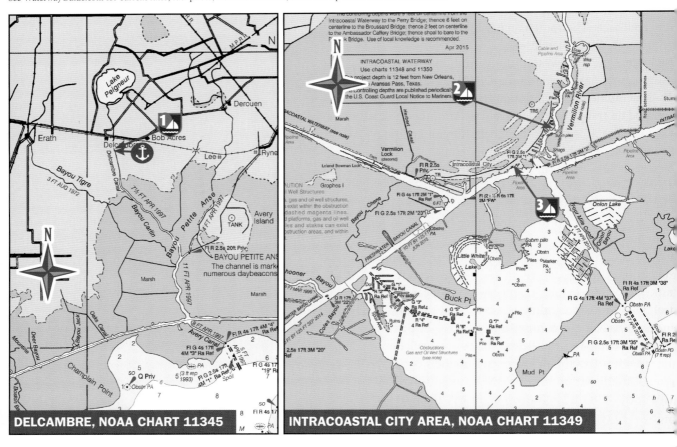

DELCAMBRE, NOAA CHART 11345

INTRACOASTAL CITY AREA, NOAA CHART 11349

# ■ TO MERMENTAU RIVER

**NAVIGATION:** Use Charts 11345, 11348 and 11350. Heading west from Intracoastal City, from Shell Morgan Landing to Mile 161 WHL, both banks are lined with petroleum-related docks and wharves. Supply boats and crew boats move in and out both day and night.

The intersection of the GIWW with Freshwater Bayou to the Gulf of Mexico can be confusing. The GIWW turns 70 degrees to the northwest from Freshwater Bayou, and the turn is easy to miss. Many westbound cruisers have proceeded straight ahead for 1 mile or more before realizing that the Leland Bowman Lock is nowhere in sight.

## Leland Bowman Lock–GIWW Mile 163 WHL

The **Leland Bowman Lock** is part of the system that prevents the intrusion of saltwater into the farming areas of the Mermentau Basin. Together with the Calcasieu Locks and the Schooner Bayou Floodgates, they retain freshwater in Mermentau Basin at a predetermined level. The Leland Bowman Locks replaced the old Vermilion Locks on the north side of the newer structure.

**NAVIGATION:** Use Chart 11350. Contact the lockmaster at the Leland Bowman Lock after passing the Freshwater Bayou Canal; quite often the locks will be standing open, and you will be asked to pass through. Go slowly through the chamber, keeping good steerageway.

## Alternate Route: Schooner Bayou– GIWW Mile 161 to Mile 167 WHL

If the Leland Bowman Lock has a long backup of traffic or is closed for repairs, the alternate route shown on your chart may be preferable. From Intracoastal City follow the Freshwater Bayou Canal south for 4 miles. The Canal intersects Schooner Bayou at the 17-foot red marker "22." Schooner Bayou only goes to the west at this intersection. Controlling depth is 5.5 feet. You will reach the Schooner Bayou Floodgate in 3 miles. Past the floodgate take the north channel 3.5 miles back to the GIWW at Mile 167 WHL. The total distance for the alternative route, from 17-foot "FW" is 10.5 statute miles. Before you begin this route check to be sure the floodgate is open.

## GIWW Mile 163 WHL to Mile 203 WHL

**NAVIGATION:** Use Chart 11350. The 40 miles to the Mermentau River is an isolated stretch through mostly swampy lowlands. It is a good time for bird watching.

The **Forked Island Bridge**, Mile 170.3, has a fixed vertical clearance of 73 feet. A tractor-pulled cable ferry connecting the rice farms at Mile 178.4 WHL operates only when needed. At Mile 201 WHL a pipeline terminal with numerous tanks is located on the south side of the waterway.

**Dockage:** It is possible to get fuel at Martin Fuel Docks at Mile 193 WHL. This is primarily a commercial facility and you should call ahead for fuel (337-785-3440). In general, they do not sell fuel in quantities of 100 gallons or less, and commercial vessels take priority. No transient slips are available, but on the south side of the GIWW, 100 yards west of Martin Fuel Dock, there is a cut, locally referred to as South Basin. Two sunken barges on the west side of the cut provide a place to tie alongside. Water depths are approximately 6 to 8 feet with some 5-foot depths reported. Tie with the bow facing the GIWW and plenty of fenders to protect from the surge created by passing tows.

## Side Trip: Mermentau River–GIWW Mile 203 WHL

The GIWW crosses the Mermentau River, 37 miles north of the Gulf of Mexico, at Mile 203 WHL. Follow the marked GIWW channel from green "1" and red "2" to red and green "M" on the north bank, just west of green "5." From here the Mermentau River goes north 15 miles to Lake Arthur. Grand Lake is to the south.

**NAVIGATION:** Use Chart 11348, which covers the river from the Gulf of Mexico to Lake Arthur. The mileage scale is reduced to one-half of that on the GIWW, and the miles are measured starting with Mile 0 from the Gulf outlet, not from the GIWW.

From the GIWW to Lake Arthur the river has a controlling depth of 9.5 feet, with generally greater depths. Some uncharted islands, a sunken shrimp boat (marked by buoys) and anchored or beached barges are scattered about.

The route south from the GIWW on the Mermentau River meanders for 37 miles through Grand Lake and upper and lower Mud Lake to a shallow Gulf Inlet. The route is shown on Charts 11344 and 11348, but boaters should seek local knowledge before making this trip.

**Dockage:** Transient slips alongside a bulkhead, and a convenience store and gas are available 7 miles north on the Mermentau River (west side) at Meyer's Landing. Meyer's Landing is primarily an RV park, with limited transient slips for $15 to $20 per night. Power is very

mited and only available through 15-amp outlets. showers and laundry are available. Call ahead (337-774-8338) for availability.

Regatta Seafood and Steakhouse, on the waterfront at Lake Arthur, has slips for customers but no overnight transient slips. On the shore side of the town docks is a nice and popular public park.

**Anchorage:** A good anchorage was reported in the river on the west bank just north of green daybeacon "1A." Another good anchorage is north of GIWW can buoys "2A" and "4" in a marshy cove at the Mermentau River mouth. Just past green daybeacon "5" on the Mermentau River, turn to starboard to anchor in the lee of the island marked "Stump PA" on the chart. Depths should be 8 to 10 feet. Charted anchorages are also available at Meyer's Landing, Lake Arthur Yacht Club and Lake Arthur.

## MERMENTAU RIVER TO CALCASIEU RIVER

This is a quiet stretch of the GIWW until you get to Mile 231 WHL at the Grand Lake Pontoon Bridge, then the Black Bayou Pontoon Bridge at Mile 238 WHL, followed immediately by the Calcasieu Lock. Plan your route carefully as you approach the Calcasieu Lock. The GIWW and the Calcasieu River do not intersect in a straight line.

**NAVIGATION:** Use Charts 11339, 11345, 11347 and 11348. At Mile 219.8 WHL you will pass under the **Creole Canal (Gibbstown) Bridge** with 73-foot fixed vertical clearance. Follow the charted channel across Sweet Lake from Mile 223 WHL to Mile 224 WHL. The **Grand Lake Pontoon Bridge** carries State Road 384. Remember, a pontoon bridge is not a swing bridge. It is a barge that is pulled open with cables that lurk under the surface even while the bridge is opening. Be sure the cables have had time to settle on the bottom before proceeding. The Grand Lake Pontoon opens on signal.

The **Black Bayou Pontoon Bridge** is just before the Calcasieu Lock, which is located at Mile 238.2 WHL. Contact the lockmaster on VHF Channel 14 before you ask the bridge tender to open the pontoon bridge. The lockmaster may instruct you to wait on the east side of the pontoon bridge, where the waterway is wider. When

the lock is available to pass through, contact the pontoon bridge on VHF Channel 13 to request that the bridge be opened. The Black Bayou Pontoon Bridge opens on signal, except from 6:00 a.m. to 8:00 a.m. and from 2:00 p.m. to 4:00 p.m., Monday through Friday when it need not open. It may open, however, at any time if traffic is light or for commercial vessels.

When you pass through the Black Bayou Pontoon Bridge, you may be required to wait in the holding area between the bridge and the **Calcasieu Lock**. The north shore is shallow and lined by rocks. The south side near the lock has 7-foot depths. There is a warning sign "Do Not Pass This Point Until," but it is a common practice when a tow is passing and you have been instructed to wait between the pontoon bridge and the east gate of the lock.

⚠ Continuing until further notice, mariners are advised not to tie off to nor allow their vessels to rest against the south chamber wall at Calcasieu Lock. This wall is unstable and vessels tying to it or exerting force on it could cause it to fail. Mariners should proceed through the structure with caution.

During low water the lock gate might be open and you may pass through if the green ball is hoisted. The lock opens on signal. Contact the lockmaster on VHF Channel 14.

Exit Calcasieu Lock and follow the channel to starboard going north around Choupique Island. In 1 mile there is an intersection with the GIWW. Turn to port on a westward heading and travel 2 miles to the wide intersection with Calcasieu River. From this intersection you can go straight ahead on a westward course in the GIWW, 12 miles north to Lake Charles, or south 20 miles to the City of Cameron and the Gulf.

**Anchorage:** There is room to anchor at the Bayou Lacassine–Short Cutoff in 4 to 5 feet at mean low water. Another anchorage possibility is Little Lake Misere (Mile 212 WHL), west of green can "1" or across the GIWW at the Bell City Drainage Canal. This is a narrow waterway with 6 to 10 feet of water.

# GIWW, Lake Charles, LA

www.snagaslip.com

SNAG-A-SLIP

EXPLORE
BOOK
BOAT

| LAKE CHARLES AREA | | Largest Vessel Accommodated | VHF Channel Monitored | Transient Berths / Total Berths | Approach / Dockside Depth (reported) | Floating Docks | Groceries, Ice, Marine Supplies, Snacks | Gas / Diesel | Repairs: Hull, Engine, Propeller | Lift (tonnage), Crane, Rail | Min/Max Amps | Laundry, Pool, Showers, Courtesy Car | Pump-Out Station | Nearby: Grocery Store, Motel, Restaurant |
|---|---|---|---|---|---|---|---|---|---|---|---|---|---|---|
| | | | | **Dockage** | | | **Supplies** | | | **Services** | | | | |
| 1. Golden Nugget Lake Charles Marina 🖥 | 337-508-4000 | 206 | – | 10/10 | – | | – | – | | | 30/100 | LPS | – | MR |
| 2. L'Auberge Casino Resort 🖥 WiFi | 337-395-7777 | 50 | – | 16/16 | 8/8 | F | – | IS | | | 30/50 | PS | – | MR |
| 3. Bowtie Marina | 337-478-0130 | – | | call/12 | – | | GD | IMS | HEP | L | – | – | – | GMR |
| 4. Bridge Point Yacht Center  241 WHL | 337-436-0803 | 50 | – | 14/16 | 40/10 | F | GD | MS | HEP | L35 | 30/30 | PS | – | GMR |
| 5. Bord du Lac Marina WiFi | 337-491-1256 | 95 | – | 38/38 | /8.5 | F | – | MS | | | 30/100 | – | – | MR |

🖥 Internet Access   WiFi Wireless Internet Access   WG Waterway Guide Cruising Club Partner  *(Information in the table is provided by the facilities.)*
See WaterwayGuide.com for current rates, fuel prices, web site addresses, and other up-to-the-minute information.

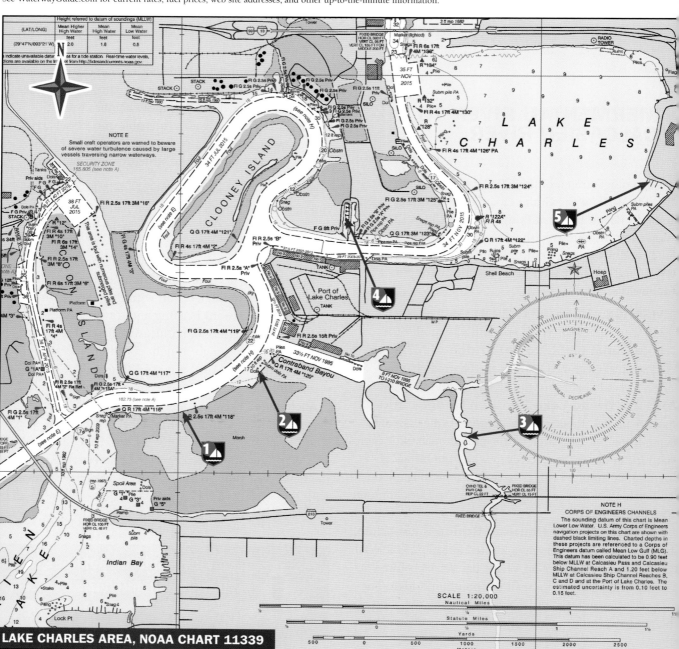

LAKE CHARLES AREA, NOAA CHART 11339

## ■ SIDE TRIP: TO LAKE CHARLES

North of the GIWW, the Calcasieu River extends 2 miles to the commercial port and casino gambling center of Lake Charles, and another 2 miles across the lake to the municipal marina in downtown Lake Charles.

This "City by the Lake" has a great white sandy beach, clear water, exciting gaming and a wide variety of restaurants and shopping delights.

**NAVIGATION:** Use Chart 11339 and 11347. Enter the Calcasieu River just northwest of Choupique Island. River depths range from 12 to 30 feet. Follow the well-marked channel as you pass through Moss Lake, Rose Bluff Cutoff and under the **Rose Bluff Cutoff (I-210) Bridge** with a fixed 127-foot clearance. After the bridge, you will pass Contraband Bayou, and follow the channel to the Port of Lake Charles. As you pass the port of Lake Charles you will see a flashing red buoy "A." Looking straight ahead you see Clooney Island, a channel to the left and one slightly to the right. Those two channels must go around Clooney Island. The channel to Lake Charles is a sharp turn to the east (120 degrees) going

past a flashing red buoy "B." Bridge Point Marina will be to port.

Just over .5 mile east of the Bridge Point Marina is the lake that gave the city its name. Stay in the marked channel and make the turn to the north at green buoy "123." To access the lake, leave the channel and cross over the spoil bank between red buoy "122" and "124." The spoil should have a 5-foot depth. Go slow and watch your depth. Parts of the spoil bank have depths as low as 3 feet. The municipal marina is on the southeast bank at a bearing of about 80 degrees, and a distance just under 1 mile. It may be easier to locate the TV tower behind the marina. Lake Charles should have a minimum depth of 8 feet to the marina.

The floating gambling casinos are on the west side of the Calcasieu River just south of the high-rise **I-10/US 90 Bridge**. These floating casinos no longer leave their docks, so cruising by them is not a problem. The casinos feature courtesy transportation to and from marinas, but check the regulations carefully before trying to dock there with your primary vessel or dinghy.

Above the **Lake Charles Railroad Swing Bridge** (3-foot vertical clearance, usually open), the Calcasieu

River is navigable for many miles and offers scenic and remote anchorage opportunities.

**Dockage:** The impressive Golden Nugget Casino is 0.8 miles northwest of the Rose Bluff Bridge, at the flashing 17-foot red "118." The casino has a marina with transient slips and all the usual amenities. To the north another 0.4 miles is the L'Auberge du Lac Resort Casino, located at the southern mouth of Contraband Bayou as it empties into the Calcasieu River. Each slip has shore power and water. The resort boasts several restaurants, a swimming pool with a lazy river, a full-service spa, shopping and an adjacent golf course.

Immediately northeast of The L'Auberge du Lac, Contraband Bayou turns to the east. A short 1-mile trip down Contraband Bayou, which has turned south, is the Bowie Marina, located on the east side of the Bayou next to a Coast Guard Station. This is a full-service marina with a mechanic, boat lift and fuel. The trip to the Bowtie Marina looks scary, but it's not if you stay in the middle of the channel where depths should be more than 6 feet. Continuing south, the bayou travels under an overhead cable with a clearance of 22 feet, followed by a fixed bridge with a clearance of 15 feet. Contraband bayou continues on for many miles.

Back on the Calcasieu River, past the 120-degree turn to starboard around the Port of Lake Charles, are the remains of an old bridge with the base on the north bank still in tack. It is in the basin here that Bridge Poi Yacht Center offers transient slips and fuel.

The Bord du Lac Marina in the waterfront promenad at Lake Charles is within walking distance of downtow restaurants and other attractions. Offices for the marina are in the Civic Center. There's a city dock nearby whe you may be able to tie up. Just be sure to ask first.

**Anchorage:** An excellent anchorage lies just a few miles upriver near the Haymark Terminal. Enter the oxbow across from flashing green "103" and proceed around to anchor in 16-foot charted depths. This is a quiet anchorage away from GIWW wakes. You may eve see a roseate spoonbill in the marsh here.

Prien Lake offers 7 to 16 feet of water with excellent holding and protection from all but north winds. Anch near the Lake Charles Golf and Country Club for best protection.

Lake Charles offers one of the finest anchorage spots along the Gulf coast, and it is the site of many celebrations and regattas throughout the summer. If yo can cross the 5-foot bar into the lake, pick your locatio for the best wind protection in 7 to 9 feet at mean low water.

# CALCASIEU RIVER TO PAVELL ISLAND

he 12-mile trip south down the Calcasieu River -enters the GIWW at Mile 241. From here the GIWW ntinues westward as a pleasant stretch of water. It is ide and deep with enough room for commercial traffic d pleasure boats.

AVIGATION: Use Charts 11331, 11339, 11342 and 1343. The GIWW swings to the west after passing the llender (SR 27) Lift Bridge, Mile 243.8 WHL. is a classic lift bridge with a 50-foot closed vertical earance. The Ellender Bridge requires a four-hour otice to open. If you require an opening, contact the lack Bayou Pontoon Bridge on VHF Channels 13 or 14. he Black Bayou bridge tender, in turn, will contact the llender Lift Bridge, and you will receive instructions to ontact them again when you are 30 minutes out from le Ellender Bridge. (Call 800-752-6706.) Leave some xtra time in your schedule so you can arrive in advance nd wait, rather than miss your opening. If you arrive arly, they may open for you if commercial traffic is aiting as well.

From the Ellender Lift Bridge, it is a fairly straight 20-plus-mile stretch to the Texas state line at Mile 266 WHL. The barge port of West Port Calcasieu is the last indication of civilization. Here, a large number of barges are stacked on the north and south banks. You may also encounter parked barge strings with no towboat. At night they exhibit a flashing yellow light on both outboard corners. The water runs straight, wide and deep, and moss-draped trees give way to grass, low scrub and low marsh.

**Anchorage:** Exercise caution here, as the east side of Pavell Island is filled with wrecks of large and small boats and a low wall of semi-submerged pilings blocks the upper end. Anchor in the west cut of the island. Be careful not to block the cut when you anchor. Some folks tie the bow up to a tree here and run a stern anchor, Mediterranean-style. This is a fairly quiet anchorage, but an occasional towboat moves through. If you have time, better anchorages can be found around Shell Island at Mile 272 WHL.

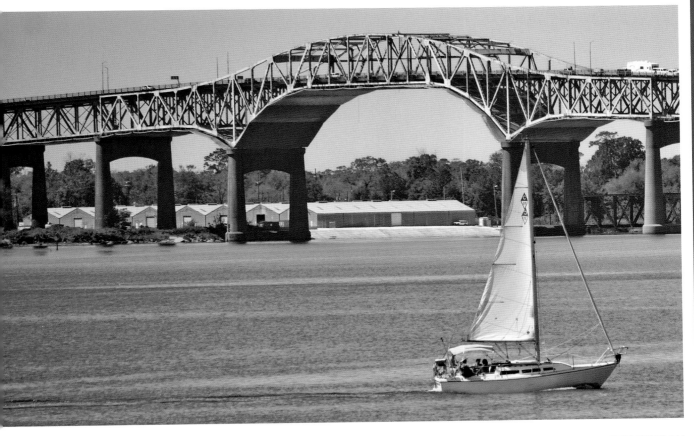

# Skipper's Notes

# The Texas Border to Freeport, TX

 Mile 265 (TX Border)–Mile 395 WHL   TX: Channel 13

**CHARTS** 11311, 11322, 11323, 11324, 11326, 11327, 11331, 11342, 11343

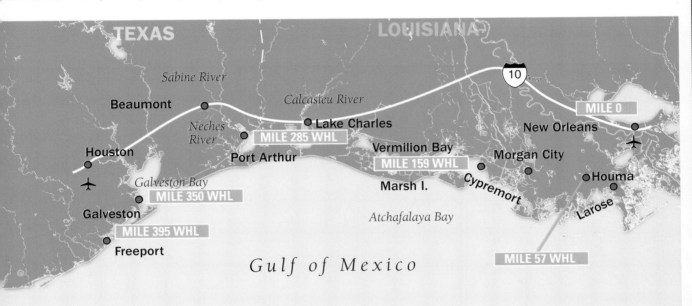

## CROSSING INTO TEXAS

From Louisiana to Mexico, the Texas coast covers over 400 miles. To the south, Padre Island with a length of 113 miles is the longest barrier island in the world. The Texas coast is a series of these barrier islands and narrow sandbars that protect the coastal prairies and plains, lagoons, bays and the GIWW. The many large rivers that run through Texas flow to the Gulf of Mexico. Because of their currents, silt from these rivers makes the waters murky along much of the upper and middle coast. Most communities along the coast are small and cruisers will find that these communities are quaint and the people are friendly.

The Texas Gulf Coast offers a varied and slowly changing vista, from alligator-laden bayous to cactus-covered bird sanctuaries. It also offers full 73-foot vertical clearance for all but one of its fixed bridges. After the relatively short Alabama and Mississippi Gulf Coast segments and the Creole-flavored Louisiana GIWW run, the long Texas coastline slowly transforms its scenery gradually shifting to the tropical.

Passes between the extended low barrier islands are scattered about 1 day's run apart. The vast majority of the coast is made up of marsh islands that are sometimes little more than sandbars or shoals. Big choppy bays run almost the entire length of the Texas coast. The bays are steeped in history and based on the waterborne commerce that created Texas Gulf communities.

Note that frequent changes to buoy numbers are made in all the bays, and charts may not show these new and altered numbers. Often buoys are missing or off station due to heavy currents or wind, so daybeacons are usually more reliable.

The upper half of the Texas coastline, from Sabine to Corpus Christi, has frequent and well-placed marinas and anchorages. This top half of the Texas GIWW is well traveled by barge and tug traffic, especially from Sabine to Freeport, where numerous petrochemical refineries are located.

# Sabine River, Neches River, TX

| | | Largest Vessel Accommodated | VHF Channel Monitored | Transient Berths / Total Berths | Approach / Dockside Depth (reported) | Floating Docks | Gas / Diesel | Groceries, Ice, Marine Supplies, Snacks | Repairs: Hull, Engine, Propeller | Lift (tonnage), Crane, Rail | Min/Max Amps | Laundry, Pool, Showers, Courtesy Car | Pump-Out Station | Nearby: Grocery Store, Motel, Restaurant |
|---|---|---|---|---|---|---|---|---|---|---|---|---|---|---|
| **COW BAYOU** | | **Dockage** | | | | | **Supplies** | | **Services** | | | | | |
| 1. Peggy's on the Bayou 🖥 📶 | 409-886-1115 | 40 | – | 1/16 | 6/5 | – | G | GIS | – | – | – | LS | – | GR |
| **BEAUMONT** | | | | | | | | | | | | | | |
| 2. Beaumont Yacht Club | 409-832-1456 | 50 | 16 | 2/81 | 5/6 | – | GD | IMS | – | – | 30/30 | LS | P | – |

🖥 Internet Access  📶 Wireless Internet Access  **WG** Waterway Guide Cruising Club Partner  *(Information in the table is provided by the facilities.)*
See WaterwayGuide.com for current rates, fuel prices, web site addresses, and other up-to-the-minute information.

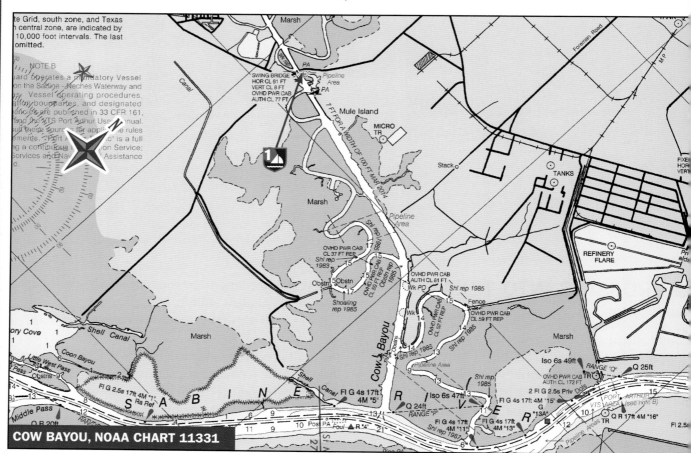

COW BAYOU, NOAA CHART 11331

The lower Texas Gulf Coast, from Corpus Christi/ Port Aransas to Port Isabel at the Mexican border, is more tropical and far less developed. Many anchorages are available, but boating facilities are few and very far between. On this lower half of the coast you will find miles of isolated waterway with very little traffic of any kind.

On the north side, the Texas border begins at the Sabine River just 2 miles downstream from Orange. However, on the south side of the GIWW, Louisiana continues until Mile 272 WHL. Pavell Island is in Texas, while Cutoff Island (farther west) is in Louisiana. The

charted course will not follow the circuitous nature of the state line, but that line is indicative of this complex and sometime confusing stretch of water. Chart your course carefully and remain aware of your location with regard to the islands, bayous, cuts, channels and rivers that intersect with the GIWW.

## Sabine River to Neches River– GIWW Mile 265 to Mile 277 WHL

**NAVIGATION:** Use Charts 11331, 11342 and 11343. At Mile 265, on the west end of Cutoff Island, is a 17-foot

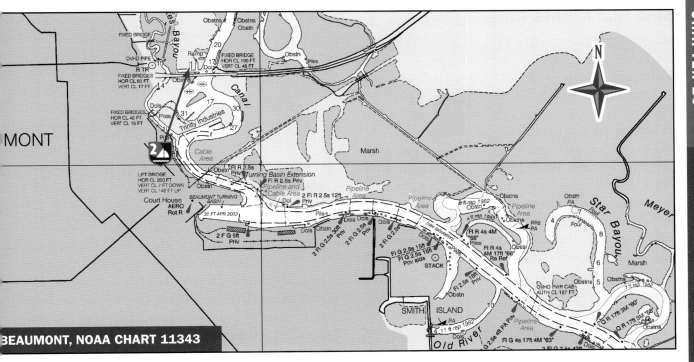

BEAUMONT, NOAA CHART 11343

ashing red "22" daybeacon. This red daybeacon is for
he channel diverging from the GIWW (Sabine River)
nd going north.

Red "22" is on the wrong side of the channel if you
re assuming it is for the GIWW. Look carefully for the
ellow GIWW markings. Take care in this area to make
ure you know your location and your intended course.
Note that the buoy and daybeacon colors are reversed
ere since ship channels are the preferred channel and
ave the red-right-returning protocol.

The GIWW runs along the northern edge of Sabine
Lake from Mile 272.5 WHL to the mouth of the Neches
River at Mile 277 WHL. The channel is 200 feet wide
nd 30 feet deep to the junction where the Sabine River
neets the Neches River.

**Dockage:** Peggy's on Old Cow Bayou is a unique and
worthwhile stop. Old Cow Bayou, north from the GIWW
about Mile 268 WHL, leads the cruiser up a winding
tream among cypress, live oak and cedar trees. Depths
are 7.5 feet in a wide channel. Peggy's is just before
he **Orange County Swing Bridge** (8-foot closed
vertical clearance, requires 6-hour advance notice to
ppen) on the east side of the bayou. They may have slips
and they sell gas. Dockside depths are about 5 feet. You
will probably tie to the back porch of the restaurant. The
lock, all 18 inches of width, is the back porch/door to
he restaurant. Power and water may be limited.

**Anchorage:** There are many good anchorages in this
rea, from Pavell Island to Shell Island. Between Pavell

Island and Cutoff Island is a great place to anchor in
10 feet of water with good holding in mud. A more
private anchorage would be difficult to find than in Old
Cow Bayou downstream from Peggy's, but note that the
mosquitoes are large here.

East Pass at Shell Island is to the south of the GIWW
at red flashing "2." East Pass circles around behind Shell
Island where anchoring in 15 to 20 feet of water can
be comfortable. Be sure to get far enough into the pass
before dropping the hook; sometimes a tow will rest in
the wide area near the mark. The pass leads to Sabine
Lake, but shallows to 2 to 3 feet before entering the
Lake; therefore, to return to the GIWW, you need to go
back to the flashing red "2."

When entering East Pass, Black Bayou is to port on
a narrow northeast course. Black Bayou has a sand bar
at the entry, so move over it slightly south of center
where there is 6 to 7 feet of water. Once past the entry
bar, there is 10 to 12 feet of water in an excellent, quiet
anchorage. If a fall or winter northerly is predicted, avoid
this anchorage; the water level could drop 3 to 4 feet,
trapping you in the bayou behind the entry sandbar.

Another possible spot to drop the hook can be found
by turning to the south at Mile 272 WHL at a spot
charted as Middle Pass. It is as deep as 25 feet in spots,
due to the strong tidal current that flows though the cut,
so anchor accordingly. It does not offer the protection of
East Pass or Black Bayou, so avoid the spot if there are
strong south or southeasterly winds.

## Side Trip: Neches River

**NAVIGATION:** Use Charts 11342 and 11343. The Neches River is navigable for 18 miles upriver from the **Rainbow Bridge** (172-foot fixed vertical clearance) to beyond the **I-10/US 90 Highway Bridge** (48-foot fixed vertical clearance) at Beaumont. This is a major petrochemical area with heavy barge traffic.

As you come up to the bridge you will see an oxbow on your port side. Avoid the northwest shore as several old ships and barge hulks lying just underwater. Stay to the east side of the Neches River in 20-plus feet of water, and then pass under the bridge. On the port side under the bridge is another submerged wreck. The starboard side is fine. Since the current is fairly strong, especially in the spring, run a bit upstream before turning to port and into the Beaumont Yacht Club channel. Stay well to the center.

**Dockage:** The 48-foot fixed vertical clearance I-10/US 90 Highway Bridge, some 17 miles upriver, limits some sailboat access to the Beaumont Yacht Club, which welcomes visiting boats and offers the calm of a deep inland marina.

On the west bank of the Neches River, under the pair of fixed bridges, a narrow canal leads to the west. If your draft can handle the entrance depth (about 4 feet), you will find inside a number of docks, a bait stand with a gas dock, as well as an antique lift on a railway. The lift can haul boats up to 30 feet, depending on the vessel's weight; call 409-962-9616 to check. (The only other lift in the area, which utilizes a crane with slings, will be found at Pleasure Island Marina on Sabine Lake.)

**Anchorage:** Frequent anchorages can be found along the Neches River banks in the lush marsh and cypress forests that line the river. The first easy anchorage is in sight of the Rainbow Bridge, just 2 miles upriver before flashing red "22." This is one of the many oxbows created by straightening out the curvy river. Depths should be around 12 feet. Bird Island Bayou, on the west side of the oxbow, can offer an interesting side tour, depending on your draft.

Another mile farther upstream is Port Neches Park. There are no facilities for large boats, but you can dinghy in to hunt for supplies. Ahead, before the next oxbow, is the narrow opening to the Bessie Heights Canal, marked by quick-flashing red "30." It may provide opportunities for anchorage in at least 7 feet of water.

The next feature running up the Neches River is the oxbow marked on the north side as "Reserve Fleet" on the chart. If the reserve fleet is not here, you may be able to drop the hook, although small outboards run through at all hours.

Farther up the Neches River, an interesting collection of dozens of huge seagoing ships from the Reserve Fleet are moored side-by-side. The security force guarding the "ghost fleet" take their job seriously so feel free to look but do not touch.

# ■ SABINE LAKE

**NAVIGATION:** Use Charts 11331 and 11342. At red "70" (Mile 275.5), Sabine Lake may be entered through a privately marked channel between Stewts and Sydnes Islands called Thousand Foot Cut. Do not cut corners here; enter when the private marks line up. Go slow, watch your depth sounder and ease into the lake. Depth in the cut change due to currents from the Sabine River. There should be 6 feet in the channel, which is partially marked by orange buoys. Keep buoys to port when entering the lake and do not cut into the channel at the can in the GIWW. The can buoy is not a channel marker for entering the lake. Proceed past the cluster piles before changing your heading.

**Dockage:** Pleasure Island Marina, operated by the city of Port Arthur, is located about 3 miles southwest of Thousand-Foot Cut on the Lake Sabine side of Pleasure Island. Pleasure Island offers camping and picnic areas, an outdoor concert park, condominiums, public beaches, fishing piers and a beach club. Pleasure Island is not accessible directly from the GIWW. You will have to enter the lake well north or south of this point.

Channel markers lead the way to the narrow entrance of the Pleasure Island Marina through the breakwater. As you enter the breakwater, there is a clear area of more than 200 yards where you can drop anchor or prepare for docking. Watch the depth sounder for some 3- and 4-foot areas bordering the channel and the approach as you enter.

If you have a yacht club membership and wish to enjoy the gracious hospitality of the Port Arthur Yacht Club (PAYC), call ahead for instructions (409-356-6253 or payc.us). The club offers the usual amenities.

**Anchorage:** A good anchorage exists off Garrison Ridge, in 5- to 6-foot depths, along the east (Louisiana) shore, where you will see a high tree-covered ridge, visible from several miles away. Another possible

anchorage is at Johnson Bayou, in 6- to 7-foot depths, also on the eastern Louisiana shore past the marina.

## Sabine Lake–South Entrance

**NAVIGATION:** Use Charts 11341 and 11342. GIWW Mile 289 WHL marks the intersection with the Sabine Neches Canal. From this intersection turn south and proceed down the Port Arthur Ship Channel to the 17-foot red "70." It is about 6 miles from the intersection to the south entrance of Sabine Lake.

To access the southern entrance to Sabine Lake, pass through **SR 82 Bridge** at Mesquite Point with a 65-foot vertical clearance and under the overhead cables with a clearance of 75-feet. (Note: Vertical clearance at the bridge may be as low as 63 feet.) There you will find 20 to 25 feet of water for a few hundred yards. Take a course of approximately 312 degrees magnetic for about 1.75 miles to the vicinity of two pilings marking a submerged wreck. About halfway to these pilings, you will note that the water is shoaling to 8 feet or less. Leave the pilings about 150 feet to port. Continue on a course that keeps you off the Louisiana side of Sabine Lake, where there is an oyster reef shoal area. Take care not to cut too close to Blue Buck Point. Then proceed

on a more northerly course to Pleasure Island Marina. There are no channel marks on either side of the bridge so proceed with caution. From this point on, the lake is generally 5 to 7 feet deep and free of underwater obstructions.

## South Sabine Lake to the Gulf of Mexico

**NAVIGATION:** Use Charts 11341 and 11342. Travel southeast from the State Route 82 Bridge (65-foot fixed vertical clearance) along the Port Arthur Ship Channel for 6 miles to Texas Point at the Gulf. The ship channel, 500 feet wide and 40 feet deep, is well marked. As you enter the jetty channel, beware of submerged and exposed wrecks on both sides. After passing Sabine Pass East Jetty at flashing green "17" and red "18," the channel opens to the Gulf with water depths of 24 to 35 feet.

Southbound from Sabine Lake, Louisiana is on your port side. A large designated big-ship anchorage area to port is filled with huge jack-up rigs. The small town of Sabine Pass on the starboard (Texas) side offers a motel about 1.5 miles from the docks at Sabine Pass Port Authority, should you need some time ashore.

# Sabine Lake and Pass

| | | Largest Vessel Accommodated | VHF Channel Monitored | Transient Berths / Total Berths | Approach / Dockside Depth (reported) | Floating Docks | Gas / Diesel | Groceries, Ice, Marine Supplies, Snacks | Repairs: Hull, Engine, Propeller | Lift (tonnage), Crane, Rail | Min/Max Amps | Laundry, Pool, Showers, Courtesy Car | Pump-Out Station | Nearby: Grocery Store, Motel, Restaurant |
|---|---|---|---|---|---|---|---|---|---|---|---|---|---|---|
| **PORT ARTHUR** | | | | **Dockage** | | | **Supplies** | | **Services** | | | | | |
| 1. Pleasure Island Marina | 409-982-4675 | 50 | 13 | call/299 | 5/6 | F | – | – | HE | C | 30/50 | S | P | – |
| 2. Port Arthur Yacht Club 🖳 WiFi | 409-356-6253 | 50 | 13 | 50/300 | 6/6 | F | GD | IS | HE | C | 30/50 | S | P | G |
| **SABINE PASS** | | | | | | | | | | | | | | |
| 3. Sabine Pass Port Authority Marina WiFi | 409-971-2411 | 50 | – | 5/87 | 20/8 | – | GD | I | – | | 30/50 | LS | P | GMR |

🖳 Internet Access  WiFi Wireless Internet Access  WG Waterway Guide Cruising Club Partner  *(Information in the table is provided by the facilities.)*
See WaterwayGuide.com for current rates, fuel prices, web site addresses, and other up-to-the-minute information.

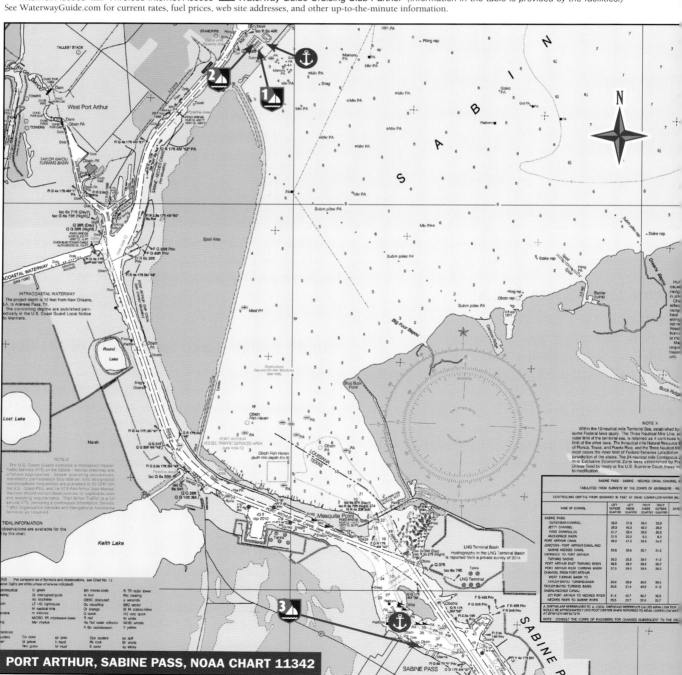

**PORT ARTHUR, SABINE PASS, NOAA CHART 11342**

**Dockage:** The Sabine Pass Port Authority maintains few slips for transient boaters. Water and power are provided, but shoreside facilities are about 1 mile away. The fuel dock, open 24 hours a day, 7 days per week, offers both gas and diesel, and is one of the few such fueling facilities in the area. Be careful, though, because they are used for commercial boats and are lined with big black tires. The slips run across the tidal current flow, so a strong ebb or flood current may press you against the dock.

**Anchorage:** Just northwest of the town of Sabine Pass is a good anchorage lying between an island and town in an abandoned large-ship channel that is used by commercial fishing boats. A strong current runs here at ebb or flood tide, so take that into account when anchoring. Be cautious, because there are a few wrecked hulks of old shrimp boats in the area.

The Coast Guard station is here, and the chart-designated anchorage is deep in the middle, carrying 8 to 10 feet of water all the way into shore. Ship and barge traffic is heavy, as are their wakes. Both of these anchorages and the town of Sabine Pass are 6 to 8 miles south of the GIWW.

# ■ NECHES RIVER TO GALVESTON BAY

It is a 73-mile run from the Neches River (Mile 299 WHL) to the wide-open and ship-filled Bolivar Roads Channel in Galveston Bay. Once you are past Taylor Outfall Canal these are easy lazy miles except for the high volume of commercial traffic. There are three fixed bridges and no pontoon or lift bridges, locks or floodgates.

## To Taylor Bayou–GIWW Mile 277 to Mile 290 WHL

**NAVIGATION:** Use Charts 11311, 11324 and 11326. When you pass green "67" and red "66" Humble Island will be on the north side of the GIWW and Stewts Island will be to the south. Immediately past the two islands the Neches River branches to starboard in a northerly direction leading to the City of Beaumont. The GIWW continues to port or south in the Neches Canal. Avoid the temptation to turn north in the Neches River if you want to stay in the GIWW. Keep Sabine Lake to port/south and stay in the Neches Canal/GIWW.

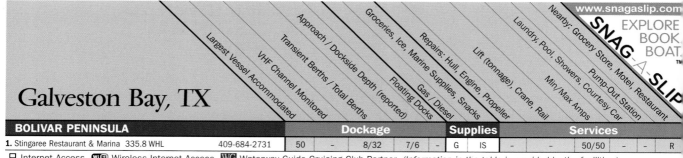

# Galveston Bay, TX

| BOLIVAR PENINSULA | Largest Vessel Accommodated | VHF Channel Monitored | Approach / Dockside Depth (reported) | Transient Berths / Total Berths | Floating Docks | Gas / Diesel | Groceries, Ice, Marine Supplies, Snacks | Repairs: Hull, Engine, Propeller | Lift (tonnage), Crane, Rail | Min/Max Amps | Laundry, Pool, Showers, Courtesy Car | Pump-Out Station | Nearby: Grocery Store, Motel, Restaurant |
|---|---|---|---|---|---|---|---|---|---|---|---|---|---|
| | | | Dockage | | | | Supplies | | Services | | | | |
| 1. Stingaree Restaurant & Marina  335.8 WHL   409-684-2731 | 50 | – | 8/32 | 7/6 | – | G | IS | – | – | 50/50 | – | – | R |

🖥 Internet Access   📶 Wireless Internet Access   **WG** Waterway Guide Cruising Club Partner  *(Information in the table is provided by the facilities.)*
See WaterwayGuide.com for current rates, fuel prices, web site addresses, and other up-to-the-minute information.

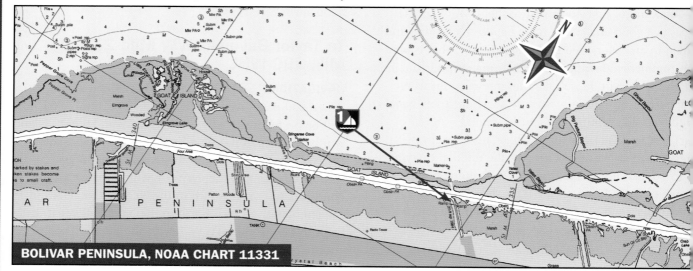

**BOLIVAR PENINSULA, NOAA CHART 11331**

Sabine Lake will be visible and open to port or south until you reach Mile 279 WHL. At Mile 281 WHL you will be in the area of Pleasure Island to the south and the City of Port Arthur to the north. At Mile 288 WHL passing by 17-foot red "50" you enter the intersection of the Neches Canal, GIWW, and the Port Arthur Ship Canal. The Port Arthur Ship Canal goes south for 13.5 statute miles to Texas Point and the Gulf of Mexico. At Mile 288.8 WHL, immediately after the intersection, the GIWW passes under the **West Port Arthur (SR 87) Bridge** (fixed vertical clearance of 73 feet).

The Taylor Bayou Outfall Canal at Mile 290.5 WHL runs north from the GIWW for almost 4 miles to a lock that the Corps of Engineers has placed to stop saltwater from moving upstream. Despite its name, the outfall canal is a drainage canal that diverts the headwaters of the Old Taylor Bayou. It does not carry any sewage or chemical discharge. It is used by commercial vessels.

At Mile 305 WHL is Salt Bayou, known locally as Spindletop Gully. There is a dark, two-story building here, and less than a .5-mile west is a harbor next to the Department of Energy Strategic Reserve Pump Station. Due to increased security concerns, this harbor is off-limits to recreational craft.

**Anchorage:** Taylor Outfall Canal is a good anchorage, and better in the fall and winter than the spring and summer due to the extra-large salt grass mosquitoes. It has between 13 and 14 feet of water to the banks over soft, blue-black mud.

An even better anchorage is available in the uncharted lateral canal that enters from the west, about .75 of a mile up the Taylor Outfall Canal. It is approximately 100 feet wide and 12 to 18 feet deep. This canal is within the Big Hill Bayou Wildlife Management Area and is alive with alligators, birds, fish and (unfortunately) mosquitoes.

## Taylor Bayou to Port Bolivar–GIWW Mile 291 to Mile 350 WHL

**NAVIGATION:** Charts 11326, 11324 and 11331. At about the halfway point between Sabine River and Bolivar Roads (Mile 319.3 WHL), you will pass under the **High Island Bridge** with 73-foot fixed vertical clearance. The 40-foot-high mound of High Island to the south of the GIWW is an ancient salt dome that is the highest spot for nearly 100 miles. As you go under the bridge, you will notice a wide, L-shaped cut to the north inside

the marsh grass. The cut has 5- to 7-foot depths. You [ca]n drop anchor here, but the barges going by push a lot [of] water in and out of this small cut.

Beyond the bridge, a long "S" turn takes 3 to 4 miles [to] unwind itself around Horseshoe Marsh and into East [B]ay Bayou. The towboat captains refer to it as the "High [Is]land Wiggles." (Not to be confused with the "Freeport [W]iggles" 100 miles to the west.) The High Island [b]ridge is the only hurricane escape route north for local [r]esidents of High Island and Bolivar Peninsula.

At Mile 325 WHL the GIWW crosses a very shallow [ar]m of East Bay (the southeast arm of Galveston Bay), [k]nown as the East Bay Washout by towboat captains. [T]he banks of the waterway are submerged here and [m]arked with buoys on both sides. Flashing green lights [m]ark the east end and flashing red lights mark the west [e]nd. Just before Mile 330 WHL the GIWW crosses [R]ollover Bay. The cut through the GIWW in Rollover [B]ay is marked the same way as the East Bay Washout, [p]lus there is a set of range markers to help guide you [t]hrough.

Rollover Pass is the only outlet to the Gulf of Mexico [f]or the entire southeast section of Galveston Bay, so the [c]rosscurrent can be significant. The pass is only good [f]or shallow-draft fishing boats. Make every effort to [c]ontact any commercial vessel prior to passing. Radio [c]onversations by towboat captains can be valuable in [t]his area.

A note on Rollover Pass: The State of Texas and [A]rmy Corps of Engineers have made plans to close the [1],600-foot manmade channel, but there is community [r]esistance to the closure and the State doesn't own the surrounding land. Rollover Pass was "a gift to the People of Texas" initiated by the Gulf Coast Rod, Reel and Gun Club, a Beaumont-based group of anglers and hunters, who purchased the land in the early 1950s. The club granted an easement to the State for construction of the channel.

From Rollover Bay the GIWW is a land cut leading down the Bolivar Peninsula to Port Bolivar, a former small commercial port with a 116-foot abandoned lighthouse, now privately owned. Port Bolivar overlooks Bolivar Roads, which is the entrance to Galveston Bay. On the eastern side of the jetties, you may spot several oceangoing freighters and tankers in a designated anchored.

Just offshore at the jetties is another holding anchorage for large ships. Then, 40 to 60 miles offshore, there is a major unloading anchorage for massive supertankers that are too huge to enter the ship channel. Lighter tankers constantly run in and out, carrying crude oil and refined products to and from the supertankers. In Bolivar Roads, ships and tugs are moving endlessly through this major intersection of the GIWW, the Houston Ship Channel, the Port of Galveston and the

**Commercial traffic** in the area of the Houston Ship Channel and Galveston Island is managed by Vessel Traffic Services, Houston Galveston (uscg.mil/vtshouston). There primary purpose is to improve maritime safety and efficiency in the largest petrochemical port in the United States. They can be contacted on VHF Channel 11 or 12. Pleasure boats are not required to contact VTS Houston Galveston and rarely do.

Texas City Ship Channel. This is a super highway of boat traffic.

Dredges are frequently working the various channels in the Bolivar Roads area and the spoil areas of the Houston Ship Channel, trying to combat heavy shoaling caused by the ebb and flow of Galveston Bay's tide and tidal currents. Throughout the Galveston Bay area, navigation lights blend in with those of ships, towboats, dredges and some of the world's largest petrochemical refineries to create a daunting light show. Picking out a slow-flashing red light in the midst of this kaleidoscope takes a keen and steady eye.

**Dockage:** At Mile 336 WHL on the south side of the GIWW is Stingaree Marina. Gasoline is available at the fuel dock to port. This is a small convenient stop with limited transient dockage at the bulkhead, alongside a small store, bait stand and restaurant. It is a good idea to call ahead and they will hold a spot open for you. Heading straight in from the GIWW depth should be around 5 feet. Electricity is available but limited.

At Mile 343 WHL, near flashing red "4" and green "3," the Bolivar Yacht Basin sits on the south side across from a large cut, called Siever's Cove on the chart, into Galveston Bay. (A small, shallow channel with private markers leads to the Galveston Bay fishing areas.) Gas, ice and limited supplies are available at the small marina dock and transient dockage is very limited. The marina caters to small fishing boats and commercial fishermen.

One mile beyond Bolivar Yacht Basin on the south shore is the development of Laguna Harbor. Laguna Harbor is a beautiful and well-protected private community just off the GIWW at Mile 345.5 WHL. Slips may be available. Prior arrangements must be made with Laguna Harbor (409-971-2573) before entering the marina facility.

From Port Bolivar, the cruising skipper has a choice of destinations: Galveston, Offatts Bayou, Clear Lake, Houston or the GIWW, southwest to the end of the line at Brownsville.

# ■ GALVESTON BAY

Galveston Bay is one of the larger bays in the United States. Average depths are 10 to 12 feet over a flat, smooth, and muddy bottom, due to centuries of shrimp trawlers dragging their kicker chains across the bottom. The bay is made up of four segments: West Bay and East

Bay border Bolivar Peninsula and Galveston Island, wh Trinity, to the northeast, and Galveston Bay, which start at Bolivar Roads, encompasses the western part of the bay all the way to Baytown.

Overall, it is more than 30 miles long from the GIWW north to Baytown and 30 miles wide from Texas City to the end of East Bay. The shores are flat and marshy in some places, with very few distinctive features.

The normal tidal range on Galveston Bay is minimal with two to four tidal changes per day. The bay is normally too rough, but small craft can anchor anywhe outside of the channel markers. Use caution when a weather front is expected. During strong winds water levels can change by 4 to 6 feet and wave heights can b significant.

Galveston is the oldest deep water Gulf port west of New Orleans, and combined with the Port of Houston, tallies up to be the largest port area in the U.S. This means constant big ship and barge traffic in the Housto Ship Channel from Galveston to Bayport and the inner ship channel under the dramatic Bayport Bridge.

## Galveston Bay West Shore

**NAVIGATION:** Use Chart 11326. Leave the GIWW and head north on the Houston Ship Channel. The channel with its well-marked flashing green and red lights, make a great reference for traveling the bay. Although the shi channel has a project depth of 45 feet, recreational boat should use the "barge shelves" along the edges in 15- to 20-foot depths.

Dickinson Bay is 7 miles north of Mile 351 WHL alon the Houston Ship Channel just past 17-foot flashing green "45" and flashing red "46." Steer southwest and follow the daybeacons and flashing lights in the bay, extending 5 miles from the ship channel. Dickinson Bay is navigable to the **Dickinson Bayou Twin Bridges** (45-foot vertical clearance). The railroad swing bridge shown on the chart has been removed. Dickinson Bay is shallow. The point on the southern tip of San Leon is aptly named, "April Fool Point."

**Dockage:** On the southern tip at April Fool Point is the Topwater Grill, a popular seafood restaurant adjacen to April Fool Marina, which caters to smaller fishing boats. Transient dockage is not available, but the marina sells gas and diesel. A vessel repair yard is located on Sa Bayou near the bridge in Dickinson Bay next door to a shrimp processor.

## Redfish Island

Redfish Island, a popular boating destination, had at one time eroded away due to storms. The Port of Houston and the Army Corps of Engineers restored the 6-acre island. A portion of the island is a bird habitat attracting barren-ground nesters like the black skimmer, Forester's tern, royal tern and gull-billed tern

**NAVIGATION:** Use Chart 11326. Redfish Island is located just northwest of the intersection of the Trinity River Channel and Galveston Ship Channel and can only be entered from the north side. As you pass HSC marker "57," locate a 17-foot-tall daybeacon with white and black diamonds located approximately .28 nm on a course of 292 from "57." When leaving the channel keep this shoal marker to port. Inside the marker depths are less than 1 foot at low tide. Continuing west, look for the other shoal marker just off the northwest tip of Redfish. Again, leave this to port.

**Anchorage:** The C shape of the island protects boaters from south, east and southeast winds as well as from wakes from large cargo and petrochemical ships in the Houston Ship Channel. It is a favorite anchorage for both local and transient boaters with depths from 6 to 8 feet or shallower as you get to the eastern shore.

## South & North Cuts

When the Houston Ship Channel was widened and deepened, Five-Mile Cut, a channel cutting across the GIWW, was permanently closed and the buoys removed. The Cut was replaced by two boater cuts called the South Cut and the North Cut. The South Cut lies just to the north of markers HSC green "61" and HSC red "62," while the North Cut is just north of markers HSC green "69" and HSC red "70." A spoil island known as the Mid-Bay Marsh lies in the old location of Five Mile Cut. The island rises several feet above the water and is considered a bird sanctuary. The marsh/island is not on older charts and chartplotters.

## Clear Lake

If you are traveling in Galveston Bay, Clear Lake is a popular place to visit, with its excellent marinas, marine services, restaurants, trendy shops and entertainment. Kemah on the south bank and Seabrook on the north bank of Clear Creek and Clear Lake are joined by the **Bayport Blvd. Bridge** (73-foot fixed vertical clearance). The Kemah Boardwalk on the south side of the entrance consists of a hotel, amusement park and many fine restaurants.

**NAVIGATION:** Use Chart 11326. Leave the Houston Ship Channel heading west at flashing green "61" using the marked South Boaters Cut. Red buoys will be to starboard with green marks to port. The entrance to the Clear Lake channel at the 17-foot flashing red "2" is 4 nm west of the South Boaters Cut marker red "8." Unless you have local knowledge of the water outside

www.snagaslip.com

SNAG-A-SLIP

EXPLORE
BOOK
BOAT

# Clear Lake, TX

Column headers (diagonal):
Largest Vessel Accommodated · VHF Channel Monitored · Transient Berths / Total Berths · Approach / Dockside Depth (reported) · Floating Docks · Gas / Diesel · Groceries, Ice, Marine Supplies, Snacks · Repairs: Hull, Engine, Propeller · Lift (tonnage), Crane, Rail · Laundry, Pool, Showers, Courtesy Car · Min/Max Amps · Pump-Out Station · Nearby: Grocery Store, Motel, Restaurant

| CLEAR LAKE AREA | | Dockage | | | | | Supplies | | Services | | | | | |
|---|---|---|---|---|---|---|---|---|---|---|---|---|---|---|
| 1. Seabrook Marina/Shipyard and Fuel Dock (WiFi) | 281-474-2586 | 125 | 16 | 20/750 | 10/9 | F | GD | GIS | HEP | L70,C20 | 30/100 | LPS | P | GMF |
| 2. Kemah Boardwalk Marina ▭ (WiFi) WG | **281-334-2284** | **115** | **16/72** | **25/414** | **10/10** | **F** | **-** | **IS** | **E** | **-** | **30/100** | **LPS** | **P** | **GMF** |
| 3. Portofino Harbour Marina (WiFi) | 281-334-6007 | 55 | - | 5/212 | 7/7 | F | - | I | - | - | 30/50 | LPS | P | GMF |
| 4. Legend Point Marina | 281-334-3811 | 50 | - | call/254 | 7/6 | - | - | - | - | - | 30/50 | LPS | P | GMF |
| 5. Watergate Yachting Center (WiFi) | 281-334-1511 | 120 | 68 | call/1200 | 9/9 | F | - | - | HEP | L35 | 30/200+ | LPS | - | GMF |
| 6. Waterford Harbor Marina (WiFi) | 281-334-4400 | 70 | 16 | 0/643 | 7/7 | F | - | I | - | - | 50/50 | LPS | P | GMF |
| 7. Marina del Sol (WiFi) | 281-334-3909 | 55 | - | 10/331 | 8/5 | F | - | I | - | - | 30/50 | LPS | P | GMF |
| 8. South Shore Harbour Marina (WiFi) | 281-334-0515 | 120 | - | call/855 | 8/10 | F | GD | IS | - | - | 30/50 | LPS | P | GMF |
| 9. Bal Harbour Marina-PRIVATE | 281-333-5168 | 45 | - | 0/133 | 5/4 | - | - | - | - | - | 30/30 | PS | - | GMR |
| 10. Clear Lake Marine Center | 281-326-4426 | 45 | - | call/161 | 6.5/6.5 | - | - | - | HE | L77,C | - | S | - | GMR |
| 11. Lakewood Yacht Club-PRIVATE ▭ (WiFi) | 281-474-2511 | 100 | - | 5/300 | 10/8 | F | D | IS | - | C2 | 50/100 | LPS | P | GMR |
| 12. Blue Dolphin Yachting Center | 281-474-4450 | 75 | - | call/237 | 8/8 | - | - | - | - | - | 30/200+ | LPS | - | GMR |

▭ Internet Access   (WiFi) Wireless Internet Access   WG Waterway Guide Cruising Club Partner   *(Information in the table is provided by the facilities.)*
See WaterwayGuide.com for current rates, fuel prices, web site addresses, and other up-to-the-minute information.

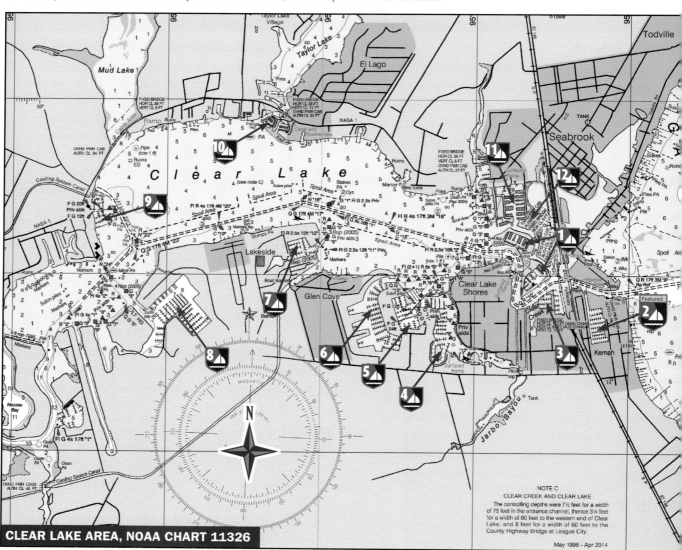

CLEAR LAKE AREA, NOAA CHART 11326

NOTE C
CLEAR CREEK AND CLEAR LAKE
The controlling depths were 7½ feet for a width of 75 feet in the entrance channel, thence 3½ feet for a width of 60 feet to the western end of Clear Lake, and 8 feet for a width of 60 feet to the County Highway Bridge at League City.
May 1998 - Apr 2014

he channel, it is advisable to stay inside the boaters
ut channel. Starting at markers "3" and "4," there are
andbars and spoil banks just outside the channel. Just
outh of green daybeacon "5" is the unmarked wreck of
n old iron barge. The old warning markers were blown
way and have not been replaced. There is generally 10
o 12 feet of water anywhere between the ship channel
nd the entry markers to Clear Creek and Clear Lake.

On weekends high-speed powerboat traffic may create
arge wakes. Entering Clear Lake at night is made easier
y several 150-foot lights at the Kemah Boardwalk
Marina. Take note that they are usually turned off by
midnight on the weekends and earlier during the week.
Check your depths, and watch your markers. Traffic is
ery heavy on weekends and holidays. The Bayport Blvd.
ridge is well illuminated throughout the night, and is
n excellent reference for navigation in this area.

**Dockage:** The Seabrook Marina/Shipyard and Fuel
Dock, on the north side of the channel, is a 55-acre
sland complex, offering complete transient amenities
nd a full-service boatyard. The Kemah Boardwalk
Marina is the only marina east of the highway bridge,
ffering floating slips with transient dockage for vessels
p to 115 feet. There is easy access to all the restaurants
n Kemah from this marina, which has slips dedicated to
estaurant traffic.

Portofino Harbour Marina is located just past the
ridge on the south side. This is a full service marina
with transient floating dockage. Further up the channel,
n the south side of the main channel, is a huge
ssortment of marinas, condominiums, restaurants and a
hipyard.

Legend Point Marina is built around condominiums,
accessible from the gated and guarded entrance by
a stone bridge. To get to Legend Point, follow the
Watergate channel until you enter the breakwater. Turn
hard to port and follow the channel around to the left
keeping close to the docks. The last Watergate dock is
covered for powerboats. Once past it you are at Legend
Point. Waterford Harbor Marina, also located here,
with a separate dedicated channel, may have transient
space; call ahead. The large Watergate Yachting Center is
entered through the Watergate channel, which is marked
by daybeacons. The marina has 1200 slips and offers
some repairs.

Continuing 1 mile west on the Clear Lake Channel,
Marina Del Sol lies on the south shore of the lake.
This is a quiet spot with transient dockage and dry

stack storage for small boats. There are no amenities or
services close by.

At the far western end of the channel on the south
shore is South Shore Harbor Marina, which is part of a
vast complex that includes a golf club, tennis courts, a
fitness center and the South Shore Hotel. The marina
itself has one of the few pump-out stations on the lake.
The marina is known as the local "hurricane hole." Dug
out of dry land, it is protected by 12 to 15 foot banks
that provide a true hurricane hole.

On the north side of Clear Lake, Bal Harbour Marina
is private. Clear Lake Marine Center has slips and offers
repairs. Back at the entrance, a channel on the north
shore marked by green daybeacons will take you to the
Lakewood Yacht Club and the Blue Dolphin Yachting
Center. Facilities at the Yacht Club are not available
without reciprocal membership or by prior arrangement.
Dolphin Yachting Center only offers long-term (month
or more) dockage.

There are many other condominium and apartment
marinas around the Clear Lake shore where transient
dockage may be available if you are able to make prior
plans.

Ad text below image

# GOIN' ASHORE: KEMAH (CLEAR LAKE), TX

| SERVICES | |
|---|---|
| **1** | Visitor Information |
| **ATTRACTIONS** | |
| **2** | Kemah Boardwalk |
| **SHOPPING** | |
| **3** | West Marine |
| **MARINAS** | |
| **4** | Kemah Boardwalk Marina |
| **5** | Portofino Harbour |
| **6** | Seabrook Marina/Shipyard and Fuel Dock |

Several coastal towns surround Clear Lake, Houston's boating capital: Clear Lake Shores, Kemah, Seabrook and League City. Seabrook, on the northeast section of the lake just east of the Bayport Blvd. Bridge, is noted for its historic district, with commercial fishing vessels, the Old Seabrook Antiques District, fresh seafood markets, hiking, biking and extensive birding trails (part of the Great Texas Coastal Birding Trails).

**Attractions:** The quaint Kemah Boardwalk (215 Kipp Ave.) features entertainment, games, carnival-type rides, shopping and restaurants of all varieties. See details at kemahboardwalk.com. The thrilling Boardwalk Bullet roller coaster is a special favorite among visitors. A short drive takes you to Houston Space Center (spacecenter.org), and *Battleship Texas*, the only battleship to serve in WWI and WWII. She was the flagship for the Omaha Beach invasion on D-Day. See more at battleshiptexas.org. From Clear Lake you can also take a car or cab to the downtown Houston area, and hop on the electric Metro trolley system, which runs fast on its tracks down Main Street.

**Shopping:** Kemah Lighthouse Shopping District at 6th Street and Bradford Avenue has an array of interesting shops and eateries to check out while you stroll and a little lighthouse park to relax in. Also, within walking/biking distance are Super Walmart, Target and Home Depot. There is an expanded Super West Marine on the south side of the lake and a regular West Marine on the north side of Clear Lake.

**Dining:** Restaurants are mostly on E. NASA Pkwy. and range from Starbucks Coffee Shop to Landry's Seafood House, Red Sushi Grill, Joe's Crab Shack, Chart House, the Flying Dutchman, the Aquarium, Saltgrass Steakhouse and the Cadillac Bar & Grill. The whole area is easily accessible to several marinas within walking/biking distance. In the Kemah area, South Shore Grille (281-334-7700) specializes in Cuban dishes and has outdoor seating.

## pper Galveston Bay

Up the Houston Ship Channel, the bustling city of Houston offers all the usual metropolitan sights and activities. Navigable all the way to the towering skyscrapers, Buffalo Bayou runs through the city from the ship channel and passes the restored *Battleship Texas* at San Jacinto Park. You must obtain U.S. Coast Guard clearance to travel past the battleship. It is advisable to call the U.S. Coast Guard before you make this trip, or call them on VHF Channel 16 to advise them of your plans.

**Dockage:** The Houston Yacht Club is situated on the west shore of Galveston Bay just 4 miles northeast, and then 2 miles northwest, of the Clear Lake entrance marker 30-foot flashing red "2." This historic yacht club was founded in the early 1900s. It is private but offers reciprocal privileges to all other yacht club members. A fuel dock with gas and diesel is available. The restaurant and lounge are located in the main club building.

To access the yacht club, stay well clear of Red Bluff Point by heading toward flashing green "73" on the Houston Ship Channel. A turn to the northwest, lining up green can buoy "1" and then 17-foot flashing green "3" to port on the Bayport Ship Channel will put you in line to approach the enclosed harbor of the yacht club. Sailboat masts inside the breakwater and the magnificent "Bermuda Pink" Houston Yacht Club building are prominent landmarks. Steer directly toward the colorful Houston Yacht Club sign on the seawall, and then turn hard to port and the entrance will open up before you.

Bayland Park Marina is located on the northeast corner of the **Fred Hartman (SR 146) Hwy. Bridge**. The channel to the marina is located just west of HSC red "100." Shoaling in the channel and at the entrance to the marina has been a problem in the past. Call ahead for updates and to let them know when you plan to arrive. Tie to the fuel dock to register if they have not given slip directions before you arrive. This marina is in an isolated location with no nearby amenities

## East of the Houston Ship Channel–Trinity Bay

**NAVIGATION:** Use Chart 11326. Double Bayou is on the east side of Trinity Bay, about 8 nm from the Boaters Cut on the north side of the spoil island. The Double Bayou Channel is about 7 feet deep. Changes to the numbering scheme and the deletion of a number of daybeacons have not improved access. The red daybeacons are currently

# Galveston Bay, TX

| | | Largest Vessel Accommodated | VHF Channel Monitored | Dockage: Transient/Total Berths | Dockage: Approach/Dockside Depth (reported) | Dockage: Floating Docks | Dockage: Gas/Diesel | Supplies: Groceries, Ice, Marine Supplies, Snacks | Services: Repairs: Hull, Engine, Propeller | Services: Lift (tonnage), Crane, Rail | Services: Min/Max Amps | Services: Laundry, Pool, Showers | Services: Pump-Out Station | Services: Nearby: Grocery Store, Motel, Restaurant |
|---|---|---|---|---|---|---|---|---|---|---|---|---|---|---|
| **SHOREACRES** | | | | | | | | | | | | | | |
| 1. Houston Yacht Club WIFI | 281-471-1255 | 70 | 68 | 90/244 | 8/7 | F | GD | I | – | L5,C2 | 30/50 | LPS | P | R |
| **BAYTOWN AREA** | | | | | | | | | | | | | | |
| 2. Bayland Marina | 281-422-8900 | 60 | – | /20 | – | F | – | IMS | – | – | 30/30 | S | – | – |

⌨ Internet Access  WIFI Wireless Internet Access  WG Waterway Guide Cruising Club Partner  *(Information in the table is provided by the facilities.)*
See WaterwayGuide.com for current rates, fuel prices, web site addresses, and other up-to-the-minute information.

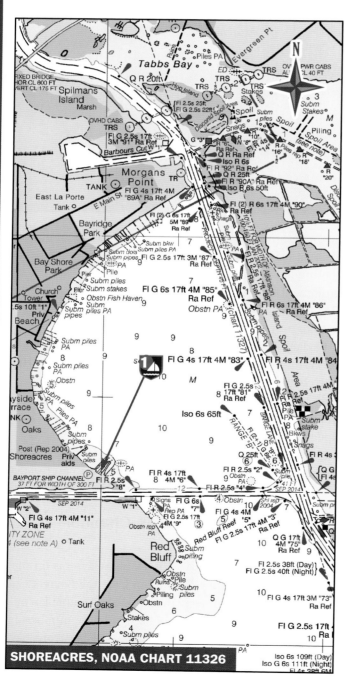

**SHOREACRES, NOAA CHART 11326**

**BAYTOWN AREA, NOAA CHART 11328**

arranged as follows: 17-foot flashing red "2," 17-foot flashing red "4," 17-foot flashing red "6," red "8," red "10," green "11" and 17-foot "red "12." There is a report that red "12" has been replaced with a daybeacon. Red "12" is at a critical turn and many boaters have come to grief here. Stay on the red side of the channel. Shallow depths should not be a problem before red "8."

 Use caution and go slowly and watch the depth sounder! Do not pass commercial traffic at the turn; it's too narrow for two.

**Dockage:** Follow the channel markers to green "15" (the last one), and then line up on the water tower to find the deepest water. The sometimes rowdy and popular bar and eating spot Marker 17 is to port. They have limited dockage and few amenities. Oak Island Complex is also located to port with slips and fuel.

Just past the Channel Marker 17 Restaurant, the bayou splits into the east and west forks. On the West Fork is Jobe Beason Park with slips for vessels to 40 feet. Next on port is the Hurricane Club & Restaurant (409-252-3269), which may have slips for smaller boats. The restaurant serves good, reasonably priced food, and there is an adjacent motel as well.

**Anchorage:** Turn right into the east fork (it looks narrow at first) and find water at least 7-feet deep for several miles. Pick a nice spot and nose into the bank. Tie your bow to a tree, or drag an anchor to the bank. Tie the stern to a tree to keep from swinging downstream. Use care not to block the bayou with either your boat or anchor rode. Depending on your draft, anchorage and bayou bank tie-ups are almost unlimited.

## Smith Point

Smith Point and the nearby Vingt-et-un Islands (French for "21") are famous for the number of birds who call the area home. The largest claim to fame at Smith Point is the incredible oyster harvest each season.

**NAVIGATION:** Use Chart 11326. Roughly 8 miles south-southeast of Double Bayou, is Smith Point. To go to Smith Point, use the Boaters Cut at red flashing "62" and then navigate through the extensive oil field located east of the Houston Ship Channel. You can also approach Smith Point from the north from Double Bayou or from the south using East Bay.

Trinity Channel was a part of a project to allow barge traffic to go to Dallas. The project was shelved in 1973 when lack of funding made it impossible. Some surveys were done and a land cut along the eastern shore of Trinity Bay was laid out. It is still shown on Chart 11326, but depths have not been maintained. There are no daybeacons or other marks.

# Channel, TX

| OAK ISLAND | | Dockage | | | | | Supplies | | Services | | | | |
|---|---|---|---|---|---|---|---|---|---|---|---|---|---|
| | | Largest Vessel Accommodated | VHF Channel Monitored | Transient Berths / Total Berths | Approach / Dockside Depth (reported) | Floating Docks | Gas / Diesel | Repairs: Hull, Engine, Propeller | Groceries, Ice, Marine Supplies, Snacks | Lift (tonnage), Crane, Rail | Laundry, Pool, Showers, Courtesy Car | Min/Max Amps | Pump-Out Station | Nearby: Grocery Store, Motel, Restaurant |
| 1. Job Beason Park | 409-267-2409 | 40 | – | 15/15 | 6/6 | – | – | GIS | – | – | 30/50 | – | – | GMR |
| 2. Oak Island Lodge (WiFi) | 409-252-4122 | 25 | – | 18/18 | 6/5 | – | GD | GIS | – | – | 30/50 | S | – | GMR |

🖥 Internet Access  (WiFi) Wireless Internet Access  WG Waterway Guide Cruising Club Partner *(Information in the table is provided by the facilities.)*
See WaterwayGuide.com for current rates, fuel prices, web site addresses, and other up-to-the-minute information.

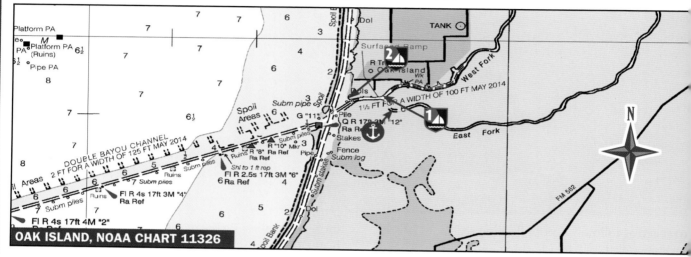

OAK ISLAND, NOAA CHART 11326

Smith Point Channel flashing green "1" marks a narrow passage used mainly by the oyster boat fleet. New buoys are in place, but local knowledge is essential for entering here. Smith Point Channel often changes and shoals appear rather suddenly. On a recent survey less than 4 feet was found at green daybeacon "3." Obtaining local knowledge to enter here remains mandatory

**Anchorage:** Although exposed from the northeast through northwest, holding is good here in 7 to 8 feet of water.

## Galveston Island

**NAVIGATION:** Use Charts 11323, 11324 and 11327. At the intersection of the GIWW and the Houston Ship Channel you can choose to go to Galveston Island using the alternate GIWW route or to the Railroad and Causeway Bridges and points west by using the main GIWW route that bisects Pelican Island.

Travel south in the Houston Ship Channel past green "27" where you can see the Texas City Dike to the west, and Port Bolivar to the east. If you are continuing west in the main GIWW route through the Pelican Island

Cut, leave the Ship Channel at green "25A" on a heading of 180 degrees and intersect the GIWW at green "3." There is plenty of water throughout this area until you reach green "3." From there, stay on the GIWW. (This route is described in detail in the "Galveston West End" section of this chapter.)

Green "25" the Houston Ship Channel makes a slight turn east. You should start to see the Bolivar Ferries transporting vehicles between Port Bolivar and Galveston Island. Continue to GR "P" where Pelican Island and Sea Wolf Park are to the southeast and Galveston Island is southwest. Take a slight turn left and exit the jetties to the Gulf of Mexico, or turn right into the Galveston Channel. Galveston Channel provides access to marinas and fuel.

You can leave the Galveston Channel by traveling back to Bolivar Roads or continuing west to Pelican Island Causeway Bridge. Contact Pelican Island Bridge to request a bridge opening and follow the channel to the GIWW at the Galveston Causeway Railroad Bridges. (This route is explained in greater detail later in this chapter.)

**Dockage:** Galveston Yacht Basin is located just west of the Bolivar Ferry landing. The Fuel Dock, just to

...e west of the Coast Guard Station (look for the big ...ell logo), offers transient dockage for powerboats ...d sailing vessels if there are slips available; most slips ...e rented by the month or year. The fuel dock opens ...om 6:00 a.m. to 6:00 p.m. every day. Galveston Yacht ...ervice, Inc. an independent repair yard located at the ...acht basin, has complete repair services. A drugstore, ...rocery, motel and eateries are within walking distance.

The Harbor House Hotel & Marina in the Pier 21 area ...as a small transient marina. The marina is a block from ...he Strand historical district. It offers electricity and ...vater, but no shower facilities, unless you rent a room at ...ne small hotel (which also gives you free dockage).

Enter and depart with caution since vessel traffic is ...eavy and tidal currents across the narrow entrance can ...e strong. There is free dockage if you are eating at one ...f the fine restaurants beside the marina. Weekends ...re fully booked in the summertime so call ahead for ...eservations.

**Anchorage:** Just east of the Galveston Yacht Basin, ...local anchorage is in the small cove formed by the ...oncrete wall sheltering the basin and some private ...omes along the shore. The Coast Guard station is just ...o the east as are the ferryboat landings. Tidal currents ...an be swift in either direction; you could consider a ...wo-anchor Bahamian style moor in this area. Although ...he commercial traffic is fairly heavy, the channel is wide ...nd riding "on the hook" is not too uncomfortable, ...lthough it will be fairly rolly when the big workboats ...nove in and out before dawn. Another option is west of ...he Pelican Island Bridge north of flashing red "2." Be ...autious of the submerged dike noted on the chart.

## Galveston West End

**NAVIGATION:** Use Charts 11322 and 11324. The GIWW ...crosses the Houston Ship Channel and the Texas City ...Channel at Mile 351.0 WHL and passes through a ...narrow cut at the northwest end of Pelican Island. ...Mooring buoys placed along the north side complicate ...the passage. It is common to find several tows tied up ...here and they appear to be in the channel. Plans to ...widen the channel are on the Army Corps of Engineers ...drawing board with no current plan of action.

From the cut to the I-45 bridges, the channel markers ...alternate with floating buoys and lighted daybeacons. ...To reconnect with the GIWW, head west along the ...Galveston Channel. The **Pelican Island Causeway Bascule Bridge** (13-foot closed with restricted openings) monitors VHF Channel 16 and uses VHF

Channel 13 for traffic. The bridge opens on signal, except from 6:40 a.m. to 8:10 a.m., noon to 1:00 p.m., and 4:15 p.m. to 5:15 p.m., Monday through Friday, when it need not open.

Once through the Pelican Island Bridge, you will see a flashing red "2" followed by a series of red nun and green can buoys. They may be difficult to see on windy days when there is chop. This route returns you to the main GIWW near Mile 356.0 WHL and follows a channel to the GIWW near the **Galveston Causeway Railroad Bascule Bridge** and the high-rise **Gulf Freeway (1-45) Twin Bridges**. Commercial traffic monitors VHF Channel 16 west of the causeway bridges, changing from VHF Channel 13 to the east. Contact the Galveston Causeway Railroad Bridge (8-foot vertical clearance) before going through. Even though it has a bridge tender, the bridge operates automatically whenever a train gets close. You must get the bridge tenders permission (on VHF Channel 09 or VHF Channel 13) to pass. The Gulf Freeway Twin Bridges have a fixed clearance of 73 feet. You will not want to be in the pass between the bridges with a barge and towboat and they will usually let you know in explicit terms.

**Dockage:** The entry to the Pier 77 Marine Service is along the west side of the Gulf Freeway Twin Bridges. While the facility doesn't have transient space, they do offer repairs and have a 88-ton lift, 110-ton crane and a railway. Payco Marina is located on the east side of the bridges. The narrow 6- to 8-foot-deep channel is unmarked, so mind your depth sounder. Payco Marina offers slips and has gas and diesel fuel. They also have a lift and repairs can be made here. You will need transportation to go to town or get to the beach. Payco Marina is primarily a fishing center, not a resort-type marina.

## Offatts Bayou

Offatts Bayou is the result of major dredging that provided landfill to raise the west side of Galveston as much as 6 feet. After the dredging, it was opened as a small boat refuge and anchorage. It cuts into Galveston Island just south of the Galveston Causeway Railroad Bridge and the Gulf Freeway Twin Bridges. Offatts Bayou offers charted depths ranging from 10 to 20 feet with good holding ground.

**NAVIGATION:** Use Chart 11322. Entering westbound from the GIWW, pass through the Galveston Causeway Railroad Bridge and Gulf Freeway Twin Bridges (Mile

# Galveston Bay, TX

| | | | | Dockage | | | Supplies | | Services | | | | | |
|---|---|---|---|---|---|---|---|---|---|---|---|---|---|---|
| | | Largest Vessel Accommodated | VHF Channel Monitored | Transient Berths / Total Berths | Approach / Dockside Depth (reported) | Floating Docks | Gas / Diesel | Groceries, Ice, Marine Supplies, Snacks | Repairs: Hull, Engine, Propeller | Lift (tonnage), Crane, Rail | Min/Max Amps | Laundry, Pool, Showers, Courtesy Car | Pump-Out Station | Nearby: Grocery Store, Motel, Restaurant |
| **GALVESTON CHANNEL** | | | | | | | | | | | | | | |
| 1. Galveston Yacht Basin WiFi | 409-765-3000 | – | – | call/497 | 10/8 | F | GD | IMS | HEP | L75 | 30/100 | LS | P | GMF |
| 2. Harbor House Hotel & Marina at Pier 21 💻 WiFi | 409-763-3321 | 80 | 68 | 9/9 | 30/10 | F | – | GIS | – | – | 50/50 | S | – | GM |
| **OFFATTS BAYOU AREA** | | | | | | | | | | | | | | |
| 3. Pier 77 Marine Service | 409-740-4000 | 71 | – | – | – | – | – | M | HEP | L88,C110,R | 30/30 | – | – | GR |
| 4. Payco Inc. Harbor and Marina  357 WHL | 409-744-7428 | 65 | – | 5/260 | 5/6 | F | – | MS | HEP | L60,C | 30/100 | S | – | GR |
| 5. Moody Gardens Marina  358 WHL | 888-388-8484 | 60 | – | 17/17 | 6/10 | – | – | I | – | – | 50/50 | LPSC | – | GMF |
| 6. Pelican Rest Marina 💻 WiFi | 409-744-2618 | 200 | 16/69 | 10/131 | 18/18 | F | GD | IM | – | L | 30/200+ | LPS | P | GMF |

💻 Internet Access   WiFi Wireless Internet Access   **WG** Waterway Guide Cruising Club Partner  *(Information in the table is provided by the facilities.)*
See WaterwayGuide.com for current rates, fuel prices, web site addresses, and other up-to-the-minute information.

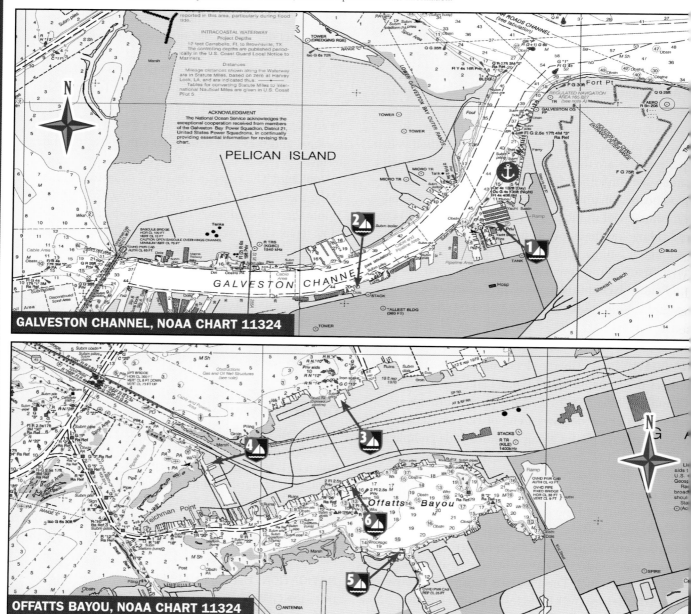

GALVESTON CHANNEL, NOAA CHART 11324

OFFATTS BAYOU, NOAA CHART 11324

57.3 WHL) and wait until you can line up the channel markers, then head southeast on the well-marked channel. Shoals form on both sides of the channel, so use caution. As you pass Teichman Point and pick up the markers indicating the main channel east into Offatts Bayou, keep to port and stay fairly close to the shoreline. There is an ever-expanding oyster reef on the south side. Do not turn south until you pass the last marker (red "28") and don't mistake red "26" for red "28." It is difficult to see the marker due to its easterly position in relation to the rest of the channel markers. If you turn south too quickly, you will run hard aground on the oyster reef, which is clearly visible at low tide. Once you have passed the last marker, your water depth increases to the 20-foot depths mentioned above.

⚠️ Placement of markers has changed in more recent NOAA charts, so make sure you have the most recent edition when navigating Offatts Bayou. Check for updates at waterwayguide.com.

**Dockage:** Past red "28" on the south shore of the bayou you will see three pyramids and a hotel that are part of Moody Gardens. There is a marina there with water and electricity but few other amenities. It is well worth the stop because it affords access to all that Moody Gardens has to offer, which includes a paddlewheel cruise boat, two theaters, a zipline course, a waterpark and a golf course. It is advisable to call ahead for reservations.

On the north shore of Offatts Bayou across from Moody Gardens is Pelican Rest Marina with floating docks and amenities. The marina features a steak and seafood restaurant and a fuel dock, as well as other resort-style amenities.

Harborwalk Yacht Club & Marina is located at Mile 362 WHL, west of Tiki Island just off of green can buoy "59." It is described in more detail in the next section.

**Anchorage:** Offatts Bayou enjoys an almost constant sea breeze from the Gulf of Mexico. This popular anchorage can be crowded on weekends, but there is always ample room. It is popular with skiers and personal watercraft operators. It is the most popular destination for those coming from the northern part of Galveston Bay, and the only sheltered anchorage in the southern part of the bay.

You can anchor almost anywhere in the bayou. The quickest and simplest location is toward Moody Gardens, where you can anchor in 15- to 20-foot depths. In foul weather the smaller part of the bayou at the southeast end might be a little more comfortable. This is a great place to exercise your dinghy while viewing the many interesting homes along the shores and canals.

In the far southeast part of Offatts you have easy dinghy access to convenience stores and the dinghy docks at Boudreaux's on the Bayou, when it is open.

# GOIN' ASHORE: **GALVESTON, TX**

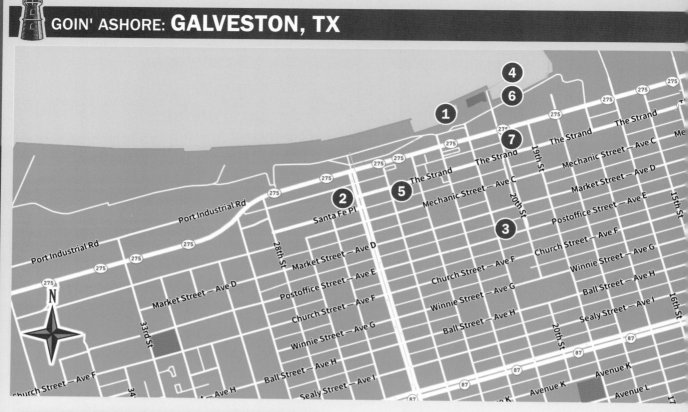

Galveston is a treasured island that the locals enjoy year round and tourist flock to by the hundreds of thousands. It is a great place to live and to visit. It has a waterfront on four sides, beautiful beaches on three, and the Galveston Channel, Wharf and Strand on the other. There is constant activity and much of it is large and bodacious. There are quiet bays and peaceful sanctuaries. There is no way to list all that there is to see and do. A good place to start is galveston.com.

From the 1830s to 1900, Galveston was the biggest and most prosperous city in Texas. Its commercial center was then known as the "Wall Street of the Southwest," and its deep port made Galveston one of the world's preeminent shipping centers. The devastating hurricane of 1900 caused more than 6,000 deaths and brought the city to its knees. The glory days were over, and Galveston endured a long and steady decline throughout the first half of the 20th century.

**Attractions:** Like many other cities, Galveston has enjoyed quite a re-emergence, and many of the architectural gems of old have been restored, including the Grand 1894 Opera House (2020 Post Office St., 409-765-1894). A wealth of information can be discovered through the Galveston History Foundation and the Galveston County Historical Museum.

Galveston has a maritime legacy, which can be best experienced with a trip along Pier 21 at Harborside Drive and 21st Street. Visit the Texas Seaport Museum (409-763-1877) and tour the restored 1877 tall ship, *Elissa*. The Museum is a worthwhile stop for history buffs and includes the Pier 21 Theater, featuring two important events in Galveston history. Scheduled each day, the "Great Storm" relates the tragedy of the 1900 hurricane, and "The Pirate Island" tells the story of Jean Lafitte's camp on the island. Also available is an immigration listing of those who came to America through this Texas port as early as the 1840s.

If you have an interest in the oil and gas industry the Ocean Star Rig Museum (409-766-7827), located on Pier 19, offers tours of a retired jack-up rig with informative lectures and gift shop.

The Strand, located one block south of Galveston harbor at Harborside Drive between the north-south crossings of 19th to 25th streets, will treat the eye with its wrought iron fringed balconies and gas lanterns lining the streets, and it can easily be toured by walking, or by catching a ride on a trolley or horse-drawn carriage. Galveston Historical Foundation developed Hendley Green, which offers a relaxing park for visitors to enjoy the sights and sounds of downtown Galveston. Seasonal programming and various food trucks are also offered. See galveston.com/hendley-green for details.

Away from the downtown area, Stewart Beach and Pavilion are great places to cool off in the green water of the Gulf. The beach offers seemingly endless stretches of sand, making it a favorite vacation place for Texans. A boardwalk extends along the beach for biking and walking, with restaurant and shopping stops along the way. The Galveston Regional Chamber of Commerce has plenty of information (galvestoncc.com) and is conveniently located across from the beach walk. The beach is well maintained and has a beach wall with a wide sidewalk on top. Pedestrians, bicycles and electric and pedal carts are plentiful throughout the summer and on winter weekends.

**Special Events:** The Galveston Visitors Center at 2328 Broadway Avenue J has information about local attractions and festivals or visit galveston.com. The city celebrates Mardi Gras in a big way, and the Dickens on the the Strand festival is a long-honored Christmas tradition.

**Shopping:** The Old Peanut Butter Warehouse (20th Street and Harborside Drive, 409-632-7165) is an 1895 building once used as a warehouse to store candy and peanut butter, now transformed into a unique shopping experience.

Katies Seafood Market on the waterfront (1902 Wharf Rd.) has fresh seafood, plus some frozen items and sauces and seasonings for cooking on the boat.

**Dining:** There are far too many dining opportunities to list them all. From the Wharf to the Strand, along the Seawall and Post Office Street there is a vast choice that is sure to please every palate and budget. Prepare ahead by visiting downtowngalveston.org.

# Galveston Bay, TX

## FLAMINGO ISLES

| | | Dockage | | | | | Supplies | | Services | | | | | |
|---|---|---|---|---|---|---|---|---|---|---|---|---|---|---|
| | Largest Vessel Accommodated | VHF Channel Monitored | Approach / Dockside Depth (reported) | Transient Berths / Total Berths | Floating Docks | Gas / Diesel | Groceries, Ice, Marine Supplies, Snacks | Repairs: Hull, Engine, Propeller | Lift (tonnage), Crane, Rail | Laundry, Pool, Showers, Courtesy Car | Pump-Out Station | Min/Max Amps | Nearby: Grocery Store, Motel, Restaurant |
| 1. Harborwalk Yacht Club & Marina 🖳 WiFi  866-435-8777 | 125 | 09 | 8/162 | 8/8 | F | GD | GIMS | – | – | 30/100 | LPS | P | GR |

🖳 Internet Access  WiFi Wireless Internet Access  WG Waterway Guide Cruising Club Partner  *(Information in the table is provided by the facilities.)*
See WaterwayGuide.com for current rates, fuel prices, web site addresses, and other up-to-the-minute information.

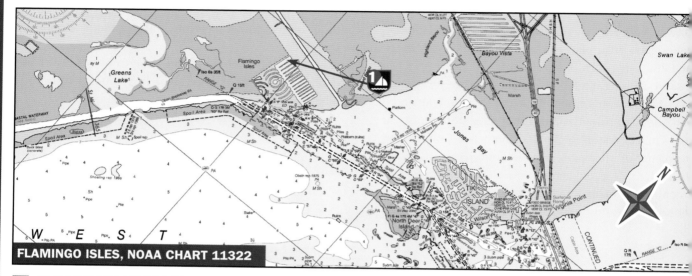

**FLAMINGO ISLES, NOAA CHART 11322**

## ◼ GALVESTON TO FREEPORT

**NAVIGATION:** Use Chart 11322. With a little planning and a mindful watch this 35-mile trip cuts through open bays and land cut channels that are easily traversed. After the bridges at Galveston, the waterway bends to starboard where a long line of floating red nun buoy have earned the name "red can bend." If the wind is over 15 knots, barge captains would prefer if you did not attempt to pass them in red can bend. The channel shoals very quickly on the green side of the channel, and it's easy to get caught aground with tows in the area. Be cautious and listen to VHF Channel 16. Talk to the tows about how they want you to proceed.

At Mile 359 WHL, green "39," a pair of buoys to the south marks an inlet into West Bay. The water in West Bay outside of the GIWW is too shallow for most cruising boats.

At 17-foot green "63" the channel bends to port and enters a land cut. At Mile 371 WHL, green "75" marks the beginning of what is referred to as the Wash-Out. West Bay has a nasty habit of washing away the

protective spoil bank here and groundings are common if you leave the channel. Efforts by the Army Corps of Engineers have improved the situation, and the large volume of barge traffic keeps the GIWW deep enough for most cruising boats.

As you get to open water at Mile 375 WHL, you have West Bay on your port and Chocolate Bay on your starboard. Heavy weather will cause a fairly stout chop and the floating aids will be difficult to see. Use the range at the beginning of the next land cut to line up the channel. Tows encountered in this and other open bay areas will appear to be using the entire channel as they slowly make their way. High winds push their bow off course, and they spend a lot of time re-centering the vessel in the channel.

Chocolate Bay has a tow channel that ends in a "Y" for barge traffic in and out of Chocolate Bayou. Pay attention to VHF Channels 16 and 13 as the tows will announce their positions in either the GIWW of the Chocolate Bayou channel and the direction they intend to travel.

The next land cut starts at about Mile 378.0 WHL and e GIWW reaches the Freeport Ship Channel at Mile 95.0 WHL.

> ⚠ Use caution at Mile 390.5 WHL. This area, known as the Freeport Wiggles, causes problems for extremely long tows and they may k you to wait to pass or cross until after they make eir turns.

**Dockage:** Harborwalk Yacht Club & Marina is part f a large planned community. The 600-yard entrance hannel is located at Mile 362 WHL, west of Tiki Island st off of green can buoy "59." Shoreside facilities clude gas and diesel and a ship store. The community also home to a restaurant with panoramic views.

## ity of Freeport

he Brazos River has played a significant part of the istory of Freeport. In the 1800s steamships and ther boats carrying passengers and goods for trade aveled the river extensively. The banks were lined by lantations and used for transportation and business. he rising and falling waters of the river caused ontinuous flooding of the towns of Freeport and alasco. Eventually, dams and a lock changed the river. inally, it was rerouted and diverted to the west leaving he Old Brazos River as what appears today as a salt ater lake. Shrimp boats and commercial boat traffic to razosport use it extensively.

**Dockage:** Just west of Mile 392 WHL, Oyster Creek eads north 2.5 miles to Kirby Marina. Depths of 6 feet re charted both in Oyster Creek and dockside in the narina; however shoaling is possible in the channel. Kirby has gas and diesel fuel, along with transient slips nd repairs. This marina is located in a rural part of reeport, which means you will likely hear cattle rather han traffic. Provisioning requires a car.

At Surfside Beach, the Bridge Harbor Yacht Club offers pleasant break and a convenient place to refuel for the ong run to Matagorda Bay and beyond. The entrance to his well-protected marina is at Mile 393.5 WHL, just rior to rounding the bend to the **Surfside Beach (SR 232) Bridge** (73-foot fixed vertical clearance). A three-story condominium building marks the south side of the entrance channel, with the fuel docks just beyond. When entering the basin from the GIWW, the fuel dock is across the first side-channel, which branches off to port. Transient slips line the west side of this side-channel. Note that getting a boat with a 6-foot draft up to the fuel

# GIWW, TX

| FREEPORT AREA | | Dockage | | | | | Supplies | | Services | | | | | |
|---|---|---|---|---|---|---|---|---|---|---|---|---|---|---|
| | | Largest Vessel Accommodated | VHF Channel Monitored | Transient Berths / Total Berths | Approach / Dockside Depth (reported) | Floating Docks | Gas / Diesel | Groceries, Ice, Marine Supplies, Snacks | Repairs: Hull, Engine, Propeller | Lift (tonnage), Crane, Rail | Min/Max Amps | Laundry, Pool, Showers, Courtesy Car | Pump-Out Station | Nearby: Grocery Store, Motel, Restaurant |
| **1.** Kirby Marina  395 WHL | 979-239-1081 | 60 | 16 | call/76 | 6/6 | – | GD | M | HEP | L60 | 30/50 | S | – | |
| **2.** Bridge Harbor Yacht Club  395 WHL | 979-233-2101 | 100 | 68 | 8/300 | 10/8 | – | GD | GIMS | – | L70 | 30/100 | LPS | P | GMF |
| **3.** Surfside Marina 🖥 📶  394 WHL | 979-230-9400 | 70 | 16 | 4/38 | 12/8 | F | GD | GIMS | HEP | L30 | 30/100 | S | – | GMF |
| **4.** Freeport Marina 🖥 📶 WG | 979-373-0800 | 150 | 16/68 | 10/149 | 13/13 | F | GD | I | – | – | 30/50 | LS | P | GMF |

🖥 Internet Access   📶 Wireless Internet Access   WG Waterway Guide Cruising Club Partner *(Information in the table is provided by the facilities.)*
See WaterwayGuide.com for current rates, fuel prices, web site addresses, and other up-to-the-minute information.

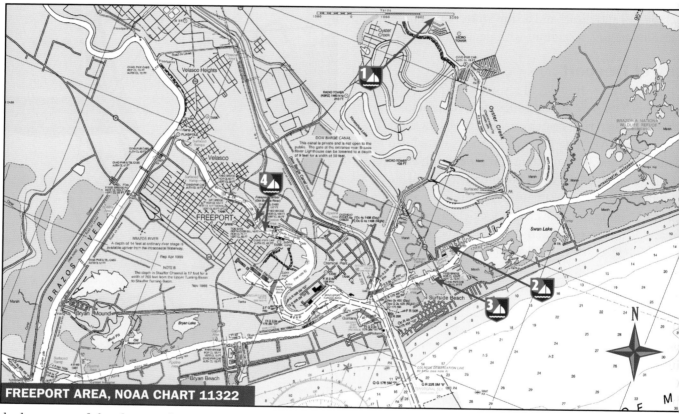

**FREEPORT AREA, NOAA CHART 11322**

docks or any of the slips can be tough during low tide. Sportfishing boats dominate the marina, which hosts fishing tournaments and other summer events. Cruisers should consider making reservations ahead of time.

The Surfside Marina is at the base of the Surfside Bridge on the east (or south) side of the GIWW. A full-service facility, the marina has stacked and floating wet slips and caters especially to large offshore fishing boats up to 70 feet. The marina has a fuel dock with gas and diesel that operates 24 hours a day, 7 days a week. The marina is on the east end of the bridge; there is access to restaurants along the beach road, some within walking distance.

The Freeport Municipal Marina has floating slips accommodating vessels up to 150 feet in length and sells fuel. It is located close to downtown Freeport on the Old Brazos River.

## Cruising Options

Continuing westward, Waterway Guide's coverage takes you all the way to Brownsville and the end of the GIWW in the next chapter, "Freeport to Brownsville."

# Freeport to Brownsville, TX

 ICW   Mile 395 WHL–Mile 682 WHL     VHF   TX: Channel 13

**CHARTS** 11301, 11302, 11303, 11304, 11306, 11307, 11308, 11309, 11311, 11312, 11313, 11314, 11315, 11316, 11317, 11319, 11321, 11322

You have to be motivated to reach the southwest end of the GIWW. It is remote, and there is no quick easy way to get there. The closest large metropolitan area is Monterrey, Mexico, 225 miles south. The closest large U.S. city is San Antonio, TX, 285 miles north, and then Houston, TX, at a distance of 367 miles. The results of this distance are evident in the culture and in almost everything you will see and do. It is uniquely beautiful and picturesque. It is the best of what you can experience in a mix of South Texas and Mexico.

For most cruising boats traveling southwest along the Texas Coast it is possible to make offshore runs during daylight hours from one coastal cut to another. Some of these cuts do not offer easy access to a marina, and it may be more practical in these areas to find a safe and comfortable anchorage. Boats making an overnight passage can easily reach a major jetty entrance with access to marine facilities. Prevailing winds can make the Texas Coast a windward shore, so be aware of wind and sea conditions before attempting these passages.

While the off-shore passages follow sandy beaches for the entire distance, the somewhat isolated intracoastal waters of southeast Texas provide frequent points of interest, abundant wildlife, ports and anchorages. The GIWW meanders through land cuts and large open bays. There is significant commercial traffic from Freeport to Port Aransas and Corpus Christi on the GIWW. Commercial traffic is almost nonexistent from Corpus Christi Bay to Brownsville.

One way to look at this stretch of coast is as it compares to the busy seaports of Houston and Galveston. The waters from Freeport to Brownsville are more like a trip to nowhere filled with incredible sights, sounds, places and people. The waters from Corpus Christi to Port Isabel are miles stretching into days of complete solitude and isolation. From east to west–Freeport to the border of Mexico–is a relaxed style of living and boating with a unique history and many interesting things to see.

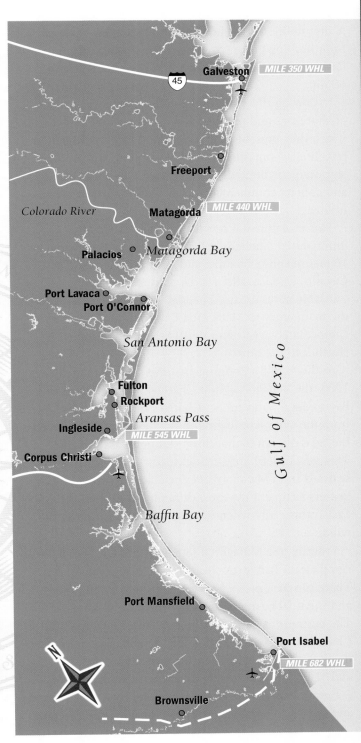

# ■ OFFSHORE: FREEPORT TO THE MATAGORDA SHIP CHANNEL

**NAVIGATION:** Use Charts 1117A, 11316, 11317, 11319 and 11321. Clearing the Freeport jetties, it is a good idea to stay offshore at least 4 nm, in 40 feet of water, to avoid the shoaling and flotsam of the Brazos River. A rhumb line with a heading of 225 degrees magnetic from flashing green "3" leaving the Freeport Channel, to flashing red "4" at the Matagorda Channel is just over 60 nm.

Following this rhumb line you will encounter many offshore rigs and platforms. With a constant and careful watch they present little danger and can be avoided by traveling 10 nm offshore in the shipping lane. Actual ship traffic is limited. Monitor VHF Channel 16 and 13, and contact commercial vessels working in the area as needed.

This coastline has few features and is mostly uninhabited. Matagorda Bay has two charted channels: Matagorda Ship Channel and, 4 nm to the east, Pass Cavallo. Pass Cavallo is a dangerous and largely unusable natural pass. The Matagorda Ship Channel is the main entry to Matagorda Bay and Port O'Conner (immediately west) and Port Lavaca and Palacios (further to the north).

Authorized by Congress in 1958 and completed in 1966, the Matagorda Ship Channel opened Matagorda Bay to deep water traffic. Changes in the discharge from the Colorado River and the new channel reduced the tidal discharge that flows through Pass Cavallo. This new (1966) jetty, that extends nearly .75 of a mile seaward from Matagorda Peninsula, is described by boaters as one of the most difficult to enter on the Gulf Coast, especially when the tide is in opposition to the wind.

Entering the Matagorda Jetties, at red marker "8," you can pick up Range "A" bearing 310 degrees magnetic. There can be a pretty heavy sea at the jetty entrance and the tidal currents normally run several knots. The currents at Pass Cavallo and The Matagorda Ship Channel can exceed 4 knots on the ebb, especially if a north wind is blowing. Once you reach markers "13" and "14," it is best to stay in the marked channel.

From offshore, there is one channel between Freeport and the Matagorda Ship Channel. Leaving the Freeport Channel at flashing green "3" on a course of 225 degrees magnetic, you reach the Old Colorado River Channel in 42.5 nm. From offshore, the first buoy you see is the 17-foot flashing red "2" at the end of the new east jetty. This channel is used exclusively by local boaters. Approach and enter with caution. The Army Corps of Engineers dredged the channel to 12 feet when it was reopened.

Travel north in the Colorado River Channel and in approximately 6 miles there is a bypass channel (Braggs Cut) that only goes east to the GIWW. The channel allows small boats to bypass the east Colorado River Floodgate. The bypass channel is for small boat traffic only. Vessels over 30 feet with drafts greater than 4.5 feet should not attempt to enter the narrow bypass channel. The Colorado River Locks are .2 nm to the north.

# ■ GIWW: FREEPORT TO MATAGORDA

It is 45 statute miles from the Freeport Intersection (Mile 395 WHL) to the Matagorda Municipal Marina (Mile 440 WHL). There are no bays or open water through this stretch of the GIWW. The channel simply follows the shore of the land cut. This stretch of the GIWW has few anchorages, navigational aids and facilities for cruising boats.

**NAVIGATION:** Use Charts 11319 and 11322. In great contrast to the open nature of the Texas coast to the south, this stretch of the GIWW has one swing bridge and two sets of floodgates to transit. Commercial traffic is fairly heavy, especially in the vicinity of Freeport, the Brazos River Floodgates and the Colorado River Floodgates. At Mile 395 WHL, the Freeport Harbor Channel (referred to as the Freeport Intersection) crosses the GIWW from the Gulf of Mexico. Ships and trawlers entering from the Gulf, towboats transiting the GIWW and commercial vessels hopping between the commercial docks within the harbor converge here creating challenging traffic situations.

Listen closely to the VHF radio before reaching the intersection; ships entering from the Gulf often move fast and are hidden by a bluff until very near the intersection. Stay clear of the submerged vessel on the south side of the GIWW at Mile 395.5 WHL.

A LNG terminal located on the southeast corner of the intersection of the channel and the GIWW will cause a lay if an LNG vessel comes to port. These vessels have moving security zone, usually 500 yards, and an armed cort. All traffic must stop while the vessel transits the hannel.

From the south side of its intersection with the eeport Harbor Channel, the GIWW leads through a eep-sided land cut to the **Freeport (Bryan Beach) ridge** (Mile 397.6 WHL, 73-foot fixed vertical earance). Three miles beyond the fixed bridge, the azos River crosses the GIWW between the **Brazos iver Flood Gates**. Call the operator of the nearest te (e.g., call the "East Brazos River Flood Gate" if estbound) on VHF Channel 13 for an opening and heck for traffic headed toward you. The floodgates sually open on signal but may remain closed when ver currents run strongly or while repairs are made. It possible and prudent to call ahead and inquire about e status of the gates at 409-233-1251(east)/-5161 west). Strong currents and floating debris are common the Brazos River. Give commercial vessels plenty of oom and proceed with caution.

The Brazos River (Mile 401 WHL) south to the Gulf not navigable and is subject to shoaling at any time. he Brazos is the longest river in Texas, stretching

1,050 miles from the city of Clovis, NM, to Freeport, TX. North of the GIWW the river is 8 feet deep with two fixed bridges (50- and 37-foot vertical clearances) and overhead power lines (57- and 47-foot vertical clearances) within the first 4 miles. Submerged pilings of unknown depths are at the first bridge. Continuing north the river carries depths of 8 feet extending to Bolivar Landing 32 miles upriver.

## San Bernard River–GIWW Mile 405 WHL

**NAVIGATION:** Use Charts 11319 and 11321. Beyond the Brazos River, the GIWW bends to port and follows the steep bank to the San Bernard River at Mile 405 WHL. The river is navigable to the north and south. Going south, a short distance to the Gulf of Mexico, the river tends to shoal on the west side, so favor the east bank. Upriver to the north carries 15 feet of water for several miles. Approximately 6 miles upriver from the GIWW is an overhead cable with a 38-foot vertical clearance. West of the San Bernard, in the GIWW, submerged pilings are charted on the north side of the waterway from Mile 404 to Mile 406 WHL.

**Dockage:** There are no overnight facilities for cruising boats on this stretch of the GIWW. One half

mile upriver, the River's Edge Motel (979-964-3814) has slips for guests staying overnight at the motel. Depths alongside are reported to be 3 feet. This is a modest motel. Call ahead for information. 2J's Café and Marina (979-964-3233) is 3.5 miles upriver from the GIWW. Call ahead for times they will be open and slip availability. Twenty miles upriver is Dido's Restaurant (979-964-3167) with slips to accommodate most cruising boats that are stopping for dinner. Call ahead to make sure room is available.

**Anchorages:** Good anchorage can be found anyplace south of the GIWW. The best anchorage in the San Bernard is close to the river entrance to the Gulf, off the beach separating the river from the Gulf. Going downriver, favor the east (port) side. Depths should be 6 feet or more. Anchor on the east side. The bottom is a mix of mud and sand. Holding is fair to good. This beach is only accessible by boat. It is a great place to walk, look for treasures and build a fire. Stay in the river. Do not attempt to enter the Gulf through this pass unless you are in your dinghy and the waters are calm. Currents are tricky, so make sure your anchor is set, as dragging anchor here could be disastrous.

You can also anchor above the GIWW in 9 feet of water with good holding in sandy mud. Boats can anchor anyplace upriver where they can find a spot away from commercial traffic transiting the river. Upriver the San Bernard is used extensively as a safe harbor from passing storms.

## To Sargent (Caney Creek)–GIWW Mile 418 WHL

**NAVIGATION:** Use Chart 11319. A No-Wake Zone is present from GIWW Mile 413 to Mile 419 WHL due primarily to residential properties on the waterway. The Farm Road 457 Bridge (also referred to as the **Caney Creek Pontoon Bridge**), crosses the GIWW at Mile 418 WHL. The bridge opens on request (VHF Channel 13 or 16). Wait until the bridge is fully open. The cables used to pull the bridge open should not be approached and be sure the cables have had time to sink to the bottom before proceeding. The south side of the bridge has a short ramp that, when lifted, provides a 13-foot-wide opening to allow small boats through. This opening is too small, however, for most cruising boats.

**Dockage:** Although there are no overnight facilities, the City of Sargent (Caney Creek) provides a rest stop for visiting boaters at a public park .75 mile west of the swing bridge. Boats are allowed to tie alongside the dock

at the park. No services are available. The dock is on th[e] banks of the GIWW and has alongside dockside depths of about 4 feet. Don't be confused by its looks; it appea[rs] to be a crew-changing zone for towboats. Nearby Crab Trap Bar and Grill (979-244-4141) is a short trip up Caney Creek with docking for very large and small cruising boats. Sting Rae's Waterfront Grill, on the nort[h] side of the GIWW (immediately west of the pontoon bridge) was closed at press time (spring 2017) but was scheduled to reopen as Hooker's in the summer.

## Matagorda–GIWW Mile 440 EHL

Matagorda is a quaint village immediately west of the municipal marina, Mile 440 WHL. It was an important part of early Texas history, founded in 1829. By 1834 it was the third largest town in Texas. The Christ Episcop[al] Church is said to be the oldest Episcopal Parish in Texa[s] dating from 1839.

**NAVIGATION:** Use Charts 11316, 11319 and 11321. At Mile 440 WHL, the entrance to Matagorda Harbor and the municipal marina is just east of the fixed **Market Street Bridge** (73-foot vertical clearance).

**Dockage:** The Matagorda Harbor municipal marina has transient dockage with a generous turning basin that can accommodate large boats. A friendly staff manages the well-protected marina. There is gas and diesel, a small store for supplies and a restaurant. More restaurants, groceries and other amenities within walking distance. Follow the road over the dike near the harbormaster's office and turn left on the main road. Spoonbills Restaurant, at 773 Cypress St. west of the marina, may offer rides from the marina and has a fine wine list and full bar (979-863-7766). It is a good idea to call ahead to see if they are open. Stanley Food Market is just 2 blocks northwest from Spoonbill's at 752 Market St.

**Anchorage:** There is all-around protection and 8 feet of water in Matagorda Basin.

## Colorado River–GIWW Mile 442 WHL

The Colorado is the longest river wholly in Texas with a length of 862 miles, stretching from West Texas to the Gulf of Mexico.

**NAVIGATION:** Use Charts 11316 and 11319. Just west of the entrance to Matagorda Harbor, the Market Street Bridge (Mile 440.7 WHL, 73-foot fixed vertical clearance) crosses the GIWW. Immediately west of the bridge is a bypass channel to the south, called Braggs

Cut. The narrow and shallow Braggs Cut allows small boat traffic to bypass the east flood gate and enter the river to the south of the Colorado River Flood Gate. Boats larger than 30 feet with a draft of more than 3.5 feet should not attempt to use Braggs Cut.

Once through the bridge, the east lock of the Colorado River stands plainly ahead. The **Colorado River Locks** open on the hour for pleasure boats. If proceeding west on the GIWW, contact the Colorado River East Lock on VHF Channel 13 to request an opening and to check for any oncoming traffic. The narrowness of the locks and the often-strong current of the Colorado River make passage across the river difficult for long tows, so stay away from the locks until the lockmaster tells you to go ahead, even when slow currents allow the locks to remain open.

The Colorado River Locks regularly close for repairs and during periods of strong currents, so you may want to call (979-863-7842, ext. 2005 ) or radio (VHF Channel 13 or 16) in advance of your intended passage. The locks are usually fully open and there is no delay. If

you are planning to go upstream or downstream tell the lockmaster ahead of time, so he can manage traffic and not open the gates of the far lock.

While in the river, keep a lookout for brush, trees and floating debris. Upstream (north) you can anchor along the banks of the Colorado when the current is light, but you will have to pick a wide spot away from the outside of a bend; tows transit the river as far north as Bay City. The South Texas Nuclear Plant, about 5 miles upstream of the GIWW, has a cooling lake 10 miles square and 10 feet deep. Water from the Colorado River was used to fill the lake; the lake now boasts its own habitat for fish, fowl, game and reptiles.

Downstream (south) the Colorado River discharges into East Matagorda Bay. This diversion channel is not navigable. Once you pass through the east gate, take the channel that branches east or to port when going down river. Along the Colorado River, private homes and fish camps line the channel's east bank. The river/channel leads nearly 6 nm from the GIWW to the jetty entrance at the Gulf of Mexico. Follow the daymarks from green daybeacon "15" to flashing red "2" and flashing green "1" at the river's discharge into the Gulf of Mexico. This channel is used exclusively by local boaters. Approach and enter with caution.

**Dockage:** River Bend Restaurant and Tavern, located adjacent to a pair of launch ramps about 1 mile south of

⚠ **View updated postings on navigation and hazards alerts**

**waterwayguide.com**

# Matagorda Bay, TX

| | | Dockage | | | | | Supplies | | Services | | | | | | |
|---|---|---|---|---|---|---|---|---|---|---|---|---|---|---|---|
| | Phone | Largest Vessel Accommodated | VHF Channel Monitored | Transient Berths / Total Berths | Approach / Dockside Depth (reported) | Floating Docks | Gas / Diesel | Groceries, Ice, Marine Supplies, Snacks | Repairs: Hull, Engine, Propeller | Lift (tonnage), Crane, Rail | Min/Max Amps | Laundry, Pool, Showers, Courtesy Car | Pump-Out Station | Nearby: Grocery Store, Motel, Restaurant | |
| **MATAGORDA** | | | | | | | | | | | | | | | |
| 1. Matagorda Harbor WiFi 440 WHL | 979-863-2103 | 120 | – | 14/222 | 14/10 | F | GD | GIS | – | – | 30/100 | S | P | GM | |
| **PALACIOS** | | | | | | | | | | | | | | | |
| 2. Serendipity Bay Resort ▯ WiFi | 361-972-5454 | 50 | 16 | 60/120 | 14/7 | F | – | GI | – | – | 30/30 | LPS | P | GM | |
| 3. South Bay Marina | 713-846-3219 | 45 | – | 20/41 | 5/5 | – | GD | – | – | – | 30/50 | – | – | GM | |
| **PORT LAVACA** | | | | | | | | | | | | | | | |
| 4. Nautical Landings Marina ▯ | 361-552-2615 | 50 | 16/68 | call/72 | 4/4 | F | – | – | – | – | 30/30 | LS | P | GMF | |

▯ Internet Access  WiFi Wireless Internet Access  WG Waterway Guide Cruising Club Partner  *(Information in the table is provided by the facilities.)*
See WaterwayGuide.com for current rates, fuel prices, web site addresses, and other up-to-the-minute information.

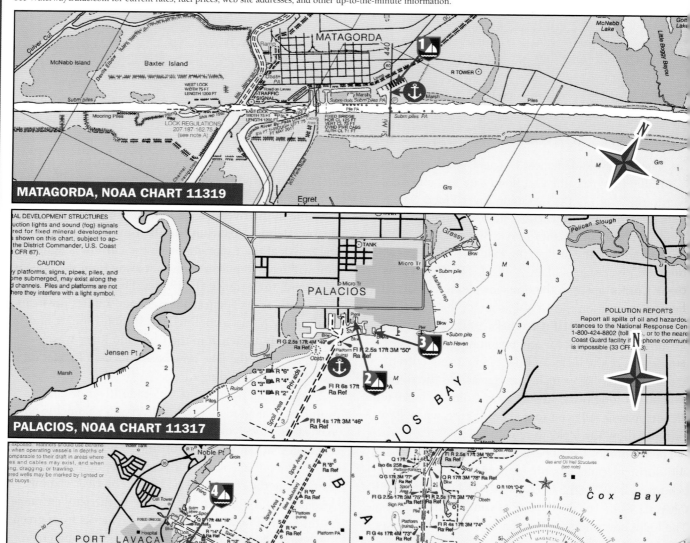

MATAGORDA, NOAA CHART 11319

PALACIOS, NOAA CHART 11317

PORT LAVACA, NOAA CHART 11317

he GIWW on the Colorado River Channel, may allow patrons to dock overnight. Call ahead (979-863-7481).

## Colorado River Channel Offshore Approach

**NAVIGATION:** Use Charts 11316 and 11319. The Old Colorado River is an improved channel that links the Gulf of Mexico with the Texas GIWW. For details, refer to information at the beginning of the chapter, "Offshore: Freeport to the Matagorda Ship Channel."Many past issues and dangers have been resolved and this recently dredged jetty entry into the Gulf opens the Matagorda area to both cruisers and sportfishermen.

# ■ MATAGORDA BAY

Matagorda Bay is rich in history. In earlier years this huge body of water may have experienced development on the scale of Galveston and Houston. However, development was prevented at that time due to the strong currents of Pass Cavallo, which were too difficult and expensive to conquer. Also, in the middle and later parts of the last century the area was ravaged by several severe storms. By any measure this bay is big. In the 1900s, Matagorda Bay and Matagorda East Bay stretched for a length of just over 50 miles.

**NAVIGATION:** Use Charts 11317, 11319, 11316. South of the Colorado River, there are no additional locks or flood gates and only two bridges until Port Isabel. (These bridges and passes will not be encountered in this section. They are on GIWW between Rockport and the south end of Corpus Christi Bay.)

Fifteen miles south of the Colorado River, the GIWW meets open bays and barrier islands. After passing through the locks, the land cut continues to Mile 455 WHL, where Matagorda Bay begins. For many years, the land cut was plagued by erosion of its banks caused by the heavy prop wash of commercial traffic until the Army Corps of Engineers placed a stone bank along the north side of the GIWW to prevent further problems.

During spring months migrating songbirds land at the nearby Mud Island Wildlife Management Area to rest after their lengthy flight. Keep an eye out; sometimes there are so many they show up on radar.

⚠ Older versions of Chart 11319 may not have the corrections that the NOAA 2006 "print on demand" paper edition has. The same be true of older chart plotters that have not been updated. Specifically, the newer chart shows a preferred alternate route north of the previous GIWW channel. Matagorda Bay Chart 11317 shows the correct route. It is especially important to follow this more northern route when conditions on the Bay are windy and rough. Refer to waterwayguide.com for daily alerts and updates.

When heading southwest from flashing red "30," you will pass one or a pair of markers at approximately 1-mile intervals. The first will be flashing red "2," then "2A," "4" and "4A." Just before reaching 17-foot flashing red "6," you can turn north to head to Palacios in the marked channel or continue on toward Port O'Connor.

At 17-foot flashing red "10," the GIWW makes a southerly turn. Just past green "13A" the GIWW crosses the Matagorda Ship Channel. The ship channel goes north to Port Lavaca and south to the Gulf of Mexico.

Continuing west to Port O'Connor, the GIWW passes green "15" and "17" as well as red "18" and "20" before reaching the number "1" and "2" buoys marking the short jetties at Port O'Connor. On approach to the Port O'Connor jetties, you will pass a green "121" buoy. Green "121" to green "111" and red "112" mark a more southerly route to the Matagorda Ship Channel. These buoys are remnants of the old more southerly channel that crossed Matagorda Bay, as discussed in the navigational alert above. They are only useful for boats making an offshore transit to and from Port O'Connor.

Boats heading east from the Port O'Connor jetties planning to go across the Bay, should take special care to look north to red "20" and not be tempted to follow green "121" through green "111".

**Anchorage:** In prevailing southeasterly winds, exit the green side of the GIWW almost anywhere to anchor in the lee of Matagorda Peninsula. The most popular spots along this stretch are just south of old channel Mile 464 WHL near Greens Bayou between the tall back range (south of green "57") and shore, and off the bulkhead near the old Matagorda Club Airfield (Mile 467.2 WHL). Stilt houses and a wrecked plane on shore are visible along this stretch.

Anchoring farther down the peninsula, nearer the inside of the jetties, is unwise due to tidal currents that run swiftly, making the frequently shifting shoals more abundant than suggested by even the latest chart.

A few private moorings have been placed outside the green side of the Matagorda Ship Channel behind Decros Island. They are rarely occupied on weekdays but should be used at your own risk. When leaving these anchorages, return to the new route across the bay; do not attempt the passage along the peninsula to the ship channel. Uncharted dangers exist here.

For more anchoring options refer to the Explorer planning page at waterwayguide.com.

## Palacios

Pronounced "Pa-lash-us," this is a small quiet location at the far northeast corner of Matagorda Bay. Palacios makes a pleasant stop for a couple of days. It offers haul-out facilities, a friendly sailing club and well-protected easily entered marinas.

It is only a few blocks to the quaint downtown area where you can find a bank, restaurants, shopping, a hardware store and Hilltop Marine Supply. One mile from the marina at Serendipity and one-half mile from the marina at South Bay is the uniquely different, picturesque and historic 110-year-old Luther Hotel. It appears to have fallen on hard times but is worth a visit and may be a place to consider for a night ashore. Nothing about these marinas or the community are "resort like" in any way, but it is an interesting place to stop and visit.

**NAVIGATION:** Use Chart 11317. The Palacios Channel, marked by a series of red daybeacons, both lighted and unlighted, meets the GIWW at Mile 466 WHL and leads north across Matagorda Bay, into Tres Palacios Bay and directly through the breakwaters of the harbor at Palacios. Westbound boaters can shorten the run to Palacios by exiting the red side of the GIWW anywhere along the stretch bound by red daybeacon "2A" and flashing red "4," and traveling across the 9- to 13-foot depths of Matagorda Bay to angle into the Palacios Channel (125 feet wide and 12 feet deep).

When taking this shortcut, be certain to pass well west of the charted Half-Moon Reef's 30-foot flashing light, which extends 3 miles into Matagorda Bay from Palacios Point. When traveling along the Palacios Channel, stay clear of the spoil areas north of the channel extending from the GIWW to Palacios.

**Dockage:** Palacios Channel passes through two parallel breakwaters and enters the harbor between flashing green "49" and flashing red "50." After passing through the outer rock breakwater, continue on a straight course past the short wooden breakwater that extends from the east side of the channel. Then turn

starboard and follow the channel a short distance to
e docks of Serendipity Bay Resort to port. Pull into an
npty slip on the central pier but be aware that some of
e slips lack adequate cleats and many boats in double
ps have strung dock lines across the vacant slip next
them (thus barring entry).

The Palacios Navigation District operates South Bay
arina, which lies just east of Serendipity Resort, next
the public boat launch. South Bay has slips and fuel.

**Anchorage:** South of Palacios, a small cove leading
Oyster Lake sometimes provides a comfortable
nchorage. However, calm winds are necessary to enjoy
. Leave the Palacios Channel between flashing red "32"
d "30" and head east toward the concrete bridge about
ree nautical miles away. If you dinghy to shore, do so
ear the bridge. The land near Hotel Point is private. It
also possible to anchor outside the Palacios Channel
5 to 7 feet in mud.

## Port Lavaca

his is a quiet community that is larger than Palacios,
nd where you will find the only hospital located
etween Freeport and Corpus Christi. The municipal
narina (Nautical Landings Marina) is in old downtown
ort Lavaca. The breakwater-protected marina is also
ome to the Port Lavaca Yacht Club. Since long time
arbor master, Jim, passed away, no single person has
een employed for the position. Currently, the parks
irector is fulfilling those duties. Contact him at 361-
84-3953 for slip assignments. Transient boats are
velcome and he is very helpful.

The shopping and dining area (about four blocks
ong) is across the street. A long walk on the road in
ront of the marina leads around the shrimp boat basin
t the end of the Lavaca Channel to the Lighthouse
Beach and Bird Sanctuary near the causeway. This
park includes a manmade beach; the elevated Formosa
Wetlands Walkway, stretching over coastal wetlands and
he tidal exchange basin; a bird-watching tower; a pier
extending out into Lavaca Bay; playgrounds; and picnic
reas. Across the street the Bauer Convention Center
s the home of the Half-Moon Reef Lighthouse. It has
esided there since retirement from service.

For adventures further afield, taxi service is available,
nd local boaters tend to be generous with rides. Many
usinesses are clustered along Highway 35 (a short drive
out a very long hike from the marina).

**NAVIGATION:** Use Chart 11317. To travel the 17 miles
to Nautical Landings Marina from the GIWW, take the

Matagorda Ship Channel into Lavaca Bay, and then
follow the relatively short Lavaca Channel.

For local boaters a shortcut through the spoils that
lie along the red side of the Matagorda Ship Channel
can cut a considerable amount of distance off the trip
to Port Lavaca from red flashing "30." However, due to
extensive dredging of the channel, some passes noted on
Chart 11317 may be closed. Seek local knowledge before
attempting to cut through the spoil areas.

Follow the Matagorda Ship Channel markers past
Indianola and Magnolia Beach to the green-over-red
intersection buoy "PL" just past markers "65" and "66."
At this intersection, the well-lighted Matagorda Ship
Channel angles to the north toward the industrial docks
of Point Comfort, and the 6- to 8-foot-deep Lavaca
Channel splits off to the west-northwest and leads to
Port Lavaca. Every other green marker is lighted, making
night entry less difficult. Foul ground lies immediately
outside the line of red markers of the entrance channel;
don't turn from the Lavaca Channel too late.

Red daybeacons for the marina entrance are topped
with white anti-bird cones, making them somewhat
confusing to a newcomer. The single piling (tacked with
reflectors) between the last of the entrance channel's
red markers and the end of the wooden breakwater may
be passed on either side. A short wooden breakwater
extends from the tall bulkhead just inside the basin and
must be kept to starboard. Be careful of the exposed
pilings and sunken vessels at the entrance to the harbor.

**Dockage:** Enter the marina through a narrow channel
between two wooden breakwaters. Once inside you will
find good floating slips with reported 4-foot dockside
depths. Wave reflection from a stepped cement bulkhead
makes the final entry into Nautical Landings a bit
rougher in southeast winds, but provides a pleasant
place to stroll, sit or fish at the water's edge in Bayfront
Park. There is also a steep boat ramp.

**Anchorage:** For boats with drafts of less than
5.5 feet, Lavaca Bay has several easily entered
anchorages. Although spoil banks line most of the red
side of the Matagorda Ship Channel, the channel may
be safely exited by heading northwest from red "56" to
anchor off Sand Point in southeast to east winds and off
Rhodes Point in north to east winds.

Boats with drafts of less than 5 feet can enter Keller
Bay for a somewhat open anchorage, with nearly
all-around protection from waves. Returning to the
Matagorda Ship Channel from any of these anchorages,
head toward the orange picnic shelters on the southeast

shore of Lavaca Bay to find the cut beside marker "56" and re-enter the ship channel.

Magnolia Beach, reached by leaving the green side of the Matagorda Ship Channel between markers "57" and "63," makes an enjoyable day anchorage and overnight anchorage in settled weather. Although usually quiet, this fine shell beach draws crowds on spring and summer weekends. Anchor out from the two-story building in depths that shoal gradually from 6 feet.

Hiking along the beach to the granite statue of La Salle and the site of the old town of Indianola is an enjoyable trip. Indianola rivaled Galveston as Texas' most important port before being devastated twice by hurricanes. The foundations of the buildings of old Indianola still lie beneath the surface of Lavaca Bay, as does the locomotive that sat on the long wharf during one of the 19th-century hurricanes. Bird watching is spectacular along the wetlands adjacent to Indianola and Magnolia Beach.

Closer to Port Lavaca, Gallinipper Point offers a pleasant anchorage with excellent protection in southeast through southwest winds. (Gallinippers are mosquitoes the size of small hawks and just as predatory. Make sure your screens are in place before dark!) To reach the anchorage, start into the Lavaca Channel from the intersection buoy in the Matagorda Ship Channel but head southwest from the Lavaca Channel once past the low range marker, head toward the house with the windmill and drop anchor in 5- to 7-foot depths near the wrecks of three scuttled shrimp boats. Dredging of the Lavaca Channel resulted in spoil being deposited in the bay between this anchorage and markers "1" through "5" of the Lavaca Channel, so you will have to leave this anchorage the same way you entered.

## Side Trip: Lavaca River

**NAVIGATION:** Use Chart 11317. For vessels with drafts of no more than 3.5 feet and mast heights of less than 35 feet, the Lavaca River offers an interesting side trip with peaceful, protected spots to drop a hook. To reach the mouth of the Lavaca River, exit the Lavaca Channel near red "8" in 6-foot depths. Locate the distant red markers before exiting the Lavaca Channel. The markers are widely spaced, so frequently sight them ahead of (and behind) your position to monitor drift and stay in the channel. Depths are quite shallow outside the channel, which turns sharply to port in

Lavaca Bay before passing under the causeway, and the turns sharply to starboard to the Lavaca River's mouth

The fixed **Lavaca Bay Causeway (SR 35) Bridge** has a 42-foot vertical clearance followed by a power line with a 69-foot vertical clearance. Rehabilitation of the bridge was underway at press tim (spring 2017).

Just before reaching the last markers in upper Lavac Bay, a bar with depths of less than 4 feet extends acros the channel. Beyond the bar, depths range from 6 to 15 feet in the river. Before making this passage toward the Lavaca River, cruisers should check for local knowledge and for navigation alerts at waterwayguide.com due to frequently changing conditions.

**Anchorage:** Although small cruising boats can nose into the bank for a quiet anchorage at several spots, the best anchorage lies by the twin bridges (one road and one railroad) that mark the end of the route for most vessels, about 10 miles up the Lavaca River.

Two sturdy dolphins by the bridge offer a convenien place to moor. Boats with heights of 10 feet or less (depending on river stage) can pass under the bridge and anchor in the 7-foot depths of the Navidad River, which enters the Lavaca River immediately beyond the railroad bridge, or they can anchor in the Lavaca River itself. When anchoring in the Lavaca River, stick well to the side and burn a bright anchor light. Outboard-powered ski and fishing boats often transit the river at high speeds.

## ■ PORT O'CONNOR TO CORPU CHRISTI BAY

### Offshore Option: Matagorda Ship Channel to Aransas Pass Channel

Aransas Pass is one of the most famous passes on the coast. It was used by Spain and Mexico to access their port on Copano Bay and to then supply the Presidios (forts) at Refugio and Goliad. The first buoyage along the Texas coast appeared at Aransas Pass in 1845 to mark the route over the ever-shifting sandbar.

**NAVIGATION:** Use Charts 11312, 11313, 11314, 11316 and 11319. On this leg, the contour of the coast changes to a more southwesterly slant. Follow a course of about 240 degrees magnetic. Dominant coastal features will be the barrier islands of Matagorda and San Jose. The

listance to run is 60 nm, and the number of oil and gas platforms diminish significantly. Pass Cavallo can be problematic due to currents but this can be avoided by giving it a wide berth of 4-plus statute miles.

Along the largely featureless shore there are two privately maintained lighthouses. The first is a slender black spire on the northern end of Matagorda Island. The second is located on the Lydia Ann Channel just east of Port Aransas. Matagorda Island is a part of the Aransas National Wildlife Refuge and consists mainly of a sandy beach backed by clumps of low bushes.

Separating Matagorda Island and San Jose Island is a pass called Cedar Bayou. It was closed during a 1979 oil well blowout in the Bay of Campeche. This short-term effort protected bay waters from oil intrusion. The extended affect had a negative impact on the waters of the bays and subsequent dredging resulted in the Pass being reopened in September of 2014. Nevertheless, Cedar Bayou is not a navigable channel accessible by cruising boats.

San Jose Island is privately owned and used primarily to graze cattle. Some buildings on the island can be spotted about 12 miles before you reach Aransas Pass.

Aransas Pass Channel is a major offshore inlet with a fair amount of large ship traffic. On approach, you will see numerous buildings, a water tower, microwave tower, the usual buoys and a lighted range mark. The jetties extend about .5 nm into the Gulf of Mexico. The

channel separates San Jose Island to the east and Mustang Island to the west.

If you enter when the tide is going out, the swells and current at the jetties can be a challenge. Immediately inside the jetties you can choose multiple destinations through waters with enough depth and vertical clearance for almost any cruising boat.

A moving safety zone surrounds LPG tankers whenever they use the channel. They unload at a terminal at the far end of La Quinta Channel.

## GIWW Option: Mile 473 to Mile 518 WHL

Port O'Connor is located on the west shore of Matagorda Bay on the north side of the GIWW. In the 19th century it was originally a fishing community called Alligator Head. The 43-mile-long run on the GIWW from Port O'Connor to Aransas Bay offers no marinas or other amenities but does provide a beautiful cruise through the Aransas National Wildlife Refuge (beginning at Mile 500 WHL)

**Note:** The GIWW actually changes direction from west to southwest and then to the south as you head to Corpus Christi and Brownsville. Corpus Christi is as far south as Tampa, and South Padre Island is comparable to the Everglades with regard to latitude. We will continue to refer to the banks as north (land side) and south (gulf side) as we continue "west" on the GIWW.

before entering Aransas Bay at Mile 515 WHL. This is a truly beautiful stretch of waterway.

Depending of the time of year, it is possible to see hundreds of birds. It can be easy to spot herons, egrets, terns, ducks, and many other birds, including whooping cranes with their 7.5-foot wing spans. For the winter months, whooping cranes migrate 2500 miles from northern Canada. In the spring they display courting rituals before flying back to Canada to nest and raise their new chicks.

**NAVIGATION:** Use Charts 11313, 11314, 11315, 13316 and 11317. From Mile 475 to Mile 485 WHL, stay mid-channel to avoid the shallow water along the banks. Starting at Mile 479 WHL the red daybeacons are placed in 2 to 3 feet of water to avoid having them knocked down by commercial towboats.

A small settlement at Mile 485 WHL has several private piers, a couple of boat ramps and dockage for shallow-draft vessels. (Space for transient boat tie-up is questionable at best.) On weekends, the area is often humming with small fishing and other pleasure boats as they cross the GIWW and disappear through a narrow cut in the spoil bank and into Espiritu Santo Bay. Just east of red daybeacon "10" to red "2E," be careful of

submerged and exposed rocks along the north bank of the GIWW.

At the east end of San Antonio Bay at Mile 491.8 WHL, red nun "2E" marks the beginning of the Victoria Barge Canal. It does not mark the GIWW; the next mark (bifurcated buoy RG "A") marks the GIWW. Over the years, the entrance to the barge canal has been the site of numerous groundings, because the buoys are often moved or removed by commercial traffic making the sharp turn into or out of the canal. Floating marks in the vicinity may be unreliable so use caution in this area. The Army Corps of Engineers has plans to remove the spoil in the "Y" which should alleviate problems here.

At Mile 501.5 WHL, on the north side of the channel, is a shallow canal leading to an Aransas National Wildlife ranger station. Five-foot depths have been unofficially reported in the canal. This is a ranger station, so if you should need refuge, be prepared to explain why you are there.

Mile 503 to Mile 504 WHL is a "wiggle," so buoys are often knocked out of position. The wiggle is marked by 17-foot flashing red "48" and 17-foot quick flashing green "53," which are firmly located on the banks. A

vee on the north bank prevents intrusion from the marshlands.

In the vicinity of Mile 507 WHL, midway along undown Bay to the north, a privately maintained channel leads south from the GIWW into Mesquite Bay. The channel and Mesquite Bay are quite shallow, with charted depths of 4 feet or less. Fishing boats, park rangers and workboats that maintain the petroleum production platforms south of the waterway use the channel. The passage and the bay are too shallow for most cruising boats.

At Mile 510 WHL, the GIWW leaves the wildlife refuge at 17-foot flashing green "1" and enters Aransas Bay for the 10-mile-long run to the Key Allegro and Rockport area. The Bay and the spoil areas are well marked; however, the Coast Guard discontinued some buoys and moved others from Mile 510 to Mile 525 WHL in April 2015. See the Waterway Guide Explorer (waterwayguide.com) for the latest updates.

Stay in the marked channel; avoid the submerged pilings to the south, and the shallow water to the north of the waterway. Petroleum production platforms are numerous and well marked.

**Dockage:** At Mile 478 WHL a 7-foot deep channel, marked with daybeacons and flashing lighted marks, extends southward from the GIWW into Espiritu Santo Bay and terminates 6 miles later at Matagorda Island State Park. A small dock with 5-foot depths can accommodate a handful of boats, but there is no shore power or other facilities. This is an unusual destination, both for its remote location and its features. Often referred to as the Army Hole, the park contains a massive WWII-era landing strip, an unspoiled (and mostly deserted) beach and a lighthouse built in 1852. It is a popular destination for local boaters. Contact the Texas Parks and Wildlife Department 979-244-6804 or 361-983-4425 for more information. Local boaters have knowledge of the passage and docks at the Army Hole and will be happy to share their experiences.

At Mile 478.5, there is a channel to the north just before red "2" that leads into a housing development with a very nice marina. Transient slips may be available. It is probably not possible to check ahead of time, so if necessary, take a vacant slip and check in if you can find someone at the office. Power, water and restrooms with showers have been available in the past.

# ■ FULTON TO ROCKPORT

A careful and cautious skipper can navigate Aransas Bay outside of the GIWW once west of red buoy "18". There are almost continuous spoil areas on the north (west) side of the GIWW. Openings in the spoil areas are marked on charts and these openings can be used to reach destinations north of the GIWW. You can leave the GIWW to the south at almost any point.

## City of Fulton

The first boating facility in the Rockport area is in Fulton Harbor. Fulton is a small, friendly community. Birding, fishing and boating provide an abundance of outdoor recreation. An annual Oyster Festival, celebrated the first week of March, crowds the harbor to capacity.

**NAVIGATION:** Use Chart 11314. Leave the GIWW between red buoy "22" and green buoy "23" and head northwest on a course of approximately 285 degrees magnetic for 2.6 nm to Fulton Harbor.

**Dockage:** The marina at Fulton Harbor is managed by the Aransas County Navigation District and has a limited number of reserved transient slips. It is home to many commercial fishing and shrimp boats. On-site Fulton Yacht Yard is a service center with a 70-ton lift and complete ship's service and repairs. The adjoining building houses Seaworthy Marine Supply (361-727-9100), a chandler who can get any boat part needed.

## Key Allegro

The 5-foot depths around the small islands in Little Bay behind Key Allegro are favored for water skiing, jet boating and partying on Tiki-hut barges equipped with bars, grills, entertainment and sunbathing platforms. If you have a rod and reel, try fishing at the docks or on Little Bay. Fishing is excellent here, especially at night.

**NAVIGATION:** Use Chart 11314. If you are going to Key Allegro or Rockport continue west in the GIWW until you come to the 17-foot flashing green "29". On the north side of the GIWW is an opening between two spoils marked by daybeacons "1" and "2." Proceed through the cut, and set a heading of about 272 degrees magnetic for 1.9 nm to the Rockport Harbor. Proceed through the cut and set a heading of about 300 degrees magnetic for 1 nm to the jetties leading to Key Allegro. Follow the marked channel for about 1 nm to the marina.

www.snagaslip.com

EXPLORE
BOOK
BOAT
SNAG-A-SLIP

# Aransas Bay, TX

| | | Largest Vessel Accommodated | VHF Channel Monitored | Transient Berths / Total Berths | Approach / Dockside Depth (reported) | Floating Docks | Gas / Diesel | Groceries, Ice, Marine Supplies, Snacks | Repairs: Hull, Engine, Propeller | Lift (tonnage), Crane, Rail | Min/Max Amps | Laundry, Pool, Showers, Courtesy Car | Pump-Out Station | Nearby: Grocery Store, Motel, Restaurant |
|---|---|---|---|---|---|---|---|---|---|---|---|---|---|---|
| **ROCKPORT AREA** | | | | **Dockage** | | | **Supplies** | | | | **Services** | | | |
| 1. Fulton Harbor  520 WHL | 361-729-6661 | 60 | 16 | 5/96 | 12/6 | – | – | IMS | HEP | L49,C100 | 20/50 | LS | P | MR |
| 2. Key Allegro Marina 🖥 WiFi  520 WHL | 361-729-8264 | 160 | 16/18 | 2/159 | 8/7 | – | GD | GIMS | – | L8 | 30/100 | LS | P | GMR |
| 3. Rockport Harbor 🖥  522.8 WHL | 361-729-6661 | 70 | 16 | 8/126 | 11/7 | – | – | GIMS | – | | 20/50 | LS | P | GMR |
| 4. House of Boats WiFi  526.5 WHL | 361-729-9018 | 50 | – | – | 12/12 | – | – | M | HEP | L50 | 30/30 | S | – | R |
| 5. Cove Harbor Marina and Drystack WiFi  525.5 WHL | 361-790-5438 | 50 | – | 15/173 | 7/8 | F | GD | GIS | – | | 30/50 | S | P | GR |
| 6. Palm Harbor Marina and RV Park  527.3 WHL | 361-729-8540 | 50 | 16 | 10/55 | 7/6 | – | GD | GIMS | – | | | LS | – | GMR |
| **ARANSAS PASS** | | | | | | | | | | | | | | |
| 7. San Patricio County Navigation Dist. Marina | 361-758-1890 | 50 | – | 1/157 | 10/12 | – | GD | GIS | – | L | 30/30 | – | P | GR |
| 8. Redfish Bay Boat House | 361-758-9000 | 100 | – | – | – | F | G | IS | – | L9 | 30/50 | S | P | GR |
| **MUSTANG ISLAND** | | | | | | | | | | | | | | |
| 9. Port Aransas Marina 🖥 WiFi  533 WHL | 361-749-5429 | 100 | 16/68 | 40/240 | 12/8 | F | – | I | – | | 30/50 | LS | P | GMR |
| 10. Woody's Sports Center WiFi | 361-749-5252 | 50 | – | – | – | – | GD | IS | – | | | | – | MR |
| 11. Island Moorings Marina & Yacht Club WiFi | 888-749-9030 | 100 | 16 | 50/350 | 8/8 | F | GD | IMS | – | | 30/50 | LPS | P | R |

🖥 Internet Access  WiFi Wireless Internet Access  WG Waterway Guide Cruising Club Partner *(Information in the table is provided by the facilities.)*
See WaterwayGuide.com for current rates, fuel prices, web site addresses, and other up-to-the-minute information.

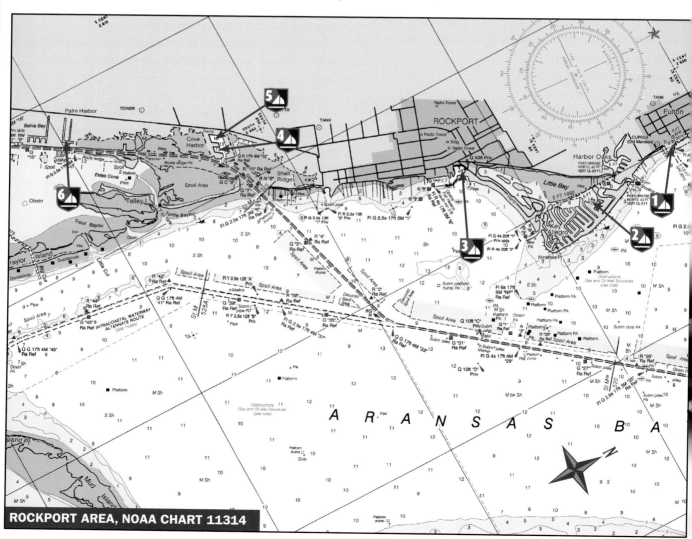

ROCKPORT AREA, NOAA CHART 11314

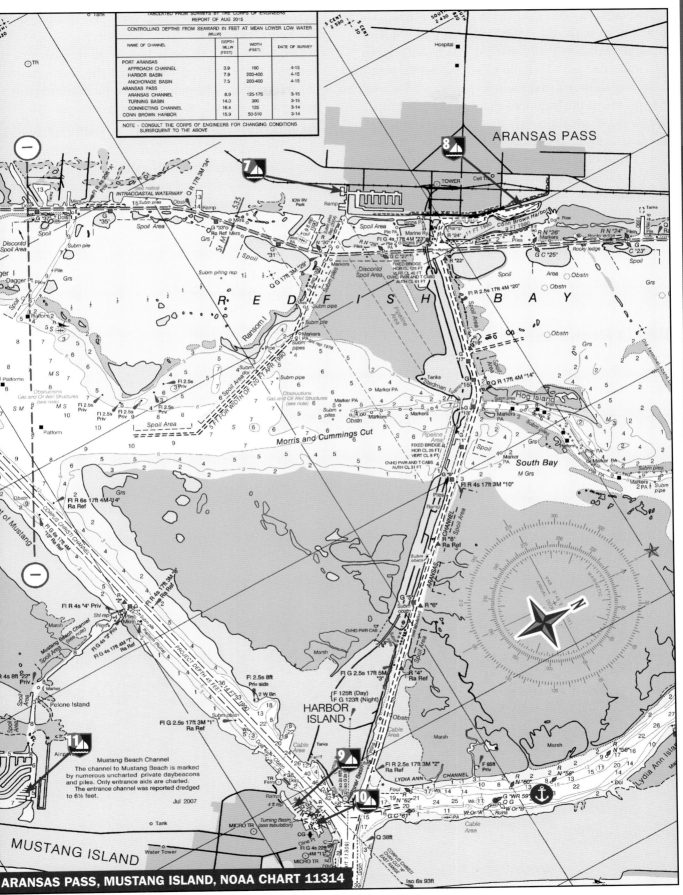

FREEPORT TO BROWNSVILLE, TX

**ARANSAS PASS, MUSTANG ISLAND, NOAA CHART 11314**

**Dockage:** Key Allegro Marina is the first marina and it will be to starboard. Enter Little Bay to Key Allegro through two short jetties marked by a flashing green "1" and a flashing red "2." Follow the channel keeping the homes to starboard and the Rockport Beach Park to port. As you round the bend into the very shallow Little Bay follow the channel markers that head directly toward the houses at the point next to the marina. Monitor your depth carefully. Key Allegro is a modern marina with quality, upscale facilities. There are no shoreside amenities or services close to the marina. Large homes and condominiums border the many canals that provide water frontage and private docking, creating a very laid-back atmosphere. The Key Allegro Yacht Club is on the island but is not accessible by water.

**Anchorage:** Behind Key Allegro in Little Bay, you can drop the hook in 4 to 7 feet with all-around protection.

## City of Rockport

Rockport is a favorite of the sailing crowd and popular with all boaters. It is also home to the Texas Maritime Museum (1202 Navigation Circle, 866-729-2469), Rockport Center for the Arts (902 Navigation Circle, 361-729-5519), the Bay Education Center (121

Seabreeze Dr., 361-749-6832) and The Aquarium at Rockport Harbor (702 Navigation Circle, 361-729-232? which are all open to the public. A cab or other ride is required for provisions. Check with the harbormaster for information. The public beach and adjacent park playground are next to the harbor to the east.

**NAVIGATION:** Use Chart 11314. On your heading of 27 degrees, Rockport Harbor is about 1 mile farther than Key Allegro. The entrance is marked by 17-foot flashin green "1" and a series of green daybeacons leading into the harbor. Keep the 17-foot flashing red "6" close to starboard when entering.

**Dockage:** A rubble dike with a concrete walkway is near the entrance to the marina at Rockport Harbor, about 1 mile from Key Allegro. Easily seen during the day, at night its lights will add to the background. The lights are bright white and fixed on tall poles, and there are also very bright fixed green lights near the water to attract fish. (Avoid a night entry if possible.) Proceed along the starboard side of the basin and keep the recreational boat dock to port. Check in at the harbor office in the small brick building behind the arts building.

Rockport Municipal Harbor is also home to the Rockport Yacht Club, whose building is adjacent to the transient slip area. Yacht club members are friendly and will be happy to provide local knowledge to visitors. They welcome other yacht club members on their docks. Fresh seafood (oysters, crabs and shrimp) can be purchased right from the boats in the harbor. Across the street is Latitude 28° 02', a local landmark restaurant serving seafood in a casual setting among works of art from the thriving local artist community.

**Anchorage:** Rockport Bight offers 8 to 10 feet of water and protection from all but the south through southeast. Across Aransas Bay from Rockport, a good anchorage can be found in an alcove at Paul's Mott, 2 miles southeast of 17-foot flashing green "21" at Mile 518 WHL, where it joins with Long Reef. This is a favored anchorage, although open to northwest winds. Seven-foot depths can be carried fairly close to shore.

A more popular spot, but equally exposed to northerly winds, is located in the bight formed by the tidal flats of Mud Island and San Jose Island to the south. Anchor outside the two private channels in 7- to 8-foot depths. Anchorages in Aransas Bay are plentiful. Anchorages should have soft mud bottoms with very good holding.

## ◼ GIWW ROUTE: ARANSAS BAY TO CORPUS CHRISTI

**NAVIGATION:** Use Charts 110309, 11312 and 11314. Near the 17-foot flashing green "33" the GIWW divides and splits into two channels marked with a bifurcated buoy, RG "N." The passage to starboard leads to a land cut, sometimes called the Rockport Cut. The passage to port leads to the Lydia Ann Channel.

The Lydia Ann Channel (to port) is used for boats going to Port Aransas and for sailboats with mast heights greater than 48 feet. This channel is covered in more detail in the next section. The two routes rejoin at Mile 539.5 WHL before the GIWW enters Corpus Christi Bay through a narrow cut aptly named the "Eye of the Needle." Because the two routes differ so obviously, reasons for choosing one over the other will vary.

The Rockport Cut (to starboard), takes the more direct route to Corpus Christi Bay. The entrance from Aransas Bay into the GIWW channel (Rockport Cut) is marked by green "7" with numerous daybeacons and floating marks beyond that point. Stay mid-channel, as shallow

water is found outside the marked passage. Note again that we are referring to the right bank of the GIWW as the north bank and the left bank as the south bank.

The Rockport Cut passes by the town of Aransas Pass, where the **Aransas Pass Bridge** with a fixed 48-foot vertical clearance at Mile 533.1 WHL limits the height of vessels using this route. Immediately before the bridge is the Port Aransas Channel with unlimited vertical height. It is included in detail later in this section.

**Dockage:** If you choose the Rockport Cut, at the first bend to port (Mile 525.5 WHL), 17-foot, quick-flashing red "12" marks the entrance to Cove Harbor where the House of Boats and the Cove Harbor Marina and Drystack are located. In this service complex are a restaurant (JD's Seafood Restaurant at the far southwest corner of harbor, 361-729-1202), fuel docks, marine supplies and other transient facilities. Full repair service is offered, and do-it-yourself repairs are permitted.

Palm Harbor Marina and RV Park, located farther west on the north bank opposite 17-foot flashing green "13" (Mile 527.5 WHL) may have transient space with very limited facilities. There is a restaurant that also has ice and limited supplies. A bulkhead, alongside the restaurant, immediately north of the GIWW, is available for customers and may be available for overnight

dockage. The entrance is narrow (maybe 16 feet) and depth is reported to be 6 feet.

Continuing on in the Rockport Cut, the busy Aransas Channel (Mile 533 WHL), used mainly by the shrimp fleet at Conn Brown Harbor and numerous small sportfishing boats, connects Aransas Pass to Port Aransas, 6 miles to the southeast. To use Aransas Channel, travel just past GIWW red nun buoy "26" then turn to port (southeast) just before the Aransas Pass Bridge and leave red daybeacon "22" to port. Remember, when entering a non-GIWW channel, the buoyage reverts to red-right-returning. (Red daybeacon "22" will be to port, because you are outbound on the Aransas Channel.)

Conn Brown Harbor is located at Mile 533 on the north side of the GIWW directly across from the Port Aransas Channel. To enter Conn Brown Harbor, pass GIWW red nun "26" and leave daybeacon "24" to starboard. Initially, Conn Brown Harbor was a commercial port for Gulf trawlers and some offshore supply boats. At the entrance to the harbor, repairs may be made at Mile 533 Marine Ways. Although they cater to large commercial vessels and use a marine railway to haul them, they also service yachts with a 150-ton lift. Diesel fuel can be found at the Ericson Jensen (361-758-5642) dock, about halfway down the harbor starboard, and gasoline at the Redfish Bay dry stack facility at the far end of the harbor (361-790-5438). Redfish Bay Boat House is full-service marina with floating docks, a restaurant and a ship store with limited supplies. Call ahead for availability.

At Mile 534.2 WHL, just before the 17-foot flashing green "29," the channel to the San Patricio County Navigation District Marina heads to the north. Do not cut the corner; a shoal encroaches on the north edge of the channel. The channel should have a depth of 6 feet; exercise caution. The San Patricio County Marina has one short transient pier attached to the concrete bulkhead in the main channel. Between the two basins, Hamptons Landing, a small private marina, has gasoline and dockage for fishing boats in the 20-foot range, and Mickey's Bar and Grill (361-758-1562).

Continuing on the GIWW Rockport Cut, once clear of the 48-foot vertical clearance Aransas Pass Bridge at Mile 533.1 WHL, the GIWW continues through the land cut to its eventual joining with the Corpus Christi Ship Channel at Mile 539.5 WHL.

## Corpus Christi Ship Channel–GIWW Mile 539 WHL

**NAVIGATION:** Use Charts 11308,11309 and 11312. From Mile 536.5 WHL (20-foot flashing red "A") to Mile 539 WHL (Corpus Christi Channel), the GIWW is marked only by green daybeacons. The Corpus Christi Channel has heavy traffic, inbound and outbound. Tows with long barge strings, Gulf-bound tankers and freighters, fast offshore supply boats, Coast Guard vessels and fishing trawlers are plentiful. Berthed tankers and large offshore production platforms under repair on the northwest bank at Port Ingleside sometimes impair visibility.

The channel to Corpus Christi and the continuation of the GIWW west are covered later in this chapter.

> **Naval Station Ingleside** closed April 2010 and cautions/warnings on Charts 11308, 11312 and 11314 concerning naval vessels no longer apply. Port of Corpus Christi has leased the property to an oilfield supply company. Expect traffic in the form of large supply vessels and other commercial traffic concerned with the offshore oilfield supply service.

# ■ ALTERNATE ROUTE: ARANSAS BAY TO CORPUS CHRISTI BAY

**NAVIGATION:** Use Charts 11308, 11309, 11312 and 11314. Until the construction of the Rockport Cut, the Lydia Ann Channel was the only route between Aransas Bay and Port Aransas (now known as the alternate route).

The route begins at bifurcated buoy RG "N" near flashing green "33" heading in a southerly direction. If your destination port is Corpus Christi, this route is approximately 5 miles longer than the Rockport Cut. Sailboats with mast heights over 48 feet must take this route, because of the height of the Aransas Pass Bridge in the Rockport Cut. Numerous lighted marks and floating buoys make this alternative route easy to follow. Land on either side of the channel, often submerged, supports marsh grasses and brush.

Near the Lydia Ann Lighthouse, an area of mangroves known as Lighthouse Lakes caters to kayakers with trails marked by buoys. The buoys help guide kayakers through the confusing group of mangrove islands. Across the channel from the lighthouse, the WWII wreck of the SS *Worthington*, marked by special "A" and "B" daybeacons, is now completely submerged. The wreck was towed to this position after being torpedoed during WWII.

The Lydia Ann alternative route ends at a four-way intersection with the Aransas Channel (Mile 534.2), the Corpus Christi Ship Channel and Aransas Pass Channel (jetties to the Gulf) at Mile 534.4 WHL. If you choose to go offshore at this point, simply follow Aransas Pass Channel between the jetties and enter the Gulf of Mexico.

To continue on the GIWW, turn to starboard/inbound and follow the Corpus Christi Ship Channel, keeping in mind the red-right-returning rule now applies. (GIWW marks continue to be identified with either yellow squares or triangles). On the south bank (the north shore of Mustang Island), the resort town of Port Aransas can be accessed through a short granite breakwater marked by flashing green and flashing red marks. Heavy ferry traffic will be encountered about one-quarter mile west of the entrance to Port Aransas.

You can continue inbound (west) on the Corpus Christi Ship Channel, through the Humble Basin. On the

# GOIN' ASHORE: **PORT ARANSAS, TX**

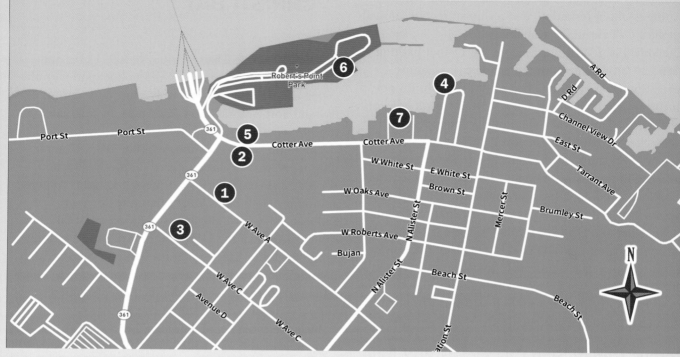

| SERVICES | |
|---|---|
| 1 | Library |
| 2 | Visitor Information |
| **ATTRACTIONS** | |
| 3 | Farley Boat Works |
| **DINING** | |
| 4 | Virginia's on the Bay |
| 5 | Fins Grill |

| MARINAS | |
|---|---|
| 6 | Port Aransas Marina |
| 7 | Woody's Sports Center |

On the northern tip of Mustang Island is the cruising destination of Port Aransas. It is a picturesque charming beach and fishing community where you will encounter a laid-back island attitude with an abundance of warm hospitality

**Attractions:** Explore the waterways and beautiful beaches in the "Fishing Capital of Texas." You will also find birding and nature walks, a professional golf resort, art galleries, dining and shopping, museums and boat building.

The cruising boater has many choices for transportation to and from their boat. For a quarter, the City Trolley will pick you up and drop you off any place in town, including the beach. The trolley itself and the Chamber Visitor Center are both easy and friendly ways to get familiar with what there is to see and do around town. This is a golf-car friendly community and there are numerous places to rent carts to drive around town, or on the beach. Beach going bicycles are also available to rent and taxi service is available.

A trip to Farley Boat Works is a must for boaters. Their doors are open and they welcome visitors. You can hear the sounds of the boat shop before you enter the building. Farley Boat Works was established in 1916 to meet a growing resurgence of interest in Port Aransas' maritime history and seafaring community. The Boat Works is expanding to offer educational programs and seminars covering various aspects of boat building.

**Special Events:** An annual WoodenPly Boat Festival is held in mid-October in conjunction with the Port Aransas Old Town Festival. Other events include the Deep Sea Roundup (mid-July) and the annual Whooping Crane Festival (the last weekend in February). For more special events, visit portaransas.org.

**Dining:** The open-air Virginia's on the Bay offers panoramic views and a full menu featuring Texas seafood and steaks. Fins Grill and Icehouse at the opposite end of the harbor has a diverse menu in a fun setting.

south side of the channel, in 2.5 miles, is the entrance to the Mustang Beach Channel leading to Island Moorings Marina.

Returning to the Corpus Christi Channel, it is then just a 5-mile run west to the GIWW before it threads the "Eye of the Needle" into Corpus Christi Bay at Mile 540 WHL. Corpus Christi Bay can be entered through the Eye of the Needle, or by continuing west in the Corpus Christi Ship Channel. The GIWW continues its westerly trek, and it is approximately 11 miles to the City of Corpus Christi on the west side of Corpus Christi Bay. (The GIWW and Corpus Christi are presented in more detail later in this chapter.)

**Dockage:** The 240-slip Port Aransas Marina, on the starboard side as you enter the harbor, has transient docks to handle boats of 100 feet and more. Restrooms, bathhouse and laundry are on site. The marina is part of a large city park complex. Port Aransas is a favorite stop for cruisers traveling the Texas Coast. Both gas and diesel are available at Woody's Sports Center on the mainland (south) side of the harbor.

Approximately 3 miles west of Port Aransas Harbor the Corpus Christi Ship Channel passes Mustang Beach Channel on the south side of the channel. This channel leads to a full service marina, Island Moorings Marina & Yacht Club. The channel is well marked and depths are 8 feet, but the cut is narrow, so stay in the middle.

As you approach the Island Moorings Marina, there are side canals that extend to private home sites. The channel to port (north) leads to the marina. The full-service marina has floating docks, gas and diesel, a ship store, a restaurant and bar and an airport next door. Beach access is less than 1 mile away, and a bus (trolley) provides transportation into Port Aransas just 3 miles away.

**Anchorage:** Across from the lighthouse on the Lydia Ann Channel, just before quick-flashing green "97" is one of the area's most popular spots to anchor. A buoyed wreck is just beyond the light. High-speed offshore fishing boats throwing huge wakes may disturb your sleep at daybreak and your leisure hour at dusk. Aside from these possible disturbances, this is an excellent anchorage with a clean sand beach and the Gulf of Mexico less than 1 mile away.

Another anchorage can be found north of the Corpus Ship Channel flashing red "14" in the old Morris and Cummings Cut. Watch the depth finder and anchor in at least 6 feet.

# ■ CORPUS CHRISTI BAY TO SOUTH PADRE ISLAND

## Corpus Christi Channel to Ingleside

**NAVIGATION:** Use Chart 11309. At the junction of the GIWW (Mile 539.5 WHL) and the ship channel, you may continue west in the GIWW by turning to port and going through the "Eye of the Needle." Moving further west in the Corpus Christi Ship Channel you cross La Quinta Channel in 1.8 miles. The channel turns to the north at red "36" terminating at the north side of Corpus Christi Bay in 4.5 miles. From red "36" the La Quinta Channel enters Ingleside Cove in 1.2 miles. The La Quinta Channel continues with depths of 45 feet and a width of 300 feet to a couple of industrial plants.

**Dockage:** There is one marina, Bahia Marina, on the south side of Ingleside Cove. The marina has a restaurant that is open on weekends only. Caution: Do not cut the corner going into the unmarked marina channel. If your vessel draws over 5 feet, call the marina for a depth check before entering.

North Shore Boat Works is located at the end of the Jewel Fulton Channel adjacent to the cove. They have a 35-ton lift and offer engine and propeller repair. Groceries and marine supplies are located on site. No transient slips are available.

## Corpus Christi Bay and the City of Corpus Christi

**NAVIGATION:** Use Charts 11309, 11311 and 11312. If you are traveling to Corpus Christi, stay in the well-marked Corpus Christi Channel and steer west, or turn slightly south (recommended route) at green "43" and enter the bay. Then stay south of the spoil areas and steer a westerly course to Corpus Christi. Strong south or southeasterly winds are common in the afternoon and the bay can be very choppy. Water depth throughout the bay average 10 to 12 feet.

If you stay in the Corpus Ship Channel and approach the enclosed basin protecting Corpus Christi's waterfront from the north, stay in the ship channel until passing 17-foot flashing green "85." Then steer south between the rocks of the protected basin and shoreline. Stay in the middle at 8- to 10-foot depths, and proceed to the marina.

The most common (recommended) and often used entrance to the Corpus Christi Marina is further south between the rock breakwater. Enter between the 17-foot red "2" and green "1". Do not cut the breakwater entrance too sharply, and do not ignore the floating green cans just inside the breakwater. They mark an obstruction. Note: Recreational vessels are restricted from entering the commercial basin north of the Harbor Bridge.

**Dockage:** Across the Bay and inside the harbor at Corpus Christi, is Corpus Christi Municipal Marina with air-conditioned showers, restrooms and laundry. A special work area is provided where tenants may do their own maintenance and minor repairs. A boat repair facility with a 25-ton lift is available for contract repairs. Both gas and diesel are available. It would be good to call ahead for reservations. The marina is the permanent home of the massive Texas International Boat Show, held every April. There are two yacht clubs in the harbor as well: Corpus Christi Yacht Club and Bay Yacht Club (private). Take a peek at the web cam atcorpuschristimarina.com/citywebcams/index.

Corpus Christi is somewhat unique among major cities on the Gulf Coast in that the downtown area is right along the water, only a few steps from the marina. The marina is part of a popular family walking and driving route, which includes the waterfront pathway of the city. On weekends, you will see a steady stream of "local tourists" out to see the boats.

## Offshore: Aransas Pass to Port Mansfield

**NAVIGATION:** Use Charts 11304, 11306, 11307 and 11312. On a course of about 190 degrees magnetic, the short Port Mansfield jetties are 78 nm. It is another 28 nm to the major shipping channel, Brazos Santiago Pass. Brazos Santiago opens into Laguna Madre where cruising boats have access to all that is offered on South Padre Island, and in the City of Port Isabel.

During the Mustang Island part of the passage, buildings, towers, hotels, RV parks, etc. are visible on shore. At night, the green and white aero beacon at Corpus Christi Naval Air Station may be visible, despite the fact that it is 10 miles inland. When the JFK Causeway, which crosses the GIWW, appears to be abeam, the features ashore begin to change, and the developments on Mustang Island and North Padre Island begin to dwindle, both in size and quantity.

About 30 miles north of Port Mansfield Channel, the Padre Island National Seashore begins and civilization ends. There are no prominent features along the shore. On a historical note, in 1553 a hurricane drove a Spanish treasure fleet ashore a few miles north of the Port Mansfield jetties. The Spaniards recovered most of the treasure later, but some of the treasure remained until discovered and recovered in 1967. It is on display in Austin, TX.

There are no offshore lights or buoys to guide a boat into the Port Mansfield Channel. The first markers are on the end of the rock jetties. The short jetties at the entrance channel are difficult to see and a boat could easily sail past and miss them entirely. This is an extremely remote area. There are no shoreside facilities or amenities. The only shelter will be an anchorage. You can continue 7 miles in a marked channel to the GIWW, or 8.6 miles to the tiny boating community of Port Mansfield.

# GOIN' ASHORE: CORPUS CHRISTI, TX

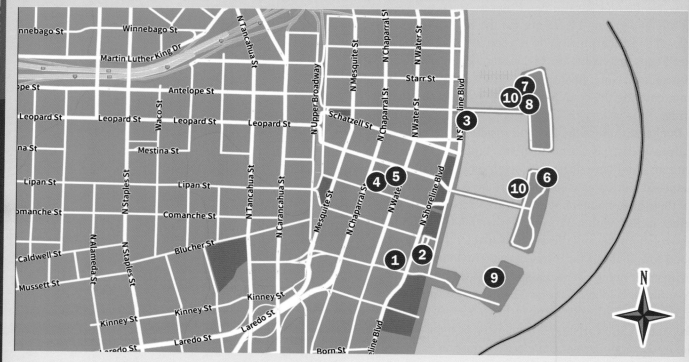

| SERVICES | |
|---|---|
| 1 | Visitor Information |
| **ATTRACTIONS** | |
| 2 | Arts Center of Corpus Christi |
| 3 | Selena Memorial Statue |
| 4 | Surf Museum |
| **SHOPPING** | |
| 5 | Water Street Market |

| DINING | |
|---|---|
| 6 | Joe's Crab Shack |
| 7 | Landry's Seafood |
| 8 | Tavern on the Bay |
| **MARINAS** | |
| 9 | Corpus Christi Yacht Club |
| 10 | Corpus Christi Municipal Marina |

After a devastating hurricane in 1919 caused incredible damage and the loss of 287 lives, Corpus Christi, with the help of the federal government, completed a massive dredging project and rebuilt the city. With the increased port traffic, the city doubled its population in 10 years and today remains a major seaport on the Gulf of Mexico at the mouth of the Nueces River. This cosmopolitan city, with all the expected amenities, is becoming a choice destination for the GIWW cruiser. Downtown is an easy walk. Many homes here are on the Texas Historic Landmark Tour, where history can be relived with a visit nine restored homes from the turn of the

20th century. Tours are offered Thursday and Friday at 10:30 a.m. The skyline view is spectacular.

**Attractions:** A boardwalk extends along the bayfront where you can walk, jog, bike, or rent a covered four-wheel bicycle for exploring. You can stop at the Selena Memorial Statue or the Selena Museum located farther down the boardwalk (5410 Leopard St., 361-289-9013), which offers a tribute to the life and contributions of the young Tejano singing star.

The boardwalk usually has a delightful breeze, making it an ideal place for windsurfing and sailing. Fishing is a popular pastime and catches are plentiful. The white sandy beaches are easily accessible and open to the public. The interesting Texas Surf Museum is nearby and explores the history of surfing and, specifically, the Lone Star State's unique place in that history through exhibits and films.

Located near the marinas, the Art Center of Corpus Christi (100 N. Shoreline Blvd., 361-884-6406) is a pleasant spot to see artists practice their crafts, with exhibits that change monthly. Grab a specialty lunch in the little restaurant, or visit the library and gift shop for an afternoon getaway. (Closed on Monday; open Tuesday-Sunday from 10:00 a.m. to 4:00 p.m.)

The South Texas Institute for the Arts, allied with Texas A&M University, is open Tuesday through Saturday, 10:00

m. to 5:00 p.m., and Sunday, 1:00 p.m. to 5:00 p.m., ith free admission on Thursday (1902 N. Shoreline vd., 361-825-3500).

The Museum of Science and History (1900 N. haparral, 361-826-4667) is home to replicas of hristopher Columbus' ships and artifacts of natural and ultural local history.

Across Oso Creek (transportation required), the South exas Botanical Garden and Nature Center (8545 S. aples St., 361-852-2100) has exhibits, a water garden, rd and butterfly trails, a wetlands boardwalk and cnic areas (open 9:00 a.m. to 5:00 p.m. daily except on ondays).

The second largest bridge in Texas, Harbor Bridge, es from the port and connects Corpus Christi Beach to e downtown area. You can get there over land from the arina three ways: 1) by taxi, 2) by ferry via the landing the marina or 3) by public bus, with a stop at the ooper's Alley T-Head. (Buses do not run on Sundays.)

The Texas State Aquarium (2710 N. Shoreline Blvd., 51-881-1200), located across the bridge, is a popular

stop. Across from the aquarium, the *USS Lexington* Museum helps you imagine life aboard one of America's most famous aircraft carriers (2914 N. Shoreline Blvd., 361-888-4873).

**Shopping:** There is no grocery store or convenience store within walking distance, so a taxi ride is necessary. The downtown farmers' market is open every Wednesday evening at from 5:00 p.m. to 8:00 p.m. at the Art Center of Corpus Christi. The Water Street Market at 309 N. Water St. is in the heart of Corpus Christi, with an open-air courtyard and a few little shops. See details at waterstmarketcc.com

**Dining:** Landry's Seafood on the waterfront (more upscale) and Tavern on the Bay at Harrison's Landing (more relaxed) are both good options for dining near the municipal marina. Closer to the yacht club is Joe's Crab Shack, a fun chain restaurant.

You can get more ideas plus a list of current events and discount coupons at the Corpus Christi Chamber of Commerce (120l N. Shoreline Blvd., 361-881-1800).

# Corpus Christi Bay, TX

| | | Phone | Largest Vessel Accommodated | VHF Channel Monitored | Transient Berths / Total Berths | Approach / Dockside Depth (reported) | Floating Docks | Groceries, Ice, Marine Supplies, Snacks | Gas / Diesel | Repairs: Hull, Engine, Propeller | Lift (tonnage), Crane, Rail | Laundry, Pool, Showers, Courtesy Car | Pump-Out Station | Min/Max Amps | Nearby: Grocery Store, Motel, Restaurant |
|---|---|---|---|---|---|---|---|---|---|---|---|---|---|---|---|
| | | | **Dockage** | | | | | **Supplies** | | **Services** | | | | | |
| **INGLESIDE COVE** | | | | | | | | | | | | | | | |
| 1. | Bahia Marina 🖥 WiFi 2NW of 540 WHL | 361-776-7295 | 50 | 16/68 | 6/56 | 6/6 | – | – | GIS | – | – | 30/50 | LPS | P | GI |
| 2. | North Shore Boat Works WiFi 2NW of 540 WHL | 361-776-2525 | – | – | – | 18/10 | – | – | M | EP | L35 | – | – | – | GM |
| **CORPUS CHRISTI** | | | | | | | | | | | | | | | |
| 3. | Bay Yacht Club–PRIVATE 🖥 WiFi | 361-356-7156 | – | – | – | – | F | GD | GIS | HEP | L,C | 30/100 | LS | P | GI |
| 4. | Corpus Christi Yacht Club 🖥 WiFi | 361-883-6518 | 60 | – | 2/ | 9/6 | – | – | I | – | – | 50/50 | PS | – | R |
| 5. | **Corpus Christi Municipal Marina 🖥 WiFi** | **361-826-3980** | **150** | **16/68** | **70/651** | **12/8** | **F** | **GD** | **IS** | **HEP** | **L25,C2** | **30/200+** | **LPS** | **P** | **GM** |
| **LAGUNA MADRE** | | | | | | | | | | | | | | | |
| 6. | Marker 37 Marina and Pier  553 WHL | 361-949-4750 | 40 | 72 | call/35 | 4/4 | – | G | GIMS | – | L | 30/30 | – | – | GI |
| 7. | Padre Island Yacht Club | 361-949-2248 | – | – | 4/30 | 4/4 | – | – | I | – | – | 30/30 | S | P | R |

🖥 Internet Access   WiFi Wireless Internet Access   WG Waterway Guide Cruising Club Partner   *(Information in the table is provided by the facilities.)*
See WaterwayGuide.com for current rates, fuel prices, web site addresses, and other up-to-the-minute information.

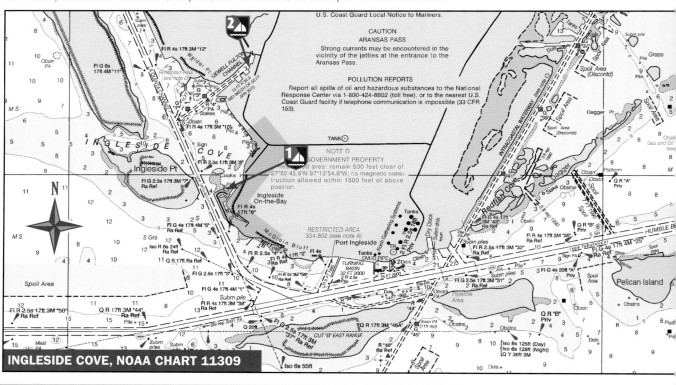

**INGLESIDE COVE, NOAA CHART 11309**

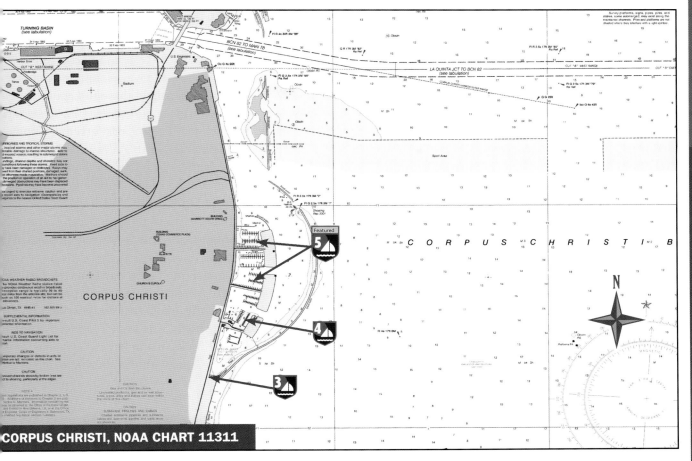

**CORPUS CHRISTI, NOAA CHART 11311**

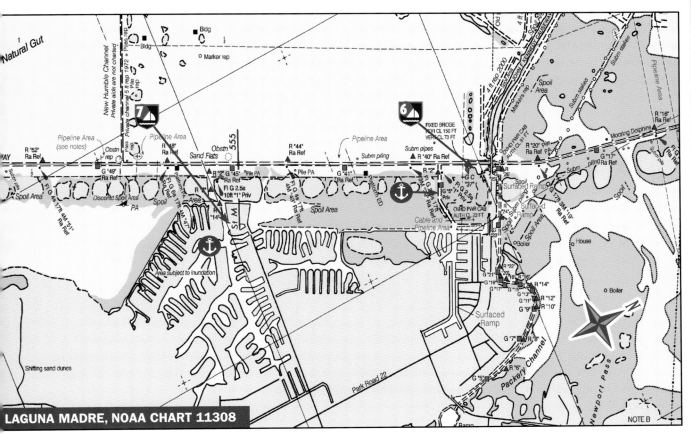

**LAGUNA MADRE, NOAA CHART 11308**

## Corpus Christi Bay to North Padre Island

**NAVIGATION:** Use Chart 11308. After crossing the Corpus Christi Ship Channel, the GIWW passes through a narrow cut ("Eye of the Needle") into Corpus Christi Bay. Shoaling occurs on both sides of the cut, and tidal currents are sometimes strong. One vessel at a time should pass through this narrow cut. The cut can be detoured by following the Corpus Christi Ship Channel west from Mile 539.5 WHL for 3 miles into Corpus Christi Bay and then turning southeast just past flashing green "43" to return to the GIWW.

Channel markers, including 17-foot-high flashing green "51" flashing red "58" and green daybeacon "61" identify the GIWW to the middle of Corpus Christi Bay. A 2-mile unmarked stretch leads past the 17-foot white flashing Morse code (A) marked with the letter "C," and ends at the 17-foot "1" that will take you through a narrow part of GIWW into the shallow waters of Laguna Madre. This begins the start of a 5-mile run to the 73-foot fixed vertical clearance **JFK Causeway Bridge** at Mile 552.7 WHL.

**Dockage:** The Marker 37 Marina and Pier is located at green can "37," just to the southwest, and almost under the JFK Causeway Bridge. A short walk around the boat ramp leads you to Snoopy's Pier and Ice Cream Parlor (361-949-8815), Doc's Seafood and Steaks (361-949-6744) and Da Boathouse, a private dock. Transient dockage is limited and depths are 4.5 feet or less. Both restaurants offer temporary dockage while dining with 4-foot depths alongside.

A private channel at green can "39" leads into a home subdivision and offers no transient facilities. Immediately past Mile 555 WHL (green can buoy "55"), a private channel leads to the Padre Island Country Club and the Padre Isles Yacht Club. Padre Isles Yacht Club welcomes visitors but has limited dockage.

**Anchorage:** The private channel at green can "39" is an anchoring possibility with 9 feet of water and good holding in mud. At green can buoy "55" is an anchorage known as Sand Dune Lagoon or Spinnaker Hole that has depths of 6 feet or more in the canals that were dug for homes yet to be built. Turn east into the channel and just past the Padre Isles Yacht Club, take a turn to starboard into the canals. Visible sand bars at some corners are easily avoided.

Shamrock Cove at Mile 544.9 EHL (behind Shamrock Island) in Corpus Christi Bay has 6 to 9 feet of water with good holding in mud.

## Corpus Christi to Port Mansfield

**NAVIGATION:** Use Charts 11306 and 11308. Numerous floating green cans, occasional red nun buoys and flashing green marks show the way along the 75-mile GIWW voyage to Port Mansfield through Laguna Madre. There are no "wide spots" to relax in, so stay in the channel. Just before Mile 565, past green can buoy "77," a marked channel to North Padre Island brings fishermen and windsurfers into Laguna Madre from the last launching ramp on the island. Submerged pilings are located from Mile 564 to Mile 587 WHL on the east side of the GIWW. There are no facilities between Corpus Christi and Port Mansfield. This is sparsely populated King Ranch country.

The marked channel into Baffin Bay joins the GIWW at Mile 579.5 WHL. Although it may look promising, Baffin Bay has numerous uncharted shallows and no facilities for cruising boats. The numerous "stars" on your chart designate rocks. Baffin Bay is navigable for 15 miles to a small marina with the alluring name of Riviera Beach, a great spot for shallow-draft fishing craft.

Traveling south of Baffin Bay along the GIWW, cruisers should be aware of many uncharted rocks in Laguna Madre. Stay in the channel for safety. From Mile 587 to Mile 612 WHL, submerged and exposed pilings populate the west side of the GIWW, and then the east side of the channel through to Port Mansfield.

The Port Mansfield water tower is prominent and can be seen from miles away. The entrance from the GIWW to the municipal marina is just 1 mile west of the diamond-shaped intersection at Mile 629.5 WHL. Turn west at flashing red "PM," and then pass between green daybeacon "29" and red daybeacon "30." Farther on, after you pass green daybeacon "31" and red daybeacon "32," you will enter the harbor between green daybeacon "33" and red daybeacon "34." If entering at night, follow the range markers since none of the daybeacons are lighted.

**Note:** Local boaters report depths in the channel to be just 3 feet; proceed with caution.

If traveling from the GIWW toward the Gulf of Mexico, start from the intersection at Mile 629.5 WHL and travel east between red daybeacon "26" and green daybeacon "25" along the channel (200 feet wide and 7 to 10 feet deep). Continue along the channel for 8.5 miles to the jetties at flashing red "2" and flashing green "3."

**Dockage:** The Port Mansfield harbor entrance channel was dredged in 2015 and depths are reportedly improved. Harbor Bait & Tackle includes a small marina that can be used by transient boats up to 60 feet. Electricity is not provided at the slips; water is available. They specialize in bait and tackle and have a well-stocked grocery, snacks and beer.

The Willacy County Navigation District Marina is located to port just beyond Harbor Bait and Tackle's docks. Both covered and open slips are available for transients up to 60 feet. The harbormaster's office is located on site. Phone the office (956-944-2325) or call "Port Mansfield Harbormaster" on VHF Channel 16 to make sure that someone is on duty.

There are a surprising number of restaurants, all within reasonable walking distance. Options include Skipper's Galley, Pelicans Cove (956-944-2848), Windjammer (956-944-2555), and Sweet Gregory P's Smokehouse and Grill (956-944-2440). There is also a liquor store and grocery store.

**Anchorage:** There is room to anchor at Mile 561 WHL (North Bird Island) between green cans "65" and "67" in 8 feet. The next anchorage possibility is 24 miles away,

at Mile 585 WHL in the Yarborough Pipeline area near green "17" where you will find 6 to 7 feet of water.

At Mile 593.6 WHL, past green "3," there is a channel with anchoring potential at Portrero Cortado in 5 to 6 feet of water. At Mile 602.9 WHL, just before green "13," is El Toro, which has 5.5 to 7 feet of water with good holding in mud. These anchorages can be difficult when spring winds are blowing. Once you reach Port Mansfield, you can drop the hook in 8 feet outside the main channel at Mile 629.8 WHL.

## Port Mansfield to Queen Isabella Bridge

**NAVIGATION:** Use Charts 11302, 11303, 11306. A little more than 1 mile south of Port Mansfield, the "GIWW West" turns to a heading of about 150 degrees. Continuing from Port Mansfield along the GIWW, the channel (12-foot reported depths) remains well marked with submerged pilings along the east side. At Mile 644 WHL, the forked entrance of the Arroyo Colorado Cutoff joins the GIWW from the west and marks the beginning of the Laguna Atascosa Wildlife Refuge (famous for having the last remaining wild ocelots in the U.S.) and the channel to Port Harlingen.

# Laguna Madre, TX

| PORT MANSFIELD | | | Dockage | | | | Supplies | | Services | | | | | |
|---|---|---|---|---|---|---|---|---|---|---|---|---|---|---|
| | | Largest Vessel Accommodated | VHF Channel Monitored | Approach / Dockside Depth (reported) | Transient Berths / Total Berths | Gas / Diesel | Floating Docks | Groceries, Ice, Marine Supplies, Snacks | Repairs: Hull, Engine, Propeller | Lift (tonnage), Crane, Rail | Laundry, Pool, Showers, Courtesy Car | Pump-Out Station | Min/Max Amps | Nearby: Grocery Store, Motel, Restaurant |
| 1. Harbor Bait & Tackle (WiFi) | 956-944-2367 | 60 | – | 14/14 | 8/8 | – | – | GIMS | – | – | – | L | – | GMF |
| 2. Port Mansfield Harbor/Willacy County Nav. Dist. (Internet)(WiFi) | 956-944-2325 | 60 | 16 | 15/124 | 12/6 | – | GD | IMS | E | – | 30/50 | S | P | GMF |

(Internet) Internet Access (WiFi) Wireless Internet Access (WG) Waterway Guide Cruising Club Partner *(Information in the table is provided by the facilities.)*
See WaterwayGuide.com for current rates, fuel prices, web site addresses, and other up-to-the-minute information.

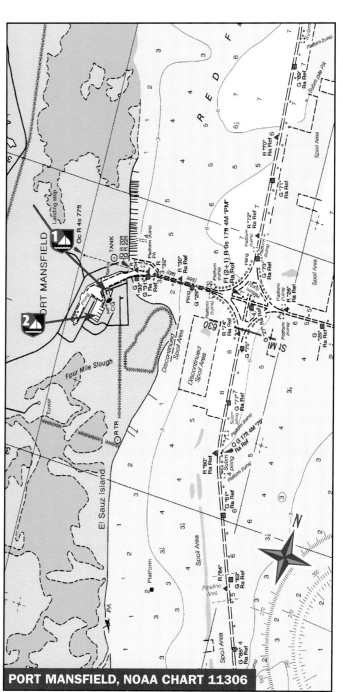

PORT MANSFIELD, NOAA CHART 11306

Near Mile 650 WHL, where fishing camps line the east bank and a large house stands prominently just west of the GIWW, the water tank and high-rise hotels of South Padre Island begin to emerge from the horizon off the po[rt] bow. The high arch of the Queen Isabella Causeway Bridg[e] comes into view. It connects Port Isabel on the mainland with the resorts and beaches of South Padre Island. A hal[f] mile before the bridge, the marked channel leads west to the Port Isabel Small Boat Basin.

To protect the ecosystem of Laguna Madre, authorization for dredging is limited. The channel from the GIWW to the small boat basin remains a problem. It is shallow and may not be navigable except with a very shoal draft. Seek local knowledge for assistance and chec[k] the *Local Notice to Mariners* and waterwayguide.com for the most current information.

There is a way into the harbor utilizing an old natural channel that parallels the shore; seek local knowledge before attempting this passage. These are shallow waters. Cruising boats drawing 4 feet or more should not attemp[t] to reach the city dock through the channel east (north) of the causeway bridge. All others should proceed with caution.

**Dockage:** On the chart, the Port Isabel Small Boat Basin looks like a pair of hands with fingers spread apart. Between the fingers are canals leading to a variety of residential dwellings from trailers to fancy stucco multi-story homes. The Port Isabel City Dock at the end of Pompano Avenue has sturdy bulkheads and slips large enough for the typical cruising vessel. Electricity and restrooms are provided.

A walk down the main street (Highway 100) from the Small Boat Basin will take you past a liquor store, a mino[r] emergency clinic, several restaurants, convenience stores, banks and the post office. West from the Small Boat Basi[n] is a Walmart and an HEB grocery store. Some marine stores are located south of the highway, including a canva[s]

pair shop, a tackle shop and a few diesel and marine
ectrical service shops. To fully appreciate all that Port
abel has to offer, a visit to the Chamber of Commerce
fice, located at the lighthouse, would be helpful (956-
3-2262).

**Anchorage:** At GIWW Mile 644.2 WHL, there is an
nchorage inside the Arroyo Colorado Cutoff Canal
ith 8 feet of water. Anchor near the spoil area located
nm from the entrance channel.

## ffshore: Port Mansfield to Brazos antiago (South Padre Island)

**AVIGATION:** Use Charts 11301, 11302, 11304 and
1306. From Port Mansfield to the pass at Brazos
intiago the course is 160 degrees magnetic, for a
stance of 25 miles. Sand dunes will be the main
oreside attraction. The first landmark to come
to sight will be the **Queen Isabella Causeway
ridge**, (73-foot fixed vertical clearance),which crosses
e GIWW and connects South Padre Island to Port
abel. Soon after, prominent buildings and the radio
eacon antenna on the South Padre Island Coast Guard
ation will guide you to the channel entrance. The
hannel is marked by a lighted sea buoy "BS," about 2
iles from the entrance to the 1-mile-long jetties. Enter
e channel close to buoy "BS" to avoid wrecks near the
tties.

## Queen Isabella Bridge to GIWW Mile 682 WHL

**NAVIGATION:** Use Charts 11302 and 11303. At Mile
665 WHL the GIWW passes under the Queen Isabella
Bridge. Just before passing under the bridge, a marked
channel runs very close to the bridge east toward Padre
Island. This shallow channel leads to the "Condo
Channel" along the backside (west side) of Padre Island.
The Condo Channel is dredged to 7 feet and provides
access to docks located near apartments, condominiums
and restaurants. Without local knowledge, this area is
better suited to a small fishing boat or dinghy than a
cruising boat.

The **Port Isabel–Long Island Pontoon Bridge**
crosses the GIWW at Mile 666 WHL in the Port Isabel
Channel. The bridge opens on signal, except Monday
through Friday, from 5:00 a.m. to 8:00 p.m., the bridge
need only open on the hour for pleasure. It opens on
signal for commercial vessels at all times and allows
recreational boats to go through with them.

Past the pontoon bridge, a series of canals lead from
the waterway into a mobile home park on Long Island.
The GIWW continues along the Port Isabel Channel
and the Cutoff Channel until the GIWW meets the
Brownsville Ship Channel at Mile 668.5 WHL. The
GIWW continues along the Brownsville Channel (250
feet wide and 45 feet deep). Pleasure vessels may use

www.snagaslip.com

SNAG-A-SLIP

EXPLORE
BOOK
BOA...

# Laguna Madre, TX

| | | Dockage | | | | | Supplies | | Services | | | | | |
|---|---|---|---|---|---|---|---|---|---|---|---|---|---|---|
| | | Largest Vessel Accommodated | VHF Channel Monitored | Approach / Dockside Depth (reported) | Transient Berths / Total Berths | Floating Docks | Gas / Diesel | Groceries, Ice, Marine Supplies, Snacks | Repairs: Hull, Engine, Propeller | Lift (tonnage), Crane, Rail | Min/Max Amps | Laundry, Pool, Showers, Courtesy Car | Pump-Out Station | Nearby: Grocery Store, Motel, Restaurant |
| **PORT ISABEL** | | | | | | | | | | | | | | |
| 1. Port Isabel City Dock  668.5 WHL | 956-943-2682 | 50 | – | – | 7/6 | – | – | – | – | – | 50/50 | – | – | GM |
| 2. Sea Ranch II at Southpoint  668.5 WHL | 956-943-7926 | 60 | 68 | 10/41 | 8/8 | – | – | GIMS | HEP | L50 | 50/50 | LS | – | GM |
| 3. South Shore Bait & Tackle  (WiFi) | 956-943-1027 | – | – | | /12 | – | GD | IMS | | | | | | GM |
| **SOUTH PADRE ISLAND** | | | | | | | | | | | | | | |
| 4. Sea Ranch Marina  668.5 WHL | 956-761-7777 | 70 | 16 | 5/64 | 6/6 | – | GD | GIMS | HP | L | 30/200+ | LS | – | GM |

⌨ Internet Access   (WiFi) Wireless Internet Access   WG Waterway Guide Cruising Club Partner  *(Information in the table is provided by the facilities.)*
See WaterwayGuide.com for current rates, fuel prices, web site addresses, and other up-to-the-minute information.

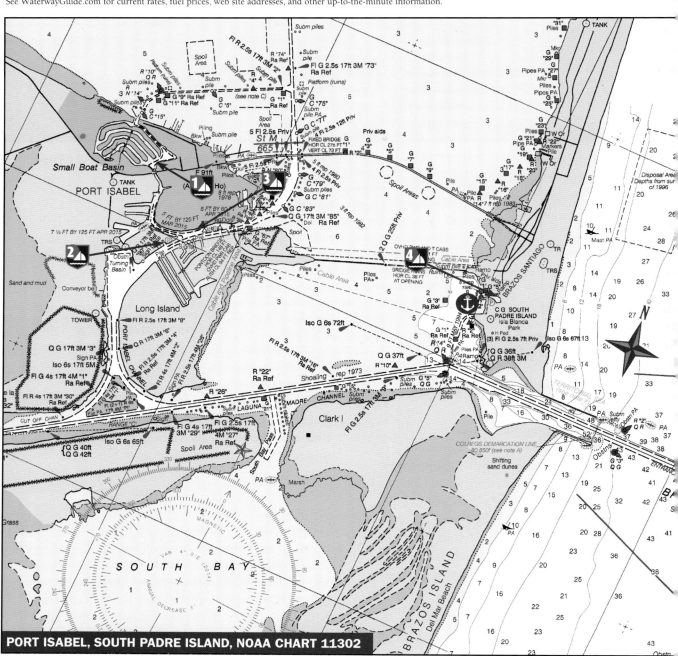

**PORT ISABEL, SOUTH PADRE ISLAND, NOAA CHART 11302**

e Brownsville Fishing Harbor at Mile 677.5 WHL
 an emergency, but dockage and other facilities are
ry limited. The channel continues to the Brownsville
rning Basin at Mile 682 WHL.

 Sea Ranch II at Southpoint lies at the "Y" of the
IWW and the back entrance channel heading to the
rt Isabel Small Boat Basin, which is restricted by a
ghway bridge with limited clearance (about 5 feet).
 South of the marina, at 17-foot quick-flashing red
0," a turning basin for commercial vessels extends
om the GIWW. The waterway then makes a westerly
rn to Port Brownsville and the end of the GIWW West,
32 miles from the Harvey Lock on the Mississippi
iver.

**Dockage:** Sea Ranch II is the largest and only full-
ervice marina in Port Isabel. It is also the home of the
aguna Madre Yacht Club and the U.S. Border Patrol.
ransient vessels can use a pump-out service on the
orner of the "Y." South Shore Bait & Tackle nearby
lls fuel. The dock location can be confusing to find
nce it requires navigation of a short side channel off
e GIWW. Check your chart! Call 956-943-1845 for
irections.

## ■ SOUTH PADRE ISLAND

outh Padre Island is famous for its white sand beaches,
arm weather, superb fishing and proximity to the Padre
sland National Seashore and the border of Mexico.
uring college spring breaks and again during Holy
Veek, when thousands of affluent Mexican tourists visit,
he island's hotels, motels, restaurants, nightclubs and
eaches fill to capacity. Isla Blanca Park, adjacent to Sea
anch Marina on the island's southern tip, and Andy
owie Park, at the north end of the city, provide popular
laces to enjoy the beach.

**AVIGATION:** Use Charts 11302 and 11303. From
Aile 668.5 WHL, travel northeast along Laguna Madre
Channel (Brownsville Ship Channel) to flashing red "4."
Vhen turning north toward Sea Ranch Marina, avoid the
vreck at flashing red "4." Steer north to green daybeacon
1" and red daybeacon "2" to the entrance of Sea Ranch
Aarina. The marina, located less than 2 miles from
3razos Santiago Pass, is the last marina and the last pass
o the Gulf from the United States.

**Dockage:** Just inside South Padre Island, a private
hannel of about 9 feet deep leads north to the Coast

Guard Station and Sea Ranch Marina, where dockage,
gas, diesel fuel and provisions can be found. Approach
and dockside depths are reported to be 6 feet or more.

**Anchorage:** An anchorage is located just north of the
marina entrance at South Padre Island. Anchor outside
the marked channel to Sea Ranch and the Coast Guard
Station in the lee of South Padre off of Isla Blanca Park
or the marina entrance. Depths in this area range from 7
to 14 feet.

Just inside of the jetties for Brazos Santiago Pass, to
the south, is a visible opening called, Barracuda Cove
that provides a well-protected anchorage with 6- to
7-foot depths. On the north side a smaller opening
called Dolphin Cove provides a place to anchor in 5-foot
depths.

## To the Gulf

**NAVIGATION:** Use Charts 11302 and 11303. If traveling
to the Gulf of Mexico from the GIWW, at Mile 668.5
WHL, steer northeast along the Laguna Madre Channel.
Pass 17-foot flashing red "28" and continue to flashing
red "4." Stay in the channel due to shoaling to the north
and submerged pilings to the south of the channel (250
feet wide and 44 feet deep). At flashing red "4," change
course to due east and run for 1.5 miles to the Gulf
through Brazos Santiago Pass.

## Cruising Options

This ends your Texas GIWW cruising experience. It
could be the beginning of your trip, but is probably
considered the end of the U.S. Intracoastal Waterway.
From here the GIWW only goes one way, or you can
proceed south along the coast Mexico via the Gulf of
Mexico.

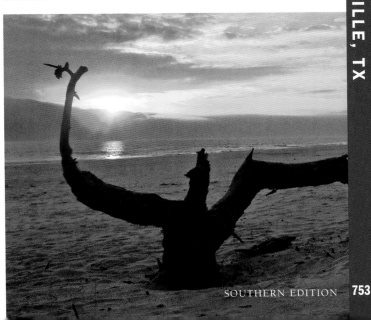

# OFFSHORE PASSES

Offshore or along the GIWW, there are no major metropolitan areas on the southeast Texas coast. Even so, this stretch of the Texas coast has six navigable inlets a cruising boat can transit to and from the Gulf of Mexico. Navigation sections for each offshore route are included within the chapter. For convenience and clarity they are summarized below from east to west.

The rhumb line from Freeport to Brazos Santiago is 200 nm. If you follow the curve of the coast it is 220 nm. From Freeport to Matagorda the coast follows a southwest by west direction for 60 nm. From Matagorda it follows a southwest course for the next 100 nm then trends south and turns to the southeast for the next 60 nm to the Rio Grande River. The entire coast is a chain of shallow bays separated from the Gulf by long narrow islands and peninsulas.

## Freeport Harbor Channel

Located at N 28°55.773' W 095°17.380'. The entrance to the inlet is 1.2 nm to the GIWW at Mile 395 WHL. The next navigable inlet is the Colorado River at a distance of 42 nm.

Freeport Harbor is 40 nm southwest of the Galveston Inlet. It is a large shipping port. It is named for the City of Freeport located west of the GIWW on the old Brazos River Channel. Locally the area is referred to as Brazosport. The area is dominated by chemical plants. Other industry is oil, natural gas, sulfur, and shrimp.

## Colorado River Channel

Located at N 28°35.469' W095°58.903'. The inlet is 6 nm from the intersection with the GIWW at Mile 443 WHL. The next navigable inlet is Matagorda Ship Channel at a distance of 21 nm.

The channel is used exclusively by local fishing boats. It is not a commercial shipping inlet. Depths are reported to be 12 feet and the channel can be used by cruising boats. There are no services in the river, but you should be able to find an anchorage.

## Matagorda Ship Channel

Located at N 28°24.920' W 096°18.930'. The inlet is 4.5 nm from GIWW Mile 471 WHL. The next navigable inlet is Aransas Pass at a distance of 60 nm.

Matagorda Bay is a large body of water separated from the Gulf of Mexico by the Matagorda Peninsula. The Ship Channel is a 22-mile-long deep water channel through a land cut to Matagorda Bay, Lavaca Bay and ending at a public terminal at Point Comfort. This is not a major shipping channel, but it is large and deep. There are very few facilities for cruising boats in this area.

## Aransas Pass Channel

Located at N 27°49.848' W 097°01.973'. The inlet is 8.8 NM from GIWW Mile 540 WHL. The next navigable inlet is Port Mansfield Cut at a distance of 78 nm.

The large shipping channel of Aransas Pass is 154 nm from Galveston and 113 nm from the Rio Grande. It is the principal approach from the Gulf of Mexico to Aransas Bay and Corpus Christi Bay. It is a busy large ship inlet.

## Port Mansfield Cut

Located at N 26°33.837' W97°16.166'. The inlet is 7.2 nm from GIWW Mile 630 WHL. The next navigable inlet is Brazos Santiago Pass at a distance of 31 nm.

This is a short channel used exclusively by local fishing boats, but is accessible to cruising boats. There are no facilities.

## Brazos Santiago Pass

Located at N 26°03.693' W 097°08.693'. The inlet is 3.2 nm from GIWW Mile 668 WHL.

This is the approach to South Padre Island, Port Isabel and Port Brownsville. It is relatively narrow, but is also a large ship inlet. It is 6 nm north of the mouth of the Rio Grande River, making it the last inlet in the U.S. From this point south all accessible ports are in Mexico.

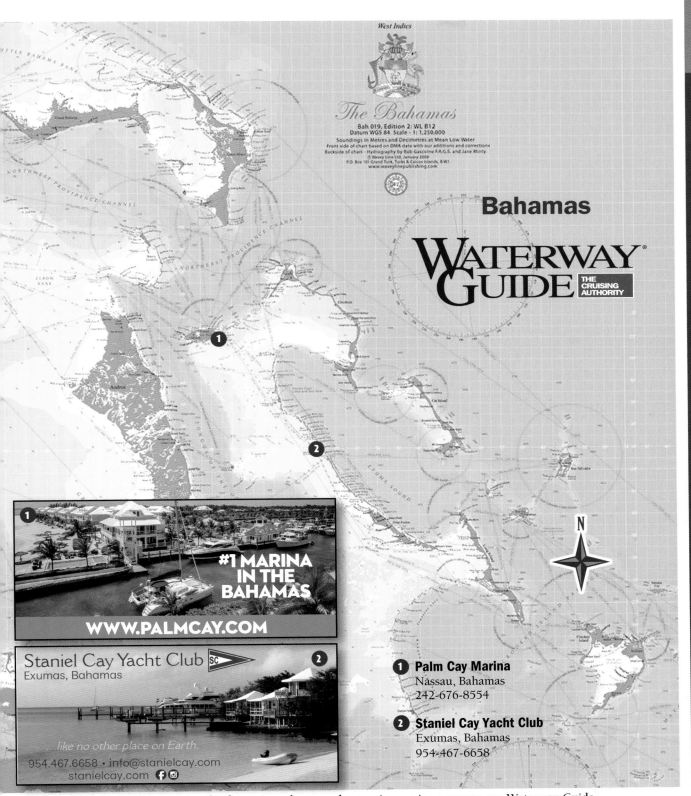

West Indies

*The Bahamas*

Bah 019, Edition 2: WL B12
Datum WGS 84 Scale - 1: 1,250,000
Soundings in Metres and Decimetres at Mean Low Water
Front side of chart based on DMA data with our additions and corrections
Backside of chart - Hydrography by Bob Gascoine F.R.G.S. and Jane Minty
© Wavey Line Ltd. January 2006
P.O. Box 101 Grand Turk, Turks & Caicos Islands, B.W.I.
www.waveylinepublishing.com

## Bahamas

## WATERWAY GUIDE THE CRUISING AUTHORITY

**1 Palm Cay Marina**
Nassau, Bahamas
242-676-8554

**2 Staniel Cay Yacht Club**
Exumas, Bahamas
954-467-6658

For detailed navigational information, charts, and extensive marina coverage see Waterway Guide
2018 Bahamas Edition. Purchase online: www.waterwayguide.com or call 800-233-3359.

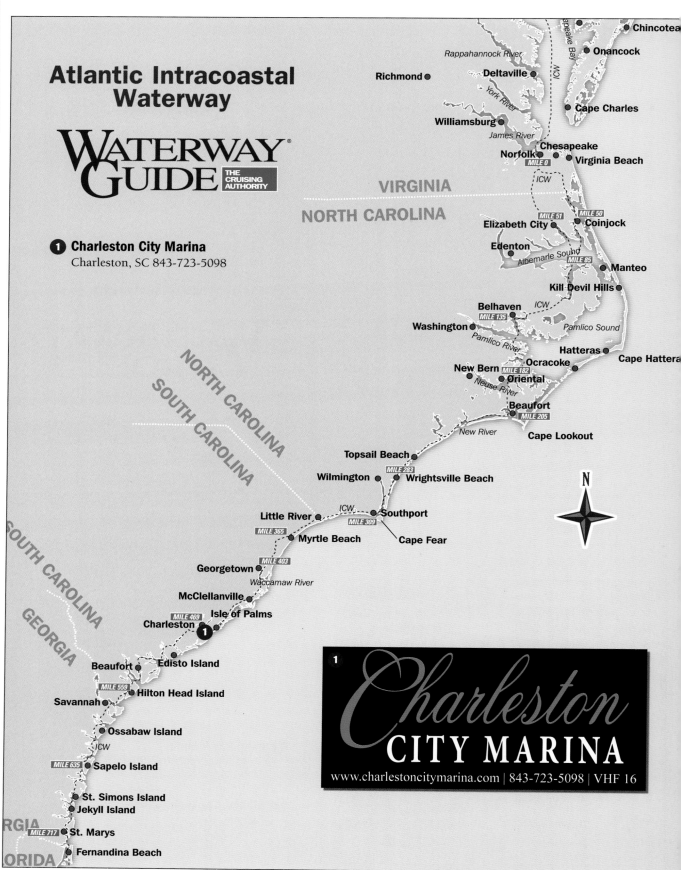

# Atlantic Intracoastal Waterway

**WATERWAY GUIDE** THE CRUISING AUTHORITY

**1** **Charleston City Marina**
Charleston, SC 843-723-5098

**Chincoteague**
**Onancock**
*Rappahannock River*
**Richmond**
**Deltaville**
**Cape Charles**
*York River*
**Williamsburg**
*James River*
**Chesapeake**
**Norfolk** MILE 0 **Virginia Beach**

**VIRGINIA**
ICW
**NORTH CAROLINA**

MILE 51 MILE 50
**Elizabeth City** **Coinjock**
**Edenton**
*Albemarle Sound* MILE 85 **Manteo**
**Kill Devil Hills**
**Belhaven** ICW
MILE 135
*Pamlico Sound*
**Washington**
*Pamlico River* **Hatteras**
**Ocracoke** **Cape Hatteras**
**New Bern** MILE 182
**Oriental**
*Neuse River* **Beaufort**
MILE 205
**Cape Lookout**
*New River*
**Topsail Beach**
MILE 283
**Wilmington** **Wrightsville Beach**
ICW
**Little River** **Southport**
MILE 365 MILE 309
**Myrtle Beach** **Cape Fear**
**Georgetown** MILE 403
*Waccamaw River*
**McClellanville**
**Isle of Palms**
MILE 469
**Charleston** **1**

N

**EXTENDED CRUISING**

**NORTH CAROLINA**
**SOUTH CAROLINA**

**SOUTH CAROLINA**
**GEORGIA**
**Beaufort** **Edisto Island**
MILE 559
**Savannah** **Hilton Head Island**
**Ossabaw Island**
ICW
MILE 635 **Sapelo Island**
**St. Simons Island**
**Jekyll Island**
**GEORGIA** MILE 717 **St. Marys**
**FLORIDA** **Fernandina Beach**

For detailed navigational information, charts and extensive marina coverage see Waterway Guide,
2018 Atlantic ICW Edition. Purchase online: waterwayguide.com or call 800-233-3359.

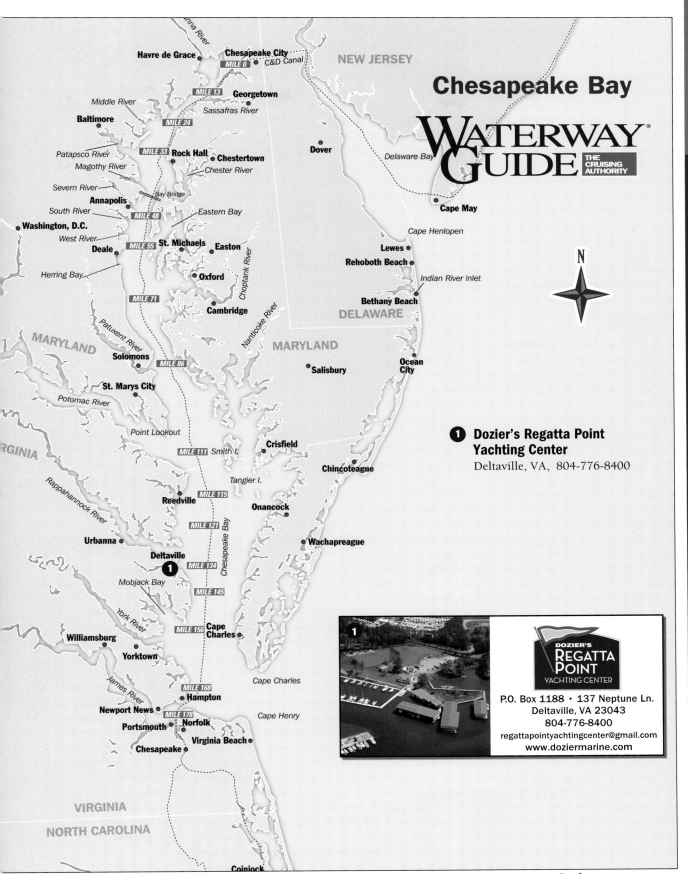

# Chesapeake Bay

## WATERWAY GUIDE®
### THE CRUISING AUTHORITY

**NEW JERSEY**

Havre de Grace
Chesapeake City
*MILE 0*
C&D Canal
*MILE 13*
Georgetown
Middle River
Sassafras River
Baltimore
*MILE 24*
Patapsco River
*MILE 33*
Rock Hall
Chestertown
Dover
Delaware Bay
Magothy River
Chester River
Severn River
Cape May
Bay Bridge
Annapolis
*MILE 48*
Eastern Bay
Cape Henlopen
South River
Washington, D.C.
West River
Lewes
St. Michaels
Easton
Rehoboth Beach
Deale
*MILE 55*
Indian River Inlet
Herring Bay
Oxford
Choptank River
Bethany Beach
*MILE 71*
**DELAWARE**
Cambridge
Nanticoke River
**MARYLAND**
Solomons
*MILE 86*
Salisbury
Ocean City
St. Marys City
Potomac River
Point Lookout
*MILE 111*  Smith I.
Crisfield
Chincoteague
Tangier I.
VIRGINIA
Reedville
*MILE 115*
Onancock
*MILE 121*
Chesapeake Bay
Urbanna
Wachapreague
Deltaville
**1** *MILE 134*
Mobjack Bay
*MILE 145*
York River
*MILE 156* Cape Charles
Williamsburg
Yorktown
Cape Charles
James River
*MILE 168* Hampton
Cape Henry
Newport News
*MILE 178*
Portsmouth
Norfolk
Virginia Beach
Chesapeake

**MARYLAND**
Rappahannock River
Patuxent River

**VIRGINIA**
**NORTH CAROLINA**
Coinjock

## N

**1 Dozier's Regatta Point Yachting Center**
Deltaville, VA, 804-776-8400

### DOZIER'S REGATTA POINT YACHTING CENTER

P.O. Box 1188 • 137 Neptune Ln.
Deltaville, VA 23043
804-776-8400
regattapointyachtingcenter@gmail.com
www.doziermarine.com

For detailed navigational information, charts and extensive marina coverage see Waterway Guide, 2018 Chesapeake Bay Edition. Purchase online: waterwayguide.com or call 800-233-3359.

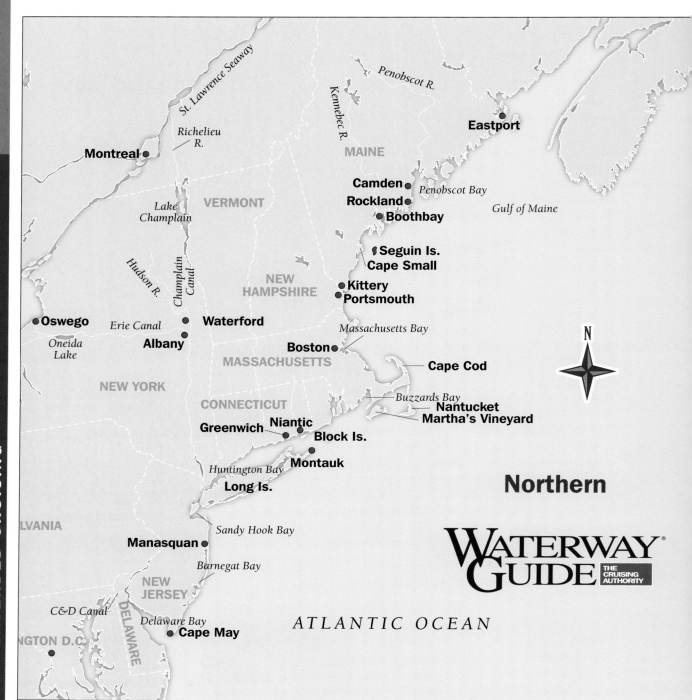

St. Lawrence Seaway

Penobscot R.

Richelieu R.

Kennebec R.

**Eastport**

**Montreal**

MAINE

**Camden**

Penobscot Bay

**Rockland**

**Boothbay**

Gulf of Maine

Lake Champlain

VERMONT

**Seguin Is.**
**Cape Small**

Hudson R.

Champlain Canal

NEW HAMPSHIRE

**Kittery**
**Portsmouth**

**Oswego**

Erie Canal

**Waterford**

Massachusetts Bay

Oneida Lake

**Albany**

**Boston**

MASSACHUSETTS

**Cape Cod**

NEW YORK

CONNECTICUT

Buzzards Bay

**Nantucket**

**Greenwich**

**Niantic**

**Martha's Vineyard**

**Block Is.**

Huntington Bay

**Montauk**

**Long Is.**

N

**Northern**

**Manasquan**

Sandy Hook Bay

WATERWAY GUIDE THE CRUISING AUTHORITY

Barnegat Bay

NEW JERSEY

LVANIA

C&D Canal

DELAWARE

ATLANTIC OCEAN

Delaware Bay

**Cape May**

DELAWARE

NGTON D.C.

For detailed navigational information, charts and extensive marina coverage see Waterway Guide, 2018 Northern Edition. Purchase online: waterwayguide.com or call 800-233-3359.

Find us on Facebook

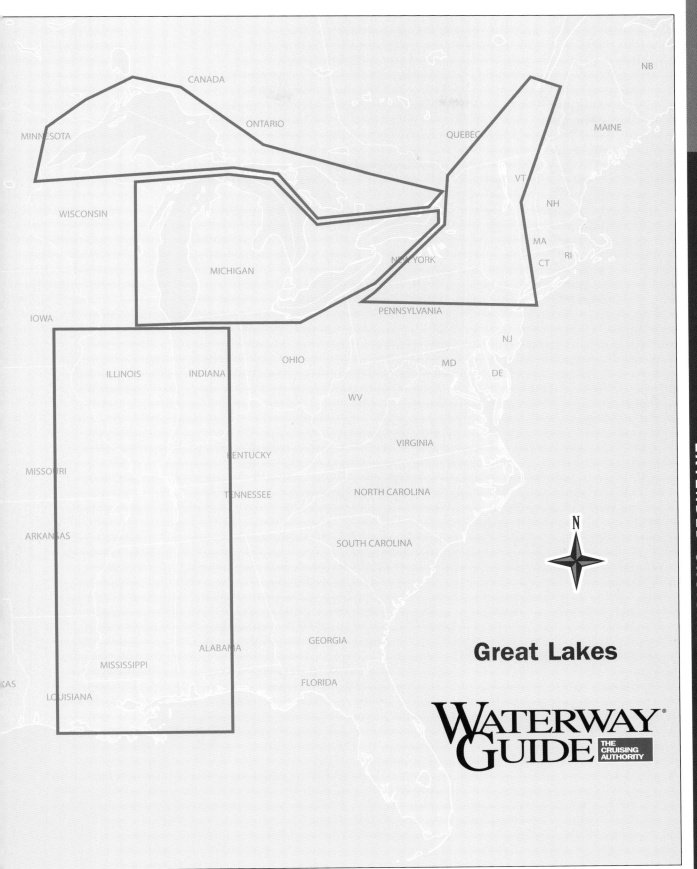

**Great Lakes**

WATERWAY
GUIDE  THE CRUISING AUTHORITY

For detailed navigational information, charts and extensive marina coverage see Waterway Guide,
2018 Great Lakes Edition. Purchase online: waterwayguide.com or call 800-233-3359.

EXTENDED CRUISING

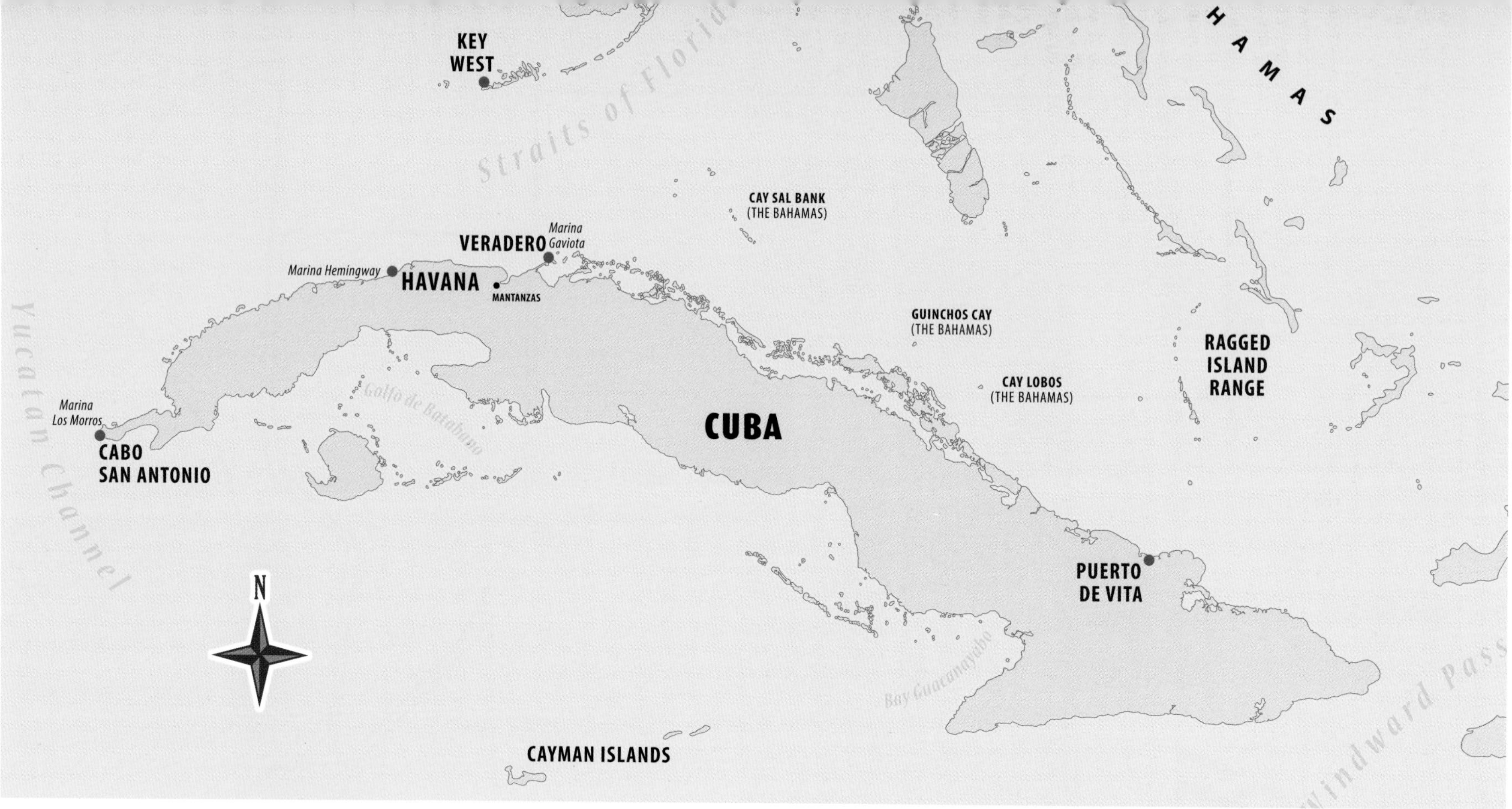

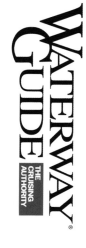

KEY WEST
Straits of Florida
HAMAS
CAY SAL BANK (THE BAHAMAS)
Marina Gaviota
VERADERO
Marina Hemingway
HAVANA
MANTANZAS
GUINCHOS CAY (THE BAHAMAS)
RAGGED ISLAND RANGE
CAY LOBOS (THE BAHAMAS)
Yucatan Channel
Marina Los Morros
CABO SAN ANTONIO
Golfo de Batabano
CUBA
PUERTO DE VITA
N
Bay Guacanayabo
Windward Pass
CAYMAN ISLANDS

# Cuba

WATERWAY GUIDE® THE CRUISING AUTHORITY

For detailed navigational information, charts and extensive marina coverage see Waterway Guide, Cuba Edition.
Purchase online: waterwayguide.com or call 800-233-3359.

# Waterway Guide
# Cruising Club Partners

Simply show your Cruising Club membership card at these participating businesses to start saving money on fuel, dockage, supplies and more.

Also receive discounts on Waterway Guide and Skipper Bob products online at www.waterwayguide.com

To sign up for your **FREE** membership call **800-233-3359** or go to **www.waterwayguide.com**

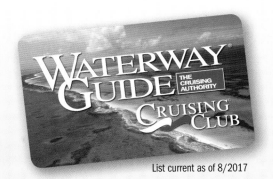

List current as of 8/2017

## Alabama

**Homeport Marina**
251-458-7135
www.homeportmarina.net

**The Wharf Marina**
251-224-1900
www.thewharfmarina.com

**Turner Marine**
www.turnermarine.com

## Bahamas

**Abaco Inn**
800-468-8799
www.abacoinn.com

**Bimini Big Game Club Resort & Marina**
800-867-4764
www.biggameclubbimini.com

**Blue Marlin Cove Resort & Marina**
242-349-4101
www.bluemarlincove.com

**Brendals Dive Center**
242-365-4411
www.brendal.com

**Davis Harbour Marina At Cotton Bay Club**
242-334-6303

**Green Turtle Cay Club**
242-365-4271
www.greenturtleclub.com

**Leeward Yacht Club & Marina**
242-365-4191
www.leewardyachtclub.com

**Marina at Emerald Bay**
242-336-6102
www.marinaatemeraldbay.com

**Master Harbour Marina**
242-345-5116
www.turnquestinvestments.com

**Port Lucaya Marina**
242-373-9090
www.portlucaya.com

**Sail and Dive**
242-577-0867
www.sailanddive.net

**Spanish Cay Marina**
242-365-0083
www.spanishcay.com

**Sunrise Resort and Marina**
800-932-4959
www.sunriseresortandmarina.com

## Connecticut

**Cedar Island Marina**
860-669-8681
cedarislandmarina.com

**Landfall Navigation**
203-487-0775
www.landfallnavigation.com

**Mystic River Marina**
800-344-8840
www.MysticRiverMarina.com

**North Cove Yacht Club**
860-388-9132
www.northcoveyc.com

**Norwalk Cove Marina**
203-838-5899
norwalkcove.com

**Saybrook Point Marina**
860-395-3080
www.saybrookpointmarina.com

**Seaview House Marina**
203-219-4693
www.seaviewhousemarina.com

## Delaware

**Indian River Marina**
302-227-3071
www.destateparks.com/marinas

## Florida

**Adventure Yacht Harbor**
386-756-2180
www.adventureyachtharbor.com

**All American Covered Boat Storage**
941-697-9900
www.aaboatstorage.com

**Always for Sail**
904-625-7936
www.alwaysforsail.com

**Amelia Island Yacht Basin**
904-277-4615
www.aiyb.net

**Anclote Isles Marina**
727-939-0100
www.ancloteisles-marina.com

**Anclote Village Marina**
727-937-9737
www.anclotevillagemarina.com

**Anglers Avenue Marine Center**
954-962-8702
www.aamcmarina.com

**Aquamarina Daytona**
386-252-6421
www.ilovemymarina.com

**Austral International Marina**
305-325-0177
www.australinternational.net

**Belle Harbour Marina**
727-943-8489
www.belleharbourmarina.com

**Bimini Bar & Grill**
941-451-8634
biminibarandgrill.com

**Boater's Edge**
321-383-4173
www.boatersedge.us

**Burnt Store Marina**
941-637-0083
www.burntstoremarina.com

**Camachee Cove Yacht Harbor**
904-829-5676
www.camacheeisland.com

**Cape Haze Marina**
941-698-1110

**Captains License Class**
888-937-2458
www.captainslicensclass.com

**City of Fort Myers Yacht Basin**
239-321-7080
www.cityftmyers.com

**Delray Harbor Club Marina**
561-276-0376
www.delrayharborclub.com

**Dolphin Marina and Cottages**
305-797-0878
www.dolphinmarina.net

**Everglades National Park Boat Tours**

**Fernandina Harbor Marina**
904-491-2089
www.fhmarina.com

**Fishermens Village Yacht Basin**
941-575-3000
www.fishville.com

**Florida Marina's Clubs**
239-489-2969

**Fort Pierce City Marina**
772-464-1245
www.fortpiercecitymarina.com

**Glades Boat Storage, Inc.**
863-983-3040
www.gladesboatstorage.com

**Good Times Motel And Marina**
352-498-8088
www.goodtimesmotelandmarina.com

**Gulf Harbour Marina**
239-437-0881
www.gulfharbormarina.net

**Halifax Harbor Marina**
386-671-3603
www.halifaxharbormarina.com

**Harbour Isle Marina**
772-461-9049
www.harbourisleflorida.com

**Hawks Cay Resort & Marina**
305-743-9000 x2
www.hawkscay.com

**Holiday Harbor Marina**
850-492-0555
myholidayharbor.com

**Holly Bluff Marina**
386-822-9992
www.hollybluff.com

**Hopkins-Carter Marine Supply**
305-635-7377
www.hopkins-carter.com

**Huckins Yacht**
904-389-1125
www.huckinsyacht.com

**Kennedy Point Yacht Club & Marina**
321-383-0280
www.kennedypointyachtclub.com

**Laishley Park Municipal Marina**
941-575-0142
www.laishleymarina.com

**Lake Park Harbor Marina**
561-881-3353
www.lakeparkmarina.com

**Lambs Yacht Center, Inc.**
904-384-5577
www.lambsyachtcenter.com

**Loblolly Marina**
772-546-3136
www.loblollymarinainfo.com

**Loggerhead Club and Marina**
561-625-9443
www.loggerheadjupiter.com

**Longboat Key Club Moorings**
941-383-8383
www.longboatkeymarina.com

**LukFuel, LLC**
305-432-3487
LukFuel.com

**Marathon Marina & Boat Yard**
305-743-6575
www.marathonmarinaandresort.com

**Marina at Naples Bay Resort**
239-530-5134
naplesbayresort.com

**Marina Bay Marina Resort**
954-791-7600
www.marinabay-fl.com

**Mariner Cay Marina**
772-287-2900
www.marincaymarina.org

**Marker 1 Marina**
727-487-3903
www.marker1marina.com

**METROPOLITAN PARK MARINA**
904-630-0839
www.coj.net

**Naples Boat Club Marina**
239 263 2774
www.naplesboatclub.com

**Nettles Island Marina**
772-229-2811
www.nettlesislandmarina.com

**New Port Cove Marine Center**
561-844-2504
www.opch.com

**Night Swan Intracostal B&B**
386-423-4940
www.nightswan.com

**North Palm Beach Marina**
561-626-4919
www.opch.com

**Old Port Cove Marina**
561-626-1760
www.opch.com

**Palm Coast Marina**
386-446-6370
www.palmcoastmarina.net

**Palm Cove Marina**
904-223-4757
www.palmcovemarina.com

**Panama City Marina**
850 872 7272
www.pcmarina.com

**Pirates Cove Resort & Marina**
772-223-9216
www.piratescoveresort.com

**Port Canaveral Yacht Club**
321-297-3441
pcyc-fl.org

**Prosperity Pointe Marina**
239-995-2155
www.prosperitypointemarina.com

**Regatta Pointe Marina**
941-729-6021
www.regattapointemarina.com

**Rivers Edge Marina**
904-827-0520
29riveredgemarina.com

**Riviera Dunes Marina**
941-981-5330
www.rdmarina.com

**RMK Merrill-Stevens**
305-324-5211
www.rmkmerrill-stevens.com

**Sailfish Marina of Stuart**
772-283-1122
www.sailfishmarinastuart.com

**Sailor's Wharf Yacht Yard**
727-823-1155
sailorswharf.com

**Sandy Beach Catamaran Sailing Charters**
954-218-0042
www.catamaransailcharter.com

**Sea Tech & Fun USA / Spade Anchor**
321-409-5714
www.spadeanchorusa.com

**Seaside Sailing**
800-569-7245
www.seasidesailing.com

**Sombrero Marina Condo. Assc.**
305-743-0000
www.sombreromarina.com

**Stock Island Marina Village**
305-294-2288
www.stockislandmarina.com

**Telemar Bay Marina**
321-773-2468
telemarbay.com

**The Jacksonville Landing**
904-353-1188
www.jacksonvillelanding.com

**The Marina at Ortega Landing**
904-387-5538
www.ortegalanding.com

**Thunderboat Marine Service Center**
954-964-8859
www.thunderboatmarinecenter.com

**Titusville Municipal Marina**
321-383-5600
www.titusville.com/marina

**Turnberry Isle Marina Yacht Club**
305-933-6934
www.turnberryislemarina.com

**Twin Dolphin Marina**
941-747-8300
www.twindolphinmarina.com

**Water Street Hotel and Marina**
850-653-8801
www.waterstreethotel.com

**Yacht Haven Park & Marina**
954-583-2322
yachthavenpark.com

**Yacht Management Marina**
954-993-9368
www.YMISF.com

## Georgia

**Fort McAllister Marina**
912-727-2632
fortmcallistermarinaga.com

**Hidden Harbor Yacht Club**
912-261-1049
www.hiddenharboryachtclub.com

**Hinckley Yacht Services**
912-629-2400
www.hinckleyyachts.com

**Hyatt Regency Savannah**
912-721-4654
www.hyattdockssavannah.com

**Isle of Hope Marina**
912-354-8187
www.iohmarina.com

**Morning Star Marinas at Golden Isles**
912-634-1128
www.morningstarmarinas.com

**River Supply Inc.**
912-354-7777
www.riversupply.com

**Sunbury Crab Co. Restaurant & Marina**
912-884-8640
www.sunburycrabco.com

**Thunderbolt Marina**
912-210-0363
www.thunderboltmarine.us

**Tybee Island Marina**
912-786-5554
tybeeislandmarina.com

## Illinois

**31st Street Harbor (A Westrec Marina)**
312-742-8515
www.chicagoharbors.info

## Louisiana

**Lake Pontchartrain Harbor Marina**
985-626-1517

**Retif Oil and Fuel**
504-349-9113
www.retif.com

**Ship To Shore Co.**
337-474-0730
www.shiptoshoreco.com

## Maine

**Edwards Harborside Inn**
207-363-2222
www.EdwardsHarborside.com

**Landings Restaurant & Marina**
207-594-4899

## Maryland

**Annapolis Harbor Boatyard**
410-268-0092
www.annapolisharbor.net

**Back Creek Inn B&B**
410-326-2022
www.backcreekinnbnb.com

**Calvert Marina LLC**
410-326-4251
calvertmarina.com

**Campbell's Bachelor Pt. Yacht C**
410-226-5592
www.campbellsboatyards.com

**Campbell's Boatyard @ Jack's Pt**
410-226-5105
www.campbellsboatyards.com

**Campbell's Town Creek Boatyard**
410-226-0213
www.campbellsboatyards.com

**Fawcett Boat Supplies**
410-267-8681
fawcettboat.com

**Galloway Creek Marina**
410-335-3575
www.dredgeanddock.com

**MarinaLife**
410-752-0505
www.marinalife.com

**Maritime Solutions Inc.**
410-263-1496
MSI-1.com

**Paradise Marina**
301-832-6578
www.Paradise-Marina.com

**Point Lookout Marina**
301-872-5000
www.pointlookoutmarina.com

**Quality Inn Beacon Marina**
410-326-6303
www.beaconsolomons.com

**Rock Hall Landing Marina**
410-639-2224
www.rockhalllanding.com

**Rockhold Creek Marina & Yacht Repair**
410-867-7919
www.rockholdcreekmarina.com

**Somers Cove Marina**
410-968-0925
www.somerscovemarina.com

**Sunset Harbor Marina**
410-687-7290
www.sunsetharbor.com

## Massachusetts

**Constitution Marina**
7-241-9640
ww.constitutionmarina.com

**reside Insurance Agency,Inc.**
8-487-0754
eside Insurance.com

**ewburyport Harbor Marina**
8-462-3990
ww.newburyportmarinas.com

**ckering Wharf Marina**
8-740-6990
w.pickeringwharf.com

**eaport Inn and Marina**
8-997-1281
ww.seaportinnandmarina.com

**neyard Haven Marina**
8-693-0720
ww.mvhm.com

## Michigan

**elle Maer Harbor**
6-465-4534
ww.bellemaer.com

**osswinds Marine Service**
1-894-4549
ww.crosswindsmarineservice.com

**etroit Yacht Club**
3-824-1200
ww.dyc.com

**arbour Towne Marina**
1-755-2218
ownemarina.com

**cobson Marina Resort, Inc.**
1-620-0474
ww.jacobsonmarinaresort.com

**nekama Marine Inc.**
1-889-5000
ww.onekamamarine.com

**rt Austin Harbor**
9-738-8712
ww.michigan.gov/
rtaustinharbor.com

**rry's Marina**
6-709-9559
ww.terrysmarina.com

**ledo Beach Marina**
4-243-3800
ww.toledobeachmarina.com

**oodland Harbor Marina**
9-743-3624
ww.woodlandharbormarina.com

## Mississippi

**iloxi Boardwalk Marina**
8-432-2628

**le Casino Biloxi**
6-834-4112
ww.biloxi.isleofcapricasinos.com

## New Jersey

**Beach Haven Yacht Club Marina**
609-492-9101
beachhavenyachtclubmarina.com

**Captains License Class**
888-937-2458
www.captainslicensclass.com

**Green Cove Marina**
732-840-9090
www.greencovemarina.com

**Hinkley Yacht Services**
732-477-6700
www.hinckleyyachts.com

**Hoffman's Marina**
732-528-6200
www.hoffmansmarina.com

**Kammerman's Marina**
609-348-8418
www.kammermansmarina.com

**Lincoln Harbor Yacht Club**
201-319-5100
www.lincolnharbormarina.com

**Marina At Southwinds**
609-693-6288
www.marinaatsouthwinds.com

**Miss Chris Marina**
609-884-3351
www.misschrismarina.com

**Riverside Marina & Yacht Sales**
856-461-1077
www.riversideys.com

**Seaboard Marine Inc.**
732 264 8910
www.seaboardmarineinc.com

**Seaside Sailing**
800-569-7245
www.seasidesailing.com

## New York

**Brewerton Boat Yard Inc.**
315-676-3762
www.brewertonboatyard.com

**Essex Shipyard**
518-963 4024
essexshipyard.net

**Ess-Kay Yards**
315-676-7064
www.ess-kayyards.com

**Glen Cove Marina**
516-759-3129
www.glencovemarina.com

**Half Moon Bay Marina**
914-271-5400
www.halfmoonbaymarina.com

**Halsey's Marina**
631-324-5666
www.seaincorp.com

**Harbor's End Marina**
315-938-5425
www.harborsendmarina.com

**Hudson River Maritime Museum**
845-338-0071 x12
www.hrmm.org

**Hutchinson's Boat Works, Inc.**
315-482-9931
www.hbwboats.com

**Hyde Park Marina**
845-473-8283
www.hydeparkmarina.com

**Minneford Marina**
718-885-2000
www.minnefordmarina.com

**New Rochelle Municipal Marina**
914-235-6930
NewRochelleNY.com

**New Whitehall Marina**
518-499-9700

**Patsy's Bay Marine**
845-786-5270
www.patsysbaymarina.com

**Pier 225 Marina LLC**
315-569-6153
pier225marina.com

**Riverside Marine Services Inc.**
518-943-5311
www.riverviewmarineservices.com

**Rondout Yacht Basin**
845-331-7061
www.rondoutyachtbasin.com

**Sell My Boat For Me LLC**
888-511-5441
www.sellmyboatforme.com

**Smith Boys Marine Sales**
716-695-3472
smithboys.com

**Star Island Yacht Club & Marina**
631-668-5052
www.starislandyc.com

**Sunset Harbour Marina**
631-289-3800
ILoveMyMarina.com

**Tappan Zee Marina**
845-359-5522
tappanzeemarina.com

**Three Mile Harbor Marina**
631-324-1320
www.seaincorp.com

**Treasure Cove Resort Marina**
631-727-8386
www.treasurecoveresortmarina.com

**Triangle Sea Sales**
631-477-1773
www.triangleseasales.com

## North Carolina

**Albemarle Plantation**
252-426-4037

**Anchors Away Boatyard**
910-270-4741
www.anchorsawayboatyard.com

**Bald Head Island Marina**
910-457-7380
www.baldheadislandmarina.com

**Bennett Brothers Yachts**
910-772-9277
www.bbyachts.com

**Cape Fear Marina**
910-772-9277
www.bbyachts.com

**Cypress Cove Marina**
252-796-0435
www.cypresscovenc.com

**Dawson Creek Boatworks**
252-617-2630
www.dawsoncreekboatworks.webs.com

**Deep Point Marina**
910-269-2380
www.deeppointmarina.com

**Dismal Swamp Welcome Center**
252-771-8333
www.DismalSwampWelcomeCenter.com

**Dowry Creek Marina**
252-943-2728
dowrycreekmarina.com

**Joyner Marina**
910-458-5053
www.JOYNERMARINA.com

**Morehead City Yacht Basin**
252-726-6862
www.mcyachtbasin.com

**Ocean Isle Marina & Yacht Club**
910-579-6440

**Page After Page Bookstore**
252-335-7243
www.pageafterpagebook.com

**Portside Marina**
252-726-7678
www.portsidemarina.com

**River Forest Manor And Marina**
252-943-0030
www.riverforestmarina.com

**River Forest Shipyard & Marina**
252-943-2151
www.riverforestmarina.com

**Sailcraft Service**
252-249-0522
www.waterwayguide.com/marina_
close-ups/sailcraft-service-inc

**South Harbour Village Marina**
910-799-3111
www.southharboursales.com/
marina.html

**St. James Plantation / St. James
Marina**
910-253-3001
www.stjamesplantation.com

**T/A Poor Man's Hole**
910-326-1953

**The BoatHouse At Front Street
Village**
252-838-1524

**Town Creek Marina**
252-728-6111
towncreekmarina.com

**Uncorked By The Sea Wine Shop
& Gallery**
910-454-0633
uncorkedbythesea.com

**Washington Waterfront Docks**
252-975-9367 ext 221
www.washingtonncmarina.com

**Whittaker Pointe Marina**
252-249-1750
www.whittakerpointe.com

**Wilmington Marine Center**
910-395-5055
www.wilmingtonmarine.com

## Ontario, Canada

**Boblo Island Marina**
519-736-1111
www.boblomarina.com

**Cobourg Marina**
905-372-2397
www.cobourg.ca/municipal-
departments/marina.html

**General Wolfe Marina**
613-385-2611
www.generalwolfehotel.com

**Rawley Resort And Marina**
705 538 2272
www.rawleyresort.com

**White Sea Resort**
705-283-1483
www.whitesearesort.ca

## Quebec, Canada

**Yacht Club Montreal**
514-789-9264
www.ycmi.com

## Rhode Island

**Apponaug Harbor Marina**
401-739-5005
www.apponaugmarina.com

**Newport Yachting Center Marina**
800-653-3625
www.newportyachtingcenter.com

## South Carolina

**Bucksport Marina & RV Resort**
843-397-5566
www.bucksportplantation.com

**Cooper River Marina**
843-554-0790

**Coquina Yacht Club**
843-249-9333
coquinayachtclub.com

**Harborwalk Books**
843-546-8212
www.harborwalkbooks.com

**Harbour Town Yacht Basin**
843-363-8335

**Harbourgate Marina**
843-249-8888
www.Harbourgatemarina.com

**Heritage Plantation Marina**
843-237-3650
www.heritageplantation.com

**Lady's Island Marina**
843-522-0430

**Osprey Marina**
843-215-5353
www.ospreymarina.com

**Pierside Boatworks**
843-554-7775
www.piersideboatworks.com

**Port Royal Landing Marina, Inc.**
843-525-6664
www.portroyallandingmarina.net

**Skull Creek Marina**
843-681-8436
www.theskullcreekmarina.com

**St. Johns Yacht Harbor**
843-557-1027
www.sjyh.com

**UK-Halsey Charleston**
Sailmakers
843-722-0823
www.ukhalseycharleston.com

## Texas

**Freeport Municipal Marina**
979-236-1221
www.myfreeportmarina.com

**Kemah Boardwalk Marina**
281-334-2284

## Vermont

**Champlain Marina**
802-658-4034
www.champlainmarina.com

## Virginia

**Bay Point Marina**
757-362-3600
www.littlecreekmarina.com

**Carter's Cove Marina**
804-438-5273
www.carterscovemarina.com

**Chesapeake Boat Works**
804-776-8833
www.chesapeakeboatworks.com

**Cobb's Marina**
757-588-5401
cobbsmarina.com

**Deltaville Marina**
804-776-9812
deltavillemarina.com

**Deltaville Yachting Center**
804-776-9898
www.dycboat.com

**Downtown Hampton Public Piers**
757-727-1276
www.downtownhampton.com

**Dozier's Port Urbanna Marine Center**
804-758-0000
www.doziermarine.com

**Dozier's Regatta Point Yachting Center**
804-776-6711
www.doziermarine.com

**Little Creek Marina**
757-971-8411
www.littlecreekmarina.com

**Mobjack Bay Marina, Inc.**
804-725-7245
www.mobjackbaymarina.com

**Norton Yachts**
804-776-9211
www.nortonyachts.com

**Ocean Marine Yacht Center**
757-321-7432
www.oceanmarinellc.com

**Regent Point Marina**
804-758-4457
www.regent-point.com

**River's Rest Marina and Resort**
804-829-2753
www.riversrest.com

**Scott's Creek Marina**
757-399-BOAT

**Signature CanvasMakers**
757-788-8890
www.SignatureCanvasMakers.com

**Smithfield Station**
757-357-7700
www.smithfieldstation.com

**Stingray Point Boat Works**
804-776-7500
www.stingraypointboatworks.com

**The Tides Inn & Marina**
804-438-4465
www.tidesinn.com

**Top Rack Marina**
757-227-3041
www.toprackmarina.com

**Urbanna Town Marina at Upton's Point**
804-758-5440

**Vinings Landing Marine Center**
757-587-8000
www.viningslanding.com

**White Point Marina**
804-472-2977
www.whitepointmarina.com

**Whitehouse Cove Marina**
757-508-2602
www.whitehousecovemarina.com

**Willoughby Harbor Marina**
757-583-4150
www.viningsmarine.com/marinas/
willoughby-harbor-marina.htm

**Yankee Point Marina**
804-462-7018
www.yankeepointmarina.com

## Washington, DC

**Capital Yacht Club**
202-488-8110
www.capitalyachtclub.com

## Wisconsin

**Harborside Yacht Center**
414-273-0711
www.harborsideyachtcenter.com

# Marina/Sponsor Index

Sponsors are listed in **BOLD**.

MARINA/SPONSOR INDEX

# Subject Index

Most relevant pages are listed in **BOLD**.

# Goin' Ashore Index

# Inlets Index